RED SOX THREADS

Odds and Ends from Red Sox History

BILL NOWLIN

ROUNDER BOOKS

Copyright © 2008 by Bill Nowlin

Published by Rounder Books

an imprint of

Rounder Records Corp.

One Rounder Way

Burlington, MA 01803

ISBN-13: 978-1-57940-157-3

ISBN-10: 1-57940-157-0

Nowlin, Bill, 1945–

Red Sox Threads

Odds & Ends from Red Sox History

1. Boston Red Sox (baseball team). History I T.

First edition

Library of Congress Control Number: 2008926883

796.357

Interior design and composition by Jane Tenenbaum

Cover design by Steve Jurgensmeyer

Back cover design by Rachael Sullivan

Printed in Canada

CONTENTS

INTRODUCTION

This is a book that's often unwieldy, was difficult to organize, and sometimes seems characterized by barely-controlled chaos. It's a very subjective book that I wrote over a period of many years, just following up on various flights of fancy—not always knowing where the research would take me. The problem was that researching one thing would lead to another, and I'd just follow the thread. And when there was a thread to follow, I often just strung the items together in a stream-of-consciousness fashion as they came up and struck me.

Other times, I'd stumble across an unconnected oddity of one kind or another—and was then faced with the question: where do I put it? I tried to find a place to work it into the flow. Sometimes I might not have succeeded as well as others.

In the course of working on the book, I became entranced with learning more about many of the more obscure players from the Red Sox past—players that many diehard fans may never have heard of, such as Regis Leheny or Clarence Winters, Vince Molyneaux or Joe Gonzalez. There are over 300 brief biographical sketches of these players.

There are maybe a couple of hundred game capsules—games like the forfeits, the tie games, the start of the 1969 season with three extra-inning games, each one longer than the one before, the time the Red Sox almost got arrested for playing a game at Fenway Park.

And several hundred vignettes, like the time as recently as 2005 when Tim Wakefield tied a major league record by giving up six home runs in one game—but won—or the last home run of Bill Buckner's career, an inside-the park homer at Fenway Park.

It's been challenging but rewarding to try and trace down the Native Americans who played for the Red Sox, or the dentists who played for Boston. It's been fun trying to think of some of the word plays that can be made with player names.

It's been nearly impossible to bring this book to conclusion. It seems as though every day something new crops up. I'm sure there are many fascinating takes on things that should have been included. I invite readers to contribute ideas of their own—and I'll be disappointed if I don't hear quite a few.

—Bill Nowlin

THE NAMING OF THE RED SOX

John I. Taylor, who first named the Red Sox.

On December 18, 1907, shortly after Boston's National League team revealed that the new uniforms for 1908 eliminated their customary red stockings, owner John I. Taylor of the Boston Americans pounced. He quickly decided that his team would adopt red hose and call themselves the Boston Red Sox. Taylor personally oversaw the uniform design, selecting red stockings because Boston's first professional baseball team—the Red Stockings—had worn them. Taylor appreciated the link with tradition. It was predicted that the name "Red Sox" would prove a popular choice.

Was Taylor imprudently putting the health, or even the lives of his players in jeopardy? Historian Ellery Clark wrote that the owners of the NL team, George and John Dovey, "decided the red dye in their club's stockings might well lead to blood infection and even worse if and when or or more of their players were cut in the leg by opposing spikes. The grand old color and the nickname were abandoned in the interests of health."

Rash though Taylor's decision may have been, generations of Red Sox players have come and gone with no documented case of red dye disease. It wasn't until the 2004 postseason that blood on the stockings played any noteworthy role in Red Sox lore.

In an October 1908 article on baseball team names, the *Boston Globe*'s Tim Murnane noted that as early as 1875, there was a shortlived team known as the Red Sox in St. Louis, and that the Cincinnati team had originally been called the Red Stockings, which "set the style for naming clubs after the color of their stockings." The Chicago White Sox and St. Louis Browns were two other such teams. He noted that "the Boston Americans took up the name Red Sox last winter, simply to have some trade mark that would be easy to write and have a baseball flavor." As a sportswriter, he was grateful: "The [use of] shorter names makes it much easier for those reporting the games or writing baseball."

Taylor's name stuck, and the team has been both beloved and bemoaned ever since: the Red Sox, the Sox, the Bosox, and sometimes "the Sawx." The Boston Red Sox are without a doubt one of baseball's greatest franchises, arguably the one that engenders the most emotion in both its fans and detractors. More people hate the New York Yankees than any other team, and the Yankees have their loyal and ardent fans, but the volatility of emotion surrounding the Red Sox might well surpass that of the Yanks simply because Boston fans themselves swing so wildly from passionate fandom to despair to disgust and back to blind faith, or yearning, once again.

The origins of those red sox

It's probably evident that the word "sox" is a breezier shortening of the word "stockings"—a covering of the foot and lower part of the leg. Sports teams in the late 19th century often included distinctively colored stockings as part of their uniform, and were often referred to by their color of stockings.

As best we can tell, the first "Red Sox" team dates back to 1875. One can find the St. Louis Red Sox—at least by nickname—mentioned as they pulled their team together for the upcoming season in the April 18, 1875 *Chicago Tribune*, which wrote, "The Red Sox, as they are familiarly known, have not yet filled their nine. They are the pick of last year's Empires and Red Stockings." A boxscore showing the Red Sox shut out by Hartford appears in the June 28, 1875 *Hartford Courant*. With Pud Galvin on the mound, the St. Louis Red Sox played a game in Reading, Pennsylvania according to a game account in the *Reading Eagle* of July 4 the following year.

It was much more common for a team to be dubbed the "Stockings" than the "Sox"—such as the National League's Boston Red Stockings of 1876. "Stockings" was a popular part of team names that year. There were two other "stockings" teams in the National League—the Chicago White Stockings and the St. Louis Brown Stockings. The Brown Stockings were sometimes dubbed the Brown Sox. In 1877, one also finds the Cincinnati Red Stockings in the league. Other teams in the league were known by the color of their stockings as well, such as the Hartford Dark Blues. They just didn't happen to incorporate the word "Sox" or "Stockings" into their team name.

There was a Boston Red Stockings team from 1876 through the 1884 season, and then in the year 1891. From that point forward, there's never been another Boston team using that particular name.

There were other teams, though, for instance the Dubuque Red Stockings in the 1879 Northwestern League—which happened to be an all-stockings league (the four-team league also included the Rockford White Stockings, the Omaha Green Stockings, and the Davenport Brown Stockings). But it proved to be a league for just a year.

One can occasionally find other colored-leg teams like the Worcester Ruby Legs (a National League team in 1880) or the Amsterdam Red Stockings of the 1895 New York State League. Perhaps because of changes in fashion or terminology, "Sox" began to supplant the more archaic sounding "Stockings" around the turn of the century.

A very early "Sox" team was the Toledo White Sox in 1894, in Ban Johnson's Western League for just the one season. The team went by three different names the following year: the Swamp Angels, the White Stockings, and—after transferring to Terre Haute on June 30, the Terre Haute Hotten Tots. And they weren't even around come 1896. The next Sox were the Chicago White Sox beginning in the year 1900.

From 1901–1904, we find the Rockford Red Sox in the Three-I League. In 1906, we find the Danville Red Sox in the Virginia League, a team which had a run through 1910, but they became the Danville Bugs for 1911. Coming in last, perhaps they thought better of the name change and reverted to the Red Sox in 1912, but moved to Bluefield and disbanded on June 16.

In 1907, the only other Red Sox team was the Greensburg Red Sox in the Western Pennsylvania League, another yearlong team.

Some books show the Boston Red Sox as beginning under that name in 1907, but given that "Red Sox" was only claimed by John I. Taylor on December 18 that year, it's misleading to indicate it as the name of the team for that season. Since 1908, though, the team's been known as the Boston Red Sox.

Other teams with red sox

A full listing of organized baseball teams in the 20th and 21st century which bear the name Red Sox, year by year:

1901–1904: Rockford Red Sox (Three-I League)
1906–1910: Danville Red Sox (Virginia League)
1907: Greensburg Red Sox (Western Pennsylvania League)
1908-present: Boston Red Sox (American League)
1909: Abilene Red Sox (Central Kansas League)
1910–1911: Superior Red Sox (Minnesota-Wisconsin League). Though retaining the same name, they were members of the Central International League in 1912.
1911–1915: Brantford Red Sox (Canadian League)
1912: Danville Red Sox (Virginia League)
1912: Spartansburg Red Sox (Carolina Association)

1913–1914: Regina Red Sox (Western Canada League)

1919–1921: Brantford Red Sox (Michigan-Ontario League)

1919: Lewiston Red Sox (New England League)

1920–1921: Redfield Red Sox (South Dakota League)

1921–1928: Jackson Red Sox (Cotton States League)

1922: Sherman Red Sox (Texas-Oklahoma League)

1927–1928: Northampton Red Sox (Eastern Shore League)

1930: Brantford Red Sox (Ontario League)

1932: Lancaster Red Sox (Inter-State League)

1933–1934: Reading Red Sox (New York-Penn League)

1934: Rayne Red Sox (Evangeline League)

1936–1940: Rocky Mount Red Sox (Piedmont League)

1936: Abbeville Red Sox (Alabama-Florida League)

1937–1938: Hazleton Red Sox (New York-Penn League)

1937–1940: Clarksdale Red Sox (Cotton States League)

1937–1942: Elizabethon Betsy Red Sox (Appalachian League)

1937–1939: Pokomoke City Red Sox (Eastern Shore League)

1937: Mansfield Red Sox (Ohio State League)

1939–1940: Granby Red Socks (Provincial League)

1940, 1943, 1946–1951: Scranton Red Sox (Eastern League)

1940: Centreville Red Sox (Eastern Shore League)

1941–1942: Greensboro Red Sox (Piedmont League)

1943–1950: Roanoke Red Sox (Piedmont League)

1944: Middletown Red Sox (Ohio State League)

1946–1948: Lynn Red Sox (New England League)

1946: Granby Red Sox (Border League)

1946–1951: Oneonta Red Sox (Canadian-American League)

1946–1951: Lenoir Red Sox (Blue Ridge League)

1946–1948: Milford Red Sox (Eastern Shore League)

1947–1955: San Jose Red Sox (California League)

1947–1948: Warsaw Red Sox (Tobacco State League)

1948: Oroville Red Sox (Far West League)

1948: Wellsville Red Sox (Pony League)

1948: Baxley Red Sox (Georgia State League)

1948: Granby Red Sox (Provincial League)

1948–1954: Morristown Red Sox (Mountain States League)

1949–1951: Marion Red Sox (Ohio-Indiana League)

1951, 1955: Hazelhurt/Baxley Red Sox (Georgia State League)

1951: Rome Red Sox (Georgia-Alabama League)

1954–1958, 1960: Corning Red Sox (Pony League, then New York-Penn League)

1956–1957: Lafayette Red Sox Midwest League)

1956: Lexington Red Sox (Nebraska State League)

1958–1960: Allentown Red Sox (Eastern League)

1961: Johnstown Red Sox (Eastern League)

1961–1984: Winston-Salem Red Sox (Carolina League)

1961–1962: Olean Red Sox (New York-Penn League)

1963–1964: Reading Red Sox (Eastern League)

1963–1965: Wellsville Red Sox (New York-Penn League)

1965–1969: Pittsfield Red Sox (Eastern League)

1965: Harlan Red Sox (Appalachian League)

1966: Oneonta Red Sox (New York-Penn League)

1966: Covington Red Sox (Appalachian League)

1967–1971: Greenville Red Sox (Western Carolinas League)
1969–1988: Winter Haven Red Sox (Florida State League)
1970–2007: Pawtucket Red Sox (Eastern League, later International League)
1971: Williamsport Red Sox (New York-Penn League)
1973–1983: Bristol Red Sox (Eastern League)
1974–1978: Elmira Red Sox (New York-Penn League)—in 1977 the team was named the Elmira
    Pioneer Red Sox
1984–1994: New Britain Red Sox (Eastern League)
1988–1994: Lynchburg Red Sox (Carolina League)
1989–2007: Fort Myers Gulf Coast Red Sox (Gulf Coast League)
1993: Fort Lauderdale Red Sox (Florida State League)
1994–2004: Sarasota Red Sox (Florida State League)

Some of the above teams were affiliated with the Boston Red Sox and some were not. A handful preceded the Boston team. Of course, there have been countless amateur, school, Little League, and community teams named the "Red Sox"—it wouldn't be possible to ever track them all. And there any number of semipro teams such as the Fergus Falls Red Sox, who played in Minnesota during the late 1940s.

One can even find such shocking matchups as the time the Knights of the Ku Klux Klan team played the Red Sox A.C. on the Arlington, Virginia Horse Grounds on April 18, 1927. The KKK team beat the Red Sox, 5–3.

The year with the most Red Sox teams

In 1948, the Red Sox had eight affiliated teams also named the Red Sox, ranking that year first for the largest number of affiliated Red Sox clubs: Lynn, Milford, Oneonta, Oroville, Roanoke, San Jose, Scranton, and Wellsville.

There were five other teams in organized baseball named Red Sox in 1948, making an overall total of 14 ballclubs with the Red Sox name attached. The other five were:

Baxley Red Sox (Georgia State League)   Morristown Red Sox (Mountain States League)
Granby Red Sox (Provincial League)   Warsaw Red Sox (Tobacco State League)
Lenoir Red Sox (Blue Ridge League)

Other shades of Sox

There have been a number of other shades of Sox. The year 1947 seems to have been the year with the widest variety of colors among Sox teams in organized baseball:

Abilene Blue Sox (West Texas-New Mexico League)
Amarillo Gold Sox (West Texas-New Mexico League)
Boston Red Sox (American League)*
Lenoir Red Sox (Blue Ridge League)
Lynn Red Sox (New England League)*
Milford Red Sox (Eastern Shore League)*
Oneonta Red Sox (Canadian-American League)*
Reno Silver Sox (Sunset League)
Roanoke Red Sox (Piedmont League)*
San Jose Red Sox (California League)
Scranton Red Sox (Eastern League)*
Sherbrooke Black Sox (Provincial League)
Utica Blue Sox (Eastern League)

Warsaw Red Sox (Tobacco State League)
Wisconsin Rapids White Sox (Wisconsin State League)
*The Boston Red Sox and affiliated teams

Other teams with colored Sox names include the following:

Montgomery Black Sox (1903, Southern League)
Santa Ana Yellow Sox Growers (1910, Southern California Trolley League)
Seattle Purple Sox (1919, Pacific Coast League)
Dublin Green Sox (1949, Georgia State League)
Everett AquaSox (1995, Northwest League)

There are, of course, numerous teams named the Black Sox, Blue Sox, etc.

With the aforementioned 1947 teams, we've thus got aqua, black, blue, gold, green, purple, red, white, yellow, and—in the Negro Leagues—the long-established Montgomery Gray Sox. The Negro Leagues also featured the Baltimore Black Sox and the Memphis Red Sox. Then there was the independent team from North Dakota, the Jamestown Red Sox, an integrated team which in 1934 featured Ted Radcliffe, a black manager overseeing players of different races. This seemingly obscure team from North Dakota even won three games in a row against an all-star team featuring several future Red Sox players such as Doc Cramer, Jimmie Foxx, Pinky Higgins, and Heinie Manush.

Some other Sox without named hues include:

Pasadena Silk Sox (1910, Southern California Trolley League)
Newark New Sox (1915, Buckeye League)
Colorado Springs Sky Sox (1950, Western League)
Miami Sun Sox (1950, Florida International League)
Toledo Sox (1954, American Association)
Yuma Sun Sox (1955, Arizona-Mexico League)
Davenport DavSox (1957, Three-I League)
Fresno Sun Sox (1957, California League
San Jose JoSox (1957, California League)
Sarasota Sun Sox (1961, Florida State League)
Clinton C-Sox (1962, Midwest League)
Middlesboro Cubsox (1963, Appalachian League)
Knoxville Knox Sox (1976, Southern League)
Niagara Falls Sox (1983, New York-Penn League)
West Virginia Coal Sox (1993, Frontier League)
Bowie Bay Sox (1994, Eastern League)

Back to the Boston Red Sox and its predecessor Boston Americans

From the founding of the franchise in 1901 until that December date in 1907, the team truly had no name other than its corporate one: the Boston American League Ball Club. Though most books on the Red Sox suggest the team had other names—the Pilgrims, the Puritans, the Plymouth Rocks, the Somersets, etc., this was never the case. True, there were various nicknames assigned the ballclub. Some may even be unprintable, but if we judge from the ones used in the newspapers of the day, we find that the team was commonly called the "Bostons" or the "Americans" (to better distinguish them from the city's National League team). It's a myth, though, that they were commonly nicknamed the Boston Pilgrims.

There follows here a lengthy discourse on disproving the myth. If you're not really interested in the methodology, please skip ahead a few pages.

THE BOSTON PILGRIMS NEVER EXISTED

In reading accounts of the 1903 World Series, I so often came across the team name "Boston Pilgrims" that I accepted this on faith as one of the names by which the team was known. I even used it myself, presenting it as fact (see page one of *Tales from the Red Sox Dugout*).

I find that I helped perpetuate a myth. That's all it appears to be: a myth.

I cannot find any contemporary indication that the Boston American League baseball club was ever known as the Pilgrims, except for a part of 1907 and that only in two of Boston's several daily newspapers.

It's a fairly widespread myth, though, as one can see by consulting a number of standard baseball reference books. For instance, the Seventh Edition of *Total Baseball* unfortunately describes the Boston Pilgrims as facing the Pittsburgh Pirates on page 280. No wonder I used the name when writing and while proofreading *Tales from the Red Sox Dugout*. No wonder other researchers do the same.

The Pilgrims keep cropping up. Burt Solomon's *The Baseball Timeline,* produced in association with Major League Baseball, consistently refers to the "Boston Pilgrims." The *Sporting News* book *Baseball*, edited by Joe Hoppel, which was also published in 2001, carelessly says the 1903 World Champions were "the Red Sox (also known as the Pilgrims, Puritans and Americans)."

Had any of these authors taken the trouble to scour the Boston newspapers of the day, they would have found nothing which even suggests a team known as the Boston Pilgrims in 1903. Or, for that matter, the Puritans. They're both wonderful names, but I can't find even a shred of evidence that they were names used in Boston at the time of the first World Series.

The team was also not named the Boston Americans. That was perhaps the most common nickname—to distinguish it from the older NL club in town—but the formal name of the team in 1903 seems to have been Boston American League Ball Club. That was the club name over which Henry Killilea signed his name when the Pittsburg and Boston clubs signed a contract to play the 1903 World Series. [Note: In 1903, Pittsburg did not have the final "h" that is currently part of the name of the city of Pittsburgh. Throughout this book, we will typically add the "h" to avoid confusion.]

Glenn Stout and Dick Johnson in *Red Sox Century*, the most definitive history of the team, do have it right. Boston's AL team owner John I. Taylor made the decision to name the team the "Red Sox" on December 18, 1907 and first ordered new uniforms with bright red stockings on that date from Wright and Ditson, the sporting goods supplier. Stout and Johnson then quote the reaction of both the *Boston Journal* newspaper and *The Sporting News*. Tim Murnane, writing in *The Sporting News*, said, "Well, what do you think of that? The Boston Americans have a new name…the 'Red Sox.'" Murnane doesn't say the "Pilgrims" have a new name; it's the "Americans" who have a new name.

Murnane actually adds more context, when he elaborates, "Ever since Boston became identified with the American League an effort has been made to give the team an appropriate nickname which would sound good in print…but no two writers will agree on any one name. It was consequently up to John I. Taylor to re-christen his bunch and he has done so effectively."

Stout and Johnson, earlier in *Red Sox Century*, noted what I found in my own reading of the several Boston daily newspapers of this era, regarding both the AL and NL teams in Boston: "Neither team had a nickname, nor would they for several more seasons. Both were simply called 'the Bostons,' although to differentiate between the two clubs, fans, sportswriters, and players commonly began referring to the NL entry as 'the Nationals,' and their American League counterparts as 'the Americans.' Other nicknames, such as the Pilgrims, Puritans, Plymouth Rocks, Somersets (so named after owner Charles Somers), or Collinsmen (after manager Collins) for the AL team and the Beaneaters, Triumvirs, or Seleemen (after manager Frank Selee) for the Nationals, were convenient inventions of the press. Their subsequent use by many historians is misleading. None of these nicknames was ever widely used by either fans or players."

Buck Freeman, wearing his "B.A." jersey.

Precisely. In fact, the nicknames were not always convenient inventions—in that *both* the Boston Nationals and the Boston Americans were sometimes dubbed the Beaneaters! Even within columns by the same sportswriter in the same newspaper, these casual nicknames were changed from day to day.

It's also true that no nickname was consistently used by the Boston press. The nickname used most consistently for the AL team—the only one which was really widely used at all—was the "Americans." Their 1902 uniforms, in fact, reflected this terminology to some extent. Photographs show "B. A." on front of the uniform. This confirms what Tim Murnane reported just a few years later.

If you want to learn more, in great (and excessive?) detail, read on. Otherwise, take our word for it and just skip to the next section of this book.

Content analysis of Boston newspaper sports coverage in 1903

The *Boston Herald* was the biggest newspaper in town in 1903. A content analysis of the game accounts in the *Herald* indicates that the team was indeed referred to by a number of names. On some occasions, more than one team name would be used in a given day's newspaper—sometimes one name would appear in the headline and another one in the body of the text.

Assuming that texts were written by reporters closer to the game, and headlines written by editors, and counting only one usage, we counted those in the text unless no name was used in the text, in which case we counted the name from the headline, if there was one. There were nine game accounts where no team name or nickname was used in either the headline or the text.

A reading of every game account for the entire 1903 season revealed that the name "Boston Americans" was used 57 times, while the term "Bostons" to describe the team was used in 54 game accounts. Interestingly, though, of the 54 game texts where "Bostons" was used in the story, 29 times the name "Boston Americans" was used in the headline or sub-head. The general impression is that the two terms were used fairly interchangeably, though with far more frequency than any other nicknames.

There were four game accounts in which the American League team was referred to as the "Beaneaters." There were two game accounts in which the only named characterization was "Bostonians" and there was one game account that referred to the team as the "Collinsites."

There were a number of other collective phrases used as aggregate descriptors to "name" the team. These were:

the locals	Collins' men	the Boston team
Collins' club	Collins' tribe	the local team
the Boston side	men from the Hub	and, of course, simply "Boston"
Boston Club		

In early September 1903, when the American League pennant seemed within their grasp, there were a couple of stories which referred to them as the "coming champions" (the sports-writers of the day were not snakebit, the way Red Sox fans have learned to become) and, once they clinched, there was at least one story referring to them collectively as the "American League champions."

How many times was this team referred to as the "Pilgrims" or "Boston Pilgrims" in the *Boston Herald*? Not one time.

Sampling of other Boston newspapers

One might conclude from this reading of the *Boston Herald* that there was no 1903 Boston team called the Pilgrims, or that for some perverse reason the *Herald* chose to ignore the name. Sampling the other Boston papers of the day by reading each of their game accounts for the month of September 1903, as the team clinched the pennant, we studied daily coverage in the *Boston Post,* the *Boston Globe,* the *Boston Journal,* and the *Boston Record.*

The *Boston Post* results were as follows:

Boston Americans—16 games	Collinsites—1 game
the Collins team—5 games	the Collins boys—1 game
Bostons—3 games	the champion Boston nine—1 game
Boston—3 games	

Analysis of the *Boston Globe's* daily coverage in September 1903 produced the following results:

Boston—18	Bostons—1	Bostonians—1
Americans—6	Collins' men—1	the Boston boys—1

There were two days where we could not find any mention at all of the team. The *Globe* seemed to be very cautious in giving the team any nickname at all. The use of the city name alone was the predominant usage.

The *Boston Journal* had very good coverage of ballgames, too. This newspaper often followed the practice of putting the nicknames of other teams into quotation marks, e.g., "Senators" and "Tigers." The content analysis in the *Journal* showed:

Boston—12	Collins' men—1	champions—1
Bostons—7	the Collins team—1	no reference—5
Americans—2	Boston American club—1	

The *Journal* also included a column composed of quotes from fans on how they rated their team's chances, but not a single fan referred to the Pilgrims, either.

The *Boston Record* always presented a header over its league standings. THE AMERICANS' RECORD was the box title for the AL standings and WITH THE NATIONAL LEAGUERS for the senior circuit. As to daily coverage of the Boston entry in the American League, the *Record's* stories broke down in these quantities:

Player/manager Jimmy Collins

Americans—11	Jimmy Collins' men—1 (the
Boston—6	same story also referred to
Collins and his pets—1	"the Boston Boys")
Collins and his charges—1	no reference—2
Boston American League baseball team—1	

How many times was this team referred to as the "Pilgrims" or "Boston Pilgrims" in these five Boston daily newspapers? Not one time.

One might note, parenthetically, that the name "Puritans" also never appeared even once in any of the daily newspapers sampled.

A survey of these five major daily newspapers in Boston in 1903 failed to turn up even one reference to the alleged "Boston Pilgrims." Where did this name come from? Agreed, it's a nice name, but it doesn't seem to have been this team's name.

Sampling of other newspapers from cities with American League Teams

We also read every September 1903 game account in newspapers from three other cities which hosted American League baseball teams by consulting the *Chicago Tribune*, the *New York Times,* and the *Washington Post*.

The *Chicago Tribune* typically used the straightforward designation "Boston" in its game stories. No other name was used more than once—except for the name "Beaneaters" which was used in three accounts. In addition, the *Tribune* described the team as Collins' aggregation, Collins' men, the American, the Bostons, the Bostonians and, in just one instance, the Plymouth Rocks.

The *New York Times* never really used any designation other than the city name: Boston. In accounts datelined from Boston itself, game stories would sometimes refer to "the local baseball team," "the local men" or, in one case, "the local Americans." After the club clinched the championship, the *Times* once referred to them as "the new American League baseball champions."

More than half the time, the *Washington Post* also simply used the city's name to describe the team. The *Post*, like the *Tribune*, employed "Beaneaters" (four times); they used "Americans" twice and "champions" twice.

After studying these eight newspapers and their coverage of the final month of the 1903 season, we find that although the team was often described as the "Boston Americans," that was more often in the headlines than in the game account. And even then, one did not get the impression that this was meant to be taken as the name of the time; it seemed more simply a way to distinguish the column presenting the AL team's coverage from that of the NL team's. Though it's convenient (and enjoyable) to have team nicknames, and the team's 1902 uniforms notwithstanding, it would be inaccurate to state definitively that the team nickname was the "Americans"—the designator "Bostons" was used as often. We are better off concluding that the team really had no nickname until "Red Sox" became established prior to the 1908 season.

All in all, the team was described in newspaper columns as "Boston" or "the Bostons" and, when more clarity was necessary, the "Boston Americans." The Boston Pilgrims, though, never existed, not in the minds of the sportswriters, nor in the minds of the fans (as best we can tell).

A thorough reading of both the *Boston Herald* and *Boston Globe* game accounts of the 1904 reaffirm that the name Boston Pilgrims did not crop up even once. Neither did the Puritans.

So where did the "Boston Pilgrims" tag come from? Was it first employed by author Frederick Leib in his 1947 book *The Boston Red Sox*, and then just used over and over by others less careful about original source material than Stout and Johnson?

Both the *Boston Globe* and *New York Times* have references to ball teams named the Pilgrims in 1905 and 1906, but they typically refer to an English "association football" (soccer) team led by Sir Henry Kirkpatrick that toured in those two years. There was a *Globe* reference to "pilgrims" in the June 19, 1905 paper, but that one referred to the Cincinnati Reds players.

Sometime in 1906, perhaps influenced by the name of the touring soccer team, the *Washington Post* began to apply the nickname "Pilgrims" to Boston's American League baseball

Cy Young with the "B. A." for Boston Americans showing on his jersey.

team and during 1907, it caught on sufficiently in some Boston newspapers to be a short-lived nickname for the team.

The first time we could find the *Globe* using the term in a Boston baseball story was an April 26, 1907 sports page cartoon declaring, "There is no joy in Pilgrimville" following a particular defeat administered by the Athletics. The *Globe*'s game account on May 15 used the nickname in both the fourth and fifth paragraph. There could be no question in context that the writer was describing Boston's American League club.

There is another mention of "Pilgrims" in the July 12, 1907 story and about another 10 uses before the year was out, more or less a baker's dozen of mentions in the one year—many fewer than in the *Washington Post*. The first use in the *Chicago Tribune* was found in the June 21, 1907 edition. The *New York Times* used the word "Pilgrims" an indicated 182 times during the 1907 baseball season, but never once in connection with baseball.

The 1907 *Boston Journal* interchangeably referred to the team as "the Americans" or "Pilgrims" throughout 1907, though more often as the Americans. The paper also referred to them as the "Bostons" on several occasions and as the "Beaneaters" once or twice. The usage of "Pilgrims" was reasonably common in May, more often than not in June, rare the first two weeks of July but then picked up again the latter half the month. The two names were used fairly equally. The *Boston Herald* used "Pilgrims" fairly frequently as well, probably a little more than half the time.

Let's suppose your time machine landed in 1903, and you were to ask, "Hey, how 'bout them Pilgrims?" Boston's baseball fanatics might not have understood the allusion. If you stuck around to catch a few more seasons, in 1907, they very likely would have—though the 1906 team (49–105) is not one that any fan found engaging. And the 1907 team suffered the spring training suicide of its manager and played under four other managers before the year was out, with only 59 wins to savor. Taylor was no doubt right in thinking it was time to refashion the team, even as to its name.

So, the Boston Pilgrims actually did exist, at least in the minds of some writers for a while in 1907. By no means is there any indication that the nickname was commonly used, though it appears it might have been sufficiently familiar to have been understood during that one season. It remains a wonderful name, but its appeal seems to have grown dramatically as the decades have passed. For clarity, Boston Americans remains unchallenged as the choice of team name until the 1908 Red Sox season.

There is another twist to the story, suggested by Kevin Vahey. The first couple of decades of the 20th century found strongly held religious views in Boston, with the city divided between Protestants and Catholics. Among the more vocal of the active Royal Rooters were Irish Catholics such as Michael "Nuf Ced" McGreevey and Vahey suggests that there might have been some antagonism reflected in the choice of nicknames such as "Pilgrims" or "Puritans," their usage designed to upset McGreevey and the Irish Catholic rooters. Vahey says, "The papers trying to stay out of ethnic wars simply referred to the teams as either Nationals or Americans." Religion did play a role, and reports indicate that neither Duffy Lewis nor Harry Hooper (both Catholics) spoke to the centerfielder that played between them, Tris Speaker, nor Speaker's pal Joe Wood. Other than Vahey's remark, we've found no indication that the use of "Pilgrims" was intended to rile Nuf Ced's bunch, but would not rule it out.

As a result of this research, first published in the Society for American Baseball Research journal *The National Pastime* in 2003, a number of online reference sources have agreed to change their data, including STATS Inc., *baseball-reference.com*, and the Baseball Almanac. Over time, the names Pilgrims and Puritans will probably tend to disappear as new books are written with more care. It seems like sort of a shame, because they are colorful nicknames. History is often rewritten, but there is merit to sticking more closely to contemporary facts. There is a fascination in reading the sportswriters of the early 1900s, how they covered games and how they occasionally labored to find alternative nicknames to describe these early teams that awkwardly lacked more formal names or nicknames.

Raising the flag for the Boston Americans' first world championship

Further in support of the idea that the 1903 team was known as the Boston Americans is the pennant which was raised before the home opener on April 18, 1904. The team erected a new 100-foot tall flagpole. Two pennants were raised before the game—one for the World's Championship and one for the American League championship. The World's Championship pennant was a large one, measuring 15 feet by 30 feet. The legend on the pennant read:

Boston Americans—1903 World's Champions

Boston's first pennant sketch, as printed in the *Boston Herald*.

A sketch of the pennant design appears in the March 18, 1904 *Boston Herald*.

The pennant was a gift from long-time supporter and local notable Arthur "Hi Hi" Dixwell. Mr. Dixwell wrote Carl Greene, secretary of the Boston ballclub, to ask "if it would be acceptable for the Boston club to receive from him a pennant emblematic of the championship of the world." Greene replied that he would be pleased and proud, so Dixwell ordered the pennant created "of the finest bunting procurable." Dixwell had just a few years earlier turned the first earth for construction of the Huntington Avenue Grounds.

Boston player-manager Jimmy Collins was in Macon, Georgia for spring training when told of the gift that Dixwell had offered, and said, "Coming from the world's greatest baseball enthusiast makes the gift more appreciated…it will always be our pleasure to point to it with pride." Apparently, on the occasion of each home victory, Dixwell habitually presented a box of cigars to the team as the players left the field.

Dixwell was arguably in a better position to know the name of the 1903 team than historians decades later. One assumes that Secretary Greene, other club officials, or the players themselves might have spoken up had the name "Boston Americans" been considered an inappropriate one.

League president Ban Johnson was present for the ceremony, as was Boston owner Henry Killilea.

There was "a grand display at opening game" with Teel's Boston Band stationed in one corner of the grandstand. Naturally, they played "Tessie" which had been featured as a rallying song during the 1903 World's Series against Pittsburgh. As the Boston players took the field for pre-game ceremonies, there was such a large ovation that "the ground fairly shook." Boston is still known as one of the best baseball cities, more than 100 years later. This was clearly true in 1903, and the *Boston Post* noted, "Never did a conquering general or emperor pass between lines of more devoted worshippers than did the Boston and Washington players yesterday."

There was such a brisk wind that even the large pennants which Collins himself raised "waved wildly in the vigorous south wind and the third baseman was called upon to exercise all his muscular energy in lifting the swaying emblems." Pitchers Cy Young and Bill Dinneen assisted Collins, as did Secretary Greene and Washington's manager Kittridge. First baseman Candy LaChance helped Collins with a final tug on the rope. The band played "Rally Round the Flag, Boys."

The second pennant read, "Boston, Champion Club, American League 1903." Dixwell was unable to attend the game, as he was suffering from rheumatism.

The wind may have also presented some difficulty to the popcorn vendor, or perhaps it was a lack of spring training. It was noted that he "seemed to suffer from a stiff arm, for he had considerable trouble throwing the sweets up to the top liners in the bleachers." (Popcorn of the era tended to be sweetened, such as Cracker Jack which had been introduced in 1896). Those bleacherites were described by the *Post* as "the real fans, the ones who pay their quarters and know baseball." Admission at the time was 25 cents.

Boston shut out Washington, 5–0.

What's the matter with the Red Sox?

FIVE REASONS.

Veteran Fan Explains the Mystery.

"What is the Matter With Boston Americans?"

Other Clubs Hear the Pennant Bee Buzzing.

The members of the Boston Americans are not home to callers these days. A conspicuous cardboard sign, hung on the dressing-room door, reads: "Positively no admittance. This means you."

It was placed there early last week, and whether it was the notice to keep off the grass, or the result of the daily meetings of the boys with opponents, the absence of fan or caller of any kind was noticeable. Most of the time after the games the door was left half open, with not a soul hanging about to take a look at the players.

The question that has long perplexed Boston fans.

It's a question pondered by generations of Red Sox fans, one that even inspired a 1973 book of that title by Al Hirshberg. In the aftermath of 2004, fans breathed a little easier—and a lot easier after 2007. One assumes that fans in 1918 were feeling pretty good after winning the World Series four times in seven years. But there were long decades of suffering defeat after defeat, and the question goes back—even to before the days they were first named the Red Sox. Witness Tim Murnane's column in the May 14, 1906 *Boston Globe* which bore the subhead "What is the Matter with Boston Americans?"

Not only does the headline sound familiar but so does the first paragraph, evoking memories of the latter years of the Ted Williams era: "The members of the Boston Americans are not home to callers these days. A conspicuous cardboard sign, hung on the dressing-room door, reads: Positively no admittance. This means you." The Red Sox had a 6–17 record at the time. This, despite this fact: "The Boston Americans are positively the highest priced team in the American league." Murnane noted that the team's player payroll was $60,000, nearly $3,000 per player.

FRANCHISE FIRSTS

The first 10 games in franchise history were away games, played on the road. The first two games were April 26 and 27, 1901 against Baltimore (the team that became the New York Highlanders in 1903, later known as the New York Yankees). Boston lost both of its two games against the future Yankees, and lost its first game against Philadelphia as well, before winning for the very first time in a 10-inning game, 8–6, on April 30. Here are some of the firsts rung up before the team found its way to its home park, the Huntington Avenue Grounds. All firsts happened in the first game unless otherwise noted.

First franchise game: April 26, 1901 (Baltimore Orioles 10, Boston Americans 6)
     Starting pitchers: "Iron Man" Joe McGinnity (Baltimore) vs. Win Kellum (Boston)
     Managers: Jimmy Collins (Boston) and John McGraw (Baltimore)
First pitch by a Boston pitcher: Win Kellum
First hit off Boston pitching: leadoff batter John McGraw doubled to right field
First run scored off Boston pitching: "Turkey Mike" Donlin followed McGraw's double with a triple
     to right. 1–0, nobody out and Donlin on third.
First base on balls issued by Boston pitching: Kellum walked Jimmy Williams, the third batter up in
     the first inning.
First strikeout: Win Kellum struck out Cy Seymour in the first, the first out recorded by Boston.
First out by a defensive player: Buck Freeman recorded the putout when Jim Jackson followed Sey-
     mour's strikeout with an out at first base
First Boston batter: Tommy Dowd, who grounded out to the Baltimore pitcher, 1–3.
First Boston hit: Jimmy Collins, who doubled in the top of the fourth
First Boston run scored: Jimmy Collins
First RBI: Buck Freeman, who singled in Jimmy Collins in the fourth
First multiple-hit game: Collins and Criger both had two hits for three total bases apiece
First double: Collins, in the fourth inning
First triple: in the sixth game of the season, May 2, Chick Stahl tripled in the third inning
First home run: in the fourth game of the year, on April 30 in Philadelphia, Buck Freeman hit a two-
     run homer off Billy Milligan in the top of the ninth to send the game into extra innings.
First player to hit two home runs in the same game: Buck Freeman (June 1, 1901 in Chicago)—Free-
     man was the first to do so in the American League.
First Boston batter to work a base on balls: Buck Freeman, in the second inning
First hit by a Boston pitcher: Win Kellum
First extra-base hit by a Boston pitcher: Ted Lewis, on May 2
First Boston pinch-hitter: Larry McLean, who doubled, batting for Kellum in the top of the ninth.
First futile Boston rally: Despite scoring two runs in the eighth and three in the ninth, Boston still lost
     the game, 10–6.
First doubleplay by Boston: Parent to Freeman, in the bottom of the first
First stolen base: none in the first two games, but Dowd walked and stole second in the first inning
     on April 29, then stole third and scored on a bad throw to third—all before the second batter
     completed his at-bat.
First Boston catcher to throw out a baserunner: unclear. It
     was either April 29 or 30, 1901. Criger got an assist on
     April 29, but contemporary news accounts don't make it
     clear how he earned it. He had three assists in the April 30
     game, and two of them were throwing out runners.
     In the third inning, Criger threw out Phil Geier.
First Boston error: Jimmy Collins
First win by a Boston pitcher: Cy Young, beating the
     Athletics, 8–6, in 10 innings on April 30, 1901, despite
     giving up 12 hits and walking one.
First loss by a Boston pitcher: Win Kellum pitched a
     complete game loss, 10–6, on April 26.
First spring training game: April 5, 1901, at Charlottesville
     VA: Boston 13, University of Virginia 0.
First mid-season exhibition game: April 28, 1901 at Wee-
     hawken NJ: Boston 5, Weehawken 2.
First extra-inning game: April 30, 1901 at Philadelphia,
     an 8–6 win in 10 innings.
First postponement: May 5, 1901 due to rain.

Scorecard from the first season, 1901.

After scoring 79 runs in its first 10 games (but only recording a 5–5 mark on the road), the team played its first home game on Huntington Avenue, on May 8, 1901. Cy Young won a 12–4 victory over the Philadelphia Athletics.

A few other franchise firsts

First ejection: Buck Freeman on May 11, 1901, by umpire John Haskell. Nabbed off second base after doubling in the bottom of the second inning, Freeman "ran at the umpire and grabbed him by the two shoulders." His ejection may have spelled the difference in a 3–2 loss to Washington. Freeman was later fined $10.

First shutout: a 4–0 loss to the Washington Senators, in Boston, on May 15, 1901. It capped the first sweep by an opponent in a series in Boston, as the Americans lost four games in a row to Washington.

First shutout win: May 25, 1901 at Cleveland, a six-hit 5–0 shutout by Ted Lewis.

First sweep of a homestand of more than two games: June 7–11, 1901. Boston swept all five games from the visiting Milwaukee team. Between June 17 and 20, Boston swept five games in a row from the visiting White Sox. In fact, Boston beat Chicago every one of the 10 games that the White Sox played in Boston in 1901. And beat Milwaukee every one of the 10 games the Brewers played in Boston. Chicago won the pennant but Milwaukee came in last.

First postseason game: an exhibition game held on September 30, 1901 at the Huntington Avenue Grounds: Boston Americans 7, Chicago White Sox 5.

The first spring training

Boston's very first games against an opponent preceded the regular season. The team trained in Charlottesville, Virginia and the team never left its Charlottesville base. The first 12 members of the team showed up on April 1 to begin the first spring training of the franchise and held a light workout on the grounds of the local YMCA. Four more players arrived the following day and that constituted the full contingent, as the plan was to field 14 players on the roster. Though the term "racially diverse" would not be used at the time, there were both black and white spectators at some of the early workouts.

There were a few intrasquad "regulars vs. subs" games and a lot of bad weather. The April 18 *Boston Globe* reported that manager "Collins is disappointed with the south as a training ground." In addition, the *Globe* remarked that the team was "unfortunate in not having any strong team in this section against whom they can play."

The only two teams the club played against opponents were both shutouts, so Boston concluded its first spring training with an aggregate score of 36–0.

4/5 @ Charlottesville VA: Boston 13, University of Virginia 0
4/11 @ Charlottesville VA: Boston 23, University of Virginia 0

The first home runs in franchise play both came in the April 11, 1901, exhibition game against the University of Virginia team, in a lopsided 23–0 win. The homers were hit by Jimmy Collins and Hobe Ferris.

It was only the second game the team ever played. Tim Murnane covered spring training for the *Globe* and it's likely he who wrote the account: "Everyone but Hemphill hit the ball. Ferris led with a home run and two singles. Close behind came Parent, with two screeching doubles and a single, and Dowd with four singles. Collins lifted the leather over the palings, besides singling."

It's virtually certain that the pitcher who surrendered the first homer was Stearns, since he pitched into the fifth—by which time Boston had already scored at least 17 runs. Stearns was Virginia's first baseman, who "tried his hand at twirling, and the professionals batted him all over the lot" according to the *Washington Post*.

BALLPARKS

The team has only had two home ballparks in its century-plus history, though a handful of home games were played at Braves Field in days long gone by.

HUNTINGTON AVENUE GROUNDS

The first home of the Boston Americans (from 1908, the Red Sox) was the Huntington Avenue Grounds. Many ballparks of the era were simply known as "league park" or the "National League grounds," but the ballpark where the Red Sox first began was the Huntington Avenue American League Base Ball Grounds. It was constructed very quickly, on the former Huntington Carnival Lot, with groundbreaking on March 7, 1901. "Hi Hi" Dixwell turned the first shovelful of dirt. The first home game for Boston was played on May 8, just two months later. Dixwell threw out the first pitch.

Boston already had a major league team—the National League's Boston Beaneaters. The competition between the Americans and the Nationals was accentuated by the proximity of the two parks. It was approximately 600 feet as the crow flies from home plate at the South End Grounds to home plate of the Huntington Avenue Grounds. It was even closer between the outside perimeters of the two parks. In between lay the tracks of the New York, New Haven and Hartford Railroad and a couple of repair sheds used to service the trains.

When the Red Sox later moved to Fenway Park in 1912, they moved less than half a mile away from the Huntington Avenue Grounds, effectively just across the Muddy River and the Fens.

The architect of the American League, Ban Johnson, had a willing financier in a Cleveland magnate named Charles Somers, who not only provided initial funding for the Cleveland Indians but the Boston Americans as well. Somers was active in shipping on the Great Lakes, in coal, and in lumber. Frederick Lieb writes that Somers also advanced $10,000 to Charles Comiskey to help him finance the Chicago White Sox and "was Connie Mack's original backer" in the Philadelphia Athletics. So Somers had his financial fingers in *four* of the eight original American League clubs. Connie Mack, owner of the Athletics, was involved with the Boston Americans, too; he headed the small group selected to find a suitable site for the AL's Boston franchise. They visited possible locations in Cambridge, Charlestown, and Boston, but finally settled on a site not far from the National League park, the South End Grounds.

The site was owned by Durand Associates and leased to the Boston Elevated Railway Company. Mack's committee (which comprised Hugh Duffy and Tommy McCarthy) asked John Dooley to speak with his partner in the J. R. Prendergast Company, a cotton brokerage. Daniel Prendergast was also a director of Boston Elevated Railway, and Dooley recalls an old newspaperman named Peter Kelley coming to his office on behalf of team owner Somers to ask that Prendergast help convince the railway company to accept a ballpark on the site. Dooley says he prevailed upon Prendergast to have the Elevated accept the offer of $5,000 for the rights to use the land. It was Connie Mack who signed the lease on the Huntington Avenue land.

John Dooley was involved in many Boston baseball booster organizations, from the Royal Rooters to the Winter League to the Half Century Club and, finally, the Bosox Club. He was father to loyal and longtime devoted Red Sox fan Lib Dooley. More about the Dooleys appears elsewhere in this book.

To say the site was unimproved was an understatement. It was, in the words of Ed Walton, "no more than an expansive wasteland made up of heavily weeded bumps and lumps." It had been used as a circus lot—even the temporary home to Buffalo Bill's traveling Wild West Circus—when a show would come to town. There was a fairly large pond on the property that children would splash into during summer months from a number of chutes they would slide down, as a water slide. In the winter, of course, people could ice skate there, but this was no high society skating pond. The area was largely bounded by rail yards, a huge Boston Storage Warehouse behind the length of the left-field bleachers, some stables, breweries, and a pickle factory. The United Drug Company was situated near enough to the park that one could often smell the chemicals at work. One thing there was not, was a baked bean cannery in the vicinity. [See the story of Baseball and Baked Beans in Boston elsewhere in this volume.] Oddly enough, though, the opera house was across the street.

The park had a very large footprint. It seated around 9,000 fans at first; more seating was added in later years. On the busiest days, several thousand more simply watched from the field itself, standing behind ropes, necessitating a change in ground rules for the day. Typically, a fair ball hit into the crowd was ruled a double, but the rules did vary some from day to day. It was 350 feet to the left field corner, 440 feet in left-center field, and some 530 feet to straightaway center. Right field was close, though, just 280 feet down the line. An expansion in 1908 pushed the right-field fence out to 320 feet, but took center field out to a staggering 635 feet. After terming it "the most mis-shapen of all the big league ballparks," Michael Gershman further emphasized the unusual center field as "the most challenging in major league history, since it featured hip-high weeds and was dotted with slippery patches of sand left over from the circus. In addition to being vast, center field sloped uphill and was made even more treacherous by the presence of a sizable tool shed in deep center." The shed was in play, though by the time any ball might have traveled that far, the batter would surely have himself an inside-the-park home run. [Gershman, *Diamonds*, p. 70]

A statue of Cy Young is positioned today on the Northeastern University campus on the very spot understood to be where the pitcher's rubber had been, facing toward home plate some 60 feet, six inches away.

The field was indeed a rough one, and Philip Lowry's *Green Cathedrals* also noted the "large patches of sand in the outfield where grass would not grow." The facility itself was striking, "built with expanded metal and roughcast cement, with a light grey tone. The roof rested on columns 28 feet in the air, hipped on all four sides," in the words of Alan E. Foulds, who quoted the *Boston Globe* as saying the structure was "covered with granite felting, toned to a soft crimson." The interior was all of pine. There were three sections of grandstands arranged in a semi-circle, each seating nearly 800 people, and large bleachers at each end. A brand new facility, the park lured patrons away from the less-attractive South End Grounds.

There were limitations, though. Gershman quotes an Associated Press article which said the "wooden seats were rickety, soot from trains in neighboring yards filled the area, and the saloon next door was a beacon for bored players—during the games."

It worked, though, and from the very first day, fans flocked to the Huntington Avenue Grounds rather than its older neighbor, the South End Grounds. It didn't hurt that the American League franchise priced its tickets at half-price (25 cents instead of 50 cents), and that Jimmy Collins and several of the National League stars had been lured to the new league.

Huntington Avenue Grounds—firsts before the home crowd

First home game: May 8, 1901 (Boston Americans 12, Philadelphia Athletics 4)
All firsts cited here happened in the May 8 game, unless otherwise noted.

Starting pitchers: Cy Young (Boston) and Bill Bernhard (Philadelphia); Cy Young got the first win.

Managers: Jimmy Collins (Boston) and Connie Mack (Philadelphia)

First pitch: Cy Young

First out recorded: Athletics leadoff batter Jack Hayden, who grounded out to third base, Collins to Freeman.

First strikeout: Cy Young struck out the second batter in the inning, Phil Geier.

First hit: Dave Fultz (a two-out single) off Cy Young in the first inning.

First Boston batter: "Buttermilk" Tommy Dowd

First Boston hit: Tommy Dowd, a first-inning leadoff single to left field

First Boston bunt: Charlie Hemphill, to sacrifice Dowd to second. Hemphill reached safely on a Philadelphia error, one of nine Athletics errors in the game.

First run scored: Tommy Dowd, in the bottom of the first

First RBI: Jimmy Collins, who drove in Dowd with a single

First home run: Buck Freeman, also in the bottom of the first inning, an inside-the-park homer that got by Geier in center. Freeman tripled and singled later in the game.

First triple: Charlie Hemphill in the fourth inning, his first of two triples on the day

First Boston double: Jimmy Collins smacked a double in the bottom of the first inning of the May 9 game.

First hit by a Boston pitcher: Cy Young, singling to lead off the second inning after Boston had scored four runs in the first.

First extra-base hit by a Boston pitcher: Cy Young tripled into the crowd in the fifth.

First doubleplay by Boston: Parent to Ferris to Freeman (6-4-3), in the second inning

First stolen base: Charlie Hemphill (Freeman was caught stealing in the third)

First Boston catcher to throw out a baserunner: Lou Criger threw out Fultz trying to take second base in the top of the first inning.

First Boston error: Buck Freeman, third inning

First run scored off Boston pitching: an unearned run in seventh inning off Young, marring the 11–0 shutout he had going.

First ceremonial first pitch: General Arthur "Hi Hi" Dixwell

Umpire for the first home game: John E. Haskell

First base on balls issued by Boston pitching: none in the first home game, but Nig Cuppy walked one batter in the May 9 game.

First hit batsman: Doc Powers hit by Cuppy on the same date—May 9, 1901.

First wild pitch: Philadelphia pitcher Chick Fraser, also on May 9, 1901.

First crowd to go home disappointed: May 11, 1901, in the third home game for the franchise, Washington beat Boston, 3–2.

First shutout: Washington pitcher Watty Lee on May 15, 1901.

First shutout win for the home team: Cy Young on July 6, 1901, shutting out Washington, 7–0.

First grand slam: the first one hit at Huntington Avenue was hit on July 8, 1902 by Philadelphia's Harry Davis, part of a 22–9 Athletics win.

First grand slam by the Boston Americans: on July 25, 1902, Jimmy Collins hit a ball "to the clubhouse" for an inside-the-park four runs in the fourth off Jack Harper of the St. Louis Browns. The phrase appears not to refer to a particular clubhouse—the Huntington Avenue Grounds clubhouses were underneath the grandstand behind home plate—but to be a generic phrase of the day meaning a very long drive.

First balk: as best we can tell, it came from Boston's Tom Hughes on July 10, 1903.

The last game at the Huntington Avenue Grounds was an 8–1 win for Patsy Donovan's Red Sox over the Senators, pitched by Charley Hall before a small October 7, 1911 gate of 840 fans. Carl Cashion was the losing pitcher. The last batter up was Kid Elberfeld. He hit into a force out.

The last run scored (and the last RBI) came on the last home run hit in the park, an inside-the-park home run hit by Boston's Joe Riggert off Charlie Becker in the bottom of the eighth.

First ballpark vendor memorialized in print

The first vendor at a Boston American League game memorialized on a newspaper page remains anonymous. Of the May 8, 1901 opening game, the *Boston Globe* noted, "It was a regular holiday attendance and the peanut man was in high glee as he sailed his paper bags among the joyous throngs in the bleachers." Aramark vendor Rob Barry, working at Fenway since 1981, has been suspended more than once for throwing peanuts, but the flair he brings to his work is part of a long tradition. Rob's story and that of scores of the folks who work at Fenway Park is told in the book *Fenway Lives*.

Unusual Road Venues

On the road, Boston played regular season games in the usual locations for the early 20th century American League: Baltimore (1901–02), Chicago, Cleveland, Detroit, Milwaukee (1901 only), New York (from 1903), Philadelphia, St. Louis (from 1902), and Washington. There were a handful of exceptions:

Canton, Ohio

On June 15, 1902, Boston played against Cleveland at Mahaffey Park, near Canton, Ohio. Appropriately, the *Boston Globe* that morning, under "American League Games Today," listed "Boston vs. Cleveland at Canton." The day before, Cy Young threw a three-hitter, beating the White Sox, 2–1. After that game, Boston took the train to Canton. The *Globe* noted that "Cleveland has thus far found the transferring of Sunday games to outside towns a successful proceeding." The Cleveland team found it could often draw large Sunday crowds in other venues.

There was such a large crowd in Meyer's Lake, just outside the Canton city limits (an estimated 6,000 fans) that fans were allowed to stand in the small park's outfield and a ball that otherwise might have been a deep fly was ruled a ground-rule double. Boston took advantage in the top of the first inning, popping three balls into the crowd and scoring two runs. The *Globe* characterized the game as a "burlesque on baseball" as fans continually pressed in, making it more of a contest between the two pitchers. Boston's George Winter came out on top, allowing Cleveland just five hits. The final score was Boston 5, Cleveland 2.

Philip Lowry, in *Green Cathedrals*, says that the ballpark, at 1,125 feet above sea level is the scene of the highest American League game ever. Cleveland played another game there on May 10, 1903, against Detroit, and then hosted Boston again on June 21, 1903. Those were the only three AL games played at Mahaffey.

In the 1903 ballgame, Boston won again. This time, the game was specifically moved due to "rigid enforcement of the blue laws in Cleveland." Again 6,000 turned out, including hundreds from Cleveland, hoping to see Cy Young pitch. It was Tom Hughes for Boston against Ed Walker. Despite four errors and 11 Cleveland hits, Hughes won, 12–7, largely thanks to the hitting of Buck Freeman who had himself a 5-for-6 game with 10 total bases, including a triple and a home run.

Fort Wayne, Indiana

Boston played an official game on meadows once used for public hangings and known as Jailhouse Flats, in Fort Wayne, Indiana?

Yes, it's true. On Sunday, August 31, 1902 some 3,500 Fort Wayne fans turned out for what proved to be an exciting 11-inning game between the Boston and Cleveland clubs, Cy Young beating Addie Joss, 3–1. Cleveland was the "home team" but the local *Fort Wayne Daily Sentinel* indicated that the crowd favored neither team. Cleveland was, after all, 230 miles away in another state. The paper noted that "there was little to arouse local pride except the presence of 'Chick' Stahl in the Boston club." Stahl hailed from Avilla, some 20 miles north of Fort Wayne. There were other players who had appeared in Fort Wayne games in the past, such as Lou Criger ("an old Fort Wayne player") and several of the Cleveland players, too. But Stahl was seen as a "Fort Wayne boy" and was featured in local coverage. His photograph was the one which accompanied a large ad for the "regularly scheduled championship game" in the *Fort Wayne News*.

A biographical feature with Chick's photo ran in the *Fort Wayne Morning Journal-Gazette*. Stahl "began his successful career on the vacant lots of Fort Wayne. It was when, as a boy, he was getting his start playing 'pig tail,' that he got the nickname that has clung to him ever since. He first appeared as a semi-professional in 1891, when the City league was formed, composed of the Dortmunders, the Pilseners, the Kaisers, and the Salvators. The clubs were backed by the two breweries here and two outside breweries, and took the names of the brands of beer produced by their patrons." Chick Stahl played with the Pilseners, both as an outfielder and a pitcher. Stahl's parents lived at 808 East Lewis Street, and his brother Perry ran a local "house of call." Chick himself was "a man of good habits, does not drink at all, smokes moderately, and saves his money." He had purchased two pieces of investment property in town the year before.

The game was held at League Baseball Park. League Park was built on a flood plain area known as Jailhouse Flats, and "as a place for hangings, homeruns, and hobos." The hangings mostly occurred in the 1850s. The Fort Wayne facility had been one of the early venues for night baseball in 1883 when the Jenny Electric Light Company rigged up an array of 17 arc lights for a ballgame. The Fort Wayne Kekiongas of the National Association had been a major league team in 1871—the team was later sold to a Brooklyn owner and became known as the Trolley Dodgers.

The price for a ticket was 50 cents, but the grandstand was "25 cents and 50 cents extra according to location of seat. These are the regular prices of the American League." Both the bleachers and the grandstand were filled and enough fans flowed out onto the field itself that several policemen were needed to keep them from encroaching on fair territory. Fans got their money's worth. There were rooters for both teams and all the Fort Wayne papers agreed that this added to the excitement. In the words of the *Fort Wayne News*, "As the rooters were divided, the enthusiasm kept at a white heat." The Bostons batted first, since Cleveland was nominally the home team. First up was Patsy Dougherty, who flied out to left. Centerfielder Chick Stahl was up next, and the game was delayed while he was presented with a gold-headed umbrella and two floral horseshoes. Stahl singled up the middle, then stole second. He took third on another out. When he tried to score on a throw down to second base, he was out by a couple of steps. It was Stahl's only hit of the game.

The Clevelands scored once in the bottom of the first, and Boston got one in the fifth when Ferris tripled and scored on Cy Young's sacrifice fly to center. At the end of nine innings, it remained a 1–1 tie. Rain threatened, but the game went on. In the bottom of the 10th, Cleveland left fielder Jack McCarthy blew a chance to win it. He hit his second double of the game off Cy Young, but took too large a lead and Lou Criger, Boston's catcher, fired a bullet to second base and picked him off. Two batters later, Bob Wood doubled—but there were two outs and no one on base. In the top of the 11th, Freddy Parent singled, and took second on LaChance's sacrifice. Ferris hit one to second, but Lajoie bumbled the ball. Parent took third on a deep fly out off Criger's bat, and scored on Young's single—Boston's pitcher had driven in both the tying and winning runs. An insurance run scored on Dougherty's double, and Young struck out the first two batters, yielded a single, then struck out the final batter, swinging on all three pitches.

The *Journal-Gazette* said the crowd "left the ground full of enthusiasm and in a drenching rain that was good enough to hold off until the game was finished." The win, combined with two losses to St. Louis by Philadelphia left Boston just one game out of first place, behind the Athletics.

Dayton, Ohio

No, the Red Sox have never played a regularly scheduled game in Dayton, Ohio. The game scheduled for May 14, 1905 was transferred from Detroit to avoid conflict with a "race meeting." After the Tigers had beaten the Bostons, 8–1 and 3–2, on May 12 and 13, both teams left for Dayton. The two teams were to square off at Fairview Park. When the game was washed out due to rain, both teams returned to Detroit to resume the series. Bill Dinneen won the next game, 6–2.

Columbus, Ohio

On July 23, 1905, an American League team from Michigan (Detroit) played a team from Massachusetts (Boston). A seemingly normal occurrence, but what was unusual was that they played this regular season game in Columbus, Ohio. It was officially a Detroit home game. Boston won the Sunday afternoon ballgame at Neil Park by the score of 6–1, Cy Young holding the Tigers to six hits. Young hailed from Peoli, Ohio, a town about 100 miles away and he drew a good number of fans. Detroit's Frank Kitson was from Michigan. The crowd was for Boston at first, but after the score was 5–1 many switched, rooting for the underdog Detroiters. Boston's Jimmy Collins was 4-for-4, all singles, and scored two runs. Boston had 16 hits, but the damage would have been far worse had Detroit shortstop Charley O'Leary not started five doubleplays.

There were two games played in Ohio's capitol; the games were deemed home games for Detroit, but Boston won them both. The July 24 game was a 7–1 win for Bill Dinneen, who allowed but three hits. Hobe Ferris hit a home run for Boston, "far over the right field fence." The ballpark was a good one, built on the same plans as New York's American League park, and fans were hoping to see Columbus become a major league city.

Before the second game, both teams visited the Ohio State Penitentiary, home to 1,700 prisoners "including a number of swell bankers."

Despite the lopsided scores, news accounts indicate nothing by way of brushbacks in the course of the two contests, though Detroit's catcher in the first game was named Drill. The *Boston Globe* indicated that the games were "too one-sided to please the spectators, who looked for a fighting, close score game."

Back in Detroit, a Wednesday doubleheader began with a Boston win, 8–3, in the first game, but Boston was shut out, 4–0, in the second.

FENWAY PARK

Coda for the Huntington Avenue Grounds

The Red Sox began to play at recently-constructed Fenway Park in April 1912. Even though the Huntington Avenue ballpark had only been used for 11 seasons, it was already the oldest park in use in the American League—only because the Tigers played their last 23 games of 1911 on the road, last playing at Bennett Park on September 10. The Red Sox played their last game on Huntington Avenue on October 7, 1911.

Pre-Fenway

After the move to Fenway Park, Roger Abrams writes, the Huntington Avenue Grounds ball-park was demolished and the lot on which it stood reverted to occasional use for traveling cir-cuses and shows. Abrams reports that the Reverend Billy Sunday, himself a former ballplayer, "built a terra-cotta brick and steel structure on the field for his evangelical crusades of 1916 and 1917. The new building had a capacity of 18,000 and cost $45,000 to erect. More than

Ed Barrow, Billy Sunday, Babe Ruth. Tampa 1919.

one-and one-half mil-lion people attended Sunday's riveting ser-mons, almost 65,000 of whom came for-ward to declare them-selves converted."

Incidentally, there was a time that Babe Ruth, Billy Sunday, and the Red Sox were all on the same field. It came on April 4, 1919 when Sunday was holding a tent re-vival on the property adjacent to the Red

Sox spring training site at Plant Field in Tampa. Sunday was invited to throw out the first pitch. Babe Ruth, leading off Boston's second inning, hit a home run off George Smith that measured 508 feet. Ruth later signed the ball and presented it to Sunday. The Babe was not converted.

The evolution of Fenway Park

In 1912, the Red Sox moved to brand-new Fenway Park (bringing over the infield sod from the Huntington Avenue Grounds) and have played there ever since, for nearly 100 years. Fenway has been described extensively in other books such as *Fenway Saved* and need not be docu-mented in depth in these pages. The park's dimensions changed from time to time over the years, with center field at 420 feet after the 1934 renovation but as deep as 550 and maybe even 593 feet in earlier times. Until 1970, there was a flagpole in center field that was situated in the ground and was in play, about five feet in front of the center-field wall, the occasional ball rolling behind the flagpole.

The left-field wall, now familiarly known as the Green Monster, was originally made of wood, but after the 1934 renovation was concrete at the base (padded only after Fred Lynn crashed hard into it during the 1975 World Series) with a structure of tin applied over a frame-work of wooden railroad ties above that. In the 1976 renovation, a hardened plastic covering replaced the tin. Even the plastic displays dents inflicted on it by hard-hit drives. In right field, the bullpens were added after the 1939 season in hopes that slugger Ted Williams would hit more home runs to right; prior to that, pitchers warmed up on the sidelines despite Fenway having the smallest amount of foul territory of any major league ballpark. Foul territory shrank further when new ownership installed two new rows of seating that encroached onto the field before the 2002 season. The lack of foul territory—more than any other feature of Fenway—makes it a difficult park for pitchers.

Janet Marie Smith is the architect who has brought about all the changes at Fenway Park since the Henry/Werner/Lucchino era began. She's added the dugout seating, the Green Monster seats above the Wall, the right-field roof deck, extensively expanded the Red Sox clubhouse, and before the 2006 season completely removed the glassed-in 600 Club behind home plate replacing it with the new EMC Club while adding more rooftop seating to the right and left.

Despite all the renovations, Pat Daley would still recognize the old park. Who's Pat Daley? Pat Daley ran the original equipment truck at Fenway Park. He started his business in the 1800s, beginning with a horse and wagon. He began with the Boston Braves, reportedly from the day the Braves began in Boston. When the American League opened in Boston in 1901, they played at the old Huntington Avenue Grounds, on the site of the Northeastern University campus. Pat Daley transported for the Red Sox as well, as did his son Milton after him.

In the 21st century, Pat Daley & Co. still transports the team's gear (and that of the visiting teams as well) back and forth from the airport. The original Pat Daley used his wagon to take the goods to the train station. There were no airports back then; there were no airplanes back then. And there was not even a loading dock at Fenway until the 21st century rolled around. Before the delivery entrance back behind Gate B was built, trucks simply pulled up to the one door by Gate D and goods had to be off-loaded and trundled down the incline inside the gate to the commissary behind home plate and to other areas around the park. The book *Fenway Lives* provides more detail on Pat Daley & Co. See the interview with Mark Tremblay.

And regardless of the structural changes around the park, as well as a couple of generations of replacement of park drainage and watering systems, the basic footprint at Fenway remains the same—it's the same infield where Ty Cobb once played and the same outfield where Shoeless Joe Jackson once roamed as visiting players; the same mound where Babe Ruth first debuted in July 1914; the outfield home to Ted Williams and Carl Yastrzemski and so many more.

The mound, of course, had been constructed several times since Ruth's debut. The mound is composed of a full five tons of clay. The field has been done over many times; during one off-season, much of the sod was stripped from the park and delivered to Carl Yastrzemski's Lynnfield house to serve as a new yard for Yaz while Boston's ballpark put in new sod. Generations of fans revere Fenway Park and consider it a cathedral of baseball, a temple to be worshipped for itself, not only as the venue for Red Sox baseball. In the final years of John Harrington's trusteeship on behalf of the Yawkey family's estate (the JRY Trust), Harrington and associates characterized Fenway as obsolete and impossible to salvage, and launched a major campaign to replace it with an ersatz Fenway across Yawkey Way. New ownership brought in a fresh appraisal, seeing Fenway as an asset, not just a decaying old facility, and the vision of Janet Marie Smith found wonderful features and possibilities inherent in the nation's oldest major league park. The future of Fenway has been guaranteed well past its 100th anniversary in the year 2012.

Through 2007, the Red Sox have sold out 388 consecutive games at Fenway. Given the largest advance ticket sales in team history heading into the 2008 season, there is little doubt but that the team will eclipse the Jacobs Field record of 455 consecutive sellouts later in the 2008 season. The team's popularity extends to their spring trainings at City of Palms Park in Fort Myers; through 2008, the Sox have sold out 73 consecutive games dating back to March 16, 2003.

Fenway's First Games

The very first game played on Fenway's sacred ground featured Harvard University challenging the Red Sox.

The exhibition game pitted the Harvard University nine against the Boston Red Sox. This was no walkover for the Sox—and this was the 1912 edition of the Bosox, which became a world championship team. It was a 2–0 squeaker, won on the strength of two RBIs by Boston's pitcher, Casey Hageman. It was Hageman's finest hour with the Red Sox.

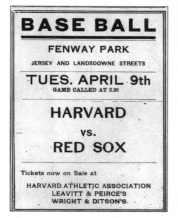

BASE BALL

FENWAY PARK

JERSEY AND LANSDOWNE STREETS

TUES. APRIL 9th

GAME CALLED AT 3.30

HARVARD

vs.

RED SOX

Tickets now on Sale at

HARVARD ATHLETIC ASSOCIATION
LEAVITT & PEIRCE'S
WRIGHT & DITSON'S

Advertisement for the first game at Fenway, from the *Harvard Crimson*.

The opening of a new ballpark is rightfully a special occasion and, despite it not being a regular season game, 4500 hardy souls braved the elements, watching in a cold "fit to test the courage of any football crowd, with a little snow on the side for good measure of discomfort." Tickets were on sale at Fenway Park itself and, for the Harvard contingent, at the Harvard Athletic Association, Leavitt & Peirce's, and at Wright and Ditson's. Hageman took the mound for Boston, squaring off against Harvard's third baseman Dana Wingate. The first batter ever to step into the box at Fenway Park took a pitch for ball one. Wingate—that first batter—struck out.

Hageman didn't bring much experience with him. He had his major league debut late the previous season and had no wins against two losses for the Sox, though with a very good 2.12 ERA in 17 innings of work. His losses were mostly bad luck. Both were complete games, and he only yielded one earned run per game—though eight runs were scored off him. He lost the first game, 4–1, and the second one, 4–2. Both were home games, at the Huntington Avenue Grounds. There were only three more games ever played at the Huntington Avenue Grounds after his second loss. Debit the defense.

He still had more experience than Harvard's starting pitcher Felton, who threw five innings before being relieved by Bartholf who pitched the final inning in what proved to be a seven-inning matchup (the game was halted after seven due to cold weather). Felton was pretty good, actually, when he got the ball over the plate. He only let up four singles, though he didn't have much control—he walked 10 Red Sox. Hageman walked three batters himself, but he only allowed one single—to second baseman Potter, the captain of the Crimson.

Harvard's student newspaper, also named the *Crimson*, noted of Felton's mound work, "Rarely does a pitcher hold his opponents to two runs when giving passes at the rate of two an inning. Felton kept the Red Sox hits well scattered and twice retired the side when the bases were full."

The Sox squad was a mixture of veterans and second-stringers. Harry Hooper, Tris Speaker, and Duffy Lewis were the outfield—as good an outfield as any team ever fielded. Not one of them had a hit, but then again, Felton was pitching around them; Speaker only had one official at-bat. Marty Krug subbed at short, so Heinie Wagner didn't have to risk his arm in the cold weather, but Larry Gardner held down the hot corner, Steve Yerkes was at second, and player-owner Jake Stahl was at first. Rookie Pinch Thomas was behind the plate.

The first hit ever made at Fenway Park was a single by Steve Yerkes in the bottom of the first inning.

Herman Nickerson, covering the game for the *Boston Journal*, recognized that "to hold the Red Sox down to a 2 to 0 score was some achievement for the Crimson nine. The boys played the game with understanding, fielding splendidly, and while they failed to hit the ball, the excuse is found in the fact that they have not faced any pitching that could be called twirling this season."

Hageman made the difference offensively as well. Two of the four Sox singles were his.

Marty Krug, born in Germany, was the rookie at shortstop. He appeared in just 20 games during the season for the Sox, then was out of major league ball for 10 years, before returning for one more season in 1922, with the Cubs. Krug, batting seventh, accepted one of Felton's free passes in the second inning. Thomas drew another walk. Felton fired to second, hoping to pick Krug off the base, but the ball skittered into center and both runners moved up. Hageman singled to score one, but neither Hooper nor Yerkes nor Speaker nor Stahl could bring in Thomas from third.

In the fifth inning, Gardner opened with a single to center. Lewis struck out and Krug walked. Thomas fouled out, but then Hageman drove in his second run of the game with a shot to center.

"Fenway Park will be a corker," commented the *Journal*. "Everyone was in praise of the new field."

In the season which followed, Hageman pitched a grand total of 1⅓ innings, despite starting in one game and appearing in another. He rang up a 27.00 ERA and that was it for his Red Sox career. 0–0. After a year off, Hageman won three and lost five in the National League, getting in 102 innings of play, but that was the end of his major league career.

One final note on Hageman: before he broke into major league ball with the Red Sox in late 1911, on September 14, 1909 he was pitching in Dayton for the visiting Grand Rapids Stags. Hageman hit Dayton second baseman Charles "Cupid" Pinkney with a pitch that led to Pinkney's death the following day.

Rev. Thomas Van Ness. Courtesy of Harvard Divinity School.

For more on other Red Sox games played against various college teams, see the appropriate section elsewhere in this book.

Fenway Firsts

It was a little tough to get regular play underway: three of the first four games scheduled at Fenway Park were postponed. The first two dates set for the park's Opening Day—April 18 and 19—were both called off due to rain, as was the game on April 22. They did manage to squeeze in a game on April 20, though, and it was a good one. Here are a number of Fenway Park firsts.

First regular season game: April 20, 1912. (Boston Red Sox 7, New York Highlanders 6—in 11 innings)
   Starting pitchers: Buck O'Brien (Boston) and Ray Caldwell (New York)
   Managers: Jake Stahl (Boston) and Harry Wolverton (New York)
First pitch: thrown by Boston pitcher Buck O'Brien
First base on balls issued by Boston pitching: Buck O'Brien to leadoff batter Guy Zinn, in the top of the first inning.
First Red Sox error: first baseman Jake Stahl, misplaying a bunt by New York's second batter.
First out recorded: Hal Chase hit a sacrifice bunt, 5–3, moving up two runners.
First hit: Roy Hartzell singled in the first, driving in Zinn
First run scored off Boston pitching: Zinn's run, on Hartzell's single.
First strikeout: Gabby Street, final batter in New York's first.
First Boston batter: Harry Hooper, who grounded back to Caldwell on the mound, out 1–3.
First Boston hit: second man up in the first inning, Steve Yerkes doubled to the incline in left field, soon known as Duffy's Cliff.
First Boston sacrifice: Harry Hooper, in the sixth inning
First Red Sox run scored: Yerkes, scoring on Speaker's double.
First Red Sox RBI: Tris Speaker doubled into the crowd, driving in Yerkes.

First home run: Hugh Bradley, on April 26,
    1912—a three-run homer over the Wall in left
    in the seventh inning off Lefty Russell. It was
    the only home run of the year for the .190
    hitter.

First triple: April 25, a first-inning triple by Tris
    Speaker

First double: Yerkes (see above)

First hit by a Boston pitcher: a ninth-inning double
    into the crowd by Charley Hall

First extra-base hit by a Boston pitcher: Charley
    Hall's double

First wild pitch by a Boston pitcher: O'Brien in the
    fourth

First balk by a Red Sox pitcher: O'Brien

First Red Sox pitcher to hit an opposing batter:
    O'Brien (Cozy Dolan)

Hugh Bradley hit the first home run at Fenway Park.

First doubleplay by Boston: third inning of April 26
    game, McInnis hit a ball off Cicotte's fingers, which became a 1-4-6-3 doubleplay

First Boston stolen base: Tris Speaker on April 23

First Boston catcher to throw out a baserunner: Les Nunamaker picked Hartzell off second base in
    the first inning.

First bases loaded walk earned by a Red Sox batter: Olaf Henriksen

First win for a Red Sox pitcher: Charley Hall

First shutout by a Red Sox pitcher at Fenway Park: Smoky Joe Wood, on May 20, 1912

First ceremonial first pitch: Mayor John F. Fitzgerald

Umpires for the first home game: Tom Connolly and Eugene Hart. Connolly also umpired the first
    game at the Huntington Avenue Grounds.

First Sunday home game: July 3, 1932. Yankees win, 13–2.

First night game: June 13, 1947. Red Sox 5, White Sox 3.

First ceremonial pitch: Mayor John F. Fitzgerald, April 20, 1912.

One could also make the argument that another Fenway first, at least in Boston, was its
very name. Owner John I. Taylor's family also had an interest in the Fenway Realty Company
and was not unhappy at the prospect of developing that part of town. As Alan Foulds points
out in *Boston's Ballparks and Arenas*, the park's name could reflect an early form of corporate
naming rights.

First grand slam: here's something different. The first major league grand slam hit by a
Boston ballplayer at Fenway Park was an inside-the-park home run hit by Rabbit Maranville
on September 26, 1914. Can't find Maranville in the list of all the players who batted for the
Red Sox? That's right. He played for the Boston Braves, and was at Fenway when he hit the
drive off Hippo Vaughn of the Chicago Cubs during one of the days the Braves used Fenway
Park as their home park.

When the park was first built, with its now-famous and very tall left-field wall, some
said no one would ever hit a ball over the wall. Hugh Bradley did so in Fenway's fifth home
game. The first grand slam hit at Fenway by a member of the Red Sox took nearly forever, it
seemed—over a decade.

On May 30, 1924, Red Sox right fielder Ike Boone hit the second home run of his career. It
came in the bottom of the fourth of the first game of the day. The score was tied 1–1 after 3½,
but before the inning was over, Boston scored seven times. Boone struck the biggest blow off
Washington starter John Martina, high up into Fenway's right-field bleachers for the inning's

final four runs. The two teams split the Memorial Day doubleheader, Boston winning 10–5 but then losing, 9–4.

Three seasons earlier, on September 3, 1921, Tillie Walker of the Athletics hit the first grand slam by a Red Sox opponent. He was a Red Sox alumnus; Walker had been with the 1916 and 1917 Red Sox. With the Athletics down 9–5 in the top of the seventh, Walker faced reliever Allen Russell with (obviously) the bases loaded and pounded a prodigious blast that cleared the left-center-field fence by maybe 20 feet. The Red Sox ultimately won the game, 11–10, largely due to Mike Menosky's high fly ball to right field that, when it came down, landed on the dirt three yards behind Whitey Witt and went for a double, tying the score and placing the winning run on third with one out.

Hosting more regular season games than any other ballpark

It almost goes without saying that the oldest park in baseball would have hosted the most regular season ballgames played within its confines. To quantify it, though, the top venues are as follows (through the 2007 season):

Fenway Park 7537   Comiskey Park (I) 6247
Wrigley Field 7386   Shibe Park 6055
Sportsman's Park (III) 7022 Forbes Field 4760
Tiger Stadium 6879   Crosley Field 4544
Yankee Stadium 6500   Polo Grounds (V) 4490

Fenway eclipsed the old total of 7,022 games played at Sportsman's Park in St. Louis on July 31, 2001 when the Anaheim Angels opened a three-game visit to the Fens. The Angels took all three games, beating Boston 4–3 in the tie-breaking game. Starting for the Red Sox was Rolando Arrojo, who left the game after seven innings, tied 2–2. Reliever Rich Garces gave up a two-run homer to Troy Glaus, and the Red Sox only responded with one.

After the 2008 season, the only two parks on the list that will remain active venues are Fenway and Wrigley. They've got the corner on tradition.

The first World Series played at Fenway Park

The 1914 World Series was the first one played at Fenway Park. 1914 saw Philadelphia's American League team play Boston's National League team, in Boston's American League ballpark. And the Braves played at Fenway the first half of 1915 as well (from April 14 through July 26), while their new park—Braves Field—was under construction. Since the new facility was even larger than Fenway, the 1915 World Series saw Boston's American League team play Philadelphia's National League team in Boston's National League ballpark. The same was true for 1916. The first time the Red Sox played in a World Series at Fenway was not until 1918.

As it happens, the Braves played a handful of other games at Fenway Park, too—April 19 and May 30 of 1913, August 1 and 8 and September 7 and 29 of 1914, and April 17 and 28, 1918.

NOT YOUR USUAL VENUES

After moving to Fenway Park, the Red Sox played a number of games at ballparks other than regular AL fields. When Sunday baseball was first permitted in Boston, a restriction on playing Sundays within 1,000 feet of a house of worship enabled play at Braves Field but not at Fenway. Until the prohibition was removed (see information on Sunday baseball elsewhere in this book), the Red Sox played Sunday home games at Braves Field from April 28, 1929 through May 29, 1932.

Over the stretch of 50 games played in the Braves ballpark, the Red Sox won 17, lost 31, and tied two games. The 17–31 reflected a winning percentage of .354, which certainly doesn't indicate any home field advantage. Of course, part of the point was that it wasn't their home field. It's also worth keeping in mind that the Red Sox weren't very good in any park during this era. Their overall winning percentages for the four years in question were: .377, .338, .408, and .279.

It wasn't the first time the Sox had played at Braves Field. They played both the 1915 and 1916 World Series at the larger facility. To prepare for the Series and their temporary "home field", they played the final doubleheader of the season on October 3, 1916 at Braves Field as well. This "gave them the chance to work under the conditions of light that they will obtain Saturday at Braves Field" wrote Tim Murnane in the *Globe*. (In 1915, their last seven games were on the road—but they had both September 29 and 30 as off-days so they took in Braves games both days at Braves Field.)

After the May 8, 1926 fire that destroyed a good part of Fenway's third base seats, the Red Sox played a number of games at the Braves' park, too.

The only other games the Red Sox played that were not at a usual American League park were two—at County Stadium in Milwaukee, both against the "home team" Chicago White Sox. The games were on August 8, 1968 and August 13, 1969.

Ray Culp pitched a four-hit complete game shutout in the 1968 game, winning 1–0 on the strength of four straight singles in the top of the second (Jerry Adair, Russ Nixon, Culp himself, and Mike Andrews).

In the game the following year (these two games were a marketing move orchestrated by Major League Baseball), Culp was the starting pitcher for Boston once more, but this time he gave up five runs in the first six innings while the Red Sox only scored three runs in the whole game.

And "the Big Egg" (Tokyo Dome) where the 2008 Opening Series was held was not at all your usual venue.

The Red Sox have played in many, many other locations when one counts exhibition games. See the separate section in this book on exhibition contests.

Fires at Fenway

The May 8, 1926 fire was perhaps a suspicious one in that the very day before there had been three other fires at Fenway, each one doused by fans with buckets of water. After the destruction of the third base bleachers on May 8, financially-struggling owner Bob Quinn elected to keep the insurance money and not replace the seats.

Just a few weeks later, on May 25, the next day's *New York Times* reported, "The first game was halted while Umpire Moriarty, Lou Gehrig and others struggled with a small fire in front of a grand stand box. Moriarty attacked the flames with his mask and Gehrig with a bat, and finally a grounds keeper rushed in with a hose."

On January 5, 1934 during an extensive renovation of Fenway Park, a spark from a cement mixing machine ignited a fire which swept through the new center field bleachers, then leapt across the street and consumed at least two neighboring buildings. A huge 110-foot boom and derrick collapsed and crashed onto the bleachers during the blaze. Damage was estimated at $250,000—big money during the Depression.

March 25, 1962: A major fire destroyed the Fenway Park press room. Did anyone check out The Splendid Splinter's alibi?

On August 4, 1999 there was a delay in admitting patrons to the park after a late morning blaze ignited by a worker's blowtorch did an estimated $25,000 in damage to a Fenway Park restroom.

Another blowtorch set off another fire on November 18, 2007 during renovations. A welder's torch sparked a fire when sparks thrown off by cutting metal ignited "a pile of construction debris on the roof of the grandstand level above the third base line." There was no dollar loss, said a Boston Fire Department spokesman after reporting that the fire was quickly extinguished.

Though not at Fenway itself, a small October 4, 1912 fire broke out in John I. Taylor's office on Washington Street.

There was a non-fire at the Hunington Avenue Grounds. On May 15, 1906 after Boston scored four runs to tie the game in the bottom of the fourth, an enthusiastic fan pulled the fire alarm. Within a minute, several pieces of fire-fighting apparatus appeared on the scene of the false alarm.

On July 7, back in 1917 during a road game in Cleveland there was a flurry of midgame excitement as somehow a fire started inside the rolled tarpaulin near the stands; the first aid crew doused it with a bucket of water from the ice tank.

The very first night game

The first night game played at Boston's AL ballpark was not the June 13, 1947 game at Fenway Park. It was the September 2, 1907 game at the Huntington Avenue Grounds. Team president John I. Taylor arranged a game between the Cherokee Indian team and the Dorchesters. The notice in the *Globe* advised, "The Cherokees bring their own lighting arrangements…lights aggregating more than 50,000 candle power are placed about the field."

Fenway's first night game

Though the team had played occasional night games on the road going back into the late 1930s, the evening of June 13, 1947 was the first night game the Red Sox played at home, and it was sold out: 34,510 fans in attendance. Boo Ferriss started and gave up 11 hits in 5⅓ innings, with a walk and a wild pitch, too. Bob Klinger relieved, and held the White Sox to two hits in 3⅔ innings. The Red Sox only managed eight singles off Frank Papish, but three of them came in the fifth inning. Combined with two walks and a Chicago error, the Sox scored five times, enough to give them a 5–3 victory.

The latest times for a Red Sox game—
home and away

These days there's an American League curfew which says that no inning shall start after 1 a.m. That wasn't always the case.

Phil Lowry reports that the "latest documented Red Sox game away from Boston" was in 1967. It ran until 1:57 a.m., the second game of a doubleheader against the Yankees on August 29, 1967. Boston won the first game, 2–1, with Jim Lonborg striking out 11 and giving up just three hits. Boston only had one more hit but, importantly also had one more run. That game only lasted 2:10—an efficient affair. Game two of the twin bill, however, saw the two teams tied and the game run to 20 innings! The game lasted 6:09, and only because the Yankees finally scored on a Horace Clarke single. The game account and box score in the *Boston Globe* are almost impossible to decipher; someone must have been very tired putting together this story, replete as it is with misspellings and (in the boxscore) misalignments of figures. That would be understandable. The Impossible Dream was in full swing; the Sox took over first place in the league with the win in game one, and even after dropping the second game were .002 points ahead of Minnesota. (The Sox and Yanks got some sleep, then played 11 innings later that afternoon—completing 40 innings of play in a 24-hour stretch.)

The latest a game ever ran at Fenway Park was, as best as we can determine, August 24, 1977. It wasn't that long a game. It was, though, the second game of a doubleheader. Game one lasted 2:26 and the Texas Rangers beat Boston, 3–0. Game two was even shorter, just 2:01. Texas won that one, too, 6–3. The reason for the 2:26 a.m. end time was a two hour, 22-minute rain delay in the top of the sixth inning during the first game. It was, Leigh Montville wrote, "the longest night." It started at 6:00 p.m. After warning patrons earlier on that the last train from Kenmore Square was at 12:45, when 12:46 rolled around, the electronic message board let everyone know that the MBTA would resume service at 5:00. "YOU JUST MISSED THE LAST TRAIN. THE 1ST TRAIN LEAVES AT 5AM." Some may have still been shaking off the double defeat, and taken that first train. Montville noted that there were only a few thousand fans remaining by game's end, but good nature prevailed. "There was even a hope, expressed often, that the second game would move into extra innings. If it's going to be bad, people said, then let's see if we can make it the worst anyone has ever seen."

In a 2:45 a.m. interview, Bernie Carbo told Montville that he'd just gotten home at 4:30 the previous morning, with the team coming in from Minnesota. He went to bed about 5:00. He was expecting to pull in around 4:00, after he left Fenway. The rain delay had run from 7:30 to 9:55. It wasn't a night that left Red Sox fans feeling rosy. "Highlights?" asked fan Len Cutler. "Sure. Watching those bananas put that tarp on the field, that was a highlight. The rain was a highlight. Watching those bananas take the tarp off the field, that was a highlight. Finding the car—that will be a highlight."

THE BALLPLAYERS

So, who are these Red Sox? Let's start with a look at the debut dates of every player who served—however briefly—with the Red Sox from the inaugural 1901 season through the Opening Series in Japan 2008. Only twice did the Sox start the season before April, in 2003 and in 2008. When David Aardsma came in to pitch the bottom of the fifth inning in the second game of the 2008 season, he simultaneously leapt to the front of the list for Sox debut dates and beat out Don Aase for first place alphabetically. Several times the Red Sox have played regular season games into October. Of all the dates between March 26 and October 7, there is only one date (May 19) on which the Red Sox have never introduced a new player into a ballgame. GM Theo Epstein has been so advised. [See note on last page of book.]

March 26
2008: David Aardsma, Sean Casey

March 31
2003: Chad Fox, Jeremy Giambi, Ramiro Mendoza, Kevin Millar, Bill Mueller, Todd Walker

April 1
1996: Wil Cordero, Mike Stanley
1998: Darren Lewis, Jim Leyritz, Pedro Martinez, Donnie Sadler
2002: Tony Clark, Johnny Damon, Rickey Henderson, Darren Oliver, Rey Sanchez.
2003: Damian Jackson, Brandon Lyon, David Ortiz, Mike Timlin, Steve Woodard

April 2
1984: Mike Easler
1997: Butch Henry, Shane Mack
1998: Damon Buford, Midre Cummings
2001: Craig Grebeck, Shea Hillenbrand, Manny Ramirez, Chris Stynes
2007: Brendan Donnelly, J. D. Drew, Julio Lugo, Hideki Okajima, Joel Pineiro, J. C. Romero

April 3
1989: Nick Esasky, Rob Murphy
1996: Tom Gordon, Jamie Moyer, Brad Pennington
1997: Chris Hammond

2005: John Halama, Matt Mantei, Blaine Neal,
Edgar Renteria, David Wells

2006: Coco Crisp, Alex Gonzalez, Mark Loretta,
Mike Lowell, J. T. Snow

April 4

1988: Brady Anderson, Lee Smith

1994: Damon Berryhill, Otis Nixon, Dave Valle

1996: Alex Delgado, John Doherty, Heathcliff
Slocumb

2000: Carl Everett, Gary Gaetti

2001: Hideo Nomo

2004: Mark Bellhorn, Cesar Crespo, Pokey Reese

2006: Josh Bard, Alex Cora, Wily Mo Peña, David
Riske

April 5

1974: Bernie Carbo, Diego Segui

1983: Tony Armas, John Henry Johnson

1993: Ivan Calderon, Andre Dawson, Scott
Fletcher, Jeff Russell

1996: Esteban Beltre, Milt Cuyler, Kevin Mitchell

1997: Steve Avery

1999: Jose Offerman

2000: Manny Alexander

2001: Frank Castillo

2005: Matt Clement

2006: Josh Beckett

2007: Daisuke Matsuzaka

April 6

1971: Luis Aparicio, Doug Griffin, Duane
Josephson

1973: Orlando Cepeda

1974: Reggie Cleveland, Terry Hughes, Dick
McAuliffe

1988: Dennis Lamp

1994: Lee Tinsley, Ricky Trlicek

1997: John Wasdin

2000: Jeff Fassero

2004: Keith Foulke, Curt Schilling

April 7

1970: Gary Peters

1977: Bill Campbell

1978: Jerry Remy, Mike Torrez

1979: Larry Wolfe

1986: Don Baylor, Joe Sambito, Sammy Stewart

1988: Steve Ellsworth, Mike Smithson, John
Trautwein

1994: Rich Rowland

1999: Mark Guthrie

2002: Carlos Baerga

2004: Bobby Jones

April 8

1971: Ken Tatum

1973: Mario Guerrero

1978: Tom Burgmeier

1979: Gary Allenson, Jim Dwyer, Mike O'Berry,
Chuck Rainey

1991: Jack Clark

1993: Scott Bankhead, Bob Melvin

April 9

1963: Jack Lamabe, Roman Mejias, Dick Stuart

1970: Mike Derrick, Ed Phillips

1975: Bob Heise

1976: Fergie Jenkins

1983: Doug Bird

1986: Ed Romero

1987: Danny Sheaffer

1989: John Dopson, Danny Heep

1990: Tony Peña, Billy Jo Robidoux

1991: Tony Fossas

1992: Frank Viola

1993: Jeff Richardson, Ernest Riles

1998: Brian Daubach, Mark Portugal

2004: Mark Malaska

2005: Ramon Vazquez

April 10

1913: Rube Foster

1928: Doug Taitt, Ken Williams

1962: Eddie Bressoud, Dave Philley, Dick Radatz

1968: Dick Ellsworth, Joe Lahoud

1976: Tom House

1978: Allen Ripley

1980: Tony Perez, Dave Rader

1981: Carney Lansford, Joe Rudi

1982: Wade Boggs

1991: Matt Young

1998: Mark Lemke

April 11

1907: Al Shaw, Denny Sullivan

1928: Charlie Berry, Ed Morris

1961: Chuck Schilling, Carl Yastrzemski

1969: Billy Conigliaro, Dick Schofield

1974: Dick Drago

1991: Danny Darwin

1992: Peter Hoy, Herm Winningham

1997: Jim Corsi

1999: Kip Gross, Pat Rapp

2000: Rob Stanifer

April 12

1909: Babe Danzig, Jack Ryan

1911: Rip Williams

1913: Dutch Leonard
1916: Tillie Walker
1922: George Burns, Joe Dugan, Joe Harris,
    Frank O'Rourke, Jack Quinn, Elmer Smith
1927: Fred Hofmann, Pee-Wee Wanninger
1955: Eddie Joost
1959: Jim Busby, Gary Geiger
1965: Lenny Green
1966: Dan Osinski, George Smith, George
    Thomas
1969: Guido Grillo, George Scott
1970: Tom Matchick
1980: Glenn Hoffman, Bruce Hurst
1981: Mark Clear, Frank Tanana
1990: Dana Kiecker
1992: John Flaherty
2006: Dustan Mohr

April 13
1909: Charlie Chech
1916: Sam Agnew
1921: Shano Collins, Nemo Leibold, Muddy Ruel
1926: Fred Bratschi, Alex Gaston, Fred Haney,
    Sam Langford, Del Lundgren, Emmett Mc-
    Cann, Rudy Sommers, Tony Welzer, Hal
    Wiltse
1928: Merle Settlemire
1933: Bob Fothergill, Bernie Friberg, Johnny
    Hodapp, Greg Mulleavy, Bob Seeds, Merv
    Shea
1954: Harry Agganis, Tom Herrin, Jackie Jensen
1963: Dave Morehead
1966: Joe Christopher, Joe Foy, Pete Magrini, Ken
    Sanders
1974: Rick Wise
1977: Dave Coleman
1983: Jeff Newman
1986: Wes Gardner

April 14
1905: Jesse Burkett
1908: Doc Gessler, Frank LaPorte, Jim McHale,
    Jack Thoney
1914: Ed Kelly, Everett Scott
1921: Curt Fullerton
1922: Alex Ferguson
1925: Turkey Gross, Rudy Kallio, Doc Prothro,
    Billy Rogell
1928: Cliff Garrison
1930: Otto Miller, Tom Oliver, George Smith, Bill
    Sweeney
1931: Pat Creeden, Ollie Marquardt, Wilcy
    Moore, Tom Winsett

1933: Johnny Gooch
1936: Doc Cramer, Jimmie Foxx, Heinie Manush,
    Eric McNair
1942: Bill Conroy, Johnny Pesky
1958: Pete Runnels
1963: Jerry Stephenson
1967: Russ Gibson, Billy Rohr
1974: Juan Marichal
1985: Bruce Kison, Mike Trujillo
2006: Julian Tavarez

April 15
1904: Bob Unglaub
1915: Carl Mays, Bill Rodgers
1918: Stuffy McInnis, Dave Shean, Amos Strunk
1920: Eddie Foster, Tim Hendryx, Mike Menosky
1921: Pinky Pittinger, Del Pratt
1924: Dud Lee, Steve O'Neill, Bobby Veach, Bill
    Wambsganss
1927: Grover Hartley
1930: Frank Mulroney
1931: Jim Brillheart, Johnny Lucas, Al Van Camp
1941: Paul Campbell, Pete Fox, Frankie Pytlak
1947: Harry Dorish, Sam Mele
1952: Don Lenhardt, Ted Lepcio, Gus Niarhos,
    Faye Throneberry
1955: George Susce
1961: Billy Harrell
1962: Bob Tillman
1966: Eddie Kasko
1969: Ray Jarvis, Syd O'Brien
1972: Danny Cater, Tommy Harper, Marty Pattin
1978: Jim Wright
1985: Steve Lyons
2004: Phil Seibel

April 16
1906: Charlie Graham
1909: Harry Hooper
1910: Duffy Lewis, Hap Myers
1921: Hank Thormahlen
1925: Roy Carlyle, Tex Vache
1926: Topper Rigney
1928: Cliff Garrison
1932: John Michaels, Johnny Reder, Bob Weiland
1935: Joe Cronin, Babe Dahlgren
1940: Dom DiMaggio
1941: Tex Hughson, Oscar Judd
1946: Ernie Andres, Rudy York
1952: Dick Gernert, Randy Gumpert, Len Okrie,
    Gene Stephens, Ken Wood
1953: Hal Brown, Ken Holcombe, Tom Umphlett
1964: Tony Conigliaro

1966: Dick Stigman
1967: Bill Landis
1968: Ray Culp
1975: Kim Andrew
1977: Bob Stanley
1988: Rick Cerone
1996: Jim Tatum
1999: Creighton Gubanich
2000: Andy Sheets
2003: Kevin Tolar

April 17
1908: Amby McConnell, Case Patten
1909: Tubby Spencer, Harry Wolter
1920: Mickey Devine, Hack Eibel
1927: Red Rollings
1933: Hank Johnson
1934: Max Bishop, Carl Reynolds, Moose Solters
1935: Bing Miller
1945: Otey Clark, Ben Steiner, Fred Walters
1951: Lou Boudreau, Bill Wight
1952: Ike Delock, Bill Henry
1955: Owen Friend, Billy Klaus
1956: Don Buddin, Mickey Vernon
1963: Felix Mantilla, Dick Williams
1964: Dalton Jones
1966: Bob Sadowski
1972: Bob Burda, Lew Krausse
1978: Jack Brohamer
1980: Skip Lockwood
1990: Jeff Reardon

April 18
1904: Jesse Tannehill
1906: Bob Peterson
1908: Gavvy Cravath
1923: Al DeVormer, Norm McMillan, Howie Shanks, Camp Skinner
1925: John Bischoff
1928: Pat Simmons
1929: Bill Barrett, Elliott Bigelow, Milt Gaston, Bill Narleski, Bobby Reeves, Hal Rhyne, Russ Scarritt, Jerry Standaert
1931: Urbane Pickering
1938: Jim Bagby, Red Nonnenkamp, Joe Vosmik
1944: Bob Johnson
1945: Jim Wilson
1950: Al Papai, Charley Schanz
1954: Tom Brewer, Tex Clevenger, Mickey Owen
1956: Bob Porterfield
1960: Ron Jackson, Tom Sturdivant, Al Worthington
1964: Bill Spanswick

1968: Gene Oliver
1970: Don Pavletich
1974: Lance Clemmons
1976: Rick Jones
1978: Frank Duffy
1979: Steve Renko
2004: Earl Snyder

April 19
1902: Patsy Dougherty, Charlie Hickman, Candy LaChance, John Warner
1904: Tom Doran
1923: George Murray, Lefty O'Doul
1928: Paul Hinson
1929: Ed Durham
1931: Walter Murphy
1934: Bill Cissell, Gordie Hinkle, Ed Morgan, Rube Walberg
1938: Charlie Wagner
1940: Herb Hash
1945: Billy Holm, Nick Polly
1947: Billy Goodman, Strick Shofner
1948: Johnny Ostrowski, Vern Stephens
1949: Walt Dropo, Tommy O'Brien
1950: Gordie Mueller
1953: Bill Werle
1960: Bobby Thomson
1964: Pete Charton, Ed Connolly
1966: Bucky Brandon, Jose Santiago
1971: Phil Gagliano
1974: Bob Didier
1996: Bill Selby
2003: Jason Shiell

April 20
1903: Duke Farrell, Jake Stahl, George Stone
1910: Louis Leroy
1914: Rankin Johnson
1920: Benn Karr
1929: Bill Bayne
1937: Bobby Doerr, Pinky Higgins, Buster Mills
1939: Ted Williams
1941: Skeeter Newsome, Mike Ryba
1945: Loyd Christopher, Johnny Tobin
1947: Frankie Hayes, Mel Parnell
1951: Ray Scarborough
1953: Billy Consolo, Bill Kennedy
1958: Al Schroll
1960: Ed Sadowski
2006: Willie Harris

April 21
1905: Art McGovern

1915: Ray Haley, Mike McNally
1916: Sam Jones
1924: Danny Clark
1934: Fritz Ostermueller
1941: Joe Dobson
1946: Mel Deutsch, Rip Russell
1951: Mike Guerra
1953: Marv Grissom
1956: Marty Keough, Dave Sisler
1958: Bill Renna
1959: Herb Moford
1960: Dave Hillman
1969: Mike Nagy
1985: Dave Sax
1998: Brian Shouse
1999: Tim Harikkala
2002: John Burkett, Ray Webster

April 22
1914: Fritz Coumbe, Squanto Wilson
1915: Ralph Comstock
1918: Wally Schang, Fred Thomas
1920: Harry Harper, Hob Hiller
1931: Gene Rye
1939: Woody Rich
1943: Garrison Ford, Eddie Lake, Johnny Lazor
1944: Joe Bowman
1946: Eddie Pellagrini
1956: Johnny Schmitz
1958: Bob Schmitz, Bob Smith
1960: Lou Clinton
1962: Hal Kolstad
1996: Alex Cole
2006: Jermaine Van Buren

April 23
1902: Bill Dinneen
1903: Jack O'Brien
1918: Joe Bush, Ossie Vitt
1922: Rip Collins
1923: Howard Ehmke
1924: Oscar Fuhr, Denny Williams
1925: Joe Lucey
1936: Jim Henry
1939: Elden Auker, Denny Galehouse
1940: Mickey Harris
1943: Lou Lucier, Tom McBride, Roy Partee
1950: Ken Keltner, Tom Wright
1950: Bob Scherbarth
1965: Jim Lonborg
1969: Joe Azcue, Sonny Siebert
1978: Fred Kendall
2004: Lenny DiNardo

April 24
1912: Pinch Thomas
1924: Joe Connolly
1933: Mike Meola
1937: Dom Dallessandro, Bob Daughters
1938: Bill Humphrey, Dick Midkiff
1939: Jake Wade, Monte Weaver
1941: Odell Hale
1943: Andy Karl, Dee Miles
1948: Mickey McDermott
1952: Hal Bevan
1953: Jack Merson
1957: Russ Meyer
1996: Rich Garces

April 25
1902: Bert Husting
1905: Myron Grimshaw
1910: Hugh Bradley
1923: Val Picinich
1924: Phil Todt
1937: Archie McKain
1938: Lee Rogers
1939: Tom Carey
1941: Dick Newsome
1942: Mace Brown
1947: Al Widmar
1948: Windy McCall
1961: Gene Conley
1969: Vicente Romo

April 26
1901: Jimmy Collins, Lou Criger, Tommy Dowd, Hobe Ferris, Buck Freeman, Charlie Hemphill, Larry McLean, Freddy Parent, Chick Stahl, Win Kellum
1902: Pep Deininger
1907: Tex Pruiett
1911: Judge Nagle
1912: Hugh Bedient, Hick Cady
1924: Homer Ezzell
1935: Moe Berg
1942: Ken Chase
1945: Bob Garbark
1946: Eddie McGah
1947: Tommy Fine, Johnny Murphy
1995: Luis Alicea, Jose Canseco, Mike Macfarlane, Alejandro Peña, Jeff Pierce, Frank Rodriguez, Mark Whiten

April 27
1901: Fred Mitchell, Cy Young
1914: Matt Zieser

1919: Roxy Walters
1927: Elmer Eggert
1930: Earl Webb
1943: Al Simmons
1996: Phil Clark

April 28
1911: Les Nunamaker
1944: Clem Hausmann
1981: Dave Schmidt
1990: Daryl Irvine
1995: Rheal Cormier, Derek Lilliquist, Keith
    Shepherd

April 29
1901: Nig Cuppy
1903: Norwood Gibson
1919: George Dumont, George Winn
1932: Pete Donohue
1935: Doc Farrell, Jack Wilson
1945: Dave Ferriss
1955: Bob Smith, Joe Trimble
1995: Erik Hanson, Mike Hartley, Bill
    Haselman

April 30
1928: Wally Gerber
1932: Smead Jolley, Bennie Tate, Johnny
    Watwood
1987: Ellis Burks
1995: Reggie Jefferson, Troy O'Leary, Steve Ro-
    driguez, Terry Shumpert

May 1
1901: Osee Schrecongost
1920: Gary Fortune
1929: Ed Carroll, Grant Gillis
1944: Joe Wood
1948: Jack Kramer
1957: Bob Chakales
1995: Joel Johnston

May 2
1901: Charlie Jones, Ted Lewis
1914: Guy Cooper
1919: Ray Caldwell
1995: Vaughn Eshelman
2005: Jeremi Gonzalez

May 3
1901: Frank Foreman
1925: Bud Connolly
1927: Buddy Myer
1944: Vic Johnson
1955: Pete Daley

May 4
1923: Dave Black
1926: Boob Fowler
1935: Dib Williams
1949: Jack Robinson
1952: Ralph Brickner
1958: Lou Berberet
1963: Jim Gosger
1965: Dennis Bennett, Rudy Schlesinger
1973: Craig Skok
1974: Rick Burleson
1990: Jerry Reed
1994: Todd Frohwirth

May 5
1926: Jack Russell
1934: Lefty Grove
1948: Ellis Kinder
1995: Brian Looney

May 6
1910: Frank Barberich
1920: Herb Hunter
1936: Johnny Marcum
1990: Tom Brunansky
1995: Stan Belinda

May 7
1904: Bill O'Neill
1994: Carlos Rodriguez

May 8
1908: Walter Carlisle
1926: Wally Shaner
1930: Cedric Durst
1949: Al Zarilla
1957: Dean Stone
1989: Joe Price
1999: Juan Peña
2005: Cla Meredith, Wade Miller

May 9
1925: Ray Francis, Paul Zahniser
1927: Herb Bradley, John Wilson
1959: Billy Hoeft
1965: Jerry Moses
1996: Brent Knackert
2000: Tim Young

May 10th
1925: Al Stokes
1937: Gene Desautels
1944: Hal Wagner
1960: Rip Repulski
1980: Keith MacWhorter

1994: Gar Finnvold
1998: Lou Merloni
2006: Mike Holtz

May 11
1933: Rick Ferrell
1939: Lou Finney
1945: Red Steiner
1950: Bob Gillespie,
      Clyde Vollmer
1969: Don Lock
1994: Andy Tomberlin
2003: Bruce Chen

May 12
1903: Aleck Smith
1911: Joe Riggert
1923: Ira Flagstead

May 13
1911: Jack Killilay
1952: Del Wilber
1994: Chris Howard
1997: Toby Borland

May 14
1910: Clyde Engle
1933: Billy Werber
1953: Floyd Baker
1995: Zane Smith
2002: Bry Nelson
2003: Robert Person

May 15
1951: Bill Evans
1960: Tom Borland
1980: Jack Billingham
1984: Roger Clemens
2004: Kevin Youkilis

May 16
1927: Cleo Carlyle
1933: Lloyd Brown
1943: Leon Culberson
1951: Paul Hinrichs

May 17
1917: Lore Bader
1933: George Pipgras
1934: Lyn Lary
1972: Bob Gallagher
1986: Rey Quinones
1987: Tom Bolton
2001: David Cone

May 18
1930: Ben Shields
1951: Les Moss
1986: Mike Stenhouse

May 19
Debuts: none

May 20
1922: Bill Piercy
1940: Joe Glenn
1950: Jim Suchecki
1960: Ray Boone
2004: Jamie Brown

May 21
1907: Bunk Congalton
1932: Regis Leheny
1961: Don Schwall
1995: Ron Mahay
1997: Mike Benjamin
2003: Rudy Seanez

May 22
1957: Jack Spring
1996: Jeff Manto
2004: Anastacio Martinez

May 23
1909: Charlie French
1929: Bob Barrett
1946: Bob Klinger
1947: Birdie Tebbetts
1991: Mike Brumley
1996: Jose Malave
1998: Keith Johns

May 24
1901: Ben Beville
1959: Bobby Avila, Ted Wills

May 25
1934: Dick Porter
1947: Leslie Aulds
1948: Babe Martin
1977: Mike Paxton
2004: Andy Dominique

May 26
1914: Del Gainer
1954: Grady Hatton
1984: Bill Buckner
1994: Greg Litton
2005: Shawn Wooten

May 27
1944: Stan Partenheimer
1979: Stan Papi
1982: Roger LaFrancois
1995: Karl Rhodes, Tim Wakefield
2003: Matt White

May 28
1935: Ski Melillo
1987: John Leister
1999: Brian Barkley
2005: John Olerud, Kelly Shoppach

May 29
1907: Jimmy Barrett
1908: Pat Donahue
1912: Marty Krug
1921: Allen Sothoron
1940: Bill Butland
1949: Frank Quinn
1993: Jose Melendez

May 30
1910: Red Kleinow
1918: Dick McCabe, Vince Molyneaux
1919: Bill James
1934: Wes Ferrell
1940: Marv Owen
1944: Jim Bucher
1965: Bob Duliba
1980: Dave Stapleton

May 31
1924: Johnnie Heving, Red Ruffing
1970: Mike Fiore
1991: Mike Gardiner
1993: Jim Byrd
1995: Mike Maddux
2000: Hipolito Pichardo
2006: David Pauley

June 1
1906: Ralph Glaze
1994: Wes Chamberlain
2003: Byung-Hyun Kim

June 2
1921: Ernie Neitzke, Sammy Vick
1926: Bill Regan

June 3
1909: Bunny Madden
1966: Lee Stange
1977: Ramon Hernandez
2000: Dan Smith

June 4
1952: Hoot Evers, George Kell, Dizzy Trout
1961: Joe Ginsberg
1966: Don McMahon
1968: Fred Wenz
1976: Bobby Darwin
1988: Zach Crouch
2003: Hector Almonte

June 5
1964: Lee Thomas
2002: Chris Haney

June 6
1923: Carl Stimson
1926: Howie Fitzgerald
1967: Jerry Adair
1989: Luis Rivera
1996: Jeff Frye

June 7
1906: Jack Hayden
1952: Johnny Lipon

June 8
1907: John Knight
1910: Ralph Pond
1935: Hy Vandenberg
1940: Stan Spence
1967: Gary Bell
1976: Tom Murphy

June 9
1910: Ed Hearn
1915: Herb Pennock
1926: Happy Foreman
1945: Randy Heflin

June 10
1938: Bill Lefebvre
1970: Cal Koonce
1975: Jim Burton
1984: Rich Gale
1988: Randy Kutcher
1990: Jeff Gray
1995: Joe Hudson
2006: Jon Lester

June 11
1909: Biff Schlitzer
1918: Frank Truesdale
1932: Ivy Andrews
1937: Ben Chapman
1952: Archie Wilson
1961: Galen Cisco

1967: Gary Waslewski
1971: Luis Tiant
1995: Chris Donnels

June 12
1920: Jigger Statz
1925: Hal Neubauer
1932: Pete Appleton (Jablonowski)
1937: Bobo Newsom
1959: Herb Plews
1960: Willie Tasby
1979: Joel Finch
2002: Juan Diaz

June 13
1979: Tom Poquette
1999: Kirk Bullinger
2001: Marcus Jensen
2003: Ryan Rupe

June 14
1939: Boze Berger
1944: Frank Barrett
1952: Sid Hudson
1960: Russ Nixon
1962: Billy Gardner
1964: Dave Gray
1966: John Wyatt
1975: Denny Doyle
2001: Doug Mirabelli

June 15
1901: George Winter
1924: Buster Ross
1932: Dale Alexander, Roy Johnson
1947: Jake Jones
1949: Walt Masterson
1952: Dick Brodowski
1960: Carroll Hardy
1972: Don Newhauser
1979: Bob Watson
1991: Jeff Plympton
2001: Sun-Woo Kim
2006: Javier Lopez

June 16
1919: Bill Lamar
1943: Babe Barna
1957: Mike Fornieles
1966: Rollie Sheldon, Jose Tartabull
1994: Sergio Valdez

June 17
1913: Earl Moseley
1926: Baby Doll Jacobson

1927: John Freeman
1966: Don Demeter
1969: Tom Satriano
1997: Jesus Tavarez
1999: Bob Wolcott

June 18
1929: Jack Ryan
1959: Jack Harshman

June 19
1907: Beany Jacobson
1911: Tracy Baker
1928: Freddie Moncewicz
1963: Bob Heffner
2006: Kyle Snyder

June 20
1906: Red Morgan
1926: Fred Heimach
1931: Bill Marshall
1943: Pinky Woods

June 21
1919: Norm McNeil
1927: Marty Karow
1936: Ted Olson
1987: Todd Benzinger
1989: Dana Williams

June 22
1949: Johnnie Wittig
1998: Billy Ashley

June 23
1931: Jud McLaughlin
1946: Bill Zuber
1977: Tommy Helms
1993: Aaron Sele
1995: Matt Stairs
1998: Carlos Reyes

June 24
1902: Doc Adkins
1908: Charlie Hartman

June 25
1908: Larry Gardner
1960: Billy Muffett
1969: Bill Lee
1972: Lynn McGlothen
2000: Israel Alcantara
2002: Alan Embree
2004: Curtis Leskanic

June 26
1994: Tim Van Egmond

June 27
1907: Jack Hoey
1916: Weldon Wyckoff
1922: Chick Maynard
1924: Hoge Workman
1936: Emerson Dickman
1945: Dolph Camilli
1951: Leo Kiely
1952: Paul Lehner
1954: Russ Kemmerer
1991: Mo Vaughn
1995: Juan Bell
2000: Morgan Burkhart

June 28
1919: Braggo Roth
1934: Joe Mulligan
2001: Bill Pulsipher
2003: Gabe Kapler

June 29
1907: Deacon McGuire
1912: Neal Ball
1926: Slim Harriss
1968: Juan Pizarro
2000: Sang-Hoon Lee

June 30
1911: Walter Moser
1918: Jack Stansbury
1919: Red Shannon
1928: John Shea
1932: Larry Boerner
1951: Karl Olson
1961: Wilbur Wood
1982: Ed Jurak
2006: Jason Johnson
2007: Jacoby Ellsbury

July 1
1941: Nels Potter
1952: Al Benton
1971: Buddy Hunter
1986: Tom Seaver
1989: Eric Hetzel
1998: Dario Veras
1999: Wilton Veras
2000: Paxton Crawford

July 2
1902: Dave Williams
1934: Red Kellett

July 3
1915: Jack Barry

July 3
1918: Walter Barbare, Red Bluhm
1953: George Schmees
1958: Duane Wilson
1967: Ken Poulsen
1974: Tim Blackwell
1994: Chris Nabholz
2002: Wayne Gomes

July 4
1904: Kip Selbach
1935: Joe Cascarella
1967: Sparky Lyle
1994: Jin Ho Cho
2000: Bernard Gilkey
2003: Todd Jones
2004: Jimmy Anderson

July 5
1920: Gene Bailey
1933: Lou Legett
1970: John Kennedy
1985: Tom McCarthy
1991: Kevin Morton
1995: Willie McGee

July 6
1909: Larry Pape
1920: Paddy Smith
1975: Jim Willoughby
1995: Rick Aguilera
1996: Tony Rodriguez
2007: Jeff Bailey

July 7
1906: Bill Carrigan
1929: Ray Dobens
1930: Charlie Small
1940: Alex Mustaikis
1950: Dick Littlefield, Willard Nixon
1999: Chad Fonville
2005: Alex Cora, Adam Stern

July 8
1922: Walt Lynch
1931: Bill McWilliams
1932: Ed Gallagher
1933: Freddie Muller
2001: Carlos Castillo

July 9
1911: Hal Janvrin
1933: Bucky Walters
1969: Ron Kline
1992: Billy Hatcher
2005: Scott Cassidy

July 10
1912: Doug Smith
1947: Sam Dente
1977: Ramon Aviles
1988: Steve Curry
1994: Steve Farr
2004: Joe Nelson

July 11
1913: Paul Maloy
1914: Babe Ruth
1921: John Perrin
1948: Mike Palm

July 12
1910: Chris Mahoney
1986: LaSchelle Tarver

July 13
1901: Frank Morrissey
1980: Bob Ojeda

July 14
1914: Ernie Shore
2005: Chad Bradford
2006: Craig Breslow

July 15
1905: Hank Olmsted
1911: Les Wilson
1927: Frank Welch
1990: Tim Naehring

July 16
1924: Chappie Geygan
1943: Catfish Metkovich
1950: Phil Marchildon
1978: Garry Hancock
1994: Stan Royer

July 17
1905: Charlie Armbruster
1929: Hod Lisenbee
1939: Bill Sayles. Sayles had previously pitched
    for the American Olympic team in Berlin
    in 1936.
1995: Jeff Suppan

July 18
1902: Tom Hughes
1958: Bill Monbouquette
1988: Larry Parrish

July 19
1909: Ray Collins

July 19 (cont.)
1937: Tommy Thomas
1958: Bud Byerly
1998: Keith Mitchell
1999: Tomokazu Ohka, Marino Santana

July 20
1914: Dick Hoblitzell
1926: Bill Clowers
1940: Earl Johnson
1958: Ted Bowsfield
1986: Calvin Schiraldi
1992: Paul Quantrill
2002: Dustin Hermanson
2005: Tony Graffanino

July 21
1928: Steve Slayton
1951: Al Evans
1959: Pumpsie Green
1967: Norm Siebern
1970: Carmen Fanzone

July 22
1918: Paul Musser
1985: Tim Lollar
2004: Abe Alvarez, Ricky Gutierrez
2006: Kason Gabbard

July 23
1972: Stan Williams
2003: Scott Sauerbeck

July 24
1930: Rabbit Warstler
1978: Andy Hassler
1998: David West
2000: Sean Berry

July 25
1902: Tully Sparks
1922: Johnny Mitchell
1928: Marty Griffin
1946: Don Gutteridge
1970: Chuck Hartenstein
1987: Sam Horn
1996: Arquimedez Pozo
1997: Brian Rose
2004: Terry Adams

July 26
1918: Eusebio Gonzalez, Walt Kinney
1922: Elmer Miller
1932: Johnny Welch
1946: Wally Moses
1963: Bob Turley

1977: Don Aase
1995: Dave Hollins
2005: Manny Delcarmen

July 27
1909: Chet Nourse
1950: Jim McDonald
1992: John Valentin
1999: Butch Huskey

July 28
1908: Frank Arellanes
1918: Jean Dubuc
1925: Jack Rothrock
1928: Carl Sumner
1959: Jim Mahoney, Earl Wilson
2001: Casey Fossum

July 29
1909: Ed Karger
1914: Vean Gregg
1918: George Cochran
2000: Mike Lansing
2003: Lou Collier

July 30
1920: Hal Deviney
1922: Chick Fewster
1954: Tom Hurd
1999: Lenny Webster
2000: Rolando Arrojo

July 31
1919: Waite Hoyt
1948: Earl Caldwell
1953: Frank Sullivan
1955: Frank Baumann
1964: Tony Horton
1987: John Marzano
1988: Mike Boddicker
1996: Darren Bragg
2005: Jonathan Papelbon

August 1
1913: Wally Snell
1959: Nelson Chittum
1995: Mike Stanton
1996: Mark Brandenburg
2001: Ugueth Urbina
2002: Cliff Floyd, Bobby Howry
2003: Scott Williamson
2004: Orlando Cabrera
2006: Bryan Corey

August 2
1913: Esty Chaney
1919: Bob McGraw, Allan Russell
1938: Jim Tabor
1998: Greg Swindell
2007: Eric Gagne

August 3
1926: Jack Tobin
1933: Joe Judge
1938: Bill Harris, Joe Heving
1940: Yank Terry
1943: Emmett O'Neill
1968: Floyd Robinson
1973: Dick Pole
1979: Win Remmerswaal
1990: Joe Hesketh
1998: Orlando Merced
1999: Bryce Florie
2004: Doug Mientkiewicz, Dave Roberts
2005: Jose Cruz
2006: Ken Huckaby

August 4
1932: Gordon Rhodes
1945: Ty LaForest
1950: Buddy Rosar
1957: Murray Wall
1964: Jay Ritchie
2000: Rico Brogna
2005: Roberto Petagine
2006: Javy Lopez

August 5
1935: Stew Bowers
1964: Al Smith
1967: Elston Howard
2003: David McCarty

August 6
1907: Cy Morgan
1920: Elmer Myers
2006: Corky Miller
2007: Brandon Moss

August 7
1911: Joe Giannini
1918: Hack Miller, Bill Pertica
1989: Jeff Stone

August 8
1911: Hy Gunning
1920: Cliff Brady
1951: Aaron Robinson
1996: Ken Grundt, Greg Pirkl

August 9
1908: Jake Thielman
1909: Charley Hall
1982: Brian Denman
2005: Mike Remlinger

August 10
1905: Pop Rising
1990: Rick Lancellotti
2004: Mike Myers

August 11
1911: Olaf Henriksen

August 12
1995: Matt Murray

August 13
1910: Billy Purtell
1932: Gordon McNaughton
1944: Rex Cecil
1955: Jim Pagliaroni
1970: John Curtis
1998: Pete Schourek

August 14
1905: John Godwin
1910: Dutch Lerchen
1918: Jack Coffey
1992: Tom Barrett
2001: Allen McDill

August 15
1947: Eddie Smith

August 16
1924: Lefty Jamerson
1951: Mel Hoderlein
1979: John Tudor
1995: Chris James
1996: Kerry Lacy

August 17
1911: Walter Lonergan
1913: Bill Mundy
1927: Bob Cremins
1935: Walt Ripley
1972: Andy Kosco
2007: Clay Buchholz

August 18
1923: Les Howe
1979: Ted Sizemore
2006: Eric Hinske

August 19
1974: Jim Rice

August 20
1938: Al Baker
1990: Mike Marshall
2001: Todd Erdos

August 21
1940: Charlie Gelbert, Bill Fleming
1966: Hank Fischer, Bill Short
1990: Phil Plantier
1991: Dan Petry

August 22
1908: Harry Niles
1993: Rob Deer
1997: Bret Saberhagen
2006: Dustin Pedroia

August 23
1910: Doc Moskiman
1967: Jim Landis

August 24
1908: Joe Wood
1910: Ben Hunt

August 25
1911: Blaine Thomas
1926: Danny MacFayden
1977: Sam Bowen
1995: Eric Gunderson
2003: Bronson Arroyo

August 26
1908: Ed McFarland
1913: Wally Rehg

August 27
1905: Ed Barry
1999: Kent Mercker

August 28
1909: William Matthews
1924: Clarence Winters
1937: Joe Gonzales
2006: Carlos Peña

August 29
1928: George Loepp
1944: Clem Dreisewerd
1967: Ken Harrelson

August 30
1924: Al Kellett
1996: Reggie Harris, Pat Mahomes
2006: Mike Burns

August 19
1986: Dave Henderson, Spike Owen
2007: Kevin Cash, Bobby Kielty

August 31
1950: Fred Hatfield
1992: Ken Ryan
1993: Luis Ortiz
1996: Nomar Garciaparra

September 1
1916: Jimmy Walsh
1931: Marty McManus
1993: Cory Bailey
1995: Dwayne Hosey
1997: Michael Coleman, Derek Lowe
1998: Mandy Romero
1999: Rod Beck
2000: Dante Bichette

September 2
1914: Bill Swanson
1932: Andy Spognardi
1957: Ken Aspromonte
1960: Marlan Coughtry, Chet Nichols
1980: Steve Crawford, Julio Valdez, Chico Walker
1990: Larry Andersen
1996: Rudy Pemberton
1998: Chris Snopek
1999: Ramon Martinez, Jon Nunnally
2001: Joe Oliver
2005: Chad Harville, Alejandro Machado, Matt Perisho
2006: Kevin Jarvis, David Murphy

September 3
1983: Lee Graham
1988: Mike Rochford
2004: Adam Hyzdu

September 4
1905: Ed Hughes
1920: Ed Chaplin
1971: Juan Beniquez, Rick Miller, Ben Oglivie
1974: Tim McCarver
1980: Luis Aponte

September 5
1932: Hank Patterson
1974: Fred Lynn
1978: Bobby Sprowl
1985: Mike Greenwell, Kevin Romine, Rob Woodward
1986: Pat Dodson
1990: Scott Cooper
1993: Greg Blosser, Jeff McNeely
2003: Andy Abad

September 6
1941: Al Flair

1970: Bob Montgomery
1975: Rick Kreuger
1977: Bo Diaz
1982: Marty Barrett
1983: Jackie Gutierrez, Al Nipper
2002: Benny Agbayani
2007: Royce Clayton

September 7
1926: Bill Moore
1931: Howie Storie
1950: Jim Piersall
1970: Dick Mills
1975: Butch Hobson
1980: Rich Gedman
1991: Bob Zupcic
2002: Shane Andrews

September 8
1925: Sy Rosenthal
1933: Mel Almada
1971: Cecil Cooper
1995: Scott Hatteberg
2001: Angel Santos
2004: Pedro Astacio, Sandy Martinez

September 9
1911: Buck O'Brien
1936: Fabian Gaffke
1974: Deron Johnson
2001: Calvin Pickering

September 10
1947: Matt Batts
1952: Dick Bolling, Hersh Freeman
1969: Gary Wagner
1972: Bob Veale
2002: Kevin Brown, Jeff Hancock, Freddy Sanchez

September 11
1905: Frank Owens
1911: Jack Bushelman
1947: Cot Deal
1976: Jack Baker

September 12
1907: Elmer Steele
1911: Swede Carlstrom
1940: Tony Lupien
1947: Merl Combs
1962: Merlin Nippert
1970: Bobby Bolin
1976: Ernie Whitt

1987: Jody Reed
1993: Nate Minchey
2000: Hector Carrasco

September 13
1907: George Whiteman
1909: Charlie Smith
1920: Ben Paschal
1924: Ted Wingfield
1931: Marv Olson
1962: Billy Macleod, Pete Smith
1968: Luis Alvarado
1970: Roger Moret
1982: Oil Can Boyd
2000: Rich Croushore

September 14
1907: Tris Speaker
1920: George Orme
1934: Skinny Graham
1942: Andy Gilbert
1943: Danny Doyle
1956: Gene Mauch
1958: Jerry Casale
1960: Tracy Stallard
1969: Tony Muser
1996: Walt McKeel

September 15
1912: Ben Van Dyke
1925: Tom Jenkins, Herb Welch
1936: Jennings Poindexter
1947: Chuck Stobbs
1956: Rudy Minarcin
1985: Jeff Sellers
2003: Adrian Brown

September 16
1909: Paul Howard
1916: Jack Lewis
1924: John Woods
1934: Spike Merena
1972: Dwight Evans
1980: Reid Nichols
1982: Mike Brown
1988: Carlos Quintana
1990: Jim Pankovits
1997: Robinson Checo
2000: Steve Ontiveros

September 17
1902: Nick Altrock
1906: Chet Chadbourne
1923: Clarence Blethen

1927: Frank Bennett, Frank Bushey
1928: Casper Asbjornson
1930: Bob Kline
1931: John Smith
1934: George Hockette
1954: Guy Morton
1955: Frank Malzone
1991: Wayne Housie
1992: Scott Taylor

September 18
1911: Casey Hageman
1919: Joe Wilhoit
1923: Ike Boone
1966: Garry Roggenburk
1966: Mike Andrews, Reggie Smith
1969: Carlton Fisk
1977: Ted Cox

September 19
1911: Tony Tonneman
1914: Larry Pratt
1922: Dick Reichle
1925: Joe Kiefer
1931: George Stumpf
1934: Al Niemiec
1948: Neill Sheridan
1959: Jerry Mallett
1964: Bobby Guindon
1981: John Lickert
1997: Curtis Pride
1998: Carlos Valdez
2001: James Lofton
2005: Craig Hansen

September 20
1906: Frank Oberlin
1929: Joe Cicero, Ed Connolly
1948: Lou Stringer
1950: Charlie Maxwell
1955: Haywood Sullivan
1978: John LaRose
1984: Jim Dorsey
2005: Hanley Ramirez

September 21
1923: Frank Fuller
1935: George Dickey
1963: Rico Petrocelli
1974: Chuck Goggin
1996: Trot Nixon
2000: Jesus Peña

September 22
1905: Joe Harris

1915: Chick Shorten
1917: Jimmy Cooney
1925: Bob Adams, Mike Herrera
1969: Mike Garman

September 23
1901: George Wilson (changed his name to
    Prentiss the following year)
1937: Johnnie Peacock
1950: Harry Taylor
1951: Bob DiPietro, Al Richter, Norm Zauchin
2006: Devern Hansack

September 24
1920: Ray Grimes
1921: Sam Dodge
1997: Jason Varitek

September 25
1907: Harry Lord
1909: Fred Anderson
1923: John Donahue
1959: Don Gile
2001: Willie Banks

September 26
1906: Heinie Wagner
1907: Fred Burchell
1951: Sammy White

September 27
1901: Harry Gleason
1902: Gary Wilson
1930: Jim Galvin
1960: Arnold Earley
1967: Ken Brett

September 28
1901: Jack Slattery, Jake Volz

1906: Len Swormstedt
1910: Marty McHale
1917: Wally Mayer
1975: Steve Dillard, Andy Merchant
1977: Bob Bailey

September 29
1909: Steve Yerkes
1935: John Kroner
1950: James Atkins
1951: Ben Flowers

September 30
1906: Rube Kroh
1951: Harley Hisner

October 1
1974: Steve Barr
1982: Marc Sullivan

October 2
1909: Jack Chesbro

October 3
1964: Mike Ryan
1999: Steve Lomasney

October 4
1972: Vic Correll

October 5
1908: King Brady
1991: Josias Manzanillo, Eric Wedge

October 6
1908: Doc McMahon

October 7
1908: Harry Ostdiek

Rooting for the laundry?

You might think that the first year of a franchise would be the year in which the most new players joined a team—after all, every single player on the team was new in the first year. There were 24 "new" players on the 1901 Boston Americans. There were 14 new players in 1902, seven in 1903, and six in 1904.

Interestingly, the early championship teams had rather few additions since the year before. As indicated above, there were seven in 1903 and six in 1904, and then eight in 1912, nine in 1915, and six in 1916. Because of the large number of players who went into military service or took jobs in war industries in 1918, there were 20 new players that year—though many of them played in rather few games. There were 11 new players in 1946, 14 in 1967, 10 in 1975, and 14 in 1986. It's no secret that recent years have seen more of a revolving door approach to player rosters, and the 2004 championship team featured 28 players who'd not been with the team in 2003. For those counting, that would be more members than in the year the franchise began.

The team won the 1904 pennant despite having a total of only 18 players for the entire season. Red Sox fans recall recent years when the team has had more than 50 players on the roster at one point or another throughout the year, but the 1904 ballclub won the pennant with only 18 all year long. One thing it does—it cuts down on the number of rings to give out.

The fewest number of new players was in 1917—the Sox already had a team which had won two World Championships in a row. Why mess with success? Oops—after winning the World Series in 2004, the Red Sox brought in 30 new players in 2005.

The largest number of new players was in 1995—a full 42 players on that division-winning team had not been on the team the previous year. Prior to then, the only two years in which more than 21 players had joined a team were 1952 (27) and 1966 (26). Even after cycling in those 42 new players in 1995, Sox management brought in 34 new men in 1996. Since 1995, the average number of new players has been 27½ . Leaving aside the obvious joke about some players not even contributing half a player's worth, this means the average number of new players over the last dozen years exceeds even the highest total in any one of the previous 94 years.

The alumni group is growing at a rapid pace.

Did someone say something about rooting for the laundry?

Thanks to F. X. Flinn for compiling the figures of new players each year.

Batting out of order to start a career

In his first major league game, in the thick of a pennant race, Dwight Evans batted out of order. It was September 16, 1972 and the Sox were trying to win the strike-shortened '72 season. Fortunately, the batting order mix-up had no bearing on the outcome.

Boston was at home and beating Cleveland 7–0, and with Luis Tiant on the mound, the game looked well in hand by the bottom of the sixth. Yaz was on second and Reggie Smith on first, and manager Eddie Kasko decided to give them some rest. He sent in Cecil Cooper to run for Captain Carl and the rookie Evans to run for Reggie. Kasko, though, told plate umpire Lou DiMuro that Evans would bat for Yaz and Cooper would bat for Smith. That was his mistake; if you come in to run for someone, you're supposed to take his spot in the order. As it transpired, neither runner scored. Come the eighth inning, it was time for Yaz (#3 in the order) to bat, and Kasko told Evans, "Go ahead up there and bat." He popped out. Indians manager Aspromonte wasn't about to protest an out. Had Dewey reached base safely—maybe even homered—he could have informed DiMuro and the batter would have been declared out. Boston won 10–0, facing seven Cleveland pitchers. The Indians faced only one; Tiant allowed but three hits.

"Dashed dreams and disappointments"—players who made the Red Sox spring training roster, but never appeared in a major league game (1946–2000)

We've only included players here through the 2000 season. Some of those from more recent years may still have a chance to make it to the majors—as Jeff Bailey finally did with the Red Sox in 2007, after more than 10 years in minor league ball.

Player Name	Spring	Hometown
Adubato, Bob	1957	Cedar Grove NJ
Beamer, Jim	1966	Roseburg OR
Betti, Richard	1996	Milford MA
Boyle, John	1964	Kent WA
Broome, Bob	1954	Summerville GA
Bryant, Pat	1998	Sherman Oaks CA

Player Name	Spring	Hometown
Buck, Eddie Joe	1955	Elmer OK
Burgess, Gus	1983–84–85	Boynton Beach FL
Busby, Dave	1962–62	Ada OK
Bustabad, Juan	1983–84	Havana, Cuba
Caruso, Joe	1964	Brooklyn NY
Chapman, Ken	1946	Mansfield MA
Ciccarella, Joe	1994	Cincinnati OH
Conroy, Brian	1993–94	Needham MA
Copeland, George	1950	Far Rockaway NY—invited to Phillies camp in 1946
Curtis, Alpheus "Al"	1955	Gaffney SC—invited to the Senators camp in 1956
Damman, Louis	1954–55	Lewiston ID
Davis, Mike	1984	Bladenboro NC—invited to the Mets camp in 1963
Dodson, Bo	1997	West Sacramento CA
Dorsch, Lewis "Jerry"	1964	Atlanta GA
Dowd, Paul	1966	Detroit MI
Farmer, Billy	1967–68–69	Auburn GA—invited to the White Sox camp in 1970
Fischer, Tom	1991–92	West Bend WI
Ford, Eddie	1977	Astoria LI NY
Fryar, John	1969	Lake Charles LA
Furfaro, Vince	1954	Somerville NJ
Gabriele, Dan	1988–89	Detroit MI
Gaines, Jack	1946	Portsmouth VA
Garcia, Cheo	1993	Maracaibo, Venezuela—invited to the Twins camp in 1992
Gonzalez, Angel	1988	Santiago, Dominican Republic
Hall, Billy	1994	Wichita KS
Hartsell, John "Jack"	1951	unknown
Henkel, Bob	1994	Dallas TX
Herron, Gerald	1966	Ventura CA
Hoban, Dick	1968	Cleveland OH
Hofmann, John	1949	Buffalo NY
Howard, Mike	1980–81	Portland ME
Howell, Lee	1960	Detroit MI
Jenkins, Bob	1956	Hagerstown MD
Jernigan, Paul "Pete"	1961–62–63	Phillips TX
Johnson, Mitch	1984 through	1998 Columbia PA
King, Jerry	1981–82	San Diego CA
Koney, Charles	1947–58	Chicago IL
Kouns, Bill	1974–75	Portsmouth OH
Krebs, Chris	1969	Jacksonville FL—invited to the Senators camp in 1970
Livernois, Derek	1991–92–93	Inglewood CA
MacDonald, Stew	1962–63	Seattle WA
Maggard, Tom	1972–73	San Gabriel CA
Malpeso, Dave	1984–85	Franklin VA
Massey, Darrell	1961	unknown
Matilla, Pedro	1990–91	Havana, Cuba
McWilliams, Stan	1953	Vallejo CA
Miller, Mike	1991	Kirkwood MO—invited to the Mets camp in 1990
Modica, Peter	1948	New Orleans LA—invited to the Pirates camp in 1950 and the Giants camp in 1954
Naudain, Gage	1963–64	Houston TX
O'Neill, Dan	1991	Holyoke MA

Player Name	Spring	Hometown
Orellano, Rafael	1996–97	Humacao, PR
Owen, Dave	1991	Seattle WA
Padilla, Roy	1997	Panama City, Panama
Parks, Danny	1982–83	Huntsville AL
Pina, Mickey	1990–91	Boston MA
Powell, Larry	1946	Dinuba CA
Richards, Lloyd Verne	1946	Portland OR
Robinson, Cecil	1966–67	Newport News VA
Ross, Charles	1974–75–76	Long Beach CA
Ross, Sean	1993	Wilmington NC
Russin, Jim	1963	Morristown NJ
Schneck, Steve	1979–80	Portsmouth VA
Schoppee, Dave	1982–83–84	Bangor ME
Schuster, Rollin	1951–52	North Bergen NJ
Sekany, Jason	2000	Walnut Creek CA
Simononis, Alphonsus	1948	Ashland PA
Simonton, Benji	1995	Walnut Creek CA
Skeen, Archie	1964	Ogden UT
Skrable, Pat	1972	San Francisco CA—invited to the Phillies camp in 1969, 1970, and 1971
Snow, Bob	1967	Portland OR
Spencer, Gerald	1976–77	San Antonio TX
Stewart, Hector	1987–88	Ponce PR
Sullivan, Mike	1995	St. Paul MN
Suter, Burke "Bill"	1979	Baltimore MD—invited to the Phillies camp in 1980
Tanner, Joe	1958–59	Newton MS
Theis, Joe	1959	Bloomington IL
Thibdeau, John	1969	Stamford CT
Tinney, Roy	1956	Altus OK
Uhaze, George	1953	Trenton NJ
Van Alstyne, Al	1954–55	Stuyvesant NY
Vasquez, Luis	1989	Bolivar, Venezuela—invited to the Reds camp in 1990 and 1991
Vazquez, Frank	1974	Ponce PR
Vezendy, Gerry	1965	Berwick PA
Vosk, Jim	1977	Red Bank NJ
Waller, Rich	1978	Passaic NJ
Washington, Ivy	1968	Independence LA—invited to the Reds camp in 1967
Wieck, Larry	1962	Evansville IN
Williams, Terry	1971–72	Ottumwa IA

Two who never played for the Red Sox—
but had a role in the 2004 championship

Two players who don't get enough credit for their role in the Red Sox 2004 World Series Championship are Jim Smith and Derek Vinyard. Neither ever played a day in the major leagues, but Derek Vinyard was the player-to-be-named later that the Sox sent to Montreal for Glen Murray on September 15, 1994. Jim Smith was the PTBNL that the Sox sent to Seattle for Lee Tinsley on the same date, completing a March trade.

Murray and Tinsley were later packaged with Ken Ryan, whom the Sox had signed as an amateur free agent, for Heathcliff Slocumb. Slocumb was subsequently sent to Seattle for

Derek Lowe and Jason Varitek. Everyone remembers how much the Slocumb trade helped the Sox, but they forget how Slocumb himself was acquired. Thanks to Tim Savage for this one.

A SURFEIT OF SURNAMES

Looking at surnames, we find that the Sox have never had a player whose last name starts with X. Only Daryl Irvine (1990–92) had a surname starting with I. There were five whose names start with Q (Paul Quantrill, Frank Quinn, Jack Quinn, Rey Quinones, and Carlos Quintana), but that is two more than the U names: Tom Umphlett, Bob Unglaub, and Ugueth Urtain Urbina—who one could say had three U's all by himself.

Perhaps not surprisingly, the initial letter of the most surnames is S, with names ranging from Saberhagen to Snopek to Swormstedt.

The most common last name among Red Sox players—perhaps no surprise—is Smith. There are 18 Smiths. They are: Al, Bob, Broadway Aleck, Charlie, Dan, Doug, Eddie, Elmer, Frank, George, George (a different one), John, Lee, Paddy, Pete, Reggie, Riverboat, and Zane.

Eleven of the 18 Smiths on the Sox served as pitchers.

There were those 18 Smiths, but there's only one Smithson, though. You remember Mike (1988–89); he was a pitcher, too.

There are twice as many Smiths as the second most common surnames—Williams and Wilson. Here are the numbers of players who share last names with others totaling at least five or more:

Smith—18	Wilson—9	Barrett—6	Harris—6 (and if you include Slim
Williams—9	Peña—6	Thomas—6	Harriss, it becomes 7)
Miller—6	Brown—7	Jones—7	Clark—5
Johnson—8			

Surprisingly, among the 93 (or 94) players represented above, there is only one pair of relatives sharing a surname: brothers Marty and Tommy Barrett. A later section of this book explores relatives who played for the Red Sox.

Needless to say, in the last couple of decades, there are names that crop up more frequently than before, names like Martinez and Rodriguez. In 1999 and 2000, brothers Pedro and Ramon Martinez were on the Red Sox roster, but in 1995, there was a Rodriguez cluster in which none of the three were *hermanos*. There were Carlos (1994–95), Frank (1995), Steve (1995), and Tony, who was in the system but first played in 1996.

In 2005, there were Miller, Mueller, and Millar. No matter how many "Millers" the Sox might have signed, it was the Pawtucket Red Sox that hold the record for most players with the same last name in one season. And Joe Kuras points out that in one game in 1995, they all played at the same time!

Rodriguez, Steve 1994–95   Rodriguez, Tony 1994–97
Rodriguez, Carlos 1994–95   Rodriguez, Victor 1995
Rodriguez, Frank 1994–95

If he'd still been around in 1995, Ruben Rodriguez might have joined them, too, but he only played in 1992, 1993, and 1994.

Two of the longest-tenured Sox players were Carl Yastrzemski—whose last name is not shared on the rolls of the Red Sox, though his son Mike was a prospect at one point—and Ted Williams, whose son John-Henry was only nominally granted prospect status in his early 30's as a courtesy to the elder Williams. Though there are more Smiths than Williams in Red Sox team history, the name Williams overshadows all others.

Who are the other Williams who played for Boston?

Other players named Williams who played for Boston...

Position players

Rip Williams (1911)—started his seven-year major league career with Boston, batting .239 in 284 at-bats. He got better. With the Senators, he hit fairly well—even reaching .318 in 1912, though he drifted back down to .239 in his final season (with Cleveland, in 1918).

Denny Williams (1924–25, 1928)—in limited playing time in 1924, he hit .365, then saw his average sink the next year to .229. He didn't play in the majors in '26 or '27, but came back in 1928 and hit .222. He died at age 30, just before spring training 1929.

Dib Williams (1935)—after five seasons with the Philadelphia Athletics, he came over to Boston early in the 1935 season, but hit a disappointing .251 (not far off from his career .267) and was out of the majors come 1936.

Dick Williams (1963–64)—better known as manager of the 1967 Impossible Dream team, Williams played for two years under manager Johnny Pesky (they were the last two seasons of his 13 as a player). He hit .257 and .159 in his two years with the Sox; he was a .260 career hitter. His 1964 year with Boston offers one unusual stat: he only had 11 hits all year long, but five of the 11 were home runs. He is being inducted into the National Baseball Hall of Fame in 2008.

Ken Williams (1928–29)—a long-time St. Louis Brown (and league leader in HR and RBI in 1922), this Williams joined the Sox for the last two seasons of his 14-year career, batting .303 and .345 in limited action.

Pitchers

Dave Williams (1902)—appeared in three games. In 18-plus innings, allowed 22 hits and walked 11 batters. 5.30 ERA. Williams contracted pneumonia while serving in the U.S. Army during the First World War and died at the Army and Navy Hospital in Hot Springs, Arkansas not long after the Red Sox had left spring training.

Stan Williams (1972)—in the last year of a 14-year career (109–94 lifetime, 3.48 ERA), this Williams also appeared in three games, pitching just 4⅓ innings. Like Dave Williams, his ERA (6.23) was higher than Ted's 4.50. Ted Williams' major league pitching career is documented elsewhere in this book.

Managers

Dick Williams (1967–1969)—260 wins, 217 losses (.545 winning percentage, 12th among Red Sox managers—but with one pennant to his credit)

Jimy Williams (1997–2001)—414 wins, 352 losses (.540 winning percentage, 13th among Red Sox managers—led the Red Sox to two AL wild cards, in 1998 and 1999)

Coaches

Dallas Williams—coached first base for the Red Sox in 2003 under manager Grady Little. When Terry Francona replaced Little, he named Lynn Jones to take over first base coaching duties.

Stan Williams—after playing with the Sox in 1972, Stan Williams served as pitching coach under Darrell Johnson in 1975–76.

Other players named Yastrzemski who played for Boston...

None. Mike tried, though.

A special case

He wasn't strictly speaking named Williams, but you've got to at least acknowledge William McWilliams who played for the Sox in 1931 and has a brief biography in the section of the book devoted to those who only ever played two games.

Terrible Ted Williams—never ejected from a game

Ted Williams was dubbed "Terrible Ted," "Tempestuous Ted," and even "The Splendid Spitter"—but he was never ejected from a major league baseball game. That's partly because he respected umpires, for doing their job the best they could. And part of it could have been strategic—his reputation amongst umpires may have won him a close call from time to time. There are numerous stories about how a given catcher would complain to an umpire who called a pitch a ball while Ted was at the plate, only to have the umpire say, "If Mr. Williams did not swing, it's not a strike."

Ted's reputation seems to have been earned by his nearly-unparalleled perception of the strike zone and his refusal to chase a bad pitch. But it was also true that he did respect umpires for the work they did. Joe Paparella told Larry Gerlach the following story: "I worked with so many outstanding players...Ted Williams stood ceiling-high. He very rarely looked back at the plate. And he would help you even to the point of getting players off your back. If you finished the season with Boston, he'd come to the dressing room, shake your hand, wish you and your family a happy winter, and thank you for being associated with the game. He was the only one to ever do that."

Consider this chart of ejections of Red Sox men named Williams:

Jimy Williams—14 ejections   Rip Williams—1 ejection
Dick Williams—7 ejections   Ted Williams—0 ejections

Dick Williams would have an eighth ejection to his credit (if that's the right word) except that one time he managed to get himself thrown out of a game that never happened. Ejected in the second inning of the June 7, 1967 game, the heavens let loose and a downpour washed the ejection from the record books.

Speaking of ejections...

Terry Francona is poised to take sole possession of the Red Sox record sometime in the 2008 season.

Most ejections of Red Sox personnel, per SABR's ejection log through 2007:

14 Jimy Williams
13 Terry Francona, Darrell Johnson, John McNamara
12 Eddie Kasko
11 Joe Morgan, Carl Yastrzemski
10 Ralph Houk, Don Zimmer
9   Sammy White
8   Jim Piersall
7   Dwight Evans, Eddie Popowski, Dick Williams

6   Buck Freeman, Grady Little, Birdie Tebbetts

5   Rick Burleson, Jimmy Collins, Joe Cronin, Butch Hobson, Jake Stahl

4   Marty Barrett, Lou Boudreau, Bill Carrigan, Tommy Harper, Deacon McGuire, Johnny Pesky, Babe Ruth, Tris Speaker, Bob Stanley, Bob Unglaub, Heinie Wagner

3   Sam Agnew, Charlie Berry, Bullet Joe Bush, Hick Cady, Jack Clark, Roger Clemens, Tony Conigliaro, Mike Easler, Dennis Eckersley, Rick Ferrell, Carlton Fisk, Bill Lee, Marty McManus, Trot Nixon, Jose Offerman, David Ortiz, Val Picinich, Wally Rehg, Reggie Smith, Chick Stahl, Jason Varitek, Joe Wood

2   Del Baker, Bill Buckner, Bernie Carbo, Ben Chapman, Tony Cloninger, Cecil Cooper, Doc Cramer, Gene Desautels, Patsy Dougherty, Dick Drago, Carl Everett, Hobe Ferris, Rich Gale, Dick Gernert, Ken Harrelson, Fred Hofmann, Bruce Hurst, Jackie Jensen, Dennis Lamp, Don Lenhardt, Derek Lowe, Fred Lynn, Rick Miller, Bob Montgomery, Buddy Myer, Skeeter Newsome, Gus Niarhos, Russ Nixon, Jim Pagliaroni, Johnny Peacock, Manny Ramirez, Jerry Remy, George Scott, Sonny Siebert, George Thomas, Mike Torrez, Charlie Wagner

1   Gary Allenson, Hector Almonte, Mike Andrews, Charlie Armbruster, Bronson Arroyo, Don Baylor, Stan Belinda, Juan Beniquez, Don Buddin, Damon Buford, Al Bumbry, Fred Burchell, Jimmy Burke, George Burns, Dolph Camilli, Kevin Cash, Frank Castillo, Lou Clinton, David Cone, Rheal Cormier, Steve Crawford, Lou Criger, Coco Crisp, Danny Darwin, Ike Delock, Al DeVormer, Dom DiMaggio, Brendan Donnelly, John Dopson, Walt Dropo, Arnold Earley, Clyde Engle, Wes Ferrell, Chick Fewster, Scott Fletcher, Cliff Floyd, Casey Fossum, Bob Fothergill, Phil Gagliano, Milt Gaston, Rich Gedman, Mike Greenwell, Doug Griffin, Eric Gunderson, Richard Haley, Charley Hall, Bill Haselman, Jack Hayden, Richie Hebner, Olaf Henriksen, Dick Hoblitzell, Elston Howard, Walt Hriniak, Joe Hudson, Ron Jackson, Reggie Jefferson, Dave Jauss, Sad Sam Jones, Gabe Kapler, John Kroner, Mike Lansing, Dutch Leonard, Darren Lewis, Steve Lyons, Mike Macfarlane, Matt Mantei, Felix Mantilla, Heinie Manush, Pedro Martinez, Eddie Mayo, Joe McCarthy, Jose Melendez, Doug Mirabelli, Jerry Moses, Mike Nagy, Al Nipper, Troy O'Leary, Spike Owen, Roy Partee, Tony Peña, Dick Radatz, Jeff Reardon, Edgar Renteria, Jody Reed, Billy Rogell, Pete Runnels, Jeff Russell, Joe Sambito, Everett Scott, Ernie Shore, Al Simmons, George Susce, Frank Sullivan, Pinch Thomas, Luis Tiant, Lee Thomas, John Valentin, Frank Viola, Tillie Walker, Rabbit Warstler, Vic Wertz, David Wells, Rip Williams, George Winter, Steve Yerkes, Kevin Youkilis

Managers

14   Terry Francona
14   Jimy Williams
13   Darrell Johnson
13   John McNamara
12   Eddie Kasko
11   Joe Morgan
10   Ralph Houk
7   Dick Williams
6   Grady Little
5   Jimmy Collins
5   Joe Cronin
5   Don Zimmer

5   Butch Hobson
4   Deacon McGuire
4   Bill Carrigan
4   Lou Boudreau

Coaches

7   Eddie Popowski
5   Don Zimmer
2   Del Baker
2   Don Lenhardt
2   Rich Gale
2   Mike Easler
2   Tony Cloninger

Players

11   Carl Yastrzemski
9   Sammy White
8   Jim Piersall
7   Dwight Evans
6   Buck Freeman
6   Birdie Tebbetts
5   Rick Burleson
4   Heinie Wagner
4   Tris Speaker
4   Babe Ruth
4   Bob Stanley
4   Marty Barrett

No Red Sox comes close to the all-time major league list, headed by John McGraw (131), Leo Durocher (124), and Bobby Cox (116). All the Red Sox managerial ejections together add up to McGraw's 131.

Some years see more ejections than others, with the counter culture years of the late 1960s and early 1970s leading the way.

Most ejections, top five years

1974: 17   1975: 14   2005: 13   1973: 12   1986: 12

Fewest ejections (zero)

1904, 1913, 1918, 1924, 1926, 1931, 1935, 1941, 1946, 1966

Since 1966, the Red Sox haven't managed to get through a year without at least one ejection. Here's the full listing:

Ejections by Year

1901: 7	1923: 4	1945: 2	1967: 4	1989: 9
1902: 8	1924: 0	1946: 0	1968: 10	1990: 6
1903: 2	1925: 1	1947: 5	1969: 2	1991: 4
1904: 0	1926: 0	1948: 4	1970: 10	1992: 9
1905: 1	1927: 1	1949: 1	1971: 5	1993: 5
1906: 2	1928: 9	1950: 3	1972: 10	1994: 6
1907: 5	1929: 1	1951: 2	1973: 12	1995: 1
1908: 8	1930: 1	1952: 8	1974: 17	1996: 3
1909: 1	1931: 0	1953: 3	1975: 14	1997: 2
1910: 6	1932: 2	1954: 1	1976: 9	1998: 5
1911: 4	1933: 4	1955: 2	1977: 3	1999: 9
1912: 4	1934: 2	1956: 6	1978: 7	2000: 8
1913: 0	1935: 0	1957: 4	1979: 4	2001: 6
1914: 8	1936: 4	1958: 2	1980: 7	2002: 9
1915: 8	1937: 3	1959: 4	1981: 3	2003: 10
1916: 1	1938: 2	1960: 2	1982: 8	2004: 5
1917: 11	1939: 1	1961: 1	1983: 6	2005: 13
1918: 0	1940: 1	1962: 2	1984: 5	2006: 1
1919: 3	1941: 0	1963: 2	1985: 5	2007: 10
1920: 3	1942: 1	1964: 9	1986: 12	
1921: 1	1943: 4	1965: 1	1987: 7	
1922: 2	1944: 2	1966: 0	1988: 9	

...thanks to David Vincent, SABR's Guru of Ejections

It is interesting to note that, as Dave Vincent wrote this author, "although some teams have non-playing personnel listed (mascots, for example) there are none of these types from Boston." Maybe Wally needs to show a little more fire!

The day Wally roughed up the president of the Red Sox

Forget about showing a little more fire, Wally was seemingly on the brink of getting himself fired on August 2, 2007. Red Sox chairman Tom Werner told the *Globe*'s Gordon Edes of how Wally approached President and CEO Larry Lucchino on the field before the Thursday afternoon day game and was unexpectedly aggressive. It was Werner himself disguised inside Wally's outfit. "I walked up to Larry and tousled his hair. He had that look on him which said, 'What the hell are you doing?' I then took three rubber baseballs that I had in my hand and fired them at his head. Now he was getting extremely irritated. I then went up to him, started to push him, and tousled his hair again. He said, 'What is going on with you?' I put

Wally on the Wall, high atop the Green Monster.
Bill Nowlin photo.

up my mitts and pretended to fight him. Now he was really getting angry…. Boy, was he about to say to Wally, 'You are so [expletive] fired.'" Werner then spoke from inside the costume: "Larry, it's me! Tom!" Lucchino later told Edes, "All I will say is that the final chapter of this dastardly deception has yet to be written."

The first Wally on the Red Sox

Speaking of Wally, who was the first Wally on the Red Sox? A meticulous search of debut dates shows us that it was Wally Snell, a catcher, who first played for Boston on August 1, 1913. He was a Massachusetts native, born in West Bridgewater on May 19, 1889. The college player from Brown only ever saw action in six major league games, all for the Red Sox and all in 1913, leaving baseball with a lifetime batting average of .250. Every one of his three hits was a single, so his slugging average was .250 as well—and so was his on-base percentage as it happens. His debut came as a pinch-hitter for Dutch Leonard in the third inning on Elks Day at Fenway; he singled but did not score. Snell had joined the Red Sox from the Hyannis ballclub and stuck with the Red Sox right to the end of the year, pinch-hitting four times, then getting two starts, September 27and his final game on October 4. He edged out another Wally contender; Snell's first game came 25 days before Wally Rehg's Red Sox debut. Snell was released to Toronto in February 1914.

Peter Mackie of Brown University informs us that "Wally Snell '13 was baseball captain in his senior year. The consummate student-athlete, he was Phi Beta Kappa, majoring in Biology."

By 1916, he was back in Providence, coaching baseball. That year, he earned a master's in botany from Brown and a Ph.D. from Wisconsin. Dr. Snell was chair of the Botany Department at Brown and taught there until his retirement in 1959, during which time he coached 48 Brown sports teams. His two published books are *Glossary of Mycology* and *The Boleti of Northeastern North America*. No doubt both are well-thumbed volumes in the Red Sox clubhouse library.

There were three earlier Walters: Walter "Rosy" Carlisle in 1908, Walter Lonergan in 1911, and Walter Moser, also in 1911. But none of the three appear to have been Wallys.

The first Wally on the Red Sox, Wally Snell. Courtesy Brown University.

Among their 32 ballplayers, the 1918 World Champion Red Sox had two Wallys, a Walter, and a Walt (and even a Weldon): Wally Mayer, Wally Schang, Walter Barbare, and Walt Kinney. And the lawyerly-sounding J. Weldon Wyckoff.

It's been a long time since the Red Sox had a Wally on the team. We've had Willie, Wily Mo, and Wil. We last had Walt McKeel in 1997 and Walt Masterson in 1951 (and Murray Wall in 1959), but the last Wally we had was Wally Moses in 1948.

Wally for a day. Do note that in late August 2004, Red Sox utilityman David McCarty was on the DL—but at one point put on mascot garb and (unknown to an unsuspecting public) served a stint as Wally the Green Monster.

Starting in 2006, there were two more mascots added to the Red Sox roster—large red sock figures named "Righty" and "Lefty." Needless to say, there are a lot of Red Sox nicknamed Lefty over the years—Mr. Grove is the first one who comes to mind. Is there a "Righty" in Red Sox annals? Not that we're come across (though presumably some Red Sox wives may feel they married Mr. Right). We do have Tom Wright (1948–51) and Jim Wright (1978–79). And Tom Wright was a lefty (at the plate), for whatever that's worth.

Red Sox players who changed their names

Some players seem to have been dissatisfied with their names, for one reason or another. Those reasons are sometimes obscure to us today. For whatever reasons, quite a number of Red Sox players changed their names over the years. No, not Bill Buckner. In some cases, it's reasonably obvious why the change. In other instances, you have to wonder what these men were thinking. In some cases, they seem not to have actually changed their names but just assumed others and were known by the other name (or maybe even both). Here's a listing of known name changes.

Hick Cady, originally Forrest Berglund.

Forrest Leroy "Hick" Cady was originally Forrest Leroy Berglund.

Bert Edgar Chaplin was Bert Edgar Chapman.

George Joseph Cuppy was George Koppe.

Joe "Gabby" Glenn was Joseph Gurzensky.

"Sea Lion" Hall's real name was Carlos Clolo—or was it?*

Pete Jablonowski played from 1927 to 1933 under his own name, and then changed it to Pete Appleton.

Albert L. Jacobson was Albin L. Jacobson.

Marty Karow was born as Martin Gregory Karowsky.

Ernest Dudley "Dud" Lee was known as Ernest Dudley.

Babe Martin was Boris Michael Martinovich.

Frederick Francis Mitchell was Frederick Francis Yapp—and, in fact, even well after his years in Boston is still listed in U. S. Census records as Frederick F. Yapp.

Johnny Pesky was John Michael Paveskovich.

Nick Polly was Nicholas Joseph Polachanin.

George Pepper Prentiss was a/k/a George Pepper Wilson.

John Picus Quinn was John Quinn Picus—or so we always thought. However, SABR's Biographical Committee learned in early 2007 that he was born as Joannes Pajkos.

James Edward "Pete" Runnels was James Edward Runnells.

Eugene Rudolph Rye was Eugene Rudolph Mercantelli.

Ray Wilson Scarborough was Rae Wilson Scarborough.

F. Osee Schrecongost was a/k/a Ossee Schreck.

Al Simmons was Aloys Szymanski.

Patrick Clement Simmons was Patrick Clement Simoni.

Frank Elmer Smith was Frank Elmer Schmidt.

Julius Joseph "Moose" Solters was Julius Joseph Soltesz.

Albert John Stokes was Albert John Stocek (though his death certificate reads "Stocek").

John Thoney was John Thoeny.

Robert Earl Wilson was Earl Lawrence Wilson, according to the record books.

Joseph "Smoky Joe" Wood was Howard Ellsworth Wood, but legally changed his name to Joe Wood. Not Joseph, just Joe.

Pretty minor changes: Jose Offerman was originally Jose Oferman. And Byron Joseph "Ty" LaForest was originally Biron Joseph LaForest.

And was Charley "Sea Lion" Hall's name originally Carlos Clolo? It says so in every record book. But it wasn't so, according to his granddaughter-in-law ReBecca Glidewell-Brown, who reports that his father was Arthur Hall and his mother Elvira Mungari. Charley was christened at the San Buenaventura Mission in Ventura, California as Carlos Luis Hall. His son was Carlos Luis Hall, Jr. It's quite possible that "Clolo" was a nickname given him as a young boy; it does seem like it could be a childlike conflation of Carlos Luis.

George Pepper Wilson won his first game, beating Ned Garvin of Milwaukee, 7–2. You'll find him in the boxscores of the day's game, but not in most record books. Reason being, he changed his name to George Pepper Prentiss for 1902 and was 2–2 for Boston, then 0–1 for Baltimore, and then died at his father's home of illness before the season was over.

According to his obituary in the *Wilmington News Journal*, Prentiss died at home of typhoid fever. The obituary mentions that Mr. Prentiss was the son of Mr. James P. Prentiss, but there is no mention of his mother or other relatives. There is no mention of his name change or the fact that he once used the name Wilson. He is listed as George P. Prentiss in the Wilmington City Directory as early as 1895 and through 1902. The likely scenario here is that, for whatever reason, he played under the name George Wilson in 1901 and then reverted to his true name, Prentiss, in 1902. It may have had to do with ducking contractual obligations in order to join the fledgling American League. Somewhere along the line he picked up the nickname "Kitten."

In 1901, he began the season with Albany as Wilson, was acquired by the Boston Americans and debuted on September 23, coming late into the second game of a doubleheader against Detroit. He pitched the final two innings of a seven-inning contest, taking over from Ted Lewis. Wilson walked a man, and then gave up a triple to Detroit's pitcher Miller—though the *Boston Globe* said that it was a hit which "Ferris made no effort to stop as it went past him." Two more runs were scored in the top of the eighth, but they aren't in the record books because the umpire called the game, already 9–2 in Detroit's favor through seven, due to darkness.

Wilson made his first and only 1901 start on September 27. He was 0-for-2 at the plate, but threw a complete game win for Boston, beating Milwaukee 9–2. According to the *Boston Globe*, he "was given a show and made a pretty good impression, having very little trouble with the visitors." It was a good enough impression that he was invited back for the 1902 season—though by the time he came back he'd changed his name.

During the 1902 season, Prentiss was not having a good season. The *Washington Post* at one point noted he was on the brink of being released due to his "uniformly poor work." Boston sold him to the struggling Baltimore franchise in July and he got in a couple of starts for the Orioles, but his season took too many turns for the worse when he became ill and returned to his father's home in Wilmington to recuperate. When he began to feel better at one point, he started pitching for the Wilmington ballclub and threw a few games trying to get back into shape. He suffered a relapse and died on September 8.

What was it with these Wilsons? And Pete Jablonowski?

In the 1960s, Red Sox pitcher Earl Wilson, we learn, changed his name from Earl Lawrence Wilson to Robert Earl Wilson. He remained known as Earl. Like George Wilson, or Prentiss, he must have had his reasons. If he changed his name. Reached in April 2006, Earl's widow Roslin flatly denied he'd ever changed his name. However, other sources indicate that the story is more complicated. While the memorial pamphlet offered at his funeral service indicates that he was the only son born to Robert Earl Wilson Sr. and Amanda Elliott Wilson, we are told that Amanda never married and that Earl was what was locally called an "outside child." Further, that Amanda was not his birth mother but rather someone who took him in. Some might feel this shameful; to us, it just sounds complicated, and we suspect we may never know the full story. Earl's son Greg Lawrence was aware of the name change, but doesn't really have an explanation for why his father changed his name. Now, how did Earl's son end up with the last name that used to be Earl's middle name before he changed it? Well, Earl's grandfather's last name was Lawrence—but that really doesn't provide a satisfying explanation. Some minor mysteries, even from relatively recent years, remain unsolved.

In Pete Jablonowski's case, newspapers of the day report that he changed his name because he was studying law and believed the name Appleton would look better on his shingle. Appleton was a rough translation of Jablonowski from the Polish. Apparently, the Baltimore Orioles of the International League were taken aback when they received a 1934 contract signed by Appleton, but had never heard from Jablonowski. Did the name change help his play on the field? Who knows? He'd had a 17–16 pitching record through 1931, came to Boston and went 0–3 in 1932, threw just two innings in all of 1933 for the Yankees, then spent time in the minors until returning in 1936 with the Senators, with whom he was 14–9. Whatever worked in 1936 wore off in 1937, though, and he was 8–15 that year. The Senators hadn't done as well in '37, but not that much worse. His law career might have paid off better, but that wasn't one he chose to pursue.

"Jabby" was a bit of a renaissance man—a 1941 clipping reported that the University of Michigan graduate was a "Mertonian," explained as a "graduate of a physiognomy school conducted in New York by D. Holmes Whittier Morton, which gives instructions on how to determine individual aptitudes through a study of facial characteristics." Pete did allow that he hadn't yet figured a way to use it to advantage against opposing batters. He'd been born in Terryville, Connecticut and set the state shotput record while starring at track and basketball as well as pitching four years of high school baseball. He threw two no-hitters for Terryville, and later an Eastern League no-hitter for Waterbury in 1926. He was an exceptionally talented pianist and his mother envisioned a musical career for him; he took special classes at the Michigan Conservatory while also taking post-graduate courses in psychology. He pitched three years for Michigan, but when not on the mound played shortstop as part of the "jaw breaker infield" of Jablonowski, Puckelwartz, and Oosterbaan.

It was only after six years in major league ball that he changed his name. His 1932 season with Boston was his sixth; he'd played with Cincinnati and Cleveland earlier. He was 0–3 with the Red Sox in 1932; he threw a total of two innings for the Yankees in 1933, and then he changed his name in 1934. Appleton earned a degree in education from Rutgers, and taught some high school during the offseasons. He attended New Jersey Law School, but appears not to have ever graduated or hung up that shingle. His obituary says that he changed his name because he had "decided that was too much of a tongue twister, especially if he embarked on a musical career, so he went to court and had his name changed." His specialty was Chopin, but Rachmaninoff was one of his favorites as well, and he played some jazz and popular melodies, too—though he preferred classical music. About his various studies, he told Cleveland writer Ralph Kelly, "Baseball isn't a bum's game any more. There's a surprising lot of shrewd and intelligent men on every team."

Let us note here the name change that wasn't: when Hugh Duffy suggested Sy Rosenthal change his last name to Rose. See the section on Rosenthal under Jewish players for detail on Rosenthal's reply.

Red Sox players who *should have* changed their names?

That might be unkind. We'll leave that question alone. We wouldn't want to make fun of anyone's name! No way.

Guys named Joe, who played for the Red Sox

Joe Azcue, 1969	Joe Dobson, 1941–43,	Joe Harris, 1905–07	Joe Lucey, 1925
Jow Bowman, 1944–45	1946–50, 1954	Joe Harris, 1922–25	Joe Mulligan, 1934
Joe Bush, 1918–21	Joe Dugan, 1922	Joe Hesketh, 1990–94	Joe Nelson, 2004
Joe Cascarella, 1935–36	Joe Foy, 1966–68	Joe Heving, 1938–40	Joe Oliver, 2001
Joe Christopher, 1966	Joe Giannini, 1911	Joe Hudson, 1995–97	Joe Price, 1989
Joe Cicero, 1929–30	Joe Ginsberg, 1961	Joe Judge, 1933–34	Joe Riggert, 1911
Joe Connolly, 1924	Joe Glenn, 1940	Joe Kiefer, 1925–26	Joe Rudi, 1981
Joe Cronin, 1935–45	Joe Gonzales, 1937	Joe Lahoud, 1968–71	Joe Sambito, 1986–87

Joe Trimble, 1955   Joe Wilhoit, 1919   Joe Wood, 1908–15
Joe Vosmik, 1938–39   Joe Wood, 1944

If we wanted, we could add Jose Canseco, Jose Cruz, Jose Melendez, Jose Offerman, Jose Santiago, and Jose Tartabull.

We might note that Boob Fowler's given name was Joseph Chester Fowler and that Gordie Mueller's was Joseph Gordon Mueller.

Joe Bush was actually named Leslie Ambrose Bush. And Joe Ginsberg was actually named Myron Nathan Ginsberg.

Managers named Joe were Cronin, Kerrigan, and McCarthy.

Joe Cicero. Courtesy of Brace Photo.

RED SOX NICKNAMES

Jablonowski or Appleton, he was still "Jake" to his teammates. Nicknames in baseball provide additional entertainment. As Steve "Psycho" Lyons once explained,

> Most guys have at least one, some have two or three—usually names unacceptable in mixed company. Still others have nicknames that even they don't know about, but everybody else does…. Most nicknames are simply the shortening of one's last name and adding a 'Y.' If the guy's last name is Anderson, he comes Andy. If it's Marzano, it becomes Marzy. If the guy isn't that exciting anyway, adding a 'Y' gets the process over with. Generally, a nickname is a form of endearment. If people just call you Bob because that's your name, it's time to start working on your personality.—Steve Lyons, *Psycho-analysis*. Sagamore Publishing

What follows is a necessarily incomplete list of Red Sox nicknames. There's no way anyone could know them all. We've left off the "Bob" for Robert or the names like Andy or Marzy, and we've left out the "Peckerhead" and other names that might not deemed acceptable in mixed company. In most cases, we've also left out the nicknames created by sportswriters to make a column more colorful and focused on the names players might call each other, even if uncomplimentary (Babe Ruth, because of perceived African features, was called "Nig" by more than a few opposing players trying to get under his skin), though there are exceptions, notably in the case of Ted Williams and Babe Ruth, where we have listed out a variety of names invented by the writers. One can be reasonably sure that no one went around calling over to Ruth, "Hey, Behemoth of Bust, you got some mail in the clubhouse." But he was in his day widely known as the "Sultan of Swat"—widely enough that other writers crafted similar handles like the "Caliph of Clout." We suspect that no one ever called Williams "Tempestuous Ted" to his face, but some players in 1938 did call him "California" during his first spring training with the Red Sox.

Bizarrely, even "Ted Williams" was a nickname itself, applied to a grey mountain lion rug that lay on the office floor of wealthy Jorge Pasquel, one of the owners of the Mexican League in the 1940s. Pasquel had shot the lion himself and the rug, with head and teeth still attached, lay on his blue-tile office floor. Pasquel gave it the nickname "Ted Williams" because he was trying to bag Ted to play for the Mexican League in 1946 as a way to give the league instant credibility. Ted (the man) reportedly refused offers that were at least triple his U.S. salary with the Red Sox.

Red Sox fans are nothing but passionate, and ready to make connections in unlikely settings. Barry Singer remembers a summer evening in the mid-1980s, when there was a free screening of *The Wizard of Oz* at the Hatch Shell, alongside the Charles River in Boston. In the scene where Dorothy meets the Tin Man, he labors to whisper "Oil can." She says, "Oil can what?" A thousand people on the lawn shouted in unison, "Oil Can Boyd!"

Notable Red Sox nicknames

Merle Theron "Doc" Adkins

Benny "Hawaii 50" Agbayani [wore uniform #50, too!]

Aristotle George "Harry" Agganis a/k/a Harry "The Golden Greek" Agganis a/k/a "Aggie"

Sam "Slam" Agnew

Israel "Izzy" Alcantara

Dale "Moose" Alexander

Gary "Muggsy" Allenson

Baldomero "Mel" Almada

Nick Altrock, "The Clown Prince of Baseball"

Ernest Henry "Junie" Andres

Ivy Paul "Poison" Andrews

Frank "Rhino" Arellanes

Bronson "Dirty" Arroyo

Robert Anthony "Casper" Asbjornson

Peter William "Jake" Appleton

Elden "Sub" Auker a/k/a Elden "Big Six" Auker, a/k/a "Mule Ears" Auker

Leycester Doyle "Tex" Aulds a/k/a "Leslie"

Lore Verne "King" Bader a/k/a "Two Pairs"

Jack Edward "Buck" Baker

Bob "Beetle" Bailey

Welby S. "Buddy" Bailey (coach)

Cornelius "Neal" Ball

Walter "Dinty" Barbare

Herbert Paul "Babe" Barna

Francis Joseph "Red" Barrett

Bob "Jumbo" Barrett

William Joseph "Whispering Bill" Barrett

Edward "Cousin Ed" Barrow (manager)

Edward "Jumbo" Barry

Frank Matt "The Beau" Baumann

Don "Groove" Baylor

William Lear "Beverly" Bayne

"Ding Dong" Gary Bell

Dennis "The Menace" Bennett

Francis Allen "Chip" Bennett

Louis William "Boze" Berger

Elliot Allardice "Gilly" Bigelow a/k/a "Babe"

John George "Smiley" Bischoff

Max "Tillie" Bishop a/k/a Max "Camera Eye" Bishop

Clarence Waldo "Climax" Blethen

Harvey Fred "Red" Bluhm

Isaac Morgan "Ike" Boone

Raymond Otis "Ike" Boone

Thomas Bruce "Spike" Borland

Stewart Cole "Doc" Bowers

Edward Oliver "Ted" Bowsfield

Dennis Ray "Oil Can" Boyd

Hugh "Corns" Bradley

James Ward "King" Brady

Darrell "Bucky" Brandon

Frederick Oliver "Fritz" Bratschi

"Steady" Eddie Bressoud

Ralph "Brick" Brickner

Hector Harold "Skinny" Brown

Lloyd Andrew "Gimpy" Brown

Tom "Bruno" Brunansky

Bill "Billy Bucks" Buckner

Frederick Duff "Lefty" Burchell

Don "Bootin'" Buddin

Tom "Bugs" Burgmeier

Jesse "Crab" Burkett

John "Sheets" Burkett

Rick "Rooster" Burleson

George Henry "Tioga George" Burns

Leslie Ambrose "Bullet Joe" Bush

"Slim" Bill Butland

Eldred William "Bud" Byerly

Orlando "The Big O" Cabrera

Forrest Leroy "Hick" Cady

Earl Welton "Teach" Caldwell

Ray "Rube" Caldwell a/k/a "Sum"

Bill "Soup" Campbell

Jose "Hoser" Canseco

Thomas Francis Aloysius "Scoops" Carey

Walter "Rosy" Carlisle

Roy Edward "Dizzy" Carlyle

Albin Oscar "Swede" Carlstrom

William "Rough" Carrigan

Thomas Joseph "Crooning Joe" Cascarella

Sean "The Mayor" Casey

Orlando "Cha Cha" Cepeda a/k/a "Baby Bull"

Chester James "Pop" Chadbourne

Robert Edward "Chick" Chakales

Frank "The Peerless Leader" Chance a/k/a "Husk" (manager)

Kendall Fay "Lefty" Chase

Frank Lane "Pete" Charton

John Dwight "Happy Jack" Chesbro

Joseph Francis "Dode" Cicero
Edward Victor "Knuckles" Cicotte
Galen "Grump" Cisco
Chalmer William "Bill" Cissell
William Otis "Otey" Clark
"Rocket" Roger Clemens
Truman "Tex" Clevenger
Michael "Prime Time" Coleman—though this
    nickname may be self-proclaimed
Harry Warren "Rip" Collins
John "Shano" Collins
Merrill Russell "Merl" Combs
Ralph Remick "Commy" Comstock
David "Coney" Cone
Tony "Tony C" Conigliaro a/k/a "Conig"
William Millar "Bunk" Congalton
Edward J. "Butch" Connolly, Sr.
Joseph George "Coaster Joe" Connolly
Mervin Thomas "Bud" Connolly a/k/a "Mike"
Allen Lindsey "Dusty" Cooke
James Edward "Scoops" Cooney
Cecil "Flash" Cooper
Guy Evans "Rebel" Cooper
Rheal "Frenchy" Cormier
Frederick Nicholas "Fritz" Coumbe
Roger Maxwell "Doc" Cramer a/k/a "Flit"
    Cramer
Clifford Carlton "Cactus" Cravath a/k/a
    "Gavvy" Cravath★
Paxton "Pac-Man" Crawford a/k/a "Pac-Dog"
    or simply "Pack"
Patrick Francis "Whoops" Creeden
Robert Anthony "Crooked Arm" Cremins
    a/k/a "Lefty"
Rick "Sunshine" Croushore
Delbert Leon "Lee" Culberson
John "Gumby" Cumberland (coach)
George Joseph "Nig" Cuppy
Hazen S. "Kiki" Cuyler (coach)
Ellsworth Tenney "Babe" Dahlgren a/k/a "Sis"
Nicholas Dominic "Dim Dom" Dallesandro
Harold P. "Babe" Danzig
Brian "Dauber" Daubach a/k/a "The Belleville
    Basher"—a sportswriter concoction
Robert Francis "Red" Daughters
Andre "Hawk" Dawson
Ellis Fergason "Cot" Deal
Otto Charles "Pep" Deininger
Ivan Martin "Ike" Delock
Sam "Blackie" Dente
Gene "Red" Desautels
William Patrick "Mickey" Devine

Baudillo Jose "Bo" Diaz
Juan "Big Thunder" Diaz
George "Skeets" Dickey
Dom "The Little Professor" DiMaggio
William Henry "Big Bill" Dinneen
Joseph Gordon "Burrhead" Dobson
John Frederick "Jiggs" Donahue
John "Dobber" Dopson
Thomas J. "Long Tom" Doran
Harry "Fritz" Dorish
Patrick Henry "Patsy" Dougherty
Thomas Jefferson "Buttermilk Tommy" Dowd
Robert Dennis "Muggsy" Doyle
Clemens Johann "Steamboat" Dreisewerd
David Jonathan "J.D." Drew
Walt "Moosup Mauler" Dropo a/k/a
    "Snowshoes"
Jean Joseph Octave Arthur "Chauncey" Dubuc
Hugh "The Little General" Duffy (coach)
Joseph Anthony "Jumping Joe" Dugan
George Henry "Pea Soup" Dumont
Edward Fant "Bull" Durham
James Edward "Pig Pen" Dwyer
Dennis Lee "The Eck" Eckersley
Elmer Albert "Mose" Eggert
Howard Jonathan "Bob" Ehmke
Henry Hack Eibel (Hack is his actual middle
    name)
Clyde Arthur
    "Hack" Engle
Dwight "Dewey"
    Evans
Walter Arthur
    "Hoot" Evers
Bibb August
    "Jockey" Falk
    (coach)
Charles Edward
    "Duke"
    Farrell

Hack Engle.

Edward "Doc" Farrell
Albert "Hobe" Ferris
David "Boo" Ferriss—you'll even find him in the
    phone book as "Boo"
William Lloyd "Chick" Fewster
Mark "The Bird" Fidrych
Henry William "Bulldog" Fischer
Carlton "Pudge" Fisk—also Carlton "The Hu-
    man Rain Delay" Fisk
Ira James "Pete" Flagstead a/k/a "Flaggy"
John "Flash" Flaherty
Albert Dell "Broadway" Flair

Leslie Fletchard "Bill" Fleming
August "Happy" Foreman
Francis Isaiah "Monkey" Foreman
Casey "The Blade" Fossum
Edward "Kid" Foster
Robert Roy "Fatty" Fothergill
Joseph Chester "Boob" Fowler a/k/a "Gink"
Ervin "Pete" Fox
Jimmie "Beast" Foxx, a/k/a "Double X"
Herschel Baskin "Buster" Freeman
John Frank "Buck" Freeman
Owen Lacey "Red" Friend
Jeff "Frito" Frye a/k/a "Small" and "Pop"
Frank "Rabbit" Fuller
Dellos Clinton "Sheriff" Gainer—also known as "Ducky"
Edward Michael "Lefty" Gallagher
Rich "El Guapo" Garces
Nomar "Nomie" Garciaparra a/k/a "Garp"
William Frederick "Shotgun" Gardner
Robert Ford "Snapper" Garrison a/k/a "Rocky"
Walter "Spooks" Gerber
Harry Homer "Brownie" Gessler a/k/a "Doc"
James Edward "Chappy" Geygan
Norwood Ringold "Gibby" Gibson
Russ "Gibby" Gibson
Don "Bear" Gile
Frank "Flash" Gilhoole
Robert William "Bunch" Gillespie
Myron Nathan "Joe" Ginsberg
Joe "Gabby" Glenn
John Henry "Bunny" Godwin
Alex "Gonzo" Gonzales
Eusebio "Papo" Gonzalez
Joe Madrid "Smokey" Gonzales
Joe "Burrhead" Gordon
Tom "Flash" Gordon
Arthur "Skinny" Graham
Craig "Little Hurt" Grebeck [this nickname may have been more confined to his White Sox days]
Elijah "Pumpsie" Green
Mike "Gator" Greenwell a/k/a "Greenie"
Sylvaneous Augustus "Vean" Gregg
Douglas Lee "Dude" Griffin
Myron "Moose" Grimshaw
Ewell "Turkey" Gross
Robert Moses "Lefty" Grove
Fermin "Mike" Guerra
Donald Joseph "Double Ugly" Gutteridge
Kurt Morris "Casey" Hageman
Arvel Odell "Bad News" Hale a/k/a "Chief"

Raymond Timothy "Pat" Haley
Charley "Sea Lion" Hall
Fred Girard "Pudge" Haney
Kenneth Smith "Hawk" Harrelson
Joseph "Moon" Harris
Maurice Charles "Mickey" Harris a/k/a "Himself"
William Jennings Bryan "Slim" Harriss
Charles Oscar "Twiggy" Hartenstein
Clemens Raymond "Clem" Hausmann
Frankie "Blimp" Hayes
Charles Judson "Eagle Eye" Hemphill
Olaf "Swede" Henriksen
Floyd Bluford "Butch" Henry
Ramon "Mike" Herrera
"Jughandle" Joe Heving
Charles Taylor "Cheerful Charlie" Hickman a/k/a "Piano Legs"
Michael Franklin "Pinky" Higgins
Shea "Hildy" Hillenbrand
Harvey Max "Hob" Hiller
Darkus Dutton "Dave" Hillman
Paul Edwin "Herky" Hinrichs a/k/a "Parson" Hinrichs
Richard "Doc" Hoblitzell
Clell Lavern "Butch" Hobson
George Edward "Lefty" Hockette
Fred "Boot Nose" Hofmann
Ralph "The Major" Houk (manager)
Paul Joseph "Del" Howard
Lester Curtis "Lucky" Howe
Waite Charles "Schoolboy" Hoyt
George "Gee" Huff a/k/a "The Professor" (manager)
Cecil Carlton "Tex" Hughson
Benjamin Franklin "High Pockets" Hunt
Harold James "Buddy" Hunter
Thomas Carr "Whitey" Hurd
Robert Leon "Butch" Huskey
Berthold Juneau "Pete" (Bert) Husting
Albert "Beany" Jacobson
William "Baby Doll" Jacobson
Charles Dewey "Lefty" Jamerson
William Henry "Big Bill" James
Harold Chandler "Childe Harold" Janvrin
Thomas "Tut" Jenkins
Adam Rankin "Tex" Johnson
Earl "Lefty" Johnson a/k/a "Stretch" and "The Earl of Emergency"
Robert Lee "Indian Bob" Johnson
Smead "Smudge" Jolley a/k/a "Guinea"
Charles Claude "Casey" Jones

Rick "Too Tall" Jones a/k/a "Tall Boy"

Samuel Paul "Sad Sam" Jones

Thomas William Oscar "Ossie" Judd

Edwin "Loose" Karger

Benjamin Joyce "Baldy" Karr

Winford Ashley "Win" Kellum

Russell Paul "Dutch" Kemmerer a/k/a "Rusty"

John "Super Sub" Kennedy

William Aulton "Lefty" Kennedy

Joseph William "Harlem Joe" Kiefer a/k/a
    "Smoke"

Leo Patrick "The Black Cat" Kiely a/k/a "Kiki"

Wendell "Wave 'Em In" Kim (coach)

Ellis Raymond "Old Folks" Kinder

Robert George "Junior" Kline

John Wesley "Schoolboy" Knight

Jack "Alice" Kramer

George "Candy" LaChance

Biron Joseph "Ty" LaForest

Joe "Duck" Lahoud

Edward Erving "Sparky" Lake

Jack "Tomato" Lamabe

William "Good Time Bill" Lamar

Elton "Sam" Langford

Mike "Lazer" Lansing

Frank Breyfogle "Pat" LaPorte

Lynford Hobart "Broadway" Lary

William Francis "Spaceman" Lee

Ernest "Dud" Lee

Wilfred "Lefty" LeFebvre

Louis Albert "Doc" Legett

Harry Loran "Nemo" Leibold

Donald Eugene "Footsie" Lenhardt

Hobert Benjamin "Dutch" Leonard

Thaddeus Stanley "Ted" Lepcio

Bertram Roe "Dutch" Lerchen

Lewis Paul "Chief" Leroy

Curtis "The Mechanic" Leskanic

Darren "D-Lew" Lewis

George Edward "Duffy" Lewis

Edward Morgan "Parson" Lewis

Johnny "Skids" Lipon

Horace Milton "Hod" Lisenbee

Claude Edward "Skip" Lockwood

James Reynold "Gentleman Jim" Lonborg

Derek "D Lo" Lowe

John Charles "Buster" Lucas

Joseph Earl "Scooch" Lucey

Ulysses John "Tony" Lupien

Elbin Delmar "Del" Lundgren

Albert Walter "Sparky" Lyle

Walter Edward "Jabber" Lynch

Steve "Psycho" Lyons

Daniel Knowles "Deacon Danny" MacFayden

Thomas "Bunny" Madden

Sal "The Barber" Maglie (coach)

James Thomas "Moe" Mahoney

Paul Augustus "Biff" Maloy

Frank "Big Frank" Malzone

Felix "The Cat" Mantilla

Henry Emmett "Heinie" Manush

John Alfred "Footsie" Marcum

Juan Antonio "The Dominican Dandy"
    Marichal a/k/a "Manito"

Albert Ludwig "Ollie" Marquardt

Boris "Babe" Martin

Pedro "Petey" Martinez

Walt "Shoe Store" Masterson

Daisuke "Dice-K" Matsuzaka

Gene William "Skip" Mauch

Charles Richard "Smokey" Maxwell

Le Roy Evans "Chick" Maynard

Carl William "Sub" Mays

John William "Windy" McCall

Joseph "Marse Joe" McCarthy (manager)

Ambrose Moses "Amby" McConnell

Maurice Joseph "Mickey" McDermott a/k/a
    "Maury"

Jimmie Leroy "Hot Rod" McDonald

James Thomas "Deacon" McGuire

Marty "Thrush" McHale

John Phalen "Stuffy" McInnis a/k/a "Jack"

Archie Richard "Happy" McKain

Justin Theodore "Jud" McLaughlin

John Bannerman "Larry" McLean a/k/a "Giant"

Henry John "Doc" McMahon

Norman Alexis "Bub" McMillan

Donald Eric "Boob" McNair

Michael "Minooka Mike" McNally
    a/k/a "Slats"

Sabath "Sam" Mele

Oscar "Ski" Melillo a/k/a "Spinach"

Michael William "Leaping Mike" Menosky

Emile Michael "Mike" Meola

James Anderson "Andy" Merchant

John Joseph "Spike" Merena

George "Catfish" Metkovich

Russell Charles "Mad Monk" Meyer a/k/a
    "Rowdy"

Wilson Daniel "Dee" Miles

Kevin "Tex" Millar

Abraham Phillip "Corky" Miller

Edmund John "Bing" Miller

Lawrence "Hack" Miller

Rick "Ram" Miller

Otis "Otto" Miller

Colonel Buster "Bus" Mills

Rudy Anthony "Buster" Minarcin

William Charles "Frenchy" Monbouquette

William Wilcy "Cy" Moore

David Michael "Moe" Morehead

Harry Richard "Cy" Morgan

Joe "Tollway Joe" Morgan (manager)

Walter Edward "Big Ed" Morris

Michael Joseph "Deacon" Morrissey a/k/a
    "Frank"

Guy "Moose" Morton

William Bankhead "Doc" Moskiman

Bill "Billy Baseball" Mueller

Billy Arnold "Muff" Muffett

Gregory Thomas "Moe" Mulleavy

Joseph Ignatius "Big Joe" Mulligan

William Edward "Swat" Mundy a/k/a "Bull"

John Joseph "Grandma" Murphy a/k/a
    "Fordham Johnny" and "Fireman"

George King "Smiler" Murray

Charles Solomon "Buddy" Myer

Elmer Glenn "Big Jim" Myers

Ralph Edward "Hap" Myers

Walter Harold "Judge" Nagel a/k/a "Lucky"

William Edward "Cap" Narleski

Louis Norman "Bobo" Newsom a/k/a "Buck"

Heber Hampton "Dick" Newsome

Lamar Ashby "Scooter" Newsome

Constantine Gregory "Gus" Niarhos

Herbert Clyde "Harry" Niles

Christopher Trotman "Trot" Nixon a/k/a
    "Volcano"

Hideo "Tornado" Nomo (maybe known as
    "No-No" because of his two no-hitters)

Lee William "Red" Nonnenkamp

Frank Rufus "Flossie" Oberlin

Thomas Edward "Obie" O'Brien

Thomas Joseph "Buck" O'Brien

Francis Joseph "Lefty" O'Doul

Jose "Offie" Offerman some fans called him
    "Awful Offerman"

Ben "Spiderman" Oglivie

Troy "Yummy" O'Leary a/k/a "O"

Pedro "Tony" Oliva

Thomas Noble "Rebel" Oliver

Karl Arthur "Ole" Olson

Marvin Clement "Sparky" Olson

Robert Emmett "Pinky" O'Neill

James Francis "Blackie" O'Rourke

David "Big Papi" Ortiz

Frederick Raymond "Fritz" Ostermueller a/k/a
    "Off" Ostermueller

Arnold Malcolm "Mickey" Owen (coach)

Marvin James "Freck" Owen

Spike Owen did not have a nickname. His real
    name was: Spike Owen

Frank Walter "Yip" Owens

James Vincent "Pag" Pagliaroni

Richard Paul "Mike" Palm

Melvin Lloyd "Marvelous Mel" Parnell a/k/a
    "Dusty"

Stanwood Wendell "Party" Partenheimer

"Donald Duck" Marty Pattin

Dustin "Pedro" Pedroia

Tony "El Gato" Peña

Herbert Jefferis "The Knight of Kennett Square"
    Pennock

Atanacio "Tony" Perez a/k/a "Doggie"

William Andrew "Solemn Bill" Pertica

Johnny "Needle Nose" Pesky

Urbane Henry "Pick" Pickering a/k/a "Brute"

William Benton "Big Bill" Piercy

Clarke Alonzo "Pinky" Pittinger

Chester Jennings "Jinx" Poindexter

Richard Twilley "Wiggles" Porter a/k/a
    "Twitches"

Erwin Coolidge "Bob" Porterfield

Arquimedez "Kimi" Pozo

Derrill Burham "Del" Pratt

Lester John "Larry" Pratt

George Pepper "Kitten" Prentiss

James Thompson "Doc" Prothro

Charles Leroy "Tex" Pruiett

Jeff "The Terminator" Reardon

Calvin "Pokey" Reese, Jr.

Robert Edwin "Gunner" Reeves

Wilhelmus Abraham "Win" Remmerswaal

Jerry "Rem Dawg" Remy (though this nickname
    was only conferred well after his playing
    days, in the early 21st century when Remy
    was a Red Sox broadcaster)

Steve "Lurch" Renko

William Beneditto "Big Bill" Renna

Eldon "Rip" Repulski

Carl "Sheeps" Reynolds

John Gordon "Dusty" Rhodes

Jim Ed Rice a/k/a "Power Plant"

Woodrow Earl "Woody" Rich

Emory Elmo "Topper" Rigney

Percival Sumner "Pop" Rising

William Joseph "Billy Jo" Robidoux

Wilbur Kincaid "Raw Meat" Rodgers

Lee Otis "Buck" Rogers
William Russell "Red" Rollings
Armando "Mandy" Romero
Vicente "Huevo" Romo
Warren Vincent "Buddy" Rosar
Chester Franklin "Buster" Ross
Robert Frank "Braggo" Roth
Herold Dominic "Muddy" Ruel
Charles Herbert "Red" Ruffing
James Edward "Pete" Runnels
Allen "Rubberarm" Russell
Glen David "Rip" Russell
George Herman "The Babe" Ruth (a/k/a
    "Bambino" and "The Sultan of Swat") Ruth
    was commonly called "Jidge" and "Honey"
    but was also called "Nig" (reference to his
    looking as though he could have African-
    American blood. Trying to rile Ruth, Cobb
    called him this all the time. He was also
    called "Tarzan" which he liked until he real-
    ized it was "…of the Apes.") The "Sultan of
    Swat" moniker was so widespread that Mark
    Halfon notes creative columnists also dub-
    bing Ruth the "Bazoo of Bang," "Behemoth
    of Bust," "Caliph of Clout," "Maharajah of
    Mash," "Rajah of Rap," "Wali of Wallop,"
    and the "Wazir of Wham."
Jack "Gulfport" Ryan
John Francis "Coffee Jack" Ryan
Dominic Joseph "Mike" Ryba
Eugene Rudolph "Half Pint" Rye (born Eugene
    Rudolph Mercantelli)
Kenneth George "Daffy" Sanders
Tom "Satch" Satriano
William "Chick" Sayles
William Cordes "Rudy" Schlesinger
Victor Joseph "Biff" Schlitzer
George Edward "Rocky" Schmees
John Albert "Bear Tracks" Schmitz
John Richard "Ducky" Schofield
Paul Frederick "Von" Schreiber
Albert Bringhurst "Bull" Schroll
Everett "Deacon" Scott
George Charles "Boomer" Scott
George Thomas "Tom Terrific" Seaver
Robert Ira "Suitcase Bob" Seeds
Albert Karl "Kip" Selbach
Edgar Merle "Lefty" Settlemire
Walter Dedaker "Skinny" Shaner a/k/a "Nig"
Howard Samuel "Hank" Shanks
Maurice Joseph "Red" Shannon
Alfred "Shoddy" Shaw

John Michael Joseph "Lefty" Shea
Neill Rawlins "Wild Horse" Sheridan
Benjamin Cowan "Big Ben" Shields a/k/a
    "Lefty"
Frank Strickland "Strick" Shofner
Ernie "Long" Shore
Charles Henry "Chick" Shorten
Norm "Smiley" Siebern
Wilfred Charles "Sonny" Siebert
Aloysius Harry "Bucketfoot Al" Simmons
Patrick "Purr" Simmons
Elisha Harrison "Camp" Skinner
Foster Herbert "Steve" Slayton
Rachel W. "Rac" Slider (coach)
Heath "Heathcliff" Slocumb
Alphonse Eugene "Fuzzy" Smith
Frank Elmer "Piano Mover" Smith a/k/a "Nig"
Lawrence Patrick "Paddy" Smith
Robert Walkup "Riverboat" Smith
Walter Henry "Doc" Snell
Julius Joseph "Moose" Solters a/k/a "Lemons"
Thomas Frank "Tully" Sparks
Tristram E. "Tris" Speaker, "The Grey Eagle"
    a/k/a "Spoke" and "Mister Spooks"
Edward Russell "Tubby" Spencer
Charles Sylvester "Chick" Stahl
Garland "Jake" Stahl
Bob "Bigfoot" Stanley a/k/a "The Steamer"
Robert Michael (Mike) "Stano" Stanley
Arnold John "Jigger" Statz
James Harry "Red" Steiner
Vernon Decatur "Junior" Stephens a/k/a
    "Buster"
Jerry "Teens" Stephenson
Howard Edward "Sponge" Storie
Dick "Dr. Strangeglove" Stuart a/k/a
    "Stonefingers"
Thomas Virgil "Snake" Sturdivant
Carl Ringdahl "Lefty" Sumner
Jeff "Soup" Suppan
James Reubin "Rawhide" Tabor
Douglas John "Poco" Taitt
Jesse Niles "Powder" Tannehill
Wilbur Arlington "Arlie" Tarbert
Henry Bennett "Bennie" Tate
Julian "Yo-yo" Tavarez a/k/a "Tornado"
George "Birdie" Tebbetts
John Peter "Jake" Thielman
Alphonse "Tommy" Thomas
Blaine M. "Baldy" Thomas
Chester David "Pinch" Thomas
Frederick Harvey "Tommy" Thomas

James Leroy (Lee) "Mad Dog" Thomas

Robert Brown (Bobby) Thomson, "The Staten Island Scot"

John "Bullet Jack" Thoney

Herbert Ehler "Lefty" Thormahlen a/k/a "Hank"

John Patrick "Jackie" Tobin

Philip Julius "Hook" Todt

Charles Richard "Tony" Tonneman

Mike "Taco" Torrez

Paul Howard "Dizzy" Trout

Robert Lee "Bullet Bob" Turley

Ugueth "Oogi" Urbina

Ernest Lewis "Tex" Vache

John "Johnny V" Valentin a/k/a "Val"

Harold Harris "Hy" Vandenberg

Jason "Tek" Varitek

Maurice Samuel (Mo) "Hit Dog" Vaughn

James Barton "Mickey" Vernon

Frank "Sweet Music" Viola

Clyde "Dutch the Clutch" Vollmer

Jacob Philip "Silent Jake" Volz

Jacob Fields "Whistling Jake" Wade

Charles Thomas (Charlie) "Broadway" Wagner

Charles F. "Heinie" Wagner

George Elvin "Rube" Walberg

Clarence William "Tillie" Walker

Cleotha "Chico" Walker

James "Snookey" Walsh

Alfred John "Roxy" Walters

Fred James "Whale" Walters

William Henry "Bucky" Walters

William Adolph "Wamby" Wambsganss [Note: at least once, in the 7–29–24 Globe, he was listed as Wamby in the box score!]

Paul Louis "Pee-Wee" Wanninger

Harold Burton "Rabbit" Warstler

John "Way Back" Wasdin

Robert Jose (Bob) "Bull" Watson

John Clifford "Lefty" Watwood

Montgomery Morton "Prof" Weaver

Robert George "Lefty" Weiland

Frank Tiguer "Bugger" Welch

Herbert "Dutch" Welch

Anton Frank "Tony" Welzer

Frederick Charles "Fireball" Wenz

William George "Bugs" Werle

George "Lucky" Whiteman

William Robert "Lefty" Wight

Delbert Quentin (Del) "Babe" Wilber

Alva Mitchel "Buff" Williams a/k/a "Rip"

Edwin "Dib" Williams

Evon Daniel "Denny" Williams

Theodore Samuel (Ted) "The Splendid Splinter" Williams a/k/a "Teddy Ballgame" "The Kid" "The Thumper" "Terrible Ted" "California" "Tempestuous Ted" "The Splendid Spitter"

George Francis "Squanto" Wilson

John Francis "Black Jack" Wilson a/k/a "Strong Boy"

Lester Wilbur "Tug" Wilson

Harold James "Whitey" Wiltse a/k/a "Pinky"

Frederick Davis "Ted" Wingfield

George Benjamin "Breezy" Winn a/k/a "Lefty"

John Thomas "Long Tom" Winsett

George Lovington "Sassafras" Winter

Clarence "Chilly" Winters

John Carl "Hans" Wittig

Joe "Smoky Joe" Wood (born Howard Ellsworth Wood)

George Rowland "Pinky" Woods

John Fulton "Abe" Woods

Harry Hall "Hoge" Workman

Allan Fulton "Red" Worthington

Carl "Yaz" Yastrzemski (Yaz's nickname before he joined the Sox was "Yeasty")

Preston Rudolph (Rudy) "The Big Indian" York

Eddie "The Walking Man" Yost (coach)

Denton True "Cy" Young

Allen Lee "Zeke" Zarilla

Norbert Henry "Norm" Zauchin

Don "Popeye" Zimmer (manager) a/k/a "Gerbil"—thanks to Bill Lee

William Henry "Goober" Zuber a/k/a "Zoom Zoom" Zuber

*Gavvy Cravath's full name was Clifford Carlton Cravath. His nickname was derived from gaviota, the Spanish word for seagull. Deadball Stars of the National League reports that a bunch of Mexican fans saw one of his hits strike and kill a seagull, forever earning himself the nickname.

Yank Terry's real name actually was Lancelot Yank Terry; he went by his middle name, but it was no nickname. And the man who seemingly sported two nicknames (Colonel Buster Mills) did not; those were his real names, too. He was given the unusual first name because his father's best friend was a U.S. Army colonel. Mills did have a nickname, though: "Bus."

"Hoot and Scoot" was a compound nickname for the shortstop/second base combination of Rick Burleson and Jerry Remy.

The best nickname for a player who didn't make the team? Maybe it was "Milkman Jim" Turner, who had a tryout for the Sox, didn't make it, but then played nine seasons in the majors for other teams, starting in 1937, with a 69–60 record and a 3.22 ERA.

Spanish nicknames *(apodos)*

Red Sox Spanish Network broadcaster Uri Berenguer and his crew report a parallel set of nicknames amongst the Spanish-speaking fan base. From the 2004 and 2007 Red Sox teams, for instance, there were:

La Pasion sin barba—Johnny Damon
El Honesto—Brian Daubach
El Verdugo—Keith Foulke
La Mega estrella—Nomar Garciaparra
Derek TerminaLowe—Derek Lowe
El hijo de la Señora Rihna—Julio Lugo
El Grande de Manoguayabo—Pedro Martinez
Don Bill—Bill Mueller
El Caballo Mayor—Trot Nixon

El Sunami Japones—Hideki Okajima
El Sexy Man (and El Gran Sexy and, of course, Big Papi)—David Ortiz
El Animal—Jonathan Papelbon
Dustin No me Digan Pequeno Pedroia— Dustin Pedroia (also called "El Pitufo mas popular"—the most popular Smurf)
El Super-Manny—Manny Ramirez
El Barbaro—Curt Schilling

Name play with nicknames

One can categorize nicknames, too.

Animal Nicknames
Don "Bear" Gile
Leo "The Black Cat" Kiely
Thomas "Bunny" Madden
Felix "The Cat" Mantilla
Rick "Ram" Miller
Tony "El Gato" Peña
"Doggie" Tony Perez
George Pepper "Kitten" Prentiss
Carl "Sheeps" Reynolds
Neill "Wild Horse" Sheridan
Julius "Moose" Solters
Thomas "Snake" Sturdivant
Mo "Hit Dog" Vaughn
Harold Burton "Rabbit" Warstler
Don "Gerbil" Zimmer

Red Sox with lambs and goats.

Aquatic Creatures
Howard Edward "Sponge" Storie
Fred James "Whale" Walters
George "Catfish" Metkovich
Charley "Sea Lion" Hall
Mike "Gator" Greenwell
Robert Ford "Snapper" Garrison
Joe "Duck" Lahoud

Birds and Insects
Bob "Beetle" Bailey
Tom "Bugs" Burgmeier
Rick "Rooster" Burleson

Andrew "Hawk" Dawson
Ewell "Turkey" Gross
Ken "Hawk" Harrelson
Tris "The Grey Eagle" Speaker
Charles "Chick" Stahl
George "Birdie" Tebbetts

Food Nicknames
Hugh "Corns" Bradley
Bill "Soup" Campbell
George Henry "Pea Soup" Dumont
Jeff "Frito" Frye
George "Candy" LaChance
Oscar "Spinach" Melillo
Wilbur Kincaid "Rawmeat Bill" Rodgers
Vicente "Huevo" Romo

Julius "Lemons" Solters

Bob "Steamer" Stanley

Mike "Taco" Torrez

George "Sassafras" Winter

William Henry "Goober" Zuber

Speaking of tacos, during Game Two of the 2007 World Series, Jacoby Ellsbury fed millions of Americans by stealing second base in the bottom of the fourth inning off Rockies pitcher Ubaldo Jimenez. The Taco Bell chain offered a promotion of a free taco to everyone in the United States if a player from either team stole a base at any time in the Series. The stolen base proved uneventful; Ellsbury was left stranded. The Red Sox won the game, but it doesn't appear the theft has yet earned Ellsbury a new nickname.

It was his last name, not his nickname, but a tip of the fork to Dizzy Trout.

Though technically more something you might ingest inadvertently rather than food per se, Ivy Paul Andrews comes to mind. His nickname was, predictably, "Poison."

And let's not forget the prospect who should have made it on nickname alone, but never did: "Pork Chop" Pough.

Beverage Nicknames include

Dennis "Oil Can" Boyd ("Oil Can" being regional slang for a can of beer)

Eldred William "Bud" Byerly

Chester "Pop" Chadbourne

"Buttermilk Tommy" Dowd

Eugene Rudolph "Half Pint" Rye

Nicknames Involving Place

Jim "Pig Pen" Dwyer

Joseph "Moon" Harris

Walt "Shoe Store" Masterson

Herb "The Knight of Kennett Square" Pennock

Jack "Gulfport" Ryan

Elisha Harrison "Camp" Skinner

Robert Walkup "Riverboat" Smith

Bobby "The Staten Island Scot" Thomson

Charlie "Broadway" Wagner

Body Parts Nicknames

Edward "Knuckles" Cicotte

Robert "Crooked Arm" Cremins

Joseph "Burrhead" Dobson

Charles Judson "Eagle Eye" Hemphill

Fred "Boot Nose" Hofmann

Donald Eugene "Footsie" Lenhardt

Eric "Boob" McNair

Johnny "Needle Nose" Pesky

Henry Emmett "Heinie" Manush

Bob "Bigfoot" Stanley

Occupation Nicknames

Roger "Doc" Cramer—to name just one of many Docs

Dom "The Little Professor" DiMaggio

Bibb "Jockey" Falk

Ralph "The Major" Houk

Waite Charles "Schoolboy" Hoyt

Edward Morgan "Parson" Lewis

Sal "The Barber" Maglie

John Joseph "Fireman" Murphy

Walter Harold "Judge" Nagel

Robert Edwin "Gunner" Reeves

Everett "Deacon" Scott

Frank Elmer "Piano Mover" Smith

Condition or "State" Nicknames

"Steady" Eddie Bressoud

William "Rough" Carrigan

Allen "Dusty" Cooke

Steve "Psycho" Lyons

John Phalen "Stuffy" McInnis

Troy "Yummy" O'Leary

Herold Dominic "Muddy" Ruel

John Richard "Ducky" Schofield—everything's just ducky

Alfred "Shoddy" Shaw

Alphonse Eugene "Fuzzy" Smith

Edward Russell "Tubby" Spence

Paul Howard "Dizzy" Trout

George Benjamin "Breezy" Winn

Color Nicknames

Walter "Rosy" Carlisle

Sam "Blackie" Dente

Gene "Red" Desautels

Harry Homer "Brownie" Gessler

Mike "Greenie" Greenwell

Mike "Pinky" Higgins

Thomas Carr "Whitey" Hurd

Jeff Gray, of course, just had that as his name, not a nickname.

Best Sox nicknames by position

1B "Dr. Strangeglove" Dick Stuart

2B "Hobe" (Albert Ferris)

SS "Rooster" (Rick Burleson)
3B "Pinky" (Mike Higgins)
LF "The Splendid Splinter" (Ted Williams)
CF "The Grey Eagle" (Tris Speaker)
RF "Dewey" (Dwight Evans)

C "Pudge" (Carlton Fisk)
SP "Smoky Joe" Wood
RP "The Steamer" Bob Stanley
MGR Bill "Rough" Carrigan, "The Major" Ralph
   Houk

Coaches
"The Walking Man" Eddie Yost—third base coach
"Needle Nose" Johnny Pesky—first base coach
Sal "The Barber" Maglie—pitching coach

Let's conclude this section with a reminder that Spike Owen's real name was…Spike Owen.

A NUMBER OF NAMES

All Toddler Team
BABE Barna
BABE Dahlgren
BABE Danzig
BABE Martin
BABE Ruth
Wally GERBER
BIBB Falk

All Presidential Team
Bullet Joe BUSH
Reggie CLEVELAND
TRUMAN Clevenger
Lu CLINTON
Reggie JEFFERSON
Earl JOHNSON (not to mention Deron, Bob, Hank, John Henry, Roy, and Vic)

Bill KENNEDY; John KENNEDY
Trot NIXON/Russ NIXON/ Willard NIXON
Jermaine VAN BUREN
BENJAMIN HARRISON Van Dyke
Earl WILSON

Other presidents reflected in Sox players' names include: Ron JACKSON, IKE Boone, Bob ADAMS, Bill REGAN, Frank HAYES, Harry TAYLOR and Scott TAYLOR and Jeff PIERCE. And they once had John TRUMAN Wasdin. Thomas Jefferson Dowd may be the only player known to be named after a President.

The Red Sox also have a few vice presidents as well: Sam AGNEW, KING Brady (William Rufus King, VP), Esty CHANEY, Tom HENDRYX (Thomas Hendricks, VP), Kevin MORTON/Guy MORTON (Levi Parsons Morton, VP), Jerry STEPHENSON (Adlai Stevenson, VP), Mike MARSHALL/Bill MARSHALL (Thomas Marshall, VP), John CURTIS (Charles Curtis, VP) and Brian BARKLEY (Alben Barkley, VP).

Then there are the presidential candidates. We could start with Art McGOVERN of the 1905 team or WILLIAM JENNINGS BRYAN Harriss (1926–28), but let's not fully unravel that thread.

Different Nationalities
SWEDE Carlstrom
Mel DEUTSCH
Charlie FRENCH
TURKEY Gross
INDIAN Bob Johnson
DUTCH Leonard
Harry Agganis, The Golden Greek
Bob Chakales, The Golden Greek
Kevin Youkilis, The Greek God of Walks
Gar FINNvold
Lou FINNey

Red Sox minor league prospect DANE Towery (2005) didn't progress past the Gulf Coast Red Sox.

All-Intellectual Team
ARISTOTLE "Harry" Agganis
ARQUIMEDEZ Pozo
Josh BECKETT
Joe CICERO
DANTE Bichette
Danny DARWIN
EMERSON Dickman
EUCLIDES Rojas (coach)

John GODWIN
ULYSSES "Tony" Lupien
Ernest NIETZKE (it's sort of like Nietsche)
Ben PASCHAL
Jinx POINDEXTER
Rick WISE
And then there's Josh BARD (as in *The* Bard—
get it?)

Most Appropriate Baseball Names Team
Matt BATTS
Neal BALL
George WINN
Al FLAIR
HOMER Ezzell
Jigger STATZ
WIN Kellum
WIN Remmerswaal
Rac SLIDER (coach)

All Edible Team
Bob VEALE
Dizzy TROUT
Herb HASH
HERB Moford
Jim RICE
Bob SEEDS
Sean BERRY / Charlie BERRY
STEW Bowers

A Couple of Rhyming Names for Pinch-Hitting
HANK SHANKS
MATT BATTS

For a relief pitcher, you might want
George WINN, though he only ever won one
game in the majors (and that one not for the
Red Sox—sadly, he beat Boston, 3–2, on September 19, 1922). Decades later, the Indians
featured a pitcher named Early Wynn, who
won 300 games. Boston also had pitcher Win
Kellum, but no major league team has ever
had a pitcher named LOSS or LOSER. Players
with names like that tend not to get signed.

All Sound-of-a-Stifled-Sneeze Team
Joe AZCUE
Fred BRATCHI
Fabian GAFFKE
Johnny GOOCH
Eric HINSKE
George HOCKETT
George HUFF (manager)
Bob NIETZKE

David ORTIZ
George SCHMEES
Bob SCHERBARTH
Steve SCHNECK
Wally SNELL
George STUMPF
Tom UMPHLETT
Bob UNGLAUB
Kevin YOUKILIS
Finally, there's YASTRZEMSKI—a true Hall of
Fame sneeze.
And, while not quite a sneeze, let's also acknowl-
edge Ken GRUNDT.

All-Syllable Teams
Carl YASTRZEMSKI
Rico PETROCELLI
Tony CONIGLIARO
Nomar GARCIAPARRA
Bill WAMBSGANSS
Osee SCHRECONGOST
Stan PARTENHEIMER
Fritz OSTERMUELLER
Pete JABLONOWSKI
Joe Foy, of course, goes to the opposite extreme,
as did Ted Cox and Dud Lee.

Animal Names
Doug BIRD
BIRDIE Tebbetts
CATFISH Metkovich
Joel FINCH
GOOSE Gregson
(coach)
MOOSE Grimshaw
Rube KROH
Jim TABOR
Dizzy TROUT
RABBIT Warstler
Larry WOLFE

Rube Kroh.

All Drinking Team
Gene RYE
Al NIPPER
PEP Deininger
HOOT Evers
And one "after drinking too much" name: Joe
HEVING
For the morning after: Jack COFFEY

Player Seemingly Most Likely To Commit An Error
Alex MUSTAIKIS
Walt DROPO

Musical Quartet
Nick ALTROCK
Pat RAPP
Dave SAX
Frank VIOLA

Guys with-names-likely-to-inspire-a-
dirty limerick team
Steve YERKES
John WYCKOFF
Tom HURD
Gordie HINKLE
Dick POLE
Jack ROTHROCK
Ted COX
Brian DAUBACH
Emerson DICKMAN

All-Girl's Name Team
BUNNY Madden
CANDY LaChance
CARMEN Fanzone
CARROLL Hardy
CHICK Fewster
CLEO Carlyle
COCO Crisp
Alex CORA
CORY Bailey
DALE Alexander
Bob DAUGHTERS
DEE Miles
Andy DOMINIQUE
J.D. DREW
FAYE Throneberry
IVY Andrews
JODY Reed
KELLY Shoppach
Byung-Hyun KIM
LEE Tinsley
LOREN Bader
Mark LORETTA
Joe LUCEY
LYNN McGlothen
Cla MEREDITH
MERLE Settlemire
PATSY Dougherty
Nick POLLY
RACHEL (Rac) Slider
ROXY Walters
SAL Maglie (coach)
TILLIE Walker
And, doubling up, BABE RUTH and KERRY
    LACY

Plant Names
Brian BARK
Charley BERRY
Red BLUHM
Don BUDDIN
Joe BUSH
Frank BUSHEY
Jack COFFEY
Steve CURRY
Ben FLOWERS
IVY Andrews
Brandon MOSS
Gene RYE
Brian ROSE
Bob SEEDS

All-Religious Team
JESUS Peña
Max BISHOP
DEACON McGuire
Gerry MOSES/ Wally MOSES
ANGEL Gonzalez
DEACON Scott
DEACON Morrissey
Blaine NEAL (as in genuflect)
Larry PARRISH
ISRAEL Alcantara
Harry LORD
…and let's not forget that Sam Mele's first name
    is SABATH

Occupation Team
Tracy BAKER
Max BISHOP
Tom BREWER
Wes CHAMBERLAIN
Lou COLLIER
Dusty COOKE
DEACON Morrissey
DOC Prothro
Hank FISCHER
Frank FOREMAN
Boob FOWLER
Wes GARDNER
Harry HOOPER
Buddy HUNTER
Joe JUDGE
John KNIGHT
Mike MARSHALL
Andy MERCHANT
Wade MILLER
Chet NOURSE
Freddy PARENT

Nels POTTER
Johnny REDER
Jeff SELLERS
Keith SHEPHERD
Camp SKINNER
Tris SPEAKER

Lou STRINGER
Scott TAYLOR
Todd WALKER
Monte WEAVER
Hoge WORKMAN
…y, en español, Carlos REYES

First and last names both unique in baseball

Which Sox players have both a first name and a last name, neither of which are shared by anyone else in baseball history? Nope, not Hipolito Pichardo. Not Josias Manzanillo. Not George Stone. Not even Covelli Crisp. These are the ones we came up (with three of them from just 2006). If you find another one, be sure to let us know.

Elden Auker
Truman Clevenger
Gar Finnvold
Kason Gabbard
Creighton Gubanich
Devern Hansack
Smead Jolley
Daisuke Matsuzaka
Dustan Mohr
Hideo Nomo
Tomokazu Ohka
Arquimedez Pozo
Osee Schrecengost
Heathcliff Slocumb
LaSchelle Tarver
Ugueth Urbina

Smead Jolley. Courtesy of National Baseball Hall of Fame.

Taking first and last names together, some interesting combinations

Shaken carbonated beverage: Pop Rising
In debt to a buddy: Owen Friend
Literate coinage: Reid Nichols
Trudge through cranberries: Wade Boggs
Thin cracker: Skinny Graham
Anti-aircraft activity: Hy Gunning
Hirsute musician: Harry Harper
Unshorn basketballer: Harry Hooper
Hairless automobile: Baldy Karr
Seeker of spices and flavorings: Herb Hunter
Search for companion: Buddy Hunter
Penis carrier: Dick Porter
Wealthy storm: Rich Gale
Designate as unblemished: Mark Clear
Grooved on winged creature: Doug Bird
Attempt to quell an unruly early St. Louis ballplayer: Mace Brown
Sad ringer: Juan Bell (alternatively: half of two bells)
High falutin' wry comedian: Tony Muser
Dispossess antlered mammal: Rob Deer
Chef covered with soot: Dusty Cooke
Send an invoice to Mr. Iacocca: Bill Lee

Toss an old British coin: Chuck Schilling
Bob Daughters—give short haircuts to female offspring
Cot Deal—a bargain on basic sleep furniture
Frank Foreman—a candid work supervisor
Happy Foreman—a jovial crew chief
Turkey Gross—144 Thanksgiving birds
Harry Harper—a hirsute harmonicat
Herb Hash—vegetarian melange meal
Bill Marshall—invoice a peace officer
Jigger Statz—manipulate baseball data
Harry Taylor—hirsute clothier

Using Mr. Gross's correct first name and last name together, inserting a comma, could sound like something truly offensive perceived by a teenager: Ewell, Gross!

In addition, the Red Sox over the years have featured a LEWIS and a CLARKE; a DARWIN and a JESUS; a COYLE and a DOYLE; a GARDNER, a FORESTER and a MILLER; a FOXX and a "Rooster;" a GILBERT and SULLIVAN, a PARENT and DAUGHTERS.

They have had players who were PESKY, WISE, and RICH. They've had a LANE, a LAKE, and a POND, both an ARROYO and a VALLE. A BUSH, some FLOWERS, and a LITTLE GROVE. Adam was STERN, but Foreman was HAPPY. One thing is a LOCK: every man has his PRICE, especially if paid in CASH. That's par for the CORSI. But they play with FLAIR, they work every ENGLE, and they do it with PRIDE. Whether SHORT or SMALL, they keep in condition. They're HALE and HARDY, and HUSKEY with plenty of HOEFT. A man of STEELE will CATER to no one. They CROUCH and they DODGE; their eyes can GLAZE over, they can fall in a HEEP while heading for HOLM. The BLUHM may be off the ROSE, but some of the scoring possibilities are fairly intriguing.

If pitcher Loren BADER fielded the ball and threw to first baseman Vic WERTZ, the play would go from Bader to Wertz!

If pitcher Alex MUSTAIKIS were to field the ball and throw to first baseman Walt DROPO, the chances for an error are doubled!

If second baseman Jim BUCHER fielded a line drive and threw to first baseman Tracy BAKER, it would be Bucher to Baker. They lacked a candlestick maker, but did have a LAMP.

If third baseman John KNIGHT threw to first baseman Max BISHOP, it would be Knight to Bishop.

If pitcher Mike PALM charged a bunt to the mound and flipped to first baseman Johnny REDER, we'd have Palm-Reder.

If Rube FOSTER whirled to pick off a baserunner and fired to Freddy PARENT, we'd have Foster-Parent.

If Odell HALE had the ball bounce off his head and ricochet to CESAR Crespo, the scorer could have called it Hale-Cesar.

If Hy Gunning fielded a grounder to his right, and fired to JINX Poindexter covering the first bag bag, it would be Hy-Jinx.

It's really too bad that prospect Seung SONG never made the team; he's got a whole name thing going all by himself. And after Keith FOULKE tired in extra-inning relief, we might have enjoyed some Foulke-Song.

If infielder Milt BOLLING tossed the ball to outfield ARLIE Tarbert, who'd snuck in behind the baserunner on second, it would be a Bolling-Arlie pickoff. Maybe it's getting time to call it a day here.

Thanks to Red Sox author Jim Prime for a great deal of help in assembling this section on names. But we're not finished yet!

Red Sox batteries

Looking at just pitchers and catchers, there are a number of combinations that might have made for some interesting batteries.

BLACK—WHITE	Dave Black—Sammy White	
BIRDIE—POLE	Birdie Tebbetts—Dick Pole	
YANK—PINCH	Yank Terry—Pinch Thomas	
PARTEE—BREWER	Roy Partee—Tom Brewer	
WAITE—LES	Waite Hoyt—Les Moss	gravity-free condition
RUTH—LES	Babe Ruth—Les Moss	amoral
WINTER—PARTEE	George Winter—Roy Partee	
PARTEE—HEVING	Roy Partee—Joe Heving	festive vomiting
BROWN—MARC	Mace Brown—Mark Sullivan	
PINCH—NIPPER	Pinch Thomas—Al Nipper	
HEINIE—NIPPER	Heinie Wagner—Al Nipper	sexual harassment?
GARDNER—MOSS	Wes Gardner—Les Moss	
CLEAR—MUDDY	Mark Clear—Muddy Ruel	
WHITE—WALL	Sammy White—Murray Wall	
ROUGH—WOOD	Rough Carrigan—Smoky Joe Wood	
BERRY—BUSH	Charlie Berry—Joe Bush	
NIXON—AGNEW	Willard Nixon—Sam Agnew	
WISE—MOSES	Rick Wise—Jerry Moses	
MUDDY—SHORE	Muddy Ruel—Ernie Shore	
BROWN—WHITE	Mace Brown—Sammy White	
PARTEE—NIPPER	Roy Partee—Al Nipper	sneaking a snort at a Mormon affair
JESSE—JAMES	Jesse Tannehill—James Wright	
PEACOCK—HUNT	John Peacock—Ben Hunt	
BEANY—BABE	Beany Jacobson—Babe Martin	
MUDDY—RHODES	Muddy Ruel—Gordon Rhodes	
YANK—RIP	Yank Terry—Rip Williams	parachute instruction
WILBER—WRIGHT	Del Wilber—Jim Wright	Orville's brother
MIKE—SHIELDS	Mike Stanley—Ben Shields	microphone baffles
FRANK—CASE	Frank Hayes—Case Patten	sausage skin
NOURSE—BABE	Chet Nourse—Babe Martin	
DEVINE—VIOLA	Mickey Devine—Frank Viola	heavenly strings
SLICK—STONE	Slick Hartley—Dean Stone	
RED—FLOWERS	Red Steiner—Ben Flowers	
WHITE—SAYLES	Sammy White—Bill Sayles	dry goods discount days
BABE—HAPPY	Babe Martin—Happy Foreman	a sex addict
HARRY—BUCK	Harry Ostdiek—Buck Newsome	
CAMP—BUDDY	Camp Skinner—Buddy Rosar	
TUDOR—DUKE	John Tudor—Duke Farrell British	royalty
SHORT—DUKE	Bill Short—Duke Farrell	diminutive royalty
PEACOCK—STEW	Johnny Peacock—Stew Bowers	dining for the effete
TUBBY—VIOLA	Tubby Spencer—Frank Viola	
ART—CASE	Art McGovern—Case Patten	
ART—CAMP	Art McGovern—Camp Skinner	
BUDDY—BARR	Buddy Rosar—Steve Barr	friendly pub
BERRY—STEW	Charlie Berry—Stew Bowers	
LES—PEP	Les Moss—Pep Deiniger	relatively sluggardly
RICH—DEAL	Rich Gedman—Cot Deal	
ROUGH—DEAL	Rough Carrigan—Cot Deal	

HACK—BERRY	Hack Eibel—Charlie Berry	
MIKE—HAPPY	Mike Ryan—Happy Foreman	giddy talk show host
LES—BO	Les Moss—Bo(bo) Newsome	gay girl slang
DEVINE—FORTUNE	Mickey Devine—Gary Fortune	
HEINIE—FUHR	Heinie Wagner—Oscar Fuhr	hairy butt
LYNCH—HUNT	Walt Lynch—Ben Hunt enraged	killer mob
BATTS—CASE	Matt Batts—Case Patten	memorabilia display
LYNCH—JUDGE	Walt Lynch—Judge Nagle	frontier justice adjudicator
RED—LAMP	Red Steiner—Dennis Lamp	prostitute signal
HARRY—BULL	Harry Ostdiek—Bull Durham	
YOUNG—BUDDY	Cy Young—Buddy Rosar	
TUBBY—HACK	Tubby Spencer—Hack Eibel	portly cabdriver
SPRING—HAYES	Jack Spring—Frank Hayes	vernal mist
BERG—SPARKS	Moe Berg—Tully Sparks Titanic	crash product
JASON—KARR	Jason Varitek—Benn Karr	vehicle pursuit
TATE—WAITE	Ben Tate—Waite Hoyt	long line at London gallery
VAL—LEE	Val Picinich—Bill Lee	
MOE—RAY	Moe Berg—Ray Culp	ocean eel
MICKEY—FORTUNE	Mickey Devine—Gary Fortune	Disney wealth
HAPPY—VALENTINE	Happy Foreman—Valentine Picinich	
CASH—SAYLES	Kevin Cash—Bill Sayles	

Some other pitching possibilities:

If Benn Karr came in to relieve Rex Cecil, we'd see the game ball going Rex-Karr.

If Gary Fortune replaced George Winn on the mound, we'd have Winn-Fortune.

Jimmie Foxx pitched an inning for the Red Sox, and if he'd handed off the ball to Ken Chase, it would be Foxx-Chase.

We could have RICK-SHAW but no pitcher named SHAW worked for Boston. Closest is RICK-SHEA.

If Arnold EARLEY…? And you'd think we could make names out of Carl MAYS or Joe BUSH. Have at it!

And that's just the batteries. Once can put together any number of other combinations. We'll start it off here, and urge readers to send in your own suggestions.

MOHR (Dustan)—LES (Nunamaker)	Derek LOWE—Joe PRICE
(J. T.) SNOW—(Doug) BIRD/Fort Myers resident	Jeff PIERCE—Ben SHIELDS
Andy ABAD—Cot DEAL/bum bargain	Dave BLACK—Bill WIGHT
AL De Vormer—Sam DENTE/Italian cuisine	Bill SHORT—Andy SHEETS
Odell HALE—Carroll HARD/healthy and sturdy	HY Vandeburg—Neal BALL
Benn KARR—Don LOCK	Steve FARR—David WEST
Curtis PRIDE—Ernest RILES	Earl WEBB—Robert PERSON/
Jake VOLZ—Tully SPARKS	Internet worker

Sox players whose names can be read as imperative sentences

Wade Boggs	Lance Clemmons	Reid Nichols
Mace Brown	Rip Collins	Chuck Schilling
Mark Clear	Bill Lee	Yank Terry

Make Your Own

Names can offer endless fascination. You can enjoy creating your own name plays. The perceptive (Mike) PALM reader can discern a clear (Howie) STORIE. And, after all, a rolling (Jeff) STONE gathers no (Brandon) MOSS.

Here are a few names to play with, pitchers or catchers or otherwise:

Josh BARD	Tom HURD	Jack SPRING
Steve BARR	TOPPER Rigney	Jake STAHL
Coco CRISP	David RISKE	Adam STERN
Johnny GOOCH	J. T. SNOW	

You could pose some connections, too, for instance from Stan PAPI to Big Papi.

Red Sox name play can be fun. You're invited to get creative and send in YOUR suggestions for plays on names, for future editions.

Anagrams

There are anagrams as well.

Boston's George Edward Thomas (1966–1971) is an anagram for an earlier player, southpaw Thomas Edward George, whose last season was with the 1918 Boston Braves.

Henry John McMahon (1908) only appeared in one major league ballgame. His full name, though, is an anagram for John Henry McMahon, who played for the 1892 and 1893 New York Giants—as long as you ignore their nicknames, Doc and Jack respectively.

Then there's Ray James Francis, whose anagramic alter ego is James Francis Ray. Mr. Francis was 0–2 for the Red Sox in 1925, worse than his 0–0 effort earlier in the year for the Yankees. He posted an identical ERA for both rival teams.

Moving away from full names to the names players were best known by, we find that Bill James (3–5 with the 1919 Red Sox) was William Henry James, but was known as Bill James (not the current Senior Baseball Operations Advisor), just as was William Lawrence James (also known as Bill James), who played for the other Boston team—also as a pitcher—and also in the same year! It must have been a bit confusing in 1919 for both Boston teams to have a pitcher named Bill James. The Red Sox got 72 innings out of their Bill, while the Braves only got 5⅓, but Bill of the Braves didn't lose any games and had a slightly lower ERA.

Wally Gerber (1928–1929) is an anagram for Wally Berger, who started the very next year with the Boston Braves. Berger was four inches taller, though, so it's unlikely the same guy coming back incognito.

Billy Werber (1933–1936) contributed nicely to the Red Sox, particularly his .321 season in 1934 when he also led the league with 40 stolen bases. Billy Brewer pitched in the 1990s, but never truly excelled.

If you start talking surnames alone, though, the list becomes extensive: Ted Lewis / Randy Wiles, Charley Graham (or Lee or Skinny) and Billy Maharg, Oil Can Boyd and Larry Doby, Frank Viola and Tony Oliva….

Keeping to surnames of Red Sox teammates alone, though, one finds that Billy Werber connects to Tommy Brewer, Rob Deer to Jody (or Jerry) Reed, Arlie Tarbert to Marty (or Bob, Frank, Jimmy, or Tommy) Barrett, Hal Rhyne to Butch Henry (or Bill or Jim, or even principal owner John W. Henry), Tex Vache to Bobby Veach, Buddy Myer to Jerry Remy, and Dennis Lamp to Mike Palm.

Shortest name / longest name

Ted Cox and Joe Foy not only have the shortest surnames, but their names and standard nicknames run just six letters in all. The seven-letter combos are

Don Aase	Jim Byrd	Ray Culp	Rob Deer
Cot Deal	Tom Fine	Les Moss	

12-letter last names

Dallessandro	Monbouquette
Mientkiewicz	Ostermueller
Partenheimer	Schrecongost (this name is often misspelled with 13 letters as Schreckengost)

First and last names combined, Jennings Poindexter looks to be the leader.

The longest first name? Arquimedez Pozo—the 5–2 ratio is tops as well.

Middle Names

One can get into middle names, too. Red Sox players have some unusual middle names, some of which are presumably surnames in the family tree. Take Aaron Helmer Sele. Without taking the trouble to research it, one could make an educated guess that it's a last name somewhere along the line. The same might well go for Bryce Bettencourt Florie. In some cases, of course, it's the middle name by which we know a player, the best case in point probably being Anthony Garciaparra.

Some of the middle names could have worked above in the lists of plays on name. For instance, players with female-sounding middle names include:

Thomas LOREN Barrett John BEVERLEY Gooch
Ellis RENA Burks Laurence MARCY Wolfe
Gary MERLE Geiger
Fred LYN Kendall—who played for Boston in 1978 but was probably never confused with teammate Fred Lynn.
Lastly, there is Clell LAVERN Hobson. Who, by the way, was Red Sox manager when Jeffrey LAVERN McNeely played for the team in 1993. Two Laverns, but no Shirley.

William CALVIN Matthews could have been listed among the intellectuals. So, perhaps, could Manuel ARISTIDES Ramirez. Mark CHRISTIAN Bellhorn might be among the more religious. Wesley POLK Chamberlain gets added to the list of Presidents. Slyveanus AUGUSTUS Gregg sounds like he was named after a combination of the early Christian apostle Silvanus and the Roman emperor.

Did Geremi Gonzalez have an older sibling? His middle name was Segundo. Did Herman Son Winningham have a sister named Hermione Daughter Winningham?

Some of the more unusual middle names include Carlos Obed Baerga, James Erigena Barrett, Elliott Allardice Bigelow, James Quinter Bucher, Jesse Cail Burkett, Esty Clyon Chaney, Cecil Celester Cooper, Covelli Loyce Crisp, Midre Almeric Cummings, Wesley Cheek Ferrell, Louis Klopsche Finney, Howard Chumney Fitzgerald, Norwood Ringold Gibson, Grady Edgebert Hatton, Darius Dutton "Dave" Hillman, Berthold Juneau "Bert" Husting, Reginald Jirod Jefferson, Todd Barton Givin Jones, Kerry Ardeen Lacy, William Harmong Lamar, Frank Breyfogle LaPorte, John Bannerman "Larry" McLean, Gerald Braheen Moses, Christopher Trotman Nixon, Wily Modesto Peña, Henry Joseph Colquit Patterson, John Picus Quinn, William Nisbeth Sayles, William Cordes Schlesinger, Albert Bringhurst Schroll, Walter Dedaker Shaner, Robert Walkup Smith, Carl Remus Stinson, Carl Ringdahl Sumner, Jose Milages Tartabull, Ugueth Urtain Urbina, Leonard Irell Webster, Frank Tiguer Welch, and—of course, the classic Denton True Young.

We may note that Carl Nettles Reynolds was no known relation to Graig Nettles.

Where's Waldo? In the middle of Clarence Blethen's name. Tickle me, Emory. Topper Rigney's name was Emory Elmo Rigney.

We already noted that Colonel Buster Mills really did have the given first name of Colonel and the given middle name of Buster. And Lancelot Terry's true middle name was indeed Yank. And Chico Walker never had a middle name, though with the first name Cleotha, the Chico is understandable.

Understandably, nicknames sometimes derive due to difficult given names, in the case of Ellsworth Tenney "Babe" Dahlgren and Percival Sumner "Pop" Rising. And Elisha Harrison "Camp" Skinner—though admittedly Camp is a pretty unusual nickname, it's still easier than Elisha. It's not surprising that Baudilio Jose Diaz was known as Bo.

One wonders about the thought that went into Homer Estell Ezzell's name. It's too bad

Rip Repulski played for the Red Sox before becoming British pop star Elton John. (If the reference eludes you, you could look it up.) Jason Alexander Shiell later starred on Seinfeld—playing an employee of the New York Yankees, no less. (That's not true.)

Let's end with a big "Yee-haw" for Rudy Caballero Seanez!

The "Z" Factor

It's just one of those things, and a reflection of the increased number of Latinos in major league baseball, but in mid-2006, a full seven of the 25 players on the Red Sox roster had names ending with "z": Alex Gonzalez, Javier Lopez, David Ortiz, Manny Ramirez, Rudy Seanez, Julian Tavarez, and Javy Lopez. Yes, the Red Sox had both Javier Lopez and Javier Lopez on the 25-man roster at the same time, even if the elder of the two Puerto Rican natives was typically called Javy and not Javier. With Javy being a catcher and Javier being a pitcher, the Red Sox lost a golden opportunity to create a Javier Lopez/Javier Lopez battery. Even just for one batter, they could have made it happen. Where was the sense of history?

The most players whose name ended in "z" who played in a given game is four. This has happened on over a dozen occasions, for instance on August 18, 2006 against the Yankees: Gonzalez, Lopez, Ortiz, Ramirez.

At the same time the Red Sox had two Lopezes, they also had two tildes on the roster: Wily Mo Peña and Carlos Peña. The possibilities were enormous.

Other letters in play

The lineup which featured the same initial letter most frequently was the June 22, 1987 starting lineup. Six Boston ballplayers had last names beginning with "B": Burks, Barrett, Boggs, Baylor, Benzinger, and Boyd on the mound. On June 25, 1969, the Sox started five "S" men: Dick Schofield, Reggie Smith, George Scott, Tom Satriano, and Sonny Siebert.

Double letters: The June 8, 1960 first game featured six Sox with double letters in their surnames: Pumpsie GrEEn, Pete RuNNels, Ted WiLLiams, Ray BOOne, Don BuDDin, and Frank SuLLivan. The second game featured seven: GrEEn, RuNNels, BOOne, BuDDin, H. SuLLivan, WiLLiams, and Dave HiLLman. The team that year also featured Chittum, Monbouquette, Muffett, Stallard, and Ted Wills—but none of them saw duty that day.

Ending with a vowel? Eight different ballplayers bore names ending with a vowel on August 22, 1971, in the day's second game. In alphabetical order by last vowel of last name: Mike Fiore, Rico Petrocelli, Carl Yastrzemski, Luis Aparicio, Billy Conigliaro, Phil Gagliano, John Kennedy, and Bob Montgomery. The first game featured six of the above, and also Bill Lee.

Six letters in a surname: Cooper, Darwin, Dawson, Melvin, Rivera, Vaughn, and Zupcic all played on June 14, 1993. The Red Sox did use two relievers while losing to the Yankees, 4–0. They could have used Greg Harris, who relieved a team record 80 games that year, but—no—they thoughtlessly chose Bankhead and Hesketh. They could also have used Dopson or Fossas, too, but manager Butch Hobson (you would have thought he would have known better) totally blew the opportunity.

The most letters in a given lineup? We can offer the names in the first game on September 7, 1970 which featured four players with 10 letters apiece in their last name: Tony Conigliaro, Rico Petrocelli, Tony Conigliaro, and Bob Montgomery. For added measure, Carl Yastrzemski played first base. But the winner was a few years later, on September 14, 1974—83 total letters in all. Beniquez, Burleson, Carbo, Cleveland, Harper, Johnson, McAuliffe, Montgomery, Petrocelli, and Yastrzemski. The total of 83 was tied on May 28, 1995 with: Chamberlain, Greenwell, Macfarlane, Naehring, Rhodes, Rodriguez, Rowland, Valentin, VanEgmond, and Vaughn.

The fewest total numbers: July 30, 1978. 49 letters. Bailey, Burleson, Evans, Fisk, Hobson, Lee, Lynn, Remy, Rice, and Scott.

On September 27, 1975 Darrell Johnson put in players whose last names contained 25 of the 26 letters in the alphabet: every letter but "X"—there never was an "X" player on the roster all year long. Johnny Pesky had gone the opposite route in the second game on August 9, 1964 using only 15 letters: even when Dick Williams pinch-hit in the top of the ninth, he didn't add a single new letter (and also flied out to right). Pesky used Horton, Jones, Malzone, Mantilla, Mejias, Smith, Stuart, Tillman, and Wilson.

RED SOX THROUGH THE AGES

First-born Red Sox

Which Red Sox player had the earliest birthdate? Francis Isaiah "Monkey" Foreman, born during the Civil War on May 1, 1863, broke into the majors in May 1884, and joined the Boston Americans in their very first season. Foreman helped coach some of the team's very first games. He also served as the starting pitcher on May 3, 1901 in the seventh game ever for the new franchise. It was Frank Foreman's one and only game for Boston in an 11-year career. The *Globe* headline read "Foreman Rusty—Old Timer Causes No Change in Collins' Luck." He gave up four runs to home team Washington in the bottom of the first, starting a complete game 9–4 loss. It was his last game for Boston, but he posted a 12–6 record for Baltimore over the course of the 1901 campaign.

Age gap

Dick Thompson wrote about Joe Cicero: "He played for the Red Sox in '29 and '30 while still a teenager and then did not reappear until 1945 with the Athletics. Might not he be the only man ever to do that, play as a teenager and as a man in his thirties, but no major league appearances while in his 20s?"

Oldest batter vs. pitcher matchup

One of the oldest batter versus pitcher matchups took place when Eddie Bressoud, 33, faced Satchel Paige, 59, on September 25, 1965. Though they knew they were seeing something very special to see Paige pitch, the 9,289 spectators in Kansas City's Municipal Stadium may not have realized the full ramifications of the unusual piece of history they were witnessing.

The oldest matchup, though, seems to be when the 57-year old Nick Altrock had his only at bat in 1933, on October 1. He faced Rube Walberg, who had turned 37 on July 27. The combined ages of the Altrock/Walberg matchup was about seven months older than when Paige faced Bressoud. Altrock had been, very briefly, a member of the 1903 Boston Americans.

Frank Malzone, 35, appeared in the 1965 game but never actually faced Satchel. Both names appear in the boxscore, but Paige only pitched the first three innings and Dalton Jones (who tapped a roller down to first on a 1–2 count in the first) was the Red Sox starting third baseman. Jones was safe on the first baseman's error. Malzone pinch-hit for Jones in the eighth inning, by which time Don Mossi was pitching for KC.

Ol' Satch was stingy, only allowing the Sox one hit, a double off the left field fence by a guy whose name was abbreviated as Yastr'ski in the *Boston Globe* boxscore.

Three innings, 10 batters, one K, no walks (Jones was thrown out on the basepaths on a passed ball that he tried to take two bases on). Paige left the game with a 1–0 lead.

The Sox struck back, though, later in the game with a Lee Thomas homer off Segui and an inside-the-park job by Tony Conigliaro. Boston 5, KC 2.

Oldest pitcher to ever start for the Red Sox

We know that Jim Pagliaroni (17) was the youngest player to see duty with the Red Sox, and that Ken Brett was the youngest pitcher to appear in a World Series game. With his August 26, 2006 start, 43-year-old David Wells completed his reign as the oldest pitcher to ever start for the Red Sox. In 2006, the Sox put on a big push to bring Roger Clemens back to Boston to finish his career. And a lesser push in 2007. Roger missed his chance to break this record, and also the lifetime record for most career wins for the Red Sox (he's tied with Cy Young with 192). Instead, he settled for a mediocre 6–6 record with the Yankees in 2007.

Boston Red Sox players born in Boston

These are the Boston Red Sox. In case you wondered about Boston-born players…

There are only 21 players who have played for the Red Sox who were actually born in the City of Boston. The Hub may be the "Athens of America" but hasn't proven to be a hotbed of baseball talent. Quite a number of players were born in surrounding communities and, particularly in baseball's first 75 years, a lot of New Englanders played the game. The only true star born in Boston, though, for any team, is Houston's Jeff Bagwell, signed to the Red Sox but traded for reliever Larry Andersen in the pennant drive of 1990, before he ever had a chance to play for Boston.

The players who made it to the majors—hardly any of whom played for the Red Sox for more than one year—are as follows:

Mark Bellhorn 2004—Bellhorn was born in Boston, but his family moved to a small town in Florida when he was just three weeks old. His father had been doing his residency as a veterinarian in Boston. Bellhorn was signed to play second base for the Sox, but found himself demoted to a utility slot even before spring training began when Boston signed Pokey Reese. Nonetheless, he found himself playing every game right from game one, when Nomar Garciaparra began the season on the DL and Reese had to fill Nomar's shoes at short. Bellhorn hit a home run in his second home game. Mark ended up playing in 138 games, with 17 HR and 82 RBIs. He had a high .373 OBP, and led the 2004 team both in walks (88) and strikeouts (177). He also had some key hits in the 2004 playoffs, including the winning home run in Game One of the World Series. After performing poorly at the plate in 2005, Bellhorn was given his release in August, and was snapped up almost immediately by the New York Yankees. Manager Joe Torre only gave him 17 at-bats; he had one single, one home run, and batted just .118. In 2006, Mark appeared in 115 games for the San Diego Padres but only managed a .190 average, and in 2007 batted just .071 (one hit in 14 at-bats) for Cincinnati.

Carlos Castillo 2001—Carlos came over in July, 2001 after three seasons with the White Sox, where he was 10–7 from 1997–9. For Boston, he pitched once at home for an inning, giving up one hit (a home run), and once away (in Chicago, in fact), where he pitched two innings and gave up two hits. Each time he gave up an earned run, so he had an ERA at home of 9.00 but a road ERA of 4.50, for a season total 6.00. His fielding was flawless—one chance, one putout.

Shano Collins 1921–1925, 1931–1932—Charlestown's Shano Collins spent the first 11 years of his career playing for the White Sox (1910-1920), then was traded to Boston, with Nemo Leibold, for Harry Hooper. Collins played infield and outfield for the Red Sox from 1921 through 1925, almost exclusively in the outfield. He posted a lifetime .264 average, managed the Red Sox in 1931 and 1932 (73–134—it was a bad time for Boston), and was Bob Gallagher's grandfather (see the section on relatives who played for the Red Sox).

Manny Delcarmen 2005—a story still unfolding, but Delcarmen first appeared for the Red Sox in July 2005. By season's end, he pitched an even nine innings in 10 games. He struck out nine, but walked seven, and yielded three earned runs for an ERA of 3.00. In 2006, Manny appeared in 50 games, all in relief. He threw 53⅓ innings, facing 243 batters, and posted an ERA of 5.06. In 2007, he truly excelled—with an ERA of just 2.05 facing 176 batters in 44 innings of relief work. His postseason was less impressive, with an ERA of 8.31 but he added the valuable experience of appearing in six postseason games to his resume.

John Frederick Donahue 1923—John Frederick Donahue was born in Roxbury on April 19, 1894. A switch-hitting 5'8" outfielder, he managed to get into every one of the last 10 games of the season and rack up 36 at-bats between his debut on September 25, 1923 and the final game on October 7. He batted a respectable .278, with four doubles (and five strikeouts), scoring five runs but driving in only one. He handled 25 chances without an error.

John Freeman 1927—Debuting in the second game of a double-loss doubleheader on June 17, 1927, Freeman was a pinch-hitter for Slim Harriss in the bottom of the ninth but we deduce that he reached base on an error (he batted, but was not charged an at-bat, and wasn't walked). On June 27, he took over in center field for Ira Flagstead and collected his two career at-bats, without a hit. He appeared in two other games, but—all told—it was no runs, no hits, no errors.

Ed Gallagher 1932—Left-handed pitcher Ed Gallagher was born in Dorchester in 1910 and debuted for the Sox on July 8, 1932. He appeared in nine games, starting three of them and losing all three. His ERA was 12.55, which explains why he didn't appear in many more games. He threw 23 2/3 innings, surrendering three homers and 36 runs, walking 28 while striking out only six. Though a switch hitter, it didn't help much. He accumulated five at-bats, struck out three times, and never did get a hit.

Paul Howard 1909—Paul Joseph Howard, who went by the nickname "Del," appeared in six games in September 1909 and mustered 18 plate appearances. Not to be confused with another 1909 Del Howard, who played in the National League, the Boston-born Boston Red Sox player had a good debut game against the White Sox on September 16. He played right field, walked, drove in a run with a double, and executed a sacrifice. In September, he walked three times and scored twice. He had three hits—two singles and a double and he has two RBIs to his name. Batting average = .200.

Herb Hunter 1920—Outfielder Hunter kicked around some (Giants and Cubs in 1916, Cubs again in 1917, and the Cardinals in 1921) sandwiched around four games and 12 at-bats for the Red Sox in 1920. For Boston, he only got one hit—a single—and thus had an average of .083. Lifetime, though, he was a .163 hitter with one home run in 49 at-bats. The 1916 inside-the-park homer for the Giants was his only extra-base hit.

Skip Lockwood 1980—Claude Edward Lockwood pitched for 11 seasons before he arrived in Boston (1980) to close out his career on a high note, with three wins and just one loss (5.32 ERA). Lifetime 3.55 ERA (57–97), he did strike out 829 batters in 1,236 innings. His first season as a pitcher was with Seattle in 1969, but he'd begun with Kansas City as a position player in 1965. That year he hit .121 in 33 at-bats and was then out of ball for the following three years. Lifetime at the plate he was .154. He never batted for Boston.

Walter Lonergan 1911—Another player who only spent one season with the Sox was Walter Lonergan. The pride of Brighton High played in semipro and company team baseball in the Greater Boston area for several years. In September 1907, Lonergan was shortstop and captain of the *Boston Globe* baseball team which won the "printer's championship of the world" in New York, which resulted in a contract with the New York Highlanders. Apparently, it didn't work out because Lonergan played for Quincy in 1910 and with Brockton in 1911. A postal worker, when Brockton's team made a run for it, he had to get an extension of leave in order to continue to compete. On August 10, Brockton traded both Lonergan and Olaf Henriksen to Boston for Tracy Baker and Joe Giannini; both players had appeared in just one game.

Walter Lonergan, born in Boston.

Lonergan debuted with an 0-for-4 day at short, played in 10 games, had seven hits in 26 at-bats (.269)—with no extra-base hits. Two RBIs. By the following spring, he was playing second base for Lowell. In 1915, he was the shortstop for Portland, Maine's New England League championship team. In 1922, we find him in the *Globe* listed as trying to round up opponents to play the Lynn city team.

Bill Marshall 1931—Bill Marshall, born in Dorchester on Valentine's Day 1911, debuted at age 20 with the Red Sox but appeared in only one game -- on June 20. He never did bat, but came in as a pinch runner in the top of the ninth and scored a run that tied the game with the Tigers at 4-4. In the bottom of the ninth, though, Detroit put one over and won the game. Marshall wasn't called on again. Three years later, Marshall turned up as a second baseman with the Cincinnati Reds and finally got some at-bats (eight of them, with one single).

Jud McLaughlin 1931–1933—Jud McLaughlin was born in Brighton, a part of Boston since the 1870s. Justin Theodore McLaughlin was born in 1912. A left-handed pitcher, he debuted on June 23, 1931 and appeared in 16 games over the next 24 months (nine in 1931, one in 1932, and six in early 1933), throwing a total of 23 2/3 innings allowing 28 runs (27 earned, for an ERA of 10.27). He struck out four and walked 17. In all those games, he only had one at-bat, a fruitless one (he struck out). He died at age 52, in Cambridge, and is buried in Belmont.

Tom "Bunny" Madden 1909–11—Thomas Francis Madden had 17 at-bats (1909), 35 (1910), and 15 (1911) before moving on to the Phillies partway through 1911. For the Red Sox he had four hits his first year (.235), 13—three of them doubles—his second year (.371), and three his third year (.200). He knocked in seven runs if you combine all three seasons' efforts. He never returned, no, he never returned and his fate is still unknown. He died in Cambridge in 1954.

Dick Mills 1970—Dick Mills was a hard guy to pin down. He was drafted by the Phillies in June 1965, a 13th round pick. He chose not to sign. He was drafted in by the Pirates in January 1966 in the sixth round of the 1966 draft. He chose not to sign. When the Red Sox drafted him in the third round in the June 7, 1966 draft, Mills signed. It might have been the third-round money, or maybe he just wanted to wait and sign with the Red Sox. He was, after all, Boston-born.

He debuted in Cleveland on September 7, 1970 coming into a game when the Indians had a 7–2 lead. Mills threw three innings in relief, allowing just one run on four hits. Six days later, he came into a game the Orioles led 7–1, inheriting a bases-loaded situation with just one out. Mills misplayed the first ball hit his way for an error allowing one run to score. He then walked in a run and hit Mark Belanger, forcing in another. He struck out Paul Blair, but then Boog Powell drove in two more with a single and then Merv Rettenmund drove in the sixth run of the inning before Brooks Robinson grounded out. Mills was not charged with even one earned run (though it was his own error that resulted in the three runs being unearned), but his performance was deemed lacking and he never pitched again in major league ball. His 2.45 career ERA is deceiving; his .500 lifetime fielding average is revealing.

Matt Murray 1995—appeared in two games, starting one. He threw a total of 3⅓ innings, gave up 11 hits and three walks and let in 10 runs. 0–1, his ERA with Boston was 18.90. Before coming to Boston, he had only appeared in four games (for the Atlanta Braves, earlier in 1995) and lost two of them. That was his career.

Mike Palm 1948—Being local, he generated a fair amount of press when he first came up with the Red Sox. Mike only appeared in three games and he pitched just three innings in all. Six hits, five walks, but just two runs. Lifetime ERA 6.00. See a separate writeup on Palm elsewhere in this book.

Eddie Pellagrini 1946–47—Eddie hit a home run his first time up in Fenway Park. He hit .211 his first year and .203 the second. He knocked in six homers in all and 23 RBIs for his hometown Red Sox, then spent six more seasons as a big leaguer with the Browns, Phillies, Reds, and Pirates. Lifetime .226, 20 homers, 133 RBIs. For many years Pellagrini coached at Boston College and he remained a popular figure in Boston into the 21st century until his death late in 2006.

Sy Rosenthal 1925–26—Sy saw service with the Sox for two seasons, playing just about every day after a September callup in 1925 and then appearing in 104 games the following year. His lifetime average is .266 with four homers and 42 RBIs. He and Jack Slattery were the only ones on this list to die in Boston, though five of the 16 are still living and therefore still eligible for the honor. See a more extensive writeup on Rosenthal elsewhere in this book.

Jack Slattery 1901—Slattery came out of South Boston and was on the very first Red Sox team in 1901, back when they were called the Boston Americans. He was a catcher but only played one game for his hometown team—on the last day of the year. In the first game of a doubleheader, he got up to bat three times, he got one hit (and also drew a walk in another plate appearance). He drove in one run with a third-inning single and scored a run in the five-run inning. A foul tip split his thumb in the ninth inning and he had to leave the game. Over the next seven seasons, Slattery was in and out of the majors, playing for four teams though not playing at all in 1902, 1904, 1905, 1907, and 1908. He graduated college with a degree in dentistry, but never practiced. Instead he coached baseball at Tufts, Harvard, and Boston College, and spent 20 years working with his brothers at Slattery Brothers, a leather firm. For Boston, a .333 hitter, lifetime he was .212. Very briefly, he managed the Boston Braves in 1928.

Andy Spognardi 1932—Called up in September 1932, Andrea Ettore Spognardi was certainly better known as Andy. He played 17 games to close out the season, batting .294 (10 for 34, with one double and one RBI). Spognardi went on to a career in medicine, serving as a doctor in the area and he died in Dedham on the first day of the year 2000.

The most at-bats that any Boston native had in a Red Sox uniform was Rosenthal with 357. Pellagrini was second with 302. Herb Hunter was third with 49. Most of the pitchers had relatively little work as well. Manny Delcarmen has already taken the lead with a total of 106⅓ innings through 2007—plus another 4⅓ in the postseason. Skip Lockwood is second with 45⅔ innings pitched. Not one of the other four Boston-born pitchers managed even four innings.

Stature in inches: Matt Murray was the tallest Boston-both player at 6'6" and Walt Lonergan the shortest at 5'7". Seven players were six feet or taller. Six players were under 5'10".

The heaviest Boston native? Do we really want to go there? Sorry, Carlos. Mr. Castillo is listed at 240 pounds.

Everett Scott, though, might have been one of the lighter-weight Sox stars ever; in *The Sporting News* of October 29, 1942, he said, "I weighed 125 pounds when I started as a regular with the Red Sox in 1914, and I never tipped the scales at more than 138 pounds in the 13 years I played in the majors." He came from Indiana, though.

Red Sox coach Richie Hebner was also a Boston native.

Ed Sprague was born in Boston, but it was only his son who played for the Red Sox. Ed Junior was born in Castro Valley, California. He hit .216 for Boston in 33 games during the year 2000 campaign.

First Boston ballplayer born in Massachusetts

The first ballplayer for the Boston Americans who was born in the Commonwealth of Massachusetts was the leadoff batter in the top of the first inning in the very first game, in Baltimore, on April 26, 1901. He had just turned 32 six days earlier. This was Tommy "Buttermilk" Dowd, born April 20, 1869 in Holyoke, Massachusetts.

Dowd, the left fielder, grounded right back to the pitcher, Joe McGinnity, and was thrown out at first base. He was 1-for-5 that first day, singling in the top of the eighth and driving in Lou Criger. Boston lost the game, 10–6.

Thomas Jefferson Dowd was a baseball veteran, first playing for the Boston Reds in the American Association, debuting on April 8, 1891. That game was also an opening day game, and also played in Baltimore. Dowd played right field and batted ninth, behind the pitcher. He was 1-for-4, singling and scoring in the eighth. Boston won that one by four runs, 11–7. After just four games, he was sent to Washington, getting in 112 games for them. He played for Washington in 1892, then the St. Louis Cardinals for 4½ years, the Phillies, then back to the Cardinals, and spent a year with Cleveland in 1899. He was out of the majors in 1900, working for more lucrative pay at a laundry business in Holyoke, then joining in American Association play for Chicago and Milwaukee. On March 29, 1901, he signed with the Boston Americans and returned for the one final year.

Dowd's last games were both on September 28, 1901 in the final day's doubleheader. He was 1-for-5 and 2-for-3. For Boston, in 1901, he batted .268—close to his .271 career mark—with three home runs and 52 RBIs.

Red Sox players who share names with Massachusetts cities and towns

There are 30 of them, of which 20 are last names.

Terry ADAMS	DENNIS Boyd	LAWRENCE Boerner	Jeff RUSSELL
Tom BOLTON	DOUGLAS Mirabelli	Bill LEE	Tubby SPENCER
Walter CARLISLE	Carl EVERETT	Mike LOWELL	Tim WAKEFIELD
CHESTER Chad-	FRANKLIN Sullivan	Fred LYNN	WARREN "Buddy"
bourne, CHESTER	Wes GARDNER	MILTON Gaston	Rosar
Nichols, etc.	Erik HANSON	Bob MONTGOMERY	Lenny WEBSTER
Lu CLINTON	Garry HANCOCK	OTIS Nixon	Al WORTHINGTON
DALTON Jones	Fred HATFIELD	Mike PAXTON	
	Joe HUDSON	Jeff PLYMPTON	

Stretching it a bit?

Barre, MA—Jack Barry or Charley Berry, Ed Barry, or Sean Berry?
Becket, MA—Josh Beckett

Bellingham, MA—Jack Billingham
Beverly, MA—Bill "Beverly" Bayne
Carlisle, MA—Cleo Carlyle or Roy Carlyle
Dudley, MA—Dud Lee
Erving, MA—Edward Erving "Eddie" Lake
Franklin, MA—Michael Franklin "Pinky" Higgins; Benjamin Franklin Hunt, etc.
Leicester, MA—Jon Lester, and Leycester Aulds
Williamstown MA—named after Colonel Ephraim Williams? Come on!

Other team personnel

Dr. Thomas GILL   WENDELL Kim   Bob TEWKSBURY

Players named the same as their home town

King Bader came from Bader, Ilinois.
Slim Love came from Love, Mississippi.
Tony Conigliaro came from Conigliaro, Massachusetts.

   (Which one of the above is false?)

FOREIGN BORN RED SOX

For the purposes of this list, Puerto Rico is defined as outside the United States. England, Scotland, and Wales are each listed separately. In each case, the year listed is the first year for which the player appeared for the Red Sox.

AUSTRIA-HUNGARY

Stefurov   John Picus Quinn (born as Johannes Pajkos) 1922

CANADA

Vernon, BC	Ted Bowsfield 1958
Moncton, NB	Rheal Cormier 1995
St. Johns, NB	Art McGovern 1905, Bill O'Neill 1904, Matt Stairs 1995
Brockville, ONT	Peter Hoy 1992
Chatham, ONT	Ferguson Jenkins 1976
Edmundston, NB	Ty LaForest 1945
Fredericton, NB	Larry McLean 1901
Guelph, ONT	Bunk Congalton 1907
Hamilton, ONT	Frank O'Rourke 1922
London, ONT	Oscar Judd 1941, Paul Quantrill 1992, Adam Stern 2005
Montreal, PQ	Eric Gagne 2007
Penetanguishene, ONT	Phil Marchildon 1950
Sarnia, ONT	Mike Gardiner 1991
Toronto, ONT	Frank Owens 1905
Waterford, ONT	Win Kellum 1901
Swift Current, SASK	Reggie Cleveland 1974

COLOMBIA

Barranquilla	Edgar Renteria 2005
Cartagena	Jackie Gutierrez 1983, Orlando Cabrera 2004

CUBA

Abreus, Las Villas	Roman Mejias 1963
Ciego de Avila	Tony Perez 1980

Cienfuegos	Joe Azcue 1969, Jose Tartabull 1966
Havana	Jose Canseco 1995, Mike Fornieles 1957, Tony Fossas 1991, Eusebio Gonzales 1918, Mike Guerra 1951, Mike Herrera 1925
Holguin	Diego Segui 1974
Marianao	Luis Tiant 1971
San Jose de las Lajas	Juan Carlos Diaz 2002
Santa Clara	Rolando Arrojo 2000

DENMARK

Kirkerup	Olaf Henriksen 1911

DOMINICAN REPUBLIC

Bani	Israel Alcantara 2000
Barahona	Julio Lugo 2007
Cambiaso, Puerto Plata	Alejandro Peña 1995
Elias Pina	Sergio Valdez 1994
Esperanza	Hipolito Pichardo 2000
Hato Mayor	Pedro Astacio 2004
Ingenio Quisquella	Esteban Beltre 1996
Laguna Salada	Wily Mo Peña 2006
Laguna Verde	Juan Marichal 1974
Monoguayabo	Pedro Martinez 1998
Monte Cristi	Tony Peña 1990, Wilton Veras 1999
Nizao Bani	Carlos Valdez 1998
Samana	Hanley Ramirez 2005
San Cristobal	Julio Valdez 1980
San Jose de los Llanos	Marino Santana 1999
San Pedro de Macoris	Manny Alexander 2000, Juan Bell 1995, Jose Offerman 1999, Rudy Pemberton 1997
Santiago	Julian Tavarez 2006, Dario Veras 1998
Santo Domingo	Hector Almonte 2003, Hector Carrasco 2000, Robinson Checo 1997, Mario Guerrero 1973, Ramon Martinez 1999, David Ortiz 2003, Luis Ortiz 1993, Carlos Peña 2006, Jesus Peña 2000, Juan Peña 1999, Arquimedez Pozo 1996, Manny Ramirez 2001, Jesus Tavarez 1997
Villa Mella, Distrito Nacional	Anastacio Martinez 2004, Angel "Sandy" Martinez 2004

ENGLAND

Berslem	Al Shaw 1907
Trowbridge	Albert "Hobe" Ferris 1901
Yorkshire	Walter "Rosy" Carlisle 1908

Note: According to the 1905 Rhode Island census and to British birth records, Ferris was born in England, though the 1910 Federal census contradicts this information, and the 1910 and the 1920 Federal census differ as to whether his parents were born in England or not. SABR's Biographical Committee has officially deemed Ferris's birthplace as Trowbridge.

GERMANY

Koblenz	Marty Krug 1912
Lundstahl	Tom McCarthy 1985
Wasseralfingen	Pep Deininger 1902
no city indicated	Tony Welzer 1926

IRELAND

Kallila	Jimmy Walsh 1916

JAMAICA
Kingston   Justin Masterson 2008

JAPAN
Kyoto   Tomo Ohka 1999,
                            Hideki Okajima 2007
Naha, Okinawa   Dave Roberts, 2004
Osaka   Hideo Nomo 2001
Tokyo   Daisuke Matsuzaka 2007

KOREA
Inchon   Sun Woo Kim 2001
Jun Ju City   Jin Ho Cho 1998
Seoul   Sang-Hoon Lee 2000
Gwangju   Byung-Hyun Kim 2003

MEXICO
Huatabampo   Mel Almada 1933
Mexico City   Carlos Rodriguez 1994
Santa Rosalia   Vicente Romo 1969

NETHERLANDS
The Hague   Win Remmerswaal 1979

NICARAGUA
Pearl Lagoon   Devern Hansack 2006

PANAMA
Colon   Ben Oglivie 1971
Los Santos   Ramiro Mendoza, 2003
Panama City   Bruce Chen, 2003

POLAND
Lublin   Johnny Reder 1932

PUERTO RICO
Aibonito   Ramon Vazquez 2005
Arroyo   Jose Cruz 2005
Caguas   Alex Cora 2005
Cidra   Luis Rivera 1989
Fajardo   Ivan Calderon 1993
Guayama   Roger Moret 1970
Juana Diaz   Jose Santiago 1966
Manati   Ramon Aviles 1977
Mayaguez   Wil Cordero 1996
Naguabo   Jose Melendez 1993
Ponce   Orlando Cepeda 1973
                        Javy Lopez 2006
Rio Pedres   Joel Pineiro 2007
Rio Piedras   Cesar Crespo 2004, Tony Rodriguez
                            1996, J. C. Romero 2007, Angel Santos
                            2001, Rey Sanchez 2002
San Juan   Javier Lopez 2006, Mike Lowell 2006
San Sebastian   Juan Beniquez 1971
Santurce   Juan Pizarro 1968, Ed Romero 1986

Matsuzaka, depicted on 2007 season tickets.

Johnny Reder, born in Poland. Courtesy of Brace Photo.

SCOTLAND

Glasgow	Bobby Thomson 1960

VENEZUELA

Cagua, Aragua	Alex Gonzales 2006
Caracas, Distrito Federal	Ugueth Urbina 2001, Alejandro Machado 2005
Cua, Miranda	Bo Diaz 1977
Cumana, Sucre	Jose Malave 1996
El Tigre, Anzoategui	Luis Aponte 1980
Mamporal, Miranda	Carlos Quintana 1988
Maracaibo, Zulia	Luis Aparicio 1971, Jeremi Gonzales 2005
Maracay, Aragua	Rich Garces 1996
Nueva Esparta	Roberto Petagine 2005
Palmerejo, Zulia	Alex Delgado 1996
Puerto Piritu, Anzoategui	Tony Armas 1983

VIRGIN ISLANDS

St. Croix	Midre Cummings 1998
St. Thomas	Calvin Pickering 2001

WALES

Machynlleth	Ted Lewis 1901

We look forward to additions to this list. The Red Sox, for instance, signed Justin Erasmus of Australia and Che-Hsuan Lin from "Chinese Taipei" in July 2007. The team has fully embraced internationalism, as witness the cover of the 2007 *Boston Red Sox Media Guide*, which depicted flags representing the natives of Canada, the Dominican Republic, Japan, Nicaragua, Puerto Rico, Venezuela, and the United States who were on the Red Sox 40-man roster.

First foreign-born player

The first foreign-born player was the starting pitcher in the franchise's very first game, Canada's own Win Kellum. Winford Ansley Kellum was born in Waterford, Ontario on April 11, 1876. In the very same game, April 26, 1901, another Canadian played as well: John Bannerman "Larry" McLean, who pinch-hit for his countryman Kellum in the ninth inning, and doubled down the right-field line. He soon scored, but Boston fell short, 10–6. McLean hailed from Fredericton, New Brunswick, born on July 18, 1881.

First player born outside North America

The first Boston player not from North America was Edward Morgan "Ted" Lewis. He debuted in the May 2, 1901 game, starting the game and benefiting from some run support from his teammates—it was 21–2, Boston, after 2½ innings. The *Boston Globe* noted that Lewis "did not pitch gilt-edge ball by any means." He went the distance, but gave up 12 runs. He still got the win.

Lewis was born on Christmas Day, 1872 in Machynlleth, Wales. Mach (as it is called locally) is a small market town, population slightly over 2,000, set in the lower Dyfi Valley about 10 miles in from the coast. It's also known as the Ancient Capital of Wales. Lewis is—so far—the only Boston player to come from Machynlleth.

The Lewis family came to America while Ted was young and he grew up in poverty in Utica, New York. Never allowed to play much baseball at home, his parents wanted him to be a minister and packed him off to college at Marietta—where he got himself on the baseball team. After receiving a scholarship offer in 1893, he transferred to Williams College and was signed to a contract with the Boston Nationals immediately on graduation. His contract specified that he would be exempt from having to play baseball on Sundays—not that this happened in Boston until nearly 40 years later—reflecting a pious outlook that saw him nicknamed "Parson" Lewis.

Lewis kept at his studies and earned a master's degree from Williams in June 1899. Promptly upon completing his 1901 season pitching for the Boston Americans, he started teaching at Columbia. For nine years, he taught elocution and oratory at Williams, later moving to become an English professor as dean of students at Massachusetts Agricultural College. In 1917, Lewis came to know New England poet Robert Frost when they met in the home of university President Meiklejohn at Amherst.

Frost had a lifelong interest in baseball (he'd been the best pitcher on his high school team in Salem NH) and dreamed that he'd pitch in the major leagues, so it was perhaps a foregone conclusion that the two would become friendly. Frost asked Lewis to show him how to throw a curveball, and recalled, "He let me into the secret of how he could make a ball behave when his arm was just right. It may sound superstitious to the uninitiated, but he could push a cushion of air ahead of it for it to slide off from, any way it pleased." On several occasions, the two enjoyed playing catch. In 1927, Lewis became president of the University of New Hampshire.

Information on Lewis and Frost can be found in Lawrence Thompson's book, *The Years of Triumph.*

First foreign-born manager

The first foreign-born manager of the Red Sox was Fred Lake (1908–09) who was born October 16, 1866 in Cornwallis, Nova Scotia, Canada. Coincidentally, the only other Sox skipper born outside the United States was the man who succeeded Lake: Patsy Donovan, born March 16, 1865 in Queenstown, County Cork, Ireland.

First foreign-born owner

The first (and last) foreign-born owner of the Red Sox is Joseph J. Lannin, who was born on April 23, 1866 in Lac Beauport, Quebec, Canada and owned the team from 1914 to 1916.

Nap Lajoie with Nova Scotia's Fred Lake, September 1908.

LATINOS ON THE RED SOX

First Latino player

The most famous Latino on the Red Sox is one few people realized was one: Ted Williams. Setting Ted aside for the moment, let's note that the first foreign-born Latin player was shortstop Eusebio Gonzales, who was a .400 hitter in the last year the Red Sox won the World Series in the 20th century, 1918. Gonzales, born in Havana, debuted on July 26, 1918—some 35 years before 26 Julio became a Cuban revolutionary holiday. "Papo" Gonzales had one single and one triple in five at-bats, appearing in just three games. He walked once, struck out once and scored two runs. He was perfect in the field. He died in Havana on Valentine's Day 1976.

Needless to say, many Latino players were born in the U.S. to families who had immigrated earlier. Let's look at some other early Latinos.

Frank Arellanes—1908–10 Red Sox

Frank Arellanes, first Latino on the Red Sox, 1908.

The first Latin player for the Red Sox was Frank Arellanes. His family first came to California in the late 1700's from Puebla, Mexico. Frank and his two brothers, Abe and Tom, both played for the Santa Cruz Beachcombers, but only Frank made it to the majors. Frank burst on the major league scene with Boston after compiling a sizzling 13–2 minor league mark for Santa Clara. He was a right-handed pitcher who debuted in a relief role on July 28, 1908. The next day's *Cleveland Press* commented "Senor Arellanes moocha caliente hombre, or in the language of the small boy, the Mexican is a 'hot number.'" A subheadline referred to him as "swarthy"—though his death certificate described his race as "white." Arellanes might have been amused; all indications are that his family had resided in California since roughly the time of the American Revolution in the late 1700s. Chances are he had a longer American lineage than most of his teammates.

Jim McGuire was the Red Sox manager, and his starting pitcher on July 28 was Fred Burchell. Cleveland had reportedly been hitting lefties well that season and southpaw Burchell surrendered three runs in the bottom of the first inning. The *Press* noted, "Burchell lasted an inning and was relieved by Frank Arellanes, the only Mexican in the big leagues. Arellanes did well until the eighth, when he fell before the Bradley, Turner, Lajoie, Stovall assault."

In the top of the eighth, Arellanes tripled for Boston. "When Arellanes made his three-base hit, Jim McGuire patted him on the back and told him how much he loved him." The score was tied at 3–3 at the time, but Arellanes was thrown out at the plate when he tried to score on a grounder to Lajoie at second. In the bottom of the inning, he got touched up for two runs and Cleveland won the game, 5–3. They only had six hits the entire game. Rhoads won for Cleveland.

On September 18, 1908, the two matched up again, but this time Arellanes was a starter. Rhoads no-hit the Sox, beating Arellanes, 2–1. The Sox pitcher only granted Cleveland five hits, but Rhoads wouldn't let Boston have any and the Clevelanders prevailed. Cleveland did make three errors, Rhoads hit a batter (Speaker), threw a wild pitch, and walked two other batters. Interestingly, Jim McGuire was now wearing a Cleveland uniform. He'd been fired as manager in Boston and replaced by Fred Lake. He coached for Cleveland during some of this game.

In 1909, Frank became—in effect—the replacement for Cy Young, who had been traded to Cleveland. A tall order, that. Frank pitched his way to a team-leading 16-win season and saved eight games as well. His record was 16–12 with a 2.18 ERA and his eight saves led the American League. He has been described as one of the first relief specialists in major league ball, largely based on those eight saves. That year, though, was the only year in which he recorded any saves and it's a year in which he started 28 games.

His addition to Boston's pitching staff helped the newly-minted Red Sox climb to the first division, as they won 88 games and competed in the hotly-contested AL pennant race with the Athletics and Tigers. His last year in the majors was also with the Red Sox. In 1910, he was 4–7, with an ERA of 2.88. His major league totals read 24–22, with over 409 innings pitched, and a career 2.28 ERA.

Final game: August 14, 1910. On August 16, he was reported as traded to St. Louis for Sacramento pitching prospect Benjamin Franklin "High Pockets" Hunt, who debuted a week later. Arellanes was officially released on the 18th. Early 1911 stories made it clear that he was sent out of town because he "failed to keep in shape" and that "quick punishment was called for." *(Washington Post)* Within a week, he pitched a 3–0 shutout against Vernon. Some jawing at the umpire saw him tossed from a game on September 21; the following day he threw a two-hit shutout against Los Angeles and on October 16 he threw a no-hitter against Vernon but lost it, 2–0, due to a number of walks.

It looked as though he'd return to the Red Sox in 1911. So reported the *Globe*'s Tim Murnane, though Sacramento owner Graham said Arellanes had truly been released and was on his team's reserve list. Arellanes did show up for Red Sox spring training, held in Redondo Beach. He drank some of the sulphur water at Redondo and developed a boil and an abscess, but he toiled on with Boston, even playing a game against Sacramento on March 21. He pitched in Denver on April 2 as the team was making its way back east, but was reported as unable even to put on his uniform due to more boils while at Lincoln, Nebraska. On April 9, he batted leadoff and played center field in Omaha, but went hitless. He traveled with the team for the first several games of the season, but saw no action and was sold back to Sacramento on April 24. By early May, he turns up in Sacramento boxscores.

Arellanes pitched well deep into the 1914 season, but was pitching for the San Francisco Missions when he was arrested in early October for statutory rape of a 14-year-old, one of several ballplayers from San Francisco, Oakland, and Portland so charged.

In early April 1915, he was pitching for Salt Lake but was let go and signed on with Denver in the Western League. After the season, he signed with Vernon. The refrain of being out of condition followed his moves. After a year with Vernon, he was cut loose the following April, 1917. On December 13, 1918, he died of pneumonia following influenza at age 36.

Charley "Sea Lion" Hall—1909–13 Red Sox

In 1909 and 1910, the Red Sox actually had two Latinos on their pitching staff—Arellanes and Charley "Sea Lion" Hall. Eighteen men appeared on the mound for the 1909 Red Sox, but 35 of the 152 starts were by either Arellanes (28) or Hall (7). Between them in 1909, they ac-

A fashionable Charley Hall, replete with Red Sox sweater.

counted for 290⅔ innings. Arellanes was 16–12 (2.18) and Hall was 6–4 (2.56). In 1910, Hall had the better record: 12–9 (1.91 ERA), with Arellanes at 4–7 (2.88).

Over the five seasons he pitched for Boston, Hall won 46 and lost 32, with an aggregate ERA of 2.93. Hall was Hispanic. It is commonly, and incorrectly, reported in many reference books that he was originally named Carlos Clolo, but mission records show that he was born Carlos Luis Hall in Ventura, California on July 27, 1884, christened at the San Buenaventura Mission. The son of Arthur Hall and Elvira Mungari, he was later described in game accounts as "swarthy." Fred Lieb's obituary in *The Sporting News* said Hall was of Mexican Indian heritage and was "weened (sic) on hot tamales." He added that "certain inelegant players referred to Charley as 'the Greaser.'" Hall was apparently sensitive to the matter, and may have tried to downplay his ethnicity. Gordon Gilmore, writing in the *St. Paul Dispatch* after Hall's death, said, "Dark and swarthy, he was rumored to be of Spanish descent but would lick any man who called him 'Carlos.'"

He originally got into baseball by "mistake", Ton Hennion of the *Ventura Daily Democrat* wrote in Hall's obituary. He went to watch a semipro game between Santa Barbara and Los Angeles in 1903, and Santa Barbara was short one man. Charley was drafted out of the stands and went 3-for-3.

He first broke into pro ball with the Pacific Coast League, playing for Seattle in 1904. He got his start in major league ball with Cincinnati in mid-1906 and pitched both that year and in 1907. With the Reds, he had won 8 and lost 10, but pitched fairly well. In 1908, he pitched for Columbus and for St. Paul, and at some point in the summer of 1909, Red Sox scout Patsy Donovan obtained him for the Red Sox. Hall's first start was on August 9, 1910—he threw a four-hit 2–1 win over the White Sox. Later in August, on the 27th, he threw a one-hitter against Cleveland; the *Boston Globe* said he was "robbed" of a no-hitter when an easy infield pop-up fell in between Bill Carrigan, Bill Purtell, and Hall during the sixth inning.

Hall was the winning pitcher in the very first game ever played at Fenway Park, on April 20, 1912. Buck O'Brien started but left after four innings; the Red Sox scored three times in the bottom of the fourth, making it a 5–4 game and Hall was asked to keep it close. He threw seven innings and won it after 11 full innings, 7–6. Hall walked and scored the tying run in the sixth, and was 1-for-3 on the day, with an uneventful double in the bottom of the ninth.

Later in 1912, Hall appeared in two games of the World Series, throwing 10⅔ innings in relief. His World Series ERA stands at 3.38.

After the 1913 season, the Red Sox released him and he returned to St. Paul in 1914. At some point, perhaps around this time, he may have suffered an injury that impaired his performance. Charley's grandson told his wife ReBecca that "one year at spring training Charley dove into the swimming pool and hit his head. He was never the same, after that."

Most of 1915 was spent in the PCL again, with the Los Angeles Angels. He was 0–4 with the St. Louis Cardinals in 10 appearances in 1916, but was sent back to the Angels. 1917 saw him start with the Angels, then go back to St. Paul. At the tail end of 1918, he appeared in the majors for the final time, getting one start for the Detroit Tigers. He had a lifetime 3.09 ERA with a 54–47 record; Ed Walton said Hall was "among the first pitchers to specialize in relief"—with 80 starts in 188 appearances. Walton says he led the American League with six relief wins both in 1910 and 1912. The record shows he led the league with four saves in 1911.

He threw four minor league no-hitters, one in 1920 for St. Paul, and pitched into the middle 1920s. His nickname was due to his "raucous penetrating voice like a fog horn at sea." (Frederick Lieb, in *The Sporting News*.) An earlier copy of the paper said he had "a voice that could wake the echoes and scare little children out of their afternoon naps a mile away from the ball yard."

Reports do indicate that Hall was fluent in Spanish. The great tragedy in his life was the loss of his three-year-old son Kenneth, killed by his own brother in a gun cleaning accident. Charley himself suffered from Parkinson's in his later years and died in December 1943.

Eusebio Gonzalez—1918 Red Sox

Eusebio Miguel Gonzalez Lopez was born in Havana, Cuba on July 13, 1892. A versatile infielder, he began his pro career with the Fe baseball club in Havana in 1910. Gonzalez was apparently spotted by Dodgers captain Jake Daubert while the Dodgers were playing a series of games in the Cuban capital; he made his U.S. debut with the Troy Trojans in the spring of 1914. Over the next few years, Gonzalez played for the Binghamton Bingos, the Scranton Miners, and the Springfield Green Sox in the western Massachusetts city, before briefly appearing for the Red Sox in three games mid-1918 (see the writeup on those games in the section of this book devoted to players with few appearances on the Sox). With the Green Sox, he also played side-by-side with his brother Ramon Gonzalez, another capable infielder. The *Springfield Re-*

publican wrote, "He has played remarkable ball for Springfield and has been the real life and hope of the club all season." Eusebio was quite popular in Springfield and the newspaper followed his fortunes with occasional stories for a year or so after his departure. Leaving Boston for Toronto, Gonzalez played there for a number of years, into the 1923 season, even marrying an Ontario woman, Audrey Jary. His last time in American professional ball was in 1928.

He came from the rough and tumble world of Cuban baseball, and returned there nearly every winter to supplement his income and remain active—until an incident in early 1924 when he was shot in the hand by sportswriter Pepe Conte during an altercation on the field. Perhaps if Ted Williams had been familiar with the story, he would have been a bit less confrontational in his approach to the "knights of the keyboard." Gonzalez recovered.

These weren't the Yawkey years. There was different ownership in Boston. During the first 20 years of the Red Sox franchise, the team had previously signed two Mexican-American ballplayers (Frank Arellanes and Charley Hall) and also a full-blooded Native American (Louis Leroy). There was no indication in the Boston press that Gonzalez, or any of these other Red Sox players, were controversial signings due to their ethnicity. Newspapers occasionally called him "the Cuban" but neither his acquisition nor his brief tenure with Boston occasioned any real comment, nor did he throughout his lengthy minor league career.

What became of Gonzalez after 1928 remains a bit of a mystery. His marriage seems not to have survived, and we know he lived his last several decades in Cuba, where he died, in Havana, in 1976. A lengthy biography of Eusebio Gonzalez appears in *When Boston Still Had The Babe: The 1918 World Series Champion Red Sox*.

Ramon "Mike" Herrera—1925–26 Red Sox

Were the Red Sox the last major league team to sign a black player? Or were they one of the first? Did the Red Sox actually have a black ballplayer long before Pumpsie Green and 22 years before Jackie Robinson debuted with the Dodgers? Havana's Ramon "Mike" Herrera totaled 276 at bats in 1925 and 1926 while serving as a second baseman for the Red Sox (an even .275 batting average). He also played for Negro League teams both before and after his stretch with Boston, one of just 11 players who played in both the Negro Leagues and major leagues before World War II.

Ramon Herrera with Babe Ruth.

Before joining the Red Sox, Herrera had played for Almendares in Havana, as well as with La Union, All Leagues, and the (Cuban) Red Sox. The Boston Red Sox purchased him from their Springfield (Eastern League) club. The *Boston Globe* termed him a "splendid prospect" and he did go 2-for-5 in his first game. Todd Bolton, asked about Herrera's history in the Negro Leagues, replied:

"In the pre-Negro League years he barnstormed in the US with the Long Branch Cubans and the Jersey City Cubans. When the first Negro National League was formed in 1920, Herrera was a member of the Cuban Stars (West), one of the inaugural teams in the league. He stayed on with the team in 1921 when it became the Cincinnati Cubans. Herrera returned to the Negro Leagues for one final season in 1928 with Alejandro Pompez' Cuban Stars (East)."

Photographs of Mike Herrera seem to show that he could easily "pass" for white, and for those who want to measure such things, he may have been more white than black. So did he have to "pass for black" when he was in the Negro Leagues? Not really, Bolton explains. There were a number of light-skinned players in the Negro Leagues and even more "white" Cubans. These players were used to playing together in Latin America. It was only in the United States that they were segregated.

Joe Gonzales—1937 Red Sox

Joe Madrid Gonzales was born in San Francisco in 1915. Claiming Spanish descent, perhaps his middle name suggests that he truly was Castilian. The right-handed pitcher debuted with the Red Sox on August 25, 1937. Contemporary coverage in the *Boston Globe* said his father was born in the Basque country of Spain. He was a star for the University of Southern California where he was undefeated his final two years.

The Red Sox had signed him and he was on option with the San Diego Padres for a few weeks, sharing space with young Ted Williams. Given a callup in August, the "young Mexican hurler" (San Diego sportswriter Earl Keller's words) debuted with Boston on August 25 as the fourth pitcher in a futile relief effort against Cleveland, as Bob Feller held the Red Sox to four hits in an 8–1 win. Gonzales pitched the eighth inning, both allowing one hit and retiring the side on just four pitches. The *Boston Herald* noted: "Thus, it was impossible to gauge how good or bad he might be. But he did seem to carry plenty of poise."

Four days later, the "coast youth" was the third pitcher in relief during a loss to the St. Louis Browns. He was second man in against the White Sox on September 2 and limited them to three hits in 5⅔ innings. Five days later, he got his first decision—a loss—after giving up four hits in one inning of relief. On September 20, he was given his first major league start. Described as Jose Gonzales, a former star athlete at the University of Southern California, Joe allowed 14 hits but won the game against the Browns, 7–5, in good part thanks to Bobby Doerr's two-run homer in the sixth.

It was Lefty vs. Lefty, and later Gomez vs. Gonzales, as Lefty Gomez beat Lefty Grove (and reliever Gonzales) in a game against the Yankees. Gonzales only gave up two hits in 3⅔ innings of work, but Gomez had let the Yankees win the game. The *Chicago Tribune* carelessly called the right-hander "Mike Gonzales." On September 26, he allowed four hits in two-thirds of an inning, in another Red Sox loss. He pitched very well against the Yankees in his second and final major league start, with the Yankees only up 1–0 after six and a half innings. Unfortunately, Gonzales tired and Joe DiMaggio hit a grand slam. That kind of did it and New York won that October 3 game, 6–1. Gonzales didn't know it at the time, but his major league career was over (1–2, 4.35 ERA). As a major league fielder, he'd been flawless. As a major league hitter, he'd been hitless, though he did sacrifice once in the October game.

He pitched for the Red Sox in spring training 1938, but was optioned to Little Rock near the end of March. In an April 9 exhibition game, he "muffled Yankee bats" for Little Rock, allowing four hits in five innings of work. On July 7, he reported to Hazleton, sent there from Little Rock. He was reportedly sold to Cleveland on August 1, 1938. Apparently back with Boston by the following year, Gonzales played with Minneapolis during the spring of 1939 (Halsey Hall called him a "Spanish-American down from the Red Sox...a horse for work"). Joe spent most of 1939 building an 11–7 record with the Padres. At the end of the year, both Gonzales and Lefty Lefebvre were sent to the San Francisco Seals in a November 12 deal so that the Red Sox could acquire one Dominic DiMaggio.

During Gonzales' six weeks with the Red Sox, the newspapers accorded no notice at all to his Hispanic heritage. It was apparently not considered a remarkable event.

Latinos on the Red Sox in more recent years

Needless to say, there has been an explosion of Latino players on the Red Sox and throughout major league baseball in recent years. By the early 21st century, a large percentage of the Sox roster was composed of players like Pedro Martinez, Manny Ramirez, and David Ortiz. Appearances can continue to be deceiving, as well: just as the name Ted Williams doesn't conjure up images of a Latino legacy, neither does the name of a Mike Lowell. Yet Lowell is of Cuban parents, speaks fluent Spanish (something that Nomar Garciaparra could not do), and is without question a Latino ballplayer. And the MVP of the 2007 World Series.

BORN IN MEXICO

Mel Almada—1933–37 Red Sox

The first Mexican-born ballplayer ever to play in major league ball was Mel Almada, who played for the Red Sox. (The Red Sox also had the first Dane ever, Olaf Henriksen, for whatever that's worth.)

Almada was born in Huatabampo in the Mexican state of Sonora. His signing to the Red Sox prompted something not seen before or since: on July 23, 1933, Alejandro V. Martinez, the Mexican consul in Los Angeles, helped host "Melo Almada Day" at Wrigley Field, Los Angeles, to celebrate the signing of Almada to the Red Sox.

Baldomero Melo Almada Quiros traced his ancestry back to Don Alvaro Vaz de Almada, Count of Abranches, who died in 1449. Descended from conquistadors, his great grandfather was said to have owned a lucrative silver mine and enough acreage in Mexico than one could fit the country of Belgium within its

Mel Almada. Courtesy of Brace Photo.

boundaries. Shirley Povich reported that one of Mel's uncles was "brutally butchered by the Yaqui Indians." The forces of Pancho Villa imprisoned another uncle for a few months and confiscated the family properties.

Melo's father, Baldomero Almada, was appointed governor of Baja California by President Obregon but the Mexican Revolution was underway. When Mel's father arrived to take over as governor, the incumbent simply refused to vacate the office—and had, Mel himself said, "a large well-equipped army, while my father's army consisted of my mother and eight children." [*The Sporting News*, September 5, 1935] Dad, he told Harry Edwards of the American League Service Bureau, "decided his family would prefer the glorious climate of Los Angeles to the excitement of trying to oust the governor who refused to be ousted." He was offered instead the position of Ambassador to France, but it seemed much too far away; he accepted instead the position of consul in Los Angeles.

His son Melo thus moved to southern California with his family at the age of one, and learned baseball as a child. While at Los Angeles High School, he reportedly set the southern California record for the broad jump (which led a *Sporting News* cartoonist late in his third season with the Red Sox to dub him a "Mexican jumping bean"). John Drohan later wrote, "Had Carranza remained president of Mexico, Mel might have become a bullfighter or possibly just another deceased hero of the cause."

Mel's older brother Louis played in the Pacific Coast League. After Mel graduated from high school, he went to hang out with his brother, who was playing with Seattle, and manager Ernie Johnson (later a scout with the Red Sox) spotted his potential, giving him a shot. Johnson told college-bound Melo that he'd be "crazy if he wasted his time on the so-called higher education." [*Collier's*, August 24, 1935] Eddie Collins signed him to the Red Sox.

Louis might well have made the majors before Mel, save for a line drive off the bat of Fred Lindstrom during batting practice at spring training with the Brooklyn Dodgers.

September 8, 1933 became the date of Almada's debut. The left-handed outfielder batted .341 in 14 games before the end of the season. He played a few games at first base as well. It was a sign of the era in which he played that *Collier's* described him as a "radio nut" and said "He even carries a portable radio with him on baseball trips, plugging it into his hotel room and listening to the programs."

At the time of his debut, the *Los Angeles Times* had noted that Almada was the third Mexican ballplayer to play in the major leagues. The prior two were born in the United States. One fact the newspaper did not note: all three played for the Boston Red Sox. The Sox had previously fielded pitchers Frank Arellanes and Charley Hall (who pitched for the Red Sox from 1909 through 1913). Would that the Red Sox had pioneered in the signing of African American ballplayers as well!

The Sox had a degree of cosmopolitanism in 1937. At one time in 1937, the Red Sox had players fluent in a number of languages on the team. Mel Almada was born in Mexico and spoke Spanish, Fabian Gaffke was German, Gene Desautels was French, and Dom Dallesandro was Italian. Multi-linguist catcher Moe Berg was able to talk reasonably fluently with each.

Almada was up and down with the Red Sox, batting .233, .290, and .253 in subsequent seasons. He wasn't being used as much in 1937, and was traded along with both Ferrell brothers to the Washington Senators on June 11 for Ben Chapman and Buck Newsom. He played out 1937 (hitting .236 for Boston, he hit .309 for Washington) but was swapped on June 15, 1938, to St. Louis. Again, he'd started slow (.244 for Washington, .342 for the Browns). St. Louis worked a mid-June transaction, selling him—again on the 15th—to the Brooklyn Dodgers, but this time Almada's average went down instead of up. After 646 major league ballgames, his career in the majors came to its conclusion. His lifetime average was .284.

Even during his time with the Red Sox, the handsome Almada got some work in Hollywood. Brother Louis had a position with Warner Bros. and Mel was cast in several movies, mostly ones released in Mexico, for Warners and Fox. In a December 8, 1935 press release from the American League, he explained, "They give me a small speaking part occasionally."

After baseball, he worked in the produce business for some time, served in the U. S. Army, and spent four years as manager of the Mexican North League baseball team based in Sonora, the Navojoa Mayos. He had four children, all Mexicans citizens. Mel Almada died on August 13, 1988 in Caborca, Sonora.

In the early 1980s, Almada lived in Tucson and told *Arizona Daily Star* writer Keith Rosenblum that he'd never experienced discrimination in baseball—but he qualified that by adding, "Humiliation? Yes. Every so often, we'd be out for a drink and suddenly someone would say, 'Hey, you goddamned Mexican…what makes you think you can act like an American?'" [August 2, 1981]

TWO MORE CUBANS FROM THE 1950S

Two more natives of Havana played for the Red Sox in the 1950s, catcher Mike Guerra and pitcher Mike Fornieles.

Mike Guerra—1951 Red Sox

Fermin (Romero) Guerra was born on October 11, 1912 in Havana and died just two days before his 80th birthday. Born in poverty, he never went to school, his first work in baseball being as a batboy in Havana. The 5′10″ righthanded catcher debuted for the Washington Senators on September 19, 1937, getting into just one game. He struck out twice in three at-bats, and had to live with a .000 major league batting average for six more seasons until the Senators gave him another shot during the talent-depleted war year of 1944. He got in 75 games and batted .281. Though he dropped to .210 the following year, he proved he had what it took and survived the return home of the many ballplayers who had been in the armed services. Guerra played for Washington again in 1946, in a backup role, then was sold to the Philadelphia Athletics that December.

Mike played for the Athletics for four years, getting more work in 1949 and 1950 and producing, with averages of .265 and .282 respectively. In December 1950, the Red Sox purchased his contract and he played in 10 early season games for Boston before being traded back to the Senators in May for Len Okrie. For the Red Sox, he was 5-for-32 (.156) with two RBIs. He completed his final season in baseball for Washington, with 214 at-bats but a disappointing .201 average. The career .242 batter managed in Havana and scouted for the Tigers in his later years, but after the Revolution "was sent to pick potatoes because of his resistance to the regime." [Gonzalez Echeverria, *Pride of Havana*, pp. 265–6]

Mike Fornieles—1957–63 Red Sox

Jose Miguel (Torres) Fornieles was a right-handed pitcher who won AL Fireman of the Year honors from *The Sporting News* in 1960, while pitching for the Red Sox. Signed by the Senators, he got his first major league work in September 1952, at age 20. Mike appeared in four games, two as a starter, threw two complete games and posted a 2–2 record with a 1.37 ERA. Despite this promise, the Senators swapped him to the White Sox that December in exchange for Chuck Stobbs. In 3½ years with Chicago, Fornieles ran up a 15–13 record with an ERA averaging around 4.00, but was then packaged as part of a six-player trade with the Orioles in May 1956.

He was 6–13 for Baltimore, traded to Boston for Billy Goodman in mid-June 1957. The Red Sox threw him right into the rotation and in 18 starts he posted a record of 8–7 (3.52). The Sox began to use him more as a relief pitcher and he began to shine. His best year was 1960, with a 10–5 record and a league-leading 14 saves. He also led the league with 70 appearances. The following year, he made the All-Star team and recorded 15 more saves. Mike was a mainstay in the Boston bullpen for several years before being sold to the Minnesota Twins in June 1963. He only threw 22⅓ innings for Minnesota, the last of his major league career. As a starter, he'd been 18–31, but as a reliever he was 45–33. Lifetime, that makes him 63–64; he had a 3.96 ERA.

First Puerto Rican native: Juan Pizarro—1968–69 Red Sox

The first native Boricuan for Boston was Juan Pizarro, born in Santurce in 1937. Juan Roman (Cordova) Pizarro was a southpaw who pitched over 2,000 innings in 18 seasons of major league work, beginning with the 1957 Milwaukee Braves. He won 131 games, lost 105, and recorded a 3.43 earned run average. After four years with the Braves—and two World Series apperances in 1957 and 1958—and six years with the White Sox (including four seasons of double digit wins), he was traded to the NL Pirates and worked a year and a half there before being sold to the Red Sox in late June 1968. His best years had been 1963 (16–8, 2.39) and 1964 (19–9, 2.56).

Though he'd largely begun to work in relief by the time he reached Boston, the Sox gave him 12 starts in 1968. His record was 6–8 (3.59 ERA). In mid-April 1969, he was traded to the Indians with Dick Ellsworth and Ken Harrelson for Joe Azcue, Vicente Romo, and Sonny Siebert. He finished his career playing for Cleveland, Oakland, the Cubs, the Astros, and the Pirates.

First Venezuelan native: Luis Aparicio—1971 Red Sox

Hall of Famer Luis Aparicio kicked off a great career as Rookie of the Year in 1956, leading the league in stolen bases (for the first of nine consecutive years), in assists (for the first of six seasons), and in putouts. From 1959 through 1966, he led the league in fielding each and every year. After seven years with the White Sox, and five with the Orioles, he was reacquired by the White Sox for three more years. Little Looie appeared in both the 1959 and 1966 World Series, and the nine-time Gold Glove shortstop was named to 10 All-Star teams.

Aparicio closed his career with the Red Sox, traded by Chicago in December 1970 for Mike Andrews and Luis Alvarado, twice making the All-Star squad. Unfortunately, one memory held by Boston fans was the October 2 game against the Detroit Tigers when Luis stumbled rounding third base and failed to score on a Yastrzemski double that would have been a triple had Aparicio not retreated to third base—only to meet Yaz arriving. The Sox lost the pennant two days later, by half a game to the Tigers. Aparicio left major league ball after a career batting average of .262, and 506 stolen bases. Luis Ernesto (Montiel) Aparicio was named to the National Baseball Hall of Fame in 1984.

First Dominican native: Mario Guerrero—1973 Red Sox

Born in Santo Domingo, DR, on September 28, 1949, Mario Miguel (Abud) Guerrero was signed by the New York Yankees at age 18, but first made the majors with the Boston Red Sox. He came to Boston as part of the Sparky Lyle trade—the Red Sox traded Lyle to the Yankees for Danny Cater and a player to be named later—who turned out to be Guerrero. In his debut game, he went 2-for-3—against the Yankees. Mario played both shortstop and second base for the Sox, but he didn't get much work since the Sox had Luis Aparicio and Doug Griffin as first-stringers at those positions. Guerrero only batted .233—an average he boosted to .246 in 1974, though Rick Burleson was Boston's main man at short. With Burleson having staked a strong claim to short, the Sox traded Guerrero to St. Louis for Jim Willoughby before the 1975 season. Mario only hit .239 for the Cardinals.

In mid-1976, he played in the minors until traded to the California Angels on May 29. He had his best two years with the Angels, batting .284 and .283 playing about half the time. In 1978, he got in a full year, with 505 at-bats, for Oakland and did well, batting .275—but committed 26 errors and only scored 27 runs all year long. After two more years with the Athletics, and despite a trade to Seattle, he was done.

Needless to say, the Red Sox have been blessed with a large number of Dominican natives since Guerrero—through the 2007 season, some 36 others in the last 30 years ranging from Hall of Famer Juan Marichal to sure future Hall of Famers such as Pedro Martinez. And that's not to mention a couple of sluggers named Ramirez and Ortiz.

JEWISH SOX

The Red Sox have fielded a few Jews over the years: Brian Bark, Moe Berg, Lou Boudreau, Happy Foreman, Joe Ginsberg, Gabe Kapler, Buddy Myer, Jeff Newman, Al Richter, Sy Rosenthal, Adam Stern, and Kevin Youkilis. Al Schacht served as a coach for the Red Sox in 1935 and 1936. [Source: Martin Abramowitz, et. al., American Jewish Historical Society baseball card set, "Jewish Major Leaguers"]

With only 12 Jews over the years, it was remarkable that three of them played in one game, on August 8, 2005. The Red Sox activated Kevin Youkilis, calling him back up from Pawtucket in one of the ongoing flurry of roster moves that seems to characterize the early 21st century Red Sox. The Red Sox had activated Gabe Kapler on July 30, back from a partial season in Japan. When Youkilis joined Kapler and Adam Stern, they became the first team to ever have three Jews on the 25-man roster all at the same time. All three appeared in the August 8 game, but none of the three made a hit.

First Jewish player: Sy Rosenthal—1925–26 Red Sox

The first Jewish player on the Red Sox was Boston-born Simon Rosenthal, who played semi-pro ball in Boston during 1920 and 1921, attracting an invitation to spring training with the Red Sox in 1922. From the sandlots in Franklin Park, Sy (as he spelled it) was signed by Hugh Duffy and sent to Hartford for more seasoning. He hit .279 with 10 homers for the Eastern League team. In late February 1923, Rosenthal was sent on option to Albany and played for Albany and Pittsfield, batting .338 with 15 homers. Sy's parents were Philip Rosenthal, who had emigrated to the United States from Russia, and Anna Gottfried, who had come from Austria.

Red Sox spring training was held in San Antonio in 1924. Rosenthal, Camp Skinner, and Dick Reichle (all of whom made the majors with Boston) had been sent to San Antonio in the fall of 1923 in a deal that brought Boone, Todt, Fuller, Gross, and Marshall to Boston. Sy started 1924 like a house afire, and the May 1 *Sporting News* reported him as "the talk of the league" with 11 consecutive hits at one point, and an average of around .750! A broken leg set him back but he hit .376 in 44 games, playing error-free outfield ball. By June 1925, still with San Antonio, he was hitting .331 with real power: 21 homers. Rosenthal's contract was purchased by the Red Sox and he appeared in 19 games starting on September 8, when he led off both games of a doubleheader against the Yankees, playing left field and having himself a 1-for-9, with one error.

Rosenthal hit for a .264 average in 72 at-bats. He hit five doubles and two triples, no homers, and drove in eight runs. He spent the 1926 season with the Sox, getting 285 at-bats in 104 games and a .267 average with four home runs and 34 RBIs. His first homer put the Sox in the lead, driving in two runs in the April 25 game against Washington, but the game went into extra innings before Boston won it. His best day came a month later, on May 25, facing the Yankees. Rosenthal hit a ninth-inning two-run homer in the first game, making it a more respectable 5–3 loss. In the second game, he hit another two-run homer, this time helping close the gap to 5–4. Boston lost both games and Babe Ruth got the headlines with his 16th homer (this was still May), with what was called the "longest homer ever made at Fenway Park"—nearly leaving the right-field bleachers.

After 1926, Rosenthal spent the rest of his baseball career in the minor leagues, beginning with the Louisville Colonels in 1927, and wending his way through Chattanooga, Dallas, Atlanta, Mobile-Knoxville (the franchise moved mid-season), Galveston, back to Atlanta, Quincy in the Mississippi Valley League, Dayton, Beckley, and ending in 1935 with Peoria. In 1931, he had a busy year, starting in February with the Atlanta Crackers, then on Galveston's roster briefly, with Mobile and Knoxville, and then back to Atlanta in December.

An injured foot hampered his performance in the big leagues, but he averaged close to .333 over the nine years in the minors. After returning to Boston, he played for the Wolf Clothiers team in the Boston Park League for a number of years.

Both Sy and his son Buddy (Irwin Rosenthal) joined to fight in World War II. Just as his son was a bit underage, so was Sy a bit over. Buddy joined the Marine Corps. Sy attempted to enlist after Pearl Harbor, but was at first turned down on account of some loose cartilage in his knee dating back to baseball days. After being rejected, he paid for knee surgery to have the cartilage removed and had some dental work done so he could pass the fitness tests, and he ultimately made the grade despite his age. "The next time I tried, they accepted me," he told *The Sporting News* on September 24, 1947. "So I liquidated my business—I had been manufacturing tin cans in South Boston—and pretty soon I found myself on a mine-sweeper."

Both Rosenthals suffered great tragedy during the war. Sy Rosenthal was inducted into the Navy on September 22, 1942.

"I had been corresponding with Buddy pretty regularly," Sy remembered, "On putting in at Norfolk in February 1944, I found a mass of my letters to him had been returned. And I had received no word from him in a long time. Then I learned of his death."

Buddy was killed in the Pacific theater on Christmas Day or the day after in 1943, during the assault to capture the airfields at Cape Gloucester on the island of New Britain in the Solomon Islands. The Marine Corps lost 325 men in the battle. Irwin's body was returned home in May 1949.

Sy Rosenthal, rendered paraplegic while serving his country.

Rosenthal later recounted his understanding of what had occurred, after his son had gone ashore with the Marines. "They went through some tall grass... and, as they went along, they couldn't locate the Japs. Finally, as a means of spotting the Japs, my boy deliberately exposed himself for an instant. The instant was too long. A second later he was dead....He was only a few months over 17."

Sy reportedly served aboard ship during the D-Day invasion of Normandy but several months later while assigned to the minesweeper *U.S.S. Miantonomah*, Rosenthal was seriously injured on September 25, 1944 when a hole was blown in the ship's starboard side, just behind the bridge, by a German mine. The ship sank just one mile off the coast of France at LeHavre, taking 58 members of the crew with her.

Rosenthal was rendered paraplegic and after three months in a French hospital returned home, confined to a wheelchair for the rest of his life. On September 13, 1947, the Red Sox held a "Day" for Rosenthal and the money raised enabled the Rosenthal Day committee to present him a deed for a new house specially fitted with wheelchair ramps and other fixtures. News stories at the time stated that Rosenthal had been a veteran of World War I as well, but given his age at the time, this seems unlikely.

During Sy's "day," a Marine Corps bugler played "Taps" from the pitcher's mound in honor of Buddy Rosenthal, and both Sy and his wife wept openly. He'd enjoyed a visit to the Red Sox clubhouse, where he greeted many players he'd known from years earlier, and admitted that his life was "Pretty tough. Oh, sure, you put on an act and say you're feeling great, but it's tough, real tough." After a moment's reflection as he glanced at his legs, he was quick to add: "As you get older, you go through life philosophically. The two kids beside me on that ship were blown to bits. I've still got my friends. Come on, let's get out to the field. I feel great."

Though of modest means himself, Rosenthal himself was known for charitable work on his own, helping raise money for a number of causes. His obituary reports two such acts. In 1952, while in the Cushing Hospital in Framingham, he learned of a Needham family whose house had been destroyed by fire, and from his hospital bed, Rosenthal offered them the use of his home.

A testimonial dinner honoring Rosenthal, given the title "Big Leaguer All the Way", drew more than 500 to the Sherry-Biltmore Hotel on April 20, 1960. A story in the *Jewish Advocate* reported that "there is barely an hour when he is free from pain" but that he devoted his life to trying to help his fellow man. The account detailed the help he had given a boy afflicted with polio, a girl who was blind, and two sisters stricken with cerebral palsy. All three cases led to his involvement in fundraising for the respective causes. He was three times president of the New England Chapter of Paralyzed Veterans of America, and active in numerous other organizations.

In 1966, he worked with the "Negro priest" Rev. Charles D. Burns to raise $55,000 for a

Vic Johnson's tribute to Sy Rosenthal.

school gymnasium at the St. Augustine seminary at Bay St. Louis, Mississippi. It was an ecumenical effort, involving a Protestant minister and a Catholic institution. The seminary was the first Roman Catholic seminary to accept African Americans, in the 1920s. Rosenthal said, "We wouldn't have to set up a Brotherhood Week if we observed the basic tenets of our faith, whatever it may be. If you have good will in your heart, you don't need a special week."

In *The Big Book of Jewish Baseball*, Rosenthal is quoted on being signed by Hugh Duffy: "Duffy wanted me to change my name to Rose because it would fit easier in box scores. But I told him that I wouldn't do it. I was born with the name Rosenthal. It won't make any difference if my name is Rose, Rosenthal or O'Brien. I'll rise and fall on my own name."

Sy Rosenthal died in the Veterans Administration Hospital in West Roxbury, Massachusetts of coronary occlusion on April 7, 1969. His funeral was held four days later at Temple Bnai Moshe, Brighton.

Happy Foreman—1926 Red Sox

August G. "Happy" Foreman was born in Memphis in July 1897. A left-handed pitcher, he broke into organized ball with his hometown team, the Southern League's Memphis franchise. He pitched both in 1920 and 1921, then left the Chicks for Clarksdale, Mississippi in the Cotton States League for 1922. The year after that, he pitched both for Shreveport and Decatur. After returning to Shreveport at the start of the 1924 season, he made his way to the Chicago White Sox and first appeared in the September 3 game, pinch-hitting for the pitcher Blankenship in the ninth inning of a game Detroit was winning, 6–4. Foreman struck out.

As a pitcher, he threw four innings in three games, walking four and striking out one, allowing seven hits but just one earned run. He got up to bat one more time and made another out.

Before the season was over, he was sent to play for the Beaumont Explorers in Texas, but was selected to join a touring team largely composed of White Sox players that left in October to play exhibition games in Canada, Ireland, England, Belgium, and Italy. In 1925, he was back with the Explorers, described by Peter S. and Joachim Horvitz as "one of the worst teams to ever play. They hadn't won a game in two or three years." Foreman pitched a great game and beat Shreveport, the team for which he'd played in 1923.

In 1926, Gus Foreman signed with the Boston Red Sox on June 8 and debuted in St. Louis on June 9. He was the third pitcher in, relieving Jack Russell by throwing 2⅔ innings in a game the Browns took, 6–4. He gave up two hits and a run; Russell was assigned the loss. He threw two hitless innings on June 12, though walking three batters. In his third appearance, he closed out the second game of a doubleheader with the Yankees, giving up two runs on one hit and a couple of walks. It was his last major league game, ending with a record of 0–0 and a 3.18 ERA in 11⅓ innings of work.

Foreman returned to the minors and played a few more years, later managing a number of minor league teams—even playing, according to the Horvitzes, for "a team of players costumed as Zulus, who played baseball in bare feet!"

Buddy Myer—1927–28 Red Sox

The Red Sox were fortunate to have Buddy Myer for just shy of two seasons near the beginning of what was a stellar 17-year long major league career, otherwise spent entirely with the Washington Senators. Myer won the 1935 batting title with a mark of .349, just edging out Joe Vosmik by virtue of a 4-for-5 final day. With a lifetime average of .303 and a total of 2,131 hits, Myer ranks as equal or better to several players enshrined in the Hall of Fame.

Myer graduated from Mississippi A&M in 1925, a multi-sport star. After playing 99 games for the New Orleans Pelicans, he was signed by scout Joe Engle of the Senators and got into four games at the end of the season. Due to Ossie Bluege's injury, he found himself playing three World Series games that year, and batted 2-for-8. Playing shortstop again in 1926, he batted .304, driving in 62 runs, but he made 42 errors, and when he started the 1927 season with five more errors in 15 games, while batting only .216, the Senators shipped him to the Red Sox for Topper Rigney on May 2. They didn't get fair value: Rigney had led the league in fielding average the year before, but he only made 36 hits for the Senators before leaving the majors for good.

Myer hit .288 for the Red Sox in 1927 and .313 the following year and he led the league with 30 stolen bases, seven more than the next man. Clark Griffith rued the Red Sox trade, but it wasn't easy getting his man Myer back: the December 15, 1928 trade cost him a full five players: Elliot Bigelow, Milt Gaston, Grant Gillis, Hod Lisenbee, and Bobby Reeves. But it got him a two-time All-Star, a batting champion, a pretty decent second baseman for 13 more years, and a solid hitter. Myer batted .300 in the 1933 World Series.

After a sub-par .252 year, the Senators released him in October 1941. Myer became a New Orleans banker in his years after baseball.

Al Schacht—coach, 1935–36 Red Sox

Leave it to the Red Sox to name a clown as their third-base coach? After seven years of semi-pro and minor league pitching (and parts of two years in the U.S. Army), Schacht joined the Washington Senators late in 1919, picking up a couple of wins. From 1919–1921, he posted a record of 14–10 with a 4.48 ERA in 53 games with Washington, played a couple of years for Reading and Binghamton, but returned to the majors as Washington's third base coach for 10 years. He coached for the Red Sox in 1935 and 1936.

He'd always clowned around a little, getting himself thrown off the team at Reading in the process, but soon built up a good act, entertaining at 25 World Series and innumerable other events—as well as before games, and even between innings from the coach's box. Schacht earned the moniker, "The Clown Prince of Baseball." In his 1955 autobiography, he acknowledged his ethnicity: "There is talk that I am Jewish—just because my father was Jewish, my mother is Jewish, I speak Yiddish and once studied to be a rabbi and a cantor. Well, that's how rumors get started."

Moe Berg—1935–39 Red Sox; coach 1939–41

One of the players Schacht coached for the Red Sox was another unique personality, catcher Morris Berg, noted for his linguistic abilities and for his later wartime work for the CIA's predecessor, the OSS. Berg was indeed a spy who contributed both in the European and Pacific theaters during the Second World War.

Before arriving in Boston, Berg had begun with the Brooklyn Dodgers in 1923, and spent time with the White Sox, Indians, Senators, and again with the Indians, almost always as back-up catcher but nevertheless accumulating 1,404 at-bats. During the off-seasons, the Columbia Law School graduate practiced law.

With the Red Sox, he had his best season the very first year, hitting .286 in 98 at-bats when he filled in for Rick Ferrell. For Boston, he batted .262, well above his career .243 mark, but he was used only very sparingly in 1938 and 1939 behind Gene Desautels and Johnny Peacock. He coached for the Red Sox in 1940 and 1941, but when World War II started in earnest, he joined the war effort. He left coaching after first being asked to tour South America as a goodwill ambassador, but then joined the OSS and served as point man in a mission to determine how far Germany might have progressed toward an atomic bomb. He was sufficiently versed in physics that he was able to converse informally with German physicist Werner Heisenberg at a Swiss conference and conclude that there was no current danger; Berg was armed and instructed to assassinate Heisenberg if the threat had loomed large. During a 1934 baseball visit to Japan, Berg had filmed several sites, apparently at the request of the U.S. government; the footage was said to have provided valuable military information. Leonard Lyons even wrote in the *Washington Post* that after lecturing at the University of Tokyo, he "helped simplify their alphabet." When he died in 1972, his last words were asking for the day's news on the New York Mets.

Berg served the United States doing intelligence work on at least four continents: Europe, Asia, North America, and South America. Much of his career has been documented by the CIA's Linda McCarthy. Those interested in learning more about Moe Berg should read Nicholas Dawidoff's biography *The Catcher Was a Spy*.

Lou Boudreau—1951–52 Red Sox; manager, 1952–54

A Hall of Famer, Boudreau was born to a father of Franco-American ancestry and a Jewish mother. At age 21, he joined the Cleveland Indians for one 1938 game and two plate appearances. The following year, Lou began to develop, batting .258 in 225 at-bats. In 1940, he broke out, driving in 101 runs and batting .295 while leading all shortstops in fielding—the first of eight seasons he held this distinction. Boudreau played for the Indians for 13 years, through the 1950 season, winning the batting title with a .327 mark in 1944. Three times he led the league in doubles, hitting 45 doubles in each of the three seasons. From 1942, Boudreau also served as manager of the Indians, first taking on the player-manager role at age 25. Among his contributions was the defensive "Boudreau Shift" employed against Ted Williams beginning in 1946.

His best year was 1948, when he drove in 106 runs and hit .355, though it was Ted Williams who took the batting title with a .369 average. Boudreau had the last laugh, though. The Indians faced the Red Sox in a single-game winner-takes-all playoff at Fenway Park and Lou practically won the game by himself. Not only did he manage the team to an 8–3 win, and flawlessly execute eight plays in the field, but he hit a home run in the top of the first inning to draw first blood, hit another home run in the fifth, and had himself a 4-for-4 day, scoring three runs. Boudreau led the Indians to a World Championship, beating the Boston Braves in six games (he hit .273, with no errors).

After the 1950 season, the Indians released Boudreau making him a free agent. Six days later, he signed with the Red Sox for 1951. Boudreau backed up Vern Stephens, but got in 260 at-bats, hitting .267. In 1952, Boudreau took over as manager. He appeared in four games and drove in two runs, though without ever recording a base hit.

Boudreau managed the Red Sox through 1954, then was the Kansas City skipper for the next three years, through 1957. In 1960, he managed the Chicago Cubs for one year. He was elected to the Hall of Fame in 1970.

Al Richter—1951, 1953 Red Sox

Norfolk, Virginia's Allen Gordon Richter was signed by the Red Sox at age 18, in 1945. Assigned to the Louisville Colonels, he got in some playing time at shortstop for both Louisvlle and Roanoke, but was drafted into the Army Air Corps and spent a year and a half in military service, only returning to Louisville in time for the 1947 season. He spent most of the next five years playing for a number of minor league teams—Lynn, Oneonta, Scranton, and Louisville. Hitting .321 for Louisville in 1951, he was called up late in the season by the Red Sox. Boston was facing its final 10 games and very much still in the pennant race. Losing 12 of their last 13 games, and the last nine in a row, didn't do wonders for Red Sox flag hopes, though.

Richter had a memorable debut, but it wasn't the kind anyone would want to remember: he was asked to pinch-hit for Les Moss in the bottom of the ninth inning. Richter hit into a double play. The Red Sox lost the game, 6–1, to Vic Raschi, who recorded his 20th win. Four days later, the Red Sox were eliminated from the race, and the next day, the Yankees clinched by sweeping a doubleheader from the Red Sox, the first game being a no-hitter thrown by Allie Reynolds. Richter's only at-bat came in the second game, again pinch-hitting for Moss. This time, he fouled out. The next day, the Red Sox faced another doubleheader with the Yankees and Richter was the leadoff batter in both games. The Sox got swept again, and Richter was 0-for-3 in the first game and 0-for-2 in the second. He did walk three times. On the last day of September, Richter started again, this time collecting a single in four at-bats. It was his only major league hit. He ended the year batting .091.

In 1952, Richter played with the San Diego Padres in the Pacific Coast League. The next year, he played in Boston's pre-season City Series with the Braves (for the first time, the Milwaukee Braves) He appeared in one more game in the big leagues, on April 21, coming in to play shortstop in the bottom of the eighth after Milt Bolling had been taken out for pinch-runner Billy Consolo. He made one putout and earned one assist, never batted, and then was sent down to Louisville.

In 1954 and 1955, Al played for Rochester in the Cardinals system, but then retired from baseball. The Horvitzes tell us that Richter went into real estate and food merchandising, and hosted "Spotlight on Sports" for seven years on television before the Sunday Game of the Week.

Joe Ginsberg—1961 Red Sox

Myron Nathan "Joe" Ginsberg played 13 years in the majors, beginning with the Tigers in 1948 and ending with five at-bats with the 1962 Mets. He was a catcher with a .241 lifetime average in 1,716 at-bats, also playing in the American League for Cleveland, Kansas City, Baltimore, and Chicago. His time with the Red Sox was limited to part of the 1961 season, after he'd been released in mid-May by the White Sox. His first Red Sox start was on June 5 in the first game of a doubleheader, and he was 2-for-4 with an RBI. He spent the rest of the season with Boston but was used only very sparingly: 24 at-bats in 19 games, with six singles and five RBIs.

Boston released him after the season. He was picked up by the Mets for 1962 but, after appearing in just two games, was cut free in May, which ended his major league career. Joe had been the Tigers regular catcher for two seasons, 1951 and 1952, and had caught one of Virgil Trucks' no-hitters in '52.

Jeff Newman—1983–84 Red Sox

Some players like Lou Boudreau had one parent who was Jewish, but was raised Christian. Jeff Newman had two Christian parents and even graduated from Texas Christian University. It was later in life that he converted to Judaism. A star in college, he also played some semipro ball in his native Fort Worth before being selected by the Cleveland Indians in the 26th round of the June 4, 1970 draft. He spent 5½ years as a catcher in the Indians system, but only made the majors after being sold to the Oakland A's after the 1975 season. He'd done time in Sarasota, Reno, San Antonio, Oklahoma City, and Salt Lake City. The A's sent him to Tucson, but he was called up in June and on June 30 appeared in his first game beginning with the seventh inning. In his one at-bat, he walked but was taken out for a pinch runner. He came in again during the seventh the next day, got one more plate appearance, this time singling in two runs.

Jeff only hit .195 that first year, without a home run, and with only four RBIs. In 1977, he popped four out of the park, drove in 15, and batted .222. He also pitched in a game. After catching for seven innings in the second game of a September 14 doubleheader in Kansas City, with Oakland losing 6–0, Newman left off the catcher's gear, grabbed a regular fielder's glove, and took the mound. He hit the first batter, Hal McRae, and gave up a single to George Brett, but then buckled down and retired the next three.

He showed some real power with Oakland, with 22 homers in 1979 and 15 in 1980, but those were the only two years he had an opportunity to play on a regular basis. He made the All-Star squad in 1979. After seven seasons with the A's, Jeff was traded to the Red Sox in December 1982, with Tony Armas, for Carney Lansford, Garry Hancock, and a minor leaguer. As the third catcher behind Gedman and Allenson, he got in rather little playing time with Boston, appearing in 83 games over the two years with only 195 at-bats, hitting an even .200. The Red Sox released him four days before Opening Day in 1985.

Newman stayed in baseball, as an instructor and coach, for many years third base coach with the Indians. He even managed for 10 games in Oakland on an interim basis, before the team hired Tony LaRussa.

Brian Bark—1995 Red Sox

Bark got a little extra pitching instruction growing up; his father was a pitcher in the minors. After college, Bark was selected in the 12th round of the 1990 draft by the Atlanta Braves. The year before, he'd been drafted by the Orioles, in the 28th round, but chose not to sign. Selected substantially higher, he signed with Atlanta. He pitched for Pulaski, Durham, and Greenville in the Braves system, then spent 3½ years playing in Triple A for the Richmond Braves—1992 through 1994, and into 1995.

That was quite a year—1995. He began the season with Richmond again, but was released on June 1. The Red Sox thought they could use a left-hander and signed him the very next day, sending him to Pawtucket. Little more than a month later, the pitcher who'd been released from the minor league Richmond Braves was pitching in the major leagues. Briefly.

On July 6, at the Hubert H. Humphrey Metrodome, Bark was brought into a game the Red Sox were losing, 6–4. He was asked to get one out, the last one in the bottom of the eighth, and did just that. On July 15, at Fenway, Bark was asked to pitch the top of the ninth in a game the Rangers were winning, 7–2. He gave up a couple of hits, but no runs. His third appearance came in Yankee Stadium, on September 8. Again, the Red Sox were losing, this time 8–0. Bark came in during the seventh inning, in relief of Matt Murray who'd already allowed three runs and had a runner on second base without recording an out. Bark retired the side.

There were no more appearances in major league baseball, despite having acquitted himself pretty well—just two singles in eight batters faced and a 0.00 ERA. The Red Sox finished in first place in 1995, a full seven games ahead of the New York Yankees.

Gabe Kapler—2003–06 Red Sox

To look at the years 2003 through 2006 makes it appear as though Kapler served the Sox for four straight seasons. Indeed, he did—but not without interruptions. After winning a World Series ring in 2004 with the Red Sox, Kapler signed to play the following year in Japan for the Yomiuri Giants. Kapler had broken in at age 22 with the Detroit Tigers, then been traded to the Texas Rangers as part of a November 1999 nine-player trade. His first year with Texas, 2000, Kapler batted .302, but slipped to .267 the following year. Mid-2002, only hitting .260, he was traded to the Rockies. He hit .311 the rest of the year, but by mid-2003 was only hitting .224 and the power he'd shown in Detroit and Texas had seemingly evaporated even in hitter-friendly Coors Field. The Rockies sold him to the Red Sox and he hit .291 for Boston in the second half of the season, breaking in big with 7-for-9 and seven RBIs in his first two games. Kapler saw some work in the 2003 playoffs but the Sox released him on December 21. They signed him as a free agent the very next day.

Kapler racked up 290 at-bats in 2004 (.272), and appeared briefly in all three rounds of the 2004 playoffs. The Sox again granted him free agency the very day after the World Series was over. His stay in Japan was disappointing and he was released by the Giants—only to re-sign with the Red Sox. A fan favorite in Boston, he hit just .247 with only one home run and just nine RBIs. His season ended abruptly in mid-September when he ruptured his Achilles tendon rounding second base on a long drive by Tony Graffanino. Tony's hit turned out to be a home run. The Red Sox released him in November and signed him again early in 2006. Recovering much more quickly than expected from such a serious injury, Kapler got in another 120 at-bats in 2006 but again without impressive average (.254) or power (two home runs). After the season, he retired from active play and became manager of the Red Sox Single-A team in Greenville SC for the 2007 season, but became tempted by the prospect of playing again and un-retired, signing with the Milwaukee Brewers for 2008.

Kevin Youkilis—2004–07 Red Sox

Billed in advance as the "Greek God of Walks" because of his patience at the plate, Youkilis was not Greek at all but of Romanian Jewish heritage. An eighth-round pick by the Red Sox in 2001, he went 2-for-4 in his first game (with a home run) and 2-for-4 in his second game. He did indeed walk 33 times in his rookie year (he also hit .260 in 208 at-bats), but he struck out 45 times. Playing exclusively at third base, save for two games as a DH, he collected a World Series ring at the end of his first year in major league ball, though the only postseason series he appeared in (0-for-2) was the Division Series. In 2005, Youk played third base, first base, and second, but only got 79 at-bats. He did improve his average to .278. Mostly working at first base in 2006, he improved his average yet again, but only by .001. He collected a full 569 at-bats, and boosted his power numbers a bit with 13 homers and a .429 slugging average. In 2007, Youk's image was printed as one of the 10 current players who were depicted on Red

Baseball card from the set of Jewish Major Leaguers.
Courtesy of Martin Abramowitz.

Sox tickets. In his first full year playing first base, he won a Gold Glove—never once making an error in the field despite handling 1,080 chances. His average jumped to .288 and he drove in a career-high 83 RBIs. He was a key player in the seven-game League Division Series against Cleveland, batting .500 (14-for-28) with three home runs and seven RBIs. His postseason batting average is .373.

Adam Stern—2005–06 Red Sox

Stern was a native of London, Ontario and a third-round pick by the Atlanta Braves in the 2001 draft. The Red Sox claimed him in the Rule V draft in December 2004, and after recovering from a fractured thumb suffered in spring training, Stern debuted with Boston on July 7, 2005. On July 22, he hit his first (and only) major league home run, in the top of the ninth inning against the White Sox. A two-run homer, but the Red Sox lost, 8–4. As indicated at the start of this section, Stern, Kapler, and Youkilis all appeared in the same game a month later, on August 8.

Appearing in 36 games, Stern only got 15 at-bats—and only one other hit. His final average was .133. Before the 2006 season began, Stern played for Canada in the World Baseball Classic and payed a major role in the Canadians' 8–6 upset win over the U.S. team. He singled, tripled, and hit an inside-the-park home run, and drove in four runs. The promise shown pre-season didn't bear out, and Stern hit just .150 in 20 at-bats. The Red Sox used him as trade bait and worked a deal with the Orioles whereby he became the player to be named later in the August 4 trade for Javy Lopez. He was sent to Baltimore on October 3. In 2007, he appeared in two games for the Orioles, playing center field but never getting an at-bat.

Craig Breslow—2006

Left-handed pitcher Craig Breslow was a 26th round Brewers draft pick in 2002 who was released two years later, but made the San Diego Padres during spring training 2005. The Yale graduate threw 16⅓ innings that year, with a 2.20 ERA but was nonetheless released after the season and snapped up by the Red Sox, where he was an all-star with Pawtucket. For Boston, he became the fourth Jew on the 2006 team, but his only two decisions were both losses; he had a respectable 3.75 ERA in 12 innings. He had one fielding chance with San Diego (error) and one with Boston (error-free), resulting in a .500 fielding percentage for his career. He grounded out (.000) in his one career at-bat, with the Padres. Breslow was an all-star with the Pawsox again in 2007. He was claimed off waivers in 2008 by the Indians, and then by the Twins.

NATIVE AMERICAN PLAYERS

There are connections one could draw between Native Americans and the Red Sox that even pre-date the franchise, as we shall see in the case of Louis Leroy. Jeffrey Powers-Beck in his book *The American Indian Integration of Baseball* devotes a full chapter to Louis Leroy, and it is perhaps fair enough to say that Leroy was the first known Native American on the Red Sox. The first with Indian ancestry, though, appears to be Case Patten.

Case Patten—1908

When Patten filled out his player questionnaire for the Hall of Fame, he declared his heritage as "Scotch, Irish, English, Dutch, and Indian" perhaps from his mother Mandana's side of the family. As far as can be determined, he was the first player of Native American ancestry to play for the Red Sox, though one suspects that rather few people knew of his ancestry. Contemporary news accounts seem not to mention a thing about his lineage in any regard. He preceded Louis Leroy with the Red Sox but was obviously of very mixed parentage and it seems safe to say that he was never clearly identified as Native American.

This left-handed pitcher was a charter member of the American League, breaking in with Washington in May 1901. Over seven seasons with Washington, he averaged over 15 wins (though, it must be said, he averaged more than 17 losses). He was a 19-game winner in 1906, with a 2.17 ERA, but seemed to falter as the 1907 season wore on and was not expected to be with the team come spring training 1908. He was brought back, though, and was used infrequently, finally being traded on May 31 to the Red Sox for left-hander Jesse Tannehill. Some thought that both pitchers could benefit from a change of scenery. Neither did all that much after the trade, though reports that Tannehill was suffering from malaria were far from encouraging.

The Red Sox didn't keep Patten for long. He appeared in just one game, on June 18, starting it and losing it, throwing just three innings and being bombed for five runs. The next day, the Red Sox put him on waivers. New York refused to waive, and therefore "under baseball law was entitled to Patten's services." (*Boston Post*) But on June 22, the Highlanders said they didn't want him and would waive their rights, in effect turning him back to Boston. Red Sox owner John I. Taylor protested to Ban Johnson, arguing that he was now New York property. "I don't know what Johnson will decide," Taylor said, but New York "refused to waive and we released Patten to [them]. That ended the matter as far as we are concerned."

Johnson proclaimed that New York management had 48 hours to change their minds, so Patten was indeed back with Boston, who clearly didn't want him. They held onto him for about three more weeks, but he was apparently unable to get into shape, so they released him unconditionally on July 10. His major league days were over. He popped up in a *Washington Post* story in 1915, driving a wagon in Westport, Connecticut and playing some local ball for Westport's town team. And he was hit hard, for 10 hits. A bizarre story involving a murderer claiming she was married to Patten had preceded Patten to the Red Sox; see the section on tragedies.

Louis Leroy—1910

Louis Leroy was almost a charter player for the franchise. Leroy was a "Stockbridge-Munsee" Indian, a group of Mohicans who relocated to Wisconsin in the beginning of the 19th century. Leroy was taught in reservation schools growing up, then continued his schooling at the Carlisle Indian Industrial School in Pennsylvania. He played baseball under famous Carlisle coach "Pop" Warner for three years, 1899–1901. Jeffrey Powers-Beck, researching his book, came across clippings in the Hall of Fame files which indicate that Leroy came to the attention of Boston ballplayer Jimmy Collins possibly as early as 1899. Boston's first manager Collins came to the American League in 1901 after six seasons with Boston's National League team.

Because he was enrolled in the government school, Leroy was not free to sign with a pro team—so he took off on his own. It was 1901. Coach Warner followed Leroy to Boston, where he found that Collins—now manager of the Boston Americans—had come to agreement with the young pitcher. Warner convinced Collins that Leroy needed to complete his education. After they returned, with Leroy still recalcitrant, Warner had him placed in a cell at the school and kept on bread and water for 57 days, confined for a longer period overall from mid-June to early September 1901—kept on the "reservation" when he could instead have been pitching for Boston.

Leroy eventually did make it to the Red Sox, but it wasn't until 1910, and then only for the briefest of stays. His first major league appearance came for the AL's New York Highlanders. In 1902, manager George Stallings signed him to a contract with the Buffalo Bison. He pitched for the Eastern League team in 1902 and 1903, then for the Montreal Royals the following two years. A 1903 clipping reflects some of the attitudes of the day, referring to Leroy as "the little red man" and with a subhead saying the "Indian warrior cut down and scalped" the opposing team. Leroy was on the "warpath"—coverage of the "heap good injun" continued on in this vein.

Late in 1905, "Chief" Leroy started three games for the New York Highlanders (later, the Yankees) beginning on September 22. He won one and lost one, with a 3.75 ERA. In 1906, he spent most of the year with Montreal again but Leroy appeared in 11 games for the Highlanders—only two as a starter—and was 2–0, with a 2.22 ERA in 44⅔ innings.

From 1907 into 1913, he pitched for the St. Paul Saints, with a brief excursion to Boston at the start of the 1910 season. Red Sox scout Patsy Donovan had spotted Leroy while on a visit to Minnesota in the summer of 1909. When he was named manager for 1910, Donovan wanted Leroy. St. Paul manager Mike Kelley had promised Leroy that he'd help him if any major league team ever wanted him, and he was true to his word. The day after his signed contract was received, the *Boston Globe* reported that the contract of "Leroy, the Indian" was in hand. The paper headlined. "Boston Club Now Has Indian Sign on that Leroy Contract."

Leroy was expert in pitching with expectoration, legal at the time. The spitballist was on his way to Boston, legitimately so this time. He joined the team for spring training in Hot Springs, but in the end played just one game for the Red Sox, and it was his last in major league ball.

His game for Boston was April 20, 1910, pitching a disastrous four innings in a game started by Charlie Smith. Smith gave up three runs in the first two innings, but Leroy gave up nine (to be fair, only five were earned) on seven hits and two walks. He struck out three. Ray Collins pitched the final three without giving up a hit, but the final score was Washington 12, Boston 4. Leroy misplayed two balls in the field, but the

Ed Karger with Louis Leroy in Hot Springs. Courtesy of Sabina Carroll.

only errors committed were four by other Boston ballplayers. He was returned to St. Paul and was 14–16 in 1910. His Boston ERA was 11.25. Lifetime, he was 3–1, 3.22 in major league ball.

Later in 1910, on July 7, he threw a no-hitter against Toledo for 9⅔ innings before a hit dropped in during the 10th inning. St. Paul scored twice and won it, 2–0. In the years that followed, Leroy pitched through 1920 with St. Paul, Indianapolis, Salt Lake City, St. Paul again, Springfield, Muskegon, Joplin, LaCrosse, St. Paul for a fourth time, Seattle, and the Mitchell Kernels in South Dakota, which team he helped lead to a league championship.

After finishing his years in pro ball, he played some semipro ball in Wisconsin while he farmed, did lumber work, and became involved in some of the tribal affairs of the Stockbridge. Readers interested in more on Leroy and other Native Americans in baseball should read the Powers-Beck volume.

William Garlow—1914 pitching prospect

In 1914, the Red Sox signed Tuscarora Indian William Garlow, a right-handed pitcher who'd graduated from the Carlisle School as captain of the team. Garlow had written the Red Sox that he was born on the Tuscarora reservation and always considered himself a "full-blooded Inidan." He also wrote, "My father and mother lived out in the woods for many years, until a few acres of wooded land had been cleared for farming purposes. There they raised a family of nine boys and four girls." The Sox took him to spring training in 1914, but he evidently did not make the team.

Indicating the absence of prejudice against Native Americans was Tim Murnane's comment in the April 12 *Globe*. If anything, it sounds as though Murnane (tongue in cheek or not) suggested it was a little *de rigeur*. "Garlow, the Indian, also will be retained as it is the proper thing to have a full-blooded Indian with every first-class major league." In the very next paragraph, Murnane writes about George Wilson [see the section on Squanto Wilson below] but there is no allusion or indication which might hint at Wilson having Native American ancestry.

Jack Stansbury—1918

Stansbury listed his background in Hall of Fame records as "American of Irish, English, American Indian." Primarily a third baseman, he came to Boston in a June 26 transaction when the New Orleans Pelicans sold three players all at once to the Red Sox: Walter Barbare, Red Bluhm, and Jack Stansbury. Neither Bluhm nor Stansbury had played in the majors. After a line drive hurt Fred Thomas' finger, and he decided to enlist in the Navy, Stansbury soon got his first chance. It came on June 30 at a game in Washington, with Walter Johnson pitching against Boston's Carl Mays.

Starting at third base and batting eighth in the order, Stansbury helped score the first run of the game in the Boston third. The first two frames saw six Sox batters up and six Sox retired. Everett Scott led off the third with a single, and Stansbury sacrificed him to second. Though Mays was thrown out, Hooper singled to right field, scoring Scott. The score was 1–0 and so it stood until the top of the ninth inning, when Boston had a chance to score but Stansbury (0-for-3 on the day) lined into an inning-ending double play. Washington tied it at the last minute with one run in the bottom of the ninth, Stansbury getting an assist on the final out. In the top of the 10th, with Dave Shean on first base, Babe Ruth hit "the longest home run ever made at the American League park here" (*Boston Globe*). The 3–1 score held for a Red Sox win. A couple of days later, on July 2, Ruth's hand was bothering him, and Stansbury had the distinction of subbing in the sixth inning for The Babe. His second game came after Ruth went AWOL a couple of days later.

Barbare was a veteran, having played in over 100 games for Cleveland since 1914. His Red Sox debut was on July 3. Philadelphia was leading 5–0, but Boston got two men on in the top of the eighth. Vean Gregg buckled down and got Scott. Barbare batted for catcher Agnew but was out. Bluhm, in his one and only major league appearance, batted for pitcher Bader, and he made an out. Barbare hit .172 for the Red Sox, but both Bluhm and he were cut before the Sox traveled to Chicago for the July 25 game. He spent two years with the Pirates and two years with the Braves, then left major league baseball.

The World War was on in earnest, and Stansbury was an attractive acquisition for the Red Sox because he was 32 years old at the time, and exempt from the new "work or fight" order that loomed over most major leaguers. He was the third of 10 different third basemen the Sox went through in 1918. Stansbury played in 19 more games, accumulating six hits (one double) and driving in two runs. His best game was on July 26 when he was 2-for-3 with a triple, alas in a losing effort. Like Squanto Wilson's run outlined below, Stansbury's triple is not in the record books, either. It's possible it was later scored a double.

Before leaving Detroit after the August 8 game, the Red Sox made a deal to pick up infielder Jack Coffey and catcher Norm McNeil, releasing Stansbury and two other players. Jack Stansbury finished his season (and his major league career) with a .128 average and a .241 on-base percentage, thanks to six walks. In 54 total chances (four in the outfield), he was charged with just one miscue. His last game was on July 29 in Chicago. The next day, in St. Louis, George Cochran took over at third base for his only time in the majors; he didn't bat as well, hitting just .117 (he didn't get in the World Series, either—that honor belonged to Fred Thomas at third).

Slim Harriss—1926–1928

This 6′6″ right-handed native of Brownwood, Texas described himself as "American-Scotch, Irish, Indian." William Jennings Bryan "Slim" Harriss pitched for the Philadelphia Athletics from April 1920 until he was part of a multi-player trade to the Red Sox for Howard Ehmke on June 15, 1926. June 29 was his Red Sox debut, winning a 2–1 five-hitter over Washington. Pitching for a last-place team, Harriss was 6–10 for the remainder of the year (4.46 ERA). That might not seem like a very good record, but heading into 1927, the April 12, 1927 *Washington Post* remarked that Harriss was "counted the ace of the Red Sox pitching staff." It's all relative. He did win 14 games in 1927, but he lost 21. The Red Sox as a team were 75–79. In 1928, he was 8–11. In nine seasons, only once did he have a winning season, 1925 with Philadelphia: he was 19–12, with an ERA of 3.49, the only time he posted a sub-4.00 earned run average. He struck out 644 batters but walked nearly as many: 630. In 1,750⅓ innings of work, he also yielded 1,963 hits. Harriss' overall record was 95–135, with a career ERA of 4.25.

Roy Johnson—1932–1935

Brothers Roy and Bob Johnson were both well-known to be Indians at the time they played. Both were were born in Pryor, Oklahoma and listed themselves as "Cherokee, Scotch, French." Roy was the eldest, born on February 23, 1903, born like his younger brother Bob on a reservation and both therefore considered "wards of the government." By the time of the first World War, the family had moved to the Tacoma, Washington area. Roy began playing ball in Tacoma, in the City League and came to the attention of scouts. His first appearance in pro ball came in Tulsa in 1925, for just 10 games and just one hit. In 1926, signed with Idaho Falls, he got in a full 451 at-bats, with 19 homers and an average of .369. That started to get attention, as did the 133 runs he scored in 119 games. He was signed to the San Francisco Seals (PCL) and was called up at the end of the year, batting .260 in 25 games. Roy played for the Seals in 1927 and 1928, hitting .306 and .360 respectively. This got him an invite to the major leagues and he broke in with the Detroit Tigers in 1929, playing a full 148 games that year, collecting 201 hits in his rookie year, and posting a .314 average while leading the league in both at-bats and doubles.

Roy played outfield throughout his career, batting left but throwing right-handed. His average dropped his sophomore year, down to .275 in 125 games. He bumped it up a bit in 1931, leading the league in triples with 19 while hitting .279. He started 1932 not at all as well, and was hitting only .251 when the Tigers traded both him and Dale Alexander to the Red Sox for Earl Webb. It was quite a good trade for Boston. Webb had set the still-standing record for doubles in 1931, with 67 two-baggers, while batting .333. He never approached those figures again, hitting 28 in '32 and just five in his final year, 1933. Alexander became the American League batting champion in 1932 and Roy Johnson hit .298 for the Sox.

Johnson continued driving his stats higher: in 1933, he hit .313 and drove in 95 runs and in 1934 he hit .320 with 119 RBIs. Run production dropped off sharply in 1935, but he batted .315. Interestingly, the Red Sox in 1933, 1934, and 1935 had Native American Roy Johnson playing left field and Mexican Mel Almada playing center. Johnson played 26 games in left in 1933, but 95 in right field and 10 in center. In 1934, he played left field exclusively (137 in 1934 and 142 in 1935). Almada played sparingly in 1933 (13 games) and 1934 (23 games), but a full 126 games in center field in 1935. It was no commitment to diversity, but reflected an openness in signings that one wishes had been extended to other players of color.

After four years averaging .313, Roy provided good trade bait and the Sox made a deal with the Senators, sending them Roy and Carl Reynolds for infielder Heinie Manush.

It was another good deal, because Roy Johnson's best days were behind him. Roy never played for Washington; one month to the day he'd been traded, the Senators swapped him to the Yankees as part of a four-player trade. Roy hit just .256, with only 147 at-bats. He got in 12 games for New York at the beginning of 1937, but a guy named DiMaggio supplanted him. Roy was placed on waivers and picked up by the Boston Bees (Braves); he finished up with them in early 1938. Roy's lifetime average was .298, but the Red Sox had him for his best years.

Ben Chapman—1937–1938

Chapman may be like a lot of ballplayers in having a degree of Native American ancestry in their bloodline; in his case, it presents irony as well. A note in January 20, 1938 *Sporting News* provided the initial tipoff. Some text under the heading "Calling the Roll of the Nations" listed Chapman as of "Irish-Scotch-Indian" descent. Was the listing correct? The listing erred in terming Bobby Doerr as of "Scotch-Irish-Indian descent." Chapman's signed Hall of Fame card, which he completed in 1960, lists himself as "Irish-English." (Another note in the Hall of Fame player file contains Chapman's response to a questionnaire he completed for autograph collector Tom Burlin. Asked "Who was the luckiest player you ever saw?" Chapman answered in two brief words: "I was.") But a lengthy *Saturday Evening Post* profile by Collie Small which ran on May 5, 1947 described Chapman as of "English, Irish, and Cherokee Indian extraction." Where does this leave us? Hard to say.

Chapman had a long career in baseball, from 1928 to 1953 (in the majors from 1930—when he broke in with the Yankees—to 1946). He came to the Red Sox from Washington with Bob Newsom in the trade for both brothers Ferrell (Rick and Wes) and Mel Almada. From midseason 1945 through midseason 1948, he managed the Phillies. In '37, he hit .307 for the Red Sox, and in 1938 he had his best year in baseball, batting .340. He played outfield throughout, save for one game at third base in '38. Trouble was, the Red Sox had a rookie coming up, fresh from winning the Triple Crown in the American Association, and he looked to be even better than Chapman. The kid's name was Ted Williams. Boston traded Chapman to the Indians for a pitcher, Denny Galehouse, and a utility shortstop they never utilized, Tommy Irwin.

The irony? When manager of the Phillies in 1947, Chapman—who'd started in baseball at batboy for the Birmingham Barons—was vocal and vicious in verbal attacks on Jackie Robinson from the Philadelphia dugout, so much so that Branch Rickey said he helped unite Robinson's teammates in Jackie's favor. Even Commissioner Ford Frick chimed in, to chide Chapman, who weakly responded that he'd baited Poles and Italians, too. Ironic it would be for one of Native American background, though Chapman's Hall of Fame questionnaire at least indicates that he didn't sufficiently identify himself as a member of a minority group.

Chapman had trouble getting along with his wife, too. In divorce proceedings when he was with the Yankees, he said he had "loved her tenderly and sincerely" while at the same time she "irritated, nagged, and hampered him" and "demanded unreasonable sums of money for clothing and luxuries" and would become "almost hysterical" when he demurred. Worse, her "annoying conversation" interfered with his sleep and spoiled his baseball playing, according to a dispatch from the Associated Press.

Arvel Odell Hale—1941

Odell Hale had a couple of nicknames. One was "Bad News" and the other was "Chief." He listed his nationality as "Irish and Indian" on the questionnaire he completed for the Hall of Fame (indicating "Bad News" as his nickname on the form itself). Coming from Caddo Parish in extreme northwestern Louisiana, he was likely a Choctaw or, perhaps, Apache. Hale married a Native American, Mabel Jane Rainwater from Oklahoma. Their daughter Dorinda confirms that he had Native American ancestry, but she doesn't know the nation(s) or tribe(s) in question. "I wish I had asked those questions a long time ago," she lamented late in 2007. Her brother Buzzy added, "He had a pretty rough childhood. His mother and dad died early. He just never talked about his childhood with us." Hale played 10 years in the major leagues,

Odell "Bad News" Hale. Courtesy of Brace Photo.

the first nine of them with the Cleveland Indians. Except for one of his 1,082 games, when he played shortstop he was either a second baseman or third baseman, or served in a pinch-hit or pinch-run capacity. A solid hitter with a lifetime .289 average and a .352 on-base percentage, his best years were 1934–36 when he averaged over .300 and drove in 101 runs twice. The Red Sox acquired him in a six-player December 1940 trade. He only appeared in 12 games for Boston, though, before being placed on waivers and claimed by the Giants, where he finished his major league career later in 1941. After a brief stint with Milwaukee, he took a position with a defense plant in El Dorado, Arkansas, a firm that was later bought up by Monsanto Chemical and where Hale worked as a senior operator until retirement.

The right-handed hitter sported a lifetime average of .289; he was apparently not that swift in that the only thing in which he ever led the majors was caught stealing (13 times in 1935). His most renowned moment in baseball was when he took part in a September 7, 1935 bases-loaded triple play against the Red Sox. Joe Cronin hit a screaming liner to third base, hit so hard that Hale couldn't get his glove up in time. The ball hit off his forehead and, seeing the misplay, the runners took off. But the ball deflected into shortstop Billy Knickerbocker's glove; he threw to second base, where Roy Hughes stepped on the bag and threw to first, doubling up both baserunners.

Ford Garrison—1943–1944

Robert Ford Garrison's contract with the Fort Worth Cats was purchased by the Red Sox in early August 1942. The outfielder soon earned comparison to his Fort Worth manager Rogers Hornsby. A native of Greenville, SC, Garrison was orginally signed by New York Yankees scout Scoop Latimer, editor of the *Greenville News*, in the fall of 1937 after he'd had a season hitting over .400. Assigned to the Amsterdam NY club, he moved up the ladder to play for Augusta in 1939 and 1940, and for Fort Worth the next two. Given a 3-A exemption from the draft, he went to spring training in 1943, the wartime year the Sox trained at Tufts in Medford, MA rather than in southern climes. He debuted with the Red Sox on April 23, playing center field and going 1-for-3. In early June, he was sent down to Louisville, hit well, and when he re-joined the Sox in mid-September, he started tearing the cover off the ball. He wound up batting a solid .279.

In early May 1944 he was traded to the Athletics for Hal Wagner. He was ultimately taken by the draft and served in the Navy during 1945 and 1946, only appearing in six games in 1945 before being inducted and nine games in 1946 after discharge. He played a number of ball-games for the Bainbridge MD Naval Training Center during his time in the service. The '46 games were his last major league games. He finished his major league career with a .262 life-time average, with six homers and 56 RBIs, but was a key player for the Newark Bears, for the Kansas City Blues, and for the Beaumont Roughnecks. He coached for the Cincinnati Reds in 1953 and, later, managed Beaumont. After baseball, he owned Ford Garrison's Building Maintenance company and lived in Pinellas Park, Florida. On a questionnaire he completed for the Hall of Fame, Garrison listed his family background as "Irish, English, and Indian." Garrison's son Jim reports that Ford's mother was half-Cherokee.

Bob Johnson—1944–1945

Bob Johnson was two years younger than brother Roy, born November 26, 1905. They over-lapped tenures in the American League and played against each other on numerous occasions. Bob batted right-handed, and played both outfield and infield positions. He broke into orga-nized ball with Wichita in 1929, promoted quickly enough to play 81 games with the PCL's Portland Beavers, which he did for 3½ years, increasingly improving as a batter: .254, .265, .337, and .330—the latter year increasing his home run total to 29 and his RBI total to 111. He was ready for the major leagues and joined the Philadelphia Athletics in 1933, hitting .290 his rookie year with 21 homers and 93 RBIs. In 1934, he hit a lusty 34 homers, increasing his average to .307.

"Indian Bob" Johnson played for the A's for 10 full seasons, averaging 104 RBIs per year. He had tailed off to just 80 in 1942, though, and was dealt during spring training 1943 to the Washington Senators for Bobby Estalella and some cash. It was another off year, with a .265 aveage—by far his lowest—and just 63 RBIs. In December, the Red Sox purchased Bob from the Senators.

It was a war year, to be sure, but Johnson had an exceptionally good season, driving in 106 runs, with a .324 average while leading the league in on-base percentage (.431), OPS (.959), and runs created (118). His last year in major league ball was 1945, tailing off to .280 with an-other 74 runs driven in. He was given his release two days after Christmas. Bob finished his career with a nearly-identical .296 average to his brother's .298.

After Bob's career, he played another four years: with Milwaukee in 1946, two seasons with Seattle, and one final year with Tacoma in 1949. Roy had similarly ended his career with sev-eral seasons after major league ball, and several of them in the same cities: two in Milwaukee, then Syracuse and Baltimore, and finally two seasons with Seattle.

See the section on baseball relatives in this book for more information on the two John-sons, and the times they faced each other while both playing American League ball. The book *Bright Star in A Shadowy Sky* by Patrick J. and Terrence K. McGrath offers a full biography of Indian Bob Johnson, with considerable material on brother Roy.

Buster Mills—1937 (coach, 1954)

The outfielder with the unusual given name of Colonel Buster Mills was named Big Six quar-terback in 1930. The Oklahoma star capped off the year scoring all the points kicking a field

Colonel Buster Mills. Courtesy of Brace Photo.

goal in the last four minutes of play in the sixth annual East-West All-Star Game. Listening to the radio at home in Ranger, Texas, Mills' father leapt up and in his excitement kicked a vase and fractured his own foot.

It was in baseball that he pursued a pro career. Self-described as "Scotch, Irish, Dutch, English, and Indian," Mills had been born in Ranger in 1908. His first year in major league ball was with the St. Louis Cardinals, and in his first six seasons of major league ball he played for a different team every year; the six seasons were spread over nine years.

Coming up from Rochester, where he'd batted .309 and led the league in getting hit by pitches (15), Mills debuted on April 18, 1934. It hadn't been a good start for St. Louis, who won their opening day game but then lost five in a row. The AP said that manager Frankie Frisch stuck Mills in the lineup on April 26 to try and "shake the jinx"—Mills made an out, but then hit two singles, a double, and a triple in his final four at-bats. On the 27th, Mills hit three singles his first three times up before finally being retired. It was a nice start, but come July 5, batting .236, he was given his release.

Given a shot with the Brooklyn Dodgers the following September 15, after another year in Rochester, he hit the first pitch he saw for a double, but ended the year with a .214 average. He spent 1936 with Rochester once again, hitting .331. In November, the Red Sox sent Dib Williams to Rochester to complete their purchase of Mills for the 1937 Red Sox. It was considered to be a "comeback" year for Buster, and he came back all right—with the best year of his career, playing a full season and batting .295 in 505 at-bats.

Breaking in on the same date as two other Red Sox, Bobby Doerr and Pinky Higgins, Mills played right field and was 2-for-4 with a triple as the Red Sox beat Philadelphia, 11–5. Though it was his best year, the Sox sought Joe Vosmik, who'd had an even better one. On December 2, Mills, Bobo Newsom, and Red Kress were traded to the St. Louis Browns to secure Vosmik. Mills had a very good 1938. In late October, the Yankees traded Myril Hoag and Joe Glenn for Oral Hildebrand and Mills, and in early January 1939, New York assigned Mills to their Newark Bears farm team. Mills began 1940 with Newark as well, but with both Jake Powell and Joe DiMaggio disabled, the Yankees brought up Mills on May 3. He hit .397 for the Yankees, but in only 63 at-bats.

Mills hit .307 for the Kansas City Blues in 1941. He was traded to Cleveland in early April 1942 for Larry Rosenthal and some money. He hit .277 in 195 at-bats and stayed in the Indians system throughout the war years, playing with the Servicemen's Team in remote locations like Guam. He appeared in nine games in 1946, until he was released on July 3, so he could begin a second career as a coach. Mills coached for the Indians in '46, for the White Sox from 1947–50, for Cincinnati in 1953 (managing the team for eight games at the end of the year), and for the Red Sox as third-base coach in 1954. When Pinky Higgins was named to skipper the Red Sox, he dropped Mills.

Leon Culberson—1943–47 Red Sox

Culberson listed "Indian" first, in his questionnaire, claiming Indian and French ancestry. He worked his way up through the Red Sox system, the final steps being from Scranton to Louisville in September 1942, and then on May 16, 1943 being sent to Boston, in a straight swap for

Tom McBride. It was a bit of a surprising promotion, given that he'd hit .286 with Scranton but only .171 in 10 games with Louisville. His debut came as leadoff batter in the second game that day, playing center field, and going 2-for-5 with a double and one RBI. Culberson played in 81 games, had 312 at-bats, and batted .272. His solo homer on June 23 beat the Athletics, 1–0. On July 3, he hit for the cycle, driving in two and scoring three against Cleveland.

Culberson played throughout the war years, rejected on more than one occasion as physically unfit for duty; he had a trick knee which had incapacitated him twice during the 1944 season. He hit just .238 in '44, but bounced back to .275 in 1945. Culberson really contributed in the pennant-winning year, 1946, with a .313 average. His most dramatic hit was a grand slam in the bottom of the 14th inning of the May 7 game against St. Louis.

In the 1946 World Series, Culberson was 2-for-7, one of the hits a solo home run in Game Five. Unfortunately, Dom DiMaggio pulled a hamstring in Game Seven trying to leg a double into a triple. This put Culberson in center field, and when Harry Walker's ball dropped in front of him and he lofted it to Johnny Pesky at shortstop, no one had any idea that Enos Slaughter was tearing around the bases from first base to score the run that won the World Series for the Cardinals.

Culberson played in 47 games in '47, but hit only .238. He was traded to the Senators in December for Stan Spence; the Sox threw in minor leaguer Al Kozar. Leon appeared in just a dozen ballgames for Washington (hitting .172) before he was traded to the Yankees (designated for their Kansas City club) to acquire Bud Stewart. The Senators sent $20,000 along, too. Culberson made headlines in July when Milwaukee Brewers catcher Frank Kerr missed a pitch and the ball lodged, stuck, in umpire Harry King's mask. Culberson saw what happened and stole second. After a couple of more years in the Yankees system, Culberson finally hung up his spikes. He did play once more in Yankee Stadium, though—for the 1946 Red Sox, who beat the 1947 Yankees in a "Not-So-Old-Timers" game on August 9, 1948. Five Red Sox pitchers combined on a no-hitter (it was a two-inning game).

Rudy York—1946–1947 (manager, 1959)

The Red Sox actually had three Native Americans on the 1947 team: Culberson, Tex Aulds, and Rudy York. York is the best-known of the bunch, named seven times to the All-Star squad, and a player who saw action in three World Series (1940 and 1945 with the Tigers, and 1946 with the Red Sox). York was part-Cherokee, perhaps ¼, perhaps ⅛—but proud of his heritage. He was often described as "the big Indian" in news accounts; Rudy was 6'1" and 209 pounds. York broke in with Detroit as a catcher, playing in three games in 1934. He made the majors to stay in 1937, playing in 104 games, with a .307 average, 35 homers, and 103 RBIs. A versatile fielder, he played 54 behind the plate, 41 games at third base, and one game at first base—where he eventually settled in as of 1940.

He improved to 127 RBIs in 1938, and drove in 134 in 1940. York's two-run homer in Game Three of the 1940 World Series broke a 1–1 tie and gave the Tigers a lead they did not relinquish.

In 1943, York led the league in homers (34) and RBIs (118). There was always additional pressure in being known as Native American. York acknowledged as much, writing, "Any time an Indian puts on a baseball uniform he becomes about six times as much of a character as any other player." And there could be a price to pay for just enjoying an evening with his teammates: "All an Indian's got to do is be seen drinking a beer and he's drunk."

York was a steady player; in a seven-year stretch (1940–46) during the days of the 154-game season, York averaged precisely 154 games per season. After driving in 936 runs for the Tigers and hitting 239 homers, he was traded to the Red Sox on January 3, 1946 for shortstop Eddie

Lake. Rudy drove in 119 runs for the pennant-winning Red Sox and contributed right away in Game One of the 1946 World Series. His solo home run off Howie Pollet in the top of the 10th inning won the first game for Boston, 3–2.

After 48 games in 1947, York was only hitting .212 and Boston traded him to the White Sox for Jake Jones, who had one of those exceptional periods breaking in, tearing up the league for a couple of weeks. York didn't tear it up for Chicago, but he did drive in 67 runs, and the trade was more or less a fair deal for both teams. At the beginning of February, 1948, York was released by the White Sox. He was picked up by Philadelphia and had 51 at-bats for the Athletics, but only averaged .157 and was released right at the end of the year.

Sometimes it's pretty hard to pin down genealogy. Terry Sloope has interviewed York's two children and offers this footnote to his ethnicity: "Rudy's supposed Native American background comes from his mother's side of the family, but that side of the family is hard to trace. Also, no one really knows exactly who in her family had the native blood, or how much, or what tribe. It's generally thought that they were part Cherokee, but there are other family members who believe it may have been Lumbee blood. But no one has any real documentation of anything…."

Ted Williams—A Tangent

No doubt there are many other Red Sox players who have some degree of Native American ancestry. Ted Williams had some Chumash in his lineage. From *The Kid: Ted Williams in San Diego*, we learn a little about his aunt Annie Cordero from Ted's cousin, Teresa Cordero Contreras. The Corderos were native Californians, she explained, and they trace the lineage back to 1765, when "the first forefather arrived here in 1765 with Father Serra as one of the leatherjackets with the Patrol Army. My forefather was a corporal. They came from Spain. They arrived in Mexico City. He married in Baja to a Mexican woman, and they came up here to California. His son married an Indian here, the princess of the Chumash Indian tribe. He was here when they were building the missions. That was in the 1780s or 1790s." So there's even a bit of royalty in the greater Ted Williams family!

Tex Aulds—1947

On January 1, 1944, Aulds had played against Texas in the Cotton Bowl for the flyers of Randolph Field, scoring his team's touchdown in a 7–7 draw. Aulds played baseball for the Randolph Field Ramblers, too, serving as batterymate for Boo Ferriss. In 1946, Tex played for Scranton. Come 1947, Aulds was in baseball, a catcher playing for the Louisville Colonels. He was spiked badly in the second game of the year, requiring 27 stitches, then went to Toronto for rehab, but was returned to Louisville on May 19. Two days later, the Red Sox released catcher Frankie Hayes and brought up Aulds to serve as third-string backstop behind Birdie Tebbetts and Roy Partee. It was a year which saw the Sox cycle through seven catchers.

Tex Aulds ("French, Indian, Irish, Scotch") played in three 1947 Red Sox ballgames. His debut came on May 25, 1947. Tebbetts was the regular Boston catcher. Another "Tex"—Sox pitcher Hughson—got hit early, as did Bill Zuber; Hughson never made it out of the first, leaving after ⅔ of an inning, one K and a runner cut down at the plate on a "great heave by [Ted] Williams." New York scored five times in the first and three more in the second. Rains held up the game for 38 minutes; when play resumed, the Yankees added two more. Down 10–0, manager Cronin sent in Tex Aulds to sub for Tebbetts.

Aulds struck out his first time up. The first Red Sox hit off Bill Bevens was Johnny Pesky's double to left in the seventh. The Sox didn't score that inning, but the Yankees did—twice more.

In the eighth, Aulds got the Sox' second hit—a single into right field. Boston posted another goose egg, though, while New York put up four more. In the top of the ninth, Pesky singled and—with two outs—Williams homered. Final: Yankees 17, Red Sox 2.

The next time Aulds had a chance to play was on May 30. Injuries and illnesses had taken a toll on the Red Sox. Williams, Pesky, Doerr, and Tebbetts were all on the casualty list. Tebbetts had wrenched his knee sliding into third the day before, but finished out the game. With a doubleheader on the 30th, it was considered doubtful he'd play, but he did start game one— veterans hated to ever leave the lineup, even for a game, in those days. He played with his knee heavily bandaged, even though trainer Win Green had urged him to rest it. The Senators jumped out to a 10–0 lead after five, and once again—down by 10 runs in a scoreless game— Tex Aulds came in to replace Birdie.

Aulds was 0-for-1 this time, with one putout, and Washington won the game, 13–6. Roy Partee caught the second game. Washington won that one, too, by the score of 5–3. Aulds didn't play again for three weeks, his final major league appearance coming on June 22, again as a sub for Tebbetts, in the first game of a twin bill. This time it was just a 5–0 lead, but this time the Indians (Cleveland) had the lead after four innings. Aulds got his fourth major league at-bat—but made an out, never batted again, and wound up his career in The Show 1-for-4. Sent down to New Orleans, he was brought back in August but saw no further action and was later released to Louisville.

Les Moss—1951

The next Native American on the Red Sox was a catcher, too: Les Moss of Tulsa, Oklahoma. Moss began his career with the St. Louis Browns in 1946, starting late in the year. He'd originally signed with the Cubs in 1942, then served in the Merchant Marine during World War II. Called up from Toledo late in the year, he made headlines in his September 16 debut game when his two-out single in the bottom of the ninth drove in the tie-breaking run which completed a doubleheader sweep of the Yankees.

The "Irish and Indian" Moss hit .371 in 35 at-bats in what remained of 1946, but had a very tough '47, batting just .157. The Browns stuck with him, and he increased his average to .257 and then .291 in 1949. He dipped a bit to .266 in 1950, and had a rough '51. In 16 games with St. Louis, he was batting just .170 when the Red Sox traded for him on May 17, sending St. Louis Matt Batts, Jim Suchecki, $100,000, and a player who was named two months later: Jim McDonald. That was quite a package. Moss hit a home run as part of a 2-for-4 day, his first day on the job for his new employers. Four days later, his May 22 grand slam won a 6–3 game from the Tigers. Overall, though, the trade was a bust for Boston. Batts hit .302 for St. Louis. Moss hit .198 for Boston. In 1952, Moss was back with St. Louis. The Sox sent him back in November, with Tom Wright, to the Browns for Gus Niarhos and Ken Wood.

Moss played about half-time in 1952 and 1953, but cropped up with Baltimore in 1954 and part of 1955 before being sent to the White Sox in another trade. Moss completed his career with Chicago, playing into 1958 (just two games) and leaving with a .247 career average in 2,234 at-bats over 13 seasons. Earlier in 1958, he'd been out with his wife and daughter in their 14-foot boat when the outboard motor conked out and the three of them went adrift for 22 hours, carried some 30 to 40 miles in the Gulf Stream before being spotted and rescued. After the season, his last, he managed Luis Aparicio's Maracaibo Rapiños in Venezuela for two years. In 1960, he managed Savannah, the White Sox Single A team.

Moss scouted for the White Sox, beginning in 1961, but also continued to manage in the system, moving to Lynchburg, and then Indianapolis. In December 1965, he was appointed manager of their Puerto Rican winter league team.

Moss coached for the big league club in the years 1967–68 and managed for two stretches totaling 36 games in 1968 after Al Lopez had an appendectomy and then developed an infection. He coached for Chicago in 1970, too, and resigned after the 1970 season. He managed for the Tigers in Montgomery in 1975 and for the Detroit club itself for 1979. He lasted 59 games, before being replaced in June by Sparky Anderson. He was pitching coach for the Chicago Cubs in 1981, and coached for Houston from 1982–89.

Al Benton—1952

This 14-year major league veteran had a lifetime batting average of .098 and just 14 RBIs in those 14 seasons. Fortunately, he was a pitcher, a 6′4″ righthander who broke in with the Philadelphia Ahtletics in 1934 and closed his career with one final Red Sox season in 1952. Was he Native American? Actually, we don't know for sure. He did not self-identify as such, but several writers referred to his ancestry as including native blood. As with Squanto Wilson (we promise we'll get to him), rather than omit him because of the uncertainty, we figured it better to include him here.

Benton's best years were with the Detroit Tigers, and he was an All-Star in both 1941 and 1942. He could start or relieve, as a closer or a long man, a versatile pitcher who appeared in 455 games, and started in 167 of them. He was the only man to pitch against both Babe Ruth and Mickey Mantle, and in 1941 (his best season) he had the distinction of successfully executing two sacrifice bunts in the same inning—the only man to ever do so. All told, his career ended with a 98–88, 3.66 ERA record. After 13 years in the majors, he spent 1951 pitching in the Pacific Coast League but was brought back by Boston for one more year, posting a 4–3 record with an excellent 2.39 ERA, all in relief.

Gene Conley—1961–1963

Aside from being a multi-sport athlete, Gene Conley was also part Cherokee. Born in Muskogee, Oklahoma in 1930, his Native American ancestry comes from his mother Eva's side of the family. Gene's wife Katie Conley mentioned Gene's Indian heritage in the biography she wrote about her husband entitled *One of a Kind,* and explained further in an e-mail: "Both of Eva's parents were half Cherokee and his ancestors were part of the Cherokee Indians that marched from the southeast to Oklahoma as gold had been found on their property. The forced march became the infamous 'Trail of Tears'. However, on his father's side, he is pure Irish and English." Mrs. Conley added that she understood Mike Higgins to have had Indian ancestry as well. When gold was found in North Georgia in 1828, the Cherokees who were native to the area were driven from the area by European settlers looking for gold and the fertile land, their seizure of the land codified in 1830 when the Congress of the United States passed the "Indian Removal Act." A series of court battles ensued, but in 1838 Gen. Winfield Scott and the United States Army uprooted the Cherokee, driving them westward. Over 4,000 died during the forced march. After settling in Oklahoma, it was several generations later that Gene Conley was born and pitched his way into Red Sox history.

Conley began his baseball career with the Boston Braves in 1952, pitching five seasons for the Milwaukee Braves after that, then for a couple of years with the Phillies before coming back to Boston, this time with the Red Sox, in a trade for Frank Sullivan. It remains one of the tallest trades in baseball history, the Red Sox trading the 6′6½″ Sullivan for the 6′8″ Conley. Gene finished his 11-year career with the Red Sox, winning 29 and losing 32. He was a double World Champion, having played for the 1957 Milwaukee Braves and the NBA champion Boston Celtics from 1959–61. He was also the winning pitcher in the 1955 baseball All-Star Game.

Was Mike Higgins Native American?

Katie Conley understood he was, but research remains to be done. Our efforts have, to date, provided no proof in this regard. If he were Native American, of course, his most famous remark as quoted by Boston sportswriter Al Hirshberg—"There'll be no niggers on this ball club as long as I have anything to say about it"—is perhaps even more shameful.

William Frederick "Billy" Gardner—1962–1963

One of the very few players in the last 50 years to be directly traded between the Yankees and Red Sox, Billy Gardner described himself as "Irish, Indian" in completing his Hall of Fame questionnaire. The June 12, 1962 trade brought Gardner to Boston, while Tommy Umphlett and some cash was sent to New York. It was the first trade with the Yankees since 1934 when the Sox got Lyn Lary for Freddie Miller and $20,000.

Gardner had a little more than eight-plus major league seasons under his belt, beginning with the New York Giants in 1954, a full nine years after he'd first been signed by the Giants. He'd been a disappointment for the Yankees, batting .212 in 1961 and 0-for-1 in 1962. With the Red Sox, he hit .271 in 199 at-bats, but tailed off in 1963 with just a .190 average in 84 at-bats. A year after being released by the Red Sox, he served as a Sox coach in 1965 and 1966. Subsequently, he coached for Montreal and Minnesota, taking over as manager for the Twins from 1981–85 and for Kansas City in 1987.

The .271 average for Boston was the best in his 10 seasons. As an Oriole, Gardner led the league with 36 doubles in 1957, but with an average of .262. His lifetime average was .237. Despite a good average with the Red Sox, in 283 at-bats, he didn't offer much power—11 doubles, three triples, and no home runs—and he drove in just 13 runs.

Billy Rohr—1967

Rohr spent just one season with the Sox, but he truly kicked off a remarkable year with his near no-hitter against the Yankees in Yankee Stadium in his very first major league start, on April 14. With two outs in the bottom of the ninth, Elston Howard looped a single to right and the no-hit bid was over. Even Yankees fans booed the hit, so intrigued they had been with the raw rookie's feat. Rohr still got the win, a 3–0 shutout. He won his second start, too, a 6–1 win against the Yankees, this time at Fenway Park. Howard drove in the lone run. They were the only two wins he would record with the Red Sox. After completing a 2–3 season with Boston, he was purchased in late April 1968 by the Indians and appeared in 17 games that year, winning one without losing any, but with an ERA of 6.87. He spent several years in the minors and seemed not to be going anywhere, so he retired and took up the law.

Rohr was "part Cherokee Indian" according to Red Sox broadcaster Ken Coleman, writing in *The Impossible Dream Remembered*. Rohr himself, though, never knew the true story. In response to an inquiry, he wrote this author, "I have been told all my life that there is Indian blood in me. However, I was adopted at birth and have zero information—let alone documentation—re my ancestry." Rohr works today as a medical malpractice attorney in California.

Jerry Adair —1967–1968

Jerry Adair's father Kinnie was a tool grinder who spoke Cherokee and played sandlot ball on company teams in the area where Jerry was born, near Sand Springs, Oklahoma. Kinnie was an active father, coaching his son in Little League and seeing Jerry letter three times in three different sports (football, basketball, and baseball) at high school. Adair was selected for all-state honors in both football and basketball, and also starred at Oklahoma State.

Adair's first entry into organized baseball was in semipro ball, playing in the Western Canada Baseball League for the Willston, North Dakota team. That sounds like a pretty remote location from which to launch a 13-season major league career, but Adair attracted the attention of scouts Danny Doyle from the Red Sox and Eddie Robinson from the Orioles. Royse Parr, whose biography of Adair in *The 1967 Impossible Dream Red Sox* provides the basis for this profile, says that Doyle offered the larger signing bonus but that Adair adroitly "figured he would move up the ladder quicker with the Orioles." Jerry signed on September 2, 1958 and appeared in 11 games with Baltimore later that very month.

In 1959, he played shortstop for the Amarillo Gold Sox, batting .309, and got a callup to Baltimore at season's end. Improving on his .105 average from 1958, he batted .314 this September, in 35 at-bats. Almost all of 1960 was spent playing for the Triple A Miami Marlins, though he squeezed in five at-bats (and hit his first home run) at the tail end of the Orioles season. It was in 1961 that he first played full-time, hitting .264 in 133 games. Though he only hit .258 over his first five seasons, Parr notes that this was "substantially above the league average for middle infielders" of the day, and that Jerry was "recognized as one of the premier fielding infielders in the American League."

Adair was traded to the White Sox in mid-June 1966. A year later, he was off to a poor start for Chicago, batting .204, but was traded to the Red Sox for Don McMahon and Bob Snow on June 2, 1967. Playing under former teammate Dick Williams may have been the tonic Jerry needed; he hit .291 the rest of 1967 and brought an extra spark (plus a few truly key hits) to the Impossible Dream team. Williams considered Adair "the ultimate professional." Author Herb Crehan paid tribute to Adair's work for the '67 Red Sox: "Role players like Adair seldom get their moment in the sun. But in the summer of '67 every Red Sox fan thought of Jerry as a hero."

1968 was disappointing. Jerry only hit .216, while filling in here and there at all four infield positions. The Red Sox chose not to protect him in the October 1968 expansion draft and Jerry was snatched up by the Kansas City Royals. He had a solid season, mostly at second base, batting .250 and driving in 48 runs. Adair wasn't used much in 1970, and was released on May 12. He played a year in Japan for the Hankyu Braves, batting an even .300 in 1971, and then retired as an active player.

Dick Williams hired Adair as a major league coach and he won three World Series rings in a row, coaching Oakland to championships in 1972, 1973, and 1974. He coached a couple more seasons for Williams with the California Angels in 1975 and 1976, but then retired altogether.

Gary Waslewski—1967–1968

Naturally, with a name like Waslewski everyone must assume you're Native American. Er, maybe not. But it appears that there were at least three members of the Impossible Dream team who were of Native American ancestry. Waslewski was aware that Billy Rohr was thought to be part-Cherokee, and they both were aware of Jerry Adair's parentage. Waslewski is not on any Indian tribal roll, though. The connection, Waslewski explained, was that "a great grandmother on my mother's side was supposed to be Cherokee. She would have been on her father's side of the family as I believe the mother was from Germany."

Connecticut-born Waslewski was a 6'4" righthander first signed by Pittsburgh but picked up by the Red Sox in the 1964 minor league draft. He debuted for Boston starting the second game of a Fenway Park doubleheader against the Washington Senators on June 11, 1967. The Red Sox were in fourth place at the time, doing better than expected but the Impossible Dream had not yet been born. By year's end, he'd started eight games and relieved in four others. He was 2–2, with a 3.21 ERA. In the 1967 World Series, he threw three innings of hitless relief in Game Three and earned himself a start in Game Six. In 5⅓ innings, he gave up just four hits and two runs and could have had the win, except that John Wyatt let the Cardinals tie it up in the seventh.

Waslewski pitched for the Sox again in 1968 (4–7, 3.67), then was traded to the Cardinals in December. He pitched for St. Louis in 1969, for Montreal in 1969 and 1970, the Yankees in 1970 and 1971, and lastly for Oakland in 1972. He never had a season with a winning record but posted a respectable career ERA of 3.44. After a couple of years in minor league ball for the A's, he retired and began work with The Hartford insurance company.

Jim Willoughby—1975–1977

An unattributed clipping in the Hall of Fame files quotes Willoughby as saying he can't understand all the fuss over the fact that rookie righthander John Henry Johnson of the Athletics is a Potawatomi Indian. "I'm descended from the same tribe. In fact, I get checks from the government every time there is a settlement for land the government took from us. And my great aunt [Mamie Echo Hawk] was the tribe's chief lobbyist in Washington for years."

The right-handed pitcher was born in Salinas, California and starred for Gustine High, drafted out of high school in 1967 by the San Francisco Giants. Willoughby pitched for Salt Lake, Fresno, Medford, and Phoenix, while finishing high school and pursuing a college degree in electrical engineering. Jon Daly's biography in '75: The Red Sox Team that Saved Baseball presents a full picture of the pitcher's life.

In 1971, he made the Pacific Coast League All-Star team, and was called up by the Giants on August 30. He threw four innings that fall, but pitched parts of four seasons for the Giants, 1971–74 (and some winter ball in Venezuela), before being sent down to Phoenix in 1974 and then traded in October to the Cardinals in a swap of minor leaguers. The sinker-slider pitcher was pitching well for Tulsa and was selected as the player to be named later in an April 4 trade to the Red Sox; three months later, Willoughby was named on July 4. With Boston, he posted a 5–2 record, with a 3.54 ERA, and found himself appearing in three games of the 1975 World Series. He was on the mound when Ed Armbrister and Carlton Fisk collided during the infamous Game Three 10th-inning bunt. He was on the mound in Game Seven, having retired the four Reds batters he faced, keeping the score tied, 3–3, after 7½ innings. Scott Cooper batted for Willoughby in the bottom of the eighth, but popped up foul to third base. Rookie Jim Burton came in, gave up a run, and the World Series was lost. Red Sox fans understand the story of a sportswriter going into a bar years later and hearing a drinker at the bar mumbling to himself about manager Darrell Johnson, "He never should have hit for Willoughby."

In 1976, Willoughby pitched exclusively in relief, throwing 99 innings in 54 games. He had his second-best season in earned runs, with a 2.82 ERA, but was saddled with 12 losses and just three wins, with 10 saves. In 1977, he was 6–2, but missed out on Boston's 1978 season, having been sold to the White Sox in early April. One more Red Sox win in 1978….

Willow was 1–6 for Chicago, traded to St. Louis after the season, released in March 1979, signed with Wichita in the Cubs system, and wound up playing for Portland in the Pirates system. Jon Daly reports that Willoughby was called up to Pittsburgh later in the year as insurance, but wasn't needed and simply sat on the bench. After going into a diabetic coma playing winter ball in Venezuela, he hung up his spikes.

In an e-mail to the author of this book, Jim writes, "I have always been proud of my ancestry—but I took it for granted. It was never played down to me or by me and likewise not much was ever said about it. It wasn't until after baseball that I became more conscious of my heritage and started doing more serious research. My grandmother was sent away to Indian schools as a child and there was a lot of prejudice against Indians. My grandmother, nearly full blood, registered my mother at half her blood. And my mother did the same for me and my sisters. They didn't want so much for our blood line to disappear as they wanted the BIA [Bureau of Indian Affairs] out of our lives and to be treated like every other citizen. I'm ⅜ CBP [Citizen Band Potawatomi] but only registered as ⅛. It's a case of parental 'passing.'"

John Henry Johnson, 1983–1984

John Henry Johnson was quoted in *The Sporting News* (May 13, 1978) as saying, "Being an Indian is important to me. It's a proud heritage. They're the ones who made America." The Houston-born left-hander was a 15th-round pick of the San Francisco Giants, but less than a month before he was ready to make the majors, he was traded across the Bay to Oakland as one of six Giants sent (along with $300,000) to acquire Vida Blue. Johnson started his first game on April 10, 1978 allowing just two hits in six innings and getting the win. He began to build toward a record of 11–10, 3.39 ERA his first season. In mid-1979, the Athletics sent him to Texas in another trade. He was 2–8 at the time. He played for the Rangers until early April 1982, the latter two years exclusively in relief. All told, he was 7–9 with the Rangers. They swapped him to the Red Sox for Mike Smithson. Johnson did not pitch in the majors in 1982, but he threw 53⅓ and 63⅔ innings in the 1983 and 1984 seasons, with four starts mixed in among his 64 appearances. His Red Sox record was 2–2, with ERAs of 3.71 and 3.53.

The Red Sox released him on April 1, 1985 and he was snapped up by the Pirates 10 days later, only to be released in turn on July 26, despite having thrown a Pacific Coast League no-hitter for Hawaii against Calgary in early May. The Brewers signed him at the end of August. There was a lot of activity but, as in 1982, he spent the year without being in major league ball. The Brewers brought him back for 29 more appearances in 1986 and 1987, but those were his last two years in big league ball.

Jacoby Ellsbury—2007

With an eye to the future, we couldn't help but note that in 2005 the Red Sox signed as a first-round pick in the amateur draft a Dine (Navajo) ballplayer, Oregon State's Jacoby Ellsbury. He was the 2005 PAC-10 Co-Player of the Year and the 23rd selection overall in the draft. NDN Sports said that Ellsbury "has already garnered early comparisons to a young Johnny Damon." In three years of NCAA play for Oregon State, Jacoby hit .330, .352, and (a figure that resonates in Red Sox Nation) .406. His on-base percentage hovered close to .500. After signing, Ellsbury played with Boston's Single A affiliate Lowell Spinners, batting .317 in 139 at-bats, with an on-base percentage of .418. In 2007, Ellsbury became the first Navajo to play big league baseball.

The very speedy Ellsbury stole 41 bases in 2006, which he began with Single A Wilmington, batting .299. He earned himself a midseason promotion to the Double A Portland Sea Dogs and hit .301 for Portland, in every way positioning himself as a center fielder for the future. Ellsbury's grandmother was a Navajo rug weaver in Arizona, and some 30 years ago his mother Marjorie McCabe Ellsbury actually designed the flag for the Colorado River Indians Tribe of which she and her son are members. Marge's sister Emily told *Farmington (NM) Daily Times* reporter Patrick Ronan that Coby has strong morals and a strong work ethic, and pride in his ancestry. "His mother taught him well," she said. "She taught him the native tongue. He can speak Navajo. He even knows how to sing some Navajo songs," she added with a laugh.

In 2007, Ellsbury got the call and debuted to fill in for Coco Crisp on June 30. He beat out what looked like a routine infield grounder for his first major league hit, and continued to both hit and steal bases throughout the season, batting .353 in 116 at-bats with three home runs and 18 RBIs. With 30 singles and eight walks—38 times he reached first base—he stole nine bases and was never caught once. In the postseason, Ellsbury batted .360 (.438 in the World Series).

Raised in part on a reservation, moving back to Madras, Oregon at age six may have made a major difference in his success playing baseball. He admits he didn't have many Native American role models when he grew up, and he's well aware that he himself may become one for younger Native Americans today. He's already developed a devoted following among Red Sox fans.

The first Native American manager

The Boston Red Sox, last team in the majors to have an African-American player on their team, may have been the first to have a Native American manager. If only for one day. Rudy York was ⅛ Cherokee, but identified as "Indian" and was understood by his fellow players to be a Native American. He managed the Boston Red Sox in 1959. For one day.

Pinky Higgins, who had skippered the Sox since the beginning of the 1955 season, saw his tenure come to an end after 73 games of the 1959 season. His fifth year as manager was the first season he'd not been in the first division, and he had his team in last place. Everyone knew he was over the edge with his drinking and it was severely affecting play. He was fired on July 3, 1959 by General Manager Bucky Harris, who then appointed Rudy York as manager for the three-game series against Baltimore. Coach Del Baker had been the first one offered the interim job, but he declined, perhaps having a closer friendship with Higgins. Harris told reporters, "Rudy will take over this series and when I get back to Boston we'll try and find a successor. This is a very unpleasant thing." Harris was close to Higgins himself.

Three hours later Harris had a new field manager—Billy Jurges.

"Naming of Jurges Astounds Players" read one Boston newspaper headline. A *Globe* columnist wrote, "Seldom has a major league manager been appointed who was less known by his new players." Jurges, though, had served as third base coach for the Washington Senators for three seasons; it wasn't as though he was a novice. Red Sox owner Tom Yawkey was reportedly as surprised as anyone by the choice, and that it had been affected so rapidly.

When York had been named, Higgins joked, "Rudy, don't tell them what your record was at North Platte." York's only previous managerial experience was a losing record for an Indians farm club—the Cleveland Indians, that is.

York, born in Ragland, Alabama, did indeed see himself as a Native American. "I'm a Cherokee Indian, and I'm proud of it," he proclaimed. The *New York Times*, in York's obituary, repeated a sarcastic comment on his fielding ability: he was "one part Indian and one part first baseman." Leon Culberson got off a good line about York, too. The first baseman hadn't arrived in camp for spring training in 1947, but this was not to be misinterpreted, Culberson explained. "Rudy says he's not holding out. He's just waiting to sign."

As manager, York was just about replaced before he started, but he did run the team for one game, the July 3 game. The Red Sox lost to the Orioles 6–1, the game lost in the bottom of the first when Baltimore piled up five runs off starter Jack Harshman, who hurt his own cause by walking three of the first four batters he faced. Willie Tasby, who came over to the Red Sox early the next year, blooped a single to right driving in one, then former Sox star Walt Dropo doubled in three more runs. After giving up five runs on just two hits, York replaced Harshman. Clif Keane, never the most politically correct knight of the keyboard in Boston, led his game account: "Manager for a day—but Rudy York was beaten tonight before he could put on his war paint." This wasn't a team anyone would really want to lead and it wasn't as though York had aspirations to manage. He was just helping out, but with the wrong team at the wrong time. It was the sixth straight loss for the Sox.

Jurges managed the Red Sox for the rest of 1959 and the beginning of 1960, winning 59 and losing 63 before he was replaced by, of all people, Mike Higgins.

What about Johnny Hodapp, the Hevings, and the Carlyles?

A number of sources cite Johnny Hodapp as a Native American. Were he, then there would have been a time the Red Sox had two on the same team, in 1933. Hodapp played 101 games at second base and 10 at first, that year (his only year with the Red Sox), while Roy Johnson played 95 games in right, 26 in left, and 10 in center. Journalist Gregory Korte, Hodapp's grandson, looked into the family lineage and reports that Hodapp was entirely German, not American Indian.

Then, there were the Hevings of Covington, Kentucky—Johnnie and Joe. They both played for the Red Sox (see the section on Red Sox relatives). In talking with Joe Heving's daughter Mary Sterling in April 2007, she mentioned that her father was of "Swedish and American Indian" parentage. The conversation was mainly on other subjects. The player questionnaires at the Hall of Fame indicate that both brothers saw their background as "German" or "American-German." Subsequent phone calls to Mary Sterling found that the number had been disconnected. The mystery remains.

And the Carlyles? Roy and Cleo? Cleo's player questionnaire indicates his ethnic background as "English and Irish" but his older brother Roy, born to the same parents, is described as "Indian and Irish."

Not a Native American—"Squanto" Wilson (1914 Red Sox)

A nickname like "Squanto" is a pretty good clue that George F. Wilson was portrayed as Native American. Newspaper stories remarked on Wilson's dark complexion and Indian nickname, though it is possible that people just dubbed him "Squanto" the way they might call another player "Nig" (Nig Cuppy, for instance) or another such name. We realized that he might not have actually been Native American—but we planned to include him here just in case he was.

Wilson was born in Old Town, Maine in 1889 and starred as a catcher for the Bowdoin College baseball team. He was signed by the Detroit Tigers after completing his junior year and appeared in five games at the tail end of the season, debuting on October 2, 1911. In 16 at-bats, he managed three hits—all singles—and got himself on base two other times by drawing a base on balls. He scored two runs, but never drove in one. His fielding left a lot to be desired, three errors in 30 chances. Wilson returned to Bowdoin and graduated in 1912.

While playing for Toronto in the International League in 1912, he suffered a serious injury in a collision and was never able to throw properly again. Switching to first base, where lack of arm strength is much less of a liability, Wilson played for Lynn, Massachusetts in the New England League, leading the league with a .365 average. The Red Sox gave him a chance, signing him for 1914. He appeared in his first game for the Red Sox on April 22, 1914. It was an interesting early-season game. The Red Sox entered the day with a record of 2–4, 3½ games behind the first-place White Sox. In the seven games they had played, Boston had scored a total of six runs—they'd been shut out three times, won games by the scores of 10- and 2–1, and had played a 1–1 tie game against Philadelphia the day before.

They played to a tie again on April 22 (see a brief narrative on the back-to-back tie games elsewhere in this book). When the Red Sox scored four times in the bottom of the fourth, it was their biggest inning of the year. Boston held a 5–1 lead only briefly; the Athletics tied it in the top of the fifth—and then took a 9–5 lead thanks to four more runs in the top of the seventh. Time was running short, because both teams had trains to catch. The umpire was former Boston pitcher Bill Dinneen. In the bottom of the eighth, Janvrin grounded out, short to first. Everett Scott drew a walk. Hick Cady flied to right, but Murphy muffed the ball and the Red Sox had runners on first and second with just the one out. Squanto Wilson was put in as a pinch-runner for catcher Cady at first. Pinch-hitter Henriksen struck out. Two down. Hooper doubled, driving in Scott and sending Wilson to third. Engle walked and the bases were loaded. On a 3–2 count, with Tris Speaker up, the outfielders were playing deep and the runners were off with the pitch. Speaker purposely tapped a ball into short left field, while the runners tore around the bases and all three scored, retying the game, 9–9. Left-fielder Daley fell, coming in to make the play, just barely stopped the ball, and was unable to throw home before all three runners scored. After Lewis flied out, the game was called by mutual agreement. Daley was not assigned an error; Speaker was awarded a double. Curiously, and correctly, all the boxscores of the day awarded Wilson a run scored, but none of today's reference works have the run recorded. We'll have to work on fixing that.

Wilson never appeared in another major league game, though he played for two years in the minors and then with a number of semi-pro and amateur teams in Maine. His photograph can be found as one of the 1922 Augusta Millionaires in Will Anderson's book *Was Baseball Really Invented in Maine?* In 1923, he signed as a player-manager with Hanover in Pennsylvania's Class D Blue Ridge League. He served as a teacher and principal at Winthrop High School in Maine for 10 years and ran a small five-store chain of retail stores known as Wilson's Dollar Stores, also located in Maine. His major league average was the .188 he hit with the Tigers. His only appearance for the Red Sox was as pinch-runner in this one game, a game neither team won.

The Hall of Fame Library helped resolve the question when they located a 1988 letter to Cappy Gagnon from Ezra Smith of Winthrop, a former employee who had known Wilson well. Smith volunteered that "a disgruntled first wife" destroyed his athletic scrapbooks, but added, "There is no evidence of him having any Indian blood. His Indian features got him the name of Squanto and as far as I know that was it. I never knew of him having any Indian friends or baseball buddies." Barring any new revelations, that's definitive enough for us.

THE FIRST AFRICAN-AMERICAN PLAYERS

It was one thing to field Latinos, Native Americans, and Jews, but another thing altogether to feature an African-American. Born in Havana? That's OK, if your complexion is light enough. You're maybe a sixth- or seventh-generation American, but showing too much African ancestry? Not welcome.

The whole question of skin color has haunted many societies, from Latin American countries to Asian ones, and certainly the United States. Approaching the mid-nineteenth century, with slavery outlawed in England for 50 years but not yet in the US, Boston was a leading center of the abolitionist movement. When it came to baseball, though, almost a century after the Civil War, almost every fan knows that, to its shame, the team which had the golden opportunity to sign the first African-American player was instead the last team to field one.

The Yankees were one of the last teams to field a black player, Elston Howard in 1955. Yankees owner George Weiss unburdened himself of a number of racist remarks of one sort or another, but it seems that above all else he didn't think that white Yankees fans would want to sit with fans of other skin colors, and clearly he didn't. Nonetheless, the times dictated change and the Yankees organization was forced to accommodate—eight years after the Dodgers.

It was still four more years before the Red Sox could bring themselves around to putting an African-American ballplayer on the field.

Jim Caple and Steve Buckley point out how the Sox hurt themselves delaying only the dozen years between Jackie Robinson's debut and Pumpsie Green's. In just those 12 seasons, "Black and Latin players won eight MVPs, nine Rookie of the Year awards, five home run crowns, three batting titles and a Cy Young."

Howard Bryant's book *Shut Out* chronicles the unfortunate facts regarding race and the Red Sox over the years, while giving credit to figures like Boston City Councilor Isadore Muchnick, ballplayer Ted Williams, and GM Dan Duquette, who each in their own way helped move the team toward greater diversity.

After 10 years of trying to bring about integration in Boston baseball—with either the Braves or the Red Sox—local journalist Mabrey Kountze was finally able to enlist a little assistance from two of the deans of the Boston sports press corps—Dave Egan and Bill Cunningham. They wrote about the need for integration. City Councilor Muchnick got on board, too; Muchnick noted that lucrative Sunday baseball was only possible in Boston by special license granted by the city government and he announced that he would see to it that the license was withheld unless black players were given a tryout.

Others have written about the subject in more detail, most notably Glenn Stout and Richard Johnson in *Red Sox Century* and Bryant in *Shut Out*. Suffice it to say here that Muchnick helped force the Red Sox to grant a tryout to Jackie Robinson, Sam Jethroe, and Marvin Williams in 1945, even though it proved a sham tryout and a greater blot on Boston when the players performed quite well, but never heard a word from the Red Sox afterward. One thing they did hear, according to the *Boston Globe*'s Clif Keane: the shout from the top of the grandstand, "Get those niggers off the field!" It strains credibility to believe that Keane truly couldn't recall who yelled it, but speculation centers on three men: Eddie Collins, Joe Cronin, or Tom Yawkey. It was almost certainly not Cronin, because he was reported as sitting in the box seats with Muchnick and African-American journalist Wendell Smith from the *Pittsburgh Courier*. In a sense, though, it doesn't really matter. The blame rests at Yawkey's door. He owned the team, all of it. A simple word from him at any point would have changed team policy. There's no getting around it: the buck stopped with Yawkey. And Robinson knew it. When the Red Sox were in the final days of the 1967 season, he said he was rooting against them: "Because of Boston owner Tom Yawkey, I'd like to see them lose," Robinson said. "He is probably one of the most bigoted guys in organized baseball." [*Chicago Defender*] Robinson may have known who it was that shouted while he was on the field at Fenway.

Ted Williams made no public statements as a player, but by choosing Pumpsie Green as his pre-game throwing partner on the sidelines in 1959, Ted conveyed by deed his welcome to Boston's first black player. Larry Doby, who had broken in a dozen years earlier with Cleveland, said that Ted had always made him feel welcome, while some of his own teammates wouldn't even speak with him. It's widely known that Ted turned a portion of his own 1966 Hall of Fame acceptance speech into a plea for the great Negro League players to be honored in the Hall. Duquette brought about, in Bryant's words, a number of "sharp, impressive changes" and earned him this accolade: "The Dan Duquette years would transform the Red Sox from a team of predominantly white players to a modern club with [the] diversity of the United Nations."

In an interesting side note, it was Hugh Duffy who both signed the first Jewish Red Sox player—Sy Rosenthal—and ran the 1945 workout for Jackie Robinson, Sam Jethroe, and Marvin Williams. Duffy praised the men afterward, but if his praise went upwards, it fell on deaf ears.

Pumpsie Green—Red Sox 1959–62

Elijah Jerry "Pumpsie" Green was the first African-American to play for the Red Sox, but there were other players who could well have had the distinction. Clearly, there was Jackie Robinson, who the Red Sox could have signed at the 1945 tryout. Robinson was chosen Rookie of the Year in 1947. There was also Sam Jethroe, snubbed at the same Sox tryout; Jethroe was voted Rookie of the Year in 1950. And there was Willie Mays, the 1951 Rookie of the Year. Imagine a team with Ted Williams, Jackie Robinson, and Willie Mays on it. That could have been the Boston Red Sox, and the number of World Championships won by the Yankees and the Red Sox might have been more in balance.

They should have played side by side for many years: Willie Mays and Ted Williams.

Willie Mays? Absolutely. In his 1973 book *What's the Matter with the Red Sox?*, Al Hirshberg explained that the Red Sox once held exclusive rights to Willie Mays, albeit indirectly, through their Birmingham Barons farm team and the team's own relationship with the Birmingham Black Barons team. One story has Red Sox scout George Digby singing praises of Mays to the deaf ears of the powers that be back in Boston; another has scout Larry Woodall being asked to check Mays out but not even bothering to attend a game before sending back a negative report. Both stories may well have been true. Whatever the facts of the matter, the Red Sox let an "inner circle Hall of Famer" slip right out of their hands. Mays told Howard Bryant in 1997, "I really thought I was going to Boston. They had a guy come down and look at me. They had a good team, with Parnell, and Stephens, and of course, Ted. But for that Yawkey. Everyone knew he was racist. He didn't want me."

One of Mays' teammates on the Barons in 1948 was Artie Wilson, whose record arguably still stands today as the last ballplayer to hit .400—Wilson hit .402 in 1948. Wilson told Eric Enders, "Some might say it doesn't count because I did it in the Negro Leagues. Well, if I hit .400 in the Negro Leagues, I probably would have hit more in the majors, because I'd have gotten better pitches to hit."

The first black ballplayer signed while Joe Cronin was GM was Piper Davis. Lorenzo Davis was nicknamed Piper, since he hailed from Piper, Alabama. He played for the Birmingham Black Barons in the Negro American League beginning in 1942, becoming a perennial all-star, and served as player-manager starting in 1948. In 1950, the Red Sox purchased rights to Davis from Birmingham and assigned him to Scranton. It was a $15,000 deal and the Red Sox paid half down to Birmingham, obligated to pay the other half if he made the team by the May 15 cutoff date. Davis played 15 games and was leading the team in the Triple Crown categories with an even .333 average, three home runs, and 10 RBIs. Apparently that wasn't good enough, and he was cut for what he was told were economic reasons.

It could have been Jackie or Willie or Piper, but it was Pumpsie Green who was first, though when the day came, it was some 12 years after Jackie Robinson's rookie year and more than two years after Robinson had retired from the game.

Green had a hard time from the beginning, reporting for spring training in 1959 and finding that Scottsdale city ordinances made him unwelcome at the team hotel; he was forced to stay at a motel 17 miles away. He had a manager in Mike Higgins who was both disdainful and alcoholic, an ominous combination. Pumpsie had never truly aspired to play in the major leagues. A native Californian, he'd had his sights set on the more welcoming Pacific Coast League—still a highly-competitive "third major league" preferred by a number of ballplayers. He never wanted to be a pioneer or a symbol, with all the extra pressure and expectation that came with it.

Though he'd only hit .253 for the Minneapolis Millers in 1958, he had an exceptional spring training, and so did the team, winning its first seven games. Green got extra playing time when first-string shortstop Don Buddin suffered an injury, and he responded, hitting as high as .449 at one point. Pumpsie hit two home runs on March 18, and another on the 22nd. He had a pinch-hit homer on March 28. The *Globe*'s Harold Kaese wrote, "Pumpsie proceeded to pound the ball much better than expected," and further noted, "There isn't any question that he can outfield Buddin, who made more errors than any other major league shortstop last year. If Green can keep up the hitting, the job is his." Green hit a slump near the end of spring training, though, both offensively and defensively (a two-base throwing error with the bases loaded on April 5 in Fort Worth). Two days later, though still hitting over .300, the Red Sox sent him on option to Minneapolis. Lee D. Jenkins, writing in the *Chicago Defender* after Green's July callup, lamented the inevitable pressure: "It's one thing to make a major league team by sheer talent but to find yourself in a position where you are almost thrust down an unwilling throat makes for a most uncomfortable state. Green was a sensation with the Red Sox during their early spring training but as the season neared the pressure began to tell in his fielding and hitting."

Green's demotion might not have prompted such reaction, had he not been the first African American player to wear a Red Sox uniform in spring training, and had the Red Sox ever had a black player on their team. The NAACP charged bias; the Red Sox said Green needed "more seasoning" and denied the charge. The Massachusetts Commission Against Discrimination (MCAD) investigated, formally inviting Tom Yawkey to defend his team against the accusation.

Kaese wrote that the club's decision to send Green to Triple A might have been wise from the strict baseball point of view, but "from every other point of view, they undoubtedly have pulled a colossal blunder." The *Herald*'s Bill Cunningham, said, "There was never a chance he could move Don Buddin" off his slot at shortstop. Right. The same Buddin who batted a lusty .239 in 1956, didn't play in 1957, and hit .237 in 1958.

The *Boston Globe* did note in a small front page story on April 14, "Red Sox Have Seven Negroes on Farm Teams." They were Pumpsie Green, Zeke King, Hubert McCoy, Jim Penny, Larry Plenty, Earl Wilson, and Tommy Williams.

Sox GM Dick O'Connell had the uncomfortable task of appearing before MCAD and defending a policy which he likely disapproved. He still managed to come across clumsily, saying he wished the Red Sox did have a black player on the team. After all, "If we had, I wouldn't be sitting here this morning." Now there's a real commitment to racial justice. O'Connell also had to defend the team's hiring process in staffing positions at Fenway Park.

On June 12, apparently mollified by promises undertaken by the Red Sox, the Commission let them off the hook. On July 3, Mike Higgins was fired; he'd once told writer Al Hirshberg, "There'll be no niggers on this ballclub as long as I have anything to say about it." Now, he no longer did, and though Higgins was to return as general manager in 1963, by then it was just too late.

A 1948 photograph of several Red Sox with racist image for Topsy's Chicken Coop, Revere Beach MA.

The Red Sox were in last place when, on July 21, Pumpsie Green made his Red Sox debut, in Chicago, pinch-running in the eighth inning and playing at shortstop. Green had been hitting .325 in Minneapolis. He started at second the next day, 0-for-3 with a walk. His first hit came in the second game of a doubleheader at Cleveland, starting at second, 1-for-2 with two walks. By the time the team came back home to Fenway, Pumpsie was 7-for-24 and still error-free in the field.

His first day in Boston, he played both halves of a doubleheader, 1-for-3 in each game, with a triple in the opener, scoring a run in both games. His first home run didn't come until September 7, contributing to a 12–4 beating of the Yankees at Fenway. By year's end, Green hit .233 with 10 RBIs, in 172 major league at-bats. Green played four seasons for the Red Sox, and one final year for the Mets. He might have flourished more had he not had so many obstacles to overcome, and had the Red Sox organization been fully supportive.

Green reflected back to Howard Bryant just over 40 years later about his experience: "Sometimes when I think of the things people like me had to go through, it just sounds so unnecessary. When you think about it, it is almost silly, how much time and energy was wasted hating."

Earl Wilson—Red Sox 1959–66

Pitcher Earl Wilson, also a Californian, was actually signed somewhat before Green (both were signed in 1953) and would have preceded him into the big leagues, but his arrival with Boston in the majors was delayed by military service. Wilson debuted seven days after Pumpsie Green. He pitched the seventh inning of the day's first game, against the Indians in Cleveland, and retired Minoso on a fly ball, then got Francona and Colavito on foul popups. Three days later, he got a start and pitched the first 3⅔ innings and he sure skated on thin ice: walking the first three batters in the first, the first two batters in the second, and the first batter in the third—in all, he walked nine, but didn't give up either a hit or a run. He let in five earned runs his next start, only recording three outs. Wilson's first decision was a win, throwing 3⅔ innings in relief against Kansas City. He stayed with the team and by year's end, he was 1–1, but with a 6.08 ERA. He batted .500, with four RBIs.

Each of the next three years, he improved his earned run average, becoming a regular in 1962 and posting a 12–8 record with a 3.90 ERA. One of his wins was a no-hitter on June 26, the first no-hitter by a Red Sox righthander since Howard Ehmke had thrown one in 1923. Wilson's bat won the game; his solo homer in the third inning was all the scoring that was needed.

His overall record with the Red Sox was 56–58, before he and Joe Christopher were traded to the Tigers for Don Demeter and Julio Navarro in June 1966. The Red Sox were a poor team in the early 1960's, but the trade may very well have been prompted by an incident in spring training where Wilson had been denied entry to a Winter Haven night spot and the reaction of Red Sox management was less to defend their pitcher than to ask him to keep mum about it. Years later, he told Howard Bryant, "Having that happen and then being told not to say anything about it was the most humiliating experience of my life." Earl kept it in for a while but when pressed by newsmen, he chose to tell the story and bear the consequences. Once the Red Sox signed a couple more black players (Jose Tartabull and John Wyatt), it became politically acceptable to send Wilson out of town.

Wilson missed out on Boston's Impossible Dream team in 1967, though he fared well in Detroit with a league-leading 22 wins (22–11, 3.27 ERA). Wilson went to the World Series for the Tigers the next year, 1968, starting and losing one game after giving up three runs in four-plus innings. One can never know how 1967 might have turned out, had Wilson still been with the Red Sox.

Except for a few appearances for San Diego in the second half of 1970, Wilson played the rest of his 11 years for Detroit, finishing up with 121 major league victories.

July 15, 1956 headline in Boston Globe. So eager, it still took three more years.

The 1967 Red Sox, with Dick O'Connell more firmly in control as GM, featured a number of players of color, from Tartabull and Wyatt to George Scott, Reggie Smith, Jose Santiago, Joe Foy, and Elston Howard. Though it seemed real progress was being made, there were long memories involved and even 30 years later the stain of racism and the resultant reluctance of numerous players to come to Boston still negatively affected Red Sox baseball. It was really only in the mid-to-late 1990s that this began to subside.

Coincidentally, after the Sox had designated Jay Payton for assignment in early July 2005 (at his request), they did not have a single African-American on the roster. There were, of course, a good number of players of color. The diversity on recent Red Sox teams had been such over the previous years that this hardly occasioned comment and raised few eyebrows. No one assumed it was anything nefarious, not like the old days.

Willie Tasby—1960

Willie Tasby broke into the majors with the Baltimore Orioles in September 1958, some eight years after he'd first signed with the St. Louis Browns. The Browns became the Orioles when the franchise moved east after the 1953 season. The right-handed outfielder hit .200 that first year, then .250 in 1959 (with 13 homers and 48 RBIs). Both he and Boston outfielder Gene Stephens were off to slow starts in 1960, and the Sox were glad to trade Stephens for Tasby on June 9. He was the first black player for whom the Red Sox had traded. Both players did better in their new environments, though the Red Sox got the better end of the deal: Stephens only improved from .229 to .238 whereas Tasby improved from .212 to .281, from three RBIs to 37 with the Red Sox, for whom he played a fairly full balance of the season of 102 games in centerfield alongside The Splendid Splinter in left.

Tasby drove in a run in his first game with the Red Sox, but then played in 20 games in a row before driving in another. When he did, it was in a July 3 game against Kansas City at Fenway. He singled to lead off the seventh, but was picked off first. Boston batted around and when he came up for the second time in the inning, he bases were full. He hit a grand slam. Probably his best day for Boston came one week later, when he went 5-for-5 against the Yankees, starting with a leadoff home run, driving in four runs and scoring three times. After completing the season with the Red Sox, he was drafted by the expansion Washington Senators team.

Tasby played for Washington in 1961 and and the first month of 1962, and for the Indians for most of '62 and 1963. He completed his time in major league ball with an even .250 average and 46 home runs.

Felix Mantilla—1963–65

Born in Puerto Rico, "Felix the Cat" had first been signed by the Boston Braves in 1952 and from 1956–61 he played for the Braves after their move to Milwaukee. In 1962, he had the honor of playing for the first year New York Mets, after being selected the prior October in the expansion draft. The third baseman had been one of the Mets' better players, hitting a solid .275. The Mets, nevertheless thought they saw a way to improve their team and traded him to the Red Sox for Tracy Stallard, Pumpsie Green, and a PTBNL (Al Moran) in the winter of 1962–63.

With the Red Sox, Mantilla had his best average in '63, but the .315 was only established in 175 at-bats. As a utilityman, Mantilla was kept very busy indeed in 1964 and appeared in 133 games, garnering 425 at-bats and posted a .289 average. He powered out a full 30 home runs. As the regular second baseman in 1965, he got even more work, though his average slipped to .275 and his HR total dipped to 18. That was respectable enough, but nothing like the year before. He increased his RBI totals, though, from 64 all the way to 92, a full 10 more RBIs than the second best producer on the club, Tony Conigliaro. The Sox traded him to Houston for Eddie Kasko; neither player broke .220 in 1966 and it was the last year as a major league player for both. Kasko managed the Red Sox for four years, and served the organization for many more.

Reggie Smith—1966–1973

Writer Jeff Angus characterized Reggie Smith's 17-year All-Star caliber major league career as "a great success that has been muddied by other people's expectations (too high) and Smith's media profile (too low)." His rookie season was a special one: 1967. His leadoff home run gave Billy Rohr all the runs he needed to beat the Yankees in that first special game of the year. The switch-hitting center fielder's best day of the year was August 20, when he hit three home runs (working from both sides of the plate in the first game) and drove in six runs to help the Sox take two from the Angels at Fenway. Reggie came in second in Rookie of the Year voting.

He improved each of his first three full years, both in average and power. In 1969, he hit .309 with 25 homers and 93 RBIs. His average dipped to .283 in 1971, but he hit 30 homers and drove in 96, leading the league in total bases. Reggie suffered a good deal of racism in Boston, though. Angus writes, "Playing in the outfield, he had to wear a batting helmet to protect himself from hard objects being thrown by his own team's fans." After the 1973 season, the Sox traded him (and Ken Tatum) to the Cardinals for Rick Wise and Bernie Carbo; it was good to get out.

He hit over .300 both of his next two years in St. Louis and made the All-Star team for the third and fourth times. Slumping badly in 1976, he was traded by the Cards to the Dodgers where he began to rebound—and then had two more excellent years (and made two more All-Star squads) in 1977 and 1978, coming in fourth in MVP voting each year. After 5½ seasons with the Dodgers, he finished out his U.S. career with a good year for the San Francisco Giants—and then played a year for the Yomiuri Giants in Japan.

He took up work for the Dodgers again in 1993, becoming minor league field coordinator. It was a step to his work as their major league batting coach, which he did from 1994 through 1999. Smith coached the 2000 U.S. Olympic baseball team that won the Gold Medal, and served as batting coach for the U.S. team in the 2006 World Baseball Classic.

When he returned to Fenway Park for the 2007 Opening Day celebration of the 40th anniversary of the 1967 Impossible Dream Red Sox, Smith revealed that current center fielder Coco Crisp had attended his Los Angeles-based Reggie Smith Baseball Centers back when Crisp was just six or seven years old.

Jim Rice—1974–1989; coach, 1995–2000

Jim Ed Rice was a first-round draft pick of the Red Sox in 1971, and both he and Fred Lynn were dubbed the "Gold Dust Twins" when the two star rookies broke into the Red Sox outfield in the same year, 1975. It was a golden year, too, all the way to Game Seven of the World Series. Sadly, Rice's left hand was broken by a Vern Ruhle pitch in the final week of the regular season and he had to miss the whole postseason. There's little doubt that having Jim Rice on the team might have made a major difference in the 1975 World Series. Fred Lynn (.331/25/105) won both MVP and Rookie of the Year, but Rice (.309/22/102) wasn't far behind—coming in second in league ROY voting and third in MVP.

After a slight sophomore slump, Rice hit his stride and from 1977–79 averaged close to .320, over 40 homers a year, and more than 125 RBIs. No other player in history had 200 hits and 35 homers in three straight years. His single best season—in which he did win the American League Most Valuable Player award—came in 1978, when he hit for 406 total bases—the most any player had hit for since Joe DiMaggio in the 1930s. He had 213 hits, 46 of them for home runs and drove in 139 runs. A broken wrist in 1980 took its toll and he never again quite reached the same heights. His .320 average and 110 RBIs helped propel the Sox to the World Series in 1986. Oddly, he hit .333 but didn't drive in even one run in the Series itself; during the ALCS against the Angels, he only hit .161 but drove in six runs.

From 1987 through 1989, Rice had to undergo knee surgery and also began to experience a deterioration of his eyesight and it had a very negative effect on his batting. After 1989, he had to retire—but has largely worked with the Red Sox in one capacity of another since retiring as a player, including work as hitting coach from 1995–2000 and as a commentator on pre- and post-game NESN broadcasts in more recent years.

Rice was a worthy left-field successor to Ted Williams and Carl Yastrzemski—and he was an individual like his predecessors as well in terms of wanting to play ball on his own terms and not have to play to the media. Because he wound up with a .298 average and 18 home runs short of 400, his determination to march to his own drummer and not be pegged as a symbol for any cause may have hurt his chances for the Hall of Fame. On the cusp of HOF consideration for many years, the point is often made that for a full decade there simply was no hitter more feared in baseball than Jim Rice.

Ellis Burks—1987–1992; 2004

By the time Ellis Burks joined the Red Sox (they selected him in the first round of the 1983 free-agent draft), it was 1987 and the Red Sox had had a number of African-American players on the team—but it wasn't as though they were over-populated with them. There had been a time as recently as that same year, 1983, that for much of the year there was only one U.S.-born black player on the Boston ballclub—Jim Rice. It's not as though there wasn't some diversity, though, in that the Sox had Tony Armas and a couple of utility players. It wasn't much of a stretch, though, for Howard Bryant to write that "the Pinky Higgins Sox of 1961 employed more black position players than the Haywood Sullivan Sox of 1983." A similar scenario presented itself for much of 1990 and part of 1991—if one ignores Tony Peña and Carlos Quintana. Burks was the only African-American on the team until Mo Vaughn joined the club in late June. All that aside, Ellis Burks was an excellent outfielder (and fan favorite) who hit .272, .294, .303, and .296 his first four years with the Red Sox, twice with 20 or more home runs, driving in good numbers and even stealing more than 20 bases each of his first three years. In 1990, he was named to the All-Star team, and earned both a Gold Glove and Silver Slugger. He hit in the .250's both in 1991 and 1992, his popularity waning with his production, and the Sox let him go.

Burks was signed by the White Sox and rebounded, then spent four years with the Colorado Rockies including the spectacular 1996 season when he led the National League in slugging, runs, extra-base hits, and total bases, hitting .344 with 40 homers and 128 RBIs. Not surprisingly, he made the All-Star team and he finished third in MVP voting. After parts of three seasons with the Giants (he again hit .344 in 2000 and had back-to-back years of 96 RBIs in 1999 and 2000) and the Indians (hitting .301 with 91 RBIs in 2002), he was signed by the Red Sox as a free agent in February 2004. He was warmly welcomed back but injuries prevented him appearing in more than 11 games in a disappointing bookend to an 18-year career—but he singled and scored a run in his last game and he does have a World Championship ring from the organization that first signed him.

When the Red Sox desegregated New Orleans baseball

Ironically, given that the Red Sox were the last team to field a black player, they help integrate a major American city when they played two spring training exhibition games in New Orleans' City Park Stadium against the Cleveland Indians on April 9 and 10, 1960. The games put an end to separate seating sections for black and white fans.

The Red Sox had played in New Orleans for years, dating back to a first game on April 7, 1904. The Crescent City even served as their spring training home for three years, 1925–27. The first game in 1925 was on March 6, after completing their first week of spring training with a workout at Heinemann Field. Melville Webb of the *Boston Globe* reported that the drill was "shortened to make way for a game between two teams of colored schools….The Sox watched a picturesque game. Each team brought its band and its contingent of girl rooters, who kept up an incessant racket. The girls were out in Spring regalia, wearing brightest colors and an assortment of chic felt headgear, reds, purples, blues and greens. The jazz music never stopped and throughout the game the rooters were dancing and swaying. It was really a great show." Webb's account of the game between "the dusky nines" makes it appear that the Red Sox team took in the whole affair before returning to their quarters at the Bienville Hotel.

Come 1960, though, times had changed. The Sox had last appeared in New Orleans in 1957, beating the Pelicans 3–0 in a March 31 exhibition game. The Pelicans, meanwhile, had lost their Southern Association standing so the city would be without professional baseball in 1960. When Pelicans president Jack Defee and local sports legend Mel Parnell (retired from his years with the Red Sox) promoted the games between the Indians and the Red Sox, there was a very positive public reaction. The game time was switched to the afternoon in order to accommodate a larger number of out-of-town visitors, too, many of whom were thought to have wanted to also take in the races at Jefferson Downs.

The Civil Rights movement was in full swing and newspapers of the day reported lunch counter sit-ins in a number of Southern states. A week before the game, the *New Orleans Times-Picayune* reported sit-in arrests in Marshall TX, Montgomery AL, Charleston SC, and other places. New Orleans mayor deLesseps Morrison said on April 1 that he "would advise

Negro students not to demonstrate in New Orleans against racially segregated lunchroom fa-cilities." A recent demonstration at Dillard University was described by the mayor as peaceful; he added that it had accomplished nothing other than to have "irritated people." The demon-strators and those that felt similarly were perhaps in some way subhuman. The tone of the mayor's remarks, though, was by no means aggressive or confrontational. The *Times-Picayune* editorialized on April 4 that "Sober thinking Negro students at Southern [University, Baton Rouge] and elsewhere, we hope, will see where they have been misled in connection with the 'sit-ins' at private eating places."

The St. Bernard Parish Citizens Council urged the public to boycott the games because they would constitute an integrated activity, which was—in their view—"in violation of prin-ciples, tradition, and heritage of our way of life in this section of our nation" given that the teams were "composed of mixed players." The council resolution added, "These games would provide a leak in the walls of Southern ways of life and traditions." Likewise, the South Loui-siana Citizens' Council opposed the games: "In the case of an integrated baseball game, we believe the urge to see such a game should be checked. It is a small enough sacrifice to make for the perpetuation of our segregated system and the future interests of our children."

The opposition was such that the Red Sox and Indians considered the possibility of hav-ing to move the games to Houston instead of playing in New Orleans. The night before the game, Parnell met the Red Sox airplane and the team walked on a red carpet into the airport terminal. "There may be a few pickets around," Parnell said, "But the advance sale has been terrific and show that the people want to see these games. I don't expect any trouble." As it transpired, the games were played and without incident.

Despite the couple of resolutions by recognizably racist groups, there was very little indi-cation in the New Orleans papers that there was any true controversy. There was no editorial comment regarding the games—before or after—and there were no letters to the editor. The game accounts in both the *Times-Picayune* and the *New Orleans States and Item* were both very straightforward. There was no reference to race or controversy, nor any indication that there was anything the least bit out of the ordinary. In the first game, Ted Williams hit a single and a double, and Frank Malzone had a couple of hits, too; they drove in two runs each. Leadoff batter Pumpsie Green, though, was 0-for-6. The Indians' Walt Bond hit two home runs and had three RBIs, while Vic Power, Russ Nixon, and Woodie Held each homered for Cleveland as well. The Indians won the Saturday slugfest, 12–8.

Sunday's game saw Tito Francona star for the Indians in a tighter 9–8 win. Francona was 5-for-5 with a double and four singles; he scored twice and drove in four. Gene Stephens was the Red Sox star, with two homers and a double; he also drove in four. It was only in the second day's account that a reference to race occurred when Bond was mentioned: "Bond, 6-foot-7 Negro rookie for the Indians, continued his sensational spring hitting with 3-for-6, including a pair of doubles."

A couple of days later, sports columnist Bill Keefe noted that the games had drawn more than 21,000 fans "for the first time saw large groups of Negroes integrating with whites here and there excepting in the reserved and box seat sections, went off without incident both Sat-urday and Sunday. White fans enjoyed the mighty hitting of Cleveland's giant Negro center fielder, Bond, and the Negro fans applauded the hitting of Tito Francona."

Keefe added, "Integrated play in any branch of sports never will become popular here or in the great majority of Southern cities and towns. Had the seating at City Park Stadium been segregated chances are there would have been a slim turnout of Negroes. On the other hand the white audiences would have been larger. Not that many remained away because of the request of the Citizens' Council to boycott the game; but there are hundreds of white sports fans who do not attend any integrated affair. The big crowds proved that New Orleans sports lovers will patronize a contest that appeals."

The Indians and the Red Sox left town and there had been a minor victory for integration in New Orleans.

Picketing Fenway Park

It wasn't only Doc Kountze and Isadore Muchnick who agitated for integrated baseball in Boston. The pressure built up over the years until it became undeniable. But on April 14, 1959 the Sox still fielded an all-white team for Opening Day. Fans flocking to Fenway encountered a Tufts student, Alvan Levenson, 22 years old of Princeton Road in Brookline, picketing outside the park with two placards, one reading "We Want a Pennant Not a White Team" and the other "Race Hate is Killing Baseball in Boston."

Levenson was a little older than your average college student, having joined the U.S. Marine Corps in 1954 and having served overseas. He wasn't part of any organized effort, hadn't any baseball background, and readily admitted when contacted in 2006 that his motives were mixed. He wasn't a diehard Red Sox fan, and though he believed in the cause, he says as much as anything he did it to impress a girl he was interested in, Paula Cohen. He was, and remains, a "conservative/libertarian" but he says the Fenway picketing did impress her. "What really melted her heart, though, was my willingness to take up a cause on her behalf."

Whatever the motives, Levenson did something that was a courageous enough act, something that put a little extra public pressure on the Red Sox. Every bit contributes. Levenson was attacked outside the park by some "goons" who grabbed the signs and tore them up—but not before a photographer captured his protest, which was depicted on the front page of the next day's *Boston Globe*. The *Globe* story was not particularly supportive, reading, "Outside, there was a minor skirmish as Sox rooters fought to destroy banner charging ballclub with discrimination." Aside from the missing word in the sentence, and the fact that there were two picket signs (placards)—not a banner—evident in the photograph, the wording implied that "Sox rooters" were on one side of the issue and Levenson the other. Levenson was quoted as saying, "For a while, I thought I was down South." He declined to prosecute.

Pumpsie Green made his debut on July 21, 1959.

ASIANS ON THE RED SOX

Wendell Kim

The 20th century was almost over before anyone of Oriental ancestry played for the Red Sox. The first such uniformed man on the field was a coach, though—third-base coach Wendell Kim.

Wendell Kim served from 1997 through 2000. Born in Honolulu, of Korean and Hawaiian descent, he'd been a prospect with the Giants in the 1970s but never made it past Triple A despite hitting .303 in the Pacific Coast League. He began his coaching career in 1980. He was—let's say—an aggressive coach at third, though—to be fair—the coach's degree of aggressiveness is set broadly by the manager.

The Red Sox have hardly ever been known as fleet afoot. Small wonder then that when late 1990s third base coach Wendell Kim sprinted across the diamond on the way to take his position, beating every Sox fielder out, some considered him the fastest runner on the team.

Jin Ho Cho—1998–99

Born in Jun Ju City, the Korean Cho first broke into big league ball with an Independence Day 1998 start against the visiting White Sox. He pitched an excellent game, giving up just one run in six full innings, but with no run support took the ultimate 3–0 loss. His second outing came in Baltimore. It was a disaster and he had to get pulled in the fifth inning, charged with seven earned runs. That got him another loss. Five days later, in Detroit, he was hammered for five earned runs and left the game in the sixth. On July 23, the Red Sox won the game in extra innings against the Blue Jays, but when Cho left the game, it was 4–0 Jays after three innings. The number of earned runs was declining from game to game, but this was clearly a pitcher who needed more work at a lower level of play. Given another opportunity in June 1999, Cho won his first two games while pitching pretty well. As June became July, he started to slip again and, though much better than the previous year, still suffered three more losses and saw his ERA climb over 5.00. Overall, he finished his MLB career 2–6, 6.52.

Tomokazu Ohka—1999–2001

In late November 1998, the Red Sox purchased this pitcher's contract from the Yokohama Bay Stars of Japan's Central League. He was no star for the Bay Stars, with a record of 1–2 and a 5.53 ERA in 32 games for Yokohama. GM Dan Duquette's scouts saw something, though, and Ohka blew through the Red Sox farm system with a record of 11–0. That earned him a callup to the slumping Sox. His U.S. debut came on July 19, 1999. It only lasted for the first inning and two batters in the second. That was enough time for Ohka to lose the game, though to be entirely fair, it was by no means all his fault. Though tagged for five runs in the one-plus inning he pitched, only two of them were earned runs. Three Red Sox errors helped pad the Marlins' run total. The final score was Florida 10, Boston 7.

Over parts of three seasons, Ohka started 25 games for the Red Sox but never had a winning record. At the trading deadline in 2001, he was swapped to Montreal for closer Ugueth Urbina. Since leaving the Red Sox, he's won 44 games (and lost 50) for Montreal, Washington, Milwaukee, and Toronto and remained in major league ball through the 2007 season.

Sang-Hoon Lee—2000

Was Bill Lee, a practicing Buddhist, reincarnated (while he's still alive) as his namesake Korean lefthander Sang-Hoon Lee? The man from Korea was the first ever player to have played professionallly in three countries: Korea, Japan, and the USA. With his long hair dyed orange, the latter Lee was introduced to the media at Fenway, and said, "Bill Lee was crazy. So am I."

Coming to Boston from Korea's LG Twins, there was a photo opportunity as Lee took the mound at Fenway on a wintry day and pretended to throw a couple of pitches over the plate. He reacted as though his first "pitch" had been smashed high over the Green Monster. He then bowed to the Wall. As he threw his second pantomime pitch, he quickly gripped his shoulder faking an injury. At this point in time, the Red Sox were cornering the market in Koreans. They had signed six of the 14 Koreans in American organized baseball. Lee debuted at Fenway, with Boston beating Baltimore in a late June game, 12–3, and gave up a home run and single while getting two outs to close the eighth. Called back up late in the season, his second outing came on September 3 against Seattle. Relieving in a game Ohka started, and lost, Lee pitched a perfect eighth but gave up a two-run homer to A-Rod in the top of the ninth. He relieved in seven more games and only gave up one more earned run, on a sac fly, finishing his first year with a 3.09 ERA. The year, though, was also his last.

Hideo Nomo—2001

It would be hard to make a better impression on your new team than to throw a no-hitter in your first game. That's what Nomo did on April 4, 2001. True, he'd come to the Red Sox with seven years of major league experience (signed as a free agent in December 2000), and he'd been both an All-Star and NL Rookie of the Year for the Dodgers in 1995. It wasn't even his first no-hitter. He'd thrown that on September 17, 1996 against the Rockies at Coors Field. After the AL no-hitter for Boston, many changed his nickname from "Tornado" to "No-No" Nomo. On May 25, only a fourth-inning double marred what would have been another no-hitter, this time against the Blue Jays. Nomo was 13–10 (4.50) with the Red Sox, but he had been signed to just a one-year deal. The Sox weren't anxious to re-sign him, but the Dodgers snapped him back up again and he won 16 games each of the next two years for L.A. After his mid-2005 release by Tampa Bay, the Yankees signed him but he has yet to appear in another big league game. His career shows 123 wins and 109 losses, with a 4.21 ERA and 1,915 strikeouts.

Sun-Woo Kim—2001–02

In the spring of 2000, Korean translator Seung-Hyun Park was kept busy in Fort Myers working primarily with Sang-Hoon Lee, but also helping out Jin Ho Cho and Sun-Woo Kim. Kim had roomed in Trenton with Ohka for a couple of months in 1999. The first of two Kims for the Red Sox hailed from Inchon, South Korea. He was signed as a free agent by Boston in November 1997. Used in relief, until given two starts in his final two 2001 experiences, Sunny Kim threw 41⅔ innings in 20 appearances (0–2, 5.83). He balanced his won-loss record, going 2–0 in 2002 but it wasn't with better pitching. His ERA was 7.45. Just before the trading deadline, the Red Sox swapped him and another Korean pitching prospect, Seung Song, to the Expos to get slugger Cliff Floyd. He's remained a big leaguer, and after the 2006 season had a record of 13–13 (including work with Washington, Colorado, and Cincinnati) and a 5.31 earned run average.

Johnny Damon—2002–05

Johnny Damon was born to a mother from Thailand and a U.S. serviceman father. While on his second tour of duty in Vietnam with the 538th Engineer Batallion, Sgt. Jimmy Damon met Yome who Dan Shaughnessy reports was working clearing up after soldiers on the U.S. base at Satahip. She was less than impressed at first sight; Sgt. Damon apparently weighed around 300 pounds at the time and Daryl Sng found a clipping from a Bangkok newspaper that quoted Yome—daughter of a Thai rice farmer—as recalling, "The first time I see [Jimmy Damon], I say, 'Oooohhh, nobody will marry with him.' I feel sorry for him, because he was real white, he had no hair." The two did come together, got married, and lived on Army bases in Okinawa and in Germany. Their second son, Johnny, was born on the base at Fort Riley, Kansas on November 5, 1973. The "Army brat" and his family finally settled down near Orlando where, according to the website *jockbio.com*, "The children in Johnny's Florida neighborhood were not particularly open-minded. They were mistrustful of a boy who was the product of a mixed-race marriage, especially with parentage from as exotic a locale as Thailand. Johnny was shy and soft-spoken, and would often stutter when he got excited. He endured his share of teasing over the years, but his positive outlook buoyed him during rough times."

If that's what it took, he certainly learned to succeed, drafted in the first round of the 1992 draft by the Kansas City Royals and making his way to the major leagues by 1995. After five full seasons with KC (and an increase in batting average each year), he was traded to Oakland as part of a complicated three-team trade embracing seven ballplayers. After only hitting .256

in 2001 for the Athletics, he was released in November and signed by the Red Sox just before Christmas.

Damon played four seasons for the Sox, becoming a fan favorite with his long hair, devil-may-care play, and his contributions to the 2004 World Championship. Knocked unconscious for several minutes during the final game of the 2003 Division Series against Oakland, he recovered in time for the third game of the ALCS, but struggled a bit. In 2004, he just was 3-for-33 against the Yankees in the replay of the League Championship Series before exploding for two home runs—the first, a grand slam—and six RBIs on three hits in the decisive Game Seven. He hit .286 with one homer in the World Series, and hit an excellent .316 with the Red Sox in 2005.

Declining to offer as much as the Yankees felt he was worth, the Red Sox parted company with one of the self-described "idiots" who won the World Series, and Damon became de-monized in the eyes of many Sox fans. It's hard to blame someone for taking such an over-the-top offer as he was given, though Sox fans felt better when his average fell nearly 30 points in his first year in New York (he did hit a career-best 24 homers, though). In 2007, he saw a further decline in production.

While the Yankees were courting Damon, so was Thai Prime Minister Thaksin Shinawa-tra—who wanted to bring Johnny to Thailand to run baseball clinics. The prime minister took Yome Damon to dinner in Washington to press his case. *Newsday* reported Johnny as saying, "She was definitely very excited" and Yome as commenting, "In my country, they don't know baseball. They want him to go to my country and show the kids how to play the game." As it happens, Thaksin announced his resignation in April 2006 after months of political turmoil amid allegations of cronyism and corruption.

Benny Agbayani—2002

Agbayani was born in Honolulu to parents of Filipino ancestry and is the only non-pitcher among the ethnically Oriental ballplayers to have played for Boston. Agbayani came to the Sox from the Mets, via the Rockies. With the Mets, he'd been an occasional star—most notable among his 35 home runs for New York being his pinch-hit grand slam in the top of the 11th inning, winning the Opening Day 2000 ballgame. The Mets had beaten the Cubs in Japan, as MLB kicked off the year in the faraway Tokyo Dome.

After four seasons with the Mets, Benny was part of a complicated three-team trade in January 2002 involving 11 players and cash. He was only hitting .205 for the Rockies when claimed on waivers by Boston on August 26. Agbayani started in left field and singled twice with three RBIs in his first Sox game. By season's end, he was batting .297 with just one extra-base hit in 37 at-bats. That proved to be the end of his time in the majors.

Bruce Chen—2003

Born in Panama City, Bruce Chen was a left-hander who'd pitched in the National League since 1998 for the Braves, Phillies, Mets, Expos, Reds, and Astros. The Red Sox took him off waivers from Houston in May 2003. He only appeared in an undistinguished five games for the Red Sox (0–1, 5.11), his final game coming on May 27. After toiling in the minors, he was granted free agency in October and signed by Baltimore; he was 2–1 in 2004 and 13–10 in 2005, before sliding to an 0–7 season he'd likely just as soon forget in 2006.

Byung-Hyun Kim—2003–04

A pitcher with more than a few moments he'd prefer to forget was Byung-Hyun Kim. The for-mer Olympic gold medalist for the 2000 Korean national team was an often-brilliant sidearm and submarine pitcher. He'd first come to national attention, though, when he was pitching for Arizona in the 2001 World Series. In Game Four, Kim gave up a ninth-inning home run to the Yankees' Tino Martinez and a game-winning homer to Derek Jeter in the 10th. The very next night, Scott Brosius hit a two-run homer in the ninth to tie Game Five. The back-to-back failures to save Series games at least didn't cost the Diamondbacks the World Championship but they left a potentially-shattered pitcher. He had saved one game in the NLDS and two in the NLCS. B.K. bounced back in 2002, though, making the All-Star team and posting an 8–3 record with a 2.04 ERA. He started off 2003 pretty poorly, with a 1–5 mark and Arizona traded him to the Red Sox at the end of May for Shea Hillenbrand. Kim was 8–5 (3.18) for the Red Sox and was signed to a perhaps unnecessarily lavish two-year deal to come back as a starter in 2004. Not much came of it (2–1, 6.23) though there were a couple of peevish moments, including him giving the finger to some fans who were giving him the business. Just before the 2005 season got underway, the Sox sent him to Colorado for Charles Johnson and Chris Narveson. In other words, they tried to get what they could. B.K. pitched for the Rockies in 2005 and 2006, losing 12 games each season, winning five and then winning eight. In 2007, he pitched for Colorado, Arizona, and Florida (a combined 10–8, 6.08 ERA).

Dave Roberts (デーブ　ロバーツ)—2004

David Ray Roberts was born on May 31, 1972, at Naha, Okinawa—part of Japan. Three months after his birth, his parents moved to the United States, but Dave remains proud of his ancestry.

A 47th-round draft pick of the Indians in 1993, he elected not to sign and was drafted by the Tigers in the 28th round the following year. This time, he signed within a week—but after four years of development in the Detroit system, was traded to the Indians, in June 1998. He debuted in the majors in August 1999, but saw only limited duty with Cleveland (165 at-bats) in his first three seasons. In 2002, he became a regular outfielder for the Dodgers after being dealt to them in a pre-season trade. Two and a half years with the Dodgers saw him get some work—and an honor in April 2004 when the team celebrated Japanese American Community Night on April 28.

"The Dodger organization is proud to honor and recognize those individuals, and more specifically, those baseball players, who have helped build relationships between the two countries," said owner Frank McCourt. "Beginning with the Dodgers' goodwill trips to Japan in 1956 and 1966 and continuing today with players like Hideo Nomo, Kazuhisa Ishii, and Dave Roberts, the Dodgers have shared a long and storied history with Japan."

Roberts was born to Eiko and Waymon Roberts, his father an African-American Marine and his mother a Japanese citizen. Both parents are members of the Okinawa Association of America and Dave himself has attended OAA events, as well as traveled on a number of occasions to Okinawa. In 2007, he told A. J. Hayes of *Asian Week* magazine, "I get so much support there, from my relatives to the Japanese people I encounter there," Roberts said. "I love going there and just hanging out. It's a special feeling—it's my heritage." Hayes added that during his major league career, Roberts has been teammates with a number of Japanese players like Nomo, Ishii, and the Padres' Akinori Otsuka. "I speak a little Japanese, but I mainly struggle with the language. Yet there has been a special bond with some of the guys. There's definitely a camaraderie that exists," Roberts said.

When signed by the San Francisco Giants for the 2007 season, Roberts said, "My mom was pretty excited about the move up here. She loves the culture of San Francisco and its Asian American influence. It's exciting because my grandparents and aunts and uncles back in Okinawa will be traveling to the States this summer to watch me play for the first time in the major leagues. I identify with my nationality and my heritage, but I am who I am. It's great to acknowledge your heritage, but I try to pride myself on being Dave Roberts. I treat people the same way regardless of where they're from." He hit .260 in 398 at-bats for the Giants.

Red Sox fans only saw Dave Roberts briefly, but there's one big play they'll never forget. He came to Boston at the trading deadline, for Henri Stanley. And played well, driving in 14 runs in 86 at-bats. He stole five bases—during the regular season. In the playoffs, Roberts had one pinch-running appearance in the Division Series, but was forced at second. His next appearance produced "The Steal." Bottom of the ninth of the fourth game of the League Championship Series, with the Red Sox losing 4–3 and facing being swept in four straight by the Yankees. Kevin Millar walked. Roberts ran for Millar. Everyone knew his assignment was to steal second. He did. And scored the tying run when Bill Mueller singled to center.

He next appeared in Game Five less than 24 hours later and, though he didn't steal as a pinch runner, he did (again) score the fourth and tying run in the bottom of the eighth, the game being resolved in the bottom of the 14th with another Red Sox win. In December, the Red Sox traded him to San Diego for three players and cash to boot. But Dave Roberts' place in Red Sox history was secure.

Red Sox players who played professional baseball in Japan during their careers

Not to mention those raised in Japan, the list includes:

Yomiuri Giants: Hector Almonte, Gabe Kapler, Shane Mack, Jeff Manto, Roberto Petagine, Tuffy
    Rhodes (also played with the Kintetsu Buffaloes), Reggie Smith, John Wasdin.
Hanshin Tigers: Jamie Brown, Rob Deer, Mike Greenwell, Larry Parrish, Andy Sheets
Seibu Lions: Greg Blosser, Scott Cooper, Reggie Jefferson, Rudy Pemberton,
Fukuoka Daiei Hawks: Morgan Burkhart, Kevin Mitchell, Bryant Nelson
Chiba Lotte Marines: Benny Agbayani, Wes Chamberlain
Hokkaido Nippon Ham Fighters: Kip Gross, Ryan Rupe
Yokohama BayStars: Mike Holtz, Lou Merloni
Willie Banks played with the Orix Blue Wave and Andy Abad played for Osaka's Kintetsu Buffaloes, as
    had Tuffy Rhodes as noted above.

And recent Red Sox fans will remember that Kevin Millar had signed to play with the Chunichi Dragons, but was pried loose by Theo Epstein and instead inspired the Red Sox to "cowboy up" in 2003 and helped win the World Series in 2004.

From 2001–04, Chang-Ho Lee served as assistant trainer for the Red Sox, the latter three seasons traveling with the big league team. He was, as well, able to help with translation work.

Daisuke Matsuzaka—2007–08

Sox fans have begun to benefit from one of the team's largest investments of all time. They guaranteed a posting fee of $51.1 million to Japan's Seibu Lions just for the right to attempt to negotiate a contract with Daisuke Matsuzaka, then signed him for a marginally-higher $52 million.

In his first year with the Red Sox, amidst an unrelenting swirl of media attention, Matsuzaka-san started 32 games and wound up with a 15–12 record (4.40 ERA) in 204⅔ innings of work. He led the team in strikeouts with 201 (and 80 walks), but surrendered 25 homers. After a 7–3 start, but a relatively high ERA, his best month came in five June starts that lacked run support (2–2, 1.59 ERA). He tired as the longer American season went on, and had a rough September. Dice-K started three playoff games (1–1 with a high 5.65 ERA), the win coming in Game Seven of the League Championship Series against the Indians. In Game Three at Coors Field, the first Japanese starter in a World Series game won the game, throwing 5⅓ innings and also batting 1-for-3, driving in two runs with a bases-loaded single to left field scoring teammates Mike Lowell and Jason Varitek with the fourth and fifth runs of a six-run inning in the 10–5 win over the Rockies. It's not surprising he was error-free throughout; he won six Golden Gloves with the Seibu Lions.

Hideki Okajima—2007–08

A bigger surprise in 2007, though, was ace relief pitcher Hideki Okajima whose was a relatively unheralded signing. Yet Okajima, with his trademark "okey-dokey" pitch, hit the Series stage before teammate Matsuzaka when he became the first Japanese pitcher to appear in a World Series game with his 2⅓ innings of flawless relief work in Game Two of the 2007 Series against the Colorado Rockies. Of the seven Rockies he faced, the left-handed Okajima struck out four. On the strength of his spectacular start to the season, Okajima-san was named to the All-Star squad but did not appear. His record for the regular season was 3–2 (2.22 ERA), throwing 69 innings in 66 games, striking out 63 batters while walking only 17. His WHIP (walks and hits per innings pitched was 0.97, the only Sox pitcher save Jonathan Papelbon under 1.

Okajima threw 11 postseason innings in 2007, with an earned run average of 2.45.

Internationalism and the Red Sox

The Red Sox have clearly come a long way and the team sometimes seems like a United Nations of baseball. For instance, look at this list of six pitchers:

Tomo Okha—Japan
Hipolito Pichardo—Dominican Republic
Rheal Cormier—Canada
Rich Garces—Venezuela
Rod Beck—United States
Derek Lowe—United States

These six pitchers, in this order, all appeared on the Fenway Park mound on the evening of September 19, 2000 helping win a 7–4 ballgame over the Cleveland Indians.

The 2007 ballclub included—not uncommonly these days—players born in the United States, Puerto Rico, Dominican Republic, Japan, Canada, Nicaragua, and Jacoby Ellsbury, a member of the Colorado River Indians Tribe of the Navajo Nation.

THE FIRST WOMAN WHO PLAYED AT FENWAY PARK

"Batting and playing first base for the Boston Red Sox: Mary Elizabeth Murphy. First base: Murphy." You can almost hear Sherm Feller announce her—the first female ballplayer for the Boston Red Sox. It never happened, though.

It's well-known that the Red Sox were the last big league team to have an African-American player. Today they have a different opportunity—the chance to pioneer by fielding the first woman ballplayer in the major leagues. To date, there has only been one woman who played baseball with a team of major leaguers in a big league ballpark. Her name was indeed Mary Elizabeth Murphy but she played against the Red Sox at Fenway Park. Her team beat the Red Sox, 3–2.

The year was 1922, and the date August 14. The occasion was Tom McCarthy Day—an exhibition game played at Fenway Park. The game was scheduled to benefit ailing but very popular former ballplayer Tommy McCarthy. The *Globe* called him "one of the greatest outfielders in the game, and who for many years has been close to the hearts of the Boston fans." As it happens, Tommy died just a couple of weeks before the benefit. Babe Ruth, who had committed to play for the All-Star team, had an operation to remove an abscess from his left leg just a couple of days beforehand; his leg had become infected after a rough slide on the basepaths. Otherwise, Babe would have played on the same team as Lizzie Murphy. The benefit proceeded nonetheless, now to create a fund to help McCarthy's daughters. Tommy McCarthy was widely admired among his fellow players and was an early Hall of Fame inductee. He was added to the National Baseball Hall of Fame in 1946.

Lizzie Murphy, the first woman to play ball at Fenway Park. Courtesy of National Baseball Hall of Fame.

Lizzie Murphy was herself pretty well known in New England at the time. This was an era where women were making great strides in a number of areas. It was in August just two years earlier, in 1920, when the 19th Amendment to the Constitution was ratified, granting women the right to vote. Women were active in sports, and newspapers of the day often featured sports page headlines regarding women's tennis, swimming, and other sports. Lizzie Murphy was a novelty, for sure, and a gate attraction. She was also a very good baseball player. A Rhode Island native, she'd played with a number of baseball teams for some years, including the Providence Independents. In 1918, she signed with semipro team owner Ed Carr of Boston, who announced on her signing, "No ball is too hard for her to scoop out of the dirt, and when it comes to batting, she packs a mean wagon tongue." With Ed Carr's All-Stars, she played a hundred games a summer, reports Barbara Gregorich in her book *Women At Play*. Lizzie played in games throughout all the New England states and the eastern provinces of Canada. She had a 17-year career and became known as the "Queen of Baseball."

At Fenway Park, though, it was to be Queen for a day. Tommy McCarthy had most recently served as a Red Sox scout and the team helped organize his "Day" working with a local committee headed by Jack Morse and John S. Dooley, chairman [see more on John Dooley elsewhere in this book]. Quite a day was prepared, including a presentation of vaudeville prior to the game—and "dancing girls" from the Love and Kisses Company. Other entries from the Bowdoin Square theater and the Old Howard entertained. When the band struck up "Sweet Adeline" the demand for Former Mayor "Honey Fitz" Fitzgerald to sing was so fervent and so persistent that he yielded to the call of the 4,000 or more in attendance, a crowd which included Mayor James Michael Curley and others. Congressman Gallivan was there and so were former ballplayers such as John Irwin and Jerry Hurley.

Nick Altrock worked the crowd, not only joining in the theatrical numbers but selling scorecards in the stands and shaking hands with several hundred children. Altrock was the star of the show, and the game.

Lizzie's appearance had been trumpeted in advance but, given the uniqueness of the situation, not extravagantly so. Paul Shannon, writing in the *Boston Post*, gave her two sentences: "Lizzie Murphy, the famous lady first baseman, will be seen in the game for a while. She won't launch any home runs but lady fans will get a peek at a sister who can cover that initial sack as many a big leaguer." Another paper called her "the brilliant woman first baseman."

As noted, Babe Ruth couldn't make it but the All-Star team Lizzie joined included: Nick Altrock, Donie Bush, and "Sheriff" Earl Smith from the Senators; Tillie Walker, Pep Young, Frank Bruggy, Bob Hasty, and Doc Johnston of the A's; Chick Shorten of the Browns; Ira Flagstead of the Tigers; Les Nunamaker and Jim Bagby of the Indians; Harry McClellan of the White Sox and Fred Hoffman of the Yankees. Every ballclub in the American League was represented. Lizzie started the game at first base, batting third in the order.

She was tested early on. The visitors, of course, were up first. Allan Russell was pitching for the Red Sox and he set down second baseman Pep Young and the shortstop Donie Bush. Lizzie Murphy stepped into the box. Two outs, no one on base. She hit a grounder to Boston's Johnny Mitchell at short and was retired. Mitchell, though, chose to showboat a bit throwing the ball first to the second baseman Del Pratt who then fired to "Tioga George" Burns at first. *Boston Globe* writer James O'Leary took him to task in his game story the next day: "It was rather ungallant of Mitchell to play it this way."

Boston batting in the bottom of the first, against Jim Bagby, her own teammate McClellan chose to challenge her as well. On a sharp grounder hit to him, he fielded it cleanly, but then deliberately held the ball until the last moment and then fired a rocket to Murphy. She caught it for the putout. Gregorich reports that McClellan walked over towards Donie Bush, nodded in the direction of first base and said, "She'll do."

Murphy played just the one inning. The All-Stars scored in top of the second. The Sox scored twice in the fifth, only to see the All-Stars come back to tie it in the sixth. Nick Altrock cut the clowning, came in to pitch, and held the Red Sox scoreless for the final four innings, the visiting All-Stars winning it 3–2 in 10 innings. Doc Johnston, who had taken Lizzie's place at first, tripled in the winning run. This was not a strong Red Sox team. In fact, they finished the season in last place, 33 games out, with a 61–93 record. No wonder, then, that the *Globe*'s sports cartoon the next day depicted Lizzie making the play and one spectator calling to another, "Attaboy! Lizzie better than the Red Sox."

Babe Didrikson Zaharias

There was one other time a woman featured as a player in a Red Sox game. It was in 1934 in spring training. The woman was premier athlete Babe Didrikson Zaharias. Unfortunately, she also played against the Sox. A gold medal Olympic track star, she excelled at other sports as well and in 1934 signed with the House of David touring baseball team. That spring she appeared in a number of preseason exhibition games, competing on the field with major league ballplayers, usually as a pitcher. In some games, she acquitted herself pretty well; in others, she did not. She may have been a better hitter, though, than a hurler. Her appearance against the Red Sox was on March 22, 1934 and she didn't last long. She was throwing for the St. Louis Cardinals in a game in Bradenton and manager Frankie Frisch gave her the starting role. The 1934 edition of the Red Sox—the team played .500 ball in the regular season to come—touched Didrikson up for three singles and a double, scoring three runs before she (apparently) completed the inning. Actually, she hadn't pitched any worse than Fritz Ostermueller of Boston who yielded three himself in the bottom of the first and another three in the second. Unfortunately, this Babe never did get an at-bat. Her replacement—Bill Hallahan—gave up four runs himself in the fifth inning. The Cardinals won in the end, though, 9–7—as Dizzy Dean blanked them the final four innings. Ostermueller walked six, Hallahan walked five. Even Dean walked two. Didrikson didn't walk a batter.

There was apparently a time when a woman actually batted on the field in the middle of a major league ball game. July 13, 1935, when the Cardinals hosted the Cubs, one of their fans named Kitty Burke snuck onto the field, picked up a bat and ran into the batter's box, where

Daffy Dean threw her a ball. She grounded out, and Frankie Frisch, Cardinals manager, argued it should count as an at-bat. Cincinnati won the game 4–3, in 10 innings, after St. Louis tied the game in the ninth. She's not in the box score, though. And it didn't count.

The Red Sox once played a game against Albert Schweitzer

No, not the famed German philosopher, physician, missionary, and humanitarian. This particular Albert Schweitzer was known by the nickname "Cheese" and was a right fielder for the St. Louis Browns. He figured in Smoky Joe Wood's July 29, 1911 no-hitter against the St. Louis Browns, batting third and going 0-for-3.

Pardon the brief interlude. We return now to our discussion of women and the Red Sox. But, no, first, one more odd twist.

Smoky Joe Wood, Bloomer Girl

One of the great Red Sox pitchers, Smoky Joe Wood, began his professional career wearing a dress—or at least wearing bloomers. As Peter Golenbock has written, "At age 16, he was paid $20 a game to dress up like a woman and pitch for the Bloomer Girls, the most famous women's team of the day." Now that's something Roger Clemens never did.

It maybe wasn't something Joe liked to talk about, but Harvey T. Woodruff uncovered the story in the November 10, 1912 *Chicago Tribune*. There was more than one team of "Bloomer Girls" that toured the country, teams of women often including a few men, who barnstormed and took on opponents along the way. In her book *Women At Play*, Barbara Gregorich reports that in the 1890s, "scores of women's baseball teams sprang up across the country, calling themselves Bloomer Girls after the clothing they wore." Named after Amelia Bloomer, this was a costume of a skirt over

Detail from sports page cartoon showing Joe Wood as one of baseball's Bloomer Girls.

loose trousers which could be used by women in athletic competitions and be sufficiently modest for the times. According to Gregorich, it seems that Boston had another championship team in 1903: the Boston Bloomer Girls won 28 games in a 26-day stretch.

Joe Wood was in Ness City, Kansas when a tour company of Bloomer Girls came into the small community about 325 miles west of Kansas City. In a September 1906 game, the barnstorming women's team was beaten, 19–1, largely because their customarily more potent bats were silenced by the 17-year-old Wood. The catcher-manager of the team, also male, approached Wood. Joe asked his father, who gave his consent. "He thought it was sort of unusual," Joe told Lawrence Ritter, "But he didn't raise any objections. I guess it must have appealed to his sense of the absurd." Wood was assigned the name "Lucy Tolton," fitted for a wig, and fitted out in bloomers. Joe was spotted by a scout for Cedar Rapids, who signed him up, soon tranferring his contract to the Hutchinson Salt Packers of the Western Association, and he was on his way to the Boston Red Sox.

Joe Wood's sister Zoe was the first woman to appear in a Red Sox team photo. She's perched on Joe's shoulder in a 1912 team photograph.

As a side note, there were occasional incidents that cropped up. In July 1911 in Providence, a visiting team beat a local ballclub, 13–11, before a "big crowd of well behaved mill operatives and country folks [who] looked on and applauded the fine fielding by the girls." Some local boys took offense at the five-cent admission charge and cut down a canvas fence that had been erected as a turnstile, and then tore down the tent in which the girls were to change. There resulted a "shower of turf, hunks of mud, stones, eggs, and all sorts of vegetables" hurled at the girls. Local businesspeople called it a disgrace and chastised the lack of proper police protection.

Zoe Wood, Smoky Joe's sister—the first woman in a Red Sox team photo. 1912. Courtesy of Mike Foster.

Bloomer Girls teams are reported into the 1950s, right up through the era of the All-American Girls Professional Baseball League (1943–1954), and one can even find a bit of a Negro Leagues equivalent: one finds the Colored Bloomer Girls playing in Chicago in 1917 and the Athenas, a "crack colored girls team" beating the Mexican Bloomer Girls in El Paso, 6–3.

And Smoky Joe wasn't even the only Red Sox player to have been a Bloomer Girl. When one or two men played with a team of barnstorming women ballplayers, they were known as "toppers", Leslie Heaphy reports, because of the curly wigs they wore atop their own hair.

Dick Hoblitzell was a Bloomer Girl, too. As author Tom Simon has written, "Dick was not getting along with his stepmother, so he accepted an invitation to join a barnstorming Bloomer Girls team to get away from her." Hoblitzell's daughter Connie Michael says that Dick's father ended up having to retrieve him somewhere in Pennsylvania and bring him back home.

Female fans

While no woman has yet played for the Red Sox, the team has a great number of female fans. The fan base has come a long way from the early days when many fewer women came to the ballpark. On normal game days as recently as the early 1960s, it would be rare to find even 10% of the fans as female.

There were exceptions, and special Ladies Day promotions were designed to attract women to the park. One such was wildy successful—the August 26, 1938 doubleheader in which Jimmie Foxx obtained his 2,000th hit. The reported attendance was 26,800 and about half of them were women, drawn in part by the 10 cents admission price. The *Globe* reported that so many women turned out that the grandstand gates had to be closed before game time. It said that the "scream day" customers "were so numerous that many men anxious to pay the $1.10 to sit in the grandstand were refused permission." An estimated 6,000 to 7,000 prospective male ticket purchasers couldn't get near the ticket windows. And "for the first time in Sox history, some of the fanettes were forced to watch their idols from seats in the pavilion and bleachers." Given that only in 2007 did the Red Sox approach restroom parity, one can only imagine the lines inside the park during the doubleheader. Though Chicago won the first game, 12–2, almost everyone stayed and were rewarded with a 9–8 victory in 10 innings in the second game.

There have been remarkable fans in days gone by, perhaps the earliest regular Red Sox female fan being one Lucy Swift of New Bedford, Massachusetts who—scorebook in hand—took in as many as four or five games a week dating back to the pre-Red Sox days in the 1880s. Donald Dewey located an unsourced clipping in Hall of Fame files which noted her death in 1943. The news item says that in 1905 she moved to Trinity Court in Boston. The clipping read: "Today in New Bedford, Miss Lucy Swift, 81, will be buried, and baseball has lost in her one of its most faithful and colorful fans. As a little girl in a whaling family of repute in New Bedford, she started going to ball games because her mother would not allow her two brothers to go unless they took along Lucy…. For several decades she had lived in Back Bay's Trinity Court, right near the depot from which the Sox and the Braves would often start their road trips through the West. Every time they left, she watched them from her apartment window, waved them goodbye and wished them luck, even though they did not know she was giving them a fare-thee-well."

Another prominent fan was Lolly Hopkins. And then there was Elizabeth Dooley, who virtually never missed a home game for over half a century beginning right after World War II. There was some overlap between the two (Ms. Hopkins died in 1959) but they were of such different personalities that one wonders if they had much contact with each other.

Lolly Hopkins was a devoted fan who commuted to Fenway from Providence for decades. Author Fred Lieb says she "buys the same reserved seat for every game"—suggesting that she didn't have season tickets, but chose instead to buy them a game at a time. Mrs. Lillian Hopkins typically attended three games a week, traveling by train from Rhode Island's capitol to that of Massachusetts and sitting in section 14, row 1, seat 24. She'd begun coming to Red Sox games with her father back in the years of the Huntington Avenue Grounds. In 1944, to reward her years of loyalty, the Red Sox presented her with a season's pass. She was maybe a bit of a loudmouth (we say that respectfully—*The Sporting News* labeled her the "Hub's No. 1 Howler") and brought a megaphone with her to ensure she could be heard—and she made sure they heard her. The megaphone was a 1939 gift from fellow fan Smokey Kelleher who thought it would save her voice. It only made her louder, and Kelleher switched his season tickets to the third base side! Hopkins kept a grayish-green megaphone at Fenway and a red one at Braves Field, stored by sympathetic ushers.

Lolly Hopkins with her megaphone. Courtesy of Bob Brady.

Lieb added, "She really gives the visiting players a going over." Tommy

Holmes was her favorite on the Braves and Joe Cronin her favorite Red Sox player until he retired from play. She then "adopted" Bobby Doerr. Johnny Pesky recalls hearing her over the crowd, "There's my Bobby!" It can be said now; Johnny adds, "Bobby would cringe." Her nickname may have derived from her practice of tossing candy to the players. Her husband would come to some games, but he said he preferred keeping out of the spotlight. Ed Walton reports that in 1950, she even purchased space on a rooftop billboard overlooking Fenway Park; the message read "Let's Go Sox." Mark Sweeney, a former crowd control supervisor at Fenway, recalls her as "a very tall woman with a Barbie-type haircut." Dan Shaughnessy reports that a number of young girls began to come to games with her and they became known as the Lollypop Gang.

Elizabeth Dooley was, by contrast, a much quieter and arguably more dignified figure. She carried a "business card" wih her name and number, and the Red Sox logo, on which she identified herself as "A Friend of the Red Sox." That she was. She worked as a public schoolteacher, but she had rarely missed a game since 1944 up until her passing in the year 2000. Did she have a favorite player? Maybe not. That was part of what it meant to her to be a "friend of the Red Sox." Tempted to boo a player? Not if you knew and respected Lib Dooley.

She was a fixture and a true Red Sox fan, seated in the very front row of Box 36 (row A, seat 3). She knew everyone, it seemed—from the players (and their families) to the umpires who might leave a water bottle in her care so they could have a drink between innings, to many of the personnel in the park who looked after her. Jack Rogers, the old traveling secretary, drove her home after every night game. She was not the longest-standing season ticket holder, but was #2. Number 1 was "Kelly" Giglio (real name Ignatius Giglio, but he used to be a tire salesman and sold a lot of Kelly Tires and this acquired a permanent nickname). Kelly's son Richard played the organ at Fenway for a number of years in the late 1990s and into the 21st century.

The Red Sox actually moved the Fenway Park on-deck circle once, because of Lib. Or, more precisely, the position where the batboy kneels during game action. The batboys would kneel right in front of her seats. They used to kneel about five or 10 feet away, but one time Lib spotted a fan reaching over the wall and stealing a couple of baseballs from the bag they keep to supply fresh baseballs to the umpires. Former schoolteacher that she was, she chastized the man for setting a bad example to his son. She also notified park security. Since she never missed a game, and never left her seat during the game, the Sox had the batboys kneel in front of her so she could keep a watchful eye.

A great friend of Ted Williams, we may never know the whole story, but she told this author that she used to have a system of hand signals for him whereby (back in his playing days) she could signal her own personal approval or disapproval of women in the stands on which he had his eye. I wanted to ask more, but decided to favor discretion. Lib continued to mail Ted gift packages of fruit throughout the years.

I visited with her often, since her seats are just about 10 rows in front of mine and a few feet over towards the dugout. She always took care of those batboys, too, with a little plastic tray she'd set on the rail. She'd put some cookies up on the tray, in case they wanted a little sweet. Later in the game, she would put up bite-size Milky Ways or other candies. She told me she didn't want to spoil them with candy before the later innings!

She was opinionated, but she shared her opinions privately. She didn't like to speak ill of the Red Sox. She remained, always, a classy woman. When Dan Shaughnessy wrote an appreciation of Miss Dooley in the *Boston Globe*, he quoted a relative regarding her thoughts about the Yankees: "'Dislike' was the word she used for the Yankees. She never used the word hate, but she felt very strongly about the Yankees." See also the section on her father John S. Dooley elsewhere in this book.

The Woman in Red

The Woman in Red: Clif Keane's front page *Boston Globe* story on April 11, 1967 was headlined "Sox Open With Hope, High Praise." The temperature at Fenway Park that day was 35 degrees, with winds gusting to 40 mph. The game was postponed due to cold. The Yankees won their game in Washington, though, and took first place. The second attempt found temperatures had risen to 46 degrees and the gusts had moderated to just 20 mph. The game went on. Some 8,324 fans braved the conditions and saw Boston beat Chicago, 5–4. Feature columnist Diane White wrote a front page story in the *Globe*, which bore the headline "Red Sox Win, Optimism Runs Rampant." White cited a good omen: the "Lady in Red" was back. Though a dedicated fan of long tenure, Mrs. Carter S. Knight of Peabody had declined to come to Opening Day in 1965 or 1966 because she was "disgusted with their half-hearted performance." But she was giving the new-look team a chance: "I like Dick Williams' style of play. They really look better under the new leadership."

Kathryn Gemme

Not all fans attend the ballpark on a regular basis, but that doesn't diminish their fandom. Take Kathryn Gemme, interviewed by this author at age 109. The paragraphs that follow were written in midsummer 2003 and are, in places, obviously dated—given the fact of the 2004 and 2007 World Championships.

Red Sox fans are renowned for their loyalty and longevity (as in "long-suffering Red Sox fan"). While it's a commonplace to cite the number of years since the Sox last won a World Series, and the "19–18" taunt is often heard during Boston visits to Yankee Stadium, there really aren't that many people still living who recall that 1918 World Series. What about someone who recalls the 1903 World Series—the first World Series ever held?

Kathryn Gemme turned 108 years old in November 2002. She was born on November 9, 1894 and was almost nine years old when Jimmy Collins, Cy Young, Bill Dinneen and others won the 1903 World Series for Boston. And in 2003, she is more of a Red Sox rooter than ever before, a knowledgeable and dedicated fan who loves to put her Sox on.

Mid-season 2002, Ms. Gemme entered the Atrium Nursing Center in Middleboro, Massachusetts and soon encountered Sharon Gosling, the center's activities director who claims for herself the title of the "second biggest Red Sox fan" in the facility.

Kathryn has a Red Sox beanie baby that she holds while watching games. Registered nurse Jan Risgin says of Kathryn, "She pops popcorn and watches the game. She watched that game last night [August 27] and was spitting nails," Risgin said [referring to a 6–0 shutout at the hands of the New York Yankees]. "She's always talking about Braves Field. She saw Lou Gehrig play and thought he was amazing. Babe Ruth, she saw him play…but then he went to *that team*."

Kathryn Gemme at age 109 with her Varitek photo. Bill Nowlin photo.

That team. She's no Yankees fan. Don't get her started. "The Yankees, they were always our enemy. I hate them. You know who I was glad to see out of the Yankees? Paul O'Neill. He was crabby. And that Clemens. I wish they'd string him up. The way he holds that ball and looks at it. What does he think he's seeing?"

"Kate" Gemme is a diehard Sox fan—and not ready to expire just yet. Once the Sox were eliminated in 2002, she said, "I must just be waiting for them to win another one." She's healthy—the only medicine she takes, reports nurse Risgin, are "baby aspirin and a vitamin."

She's followed baseball for years and years. And years. If there's a game on, it's a priority. "Something gets ahold of you. The radio, the announcing…you could picture yourself at the game. Even when I was at home in my 80s, if people came calling, I'd have to tell them, 'There's a game on, you know.' I'd be listening to the game, not listening to what they were saying."

She has her favorite Red Sox players these days and she shows a real understanding of the game. Two favorites of today are Nomar Garciaparra and Jason Varitek. Of Nomar, she says "Nomar—that's MY exercise! Heel and toe. Heel to toe! Nomar. We have accepted Nomar. He is everybody's favorite, he's a natural at what he does, he doesn't thump his chest, and he makes watching baseball thrilling."

Catchers have always fascinated her. Sharon Gosling explains that Kathryn admires them for the role they play in the game, "calling the throws, the continuous movement, well, just the responsibility in general. She admires Jason Varitek for his confidence, the way he portrays himself, his positive attitude, and the fact he is always ready." Sharon and Kathryn share a private joke about Varitek and the way he squats behind the plate, a bit of private humor shared between two women. "Varitek. I just like him," Kathryn says. "When he squats. He seems so confident. I like the way he calls the pitches. They don't shake him off very often."

That's perceptive, and accurate. Pitchers rarely do shake off Jason Varitek. She's observant about other matters, too. "Did you notice what Daubach does before he hits? Takes his hat off and rubs his head three times." This is a woman who's tuned in to the Red Sox.

How long has she been a Red Sox fan? At first, she followed the Boston Braves. "Since I knew anything about baseball, I've followed it. Since I was 14 years old. It was the Braves, the Braves. I was born in Chicopee Falls, my home town. I went to school with Rabbit Maranville. He went to Springfield High School and I was in Chicopee just on the border. We got to know each other. He was a cute little guy. And he had that vest pocket catch!

"Back then, baseball was just a game to me. Hitting the ball and running. It wasn't until I got older that I realized why they would pass anybody [give an intentional walk]. I used say to myself, 'The damn fool put him on base for nothing.'"

Kathryn does recall the first World Series, though only dimly. "Rah-rah-rah. I knew about it. When you're nine years old…until I was 14, you don't pay attention." She has similarly vague memories of the Red Sox triumphs in 1912, 1915 and 1916—and if she's right about being 18 at the time, she attended her first game the year after Fenway Park opened. "We were young kids. 18 years old. We went on a trolley car. I just know they won a lot of them—but they haven't won for a long time. In 1918, I was 23 and I was raising my children, but I listened to the game on the radio when my husband tuned in. I never forgot the Red Sox. We saw Babe Ruth play. He was a pitcher. I remember him in knickers, and the little steps running to first base. It's a vivid memory. If Babe Ruth was alive today, he'd be my age.

"My mother was just a plain ordinary woman. She died very young at age 39. My dad was a mechanic. He was a Stevens-Duryea mechanic, the automobile. No college graduate, but he had a lot of logic. That's my father. My dad got remarried again, which was a no-no then. There were only two children, myself and my sister.

"My husband was a machinist. Ovella Gemme. During the war, he made guns. Stocks. In Springfield. He had to stay home. We had the two children. Stevens Arms and Tools. Gemme—French. Mine was a French name, too—Moreau, although my mother was Irish.

"I was just plain common Lizzie. I'll tell you, though, I did my share during the war. I helped to assemble parachutes. World War II. They didn't have parachutes in the first World War. They wanted married women to work. You know how big a parachute is. We had to string them and be sure they were strung right, because if they weren't perfect, they wouldn't open. The only time I ever left the house was during the war, to do those parachutes at the Shawmut Woolen Mills."

Though more interested in the Braves than the Red Sox, Kathryn switched loyalties about five years before the Braves left town. Those were some great Red Sox years, starting in 1946, but it was a catcher who caught her eye. "I've been interested in the Red Sox since Birdie Tebbetts."

Today, baseball plays an important role in Kathryn's life. "I watch as often as I can. I would say every game. I've lost some of my eyesight—the corners are cut off—but I still watch every game. Sometimes I can lose track of the ball, lose the flight of the ball, but my eyes are glued to it. I love baseball."

Her family pays for NESN so she needn't miss a single game. At the nursing home, she'll follow every play—though she has to be respectful of her roommate. "But when she's out, I turn it up." What about those late night West Coast road trip games that don't even start until after 10 p.m. Boston time? "I don't take a nap, but I stay with it. I wait till it's over."

Baseball has taken on more significance since she turned 100. "The last 8 years, I can't read. Baseball always thrilled me. Now it's the only pleasure I have. It's what I like to do. I don't care if other people like it or not. I love it. When I was growing up, I didn't realize [all the strategy]. I just knew I always liked it. I liked the Red Sox. I went to games way back when I didn't know my ear from my elbow. I won't live long enough to learn all there is to know about baseball!"

What about off days during the season? "No game tonight? I'll watch a ball game, though. The National League. Once in a while, I'll watch Maddux pitch. I'll watch something. As long as there's action. I'm ashamed to say, but I like boxing, too."

Does Kathryn have other interests besides sports? "To tell you the truth, there not much. I had to leave the organ. My son-in-law gave me an organ. I played the organ until about 6 months ago. I'm stuck here. The Red Sox are my Godsend."

Some capsule comments from Kate:

Ted Williams: Ted Williams? That's a foregone conclusion. He was the Splendid Splinter. I'd just have to say he was the best ever. I saw him play. I can see that tall, lanky running kid. He kind of loped. I'd never leave my seat, even to go to the bathroom. You had to admire Ted for what he did. I guess he wasn't very sociable, but he was marvelous with no question.

You know who stands out in my memory? The guy who ran backwards to first base. Jimmy Piersall. I always admired him.

Also, another one—I can picture him pushing his home run. Carlton Fisk. I liked him. Big square jaw. Determination right there.

Varitek is right up there with Nomar, but with half the recognition.

Roger Clemens—He registers nil with me because of his poor personality, but he is an excellent pitcher.

Jim Rice—I absolutely loved him. Besides being a handsome man, he was a handsome player. He was a lot of fun to watch.

Wade Boggs—When he got up, I was sure he was going to get a hit.

Mo. I liked Mo Vaughn.

Canseco, he was a crybaby.

Johnny Pesky. From Doerr to Pesky, I remember that. And he played the hot corner, too.

I liked that nice pitcher for the Red Sox, Luis Tiant.

Even now, I try to remember the replacements on the Red Sox. If you remember your own name at 108, you're doing good.

Sharon Gosling wrote a letter to the Red Sox about Kathryn Gemme and they responded with a package containing a letter (unsigned) and photos of Nomar Garciaparra (signed), Jason Varitek and Brian Daubach. "I couldn't believe it—for *me*?" She showed it to all her new friends at Atrium, but they didn't seem that excited. "I thought they'd go ga-ga over it. I love it. There's no doubt about it." Weeks later, Kathryn was still pleased and excited that the Red Sox had sent her these items. They are minor treasures she keeps with her throughout the season.

I reached out to Kate the day after the Red Sox won the World Series, and Sharon Gosling wrote me back on October 28, 2004: "She is pleased, and now that her goal is met, she is ready to go."

As it happens, she made it to another game, appeared on the field in 2005, and even got a kiss from Johnny Pesky. Ms. Gemme died on December 29, 2006, at age 112.

Doris Kearns Goodwin

Another fan of note is Pulitzer Prize-winning historian Doris Kearns Goodwin, who has written so movingly about her own childhood as a fan of her hometown Brooklyn Dodgers in her book *Wait Till Next Year*. Transplanted to Boston, she adopted the Red Sox as her new team. The Dodgers, of course, had meanwhile moved to the West Coast. "Living up here and having my children, I think it was absolutely natural that I became a Red Sox fan because then I could share with my own sons the relationship I had with my father through baseball. In some ways it's the other end of that generational scale where the love of baseball started with my

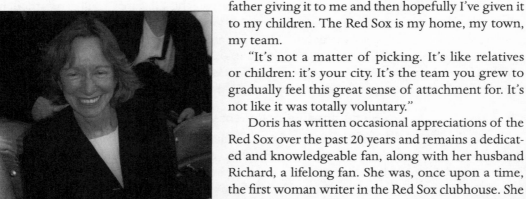

father giving it to me and then hopefully I've given it to my children. The Red Sox is my home, my town, my team.

"It's not a matter of picking. It's like relatives or children: it's your city. It's the team you grew to gradually feel this great sense of attachment for. It's not like it was totally voluntary."

Doris has written occasional appreciations of the Red Sox over the past 20 years and remains a dedicated and knowledgeable fan, along with her husband Richard, a lifelong fan. She was, once upon a time, the first woman writer in the Red Sox clubhouse. She was working on an article for *Life* magazine about George Scott and Joel Finch, a story about a veteran player and rookie trying to make the team, and the different pressures they each faced.

She earned entrée in part due to a lawsuit filed by *Sports Illustrated* on behalf of its writer Melissa Ludtke. "I was sitting on the bench out in front of the [Winter Haven] locker room where a lot of the

Doris Kearns Goodwin at Fenway. Bill Nowlin photo.

reporters and journalists used to sit and they had just come down with the ruling that said that women had to be allowed in the locker room. I was sitting next to Haywood Sullivan...this would date it...and he said, 'Go in.' When you're not allowed into something, it creates some great magical...you think it's going to be some palace inside." Her reaction to her first visit to the Inner Sanctum was to be underwhelmed. "This is it?"

As a fan, she has no superstitions. After all, "whatever the range of superstitions would have been, we all would have used them up by now!" She admits a little sheepishly, though, "Something has happened to me of late. It's become embarrassing. I can watch the whole game when I'm at the park but when I'm home I find it hard when the other team is up. I get nervous and I tend to leave the room a lot. I would never leave when the Red Sox are up, because I want to see the good things—but I'm glad to take a break in case something bad happens, I like to miss it. That's really stupid and I'm not happy about that."

As a Red Sox rooter, Doris has developed a strong sense of pride. She does not like to see Sox fans come across looking poorly. "Every time I see this 'Yankees Suck' thing, it just drives me crazy. It makes us seem like we're really irrational." Boston fans should be better than that. "You just don't want to have us thought of that way—I don't think we are those kinds of people. The fans are passionate. They're knowledgeable. They go to the games. They know about it. They care about it. That's part of what sports is about. And it's great to have that connection with anybody, when you see them, there's a deeper sense. When you see a fellow Red Sox fan, I think that something connects more deeply than if a Yankee fan sees a fellow Yankees fan. What's connecting is all the history of waiting and hoping."

Except those who legitimately grew up in New York, with a lot of Yankees fans, "you just have a feeling that they have picked the winner."

Women in the press box

There were other women who covered the team professionally. In 1957, the *Cleveland News* assigned Doris O'Donnell to take an eastern swing with the Indians and write a number of feature articles. She was received well enough in Baltimore and Washington but found herself banned from the press box at Yankee Stadium and at Fenway Park. She'd become the story. "At Yankee Stadium, I didn't get to first base," she wrote. "At Fenway Park, I got to the gate, where I was stopped cold. [The baseball writers] voted 5–4 to keep me out. It never even occurred to me that they wouldn't let me in. I was a member of the Newspaper Guild like the rest of the guys." She was denied entry, though, and ended up in a skyview seat, which was near the press box—but wasn't the press box.

Dick Bresciani tells some entertaining stories about these days. He can't recall her name but remembers that a female reporter from Chicago came to cover games at Fenway Park and, as with Doris O'Donnell, was not allowed into the press box, which was a male preserve at the time. Apparently, the Red Sox actually built her a separate adjunct press box, and the old press steward Tommy McCarthy (now deceased) set a little table for her with a tablecloth and a rose, outside somewhere on the roof.

Another early reporter was Canada's Alison Gordon. "I was the first female member of the Baseball Writers Association of America," she explained in a March 2002 interview. She was spoiled in Toronto, where she says that Blue Jays GM Pat Gillick made sure she was treated correctly. "Gillick, in the media meeting they have with the players in spring training, evidently told the players the most remarkable thing: that they would like the players to treat me the way they would like their wives or sisters or mothers to be treated in the same situation. They took a kind of perverse pride in doing it right.

"I had more trouble in the press box than I had in the locker room. With some stunning exceptions. I wasn't really invading player turf; I was invading male sportswriter turf.

"The Red Sox were a very difficult team to cover, for a woman. In the first year, the one friend I had in the Red Sox clubhouse was Larry Whiteside. We had something in common; we were both tokens. And we both sort of saw it like that. And we both felt like we were carrying our entire—in my case, gender, and in his case, race—on our shoulders. I couldn't get away with asking some sort of dumb rookie mistake question. It wouldn't just be, 'Oh, she's new and doesn't know'—it would be, 'See? Women can't do it!' It would just be seen as proof of the fact that women should not be doing this job.

"Boston was a tough place to go. But it did improve. They did figure out that I was actually trying to do a job, the same job they were trying to do, and they cut me a bit of slack. It took a while, but they all did finally come around."

This was at a time when, according to Lesley Visser, "a media credential actually said that no women or children were allowed in the press box." [*Boston Baseball*, May 2007]

In "Sharing the Beat," writer Diane K. Shah recalled being assigned to cover some games at Fenway Park for the *National Observer* in September 1972. Red Sox PR man Bill Crowley was hesitant about providing credentials, mentioning "We don't let women on the field, and the Baseball Writers Association runs the press box." The head of the Boston chapter of the BWAA "sort of stutterered and put me on hold for a long time, and then he said he couldn't do it." After the publication's attorney called the Red Sox, there was a little more compliance. "When I got up there all I'd heard was 'Well, that girl can come in if she behaves herself,' and I didn't know what that meant. Bill Crowley had told me he'd get me a box seat and said he'd bring players there for me to interview. I said, 'You mean you'll bring Carl Yastrzemski to see me in the stands right after a game?' and he said, 'Well, I'll try.'"

Shah got a field pass but found that none of the players would talk to her. There had apparently been a team meeting and the players were told to "watch their language"—a quaint notion that most of them took to mean they shouldn't talk to her at all. She later got in a word with Carlton Fisk and pitcher John Curtis.

Dick Bresciani can laugh about it today, but it was clearly an awkward time. Shah remembers, "Before the game, Dick Bresciani, the assistant public-relations man, took me up on the roof, where the press box and the pressroom are. I could see he was terribly uncomfortable about something, and when we got there he explained that I could come into the press box but that the pressroom was a social place, for eating and drinking, and no women were allowed in there. I saw that they'd set up a little ice-cream table outside the pressroom, with one chair and one place setting, and there was a little folder on it with 'Ladies' Pavilion' written across it. I didn't eat at all that night. I just ignored it." Bresh remembers a little picnic table set with a white tablecloth and a small vase with a red rose in it. The Red Sox were trying, in their own way. Gallantry and pleasantries, though a separate but equal approach that wasn't going to work in the long run. The next night, the pressroom was open and, seeing no one sitting with Shah, owner Tom Yawkey invited her over to his table. Shah summed up the experience, "The strangest thing of all, when I look back on it, is that none of this seemed to have been done with any malice. They were all polite, in a distant sort of way. They just didn't know what to do about me." [Shah quotations come from Roger Angell, *Late Innings,* NY: Simon & Schuster, 1982]

Players' wives

There have been any number of interesting stories involving players' wives, from Ted Williams' wives to Joe Cronin's wife to Debbie Boggs to the wives of today who are so active in area charities (wives such as Kathryn Nixon, Shonda Schilling, Dawn Timlin, and Karen Varitek have been especially active in recent years with a number of causes and helping bring together a couple of books, an annual food drive, and more).

It's interesting to note that at least one player's arrival with the Red Sox—Tommy Fine—was delayed as much as seven years because of a "Bosox Camp Ban on Wives." Fine was due to report to Sox spring training in February 1940 and received a letter the month before asking if he was bringing his wife so the team could arrange accommodations. He was just getting married, and he felt great that he could bring his new bride to spring training. Then came another letter, just two days before he was to depart. The Sox had apparently changed their mind, and wives were no longer welcome. He'd already sent some belongings ahead. "Our trunk had gone," he told Roger Birtwell. "And besides—I just didn't have the heart to tell my wife. She had set so much store on the trip." When the pair arrived in Florida, no one said a word but Fine felt like he got a very cold shoulder. He tried to bear down but that only made his pitches wilder. He sank in the minors as he tried even harder. The next year, his appendix burst, then the war saw him in the Army Signal Corps. He mustered out in time to play well for Scranton in 1946, and finally made the majors on April 27, 1947. He only appeared in nine games for the Red Sox (1–2, 5.50 ERA), and in the final days of the season was traded to the San Francisco Seals. [*The Sporting News*, May 14, 1947]

Jean Yawkey

After Tom Yawkey died, his second wife and widow Jean Yawkey became, in effect, the owner of the Boston Red Sox, although it was a complicated and sometimes stormy ownership due to the actions of some of the others in the ownership group. There was, for instance, the "coup LeRoux" when co-owner Buddy LeRoux announced that he was taking over the ownership of the team—only to see his grasp on power erode rather quickly. We won't go into that here, nor will we opine at any length on Mrs. Yawkey's regime other than to note that after her passing, the organization began to move more quickly toward a more rational and more modern approach toward doing business. She herself never brought the Bosox out of the shadow of her husband. There remains, of course, Yawkey Way—the stretch of Jersey Street which passes by the ballpark. And there remain the Morse Code letters on the scoreboard which spell out the initials of Thomas A. Yawkey and Jean R. Yawkey.

Helen Robinson

Another forceful female personality who made her presence felt at Fenway for six decades was switchboard operator Helen Robinson. Originally hired by Eddie Collins, she started work on September 2, 1941—the month that Ted Williams secured his status as the last major league batter to hit .400. Months later, Robinson began filling the time between fielding calls by knitting sweaters for all the Boston ballplayers who were off to war. It was also Helen Robinson who used to sew the uniform numbers on the backs of the players' jerseys.

If you never heard her, you wouldn't understand, but she had the crispest—even off-putting—way of answering the phone. All she said was "Red Sox"—but it was the way she said it. She arrived on time, left on time, and stayed until the end of every game, right up to the day she died. It was said that she knew everybody—and knew where all the bodies were buried, maybe more knowledgeable than many of the team's executives. She steadfastly, and

Lou Gorman helping honor Helen Robinson at a Bosox Club luncheon. Bill Nowlin photo.

consistently, declined all requests for interviews. As Rod Oreste once wrote, "She is a picture of discipline and tact, never talking about anyone else's business and shunning any action that would make her the center of attention." Dan Shaughnessy dubbed her "one of the most powerful people at Fenway."

Elaine Weddington Steward

One of GM Lou Gorman's appointments remains a major executive with the ballclub today. Elaine Weddington. She began work for the Red Sox in 1988 as associate counsel and became assistant general manager two years later. She currently serves as Vice President and Club Counsel, and is one of the highest ranking females in organized baseball.

"Baseball Annies"

Then there was a fan named Margo. We prefer not to spoil this section by writing about her, but a brief acknowledgement seems necessary. If you followed baseball in the late 1980s, you would have known the story of this Southern California mortgage banker who was a particular fan of one Red Sox player, Wade Boggs, for four years. A palimony lawsuit was settled in court, but both parties were sworn to keep the content confidential. Roger Clemens and Mindy McCready? Let's wait and see.

Managing women ballplayers

Marty McManus and some South Bend Blue Sox ballplayers. Courtesy of Mary Pratt.

When women began to play baseball during the World War II years with the launch of the All-American Girls Professional Baseball League, a few Red Sox alumni became involved as well. Red Sox manager Marty McManus (1932–33) was hired to manage the South Bend Blue Sox, and did so in 1945 and again in 1948. AAGPBL alumna Mary Pratt recalls playing for McManus on the Kenosha Comets in 1944. Jimmie Foxx, with the Sox from 1936 to 1942, managed the 1952 Fort Wayne Daisies. And Bill Wambsganss (with the Red Sox in 1924 and 1925) managed the 1945 Fort Wayne Daisies—which included Bill Lee's aunt Annabelle Lee. Wamby managed Fort Wayne again in 1946, and the Muskegon Lassies in 1947 and 1948.

McManus related something interesting to Pratt pertaining to his time managing the Red Sox. "One day he told me that he was sitting on the bench, and he had positioned all the players, and all of a sudden he saw them all moving. He went and he walked up to the top of the dugout steps and he looked up into the pressbox, and there was Eddie Collins pushing every one…I've contended that's what's been wrong with the Red Sox all these years. The managers don't run the club; it's all up the top there." [Interview with Mary Pratt, April 2006.]

Raising Red Sox

Of course, in the raising of the many Red Sox players over the years, many women have played important roles. In the course of many interviews, one learns that it was not infrequent for the mother to have been the one who encouraged the son. Kim Andrew of the 1975 Red Sox, for instance, says of his mother, "She played a little bit, softball and that sort of thing. She was the one who was actually the athlete over my father, who was always more of an artist and that sort of thing. I think part of my athletic ability may have came from her side." Another ballplayer from the '75 Sox was pitcher Bill Lee. He credits his aunt Annabelle Lee, also a lefty, who pitched for nine years in the AAGPBL. In his autobiographical *Have Glove, Will Travel*, Bill Lee notes his aunt's lifetime 2.19 ERA, her two no-hitters, and her perfect game and writes, "My aunt worked on my control and mechanics and taught me how to change speeds. She also smoothed my delivery and insisted I throw every pitch from the same release point and with the same motion. 'That way,' she would remind me, 'the batter can't read your motion and figure out what you're going to throw.' Annabelle and my father were the best pitching coaches I ever had."

There might truly have been a time when Red Sox could have benefited from a pitcher on staff like Annabelle Lee. We'll never know.

Gina Satriano

How close might we have come to a father / daughter pair of relatives? Maybe fairly close. Tom Satriano had a 10-year career in the major leagues, with his last year and a half as a catcher (and third baseman and

Annabelle Lee and her nephew Bill, 2008. Courtesy of Diana Lee.

utility player) for the Boston Red Sox. Two of his daughters played professional baseball as well, and Gina Satriano appeared with the Colorado Silver Bullets at Fenway Park while on tour in 1994 and 1995.

Tom spent most of his career with the Angels—first with the Los Angeles Angels beginning in 1981 and then, when the team moved to Anaheim, with the California Angels right into the middle of the 1969 season when he was traded to the Red Sox. He appeared in 47 games for Boston that year, batting a disappointing .189 (he'd been having a decent year with the Angels, at .259). In 1970, his final year, he hit .236 in 165 at-bats. After 674 games, though, his knees were giving out and it was time to retire.

He'd already received his bachelor's degree from USC, and went on to take his CPA exam. Tom worked for Price Waterhouse for a while, then opened his own firm which he sold in the first years of the 21st century. He works when he wants to now, pretty much semi-retired.

When he came to Boston, he brought his family with him, though. Gina, who was not quite five years old when her dad retired from the game, has some fleeting memories. "I remember always having a baseball. I have a vision of sitting in the stadium, seeing the players and seeing my dad on the field. I have memories of running up and down the stairs of empty ballparks, with a baseball in my hand. Tossing it up and catching it."

Gina and her sister Lisa—about 21 months younger—both played pro baseball. Younger brother Nick played four years of Division One baseball with U.C. Santa Barbara, and went to some tryouts but never went on from there. Today both Lisa and Nick are in the movie business, both working as first assistant directors. Gina herself is a deputy district attorney with the Los Angeles District Attorney's office and has made occasional headlines with high profiles cases such as the Paula Poundstone child abuse case in 2001, the Courtney Love assault case in 2005, and the Mel Gibson drunk driving case in 2006. Both Gina and Lisa played for the Log Angeles Legends in 1997—Lisa playing second base and center field and Gina as starting pitcher and shortstop.

Tom Satriano definitely devoted time to teaching his children what he could. With tax season being right in the middle of baseball season for Little Leaguers, though, he could never really be the main coach on a team. "But he helped us when he could," Gina recalls. "He'd go to the cages with us. He'd play catch with us; he supported us at our games." Mom, though, was the one who put in the long hours. "Aside from going to watch my dad, my mom really gets the credit at the beginning for my love of baseball. My mom had the time and was out there every day encouraging me when I broke into baseball."

There were not at all easy times, Gina reflects. "It was a little scary at that time. Some scary things happened when I first broke in; we had to threaten lawsuits and all that stuff. Other parents were threatening us. She kept most of that from me, but she encouraged me to keep playing—being the only girl out there.

"This was when I was seven. 1972 or '73. That was pre-Title IX and we had to challenge the Little League in order to allow me to play. My mom. I didn't even know about it until later. She had threatening phone calls in the middle of the night. We had palms—like from a palm tree—burned on our lawn in the form of a cross. We had some interesting things happen.

"It got easier. Well, yes and no. It was harder for them to keep me out, but I still took a lot of criticism at the time. Even in Pony League, we had players quit teams, and teams quitting leagues, because they refused to play against a team that had girls on the team. I tried out for the men's baseball team at U.C. Davis, where I went to college and did my undergrad work. The coach allowed me to try out. He didn't stop me from trying out. Looking back on it, you gain some wisdom. I don't know that he ever seriously considered me as being part of his team. I think he was just avoiding conflict. I wasn't ever involved in any of the clubhouse discussions. I was just thrilled to be there at the time. I didn't have the mind of a lawyer then. I thought I was being given a fair shot because when I said I wanted to try out, he didn't hem or haw. He said OK. I also had friends who made the team who told me that he talked about it and that he never intended to put me on the team."

The first time Gina ever had another girl join her as a teammate, it was her sister Lisa. After her parents divorced, their mother adoped another girl and she, too, played baseball. Bridget Satriano, though she sometimes went by her legal name Bridget Wold. "She ended up being the only female manager in the women's pro league. She managed the Legends in '97 and '98. The Legends relocated to Miami in 1998. That's why I didn't stay with them; I went to the Long Beach Aces. So my sister managed the Legends in Miami and I played for the Aces against her."

Gina's first professional team, though, was the Silver Bullets, and she played with them in 1994 and 1995. "We trained for one year at Winter Haven, which is where my dad went for spring training. That was kind of fun. And when we got to Fenway, I just thought, 'Man, my dad spent so much time here. More time in the bullpen than out on the field. At that point he was at the end of his career.'

So both father and daughter played professional baseball at Fenway Park. Daughter Gina's team didn't fare well at Fenway. They lost the July 21, 1994 game to the Boston Park League team, by a score of 6–0. The next year, their game was on July 1 and they lost to Hanscom Air Force Base, 4–2. Gina was 0–4 as a pitcher in 1994, with an ERA of 5.05 (second best on the team) and she was 0–2 the following year, with a 5.82 ERA.

The D.D.A. sounded a bit wistful wrapping up the July 2002 interview: "There's no women's pro ball anymore—so IT retired ME rather than me retiring. If there was any choice, I'd still be playing."

Dale Keough

An earlier possibility might have been Dale Keough, daughter of Marty Keough (1956–1966). It was quite a baseball family, with Marty's brother Joe Keough playing for three American League teams from 1968–1973, and Marty's son Matt playing for five different teams from 1977–1986. Matt's sister Dale played center field for the Fullerton Royals in the Pacific Coast Women's League in 1975, and sportswriter Eddie West of the *Santa Ana Register* in May of that year, "Dale might be the first woman to break the ol' baseball barrier. She has the background."

Matt's son Shane Keough was a 36th round pick by Oakland in the June 2005 draft.

Janet Miller

Johnny Pesky says that Rick Miller's wife Janet played in Red Sox Fantasy Camp and, he wrote in *Diary of A Red Sox Season*, "She's pretty good." Janet comes from good lineage. Her brother Carlton Fisk was a pretty good catcher for the Red Sox.

Whitney Mollica—Don Zimmer's grand-daughter

Sure, it's softball, but keep an eye on U. Mass. third baseman Whitney Mollica, Don Zimmer's grand-daughter. He's been following her progress closely, and her team won the Atlantic 10 championship in May 2007. In 2006, the freshman won both Rookie of the Year and Player of the Year honors in the conference. She was a .394 hitter, who played every game all season long. Mollica hit .556 her senior year at Salem NH High School, and pitched, too, with a 13–3 record.

Jacqui Robinson? Will the Red Sox field the first female major leaguer?

Early in 2007, Major League Baseball adopted its first changes to the rules since 1996. Among them was this reference to gender-neutral language:

Any reference in these Official Baseball Rules to "he," "him" or "his" shall be deemed to be a reference to "she," "her" or "hers," as the case may be, when the person is female.

The Red Sox will have the opportunity to field the first female major leaguer, balancing to some degree the shame of having been the last to field an African American ballplayer.

UTOPIA, TEARS AND FAMILY AFFAIRS— RELATIVES WHO PLAYED FOR THE SOX

First Red Sox player to grow up in a communal utopian society

Bill Zuber was born and raised in the Amana Colonies, a communal society established in eastern Iowa prior to the Civil War by a religious group known as the Community of True Inspiration.

Zuber was first discovered by a Cleveland Indians scout who, according to baseballroadtrip. net, found the 17-year-old boy "helping with the onion harvest in the kitchen gardens. With no baseball available, the scout selected a large onion and asked Bill if he could hit a nearby barn. The obliging young man promptly threw the onion over the barn roof—and an illustrious baseball career was launched."

In mid-September 1936, "Goober" Zuber broke in with the Indians. He played with Cleveland until he was purchased by the Washington Senators at the start of the 1941 season. In January 1943, he was traded to the Yankees. After throwing just 5⅔ innings in 1946, the Red Sox bought him from New York and he posted a 5–1 record, by far his best year in major league ball. His first start resulted in a 3–0 three-hit shutout of the Indians. He even had the chance to pitch two innings in the 1946 World Series.

In 1947, Zuber appeared in 20 games, all but one in relief. His record was 1–0, the one win coming when he pitched the final four innings of the May 13 game, allowing just two runs while the Red Sox helped him out with 14 runs in their last three innings. This was a game in which Bobby Doerr hit for the cycle and Ted Williams hit two homers into the left-field screen—said to be the first two homers Ted had ever hit to left at Fenway. Zuber was 0-for-1, with two sacrifices. His 5.33 ERA wasn't good enough, and Zuber was released shortly after the season ended. He returned to Homestead, Iowa and founded Bill Zuber's Restaurant and Dugout Lounge, which served meals from 1949 through 2006, and let patrons test their arms with a ceremonial onion toss. Now it's an "Iowa prairie-themed hotel" named Zuber's Homestead Hotel.

Crying in the press box?

They say there's no cheering in the press box, but after Fred Snodgrass's muff that gave the 1912 World Series to the Red Sox, Frederick Lieb reported that one of the New York writers, Sid Mercer, was "so overcome with emotion that tears of chargin coursed down his handsome cheeks as he dictated the tenth inning to his telegraph operator."

Relatives who both played for the Red Sox

Big Ed Delahanty and his four brothers all played major league baseball. Ed, Frank, and Jim all played against the Red Sox, but not one of the five played for the Sox. There were brothers who did, though, and some father/son combinations, and some other related pairings as well.

BROTHERLY LOVE

Long Tom Hughes and Ed Hughes

Thomas James "Long Tom" Hughes was a pitcher who started his 13-year major league career with the Chicago Cubs in 1900 and 1901. Boston acquired him from Baltimore partway into 1902, and he went 3–3 with the Boston team.

In 1903, though, Hughes won 20 games (five of them shutouts) while only losing seven, with a 2.52 earned run average. His record earned him a start in Game Three of the first World Series ever held, a home game in Boston against Deacon Phillippe and the Pirates. After yielding three runs (two earned) in two-plus innings, letting the first three batters reach base in the top of the third, manager Jimmy Collins called on Cy Young for relief but it was too late: Pittsburgh won, 4–2. Hughes' World Series record is 0–1, with a 9.00 ERA. It was his only appearance and Young's biographer Reed Browning asks, "Could the gamblers have gotten to Hughes, and might Collins have suspected as much?" Speculation, of course, but apparently Hughes never suited up the rest of the Series and the 20-game winner was traded after the season.

Hughes was swapped to New York for lefthander Jesse Tannehill, who'd been in the majors since 1894. Hughes joined the New York Highlanders (later Yankees) where he didn't fare as well as in Boston—going 7–11—and later in the year was sent on to Washington, where he fared even worse (2–13), though the year's ERA was a respectable 3.59. Washington kept him and he played eight more seasons there. (Boston actually got the better of the trade; Tannehill played four full years and won 62 games while losing 38.) Tom Hughes played organized baseball for 23 years, 1900–1923, 13 of them in the major leagues. "Trouble with the game today is that the boys are too gentle," he said in 1935. "I wouldn't say they're all sissies because they're certainly not. But a good sock in the chin occasionally would stir up a little enthusiasm. I wouldn't uphold rowdyism, but more aggressiveness would help." He came from the days when "it wasn't uncommon for the players to leave the ball parks with bats in their hand for protection." [*The American*, May 16, 1935] Then again, the last game he pitched was against Jim Vaughn and the Fairies!

Younger brother Ed Hughes began his career with the other Chicago team—the AL entry—on August 29, 1902 in a game against Detroit. He just played that one game, with a single in four at-bats. That was it, until 1905 when he joined the Boston Americans (later Red Sox) and finally got his chance to pitch. That year he appeared in six games, winning three and losing two in 33⅓ innings, with a disappointing 4.59 ERA. At the plate, he got three hits, scoring twice and even knocking in a couple of runs. They brought him back again for an encore season in 1906 but he didn't contribute anything helpful: he threw 10 innings without a decision (all in relief) with a 5.40 ERA—Ed got up only two times in two games and didn't get a hit at all. His lifetime .222 plunged to just .190 and he was out of the majors for good.

Had he ever faced brother Tom, who was twirling for the Senators, in either year? How did each do facing the other team?

The two teams faced each other 20 times in 1905. Washington took seven of the first eight, but only won two of the final 10 meetings. Tom Hughes faced his former teammates for the first time late in the season, on September 9. The starting pitcher, he was paired with Tannehill and it was expected to be a pitchers' duel but Boston tied it in the ninth with three runs, as Hughes was chased, and won it in the 11th, 8–7.

Two days later, Ed Hughes pitched in game two of a doubleheader. Boston took the first game, but Ed blew it early in the nightcap, and was gone before the first inning was over, charged with four runs. Norwood Gibson wasn't any better—and Gibson was left in to pitch the entire rest of the game, a 14–0 defeat.

A week after that, Tom pitched a 4–2 victory for the Senators over Boston's Norwood Gibson; it was Tom's first win over Collins' men. On the 20th, in the words of the *Boston Post* writer, "Eddie Hughes, brother of 'Long Tom,' pitched a great game for the Boston champions today, and were it not for a little letup in the second inning Washington would have been shut out." The final score was 7–1.

In 1906, Ed only appeared in two games. On May 31, he came on in relief of Jesse Tannehill and Cy Young in a game Boston lost 9–2. Boston scored twice in the first but then was stopped cold. Tannehill lasted a little over one inning and Young pitched through the sixth. Ed Hughes finished the game, yielding just one run in three innings. His other appearance was not against Boston.

Tom had pitched against Boston on May 4, and the colorful language of *Boston Post* writer Frederic P. O'Connell is a treat: "Long Tom Hughes, who once pitched for Collins, was in the box for Washington, and he pitched rings around Dinneen, whom Collins thought big enough to 'skidoo' the hoodoo that has the locals in its grasp."

Tom Hughes pitched on June 2, losing 6–2, and again on July 4, losing to Cy Young, 9–3. The last time that year he faced Boston, on September 8, he won, 9–2.

So the two brothers never went directly up against each other, and both enjoyed mixed success against their opponents. Did fraternization rules apply to truly fraternal siblings?

The brothers were two of the six sons of Irish immigrants Mr. and Mrs. Patrick Hughes. Father Patrick worked in the steel mills. After baseball, Ed was a member of the Chicago Police Department for nearly 20 years, living with his mother, and died at age 48 of a pulmonary hemorrhage. He was remembered as a hero for an incident 11 years earlier. Off-duty, he had happened on an incident involving Henry McIntyre, who had barricaded himself in his house and killed four people, including a police sergeant. Three other policemen had been wounded. The captain ordered Hughes to leave the area, but instead the former catcher walked into the house. McIntyre fired at him but missed, whereupon Hughes shot twice and killed the man.

Long Tom ran a saloon in Chicago and stayed active playing Sunday ball in the Midwest League. In 1953, Ford Frick invited him and the other participants of the original 1903 World Series to the Golden Anniversary celebration.

Johnnie Heving and Joe Heving

John Aloysius Heving was born in 1896 in Covington KY and served eight years in the majors, five of them with the Red Sox.

Johnnie's career began late September (the 24th) 1920 with the St. Louis Browns, with a one-game, one at-bat first season. He didn't get a hit. For the next three years, he may have wondered if that would be his career line—.000 in one plate appearance, but in 1924 he caught on with Boston and got 109 more at-bats, batting .284. It was an on-again, off-again relationship with the Red Sox—Heving played in 1924 and 1925, but did not in 1926 or 1927, then came back and played in 1928–1930.

He hardly ever made the headlines, but played solid enough ball. In 1929, he hit .319 in 188 at-bats and one of them was big: his bases-loaded single in the bottom of the ninth won the September 8 game against the Browns, 4–3. Probably his best day of all came the following year, on April 19, 1930. The first game of the Patriots Day doubleheader against the visiting Yankees stretched to 15 innings until Johnnie ended it with a single to center, driving in Bill Regan from second base. Johnnie was 4-for-7 on the day.

His last two seasons were with the Philadelphia Athletics and he even got himself a pinch-hit at-bat in the 1931 World Series. He made an out in that one plate appearance, just as he had in his one at-bat with the Sox back in 1920.

After eight years in the major leagues, Johnnie had a .265 lifetime average, with 261 hits in 985 at-bats. He had just one career home run, with Philadelphia. His best year is reflected in the .319 he hit in 1929. It was one of the Red Sox' worst years, though, with the team winning just 58 games and finishing 48 games out of first place.

Joseph William Heving was born (1900) and died in Covington, KY. The *New York Times* described him as "a Kentuckian who loved to tell hillbilly stories."

Joe Heving was born four years later than his brother Johnnie, but debuted 10 years afterwards, on April 29, 1930 with the New York Giants. This Heving heaved for a living—he was a right-handed pitcher. Joe appeared in 63 games for the Giants in 1930 and 1931, winning eight and losing 11 in 132 innings, almost exclusively in relief. He did not play in the majors in 1932, but returned in 1933 with the White Sox.

There was one season when both brothers were in the majors at the same time—1930. Joe pitched for the Giants while Johnnie played with the Sox. They never stood a chance of facing each other. The Red Sox and Giants didn't face off in exhibition games between 1928 and 1935. There was no All-Star Game—the first one was held in 1933. In any event, a 7–5 pitcher with a 5.22 ERA would never have made the All-Star squad in the days before it became practice that each team would have at least one representative. And though Heving was second in the league in saves (with eight), there was no way he'd outclass Bill Terry or Mel Ott that year as a Giant. There was also no way they'd meet in the World Series, not with the Red Sox again in last place, 50 games out of first. The Giants had more of a shot, but finished in third place.

Joe Heving was an early relief specialist and after he came to the Red Sox in 1938, he won eight and lost just one, then led the league in relief pitching both in 1939 (11 wins and just three losses) and again (eight more wins as a reliever, four as a starter) in 1940. He put his name in the record books, with one of the wins in 1939. On July 13, the Red Sox played the first road night game in history, in Cleveland. The game went 10 innings, and the Red Sox won it, 6–5. The winning pitcher was Joe Heving.

Peter Golenbock reports Doc Cramer as having said, "Cronin wanted to use him every day, and Joe Heving couldn't stand it. He was too old for that." Perhaps Golenbock didn't know was that Joe Heving was already a grandfather at the time; he'd married early, and became a grandpa in 1938 while with the Red Sox. He was the only grandfather among major league players of his day. Heving served with the Indians from 1941 through 1944, and then finished his career with one more year in Boston, this time with the Braves. He compiled an excellent 76–48 record, often pitching for teams that weren't that strong.

Roy Carlyle and Cleo Carlyle

Roy and Cleo Carlyle grew up in Norcross, Georgia, where their father Will ran a grocery store that had the only ice box in that part of town. When they weren't working in the family store, the Carlyle brothers were out playing ball.

Roy "Dizzy" Carlyle broke into major league ball early in 1925 with the Washington Senators, appearing in just one game, in which he had just one at-bat (a strikeout). He was soon traded to Boston. He played in the 1925 Red Sox outfield under manager Lee Fohl, and Roy did very well for a last-place team. Sometimes today's Red Sox fans forget how bad the team really was in the post-Ruth, pre-Yawkey era. The 1925 team won just 47 games and finished 49.5 games out of first place. Had he stuck with the Senators (was that strikeout so unforgiveable?), he might have played in the World Series that year. The rest of the Washington team did.

Roy hit .326 with seven home runs and 48 RBIs in 276 at-bats. In 1926, he hit .285 but then was claimed off waivers by the Yankees where he finished out the season hitting .385 for New York. Roy left the majors after the 1926 season—but his younger brother Cleo (Cleo was his middle name, which he preferred to his given first name, Hiram) entered in May 1927, the very next spring. Cleo's debut was May 16, in a pinch-hitting role. He started well, doubling down the first-base line. Cleo was an outfielder and had really shone in spring training that year but pulled a ligament in his leg—hence the late start. His leg was still subpar and he was replaced by pinchrunner Ted Wingfield who, on a succeeding play, was thrown out at the plate. Two days later, Carlyle got another chance to hit and again came through—pinch-hitting for Wingfield in the seventh inning. He singled to the opposite field and was again replaced by a pinch-runner, Billy Rogell. This time his replacement runner scored, but in a losing cause. Another 48 hours passed and Carlyle was brought in to bat for pitcher Danny MacFayden, who had homered in the third inning but wasn't getting the job done on the mound. Carlyle proved all too human himself and made an out.

The second, and younger, Carlyle played for the Red Sox just the one year, in 95 games hitting a very mortal .234.

Roy Carlyle kept playing ball for a few years after he left the majors, and is said to have hit baseball's longest tape-measured home run (618 feet). On July 4, 1929, Carlyle hit a tremendous drive clear out of the Oakland Oaks' old ballpark in Emeryville. The ball went over the outfield fence, the parking lot, and two buildings before it crashed into the gutter of a house, leaving a big mark on the metal. One of his teammates saw the impact, and was thus able to measure the distance. A week later in Salt Lake City, he hit a drive reportedly measured at 605 feet.

Thanks to Will Hammock of the Gwinnett Daily Post *for some of the information contained in this writeup.*

Alex Gaston and Milt Gaston

Brother against brother? The brothers united as batterymates? *Les frères* Gaston faced both scenarios. They played against each other in 1926 when Alex Gaston was a catcher with the Red Sox and brother Milt was a pitcher for the St. Louis Browns, and they were batterymates when brother Alex caught Milt in 1929.

Someone liked the name Nathaniel. It was Alex's middle name and Milt's true first name. Both started with New York teams. Alex was the eldest, and he began his career first, with the

New York Giants in 1920. A catcher, he was in and out of the majors. He saw limited duty with the Giants for four straight seasons, but after 1923 he was gone. The next year, 1924, younger brother Milt began his major league career with New York's American League team—the Yankees. Milt was a 6'1" right-handed pitcher, four inches taller than his older brother. He pitched for the Yankees the one year, then moved to the Browns for three, to Washington for one, and then to Boston for the 1928, 1929, and 1930 seasons (a 20-game loser, he led the league in losses in 1930). He wound up with three years pitching for the White Sox. Lifetime, Milt

was 97–164 with a 4.55 ERA, in part reflected in a poor strikeout to walk ratio—he walked 836 but only struck out 615. Milt hardly ever had a winning season.

After a couple of years out of the majors, Alex resurfaced in 1926 with the Red Sox. He hit .223 in 301 at-bats. How did he do when the Sox catcher faced his younger brother?

In 1926, the Red Sox played the Browns 22 times, with Boston winning 11, and the Browns winning 11. There was one tie game (5–5, the second game of a July 24 doubleheader) called at the

Alex and Milt Gaston, brother battery for Boston.

6:00 p.m. Sunday baseball curfew time. The Sunday games were played at Braves Field, since Fenway was off-limits to Sunday baseball at that time. These were not stellar teams. Boston finished the season in last place with just 46 wins and St. Louis was next to last with 62 wins.

How did Alex and Milt fare when the two brothers squared off against each other? Alex did OK generally against the Browns, but beat up on his brother a bit. Alex played in the first two meetings of the clubs, but Milt did not pitch either game. Neither of them played in the third and fourth meetings. Milt pitched in the fifth and threw 10 full innings. The game was knotted 2–2 after nine, but then Boston scored a run in the top of the 10th off Milt. The Browns

came back and won it in the bottom of the 10th, but Alex never appeared in the game. Several more meetings came to pass, and still the brothers hadn't played in a game against each other. In fact, the two teams faced each other 16 times (including the tie) before the time came when Alex dug into the batter's box to face brother Milt. It was the second inning of the second game of the August 16 doubleheader, at Fenway Park. And the bases were loaded at the time. The Red Sox had lost the first game, 6–1. Ford Sawyer, in the *Globe*, wrote, "On the sun-baked diamonds of our national pastime sentiment is unknown and brotherly love is a thing not recognized. Many must sometimes battle against his dearest chum for a regular's post, cousin struggle

Detail, sports page cartoon.

with cousin for the same playing berth, brother contends against brother for the old ball game." There was one out and no score in the game. "No brotherly love stuff now!" a fan reportedly cried out. No worries. Alex banged a triple to left center, clearing the bases, and providing all the runs Boston needed to defeat brother Milt, 7–1.

They faced each other once more on September 12. Again it was a doubleheader, this time in Sportsman's Park, St. Louis. Alex went 3-for-5 in the first game, which Boston took, 11–3. Milt started game two and held the Red Sox to just two hits in a 1–0 complete game win. Only one Bosox reached second base. Of the two hits, though, the first one was by brother Alex, a single in the third inning. Milt got the win, though, so perhaps we could call it even.

After the 1926 season, Alex disappeared from the record books for two more years. This time when he came back onto the page, it was 1929 and both he and Milt were on the same team—the Red Sox. Alex appeared in 55 games and Milt in 39. Milt won 12 and lost 19 that year—his .387 winning percentage, though, was better than the team's. Boston came in dead last again that year, with a record of 58—96, a .377 percentage. Alex did his best to help the cause; he improved on his 1926 average, but by the slimmest of margins: he hit .224 instead of 1926's .223. He did bang in two of his three career home runs, but that was it for Alex. Milt soldiered on for another five years.

How often were Alex and Milt batterymates and how did the team fare when the brothers teamed up? The first time Milt and Alex were the battery, it was Milt who got battered. Milt's first start for the Red Sox was not an auspicious one. It was May Day 1929 and a distress call went out early in the game. Milt lost to the Athletics, a game with a final score of 24–6 which occasioned a *Globe* subhead, "All Fenway Park Hitting Marks Smashed." Gaston (Milt) was gone after 1⅓ innings, having given up eight hits and walking two. He took the loss. The Red Sox used 23 players in the game, but the only one to play the entire game was Alex Gaston, who went 3-for-5 and actually had himself a good game—except, possibly, in terms of calling the game from behind the plate.

Milt took the mound again on May 6. This time he gave up nine hits and a walk (and five runs) in six innings. Harry Heilmann was responsible for all five runs—a two-run homer in the first, an RBI single in the third and another two-run homer in the fifth. Final score: Detroit 8, Boston 4. Milt managed to secure a single for himself in the game, and brother Alex went 1-for-3.

Just three days later, on May 9, Milt was pleased when the Sox scored twice in the first and added another run later, but the Indians tied it up 3–3 in the sixth and won 4–3 in the ninth. Alex didn't help much. He went 0-for-3.

Milt lost his next two starts, too. Alex didn't play in either or those, not did he play on May 28 when Milt finally earned himself a win.

It was June 13 before they appeared as batterymates again, this time because Sox catcher Charlie Berry had been ejected. Alex was 0-for-1, with a sacrifice. Milt got himself a 4–1 win. June 17: both started in game two of a doubleheader, Alex going 1-for-3. They lost, Milt yielding 13 hits and three walks in seven innings. On June 22, Milt pitched in the first game and lost, walking in the winning run in the 10th inning. Alex appeared in the second game, taking Heving's place, but didn't get an at-bat. Milt continued to pitch—got himself a homer on July 4 off Lefty Grove (in a 3–1 Philadelphia win); his error on July 20 cost the Sox that game. The next time the Gastons played together was July 26, Milt suffering a 4–1 defeat to Detroit. Alex spelled Berry mid-game and went 0-for-1 but scored the only Sox run. On July 31, Alex played in game one but only pinch-hit in the second game (unsuccessfully) as Milt absorbed another defeat.

On September 2, Milt pitched and won game two on that day's twinbill, but the only game brother Alex played in was the first. On September 8, they played at Braves Field (it being Sunday). Just as back on July 24, 1926 when the two brothers squared off against each other, this game was also called a few minutes before the 6:00 p.m. curfew. Milt started and held St. Louis scoreless through 10 innings. Since the Red Sox had managed only three hits (two of them by

Alex) and failed to score as well, the game ended 0–0. Both ties involved the St. Louis Browns; the 1926 game had Milt pitching for them and this one had Milt pitching against them.

On September 14, Milt only gave up five hits (though he walked six batters and threw a wild pitch), losing to the Tigers, 2–1. Both brothers batted three times; neither got a hit. The last game they both appeared in was on September 19, Alex went 0-for-2 but Milt helped his own cause. Alex was safe on an error in the fifth. The next batter made an out, and then Milt doubled. A couple of batters later, Milt himself scored with what proved to be the winning run. All in all, not that inspiring a collaboration. Alex never returned to big league ball. Milt was 12–19 in 1929, 13–20 the next year and then a dismal 2–13 for Boston in 1931. He pitched three more years, for the White Sox, and then left the game. He died in 1996 in Hyannis, MA at age 100.

Rick Ferrell and Wes Ferrell

The Ferrell Brothers were quite a pair. Rick ended up in the Hall of Fame, yet Wes was so impressive that many critics argued they'd inducted the wrong Ferrell. After appearing over seven seasons with the Indians, pitcher Wes Ferrell was traded to the Red Sox in May 1934 where he joined his brother Rick, who'd been traded from St. Louis to Boston in May 1933. Rick was a catcher, so the Sox had themselves an all-Ferrell battery. *The Sporting News* of July 9, 1936 reported that they roomed together when traveling with the team, "though rather contrasting types."

Rick was an eight-time All-Star, catching the first All-Star Game ever, in 1933. In his first four years with the Browns, he'd improved his average each year, hitting a high of .315 in 1932. His low with the Red Sox was .297, and he accomplished the same feat in four seasons with the Sox, increasing each year to a high of .312 in 1936. On June 11, 1937, both Ferrells were traded to the Senators, with Mel Almada, for Ben Chapman and Bobo Newsom. It stands as the only time two brothers were dealt in the same transaction. Rick was widely admired; Wes was a piece of work. Boston manager Joe Cronin said as much in his comment on the trade, which acknowledged Wes only indirectly: "Funny the difference between those two brothers. I sure hated to lose Rick—good ballplayer, hard worker, easy to get along with."

Rick played with Washington for four years, then was traded back to St. Louis in early 1941, only to be re-dealt to the Senators just before the 1944 season. In all, he played 18 seasons, with a career batting average of .281, with 28 homers and 734 RBIs.

Though a pitcher, Wes hit 10 more homers in his 15 years than his brother Rick in his 18, and he was just one point behind Rick in average (.280 in 1,176 at-bats). He pitched 2,623 innings with a career 4.04 ERA (the first half of his career was markedly better than the latter half), with a 193–128 won-loss record. A little over a year after arriving in Washington, Wes was released, signing two days later with the Yankees. Released by New York in May 1939, he was signed the following winter by the Brooklyn Dodgers, only to be released in May. The same pattern obtained in 1941: signed by the Braves in February, released in May.

The lives of Wes and Rick (and other talented Ferrells) are recounted in Dick Thompson's book *The Ferrell Brothers of Baseball*, and the colorful Wes often crops up in other books on the Red Sox. He had a flair for the dramatic, with flashes of anger at himself that ranged from walking off the mound in the middle of the game to knocking himself out with a punch to his own head in August 1934. He just missed a no-hitter with the Indians in 1932. His best season with Boston was 1935, when he was 25–14; the Red Sox only won 78 games that year. On July 31, 1935, Wes hit two home runs in Washington for one of those wins. Not one player on the Washington team hit more than one home run at home all year long.

Rick and Wes combined for homers for the first time on July 19, 1933. The following year,

Wes had a few big hits: his August 11 pinch-hit homer won a game against the Yankees in the 13th inning, and his two homers both tied and won the August 22 game in the bottom of the 10th inning. In the space of a week and a half, he'd twice thrilled Red Sox fans with walk-off homers. On the mound for the Red Sox, Ferrell won 62 and lost 40.

Roy Johnson and Bob Johnson

The Johnson boys aren't so well known today. Both outfielders, Roy was the elder—a Sooner, born in 1903. He started his 10-year career with the Tigers and then came to Boston in the early part of the 1932 season. For the Red Sox, for whom he played 94 games that year, he hit .298. His tenure in Boston carried him through 1935 and then he was off to the Yankees, where he saw only part-time work in 1936 and a few games at the start of the 1937 campaign, when he was traded back to Boston—the National League team. For the Red Sox, these were interesting times. When Roy came in, it was in the 43–111 season of 1932. Tom Yawkey bought the club, renovated Fenway Park and by 1935 the team was over .500. Roy Johnson contributed. He hit over .300 the three full seasons he played for Boston, and .298 the year he arrived mid-season. His four year totals were 611 hits in 1,954 at-bats, for an average of .313. He hit 31 homers and knocked in 327 runs, with 119 of them in 1934.

Bob, now. He'd already played against the Red Sox for 11 seasons before he came to Boston, for Philadelphia and Washington. "Indian Bob" was three years younger than Roy, and entered the big leagues four years behind him. His two years with the Red Sox were the war years of 1943 and 1944. Bob was playing for the Athletics, though, for three years that Roy was playing for Boston—1933, '34 and '35. Bob hit for more power (288 HR to Roy's 58, for instance) but, remarkably, both brothers wound up with identical .296 averages. If they really wanted to get down to it, though, Roy could lord it over his brother just a bit in batting average: Roy hit .2963982 and Bob came in second with .2963872.

The first time the two brothers faced each other in major league play came on April 23, 1933 when the Athletics visited Fenway Park. Bob played right field for Philadelphia and batted fifth in the order, following Jimmie Foxx. He was 0-for-5 on the day, batting against an unrelated Johnson, Red Sox pitcher Hank. Roy Johnson batted second for the Red Sox, playing center field. He had a 2-for-5 day, with one RBI and one run scored. He committed two errors. The Red Sox won. Both Johnsons had two RBIs the next day, with Roy enjoying another 3-for-5 day, and Bob settling for a double and three runs scored.

Their paths would cross more than a few times in the four seasons they each played American League ball, and occasionally their paths would meet. They never played for the same team at the same time, but after the June 17, 1933 doubleheader in Boston, the two teams shared the same train west—the Red Sox heading to Cleveland and the Athletics to Detroit.

The following year, Bob hit a pinch-hit homer that gave the Athletics the lead in a game they won, 12–11. The four RBIs that Roy drove in kept the Red Sox close, but it was Bob's hit that made the difference. There are numerous other times both played in the same game, but being on opposing teams didn't affect their closeness. The two often spent time together in the off-season hunting and fishing.

For more information on the Johnsons, see the section on Native Americans.

Ed Sadowski and Bob Sadowski

There were three Sadowski brothers who played major league ball, all more or less around the same time.

There was Ted, there was Ed, and there was Bob—none of whom should be confused with who we will call the "other" Bob Sadowski, a utility infielder who also played at the same time. This "other" Bob came from Missouri and was no relation whatsoever. And none of them should be confused in any way with Ray Sadecki. Just to complicate matters a bit more, there was also Jim Sadowski—but he didn't play until 1974 with the Pirates, only appearing in four games.

Ted, Ed, and the "other" Bob all began their major league careers in 1960, Ted Williams' final year.

Ed Sadowksi was the eldest of the brothers, born in 1931. He was a catcher who was in the Red Sox system since just prior to the 1951 season, finally making the major league team in 1960. His first game was at Fenway against the Yankees, entering the game in the top of the second when Haywood Sullivan was hit by a foul tip. Ed walked his first time up, and later doubled in the final run of a 7–1 win for Jerry Casale. Six days later, in Yankee Stadium, he hit his first home run—off the same New York pitcher, Art Ditmar. In June, he had the only hit in a game against the Indians, but he played until July when Jim Pagliaroni was called up and Ed sent to Spokane.

Ed was just with Boston the one year, appearing in 38 games and batting .215 with three homers, four doubles, and four triples. After the season, Ed was selected by LA in the expansion draft and spent three years with the Los Angeles Angels. In 1964 and 1965, he was out of the majors, but he resurfaced briefly with the Atlanta Braves for three games in 1966. While with the Angels, one of his teammates was the man we've dubbed the "other" Bob Sadowski. One can only imagine how strange it was to be teammates with a Bob Sadowski who was not your brother Bob Sadowski—and in the very same year that your brother Bob was beginning his career with Milwaukee (perhaps fortunately, Milwaukee was in the other league). Ed's last year was 1966; he was a lifetime .202 hitter.

The middle of the three brothers was Ted Sadowski. Ted was five years younger than Ed, but broke in the same year, pitching for the Washington Senators. From 1960–62, he appeared in 43 games for the Senators and the Twins, with a career record of 2–3, 5.76 ERA. Ted faced the Boston Red Sox, but never played for them. While with Washington, Ted appeared in just 17⅓ innings. Did he ever face his brother Ed, who began with the Red Sox in 1960? He did not. The two teams faced each other 20 times in 1960, but while Ed had a few scattered plate appearances against the Senators, Ted first pitched against the Red Sox on September 2 (his major league debut). By this time, Ed had been sent back down to the minors. Ted's debut came in the second game of a twi-night twin bill. Pedro Ramos started and went six full innings, scattering five hits, and left with the Sox ahead, 2–1. Ted Sadowski came in and threw three innings in relief, benefiting from two runs the Senators scored off Mike Fornieles, and walked off with the win, the final score 3–2. The *Boston Globe*'s account said, "And the winning pitcher—seeking revenge, perhaps, because the Red Sox shipped his brother to the bushes—was Ted Sadowski, 24-year-old righthander who joined the Senators from Charleston, West Va., before the game." Ted didn't let a runner past second, and in the ninth inning with one out and a man on first, he struck out another Ted—Ted Williams.

Twice later in the 1960 season, Ted faced the Red Sox. On September 4, he pitched an inning and let in a run, with a double by Pagliaroni and a triple by Don Gile. On the 18th, he threw one inning of no-hit relief in a game the Red Sox won.

The year after Ted Sadowski left major league play, Bob entered. Bob Sadowski was the youngest of the three brothers, born in 1938. Originally signed by the St. Louis Cardinals, he was traded to the Milwaukee Braves, and four days later played in his first game on June 19, 1963. Had Ted hung on one more year, all three brothers would have been playing at the same time.

Bob was also a pitcher. He played with the Braves for three seasons—1963–1965—but when the Braves left Milwaukee after the 1965 season, it was the Atlanta Braves who traded Bob to Boston—from whence the Braves had come, back in 1953. Bob and Dan Osinski were traded for Lee Thomas and Arnold Earley and Jay Ritchie, named a month later. With the Red Sox, he won one and lost one, throwing 33⅓ innings and posting a 5.40 ERA. Independence Day was his last day on the field. When Dennis Bennett came back from surgery on July 13, Bob was sent to Toronto to make room for Bennett on the roster. It was Bob's last time in MLB. Too bad he wasn't around for '67. He won 20 major league games and lost 27, with a career ERA of 3.87.

So, catcher Ed Sadowski began his major league career with the Red Sox, while his brother Bob—a pitcher—finished his major league career with Boston. Ed finished his career with the Atlanta Braves in 1966—Bob had started his career with the Braves three years earlier, when the Braves were still in Milwaukee. The year after Bob left the Braves (1965), Ed joined them (1966).

Nephew Jim Sadowski was, like his three uncles, also born in Pittsburgh, in 1951. He played in 1974 for the Pirates, appearing in four games. Jim said that there was another uncle who could well have signed, too, but he married young and then World War II intervened and he just never did play pro ball. Jim recalled seeing his uncle Bob pitch for the Braves against the Pirates at Forbes Field while he was growing up. Of his uncle Ed, he remembered, "When he was with the Red Sox, he would spend some time in town in the off-season and I had a chance to shag some balls for him and that sort of thing. They would all come home and work out at the local field right behind my grandmother's house." Jim recalled that uncle Ted "used to brag about striking out Ted Williams."

Though truly tangential, "the other" Bob Sadowski spent four years in a row, each with a different team, and he recalls, "I played on the Angels with Ed. Bob and I came out of the Cardinals organization, but then he quickly went to Milwaukee. We often got our mail mixed up, Bob and I. In fact, we got our bubble gum cards mixed up. They'd send me his and he'd get mine. I don't know if he got any of my checks, though!"

Tony Conigliaro and Billy Conigliaro

Tony and Billy Conigliaro.

The Conigliaros in their day rivaled Pedro and Ramon Martinez in theirs. Sadly, in the Conigliaros' case it was fame and misfortune. Like Pedro and Ramon, there was a period of time when Tony and Billy were both on the 25-man roster, both playing for Boston at the very same time.

The Conigliaro family was always a tight and loyal one, and with brothers Tony and Billy both signing with their home town team (they were born in Revere and grew up in East Boston), baseball was a family affair. Born 2½ years apart, Tony and Billy were close as kids and both loved playing baseball. As Tony wrote in *Seeing It Through*, "We had two baseballs, all taped up because they were so worn out, and a grubby old bat...Billy would throw me the two baseballs and I'd hit them...as far as I could, go get them, come back, then I'd pitch the two balls at him....We'd do this back and forth all day long."

Tony got a very early start. The 1964 Red Sox were a bit of a lackluster team and manager Johnny Pesky gave a local kid a shot, telling Tony's father Sal at the end of spring training that the kid had earned himself a spot. Tony C was just 19 years old. The very first pitch he saw at Fenway Park, he hammered for a homer. By the end of his rookie year, he'd hit 24 home runs and batted .290. In so doing, he set a major league record which still stands today for the most home runs by a teenager.

Tony's stance was an aggressive one, right up on home plate. He suffered two separate fractures in 1964, his wrist and his ulna.

In his sophomore season, Conig was the home run champion in the AL with 32.

Billy Conigliaro signed with the Sox in the summer of '65 after graduating from high school, and the two brothers were at spring training together in the spring of '66. By this time, though, Tony was an established celebrity with a couple of pop recordings to his credit, and simply traveled in different circles than his younger brother. Billy needed seasoning as a ballplayer and first joined the big league ballclub in 1969.

Of course, by then, the Impossible Dream Team of 1967 had come and gone. Tony C helped spark the club that magical year for the first 4½ months, in the process becoming the youngest American League player ever to reach the 100 home run plateau. He was also named to his first (and, as it happened, only) All-Star squad. But he still crowded the plate, almost as an article of faith. In spring training, Tony suffered a shoulder blade fracture during batting practice—certainly no "purpose pitch" or brushback. On August 18, 1967, a Jack Hamilton pitch struck Tony square on the spot where the eye, the cheek and the temple all come together. It was such a serious injury that the last rites were administered to the young star right-fielder. The very evening before, Ted Williams had sent a message through one of Tony's rock and roll business partners that Tony should back off the plate a bit. Ted said he was crowding it too much. Tony was in a slump, though, and Billy (at the August 18 game, since he was out with an injury from his work in the minors) reported that Tony's response was that "he was going to get closer." He didn't want to be perceived as giving in, and he didn't want to yield any advantage.

The resulting tragedy cost Tony the rest of the '67 season (and probably cost the Red Sox the Series, just as Jim Rice's broken arm in 1975 probably spelled the difference in that one; both Series had gone to the full seven games). Tony lost all of 1968 as well. Most people doubted he would ever play again, but he persevered—even working out to see if he could make the team as a pitcher (at age 11, the Little Leaguer had gone 8–0 with two no-hitters).

In 1969, both Conigliaros saw time with the Sox. It was Billy's rookie year and, like his brother, he opened in Boston with a bang. Two of them, in fact. Billy had earned a spot midway through spring training; he had appeared briefly in a couple of early-season road games and was 0-for-1. But his first Fenway start came on April 16—ironically as a sub for brother Tony, who'd suffered a minor knee injury a day or two earlier. Though he made an out his first time up, when Billy came to bat in the third inning, he slammed a Dave Leonhard 2–2 slider into the left-center screen. Next time up, in the sixth inning, Billy hit another home run into the same place, off the same Orioles pitcher. This time it was a fast ball. Two solo shots. Rico Petrocelli got on Billy C when the youngster seemed too glum for the photographers after the 11–8 loss to Balitmore. "Come on, Billy, smile." "We lost," countered the competitive Conigliaro, but then acquiesced. The home debut accounted for half of his homers that year. Conigliaro dad Sal missed the game; he was at work at Triangle Tool and Die.

Tony was named Comeback Player of the Year in 1969, homering in his first game and ending the year with a total of 20. Billy fared well, batting .287 in just 80 at-bats, with the four home runs. 1970 was a year when both brothers did well—Billy batted .271 but had 18 homers and over 400 plate appearances. Tony doubled his younger brother's home run total, with 36, hitting .266. With Billy's 18 and Tony's 36 that year, the two combined for 54 roundtrippers. That's a single season record for home runs by a brother combination. One incident saw both brothers involved, in a fashion: Tony was hit by a pitch, attacked the pitcher, and was ejected. Billy took Tony's place in the lineup and when his turn came around, homered into the upper deck. When Billy got back to the clubhouse, he said that "Tony was jumping up and down."

But Tony's eyesight was not getting better. Remarkably, he admitted later on that he'd accomplished all that he had in 1970 with pretty much just one eye, compensating for the other one. The stats didn't show it, but the Sox suspected that his vision was actually getting worse, and so traded Tony to the California Angels after the season was over. Billy stayed on with Boston. David Cataneo, author of the excellent book *Tony C*, quotes Billy, seated in the Red Sox dugout: "It was very strange seeing him in another uniform, playing against the home team. You thought things like that didn't happen."

Tony had a poor year in a more limited role. Billy did OK (.262, 11 HR) but was traded, too, to Milwaukee. He had acquitted himself well, but his was clearly a career overshadowed by his brother's tragedy. Billy's average dropped progressively for each of the five seasons he played.

Tony came back to Boston in 1975 for one last try, after three years away, and made the team. But he wasn't productive. This was, like 1967, another year the Red Sox won the pennant, but this time Tony's .123 average, his two HR and nine RBIs over 21 games was really not a factor. He wasn't doing the team or himself any good, so he retired for good.

Ironically, Tony C was on both pennant-winning teams (1967 and 1975) but never saw postseason play. Brother Billy did. It was nothing to write home about, though. Billy's last season was with the 1973 Oakland A's. He hit an even .200, without even one home run. In the ALCS, he went 0-for-4 with two strikeouts in the one game he played. In the Series, Billy appeared in three games and went 0-for-3 in pinch-hitting roles.

Several years later, when both brothers were long out of baseball, Billy drove Tony into Boston so Tony could interview for a broadcasting job with the Red Sox. On the way home, Tony C suffered a heart attack (he was only 37) which left him bedridden for life. His incredibly loyal brother Billy—indeed the whole Conigliaro family—bore the burden of seeing Tony nearly totally incapacitated. After eight long years of struggle and suffering, Tony Conigliaro slipped away, dead at age 45. It was a merciful end to a long and painful period. Author Cataneo reports that Billy shed tears, "joyful that Tony's torture was over."

Marty Barrett and Tommy Barrett

Marty Barrett and Tommy Barrett were both second basemen for Boston. Marty, the eldest brother, had the more successful career, nine years with the Red Sox and a final few games with the Padres afterwards. Marty hit a solid .278 for Boston and played his position well, twice leading the league in fielding at second base. He typically batted second in the order, and was one of the league's harder batters to strike out. In 1986, he was the MVP of the American League Championship Series against the California Angels (batting .367 with five RBIs and four runs scored, and 80 chances in the field without an error). He hit even better in the World Series, but pitcher Bruce Hurst was due to get the nod—before Boston's hopes all fell apart late in Game Six. Barrett hit .433, with an on-base percentage of .514, again without an error, only scoring once—in large part because between them Bill Buckner and Jim Rice only drove in one run all Series long.

Barrett felt his best year was 1988; though not the year he hit for the highest average, he drove in more runs (65) than in any other season. He was a steady fielder, rarely missing a game prior to his right knee injury. See the section in this book on hidden ball tricks. Marty pulled off the trick three times, tying him with Johnny Pesky for the most by a Red Sox player.

Unfortunately, Marty's career ended sooner than he would have liked, due to a midsummer ACL tear in 1989. He sued the Red Sox and part-owner Dr. Arthur Pappas for medical malpractice—not providing the proper medical advice and treatment. The suit was resolved in 1995 with a settlement reported as $2.4 million.

Though less than two years younger, Tommy Barrett originally signed with the Yankees in 1982 but didn't crack the majors until he was 28—and then it was with the Phillies, in 1988. He played a few games in '88 and '89, but it wasn't until 1992 that he made it back to The Show. In 1992, Tommy appeared in four games for the Red Sox, ensuring him a permanent place on the list of relatives who both played for Boston. In five plate appearances, all in a three-day stretch from August 14–16, he walked twice but went 0-for-3 officially. He did score once, with the go-ahead run coming in on a Wade Boggs single as a pinch-runner for Jack Clark.

Pedro Martinez and Ramon Martinez

Which two brothers between them hold the most Cy Young Awards?

Ramon Martinez (his first name is Nomar spelled backwards) had four years of major league ball under his belt before brother Pedro (Ordep spelled backwards) followed in his footsteps. Ramon had done well for the Dodgers, and been a 20-game winner in 1990—with a league-leading 12 complete games. Both brothers have the same middle name: Jaime. For 1992 and 1993, the two brothers were on the same Dodgers team, but Pedro was dealt before the 1994 season began. Pedro put in four seasons for the Montreal Expos, while Ramon soldiered on with Los Angeles. Ramon's 123–77 record with the Dodgers is testimony to how good he was, until a serious injury during 1998 shelved him for more than a year.

Pitching for opposing teams in the same league, Pedro and Ramon Martinez only faced each other once as starting pitchers, on August 29, 1996. It was quite a game. Ramon was working for the Dodgers and was 10–6 on the season; Pedro was 11–8 with the Expos with a somewhat higher ERA. They were actually the sixth set of brothers to face each other in major league ball. The Madduxes, Niekros, and Perrys had, and so had Virgil and Jesse Barnes and Tom and Pat Underwood. Pedro took the 2–1 loss, despite a complete game effort with 12 Ks and just one walk. He yielded two runs on six hits, two of which were back-to-back homers for Mike Piazza and Eric Karros. Ramon threw eight, and walked five batters but he only gave up three hits and one run. He struck out seven. When Pedro was traded to the Red Sox after winning the Cy Young Award in the 1997 season (too expensive for the Expos to re-sign), the only time they'd likely face each other would be in the World Series. That chance never came.

The two brothers once again put on the same uniform, though, three years later in 1999. Ramon was coming off some serious shoulder surgery (rotator cuff) and it was his first start in 15 months. It was Pedro's third year with Boston and he'd won himself a second Cy in 1999, unanimously, with a 23–4 record, 313 strikeouts, and a 2.01 ERA. Pedro also hit a stretch in August and September where he struck out at least one batter in 40 consecutive innings. During the stretch, he fanned at least 10 batters in eight consecutive games. Ramon had to continue his rehab most of the year, but come September 2, 1999, the Red Sox gave him his first start in more than 14 months. 31-year-old Ramon was shaky and he got his younger brother shook up, too. After the game, Ramon told reporters that in the second inning, "Pedro got nervous when I got the bases loaded and no outs. I said, 'Hey, relax. I've been through that before.'" He got out of that inning without damage but, all told, he let up four runs (three earned) in three-plus innings and the Sox lost, 4–2. Given a couple more starts, Ramon the Elder won third time out, a 4–1 win in seven innings. On October 2, Ramon threw six scoreless innings—and then he threw 5⅔ solid innings in Game Three of the playoffs. Pedro had shoulder pain himself in Game One and had had to exit after the first four innings.

Everyone hoped 2000 would see both brothers blossom. No one expected Pedro could do better than he had in 1999—but in fact, he did! Opposing batters only hit .167 off him

(the major league single-season record) and he posted the lowest on-base percentage against (.213) in over 100 years. His ERA was just 1.74 in a year when the league average was 4.91. For the second year in a row, the Cy Young was awarded him—again by unanimous vote. Ramon, though, struggled. He'd acquitted himself well enough at the tag end of 1999, but in 2000 his record was 10–8. Worse, his ERA was a fairly poor 6.13. That was it for Ramon. He called it a career. Quite a good one (135–86, with a 3.62

Pedro Martinez poking Ramon during the National Anthem, Santo Domingo spring training game, 2000. Bill Nowlin photo.

lifetime ERA), but with a disappointing end in his 13th season in the big leagues. There was hope that younger brother Jesus Martinez could make the team, but he did not.

In the meantime, Pedro continued to pitch well. 2001 saw him suffer some, and Red Sox Nation began to hold its breath every time he took the mound with a typically Red Sox sense of foreboding that any pitch could be Pedro's last. In 2002, though, Pedro came back strong, with a 20–4 record and a 2.26 ERA, second only to Barry Zito in the Cy Young Award voting. Pedro lowered his ERA further, to 2.22, in 2003 and helped take the Red Sox to the seventh game of the American League Championship Series with a 14–4 season. He seemed to have Game Seven sewn up, and left the field to the congratulations of his teammates, staked to a 5–2 lead after David Ortiz hit a home run in the top of the eighth—only to be unexpectedly sent back out to pitch again by manager Grady Little. Pedro was bombed for three runs, and the Red Sox ultimately lost the game and a trip to the 2003 World Series.

In 2004, Pedro helped bring the Red Sox to the Promised Land, with a sub-par season (16–9, 3.90 ERA), but with two key wins in postseason play. His contract completed, and the Red Sox brass believing his best years were behind him, the New York Mets offered much more than the Red Sox and Pedro left for greener pastures in New York.

FATHERS AND SONS

Smoky Joe Wood and Joe Wood Jr.

It's one of those clever trivia questions. What father/son brace of Boston pitchers won 116 games and lost 57 for the Red Sox?

The answer is Smoky Joe Wood and Joe Junior. Joe was 116–56 for Boston and Frank was 0–1. "Smoky Joe" was, of course, spectacular with a *career* ERA of 2.03. His best year for wins and losses was 1912 when he was 34–5 and his best year for ERA was 1915 when he posted a league-leading 1.49 ERA (15–5). In both years, the Red Sox won the World Series. Wood won three Series games in 1912 and lost one; he didn't pitch at all in the 1915 Fall Classic. He'd gone 15–5 that year but was hurt to the point where he couldn't even lift his arm. Manager Bill Carrigan came to him, explains his son Bob, and asked, "How's your arm, Joe?" "If you need me,

I'll be in the bullpen, but my arm is bad. I'm in the bullpen. That's the best I can do." He didn't play at all in 1916, still suffering the bad arm. There may have been a little contract disagreement as well, but it was really the arm which kept him out the full year. He'd been getting treatments from doctors, but nothing much helped.

He contacted Tris Speaker, his old roommate and Red Sox buddy and now player-manager with the Indians, and they decided he'd come over to Cleveland and try out. He thought his arm was going to be OK but it never was. He appeared only briefly in 1917, but when 1918 rolled around, there were so many ballplayers in military service that the team was having difficulty creating an outfield. Someone suggested, "Why don't you put Joe out there?" and he made it well enough (.296 in 422 at-bats) that he played five seasons as an outfielder—batting a very impressive .298 from 1918 through 1922. Speaker had him platooned with Elmer Smith in 1919, 1920, and 1921 but made Joe the regular outfielder in 1922. He hit .297 in his final season. "He'd proved everything to himself, and everybody else, and he had an offer to go to Yale and coach the Yale team, and he decided he'd better take it," recalls son Bob.

As a pitcher, Joe was 0–1 for Cleveland, appearing for them only briefly in 1917, 1919, and 1920.

How could he have a son known as Joe Junior, when he was born Howard Ellsworth Wood, and the record books show his son's name as Joseph Frank Wood? Good question. Bob Wood, Joe Junior's brother, explains: "He wasn't really a junior. My father's name wasn't really Joe, either. He legally had his name changed to Joe Wood. Joe. Never Joseph." And, while we're at it, Bob Wood explains, it was always Smoky. Never Smokey. And, he further adds, "My brother was Joe. Not Joseph. His birth certificate was Joe. Joseph Frank Wood? No, that's not right."

Joe Junior was called Joe Junior, whatever his given name, but he was hardly a chip off the old block. His brief three-game career took place in one of the war years, 1944, when he was 28. Joe Junior's debut was on May 1, 1944. The game was an 11–4 rout of Boston by the Senators. Yank Terry yielded six hits in 1⅔ innings. Clem Hausmann gave up five in 2⅓ innings. The Senators were up 6–0 after they completed their half of the fourth inning. "Only Joe Wood Jr., bearer of an illustrious baseball name, could stop the Nats. He held them to one run in three innings, then departed [in the seventh] for a pinch-hitter [who didn't hit safely]. Oscar Judd replaced him in the eighth and yielded seven hits in the last two frames," wrote the *Globe* sportswriter.

Joe Jr. appeared in just three games, with just one start. He carried a lifetime mark of 0–1, 6.52 ERA, having pitched a total of 9⅔ innings, and surrendered 13 hits and three walks. He struck out five. Given that it was wartime, with depleted rosters, why didn't he get more of a shot? He'd signed in 1941 with the Red Sox and was successful in Scranton over two seasons, his Scranton stint including a no-hitter. He played in 1943 with Louisville in the American Association. He never went into the service, as he had a wife and child. While in Boston for his cup of coffee, he developed a bad arm and was sent down to Louisville; he finished that season with the San Diego Padres in the Pacific Coast League (5–4, 2.50 ERA, in 79 innings). He finished his career with Sacramento, hurting his arm with what years later he decided must have been a rotator cuff injury. "They can fix them now, but they couldn't back then," he told Bill Swank in *Echoes from Lane Field*.

There could have been other Woods in the big leagues. Bob Wood was a left-handed first baseman and pitched occasionally. He played a "lot of college ball, a lot of semipro ball and then I went in the service and played a lot of service ball. Unfortunately, the Army got me before I was able to sign. I had an opportunity to sign, but didn't." Bob got his commission and served in the medical corps, spending a fair amount of time playing both basketball and baseball in the service. The scouts talked with me but I went in the service instead." He

Joe Wood "Junior" and Smoky Joe, 1941. Courtesy of Bob Wood.

was invited to work out with the Red Sox, who held their spring training at Tufts College in Massachusetts in 1943, and he would have joined Joe Junior there, but for the fact that the particular day he was invited to work out was the day of his wedding luncheon. Bob went on to a lifetime career in hospital administration—with a sideline in antiques. Bob often attends baseball memorabilia shows; he was doing as many as 42 a year, but in his early 80s has cut back to maybe 16 a year.

There was yet another brother, Steve. He was a pitcher, and played college baseball at Colgate with Bob. Steve actually did sign with the Red Sox and went to Scranton and then on up to Louisville, "but that's as far as he got. He was moving up the ladder, but then he went in the service. We were both at Ford Devens," Bob remembers, "we played ball there. Then he went overseas."

A father who was one of the bigger stars in the Red Sox sky, with two sons who signed with the Red Sox (one who made it briefly) and a third son who talked to Red Sox scouts. It could have been quite a family affair. Only Bob's twin sister never played ball. Maybe she should have contacted Marty McManus and tried out for the All-American Girls Professional Baseball League. (See information about Red Sox manager McManus and the AAGPBL elsewhere in this book.)

Was Smoky Joe a good teacher as a father? As with any father in baseball, he was away a lot, working. Away during the springs and summers and early fall. Even after he retired, Bob recalls, "When we were playing ball at Deerfield Academy or in college, he had his team [he coached for Yale for 20 years] playing games, too, so he didn't see too many of ours, but during the summer he was always there. After his season was over in June, he always got to our games around Connecticut. He never really put it to us [as a teacher] but if we had anything we wanted to ask him about or if he saw anything we were doing that he wanted to comment on, well, he certainly did that."

Ed Connolly, Sr. and Ed Connolly, Jr.

Ed Senior was a catcher who played for the Red Sox beginning in 1929. A native of Brooklyn, "Butch" Connolly was signed by the Red Sox in 1928 and assigned to the Pittsfield club in the Eastern League. There he was rated an excellent receiver but only a fair hitter.

He joined the Sox late in 1929 and appeared in five games, with eight at-bats but nary a hit. The following spring, manager Heinie Wagner suggested he might be better off if he batted from the other side of the plate. He'd come up as a right-handed hitter and so he appears in the record books. "I was a left-handed hitter when I started playing all in school, and my coach made me hit right-handed," Connolly told his manager. "He said I would never get to the major leagues as a left-handed hitting catcher, that the big leagues wanted catchers who batted right-handed." Wagner told the 21-year-old backstop, "He was wrong…The big leaguers want catchers who can hit, and they don't care whether they bat right-handed or left-handed. Go back to hitting left-handed."

From .000 in 1929, there was really only one way to go—up. Whichever way he hit (the record books don't acknowledge the probability that he switched to the other side of the plate after his first year), he did hit better. In 48 at-bats, he made nine hits including a couple of doubles and knocked in seven runs, for an average of .188. In '31 he got almost twice as many at-bats but had fewer hits; his average was but .075, surely one of the lowest for a player with 93 at-bats. Connolly never saw much duty—the most time he saw was during the nadir of the Red Sox in 1932 when the team only won 43 games all year long. Ed hit .225 and drove in 21 runs that year—his last—but his career mark was just .178. He never hit a home run. He drove in 31 lifetime. He wasn't all that good fielding a catcher at the major league level, with a fielding average of .966.

After the Red Sox, Ed stayed in pro ball a while longer, playing for Jersey City, Kansas City, Galveston, and Reading before retiring in 1934. He was a tough one. In a Texas League game, he was knocked down by a young prospect for the Indians. He warned him not to do that again, and the pitcher threw another close one, whereupon, in the words of writer Jimmy Murphy, Ed "strode out to the mount and hit him flush on the chops and dropped him cold."

Late in 1963, Ed died unexpectedly, in Pittsfield, Massachusetts—the town where he began his career. He was employed by the Massachusetts Natural Resources Department at the time of his death.

Had he lived just six months longer, he would have seen Ed Junior begin his career with the Red Sox. Junior had been born in 1939 so he never had seen his dad play, either, even when a toddler. Junior was born in Brooklyn, too, and he was a left-handed pitcher—though not the best of pitchers. Were he and his father backyard batterymates, as Ed Junior grew and developed into a prospect himself? Sports columnist Murphy wrote that the elder Connolly "had groomed his son to be a big leaguer." Son Ed also passed through Reading, where Eddie Popowski was impressed with him and talked major league manager Johnny Pesky into giving him a spring training invite. Connolly was raised a Red Sox fan, so this was the fulfillment of a lifelong dream.

Ed Junior—dubbed The Curver—got 15 starts but only won four while losing 11 in 1964 under manager Pesky (ERA 4.91). Early in the 1964 season, Connolly's spring training roommate was another Red Sox player to have a relative on the team—Tony Conigliaro, whose brother Billy later played for Boston. Ed's first game was April 19, 1964—the Red Sox were 2–1 and Eddie Connolly got the fourth start of the young season. He struck out six batters, while walking five. He didn't let up a hit his first three innings, then gave up a single in the fourth. One hit through four, and he got the first batter in the fifth with a strikeout. Then the runs began. First came a perfect bunt by Don Buford, which Malzone had no chance with and so let roll; it stayed fair. A single followed, and then a wild pitch let in a run. Another walk, but then came a tailor-made double play grounder to Malzone at third. The ball took an unexpected hop and went for a single, another run scoring. A squibber to the right of the mound drove in the third run of the inning and then another unintended infield dribbler brought in the fourth. There was a good bunt and one solid hit in the inning, but four runs had come across by the time it was over. Connolly showed promise, though, and Pesky gave him a fair shot. He did throw one complete game shutout, but it wasn't an impressive year. He struck out 73 in 80⅔ innings, but walked 64.

The following spring, Billy Herman had become the manager and Connolly was wild in both of his two preseason starts. He traveled north with the team, though, and stayed with the big league club for 45 days but was eventually sent down to Toronto. The Indians drafted him after the season was over and he reappeared in the majors with Cleveland in 1967; he was 2–1 that year but with a poor 7.48 ERA. In the off-season, he was a player-to-be-named later in a trade to the Angels, but didn't make the big league team in spring training, so he quit.

He found far greater success as a stockbroker with Kidder Peabody in Pittsfield, making more money after one year than he ever had in baseball, and rising to become a senior vice president at Paine Webber in New York City. Ed Junior died in 1998.

Walt Ripley and Allen Ripley

Unlike Ed Connolly, Sr., Walt Ripley not only had a chance to see his son break in with Boston. He had the opportunity to follow his son's entire major league career through retirement. Walt himself was born in Worcester, but was first noticed at Mansfield High School. At age 18, after his first year at Deerfield Academy, his parents officially signed his contract for him at Fenway Park. Walter Ripley got into his first game at age 19. This was early in the Yawkey years, in 1935. In his August 17 debut, he pitched in game one, a double defeat in a twinbill against the Browns. The Sox lost 11–7, and then were shut out in the second game, 7–0. All in all, he only appeared in two games, both times in relief, for a total of four innings for the Red Sox. He gave up seven hits, though, and three walks. His ERA rests at 9.00. Before he turned 20—though he didn't know it at the time—he had completed his career in major league baseball.

Son Allen was born in 1952, in Norwood. He saw more major league service time. On April 10, 1978, nearly 43 years after Walt Ripley's Sox stint, his son Allen started for the Red Sox and went eight innings, allowing four runs "only one of which…was his total responsibility" wrote the *Globe*. Victimized by two Jerry Remy errors, the inning should have been over before he gave up a three-run homer to Andre Thornton. "He could have had a shutout. He pitched like hell" said Don Zimmer. "It's a shame to get pitching like that [and not win]," commented Carlton Fisk. When Ripley departed after eight, the score was tied. Reggie Cleveland yielded a run in the ninth and the Sox lost, 5–4. Allen Ripley won two and lost five that year. Had he won three and lost four, of course, there never would have been a Bucky Dent game. Ripley was 3–1 the following year with about the same amount of playing time. He cracked 100 innings with the Giants in 1980 and played with them and the Cubs. His last year was 1982. With Boston, he was 5–6. Lifetime, 23–27 with an ERA precisely half that of his father: 4.50.

Did his father work with him on his pitching in the backyard? Tutor him in the ways of the game? Help him get signed with the Red Sox? We don't know. Allen was signed to the Red Sox by Lefty Lefebvre, who lived at the time in Seekonk, the next town over from where Allen played ball. Lefebvre saw him pitch, liked what he saw and signed him. Asked about Walt Ripley's involvement in the process, Lefebvre said, "I only met his father once, I think." There was definitely no active paternal involvement in the signing. Word is that Allen fell in with some unfortunate company and got himself in some personal difficulties and has pretty much chosen to keep to himself in recent years. We wish him well.

Dolph Camilli and Doug Camilli

Adolph Louis Camilli broke into big league ball late in 1933 after several seasons with San Francisco and Sacramento in the Pacific Coast League. Purchased by the Cubs, he spent the first 11 of his 12 seasons in the National League with the Cubs, Phils, and Dodgers. Camilli's best year was 1941, with the Dodgers, when he led the NL in both home runs (34) and RBIs (120); he was an All-Star both in 1939 and 1941 and overwhelmingly won the National League's MVP Award in 1941. He appeared in five games of the 1941 World Series, but only had three hits in 18 at-bats and struck out six times.

Camilli was a compact 5′10″ power hitter. One remarkable game came on August 23, 1942, when Doug drove in all six runs, finally beating the New York Giants with a grand slam in the bottom of the 10th inning. Branch Rickey discussed a managerial role with Dolph in early 1943, but there was no interest. Traded to the Giants in August, he chose instead to retire, characterizing himself as "washed up" and saying he'd retire to his cattle ranch in California though it meant giving up the very considerable salary still due him for the balance of the 1943 campaign. The veteran Dodger's decision to quit was at least partially a partisan one: "I hated the Giants. This was real serious; this was no put-on stuff. Their fans hated us, and our fans hated them. I said nuts to them, and I quit." [*The New York Times*, October 22, 1967]

In late December, he signed a two-year deal to serve as player-manager for the PCL's Oakland Oaks, though the deal had to be approved by the commissioner, given Camilli's refusal to report to the Giants. He was one of the best hitters in the league before an August foot injury forced him to focus exclusively as manager.

Fired in June, 1945, the left-handed first baseman was approached by the Red Sox and signed on for a final season, his first in the American League. Camilli played 63 games for the Red Sox, hitting just .212 with two home runs against pitching depleted by war. It was his worst season in a career where he averaged .277 and hit 239 homers. It was time to get out. Both he and Bob Johnson were released on December 29.

Dolph Camilli stayed in baseball, managing teams in the PCL and in the Indians system, coaching some, and becoming a scout for the Phillies, Yankees, and Oakland Athletics. One other day of note occurred on August 4, 1962. In an exhibition game which featured Dom DiMaggio in left, Joe DiMaggio in center, and Vince DiMaggio in right, Dolph played for San Francisco as well, putting in a little time at first base. Dolph Camilli died in 1997.

Dolph and his wife had five sons, all of whom played baseball, but it was son Doug who made the majors. Two daughters were involved in athletics as well. In 1961, both Dolph Jr. and Bruce Camilli signed bonus deals with the Yankees on the same day, but Doug had already made a few headlines as a prospect in the Dodgers system.

Doug Camilli was born in Philadelphia at the end of Dolph's 1936 season. He was nine when his father bowed out of baseball. Did his father

Dolph Camilli and Doug Camilli. Courtesy of Brace Photo

have something to do with his becoming a ballplayer? "Early on. I think it had something to do with it, sure," he says. Doug became a catcher, though. "He didn't have anything to do with that part of it." Doug started his own career at the tail end of November 1956, signing with the Dodgers—who had now moved to Los Angeles. His first game with the big league club came on September 25, 1960; he singled in four at-bats, after taking over for catcher John Roseboro. Doug played five seasons with the Dodgers, appearing in 163 games all told. With the start of the 1965 campaign, he migrated to the AL, too, sold to the Washington Senators in November 1964.

With Washington, he appeared in 149 games over three seasons. When he broke his thumb in a game against the Yankees in July 1966, Joe Pignatano took over and Doug only got into three more games, in September. He was used throughout the 1967 season, but only appeared in 30 games, batting .183. He was sold to Hawaii at the very end of the season. As late as

March 1968, he still hoped to hook on for another season as catcher with the Senators, but it was not to be, and Doug took a coaching position with the Senators where he served under manager Jim Lemon for the 1968 season. Lemon managed the Senators for just the one year.

In 1969, Ted Williams took over as manager of the Senators and Camilli served as Ted's bullpen coach. "I kind of came with the ballclub," Doug explains. "I was under contract." Interestingly, the record books show Doug as appearing in one game that year—three AB with a single. The team had put Camilli on the active roster a couple of days ahead of time. "It was at the end of the year and one of the catchers had a bad hand. They wanted…just in case. It was a mopping up game. We tied it and we went into extra innings."

The game was on September 14, 1969 against Detroit and starting catcher Jim French popped foul to Norm Cash in his one at bat. He was lifted for pinch-hitter Versalles, but in vain. Camilli came in behind the plate to start off the seventh. The second batter up was Al Kaline, and Camilli snared his foul popup. At the plate, though, Camilli whiffed in the bottom of the seventh, ending the inning for the Senators. He came up again, with one out, in the bottom of the ninth. He was caught looking and struck out again. The Tigers scored two in the top of the ninth and the game went into extra innings. Doug Camilli came up again in the home 11th, with two outs and Del Unser having just singled. Camilli drove a single himself, moving Unser to third, but the Senators rally ended there, and the Tigers scored three in the top of the 12th to win it.

So Doug Camilli hit .333 in his final season as a major league ballplayer. Though Washington played 15 more games that year, Camilli never got another shot.

Doug came back to Boston and served as bullpen coach for four seasons under Eddie Kasko, signing in December 1969. He stayed in the organization for another dozen years afterward, in his words, "Managing and coaching. Coached mostly. In the minors. Traveled some, like a roving instructor sometimes. Managed in Greensboro. Two years in Winter Haven. There was a couple of years in between there. My last year with them was '92."

Dolph's brother and Doug's uncle Frankie Camilli was a heavyweight prizefighter who fought under the name Frankie Campbell until he was killed due to injuries to the head sustained in his fight against Max Baer on August 25, 1930.

Haywood Sullivan and Marc Sullivan

At 6'4" and 215 pounds, Haywood Sullivan was a formidable backstop when he broke in with the Red Sox on September 20, 1955. He didn't get to play all that much, though—just six at-bats in '55, only one in '57, and but two in '59. The astute reader will note that he did not play for Boston at all in even-numbered years. After three "seasons" and a total of nine at-bats, he had yet to make a hit, though he did reach base on a walk in 1959. In 1960, though, Sullivan broke through on his 17th plate appearance, singling to left. He played in 52 games and accumulated 124 at-bats. Unfortunately, his hitting (.161) didn't set any worlds on fire.

Sullivan did play three years for the Kansas City Royals, 1961–63, where he hit .240. Somehow this is the player who the Yawkeys seemed to "adopt" as a favorite. In fact, Jean Yawkey seemed to like him so much that he was given co-ownership of the Red Sox team in 1978 and he remained a co-owner through the 1993 season.

Marc Sullivan was born during one of those even-numbered years (1958) and he made the big league club himself, right at the end of the 1982 season, and went 2-for-6 in two games. The same height as his father—who was general manager of the Red Sox at the time—Marc weighed 10 pounds less but he seemed to start off as though he were determined to reverse the pattern of the years with his father. They did share the same middle name. Marc played in 1982 but not the odd-numbered year 1983, then came back again in 1984—where he again played in two games, again had six at-bats. This time, though, Marc hit safely three times.

This may have impressed GM Lou Gorman, who—breaking the obverse mold—brought Marc back in 1985. The elder Sullivan remained an owner of the team throughout the Gorman years. In '85, Marc hit .174 in 69 at-bats, a record he improved to .193 in 119 at-bats the following pennant-winning year. The young catcher played in 60 games with 160 at-bats in '87 but his average tailed off to .169, despite again matching his career-high two home runs.

With the two-day player strike in August 1985, Marc Sullivan became the first player in all of baseball to go on strike against his own father.

During Haywood Sullivan's six seasons as GM, only in the last year did the team win less than half their games. Overall, his record as GM stands at 499–416, a .545 winning percentage. These were the Zimmer/Houk years, pretty good years overall. They might have been better but for Sullivan's failure to renew the contracts of two Red Sox stars after the 1980 season—Carlton Fisk and Fred Lynn. They just walked away and became free agents when the general manager failed to tender them new contracts within the mandated period. It was what you might call a "negative draft."

Dick Ellsworth and Steve Ellsworth

Dick Ellsworth is the dad. He pitched one year for the Red Sox, 1968, and a brief couple of appearances in 1969. Steve Ellsworth is the son. He pitched just one year for the Red Sox, too—some 20 years after his father, in 1988. Dick hailed from Wyoming, though raised in Fresno, California; he broke in with the Cubs at age 18, fresh out of high school. He spent eight seasons with the Cubbies, including a 22–10 season with a 2.11 ERA in 1963. No Cubs lefthander has won 20 games since Ellsworth. The 1966 season, though, was a rough one. Even though the Cubs did reasonably well, Dick had a very disappointing 8–22 year, albeit with a decent 3.98 ERA. In December 1966, he was traded to the Phillies for Ray Culp and some cash. 1967 wasn't a good year for him, either, but when he was traded to the Red Sox in December 1967, he did very well indeed. Ellsworth posted a 16–7 record in 1968, with a 3.03 ERA. The team was lackluster, but Ellsworth stood out. (He says he might have won 20 games, but the son unintentionally undermined the father: Dick caught mumps from his son Steve and missed at least five starts in August.) Soon after the start of the 1969 season, both he and Ken Harrelson were traded to the Indians. He pitched for Cleveland and Milwaukee for the next three years, until he was released at the end of June in 1971.

In 1968, while with the Red Sox, Dick brought his son Steve to the annual Fathers and Sons game. Steve turned eight that year. Twenty years later, he was wearing a Red Sox uniform again and pitching at Fenway Park once more, this time for real. His father was tall—6'4"—but Steve had four inches on his dad. He didn't fare as well, though. Steve, a right-hander, ran up a record of just one win against six defeats, with an ERA of 6.75.

Both father and son live in the Fresno area, and Steve has three sons. Dick told Ron Marshall of *Boston Baseball*, "At least one of them is going to be a good ballplayer, I can see that already. I don't know who is scouting for the Red Sox in the San Joaquin Valley, but they better put him on alert!" Maybe someday, we'll see the first three-generation line among the fraternity of Red Sox players.

FATHERS AND DAUGHTERS

It hasn't come to pass yet, but earlier in this book we have seen the story of Tom Satriano and his daughter Gina Satriano, in the section devoted to women and the Red Sox. Both have played professional baseball at Fenway Park.

OTHER RELATIVES WHO SERVED THE SOX

Shano Collins and Bob Gallagher

A native of Charlestown, Massachusetts, who as a kid used to sell peanuts at the Walpole Street Grounds, John "Shano" Collins was a versatile outfielder with the Red Sox from 1921 through 1925. After 11 years with the Chicago White Sox, he came to Boston in a trade for Harry Hooper. Shano was the leadoff hitter on the "Black Sox" team of 1919, along with fellow outfielder Shoeless Joe Jackson, but neither Shano Collins nor similarly-surnamed Eddie Collins were ever accused of being in on the plot to throw the Series. Shano hit .250. He'd already been one of the World Champions in 1917, when the White Sox won it all. In that Series, he hit .286. Lifetime, his regular season average is .264. Shano played all fields—right, center, and left. He passed away in 1955. His name lives on in Bob Gallagher's middle name—Collins, named after his uncle Robert Collins, Shano's son. Robert Collins was killed on Iwo Jima.

Bob Gallagher was Shano's grandson—his mother was Shano's daughter and (born in 1948) he still retains faint memory of sitting on his grandfather's knee. Bob signed with the Red Sox and his first game was May 17, 1972 when he was inserted as a pinch-hitter. He didn't get a hit. That year he only had four more chances to bat and he struck out three of his five at-bats, never getting a major league hit. It must have been a frustrating off-season, wanting to come back and get that hit. He never did, for Boston. When he did, it was with Houston—the very next year, 1973. In fact, he racked up 39 hits (six for extra bases) and hit .264 for the Astros. Bob played in '74 with the Astros and '75 with the Mets, and left with a .220 average.

Gallagher's father might have made the majors, too: "My dad made the hall of fame in basketball at Providence College. He was going to play baseball but he played in the Cape Cod League and he broke his thumb sliding. He got hurt, and it because a problem so he ended up just being a 90-day wonder who ended up going into the service in World War II. He was a good mentor, though. A good motivator. He was certainly my director." Of grandfather Shano Collins, he said, "He was a little better than I was, but I was received very well because of him. A lot of people remembered him…respected that background. There's such lore in Boston. I got more attention than I deserved. I was seven when he died. I remember sitting on his knee at the house, but I didn't talk baseball. At age six or seven, I didn't have that picture. I wish I could go back and ask some questions."

Gallagher's son Zachary showed some talent at baseball, too, but he "wasn't fast enough, wasn't strong enough. It wasn't going to be his sport, not professional. So he just went with what he enjoyed. He went to Stanford as a water polo goalie and played in the NCAA championships for Stanford."

George Susce and George Susce

The father pays for the sins of the son. When pitching prospect George Daniel Susce chose to sign with the Red Sox in 1950, the Cleveland Indians fired his dad, coach George Susce, on January 10. George the elder Susce had been with the Indians since 1941. George Daniel wasn't a junior, though; his father—who bore the nickname "Good Kid"—was named George Cyril Methodius Susce. So the Sox hired G. C. M. Susce. He coached for the Red Sox from 1950 through 1954.

The season after Dad left the Red Sox, the younger Susce pitched for the Red Sox, for whom he worked in parts of four seasons (1955–58), compiling an 18–14 record. In his rookie year, 1955, he threw a one-hitter against the Kansas City A's on July 20. His dad was a coach for KC in 1955, and must have been proud of his son's accomplishment.

Both George Susce, Jr. and Dave Sisler were teammates on the Red Sox (1956–58). Both of their fathers had played major league ball. One other Sox team that included two pitching sons of big leaguers was the 1963 Red Sox which included Chet Nichols, Jr. and Jerry Stephenson.

Dom Dallessandro and Dick Gernert

Dom Dallessandro broke into major league ball with the Red Sox in 1937. The young 23-year-old outfielder had a chance to play, but only garnered a .231 average with 34 hits in 147 at-bats. He needed a little more seasoning. After the 1937 season, the San Diego Padres assigned Ted Williams to the Boston Red Sox in exchange for Dallessandro, Al Niemiec, two minor leaguers, and a sum of money reported between $25,000 and $35,000. In 1938, Dallessandro hit .309 with 22 homers and in 1939 he led the Pacific Coast League with a .368 mark. Dallessandro, known as the "Mighty Mite" in San Diego (he was 5'6" tall), had earned his way back into the major leagues; he began the next year with the Cubs and spent seven seasons there, ultimately compiling a .267 career average. Ted Williams won the Triple Crown in the American Association in '38 and then went on to serve the Red Sox for many years to come. Dallessandro could always say he was traded for Ted Williams.

"Dim Dom" Dallessandro had a nephew who played ball: Dick Gernert. Both were born in Reading, PA, though 15 years apart. Dallessandro was married to Gernert's mother's sister. Was his nephew inspired by him in some way? "We used to go see him play whenever he came to Philadelphia," remembers Gernert, who broke in with the Red Sox just five years after uncle Dom had retired from the Cubs following the 1947 season. Gernert, a 6'3" slugger and first baseman for the Sox, played both for Boston and, briefly, the Cubs—even though they shared the diamond more than once in 1950. After leaving the Cubs, Dallessandro played in the American Association for a few years and was with Indianapolis in 1950, the same year Dick Gernert played with Louisville. The families apparently were not close, and divorce took them further apart in years to come. Though uncle and nephew played against each other, trading positions at the half innings, Gernert doesn't recall talking baseball with his uncle either then or later in his career.

Matts Batts and Danny Heep

Another uncle/nephew combination involves catcher Matt Batts (with the Red Sox from 1947–1951) and his nephew, outfielder Danny Heep (with the Sox in 1989 and 1990). Both are natives of San Antonio, though Batts has long made his home in Baton Rouge. Matt's half-sister Eva married Jake Heep, who worked for the Air Force at Kelly Field in San Antone.

Jake Heep himself was a pretty good ballplayer (in his brother-in-law's estimation), but had to work to make a living. Perhaps he saw his dream come true through his son Danny, who played 13 seasons of major league ball.

Matt Batts was signed by the Sox while at Baylor, signed with a $2,500 bonus by legendary University of Texas coach and scout for the Red Sox Billy Disch, but this was 1942 and Matt ended up in the service like so many others. He served in the Army Air Corps (later the U.S. Air Force) as a crew chief working on planes at Randolph Field. After the war he entered the Red Sox farm system and made the big league club as a backup catcher (to Birdie Tebbetts) in 1948, hitting .314 in 118 at-bats. He'd opened some eyes in a brief September 1947 debut, hitting an even .500 in 16 at-bats. Despite getting a few more at-bats, Batts had a sort of sophomore slump in 1949, dipping to .242, while beginning to feel a little frustrated at not playing regularly.

Adjusting to the role, perhaps, he rebounded to .273 in 1950—close to what proved to be his career batting average of .269. When the Red Sox brought in manager Steve O'Neill to take over for Lou Boudreau, Batts got much less work. "O'Neill didn't like me for some reason," he says, still surprised, as he'd been friendly with two of O'Neill's children. Early in 1951, he was traded to the St. Louis Browns. Batts played for the Browns, the Tigers, the White Sox, and the Reds—always as a backup backstop. After 10 seasons, he retired after the 1956 season to work in the district atorney's office, eventually leaving that work to go into the printing business that another attorney and Matt launched, and which Matt's wife Arlene ran. Arlene and Matt had two daughters, and there's another thread one could explore someday: one of their daughters married *Boston Herald* baseball writer Larry Claflin.

The year after Matt retired, Daniel William Heep was born—1957. Like his uncle, Heep played for five different major league clubs, but he was an outfielder. Like his uncle as well, Danny's role was a backup role. He played baseball at Lee High and became a college star at San Antonio's St. Mary's University, a two-time All-American (1976 and 1978)…as a pitcher. Drafted by the Houston Astros in the 1978 second round, he saw his first action the very next year, though just with two base hits in the 14 at-bats that year. After playing part-time the next three seasons, he was traded to the New York Mets for pitcher Mike Scott. He got in four years with the Mets, two mediocre ones and then two pretty good ones (hitting .280 and .282). He'd set a major league record in his second year, hitting four pinch-hit homers all in the same season. Uncle Matt says that, while he played a little catch with his nephew, they never spent time working together.

After the 1986 season (he was 2-for-15 in the playoffs), the World Champion Mets let him go. He signed on the following summer with the Dodgers and played for a year and a half before they, too, gave him a release. The 1989 Red Sox took him on in February; with a number of minor injuries to their outfield, Danny got some real playing time (320 at-bats) and he really came through with his best year in pro ball, batting an even .300 with a career-high 49 RBIs. He even appeared in 19 games at first base.

Relegated to just 69 at-bats the following year, he hit a disappointing .174—though he did have the distinction of pitching the last inning of a game against the Twins; Minnesota was up 15–0 when Danny threw the ninth. The final score was 16–0; he'd given up fewer runs than any of the four other Red Sox pitchers. (He'd thrown the last two innings of a blowout game for the Dodgers in 1988.) He failed twice in pinch-hitting roles against Oakland in the 1990 playoffs—but other than Wade Boggs, almost no one else was hitting either, and the A's swept all four games. It was one of four times Danny played in the postseason.

Released by the Red Sox in November, he signed on with the White Sox in April 1991, but was traded to the Braves before seeing any action. Despite hitting .417 in his last year (5-for-12), he wasn't being used much and was released by the Braves in June.

Since 1992, Heep has been teaching baseball to the quite successful University of the Incarnate Word Cardinals in San Antonio. He's married and has two children.

Jack Ryan and Mike Ryan

Mike Ryan, a Red Sox catcher from 1964 through the Impossible Dream season of 1967, had a uniformed relative on the Red Sox: his grandfather's cousin was Jack Ryan, who served as a Sox coach for five years, 1923–27, working under both managers Frank Chance and Lee Fohl. Mike was a defensive specialist who played major league ball from 1964 through 1974. Jack Ryan broke in with Louisville of the old American Association way back in 1889. He later caught for a Boston baseball team, but it was the National League Boston Beaneaters from 1894 through 1896. After his playing career, he coached at the University of Virginia for nine years and then was hired as pitching coach for the Red Sox in March 1923. Though Jack Ryan died in Boston in 1952, Haverhill's Mike Ryan does not recall ever meeting him. Neither Ryan was related to pitcher Jack "Gulfport" Ryan.

Danny Doyle and Denny Doyle

Then there are a couple of Red Sox who *think* they're related, but might not be. Danny Doyle was a catcher, called up right at the end of the 1943 season. He appeared in 13 games but then got a callup of another sort and served in the United States Army in 1944 and 1945. With the onset of diabetes, and all the veteran Sox servicemen returning in 1946, he never saw duty again as a major league ballplayer—though he signed a number of players as one of the most effective Red Sox scouts. Before Pedro arrived, Doyle could laugh that he signed every Sox Cy Young winner—Jim Lonborg and Roger Clemens. In 1988, Danny Doyle was named Midwest Scout of the Year by the Scout of the Year Foundation. Danny lost his sight in his final years, and passed away on December 14, 2004.

Denny Doyle came over to Boston partway into the 1975 pennant-winning season, and hit a solid .310 in 310 at-bats. During the 1975 World Series, the two Doyles met for the first time, though Denny had learned about Danny in an unusual fashion—receiving shipments of bats from Hillerich and Bradsby with "Danny Doyle" inscribed on them. "At the very beginning of my career with the Phillies, they would order my bats from the Louisville Slugger bat company and every so often I would get a shipment of his signature bats. They pulled the wrong guy. I thought it was a joke at first, then I started thinking…ah, no way, so I asked them and they said, 'There's a scout in the Red Sox organization.' I was with the Phillies then. When I came to the Red Sox, I got a few chuckles out of it from a few people."

In fact, there is a strong physical resemblance between the two Doyles. Danny's son Tom is only a few months older than Denny, and he says, "Denny and my dad look quite a lot alike—their complexions. When Denny got traded from the Angels back to Boston, the trainer insisted on calling him Danny. He'd say, 'My name is Denny" "Yeah, right, Danny." Tom's sister Dana Nelson adds, "I can't tell you how much they look alike. There is a great similarity there. Denny Doyle could be my uncle Bill's son; they look so much alike it's uncanny."

Knowing that both families come out of Kentucky, Dana has done some genealogical research back to 1803 but hasn't yet determined any connection. Denny Doyle was born in Glasgow, and Danny's father was born in Mt. Sterling—but the two communities are 169 miles apart. At their first meeting back in '75, Dana laughs, "Denny Doyle used to call my mom 'Mom' when they met in Boston." Denny and Danny talked more when they met in 2001 at the celebrations held in honor of the 100th anniversary of the Red Sox. Danny himself added, "We are related, I'm sure. At that last meeting, we rode to the park and back on the bus. It turns out in the conversation, we're pretty sure that we are related. We come from Ireland; he has some relatives that come from about the same places ours did, but I don't have any definite information. He thinks we are related and I do, too. I went back to Ireland and visited some of the places that my people come from, and kissed the Blarney stone and all that stuff."

Denny, for his part, understands that they may never know what relationship there might be. "It's a stretch at this point, a dead end. It's the type of story you want, but I don't like to throw anything out there unless it's for sure." Denny Doyle remains active today running a number of youth development, coach certification, and parent awareness programs. His company, which he runs with his brothers Brian and Blake out of Winter Haven, certifies somewhere around 25,000 or more coaches a year. Some Red Sox fans will remember Brian Doyle, who got involved with the Yankees in 1978, the year after Denny left the majors. It was also the year the Yankees beat out Boston for the pennant in the infamous one-game playoff. Brian was added to the roster in place of the hurting Willie Randolph, and he starred in the Series, batting .438; he and Bucky Dent combined for five RBIs in the final game victory. "It was interesting to watch, I'll tell you that," Denny recalls, then adds, "And I don't even like the Yankees!"

Chris Haney and Mike Cubbage

When Chris Haney joined the Red Sox early in the 2002 season, he became half of a recent pair of Red Sox relatives. Chris, a left-handed pitcher, is a "distant cousin" of Sox third base coach Mike Cubbage. Haney was a 10-year veteran who started with the Montreal Expos in 1991 but spent most of his career with Kansas City. He'd built up a 38–52 record, with a 5.11 ERA. In 2001, he played in Japan, but he was signed to a minor league contract by the Red Sox early in 2002, as the team was looking for a backup southpaw reliever. His father is Larry Haney, who played from 1966 to 1978 for four American League clubs and, in the middle of his career, appeared in two games for the National League's Cardinals. No relation to Fred Haney or Todd Haney. But he is related to Mike Cubbage. "More than anything," Chris says, "I saw him at church all the time. There's a lot of Haneys in that church."

Cubbage played eight years for three clubs, with a lifetime .220 average in 1,951 at-bats. Cubbage's career and that of Chris's dad Larry overlapped, and Chris says, "I grew up in a baseball family, but this [June 2002] is the first time I've been in pro ball with family. I knew him when he played for the Twins. My dad was still on the field as a coach in my rookie season but that was his last year as a coach, in '91. He was with the Brewers and I was with Montreal. But I always knew where Mike was. We all disappeared in the summer and then we'd all get back about the same time." Haney was referring to how ballplayers tend to leave home for months at a time. He reports that his father helped tutor him all he could, but he was out playing ball. His mom, he says, "was the one who caught and flipped and all that." During the summers, the family would join up and he had the chance to observe "how guys at his level did things, how they went about their work."

Sox coach Cubbage's mother was a Haney, Margie Haney, "from the small town in Virginia that Chris is from. Barboursville. I think my mother and Chris's father were second or third cousins. I don't know what that makes Chris and myself. We live in the same development. We live on the same golf course. Our wives are good friends. It's nice to be on the same team."

Anastacio Martinez and Sandy Martinez

Two cousins played on the 2004 World Champion Red Sox. Neither is related to Pedro, the third Martinez on the '04 team.

The clue to their family ties rests in their place of birth. Anastacio Martinez was listed as being from Villa Mella, Distrito Nacional (Dominican Republic) and Angel "Sandy" Martinez was listed as being from Villa Mella, Distrito Nacional (Dominican Republic). Hmmmm. Sandy was eight years older, a catcher, and in his eighth season as a major leaguer. Anastacio was a pitcher, in his debut year.

True, Martinez is a very common surname—so common that Sandy's mother bore the same surname as his father. But this was worth checking out. Jorge Sainz, player agent for both men, confirms that the two are cousins. No, it never happened that one caught the other in a major league game. Sandy only played for the Red Sox in three very late-season games, with four fruitless at-bats. Anastacio's tenure lasted from his debut on May 22 to his last game on July 2. He won two games and lost one, but had an unimpressive 8.44 ERA.

For both, it was their last year in the majors.

John Olerud and Dale Sveum

John Olerud and Red Sox third base coach Dale Sveum both served with the 2005 Sox. They both agreed they are second or third cousins but neither was that clear on the precise lineage. When John's grandmother back in North Dakota learned there was a Sveum in baseball, she told John that there were Sveums in their family. Asked about the family lineage while the Ole-ruds were visiting their son at Fenway Park in late August 2005, John's father John explained how they realized there had been a connection. "Sveum is not a real common name," he noted. Dale Sveum broke in a few years before Olerud, and the name was a familiar one in the family: his grandmother had been Thora Sveum. Mr. Olerud called his mother on a cellphone right from Fenway and got the lowdown. His grandmother was Thora Sveum and her brother Clifford was Dale Sveum's grandfather.

The Red Sox first signed John Olerud on May 1, 2005—to a minor league contract. Playing for a brief stretch with Pawtucket, it was the first time the longtime veteran Olerud had ever been in the minors. When he first arrived in the majors in 1989, he'd never spent a day in minor league ball. Olerud had 16 years under his belt before coming to the Red Sox. He'd played with Toronto, the Mets, Seattle, and the Yankees. He said that Boston was the best organization he's been with as far as taking care of family.

1993 was Olerud's best year, winning the AL batting crown with a .363 average and coming in first in on-base percentage with a .473 mark. In his final season, John batted .289 for Boston, in 173 at-bats. After 2005, he chose to retire from baseball, leaving the game with 2,239 hits and a lifetime .295 average.

RELATIVES WHO TRIED TO MAKE IT

There are, as well, those relatives who almost made this list. For instance, John Malzone, 2002 coach for the Sox single A affiliate Lowell Spinners club, whose father is Frank Mal-zone, a member of the Boston Red Sox Hall of Fame. John played seven years in the Red Sox system, reaching as high as triple A—but never made it to the big league club.

And then there's John-Henry Williams, son to the Splendid Splinter, who (at age 33) signed with a Red Sox farm club for a try-out. Born in 1968, John-Henry's first serious attempt at baseball came in 2002; he signed with the Gulf Coast Red Sox in late June. The club was an affiliate of the Boston Red Sox and most observers assumed that the only reason John-Henry was signed was out of respect for his father, the greatest Red Sox player of all time. He never did get a hit for the Gulf Coast team and, in just the second game he played, John-Henry broke a rib chasing a foul ball that fell in the seats. Give him credit for effort. Eight days later, Ted Williams died.

The following year, John-Henry enlisted the help of a full-time hitting instructor and worked out with expensive equipment. Ted's son gave it all he had and hooked on with a couple of independent league teams in 2003, the Selma Cloverleafs in Alabama (a team that

Fathers and Sons day photo, with two generations of Ferrisses. Courtesy of Boo Ferriss.

had no home park and consequently played all its games on the road) and the Baton Rouge River Bats in Louisiana. Though no one felt a player just starting out at such an advanced age had much of a future, John-Henry hit .190 for the River Bats as a first baseman and DH. Wearing #30, the 6'5" 220-pound Williams's stats read:

	AVG	G	AB	R	H	2B	3B	HR	RBI	BB	SO	SB	CS	SLG	OBP
Williams, John, DH	.273	13	33	3	9	0	0	1	4	13	0	1		.333	.400
Williams, John, 1B	.153	26	72	3	11	3	0	0	2	9	33	0	2	.194	.274

The River Bats won the 2003 South Eastern Professional Baseball League playoffs, but by the time they entered post-season competition, John-Henry was no longer with them. Something was wrong. He was becoming too fatigued. Come October, he was diagnosed with acute myelogenous leukemia, a particularly deadly form of the cancer. Less than six months after diagnosis, despite a bone marrow transplant from his sister Claudia, John-Henry Williams succumbed to cancer. Material on John-Henry Williams comes from *The Kid: Ted Williams in San Diego* (Rounder Books).

J. B. Brillheart appeared in 11 games for the Red Sox in 1931, his fourth year in the majors dating back to 1922 (he was out of the majors more than in them, playing in 1922, 1923, 1927, and 1931). Jim appeared in 11 games for the Red Sox, with a record of 0–0 (5.49 ERA). He brought his younger brother Jerry to Sox spring training in 1931, but Jerry didn't make the team, and was released to the Richmond ballclub. Too bad—the Sox could have had yet another brother combo.

Bill Fischer and Tom Fischer

In 1991, Red Sox pitching coach Bill Fischer had a prospect to look over during spring training in Winter Haven—his nephew Tom Fischer. Tom had been the #1 draft pick of the Red Sox in 1988, and the number one pick was never a courtesy pick the way, say, a 35th round pick might be (see Erich Cloninger below). Tom Sr., Bill's younger brother, had spent four years in the White Sox system but never advanced to the major leagues. There were some baseball genes in the family, though. His third year in the Red Sox system, Tom Jr. had won 13 games with the Double A club in New Britain (13–10, 4.19 ERA). The left-hander got his own baseball card, in the minors, but never made it to big league baseball.

Bill Lee and Andy Lee

Bill Lee's son Andy is also a southpaw. Andy played in the Cape League in 1997 and did well enough that some commentators—including Peter Gammons on "Baseball Tonight"—thought he'd be drafted. But, he says, he sat by the phone a couple of days and nothing happened. "My dad helped me get a couple tryouts in South Florida, so I packed up my girlfriend's Toyota Tercel and drove 23 hours to Jupiter, Florida." He worked out for the Expos, then the Mets, and finished up with the Red Sox. They all felt he did well, but it was "just a numbers thing"— they had too many kids in their system after the draft. He went back to school and finished his degree that fall.

He signed with the Red Sox in 1999 and got invited to spring training. He made it right to the final day of the spring and thought he was on his way to Augusta but ended up getting cut. Andy returned back home and started working, then got an unexpected call from the minor league director asking if he could be in Lowell in three days to play A ball. He spent a couple of weeks playing for the Gulf Coast League and one season with the Lowell Spinners. "Put up good numbers. Age and lack of velocity got me," he says. Today, Andy coaches ball at Hinds Community College in Mississippi.

Joe (Sr.) and Joe (Jr.) Kerrigan

The Red Sox show a pattern of drafting the offspring of coaches and managers working in their system. It's a nice gesture of courtesy that may one day pay off. In recent years, among the offspring the the Red Sox have drafted is Joe Kerrigan, Jr., son of Red Sox pitching coach (and, briefly, manager in late 2001) Joe Kerrigan.

Jimy and Brady Williams

Kerrigan's colleague and immediate predecessor Jimy Williams, manager from 1997–2001, was no doubt pleased when the Red Sox drafted his son Brady. Jimy himself had initially signed with the Red Sox in 1964, many years before ultimately suiting up with them at Fenway as field manager. In early 2007, Brady was coaching with the Devil Rays.

Tony Cloninger and Erich Cloninger

On the second day of the 2003 Major League Baseball draft, Liberty University's Erich Cloninger was selected in the 35th round by the Boston Red Sox. Cloninger, whose grandfather was Red Sox pitching coach Tony Cloninger, was the 17th pick in the round, and the 1,044th pick overall.

Cloninger had his best season as a Liberty Flame in 2003, finishing third on the team in hitting with a .329 batting average. He was also second on the team with 24 RBIs.

Brad Mills and Beau Mills

Fresno State third baseman Beau Mills, the son of Red Sox bench coach Brad Mills, was drafted by the Red Sox in 2004 and played in the Cape Cod League in 2005. Another son drafted in '04: Nick Francona.

THE NON-RELATIVES

Then there were the non-relatives. Many assumed that Chick Stahl (1901–06) and Jake Stahl (1903, 1908–13) were related, and many newspapers of the day reported it as fact. Even respected writers such as Ed Walton and Neft and Cohen took them to be related, at least in their earlier published work. The Stahls may both may have been men of steel, but they weren't related.

In 1903, the two non-relatives played together and there were occasions like the July 29 game against New York where they batted back-to-back. New York was leading 15–13 in the bottom of the ninth when Chick batted for Lou Criger and struck out. Next up was Cy Young, who had given up all 15 of New York's runs. (This was not one of his best days.) Collins finally decided to take him out, and Jake Stahl came in as a pinch-hitter. It was back-to-back Stahls. Jake hit a fly ball to left, but Tannehill failed to negotiate the embankment in left and let the ball drop, where it went for a triple. He scored on the next play, but the New Yorkers won, 15–14.

The Newsomes

Though both Dick Newsome and Skeeter Newsome had the "e" on the end of their name (unlike Bobo Newsom), and even though both were Southerners, they had "different drawls." As far as they knew, there was no relation and indeed they had never met until spring training in 1941.

RELATIVES IN THE FRONT OFFICE

Not surprisingly, there have been relatives in the Red Sox front office, too.

After John Quinn graduated from Boston College in 1932, he became secretary of the Red Sox. His father Bob was owner and president of the Red Sox at the time. John stayed with the Sox for a couple of years after Bob sold the Sox to Tom Yawkey, but in 1936 Bob asked for his release so he could come to Boston's National League club. He became secretary to the Boston Bees (Braves) while he also headed up their farm system.

The Kenney family probably has the longest thread of front office tenure, spanning three generations (and perhaps looking ahead to a fourth). The story is told in more detail in the book *Fenway Lives*, but it is one of the more impressive family lineages in Red Sox history. Edward P. Kenney was Assistant General Manager of the Red Sox until September 2000. His grandfather Tom began the family Fenway dynasty on the grounds crew back in the 1920s. After new ownership came in, Tom Kenney did some driving for Tom Yawkey and Eddie Collins. Grandson Ed says, "He was more or less like a personal assistant. I don't know if there was an exact title. He was just around the ballpark."

Tom son's Edward F. Kenney worked from the early 1940s until he retired after 45 years of service. He worked his way up from the grounds crew to become head of the farm system, and was titled Vice President for Player Development. While working at Fenway, he met his future wife Anna, a secretary, and they married in 1948 and Edward P. was born some time later. Edward F. recalls coming to Fenway as early as 1934. When Joe Cronin came to the Sox, "He let me work out with the team. I used to go out in batting practice and all. Hughie Duffy was a great man there and I used to work out with him in the morning before the regular players came in." Duffy actually signed him to a Red Sox contract, but World War II intervened and after the war whatever talent Ed had had succumbed to a sore arm in spring training. Instead, he took a position working in the ticket office during the hot 1946 season. Within a year or two, Cronin started sending Ed out around the country holding tryout camps and looking at prospects.

The younger Ed, third in the lineage, recalls, "I grew up around the ballpark, with some other young kids like Marc Sullivan who were around the ballpark and in the same age group." He spent a lot of time working in Bristol for the Sox Double A team there, eventually becoming an assistant in the minor league scouting office, assistant farm director, and Director of Minor League Operations. "I guess you could say it's in my blood."

One finds a number of similar lineages amongst employees who work for the concessionaire at the ballpark, and several of these are detailed in *Fenway Lives*.

Of course, there are also relatives by marriage. Rick Miller, for instance, married Carlton Fisk's sister Janet Marie after the 1973 season, and so the two teammates became brothers-in-law. Fisk later commented, "He's just really lucky that he met me, because if he didn't meet me, he wouldn't have met her."

Theo Epstein's tie to Teddy Ballgame

Theo Epstein's aunt Barbara was married to sports photographer Fred Kaplan, a friend of Ted Williams. Their son, Lee Kaplan, was the young boy who—at about age four—was getting antsy sitting around Ted's Boston apartment before a game, and coined the nickname "Teddy Ballgame." A photograph of toddler Lee with Ted Williams appears on page 134 of *Ted Williams: The Pursuit of Perfection*.

IN THE YEARS TO COME

There is always hope that we'll be able to add other names to the list. The Sox missed out on Michael Garciaparra, Nomar's younger brother, taken by the Mariners as their top selection in the 2001 draft. But in the 19th round of the 2006 draft, the Chicago Cubs took pitcher Jeremy

Papelbon. Jeremy's twin brother Josh Papelbon was selected in the 48th round by the Boston Red Sox and began his career with the Lowell Spinners.

David Laurila asked Josh Papelbon, "The Alou brothers, Felipe, Matty and Jesus, once patrolled the outfield together for the San Francisco Giants. If the Papelbon brothers were outfielders, who would play where?" Josh answered, "It would have to be me in left, Jeremy in center, and Jonathan in right. That would be kind of ironic, too, because from left to right it would be in inverse order of our birth. There'd be communication errors if we played together out there, though. Jonathan wouldn't want to take directions from his younger brother, even if he was the centerfielder, and I wouldn't let Jeremy call me off either. It would be a real power chain, and whoever got there first would get the ball. That's how it's always been with us. We all want to be the one who wins." Maybe the Red Sox can trade for Michael Garciaparra and pick up Jeremy Papelbon for a future team as well. They could have a Papelbon start the game, another come on in relief, and the third one close the game.

In back-to-back games on September 25 and 26, 2007, Julio Lugo stepped into the batter's box to face his younger brother Ruddy, a pitcher for Oakland. It was the first time brothers had faced each other anywhere in the majors for more than five years. Julio drew out his at-bat for eight pitches before drawing an eighth-inning walk. He scored two batters later. The next night Ruddy got his brother to fly out and end the sixth.

HOME RUNS BY BROTHERS

Tony Conigliaro (36) and Billy Conigliaro (18) totaled 54 homers for the 1970 Red Sox, edging the Aarons by one and predating the Giambis by 21 years. Billy is ofttimes overlooked, but he had some pop. The best found for two brothers in the same year not on the same team was the year before: Lee (38) and Carlos (18) May, for 56.

Billy and Tony twice both hit home runs in the very same game. It's been done 20 times by brothers in history. The two times the Conigliaro brothers did it were July 4, 1970 and September 19, 1970.

It has also been done 10 times by brothers in the same game, with the brothers on opposing teams. On June 30, 1950, Dominic DiMaggio hit one out in the second game of the doubleheader and so did brother Joe. The other time this involved a Red Sox player is when Boston's Rick Ferrell and Cleveland's Wes Ferrell each hit a home run in the very same inning of the July 19, 1933 ballgame.

ROYALTY AND THE RED SOX

At the risk of repeating ourselves a bit, two players who began in the 1930s seem to have had a bit of royal blood.

Mel Almada. July 24, 1933 Alejandro V. Martinez, the Mexican consul in Los Angeles, helped host "Melo Almada Day" at Wrigley Field, Los Angeles, to celebrate Almada's signing to the Red Sox. September 8, 1933 became the date of Almada's debut. Almada traced his ancestry back to Don Alvaro Vaz de Almada, Count of Abranches, who died in 1449. Descended from conquistadors, his father was offered an ambassadorship to France but declined, accepting the post of consul in Los Angeles in 1914. His son Melo thus moved to southern California at the age of one, and learned baseball as a child.

Ted Williams. Ted's cousin Teresa Cordero Contreras was the daughter of Mary Venzor Cordero, sister of Ted's mother May Venzor. Teresa explained how The Splendid Splinter was related to royalty. When the first Cordero arrived in California in 1765, he had married a Mexican woman in Baja California. Their son married an Indian, "the princess of the Chumash tribe" in the late 18th century. More information on the Ted Williams lineage is found in *The Kid: Ted Williams in San Diego*.

At the Chelsea Football Grounds, in England on February 26, 1914, 18-year old Cambridge, Massachusetts native Tom Daly (later a Red Sox coach) played in an exhibition game for the edification of King George V and some 30,000 Englishmen in attendance. It was the final game of a round-the-world tour between the Giants and White Sox, using some borrowed talent like Daly.

Tris Speaker was on the tour, playing as a member of the White Sox team, thus being the first member of the Red Sox to play before the King of England. Apparently, the King had asked Daly to hit a homer. "I'll do the best I can, Your Majesty," he replied, and hit the first pitch of the 11th inning out of the park for a White Sox win. His Majesty stayed for the whole game. Daly served as a coach for the Red Sox from 1933–1946.

The Red Sox had a player named King Bader, from Bader, Illinois. Lore Verne Bader started his career with the New York Giants in September 1912 and won two games, recording an earned run average of 0.90. Though a 22-game winner for Dallas in 1913, and though he rolled up a record of 81–45 for Dallas and Buffalo, he didn't get another shot at major league ball until coming to the Red Sox in 1917. He threw 38 innings in 15 games, had a 2–0 record and an ERA of 2.37. In 1918, though, he was 1–3 in just five games. They were his last in the major leagues, though he played several more years in the minors.

In 1942, Elden Auker pitched a game watched by the former King Peter II of Yugoslavia but he was pitching for the Browns at the time.

The Red Sox really haven't had players named Queen or Prince, and certainly not Princess. They've had a few Earls, though: Caldwell, Johnson, Snyder, Webb, and Wilson. They had Duke Farrell.

And they did have two Latino kings—Rey Sanchez and Carlos Reyes.

For those who've studied Latin, there are Regis Leheny and Rex Cecil.

Carney Lansford once said that he was related to Sir Francis Drake.

In terms of imperial leaders, we have to at least note Julio Cesar Lugo.

Merlin Nippert—well, Merlin wasn't really royalty, but…

And, finally, apropos of rather little, there was The Kingdome—the Red Sox did pretty good there: 61–50 on the road when visiting Seattle, before the Kingdome was imploded on June 27, 1999.

ONE FINE DAY

"A guy who's played one game in the pros is like a former state senator, a big man in most neighborhoods and any saloon as long as he lives."—Wilfred Sheed

Charlie Hartman—June 24, 1908

There are a number of players who appeared in only one game at the major league level, for the Red Sox. The earliest such one-game performance was that of Charlie Hartman. Hartman is enough of a mystery that some standard sources don't indicate whether he batted left or threw left. As it happens, he never batted at all, in major league ball. He did pitch, once, throwing the last two innings in the June 24, 1908 game against the Senators. And he threw left-handed, according to both the *Boston Journal* and the *Boston Globe*.

Hartman was born in Los Angeles on August 10, 1888 and was purchased by the Red Sox from Connie Mack's Philadelphia Athletics. He'd gone to spring training with the Mackmen but they had a strong enough staff that he was expendable. The story announcing his signing indicated that he was a left-hander who had pitched well for the Portland club in the Coast League, but named him Claude Hartman. A *Globe* photograph in May was captioned Claude as well, but later census records confirm him as Charles O. Hartman.

His first appearance for the Red Sox came in a May 17 exhibition game in Providence where the Red Sox beat the Worcester championship club, 8–0. Hartman started, and Ralph Glaze took over later. His official major league appearance (the one and only) came in a game the Sox were losing, 7–1. The third pitcher of the afternoon, he "looked good"—giving up just one hit, a single by George McBride that followed a walk and a throwing error by Ed McFarland. Charging Hartman with an earned run doesn't seem right. Bill Carrigan pinch-hit for him in the bottom of the ninth. The *Journal* wrote, "There was nothing really to commend or criticize in the youngster's work." The *Boston Post* said that Hartman, "although pretty wild, made a fairly decent showing."

In January 1909, Hartman, Doc McMahon [see next entry], and 10 other Red Sox players were placed on waivers. McMahon was claimed by Wilkes-Barre and Hartman was claimed by Portland of the Pacific Coast League.

Doc McMahon—October 6, 1908

Doc McMahon pitched and won the only game in which he ever appeared, a game against the New York Highlanders. The date was October 6, 1908. McMahon threw a complete nine-inning game, striking out three and walking no one. He gave up three runs on 14 hits and ended the season (and his major league career) with an undefeated 1–0 record.

It was the next to the last day of the season. Eddie McMahon faced New York's Andy O'Connor, a "Roxbury lad" who also making his major league debut. Like McMahon, this was O'Connor's one and only appearance in the major leagues. Another Massachusetts native, O'Connor also threw a complete game. He struck out five, but he walked seven, hit three batters, yielded 15 hits and was tagged for 11 runs. For the next 72 years (O'Connor died at age 96 in 1980), the New York pitcher must have looked back with regret at his one line in the record books.

McMahon, on the other hand, could recall with pride the one shot he had. He also acquitted himself pretty well at the plate. He went 2-for-5, both singles, and so goes down in history as a lifetime .400 hitter.

Henry John McMahon was born in Woburn, Massachusetts on December 19, 1886. McMahon had been one of the outstanding scholastic pitchers in the state, helping bring his team to victory in the old Middlesex and Mystic Valley leagues. After graduating from Woburn High, McMahon attended Holy Cross from 1906 to 1908 where he played ball with Jack Barry, captain of the 1908 team as a sophomore. Holy Cross records indicate that McMahon did not have a particularly impressive baseball career at Holy Cross. He never graduated from Holy Cross; he moved on to Tufts Dental School, where he earned a degree in dentistry.

Nearly 100 years later, how he ended up with the Red Sox remains a bit of a mystery. But he was not only signed, he got a chance to start.

Doc McMahon had stayed for much of the year with the Boston team, after which he was sent to minor league teams in Syracuse NY and Reading PA for seasoning. His contract was sold to the Wilkes-Barre club on December 29, 1908, according to the *Woburn Times*. His fellow students at Tufts presented him with a "traveling bag" in March 1909 as he left for Wilkes-Barre, and the *Times* noted that, "He is practically a member of the Boston Americans and may be 'resold' to Boston before too long." He did not rate his prospects highly, though, and before too long "he abandoned his baseball ambitions and took up the practice of dentistry in this city," explained McMahon's obituary. McMahon later became a coach at Woburn High, and continued playing semipro ball. An August 1917 news account had McMahon pitching for Manchester-by-the-Sea, saying he "whipped United Shoe at Manchester" in a 1–0 shutout which ran his scoreless innings streak to 21 straight innings.

The former pitcher turned dentist settled into the family home at 3 Border Street and enjoyed life in his hometown. Doc McMahon died of heart trouble on the couch in his own living room at age 41, leaving a wife and three children.

Ralph Pond—June 8, 1910

Ralph Pond was a product of the University of Maine who seems to have joined the Red Sox on the road in Chicago right after completing the school year at the University of Maine. Pond was an outfielder and the very day he joined the team, he saw service. June 8 was a big day for youngsters joining the Boston team—not only did Ralph Pond come up that day but so did fellow U. Mainer Marty McHale and "Hap" Myers, a first baseman.

It was a rough outing, not just for Pond but for the team in general. Filling in for Tris Speaker for the day, our man Pond started in center but failed to get a hit off veteran White Sox hurler Frank "Piano Mover" Smith. He struck out his first time up, leading off the second, though the Sox scored later that inning when Duffy Lewis drove in Larry Gardner. Chicago came back with two in the bottom of the third, though. With one away, Sox shortstop Harry Lord booted pitcher Smith's grounder. Leadoff hitter Charlie French flied to center but Pond misjudged it and the ball got by him enabling Smith to scamper all the way around from first. Pond threw the ball in to Lord, covering second but Lord mishandled the ball and French took third, scoring when the next batter White flied to Harry Hooper in right.

In the fourth, Pond slapped a hot shot back to the mound and Smith fired to first for the out.

In the fifth, Boston took the lead again, with two runs of their own. Lord made his third error of the game in the third and French was safe. He made it all the way from first to third on a 5–3 sacrifice by White, because Sox pitcher Charley Smith (who'd run over to cover third) dropped the ball fired back across the diamond. French scored by taking a huge lead off third, and when catcher Carrigan fired down to third base to pick him off, the third baseman threw the ball back in the dirt as French ran for the plate. Dougherty hit a double into center and Pond chased after it, inadvertently kicking it all the way out to the center-field wall in the process. Pond singled in the sixth and stole a base—qualifying him for momentary membership in that year's "Boston Speed Boys"—but that was about all he had to show for the day. When he came up to bat for his final time in Boston's eighth, the Red Sox had already scored one run and had Hugh Bradley on second. Pond, unfortunately, lined to Chick Gandil at second and Bradley was doubled off in an inning-ending double play. Charley "Sea Lion" Hall—a pitcher—replaced Pond in center for defensive purposes when the White Sox came up in the bottom of the eighth. Pond was "given the G. B." wrote the *Boston Post* (given the grand bounce). If so, it proved to be a permanent G. B. from major league ball.

"Weird Fielding Lost Game for Red Sox" headlined the *Post*. Final score Chicago 5, Boston 4. Commenting on Pond's performance that day, the *Boston Globe* presciently noted, "Just at the present the sturdy collegian won't do, for he loomed up sadly deficient in the fine points of middle fielding." The Sox made seven errors that day. The *Chicago Tribune* was a little rougher on him. "A bum finger kept [Tris] Speaker out of the game and a recruit named Pond started to fill his shoes. The youngster may be a Pond in Maine but he was hardly a puddle in center field. In fact, he did not cover much more ground on fly balls than a good sized raindrop. After he had misjudged two which went for hits Pitcher Hall was sent out there in the eighth." One of the misjudgments was counted an error for Pond; it was the only fielding chance he ever had. He's one of the 43 major leaguers (and the only one on the Red Sox) who fielded a ball in the 20th century but left baseball with a lifetime fielding average of .000.

Unlike Pond, McHale had to bide his time and did not make his first appearance in a game until September 28, right at the end of the year. McHale squeezed in two starts and lost them both. Next year, though, McHale was back and Pond was not. McHale pitched in 64 games for the Red Sox, Yankees, then the Red Sox again, and finally the Indians—a career that lasted into 1916, though not once did he have a winning record (11–30 lifetime, despite a 3.57 career ERA). Hap Myers had been with the team in April very, very briefly but rejoined it on June 8. He, too, stuck for a few years, appearing in three games for Boston in 1910 and 13 more in 1911 (after seeing 11 games of duty with the St. Louis Browns earlier in 1911). After 81 at-bats, he had a .333 average and joined the Boston Braves for the 1913 campaign, where he got a chance to play fulltime, racking up a .273 average in over 500 plate appearances. In 1914 and 1915, Pond played for Brooklyn in the Federal League and when that league shuttered, his career in major league ball was over.

Pond's lifetime average was .250—he had a major league hit (and that stolen base) to reminisce about for the next 37 years until his death in 1947.

Tracy Baker—June 19, 1911

Just as Patsy Donovan had given Pond a day in the sun in 1910, he gave Tracy Baker one just about a year later in 1911. Boston was in New York, playing the Highlanders (a couple of years before they took on the name "Yankees.") Smoky Joe Wood was on the mound for the Red Sox, and he'd shut the New Yorkers out twice in one series the last time he'd faced them in New York. Like Pond, Baker was a college kid, too, just in from Washington University of Seattle. Baker started the game at first base. Like Pond, he showed some inexperience in the field, though he played well at first, recording four putouts over the first two innings while Boston built up a 4–0 lead. Baker shows up as 0-for-0 lifetime, but his one plate appearance was a sacrifice and helped in the three-run second. But then in the bottom of the third, Heinie Wagner fired the ball so hard and fast from short that Baker couldn't handle it and the ball shot all the way to the stands. He wasn't actually charged with an error (the *Post*'s Paul Shannon called it a "savage throw"), but the other Boston players spoke up ("a yell from the Boston players caused manager Donovan to make a quick change") and Clyde Engle came in to finish the game at first. Boston won 6–3, and Joe Wood notched another victory. Tracy Baker had had his day, though.

Joe Giannini—August 7, 1911

Was Joe Giannini potentially the wealthiest player ever to appear in the Red Sox lineup? Joseph Francis Giannini was born in San Francisco on September 8, 1888. He had played for San Francisco in 1910, in the California League. The Bank of America grew out of the Bank of Italy founded by A. P. Giannini in San Francisco. At the time of his 1942 death in San Francisco, Joe Giannini was an assistant manager at the Bank of America. Coincidence? Apparently. Librarians at the San Francisco Public Library have been unable to trace any connection, despite consulting the various resources available to them.

What we do know about Joe is that he played one game in major league baseball, on August 7, 1911, against Cleveland. Smoky Joe Wood was pitching for the Red Sox. It was his second start after his July 29 no-hitter. Steve Yerkes was out after hurting the index finger on his throwing hand on August 6, so Joe Giannini started the game at shortstop.

He had a tough day at the park. The *Herald* claimed, "It was his general all around weakness that allowed the Naps to secure the majority of their half a dozen runs tallied in the sixth inning."

Second time up, he took four balls and was entitled to a walk, but the umpire had lost track of the count and denied him the base. Joe grounded out short to first on the next pitch.

Next time up, in the fifth inning, he slashed a double down the third base line. He "almost knocked the pins from under Neal Ball," wrote the *Herald*. Wood walked, and Hooper walked and the bases were loaded. Engle grounded to third, and Ball stepped on the bag forcing Wood at third, then threw home to Cleveland catcher Gus Fisher at the plate, who tagged Giannini. The *Globe* faulted Joe, saying he "failed to run with the pitch."

In the field, Giannini was charged with two errors, both in the sixth inning. The Indians scored two runs on Lajoie's inside-the-park home run. Then, with one out and two men on base, Fisher hit a tailor-made double play ball to Giannini. Joe threw wildly to Wagner at second and the bases were loaded. The next batter hit a grounder that reporters thought Giannini should have reached, but did not. Two runs scored. A double steal moved the runners up. A grounder hit right at Giannini went through his feet, and he was charged with his second error of the inning, while the fifth and sixth runs of the inning crossed home plate. After Wood struck out the final batter, a change was made at short and Joe G was given the rest of the day off. The *Herald* noted, "Purtell was played after that disastrous showing, and was a big improvement."

Doug Smith—July 10, 1912

Massachusetts native Douglas Smith was born in Millers Falls on May 25, 1892. He starred at Miller Falls High school, averaging 13 strikeouts a game. Red Sox scout Patsy Donovan signed the left-handed phenom who in the spring of 1912 threw three no-hitters—against Greenfield, Westfield, and Chicopee. In the Chicopee game, Smith struck out 20 batters in just eight innings, the game being played in Millers Falls.

The St. Louis Browns were beating up on Red Sox pitching in the July 10 game, and Smith was the last of four Red Sox pitchers called upon. The *Globe*'s Mel Webb wrote that his "left-handed service looked mighty good. Smith was a little nervous (as well he might be his first day in fast company), but the high school boy came over the shoulder nicely on his delivery and seemed to have a lot more on the ball than mere speed." Doug threw three innings, giving up four hits and one ninth-inning run. He was pinch-hit for in the ninth, so never stepped into the batter's box.

The Philadelphia Phillies contested Smith's signing, arguing that they had signed him. On July 17, the National Commission ruled in favor of the Red Sox, noting that the Phillies claim was based on an unsigned contract that had a statement by Smith's brother and guardian written on its back. On August 13, Smith was released to the Lowell ballclub. The only other time he appeared in the *Boston Globe* was as an author of a February 11, 1913 piece on the greatest play he'd ever seen on a ballfield. He named Hooper's catch in the final game of the 1912 World Series.

Red Bluhm—July 3, 1918

Red Bluhm's debut was inauspicious, and certainly overshadowed by other developments. World War I was in full fury, with a major offensive dominating the news, but that didn't keep Babe Ruth from the front pages. "Babe Ruth Quits Red Sox in Huff" proclaimed the *Chicago Tribune*, explaining that Ruth had said he'd enter the shipyard at Chester, Pennsylvania to play for the Bethlehem Steel Company ball team. Joe Jackson and others had apparently already done so as well.

Boston owner Harry Frazee was more than a little ticked off at his star southpaw and indicated he would fight the defection in federal court, if necessary, getting a restraining order to prevent Ruth from enlisting with another team while Ruth was under contract to Frazee's Boston club.

The dispute began between Ed Barrow and Ruth during an earlier game. Manager Barrow had criticized Ruth for swinging at bad pitches and striking out twice, then removed him from the game when the exchange between the two got heated. Ruth's performance was ascribed to "stomach troubles"—sometimes a euphemism for excessive consumption of alcohol. Ruth turned up at his bar in Baltimore. After the Washington series, he'd been given the off day off, but he failed to rejoin the team as planned in Philadelphia and talked about signing with the steel company. The *Boston Globe* indicated that "Not a single player on the team is in sympathy with him, and the Red Sox first and last are disgusted with the actions of a man whom they say had his head inflated with too much advertising and his effectiveness impaired by altogether too much babying."

Ruth apparently thought better of it and wired that he would catch up with the team. For his part, Red Bluhm was very glad to be with the team and harbored no hopes to leave. The Red Sox, though, were in danger of falling from the first division, "slipping fast." Fred Thomas and Amos Strunk were both injured and Dave Shean's foot had become infected. To top it off, ace pitcher Carl Mays (a 21-game winner in 1918) had just received formal notification from his draft board that he was subject to call at any moment.

The "Mackmen" beat the "Barrow brigade" that day. Philadelphia scored once in the first and twice more in both the third and the fifth. Wally Schang's three errors didn't help; the A's scored two runs without the benefit of a hit. With two hits of their own, Boston mounted a bit of a threat in the eighth, but "Dinty" Barbare batted for the catcher Agnew and failed, so Barrow sent in Bluhm to hit for the pitcher, Lore "King" Bader—also to no avail. Boston was beaten, 6–0. Ruth came back. Mays was never called up, nor was Bluhm called upon ever again.

In fact, he was almost never heard of again in baseball. Maury Bouchard reports that the record of Bluhm's appearance, though printed in the Boston newspapers, was never entered on the scorecard which was turned into the American League office. It was only 44 years later, in 1962, that his name was entered into the record books—some 10 years after his passing.

Hal Deviney—July 30, 1920

Another pitcher who just saw action in one game was Hal Deviney of Newton, Massachusetts, a right-hander born on April 11, 1893. He first turns up in a *Boston Globe* boxscore in July 1914, pitching for New Bedford (Colonial League). He pitched for New Bedford the following year, too, later turning up in 1919 with the Buffalo Bisons of the International League, throwing a three-hitter against Newark on "Pat Donovan's Day." The former Red Sox manager (Donovan) scouted some, and likely recommended Deviney to Boston.

In May 1920, Buffalo gave Deviney his release. On June 30, the Sox signed him. He traveled with the team, but his first entry into a game was in Cleveland on July 30, 1920. Joe Bush started for Boston, but gave up seven runs in five innings. After five, it was 8–0, Indians. Deviney came in and pitched the last three innings, giving up seven hits and five more runs. He walked two and struck out none, but did finish the game—not surprisingly an Indians win, 13–4.

Deviney might have fared better as a batter. He singled to right his first time up, in the eighth, and tripled in the ninth, leaving him with a 1.000 batting average and a 2.000 slugging average as counterpoint to his 15.00 ERA. He never got another shot, though he kept playing baseball for years, last attracting newspaper notice when optioned in 1928 from Bridgeport

(Eastern League) to the Salem, Massachusetts (New England League) team. The 1928 Salem Witches are considered by some to be the first farm team in the Red Sox system, but Deviney never got another look.

Lefty Jamerson—August 16, 1924

Charles Jamerson came to the Red Sox at age 24, in 1924, having played semipro baseball and professional football for the Milwaukee Badgers. The left-hander signed on August 16 and got into a game the very same day. The Browns were visiting Boston and took two from the Red Sox, 10–2 and 6–4. Jamerson came in during the first game, with the Sox already behind St. Louis, 8–2. He walked three and gave up a hit, allowing two earned runs. Veach pinch-hit for him in the bottom of the ninth.

The following February, Jamerson had some tough competition in spring training camp, being just one of numerous pitchers trying out for the team (Oscar Fuhr, Rudy Kallio, Joe Kiefer, Joe Lucey, Pay Noonan, Charles "Red" Ruffing, John Schelberg, Harold Sherman, Louis Temple, Harold Wiltse, Ted Wingfield, and John Woods). Most of them made it to the majors, though for most it was but a brief stay. Jamerson never made it back. He played for Hartford, Pittsfield, and Waterbury in the Eastern League, but apparently didn't quite have what it took, even to pitch for the perennially last-place Red Sox of the 1920s.

John "Abe" Woods—September 16, 1924

Pitcher Abe Woods, back in 1924, appeared in just one game and threw just one inning. It was late in the season, September 16 of that year, when the 6-foot, 175 pound Woods (born John Fulton Woods in Princeton, West Virginia) was called on to pitch the eighth inning for Boston. The White Sox, playing at Comiskey, already had an 8–4 lead, and had knocked an unusual number of Red Sox hurlers out of the game, beginning with Howard Ehmke, who gave up four runs in the bottom of the first. Boston manager Lee Fohl pulled Ehmke in the third, after he'd given up another run in the second and gave up two straight singles in the third. Reliever George "Smiler" Murray let the two inherited runners score, and then closed out the inning. Red Ruffing came on for Boston in the fourth and was unscathed until he yielded a run in the seventh. Woods then made his debut, getting the first man out—but then gave up three straight walks before getting the next man (former Red Sox rightfielder Harry Hooper) out. Eddie Collins then flied out to Ira Flagstead for the final out of the inning. Woods didn't let up a hit, and sports a lifetime ERA of 0.00—but those three walks didn't impress and he never got another call. He died on October 4, 1946 in Norfolk, Virginia, just two days before the Red Sox opened the 1946 World Series.

John Shea—June 30, 1928

John Michael Joseph Shea was another lefty who couldn't stick, even in the pitching-deprived Red Sox teams of the 1920s. A native of the area, born in Everett two days after Christmas 1904, he was discovered pitching for Boston College. Beating Notre Dame, 8–1, on June 7, 1928 may have caught the eye of Red Sox scouts. Shea was signed on June 19.

A large crowd, some 25,000 fans, came out to Fenway for a doubleheader with the Yankees. Even five pitchers couldn't stop New York from piling up an 11–4 win in the first game. Allan Russell started and kept it close; it was 4–3 in New York's favor after six. Removed for a pinch-hitter, Pat Simmons was asked to pitch, but after he walked the #8 and #9 batters in the Yankees lineup, he was pulled. Big Ed Morris came in, but he'd not had time to warm up and got pounded. Three hits, three runs, and Herb Bradley got the call. Shea, whom the *New York Times* called "a late scholar at Boston College," pitched the ninth, allowing one hit, one walk, but two runs. He never allowed another run in major league ball, but that was because he never had the opportunity.

Hank Patterson—September 5, 1932

Born in San Francisco, Patterson was an All-City catcher for three years and captain of the Lincoln High School team in Los Angeles. He played guard on the football team, was class president, and also reportedly won most of the waltz contests at Lincoln school dances. He played for St. Mary's College in Kansas, and was signed on February 3, 1932 by the Red Sox.

Patterson appeared in just one game, the second game of a doubleheader in Washington on September 5, 1932. Bennie Tate was the starting catcher for Boston. The Red Sox had lost the first game, 6–2. They were losing the second, 9–3, and Tate may have been tiring; he was 1-for-6 on the day. So Patterson was given a look. He was 0-for-1 at the plate, and seemed to have done well enough behind the plate. No runs were scored on his watch. It was the only look he got in major league play.

Still signed to the Red Sox, Hank was sent on option to the Hollywood Stars on January 17, 1933. Patterson played with the Sheiks in the early springtime, but was released in mid-April. The idea had been to send him to Albuquerque, but "the proposed West Texas League blew up," leaving him without a team. When the Red Sox truly cut him loose is unknown.

Red Daughters—April 24, 1937

Robert Francis "Red" Daughters appeared in a game against the Yankees on April 24, 1937 and for over 50 years could always say he played with Bobby Doerr, Joe Cronin, Pinky Higgins, and Doc Cramer against Gehrig, Dickey, Crosetti, Rolfe, and Lazzeri. The game was the home opener of the '37 season.

Originally scheduled for the 23rd, Boston's opening day was postponed due to cold. Some "big crisp flakes" of snow fell in the morning before the 3:00 p.m. game was finally called at 12:30. The minute the game was called, manager Joe Cronin had his team work out for an hour. "The Yankees didn't even budge from the warmth of their hotel," the *Globe* noted. Cronin was credited with inspiring his troops to new enthusiasm. "A year ago, you probably couldn't see the athletes for the dust as they beat it back to their various domiciles upon hearing the news of a postponement."

When they played the next day, the Yankees jumped out to a two-run lead off Lefty Grove in the top of the fourth. Grove yielded another run in the sixth and Grove was lifted for pinch hitter "Dim Dom" Dallessandro in the bottom of the sixth. Dallessandro walked and scored, one of the three runs the Sox scored to tie the game. In the eighth, New York took the lead but Boston came right back to tie it back up. The Sox stood a chance to win in the bottom of the ninth, but Bobby Doerr was caught off second base and the inning ended fruitlessly.

Fritz Ostermueller had blanked the Yanks in the ninth, but they got two runs off him in the top of the 10th. In the bottom of the 10th, the Sox started to come back. Higgins led off with a double, then Rick Ferrell walked. Red Daughters was sent in to run for Ferrell. Buster Mills forced Higgins, pitcher Murphy firing to Red Rolfe at third. Mel Almada drew a walk, loading the bases, and pushing our man Daughters to third. Bases loaded, one out. McNair batted for Ostermueller and grounded to Crosetti at short; his throw to Lazzeri at second forced Almada. Daughters scored, and Mills advanced to third. Bobby Doerr flied to John Powell in left to end the game. Boston lost it, 6–5.

Daughters' career in the majors was over. He'd never had an at-bat, but he had acquitted himself well on the basepaths, advancing a base at a time, and he experienced the thrill of scoring a run in an extra-inning Opening Day game against the Yankees.

Red was a third baseman and centerfielder. Born in Cincinnati, he moved to Watertown, Massachusetts at a relatively early age and grew up there, attending Holy Cross and Boston College. He played for a number of years after his stint with the Red Sox, spending a fair amount of time with the Rutland Royals. He also played for Chatham in the Cape Cod League. At one point during his time in minor league ball, he got a hit off Satchel Paige and family members recall that as "the biggest triumph of his life." He was particularly close to Moe Berg—not something many players could say—sometime after World War II, when Berg was on the street due to alcoholism, Red brought him in to live with his family and he stayed for a couple of months, getting himself back together again. Coincidental or not, Red's brother Don was active in WWII intelligence work and spent most of his life in South America after the war. Red had served as a lieutenant in the Navy, on board ship, and worked on the side doing athletic things to keep the men's morale up. He worked for Union Carbide and Burlington in the postwar era and family members say he kept his hand in with a little scouting.

Bob's daughter Mary Kay Daughters Brown reports that her father pulled out his arm or broke his collarbone during his time in Boston and he couldn't throw well enough after that. He tried to come back, playing in the minors for a few years—and then he went off to war. He later told his brother Don, "I couldn't swing my bat fast enough; they were just too fast for me." He coached for some time before taking up a position as a general sales manager for a couple of companies in New York. Daughters retained an avid interest in baseball—"a fanatic his entire life" according to his nephew Don Daughters, Jr. "He had these great connections and he'd get great seats." Don Jr's daughter Emily, a lawyer in Boston, brings things full circle. She herself is a fanatic Red Sox fan.

Red remained a huge baseball fan his entire life—and always a Red Sox fan.

Bob Scherbarth—April 23, 1950

Bob Scherbarth was a catcher for the Red Sox. He, too, played in just one game—and never did get a chance to bat. His "cup of coffee" came on April 23, 1950 in the first game of a double-header against the Philadelphia Athletics. "I went up there for a month," he recounted in a 2001 interview. "Birdie Tebbetts and Buddy Rosar both got injured. Birdie busted his little finger and Rosar had some busted ribs or something. Matt Batts was in the bullpen and they brought me up there from Louisville until they got well." Tebbetts had an "incomplete fracture" of one finger.

Joe Dobson was pitching for Boston but didn't have a good day and gave up runs in the second and third, then got touched up for four more in the fifth, suffering from some unfortunate Red Sox fielding on a very wet Philadelphia field. Ted Williams was out with a cold, but a Pesky single and Stephens triple saw Boston draw first blood. Birdie Tebbetts started the game behind the plate, but Joe McCarthy pulled him late in the game (Tebbetts was 0-for-3) and inserted rookie Scherbarth as catcher. The rookie played ever so briefly, and when it was his turn to hit in the eighth inning, McCarthy sent up Merl Combs as a pinch-hitter. Combs drew a walk. McCarthy then had Tom Wright pinch-hit for the pitcher Mueller, and Wright singled, driving in a run. The Red Sox still lost the game, 9–4, but came back and won the second game, 12–2. Matt Batts caught the second game, going 1-for-2. Scherbarth never played in another major league game.

Scherbarth won't ever forget it, though. "That was really something! I was in the bullpen and all of a sudden, the coach [George Susce] says, 'Scherbarth, you're in there!' The managers and coaches said they were really grateful that I came up to help them out. Even though I didn't play or anything, they got me in one inning just so I'd get my name in the book."

Interestingly, the base on balls was the only appearance Combs had for the Red Sox in

1950. He left with a 1.000 OBP, traded to Washington about two weeks later. The game was also notable because it provided a first for Tom Wright. Wright had appeared in three games in 1948 and five in 1949, but it wasn't until this game in 1950 that he made his first major league putout, after he entered the game in the eighth. He singled in the inning, pinch-hitting and then went 3-for-4 in the second game.

Scherbarth had spent six years in the minors—Roanoke, Scranton, and Louisville. After a week or so longer with the Red Sox, he returned to Louisville for a couple of years. He later played for El Paso, San Jose, and Albany. He scouted for the Mets for 11 years, but built a career as an artist in lithography. "I have definitely remained a Red Sox fan. It was the greatest thing that ever happened to me—just to put on the Red Sox uniform. The Red Sox, they treat you like you're a...I never felt so good in my life as I did when I got up there."

Jim Hisner—September 30, 1951

Another Bosox player who saw action in just one game was Harley Parnell "Jim" Hisner. The year was 1951. He can legitimately say he teamed up with Ted Williams, Bobby Doerr, Johnny Pesky, and Dom DiMaggio. Called up in mid-September, he watched Allie Reynolds throw a no-hitter against the Red Sox on the 29th, the next-to-last day of the season. The final day of the '51 season fell on September 30 and Hisner got the start for the Red Sox.

Almost all the Red Sox regulars were given the day off. Ted didn't play, and neither did Dominic, not Bobby, nor Walt Dropo or Vern Stephens. The Yankees, though, played all their regulars—and six of them later became Hall of Famers—Mantle, Rizzuto, DiMaggio, Mize, Bauer, and Sain. Jerry Coleman is recognized today in the Hall of Fame for his work as a broadcaster. Joe DiMaggio's single early in the game proved to be his last regular-season hit as a major leaguer.

With Sammy White catching, Jim Hisner pitched six full innings, giving up three runs on seven hits, all singles. He struck out three and walked four. He can claim the distinction of having twice struck out Mickey Mantle. The Sox lost, though, 3–0. Yankees pitcher Frank Shea threw the first five and Johnny Sain closed out the shutout in relief. The Yankees went on to win the World Series, beating the Giants four games to two.

American League pitchers still batted in those years, and Hisner went 1-for-2 at the plate. In the seventh inning, Johnny Pesky pinch-hit for him, but grounded out. In spring training 1952, Hisner lockered next to Williams, but was cut from the team "two hours before the end of spring training" by new manager Boudreau. He never made it back to the bigs. Three more years in pro ball, and another few in semipro, and that was it. He worked for more than 30 years as a machinist in the Fort Wayne area. When Richard Tellis interviewed him for the book *Once Around the Bases*, Hisner was retired and driving a fertilizer truck part-time, and reported that he was still asked for autographs now and again.

Guy "Moose" Morton—September 17, 1954

Guy "Moose" Morton, Jr. had his major league debut with the Red Sox in 1954. His father—the "Alabama Blossom"—pitched in the majors for 11 years for the Indians, winning 98 games. Guy Jr., whose stocky 6'2", 200-pound frame earned him the nickname "Moose," started as a pitcher, but it was his bat that caught the eye of the scouts. He turned to catching, and still remembers visiting the Red Sox at Fenway in late 1949 and hitting nine of the 10 batting practice pitches he was thrown over the Wall in left.

Morton played in the minors, but was called to duty from the National Guard as the war in Korea heated up. He was put to work training new recruits, but got in some time playing for the base team at Camp Atterbury, Indiana. His service complete, he hit just over .300 for Roanoke in 1953 and then .348 for Greensboro in 1954, with 120 RBIs and 32 home runs. He told Richard Tellis, "Ted Williams and I are the only ones to ever to hit one over the flagpole in center field in Birmingham."

He looked like a prospect and got a late September call-up. As it happens, he was assigned the locker next to Ted. He traveled with the team and took batting practice at Fenway. On September 17, the Red Sox were in Washington, down 4–0 after just two innings. The two teams and Detroit were all bunched together, fighting for fourth place. In the third inning, manager Lou Boudreau sent Morton to the plate to bat for pitcher Frank Sullivan. "I remember going up," he told Tellis. "I had a lot of confidence. I wasn't scared. It was just another time at bat. I was well schooled and had done this before. I just didn't do it….I saw the ball well, and I had good cuts." Facing lefty Dean Stone, Morton struck out on three straight pitches. "I swung at them all—one, two, three. I think the last one was a slider above the belt. I was a high-ball hitter, and I swung over it. I didn't feel anything particularly about it. It was just another day's work. I had struck out before." It turned out to be his one and only at-bat in the majors. The final score was 8–0.

Morton spent four more years in minor league baseball, before he decided to hang up his spikes. He played for Louisville in 1955, with a kind of average season, and the Sox traded him to Washington at the end of the year. He earned his master's in education and worked as a high school coach in Alabama. Moving to Ohio, while teaching at junior high, he started a little church in his own home, did a little street-corner preaching, and was invited to fill in at a church in Wooster. "Moose" Morton became a Christian pastor and has followed that calling for over a third of a century. "Baseball is the greatest game of all," he says, "but serving God is the real major leagues."

Bill "Rudy" Schlesinger—May 4, 1965

In the only major league boxscore in which he'll ever appear, Bill Schlesinger can't even find his whole name. It was shortened to Schles'ger. The space taken by the apostrophe replaced the "n"—leaving his name actually shortened only by the width of the typset letter "i." Conigliaro got his full name in the same boxscore, but Carl Yastrzemski had to settle for "Y'trz'ski." The boxscore appeared in the *New York Times*. Since the game was a West Coast game, there was no boxscore in the *Boston Globe*—nor did they run one the following day. And the record books show Bill's name as "Rudy Schlesinger" not Bill.

He explained about the nickname in a 2003 interview. "Rudy? That's a slang word. When I was playing, when somebody would get mad, when he was always upset about striking out, breaking up water coolers, breaking up bats and all that—they would always say that you're a red-ass. They just called me Rudy Redass."

May 4, 1965 was first baseman Bill Schlesinger's major league debut. It was also his last appearance. Dave Morehead started the Tuesday night game in Chavez Ravine and only allowed two hits before the fifth, when he surrendered a grand slam home run to California Angel Costen Shockley, a .150 hitter. It was Shockley's first American League home run, hit into the right field bleachers. (Shockley had hit one home run the year before for the Phillies, had one later in 1965 for the Angels, and then his career was over.) The final score was 7–1 so Morehead bore the loss. Later in the game, Dennis Bennett threw a couple of innings for the Red Sox. He had one rough inning, giving up four hits and two walks and was lucky to escape with only having yielded two runs. He escaped by fielding a pop bunt which he turned into a double play. It was Bennett's first appearance for Boston. He had come over from Philadelphia himself in a trade for Dick Stuart. The winning pitcher was Marcelino Lopez, a Cuban refugee southpaw. The lone tally for Boston was a solo home run by Lenny Green. Schlesinger appeared as a pinch-hitter in the game. One at-bat.

He'd had about as unorthodox an entry into baseball as one can get. He didn't play Little League. He went out for his high school team, but couldn't make the team. He tried again with the University of Cincinnati, but got cut there, too. But his father ran a retail hardware store in Cincinnati and befriended a number of ballplayers, employing men like Ted Kluszewski, Roy McMillan, Johnny Temple, and Gus Bell in the winters. Yankees scout Pat Patterson was a frequent lunchtime companion of Bill and his father, and he saw Bill playing in a local Sunday beer league (Bill was 20 at the time), and Bill offhandedly said he'd like to play pro ball. The Yankees didn't even want to give him a look, but Patterson's friend Denny Galehouse was a scout for the Red Sox and he offered $1,000 as a bonus, even though Bill said, "I really wasn't that good. I had a lot of power and speed but that's about it. Power and speed together is kind of unusual." Never having played organized baseball, Schlesinger signed a contract with the Boston Red Sox.

He played in the minors for the Wellsville Red Sox, and recalls hitting 37 homers, batting .350, and stealing 45 bases. In 1965, he broke with the big league club, heading north out of spring training. He never saw any time, just sitting on the bench, and even got out of the habit of bringing a bat to the dugout. On May 4, he was eating a candy bar on the bench when Billy Herman approached him: "I'm sorry to interrupt here, but I want you to pinch-hit."

Schlesinger scrambled, while the clubby ran to get his bat, bringing it up with a donut on it. "The first thing I did," Schlesinger remembers, "there's three steps going up out of the dugout. Well, I tripped there and I fell on the third step and skinned up my knee. So now it's time for me to go up and hit because the guy just made the second out. I'm walking up to the plate with this donut and I keep pounding that bat on the ground, trying to get that donut to come off, and it wouldn't come off. I'm getting closer and closer to home plate and this umpire's looking at me and he says, 'Come on, come on! It's 7 to nothing here and I've got a dinner date one hour from now.' He says, 'Do you need help with that donut, getting it offa that bat?' I said, 'Yeah, kinda….' So the umpire takes the bat and gets the donut off the bat. And all these guys over on the Red Sox bench, and I guess the Angels bench, too, they were all laughing and screaming at me. So I finally get up to home plate and this catcher says, 'You're a fastball hitter, aren't you?' I said, 'Yeah,' and he says, 'Well, it's gonna be all fastballs.'

"So the first pitch was a curveball. And I looked at the catcher and I said, 'What's going on here?' He says, 'Well, so I lied. So what?' He started throwing me fastballs. So I grounded out to the catcher. That's what I did. It just went off home plate, and it went up real high and he got me by about a half a step at first base. And then that was it." Three days later, when the Sox were back in Boston, Schlesinger was traded to Kansas City's farm club in Lewiston, Idaho. He soldiered on, playing for five more seasons in a variety of locales for a number of teams (twice more he was Red Sox property, playing in Winston-Salem and Pittsfield, but in 1970 he was hit hard in the face with a pitch and lost about 40% of his vision. It was time to retire. Bill works today at Pleasant Ridge Hardware in Cincinnati, inherited from his father in 1972. (A more complete version of Bill Schlesinger's oral history appeared in *NINE* magazine's Spring 2007 issue.)

John Henry LaRose—September 20, 1978

A native of Pawtucket, John LaRose was first called on in relief against the Tigers, as the Red Sox and Yankees battled to the wire. With just 11 games on the schedule, and the Yankees holding a slim two-game lead, the pennant was up for grabs and every game counted. LaRose had almost been a Yankee, drafted in the third round fresh out of high school in 1969. The Yankees withdrew their offer when LaRose pulled a muscle in his arm while the dickering over signing bonus was underway. In the second round of the draft, that winter, the Red Sox signed him for a sum far less than New York had offered.

In 1970, he threw most of the season for Jamestown and did well, earning two late-season starts with Pawtucket—and pitched a complete game shutout each time. In 1971, he couldn't even make the team, and was assigned to Single A Winston-Salem. It was pretty much a lost year, with six months spent in the National Guard. For the next two years, he put in his time building experience but his record didn't show a lot of progress. Despite a good 1974 season, the Red Sox chose not to protect LaRose and the Twins claimed him, but returned him before the '75 season got underway. He had quite a good year (8–1, 2.42) and Bristol won the championship. He didn't get called up—but his manager did. Dick McAuliffe appeared in seven late-season games as the Red Sox won the pennant.

1976 was "not a particularly memorable year," he told Richard Tellis. 1977 was a break-out year, though, pitching for Triple A Pawtucket. Primarily working as a starter, he posted a record of 11–7, with a 3.04 ERA, and made the International League All-Star Game. In 1978, Pawsox manager Joe Morgan designated LaRose as the closer. He was superb, appearing in 51 games, saving 15, and even winning 10. He even shut down the Red Sox in an exhibition game, with a 1–2–3 ninth inning that preserved a 2–1 victory for Pawtucket.

Called up in mid-September, he joined the team in New York but first got the call in Detroit. It was a night game on September 20. The Sox were in a tight pennant race, just 1½ games behind the Yankees. Mike Torrez had started but given up three runs in the first four innings. A walk and a single put runners on first and second with nobody out, and Don Zimmer called on LaRose to try and keep the game close. The rookie walked Shawn Kemp on a 3–2 count, but catcher Carlton Fisk claimed the ump had blown the call. Based loaded, nobody out. LaRose got Milt May to hit a grounder to Jerry Remy at second; Remy fired to Fisk and cut down the lead runner. Pinch-hitter John Wockenfuss hit into a 6–4–3 double play. Albeit not a save situation, LaRose had done the job a closer is asked to do, getting out of the inning without letting in a run.

Rather than turning to a long reliever, and perhaps forgetting that LaRose had been up and down in the bullpen several times during the game before the fifth, Zimmer sent LaRose out again, and he was hammered for three runs on a double, a walk, and a three-run Lou Whitaker homer. He got out of the sixth without further damage, but started the seventh with a single and a walk before being relieved. Both runners scored, so LaRose was charged with five earned runs on three hits in two full innings. He'd walked three and not struck out a batter (since the umpire hadn't given him the call on the 3–2 pitch to Kemp).

"After that game," LaRose told Tellis, "I never even warmed up." Until the October 2 single-game playoff against the Yankees, with the pennant at stake. The Red Sox were leading 2–0 after six innings and the Fenway faithful were cautiously optimistic. With one out in the seventh, two Yankees hit singles and Zimmer had a call placed to the bullpen to get both LaRose and Bob Stanley warming up. Torrez retired pinch-hitter Jim Spencer for the second out. Then Bucky Dent hit a three-run homer. Mickey Rivers walked, and Stanley was called in. "LaRose, sit down." That was it. Could he have done any worse if he'd pitched to Dent?

In spring training 1979, he'd pitched a grand total of two innings in the big league camp. That year and in 1980, LaRose pitched for Joe Morgan in Pawtucket. Neither year was particularly distinguished. He left the game, kicked around at a number of jobs for a few years, even playing for two years with Bill Lee, Cecil Cooper, and other players in the Senior Professional

Baseball League. In 1992, he settled down, taking full-time employment as a blackjack dealer at Foxwoods Casino.

John Lickert—September 18, 1981

Another name which flickered momentarily in one box score, and then was never seen again is that of John Lickert, who in 1981 appeared in one game behind the plate but never stepped into the batter's box as a hitter.

An All-American his last three years in high school, John was a 10th round draft pick for Boston in 1978. He'd done very well indeed in spring training, but was the first one cut. "You've got to have a chance to play every day," he was told. He did play and played well; by the time he hit the playoffs, he had thrown out 94 runners in 109 games. Called in early September, right after the playoffs were over, he joined the Red Sox in Detroit—though he had to wait outside Tiger Stadium for an hour and a half before the Tigers opened the park and let him in. About 10 days later, he was in a game—if only briefly.

Playing at home on the 18th, Mike Torrez of the Red Sox had given the Yankees one run in each of the first four innings while Ron Guidry had yielded just one. The score stood 5–1 when the Sox came up in the bottom of the eighth. Ron Davis had taken over, relieving Guidry. He got off to a fine start, with Jerry Remy grounding out and Dwight Evans whiffing. Then the roof fell in. Rice singled off the Wall, Yaz worked a walk and Lansford singled to left, plating Rice. Stapleton doubled down the first base line, scoring Yastrzemski—and Lansford came all the way around from first on Reggie Jackson's error bobbling the baseball. Tony Perez walked. Catcher Gary Allenson was due up and was 1-for-3, but Rich Gedman was announced as pinch-hitting for Allenson. The Yankee skipper countered with lefthander Dave LaRoche. Sox manager Houk called Gedman back and put up righthanded veteran hitter Joe Rudi in his place. Rudi came through, singling to right and driving in Stapleton. The game was tied. Reid Nichols was put in as a runner for Rudi, and Rick Miller sent his second home run of the year into the Boston bullpen, a three-run homer giving the Red Sox an 8–5 lead. Remy struck out to end the inning.

John Lickert was on the expanded September roster. He'd hit .270 at Bristol with five HR and 57 RBIs. Bristol had won the playoffs and Lickert was second only to Jim Gentile's 59 RBIs in that department. Roger LaFrancois was the catcher at Pawtucket, but the 21-year-old Lickert had gotten the callup. (LaFrancois had his day in the sun in 1982 and batted .400 in 10 at-bats.) In the top of the ninth, with Allenson and Gedman both out of the game, defensive duties fell to the untested John Lickert.

This was an important win for the Red Sox, leaving them just one game behind in the second half standings of that unusual strike-interrupted season. The battery of Mark Clear and Lickert held the Yankees scoreless in the top of the ninth, allowing just one hit while striking out one.

"It was the Game of the Week—Saturday," Lickert recalls. "My parents, all my buddies in high school seen it. I got all kinds of letters, telegrams, calling me, congratulating me, so at least everybody seen it when I did play. That was good."

The next spring, he was certainly hoping to come back and he says he hit 8-for-16 and led the team in home runs, RBIs, and stolen bases—but this time he was cut on the final day and sent to Pawtucket. Again, to get a chance to play every day. The Sox had Gedman and Allenson, though, and General Manager Haywood Sullivan's son Marc was in the system, too. Marc himself got into 137 games over the next several years, batting .186. John Lickert had appeared in a game but never had even one official at-bat.

"I knew I was good enough to play with the guys because I did in spring training and I did very well. You finally get called up—but I never got a chance to play. I couldn't understand the last three games of the season. My parents drove all the way up to Cleveland and he [Houk] didn't play me, Garry Hancock, or Bobby Ojeda. My father went in there and had a talk with him afterwards. By that time, they were out of it. Even Carl Yastrzemski came up to me and said, "John, I can't believe that you guys are not playing today."

John served four more years in the minors, and says he caught every game Roger Clemens pitched in Pawtucket. "I caught a Hall of Famer. That's one thing they can't take away from me." Finally, he left the game. Today, John is a truck driver for Ryder. He also runs a non-profit organization called the Rhode Island Hurricanes which raises money so that young girls who cannot otherwise afford it can receive financial support to participate in girls' basketball. "I'm glad the Red Sox drafted me and gave me the opportunity. That's why I try to give back to the kids." There's a part of him that still misses baseball, though, and when interviewed late in 2001, he'd begun to develop his resume with an eye toward trying to get back into some area of baseball management.

Steve Lomasney—October 3, 1999

More recently, Peabody's Steve Lomasney played in just one game for the Red Sox, on 10/3/99. Unlike the others on our list Steve was still working hard when interviewed in October 2001 and hoping to get back in there and add to his stats in the record books.

October 3, 1999 was the last game of the 1999 season. The Red Sox had already clinched the wild card slot. You'd think that a game this late in the season, with all the races already decided and the Orioles basically 20 games out of first place, would have been a relatively quiet contest. It wasn't. The game was at Camden Yards and featured a war of brushback pitchers as the two pitching staffs continued a battle which had broken out several days earlier. Although no one could appreciate it at the time, it was in this earlier game that Nomar Garciaparra had been hit in the wrist by by an Al Reyes pitch. Nomar played through the 2000 season, admirably, but was forced to take off almost the entire 2001 season when the wrist failed to fully heal.

Boston won the game 1–0 in 10 innings. Jimy Williams used 27 players. Varitek started behind the plate, was replaced by Steve Lomasney (in his first major league appearance) and finally Hatteberg closed out the game. Steve's dad Ed was charged up. "I saw it on TV. What a thrill that was. I think he caught about seven innings. He threw out two runners, but he struck out twice. He looked real good defensively."

Steve had a lot of hard luck and never got a chance to come back in 2000 or in 2001. A broken toe, torn hamstring, and a serious eye injury all conspired to keep him on the disabled list for far too much of the time. As the fourth catcher in the Red Sox organization, he didn't even really get the chance to make his mark at Pawtucket.

He still recalls his one major league game, though. "Unfortunately, offensively, I didn't do as well as I wanted to. I struck out both times. I'm in the books right now as 0-for-2 with two strikeouts. Defensively, I threw out a couple of guys. I struck out my first at-bat; I was just so over-anxious. I chased a 3–2 count fast ball that was out of the zone. Then I got to another 3–2 count and I thought the pitch was a ball, and he rung me up on it. I thought I had good at-bats. The outcomes weren't good, but it wasn't like I got up there and struck out on three pitches. I fouled off a couple of balls. They were decent at-bats."

How much does Steve want to get back to the major leagues? "Oh, it's unbelievable. It really is. I'm still a young age. But to get the taste when I was 22, it seemed like so long ago, and I haven't been back there and knowing that if I hadn't had these injuries the past couple of years, I might be there…but it's going to make it all that much more sweet when I get there."

What would it be like if it just didn't work out, if he just never did get another chance to return? "Well, I'm not thinking that way right now. I'm confident in my ability that I'll get there. I hope it's with the Red Sox. I think I'm talented enough and I'm confident enough in myself that I'll be there. [But if I don't…] I couldn't even imagine. I couldn't even imagine."

In 2002, Lomasney played for the Red Sox' Trenton affiliate, caught very well but only hit around .210 without a great deal of power (eight home runs). He led the league in strikeouts with 132, and was not found among the September callups. Through the 2007 season, Steve has still not had another major league appearance.

Postscript: There was an earlier game, during the regular season, in which Steve played for the Boston Red Sox—and he hit a home run, a double, and a single. It was an exhibition game against Pawtucket held at McCoy on June 3, 1999. Steve was on loan from the Sox' Single A team in Sarasota.

Players who appeared in just one game in a given year

In 2004, Earl Snyder and Abe Alvarez each played one game for Boston. Snyder had already been in 18 games for Cleveland a couple of years before. Mike Stanton appeared in just one game for Boston in 2005, but had previously appeared for Boston in 81 other games (not to mention some 1,108 other games in all, for some six other teams). Abe Alvarez came back with Boston in 2005 and got in twice as many games, though pitched fewer than half the innings. In 2006, he appeared for the Red Sox again, just for one game. Three years, four games, 10⅓ innings.

Consider the following list.

* played just one game ever for Boston, but did play other games for other teams
** played only one game for Boston in this particular year, but played in at least one other year for Boston, too
*** played only this one major league game ever

In some years, there were no players who played in just one game.

1901—Frank Foreman* / Harry Gleason ** / Frank Morrissey* / Jack Slattery * / Jake Volz*
1902—Bert Husting* / Fred Mitchell **
1903—Nick Altrock*
1905—Yip Owens*
1906—Rube Kroh**
1908—King Brady* / Charlie Hartman*** / Deacon McGuire** / Doc McMahon*** / Harry Ostdiek* / Casey Patten* / Jesse Tannehill** / Jake Thielman*
1909—Fred Anderson** / Jack Chesbro*
1910—Louis LeRoy* / Ralph Pond***
1911—Tracy Baker*** / Joe Giannini*** / Charlie Smith** / Frank Smith**
1912—Doug Smith***
1913—Esty Chaney*
1914—Squanto Wilson*
1915—Guy Cooper**
1916—Richard Haley*
1917—Weldon Wyckoff**
1918—Red Bluhm*** / Bill Pertica* / Weldon Wyckoff** [again]
1920—Hal Deviney*** / Ray Grimes*
1921—Sam Dodge** / Hob Hiller**
1924—Lefty Jamerson*** / Al Kellett* / John Woods***
1925—Bobby Veach**
1926—Sam Langford* / Buster Ross**
1927—Fred Bratschi* / Frank Bushey**
1928—Frank Bennett** / John Shea***
1930—Bill Bayne* / Bob Kline* / Tom Winsett*

1931—Bill Marshall*

1932—Johnny Lucas** / Jud McLaughlin** / Hank Patterson***

1933—Greg Mulleavy *

1936—Emerson Dickman**

1937—Stew Bowers** / Bob Daughters***

1938—Bill Lefebvre**

1939—Fabian Gaffke**

1941—Paul Campbell**

1942—Tom Carey**

1944—Stan Partenheimer*

1946—Jim Wilson**

1947—Bill Butland**

1948—Windy McCall** / Johnny Ostrowski*

1949—Johnny Wittig*

1950—James Atkins** / Merl Combs** / Dave Ferriss** / Bob Gillespie* / Phil Marchildon* / Frank
    Quinn* / Bob Scherbarth***

1951—Ben Flowers* / Harley Hisner***

1952—Hal Bevan* / Len Okrie*

1953—Jack Merson* / Al Richter** / Clyde Vollmer**

1954—Moose Morton***

1955—Jim Pagliaroni** / Bob Smith*

1957—Milt Bolling** / Russ Kemmerer** / Jack Spring* / Faye Throneberry**

1960—Jim Busby**

1961—Tom Borland**

1962—Billy Muffett** / Pete Smith** / Tracy Stallard** / Ted Wills** / Wilbur Wood**

1963—Rico Petrocelli** / Jerry Stephenson**

1964—Mike Ryan**

1965—Rudy Schlesinger***

1966—Gary Roggenburk**

1967—Ken Brett**

1968—Fred Wenz**

1970—Jack Curtis**

1972—Vic Correll* / Mike Nagy**

1973—Ken Tatum**

1974—Steve Barr**

1975—Steve Dillard** / Buddy Hunter**

1976—Andy Merchant**

1977—Ramon Aviles* / Jim Burton** / Rick Krueger**

1978—Reggie Cleveland** / John LaRose***

1980—Stan Papi**

1981—John Lickert***

1986—Wes Gardner**

1988—Rob Woodward**

1991—John Dopson** / Josias Manzanillo* / Eric Wedge**

1996—Ken Grundt** / Walt McKeel**

1997—Brian Rose** / Jason Varitek**

1999—Steve Lomasney***

2000—Sean Barry*

2001—Marcus Jensen*

2004—Abe Alvarez** / Earl Snyder*

2005—Scott Cassidy* / Matt Perisho* / Mike Stanton** / Shawn Wooten*

2006—Abe Alvarez** / Corky Miller*

TWO-TIMERS AND OTHERS WE MIGHT HAVE MISSED

PLAYERS WHO PLAYED IN JUST TWO RED SOX GAMES AND NEVER APPEARED IN ANOTHER MAJOR LEAGUE BALLGAME

Ed Hearn—June 9 and 10, 1910

"Hearn, a California recruit, played shortstop for Boston, and performed well in the field." So read the note in the *Washington Post* the morning after Hearn's error-free debut. Hearn batted eighth, filling in for Heinie Wagner by playing short behind Frank Arellanes. He was 0-for-1 at the plate, despite playing the whole game. He even made the subhead in the *Post*: "Hearn Plays Well." Even Hearn's walk leading off the third came to naught, as the White Sox won, 3–0, behind the pitching of Irving (Young Cy) Young, a former Boston NL pitcher.

The player, spelled Hearne in the *Boston Globe*, couldn't have been too pleased for his future prospects in the subhead after his June 10 game: "Hearne Like a Sieve." Oops. Two runs ultimately scored on his fumble of an "easy grounder" but only because Harry Lord misplayed the next ball, throwing it into the stands. Another run scored when a ball scooted through Hearn's legs in the Cleveland third. And those were all the runs the Naps needed for a 3–1 win. Despite having a bad leg, Wagner played the rest of the game starting in the fourth "and it closed a big hole," remarked the *Globe*. Two games, two at-bats, one of them a strikeout.

Blaine Thomas—August 25 and September 5, 1911

Thomas was born in August 1888, but no one has yet been able to turn up the date. His debut is easy to pin down, though. He started the second game in St. Louis on the 25th and "lasted just long enough to allow the Browns to score their two runs." He pitched well for the first three innings, but walked the first batter in the fourth. Second man up tapped the ball back to the mound, but first baseman Hack Engle didn't cover the base. A sacrifice moved both runners up. Again, a ball was hit back to Thomas on the mound, but Engle failed to handle the throw and a run came in on his error. The second run came in a couple of batters later when Thomas had his third chance, but muffed the throw himself. Charley Hall finished the game and got the 3–2 win.

On September 5, Thomas got another start, against New York. It was a short start. He hit the leadoff batter with his very first pitch. He walked the next man up. Catcher Les Nunamaker fielded a bunt and forced the lead runner at third. Hal Chase hit to third, and again the lead runner was retired. When Thomas walked the next batter to load the bases, he was pulled. Permanently. Hall got out of the inning, but Boston lost the game, 3–2.

Swede Carlstrom—September 12 and 13, 1911

It wasn't an auspicious debut. The *Boston Globe* noted that Carlstrom, "late of the Lawrence club" had a difficult game at shortstop. "The young fellow fell down badly. He acted very nervous; on the first ball he picked up he fell flat on the ground as he went to throw the ball, and later in the game he ran over and knocked the ball out of Yerkes' hands after Yerkes had taken a fly." He also made a "wild throw to first" in the fourth and a runner reached first base in the sixth on a "fumble by Carlstrom." Oddly enough, the Red Sox committed five errors but none were charged to Carlstrom. He singled, 1-for-3 at the plate.

He got another chance, the very next day. This time he was 0-for-3, and Tim Murnane, covering the game for the *Globe*, listed a litany of bumbling plays in the field: in the first inning, Washington scored a run due to "Carlstrom's failure to stop a grounder." This came after Pape had fielded a ball hit back to the mound, with a runner on first, but when he turned to throw to second to start a double play, he "found Carlstrom and Gardner mixed up on the base." In the second inning, he "threw to second too late to get the runner." Washington got another run in the sixth, when the leadoff batter was safe "as a ground ball went through Carlstrom." The hapless Swede was lifted for a pinch hitter in the ninth. Again, he wasn't assessed an error, but he definitely didn't get any more chances.

Tony Tonneman—September 19 and 22, 1911

Tonneman was a catcher. He was 0-for-3 at the plate, but made 10 putouts catching Ray Collins. One of them was the play of the game in the top of the ninth. The Red Sox held a 2–1 lead over the visiting Tigers. A single and a sacrifice had one out but a fast runner, Jim Delahanty, on second. Collins struck out a man for the second out. Then George Moriarty singled over second base, but Tris Speaker was running in all the way, picked it up, and fired it home to Tonneman at the plate. "Straight as a rifle bullet it came and landed in Tonneman's mitt a fraction of a second before Del slid in, feet first. Tonneman snapped the ball onto him before he touched the plate, completing as brilliant an all-around play as was ever made at the Huntington-av grounds." [*Boston Globe*]

Detroit scored first, with four runs in the top of the fourth, on the 22nd. Ty Cobb singled, stole second and kept on trucking to third as Tonneman's throw to second base went wild. In the bottom of the fourth, Tony T. doubled to right-center and drove in a pair. When Hooper singled, Charley Hall—serving as third-base coach—had to grab Tonneman by the head (!) to hold him up so he wasn't thrown out at the plate. Later in the game, he successfully sacrificed and drew a walk as well, officially 1-for-2 at the plate. He did make a couple of errors.

Reports have Tonneman signing with the Red Sox in October, but he turned up playing for Memphis in 1912, and was sold to Vernon of the Pacific Coast League in January, 1913. The *Atlanta Constitution* said his "belligerency" was the reason he was sent out from the Southern League. He continued to move from club to club, and then disappears from the historical record.

Paul Maloy—July 11 and July 22, 1913

Maloy was a "new find from the wilds of Michigan" who pitched the top of the July 11 ninth with a 5–1 Sox lead over St. Louis. He hit the first batter, but retired the next three, each one on a ground ball. Tim Murnane allowed as how he, "after good coaching, may prove of American League timber."

Eleven days later, with Cleveland leading, 6–4, after six innings, Maloy took the mound and found rough going. He walked the first man, hit the second, threw the ball away on the third batter, then gave up a double and a triple. He finally got out of the frame, but Murnane's judgement now had him a "toy pitcher." In early August, he was sold to Worcester.

Esty Chaney—August 2, 1913

Did he play one game in the majors—or two? Esty Chaney made his debut for the reigning World Champion Boston Red Sox on Elks Day 1913—August 2. Boston had lost four games in a row to the Naps (as the Cleveland Indians of the day were often known). Chaney came in and pitched the ninth inning of the second game of a doubleheader, Boston already trailing 6–0. He gave up one hit and two walks, letting in one run. Manager Carrigan kicked about a play involving Nap Lajoie, but predictably to no avail—though Carrigan did manage to get himself ejected. Chaney finished out the inning, but never got in another major league game—or did he?

The next year, Chaney appeared in one more game in the "majors"—with the Brooklyn Tip Tops in the Federal League. It's in the books, and most baseball researchers deem the short-lived Federal League a major league. One game, four innings, seven hits, two walks (and one strikeout), yielding three runs. Call it a career; that was it.

Matt Zieser—April 27 and May 11, 1914

"Kept the Senators Scoreless, Once He Got Into His Stride"—headline on *Globe* photograph. The right-hander came in after George "Rube" Foster was bombed for four runs in the bottom of the Senators second. Zieser was hit hard in the third, and gave up a couple of runs, but settled down and threw five scoreless innings to complete the game. Boston lost, 6–1.

A couple of weeks later, Zieser entered a game against New York in the sixth, and again had troubled getting started: he walked three men, threw a wild pitch, and hit a batter. "With these little peccadillos were mixed up a passed ball and a base hit, the combination being good for the two runs scored off Zieser." He lucked out when Jeff Sweeney tried to block the catcher on a two-strike pitch to try and help Harry Williams steal home—but he mistakenly bunted the ball foul and was called out. Zieser only allowed three hits in four innings, but the game was out of reach.

Paddy Smith—July 6 and 7, 1920

Paddy had back-to-back games in Philadelphia, and then was gone. The Red Sox had an 11–0 lead, so manager Ed Barrow gave catcher Roxy Walters a bit of a breather before the second game. Smith was 0-for-1 at the plate, catching Sad Sam Jones. Boston lost the nightcap, 5–1.

Losing 6–0 in the next day's game, Barrow had Smith pinch-hit for McNally in the ninth inning. He made an out. The Sox were shut out in the day's second game, too, 1–0. Lifetime average: .000.

Carl Stimson—June 6 and July 7, 1923

Ten earned runs in four innings of work. This switch-hitting right-handed pitcher was brought into an "irretrievably lost" game against Cleveland, for two innings of experience, but "took matters too seriously" and was "overanxious, which tied him up and was as wild as a hawk." Red Sox fans, already upset at the 10–1 deficit, gave him the business. He walked three, threw a wild pitch, hit a batter, gave up six hits, and allowed seven more runs. He didn't even get a chance to bat, pulled for a pinch-hitter in the bottom of the ninth—as the Red Sox scored three times to make the final 17–4.

Still suiting up with the team, Stimson came into another game a month later against the Indians that was even more of a lost cause, the July 7 game in which Lefty O'Doul was punished by his manager (and the Tribe) by being left in, and in, as he surrendered 13 runs in the sixth inning and was not removed until after he finally closed out the inning. O'Doul had come on in relief of Fullerton, who had given up eight runs in the first three innings. The 24–2 game was turned over to Stimson, and he let in six hits and three more runs—one in the seventh and two in the eighth. Career ERA: 22.50. A special dispatch to the *Globe* observed that Stimson's was "considered a remarkable performance when that of his predecessors was taken into consideration." What an epitaph.

Bob Adams—September 22 and 23, 1925

Back-to-back games for Holyoke, Massachusetts pitcher Bob Adams. He was the third and final pitcher in an 11–8 home loss to the Tigers. Ted Wingfield started, relieved by Buster Ross—who had his nose busted by a bouncing ball off Al Wingo's bat. Adams threw 1⅔ innings, giving up four hits and giving way to a pinch-hitter in the ninth—but not before he'd had one at-bat for a single.

Adams entered the next day's game, too, again as the third pitcher in a game Detroit won, 15–1. Ehmke started, Fuhr couldn't hold them, and Adams was knocked around for six hits (including a Harry Heilmann homer) and five runs in four innings of work. A "lifetime" ERA of 7.94 and a career batting average of .333. He had five assists in five chances, for an error-free 1.000 fielding percentage.

Bill Clowers—July 20 and 21, 1926

The Texan was a right-hander pitcher who contributed ⅔ of an inning against the White Sox at Fenway, in a disaster of a game which saw Chicago with a 13–1 lead after 3½ innings. Red Ruffing started and threw 1⅔ innings, relieved by Del Lundgren, who similarly lasted 1⅔. Clowers closed out the fourth, allowing just one hit, a single by Schalk that brought in two inherited baserunners. Jack Russell pitched the last five innings without letting in a run. Final score, 13–2.

The very next day, there was another blowout. By the time the ninth inning began, the Browns already held a 10–1 lead. Clowers came into the game, and allowed one more hit (as well as throwing a wild pitch). It wasn't as though the last-place Red Sox were overloaded with pitching talent, but despite his 0.00 ERA, Clowers never appeared in another game and was sold to the Mobile ballclub on August 9.

Frank Mulroney—April 15 and June 24, 1930

Mulroney came from Iowa, a right-hander. His debut game was one inning of hitless relief against the Washington Senators, after Ruffing threw the first eight (and gave up six runs). The Senators' Joe Cronin had hit a three-run homer and driven in a fourth run with a sacrifice fly. Mulroney struck out one.

More than two months later, our man Mulroney pitched the final two innings, in a game the Red Sox had already tied three times. After scoring two times in the bottom of the eight, in came Mulroney. The score was 6–6. Every one of the first six Detroit runs had come in after being granted first base on walks from starter George Smith. Mulroney didn't walk a batter, and he held the Tigers scoreless in the ninth. In the top of the 10th, though, an error by Hal Rhyne and a sacrifice fly brought in two runs. Mulroney gave up two hits and was charged with one earned run. Boston scored but once in the bottom of the 10th.

Jim Galvin—September 27 and 28, 1930

Somerville, Massachusetts native Jim Galvin played the last two games of the 1930 season. He pinch-hit for pitcher Ed "Bull" Durham in the eighth inning of the September 27 game against visiting Washington. The Yankees came to town the next day for the final game of the year. Galvin pinch-hit for Jack Russell in the bottom of the ninth. He failed to get a hit either time, and never did end up putting on a glove in a major league game. The pitcher who retired Galvin in the game against New York was none other than Babe Ruth, who threw a complete game 9–3 victory. It was the first game Ruth had pitched since 1921.

Walter Murphy—April 19 and 21, 1931

The game at Griffith Stadium was pretty much a lost cause, after the Senators had scored eight times in three innings off starter Danny MacFayden and Jim Brillheart. Murphy was the fourth pitcher in the game, and he threw a scoreless eighth, touched for just one hit.

While still in Washington, Walter was again the fourth pitcher and once again pitched the final inning. The Senators already had an 11–2 lead. Murphy walked one and gave up three hits; the Senators scored two more runs. It wasn't *that* bad, was it? Murphy never worked for the Red Sox again.

Bill McWilliams—July 8 and 11, 1931

McWilliams came out of Iowa, and came into the second game of a doubleheader at Yankee Stadium. Babe Ruth had helped win the first game with his 21st homer of the season; New York won, 13–3. New York had a 6–1 lead after seven. Boston scored two runs in the top of the eighth, and McWilliams had a chance to help add to the total, but when he pinch-hit for Ed Morris, he made an out.

William McWilliams. Courtesy of National Baseball Hall of Fame.

The Red Sox moved on to Washington and had another doubleheader, against the Senators, on July 11. Boston lost both of those games, too. In the first game, McWilliams pinch-hit for pitcher Bob Kline in the top of the ninth. Again, he made an out. Boston lost, 7–1. McWilliams lost his chance to impress, not that he was given that much of a chance. He did turn up three years later playing for Detroit—the Detroit Lions of the National Football League.

Regis Leheny—May 21 and 22, 1932

Left-hander Regis Leheny was seen as a real prospect, but he never quite panned out. The son of a Pittsburgh police lieutenant, Leheny joined the Pirates in their four-day train trip across the country to Paso Robles for spring training in 1928. He didn't make the big league club but was farmed out to Salisbury for more experience. He bounced around the minors for a few years, until he hooked on with the Boston Braves in spring training 1931. Burt Whitman, in *The Sporting News*, said Leheny was "going great guns" and that Braves manager Bill McKechnie was "willing to go on record to the effect that Leheny will be a good and winning pitcher this year." He faced the Yankees at least twice during the exhibition season, pitching much better the second time around against Ruth, Gehrig, and company. He opened the season with the club but was released by the Braves on May 13. Given another look in 1931, he still didn't make the grade, but on May 12, 1932, he was signed by the Red Sox as a free agent.

Quickly brought on board, he first saw major league action against the Philadelphia Athletics in the first game of a doubleheader swept by the A's. Leheny was the fifth of six pitchers in the 18–6 first game and surrendered three hits in ⅔ of an inning. He got the last out of the third inning and the first out of the fourth, but the runs kept coming and he was charged with four of them. It wasn't an impressive debut. His name was misspelled as "Leheney" in most boxscores but omitted entirely from the *Washington Post*'s. Moving on from Philly to D.C., Leheny was called upon the very next day to pitch the final two innings in a 7–1 loss to the Washington Senators. One more run was recorded next to his name. He'd appeared in two games and faced 16 batters. He threw 2⅔ innings, striking out one, but walking three and surrendering five hits, charged with five earned runs. His ERA is thus 16.88. He had one at-bat, but failed to get a hit. He had two chances in the field and performed to perfection. It was the pitching that was the problem—even for the 1932 Red Sox.

He was found back in Florida in the spring of 1933. The *New York Times* reported that "he is supposed to be trying for a job with the Cincinnati Reds over in Tampa, but when he warms up at all it is with the Boston Braves." John Kieran described him in the *Times* as "a man without a country" and told a tale that appears to be related to his brief tenure with the Braves, saying that Leheny was "put on the blacklist by the other players for something that was not his fault. The train on which the team was traveling pulled into Pittsburgh at 4 a.m. and the Pullmans were side-tracked to allow the players to continue their slumbers undisturbed. But a brass band was there to greet Regis, the home-town hero, and the musicians banged away until the outraged ball players tossed Regis off the train and told him to take his greeters with him."

After baseball, Leheny became a candidate for the Pennsylvania state legislature, running from Pittsburgh's Fourth Ward. We don't know how he fared. We just know that he died in Pittsburgh, to little fanfare, in November 1976.

Walt Ripley—August 17 and September 11, 1935

Ripley was a Worcester boy, who went to Deerfield Academy in Western Massachusetts and attracted attention when he threw a no-hitter in a May 25, 1935, game against the Williams College freshmen. Ripley struck out 17, didn't walk a batter, and only an infield error in the seventh stood in the way of a perfect game. The Red Sox signed him—he was 19 at the time—and his first appearance came in Battle Creek, Michigan in an August 12 "Boy Scout Day" exhibition game against the St. Louis Cardinals. Ripley walked three and gave up seven hits—but still got invited into a major league game five days later.

His debut was against the other St. Louis team, the Browns, in St. Louis. He came in to pitch the bottom of the eighth, walking two and giving up one hit and one run. The Red Sox lost, 11–7. That was a better outing than his second game, a September 11 home game. The White Sox had an 8–2 lead after six innings. Ripley pitched the last three innings, hammered in the seventh with a walk, two doubles, and a single bringing in three more runs. Ripley fared better in the eighth and ninth, keeping Chicago scoreless despite allowing another three hits.

Ripley stayed in the Red Sox organization through the 1937 season. His son Allen pitched for the Red Sox in 1978 and 1979. See more information on the Ripleys in the section on relatives who played for the Red Sox.

Bill Humphrey—April 24 and May 4, 1938

The Red Sox threw four rookie pitchers into a game against the Athletics, in Philadelphia. Emerson Dickman started, relieved by Charlie Wagner, Dick Midkiff, and Byron William Humphrey. Dickman took the loss. The 6'0" right-handed Humphrey closed the game, getting the last two outs (though giving up a couple of hits before doing so). It was a 10–4 loss. The AP boxscore called him "Humphreys."

All in the same May 4 boxscore, the AP labeled him H'phreys, Humpreys, and Humpries. The accompanying text called him Humphreys. Starter Jack Wilson did enough damage, giving up three runs. Humphrey gave up another in the ninth, on three hits. On May 12, the Bosox cut their squad to the 23-player limit by selling Humphrey to the San Diego Padres. Until his dying day, the Missouri native never saw his name spelled correctly in a major league boxscore.

Neill "Wild Horse" Sheridan—September 19 and 26, 1948

Sheridan couldn't make the Sacramento High School team. Asthma saw him discharged from the Marines during World War II. A friend of Lefty O'Doul's got him a tryout with the San Francisco Seals and he made the team in time to collect one at-bat in 1943. He had 150 at-bats the next year, though, batting .293, and he played for the Seals through 1947 (with a brief stay in Chattanooga). Traded to the Red Sox, he was sent to Seattle in 1948, coming up to the big league team at the end of the year when outfielder Sam Mele hurt his ankle.

Wild Horse Sheridan was put in as a pinch-runner for Bobby Doerr in a 6–6 game on September 19. No one knocked him in, and the Tigers scored twice in the seventh to win the game. His second appearance came one week later, pinch-hitting for Boo Ferriss in the top of the ninth of a game the Sox were losing to the Yankees, 6–2. He slammed the first pitch out of the ballpark, but foul. He was called out on strikes. Birdie Tebbetts, on second base, told him it was no strike, but there was nothing to be done. He stayed with the Red Sox through the end of 1948, including the playoff game, but never got in another major league game. In six subsequent seasons, Sheridan played for Seattle, San Francisco, San Diego, Minneapolis, Toronto, San Antonio, Oakland, Sacramento, San Francisco, Victoria, and Vancouver. Feeling his prospects as a ballplayer were limited, he retired from baseball and went to work for a California grocery store, running the liquor department.

Duane Wilson—July 3 and 12, 1958

Initially signed as a free agent by the Red Sox back in 1952, Duane Wilson finally got a crack at the big time six years later. He started the game on July 3 against the Baltimore Orioles and escaped with only one run charged against him, despite giving up eight hits and five walks in the six full innings he pitched. The game went on and on. Tied 2–2 after nine, it looked like it was over when Leo Kiely gave up three runs to the O's in the top of the 10th, but the Red Sox scored three, too. In the top of the 15th, Baltimore scored two unanswered runs off Murray Wall and the whole thing was over. Wilson's one official at-bat was a whiff. He'd laid down a successful sacrifice bunt in the fifth inning, but the runner never scored.

After the White Sox had dealt a 7–4 loss to Boston in the first of two on the 12th, Wilson started the second game but didn't last long. He got one out, but gave up two walks and two hits and four earned runs, the latter two coming when Earl Battey greeted reliever Mike Fornieles with a three-run homer. It was Fornieles tagged with the ultimate 11–5 loss, but two days later the Red Sox called up rookie Bill Monbouquette from Minneapolis and sent Wilson to the Millers. Wilson was recalled on September 1, but saw no further action.

Bill Macleod—September 13 and 22, 1962

Pete Smith started for his hometown team, but was shellacked for eight runs in 3⅔ innings. Finally, Billy Macleod was brought in to put out the fire. He faced one Tiger, Bill Bruton, and got him to ground out, short to first. With runners on first and second in the top of the fifth, Pumpsie Green pinch-hit for Macleod but he grounded out, too. Green stayed in the game, homering and accounting for three RBIs, but the Red Sox lost, 14–6.

Macleod's second and final appearance for his hometown team (Macleod was from Gloucester, Smith from Natick) came on September 22. Unfortunately, this time he took the loss. The score was 3–3 after 10 innings. The Red Sox failed to score in the top of the 11th, but they'd taken out the pitcher for a pinch-hitter. The game was in Washington, so a run meant the ballgame. Macleod gave up a single in the 11th but struck out two and was otherwise unscathed. After getting the first out in the bottom of the 12th, he gave up a single, a single, and a double. End of game.

Dick Mills—September 7 and 13, 1970

Mills was a 6'3" right-handed pitcher who appeared twice in 1970. Originally selected by the Phillies in the 13th round of the June 1965 draft, he elected not to sign and was chosen by the Sox the following June. After five years in the minors, Mills was brought to the Red Sox.

It was September in Cleveland, the second game of a doubleheader by the lake. The Red Sox won the first game, 4–3. Cal Koonce started the nightcap, giving up six runs in four frames.

Mills pitched the sixth, seventh, and eighth innings, giving up one run on four hits. He walked two and struck out two, and threw a wild pitch. The Indians won, 8–2.

His last appearance came in Baltimore six days later. He came into a bases-loaded, one-out situation in the bottom of the seventh. The O's already had a 7–1 lead. Andy Etchebarren hit the ball back to Mills, who committed an error. One run came in, bases still loaded. A walk forced in another. Mills hit Mark Belanger with a pitch, forcing home another run. After striking out Paul Blair, Boog Powell singled in two and Merv Rettenmund singled in the sixth run of the inning. Brooks Robinson grounded out. None of the runs were charged to Mills as earned runs, even though it was his error that set them all up. Not an impressive showing. John Kennedy batted for Mills in the eighth and Roger Moret came in to pitch a 1–2–3 bottom of the eighth in his major league debut.

Kim Andrew—April 16 and 22, 1975

Kim Andrew played early in the pennant-winning season of 1975. He appeared in two games—the first being April 16—and managed to hit .500, but he only got two at-bats in the majors. The Sox were just a week out of spring training. The team had finished third the year before, not that much over .500 themselves with an 84–78 record. Playing in Yankee Stadium, Yaz greeted Pat Dobson with a two-run homer in the first. In the third, Fred Lynn led off with a solo home run. Later that inning, Yaz walked, stole second and then took third on Munson's errant throw, but he jammed his left ankle into Munson's shin guard trying to score later in the inning. He had it taped and stayed in the game. Doug Griffin, though, had a right hip which was bothering him pretty badly and he sat out the game.

Lynn led off the fifth as well, and hit another one out. The Red Sox won the game, 4–2, with those three home runs accounting for all of their scoring. Andrew entered the game defensivly in the bottom of the ninth, but the balls were hit to other fielders and he saw no action.

Kim Andrew's next appearance was on Patriot's Day, Monday April 22. Bill Rodgers won the Marathon with a record 2:09:55. The Sox were hosting the Yankees this time, Dobson again getting the start for New York. Bill Lee started for Boston, but got hammered for four runs in the top of the first and got charged with four more in the fourth. Boston was losing 11–0 after six. Griffin had started the game and went 0-for-2, but then left after the sixth inning and Andrew took his place at second.

His first time—his first at-bat in the major leagues—he made an out, but in the ninth he made his mark. The Sox were down 12–0 and at risk of being shut out, at home, before the holiday home crowd. Tim Blackwell, who'd come in to the game to spell Bob Montgomery, led off the top of the ninth with a double to right. Rick Burleson grounded out to Nettles, but then Andrew singled to deep short. Bob Heise singled to left, scoring Blackwell, and Bernie Carbo hit into a double play to end the game. Sox lose, 12–1. Kim Andrew was batting .500—and that remains his lifetime average.

He spent time in Pawtucket, and Bristol, but tired of feeling like a yo-yo, so he left baseball after the 1977 season—only to be surprised by an invitation to play in Italy for Bollate in Milano. That was intriguing, and enjoyable, but Kim then left pro ball completely and has worked for Federal Express for some 25 years. A longer biography of Kim Andrew appears in the book *'75: The Red Sox Team That Saved Baseball*.

Jim Byrd—May 31 and June 1, 1993

Jim Byrd appeared in two games for Boston, but ever so briefly. His first game was on the last day of May in 1993. His second was on the first of June. Byrd was a switch-hitting shortstop, who hadn't exactly torn up the International League playing for Pawtucket. He was hitting .175 with 12 errors in just 45 games—but Luis Rivera had hurt his hand and Mike Greenwell was a couple of days from coming off the DL. Both Cheo Garcia and Steve Lyons would probably have been chosen over Byrd, but both of them were injured as well. Pitcher Ken Ryan was sent down to Pawtucket to make room for Byrd, who (like more than a few Red Sox players) got lost trying to find Fenway Park. "I ended up somewhere downtown and I had to ask some guy where Fenway was," he told Nick Cafardo of the *Boston Globe*. It was never intended that Byrd would stay more than a few days, but he did see action the very first night, put in as a pinch-runner for Andre Dawson in the eighth inning. The box score reflects Byrd as pr-dh. The Sox scored two runs that inning, but neither of them was Byrd, though he did make it as far as second base on a wild pitch by Royals pitcher Mark Gubicza. Boston lost, 5–3. The next day, Boston lost, 4–3. Again, Byrd came in to run. Again, he didn't score. Immediately after the game, Greenwell was activated and Byrd was sent back to Pawtucket.

Keith Johns—May 23 and 26, 1998

Johns was drafted by the Cardinals in 1992, traded to the Brewers as part of a three-team trade early in 1997, then sent to the Orioles in August, 1997. The following spring, the Orioles traded him to the Red Sox for minor leaguer Bo Dodson. Two months later, he pinch-hit for Sox DH Jim Leyritz at Fenway Park and drew a walk. That was his contribution to the May 23 game against the Yankees.

On May 26, Johns came into the game later, defensively, playing second base. Lou Merloni had started at second, but when Midre Cummings pinch-hit for Lou, the Sox needed a second baseman. Keith Johns got the call. He made a putout and an assist, taking part in a double play.

Johns was released in October, "granted free agency" as the saying goes. No official at-bats. He did his job well in the two games he played, and he can certainly take pride in that, but it just seems to lack a little in the bragging rights department. Still, compared to many of our short-timers....

Juan Peña—May 8 and 14, 1999

Misfortune. What a great start to what Sox fans hoped would be a long and promising career. You couldn't ask for a much better beginning. Bret Saberhagen was put on the disabled list, and 21-year-old Dominican Juan Peña was called up. The young pitcher had led the International League in 1998 with 146 strikeouts, with a no-hitter under his belt, and was off to a 3–1 start with Pawtucket.

Peña pitched the first six innings of the May 8 game at Fenway Park, limiting the Angels to just one run on three hits, while striking out eight and only walking one batter. Six days later, at Skydome, he did as well or better in his second start. This time, he threw seven shutout innings with six hits, struck out seven and walked two. Boston won the two games, 6–1 and 5–0, with Tim Belcher and David Wells taking the losses.

A sore right shoulder forced Peña onto the disabled list and he never came back. He pitched in spring training 2000 but had to go back on the DL, first the 30-day list and then the 60-day list. The Sox signed him again in March 2001, but he could never get back on track and such a promising start petered out into disappointment.

Phil Seibel—April 15 and 18, 2004

A member of the 2004 World Champion Boston Red Sox, it could be too early to count Seibel out as someone who will never appear in the majors again. The left-hander had pitched for the University of Texas and was drafted in 2000 by the Montreal Expos in the eighth round. In early April 2002, he was traded to the Mets as part of a seven-player trade, and ultimately selected off waivers by the Red Sox in November 2003.

His major league debut came the evening of April 15 at Fenway Park. Pedro Martinez started the game, but was bombed for seven earned runs in five innings, walking four and only striking out three. Seibel was the seventh of eight Red Sox relievers brought in to try and stem the tide. The game was tied 7–7 and went into extra innings. Bronson Arroyo took the mound in the top of the 11th and promptly gave up a homer to Miguel Tejada. Five batters later, there was one out, another run had scored, and the bases were loaded. Seibel came in to face Larry Bigbie, who reached first base on Kevin Millar's error at first base as a third run scored. Seibel then walked Brian Roberts, forcing in the fourth run of the frame. He was pulled in favor of Frank Castillo, who gave up a single (seeing a fifth run score) before getting Tejada to ground into a double play. Baltimore won, 12–7.

Three days later, Seibel faced the Yankees on Sunday afternoon. Starter Derek Lowe had given New York seven runs in just 2⅔ innings. Mark Malaska kept the Yankees scoreless through the fifth, and Seibel came on to pitch the sixth. He threw 3⅔ hitless innings, though walked four—two of them in the top of the ninth, which brought about his removal. Castillo came on, and walked Bernie Williams, but then retired Alex Rodriguez on a bases-loaded fly ball to center.

Near the end of the season, Seibel was released by the Red Sox, only to be re-signed on the first day of the ALCS. In 2006, he pitched for Red Sox affiliates in Greenville, Portland, and Pawtucket, throwing 80 innings with a 1.24 ERA. He's never given up a hit in major league play, and sports an error-free record in the field as well.

An exception: Devern Hansack—September 23 and October 1, 2006

Originally scheduled to be included in this section, but after he appeared in three more games in 2007, he no longer qualifies. But we had it written up anyhow, and rather than delete it….

It was quite a week for the first Nicaraguan native to play for the Red Sox. Signed back in 1999 by the Houston Astros, and released in 2003, right-handed pitcher Devern Hansack had reportedly given up on baseball and taken up work as a lobster fisherman in Nicaragua. He did a little barnstorming in Nicaragua, though, and Red Sox scouting executive Craig Shipley saw him pitch at a Fall 2005 baseball tournament in The Netherlands. He was signed by the Sox in December and pitched for the Portland Sea Dogs in 2006 (8–7, 3.26 ERA, with 124 strikeouts and just 36 walks in 132⅓ innings). Hansack pitched eight innings in the September 17 Eastern League Championship game as the Sea Dogs beat Akron to win the playoffs. Six days later, he appeared in his first major league game, starting against the Blue Jays in Toronto.

After three scoreless innings, he got touched up for two solo homers in the fourth and another run in the bottom of the sixth before being relieved. The Boston bats were fairly quiet and the three earned runs gave him the loss. The last game of the year fell on the first of October and, after a rain delay of three hours and 23 minutes, Hansack got his second start—and threw a no-hitter! The Baltimore Orioles sent up 15 batters over the first five innings. Only one reached base, on a walk, and he was retired on a double play. The Red Sox scored nine runs on seven hits. Not one Oriole managed a hit off Hansack before the rain resumed and the five innings of play constituted an official game.

Under a questionable ruling by the Commissioner's office in the Fay Vincent years, Hansack's rain-shortened gem doesn't count as an "official" no-hitter. He did get the win. It does count as a shutout. It does count as a complete game. It was a compete game win in which the defeated team was held hitless, but somehow it's deemed to not be a no-hitter. In this book, it is.

Another no-hitter that wasn't official belongs to Matt Young, on April 12, 1992. He lost that game to Cleveland, 2–1, but never gave up a hit. Since he only threw eight innings, and since he lost, he was denied no-hitter status.

SOME OTHER SHORT-TIMERS: THOSE WHO PLAYED JUST THREE GAMES

Ben Beville—May 24, May 30, and June 2, 1901

Clarence Benjamin Beville was a pitcher on the first-year team of the franchise. Controversy preceded him to Boston. The *Los Angeles Times* on the second of February described the right-hander as a "star twirler of the Oaklands [who] is now debarred from the California League for jumping his contract and signing with the Montana aggregation." He'd played some for Butte in 1900. He played some right field for San Bernardino in February and some left field in March, batting .162 at the end of the Southern California Baseball League season, which ended in March. He was playing for Kansas City in the Western League in early May. As of May 15, he was reported in a Boston Americans uniform, though described by the *Chicago Tribune* as "at least ten pounds overweight and will not be in form for some days."

Beville debuted on May 24, and he pitched acceptably, but the Bostons were shut out by the Tigers in Detroit, 3–0. Beville allowed seven hits and five walks, and suffered three errors. The *Globe* said he was "not hit hard, but was as wild as a hawk." On May 30, Beville started again in the morning game of two on Memorial Day. He walked the first two batters but escaped further damage in the first. An error behind him gave Chicago a baserunner to lead off the second. There followed a walk and then a double down the third baseline past Collins. "Beville lost his bearings completely here," reported the *Tribune*. He threw eight straight balls, and was yanked from the game in favor of Cuppy. Boston lost, 8–3.

In the fifth inning of the June 2 game in Milwaukee, umpire Haskell banished both Jimmy Collins and Buck Freeman, so Dowd was brought in from left field to play third and two pitchers were inserted as fielders—Cuppy in left and Beville at first base. Ben came through well enough at the plate, though he made an error in the field. With the score 4–2 in favor of Boston after eight, Beville kicked off a two-out rally in the ninth with a double into the crowd in left field. Parent hit a home run, and the hits just kept coming. Beville came up a second time and doubled again. They were the only two hits he ever had—and in the process he'd set a record that still remains today for the most doubles in an inning. It's been tied by several others, including six other Boston batters. Before the third out could be secured, Milwaukee had given up nine runs. Earlier in the game, Beville had walked and come around to score in the sixth. Not a bad day at all—but he was released on June 10 when Boston prepared to bring in George Winter whose debut on the 15th was the first of 213 appearances for Boston.

Dave Williams—July 2, July 18, and August 3, 1902

Doc Adkins pitched the first inning and didn't fare well: three Washington runs. Williams, a left-hander, took over starting in the second. Four runs scored in the third, but the *Globe* correspondent suggested a bad umpiring call cost three of those runs. (The *Globe* also suggested that "fatty Adkins" needed to lose about 30 pounds.) Williams gave up seven hits in eight innings and walked one. He singled, 1-for-4 as a batter. Washington won, 8–3.

July 18. Hughes, who hadn't pitched in months, got the start. He wasn't ready, and "he suffered intense pain with every ball he tried to work toward the plate." Williams got roasted, by the fans and by the newspaper: "he has a lot to learn about pitching and should be in a primary league." He walked five, struck out five, and hit a batter, and by the time the game was over, it was 14–4, Cleveland. The game story says Williams singled in the second and singled in the fourth, both times apparently driving in a run, but the boxscore shows him as 0-for-4. Something to be reconciled there.

On August 3, Williams made his third appearance, in relief of Bill Dinneen. Detroit had an 8–3 lead after five. Williams took over in the sixth and let in one run each inning. Five walks and a wild pitch overshadowed the two strikeouts. Williams went back to school. In March 1903, he was a student at the University of Pennsylvania. He signed with Kansas City but we won't try to track him any further.

Gary Wilson—September 27 and 29, 1902

James Garrett Wilson came from Baltimore, born in 1879, a 5'7" righthanded second baseman. Wilson played on just two days, but actually played in three games. His debut came on September 27, 1902, when he started at second and played both games on a road date doubleheader in Baltimore, Wilson's home town. Batting seventh in the order, Wilson was 1-for-4 with a single in the first game and 1-for-3 with another single in the second. The *Boston Globe* boxscore says he hit a home run, but closer analysis shows him with just one total base, while Baltimore's Hal Wiltse has five TB on two hits. Wilson did drive in two runs, but it was a result of a ball misplayed by Baltimore second baseman Tom Jones, he of the four errors on the day. Wilson was almost as shaky in the field, with two errors in game one and one error in game two. Fortunately, Boston won both games, 9–8 and 4–2. Wilson did take part in two double plays.

On September 29, Wilson was 0-for-4 and made another error. Boston beat Baltimore this game, too, by the score of 9–5. It was the last game ever played by the Baltimore team, which relocated to New York the following year and became the New York Highlanders (later, the New York Yankees). Apparently, Wilson wasn't impressive enough to be invited back to the 1903 Bostons.

Hank Olmsted—July 15, July 19, and July 26, 1905

Boston president John I. Taylor enjoyed traveling and signing players for the team. In August 1904, he signed up Henry Olmsted, a pitcher who'd played for Milwaukee in 1902 and Peoria in 1903. The *Globe* noted that "a great future is predicted for him" and, though his signing from the Columbus club was contested, his was one of several the national baseball commission allowed.

"Young Olmstead Proves A Puzzle" read the *Globe* headline on July 15. The paper ran a good-sized photograph, too, helping highlight his five-hit debut against the Browns in St. Louis. It was a crisp 2–1 win, a "close call, but young Olmstead delivered the goods." The paper spelled his surname with an "a" and even called him Ned Olmstead at one point. Apparently, he had a deceptive delivery, with his "slow ball" hard to hit squarely. Olmsted was 1-for-3 with a single.

His next start came four days later, in Cleveland, and he gave up just seven hits in a complete game effort, but lost the game, 5–1. He "pitched well, but failed to field his position," concluded the *Globe* correspondent. No errors were charged to the young right-hander, but he exhibited a "failure to keep his eyes open" which we can conclude must indicate that he simply never got to balls he should have.

When Boston played a regularly scheduled game in Columbus, the fans asked that Olmsted get a start; he was a local favorite after his past play in the Ohio capitol. He was held until Detroit, though, and started his third game. He held the Tigers to just six hits, but walked five and gave up four runs. Since Boston didn't score one, he lost again, though this time the *Globe* allowed that he "looked pretty good."

Not good enough, though. The long western road trip over, the fans back home never got to see Hank Olmsted play. His ERA was 3.24, with a 1–2 W-L record. In January, 1906, Taylor paid big money ($3,000) to purchase an outfielder named Clay, and "threw in pitcher Olmsted for good measure."

Walter Carlisle—May 8, 9, and 11, 1908

He came from Yorkshire, England when he was two years old. Living in Minneapolis, he played amateur ball there for three years before joining the Millers in 1902. He played for Crookston from 1902–04 and for Rock Island from 1904–06. Boston had been after him since 1905, competing with Cleveland to secure him from the Rock Island ballclub. Interest only increased in May and June 1907, when he made a "world's record" by hitting five home runs in a 20-game stretch for the Los Angeles Angels; the team won the PCL pennant and Carlisle was sold to Boston for $2,500. The *Los Angeles Times* declared, "Boston certainly gets a jewel in him, for he can hit, field, run and play almost any place. The Champions will look a long time to find his equal."

Carlisle played left field for Boston and he batted leadoff. He was 1-for-4 in his first major league game, with a single in the sixth. The Red Sox lost to the visiting New York team, 3–0. New York won again, 2–1, the next day. Carlisle led off again, but was 0-for-4. The *Globe* described a "beautiful throw from left field" on Kleinow's single, "picking up the ball on the dead run and sending it to the plate like a rifle shot." With a shoestring catch, the paper adjudged him "pretty near filling the bill as a throwing outfielder and a fast man on the bases."

New York won yet another one, 3–0, on the 11th. Carlisle was 0-for-2, striking out twice and being replaced by Jim McHale in the seventh. On May 29, he got the word that he'd been dealt to the American Association team in Kansas City. Later reports had him "receiving great praise" for his work in KC. The *Globe* gave him a nice sendoff, with what proved to be his major league obituary: "Carlisle is one of the finest outfielders in the profession. He is a beautiful thrower, and very speedy, but he failed to show good form at the bat in the few games that he played with the Red Sox."

He did pop up on July 19, 1911, as a center fielder for Vernon in the Coast League. Running in from center, he caught a ball, crossed the second base bag, thus doubling off the baserunner, and momentum carried him to first base, where he tripled off that runner for an unusual unassisted triple play. He led the league in RBIs for five seasons.

Chet Nourse—July 27, July 30, and August 4, 1909

Nourse was an Ipswich native and a pitcher for Brown University who shut out Harvard on a two-hitter in 1909 and began to attract attention. In April, it was announced that he would join the Cubs after he graduated from college—but it wasn't Nourse who made the announcement. In fact, he'd agreed to join the Red Sox but asked them to withhold the news until after graduation. He was a catcher as well as a pitcher in high school, but focused on mound work in college, and in four years never yielded more than six hits a game.

Biff Schlitzer began the game against New York, but he couldn't get out of the second. Nourse made his debut and pitched better in 2⅓. Pape followed Nourse, but didn't pitch all that well, either. "Nourse was not hit as often as his colleagues, but he was weak and manager Fred gave him short shrift." (*New York Times*) New York won, 6–0.

He relieved again three days later, coming in for Collins in the eighth, but let in one inherited run and four more for which he bore responsibility. That put the icing on a 10–4 St. Louis victory.

On August 4, Nourse was the third pitcher in a game against the Tigers. He didn't shine this time, either. Three chances, five innings, five hits, five walks, and a 7.20 earned run average. Nourse was farmed out and kept in the system—he was with the Red Sox spring training traveling party that traveled to Redondo Beach, California in 1911—but he definitely did not reappear on the rolls of major league records.

Chris Mahoney—July 12, September 28, and October 8, 1910

Two appearances as a pitcher and one as an outfielder.

Mahoney and his catcher McDonald, from Fordham University, had played in Pittsfield in the summer of 1908, pitching a full 16 innings against North Adams, before losing to the battery from Holy Cross, 2–1. When he made the majors In 1910, he entered a July game well under control. Boston had a 14–0 lead over the Indians and Eddie Cicotte seemed certain to get the win. Mahoney came in to pitch the last three innings and he struck out Lajoie, the third batter he faced. He let up five hits and five runs; at the plate, he was 1-for-1 with a single. He scored on Tris Speaker's triple.

In the September game, Mahoney played right field for the full game, 0-for-2 batting third in the lineup, without any action at all in the field. Boston's three runs in the 4–3 loss to Cleveland, in Cleveland, all came on errors.

In his October game, Mahoney started the last game of the year, in New York against the Highlanders. He pitched the whole game, striking out four and walking two. Both teams had 11 hits, but the Red Sox left 10 men on base and the Highlanders left just five. Though 0-for-3 at the plate, and trailing by just one run with a runner on second, Mahoney hit for himself. He flied out to left. Harry Hooper rolled out to second base and Mahoney lost his only decision.

Mahoney had batted cleanup in college, and showed some "fine hitting" for Fort Worth in 1911, playing often in the outfield, and sparking the interest of manager Donovan and owner Taylor, but nothing seems to have come of it.

Ed Kelly—April 14, 20, and 22, 1914

Kelly was a right-hander, born in Pawtucket. His first appearance was flawless, three outs in the ninth inning against Washington. He gave up a hit his second time out, a brief two-thirds of an inning against Philadelphia, and walked one. He mopped up in a six-run top of the 10th after Bedient had been unable to hold back the A's. The third game he was in ended as a 9–9 tie, again against Philadelphia, as the Sox scored four times in the eighth after Kelly had held them hitless in the top of the inning.

He wasn't all that impressive, deemed to need some more work. He never came back, but he nevertheless has a lifetime 0.00 ERA.

Kelly became a miner and died at age 40 in Red Lodge, Montana following surgery for an unspecified illness.

Eusebio Gonzalez—July 26, July 28, and August 6, 1918

"Gonzalez is a Cuban who was obtained from the Springfield, Mass. Team. Being a citizen of Cuba, he is not subject to military service in the United States."—Boston Globe

Given how decimated the major league rosters were, due to the World War, this was understood as a considerable advantage. The infielder came in for Everett Scott at shortstop during the game in Chicago (the Sox were losing, 7–1) and tripled his first time at bat, scoring a moment later when Stansbury followed with a single. Two days later, Gonzalez again filled in for Scott in the later innings. He made an out in his one at-bat. Batting .500, though.

The third game came in Detroit, and he played a full game at the hot corner. He was 1-for-3 in a game tied 4–4 after nine innings. Gonzalez led off the 10th and drew a walk. Carl

Mays walked, too, and Schang got on due to a Detroit error. Bases loaded. Tigers pitcher Rudy Kallio fielded Hooper's grounder and threw home to cut down Eusebio and start a double play, but the throw went all the way to the backstop and two runs scored as the Red Sox took the lead. Shean drove in another run. Mays gave up one run, but the Red Sox won, 7–5.

He made no errors in the field, batted .400 with a triple, and scored two runs, but Gonzalez never got another chance to play in the big leagues.

Walt Lynch—July 8, 12, and 17, 1922

When both Roxy Walters and Ed Chaplin suffered injuries, the Red Sox were left with just one catcher—Muddy Ruel. They needed a backup so they recalled Walt Lynch, who'd been farmed out to Richmond. He'd come from Buffalo, signed while playing semipro ball there. He spelled Muddy in the second game against the first-place Browns, working the last three innings. Boston won the first game, 2–1. Lynch had one at-bat, singled, and scored.

Again, on July 12, he came in late. This time, when he was due up in the ninth, he was pulled for a pinch hitter, who singled and helped spark a six-run Red Sox rally, but Boston still fell short to the visiting Indians, 11–7.

The Red Sox got five runs in the first, but were swamped by 16 Detroit runs (Cobb had a 5-for-5 day, including a three-run homer in the ninth). Lynch had an 0-for-1 game. And with injuries sufficiently healed, there wasn't need for Walt any longer, though he'd acquitted himself well.

Paul Hinson—April 19, May 7, and May 30, 1928

Hinson, 23, from Vanleer, Tennessee presents a bit of mystery. An initial look at boxscores of the day shows that he made his major league debut as a pinch runner on April 19 in Boston, running for Johnnie Heving in the bottom of the eighth inning. Heving had batted for Slim Harriss and singled. Hinson scored as part of a four-run eighth that converted a 6–3 deficit into a 7–6 win over the Yankees. Ruffing shut down New York in the ninth. The Red Sox win knocked the Yankees out of first place for the first time since May, 1926 (if one doesn't count Opening Day 1928, when the only game played had the Sox temporarily in first, thanks to their 7–5 win over Washington.

On May 7, Hinson was again sent in to run, in the bottom of the ninth, running for catcher Charlie Berry, who had singled. Hinson was left on base. Boston lost to Cleveland, 4–2.

Hinson repeated as a pinch runner for Berry in the ninth of the May 30 game, after Berry pinch-hit a single for Al Simmons in the bottom of the ninth. Again, Hinson was left on base. It was the second game of a doubleheader against Philadelphia and Boston lost both games. Our pinch-running specialist then walked off the major league stage, never to be heard from again. We know he was an infielder, but he never had the chance to field. We know he batted right, but he never got a chance to bat. He did contribute, though, to one Red Sox win in a decade where the Red Sox had precious few.

Tangent: The all-time leader among Red Sox for games played without an at-bat is many more than Paul Hinson's three. It is Bob Stanley, who from 1977 through 1989 appeared in 637 games without a single regular-season at-bat. He did go 0-for-1 in postseason play; Steamer struck out in the ninth inning of Game Two of the 1986 World Series. The Red Sox won the game, and Stanley got the save.

Freddie Moncewicz—June 19, June 20, and July 3, 1928

A shortstop for Boston College for four years (1925–28), the pride of Brockton, Moncewicz entered his first game in Washington, giving Wally Gerber a rest late in the second game. Gerber was 2-for-5 on the day; Freddie was 0-for-1 but got his feet wet as Boston went down to a 16–7 defeat (they'd won the first game, 5–1).

Same thing the next day—a late-inning substitution for Gerber at short. This time, E. Garland Braxton shut out the Sox, 8–0. Mr. Moncewicz never got up to bat.

His third game, Freddie ran for Red Ruffing in the seventh but had no chance to score. That's about it. In the end, Moncewicz went back to Brockton, where he died in 1969. He was 0-for-1 in three major league games. All he ever did was strike out. Well, that's not exactly fair. He did make two plays without an error.

Al Baker—August 20, 26, and 29, 1938

The immortal Al Baker was a Mississippian. He pitched two innings in his first game, helping hold a win over Washington for Archie McKain, though giving up six hits in two innings (at least he didn't walk anyone).

On the 26th, Bagby got hit hard by the White Sox and couldn't finish the third; Baker came on and induced a double play. After giving up a leadoff single in the sixth, he was yanked. Four hits in all, and a walk.

Baker's last action came in a game he entered after it was Detroit 11, Boston 1. He pitched the last three innings and gave up four more hits. His ERA was 9.39.

Joe Wood Jr.—May 1, 5, and 14, 1944

Not entirely a chip off the old block, Wood was not really Joe Jr., since Smoky Joe's real name was Howard, not Joe. And he never won 34 games in a season. In fact, he never won any. He only got one start. His first time in was to throw more or less the middle three in an 11–4 loss to the Senators. Then he pitched the seventh and eighth innings against the Yankees, in a game Tex Hughson started (and lost). The AP story said it was Charlie Woods pitching, but we know better. Lastly, he secured a start on May 14. That didn't work out, either. He was gone in the fifth, after giving up a total of eight hits in 4⅔ innings. He took the loss.

His start was in the first game of a doubleheader hosting the Tigers. To confuse matters a bit, the first Red Sox reliever in the second game was George "Pinky" Woods. At least this was 1944; in 1943, the Tigers had an infielder named Joe Wood. For more information on Joe Wood Jr., see the section on relatives playing for the Red Sox.

Mel Deutsch—April 21, April 23, and May 7, 1946

The 1946 Red Sox won 21 of their first 24 games, and never looked back. They started with four in a row, but Boo Ferriss was battered for seven Philadelphia runs in the first three innings of the first April 21 game. Right-handed reliever Mel Deutsch came in to get out of the third and took it through the seventh, lifted for a pinch hitter. In 4⅓ innings, he breezed until getting hit in the seventh for three runs. Boston had scored five in the sixth, closing the gap. In the bottom of the ninth, the Red Sox unloaded for six runs and tied the game, winning it 12–11 in the 10th when Ted Williams hit a bases-loaded single.

Deutsch had been a prospect in 1944, taken into the service and missed the 1945 season. The rookie's second role was in relief of war hero Earl Johnson against the Senators, brought in when Johnson got in trouble in the eighth. Mel recorded two outs, with no hits, but Washington scored six runs off Clem Dreisewerd, Mike Ryba, and Jim Wilson in the top of the 11th.

His third game was also an extra-inning affair and, once again, he was gone well before the final resolution. In Boston, St. Louis scored four early runs off Tex Hughson. Deutsch came in to help his fellow Texan in the third, and pitched the fourth inning, too, allowing two more runs. The Red Sox bats tied it, though, and it was 6–6 after nine. And after 13 innings, too. In the bottom of the 14th, Rudy York walked, Dom DiMaggio singled, and Hal Wagner was intentionally passed. Leon Culberson hit the first pitch he saw for a grand slam. It was their 12th win in row. The next day, the Red Sox trimmed the roster sending Deutsch and Wilson and outfielder Andy Gilbert to Louisville.

Leslie "Tex" Aulds—May 25, May 30, and June 22, 1947

See Aulds' profile under Native Americans.

Mike Palm—July 11, 18, and 21, 1948

This cup of coffee player starred for Belmont High and made the Red Sox while in high school, signed out of a baseball school tryout at Fenway Park. He was a real fan, whose father had pitched industrial league games in the Boston area and often taken young Mike to both Braves Field and Fenway Park. During the war, Palm spent time in the Army Air Corps both in North Africa and in India. After time with Roanoke and Birmingham, he was leading the Southern League in ERA before getting called up to Boston.

On July 11, 1948, the Sox won the day's first game, 9–8, in 10 innings when Dom DiMaggio doubled home Billy Goodman. In the second game, DiMaggio homered again and Johnny Pesky hit a three-run homer, but the six-run inning off Mickey Harris did in the Red Sox. Palm relieved Harris with two outs in the bottom of the sixth, and surrendered three hits before getting out of the inning. Parnell took over in relief, come the seventh. The game ended after 7½ innings because of Philadelphia's Sunday curfew law. Palm recalls, "I was a little wild, you know—nervous as hell…in a big league uniform." He roomed with Ferriss on the road and stayed with his own family in Belmont while the Red Sox were at home.

Palm's second game was a week later, in Boston, on the 18th—again, a doubleheader, this time against the visiting St. Louis Browns. Boo started for Boston but gave up seven hits in his 2⅔ innings of work. The Red Sox were behind, 4–0. Mike Palm closed out the third inning and pitched the fourth, allowing just one hit though he walked three batters. At the plate, though, the Red Sox came alive and scored six times in the bottom of the fourth. With a 6–4 lead, McCarthy brought in Earl Johnson to pitch. He scattered three hits in five innings of work, letting in just one more run. The six more runs the Red Sox scored in the sixth proved pure gravy. Johnson was awarded the win, even though Palm had left with the lead.

The last time Palm pitched in the major leagues was in yet another twinbill, a day/night doubleheader against the White Sox at Fenway Park on July 20. Boston won the afternoon game, 3–1. In the night game, Ferriss again fared poorly, hammered for six hits in 1⅔ innings. The White Sox scored five runs in the second, and Palm was once more brought in to close the inning. He allowed two hits and walked two in 1⅓ innings, giving up one run in the top of the third, but once the Red Sox had scored five runs in the bottom of the third and made it a close game, he gave way to Earl Johnson. Palm was again hitless at the plate. Chicago scored three more runs, but the Red Sox scored once in the eighth and three runs in the bottom of the ninth to take the game, 10–9.

Palm was sent back to Birmingham, which won the Dixie Series. Mike won four games in the playoffs. In early 1949, Red Sox manager Joe McCarthy cited Palm as a prospect but he spent two years with Louisville and then was sold to Sacramento. He told this author, "I figured I wasn't going to be in the Hall of Fame. It was time to go to work."

Jack Robinson—May 4, 5, and 11, 1949

His name was John Edward Robinson, and his nickname was Jack. Jack E. Robinson? A Red Sox player? The man was a right-handed pitcher from New Jersey. When Mickey Harris was pounded for 14 hits and five runs in Detroit, Robinson got the last out of the sixth and pitched the seventh, allowing just one hit. Combs flied out, batting for him in the eighth. Robinson never did get a chance to bat in major league ball. Virgil Trucks beat Boston, 5–1.

The next day, the Sox faced Bob Feller in Cleveland. Jack Kramer started for Boston, but gave up a second-inning three-run homer to Ken Keltner (in the first game the two teams had played since Keltner did the Red Sox in with a three-run homer in the October 4, 1948 single-game playoff that gave the Indians the pennant) and another to Minnie Minoso. After two singles, Robinson came on in relief, inheriting the two runners. He threw a wild pitch, then walked Larry Doby. Lou Boudreau knocked in two more runs with a bases-loaded double, Doby being cut down at the plate. Robinson got out of the inning, then pitched the third before giving way to Dorish to start the fourth.

Jack Robinson's final game was in Chicago. Again the Red Sox lost. Again, it wasn't his fault, though he did add a balk to his record. Robinson pitched one inning and gave up one hit. It was a game in which the White Sox scored in each and every inning, fortunately a home game for them or the tally might have been worse than the 12–8 final. Robinson returned to minor league ball, with a career 2.25 ERA in the majors.

Pete Magrini—April 13, April 27, and May 9, 1966

Magrini was signed by the Twins in 1964, but selected by the Red Sox in November that year in the first-year minor league draft. The right-hander came into a game the Orioles led, 4–1, and enabled them to run it to an 8–1 lead. He took over with one out in the eighth and hit the first batter he faced, future Hall of Famer Frank Robinson. Robinson stole second. Another future Hall of Fame Robinson, Brooks, walked. Boog Powell singled. We'll spare you the details, but he did get both Robinsons in a 1–2–3 ninth.

Two weeks later to the day, at Fenway facing the White Sox, Pete came in to relieve Jerry Stephenson in the third, allowed one inherited run to score and gave up another before settling down again—though he did make an error in a fifth-inning rundown after he'd picked Frank Robinson off first.

On May 9, at Kansas City's Municipal Stadium, he got a start but only lasted three innings and part of the fourth, giving up four runs on three hits, with four walks and a wild pitch mixed in. He was sent to the minors and, in August 1967, sent (along with Ron Klimkowski) to the Yankees for Elston Howard. ERA = 9.82. 0-for-3 at the plate.

Andy Merchant—September 28, 1975, and June 2 and 10, 1976

Andy Merchant, a catcher, got the start on September 28th, catching Dick Pole. "I'd gone up several times, in fact. They'd call when someone got an injury. They'd call me up for a little while. I was kind of the next catcher in line. I was back and forth." It was the last game of the season, a Sunday game, and the Red Sox had already clinched the pennant on Friday night after New York had beaten Baltimore. The *Boston Globe* headlined their game story "Red Sox scrubs bite dust, 11–4." Butch Hobson played third base, only his second major league start; he went 1-for-4. Steve Dillard was at second, his debut. Dillard went 2-for-5 and scored two runs. And Andy Merchant got the start behind the plate, batting third in the order. Dillard singled and then stole second in the first inning. Merchant flied deep to center, and Dillard tagged up and took third on the play. He scored on Carbo's single which followed and the Red Sox took a 1–0 lead. The Indians scored twice in the second, but Boston came back in the third. Dillard singled to left and Merchant singled to right. Carbo singled again and picked up another RBI. Rick Miller drove in Merchant and Carbo and Boston was now up by 4–2. That lead was erased by the six runs the Tribe scored in the fifth. Merchant picked up another single later in the game, and wound up 2-for-4 on the day. The season was over and there was no postseason for Merchant or Hobson, nor was there for Dillard. Andy didn't even stick around to watch the World Series. "I just went home and watched old Carlton on TV like everybody else."

Merchant did appear briefly in 1976. Again up and down a couple of times, he saw limited duty in two games for a total of two at-bats—but he didn't manage another hit, striking out both times. His major league career average plunged from .500 to .333, and there it stands today.

Postscript: Merchant had been in the organization for a few years by this time, starting out at Single A in Winston-Salem. He spent most of his career at Pawtucket. In 1977, he reports, "I was supposed to show up with the big league club to work out with them in spring training but I never got a letter or anything. So I thought I was going back with the minor league club at a later date [minor league players reported later.] I got a phone call from one of my roommates [with the Red Sox] who said, "Your uniform's in your locker and they're waiting on you. They said, can you call Ed Kenney?" So I did. I called him and I said, "Well, you all going to pay me for the week I missed? I'll catch the next flight." But they wouldn't do it. Anyway, we got a bad connection on the phone and I missed him. He never called me back and I never called him back. I never got a release from Boston or anything. That's where it ended. It was really weird; that's the way it ended, right there.

"I ended up with Alabama Power Company. I was a line-clearing specialist. I'm retired from there now. I enjoyed it [the majors], though, I'm glad I got there. I got overlooked a little bit. It's part of life. I enjoyed a cup of coffee and then went on about my way." A longer biography of Andy Merchant appears in the book '75: The Red Sox Team That Saved Baseball.

Zach Crouch—June 4, 5, and 10, 1988

When pitcher Wes Gardner was placed on the DL with an infected finger, the Sox summoned the left-handed Crouch from Pawtucket. He'd been with the Red Sox since the 1984 draft. Zach saw first duty as the second of the three pitchers it took to get the Blue Jays out in the top of the ninth at Fenway. Smith was charged with six runs (three earned) and Crouch with one, but since Roger Clemens had given up three and the final score was 10–2, Roger got the loss. Crouch got the first batter he faced, but then walked a man, gave up a double, and was removed, charged with one earned run.

The very next day, the Jays scored 12 runs, none of them charged to Crouch, though he had little to be proud of. Inheriting a bases-loaded situation, he doled out three straight singles before restoring order thanks to a brilliant 6-2–5 double play.

Meeting Toronto for a third time, this time at Exhibition Stadium, he was called on with two outs and two on in the bottom of the sixth. He faced one batter, Lloyd Moseby, and walked him. When Cecil Fielder was announced for Rance Mulliniks, manager McNamara called for Mike Smithson to take over for Crouch. Then Leach was brought in for Fielder and Smithson struck him out. Jays 3, Red Sox 0. Crouch was sent back to Pawtucket on June 13, when Gardner was reactivated.

Steve Curry—July 10, 18, and 23, 1988

Curry was another right-hander, another 1984 Red Sox draft pick. His first game was a start in Chicago. He gave up two runs in the first, another in the fourth, and left with two men on base in the fifth. Mike Smithson bailed him out. Curry had walked nine men in $4\frac{1}{3}$ innings. He was tagged with the loss. He started again, at home, on the 18th, and again lasted $4\frac{1}{3}$ innings, but this time just gave up two runs, leaving with two men on. And the Red Sox won, but the win went to Dennis Lamp.

His last start was more truncated, terminated after $2\frac{1}{3}$, and after five earned runs on four hits and four walks, a walk, and a balk. Smithson took over and got the win when the Red Sox scored twice in the third, four times in the fourth, and sprinkled in another five runs.

Brian Bark—July 6, July 15, and September 8, 1995

See Bark's profile under the section on Jews on the Red Sox.

Ken Grundt—August 8, 1996, May 13 and 20, 1997

He'd been in the Giants and Rockies systems, but was released by both teams and signed as a free agent with the Red Sox in November 1995. The Red Sox released him, too, a year later. He'd appeared in just one game, at Fenway Park on August 8, 1996. He got one out in the ninth, but also gave up a run thanks to a John Olerud double.

Maybe having second thoughts, the Sox signed Grundt again in January 1997. He appeared for a second outing as the middle of five pitchers in a Kauffman Stadium game in KC on May 13. In one inning, he gave up two runs. Kansas City already had seven runs at the time, and the Red Sox never got any.

It was another five-pitcher game for the Red Sox, as Chicago piled up a 10–1 win at Comiskey. Grundt was fourth of the five, throwing two innings and giving up another run. After the season was over, the Red Sox released him for a second time, in October 1997.

David Pauley—May 31, June 6, and June 11, 2006

Pauley is a right-hander originally drafted by the Padres in 2001. The Red Sox picked him up in December 2005 as part of the Dave Roberts trade. Roberts went to San Diego and the Red Sox got Jay Payton, Ramon Vazquez, Pauley, and some cash.

He got his first start in Toronto on May 31, an 8–6 Red Sox win. But Pauley didn't perform well, giving up six earned runs in 4⅓ innings on 11 hits and three walks. Even though the Sox were leading 7–6 when he left the game, he hadn't thrown the requisite five innings to get the win as a starter.

Pauley got thrown to the wolves on June 6, asked to start in Yankee Stadium. There he pitched very well, giving up just two runs in 6⅔ innings—one on a solo homer to Bernie Williams, the other coming after he turned over a bases-loaded situation to Rudy Seanez, who walked home what proved to be the winning run in a 2–1 Red Sox loss. His third and last start came on June 11 at Fenway Park. As in his first game, he again gave up six earned runs, this time in five innings, and this time the Red Sox didn't fully bail him out. Texas won 13–6. Pauley's three starts left him 0–2, the two games with six earned runs each bookending a very good game in New York. In March 2007, he was optioned to Pawtucket. Oops, he returned in 2008. Oh, well. Nobody's perfect.

Jeff Bailey—July 6–8, 2007

He wouldn't have meant to be unkind, but Gordon Edes of the *Boston Globe* led his game-after story by writing, "The Tigers rolled out the major leagues' most potent offense. The Red Sox rolled out Jeff Bailey, not to be confused with Buddy, Bob, or Beetle." The Tigers won the game at Comerica Park, 9–2. Bailey played first base in his big league debut. Jeff hit a long fly ball to center field in the third that should have resulted in his first RBI, but Wily Mo Peña was cut down at home plate on a "terrific throw" by Curtis Granderson—so Bailey was charged with hitting into a double play instead. He wound up 0-for-4, leaving three runners on base. He played the next game, too, going 0-for-2. And the day after that, with which he wound up his season with totals of 1-for-9 (.111)—but the one hit was a home run off Detroit's Nate Robertson on the 8th, so he finally collected that RBI. "[It feels] pretty good," said the 28-year-old Bailey, who had labored 11 seasons in the minor leagues before finally getting his shot in

The Show. What the future may hold for him remains to be seen. He'll always be able to say he hit a home run in major league baseball. And a ring, for being on the 2007 team.

Zero games—but a World Championship ring

Then there were the guys who played zero games for the Red Sox, but were on the 25-man roster and spent some time with the team. The list would be too difficult to compile here, but it's probably safe to say that the happiest among them would be Brandon Puffer. Puffer was a pitcher, a right-hander who'd broken in with Houston in 2002. Unlike the players above, there was a difference: Puffer had appeared in other major league games, some 85 of them—with Houston in 2002 and 2003, with San Diego in 2004, and very briefly with San Francisco in 2005. He played in the Pacific Coast League in 2006 and in the Double A Texas League in 2007.

On July 2, 2004 the Red Sox purchased him from the Padres. They granted him free agency on October 15, 2004. He never got in a game for the Red Sox—but he did get himself a World Championship ring. Ownership awarded rings to everyone on the team, whether they played or not, the theory being that they could have played if called upon and even Puffer's presence on the roster—ready to pitch—might have made a difference.

What happened is that, before Puffer could pitch, the Sox acquired left-hander Jimmy Anderson. It was the same day, swapping minor leaguer Andrew Shipman to the Cubs. With Anderson's arrival, Puffer was surplus and so was optioned to Pawtucket. When the rosters expanded in September, Puffer was promoted to the big league bullpen; Anderson was already gone, released on August 1 after six innings of work. Anderson collected a ring, too, of course. Puffer spent one night with the Red Sox, recalled for the game on the evening of September 2, and then was designated for assignment the following day to clear room for Adam Hyzdu to play the outfield.

Joe Nelson had been designated for assignment to make room for Puffer. He's another story. He'd pitched two innings for the Braves back in 2001, giving up eight earned runs. A week after they released him in 2002, the Sox signed him—only to let him go 18 days later—and then re-sign him some 581 days after that. The re-signing came on March 30, 2004. Nelson pitched 2⅔ innings in a 10-day stretch in mid-July, recording two more outs than he had for Atlanta while "only" giving up five runs. He got a ring, too. In 2005, Nelson moved around, never making the majors but in the Mets organization, the Devil Rays, the Cardinals, and the Royals—all in one calendar year.

Other lesser-known members of the 2004 World Champion Red Sox (10 appearances or less) include Abe Alvarez, Pedro Astacio, Jamie Brown, Frank Castillo, Andy Dominique, Bobby Jones, Byung-Hyun Kim, Sandy Martinez, Phil Seibel, and Earl Snyder.

Puffer actually did pitch at Fenway Park in 2004—but it was *against* the Red Sox. He came into the June 10 night game, in relief of Ismael Valdez. It was the fifth inning and there were runners on second and third, no one out, with the Sox holding a 4–1 lead over the Padres. Two inherited runners scored, and two runners that Puffer let on scored, too. The game was 8–3 Boston when he left after three full innings, the final score 9–3. So the only action he saw involving the Red Sox was to oppose them, which he didn't do all that effectively. "I think I could have been a great idiot," he said when it was all over, in reference to the 2004 Sox team, who were self-described as a "bunch of idiots."

It's got to be a bit unusual to be awarded a World Championship ring by a team you opposed on the field, but never played for. Puffer is appreciative. In a December 2007 e-mail, he added, "The Red Sox were extremely gracious including me in the lucky group of people to receive such a special momento to 'The Nation'."

Not the most compelling performance, but a ring nonetheless

In 2007, Royce Clayton won himself a World Championship ring. The well-traveled infielder also set a record, playing for his record 11th major league team. At the plate, his contribution to the Red Sox was a negative 100 OPS. He had six at-bats, without a hit, struck out three times, and grounded into two doubleplays. But he did score a run. And was perfect in the field with two assists in the only two chances he got.

PHANTOM PLAYERS AND A FANTASY

And then there were the phantom players. First up, McClean. Check the boxscores for April 27, 1901. McClean batted for Kellum in the ninth. McClean? The Red Sox have no one by that name in their records, nor does Mr. McClean appear in any of the baseball encyclopedias or record books. But that's really an easy one. It was pretty obviously Larry McLean, and a simple misspelling in the boxscore, a not-infrequent occurrence 100 years ago. Contemporary game accounts verify it was McLean, not McClean.

Al Olsen

The May 17, 1943 newspapers carried boxscores of the doubleheader the Red Sox played against the White Sox in Chicago. The White Sox won the first game, 4–2, and lost the second

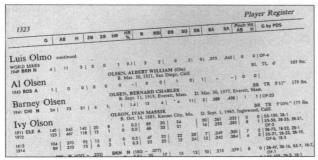

game to Boston, 4–2. Neither was an exceptionally interesting game, but the boxscore reflects a player named Olsen pinch-hitting for Red Sox pitcher Dick Newsome in the seventh inning. Olsen then stole a base, but he never scored and Joe Dobson came on to pitch the bottom of the seventh. Olsen would have been Al Olsen, who was indeed listed in editions of both A. S.

Al Olsen's listing in the *Baseball Encyclopedia*.

Barnes and MacMillan's *Baseball Encyclopedia* for some 35 years. Albert W. Olsen, one of the "cup of coffee" players who had appeared in just one major league ballgame. The only trouble was: it couldn't have been Olsen.

Though Olsen had gone to spring training with the Red Sox in 1943, he was sent to the San Diego Padres the day before the season began and played the full year in the Pacific Coast League as a left-handed pitcher. That in itself wouldn't have precluded him pinch-hitting but Coast League records and boxscores make it clear he was playing there, not in Chicago, not even for just that one day.

Most of the boxscores were distributed by the Associated Press and picked up by various newspapers around the country, so it's not surprising that papers in Los Angeles, New York, and Washington include Olsen in their boxscores. So did the Chicago and Boston newspapers, with the exception of the *Boston Post*. The *Post* listed "Culb'son" as the pinch-hitter, clearly Leon Culberson, who debuted that very day. Trouble is, game accounts are clear that Culberson's debut came in the second game, and that's what Culberson himself reported when asked about it by Red Sox historian Ed Walton in 1986.

The most likely scenario is that the pinch-hitter was Johnny Lazor. Olsen had worn uniform #14 during spring training. Lazor wore #14 during at least part of the 1943 season, and Lazor was used for pinch-hitting duties. Cliff Kachline pointed out that scorecards were often not kept up to date as to uniform numbers and that some of the spring training names and numbers would often include incorrect attributions; in fact, Kachline located a scorecard from the very week before, when the Red Sox had played in Washington on the same roadtrip and Olsen was listed as #14 despite the evidence that he was indeed with the San Diego ballclub. Ira Berkow of the *New York Times* called Lazor to ask him in 1990, but it was "so many darn years ago" that his memory was far from certain. At this distance, it seems a safe enough guess that the "phantom" player was Johnny Lazor, and Al Olsen has been expunged from American League records.

Wright, RF

Our friend Mr. Lazor pops up again just two years later in another wartime mystery. Check the boxscores of the doubleheader in St. Louis on July 1, 1945. The Browns had won the first game, 7–3, and had just taken a 3–2 lead in the second game after eight innings. The first two batters in the top of the ninth were both retired. Then Ben Steiner tripled. Dolph Camilli singled in Steiner to tie the game. Bob Johnson singled. Tom McBride pinch-hit for Lazor and he singled, scoring Camilli. Newsome (this was a different Newsome from 1943, this being infielder Skeeter Newsome) then pinch-hit for Tobin, and he singled, too, driving in two more runs, taking second base on the play. Culberson was intentionally walked, and Bob Garbark doubled Newsome home. The Red Sox scored five runs and took a 7–3 lead.

The Sox took the field for the bottom of the ninth and all the boxscores show "Wright, rf"—but who was that? The Red Sox never had a player named Wright until September 15, 1948 when Tom Wright made his major league debut. He'd been signed by the Red Sox before the war, but in 1945 he was serving in the South Pacific with the 13th Air Force. After being mustered out, he played 1946 with Durham and 1947 with New Orleans. He played 151 games with Louisville in 1948 and only had three brief appearances for the Red Sox late that year. So here's a game with a Culberson (already in the game in center field), a Newsome (already in the game, playing third base), and a Lazor (removed so McBride could hit). But who was Wright? Who was the right man for the job? Who played right field? Was there another Wright in the majors who somehow spent a day in St. Louis for the Red Sox?

Ed Wright played for the Boston Braves that year, but his first game in town wasn't until July 29 and he only came over from Indianapolis on July 20. The idea that he somehow suited up as a Red Sox and scooted out to right field is too far-fetched. Taft Wright of the White Sox had been reported as shipping out from Oahu to outlying islands in a June 25, 1945 news report. The Buffalo Bisons sold Ab Wright to the Baltimore Orioles in early June, but he probably hadn't snuck out to St. Louis; he was still with Baltimore in August.

Hall of Famer George Wright had actually played for Boston, but that was between 1871 and 1881, in the other league and—besides—he'd died in 1937. Equally unlikely was Harry Wright, since he'd died way back in 1895.

A better guess would be that it was a player actually on the Sox who was simply misidentified. There were 13 other players accounted for in the boxscore, leaving the most likely candidates (the only other Red Sox shown as having played outfield in 1945) as Pete Fox, Loyd Christopher, or George Metkovich. We can cross Christopher off the list, though, since he was claimed off waivers by the Cubs about five weeks earlier. Fox missed some games starting in mid-June due to a tooth extraction, Lazor taking his place. From June 15 to July 4, the only two men found playing right field in other boxscores were Lazor and McBride. On July 4, Metkovich played both halves of the Independence Day doubleheader. The next time Pete Fox filled in was July 7, as a defensive substitute in right field. So our money's on it being either Metkovich or Fox in right, and maybe as silly an explanation as the person filling out the boxscores having been thinking "right" as in right field and thoughtlessly entering "Wright" in the slot provided.

Lou Proctor

Playing against the Red Sox in 1912, supposedly, was Lou Proctor who batted for pitcher Jack Powell of the St. Louis Browns, pinch-hitting in the five-run seventh inning the Browns put together in a futile attempt to overcome Boston's 11–4 lead. Cliff Kachline notes, though, that "a Boston newspaper referred to the pinch hitter as Albert 'Pete' Compton, a catcher with the Browns that season (whose real first name was, of all things, Anna)." The story that emerged—urban folklore or not—was that a Western Union telegrapher named Lou Proctor had a little bit of fun and inserted his own name into the boxscore in an innocuous fashion— he didn't claim a base hit and was content with a lifetime .000 batting average.

The game was in Boston, though, and Proctor appears in the very respected Tim Murnane's game account in the *Globe*, as well as the *Globe* boxscore, so the telegrapher story doesn't quite hold water, unless the telegrapher altered Murnane's account. Compton pinch-hit for the Browns quite often in 1912, and chances are that it really was Compton who walked.

Bob Dunbar

There was even a phantom sportswriter in Boston. Bud Collins wrote a memoir in the November 2004 issue of *Boston* magazine, which appeared under the subhead: "You think faked stories and faked documents are a scandal? In Boston, some of the journalists themselves were made up."

Collins had worked at the *Boston Herald* and one night was told by his copy editor, "My boy, tonight you are Bob Dunbar." One of the more popular columns in the *Herald*'s sports pages was written by Bob Dunbar and had been for years. Dunbar, though, well, there never was a Dunbar. He was a convenient fiction that allowed the *Herald* to run a column for years without any one person ever having to suffer repercussions. Collins drew the assignment, as he put it, of "ghosting for a ghost."

Speaking of repercussions, Collins says that Ted Williams complained (as only Ted could do) one day in the clubhouse, "Why doesn't that bastard have the guts to show up here?"

Collins says he commiserated with Williams, "He's pretty old and not too well. But you're in good company. Bob's knocked everybody, even Babe Ruth."

Bob got mail at the *Herald*. More than once, Collins says, someone he encountered would ask him to give their "regards to Bob when you see him." Collins even filed an expense report once for Dunbar, but that didn't play too well at the paper. At last, one day in 1967, a new sports editor joined the *Herald*. The column stopped running near the end of the baseball season and Collins—now employed by the *Globe*—ran into the new sports editor. He asked after Bob's health and was told, "Haven't you heard? Bob's dead." Collins wrote Bob Dunbar's obituary as his next column.

Found! Clarence Winters—the last missing Red Sox player

SABR's Pictorial History Committee set itself itself the task to locate at least one photograph of each man who ever played major league baseball. The committee was born when Tom Shieber pitched the idea to the board of directors in the summer of 1994. The committee was formed later that year and its first newsletter was issued in January 1995. From 1994 until the summer of 2000, Tom chaired the commitee and acted as the PHC Newsletter editor. Mark

Rucker was chair for a short while afterward. Since then, the committee has been led by Bill Hickman. The committee has been able to catalogue images for about 96% of the players who have been in the majors since the beginning, 1871. The Player Image Index currently consists of more than 26,000 records describing image sources for over 15,800 major league players.

In December 2005, curious to know which former Red Sox players might be lacking photographs in the log of photo references maintained by the committee I sent an e-mail to the chair. Bill sent me an Excel spreadsheet labeled "PLAYERS MISSING FROM THE PLAYER IMAGE INDEX." There were only two Red Sox players missing—even including the Boston Americans (1901–07). They were Bob Adams (who appeared in two games in 1925) and Clarence Winters (who appeared in four games in 1924). Both were pitchers.

I tucked Bill's response away and only rediscovered it in March 2007 when trying to wrap up this book. I wrote Bill on March 25 to ask if this was true, that just these two players were missing and to ask if they were still missing. Bill wrote back the same day, advising me:

Bob Adams. Courtesy of SABR.

"You're correct on both counts. Adams and Winters are the only missing Red Sox players, and no one has yet reported an image representing them. However, Marc Okkonen may have found an image of Adams. He sent me a list of those players whose images he still needs for his *2000 Cups of Coffee* book. Adams was not on Marc's list, but Winters was. (Both had short-enough major league careers to qualify as coffee cups). But if Marc has an image of Adams, he has not yet told me about it." I wrote Marc about a week later, and asked him if he did have an image of either player. Marc wrote back almost immediately to report that, yes, he had very recently received an image of Adams. He said he would be glad to send me a copy, then added, "I also received an image of a pitcher Winters in a team photo of Hartford of the 1923 Eastern L but I have my doubts that this is Clarence Winters. I have been unable to find a first name for this guy but Clarence Winters had a pretty full season with Saginaw in 1923, so I don't believe this was Clarence." He added that both pictures came from Rich Ulrich and Marvin Scott. Scott wasn't quite sure where he'd originally turned up the Adams photograph, but that it may have been from the collection of Ed Koller, which he had inherited.

Three days later, Bill Hickman wrote that he'd just received a submission from Marvin and Rich Ulrich, who reported that it "shows Clarence Winters in a 1923 Hartford team photo as published in the 1924 *Spalding Guide*. They think it's Clarence, at any rate. The caption simply says Winters. *The Sporting News* reserve lists for Hartford for 1923 and 1924 don't list a Winters, so that's no help in finding the first name. But given the proximity of Hartford to Boston and the timing of the appearance of Winters with the two teams, it seems likely that it is Clarence." If this were Clarence, the Red Sox player image list would be complete.

I asked Ray Nemec for information on Winters' minor league career, hoping to find some possible clues that might confirm the Hartford image or otherwise track him down. Ray sent me the Winters stats, and they confirmed what Bill had reported: he did not play for Hartford at all—ever. And Bill had found that he wasn't even on Hartford's reserve list. Winters had played for San Antonio in 1924, some 32 games, and then for Boston. In 1925, he returned for another season in San Antonio and even appeared for a very few games in 1926 before leaving professional baseball. Neither Tom Kayser nor David King were able to locate photographs in San Antonio.

Winters had been born in Detroit and died in Detroit, and played in the Michigan-Ontario

League from 1920 through 1923. Noting that he'd pitched in 38 games for Saginaw (17–10, 3.34 ERA) in 1923, I figured maybe there'd be stories in the Saginaw papers that year, or when he'd made the major leagues in 1924.

I used the search function in the online SABR directory looking to see if SABR had any members in Saginaw. We do—one. His name is Joe Heitkamp, a retired educator (a good sign—maybe he'd have some spare time) and (an even better sign) he listed one of his areas of interest as "Minor Leagues in Saginaw, MI." And he has e-mail. I wrote Joe a note on April 8 and just under 48 hours later received a note back from him with two different photographs of Winters from the *Saginaw News Courier*. A former high school history teacher, Joe had visited the Hoyt Library and while I was at Fenway enjoying Opening Day, the images came through on my Treo.

Clarence Winters at Saginaw—thanks to Joe Heitkamp.

There was no question that this Winters was Clarence Winters. It said so in the captions and accompanying story. But had Winters also been at Hartford, long enough to appear in the team photo that Rich Ulrich had offered? On my way home the day after watching the Red Sox play a late April game in Yankee Stadium (the Red Sox won, 11–4), I stopped in at the Hartford City Library and perused *Hartford Courant* microfilm for the 1923 season. The Winters in question turned out to be Jess Winters, not Clarence. He was one of their two star pitchers that year, when Hartford won the Eastern League pennant. It's the same Jess (Jesse in most record books) Winters who was with the Phillies earlier in the year, described more than once in the *Courant* as the "tall Southerner." Jesse came from Texas.

The important thing is that the player image list for the Red Sox is complete. The image Joe Heitkamp supplied completed the list. The Red Sox are the first team to have a complete set of images available, though several others were very close at the time. As of the time this book goes to press, the committee lacks only one Cleveland player: Charles "Shorty" Gallagher (OF, 1901), and one New York AL player: Ed Wilkinson (OF, 1911). Washington AL still needs Grier "Skipper" Friday (P, 1923) and Ed C. Johnson (OF, 1920). The other teams need three or more players. Anyone interested in becoming a photo detective and wanting to try to help locate images of the "missing players" can contact the author of this book through the contact information at the end of the book.

Clarence Winters

Winters himself was a right-handed pitcher from Detroit, who broke in with Battle Creek in the Michigan-Ontario League in 1920. He posted an ERA of 2.88, winning 13 and losing 13. He stayed in the league three more years, two with Port Huron-Sarnia, for whom his 1921 ERA ballooned to 4.50 as he led the league in earned runs and runs allowed. His record was 12–16. He got matters back under control a bit in 1922, with a 2.91 ERA and a 16–18 mark. In 1923, he pitched for Saginaw. He won 17 while losing 10, with a 3.34 ERA. This apparently got him noticed, and a contract with the Texas League playing for San Antonio. He won 13 games and lost 11, but his 7.62 ERA hardly seemed worthy of getting him a promotion to the major leagues. Yet on August 17, the Red Sox acquired him, trading Oscar Fuhr to San Antonio. What they were thinking is hard to grasp.

Fuhr was a left-hander with a 3–6 record and a 5.94 ERA that year (he came back to Boston in 1925 and was 0–6). The Red Sox were entering a stretch where they played five doubleheaders in seven days.

Winters donned a Red Sox uniform, but his August 28 start was inauspicious. It was the second game of two, in Philadelphia. He had everything going for him, with his teammates scoring seven times in the first inning—and he held the Athletics to just one hit in his first three innings—but then it all fell apart. The *Boston Globe*'s James C. O'Leary was kind; he wrote, "They began to treat him roughly." Winters gave up a double, a single, saw a screaming line drive mishandled, then surrendered another double, and another—and was sent to the showers. He started again just two days later, on August 30. The A's scored once in the first, but the Sox scored twice in the second. Then, after getting one out in the second, "Chilly" Winters walked a batter, was hit for a triple and a single, struck out a man, yielded a double and a single, and was pulled. He was charged with all five runs—plus the one he'd given up in the first. He took the loss. Two days later, he faced the Yankees on September 1. Jack Winters (as he was also known) came on in seventh-inning relief and saw Wally Pipp drive in the two base-runners he'd inherited. He got an out, then doled out a base on balls and two singles, and—with Lou Gehrig coming to bat—was pulled. The *Boston Post* said, "He was kicked around the diamond and left for dead in no time at all."

Winters pitched for the last time on September 4. Pitching against a dominant Washington ballclub, he came on to pitch the seventh and was "treated to a bombardment that netted a trio of tallies, when the Senators batted around." (*Boston Globe*) He gave up seven hits in two innings, walked one, and struck out two.

After four appearances in a nine-day stretch, by the time his brief big league career was over, he'd faced 48 batters and given up 22 hits and four walks. His ERA was 20.57 (but at the plate he was 1-for-3). The Red Sox bought Ted Wingfield from Chattanooga on August 30, and slotted him into the role Winters had tried to hold down.

Winters reappeared in San Antonio in 1925 and was 11–11 (4.72), then appeared in a handful of games in 1926—so few that records were not compiled. He died at a fairly young age in Detroit on June 29, 1945.

Bill Nowlin's debut at Fenway

Hey, as long as we're talking about phantom ballplayers, what about indulging a fantasy? Unlike Al Olsen's story, though, this actually happened and it happened at Fenway Park.

Baseball's record books are replete with "cup of coffee" players, who had but a brief opportunity to play a few games in the major leagues. Many a baseball fan has mused about a shot at getting just one at-bat. Go to any batting cage, though, and try to hit against a "fast" machine. Typically, the "fast" machine throws at around 80 miles per hour—and that's just a changeup in the majors. It's a humbling experience for most.

What's next best? Playing ball in a major league ballpark? That rates up there. Every year, thousands of fans line up at Fenway Park all summer long and pay $12.00 to take a 45-minute tour, the highlight of which is to sit in the dugout, walk along the warning grass (don't even *think* of putting a foot on the grass, though!), peer into the bullpens, and touch the Green Monster in left.

On July 16, 2002, I had the opportunity any true blue Red Sox fan would give…well, a lot for. I was invited to play softball with bankers from Fleet Bank and selected customers—on the field at Fenway. I lucked into this because I'd co-authored *More Tales from the Red Six Dugout* with Jim Prime, and the book had just been published. I had a few friends at Fleet from days when my company Rounder Records worked with Brian O'Connor and their middle market group. Brian's mother even provided a story for another book Jim and I have out, *Ted Williams: The Pursuit of Perfection*. Fleet Bank, as it happens, was a sponsor of Major League Baseball.

It wasn't my first time in the batter's box at Fenway. On three earlier occasions, I had hit against a batting machine there in charity events—the Jimmy Fund's Fantasy Day at Fenway. In 2001, after former Red Sox announcer Ken Coleman had intoned "#9, Bill Nowlin," I embarrassed myself on the first swing corkscrewing so badly I fell to the ground, my helmet flying off my head. Once I stopped laughing, I steeled myself for action again and felt a lot better about a hard foul drive into the seats up in section 30. Then I really acquitted myself with a long liner down the line in left, which bounced off the warning track and one-hopped the Wall hitting above the padding. A sure single in any league. Maybe two bases.

July 2002, though, was the first time I ever got to actually bat against live pitching (even if it was softball) and play a game at Fenway Park.

Game time temperature was 82 degrees, the wind blowing out at about five miles per hour. (Actually, I just made that up, but it's pretty close. It was a nice, sunny day, not too hot, not too humid. A perfect day for baseball.)

Everyone had special uniform shirts that looked a lot like Red Sox ones. Fleet All Stars. Very thoughtfully, Rachel Goodrich from Fleet saved #9 for me. (They gave my son Emmet a #2 shirt.) Rachel wore #5—she was a huge Nomar fan.

First time up, I hit the ball hard but flied out to straightaway left. Second time up, I took two balls outside and then got a little anxious, I guess, lunging a bit at the third pitch and popped up to the shortstop. I was facing humiliation. Would I debut at Fenway and find myself with an 0-for-3? There was a lot on the line as I stepped in a third time. Toeing the rubber was relief pitcher Ralph Sillari. I told myself to keep loose, to just meet the ball and try to hit it on a line. I took one pitch. Then I drilled a hard shot over the third baseman's head, between short and third, into left field and got myself a single. I was batting .333 in a big league ballpark.

I took second on the next play and scored on the one after that. I also played left field, which was a treat. After Ted Williams had died, the Fenway grounds crew had mowed a huge "9" into the grass in left. I played right in the middle of that 9.

Unfortunately, late in the game I pulled a hamstring while running to cut off a ball hit hard down the line past the third baseman. I had to take myself out of the game and go on the 365-day disabled list. I wouldn't have to worry about seeing my average drop under .300, though. Several years later, I look back and realize: I have a lifetime .333 batting average in games at Fenway Park.

AN ODD TURN ON THE MOUND

The outfield trio of Duffy Lewis / Tris Speaker / Harry Hooper was a true "golden outfield." The three, in 1913, formed what may well have been the best defensive outfield in baseball history.

Harry Hooper and Duffy Lewis—October 3, 1913

On October 3, 1913 both Lewis and Hooper pitched in the same game! It was the second game of a doubleheader versus the Washington Senators in D. C., the next to last game of the year. Boston won the first game, 2–0, with a Dutch Leonard two-hitter, which guaranteed the Red Sox a fourth place finish in the process. Washington won the second event, 11–3, and secured second place for themselves.

Sox starter Earl Moseley "was as wild as a suffragette orator" in the dated words of the *Boston Post* writer. He gave up nine runs on nine hits, but "to add to his misery, the Senators stole nine bases on catcher [Chet] Thomas"—including five stolen bases in the first inning alone. Moseley got through the fifth, but manager Bill "Rough" Carrigan called on Harry Hooper to pitch the sixth in relief. The crowd was reported "surprised but highly amused" when Hooper was announced. He did well enough, though. Clyde Milan was first up and Hooper walked him. He immediately stole second, perhaps suspecting Hooper hadn't perfected his pickoff move. Foster flied to Hack Engle in center, who earned an assist doubling up Clyde Milan. First baseman Bill Mundy retired Chick Gandil unassisted.

Carrigan sent Hooper back out in the seventh. Ray Morgan was 2-for-2 in the game but Hooper got him. Ainsmith singled. Acosta flied out to Reng in right. McBride hit a Texas Leaguer to left, but Ainsmith was retired trying to take third on the play. In his only major league pitching appearance, Hooper had given up two hits and a walk but not allowed a run in two innings.

Carrigan shifted defensively in the eighth, swapping Hooper with Duffy Lewis. Hooper was sent out to play left field and Lewis was brought in to pitch. Lewis "laid a small wager with Griff [Senators manager Clark Griffith] that he, too, could shut the Senators out." [*Post*]

Pitcher Carl Cashion pinch-hit for fellow hurler Rex Dawson, and he touched up Lewis with a "smacking double." Danny Moeller hit one which third baseman Larry Gardner muffed. Cashion scored, Moeller taking second. Lewis lost his wager. Lewis fanned Gedeon, though, and Foster lined to Hal Janvrin at short. Chick Gandil singled and Moeller scored. Gandil was caught off first, apparently having taken too wide a turn. Instead of a simple rundown, the Red Sox threw the ball all over the field and Gandil kept moving up until he found himself between third and home and was finally tagged out at home plate. The *Post* commented that it "looked very much as if the Sox wanted to 'show up' the aspiring Lewis."

Tris Speaker—October 7, 1914

Tris Speaker hadn't played in that final doubleheader of 1913, but he had his moment of last-game hijinks on the mound a year later. The Red Sox and the Senators again squared off at the very end of the year. Only 832 people paid to see the final game, but they got to see "The Grey Eagle" in his combination pitching debut and swan song. The Sox were solidly set in second, but the Senators were battling for third place money. They won—and had amassed a 10–4 lead after seven. Speaker kicked off the day's scoring with a double in the first, driving in Janvrin, who'd singled before him. Speaker tried to steal third but was erased. Lewis, up next, singled to center, stole second and then tried to steal third but he, too, tried in vain. In the second, Gardner doubled and then Cady doubled. For some reason, catcher Cady was batting and baserunning with his pad and shin guards on and was picked off second, caught flat-footed. The few fans there were angry and shouted for the Sox to "play ball."

Hugh Bedient started. He was lifted for a pinch-hitter in the fourth: Smoky Joe Wood! And who took Smoky Joe's place on the mound? A young rookie named George Herman Ruth. Guy Cooper took over for Ruth in the seventh.

The ninth inning presented a real spectacle. Shanks had led off the ninth and doubled. Pitching for the Red Sox after the double was Tris Speaker. Chet Thomas took up play at first. Acosta singled, sending Shanks to third. Henry was out, Speaker looking Shanks back to third before he tossed to Thomas at first. Though McBride was already 2-for-4 in the game, Washington manager Clark Griffith put himself in the game. Speaker laughed when Griffith stepped in and Spoke waved his outfielders in very close to the edge of the infield. Griffith had the last laugh, though, as he doubled to left and knocked in a run, the 11th for the visitors. When Griffith tried to steal third on Speaker's delivery, he was nabbed by Cady's throw to third. Speaker got out of the inning with two hits and one run charged to him, according to the record books.

Doug Taitt—July 25, 1928

Taitt was a Southern California slugger the Sox sought in the late 1920's. He first drew notice as right-fielder with the Los Angeles Angels of the Pacific Coast League, but first made his mark after being sold to the Nashville Vols in early 1927. "Taitt, when he connects, sends the apple on long journeys," wrote the *Atlanta Constitution*. He hit .350 that year in Southern Association play. Of interest as well was a stint on the mound for Nashville against the Birmingham Barons on August 8. The Vols were losing big, when Taitt was moved in from center field and asked to pitch the last five innings; he gave up just three hits and one earned run.

After their season, Nashville sold "Poco" Taitt to the Red Sox on September 10. What first was reported as just a cash transaction was later revealed as involving quite a heavy price in players to be named later: the *Washington Post* reported that Boston sent two players named Knox and Unglaub, and pitchers Del Lundgren and Ted Wingfield. In October, Taitt kept fit barnstorming as part of the Bustin' Babes as Babe Ruth's team barnstormed against Gehrig's Larrupin' Lous.

Taitt played 1928 with the Red Sox, kicking off the year with an infield single on Opening Day. It was on July 25, 1928, though, that he was asked to pitch in a major league ballgame. The Sox were in seventh place, 28½ games out of first, and facing Cleveland. The Indians beat Boston 10–2 in the first game of a doubleheader, and were leading 12–5 after seven innings in the second, when Taitt was brought in from right field. Manager Bill Carrigan had already blown through five pitchers on the day, and likely knew that Taitt had pitched for Nashville (or Taitt told him). Taitt got through the last inning, giving up two hits and walking two, while striking out one batter. The Indians scored three earned runs off him, but his place in the record books was secure.

At the plate, he hit .299 on the year. In late May the next year, Taitt was traded to the White Sox for Whispering Bill Barrett. His final year in the majors was 1932 with the Phillies, and then he bounced around the minors from Dallas to Hollywood to Jersey City, later managing in Tyler, Texas in 1938.

Jack Rothrock—September 24, 1928

The next time Bill Carrigan wanted a position player to pitch, he turned to Jack Rothrock instead. The situation practically demanded he be used. In 1927, Rothrock had played all four infield positions and in 1928, he'd played all three outfield slots, sometimes playing more than one position in a given game. Pitching and catching were the only two positions remaining.

The 404 Motor City fans who came to the September 24 game saw Sam Gibson throw a five-hit, 8–0 shutout for the Tigers. Rothrock played the outfield (lf), the infield (ss), and pitched the final inning of the game (without letting a runner reach base).

Five days later, Rothrock strapped on the "tools of ignorance" and caught an inning in the game, playing his ninth field position. Rothrock finished the season, his fourth with the Red Sox, batting .267. The next year, 1929, he hit an even .300.

After being sold to the White Sox on the last day of April in 1932, Rothrock played through the 1937 season.

Bobby Reeves—September 7, 1931

Bobby Reeves started his career with the Senators, but after three seasons—the third batting .303—he was one of five players traded to the Red Sox so that Washington could reacquire shortstop Buddy Myer. Reeves played three seasons for the Sox but progressively declined at the plate: .248, .217, and .167 in 1931. Near the end of the 1931 season, on September 6, the

Sox were—typically in this era—in last place, 43 games out of first place. Second baseman Reeves was not having a good year; by year's end, after 84 at-bats, he'd knocked in a total of one run. The *Washington Post* suggested that his major contribution had become pitching pregame batting practice.

On September 7, the Red Sox hosted the Senators for a Labor Day doubleheader. Washington took the first game, 7–5, but struck early and hard in the second game with four runs in the top of the first and eight runs in the top of the second. There didn't seem to be anything the Sox could do to stem the tide. Jack Russell was Boston's starting pitcher and he got through the first, but couldn't get anyone out in the second. In came Ed Morris, who got one out, but only one, and then came Jud McLaughlin, who also got just one out. Finally, the *Post* wrote, "in great desperation," Boston manager Shano Collins pulled in second baseman Reeves.

Reeves retired the first batter he faced, closing out the second inning. He allowed two runs in the third inning, and another one in the fifth, but in 7⅔ innings he faced 29 batters, walking one but only letting up six hits. The final was a 15–1 Washington win.

Reeves wasn't hitting and he was 0-for-4 at the plate. His fielding was pretty poor, an overall career .911 (though he was perfect in three chances off the mound). This was the last year of his major league career. He was sold to Portland in early 1932, and he played for the Beavers for a couple of years, then with Albany, and faded from the scene, making his way back to his native Tennessee.

DOC CRAMER, JIMMIE FOXX, AND TED WILLIAMS: WHAT WAS IT WITH JOE CRONIN IN AUGUST?

Cronin put 1938 All-Star center fielder Doc Cramer on the mound on August 30, 1938. The following year, Jimmie Foxx stepped on the rubber on the sixth of August. And the year after that, Ted Williams threw two innings on August 24, 1940.

Doc Cramer—August 30, 1938

Cramer was a lifetime .296 hitter over 20 years in major league baseball. In his five years with Boston, he hit .302, averaging 188 hits a season. A lot of position players pitched earlier in their careers, and Cramer had broken into pro ball as a pitcher for Martinsburg in the Blue Ridge League. He'd kept up his interest in throwing, and sometimes experimented with trick deliveries during pregame warmups. There had been some talk earlier in 1938 about using him in relief. The Red Sox were only in second place (though 18 games behind the Yankees) on August 30, when less-than-stellar performances from Joe Heving and Dick Midkiff saw the St. Louis Browns with a 7–1 lead over the Red Sox after five. Two other Sox moundsmen—McKain and Baker—had been hit hard the day before, and Jim Bagby had just come down with a sore arm. Emerson Dickman had pitched 10 innings two days earlier, on Sunday. Cronin wanted to save Bill Harris and Fritz Ostermueller for the upcoming couple of games. So Cronin went and talked to the skeptical home plate umpire, Lou Kolls. Kolls assented and Doc Cramer came in from center, replaced by Red Nonnenkamp.

Cramer started the sixth and fanned Browns pitcher Ed Cole. Mel Almada and George McQuinn both grounded out. Three up, three down. Boston actually scored twice in the bottom of the sixth, but Cramer gave one back in the seventh. Buster Mills, who'd been Cramer's Sox teammate in 1937, singled off him, then moved to second on a walk to Clift. Bell made an out, but Cramer wasn't as adept at holding on the runners, and they pulled off a double steal, with Mills scoring on a liner to Vosmik in left. Cramer retired Browns backstop Sullivan to end the inning.

The Sox got back in the game, then closing to within three runs, 8–5, but the Browns scored once more in the top of the eighth, as another former Sox player, Mel Almada, singled past Foxx at first. He stole on Cramer, too, and soon scored when Mills again touched up Cramer, this time for a double to right center. Cramer got out of the ninth without incident, yielding just one walk.

Where the other two Boston pitchers had yielded seven runs in five innings, Cramer only gave up two in four innings. Three hits (two by Mills), three walks and one strikeout, he goes down in history with an ERA of 4.50.

Jimmie Foxx—August 6, 1939

Less than a year later, Joe Cronin sent Jimmie Foxx to the mound. Double X was in his fourth year with Boston and led the league in home runs in 1939, the fourth time he'd done so. (In 1932, Philadelphia's Foxx had out-homered the entire Red Sox team, 58–53.) The Hall of Famer got his shot in front of one of the largest Fenway crowds ever—police estimated that as many as 15,000 fans were turned away. Boston was getting shellacked, though, and were down 10–1 after eight innings.

Denny Galehouse, Woody Rich, and Jake Wade were all pounded by Detroit for 17 hits, giving up two in the second, three in the fifth, two more in the sixth, and another three in the eighth. Hutchinson actually drove in two of Detroit's runs, and Galehouse the only one for the home team.

Joe Cronin had a sense of how to offer the fans a bit of a treat. He sent Foxx out to the bullpen to warm up during the bottom of the eighth. "Get hot," Cronin told the Sox slugger, "because you're going to pitch the last inning." Foxx had pitched for Sudlersville High School, back home in Maryland. Once in his junior year, he struck out 18 opponents on the Centreville team. He was scouted by team manager Frank "Home Run" Baker of the Easton Farmers team (Class D) in its first year in the Eastern Shore League.

He got a wild ovation as he strode to the mound to pitch the ninth. "Mixing up his stuff like a veteran chucker, he quickly fanned his old roomie, Mike Higgins, forced Birdie Tebbetts to lift an easy foul to [Sox catcher] Johnny Peacock and finally retired Pete (Single X) Fox on a harmless roller to Boze Berger, who was playing at shortstop at that stage of the game." Detroit didn't have any substitutions in the lineup; Foxx was ready to face the same nine who had already scored 10 runs on 17 hits—and they couldn't get the ball out of the infield off him.

The Phillies were Foxx's next team; in 1945 he pitched in nine games for them. Over 22⅔ innings, Foxx posted a 1.59 ERA.

Foxx as catcher

As if it weren't enough to have Foxx firing fastballs, Joe Cronin used him behind the plate several times. He'd caught fairly often for the A's in 1935, and offered to do so again in 1940. Lou Finney was hitting so well that Cronin wanted to keep him in the lineup, so

Foxx and The Kid with a stewardess. Courtesy of the Boston Public Library.

he experimented a bit letting Foxx catch. The first game was July 31, and Foxx had two singles and a walk, knocked in two and scored twice. After three games as catcher, it was reported that he had "an ulcerated tooth and his upper legs are sore from the catching stances" but it didn't stop him from banging out his 23rd homer and, two days later, his 24th. The record books show Foxx as catching in 42 games in '40. And he played third base once, too.

Ted Williams—August 24, 1940

Then August 1940 rolled around. The Red Sox had a player on the team who'd been a real mound ace in high school. Ted Williams starred as a pitcher for Hoover High School in San Diego. Several times, Ted struck out a dozen or more batters and some reports say he set the high school record by striking out 20 batters in a game. He was the winning pitcher, allowing just three hits to rival San Diego High in the first American Legion championship tourney.

Knowing Ted, he probably let everyone in the Boston clubhouse know how he could pitch. He had told Cronin he really wanted the chance to try it sometime. In the first game of the August 24 doubleheader against Detroit, Boston was being beaten 11–1 in front of a home-town crowd of 29,200. After seven innings, Cronin shouted in the dugout, "Who the hell we got to pitch?" Ted spoke up quickly. "Me. I'll pitch." Cronin said, "Okay, Kid. Let's see if you're as good as you say."

Frank Croucher, having a bad year (with a .105 average, it seems surprising he came back the next to hit .254), singled to lead off the eighth. Next up was Tiger pitcher Tommy Bridges, who bunted. Ted pounced, spun, and fired "a bullet peg" cutting down Croucher at second. "A good play even for a regular pitcher," noted the *Herald*. Pete Fox hit one down the line but first baseman Finney fielded the ball and threw to Cronin covering second, forcing Bridges. Barney McCosky ended the inning with a fly ball to Dom DiMaggio in center field.

In the ninth, again the first batter singled to center—it was Mike Higgins, who no doubt would have been mortified had he been struck out by Foxx in 1939 and again by Ted Williams in 1940. Hank Greenberg followed with a single to right, Higgins taking third. Ted struck out Rudy York, though, on a called third strike. York hit .316 that year, with 134 RBIs and he was hot that day. York had already knocked in five runs in the game on four hits, including a double and a home run. In the second game, he went 2-for-5—including another homer—and knocked in two more runs. He was definitely seeing the ball well. Ted struck him out on three pitches.

Dutch Meyer was up next. He already had two RBIs in the game, having hit two singles in four at bats. He grounded to third. It looked to be a game-ending double play, but Charlie Gelbert (who'd come over from Washington mid-season) juggled the ball. Higgins scored on the play as Gelbert's only choice was to throw across the diamond and settle for getting Meyer at first. The next batter was Birdie Tebbetts, who rapped the ball right back to Ted on the mound. Ted threw to first for the third out.

"My greatest claim to fame was striking out Rudy York with two men on," Ted wrote in his autobiography. "I gave him a good sidearm curve, it broke about a foot, right over the plate, and he took it. I guess he didn't know what to expect, whether I would throw it over the backstop or what. To this day, York claims I quick-pitched him. I didn't, but he always says, 'You quick-pitched me.'" The final out was a strikeout, fouled into Joe Glenn's glove. Notably, Glenn had also caught Babe Ruth.

Williams, like Cramer, boasts a 4.50 ERA, not bad by today's standards. Two innings, three hits, one run, one K, no walks. Had Gelbert handled Meyer's ball cleanly, though, Ted would have been out of the ninth without letting up a single run. The real Red Sox pitchers had already yielded 11.

OTHER POSITION PLAYERS WHO PITCHED FOR THE RED SOX

Eddie Lake—May 17, June 2, June 23, July 5, July 9, and July 16, 1944

Eddie Lake was primarily a backup shortstop who played from 1939 through 1950, with the war years (1943–5) being his time in Boston. In 1943, he had 216 at-bats with the Red Sox and hit just .199. He did marginally better in 1944, hitting .206—but had the uncommon opportunity to actually pitch not just one time but in six games. The 5'7" infielder had thrown a half-hour of batting practice on May 17, but Joe Cronin stuck him on the mound in the sixth inning of the second game of that day's doubleheader, after the Browns had posted nine runs.

Lake pitched 2⅓ innings. He gave up three hits, walked two, struck out one, and made a fielding error as pitcher. Three runs scored, but the *Boston Globe*'s Harold Kaese was impressed: "Compared with most Sox pitchers, Lake has a lot of stuff on the ball and if handled like a pitcher, he probably would prove as effective a game-finisher as Cronin has." The *Globe* ran a story the next day headlined, "Cronin Sees Eddie Lake as Sox Mound Prospect."

A couple of weeks later, on June 2, Lake was called upon again and pitched no-hit ball for two innings. On June 23, he threw the final four innings, yielding three hits, one run. He got a double at the plate. His longest mound stint was on July 5, when he pitched the final six innings; in the process, though, he yielded six hits and three runs.

On July 9, "Sparky" Lake pitched the final three innings. Five hits, three runs. And in his last time on the mound—July 16, he threw the final two innings. He let up two hits, and he hit two batters.

All told, his line as a pitcher was 19⅓ IP, 20 hits, two HRs, 11 BB, seven K, and a respectable 4.19 ERA. (The league ERA was 3.40.) In 1945, Eddie played regularly (473 AB) and he hit .279, actually leading the league in on-base percentage—other than Ted Williams and Roy Johnson (in 1944), Lake was the only Red Sox player to do so since Jimmie Foxx in 1939. The next was Yaz, who led the AL in 1963. 1945 was Lake's best year.

George Schmees—September 17 and 20, 1952

Schmees spent one season in major league ball. Right after the war, he was signed by the Cincinnati Reds before the 1946 season. A year later, the Reds sent him to the Dodgers and he played in the Dodgers system through 1951, when he was selected by the St. Louis Browns in the Rule V draft. He debuted for the Browns on April 15. Though he'd hit .328 for the Hollywood Stars in 1951, he didn't exactly tear up Sportmans Park; he was hitting just .131 (8-for-61, with one double, one triple, and three RBIs) when St. Louis put him on waivers.

The Red Sox claimed him on June 30, paid the $10,000 waiver price for him on July 1, and put him in a game playing right field on July 3. Schmees was 0-for-2 in his Red Sox debut, but had a nice 2-for-4 day on July 4. Come September, manager Lou Boudreau didn't just stick Schmees into a lost cause game; he gave the left-hander a start on September 17 against his former team. The game in St. Louis drew just 1,250—the smallest gate of the year—and it might have been smaller yet but for the novelty. Rocky, as George Schmees was known, gave up four hits and two earned runs in two innings of work before he was replaced by Ike Delock. The Browns won, 10–4, as the Red Sox used five pitchers in all. Both Delock and Hersh Freeman gave up more runs. Schmees got a single his only time up.

Why did Schmees get a start? The Red Sox staff was a little over-worked, but newspaper accounts don't indicate them as being that fatigued. The Associated Press wrote: "Manager Lou Boudreau took a long chance here when he chose as his pitcher George Schmees, an outfielder without previous major league experience as a hurler. Schmees, a lefthander, has been such a disappointment as a batter than Boudreau was willing to take the pitching gamble. Schmees

pitched only briefly back in the low minors, five years ago." If being a disappointment as a batter was the only criterion, Boudreau would have had a large pool of available talent.

Boudreau did say he was "satisfied" with pitcher Schmees. Three days later, Boudreau put
his man in again, this time in relief, pitching the last four innings of a game in Washington, won
by the Senators, 10–6. Schmees was again 1-for-1 at the plate, and scored. He walked two, struck
out two, kicked off a 1–6–3 double play, and allowed five hits—but he didn't allow a run.

In early December, the Red Sox sold Schmees to the Seattle Rainiers. He started off the
year nicely, with three home runs in an exhibition game at Palm Springs, but only rarely
turned up in game accounts after that.

Danny Heep—May 25, 1990

It was nearly 40 years before another Red Sox position player took the ball, toed the rubber,
and faced opposition batters. It was one of those games. The Twins were beating the pants
off the Red Sox, 15–0, at the Metrodome. Eric Hetzel started and gave up seven runs (three
earned), and relievers Dennis Lamp, Wes Gardner, and Jerry Reed had given up two earned
runs apiece. What was manager Joe Morgan to do?

Heep had already pitched once before, for the Dodgers, on July 30, 1988. He'd closed out
the last two innings of that game, letting in two runs in a game that was 12–4 Astros when he
entered.

Morgan had put Heep into right field to take over for Tom Brunansky in the seventh. For
the bottom of the eighth, he brought Heep in from right (Randy Kutcher took over there) and
gave him the ball. Heep gave up a leadoff double, a single, got one out on a force play, then
gave up two more singles. No further damage was done after Shane Mack grounded into a
6–4–3 double play. His ERA with the Dodgers was 9.00 and he'd matched it in this brief inning with the Red Sox. Though he'd hit .300 the year before, in 320 at-bats, he saw much less
playing time in 1990 (and no more pitching time) and ended the season with a .174 average.
In November, he was released by the Red Sox. He was signed in mid-April 1991 by the White
Sox, traded to Atlanta, but released by the Braves in mid-June.

Steve Lyons—July 21, 1991

Just a year later, Steve "Psycho" Lyons pitched for Boston. He, too, had done it before, with
the White Sox on June 16, 1990. He closed out that game, allowing just the final run in a 12–3
beating administered by Oakland. He walked four and struck out one, gave up a pair of hits,
and one earned run.

Lyons improved his pitching line, with the Red Sox. It was the 21st of July at Fenway. As in
the Heep happening, the Sox were playing the Twins. Joe Morgan was still managing. Tom
Bolton, Kevin Morton, Dennis Lamp, and Tony Fossas had all given up two or more earned
runs. Dana Kiecker shut down the Twins in the eighth, but Morgan brought Lyons in from
center field to pitch the ninth. It wasn't by pure chance; Morgan was aware that Lyons had already played every infield position and every outfield position so far on the season, and DH'd
as well. Lyons had done the same thing for the White Sox in 1990. (He'd even played all nine
positions in a 1990 White Sox-Cubs exhibition game—and had even won a game once back in
1983 for the Double A New Britain Red Sox.)

Psycho retired the first two Twins when Leius flied out and Knoblauch struck out, but
Jarvis Brown singled and Chili Davis doubled. Lyons buckled down and got Brian Harper to
fly out to center field. He says his sinker was clocked at 88 mph and that he got Knoblauch—
one of 1991's toughest strikeouts—on a slider down and away. "My mechanics were brutal,"
Lyons wrote in his autobiographical *PSYCHOanalysis*. "No wind-up to speak of, lousy exten-

sion, and I short-armed the ball." What he values the most is "the fact that I got a chance to stand out there, straddle the mound, challenge a big-league hitter, and shake off a sign. The fact that I threw one pitch as a major leaguer will forever be noted." And his lifetime ERA ain't bad: 3.00 after facing 17 major league batters, with four hits, four walks, two strikeouts, and two earned runs in three innings of work.

For whatever reason, Lyons never caught a game for the 1990 White Sox (though he had in both 1988 and 1989), and for whatever reason, Joe Morgan never put him behind the plate in 1991, either. Lyons had to wait until September 8, 1993 before he got his shot at catching for the Red Sox, finally playing his ninth position in what was his fourth stint with the Red Sox. (The record books show three stints, but Lyons was a Chicago Cub for most of spring training 1993 before being signed again by the Red Sox.)

Andy Tomberlin—May 20, 1994

Wouldn't you know it was the Twins again, the next time the phenomenon presented itself? Butch Hobson was Boston's manager. The score was 21–1, Twins—mercifully, the game was in Minneapolis. Every run was an earned run—starter Joe Hesketh gave up four and Paul Quantrill two. Todd Frohwirth gave up nine in three innings of work, and Greg Harris six. Both Quantrill and Harris only ever got one Twin out. Ken Ryan actually survived 1⅓ without giving up a run and yielding just two hits, while striking out three. But Hobson asked Andy Tomberlin to pitch the bottom of the seventh and he did so well he threw the eighth as well. Tomberlin had pitched before; he had a 34–3 record in high school with a few no-hitters to his credit. No runs on just one hit.

Two hits, no runs, one walk, one strikeout. The final score was 22–2, but it could have been worse had not Ryan and Tomberlin plugged the dike.

Tomberlin had hit .286 for the Pirates in limited action in his rookie year, 1993. They turned him loose in October, and he signed with the Red Sox in February 1994. He saw even less playing time with Boston, just 36 at-bats playing left and right field and DH'ing a bit. He had seven hits, his only RBI coming on a solo home run on May 30 against Kansas City—the eighth-inning two-out pinch-hit homer stayed just fair, and just cleared the Green Monster, but tied the game for the Red Sox, 5–5. In the 10th inning, with one out, Scott Cooper singled and Tomberlin singled, moving Cooper into scoring position. Damon Berryhill doubled off the Wall and won the game.

Tomberlin's parents had a satellite dish at home. Immediately after the game, the *Globe*'s Marvin Pave asked Tomberlin about his second major league home run: "I think they saw this one, but since I was hitting .167 my dad might have changed the station before I got up. I'll be calling them soon."

Though he went on to play for Oakland, the Mets, and the Tigers, and compiled a career .233 batting average, he never pitched in another game. His career pitching line shows two innings of work, with one hit, one strikeout, and one walk—a lifetime ERA of 0.00.

Mike Benjamin—June 21, 1997

Sox starter Vaughn Eshelman started pretty poorly, giving up six runs to the Tigers in the first two innings. Joe Hudson pitched the third through the fifth frames, allowing just one hit and no runs. Mark Brandenburg pitched the sixth, allowing four runs, and Kerry Lacy pitched the seventh, allowing five more. It was 15–3 after 7½, so the Sox mixed things up a bit, bringing Darren Bragg in from center field to play third base for the first time in his career and bringing Mike Benjamin in from shortstop to pitch for the first time in his. Jesus Tavarez took over in center and Jeff Frye at short.

Benjamin faced three Tigers and retired them all, 1–2–3. He was the only one of the five Red Sox pitchers to complete his assignment unscathed. "I don't like to degrade the game," said Red Sox manager Jimy Williams. Benjamin was 31 years old, with eight years of major league experience behind him, but the last time he'd pitched was in junior college when he'd pitched against his old high school team in an alumni game. Williams was facing a situation where he'd used nine pitchers in the last 27 hours.

It took Benjamin just nine pitches to shut down the Tigers, but when asked if he was looking forward to trying it again, he told Gordon Edes, "Oh, no," he said, "because if I get back out there, that means we're playing like [expletive]."

Though he played four more years in the majors, for the Red Sox and Pirates, he never had an encore performance to go with his .233 lifetime batting average.

David McCarty—April 9, June 12, and October 3, 2004

Unlike most of the others above, David McCarty announced at the start of spring training 2004 that he wanted to pitch. He was nearing what looked like the end of his career, and thought he might give it more life if he expanded his repertoire to include pitching. The idea might have been prompted by Milwaukee Brewer Bruce Kieschnick, who threw 53 innings in relief in 2003, and batted an even .300 in 70 at-bats. (Kieschnick repeated again in 2004.) "My primary job is as a hitter, but if I can go out there and *pitch* some time, too, especially throwing left-handed, that's a big plus," he told Bob Hohler.

McCarty had broken in with the Twins back in 1993 and had eight major league seasons under his belt. He nearly overdid it in spring training, trying hard to prepare himself for both tasks. He couldn't have gotten into a game much faster than he did. In the fifth game of the year, the home opener, manager Terry Francona brought him in to close out the ninth inning of a game the Red Sox were losing, 8–5. After getting the first batter to ground out back to the mound, a walk, a wild pitch, and a double saw one inherited run score and McCarty charged with one of his own before getting the final out.

In the May 27 game, another blowout (15–2), McCarty was already in the game as DH, but ran out to the bullpen to warm up in both the eighth and ninth. Anastacio Martinez closed out the two innings of one-hit ball, so David was never needed.

A couple of months later, the Sox found themselves down 14–5 to the Dodgers at Fenway. Manny Ramirez had been pulled out of left field, and McCarty replaced him there, but was brought in to pitch the ninth. Ground out, strikeout, ground out. 1–2–3, side retired. He certainly had a better day than any of the four Red Sox pitchers who had preceded him.

His final appearance came in the final game of the season, October 3. This was a close game, but not one that affected the standings. The Sox were losing to the Orioles, 3–2, and McCarty threw the seventh and the eighth, allowing just one hit while striking out three. He batted .500 in limited action in 2005 (2-for-4), but didn't take the mound.

McCarty also saw action of another sort in 2004—and while on the 15-day disabled list. Unknown to the public, he suited up as Wally the Green Monster and went out on the field during the last couple of weeks in August.

From an idol to an agent

When David McCarty was growing up in Houston in the late 1970s, his idol was left-hander Joe Sambito of the Astros (Sambito ended his career with the Red Sox in 1986–87). Who was McCarty's agent during his 2003–05 stint with the Red Sox? Joe Sambito.

Playing with an idol and an idol's son

Roger LaFrancois is perhaps the only ballplayer to both play on the same team as his child-hood idol and his idol's son. LaFrancois played with Carl Yastrzemski on the 1982 Red Sox and with Yaz's son Mike Yastrzemski on the 1985 Durham Bulls.

Mike Greenwell as catcher

Mike Greenwell played all the outfield positions, more than once, and he also caught one game, for one inning. It was on July 17, 1987, a home game at Fenway Park. The Oakland A's were leading 4–1 until the Red Sox scored three times in the bottom of the ninth to tie the game. Greenwell had walked and scored the first of those three runs. Catcher Danny Scheaffer had come in to catch in the top of the ninth, replacing Todd Benzinger, who'd pinch-hit for Marc Sullivan in the Red Sox eighth. Greenwell had been the DH, but changed "positions" to catch in the Athletics' top of the 10th. There were quite a few other changes as well.

As a catcher, Greenwell recorded all three putouts in the one inning he caught. But that was far from the full story. During the inning, he caught a total of four pitchers (Bob Stanley, Joe Sambito, Calvin Schiraldi, and Wes Gardner) as the A's scored seven times. Greenwell was charged with one error, fielding a sacrific bunt. Strikeouts were recorded by Sambito and Gardner (2).

We're not sure what pitches Greenwell signaled, but in addition to the three K's, the A's got five hits, walked twice, stole two bases, and even had back-to-back home runs by Mark McGwire and Carney Lansford.

Though the Sox had imploded defensively, they came back and scored two runs in the bottom of the 10th, Greenwell scoring the second of the two (he'd singled), but the final score was Oakland 11, Boston 6.

Talk about a utility player

He played the outfield, played the infield, and he pitched, too! Henry Hack Eibel broke in with the Cleveland Indians as a first baseman and outfielder on June 13, 1912—but only ever played that one day. He got three at-bats but didn't get a hit. For nearly eight years he went… somewhere. In 1920, though, the Boston Red Sox gave him a shot and he made his return to the major leagues as a utility player, appearing in some 29 games. He mustered eight hits in 43 at-bats, for a .186 mark.

He must have had some talents (the name "Hack" seems to have been his legitimate middle name and not a nickname) because on June 22, Sox manager Ed Barrow used him three times as a pitcher in a 16-day period. He was effective, with a career 3.48 ERA based on 10⅓ innings in three relief appearances.

On June 22, Bullet Joe Bush started the game against the Indians, but was shelled for 11 hits in four innings, and Gary Fortune gave up five hits in just ⅔ of an inning. Barrow sent in Eibel to close out the Cleveland fifth and he struck out the first man he faced, Tribe first baseman Doc Johnson (a .292 hitter that year). Maybe he remembered something from years earlier—Johnston had been one of Eibel's teammates on the Cleveland team back in 1912. Eibel finished the game, 3⅓ innings of work in which he yielded just four hits, striking out three and walking just one. The *Boston Globe* sportswriter remarked, "Eibel made the best showing of the trio…. Today he showed enough pitching ability to stop the Indians' fifth inning rally and hold the tribe to two runs." The Indians won the game, 13–5. While closing out the game, Eibel came up to bat twice. He singled once and doubled the other time.

On July 1, Walter Johnson held the Red Sox hitless for 8⅔ innings. Facing a no-hitter,

Barrow sent Eibel up to bat for Sox starter Harry Harper, who'd pitched a nice game himself, limiting the Senators to just one run. Eibel almost came through. The game writeup indicated that only a "great play by Judge and Johnson, the last one of the day, killed off a base hit and was the only difficult fielding chance the Senators had in the entire game."

The next day, Boston was down 9–2 in the sixth inning, but came back to tie it and won in the 10th on a Harry Hooper (Hooper, not Harper) homer. Eibel pitched the seventh and eighth innings for Boston, having relieved "Sad Sam" Jones. He gave up just one hit in the two full innings, and was lifted for a pinch-hitter in the eighth.

His final appearance as a pitcher came on July 7. The Sox were shut out twice by Philadelphia, 6–0 and 1–0. Eibel came in to close out a five-run fourth inning, as "Baldy" Karr was getting hammered. He scattered five hits in 4⅓ innings and closed out the game. Dave Keefe actually had a no-hitter going against the Sox into the eighth and only let up four hits total—Eibel had two of them.

Why Barrow never used Hack again remains a mystery. He seemed to pitch well, and he made half of his lifetime career hits during the games he pitched. Nonetheless, he never pitched another inning.

THE GUYS IN CHARGE: MANAGERS, CAPTAINS, AND OWNERS

MANAGERS

In baseball, a batter is highly rewarded if he consistently hits .300—in other words, he only makes outs 70% of the time. In electoral politics, anything over 55% of the vote is considered a landslide. Major league managers are expected to win *every* game—just ask the fans (and more than a few owners)—but, of course, very few actually win more than 55% of the games they manage.

Of the 44 men who have served as manager for the Boston Red Sox (or Boston Americans), there were four who are deemed interim managers (Eddie Popowski, Pete Runnels, Rudy York, and Cy Young). The other 40 are considered regular managers by the *Red Sox Media Guide*. Some of them had pretty short tenures, for instance, George Huff, who managed for just eight games (2–6) in 1907 before returning to the groves of academe.

The winningest manager the Sox ever had was Jake Stahl, with a .621 winning percentage over 235 games in 1912–13. It may have helped that Stahl was that rarest of creatures: the player-owner. During the years he led the Bosox to a 144–88 mark (with three ties), Stahl owned a 5% stake in the ballclub. He was replaced in mid-1913 by Bill Carrigan. *Red Sox Century* says that Jimmy McAleer feared that Stahl was planning to take over from him as club president, so he pre-emptively fired Stahl on July 14 and brought in Bill Carrigan.

The losingest manager was Rudy York. Of course, he only managed for one game—and the Sox lost the game. He'd never wanted the job, and wasn't even the first choice for the position. Tom Yawkey finally realized he had to rid the team of Mike Higgins, so had Bucky Harris fire him. Harris asked Del Baker to take over as interim manager, while they sought someone else, but Baker declined. (The following year, when Jurges was released, Baker did fill in for seven games until the second coming of Pinky Higgins.)

Bob Unglaub hadn't exactly lobbied for the job, either, and his win percentage of .310 in just 29 games back in 1907 was nothing to write home about. Chick Stahl—the other manager named Stahl—didn't fare as well as Jake, winning an even 35% of his games in 1906. Lee Fohl had a long time to work his way out of the rut, but he fell even a bit shy of Stahl, winning only

.346 in 1924–26. It took 463 games before the move was made, and Bill Carrigan enticed back for another stint.

One thing about Rudy York having managed for a game—the Red Sox may hold the distinction of being the first team in baseball to have a Native American as field manager. See the separate section in this book that describes York's brief tenure.

Winning percentage—Red Sox managers

Based on a 162-game season, a winning percentage of 55% translates to 89 wins. A manager would have to see his team win 97 games to approach a .600 record.

Wins percentage as Red Sox manager, 150 or more games, through 2007	Red Sox managers winning less than half their games
Jake Stahl .621 (144–88)	Lou Boudreau .497 (229–232)
Joe McCarthy .606 (223–145)	Bill Carrigan .494 (489–500)
Steve O'Neill .602 (150–99)	Butch Hobson .472 (207–232)
Jack Barry .592 (90–62)	Johnny Pesky .451 (147–179)
Grady Little .580 (188–136)	Deacon McGuire .443 (98–123)
Terry Francona .579 (375–273)—a work in progress	Hugh Duffy .442 (136–172)
Fred Lake .579 (110–80)	Billy Herman .413 (128–182)
Don Zimmer .575 (411–304)	Frank Chance .401 (61–91)
Kevin Kennedy .559 (171–135)	Marty McManus .383 (95–153)
Jimmy Collins .548 (455–376)	Shano Collins .353 (73–134)
Dick Williams .545 (260–217)	Lee Fohl .346 (160–299)
Jimy Williams .540 (414–352)	Heinie Wagner .338 (52–102)
Joe Cronin .539 (1071–916)	
Eddie Kasko .539 (345–295)	
Darrell Johnson .539 (220–188)	
Joe Morgan .535 (301–262)	
Ralph Houk .525 (312–282)	
John McNamara .521 (297–273)	
Patsy Donovan .520 (159–147)	
Ed Barrow .512 (213–203)	
Mike Higgins .502 (560–556)	
Bucky Harris .500 (76–76)	

Though it usually seems that way, it's not all wins and losses. In Red Sox history, there have been 82 tie games. Joe Cronin had a wins percentage of .539, but he also skippered a full 20 tie games. Second on the tie games list is Bill Carrigan with 14—and it's interesting to note that Carrigan (honored in the Red Sox Hall of Fame, for good reason) had a sub-.500 wins percentage as a manager. If he hadn't been enticed back for those three seasons in the 1920s, though, he would have been far better off. From the time he took over in 1913 through the end of the 1916 season (his first managerial stretch), Carrigan had a .616 wins percentage.

The most dramatic turnarounds in AL history

The 1967 Red Sox leapt from ninth place—just a half-game out of the cellar in 1966—to first place and the pennant. The '66 Sox won 72 games and the '67 Sox won 92, for an improvement of 20 games. In terms of an improvement in games won, it was not at all the best turnaround even in Red Sox history. That honor goes to the 1946 Red Sox, who posted a plus-33 figure: 71 wins in 1945 versus 104 wins in 1946. The 1995 Red Sox won 86 games, 32 more than the 1994 team. That same year, though, the Cleveland Indians won 100 games, 34 more than in 1994. The Red Sox won 96 games in 2007; they could take first place (in more ways than one) if they could win 35 games more in 2008 than they did in 2007. That would make for a nice and tidy 131–31 record.

Managing into the playoffs

Bill Carrigan brought the Red Sox into the World Series two years in a row: 1915 and 1916. Joe Morgan took them into the playoffs twice, in 1988 and 1990. And Jimy Williams had a pair,

Manager Terry Francona in the dugout wearing his rarely-seen uniform jersey. Bill Nowlin photo.

too, in 1998 and 1999. But no Red Sox manager ever brought the team into the playoffs three times—until Terry Francona turned the hat trick in 2007. With a World Series win in his first year at the Hub team's helm in 2004, and a desultory 2005 postseason, Francona saw the 2006 campaign implode due to a spate of injuries, but took another trip to the Promised Land in 2007. The Sox never let go of first place from April 18 on. Despite a few scares, particularly in the League Championship Series against the Indians, the Red Sox won the World Series against the Colorado Rockies in Francona's second straight Series sweep. After his first four seasons, he not only boasted a perfect 8–0 record in World Series play (and an enviable 22–9 record in the playoffs) but had a total of 375 regular-season wins—the most of any Red Sox manager in his first four seasons. Only Joe Cronin among Red Sox managers had managed more than five consecutive seasons; Francona's new contract would take him to 10 full years if the team exercised its option following the 2011 campaign.

Red Sox managers—100 wins/100 losses

Only three Red Sox managers have won 100 or more games in a season:

Jake Stahl (1912) 105–47   Bill Carrigan (1915) 101–50   Joe Cronin (1946) 104–50

No one's done it since Cronin, though Don Zimmer's 1978 team came closest, with 99 wins. As we recall, that was one short of the number needed to make the postseason that year.

Sox managers who lost 100 or more games in a season:

Jimmy Collins/Chick Stahl (1906) 49–105   Bill Carrigan (1927) 51–103
Lee Fohl (1925) 47–105   Heinie Wagner (1930) 52–102
Lee Fohl (1926) 46–107   Billy Herman (1965) 62–100

Since the season expanded to 162 games, even with the additional opportunity that presents, no Sox manager has lost 100 games.

Most major league managers on one major league team

The 1908 Boston Red Sox had 10 past, present, and future managers on the team: Bill Carrigan, Gavvy Cravath, Doc Gessler, Harry Lord, Deacon McGuire, Tris Speaker, Jake Stahl, Bob Unglaub, Heinie Wagner, and Cy Young. Gessler and Lord managed in the Federal League. The total of 10 gvies them one more than the 1956 St. Louis Cardinals.

The longest-serving Red Sox manager was Joe Cronin, who served for 13 years, from 1935 through 1947. Mike Higgins served for most of eight seasons, and Bill Carrigan for seven. The very first manager, Jimmy Collins, served for most of six seasons, and both Jimy Williams and Don Zimmer for most of five. As is expected, many managers fell short of finishing out their final year. It's not a job that typically offers long tenure.

Co-managers?

Hugh Duffy, who is credited with hitting .440 for the Boston Beaneaters in 1894, only won a slightly higher percentage of the games he managed (.442). He almost became the first co-manager in 1921, the first of his two years at the helm. The March 26 *Washington Post* reported that the team would be managed jointly by coach Jimmy Burke and by Duffy. Burke had managed the St. Louis Browns the preceding year. "That is the working agreement we have drawn up," Duffy said. "We are veterans of the game, and neither of us seeks any individual glory. All we want to do is to win ball games. That will be glory enough." A glance at the standings shows there wasn't a lot of glory going around in 1921 and 1922.

Player-managers

The player-manager is an extremely rare commodity today but, then again, a pitcher rarely throws a complete game anymore. This is the age of specialists and having players play and managers manage was one of the first moves toward specialization. The earliest managers didn't even have coaches—John McGraw was the first to have a full-time coach; that innovation took place in 1909. As late as the 1950s, minor league managers in the Red Sox system did without coaches. For taking on managerial duties, the player-manager got paid extra, so there was incentive provided.

In the first half of the 20th century, the Red Sox more often than not had player-managers; since 1944, they have not had one (Cronin's appearance in just three games in 1945 is not deemed sufficient to count).

The following Red Sox served as player-managers:

Jack Barry—1917
Lou Boudreau—1952; served two more years as manager only
Bill Carrigan—1913–16; served a second stint as manager only in the 1920s
Jimmy Collins—1901–06
Joe Cronin—1935–45; served two more years as manager only
Deacon McGuire—1907–08
Marty McManus—1932–33
Chick Stahl—1906
Jake Stahl—1912–13
Bob Unglaub—1907
Cy Young—1907

The years cited are the years these men managed. They were not player-managers each year. The narrative below summarizes some of their work.

Jimmy Collins was the first manager for Boston's American League franchise, and he was a steady anchor at third base for six years, until he was replaced during the 1906 season by a fellow player, Chick Stahl. Collins was a hugely popular player in Boston for the National League team and when Ban Johnson determined to create a rival franchise to compete in the Boston market, he induced team owner Charles Somers to bring Collins on board. Collins, as anticipated, brought over several players with him. It wasn't hard to do when you had a bigger purse at your command. From the beginning of the franchise, the team that became the Red Sox was known for paying well. In the earliest of days, that was how the AL as a whole established itself. Collins successfully helped develop and shape the franchise, and captained the Americans to win the first World Series played in the modern era—1903. When the New York Giants refused to play in a Series the following year, the title remained with Boston. After John I. Taylor bought the ballclub, it rapidly began to fall apart; communication between Taylor and Collins couldn't have been worse. Collins was saddled with an owner who wouldn't make the moves it took to renew the pool of talent and the two ended up not even speaking. As the 1906 season progressed, things went from bad to worse when Boston hit a losing streak which almost lasted the entire month of May. Starting May 1, the team didn't win a game until May 24, and lost a total of 20 straight games. It would be an understatement to note that the team was not playing well; even Cy Young himself lost five games in a row during the stretch.

Finally, Collins just couldn't take it any longer and when they lost back-to-back-to-back games the first week of July (with the team committing nine errors in the July 7 game), Collins went AWOL after the game and couldn't be found for a week. **Chick Stahl** became acting manager in Collins' absence. Collins came back, but played for Stahl—and even lasted through the winter, opening the 1907 season in Boston before being traded to Philadelphia.

Named Boston's manager at the end of 1906, Stahl lasted through the winter—but just barely. He killed himself in spring training. As player-manager, though, he'd done pretty well. A lifetime .305 hitter, his lifetime cut short by suicidally drinking carbolic acid, he'd hit a solid .286 in '06. In the 40 games he'd managed, the team was 14–26 and (after the 1906 debacle) could hardly be expected to do worse.

With Stahl departing this earth on March 28, Boston's owner Taylor had to move fast to find a replacement. It's perhaps not surprising that 1907 was an unsettled year—and Boston ran through four managers in just the one season. In fact, given that Collins and Stahl had shared the position the previous year, the team really had six managers in just about a 12-month period. **Cy Young** managed for the first six games of '07, until Taylor could hire a permanent manager Taylor's first hire was George Huff, a college athletic director who'd never been involved in major league ball. No player-manager was Huff; in fact, he wasn't much of a manager at all. After eight games, he was gone. Taylor had now had Collins, then Stahl, Young, and then Huff. Now he settled on **Bob Unglaub**, the team's first baseman. Though only 25, Unglaub must have had some leadership qualities; Huff had named him team captain, though that could equally well have branded him suspect for that very reason. Unglaub had played some in 1904 and 1905 but wasn't in the majors in 1906; he entered the 1907 season with a .216 career batting average. As player-manager for 29 games (9–29), he hadn't done much better than Huff. Now Taylor turned to a pitcher, **Deacon McGuire**, to take over as manager. Under McGuire, the team finally stablized, though the effort must have worn on them. A September swoon saw a 16-game winless streak lasting from September 12 through October 2 (they did manage to tie two games in the stretch).

McGuire did decently and was invited back for another year as manager—the first man to actually manage the Boston Red Sox. During the offseason, the team had adopted the name Boston Red Sox. Taylor kept selling off players and sold off Hobe Ferris, Freddy Parent, George Winter, Jesse Tannehill, Gavvy Cravath, and, eventually, even his manager, McGuire. The new head man was Fred Lake, a Nova Scotian who had played in 1891 (for Boston), 1894, 1897, and—breaking the every-third-year pattern—again in 1898, though only racking up 124 at-bats in the four seasons. Lake did quite well, managing to a .579 winning percentage in 1908 and 1909. Then he moved across town, to the team he'd broken in with in 1891, and managed the Boston Nationals in 1910, even appearing in three games for them, though without a hit in his sole at-bat. Managing the Red Sox in 1910 and 1911 was Patsy Donovan. He'd pretty much wrapped up as a player in 1904, but did have nine years of managing experience, mostly as a player-manager.

1912 saw something different—a player-manager-owner. **Jake Stahl** had been on the first pennant-winning team back in 1903. He went to Washington in 1904–6, and was player-manager the last two seasons. In 1907 he was out of the majors, then returned with New York for the first half of 1908 before coming back to Boston. He played 1909 and 1910, but then took off 1911 to pursue his other, more lucrative career in banking. In 1912, though, he was part of James McAleer's group which bought the Red Sox from John I. Taylor. Stahl reportedly held a 5% ownership share. Perhaps to better manage his assets, he returned as player-manager, playing a little more than half the time, batting .301 and led the team to a World Championship. Stahl stuck it out into 1913, but apparently his principal partner—former player

John McGraw and Jake Stahl at the 1912 World Series.

Jimmy McAleer—feared Stahl was mounting a coup of sorts, and McAleer fired him, handing the reins to "Rough" Carrigan, a hard-nosed catcher (who, as it happened, also pursued a career in banking which took him away from baseball).

Bill Carrigan at least lasted for a few years, finishing out 1913 and managing the next three years, bringing the Red Sox two more World Championships, in 1915 and 1916. It's been argued that catchers make the best managers, since they call the pitches and are the only defensive player who sees all his teammates arrayed in front of him face-to-face. Carrigan caught and managed, and it's hard to argue with his success, in his first incarnation. From 1913 through 1916, his teams had a winning percentage of .616, and the team progressed from fourth place to second place to back-to-back World's Championships. Carrigan went out on top. He'd played 10 seasons with the Sox, but played progressively less each year after assuming managerial duties. He retired to pursue lucrative business interests in Maine, declining to return even when approached by new Red Sox owners. Ten years later, though, he was lured back to help turn around the team in 1927, but was unable to do so. The team finished last each one of three years, with records of 51–103, 57–96, and 58–96. That part of his career is best swept under the rug.

Succeeding Carrigan after the 1916 season was **Jack Barry**, who managed just the one year, 1917. Barry played 11 seasons in the majors, the last 3½ with the Red Sox. He managed all 157 games in 1917 (90–62—there were five ties in just the one year, and the team finished in second place). Barry himself hit just .214 in 388 at-bats, but that wasn't necessarily due to the distraction of managing (he'd hit .203 the year before under Carrigan). He hit two of his 10 career homers and drove in 30 runs. A second baseman, he made 14 errors the year he managed but that was a relatively low total for him. When 1918 rolled around, Barry was in the military along with a lot of other Red Sox players.

The president of the International League, **Ed Barrow**, took over, and served for the years 1918–20 until he found greener pastures with the Yankees. He wasn't a player-manager. In fact, he'd never been a player. As the *Chicago Tribune* noted: "his first experience in baseball was in handling peanuts and popcorn when he worked for Harry Stevens at Pittsburgh in the early days."

Hugh Duffy managed in 1921–22 and Boston won .442 of its games in those two years— just barely better than Duffy's own .440 best-ever single-season batting average for the other Boston team back in 1894. Duffy had four seasons as a player-manager himself, but it had

Frank Chance.

been 10 years since he'd managed and even longer since he played. Duffy was succeeded by **Frank Chance**, who won just .401 of his games in 1923, winning 61 and losing 91, and finishing in last place. It was the only year Chance did not serve as player-manager. Given the talent-depleted staffs that were the legacy of the Frazee years, some of these managers might have been doing well to win as many as they did. "The Peerless Leader" had 10 years as player-manager for the Cubs and Yankees, but hadn't had an at-bat for 10 years.

1924 brought **Lee Fohl**. He'd had a brief career as a player in the National League, with three at-bats in 1902 and 14 in 1903. He had good managerial experience, too—two years in Cleveland and three in St. Louis. His winning percentage over a full three-year stretch was a dismal .346 (and if it hadn't been for a .435 mark in 1924, it would have looked far worse). Fohl's team lost over 100 games two years running (47–105 and 46–107), just barely edging .300 each year.

Given how the team fared under Fohl, it seemed like time to reach into the past for inspiration. After a full decade out of the game, Bill Carrigan was enticed back in time for the 1927 season. Boston had finished dead last in 1922, 1923, 1925, and 1926 and just missed being last in 1924 by finishing ½ game ahead of the White Sox. Carrigan's Second Coming alone couldn't turn the tide. Boston stayed in the cellar all three years of his second stint: 166 wins against 295 losses (.360). When he left to return to Maine, it really was the great depression.

Heinie Wagner didn't do any better in 1930. In fact, he did worse. The Sox still settled for last place, but he only won 52 and lost 102 (.338). Shano Collins took over in 1931. His team won 62 and lost 90 in '31, but '32 was a disastrous start. After 55 games, the Sox had only won 20%—11 wins to 44 losses. Shano was supplanted by **Marty McManus**, who resumed the tradition of the player-manager. McManus had only arrived in Boston (from Detroit) late in the 1931 season. He finished out 1932 with a .323 mark (hey, that was a real improvement over Shano's start) and then boosted the winning percentage an even 100 points to .423 in '33. Then it was time for Tom Yawkey to take over—and McManus went across town to play for the Braves.

Yawkey brought in Bucky. Bucky Harris had been a player-manager in his day, but his days as a player were finished. Harris accomplished what must have seemed impossible to Sox fans back then—he led a .500 ballclub. "We'll win as many as we lose" might have been his mantra. Harris left Boston after the one year, but went on to manage 18 more seasons in the majors (leading the Yankees to a World Championship in 1947), and later served as Red Sox GM in 1959–60.

Tom Yawkey was ready to buy himself a ballclub, and he started with player-manager **Joe Cronin**, who skippered the Senators to a pennant in 1933, only to see them plunge to seventh place the following year. Yawkey wanted Cronin, though, in the worst way and opened his checkbook, and wrote a check for $250,000 to Clark Griffith (and sent shortstop Lyn Lary to Washington, too) to obtain Cronin's services. Cronin was on his honeymoon at the time—married to Griffith's daughter. He was player-manager for the Red Sox from the year he arrived and the money Yawkey spent on any number of players began to produce results. By 1938, the Red Sox reached second place.

And Cronin stuck around, too—he managed 2,007 games for Boston, almost twice as many as second-place Pinky Higgins. Cronin's win percentage for the Red Sox was .539, well above average. He was a player-manager and during his years as manager he played in 1,055 of those 2,007. Injuries limited him to just 81 games in 1936 but he was otherwise a very steady player from 1935 through 1941, playing in over 140 games every year save '36. He cut back to just 79 at-bats in 1942, 77 in '43, and 191 in '44. He only had eight at-bats in 1945, having broken his leg in April (but he batted .375 in those final eight times up) and none in his final year, 1946. As a player, he wound up with a .301 lifetime average, though he was never a particularly good fielder. A number of Red Sox pitchers disliked working for him because Cronin himself would often call the pitches, rather than leaving it between the catcher and pitcher. It wasn't easy being both management and player; Cronin's involvement in negotiating salaries alienated him from some of his teammates. After his years as manager were done, Joe Cronin served as VP of the Red Sox and, later, president of the American League.

After stints by Joe McCarthy and Steve O'Neill, Yawkey selected **Lou Boudreau**, who managed from 1952 through 1954. Boudreau came to the Red Sox from Cleveland, where he had served as player-manager and shortstop for nine seasons. His first year with Boston was his last year as player-manager, 1952. The Sox finished sixth, winning 76 and losing 78 for a .494 winning percentage. Though listed as player-manager, he didn't play much, appearing in just four games, with three plate appearances and a .000 batting average. He did drive in two runs, though, and scored one. He appeared in one game at short and one at third base. Boudreau's 1952 campaign was the last that saw a player-manager for the Red Sox.

Others who managed the Red Sox solely as managers but who had previously served as player-managers for other teams include: Patsy Donovan, Hugh Duffy, Bucky Harris, Billy Herman, and Fred Lake.

Other books have detailed the stories of other Red Sox managers, but Boudreau was the last of Boston's player-managers.

Red Sox managers who were pitchers

Throughout baseball, for whatever reasons, it's rare that pitchers become major league managers. Of the 43 men who have served as manager of the Red Sox, only four ever saw major league playing time as a pitcher. Cy Young put in a little time as a pitcher—he appeared in 906 games over 22 seasons. And in 1907 he managed six games for Boston; the team won three and lost three. Deacon McGuire was another who had pitched—but it was only one four-inning stint way back in 1890 for Rochester. McGuire gave up 10 hits and five runs, walking one but getting himself a strikeout, too. He played 26 seasons but that was the only time he pitched. Chick Stahl was another one-game wonder. He threw two innings for the Boston National League team in 1899, and gave up two runs on three walks and two hits. Joe Kerrigan was in his fifth year as Red Sox pitching coach when he was appointed successor to fired manager Jimy Williams; Kerrigan had thrown 220 innings, appearing in 141 games beween 1976 and 1980.

Red Sox managers who never played major league ball

There were seven Red Sox managers with no player experience whatsoever at the major league level.

Ed Barrow managed for three seasons from 1918–1920, long enough to see the transfer of Babe Ruth to the Yankees before he moved to New York to become general manager there. He had never been a player, but was certainly an astute baseball businessman.

George Huff was never a player, either. He was the athletic director at the University of Illinois and his only contact with major league ball was that he was a part-time scout for the Cubs. He was selected on short notice; manager Chick Stahl had committed suicide near the end of March. Cy Young filled in, reluctantly, as an interim manager and the team got off to a 3–3 start during the six games Cy skippered. Then Huff was named. Stout and Johnson say that the team was "shocked. They didn't think that Huff, who they disdainfully called 'the Professor,' was remotely qualified for the job." Thirteen days later, sporting a 2–6 record, Huff took the train back to Illinois. Boston owner John I. Taylor generously kept him on the payroll as a scout—which paid off when Huff signed both Tris Speaker and George Whiteman later that year.

Eddie Popowski, like Huff, only had a brief tenure as Red Sox manager. Both times he managed, in 1969 and 1973, it was as a fill-in. The Red Sox seem to have often fired their manager just a few days before the end of the season. Popowski filled in the last eight games of 1969, after Dick Williams had been let go. Eddie Kasko kicked off the 1970 season, but he, too, was fired before the game on the final day of the 1973 campaign. Popowski managed that game as well. Johnny Pesky was fired two days before the end of the 1964 season, and Billy Herman stepped in. Though never a Red Sox player, Popowski served with the Red Sox from 1937 to 2001. For 21 years he was a manager in the minors for the Sox; his debut in the big leagues was as third base coach in the 1967 Impossible Dream season. After 10 seasons as coach, he returned to the minor league system for 25 years as an instructor.

After 13 years with Joe Cronin as manager, the Red Sox made a move before the 1948 season, hiring veteran manager **Joe McCarthy**. "Marse Joe" was the first manager to win a pennant in each league, and he boasted a total of nine pennants all told, and seven World Championships. He'd played as an infielder for 15 years in the minors, mostly at second base, and managed in the minors for several years before taking over as Chicago Cubs skipper in 1926. After five years with the Cubs, he managed the New York Yankees for 16 seasons. The Red Sox enticed him out of retirement and Boston had three very strong seasons, losing the pennant on the very last day of the season both in '48 and '49, and coming close in 1950. McCarthy's penchant for alcohol may have taken a little too much of a toll on him; for whatever reason, the Sox fell short all three times.

Like Grady Little, **John McNamara** is remembered as a Red Sox manager who, having made just one move, might have won a World Championship for the Red Sox. In McNamara's case, he kept Bill Buckner at first base in Game Six of the 1986 World Series, instead of putting in Dave Stapleton for defensive purposes late in the game—as the record shows he had consistently done before the game that looked like the grand finale. He more or less admitted that he felt Buckner deserved to be on the field when the Sox won it. Rather than doing his star first baseman a favor, he created a monkey on Buckner's back that endured some 18 years. McNamara had been a catcher in the minors for a number of teams, and also worked for a plethora of teams as coach (Oakland, San Francisco, and California) and manager (Oakland, San Diego, Cincinnati, California, Boston, and Cleveland).

Kevin Kennedy, whose greatest sustained success has been as a television analyst and commentator for Fox Sports and XM Radio, was a minor league catcher for eight seasons, then was a minor league manager in the Dodgers system for another eight seasons. In 1992, he worked for the Expos as bench coach, working as farm director as well. In 1993–94, he managed the Texas Rangers and in 1995–96 he managed the Red Sox.

Grady Little had brought the Red Sox to Game Seven of the 2003 American League Championship Series, and the Sox were poised to take the game from the Yankees and make it to the World Series for the first time since 1986. Like John McNamara, it all came down to just one move: in this case, it was asking Pedro Martinez to go back out and pitch another inning, when both Pedro's accumulated experience and body language indicated he was done.

You all know the story. Let's not drag it out again here. Little had been a ballplayer in the Braves system and played in the minors for the Yankees as well. Starting in 1980, he began managing in the minors, and put in a full 15 years before getting his first gig as a major league coach with San Diego in 1996. A very popular coach with the Red Sox from 1997–1999, Little coached for California in 2000, but was brought back to Boston in 2002 and managed the team for two seasons with an excellent won-loss record. It all came down to one bad move.

Alan Foulds had a good point when he wrote that, "When the Boston Red Sox change managers the public interest generated is at least equal to that of choosing a new mayor."

Joe Morgan

Speaking at the 2007 gathering of the Boston Braves Historical Association, Joe Morgan claimed a certain distinction among ballplayers, saying that his record constituted a bit of trivia: He'd played for the most teams while getting into the fewest games: Joe appeared in 88 major league games but did play for five teams in the process (Milwaukee Braves, KC Athletics, the Phillies, the Indians, and the Cardinals). He asked those attending the luncheon, "Now that's hard to do, right?"

CAPTAINS

"When Jason Varitek was named captain of the Red Sox on the day before Christmas 2004, it was said that he was "just the third team captain since 1923...only Carl Yastrzemski and Jim Rice have borne the title of captain in the last 81 years."—CBC Sports

In earlier days, there was almost always a captain and captaincy was more than just an honorary title bestowed on a player to whom others looked up. Howard Rosenberg explains that in the 19th century, the captain was typically "in charge of arguing rules interpretations... as a matter of practice, if a team had a manager and a captain, the manager usually set the lineup, and the captain was in charge after the game began."

Captain Jason Varitek. Bill Nowlin photo.

By the 20th century, the manager would be the one to speak up when argument was called for. There was a considerable number of player-managers in the first few decades of the century, so a manager like "Deacon" McGuire (1908) played almost not at all but still could be said to hold the additional title of captain "by virtue of still being an active player." The *Boston Globe*, though, indicated in a January 19, 1909 story that when manager Fred Lake had taken over during the 1908 season, he found that "there was no one holding the title of captain." He said it looked that Jake Stahl was providing good leadership, so he didn't feel compelled to name a new captain. In looking ahead to 1909, though, he thought about the players he would be leading and named Gessler as captain. The extra responsibility meant some extra money for Gessler, and the right fielder welcomed being designated as Lake's "running mate."

While Gessler was ill during some of the early 1909 season, Harry Lord assumed his duties as captain. In midyear, Lake began to play Harry Hooper as his right fielder, and Lord took over as captain for the remainder of the season. The January 1, 1910 *Globe* reported that incoming manager Patsy Donovan had officially named Lord as captain for 1910.

Lord didn't last the year, though, and on August 6 he was "relieved of the captaincy" and Heinie Wagner took over. Shedding the extra duties lifted a burden from Lord's shoulders.

Lord was traded to the White Sox and, lo and behold, by 1911 he was captain of the Chicago team. By the end of 1911, Tris Speaker had become captain of the Red Sox, taking over in mid-September when Wagner was out due to injury.

Jake Stahl clearly supplanted Wagner for a year, but Stahl missed a lot of time, had a foot operation early in the year, and was barely around in 1913. Wagner resumed his role as captain late in the 1912 season, and was reappointed as such for 1913 in January. Wagner served through the 1915 season, but by spring training 1916, Jack Barry had been named as Carrigan's captain.

A player/manager was not always captain. Bill Carrigan, for instance, was an active player/manager, but not the field captain. He asked Jack Barry to perform those duties. When Carrigan retired after the 1916 World Series, Jack Barry was named manager for 1917 and served as captain as well. By November, though, he was in the U.S. Navy. In March 1918, manager Ed Barrow named first baseman Dick Hoblitzell the new captain of the Red Sox.

In July 1920, captain Harry Hooper underwent an operation after being hit in the shin by a foul ball, but came back before the end of the season. In December, the ballclub announced that he would captain the team again, but three months later, in early March 1921, he was traded to Chicago. A week later, Everett Scott was named the new captain. Several months after Scott was traded to the Yankees in December, Derrill "Del" Pratt was designated captain in early April 1922.

George Burns was captain for 1923, taking over partway through spring training. The *Washington Post* noted Mike Menosky "acting as captain" for the last day of the 1923 season, October 7. No doubt there were other such instances of filling in from time to time.

Then there was the "silent captain"—Bobby Doerr. When Doerr was elected to baseball's Hall of Fame, Ted Williams told Joseph Durso of the *New York Times*, "We never had a captain, but he was the silent captain of the team."

Rosenberg also unearthed the following anecdote in the preseason of 1929. The Sox had new infielder Bill Narleski, who, "as he goes through his paces, tells the other infielders, 'this is the way to go get 'em.' Kidding Narlesky [sic] back, they nicknamed him 'Captain.' Narlesky likes the nickname and now bosses the other players. Even Manager Bill Carrigan has joined the other players in calling Narlesky 'Captain,' for he likes the spirit of the rookie and will think a long time before giving any one [sic] else the call over him."

Yaz was captain in 1966, but when Dick Williams took over as manager, he declared that he didn't want a captain on the team, so there was no captain until Darrell Johnson took over for Williams in 1969 and Yaz resumed the role.

Red Sox Captains

Jimmy Collins 1901–05	Tris Speaker 1911	George Burns 1923
Chick Stahl 1906	Jake Stahl 1912	Mike Menosky 1923
Bob Unglaub 1907	Jack Barry 1915–17	Jimmie Foxx 1940–42
Deacon McGuire 1908	Dick Hoblitzell 1918	Carl Yastrzemski 1966, 1969–83
Doc Gessler 1909	Harry Hooper 1919–20	Jim Rice 1985–89
Harry Lord 1909–10	Everett Scott 1921	Jason Varitek 2005–
Heinie Wagner 1910–11, 1912, 1913–14	Del Pratt 1922	

OWNERS

Player/owner Jake Stahl

1912 saw something different for the Red Sox, and indeed all of baseball—a player-manager-owner. **Jake Stahl** had been on Boston's first pennant-winning team back in 1903. He went to Washington in 1904–6, and was player-manager the last two seasons. In 1907 he was out of the majors, then returned with New York for the first half of 1908 before coming back to Boston.

He played 1909 and 1910, but then took off 1911 to serve as a banking executive in Chicago. He returned in 1912 as a player/owner. He was part of Jimmy McAleer's group which purchased the Sox. McAleer and Robert McRoy were listed as co-owners. Stahl was said to have held 5% of the corporation. He also played first base—and hit .301.

In November 1913, Joseph Lannin bought the 50% of Red Sox shares owned by McAleer, McRoy, and Jake Stahl.

Two bellhops in a row owned the Red Sox

When New Yorker Joseph Lannin bought the half of the Red Sox shares owned by McAleer, McRoy, and Stahl, the sale was—no surprise—more or less dictated by AL architect Ban Johnson, angry that McAleer had dismissed Jake Stahl as manager in mid-season. Canadian-born, Lannin had been a bellhop in a Boston hotel, rose in the ranks, and eventually came to own three New York hotels. Lannin became President of the Red Sox. An indication of Johnson's involvement was how McAleer learned of the sale. Joe Cashman told Peter Golenbock that McAleer received a telegram reading, "You have just sold the Red Sox to Joseph Lannin. Ban Johnson." Interestingly, Lannin ultimately sold the Sox to another former bellhop, from Peoria: Harry Frazee. General Charles H. Taylor and his son John retained ownership of their half of the shares.

Charles Somers

The very first owner of the team was one Charles W. Somers of Cleveland, Ohio. He was awarded the franchise in a meeting of American League magnates on January 29, 1901 as the league was first formally organized and prepared to play its first season. Somers didn't just own the Boston team; he also owned the Cleveland franchise, and had an interest in the Philadelphia and Chicago clubs, too! Why the heck not? The league was just being built and some of the magnates played more than one role. Connie Mack of Philadelphia, for instance, represented the league in negotiating the lease of land for Boston's Huntington Avenue Grounds ballpark. Mack also made the initial salary offer to hire Jimmy Collins away from Boston's National League team to become manager (and third baseman) for Boston's new AL ballclub. All of the leases and 51% of the capital stock of each franchise were placed in trust of league president Ban Johnson, who declared, "It's war with the National League."

In July, Somers raised the idea of playing the National League leader, or at least the Boston Americans playing the Boston Nationals, after the regular season was over.

Matthew R. Killilea, described as "Johnson's legal adviser and business counselor" (*Washington Post*) was president of the Milwaukee ballclub in 1901. Henry J. Killilea, an attorney from Milwaukee, sold the Milwaukee franchise to his brother Matt and Fred C. Gross in December; the team moved and became the St. Louis Browns beginning in 1902.

On January 26, 1902, the Killileas sold off their interest in the Browns to "a number of St. Louis capitalists." Two days later, it was revealed that back on August 10, 1901, Somers had sold controlling interest in the Boston club to the two Killileas. Somers retained a very few shares, so that he could remain as president—with maybe as small a stake as one $10.00 share. Ban Johnson commented that the Killileas were backed by a "wealthy man who may later appear as a baseball man." (*Boston Globe*) Later news reports indicate that the mysterious man may well have been Johnson himself.

Henry J. Killilea

The Milwaukee lawyer bought the remaining shares of the Boston club in March 1902, save for Somers' share. His brother Matt died at age 45 of Bright's disease on July 27, 1902. This left

Henry in charge of the ballclub. He hired Charles Baird, the athletic director of the University of Michigan, as his business manager but a petition from students at the university caused him to release Baird from his contract. He then thought to hire a sportswriter from Milwaukee, either Friese or Andrews, but settled on Joseph Smart, a young Milwaukee man in the publications business. Killilea did come to agreement with Pittsburgh owner Barney Dreyfuss and the first World Series was played in October 1903, after the owners also came to terms with their own players as to the disposition of the proceeds from the games.

In November, there were rumors that Killilea had sold the club to a group from Boston. He denied them, but in December the *Los Angeles Times* reported that he was "disgusted at the way he has been treated by some of the members of the team" and that "his cup of indignation is full to overflowing." The word was that the Boston team would be "disintegrated"— shut down, disbanded, no more. In January, though, Killilea took out a seven-year lease on the Huntington Avenue Grounds. In March came word that Congressman John F. Fitzgerald had bought the ballclub. He'd offered $100,000 and Killilea was willing to accept, John Dooley reported, but Ban Johnson "would not agree to Fitzgerald as purchaser." *Boston Globe* sportswriter Tim Murnane put in an offer of $125,000, acting on behalf of *Globe* publisher Charles Taylor. New ownership was announced on April 18, 1905 and John I. Taylor, the publisher's son, became president. Ownership of the team was, for the first time, in local hands.

John I. Taylor

The son of the *Globe*'s General Charles Taylor had worked for a time as the advertising manager of the newspaper, but by the time of the purchase was no longer employed. He was, instead, a "well-known amateur sportsman" with membership in local golf and yacht clubs. Taylor was a big baseball fan who had attended most of the games in the first few years of the franchise. He owned the club through 1911 and, as seen, was the one who gave it the name "Red Sox" in December 1907. He was also instrumental in preparing the club to move to a new facility on land in the Fenway, land which belonged to the Taylors. Taylor owned an interest in the Red Sox until May 14, 1914 when he sold his shares to Canadian real estate and hotel man Joseph Lannin, one of the former bellhops. It is not our intention here to write about each owner so we will forego much on Lannin and his successor, Harry Frazee, though we will note that Lannin died falling out of a hotel room window in Brooklyn some 14 years and one day later.

And some 88 years later, the *Boston Globe* again became a part of the Red Sox ownership structure, when the parent company *New York Times* purchased a 17% share in collaboration with John Henry, Tom Werner, and others.

Bob Quinn

After Frazee, J. A. Robert Quinn was lead man for a Columbus, Ohio syndicate that bought the club on August 1, 1923 and owned it for 10 years. Quinn himself had a background in baseball and was at the time the business manager for the St. Louis Browns. Boston fans were thrilled to have seen the last of Harry Frazee, forever to be known as the man who sold Babe Ruth, and greeted Bob Quinn's arrival with glee. A subhead in *The Sporting News* even speculated, tongue in cheek: "Hub May Make Date of Red Sox Sale New Holiday." Unfortunately, the finance man in the Quinn group was manufacturer Palmer Winslow and he died in April 1927, leaving Quinn with insufficient funding to run the team, which had—in any event—sold off most of its best players during the Frazee years. Quinn had to contend with the first years of the Depression to boot. When Sunday baseball was approved at Braves Field, yet prohibited at Fenway due to its proximity to a house of worship, Quinn considered selling Fenway Park and working out a deal to play the Red Sox home schedule at Braves Field. Giving up the struggle, on February

5, 1933, Quinn sold the Red Sox for a reported $1,500,000 to young Tom Yawkey.

When Yawkey (and his general manager Eddie Collins) took over, they brought about a radical transformation of the team. Not one 1931 player remained on the 1934 team. Come to think of it, though, how many Red Sox players from the 2004 World Champion Red Sox were on the 2007 team?

Eddie Collins, Babe Ruth, Ted Williams.

Haywood Sullivan

If two different graduates of bellhop work could become owners of the Red Sox, the story of Haywood Sullivan isn't as strange as it might otherwise seem—though it isn't every day that a team's backup catcher is anointed owner. Signed by the Red Sox in 1952, three times he was called up to the big league club but in none of those times did he stick. He'd only earned enough of a look to accumulate nine at-bats and never managed to get a hit once—not in 1955, 1957, nor 1959. After Sammy White was traded to the Indians for Russ Nixon in March 1960, Sullivan got his chance—not to become the regular catcher, but to back up Nixon. His first hit finally came in a game at Fenway which the Sox were losing 8–3 to the Yankees. Maybe it seemed momentous to the Yawkeys that Sullivan singled in the bottom of the ninth after three fruitless at-bats. Showed some spunk. On his 21st at-bat, he hit a double and had himself a two-hit game. It was one of only two times in his Red Sox career that he managed two hits in the same game. The second came in the midst of a seven-game hit streak that began in July. No threat to Joe DiMaggio, though; Sullivan ended his one significant season with the Red Sox batting .161.

The year after Tom Yawkey died (July 9, 1976—the 16th anniversary of Sullivan's two-hit game against the Yankees—no runs scored, no RBIs), the trust serving as owner put the team up for sale. They turned down an eminently qualified bid by a group headed by respected business leader Dominic DiMaggio, instead giving it to a group owned in part by Haywood Sullivan (then a Red Sox VP) and the team's trainer, Buddy LeRoux. This, despite the fact that they didn't have enough money to pay the price, and were sure to be turned down by the magnates of the American League, who had to approve any sale. Why would a trust want to sell to a group that hadn't enough money? Eyebrows were raised. They were raised even higher when the group consummated the purchase—because Yawkey's widow Jean joined the group and provided the necessary financing. In effect, she sold the team to herself but in the process loaned money to two men so they could then become her partners.

Nice work if you can get it. Here's a guy who hit .161 with the team and had no money beating out at least one other group led by a respected businessman who did, and was a bonafide Hall of Fame candidate and Red Sox alumnus to boot. Suspicions were that Haywood Sullivan had become something of a surrogate son to the Yawkeys. Maybe he was a good drinking companion to the old man; was he something more to Jean Yawkey? Maybe he was just a good ol' boy with a nice courtly manner. Nothing about his reign at the helm of the Red Sox suggests there was exceptional talent involved. Competent, probably—though occasionally less than that, such as the time he lost Carlton Fisk by forgetting to mail him his contract renewal on time. He obviously had something to recommend him but, so far as we know, he hadn't worked as a bellhop in his youth.

Carlos Baerga—player/owner on both sides of labor/management

Another oddity of labor/management relations is represented by Carlos Baerga who played in 73 games and hit .286 for the 2002 Red Sox. He'd been a big name in the early 1990s as a three-time All-Star second baseman for the Cleveland Indians (1992, 1993, and 1995). A switch-hitter, he did something no player had ever done: on April 8, 1993 he hit two home runs in the same inning, one from each side of the plate. After six seasons with the Tribe, he'd posted a .305 career average and 505 runs batted in. Then he began to decline. He put on weight after the 1995 season and seemed to lose some competitive fire. In mid-season 1996, he was traded to the Mets, for whom he hit only .193.

Baerga bounced around, and over a four-year span suffered several injuries while serving with five different organizations: the Mets, Cardinals, Indians, Padres, and Mariners. The Cardinals signed him in February 1999 but cut him before he played a single game. In 2001, he was a spring training invitee with the Mariners but didn't make the cut. Baerga began to re-evaluate his career, and almost retired.

He'd done well and saved some money, so he bought a baseball team for himself in Puerto Rico, the Vaqueros de Bayamon. Coming off knee surgery, he explained, "I was going to retire. I wasn't going to play any more because I was getting hurt. I had knee surgery. So I said, well, let me buy this team and I'll stay in baseball." But he still had it in him to make one more try, with renewed determination. He began the long trek back with a team others might initially mock: the Long Island Ducks.

Carlos made the all-star team for the Ducks, but got a very attractive offer mid-season from the Samsung Lions in Korea and the Ducks gave him permission to take advantage. He got back in condition and his confidence returned, too. Returning to Puerto Rico, he played for his own Vaqueros (Cowboys), one of the few player-owners in baseball history. And he tore up winter ball, finishing second in the league with a .346 mark. The team he owned won the play-offs in Puerto Rico and became the island's entry in the early 2002 Caribbean World Series.

Carlos Baerga. Bill Nowlin photo.

Red Sox Director of Player Development Dave Jauss saw Baerga play and said, "He had an outstanding winter ball season in Puerto Rico as the owner of his club, which impressed us the most. He also showed that he had gotten back into excellent shape, demonstrating his dedication and determination." The Red Sox invited him to 2002 spring training—an invitee for the second year in a row. Despite not playing a game in the majors since 1999, he made the Red Sox.

He'd seen an awful lot of baseball's ups and downs. Serving as an owner, here he was signing with the Sox to become a player. "Now I appreciate what an owner has to go through to maintain a team. You have to care about 30 people—the players and coaches. How to keep them happy, how to keep the fans happy. It takes hard work." Carlos joked around with new principal owner John W. Henry about being an owner himself. It makes for strange situations—an owner of one team vying to make another team as a spring training invitee. After he made the Red Sox, he was on the payroll as an employee—and a member of the player's association. And one of his Red Sox teammates was Rey Sanchez, a player Carlos recruited and hired (as owner of the Vaqueros) for Bayamon.

Did he offer John Henry a spot as an invitee to pre-season training with the Vaqueros de Bayamon? That's not known, but Henry is such a baseball fan, he might have taken Baerga up on it!

John W. Henry

The principal owner of the Boston Red Sox was active in ownership of other teams prior to coming to the Red Sox. Disposing of a share in one team can take time, and isn't always the easiest thing to effect. It's an historical quirk that at one point in time, John Henry owned portions of the New York Yankees, the Florida Marlins, and the Boston Red Sox. Shades of Charles Somers in 1901. By August 2003, the sale of his 1% share of the Yankees complete, Mr. Henry became a one-team owner. Imagine heading into the 2003 and 2004 ALCS owning parts of both teams.

And what about Tom Werner? Had the Red Sox found themselves playing the Padres in the postseason at any time from 2002 through 2006, Red Sox chairman Werner would have held an interest in both teams. It was only in January 2007 that he finally sold his 10 percent stake in the San Diego team to principal owner John Moores.

OH, THE PLACES YOU'LL PLAY!
SPRING TRAINING, THE RED SOX, AND GEOGRAPHY

The Red Sox have trained in a number of locales over the years, with spring training headquarters being based in the following:

1901 Charlottesville, VA.	1920–23 Hot Springs, AR.	1943 Medford, MA.
1902 Augusta, GA.	1924 San Antonio, TX.	1944 Baltimore, MD.
1903–1906 Macon, GA.	1925–1927 New Orleans, LA.	1945 Pleasantville, NJ.
1907–1908 Little Rock, AR.	1928–29 Bradenton, FL.	1946–1958 Sarasota, FL.
1909–1910 Hot Springs, AR.	1930–1931 Pensacola, FL.	1959–1965 Scottsdale, AZ.
1911 Redondo Beach, CA.	1932 Savannah, GA.	1966–1992 Winter Haven, FL.
1912–1918 Hot Springs, AR.	1933–1942 Sarasota, FL.	1993- Fort Myers, FL.
1919 Tampa, FL.		

Payne Park, Sarasota spring training home of the Red Sox.

The Boston Americans held spring training their very first year in Charlottesville, but that was a bit unusual at the time. Most teams simply prepared for play in their own home cities: for instance, Baltimore, Cleveland, Detroit, and Philadelphia all stayed home. Washington traveled only as far as Phoebus VA, near Newport News. Chicago and Milwaukee both wound up spring training in Excelsior Springs MO, near Topeka. To travel to another location for spring training was by no means the norm. Of course, the new ballpark wasn't ready yet in Boston so training there was never an option. By and large, ever since, they have trained in Southern locales where the climate is better for baseball in February and March, though in the early years before the expanded 162-game schedule kicked in with the 1961 season, spring training rarely began before March and often lasted into mid-April.

There was some degree of competition between communities hoping to entice teams in the early years, but nothing like the long-term undertakings in the latter years of the 20th century which would involve towns building ballparks for teams and offering other incentives as well. There were extensive and complex negotiations between the Red Sox and both Winter Haven and Fort Myers leading up to the decision to relocate to Fort Myers beginning in 1993.

The 1911 visit to Redondo Beach seemed like a good idea at the time, but an unusual amount of rain that spring dampened Sox enthusiasm for a return. The Red Sox split into two teams and played their way back east, allowing Red Sox baseball to be played in any number of seemingly odd locations like Lincoln, Nebraska. There was even serious talk in that era of training in Hawaii. In the days before air travel, that truly would have been something.

During World War II, teams helped the war effort by holding training much further north and thus not riding the rails any more than necessary. For three years, this wasn't Grapefruit League or Cactus League play, but rather the Frostbite League.

Frostbite League spring training / 1943–1945

As World War II progressed and the war effort lay greater and greater claim to American resources, every industry tightened up as best it could. One adaptation that baseball made was to schedule spring training nearer the cities which the teams would ultimately have as a home base. The Red Sox, then, instead of taking the train to Sarasota, Florida, held 1943 spring training in Medford, Massachusetts. Red Sox spring training headquarters was at Cousens

Gymnasium of Tufts College, just 8.07 miles from the Yawkey Way address of Fenway Park.

The student newspaper, the *Tufts Weekly*, announced the plan and then remarked that "spectator accommodations are very limited in the Cage" and only Tufts students would be admitted. "Students will be able to see the practice only from the balcony and will not be allowed on the Cage floor level during the practice." Cousens cage was a large two-story

Gene Mack depicting spring training at Tufts in Medford, Mass. 1943.

indoor facility, with netting draped from the ceiling. Batters could hit the ball into the netting while taking batting practice. A large Gene Mack cartoon in the *Boston Globe* gives the picture of the team working on hitting and infield play in the cramped confines. Mack's cartoon was signed "Gene Mack, Sarasota" with the place named crossed out and changed to Medford.

Early in March, manager Joe Cronin had some speaking engagements around New England. He dropped in at Amherst College and visited 1942 stars Johnny Pesky and Ted Williams, who had both begun soloing as Naval aviation cadets. Cronin commented that they had "their minds 100 per cent set on the Navy flying game." Six days later, a Sox delegation including

Cronin, a couple of coaches, equipment manager Johnny Orlando and the superintendent of Fenway Park visited Pop Houston, Tufts athletic director. They planned to work out at Tufts for just nine days or so in an abbreviated spring training session before heading to Baltimore to play a very limited number of exhibition games. To cut down further on travel, the 1943 schedule included 14 home doubleheaders.

On March 15, several Sox players began informal workouts at Tufts. Cronin and coaches Hugh Duffy, Tom Daly, and Frank Shellenback worked out with players Tony Lupien, Jim Tabor, Skeeter Newsome, and Pete Fox. They "had a drill on a baseball surface which did not remind them of Sarasota, Florida, the least little bit." They were nonetheless able to work on bunting, played pepper and calisthenics—led after the first day or so by a volunteer, chief petty officer Harold Knight. The early arrivals planned a week of easy workouts before the regulars came on the 22nd. Lupien and Newsome had already been working out at Harvard. The Boston Braves worked out at the Choate School in Connecticut.

Most of the players reported on time, with just Doerr, Judd, and Terry missing.

Cronin turned down the offer of a "tally-ho coach" to take the team back and forth from the Kenmore Hotel near Fenway Park. Tufts hung a green baize batting background to help, and blocked off one window which was in the batter's line of vision. When the weather improved, the team moved outdoors to work out, but the College Acres field across the street was adjacent to an active railroad line and the *Globe* noted that "the field is so close to the railroad tracks that many of the boys got locomotive cinders in their eyes."

On March 26, over 500 fans came to watch the workout, with "quite a few of them... school children who had never seen a big league team practicing." Cronin was pleased that the weather had been decent, and he put the best spin on matters, noting that in any event the weather was much as the first few weeks of the season would likely be. He expressed satisfaction with the way the players were getting in shape. The next day, though, Eddie Lake came down with German measles and was quarantined in his Brookline home. Fortunately, despite having worked together in close quarters with his teammates, the disease did not spread.

The weather turned worse, but the team had gotten in five outdoor practices and Cronin felt the pitchers were in decent early season condition. Newspaper accounts report on how the various players were coming along. When they headed southward on April 2, Cronin acknowledged, "There's no substitute for the sun. But the next best thing to the sun is this." Most of the players agreed, but sportswriter Harold Kaese still felt training in New England was a handicap. Among other things, explained coach Tom Daly, is that there is less air resistance indoors so both pitching and hitting were different experiences. The indoor cinder track was a harder surface not as suited to baseball cleats as to track spikes, and it was impossible to put a mound in the cage, which understandably make life tougher on the pitchers.

All in all, concluded Kaese, "There wasn't much glamour for the Red Sox at Tufts, but, as somebody pointed out, there wouldn't have been much glamour in Florida or anyplace else—not this Spring." They weren't above a little levity, though, and while Cronin and others were thanking C.P.O. Knight for leading them in calisthenics, Newsome and Mace Brown and a couple of others doused the drill master with four buckets of water.

The Sox entrained to Brooklyn for the first game of the exhibition season, which instead of an "atmosphere of orange groves, flamevine and hibiscus, opens in the smoke and grime of Flatbush." The Yawkeys beat the Rickeys, 5–0. They also shut out the Orioles the next day in Baltimore, 8–0. Though further south, the next day's game was called off due to cold temperatures and high winds. The third game of the young season was again a shutout, this time Sox 11, Orioles 0. Lest any fans back in Boston get too excited by a spring training season with three consecutive whitewashes, the *Globe* reminded readers that the games with the Orioles were only valuable as workouts. Finally, playing on the grounds of Plainfield High School, the Sox staff yielded two runs, as Boston beat the Newark Bears 5–2, taking the next game 9–1. After five straight Red Sox wins, Mel Ott's Giants beat Boston at the Polo Grounds 3–2.

On April 14, the team beat it back to Boston and played Boston College at Fenway Park for about 1,000 fans, edging the Eagles 17–2. It was the first game at Fenway in '43, and Al Simmons hit a home run into the net, but pulled a ligament in his right calf "while watching the flight of the ball." He blamed the accident on his "elastic garters." The Sox planned a game against Harvard on the 16th, to avenge the 1–0 loss to the college team some 27 years earlier. Mission accomplished: Red Sox 21, Harvard 0.

Ted Williams may have inspired the Sox, too. He stopped by the park before the game and swore that he was going to bring some of his Naval slide rule studies to the science of hitting a baseball. "Density of ash and the resiliency of a baseball—that's what I want to find out," he said. "Gimme that, and I've got the answer to how much energy I can save hitting a home run if the wind's with me."

The Red Sox then wrapped up the spring season taking the annual City Series from the Braves two games to one. The full proceeds of the first game were donated to the Red Cross. The Sox lost the second game 6–1 on the strength of five Braves runs in the top of the 10th inning. The game on the 21st was called on account of mud. The final game in what Jim Bagby called the "frostbite league" was a 1–0 Tex Hughson two-hit win.

The Medford site was the northernmost of all spring training sites. Early in 1944, the *Tufts Weekly* took a moment to note that, in 1943, some said the Sox' poor showing "was in part due to the poor start that the squad got at Tufts College." Columnist Ed Shea reported, however, that GM Eddie Collins said the club had been fully satisfied with conditions and that the Sox would return in 1944.

In 1944, the Sox indeed started the spring at Tufts again, eight afternoons of conditioning drills for a limited number of players beginning March 17. In fact, the *Globe* headline on the 18th read "Executives Outnumber Players as Red Sox Begin Training." Cronin batted balls against the netting, then hit grounders to the four players present. The paper noted the informality of the drill, none of the ballplayers wearing Sox caps. "Last year's caps were given to pilots in the South Pacific area. New ones may arrive today." The weather was not as welcoming in '44. The March 21 paper ran a story headlined "Red Sox Work Outdoors—Shoveling Snow." They had to shovel driveways and put on snow chains to get to practice. "This is the first time I ever wore overshoes to Spring training," complained Cronin as he showed up late himself.

Admiral R. A. Theobald, commandant of the 1st Naval District dropped by on the 23rd, and offered a little advice to Tony Lupien, urging the left-handed hitter to hit to the opposite field. Watching Joe Wood, Jr. work out, the admiral notes, "I saw his father when he beat Walter Johnson in that famous 1–0 game." On the 25th the team took the train to Baltimore where the full squad assembled. Weather conditions there saw them working out indoors at the Gilman School cage.

The first exhibition game was on April 1, and it was no joke. The game featured the talent-depleted but nonetheless major league Boston Red Sox against Dick Porter's Coast Guard "Cutters" at Curtis Bay Navy Yard. Porter had closed out his career, playing briefly for the Sox back in 1934. The Coast Guard won, 23–16, kicking off the game with 12 runs in the bottom of the first inning. It was Joe Wood, Jr. who started poorly, giving up four hits and five walks and leaving the bases loaded for reliever Mike Ryba. Hank Sauer tripled all three in. Red Sox players also committed eight errors.

The Sox got back on track, though, on April 3, defeating the Naval Academy team at Annapolis, 7–3. Things were evened up a little, though, with an exchange of batteries. Vic Johnson, Yank Terry, and Wood pitched for the Midshipmen, throwing three innings each, while Roy Partee caught part of the game. USNA pitchers Conway Taylor and "Happy Haynes" held their own Navy team to seven hits, with their catcher Victor Finos (of Everett, Massachusetts) behind the plate. On 4/4, the Sox routed the Orioles 19–3; the next day's game with the Giants was snowed out. The team got in several games but then freezing rain brought the 4/11 game to a halt. The next day's game versus the Braves in Hartford was also scrapped. By the time the official City Series began, the Sox had only played seven exhibition games.

This year's City Series was re-christened the "Chilblain Championship." The Red Sox won the first two games, and therefore the series, which was just as well since the third game was rained out. Game Two was played at Fenway Park in 43 degree temperature, with rain and even hail.

Opening Day 1944 was the April 18 game at Fenway where the Yankees' Hank Borowy beat Yank Terry 3–0, and the season was underway.

In 1945 spring training was held in Pleasantville, New Jersey at the high school, some six miles from Atlantic City. Sox traveling secretary Phil Troy announced that the players "will have better locker accommodations than we had down at Sarasota—and they were all right down there." The high school field needed some prep work—third base was 14 inches (!) out of alignment. Some rolling needed to be done, but the field was ready on time for the March 15 official start. There were no workouts at Tufts in '45. U.S. forces had crossed the Rhine and defeat of Germany was clearly on the horizon. For the second year, though, baseball agreed to voluntary measures to curtail travel—the Senators, therefore, would not travel as far as 45 miles to play the Athletics, but with the Red Sox and Yankees both within a few miles of each other at Pleasantville and Atlantic City, inter-team play was fine and nine games between the two teams were scheduled. Because the war was going well, the War Manpower Commission ruled that players could return to the game from offseason employment. "There is considerable evidence that it adds to the morale on the homefront in wartime and that, therefore, there is real justification for this action," stated WMC chairman Paul V. McNutt. 1945, though, remained a year where very few veterans from 1942 returned to play ball. There were so many new players in 1943–45 that on Opening Day, Harold Kaese wrote, "If Ted Williams stepped into the Red Sox batting order today, half the Yankees would not recognize him."

March 24 was the first intrasquad game, with Captain Bob Johnson's "Regulars" beating Joe Cronin's "Yannigans" 3–2, in six innings. Bases on balls were ruled taboo, so every hitter could hit, but strikeouts were not banned and there were 10 Ks. The Yannigans (second-stringers) lost again the next day, 5–4, despite Cronin's two home runs to help out his charges. Once the Sox—Yanks contests began, there were some high-scoring affairs. Sox 12, Yanks 6 was the first score, though New York beat Boston 13–2 and 15–14 the next two games. The Red Sox played and dominated "a non-descript" all-service team at Pleasantville, 20–4. Boston won five games and New York won four before they broke camp. The 1945 City Series saw the Sox swept in the first two games, both played at the "Wigwam" (the National League field). The series was interrupted for two days for the funeral of President Franklin D. Roosevelt, and then the Red Sox won the final game on April 15. The next day, the Red Sox gave at least the appearance of a tryout to three black players at Fenway Park—Jackie Robinson, Sam Jethroe, and Marvin Williams. "Pretty good ballplayers," said Hugh Duffy. "Get those niggers off the field!" shouted an unattributed voice from up near the door to the Red Sox front office.

The next day, April 17, was Opening Day. Catfish Metkovich set a record with three errors in one inning and the Red Sox lost 8–4. The new season was underway. The Red Sox lost every one of their first eight games for the worst start in franchise history.

Post-war spring training

In the first year after the war, the Red Sox immediately took advantage of the end of travel restrictions and scheduled a couple of exhibition games in Havana, Cuba. In the spring of 2000, the Red Sox played two games against the Houston Astros in Santo Domingo. The Red Sox have also crossed both southern and northern borders, to play exhibition games in Mexico and Canada. There was talk of playing in England, Ireland, or Italy, though that has yet to come about, though individual members of the Red Sox have visited other lands as far back as Tris Speaker playing (in 1913–14) before King George V of England in London and Abbas II (the last khedive of Egypt) in Cairo, and as recently as during 2006's inaugural World Baseball Classic.

In 2008, the Red Sox played exhibition games against both the Hanshin Tigers and the Yomiuri Giants, winning both games, and then opened the season with two games in the Tokyo Dome against the Oakland Athletics.

Ted Williams and Cuba

"I'll tell you something I haven't told many people. If Castro hadn't taken over Cuba, I wouldn't be in Florida today. I'd be living in Cuba. That's right. I had a spot picked out at Varadero Beach. I had plans to fish all those miles of bonefish flats. I couldn't go there now, but that's one of my dreams that didn't come true—living at Varadero Beach and fishing those bonefish flats."—interview with Jim Hardie in The News *(October 30, 1988) when Ted was 69 and had just sold his house and boat in Islamorada to move to Citrus Hills. "It got so there were more boats than fish in the Keys. All gone downhill."*

In the 1950s, Ted WIlliams often said that after he finished playing ball, he'd like to head to Cuba, buy a boat and just enjoy fishing. Needless to say, after Fidel Castro, Camilo Cienfuegos, and the other Cuba revolutionaries took over in 1959, the idea lost its attraction to Ted—despite the revolutionaries' obvious love of baseball.

Ted retained a few Cuban connections of sorts. In 1999 I began working on a long-term project, interviewing people who work in and around Boston's Fenway Park. Naturally, I included the usher who works the section where I have my season tickets. He is Rodolfo Cid and he began working as an usher at Fenway on Opening Day in 1975. Cid is a Cuban refugee, who left the island in 1962 with his family after a short stay in jail and after seeing his young daughter marching in the street singing the "Internationale." During the interview, he told me that as a young employee of the railroad he had used his rail pass to travel halfway across Cuba in March 1946 to catch the two spring training games between the Washington Senators and the Boston Red Sox. And he wasn't disappointed: he'd seen Ted Williams hit a home run.

When I traveled to Cuba for a week of baseball in March 2001 with Cubaball Tours, I decided to research more about this two-game weekend visit in 1946. I'd read the *Boston Globe's* accounts and they didn't mention any home run by Ted. In Havana, I visited the Biblioteca Nacional and got myself a library card. I don't really read or speak Spanish very effectively, never having studied it and just having picked up what rudimentary skills I have while traveling. The woman who issued me the card, though, was a baseball fan and she pointed me in the right direction.

I called up a few newspapers—Havana had quite a number of daily papers in 1946—and both a couple of weekly and monthly publications as well. Most of the dailies did not publish Monday editions, so I began to worry about finding Cuban coverage of the Sunday game. The first four or five newspapers I checked provided no coverage of the Sunday game. *El Crisol* did publish on Mondays, though, I found on my second visit.

The Senators, fairly frequent visitors to Cuba in those days, arrived on the 7th of March and held a practice on the 8th. The Red Sox came in on a charter flight at 5 p.m. on the 8th. *Informacion* wrote that Williams was the "attracion maxima" of the two-game series. Considered the best hitter in the American League, Williams ("el formidable jonronero") had returned to baseball after serving three years in the armed forces of "Tio Samuel." This newspaper ran a large cartoon on the sports page depicting an attractive young woman hiking up her skirt to put on her silk stockings, telling a Cuban ballplayer, "De eso nada, ahora estoy con las grandes ligas."

Eddie Collins traveled with the Red Sox party, as did manager Joe Cronin and AL president William Harridge. The Red Sox player contingent was, in alphabetical order: Ernie Andres, Paul Campbell, Dominic DiMaggio, Bobby Doerr, Danny Doyle, Boo Ferriss, Andy Gilbert, Mickey Harris, Tex Hughson, Sam Mele, Catfish Metkovich, Eddie Pellagrini, Johnny Pesky, Freddie Pytlak, Charlie Wagner, and Ted Williams. Coaches Paul Schreiber and Larry Woodall joined the party, led by traveling secretary Tom Dowd. Eddie Collins traveled with the Red Sox as did manager Joe Cronin and American League president William Harridge. Commissioner Chandler was present as well.

Collins, in remarks at the airport, said he was happy to return to Havana, where he had visited often as a player with Connie Mack's Athletics. Collins, who had signed Ted Williams and Bobby Doerr for the Red Sox, also remembered by name Armando Marsans as one of the greatest outfielders he'd seen, pitcher Jose Mendez and a few others. *Informacion*'s sportswriter felt the Red Sox had a good chance for the pennant in '46 with the Pesky/Doerr combination at second, Williams back with Dom DiMaggio in the outfield, the addition of Rudy York at first and some good pitchers in Ferriss, Hughson, Harris, and Dobson.

The first exhibition game was scheduled for Saturday, March 9 and the gates opened at noon. Game time was 3 p.m. at Stadium Cerveza Tropical, a capacious ballpark in downtown Havana. That evening at 9 p.m., Gavilan Kid (known in the U.S. as Kid Gavilan) boxed against Sosa (any relation to Sammy? wouldn't that be something?) at the Palacio de los Deportes. Gavilan won on points. Rodolfo Cid grew up with Gavilan as a neighbor in Camaguey.

In the ballgame, though, despite an eight-run Boston fourth inning, Washington won the game 10–9 with a dramatic six-run bottom of the ninth, the big blow a Robertson triple. Earlier in the game, Williams, Pesky, and Doerr had all tripled as well. Pitching for Boston were Dobson, Brown, and Wagner. Wagner took the loss. Max Wilson, whose major league career record was 0–1, got the win in this one. The Sox earned nine runs on 10 hits, but the Senators had 15 hits and that all-important 10th run. Ted was the only Boston player with more than one hit; he went 3-for-4 in the game with one "carrera empujada" (run batted in). Time of the game was two hours and 55 minutes.

The stadium opened at noon the next day—Sunday—for Clark Griffith Day ceremonies. The Red Sox came back on and beat the Senators 7–3. This time Boston scored first, with three runs in the third, adding single runs in the fourth, fifth, eighth, and ninth. Williams had yet another triple, as did Dom DiMaggio. Rodolfo Cid's memory was incorrect. Ted had tripled in both games but not hit any homers during the actual contest. News coverage in *Hoy*, the paper of the Communist Party, indicated "Ted Williams bateo un tribey y dos hits, y en las practicas al bate se llevo en claro la cerca del right en tres occasiones, una de ellas por sobre la valta anunciadroa, en un batazo de proporciones similar al famoso homer de Dick Sisler." Perhaps it was one of those batting practice drives that Rodolfo Cid recalled. Those three balls Ted hit out of the park in right field would have been tremendous drives. This was a huge park (Tropical still stands today, used as a track and field facility).

Ted's triple in game two was hit off Wolff, deep to left field right down the line and, following as it did an error, as Heath dropped Campbell's fly to left, kicked off the three-run third inning rally. Doerr followed with a double right down the line as well, and then Dominic singled to right. The paper acknowledged that Ted had just one hit, 1-for-5 on the day, "pero eso fue un largo triple por lo ultimo del left field que inicio el rally de tres carreras." It was Dom's day, 3-for-5—also hitting a triple and driving in two. Doerr got that double and a single in five trips to the plate. Hughson, Ferriss, and Harris pitched, with Tex Hughson picking up the win, and Wolff bore the loss. Pesky and Doerr were cited for their defense. *Cuba Deportiva* said that Williams made a beautiful catch of a foul fly early in the game. The game lasted but 2:05.

This wasn't the Red Sox' first visit to Cuba. In 1941, they'd played three games against the world champion Cincinnati Reds on March 28, 29, and 30. Boston won the first game 9–2, but then lost the next two 6–3 and 2–1. All three games were also played at Tropical. Ted was supposed to make the trip, but at the last minute he did not. Preceding the three contests against the Reds, Boston played a local Cuban team and was defeated 2–1. Juan Decall, who strung telephone wires for a living, only gave up the one run on a Stan Spence sacrifice fly. The Boston press praised the level of play and noted that the local crowd was "highly enthusiastic...so exultant at the finish they threw seat cushions onto the field, an old Havana custom." (Some of us recall Seat Cushion Night at Fenway Park a few decades later. That was a disaster never to be repeated.)

The Boston Red Sox were being courted by the University of Havana, which was hoping that the Red Sox would hold their regular spring training at the high quality university facilities beginning in 1943. As it happens, war broke out and the Red Sox found themselves training much closer to home, ironically at another school of higher learning—Tufts College in Medford, Massachusetts.

TED WILLIAMS

Ted Williams in Cuba. Sensacion premium, courtesy of Cesar Lopez.

Ted Williams is still remembered in Cuba today. I'd heard that his photograph still hung in the lobby of the Hotel Sevilla, where the Sox had stayed in 1946. The Mexican League magnate Bernardo Pasquel frequented the lobby during the Sox stay, and roamed the corridors buttonholing Red Sox stars. Pasquel's brother Jorge had reportedly cabled just hours earlier to make an offer to Williams of a tax-free $100,000, for three seasons in Mexico.

Bernardo Pasquel asked one of the writers who accompanied the Red Sox to introduce him to Williams. Ted and Pasquel sat down to chat in the bar "Criollo", when Joe Cronin strode up and inserted himself in the conversation, saying, "I'm the manager of this gentleman. You should be talking to me, not to him." Pasquel turned to Williams and asked, "¿Y usted un hombre libre?" ("Are you a free man?") Pasquel didn't wait for a reply but told Cronin that he wanted to talk with Mr. Williams and that if he did not sign to play with Boston, he would make a great offer to Williams.

Ted replied that he was glad that baseball was so well established in Mexico that they wished to compete against U.S. baseball, but that before he made the trip to Havana he had indeed signed to play for Boston. Ted spoke for himself and the writer for *Bohemia* said that Cronin left like "un perro depresa" ("a sad dog").

Ted's photo does indeed still grace the lobby of the Sevilla early in the 21st century, as part of a photo gallery of hotel guests which also includes Joe Louis, Perez Prado, Errol Flynn, Georges Simenon, Luis Angel Firpo, Graham Greene, Enrico Caruso, Gloria Swanson, Santos Traficante, Irenee Dupont, and Al Capone.

I asked bookstall vendors at the Plaza de Armas if anyone had photos of Ted for sale. I already owned Ted's sole Cuban baseball card (the 1947 Propagandas Montiel card) and a Cuban magazine which had featured Ted. I was able to purchase a print of Ted visiting the original Sloppy Joe's, a 1950s photo. Sloppy Joe's was owned by Jose Abeal Y Otero, a Spaniard who had come to Cuba in 1906.

Later, at the home of a Cuban baseball aficionado, I was able to buy an original photo of Ted in the batter's box at Tropical during those 1946 games against the Senators. Ted posed as well for *Información*'s Ramon Fernandez at Tropical and Mark Rucker later supplied me with a copy of that photograph.

A photograph of Ted also hangs in the Hotel Nacional.

Places the Red Sox have played baseball

The Red Sox 2004 Trophy Tour visited each one of the 351 cities and towns in Massachusetts. The 2007 trophy has already been to Nova Scotia and to Japan.

Wouldn't it be nice if the Red Sox could become the first major league team to play in all 50 states—to suggest that the team in this regard was truly "America's team."

The Red Sox themselves have played baseball in 42 states so far, plus the District of Columbia, Canada (three Canadian provinces), and three other countries (Cuba, the Dominican Republic, and Mexico), plus both Puerto Rico and the Virgin Islands. A fourth country was added to the list when the Red Sox opened the 2008 season in Tokyo, Japan.

The states where the Sox have yet to play baseball are:

Alaska	Montana	South Dakota
Hawaii	North Dakota	Wyoming
Idaho	Oregon	

It would take some scheduling and be costly, but with a commitment to play at least one game in each of these eight states, the Red Sox could become the first major league club to have played in all 50 states.

They have played in more Florida communities (33) than those of any other state. California is next, with 17. New York has 16 communites and Massachusetts has 15; North Carolina and Texas both follow with 12. They have played in 11 different Connecticut and New Jersey locales.

All told, through 2008, the Boston team has played in 2,608 preseason exhibition games, 231 in-season exhibition games, and 41 postseason exhibitions. The two games in August 1981 played to tune up for the "second half" of that year's split season are included here as in-season games, as are the three games in Los Angeles in 2008. Except for the 2005 Cooperstown game, and those three L.A. games, there have been no midseason exhibition games since 1999. The last postseason exhibition game was in 1946 as the club wanted to keep tuned up for the forthcoming World Series. The last time the Red Sox played after their year's work was entirely done—postseason play and all—was in 1920.

Of the preseason games, Boston has a W-L record of 1,412–1,145 with 51 ties. The inseason record is 137-84-9, with a tied intrasquad game at Cooperstown in 1989 when the Cincinnati team failed to show up. In postseason play, they are 32–8 with one intrasquad game played in Burlington, VT on 10/10/1910.

In the following listing, the game noted is the first-known game played by a Boston Red

Sox or Boston Americans team in the locale indicated. Some are intrasquad games but most feature opponents. Included are preseason exhibition games, midseason exhibition games, postseason exhibition games, regular season games, and postseason championship games (e.g., the first World Series game in Pittsburgh).

Many of the games were played by second-string teams, particularly during 1911 when there were two touring teams created. The "second team" that year was often dubbed Carrigan's Colts. They were, nevertheless, comprised of Boston Red Sox players and are hence listed here. In any given game, particularly the less-meaningful spring exhibition games, the goal is to play baseball and not necessarily to win. One does wonder about some of the pairings, such as the June 20 game against the Father Mathew Temperance Society in 1904 or the two September 1919 games against the Klein Chocolate Company, but one presumes there's a story behind the story involving a personal connection with an executive or player of the Boston ballclub. In the case of the Father Mathew Temperance Society game in Elmira, the game was won by the temperance advocates 6–5 in 10 innings, but one wonders about the sobriety of the official scorer. See the full story on this game below. In the case of Klein Chocolate, the Red Sox got their revenge the next day with a 3–1 win over the company team that had shut them out 4–0 on September 25.

Boxscore of the 1904 game against the Father Mathew Temperance Society.

There were intrasquad games almost every year, preceding games against other teams, but only counting preseason games against outside opponents, Boston won each one of their first 20 preseason games before being defeated in their third spring season by Louisville in Macon, Georgia on April 6, 1903. They didn't have their first losing spring, though, until 1917.

All told, using the same criterion, through 2007, the team has won 1,381 and lost 1,129 preseason exhibition games. There were 47 tie games. Understandably, given that these were training exhibitions and not championship games, there was less necessity to have a game result in a win. There were, however, some 148 preseason games played into extra innings. Of these, Boston won 60, lost 69, and saw 19 result in ties. In 2007 alone, the Sox played four games to ties.

If we omit the 1901 season when the franchise was just getting underway, the number of games played in a typical preseason exhibition year has been more or less around 30 games, but it has ranged as low as four in 1912 and as high as 64 (!) in 1911.

There remains one game that's a bit of a mystery. The *Boston Globe* says it took place in Macon, Georgia on March 14, 1904. Newspapers in Boston reported that the game lasted 15 innings, but neglected to name the opponent and never indicated whether the game remained tied or was resolved with a winner and a loser. The *Macon News*, however, reported it as a practice, not an exhibition game and noted that "after nine innings had been played, the score stood 10 to 6, and this time it was in Mercer's favor." Did they simply keep on playing until 15 frames had been played? Even the Macon newspaper doesn't make that clear. We're forced to agree that it wasn't truly an exhibition game and not include it in our tabulations.

Boston's first midseason exhibition game ever was played after the franchise only had two regular season games under their belts—neither of which they won. They played the West New Yorks at Weehawken, New Jersey and won, 5–2. Their next exhibition game came on August 4, 1901 on the St. George Cricket Grounds in New York, and the Boston Americans beat the Hoboken nine, 9–4. Hoboken turned the tables in 1902 with a 7–4 win on the Cricket Grounds on July 13.

The first postseason exhibition games came six days in a row, from September 30 through October 5, 1901 playing in Boston, Greenfield, Lynn, and Marlboro, Massachusetts and in Manchester and Nashua, New Hampshire.

In all, the Red Sox have played in 264 different communities in the United States (267 if you include each borough of New York City as a separate community, since the Red Sox have played in Manhattan, The Bronx, Queens, and Brooklyn). They have played in 14 other communities, outside of the United States proper.

Alabama
Birmingham 4/9/1918 Brooklyn 3, Boston 1
Decatur 4/1/1927 Minneapolis 12, Boston 9
Dothan 4/1/1941 Boston 10, Cincinnati 4
Mobile 4/1/1904 Boston 6, Mobile 1
Montgomery 3/31/1904 Boston 2, Montgomery 1
Selma 4/5/1946 Cincinnati 4, Boston 2 and
    Cincinnati 2, Boston 1
Tuscaloosa 4/6/1934 Boston 11, University of
    Alabama 3
The game in Gadsden scheduled for 4/4/1941 was
    called off due to wet grounds. The Red Sox have
    yet to return for a game in Gadsden.

Arkansas
Hot Springs 3/20/1909 Boston 14, Memphis 2
Little Rock 3/18/1907 Boston 2, Little Rock 1
Pine Bluff 3/28/1922 Boston 6, Pittsburgh 2

Arizona
Apache Junction 3/14/1963 Houston 12, Boston
    11 (10 innings)
Mesa 3/28/1957 Boston 5, Chicago Cubs 3
Phoenix 3/27/1957 New York Giants 5, Boston 2
Scottsdale 3/8/1959 Boston 12, Chicago Cubs 8
Tucson 3/29/1957 Cleveland 7, Boston 1
Yuma 3/27/1911 Boston 17, Yuma 5 (despite
    Bedient, Kleinow, Purtell, and Duffy Lewis
    all playing for Yuma)

California
Anaheim 5/13/1966 California Angels 4, Boston 1
Bakersfield 3/15/1911 Boston 1, Bakersfield 0
Hanford 3/14/1911 Boston 9, Hanford 3
Hollywood 3/25/1957 Boston 3, Hollywood Stars
    0
Los Angeles 3/1/1911 Boston 6, Los Angeles 5
Modesto 3/13/1911 Boston 5, Modesto 0
Oakland 3/8/1911 St. Mary's 1, Boston 0
Palm Springs 3/20/1961 Boston 8, Los Angeles
    Angels 7
Pomona 3/20/1911 Boston 7, Pomona 0
Redlands 3/6/1911 Boston 7, Redlands 3
Redondo Beach 2/28/1911 Yannigans 5, Regulars 1
Riverside 3/22/1911 Boston 5, Riverside 0
Sacramento 3/21/1911 Boston 2, Sacramento 1

San Bernardino 4/1/1963 Chicago Cubs 13,
    Boston 3
San Diego 3/13/1959 Boston 8, Cleveland 5
San Francisco 3/11/1911 Boston 6, San Francisco 1
San Jose 3/20/1911 Boston 3, Santa Clara
    College 2

Colorado
Denver 4/1/1911 Denver 6, Boston 3
Pueblo 3/31/1911 Boston 10, Pueblo 4
The game originally announced for Grand
    Junction on 3/30/1911 was then changed to
    Salida, but was then called off because a train
    wreck on the line held up the train carrying the
    Red Sox too long.

Connecticut
Bristol 9/21/1919 Boston 6, New Departure 2
Bridgeport 4/28/1918 Boston 7, Bridgeport
    All-Stars 0
Hartford 4/16/1902 Boston 13, Hartford 2
Meriden 10/10/1908 Philadelphia 7, Boston 2
New Haven 4/21/1903 Boston 9, New Haven 2
New London 8/27/1945 Boston 12, Coast Guard
    Bears 8
Thompsonville 6/24/1923 Holy Cross 5, Boston 4
    (10 innings)
Torrington 8/15/1920 Torrington 7, Boston 4
Waterbury 4/15/1902 Boston 18, Waterbury 7
Willimantic 9/18/1921 American Thread 2,
    Boston 1
Windsor Locks 7/9/1922 Boston 8, Windsor Locks
    Collegians 7

Delaware
Wilmington 4/6/1944 Boston 8, Phillies 6

District of Columbia
Washington 5/3/1901 Washington 9, Boston 4

Florida
Arcadia 3/25/1938 Louisville 7, Boston 0
Auburndale 3/14/1928 Boston 4, Baltimore 4 (tie)
Avon Park 3/20/1928 Boston 11, St. Louis
    Cardinals 8
Baseball City 3/8/1988 Kansas City 4, Boston 3
Bradenton 3/3/1928 Regulars 4, Yannigans 2

Clearwater 3/24/1933 Boston 12, Newark 3

Cocoa 3/15/1968 Boston 3, Houston 1

Daytona Beach 3/24/1942 Brooklyn 4, Boston 3

Fort Myers 3/16/1935 Philadelphia Athletics 4,
Boston 1

Fort Pierce 3/16/1954 Pittsburgh 2, Boston 1

Gainesville 4/7/1919 Boston 4, New York Giants 2

Jacksonville 3/31/1905 Boston 5, Cincinnati
2—first exhibition game played against a
National League team

Jupiter 3/13/2000 Boston 8, Montreal 6 (10
innings)

Kissimmee 3/16/1986 Boston 8, Houston 5

Lakeland 3/30/1935 Detroit 3, Boston 0

Leesburg 4/3/1946 Cincinnati 9, Boston 8 and
Boston 2, Cincinnati 1

Miami 3/13/1935 Boston 7, New York Giants 5

Miami Beach 3/26/1941 Boston 11, Philadelphia
Phillies 7—Bobby Doerr hit three home runs

Orlando 3/30/1933 Montreal Stars 8, Boston 2

Palm Beach 3/31/1941 Boston 2, Rochester 0

Palmetto 3/28/1929 Buffalo 9, Boston 4

Pensacola 3/9/1930 Boston 16, U. S. Navy Base 4

Plant City 3/301988 Boston 6, Cincinnati 1

Pompano Beach 3/22/1966 Washington 8,
Boston 7

Port Charlotte 3/16/1989 Texas 10, Boston 4

St. Petersburg 3/19/1928 Boston Braves 4, Boston
Red Sox 1

Sarasota 3/18/1928 Buffalo 10, Boston 6

Sebring 3/25/1936 Boston 9, Newark 7

Tampa 4/4/1919 Boston 5, New York Giants 3

Tarpon Springs 3/31/1929 Boston 9, Tampa 3

Vero Beach 3/22/1971 Boston 10, Los Angeles
Dodgers 5

West Palm Beach 3/15/1935 St. Louis Browns 15,
Boston 2

Winter Haven 3/8/1928 Boston 4, Philadelphia
Phillies 3

Georgia

Atlanta 3/28/1904 Boston 15, Atlanta 5

Augusta 4/5/1902 Boston 11, Warner's Team
1—this was really a Regulars vs. Yannigans game

Columbus 4/8/1930 Columbus 8, Boston 6

Macon 3/19/1903 Boston 5, Mercer University 2

Moultrie 3/31/1939 Boston 13, Moultrie Packers 3

Savannah 3/27/1905 Savannah 7, Boston 5

Thomasville 4/3/1936 Chicago Cubs 8, Boston 6

Waycross 4/2/1953 Phillies 9, Boston 8 (10 innings)

Illinois

Champaign 4/2/1913 Boston 10, University of
Illinois 0

Chicago 5/30/1901 Chicago White Sox 8, Boston
Americans 3

Danville 4/5/1908 Boston 6, Danville 0

Great Lakes 5/23/1944 Great Lakes Naval
Training Center 3, Boston 0

Peoria 4/3/1917 Brooklyn 13, Boston 5

Springfield 4/17/1951 Boston 5, Springfield Cubs 2

Indiana

Elkhart 6/17/1904 Boston 10, Elkhart 0

Evansville 4/11/1903 Evansville 6, Boston 5

Fort Wayne 4/7/1908 Boston 5, Fort Wayne 0

Indianapolis 4/3/1908 Indianapolis 4, Boston 1

Lafayette 4/4/1917 Boston 8, Brooklyn 5

The 3/27/1907 game at French Lick was rained
out.

Iowa

Davenport 4/2/1917 Boston 5, Brooklyn 1

The 4/6/1911 and 4/7/1911 games scheduled at
Sioux City were both rained out. Dubuque had
invited the Red Sox and Phillies to play in the
1915 post season, as part of a projected tour to
the Pacific coast, but Red Sox insistence on a
guarantee plus expenses scotched the tour.

Kansas

Topeka 4/5/1911 Boston 7, Topeka 0

Wichita 4/2/1911 Boston 5, Wichita 4

Kentucky

Bowling Green 4/7/1922 Goofs 6, Regulars 1
(intrasquad)

Dawson Springs 4/6/1923 Boston 5, Louisville 1

Lexington 4/8/1903 Boston 25, State College 3

Louisville 4/4/1903 Boston 7, Louisville 1 Two
days later, Louisville beat Boston 8–6 for the
first-ever exhibition loss after 14 wins in a row
(despite Boston pitching Cy Young)

Madisonville 4/7/1923 Boston 13, Louisville 10 (10
innings)

Owensboro 4/8/1941 Boston 5, Cincinnati 2

Paris 4/8/1922 Regulars 14, Goofs 10 (intrasquad)

Louisiana

Destrehan 3/19/1925 Boston 4, Mexican
Petroleum Corp. 0

New Orleans 4/7/1904 Boston 1, New Orleans 0

Shreveport 4/5/1924 Boston 9, Shreveport 0

Maine

Bangor 7/15/1935 Boston 8, Maine All-Stars 1

Portland 10/5/1909 Boston 3, All-Maine 0

Sanford 10/1/1919 Boston 4, Sanford 3

Maryland

Annapolis 4/3/1944 Boston 7, U.S. Naval Academy
Midshipmen 3

Bainbridge 6/19/1944 Bainbridge Naval Training
Center 5, Boston 2

Baltimore 4/26/1901 Baltimore 10, Boston 6

Cumberland 7/12/1937 Boston 5, Cumberland
American Legion 1

Curtis Bay Navy Yard 4/1/1944 U. S. Coast Guard
Cutters 23, Boston 16
Fort Meade 7/14/1943 Boston 8, Washington 3

Massachusetts
Beverly 10/10/1919 Boston 2, Marblehead
0—Babe Ruth's last game in a
Red Sox uniform
Boston 5/8/1901 Boston Americans 12,
Philadelphia Athletics 4
Brockton 6/18/1909 Brockton 2, Boston 1
Cambridge 6/26/1925 Boston Red Sox 13, North
Cambridge 6
Camp Myles Standish 8/5/1943 Boston 8, Camp
Myles Standish 3
East Douglas 9/26/1946 New York Yankees 8,
Boston 7
Fitchburg 9/27/1922 Boston 7, Fitchburg 4
Fort Devens 6/12/1942 Boston 11, Fort Devens 5
Greenfield 10/4/1901 Boston 3, Greenfield 0
Lowell 4/18/1908 Boston 3, Lowell 2 (10 innings)
Lynn 10/1/1901 Boston 8, Lynn picked team 5
Marlboro 10/5/1901 Marlboro 4, Boston 3
New Bedford 6/19/1905 Boston 12, New Bedford 0
Pittsfield 8/11/1921 Boston 10, Pittsfield Hillies 9
Springfield 8/20/1934 Boston 14, Milton Bradley 1
Worcester 4/18/1902 Boston 5, Worcester 3

Michigan
Battle Creek 8/12/1935 St. Louis Cardinals 9,
Boston 8
Detroit 5/22/1901 Boston 9, Detroit 5
Flint 8/29/1921 Boston 12, Flint 7

Minnesota
Minneapolis 5/5/1961 Minnesota Twins 5, Boston
Red Sox 1

Mississippi
Greenville 3/30/1920 New York Giants 8, Boston 2
Gulfport 3/29/1926 Boston 3, Gulfport 3 (tie)

Missouri
Caruthersville 4/2/1922 Boston 2, Milwaukee 0
"played on a race track enclosure"
Kansas City 4/8/1911 Boston 4, Kansas City Blues 3
St. Joseph 4/6/1911 St. Joseph 5, Boston 4
St. Louis 6/7/1902 St. Louis Browns 4, Boston
Americans 3

Nebraska
Lincoln 4/5/1911 Lincoln 8, Boston 7—former
Red Sox player and manager Bob Unglaub
played second base for Lincoln
Omaha 4/8/1911 Omaha 5, Boston 2

Nevada
Las Vegas 3/20/1960 Chicago Cubs 3, Boston 2
Reno 3/27/1911 Boston 14, University of Nevada 4

New Hampshire
Manchester 10/2/1901 Boston 6, Manchester 1
Nashua 10/3/1901 Nashua 6, Boston 2

New Jersey
Atlantic City 3/31/1945 New York Yankees 15,
Boston 14
Camp Kilmer 9/17/1943 Boston 9, Philadelphia
Athletics 4
Clifton NJ 5/5/1918 Boston 3, Doherty Silk Sox 1
Fort Monmouth 6/21/1943 Boston 8, Signal Corps
All-Stars 0
Jersey City 9/16/1917 Boston 4, Jersey City
Skeeters 4 (tie, 10 innings)
Long Branch 6/28/1914 Boston 2, Long Branch
Cubans 0
Newark 4/24/1904 Boston 4, Newark 3
Paterson 6/2/1919 Doherty Silk Sox 6, Boston 5
(10 innings)
Plainfield 4/8/1943 Boston 5, Newark 2
Pleasantville 4/1/1945 Boston 20, All-Service
Team 4 "a nondescript team made up of service
men"
Weehawken NJ 4/28/1901 Boston 5, Weehawken 2

New Mexico
Albuquerque 4/5/1961 Boston 4, Chicago Cubs 3

New York
Brooklyn 4/6/1916 Boston 6, Brooklyn 0
Buffalo 4/18/1903 Boston 8, Buffalo 7
Camp Shanks 8/31/1943 Boston 10, Camp Shanks
1
Camp Upton 6/11/1945 Boston 7, New York
Yankees 6
Cooperstown 6/13/1940 Chicago Cubs 10, Boston
9—annual Hall of Fame game at Doubleday
Field
Elmira 6/20/1904 Father Mathew Temperance
Society 6, Boston 5 (11 innings)
Geneva 8/15/1921 Boston 13, Standard Optical 3
Gloversville 7/5/1907 Boston 8, A. J. & G. 3
Jamestown 7/30/1902 Jamestown 3, Boston 2 (10
innings)
Long Island City 10/5/1913 Boston 6, Long Island
City 1
Malone 7/11/1934 Boston 8, Malone 0
Mitchel Field, Uniondale L.I. 5/4/1944 Boston 18,
Mitchel Field service team 6
New York 6/1/1903 Boston Americans 8, New
York Highlanders 2
Rochester 6/22/1908 Boston 9, Rochester 2
Sampson 6/5/1944 Sampson Naval Training
Center 20, Boston 7
Syracuse 6/3/1906 Syracuse 7, Boston 3

North Carolina
Charlotte 4/4/1929 Boston 11, Charlotte 1

Durham 4/10/1938 Boston 10, Cincinnati 9

Gastonia 4/13/1937 Boston 8, Washington Senators 3

Greensboro 4/10/1934 Boston 9, Greensboro 5

High Point 4/7/1952 Philadelphia Athletics 12, Boston 6

Lexington 4/7/1939 Boston 7, Cincinnati 2

Raleigh 4/7/1920 Boston 9, Buffalo 1

Rocky Mount 4/14/1937 Cincinnati 10, Boston 5

Statesville 4/4/1940 Cincinnati 13, Boston 7

Wilmington 4/1/1932 Boston 13, Wilmington Pirates 6

Wilson 4/11/1956 Boston 6, Phillies 4

Winston-Salem 4/6/1920 Boston 6, New York Giants 0

The 4/5/1920 game in Asheville was rained out.

Ohio

Canton 9/8/1936 Canton Terriers 7, Boston 4

Cincinnati 4/12/1905 Cincinnati 5, Boston 3

Cleveland 5/25/1901 Boston 5, Cleveland 0

Columbus 4/17/1903 Boston 2, Columbus 1

Dayton 4/3/1907 Boston 5, Dayton 3

Sandusky 9/23/1906 Boston 3, Sandusky Stars 0—Cy Young pitched a one-hitter

Springfield 4/6/1907 Boston 2, Springfield 0

Toledo 4/4/1908 Boston 1, Toledo 0

Youngstown 5/26/1921 Boston 7, Youngstown McElroys 4

Oklahoma

Oklahoma City 4/1/1911 Boston 16, Oklahoma City 1

Tulsa 4/5/1952 Boston 5, Tulsa 3

Pennsylvania

Connellsville 7/24/1922 Boston 9, Connellsville 2

Greensburg 9/30/1908 Greensburg Elks 2, Boston 0 (the Elks club one-hit the Red Sox)

Harrisburg 9/25/1919 Klein Chocolate Company 4, Boston 0

Lancaster 9/26/1919 Boston 3, Klein Chocolate Company 1

Philadelphia 4/29/1901 Philadelphia 8, Boston 5

Pittsburgh 10/6/1903 Pittsburgh 5, Boston 4

Reading 7/6/1933 Boston 6, Reading 3

Scranton 4/26/1908 Scranton 2, Boston 0

Wilkes-Barre 4/11/1909 Boston 1, Wilkes-Barre 0

York 5/28/1919 Boston 10, American Chain Company 3

The September 8, 1921 game in Jonestown was canceled because the Red Sox never showed up.

Rhode Island

Berkeley 10/3/1909 Boston 4, Berkeley Mill 4 (tie)

Bristol 5/14/1922 Boston 17, Bristol 1

Davisville 6/27/1944 Boston 3, Camp Thomas 1 and Boston 5, Camp Endicott 2 (two games)

Newport 9/19/1909 Boston 14, Newport 1

Pawtucket 4/22/1982 Boston 3, Pawtucket 1

Providence 9/13/1903 Boston 7, Fall River 3

Quonset 6/9/1943 Boston 8, Quonset Naval Air Station 2

Warwick 4/23/1905 Boston 8, Providence Grays 6

Woonsocket 7/14/1918 Boston 5, Queen Quality of Jamaica Plain 2

South Carolina

Bamberg 4/5/1921 Boston 9, Rochester 8

Charleston 4/6/1921 Boston 8, Rochester 0

Columbia 4/9/1919 New York Giants 7, Boston 2

Darlington 4/7/1921 Boston 11, Rochester 6

Florence 4/6/1939 Boston 18, Cincinnati 18 (tie) !!

Greenville 4/4/1955 Boston 9, Phillies 7

Spartanburg 4/10/1919 New York Giants 4, Boston 1

Tennessee

Chattanooga 3/29/1931 Boston 6, Chattanooga Lookouts 2

Clarksville 4/6/1922 Boston 5, Minneapolis Millers 2

Dyersburg 4/3/1922 Boston 5, Minneapolis Millers 2

Jackson 4/5/1922 Boston 10, Minneapolis Millers 6

Kingsport 4/9/1947 Boston 17, Cincinnati 6

Knoxville 4/3/1920 New York Giants 5, Boston 0

Mascot 4/3/1921 Regulars 6 vs. Yannigans 3

Memphis 3/26/1908 Boston 7, Memphis 0

Nashville 4/11/1905 Boston 4, Nashville 4 (tie)

Texas

Abilene 3/29/1911 Boston 19, Abilene Redbirds 7

Arlington 4/28/1972 Texas Rangers 9, Boston Red Sox 6

Austin 4/4/1918 Boston 10, Brooklyn 4

Corpus Christi 4/6/1959 Boston 11, Chicago Cubs 3

Dallas 3/30/1911 Boston 4, Dallas 0

El Paso 3/28/1911 Boston 9, El Paso 1

Fort Worth 3/31/1911 Boston 4, Fort Worth 2

Houston 4/5/1918 Brooklyn 5, Boston 3

San Antonio 3/25/1920 Boston 3, New York Giants 0

Victoria 4/7/1959 Chicago Cubs 8, Boston 7

Waco 4/2/1918 Brooklyn 2, Boston 1

Wichita Falls 3/22/1920 New York Giants 14, Boston 8

Utah

Salt Lake City 3/28/1911 Boston 9, Salt Lake City 2

The game originally announced for 3/28/1911 in Ogden was played in Salt Lake City instead.

Vermont

Burlington 10/10/1910 Gardner Team 4, Collins Team 1—an intrasquad game by two Red Sox squads

Rutland 10/5/1919 Boston 6, Rutland 2

Virginia

Charlottesville 4/5/1901 Boston 13, University of Virginia 0—first spring training game for the Boston franchise

Danville 4/12/1938 Boston 14, Cincinnati 13

Lynchburg 4/8/1952 Philadelphia Athletics 4, Boston 3

Norfolk 4/8/1920 New York Giants 7, Boston 5

Petersburg 4/8/1921 Boston 7, Petersburg Trunk Makers 4—three Syracuse Stars players joined the Trunk Makers

Portsmouth 4/7/1955 Phillies 4, Boston 3 (10 innings)

Richmond 4/13/1915 Boston 5, Richmond 0

Roanoke 4/12/1939 Boston 17, Cincinnati 14

Washington

Seattle 6/19/1961 Boston 5, Seattle Rainiers 4

West Virginia

Bluefield 4/7/1954 Boston 7, Milwaukee Braves 5

Charleston 4/10/1940 Boston 2, Cincinnati 1

Wisconsin

Milwaukee 6/2/1901 Boston 13, Milwaukee 2

Playing in other countries

CANADA

New Brunswick: St. John 8/26/1930 Boston 7, St. John 5

Ontario: London 8/30/1921 London Champs 5, Boston 3

Toronto 7/24/1916 Boston 5, Toronto 5 (tie)

Quebec: Montreal 6/8/1970 Montreal Expos 8, Boston 6

CUBA

Havana 3/27/1941 Cuban Stars 2, Boston 1

DOMINICAN REPUBLIC

Santo Domingo 3/11/2000 Houston 4, Boston 3

JAPAN

Tokyo 3/22/2008 Boston 6, Hanshin Tigers 5

MEXICO

Nogales 3/26/1965 Boston 15, Cleveland 9

PUERTO RICO

Bayamon 3/21/1978 Boston 5, Pittsburgh 4

Ponce 3/27/1966 Boston 5, Minnesota 1

San Juan 3/25/1966 Minnesota 9, Boston 0

VIRGIN ISLANDS

St. Croix 3/31/1967 New York Yankees 3, Boston 1

St. Thomas 4/1/1967 Boston 13, New York Yankees 4

Also played outside the actual United States:

ARIZONA TERRITORY

Yuma 3/27/1911 Boston 17, Yuma 5

Thanks to Walter LeConte for locating a couple of dozen in-season exhibition games.

Places in America still waiting for the Red Sox

The following 10 communities once had a Red Sox game scheduled, but for one reason or another (usually, weather) the game was never played—and residents are still waiting to see the Red Sox in their home town.

Terre Haute IN (1903)

French Lick IN (1907)

Grand Junction CO (1911)

Salida CO (1911)

Ogden UT (1911)

Sioux City IA (1911)

Asheville NC (1920)

Jonestown PA (1921)—On November 6, 1922, the Red Sox were ordered to pay $534.05 to Henry Molliter of the Jonestown PA independent baseball club. An exhibition game had been planned for September 8, 1921, but the Red Sox never showed. The ballclub said that the game had been called off when two of Jonestown's players were ineligible; it turned out they actually were eligible. No damages were assessed, but the Red Sox were ordered to cover Jonestown's expenses.

Gadsden AL (1941)—The game scheduled for April 4, 1941 was called off due to wet grounds. The Red Sox have yet to return for a game in Gadsden. Some fans may still be holding that rain check.

Redondo Beach CA (1911)—A little shortchanged? The spring training home of the Red Sox was in Redondo Beach, California. It was the year in which the Sox crossed the country, playing with two squads and playing an astonishing 64 preseason games in 11 states, including 40 in 12 different California communities. They played three intrasquad games in Redondo Beach but never took on a competing team at their spring training home.

EXHIBITIONS AND THE OPPOSITION—COLLEGES, THE MILITARY, AND COMPANY TEAMS

The City Series

One recurrent rival in early exhibition play was the Boston Braves, with a "City Series" often played in The Hub in the final days before the regular season began. Since the Braves moved to Milwaukee, the idea of a City Series simply no longer made sense. When MLB introduced interleague play, though, one of the first pairings was to match the Braves (now based in Atlanta) with the Red Sox.

In the years 1905 through 1953, there were 31 series played. Frank J. Williams tabulates 13 series that went in favor of the Red Sox, seven in favor of the Braves, and 11 series that were tied. All in all, the Sox won 62 games and the Braves won 38. There were four ties. Since the Braves left Boston in 1953, there have been other games between the two. The teams played each other two games in Florida in 1954, and barnstormed for six more at the end of spring training. In the 38 exhibition games since 1953, the Red Sox won 25 and the Braves won 12. There was one tie in 1956. In interleague play, which began in 1999, the Atlanta Braves have won 23 and the Red Sox 16.

These days, Boston's most frequent spring training rival is the Minnesota Twins, because both the Red Sox and Twins call Fort Myers home, each team having its own facility in the "City of Palms."

The Red Sox press release for March 3, 2005 was particularly humorous in regard to the Lee County competition: "The defending Mayor's Cup (and World Series) champion Boston Red Sox begin their 2005 Grapefruit League campaign tonight as they host the Minnesota Twins at City of Palms Park…the Red Sox, who last year captured their first Mayor's Cup championship since 1999 (and their first World Championship since 1918) send newly acquired righthander Matt Clement to the mound tonight in the first of 6 spring meetings between the cross-town rivals…according to the original Mayor's Cup charter, written by Ban Johnson in 1903 and recertified this winter by newly re-elected Fort Myers Mayor Jim Humphrey, a tie in the spring series keeps the coveted Mayor's Cup in the possession of its current owner, so the Red Sox must win 3 of 5 from the Twins to maintain Baseball's Holy Grail."

Sox vs. colleges (St. Mary's, BC, Harvard, Northeastern, Mercer, and more)

In recent years, the Red Sox typically start off the season with a game or two against Boston-area college teams that travel to Florida. Though there were long stretches of time without such exhibitions, play against college teams dates back to the earliest years of the franchise. As we've seen, the first game the team ever played was not against major league competition.

While preparing for the inaugural 1901 season, the Bostons played the University of Virginia nine—and did pretty well, shutting them out 13–0 and then, six days later, 23–0.

In 2008, it was a 39–0 day as the World Champion Boston Red Sox beat both Boston College and Northeastern to open the year's exhibition season. BC got one hit, Northeastern managed three. The Red Sox took 27 walks and got 30 hits on the day.

Surely the major league baseball Boston Red Sox would walk all over any college team that ever dared challenge them to a ballgame, right? Not always.

Although Connie Mack's Athletics dominated in 1910 and 1911 both, the Red Sox played over .500 ball both years. Yet on March 8, 1911, the baseball team from little St. Mary's College of Oakland, California held the Sox scoreless and beat them 1–0. The whole college had a total enrollment of 238 in 1911. From those 238 students emerged nine who beat the Bosox. And nine was all it took.

St. Mary's has a long history with baseball. Over the years, this one small college has produced an astonishing number of major league ballplayers—63 in all! The most recent ones are Mark Teahen, James Mouton, and Tom Candiotti. The Red Sox alone count the following former St. Mary's men among their own alumni: Frank Arellanes, Bill Fleming, Harry Hooper, Bill James, Earl Johnson, Dutch Leonard, Duffy Lewis, Jim McHale, and Emmett O'Neill.

When they beat Boston, the Red Sox were just opening spring training. After four years of training in Arkansas, the team decided to train at Redondo Beach, California in 1911. As it happens, they returned to Hot Springs in 1912 and spent the next seven springs there. This was the first game of the season for the Red Sox; the collegians had been playing all winter. There had been rain for some days and the field was (according to the *Boston Post* story) "slow and rather muddy, making snappy playing next to impossible."

Two youngsters pitched for Boston at Freeman's Park—Pierce from Augusta (his first name was not recorded by the *Post* or the *Globe*) pitched the first five frames and then Hugh Bedient took over, showing a bit of the promise that would propel him to the majors a year later, when he went 20–9 and even won Game Five of the World Series for the World Champion Red Sox. The Bosox box men held St. Mary's to just five hits, four off Pierce and just one—the fatal one—off Bedient, but "Brick" (a/k/a "Tiny") Leonard took the mound for the "Phoenix" team from St. Mary's and himself held the Sox to five, two of them by Tris Speaker, a single and a double. He struck out Gardner and Speaker (on three straight strikes) in the first, and struck out two more Sox in the second. Leonard wasn't in top form, either—he'd reported a sore arm before the game. Neither team scored for eight innings.

This Sox team was stocked with good players. Larry Gardner led off and played second base. Harry Hooper batted second and was in right, with Speaker set in center and Duffy Lewis in left. Readers who have a memory stretching back three paragraphs may note that ⅔ of the Red Sox outfield were St. Mary's alumni. Team captain Heinie Wagner was at short and Hugh "Corns" Bradley at first—Hugh hit .317 in 1911. About the only nonentity was Nebinger at third; he never made it (though he had one of the hits off Leonard). Pierce never made the majors, either. Catching duties were split by Rip Williams and Pinch Thomas.

Leonard struck out six Sox and never did let in a run. The game was decided in the ninth, when St. Mary's third-bagger Billy Wallace—who had already singled once and been hit by a pitch—got ahold of a Bedient curveball and shot it straight down the first base line, fair by inches. Hooper hustled over to get it and made the long throw in, while Wallace streaked around the bases. He ran through the third base coach's sign and scored as Heinie Wagner juggled the ball momentarily. The *Post* gave Wagner an error on the throw; the *Globe* awarded Wallace a home run.

St. Mary's, despite being the home team, was batting in the top of the ninth. The Red Sox had one last chance in the bottom of the inning. Speaker singled and then Duffy Lewis slashed what looked like a sure double to left, but leftfielder Norman Lynch leaped to snag the ball in foul territory with his bare hand and instantly fired a shot to the plate to snare Speaker, who had tagged up and tried to score.

The shutout cost Patsy Donovan a hat. St. Mary's (Leonard pitching) had beaten the White Sox the year before, 6–0. This was becoming a habit at the Catholic school. Boston manager Patsy Donovan didn't exactly offer to eat his hat if the Sox were shut out, but he'd bet a hat if they were and he had to make good on his lost wager.

The Sox rested, but St. Mary's played another game right afterwards and Phoenix pitcher Mike Cann threw a no-hitter against the University of California team from Berkeley, 4–0.

Given that there were St. Mary's alumni on the Sox team, too, the small college in Oakland had both sides covered. St. Mary's furnished a number of players to major league ball in the early 20th century. Hooper had also won the gold medal as the most exemplary scholar in 1906. Hooper had starred on the 1907 team, which boasted a 26–0 record; Lewis played on the second team, never making the college's first team—but the didn't prevent him from becoming a star, driving in the winning run of Game Three of the 1915 World Series, with two outs in the bottom of the ninth. Students sent a telegram to Lewis reading, "St. Mary's is proud of you." Not wanting to forget Hooper, the man Lewis drove in, they wired him, "St. Mary's offers congratulations." Nor did they ignore Sox starter Dutch Leonard, who won the game 2–1, wiring him "Hurrah for the old school." The Phillies were not without their own man in the game: catcher Eddie Burns was also a St. Mary's graduate and he scored the only run for the Phils in their defeat. Philadelphia manager Pat Moran had another St. Mary's man on the bench, pitcher Joe Oeschger. Had Moran used Oeschger—which he did not—it might at least have evened the teams a bit in the eyes of *Baseball* magazine's C. P. Beaumont. With three St. Mary's players on the Red Sox to two for Philadelphia, perhaps Moran could have evened the odds on the Series, which Boston took four games to one.

Connie Mack's Athletics scouted and signed three of the players on the St. Mary's team and Elmer "Tiny" Leonard did debut for the A's later that year, appearing in just five major league games (2–2, 2.84 ERA). Tom Fitzsimmons, the Phoenix shortstop, had four at-bats for Brooklyn in 1919 but nary a hit.

In 1916, another college team beat the Red Sox. Unlike the 1911 Sox, this was a dominant Red Sox team. The 1915 Red Sox won the World Series over the Phillies and the 1916 edition beat the Brooklyn Robins in just five World Series games as well. But on April 10, 1916, Harvard College beat the Red Sox 1–0. Harvard hadn't even begun to cut down its team for the spring season, but the reigning World Champion Red Sox were back from spring training, ready for the season to begin, and fielded their regular lineup behind Vean Gregg. Three Boston hurlers held the Harvards to five hits, but the lone run of the game was scored on a Larry Gardner error, single, and an infield roller. The Red Sox made three errors. Harvard did well in 1916, too, with a 22–3 season. Helping hold the Sox scoreless was pitcher Eddie Mahan from Natick, relieved (like Gregg) after five innings. The *Harvard Crimson* termed it a "brilliant 1–0 victory from the World's Champion Red Sox," adding that the game "was not a gift from magnanimous professionals; the Crimson players simply played better ball. The offensive work of the two nines was about on a par, but in the work in the field the University was decidedly superior, playing without error and pulling off three sensational double plays, the last of which effectively nipped the Red Sox' ninth inning rally and ended the game."

Perhaps Harvard was avenging the 2–0 defeat at the hands of the World Champion 1912 Red Sox; that was the first game ever played at Fenway Park. The new facility opened on April 9, 1912, and the first batter ever was a sophomore from Harvard University named Dana J.P.

Wingate. He struck out, as did the second batter to face Hageman. The third popped up to Yerkes at second base. In fact, Hageman threw a one-hitter. Only Bob Potter hit safely for Harvard, leading off the fifth inning, singling between third and short. Moments later, he was picked off first by Hageman but broke for second base and got in safely when shortstop Marty Krug dropped Jack Stahl's throw from first. Potter thought he was out, though, and stepped off the bag. He was tagged, and then he truly was out.

Harvard has played seven games in all against the Red Sox. The first two games were played at the Huntington Avenue Grounds. The April 12, 1910 match was billed in the *Harvard Crimson* as somewhat educational: "Today for the first time in 14 years the University nine will meet a professional nine on the diamond. This is one feature of a general awakening on the part of the athletic authorities, who seem to have come to realize that there is a certain satisfaction in winning, and that it is worth while to give the teams every opportunity for development. The nine will learn much from even one professional game...." The score was Red Sox 4, Harvard College 1. One wonders about the lessons learned in the 21–0 defeat in 1943, however.

4/12/1910—Red Sox 4, Harvard College 1	4/10/1916—Harvard 1, Red Sox 0
4/11/1911—Red Sox Colts 4, Harvard College 2	4/16/1943—Red Sox 21, Harvard 0
4/9/1912—Red Sox 2, Harvard 0	4/4/1987—Red Sox 8, Harvard 0
4/8/1913—Red Sox 5, Harvard 0	

Interestingly, as Dan Shaughnessy pointed out in the April 5, 1987 *Boston Globe*, after Roger Clemens' start in the fated Game Six of the 1986 World Series, the very next team he faced was Harvard! The competitive Clemens mowed them down—10 Ks, no hits in six innings. As Dick Thompson wrote, "Everyone knew Harvard had no right being on the same field as the Red Sox."

One of the players facing Clemens was Frank T. Caprio, currently Treasurer of the State of New Jersey. He told the *Providence Journal*'s Bill Parrillo, "I couldn't believe it. You see him on TV and you think of the MVP awards and the Cy Young and all that. And now there he is and you're trying to get a hit off him. It was hard to believe. His fastball was as fast as any pitch I had ever seen. But what made him great was his other pitches were that much better than any other curveball or slider or changeup that I had ever seen, and he had total control." Clemens wasn't the only Sox star present; Ted Williams was watching from the bench.

The Sox held pretty good records against other college teams as well. Their first two games ever—even before they played their first American League game—were spring training exhibitions in April 1901. At Charlottesville, the Boston Americans beat the University of Virginia by back-to-back scores of 13–0 and 23–0.

The team from Hobart College passed through Georgia in 1902 to play the University of Georgia team in Athens, and wanted to play Boston, but wished to share the receipts from the game and Boston manager Jimmy Collins would not agree. Consequently, Hobart has never yet played a game against Boston.

The next college team they faced was in 1903—Mercer College. In the early days of the 20th century when the team had its spring training base in Macon, Georgia, the Mercer boys lost 21 games in a row to Boston. This despite Cy Young's work as coach for the Mercer nine—and even his pitching for Mercer in a March 27, 1903 game, which Mercer lost 19–6.

The composite score was Boston 286–Mercer 52. The last of the 21 losses was a close one, though, a hard-fought 11-inning game which the Red Sox just barely won, 2–1, on March 23, 1906. Were the Red Sox getting worried? Cause and effect? The Red Sox never played another game against Mercer and so preserved intact their undefeated record.

Against the Boston College Eagles, the Sox hold a record of 19–0.

1916 Red Sox 9–1	1997 Red Sox 13–0	2003 Red Sox 9–6
1933 Red Sox 9–2	1998 Red Sox 10–1	2004 Red Sox 9–3
1943 Red Sox 17–2	1999 Red Sox 4–3—becoming	2005 Red Sox 11–5
1993 Red Sox 2–0	uncomfortably close	2006 Red Sox 10–0
1994 Red Sox 12–1	2000 Red Sox 8–3	2007 Red Sox 9–1
1995 Red Sox 19–0	2001 Red Sox 11–5	2008 Red Sox 24–0
1996 Red Sox 22–0	2002 Red Sox 2–1—a squeaker	

In another college game of note, five Red Sox pitchers combined to throw a spring training no-hitter against Northeastern University on March 4, 2005. The score was 17–0. On top of Northeastern's 7–0 defeat just the year before, it wasn't an impressive showing by the Huskies, but they fought back and in 2006 lost by a more respectable 9–2 final score.

The Sox played the Waterbury Collegians in August 1917; the Collegians (who lost the 6–1 game) were a semipro team largely made up of college players—a common practice of the time. On July 9, 1922, they played the Windsor Locks Collegians at Windsor Locks, Connecticut (and won in 13 innings, 8–7). A pitcher from Holy Cross pitched for Windsor Locks, a summer team that lasted four or five season and was largely made up of ballplayers from Holy Cross, Boston College, and Harvard.

Other colleges and universities the Red Sox have played are: State College (Kentucky), St. Mary's, Santa Clara College, University of Nevada, University of Illinois, Holy Cross, University of Arkansas at Fayetteville, Randolph Macon College, Virginia Medical College, Maryville College, Spring Hill College, University of Alabama, University of Florida, Providence College (which was a May 24, 1932 game only won 9–8 by scoring five runs in the ninth inning), and "an all-star team made up largely of college players" at Bangor, Maine on July 15, 1935. That score was Boston 8, Maine All-Stars 1. The only college teams to ever beat Boston were: St. Mary's (1911), Harvard (1916), Holy Cross (1923 and 1938), Providence College (1932), and Yale (1934). Though the Red Sox spring training home in 1943 was Tufts College in Medford, Massachusetts, they have never yet played the Tufts team.

The Red Sox vs. the United States armed forces

As it happens, the Sox also played a number of military teams. Here's what we believe to be a complete list:

1930

3/9 @ Pensacola FL: Boston 16, U. S. Navy Base 3
3/12 @ Pensacola FL: Boston 4, Naval Air Station 3
3/23 @ Pensacola FL: Boston 6, Pensacola Flyers 3
3/26 @ Pensacola FL: Boston 8, Pensacola Flyers 2

1937

7/12 @ Cumberland MD: Boston 5, Cumberland American Legion 1

1941

7/8 @ Brockton MA: Boston 7, Camp Edwards 5

1942

6/12 @ Fort Devens MA: Boston 11, Fort Devens 5
9/4 @ Camp Edwards MA: Boston 3, Camp Edwards 2

1943

6/8 @ Quonset RI: Boston 8, Quonset 2
6/11 @ Fort Devens MA: Fort Devens 6, Boston 5

6/14 @ Boston MA: Boston Red Sox 14, Boston Coast Guard 8

6/21 @ Camp Wood, Fort Monmouth NJ: Boston 8, Signal Corps All-Stars 0

7/19 @ Norfolk VA: Norfolk Naval Training Station 4, Boston 3 (10 innings)

8/5 @ Camp Myles Standish MA: Boston 8, Camp Myles Standish 3

8/31 @ Camp Shanks NY: Boston 10, Camp Shanks 1 (7 innings)

1944

5/4 @ Mitchel Field, Uniondale, L.I., NY: Boston 16, Mitchel Field service team 6

5/8 @ Quonset RI: Boston 8, Quonset Naval Air Station 3

5/23 @ Great Lakes IL: Great Lakes Naval 3, Boston 1

6/5 @ Sampson NY: Sampson Naval Training Center 20, Boston 7

6/12 @ Camp Myles Standish MA: Boston 6, Camp Myles Standish 4

6/19 @ Bainbridge MD: Bainbridge Naval Training Center 5, Boston 2

6/27 @ Davisville RI: first game: Boston 3, Fort Thomas 1; second game: Boston 5, Camp Endicott 2
   (two seven-inning games played on adjacent fields)

8/24 @ Fort Monmouth NJ: Boston 9, Fort Monmouth All-Stars 7

1945

5/7 @ Sampson NY: Boston 6, Sampson Naval Training Center 3

6/26 @ Great Lakes IL: Great Lakes Bluejackets 3, Boston Red Sox 2 (Bob Feller strikes out 9 Sox for
   Great Lakes)

8/27 @ New London CT: Boston 12, Coast Guard Bears 8

Playing against the U.S. armed services, the Red Sox appear to hold a 20–6 record.

They did play some games to benefit veterans, such as the June 25, 1951 game at Fenway Park for the New England Hospitalized Veterans Fund. The score: New York Giants 5, Boston Red Sox 4.

Playing company teams

The Sox have also played a number of company teams at one time or another. This is the listing we have compiled:

1909

10/3 @ Berkeley RI: Boston 4, Berkeley Mill 4 (tie, 11 innings)

1913

9/8 @ Manchester NH, on the grounds of the Amoskeag Textile Club: Boston 3, Manchester Manufacturers' Baseball League All-Stars 1. A team selected from the various company teams in the league named.

1918

5/5 @ Clifton NJ: Boston 3, Doherty Silk Sox 1

7/14 @ Woonsocket RI: Boston 5, Queen Quality of Jamaica Plain 2

1919

4/14 @ Richmond VA: Boston 9, Bankers 1 ("the State and city bank nine")

5/28 @ York PA: Boston 10, American Chain Company 3

6/1 @ Paterson NJ: Doherty Silk Sox 6, Boston 5 (10)

9/7 @ Baltimore MD: Boston 10, Baltimore Dry Docks 6

9/21 @ Bristol CT: Boston 6, New Departure 2

9/25 @ Harrisburg PA: Klein Chocolate Company 4, Boston 0

9/26 @ Lancaster PA: Boston 3, Klein Chocolate Company 1

1920

7/4 @ Paterson NJ: Boston 7, Doherty Silk Sox 6 (10)

8/29 @ Meriden CT: Boston 4, Schenck Castermen 2 (The H.B. Schenck Company manufactured casters.)

1921

6/12 @ Warwick RI: Boston 9, International Culinary Institute 2

8/12 @ York PA: American Chain Company 6, Boston 1

8/15 @ Geneva NY: Boston 13, Standard Optical 3

9/18 @ Willimantic CT: American Thread 2, Boston 1

1922

4/23 @ Paterson NJ: Doherty Silk Sox 5, Boston 4

7/16 @ Bristol CT: Boston 9, New Departure 2

1923

6/10 @ Hartford CT: Boston 12, Hartford Dixie Gas and Oil Dixies 1

1925

3/19 @ Destrehan LA: Boston 4, Mexican Petroleum Corp. 0

1934

6/11 @ Portland ME: Boston 7, Burnham & Morrill 1 (B&M was the leading canner of baked beans; the Governor of Maine attended, as did Rudy Vallee. Bill Carrigan umpired.)

7/9 @ Brockton MA: Boston 8, Taunton Lumber Company 1

8/20 @ Springfield MA: Boston 14, Milton Bradley 1

1935

7/8 @ Brockton MA: Boston 10, Taunton Lumber 1

1938

7/6 @ Brockton MA: Taunton Lumber Company 10, Boston 5

1940

7/9 @ Brockton MA: Boston 20, Taunton Lumber Company 2

Though a wonderfully named aggregation, the Petersburg Trunk Makers were a Virginia League team and not a company team; the Red Sox beat them in 1921. Likewise, the Moultrie Packers—beaten 13–3 by Boston in 1939—were an entry in the Georgia-Florida League.

Games played against religious organizations

1931

3/21 @ Pensacola FL: Boston 15, House of David 2

3/22 @ Pensacola FL: Boston 14, House of David 4

Fraternal societies

The team has done rather poorly against fraternal societies, though in reality they actually won the first game. See that story elsewhere in the book.

1904

6/20 @ Elmira NY: Father Mathew Temperance Society 6, Boston 5 (11)—despite actual score being 5–4 Boston after nine innings, and both teams scoring six runs after a full 11.

1908

9/30 @ Greensburg PA: Greensburg Elks 2, Boston 0 (umpire: John K. Tener) The Elks one-hit the Red Sox!

OPENING DAYS

The Red Sox have opened as early as March 25 (2008) and as late as April 23 (1919), with home openers as early as April 1 (2002) and as late as May 8 (1901). Of the home openers, Boston has won 62 and lost 46—through 2008. Prior to the climate-controlled Tokyo Dome opener in 2008, the earliest opening day had been March 31 in 2003.

They won 10 of their first 12 home openers; they had a 9–2 record at the Huntington Avenue Grounds. The Fenway mark is thus 52–44.

The team won six opening games in a row from 1907 through 1912, and again from 1938 through 1943. The worst losing streak was five (1924–1928). There were five shutouts they won, and five shutouts they lost. The biggest margin of victory was their 14–3 win over the Yankees in 2007, the worst margin of defeat the 9–2 loss to the Tigers in 1968.

Their best home opener record was against the Washington Senators (11 wins-6 losses) followed closely by the Philadelphia Athletics (13–7), while their record against the Yankees stands at 12–12.

In 1918, the Red Sox continued on to win their first six home games and in 1920, they won their first six—which total they matched again in 1998. In 1957, they won the first five road games.

In 1944, unfortunately, the Sox were shut out in both their home and road openers.

The following year, the Red Sox drew only 3,489 to their first game at Fenway—the lowest attendance ever for a home opener. Of course, there was a war going on.

Needless to say, some seasons started better than others. There hasn't been a worse start than 1945, when Boston lost its first eight games, and there hasn't been a better start than the next year—1946—when the Sox got off to a 21–3 start. One of the odder seasons was 1969, which kicked off with three consecutive extra-inning games, each one longer than the one before. Boston won the first game of the year, 5–4 in 12 innings. The second game ran 13 innings, but Boston lost, 2–1. The third game of the year lasted 16 innings before George Thomas's pinch-hit grounder to second scored Petrocelli from third to give the Red Sox a win.

As noted, in 1918, the Sox won their first six games, all at home, and started the season 12–3 before dropping six straight on the road. In 1920, playing Ruth-less ball, Boston won its first seven home games, a feat they matched in 1998. 1957 saw the Red Sox win their first five road games.

One would think that by the law of averages, the Red Sox would open as frequently at home as on the road. There's been an imbalance in season openers, though, with only 38 of them in Boston and 69 on the road. It's been an imbalance that has increased over time; 11 of the first 26 season openers were in Boston, but only 27 of the following 81—this despite a stretch from 1971 through 1986 when there was a strict alternation. Schedulers may have come to feel that it makes more sense for a team in the northeast to open the season in somewhat warmer climes; we couldn't disagree. Only five times have the Sox opened seasons at home in back-to-back years; never have they opened more than two seasons in a row. The longest stretch of road season openers was seven (1927–1933), though as recently as 1996–2001 saw six season openers on the road.

The most games the ballclub has played while starting the season on the road before returning home is 10, in 1901, but that's because they didn't yet have a home to come to—the Huntington Avenue Grounds was still under construction as the season began. The team had a 5–5 record before playing their first game at home. In 2003, the Red Sox also played 10 road games before the first home game; they had a 6–4 record. In 1984, 1997, and 1998 they played eight road games kicking off each year, with a combined 10–14 record. The most home games that the Red Sox have played before taking to the road is eight, which they have done twice: 1914 (2–4), with two ties) and 1918 (7–1).

The Red Sox also played at ballpark openers in Philadelphia (Shibe Park, 1909), in Washington (Griffith Stadium, in 1911), and New York (Yankee Stadium, in 1923). Graciously or otherwise, they lost each one of those games.

Only two pitchers ever made their major league debuts in an Opening Day start for the team: Win Kellum in 1901 and Jim Bagby, Jr. in 1938.

When Daisuke Matsuzaka opened the 2008 season in Japan, he became the first foreign born player in American League history to start on Opening Day in his native land. The first foreign-born pitcher to start a season for Boston was also the first pitcher to ever

The first starter ever, Win Kellum. Courtesy of National Baseball Hall of Fame.

start for the team: Win Kellum of Waterford, Ontario. He threw Opening Day for the franchise on April 26, 1901.

The second was Jack Quinn, a native of Stefurov, Austria-Hungary. Born as Joannes Pajkos, he began (and lost) the 1922 opener. The next foreign-born starter was from Marianao, Cuba in 1973's opener: Luis Tiant. That year, the Sox started a five-year string of foreign-born starters. It was Tiant again in 1974; Holguin, Cuba native Diego Segui relieved Luis and took the loss. In 1975, Tiant started for the third year in succession, and in both 1976 and 1977 it was Ferguson Jenkins of Chatham, Ontario.

From 1998–2004, Pedro Martinez pitched in seven consecutive Opening Day starts.

Among Boston's Opening Day starters, the man with the most is Roger Clemens with 10 (five wins, two losses, and three no-decisions). Pedro pitched the seven indicated (3–1, with three no-decisions). Cy Young started six and was 3–3. Dennis Eckersley drew five starts (2-1-2). Mel Parnell started four, as did Bill Monbouquette. A number of Sox threw three each: Smoky Joe Wood, Babe Ruth, Howard Ehmke, Danny MacFayden, Wes Ferrell, Tex Hughson, Frank Sullivan, and Luis Tiant.

Only three pitchers in Red Sox history have won three Opening Day contests in a row. They are: Babe Ruth (1916–1918), Wes Ferrell (1935–37), and Pedro Martinez (1998–2000.)

Ted Williams batted in 15 Opening Day games, batting .433 (23-for-53) with 42 total bases and 15 RBIs.

Seven U.S. presidents have attended Red Sox openers, in Washington DC: Taft, Harding, Coolidge, Hoover, Roosevelt (Franklin), Eisenhower, and Lyndon Johnson.

Some special home openers—the wins

April 20, 1912—Boston 7, New York 6 (11 innings)
The first game ever played at Fenway Park has been covered elsewhere in this book.

April 22, 1915—Boston 7, Philadelphia 6
They probably couldn't have done it without the five (yes, 5) errors by one of the game's great batters, Nap Lajoie, Philadelphia's second baseman. The hometown Royal Rooters "worked much more vigorously than the Boston players" and the band played "Tessie" over and over the

final six innings of the game, but with the Athletics holding a 6–2 lead after six innings, it wasn't looking good for the Red Sox. They nudged the score up to 6–5, but it was "Murphy's Muff" that cost Philadelphia the game in the ninth as two runners scored while the A's third baseman watched Wagner's high infield fly ball come down—and tick off the side of his glove.

April 12, 1916—Boston 2, Philadelphia 1
Babe Ruth got the first of his league-leading 41 starts in 1916, pitching for the reigning World Champions through 8⅓. The Sox scored single runs in the sixth and seventh off reliever Bullet Joe Bush. There were just nine hits in the game, five by Boston and four by the visitors.

April 21, 1921—Boston 1, Washington 0
It was, as the *Globe*'s James C. O'Leary confidently predicted when the season was just a few days old, "as fine a game of baseball as will be played this season." Sad Sam Jones started for the Sox and held the Senators to just two hits. He also knocked in the lone run of the game in the bottom of the second inning, on a freaky combination of events. McInnis doubled, but was then tagged out on his way to third base on a grounder. The Senators let a weak roller trail along the third base line, but it stopped unexpectedly in fair territory. Then Jones hit another ball right down the line, harder. This one hit the bag and eluded the third baseman on the bounce, letting Everett Scott score on the play. It was a crisp error-free affair that, from start to finish, only required 77 minutes to play to completion.

April 20, 1946—Boston 2, Philadelphia 1
"Pesky Steals Show." After three straight road wins to start the season, the Sox came home and opened before the "largest American League opening day attendance in Boston history." Tex Hughson allowed the Athletics seven hits but just one third-inning run. Philadelphia's Dick Fowler only allowed two hits—the first run came in the first without benefit of a hit when Johnny Pesky scored, running home from second base as the A's fell just short of completing a double play. In the bottom of the ninth, Pesky homered just 10 feet to the left of the right-field foul pole and maybe three rows deep. That made it 2–1 Red Sox and the score held.

April 18, 1952—Boston 5, Philadelphia 4 (10)
The Athletics led 3–0 after five, but Boston scored once in the sixth and tied what had become a 4–1 game with three runs in the bottom of the ninth. A walk and a single set it up for Clyde Vollmer to win it in the bottom of the 10th; his one-out single to left brought home Faye Throneberry with the winning run.

April 8, 10, and 11, 1969—Sox start the 1969 season with three extra-inning games, each one longer than the one before
Opening Day, April 8, 1969, was the first game of a comeback for Tony Conigliaro. After striking out in his first major league at-bat since his beaning in '76, Tony C worked a walk, singled, flied out deep, homered in the 10th to re-tie the game, and then walked and came around to score the winning run two innings later. Bases loaded, 12th inning, no one out, Russ Gibson flied to Rettenmund in right field, but it wasn't deep enough. Dalton Jones pinch-hit and hit the ball to Rettenmund again, but this time it was deeper into right and Tony scored. Juan Pizarro retired the side for the Red Sox. Boston 5, Baltimore 4 (12 innings).

In an interesting side note, Fred Wenz had come in to relieve back in the 10th, after Sparky Lyle had given up a two-run home run to Frank Robinson, which had re-tied the game, and then Rettenmund had doubled after the homer. Wenz walked Brooks Robinson intentionally to fill the empty base at first, and then got Davey Johnson to loft a pop up to Scott. At this point in his brief career, Wenz had pitched in two seasons for the Sox without ever letting an opposing batter hit a fair ball off him. His first major league appearance was for Boston on June 4, 1968. He worked one full inning, walking two but striking out three. No one had hit a fair ball off him in '68, since that was his one and only appearance. Since he didn't throw the 11th inning of this 1969 opener, he'd seen his second stint in the majors also end without a ball hit into fair territory. It was a record that wouldn't last.

The second game of 1969 ran even longer—13 innings instead of 12. This time Baltimore came out on top, 2–1, after nine innings of scoreless ball. Ray Culp and Mike Cuellar both threw the first 10 frames, despite a 35-minute rain delay. The Boston loss was blamed on a bad umpiring call. Frank Robinson had led off for the hometown O's with a double right down the right field line—according to umpire Emmett Ashford. The close call infuriated Dick Williams and the Red Sox, and proved fatal when Boog Powell singled in Robinson as soon as play resumed.

The Boston teams moved on to Cleveland, and the innings ran even higher—first 12 innings, then 13 innings, and on April 11, the third game of the season ran to 16 full frames. This time, Boston came out on top when pinch-hitter George Thomas dribbled a little squib so slowly to second that the Indians couldn't pull off the double play that could have closed out the top of the 16th, and a run scored. Cleveland's Larry Brown missed hitting a ball out by three inches; it hit the top of the wall and bounced back in play, and Brown was held to two bases. Three strikes later, the game was over. The Indians had men in scoring position in the 10th, 11th, 12th, 13th, and 16th but never once scored since way back in the second inning. Final score, 2–1 Boston. For the third game in a row, questionable umpiring plagued the game, this time including a called strike on a pitchout!

After 41 innings in three games, the Red Sox were anticipating an 18-inning game for the season's fourth game. It didn't happen. It took two games to play out the next 18 innings.

Note: for what it's worth, which is practically nothing, it wasn't until the fourth game of the 2007 exhibition season that the Red Sox played a game in less than 10 innings.

April 6, 1973—Boston 15, New York 5

In the first major league game to feature the designated hitter, New York's Ron Blomberg earned a run batted in his first time up by not hitting. He took a bases-loaded walk, part of a three-run top of the first for the Yankees. Blomberg ended the game 1-for-3, while Boston's DH Orlando Cepeda went (ahem) 0-for-6. But Yaz hit a homer in the bottom of the first, and 1972 rookie of the year Carlton Fisk drove in six runs on the strength of a two-run home run, and a grand slam. With a double and a hit-by-pitch, Fisk scored four times. The Sox hammered out 20 hits and won with ease. Three games later, they were 4–0 on the season, each win earned at the expense of the Yankees.

April 14, 1978—Boston 5, Texas 4 (10)

After a 3–3 road start, Boston opened at home, but gave up a run to Texas in the second and another in the third. They evened it up, only to see the Rangers score again, one in the seventh and one in the eighth. Butch Hobson homered in the bottom of the eighth and Jim Rice singled in Jerry Remy to tie it again. Dennis Eckersley pitched through 9⅔, relieved by Dick Drago—who promptly threw a wild pitch putting two Rangers in scoring position. He buckled down and struck out Toby Harrah. Hobson singled to lead off the 10th, took second on a sacrifice bunt, took third on another ground out, and finally scored on Rice's second RBI single of the game.

April 26, 1995—Boston 9, Minnesota 0

With the season starting late due to the player strike that had forced cancellation of the 1994 World Series, the Twins came to Boston for the season's first game—on April 26. Aaron Sele threw the first five, and four relievers took one inning apiece, combining to shut out Minnesota on just two hits. In the meantime, the Red Sox feasted on Twins pitching, the seven-run sixth stacking up runs to spare.

April 10, 1998—Boston 9, Seattle 7

One of the most exciting home openers ever came on April 10, 1998. The Sox had already played eight games before their first Fenway game, and had a disappointing 3–5 record. They started New Bedford native Brian Rose against Randy Johnson and the visiting Seattle Mariners. Damon Buford's two-run homer gave the Red Sox the first runs of the game in the bottom of the fourth but Rose got chased in the top of the sixth as Seattle scored three. The Mariners added two in the eighth and two more in the top of the ninth. It was Seattle 7, Boston 2 when reliever Heathcliff Slocumb took over from the Big Unit. A single, a walk, and a double, and Slocumb's day was done. Tony Fossas—another former Red Sox pitcher—walked the one batter he faced. The bases were loaded and future Red Sox pitcher Mike Timlin was brought in. Nomar singled, reducing the gap to 7–4. Timlin hit John Valentin, making it 7–5. There was still nobody out and the bases were still loaded. A sacrifice fly would tie the game. The fourth pitcher, Paul Spoljaric, had to pitch to Mo Vaughn. He did. Mo hit it out—grand slam! Game over. The Red Sox won, 9–7. Immediately after the slam, an inspired control room operator played "Dirty Water" by the Standells, and a new Fenway tradition was born. For the full story on the Red Sox victory anthem, please see the book *Love That Dirty Water*.

Selected Red Sox wins in road openers

April 23, 1919—Boston 10, New York 0

The Yankees had their secret weapon of 1918 starting for them, George Mogridge. The left-hander had started six games against the Red Sox and won every one of them. But come 1919, the World Champions were not to be denied. Carl Mays shut out the Yankees on four hits with his "queer pitching" (*New York Times*), while Babe Ruth kicked off the season for the Red Sox with a two-run home run in the first. Ruth's liner bounced over center fielder Duffy Lewis' shoulder and just kept on going while Ruth chugged around the bases for an inside-the-park home run. Mogridge was down 4–0 after eight, and was left in to suffer six more runs scored against him in the top of the ninth.

Babe Ruth, homered in New York to start the 1919 season.

April 16, 1935—Boston 1, New York 0

Opening the season for the Red Sox was newly-acquired starter Wes Ferrell who, pitching to his batterymate brother Rick Ferrell, held the Yankees to just two hits—one in the fourth and one in the seventh. Lefty Gomez pitched brilliantly, too, the only Red Sox run coming in the top of the sixth after Billy Werber doubled. A bad pickoff throw allowed Werber to take third. Gomez struck out Boston's Carl Reynolds, but Bill Dickey dropped the third strike and had to throw to first. Werber tore home and scored under the return throw to the plate.

April 17, 1936—Boston 8, New York 0

On his way to the seventh of nine seasons in which he led the league in earned-run average, Lefty Grove, pitching to Rick Ferrell, held the Yankees to just two hits—one in the fifth and one in the seventh. Both singles were provided by one Lou Gehrig. Former Red Sox pitcher Red Ruffing took a beating, tagged for all eight Red Sox runs.

April 16, 1940—Boston 1, Washington 0

The spring after completing the ninth of the nine seasons in which he led the league in earned-run average, Lefty Grove held the Senators to just two hits—one in the eighth and then another in the eighth. Grove had thrown a perfect game for the first seven innings, faltered in the eighth, but held on to the shutout. In doing so, he spoiled an excellent effort by Washington's Dutch Leonard. Leonard walked Doerr to lead off the second. On a comebacker, he had to throw to first as Doerr took second. Desautels popped up to Rick Ferrell, who was catching for the Senators. Grove was up and the lifetime .148 batter hit a hot drive off Jimmy Bloodworth's glove that allowed Doerr to score the game's only run.

April 22, 1943—Boston 1, Philadelphia 0

Philadelphia's Jesse Flores held the Red Sox to just two hits before a small Shibe Park Opening Day crowd of just 4,553. Red Sox rightfielder Pete Fox's fourth-inning double set him up to take third on Bobby Doerr's sacrifice and then score on Johnny Lazor's infield grounder. Johnny Peacock singled for the only other Boston hit. Tex Hughson allowed three hits, but no runs—though he flirted with disaster by walking the bases full in the bottom of the eighth before securing the third out on an easy ground ball hit back to the mound.

April 16, 1964—Boston 4, New York 3 (11)

The Red Sox opened up an early 3–0 lead off Whitey Ford, then gave back two in the bottom of the third but Bill Monbouquette otherwise held firm through 6⅓. Dick Radatz gave up the tying run in the bottom of the eighth, but won it in the 11th when Boston catcher Bob Tillman hit a one-out triple and pinch-runner Roman Mejias scored on Ford's wild pitch. Two K's and a groundout later, Radatz had his first win of the year. He'd go on to win 16 games, all in relief.

April 6, 1969—Boston 5, Baltimore 4 (12)

It was Tony Conigliaro's first game in a year and a half since his August 1967 beaning. The game was tied 2–2 and went into extra innings. Conig hit a two-run homer in the top of the 10th. But the Orioles tied it back up. Tony led off the 12th with a walk, moved to second on Scott's single, to third on Petrocelli's walk, and scored two batters later on Dalton Jones' sacrifice fly.

April 11, 1975—Boston 6, Baltimore 5 (12)

Capping their first road game of the year, Carl Yastrzemski hit a home run in the top of the 12th, giving the Red Sox a 6–5 win over the Orioles. Three innings of scoreless relief earned Diego Segui the win, after starter Rick Wise had gone nine. The very next day, Reggie Cleveland pitched 12 innings for the Red Sox and got a 2–1 win when Boston scored in the top of the 13th. Dick Drago saved the game.

April 4, 2000—Boston 2, Seattle 0

Pedro Martinez pitched a two-hit gem, just a third-inning single by Carlos Guillen and a fourth-inning single by John Olerud in the hits column. Pedro struck out 11 and walked two, and turned it over to Derek Lowe after seven. The Sox scored once on an RBI single by Troy O'Leary in the sixth and an RBI single by Jose Offerman in the seventh. Boston then lost its next four games, until Pedro pitched once again.

March 25, 2008—Boston 6, Oakland 5 (10 innings)

One couldn't actually get from Boston to Tokyo by road. That point settled, the 6–5 win in 10 brought the Red Sox record in Opening Day extra-inning games to 3–9–1. Daisuke Matsuzaka stood to gain the win when he left, but Kyle Snyder's gopher ball allowed the win to ultimately go to fellow Japanese native Hideki Okajima.

First game losses

Sadly, the Sox lost some Opening Day affairs. While we don't want to dwell on these disappointing days, we will point out that the Red Sox lost their first games of 1986, 2004, and 2007 (as well as 1904 and 1915). The other seven opening games of pennant-winning years saw Red Sox victories. Some of the first game losses are presented here.

April 14, 1906—New York 1, Boston 0

Cy Young pitched a 12-inning gem but Jack Chesbro pitched a better one. Despite giving up 11 hits, Chesbro didn't let up even one run. A double and a single plated New York's winning run in the bottom of the 12th. It was the first of 105 losses for Boston that year.

April 10, 1913—Philadelphia 10, Boston 9

The reigning World Champions put up a fight but having Smoky Joe Wood (34–5 in 1912) battered out of the box after giving up seven runs in five innings, they had some ground to make up. Facing a 10–5 deficit, Boston scored four times in the bottom of the sixth, but neither team scored after that. The run that made the difference scored on a weird play involving Athletics batters on the basepaths and an errant throw when one of the baserunners needlessly tried to retreat all the way from second to first.

April 14, 1925—Philadelphia 9, Boston 8 (10)

After six innings, the Red Sox led 6–0, but the pitching quartet of Ferguson, Ross, Wingfield, and Kallio gave up eight runs while the Sox scored just once more in the eighth and once in the ninth on solo homers by Flagstead and Harris. Tied in the 10th, Rudy Kallio allowed three hits and lost the game.

April 13, 1926—New York 12, Boston 11

New York had leads of 4–0, 5–1, and even 11–1, but then had to hold on as the Red Sox kept scoring—two in the fifth, five in the sixth, one in the seventh, and two in the eighth. They crept to within one of tying, but couldn't score in the bottom of the ninth.

April 11, 1932—Washington 1, Boston 0 (10)

President Hoover threw out the first ball, but left after seven scoreless innings. The Red Sox singled twice in the top of the 10th, but stuck with starting pitcher Danny MacFayden—who struck out on three pitches. MacFayden walked Buddy Myer in the bottom of the 10th and then lost the game on Heinie Manush's long double.

April 17, 1934—Washington 6, Boston 5 (11)

In the bottom of the 11th, Joe Cronin doubled, and the Senators loaded the bases with two outs. A "dinky grounder" to third base by Dave Harris brought home the winning run when Bucky Walters couldn't get a grip on the ball and the tiebreaker scored.

April 17, 1942—New York 1, Boston 0

34-year-old rookie Oscar Judd (he'd only thrown 12⅓ innings in 1941) threw a whale of a game, a five-hitter, allowing just one run in the bottom of the fourth on a single, an error, and a single. Tiny Bonham threw a six-hit shutout.

April 18, 1948—Philadelphia 5, Boston 4 (11) (first game)
Philadelphia 4, Boston 2 (second game)

A morning/afternoon dual admission Patriots Day doubleheader saw the Athletics take two from the hometown Boston Red Sox behind the pitching of two war heroes—Phil Marchildon and Lou Brissie. The first game took 11 innings, Philadelphia scoring twice in the top of the

11th and Boston coming back with just one in the bottom. Had the Sox won either game, they wouldn't have faced a single-game playoff for the pennant.

April 18, 1950—New York 15, Boston 10

The Red Sox were cruising, with a 9–0 lead after four innings and the Fenway faithful were feeling giddy—and then the roof fell in. The Yankees got four in the top of the sixth—not that big a deal—but then added nine more runs in the eighth, and that spelled doom for Walt Masterson, who'd only ever retired one man in relief of Parnell. By the time it was all over, the hometown crowd was crushed.

April 17, 1951—New York 5, Boston 0

The Yankees' Jackie Jensen hit a two-run homer in the third inning, all they needed as Vic Raschi limited the Red Sox to six singles. Jensen doubled to lead off the sixth and scored on the first run batted in of Mickey Mantle's career. Bill Wight, Ellis Kinder, and Mickey McDermott pitched for Boston.

April 18, 1960—Washington 10, Boston 1

Batting fifth, Ted Williams hit an Opening Day home run in the second inning, but the rest of his teammates weren't able to solve Camilo Pascual, who threw a three-hit shutout as the Senators pounded Tom Sturdivant and Al Worthington for 10 runs at Griffith Stadium.

April 12, 1966—Baltimore 5, Boston 4 (13)

It's almost too painful to write up. Jim Lonborg was pitching his fourth inning in relief. There were two outs, but a single and two walks (the first one being intentional) loaded the bases—and Lonborg balked. The go-ahead run crossed the plate.

April 11, 1974—Baltimore 7, Boston 6 (11)

When the Orioles scored three times in the top of the fourth, it was tied 3–3. They went up 4–3 in the top of the seventh, and fell behind 5–4 in the bottom of the seventh. They re-tied it in the eighth and the game went into extras, 5–5. Baltimore scored once in the top of the 10th on an error and a double, but Juan Beniquez tied it up once more with a home run. In the top of the 11th, Baltimore scored yet again on a force play. The Sox got two men on base, but failed to score.

April 1, 2002—Toronto 12, Boston 11

Both teams started scoring early: Toronto scored 3, 4, and 1 in the first three frames, and the Red Sox scored 1, 2, and 3—and added 5 in the fourth. Pedro Martinez was charged with eight runs through three innings, one of the worst outings of his career—and not the way he wanted to start the season. Toronto came back with three in the top of the fifth off Darren Oliver and it was 11–11, where it remained through eight. Ugueth Urbina started the ninth and (after one out) gave up a walk and a single, suffered a double steal, and then issued an intentional walk. A sacrifice fly broke the tie, and Boston failed to score.

Neither a win nor a loss—April 14, 1910: Boston 4, New York 4 (14)

The road opener in 1910 ended in a 4–4 tie with New York, in a game called due to darkness after 14 innings. Before 25,000 fans—said to be the largest at the time to have seen the Highlanders play—the two teams battled until they could play no more. Cicotte and Wood each pitched seven innings, facing off against New York's Vaughn, who threw all 14. For a game called on account of darkness, it's perhaps ironic that the two New York runs that tied it up scored during a seventh-inning rally just after rightfielder Harry Niles discarded the sunglasses he'd worn for the first six. He misplayed a liner and New York was able to build on the miscue.

Last game of the year

For what it's worth, the team has played 61 of its final games at home and only 46 away. Of the ones at home, they have a 34–27 record. Of the road games that closed a season, the record is 14–31–1. Mathematically-inclined readers may notice that, overall, the record stands at 48–58–1. This listing only tabulates the absolute last game of the year—in a doubleheader, it ignores the first game and only counts the second.

Sox vs. Yanks opening days

Over the 108 years of the Boston franchise, there have been 20 times that Boston kicked off the campaign playing in New York, the most recent in 2005.

When the league comprised just seven other teams, this happened more frequently; in the first half of the years of Red Sox existence (1901 through 1951), Boston played their first game of the year in New York some 14 times. Since that time, there have only been five such occasions. And there has only been one time since 1970: 1992's Opening Day (a 4–3 loss).

In the 20 times the Sox started the season in New York, Boston has won but six of them and lost 13 times. The 1910 opener ended in a 4–4 tie.

The first seven times the two teams met in an Opening Day, the venue was in New York. Finally, in 1924, Boston hosted New York for the first game of the year.

When the true Opening Day was held in Boston, with the New Yorkers the visitors, the results have been more even. Unlike the 20 times the two teams met in New York, there have only been eight occasions they started in Boston. Boston lost the first two of those (1924 and 1926), but has won the last three times (1971, 1973, and 1985). Over all eight games, each team has won four times.

Then there are the years when both teams hosted the other for their respective openers. That was the case in 2005, but the last time it had happened was 1973. Boston won Fenway's Opening Day, beating the Yankees 15–5, then both teams met in the Yankee Stadium opener and the Red Sox won that one, too, 3–1. In 1970, Boston also won the two Opening Days. Prior to 2005, those are the only two years since 1935 that the teams have swapped Opening Days. In earlier years, this happened in 1906, 1912, 1917, 1919, 1923, 1924, 1926, 1929, 1931, 1933, and 1935. It happened 11 times in the first 35 years, then just two times in the following 68 seasons.

The earliest Opening Day in the rivalry was 2005's April 3 start, which the Yankees took handily. Prior to 2005, the earliest was April 6 (both 1971 and 1973). The latest date for an Opening Day was, perhaps not surprisingly, the war year of 1943, when Opening Day was on April 27.

Cumulative run totals for true Opening Day games are: New York 165, Boston 148. There was the 4–4 tie, as noted. There were nine shutouts—five by the Yankees and four by the Red Sox. None of the games were extra-inning affairs, other than the 4–4 tie on Opening Day in 1910, which ran to 14 innings before being called due to darkness.

SPECIAL DAYS

Patriots Day games

The morning baseball game on Patriots Day is a unique aspect of Boston baseball, the one fixed date on the American League schedule: the Red Sox have to be at home on Patriots Day for an 11:05 a.m. game timed to end just about the time the Boston Marathon runners race through Kenmore Square two blocks away (and about one mile from the finish line). Patriots Day was always celebrated on the anniversary of the first battles of the American Revolution in Lexington and Concord on April 19, 1775. Since 1894, it is a full state holiday both in Massachusetts and Maine. With the decision to celebrate many holidays on Mondays, since 1969, the actual date of Patriots Day has been celebrated on the third Monday in April. The Boston Marathon has been run on Patriots Day since 1897. Boston's National League team, the Boston Beaneaters, lost a home opener that day to the Philadelphia Phillies, 6–5, but went on to win the 1897 pennant. Four of the 1897 Beaneaters later played for the Boston Americans: Jimmy Collins, Charlie Hickman, Ted Lewis, and Chick Stahl. Hugh Duffy, Fred Lake, Chick Stahl, and Jimmy Collins managed the Americans at one time or another.

After the Americans launched their franchise in 1901, the two Boston teams found themselves competing for the lucrative Patriots Day gate. In 1901, the AL season didn't even start until April 26, so it was a non-issue, but in 1902, the Americans' home opener was scheduled on the 19th and the Beaneaters had a home doubleheader the same day. This was three ballgames held on the two league parks, separated only by a railroad line—a little much. In 1903, the Americans scheduled an even earlier start to get a jump on the Nationals, playing a 10:00 a.m. game as the first of two separate admission games (with the Marathon finish in between). They quadrupled the attendance at the Beaneaters' first game and beat them more than 7-to-1 in the afternoon affairs, some 27,658 to 3,867.

Starting in 1904, the two teams worked out a schedule more or less alternating games from year to year with the Americans in town on the even-numbered years. On April 18 of that year, the day before Patriots Day, John I. Taylor bought the team he would later dub the Red Sox, and over 28,000 fans crammed into the Huntington Avenue Grounds to see the Americans take two from Washington.

Of course, when the Boston Braves (previously the Beaneaters) left Boston, this was no longer an issue and from 1953 onward, the Red Sox have almost always played at home on the odd-numbered years as well. There have been rainouts, of course, as in 1955, 1965, and 1967, but the last time the Red Sox were not at home to play on Patriots Day was in 1958; the Marathon was run on the 19th, but the Red Sox were out of town, losing to the Senators in our nation's capitol, 4–3. The 1959 game was a nice one, a 5–4 win in the bottom of the 12th when the inning's leadoff hitter, Frank Malzone, homered off reliever Ryne Duren of the Yankees.

Other than the rainouts, the Red Sox have played at home on Patriots Day every year since 1960, except for the year the players were on strike, 1995. The games are typically held at 11:05. With the increased popularity of Red Sox baseball in the aftermath of 1967's Impossible Dream team, Patriots Day doubleheaders were discontinued from that point forward.

The morning game is the only morning game on the major league schedule. The Players Association forced it to start at noon for one year, in 1987, but by the next year they agreed to revert to the customary 11:05 start. With the Boston Marathon start time moved up to an earlier hour, the 2007 game was scheduled to begin at 10:05, but rain delays pushed it back for a little more than two hours.

Ted Williams, Dick Gernert, and Jim Rice each have three Patriots Day home runs, leading the team in that department. Cy Young leads all pitchers with four wins in Patriots Day games.

Thanks to David Nevard and to Graham Knight of www.redsoxconnection.com for assistance in this section.

Friday the 13th games

There used to be suggestions that the Red Sox were cursed. Remember those days? Something about a Bambino? Of course, looking at the injury reports for the 2006 Red Sox, one might well come to the conclusion that there was indeed a curse. One thing we can put to rest, though, is any notion that Friday the 13th adversely affected play on the field.

The Red Sox have played 73 games that fell on a Friday the 13th and they won 44, lost 29, and one game (in 1907) ended in a tie. In all, the Red Sox scored 384 runs while surrendering 312.

At home, the Sox record is 27–17. Its record on the road is 17–12.

The longest streaks are eight wins in a row (September 1991 through July 2001) and three losses in a row (this happened twice, once in the very early 1940s and once from 1969 to 1973).

There were 12 shutouts, split equally into six wins and six losses. In one-run games, Boston won 10 and lost seven. They played five doubleheaders and split all five of them.

There was never an opening day on April 13 nor has there been a post-season game on a Friday the 13th. However, the Red Sox did clinch the pennant once on a Friday the 13th, with their 1–0 win over Cleveland on September 13, 1946.

Games played on Friday the 13th

September 1901, at WAS, won first game 5–1, lost second 5–3

June 1902, at CHI, lost 9–0

May 1904, won 2–1 over Detroit

July 1906, loss 8–1 to St. Louis Browns

Sept 1907, 6–6 tie in Philadelphia

August 1909, won 7–2 over Cleveland

May 1910, won 8–1 over St. Louis

June 1913, won 7–6 over St. Louis in 13 innings

August 1915, won 3–2 over Washington

July 1917, lost 1–0 in Detroit

June 1919, won 6–1 over Chicago

August 1920, at PHI, lost 3–1, then won 7–0

May 1921, won 16–8 at Chicago

July 1923, at DET, won 6–4

June 1924, at CLE, won 8–3

May 1927, at CLE, won 7–0

April 1928, lost 6–4 to Cleveland

June 1930, lost 1–0 at STL in 11 innings

July 1934, won 7–2 over St. Louis

September 1935, won 13–4 over St. Louis, then lost 4–2

August 1937, lost 3–0 at Washington

May 1938, won 10–0 over Washington

September 1940, lost 1–0 at Cleveland

August 1943, lost 3–2 at Chicago

July 1945, at NY, lost 4–2, then won 8–4

September 1946, won 1–0 at Cleveland—clinching the pennant

June 1947, won 5–3 over Chicago

August 1948, at Washington, won 6–2

July 1951, lost in Chicago in 19 innings, 5–4

August 1954, lost in New York, 8–2

May 1955, won 4–3 over KC

July 1956, won 5–4 over CHI

September 1957, lost 13–6 to Cleveland

June 1958, won 9–3 over KC

July 1962, won 11–10 at KC in 15 innings

September 1963, won 7–3 at KC

August 1965, won 3–2 over CHI

May 1966, lost 4–1 in California

September 1968, won 3–0 over Minnesota

July 1969, lost 3–1 to Oakland

August 1971, lost 5–1 vs. KC

July 1973, lost 4–1 to Texas

September 1974, won 8–5 in Milwaukee in 10 innings

June 1975, won 10–4 at KC, then lost 6–5

August 1976, lost 2–0 at Oakland

May 1977, won 7–5 at Seattle

July 1979, lost to Texas, 12–7

June 1980, won over CAL, 3–0

August 1982, won 5–2 over BAL

April 1984, lost 13–9 to Detroit

July 1984, won 9–5 at Seattle

September 1985, lost 6–3 at Milwaukee

June 1986, won 5–3 over Milwaukee

May 1988, won 14–8 over Seattle

April 1990, lost 9–5 to Milwaukee

July 1990, lost 5–3 to KC

September 1991, won 5–4 at NY

August 1993, won 5–3 over Toronto

May 1994, won 5–3 over Toronto

September 1996, won 9–5 over Chicago

June 1998, won 8–4 over New York Mets

August 1999, won 11–6 over Seattle

April 2001, won 3–2 over NY Yankees in 10
    innings

July 2001, won 3–1 over NY Mets at NY

September 2002, lost to Baltimore, 8–3

June 2003, won 4–3 over Houston

August 2004, lost 8–7 to Chicago

May 2005, lost to Seattle, 14–7

April 2007, won 10–1 over Los Angeles Angels
    of Anaheim

Caught four fall balls at one game

Luck, or what? Many of us have been to hundreds of ballgames and never caught a foul ball. Two friends took Jonathan Plaut, a litigator in Boston, to a Sox game against the Blue Jays on July 2, 2005. They sat three seats away from the backstop screen, on the third base side. During the course of the game, Plaut caught four foul balls. All were pitched by David Wells, all were off Toronto's bats. Mr. Plaut commented for *Red Sox Threads*, explaining, "I fielded them all cleanly without a glove and without dropping any of them. There were no struggles for the balls."

How'd you like to win a bear from the State of Maine?

Luck, or what? August 14, 1955 was State of Maine Day at Fenway Park. Janet Zauchin of Bessemer, Alabama recalls the time that her husband Norm Zauchin won a black bear named Homer because he hit the first home run for the Red Sox in the game. In fact, he hit two homers—but only won one Homer. The Zauchins didn't take Homer home, but requested that he be shipped to a zoo in Birmingham, Alabama, not far from their home. Homer lived in the zoo until he eventually expired of old age.

The Boston Red Sox of Maine?

These are times when we have a team named the Los Angeles Angels of Anaheim. It might have even been more accurate for the Red Sox to have named their team the Boston Red Sox of the State of Maine. Even before they were the Red Sox, the team was at its inception organized and incorporated under the laws of the State of Maine. On January 22, 1901 plans were put in motion when Ban Johnson and Charles Somers met at Young's Hotel with the architect for the planned grounds at Huntington Avenue and Michael J. Moore, the attorney for the new franchise. "It will be organized under the laws of Maine," reported the *Chicago Tribune*. One of Boston's biggest fans, Arthur "Hi-Hi" Dixwell placed an order for 100 season tickets.

Kind of gives a different meaning to State of Maine Day at Fenway Park. Of course, Maine used to be part of Massachusetts and only became a state of its own in the year 1820.

It does seem as though the Red Sox remained in Maine for a considerable portion of its existence. In one of its incarnations, the Boston American League Base Ball Company was organized at Portland, Maine on July 25, 1923 and was only dissolved and terminated on May 2, 1960 by Justice Walter M. Tapley, Jr. of the state's Supreme Judicial Court.

Doubleheaders discontinued

The only doubleheaders that happen these days come about due to postponements in the schedule.

The last time the Red Sox swept a doubleheader was October 2, 2004 and they beat Baltimore at Oriole Park by identical scores, 7–5 and 7–5.

May 1 that year was a double defeat, though, as Boston lost two games to the visiting Texas Rangers, 4–3 and 8–5. Just two days before, the Sox had taken two from Tampa Bay, 4–0 and 7–3.

HELLO/GOODBYE—SOME MEMORABLE DEBUTS AND DEPARTURES

Debuts

Some of the more interesting Red Sox debuts by players are presented here.

July 6, 1909: Red Sox rookie **Larry Pape** made his debut with a 2–0 win over the crippled Washington Nationals, in the second game of a doubleheader sweep. Of the seven Sox pitchers who threw shutouts in their first start, Pape was the only one to do so at home (in this case, Boston's Huntington Avenue Grounds). No one has ever done it at Fenway Park.

April 12, 1913: **Dutch Leonard** debuted with the Red Sox, entering the game in the second inning, in relief, and giving up just one run. Leonard, who led the league with a 0.96 ERA the following year, had forsaken a career in music to play baseball. The Leonard family of Fresno was a musical family, each playing different instruments. Hubert ("Dutch" to his baseball friends) "put over all the tricks of the trap drummer" according to the *Los Angeles Times*, and had been considering professional orchestra work when he hooked on as a ballplayer.

June 4, 1915: Red Sox second baseman **Bill Rodgers** had a most unusual debut—pinch-running for Tris Speaker in the first inning of the ballgame, then leaving the lineup only to return pinch-hitting in the eighth inning for Ernie Shore. Speaker was beaned and Chicago manager Pants Rowland allowed Rodgers in as a courtesy runner. He was left stranded on the basepaths. In the bottom of the eighth, down by a 2–0 score, Pinch Thomas (hitting for Hick Cady) singled with no outs. With the pitcher Shore due up, manager Bill Carrigan brought Rodgers into the game a second time. Rodgers drew a base on balls, but the Red Sox failed to score. Rodgers had come to the Red Sox in an odd way. He'd played for Cleveland earlier in the year, but been released to Portland in the Pacific Coast League. Not pleased, he refused to report and approached Boston's Carrigan, asking for a job. He was told he had to get his unconditional release first. Portland told him he could purchase his own release for $2,500, and wired the Red Sox that they could have him on a free trial if they promised to pay the Beavers should they keep him. The Sox said they didn't want him, but nonetheless wound up with him just eight days later. They sold him to Cincinnati on July 8.

September 17, 1934: **George Edward "Lefty" Hockette** made his major league debut a memorable one, pitching a no-hitter through seven innings in St. Louis, as the Red Sox built up a 3–0 lead. A single by Grube in the eighth and another by Bejma in the ninth proved the only hits, and Hockette had himself a two-hit 3–0 shutout. He was one of just seven Sox starters to shut out an opponent in their debut game. The others were: Rube Kroh, Larry Pape, Buck O'Brien, Dave Ferriss, Dave Morehead, and Billy Rohr.

August 13, 1944: 27-year-old rookie pitcher **Rex Cecil** flew all the way cross-country from San Diego—a bit of an ordeal in those days (and now often an ordeal again)—and stepped right into his major league debut. He'd never seen a major league game, and never even been in a major league ballpark. Boston scored a run in the bottom of the ninth, and tied the game at 6–6. Cecil arrived at Fenway Park, was fitted for a uniform, and shown to the mound. He got out of a bases-loaded jam, and kept the Browns scoreless for four innings until Bobby Doerr hit a home run to win it in the bottom of the 13th.

April 29, 1945: In his major league debut, Mississippi's **Boo Ferriss** of the Red Sox survived a horrific first inning. Every one of his first 10 pitches missed the strike zone. In all, he threw

17 first-inning balls and loaded the bases, but escaped without surrendering a run, and then proceeded to whitewash the A's with a 2–0 shutout. He was no slouch at the plate, either, hitting 3-for-3. Ferriss threw a shutout his second game, too, against the Yankees, and got almost halfway into his third, against the Tigers, before giving up his first run. He started his career throwing 22 consecutive scoreless innings. He won his first eight decisions in the majors, beating every opponent in the league the first time he faced them.

April 22, 1946: Local boy makes good. Boston's **Eddie Pellagrini** made his major league debut in the fifth inning after Johnny Pesky was beaned by a Sid Hudson fast ball. Pelly came up in Pesky's slot in the lineup in the seventh inning and hit a game-winning home run over the left-field Wall in his first at-bat. The Red Sox beat Washington, 5–4. Pellagrini recalled that Ted Williams congratulated him, but warned, "Eddie, that's the worst thing you could have done because now they're going to pitch you like they pitch me!"

It was sure a good way to make an impression on your new team. June 15, 1947: **Jake Jones**, in his first game with his new team (the Red Sox) beat up on his old team (the White Sox). His first appearance for Boston came in a doubleheader. Jones homered in the first game, a solo shot that helped Boston beat Chicago, 7–3. In the second game, he came up with two outs and the bases loaded in the bottom of the ninth, the game a 4–4 tie. Bam! Slam! Thank you, Jake.

August 13, 1955: **Jim Pagliaroni** made his major league debut, at age 17 the youngest player to ever appear for the Red Sox. When the Senators built up a 17–6 lead over the Sox, he was put in to spell Sammy White behind the plate and caught a couple of innings. He never did get an at-bat, but he picked up an RBI with a sacrifice fly. It was more than five years later before he appeared in another major league game, but ended up playing 11 years in major league ball.

September 17, 1955: **Frank Malzone** debuted as a pinch-runner in his first game, and was left on base. The first time he got a chance to bat was in the September 21 doubleheader; he hit into a force play his first time up—but then hit safely six times before the day was done (though the Sox lost both games to Baltimore).

April 15, 1959: It was quite a debut for Red Sox rookie pitcher **Jerry Casale**, who held the Senators to three runs on seven hits, and in the bottom of the sixth inning hit a Russ Kemmerer curve ball for a three-run homer all the way over Fenway's left-center field Wall and screen, landing atop a Lansdowne Street building. Casale had strong feelings about what he saw as the anti-Italian prejudice of Joe Cronin and Mike Higgins. About Higgins, he noted, "I don't like to say things like this, but the son of a bitch was always drunk. And he'd never talk to you." Casale felt that Frank Malzone would have come to the majors a lot earlier, Billy Consolo deserved more of a chance to play, and both Ken Aspromonte and himself never got the shot they merited. (See Casale's comments in *Red Sox Nation*.)

April 13, 1963: It's **Dave Morehead**'s debut and he shut down the Senators, 3—0. The last time any Red Sox rookie debuted with a shutout was Dave "Boo" Ferriss back in 1945.

April 17, 1964: It was a Fenway fundraiser for the John F. Kennedy Memorial Library, and also the major league debut for 19-year-old **Tony Conigliaro**. He pounced on the very first pitch he saw, a fastball from Chicago's Joel Horlen, and drove it over the Wall, over the screen, and out of the park. Manager Johnny Pesky was pleased, and so was 91-year-old John Dooley, witnessing his 71st Opening Day at a Boston baseball game, a record pre-dating the Red Sox back into the 19th century. Jack Lamabe pitched his first complete game, his third major league start, a 4–1 win.

May 4, 1965: The only major league appearance of **Bill "Rudy" Schlesinger** came in a pinch-hitting role on this day. Heading for the on-deck circle, he stumbled coming up the dugout steps, couldn't get the doughnut off his bat, then dropped a little ball a few feet in front of the plate for an easy out: "It just went off home plate, and it went up real high and he got me by about a half a step at first base."

May 9, 1965: Five days later, **Jerry Moses** had his debut, pinch-hitting in the first game of two against the Indians. He struck out. Second time up, May 25, he pinch-hit and homered. Third time up, he pinch-hit for Dick Radatz. He made an out to second base. Last time up, he pinch-hit on June 16 with the bases loaded. He struck out. He didn't get into another big league game until three years later. In the end, though, he appeared in 386 games.

April 14, 1967: In his major league debut, rookie **Billy Rohr** sustained a no-hitter against the Yankees, in New York, for 8⅔ innings. Yankees catcher Elston Howard singled to right-center field to spoil the no-no, but Rohr still had himself a superb 3–0 one-hit shutout against Whitey Ford. Reggie Smith scored the only run needed with his leadoff home run. Rohr had lost a no-hitter on the final pitch of a June 24, 1965 seven-inning game, pitching for Boston's Toronto farm club. Rohr had thrown 10 no-hitters in high school and sandlot ball.

June 4, 1968: After pitching in both 1968 and 1969 for the Red Sox, righthander **Fred Wenz** still had not yielded even one fair ball, much less a hit. In his June 4, 1968 debut he struck out three of the four batters he faced; the other worked a walk. His second ML appearance was on April 8, 1969 and he was asked to walk Brooks Robinson intentionally to pitch to Davey Johnson, who he retired on a foul popup. Only in the 12th inning of the April 11 game did he allow a fair ball—two of them. After striking out the first two he faced, Tony Horton singled. Then Wenz pitched to four more batters before Lee Maye grounded back to him on the mound.

May 4, 1974: It wasn't quite as bad as Johnny Pesky making four errors in front of 8,000 fans at the first City Series exhibition game during his rookie year, but **Rick Burleson** made three errors in his major league debut. It tied a major league record.

June 28, 1976: He'd appeared in two road games in 1975, but **Butch Hobson** marked his Fenway Park debut with a double off the center-field wall and an inside-the-park home run, helping the Sox win, 12–8, over Baltimore.

September 18, 1977: The Red Sox beat Baltimore 10–4, and part of the reason was **Ted Cox**. It was the 22-year-old's debut, and he not only went 4-for-4 but was in the on-deck circle with a shot at a fifth hit, when Rick Burleson grounded out to end the game. The next day, at Fenway, he singled off New York's Ed Figueroa his first time up. He was second up in the third and singled again—six hits in his first six major league at-bats.

April 12, 1992: Pitcher Matt Young walked Indians leadoff batter Kenny Lofton, who then stole second. As Young struck out Glenallen Hill, Lofton proceeded to steal third. He scored when Luis Rivera committed an error on Carlos Baerga's grounder. The Indians had an early lead, 1–0. In the third inning, Cleveland got another run when Young walked the first two batters. The runner on second moved to third on one force out, and scored on the second. Young was losing the game 2–0, and he hadn't given up a hit. He never did. He threw eight full innings, never allowing the Indians a single hit. The game was in Cleveland, and the Indians had a 2–1 lead after 8½, so there was no need to pitch the bottom of the ninth. Young had thrown a no-hit game and lost. Some years later, Major League Baseball declared that it didn't count as a no-hitter because he only pitched eight innings. Regardless, he pitched the full game and never yielded a hit. Most people would agree that's a no-hitter. "The game's over and they don't have any hits," noted Young. Catcher **John Flaherty** had caught a no-hitter in his major league debut…except, well, MLB said it wasn't one. Even if it was.

May 2, 1995: V for Victory. There had been times that a grand slam accounted for all the runs in a 4–0 win, but Boston's 8–0 defeat of the Yankees was the first time that two grand slams accounted for all the runs in a ballgame. Seton Hall teammates John Valentin (third inning) and Mo Vaughn (fourth inning). All in all, a pleasant debut for Sox pitcher **Vaughn Eshelman**.

July 27, 1999: A six-run fifth helped the Sox overcome a 7–3 deficit and beat the Blue Jays in a wild 11–9 game, in which newcomer Butch Huskey had his Red Sox debut with three hits including a phantom home run ruled a single. Replays clearly showed the ball had hit in the bullpen and bounced back onto the field. Huskey got two shots in the following day—a sixth-inning grand slam and a ninth-inning solo shot in an 8–0 shutout of the Jays.

April 4, 2001: Pitching in his Red Sox debut, **Hideo Nomo** threw a no-hitter. It came in Baltimore, on the second day of the season. Nomo walked three and there was one Red Sox error, but not a single Oriole managed a hit in Camden Yards that day.

April 1, 2002: The Red Sox open at home and host the Blue Jays, who command an early 7–1 lead after 1½ innings. Pedro Martinez lasts but three innings, leaving with an 8–3 deficit. Darren Oliver is tagged for three more, and the score is 11–11 after 4½. Another Darrin, name of Fletcher, has three RBIs in the game, then adds another with a game-winning sacrifice fly in the ninth. 12–11 final, Jays. The game was also marked by the Red Sox debut of slugger **Tony Clark**, who created a wonderful first impression, going 3-for-5 with a home run and three RBIs. In the whole rest of the season, he only hit two more homers and batted just above the Mendoza line, at .207.

June 28, 2003: **Gabe Kapler** had an impressive debut for the Red Sox. Fresh in from the Colorado Rockies, Kapler went 4-for-5 with three RBIs. The next day, June 29, he was 3-for-4 with two homers off Brad Penny and a total of four more RBIs. Add it up: 7-for-9 and seven RBIs in his first two games.

May 8, 2005: The major league debut of pitcher **Cla Meredith** could have been worse, but not much worse. With a depleted pitching staff and a dual-admission doubleheader, the Sox called up Meredith and threw him into the seventh inning of a tie game with two outs and a runner on second. Meredith had risen incredibly fast in the Red Sox system, spending all of 72 hours at AAA. He had never given up a home run at any stage in all of his 42 prior pro appearances. He walked the first batter, and the second, then gave up a grand slam to Seattle's Richie Sexson, and gave up a double to straightaway center before finally getting an out on a fly to left-center. The Red Sox got two back, but lost, 6–2.

September 19, 2005: **Craig Hansen** became the first person to be drafted and reach the major leagues in the year he was drafted. He was selected by Boston in the first round (26th pick) of the 2005 amateur draft, and signed on July 26. Just 55 days later, he pitched the fifth inning of a game at Tropicana Field and retired the side 1–2–3, with two strikeouts.

April 5, 2007: When **Daisuke Matsuzaka** struck out 12 while walking just one, on his way to a 4–1 victory over the Royals at Kauffman Stadium, he became only the fourth pitcher in Red Sox history to whiff 10 or more batters in his first appearance for the ballclub.

Sox pitchers who gave up a home run to the first
batter they faced in the major leagues

It's only happened thrice.

Charlie Mitchell came in to pitch the eighth inning of the August 9, 1984 night game at Arlington Stadium. First Ranger up was first baseman Pete O'Brien, who homered. Mitchell then retired the next three batters. It was one of only two home runs Mitchell ever surrendered—but then again he only ever pitched 18 innings in the major leagues.

Jeff Suppan built a long career in major league ball, but it started with a leadoff homer by Kansas City second baseman Keith Lockhart on July 17, 1995 at Fenway Park. Suppan got out of the inning, and pitched 5⅔ innings but bore the loss as the Royals won the game, 4–3.

Hideki Okajima's came in relief on Opening Day 2007. Taking the ball to throw the bottom of the sixth, he threw his first pitch to Kansas City catcher John Buck—who drove it out of the park.

Monbouquette thrown in holding cell at Fenway,
the day he signs his first contract

"I remember sitting out in the right-field stands at Fenway watching a game with my mom and dad right after I signed. These two guys behind us were swearing and drinking, and they spilled some of the booze on my mother. I looked at my father, he just nodded, and we proceeded to take care of these two guys. The next thing you know two cops came along, and they take my father and I into some kind of holding cell in the bowels of the ballpark. This big cop is trying to pronounce my name, and he keeps getting it wrong. I asked him to please call upstairs to Johnny Murphy, the Sox farm director, and when he still can't pronounce my name I ask if I can talk to him. I get on and say, 'Mr. Murphy, I'm down here in this holding cell with my dad,' and then I tell him what happened. He says, 'I'll be right down,' and we get out. That was my first day with the Red Sox!" *[Boston Braves Historical Association Newsletter, Fall 2003, p. 3]*

How some Sox players first broke into the hits column

It was only in his eighth big league game that **Mike Greenwell** finally got a hit, but every one of his first three hits were home runs. In the top of the 13th inning of the September 25, 1985 game in Toronto, Bill Buckner doubled and Greenwell followed with a homer off John Cerutti. His hit won the game.

The next day, facing Doyle Alexander and with the Sox down 1–0, Mike Easler singled and—after Dave Stapleton struck out—Greenie homered again, another two-run home run. This one also won the ballgame, a 4–1 final.

After three more games, Greenwell had another hit on October 1—a ninth-inning solo home run. This time it made no difference at all, boosting the Sox lead over the Orioles to 10–3. All three hits had been on the road. He had three more hits in Baltimore, but his first hit at Fenway was a homer, too, on October 4. He'd entered the game in the ninth and was walked intentionally in the 10th. The score remained tied. Both teams had scored three times in the 11th. It was in the bottom of the 12th inning, but no one was on base and the Brewers had scored twice in the top of the 12th. When no one else produced, the Sox fell short, 8–7.

As with Greenwell, **Creighton Gubanich** had to wait a bit for his first hit but when it came, it was a big one. Gubanich appeared in two early-season games in 1989, first as a defensive replacement without an at-bat and second as a starting catcher (0-for-3). On May 3, he got his second start and hit a grand slam home run in the top of the first inning in Oakland. He also got hit by a pitch and singled, scoring two runs before being replaced by Jason Varitek later in the game. It was the only home run he ever hit in his brief 18-game major league career.

Late in the 1976 season, **Jack Baker** stepped to the plate for the Red Sox and his first major league hit was a home run into the screen at Fenway. Was this a new "Home Run" Baker in the making? Perhaps so, but this Baker hit a detour somewhere along the way. In 22 other at-bats at the tail end of 1976 and in three more in 1977, this Baker only managed two other hits. The career .115 hitter moved on to another career.

September 27, 1950: In his first major league at-bat, **Jimmy Piersall** stepped into the box in a pinch-hitting role. It was the third inning of the day's second game. Senators pitcher Gene Bearden threw a "baffling knuckle ball…and I was so scared that I threw the bat over the third-base dugout and into the grandstand the first time I ever swung at a ball. Imagine my embarrassment when I found myself standing at the plate without a bat in my hand." Piersall walked over to the on-deck circle and whispered to Bill Goodman, "What do I do now?" Goodman gave his bat to Piersall, who ran the count to 3 and 2 and then singled to right.

Billy Conigliaro was another player whose first hit was a homer. So was his second. They both came in the same game—his third—on April 16, 1969. And, like Mike Greenwell, so was his third, the following day. In the process, he struck out five times, but what the heck. His fourth hit was a mere single, but then he doubled later in the game.

How some of the Sox greats broke in

Cy Young—April 27, 1901

He did have 287 wins in the National League, but in his first start for Boston in the brand-new American League, Cy got slammed. He gave up three runs to Baltimore in the first inning, three more in the third, another two in the fourth, and he finally got himself taken out of the game in the sixth as the Orioles scored three more. The final score was 12–6. He won his second start, three days later, but it wasn't easy, taking 10 full innings and by the score of 8–6. Young had an amazing first three seasons with Boston, winning 93 games (an average of 31 wins per season).

Tris Speaker—September 14, 1907

After Boston dropped the first game of a doubleheader to Philadelphia, they tried out two new acquisitions who'd come to the team from Texas in the same deal: Tris Speaker and George Whiteman. In the eighth inning, with the A's leading 3–0, Boston got a man on first. Boston pitcher Morgan was due up. "Speaker, the young Texan, went to bat for Morgan and struck out, making a weak showing." [*Boston Globe*] Whiteman, pinch-hitting in the ninth, grounded back to the pitcher. In 19 late-season at-bats, Speaker hit safely just three times for a .158 average. Boston didn't even bother to send him a contract for 1908, but things worked out, he got some playing time, though only hit .224. Starting in 1909, he hit over .300 seven years in a row, before being traded to Cleveland.

Joe Cronin—April 16, 1935

When Joe Cronin debuted for the Red Sox, it was as a player-manager. After helping Yankees manager Joe McCarthy hoist the flag on the Yankee Stadium flagpole before the game, he happily watched Wes Ferrell throw a two-hit shutout against New York and saw the Red Sox win, 1–0, on Billy Werber's sixth-inning double and two Yankees errors. Cronin was 1-for-4 at the plate and handled six chances without an error.

Bobby Doerr—April 20, 1937

Playing in Philadelphia, Bobby Doerr was the leadoff hitter in the top of the first for Red Sox Opening Day 1937. He had himself a 3-for-5 day (all singles) and finished the day with a .600 batting average and an .800 fielding average (he made one error in five chances). The Red Sox gathered 18 hits in all, and drubbed the A's, 11–5. Wes Ferrell got the win.

Ted Williams—April 20, 1939

The Kid broke in against future Hall of Famer Red Ruffing, during the Yankee Stadium opener. Playing right field, he was credited with three putouts but a run scored on a fifth-inning Jake Powell triple of which the A.P. said Williams "played the rebound poorly." In his debut at the plate, batting sixth, Ted fouled off a curve, fouled off a curve, and then struck out on a high fastball. Second time up, same thing: a foul off a curve, a foul off a curve, and a strikeout on a high fastball. Six pitches, six strikes, two outs. In the dugout, Ted fumed and he pointed to Ruffing, telling his teammates, "This is *one* guy I *know* I am going to hit, and if he puts it in the same place again I'm riding it out of here." Ruffing served up the high fastball, and Ted hit it off the right-centerfield wall one foot below the top of the wall for a two-base hit. He finished the day batting .250, and the Yankees won, 2–0. The run that scored in the fifth was the second of the two.

Carl Yastrzemski—April 11, 1961

The man who took Ted's place began his career on Opening Day at Fenway Park and saw the Kansas City Athletics win, 5–2, on four Boston errors and with just one of the runs being earned. None of the errors were Yaz's, though; he handled two chances without a miscue. Yaz singled his first time up, but was caught attempting to steal second. In the end, he struck out twice and had a generally mediocre 1-for-5 day at the plate. He was 2-for-3, with a triple and two RBIs in his second game. The Red Sox beat the Angels, 3–0. That one felt a lot better.

Carlton Fisk—September 18, 1969

The Red Sox were 24 games out of first place as they prepared for a day/night doubleheader against the Orioles. Carlton Fisk was the starting catcher in the first game. He grounded out to first his first time up, grounded out to short the next time, and struck out his third time up. Final time up, he hit to the second baseman for an out, 0-for-4 in the game. Baltimore won, 6–4. Boston took the night game, 5–0, with Gerry Moses catching, doubling, and driving in the third Red Sox run. Fisk never did get a hit in 1969, and spent the winter looking back in disappointment. He spent almost two full years staring at his 0-for-5 line in the major league record books, before he got into another game in September 1971. The line soon grew to be 0-for-12, until September 12 when he came in to take over for the injured Duane Josephson in the bottom of the first inning of a game in Detroit. His first time up, in the top of the third, he hit a solo home run. He ended the game 2-for-3, and had two-hit games in three of his next five games.

Roger Clemens—May 15, 1984

When Roger Clemens was given his first start, the Red Sox were really having a rough season. They were in last place, 14 games out of first, even though it was only mid-May. The rookie Clemens offered no immediate turnaround. His first game was a night game in Cleveland and he retired the first two batters, on a groundout to first and a foul fly to left field. Then Pat Tabler singled, and stole second. Andre Thornton singled in Tabler, and then Tabler stole second. He escaped from the inning with just one run, but in 5⅔ innings gave up five runs (four earned). Reliever John Henry Johnson was given the loss. Clemens didn't do any better in his first month on the job. In his first six starts, he surrendered the following number of earned runs per start: 4, 4, 5, 3, 6, and 6. He won two of the games, but had an ERA of 7.13 after the June 12 game against the Yankees at Fenway. It was the second start in a row he'd been tagged for six earned runs, and he only got off the hook when Dwight Evans hit a leadoff triple, and scored, in the seventh, and a three-run homer in the bottom of the eighth to give the Red Sox a win. Roger was long gone; he hadn't survived the fourth.

Pedro Martinez—April 1, 1998

Unlike Clemens, Pedro came to Boston with a 1997 Cy Young in his back pocket and a $75 million contract in the bank. He'd come a long way from the dirt floor/tin roof house where he was raised. And he produced immediately. The first game he pitched for Boston was Opening Day 1998. He mowed down the first 11 Oakland batters he faced, and by the time he left the game, he'd pitched seven full innings, struck out 11, and only given up three hits. He won the 2–0 shutout, both Sox runs coming on sacrifice flies. It was only after Pedro's sixth start that his ERA climbed over 2.00; he only gave up one run total in his first three starts. After his first 10 starts, he was 5–0 with a 1.74 ERA. He finished the year 19–7, with a 2.89 ERA, and helped the Red Sox into the postseason, where he won the only postseason game in which he appeared.

Leaving in style—memorable exits

Most Red Sox fans know that Ted Williams homered in his final at-bat in the major leagues. He's just one of three Boston players who ended their careers with a home run.

October 6, 1906—Chick Stahl

Chuck Stahl batted 5,069 times in the major leagues, and 595 times in his final season, 1906. He played in every one of that year's 155 games. A lifetime .305 hitter whose career was split between the Boston Nationals and the Boston Americans, Stahl was coming back for another season in 1907 when he took his own life on March 26. That story has been told elsewhere, but what interests us here is that on that 595th at-bat in 1906, Chick Stahl hit a home run.

Boston finished the 1906 season dead last, 45.5 games out of first place, with a miserable 49–105 (.318) record. (Stahl's former team in the other league also finished last, 66.5 games behind first place Chicago.) And Stahl's home run didn't even help his team win the game; the final score on the October 6 game was New York 5, Boston 4. "The game was a doleful one," wrote the *Boston Post*. "The players played because they had to, the spectators attended because the force of habit was potent, and nobody seemed to care how the game resulted." Stahl's home run provided almost the only ripple of excitement for the Huntington Avenue home crowd. Shortstop Chadbourne had walked and then Stahl hit his eighth-inning homer toward (but not into) the center-field seats. Chadbourne scored and Stahl circled the bases, "by the grace of some very slow fielding" by the New York team. In other words, it was an inside-the-park home run.

Like Ted Williams, Chick Stahl had hit a home run in his last time at bat in the major leagues. He couldn't have known it at the time, and no one has ever suggested that he wanted to leave this life holding that distinction. But hit it, he did—one of four homers he hit in 1906, and one of 36 in his career.

September 28, 1960—Ted Williams.

The story is well enough known that we need not devote too much space to it here. It's never discussed, but Ted could have had a backup plan, had he wanted one. Homering in front of a Boston audience, in his last possible at-bat is pretty hard to top, but the Red Sox did go on to play three games in New York. Had the ball traveled a slightly shorter distance and had Ted been robbed by Pilarcik reaching over the bullpen railing to snag that last home run, Williams could have gone on to New York and gunned for a game-winning homer there, and then retired. The Sox lost all three of those games, two of them by one run and the other one by two runs. A Ted Williams homer could have made a difference, though it could in no way have salvaged the 1960 season. Boston finished up 65–89. That's one of the reasons so few fans turned out to actually see Ted's dramatic home run. The 10,454 who did represented a good crowd for the year, but imagine the hype a game like that would receive today. There might be 10,454 fans turned away from a filled-to-capacity Fenway, all looking for last-minute seats and just wanting to be in the environs for Ted's last game.

To be fair, though, Ted had told Curt Gowdy beforehand that it was going to be his last game, and fans in Boston knew it would be their last chance to see The Kid in a ballgame.

September 30, 1962—Don Gile

Don Gile became the third Red Sox player to homer in his last at-bat. Like Stahl, Gile didn't know it was going to be his last at-bat. Only Ted knew that. Gile was winding up his fourth year in the record books (though he'd only batted 10 times in 1959 and 18 times in 1961). Brought in late-season to fill in for Pete Runnels, Gile wasn't having a very good year. In fact,

he was having a terrible year at the plate. It couldn't have been worse. Before the final day of the season, Gile had batted 34 times in 1962 and hadn't managed even one hit all year long. An 0-for-34 streak (an 0-for-34 season at that point) was not the way to impress your employers with your prospects for the following year. He had walked three times, but even if there were some executive studying on-base percentage back then, it wouldn't have warranted attention.

Don Gile posing...

The last day of the year featured a doubleheader against the visiting Washington Senators. They were in last place, with a record even worse than the eighth place Bosox. Runnels won the batting title that year, with a .326 mark—five points ahead of Mickey Mantle's .321. But he wasn't feeling well that final day—he had a cold and a fever, so he sat out the games. "Bear" Gile filled in at first base for both games

...and homering. Courtesy of Don Gile.

and bookended the doubleheader with hits. His first time up in the first game, he "blooped a fly to short centerfield that fell in safely." (*Herald*) He made outs his next five times up, twice more in game one and the first three at-bats in game two. Boston lost the first game 3–1. In the second game, the Senators had scored once in the first and the Red Sox had matched that courtesy of a Gary Geiger solo homer in the third. It was tied 1–1 going into the bottom of the ninth. Jim Pagliaroni walked and pitcher Earl Wilson was put in as a pinch-runner. In stepped the 6'6" Gile, with his .025 average. Jack Jenkins, just 19, had pitched wonderfully in his first major league start. The first pitch he threw Gile, though, was drilled into the nets atop the Wall and Boston won the game, 3–1. Gile won the game and felt a bit better. Referring to the two hits right after the game, he said, "I thanked them for letting it [the first one] fall in, but I thought I should have one really legitimate blow for the record book."

You can see it today, in the record book. One home run, in his final at-bat. (Gile was not invited back, despite having raised his lifetime average to .150 with the two hits.) In a March 2007 e-mail, Gile allowed, "Sure wish I had known that was going to be my last at-bat in the majors…I might have pulled a 'Piersall' and finished it all off with a hook slide into home!"

October 2, 1982—Brian Denman

Brian Denman threw a six-hit shutout against the New York Yankees in his final big league game with the Boston Red Sox. It was a Saturday afternoon game in Yankee Stadium, matched against Dave Righetti. The Red Sox were solidly in third place in the AL East. The Yankees were in fifth place. It was the next-to-last game of the season. Brian gave up two doubles to Barry Evans in the early innings but those were the only hits in the first four frames. The Red Sox scored their first run—the winning run—in the top of the fifth when Righetti hit Dave Stapleton with a pitch, and Wade Boggs doubled him to third base. Ed Jurak hit a sacrifice fly to left, scoring Stapleton.

Denman finished the season 3–4, his first and only season of major league ball. He'd started every one of the nine games in which he appeared, facing 206 batters while throwing 49 innings, and had a 4.78 ERA. He never made an error in the field. But what a nice way for the 26-year-old right-hander to go out.

And then, the very next day…

October 3, 1982—Roger LaFrancois

The last man to play with a major league club for an entire season and hit .400 was not Ted Williams, but it was a fellow Red Soxer: Roger LaFrancois. Roger used to go to Red Sox games as a kid. He signed with the Red Sox and came up in their system, even receiving instruction

from Ted Williams during spring training at Winter Haven. In 1982, it all paid off. Roger made the club out of spring training as a backup catcher behind Gary Allenson and Rich Gedman and he spent the full 162-game season with the Red Sox, making every homestand and every road trip. He didn't miss a game.

Unfortunately, he also didn't get to play in that many of them. The first time he appeared in a game was May 27, and by that time the Boston papers had already begun to run photos of him with captions such as "Day 32: do you know who this man is?" Ralph Houk was from the old school and, as LaFrancois says, "played nine." He really didn't utilize his bench the way managers do today. LaFrancois appeared only very briefly and had only been in seven games as he approached the final day of the season, October 3. He had only been in seven games, with five at-bats and only a double and a single to show for it. Still, he *was* batting .400.

.400 hitter Roger LaFrancois waiting a good pitch to hit. Courtesy of Roger LaFrancois.

Then Houk gave him the opportunity to start the season's final game, and Roger faced a dilemma like the young Ted Williams faced in 1941. Should he sit out the game and preserve his .400 average, or should he go for it? "There was a lot of pressure on me that last day, but I didn't want to sit on my average," Roger quipped in a November 2001 phone call. "I decided to play." It turned out to be an 11-inning affair against the Yankees in the Stadium. Roger hit a solid single up the middle earlier in the game but then saw his average sink to .333 as the game went into extra innings and he'd gone 1-for-4. He was 3-for-9 on the year, and in his major league career.

In the top of the 11th, though, the young catcher came up to the plate one more time. A walk would preserve his average at .333, but an out would drop it to a less-distinguished .300. Instead, LaFrancois jumped on a 1–2 Rudy May breaking ball and bounced it over the pitcher's head for an infield hit. Three batters later, Roger scored what proved to be the winning run of the game on a Rick Miller single. After suiting up for 162 games with the 1982 Red Sox, his average for the year stands in the record books at an even .400 today.

October 5, 2001—Calvin Pickering, who gave up the distinction
On October 5, 2001, Calvin Pickering didn't think it was going to be his last game. Gile might have made a fair guess that it would be his, given his .049 average in 1962, but Pickering was actually not doing badly. He'd hit .280 at season's end—14 hits in 46 at-bats, with three home runs and seven RBIs.

His last time up was in the last game of the season. There were two games that day, a split doubleheader between Boston and Baltimore. Pickering had played first base in the first game and gone 1-for-4 with a run batted in. Taking second place was going to get each player an extra $12,000 in 2001, and the Red Sox were able to take second by winning their final five games. Boston took the first game 5–0, and Pickering's RBI was the fifth of the game, on a single in the eighth. In the second game, Daubach played first and Pickering grabbed some bench. Boston scored first, with one in the second, but Baltimore tied it up and took a 3–2 lead by the end of six. O'Leary and Burkhart each made an out to start the Sox seventh, but then Hillenbrand singled and Mirabelli walked. Manager Joe Kerrigan called on Calvin to pinch-hit for second baseman Santos, and Pickering pounded "Way Back" Wasdin for a three-run homer to center field. Boston led 5–3, and Pickering might have won the game, but Tim Raines hit a two-run homer off Tim Wakefield to tie. The game went into extra innings, but mercifully just one: Trot Nixon hit his own two-run homer in the bottom of the 10th and everyone went home. At least Calvin Pickering could say he went out with a blast.

But not any more. After spending 2002, 2003, and most of 2004 out of the majors, Pickering may have lost his chance at baseball immortality by coming back in late August 2004 for 35 games with Kansas City. He did hit a home run on October 2, with just one game to go, but he accumulated seven more at-bats without hitting any more homers. In 2005, he hit a home run his last time up in the first game he played, but then went on to appear in six more games without any homers. He hasn't played major league ball since 2005.

October 1, 1995—Chris Donnels
Speaking of Pickering, that reminds us of Chris Donnels. He gave up his chance for immortality, too. On October 1, 1995 Donnels took over at second base for Luis Alicea late in the game, and had one at-bat, in the ninth inning. Donnels hit a home run off Milwaukee's Scott Karl, in a game the Sox dropped, 8–1. It was his last at-bat in the major leagues—until five years later, when he hooked on with the Dodgers and Diamondbacks for another 202 at-bats (which included 10 more homers). His last at-bat was a fly out to center.

ALL-STAR GAMES, HALL OF FAME GAMES, TIES AND FORFEITS, AND OTHER ODD GAMES

All-Star games—at Fenway

The tradition of holding an exhibition game pitting the stars of the American League against those of the National League began in 1933. The game moves from major league city to major league city; the fourth such game was played in Boston—at Braves Field. The first one scheduled for Fenway Park came in 1945, but a desire to comply with wartime travel restrictions on unnecessary travel led baseball to encourage each club to schedule a game in its home park rather than have players traveling around the country. It would hardly have taxed our national transportation network to have 30 or 40 ballplayers traveling (All-Star rosters were much smaller at the time), but baseball wouldn't have wanted to do anything seemingly out of step with the war effort. The 1945 All-Star Game at Fenway Park was canceled. Instead, it was held the following year.

The first time the game was held at Fenway Park, most of the stars who'd served in the armed forces were back, and (fittingly for a Fenway affair) the All-Star among All-Stars was one Ted Williams.

First, though, let's set the stage by harking back to Ted's earlier record in All-Star Games.

Ted's first starring role—July 8, 1941

Ted's first starring role had come in the 1941 game, in Detroit, midway through Ted's .406 season. It's the game which Ted always said provided the biggest thrill of his long career.

There's no doubt that Ted had been excited about his first All-Star Game the year before in 1940. Coming off a spectacular rookie year, where he knocked in a record 145 RBIs, he was a natural for the team. The manager was teammate Joe Cronin, and other Sox players Jimmie Foxx, Doc Cramer, and Lou Finney all traveled to St. Louis with Ted. It wasn't a memorable game for "toothpick Ted," though. He walked in the first, but grounded out twice and was replaced by Hank Greenberg late in the game. The whole AL team only mustered three hits against a dominant National League pitching staff and lost 4–0.

In the 1941 game, Ted walked in the second, then doubled in a run in the fourth. He flied out his next time up, in the sixth. The Cubs' Claude Passeau struck him out in the eighth on a called strike, one that Ted thought was a bit low. Jimmie Foxx reported that for a couple of weeks Ted had been saying that he wanted to hit one out, but it wasn't looking like a truly special game for the young star.

The AL was behind 5–3 in the bottom of the ninth, and the bases were loaded. Joe DiMaggio grounded a ball for a fielder's choice, and knocked in one run. Ted was up for the fifth time in the game now, with runners on first and third and two outs. Passeau was on the mound, hoping to strike Ted out once again. Not too many pitchers struck Ted out twice in a row, though. The first pitch was a ball. Ted fouled off the next, down the first base line. Then came ball two. There was a pretty strong wind blowing, across the field, but Ted hit Passeau's next pitch off the front of the press box built on top of the third deck, nearly out of Briggs Stadium, for an ending Hollywood couldn't have topped. Come from behind, two outs in the ninth, to win the game 7–5.

We've all seen the film of Ted galloping around the bases, clapping his hands as he ran, laughing and smiling. The *Boston Globe* reported that "hardened veterans like Joe DiMaggio, Bob Feller (already changed into street clothes but out on the field to greet him), Joe Cronin, and Jimmie Foxx were suddenly transformed into boyish hero worshippers." Ted never stopped running until he reached the dugout, an act perhaps of self-preservation as he was mobbed both by his fellow teammates and spectators who ran onto the field. "I just shut my eyes and swung," Ted said. "I had a feeling that if I got up there in the ninth, I'd go for the Downs. Boy, I feel good. There ain't nothin' like hittin' a home run.... Do you know the biggest kick I got out of the whole thing? I'm tickled for my mom's sake because she was listening." Then Ted started in talking, not about his game-winning homer but about a great throw he'd made (a "tremendous heave" according to news reports) which had prevented a run from scoring earlier in the game.

July 9, 1946—American League 12, National League 0

The Red Sox were such a dominant team in 1946 that fully ⅓ of the All-Star squad came from their ranks—and it wasn't to economize on travel. Dom DiMaggio, Bobby Doerr, Johnny Pesky, Rudy York, Hal Wagner, Ted Williams, and pitchers Mickey Harris and Dave Ferriss were all selected. The Sox could have fielded every starting position except third base.

Our old friend Claude Passeau—still a great pitcher—was the NL starter. He worked very carefully to Williams and finally walked Ted on a 3–2 pitch. One could argue that it was the only damage Ted didn't do all day—but a walk's as good as a hit and Ted was on base for Charlie Keller's home run and scored the first American League run. The AL began building what became a 12–0 shellacking of the National Leaguers. Ted hit a solo homer his next time up, singled in the fifth, knocking in another run, singled again in the seventh, and then homered for three more RBIs in the eighth.

That final home run was the first anyone had ever hit off of Rip Sewell's famous "eephus pitch"—a pitch thrown in a roughly 20-foot high trajectory and which came down over the plate. The Pirates' Sewell saw Ted as a challenge, saying of the Splendid Splinter, "He just loves to bat. He doesn't walk up to the plate. He runs up to it." The first pitch Sewell threw was an eephus, which Ted fouled to third. "That was my first look at the eephus or the oophus or whatever you call it," Ted said. "I stepped back and tried to push [it] to left." A fast ball followed, strike two. The third pitch was another eephus, way outside. Ted correctly anticipated the next pitch. "I stepped into it and gave that last one all I had." He strode forward, coming out of the batter's box in his eagerness. "The ball took about five minutes getting up there, and he had plenty of time to think it over," remarked Tex Hughson. Williams hit it into the bullpen in right, where pitcher Mickey Harris caught it.

Ted went 4-for-4, with a walk, two singles, and two home runs, for 10 total bases. The rest of the team together accounted for just 14 more.

It was one of the greatest displays of hitting in All-Star history, and in front of the home crowd to boot.

Ted Williams—18 times an All-Star

In the 1947 All-Star Game, Ted got a bit of revenge against the Cardinals' Harry Brecheen (who'd shut down Boston's offense so effectively in the 1946 World Series) going 2-for-2, a single and a double. He was 2-for-4 in the game. One of the outs was on a called third strike, and the following year umpire Jocko Conlan apologized to Ted for missing the call.

In 1948, due to a rib cartilage which had torn loose in a game in Philadelphia beforehand, Ted couldn't start. He did pinch-hit in the sixth and drew a walk. The 1949 game was unremarkable, Ted coincidentally suffering from a cracked rib beforehand. Williams went 0-for-2 but got himself on base twice, drawing another couple of walks. Ted also made a great over-the-shoulder catch which "helped save the game" according to Lou Boudreau.

The 1950 game came close to ending Ted's career, and cut short what could have been a tremendous season. Ted was off to his best start ever, with 25 home runs and 83 RBIs before the All-Star break. Playing left, Ted make a great catch off Ralph Kiner in the first, snagging the ball over his shoulder and then crashing hard into the unpadded wall at Comiskey. The first edition of the *Boston Globe*, composed while the game was still in progress, had a full-page headline, WILLIAMS' SPECTACULAR ONE-HAND CATCH ROBS KINER. Ted made another "difficult catch" off of Kiner a couple of innings later. At the plate, he grounded out, flied out, singled to drive in a run in the fifth to put the AL team in the lead, and struck out looking in the seventh. Ted played the whole game until he was taken out, now in considerable pain, in the ninth. He'd actually broken the radius, near his elbow, but gritted it out and acquitted himself well. It was two months before he could come back after undergoing an operation.

Called to military service once more, Ted did not play in either the 1952 or 1953 games though, just home from Korea, Marine Capt. Williams attended in uniform to throw out the first pitch in the 1953 contest. In 1951, he had gone 1-for-3, a triple, and drawn a walk. 1954 saw Ted strike out twice, a rare phenomenon for any game. He drew a walk, too. The 1955 All-Star Game saw a 1-for-3, with another walk. Willie Mays ran down and snared a long ball which would have gone out. Ted played in seven more All-Star Games (two were held each year in 1959 and 1960) but with the exception of a home run off Warren Spahn in the 1956 game, he did nothing really special. In 16 plate appearances those last seven games, he got that one homer and singled once, walking just twice. The single, slashed hard to right field, was a pinch-hit in his final All-Star appearance, in 1960.

Before that final game, at Yankee Stadium, Ted was given a great cheer which the *Boston Globe* writer described as "reminiscent of the famous farewell salute Boston fans gave Yankee Joe DiMaggio several years ago in Fenway Park."

All told, Ted Williams batted .304 in All-Star competition (excellent, but not compared to his lifetime .344 total) with four home runs and 12 RBIs. Disciplined at the plate as always, he drew 11 walks and so increased his on-base percentage to an impressive figure of .431. Anyone else would be pleased. Though all told Ted's performance was subpar by his own standards (his lifetime on-base percentage was a staggering .482—the greatest ever accomplished by any hitter) the 1941 and 1946 games were such dramatic and spectacular accomplishments that they overshadow the lesser games. Would that all hitters had two such games to look back on! Would that Ted hadn't been injured just before the 1946 World Series, or had been able to transfer his All-Star Game production to that year's Fall Classic.

July 31, 1961—American League 1, National League 1

After the 1946 game, the next time the All-Star Game was held at Fenway was for the second of the two games staged in 1961. It was the first year after Ted Williams' retirement in September 1960. And Yaz hadn't yet begun to shine as brightly as he would. In the first 1961 All-Star Game, the only Sox player was Mike Fornieles who came on to pitch in the eighth inning of a tight game the NL was leading, 2–1. This was an era when, quite frankly, the Red Sox had rather few stars. Fornieles promptly surrendered a home run to George Altman. He got Willie Mays out on a fly to center, but then Frank Robinson singled, and he was pulled from the game. The AL tied it back, but lost in 11 innings, 5–4.

The game at Fenway, though, ended in a tie after nine innings, when rain prevented it also going into extra innings. Rocky Colavito's first-inning homer provided the one AL run. Boston rookie pitcher Don Schwall was the only Red Sox player in the game. Schwall threw the middle three innings of the game for the Americans, sandwiched between Jim Bunning and Camilo Pascual. He gave up just one run, but it was enough to tie the game. Eddie Mathews walked. Schwall retired Aaron before Mathews and Mays after, but then hit Cepeda with a pitch, and Bill White singled Mathews home.

July 13, 1999—American League 4, National League 1

The only ASG played at Fenway at night will long be remembered more for the pre-game activities, as MLB celebrated the last game of a year beginning with "19" by assembling a collection of the greatest living players of the century. The players each took a spot along the baselines, stretching all the way from first base to third base. Last to be introduced was the hometown hero, Ted Williams, driven in from center field in a utility cart. When he reached the mound, the great stars of the past broke from the script and spontaneously all made their way to the mound to greet Ted. It was an incredibly emotional moment.

When the game belatedly got underway, Boston's ace Pedro Martinez took the mound—and struck out the side. In succession, he struck out Barry Larkin, Larry Walker, Sammy Sosa, and Mark McGwire. Matt Williams reached on an error, and then Pedro struck out Jeff Bagwell while Williams was cut down stealing second on a strike-him-out, throw-him-out play. The five strikeouts tied the AL All-Star record. It was a dominating performance, but Pedro struggled some as the season continued. You'd never know it from his stats that year, but he wasn't fully the same pitcher he had been for the rest of the season. He got the win during the 1999 game, though; some guy named Schilling, working in the other league at the time, took the defeat.

Other Red Sox in other All-Star Games

The first All-Star Game was held at Comiskey in 1933. The only Sox Star was catcher Rick Ferrell, Wes's brother. He flied to right, flied to right, set up a run with a sacrifice bunt, and grounded out, officially 0-for-3. Future Sox players in the game were Ben Chapman, Al Simmons, Joe Cronin, and Lefty Grove.

Cronin, playing for the Sox by 1935, hit a sacrifice fly and produced the first RBI by a Red Sox player. Lefty Grove started the 1936 game and gave up only two runs but was still tagged with the loss in the 4–3 defeat. Jimmie Foxx singled as a seventh-inning pinch hitter and set up the second run, scoring the third himself two batters later. Cronin was 1-for-4 with a double in the 1937 game; Foxx pinch-hit but grounded back to the pitcher. Cronin doubled again in 1938, going 2-for-3 with an RBI. Foxx, Grove, and Doc Cramer all represented the Red Sox as well, but without great distinction.

In 1939, Cramer and Cronin each went 1-for-4. The 1940 game saw Ted Williams' first All-Star appearance; Lou Finney took his place in the order in the sixth inning. Neither got a hit, nor did Foxx. The AL collectively only managed three hits. Ted's role in the 1941 game is described above; other Sox were Bobby Doerr and Jimmie Foxx. Dom DiMaggio singled, driving in his brother Joe in his only at-bat. Ted was the only Red Sox player who saw action in 1942. He singled once in four at-bats.

Doerr's three-run homer in the second inning of the 1943 game was key to the 5–3 win, and Tex Hughson earned the save, though not without a little shakiness. The same two players came back for the fray in '44. Doerr was 0-for-3, and Hughson took the loss, giving up four runs in an inning and two-thirds. As noted above, the '45 game was canceled and Ted Williams dominated the 1946 game at Fenway.

Come 1947, Ted was 2-for-4 and Bobby was 1-for-2. Doerr's seventh-inning single resulted in the winning run in the 2–1 game. With one out, Doerr singled, then stole second. He was effectively picked off second, but reached third when Johnny Sain's pickoff throw went into center field. He scored the go-ahead run on Stan Spence's single. Vern Stephens got the only

Sox hit in 1948, though Ted, Bobby, and Birdie Tebbetts each had a chance. Tebbetts and Dom DiMaggio each hit a single and a double in 1949; both Stephens and Williams failed to hit safely, though Ted walked and scored.

The 1950 game was the one in which Ted Williams broke his elbow making a great defensive play in the first inning, and went on to have a 1-for-4 game with an RBI. Walt Dropo tripled. Doerr and Dom D both played, but failed to hit. In 1951, three teammates (Dom, Bobby, and Ted) all had one hit (Ted's was a triple), and Mel Parnell threw one inning of work, giving up one run.

In his sixth All-Star Game, 1952, sole Sox representative Dom DiMaggio doubled and drew a walk in three plate appearances. Billy Goodman was 0-for-2 in 1953, and Ted Williams was also 0-for-2 in 1954, but Ted scored a run after leading off the fifth with a walk. Pitcher Frank Sullivan lost the game in 1955, though he'd only given up one run in 3⅓ innings of work—a walk-off 12th inning home run to Stan Musial. Ted and Jackie Jensen both played for Boston; Ted scored once, after a walk, on a Mickey Mantle home run.

Tommy Brewer gave up all three runs in the 1956 game, but the AL won anyhow, 7–3. Ted hit a two-run homer. Mickey Vernon started at first, but was 0-for-2. In 1957, the AL pulled out a 6–5 win with three runs in the ninth. Both Ted and Frank Malzone both played, but neither hit safely. Once again, Ted walked and scored. Jackie Jensen drove in a run on a groundout but was 0-for-4 in 1958. Ted was 0-for-2; Malzone 1-for-4. In 1959, Frank Malzone's second inning solo homer was the sole bright light for the Red Sox. Pete Runnels and Ted Williams both went 0-for-3.

The first 1960 game was a disaster. Bill Monbouquette started, gave up four runs in two innings, and took the loss. Malzone, Runnels, and Williams all tried to produce at the plate, but fell short. There was a second All-Star Game in 1960, and Ted Williams singled in a pinch-hitting appearance, the last All-Star at-bat of his career. The AL was shut out, though. Runnels and Malzone were both held hitless again.

There were two games again in 1961, and the story of both games is told above in the section on All-Star Games at Fenway.

Not a single Sox player saw action in the first 1962 game, and the only one who did in the second game was Pete Runnels. He hit a pinch-hit home run leading off the third inning. Returning to the format of one game per year, Frank Malzone singled and later scored in his one at-bat in the 1963 game. Yaz made his first appearance in the ASG, going 0-for-2. Dick Radatz closed the game, allowing one run in two innings. The Monster was the only Red Sox in the 1964 game, but he probably wished he hadn't been. After pitching 2⅔ innings, he let the Nationals tie up the game, 4–4, in the bottom of the ninth and then surrendered a pinch-hit three-run homer to Johnny Callison. It wasn't until 1967 that the Red Sox saw another player in an All-Star Game, and that was Tony Conigliaro, who had a disappointing 0-for-6 game. Carl Yastrzemski had a very good 3-for-4 game, and Rico Petrocelli saw action as well, though he popped to second in the one at-bat he had. The AL only mustered three hits in the '68 game, and neither Yaz (in four at-bats) nor Ken Harrelson (in one) got any.

Ray Culp pitched a hitless ninth to close the 1969 game, but the NL won, 9–3. Reggie Smith pinch-ran and scored, but failed to hit in two subsequent at-bats. Rico was 1-for-3, Mike Andrews and Yaz both hitless in one at-bat apiece. In 1970, Yaz had his second big game as an All-Star, going 4-for-6, driving in Ray Fosse with the first run of the game in the sixth, singling and scoring in the eighth—but the NL scored three times to tie it in the ninth and won it in the 12th. Luis Aparicio joined the Red Sox starting in 1971 and scored once, batting 1-for-3. Yaz was hitless in three at-bats. Carlton Fisk appeared in his first game, singling and scoring in two at-bats; Yaz was 0-for-3 and Reggie Smith made an out in another pinch-hitting role. Fisk was 0-for-2 in '73 and Yaz was 0-for-1 in '74. Luis Tiant was hit hard and took the loss in the '74 game, giving up three runs in two innings of work.

In 1975, Yastrzemski hit a three-run homer off Tom Seaver for his only home run in All-Star play; Fred Lynn was 0-for-2. Tiant threw two scoreless innings in the 1976 game. Fred Lynn got one of the five AL hits, and scored. Yaz (two AB) and Fisk (one) were hitless. Bill Campbell pitched a hitless inning, and Yaz, Lynn, Rice, Fisk, and Burleson all played in the 1977 game, but only Rice hit, a single in the eighth. Lynn walked and scored in the sixth. Fisk drove in the first run of the 1978 game on a sacrifice fly, but was the only Red Sox player to truly contribute (Rice 0-for-4, Evans 0-for-1, Fisk 0-for-2, and Lynn 1-for-4).

In 1979, Lynn hit a two-run homer in the first off Steve Carlton, in his only at-bat. Yaz was 2-for-3 with a run batted in, Rice doubled in five at-bats, and Rick Burleson was 0-for-2. Bob Stanley pitched two innings and gave up one run. Fisk hit another two-run homer in the 1980 game (off Bob Welch). He was 1-for-3. Fisk was 0-for-2. The 1981 game saw Lynn drive in another run with a sixth-inning single. Evans was 1-for-2 and scored a run. Fisk was 1-for-3 and scored a run. Burleson was 0-for-1 and didn't.

Dennis Eckersley started the 1982 game, in Montreal, but gave up three runs in three innings and lost it. Lynn, Evans, and Yaz were all hitless. Finally, after losing 11 All-Star Games in a row, the American League won one thanks to a 13–3 rout by the 1983 squad. Fred Lynn hit the only grand slam in All-Star history, off Atlee Hammaker in the third inning. Jim Rice had led off the same inning with a solo homer off Hammaker. Rice was 2-for-4. Yaz batted once but made an out. Bob Stanley threw two scoreless innings.

Only Rice played in 1984 and he was 0-for-1. Rice was 0-for-3 in 1985; Wade Boggs got in one plate appearance and walked, but Rice struck out, Rich Gedman struck out, and the game was over.

Roger Clemens started the 1986 game and threw three perfect innings; he was given the win. His one time up, he struck out. Boggs was 1-for-3, Rice was 0-for-1, and Gedman caught but didn't bat. The 1987 National League team scored twice in the top of the 13th to break a 12-inning tie shutout. That Dwight Evans had gone 2-for-2 was in vain. In 1988, Boggs was 1-for-3. Clemens pitched again, one scoreless inning. In 1989, Boggs was 1-for-3—a first-inning home run. Mike Greenwell got an at-bat, but was 0-for-1.

Boggs was 2-for-2 in 1990, the only Sox player in the game. Wade Boggs was 1-for-2 and scored a run in 1991; both Clemens and Jeff Reardon pitched in relief. For three years in a row, 1993–95, not one player wore a Red Sox uniform. In 1995, Mo Vaughn played first and was 0-for-2 at the plate, striking out both times. Vaughn collected a hit in 1996, though, a double in the first of his three at-bats. Nomar Garciaparra hit into a force play in the eighth inning of the 1997 ASG, the only Red Sox star to play. Tom Gordon pitched an inning in 1998, giving up three hits and two runs (one earned) in one inning of work.

The 1999 game was held at Fenway and is covered above. In 2000, three Boston players saw some action. Carl Everett was 0-for-2, but drove in a run with a bases-loaded walk. Nomar was 1-for-2; he singled and scored in the ninth, though he also committed two errors. Derek Lowe threw a hitless sixth. 2001? Manny Ramirez, 0-for-1. That was it.

In the infamous 2002 game that was suddenly stopped by the Commissioner, tied 7–7 after 11 innings, due to a lack of pitchers and an unwillingness to ask the last man in to pitch another inning or two. Shea Hillenbrand started at third base and went 0-for-2. Nomar pinch-hit, to no avail. Johnny Damon was 1-for-2 and scored. Manny Ramirez had a 2-for-2 game, two singles with one RBI. Garciaparra was 0-for-1, the only Boston player in the 2003 game despite the team taking it to the seventh game of the 2003 ALCS.

The 2004 season as a whole was a pretty good year for the Red Sox. The same was true in the All-Star Game. Manny Ramirez hit a two-run homer in the first inning off former Red Sox pitcher Roger Clemens, who let in six first-inning runs. David Ortiz hit his own two-run homer in the sixth, off former Sox prospect Carl Pavano. Under new rules promulgated in the wake of the 2000 game, the AL win in the 2004 game gave Boston the home field advantage in the World Series. And did so again in 2007. The 2005 game will not be remembered for Matt Clement's performance, but he'll likely always remember it with justifiable pride; he threw one inning without giving up a hit. David Ortiz was 2-for-3 with an RBI single in the third. Johnny Damon was 1-for-2, Manny was 0-for-2, and Jason Varitek was 1-for-1, scoring a run later in the game after working a walk.

NL pitchers finally shut Ortiz down in 2006; he was 0-for-2. So was the second baseman from the Sox, Mark Loretta. Manny was injured and didn't play; Jonathan Papelbon was there but didn't see duty. In 2007, six Sox went to San Francisco for the Midsummer Classic and the AL won its 10th consecutive game (not counting the tie game), with the win awarded to Boston's Josh Beckett who pitched two innings of one-hit ball. Papelbon pitched an inning, with one hit and no runs. Mike Lowell was 1-for-1. Both Ortiz and Ramirez hit, but were 0-for-3 between them. Reliever Hideki Okajima warmed up, but was not needed.

Most RBIs in All-Star play for a Red Sox batter

Ted Williams, 12

5 each: Fred Lynn, Carl Yastrzemski

3 each: Bobby Doerr, David Ortiz, Manny Ramirez

2 each: Joe Cronin, Dom DiMaggio, Frank Malzone, Goerge Scott

1 each: Wade Boggs, Scott Cooper, Carl Everett, Carlton Fisk, Jackie Jensen, Jim Rice, Pete Runnels, Birdie Tebbetts

Most hits in All-Star play for Red Sox batters

Ted Williams, 14	Wade Boggs, 7	Joe Cronin, Fred Lynn, and
Carl Yastrzemski, 10	Dom DiMaggio, 6	Jim Rice, 4

The Red Sox in the annual Hall of Fame games at Cooperstown

Beginning in 1940, the National Baseball Hall of Fame has hosted an annual exhibition game at Doubleday Field, Cooperstown between two major league baseball teams. The Cubs and the Red Sox met in the first such game, and the Sox have been involved in eight games in all, winning four and losing three. The 1989 contest was an unusual tie game in which the Red Sox played against themselves. These games have not always been hard-fought affairs, the way the All-Star Games used to be, but the 2005 event was definitely more of a spectacle than a true baseball game.

June 13, 1940: Chicago Cubs 10, Boston Red Sox 9. The first game was tied 4–4 after four innings, but the Cubs scored six times in the top of the seventh, then saw the Red Sox come back with five runs of their own in the bottom of the seventh. The game was then called due to rain. There were six home runs banged out of the cozy confines of Doubleday Field, four by the Cubs and two by Ted Williams, a solo homer in the third and a three-run job in the seventh. Dom DiMaggio was injured and had to leave the game after crashing headfirst into the stands as he caught a Billy Rogell fly ball.

July 24, 1950: Boston Red Sox 8, New York Giants 5. The Giants led 5–2, after five, but the Sox narrowed it to 5–4 as Johnny Pesky and Vern Stephens both homered in the seventh.

Boston scored four runs in the top of the eighth and took away an 8–5 win. Dick Littlefield pitched a complete game win. Ted Williams did not play, since he had broken his elbow just 13 days earlier in the All-Star Game. There were six errors in the game, played in a light rain, and the Red Sox left a full 15 runners on base.

July 25, 1955: Boston Red Sox 4, Milwaukee Braves 2. In a matchup facing the former Boston Braves, the Red Sox triumphed, 4–2, the first of three runs scored in the top of the first coming on Ted Williams' home run. Ted left after just the one at-bat; Ted Lepcio hit a homer in the eighth.

August 5, 1963: Boston Red Sox 7, Milwaukee Braves 3. As in 1940 and 1950, there was again a little light rain. The Red Sox played the Braves again, and won again, this time 7–3. Billy Gardner led off with a home run, Russ Nixon's sixth-inning single drove in the winning run, and Dick Williams hit a three-run homer as the icing on the cake for manager Johnny Pesky. Hank Aaron hit a homer for the Braves.

August 18, 1975: Boston 11, San Francisco Giants 5. Both Fred Lynn and Dwight Evans hit two-run homers in the top of the first. Fisk hit a solo shot in the third, and Denny Doyle hit a two-run homer in the sixth. Despite three errors, the homers helped the Sox win handily.

July 29, 1985: Houston 5, Boston 3 (10). Roger Clemens allowed just one run in the first five, and both Marty Barrett and Steve Lyons homered for the Red Sox, but the Astros scored twice in the ninth to tie it, and game went into extra innings. Back-to-back Houston homers sank the Sox in the 10th.

July 24, 1989: Boston 4, Yastrzemskis 4. The game was a tie, called to a halt after seven innings. It turned into a split-squad game with two teams of Red Sox vying against each other, after the Cincinnati Reds failed to arrive for the Hall of Fame game due to a hydraulic problem with their airplane in Montreal. Carl Yastrzemski had been inducted into the Hall of Fame the previous day, so the teams called themselves Boston versus the Yastrzemskis. Four Red Sox hit homers in the game—Wade Boggs, Jim Rice, Nick Esasky, and Eric Wedge. Foreshadowing the 2005 game, coach Al Bumbry got in the game—and excelled. He had a 2-for-3 day and stole a base.

May 23, 2005: Detroit 6, Boston 4. Cooperstown was like one big block party as thousands of still-delirious Red Sox fans strolled up and down Main Street, celebrating the reigning World Champions. The Sox took the game a little less than seriously, with pinch-hitting appearances by third base coach Dale Sveum and even Media Relations Coordinator Peter Chase—who, frankly, could have been a little more coordinated himself. Still, who wouldn't want to play baseball at the Hall of Fame? The Tigers took a 4–1 lead, but Boston tied it in the top of the seventh. Pawtucket prospect Mike Lockwood drove in two, while future Sox player Carlos Peña was the MVP for the Tigers, going 4-for-4, scoring twice and driving one in. The Tigers won it in the bottom of the ninth with a two-run walk-off home run by Derek Nicholson.

Tied games, forfeited game, and no-decision games

In the 100-plus years of Red Sox baseball, there have been a number of games which were—at least at first—nonconclusive. Tie games used to be much more common than they are today. In the early years of the 20th century, there were usually one or two per year. There have been 82 tie games in Red Sox history, but only six since 1950, and the last one was back in 1985. There have been three games that were forfeited. And one game that ended in a no-decision. Individual records (home runs, strikeouts, etc.) count when games are tied, but ties are not reflected in the standings, and so have to be replayed—that is, unless the teams decide not to replay them. There used to be a lot more flexibility in such matters than there is today.

How much more interesting the earlier seasons sometimes seemed. Consider this list of the number of games played each year by the Boston franchise, and notice the variations:

1901	138	1923	154	1945	157	1967	162	1989	162
1902	138	1924	157	1946	156	1968	162	1990	162
1903	141	1925	152	1947	157	1969	162	1991	162
1904	157	1926	154	1948	155	1970	162	1992	162
1905	153	1927	154	1949	155	1971	162	1993	162
1906	155	1928	154	1950	154	1972	155	1994	115
1907	155	1929	155	1951	154	1973	162	1995	144
1908	155	1930	154	1952	154	1974	162	1996	162
1909	152	1931	153	1953	153	1975	160	1997	162
1910	158	1932	154	1954	156	1976	162	1998	162
1911	153	1933	149	1955	154	1977	161	1999	162
1912	154	1934	153	1956	155	1978	163	2000	162
1913	151	1935	154	1957	154	1979	160	2001	161
1914	159	1936	155	1958	155	1980	160	2002	162
1915	155	1937	154	1959	154	1981	108	2003	162
1916	156	1938	150	1960	154	1982	162	2004	162
1917	157	1939	152	1961	163	1983	162	2005	162
1918	126	1940	154	1962	160	1984	162	2006	162
1919	138	1941	155	1963	161	1985	163	2007	162
1920	154	1942	152	1964	162	1986	161		
1921	154	1943	155	1965	162	1987	162		
1922	154	1944	156	1966	162	1988	162		

Through 2007, there have been 16,559 regular season games.

The first time the Red Sox switched to the 162-game schedule in 1961, they played 163 games. In fact, it took them four years before they finished with the intended 162 games. The first time they hit 154 games, it was 1912. During the remainder of the 154-game era (one has to exclude war-affected years 1918 and 1919), there were only 19 times they actually played 154 games. In the 47 years of the 162-game era, they hit 162 on the nose 32 times, with an eight-year streak from 1964–71.

The distribution of number of games is:

32 seasons—162 games
20 seasons—154 games
13 seasons—155 games
5 seasons—153 games and 157 games
4 seasons—152, 156, 160, and 161 games
3 seasons—138 games and 163 games
1 season each of 108, 115, 126, 141, 144, 149, 150, 151, 158, and 159 games

Forfeited games

June 28, 1902

There have been three forfeited games in which the Red Sox (or Americans) were involved. The first was on June 28, 1902—a game where the visiting Boston Americans played the Baltimore team, the very same team which the following year became the New York Highlanders and, ultimately, the New York Yankees. Boston won the game, courtesy of a forfeit awarded them by umpire Tom Connolly. Boston scored once in the first and Baltimore answered with one, adding single runs in the fourth and fifth as well. Boston scored four times in the top of the sixth, and Baltimore got back one. 5–4, Boston was up by one. Then Boston got three more runs in the seventh and another one in the top of the eighth, and the game was not looking good for Baltimore manager John McGraw. Cy Young was pitching well for Boston, but an error he made and three more by his fielders led to some of the scoring. Baltimore had Seymour on first and McGann on second with nobody out, when Bresnahan hit to Collins and McGann rounded third, then got in a rundown between third and home. Seymour meanwhile scooted all the way around third himself and started for home. McGann actually made it back to third, and Seymour had to streak back toward second—which he reached. It seemed like all the runners were safe, but Seymour hadn't touched third on his way back to second. Collins called for the ball to be thrown to Parent, who tagged Seymour with it and Connolly called Seymour out. McGraw got hot and so did Connolly, who later said that McGraw had called him a "robber and a thief." Whatever words were exchanged, McGraw was thrown out of the game and off the grounds. He refused to go, whereupon Connolly forfeited the game to Boston, 9–0.

The Baltimore players agreed that Connolly's call on Seymour was correct, but they felt he too hastily tossed McGraw, not giving him enough time to cool down and depart. The score was 9–4 at the time. The forfeit should have made it 9–0, but the record books nonetheless show it as 9–4 with the game ending with one out (Seymour) in the bottom of the eighth inning.

September 3, 1939

It was over 37 years before there was another forfeit. That occured on September 3, 1939—though the forfeit was later overturned and the game ruled a 5–5 tie. Starting pitcher for the Red Sox was Charlie Wagner, then in his second year of play—and still with the Red Sox into the 21st century. Boston beat the World Champion New York Yankees for the seventh straight time in the opener, 12–11, but the second game was declared a 9–0 Yankees victory by forfeit, so declared by umpire Cal Hubbard. The game was at Fenway Park. Hubbard's forfeit was prompted by what *Globe* writer Gerry Moore termed "a shower or straw hats, pop bottles and other stray refuse thrown onto the playing field by part of the rabid 27,000 crowd who desired to delay the contest until the Sunday curfew law could be exercised to save the Sox a 5–5 tie." The fans were already at "fever pitch" because five times during the afternoon the Red Sox had come from behind. In the bottom of the sixth of the second game, the Sox scored twice on homers by Ted Williams and Joe Cronin to take the lead, but Joe Gordon hit one for New York in the top of the seventh. Both teams had their eyes on the clock, as the 6:29 p.m. Sunday curfew approached. In the top of the eighth, the Yankees scored twice off Joe Heving and Cronin did what he could to have the Sox slow down play in hopes the curfew would take effect before the inning could be completed—thus the final score would be that of the last completed inning, which was 5–5. There was one out but there were Yankees on second and third; Cronin took his time having Heving intentionally walk Babe Dahlgren.

Here's where the Yankees started trying to speed things up. Feeling good about the two-run lead and wanting to get into the bottom of the inning as quickly as possible, Dahlgren started swinging at the intentional pitchouts. Hubbard called a strike after the first aimless swing and Cronin objected, then announced he would play the rest of the game under protest. On Heving's next wide pitch, George Selkirk (the runner on third) ran home half-heartedly and was tagged out by Boston catcher Johnny Peacock. On Heving's third pitch, Joe Gordon did the same thing (he'd moved from second to third while Selkirk was being tagged out. So the Yankees were out of their half of the inning. The crowd objected and "from almost every sector of the enclosure, articles ranging from Summer skimmers to undevoured hot dog rolls were thrown until the park was beyond playing condition. The barrage lasted for fully three minutes." Hubbard conferred with the other umpires and the two managers and declared a 9–0 forfeit to New York. The Red Sox objected that the umpires precipitated the crowd reaction through their neglect, their failure to deal with the Yankees' unacceptable conduct. Cronin later said that even New York manager Joe McCarthy suggested declaring the game a 5–5 tie during their conference. The forfeit was later overruled, the game declared a tie, and the New York players were reportedly fined.

August 15, 1941—ultimately forfeited

Not quite two years later, on August 15, 1941, there was another forfeit. The game was reported in all the next day's newspapers as a 6–3 home win for the Washington Senators. Boston had a 3–1 lead when heavy rain began to fall; the Sox gave up three runs in the fifth and solo runs in both the sixth and seventh, and then the umpires called the game. *Boston Globe* writer Gerry Moore commented, "Any chance of continuing had been cagily prevented by the Griffith Stadium ground help, who at no time made an effort to put a covering of any kind on the diamond." Cronin protested the game on the basis of "the negligence of the Washington baseball club" to cover the field. By the time the game was called, the rains had already stopped and the game could easily have continued, except for the fact that the grounds were now in unplayable condition. When they'd ordered Senators manager Bucky Harris to cover the infield, the umpires had been told that there wasn't a sufficient crew to comply with their request. The Senators outsmarted themselves; American League President Harridge later forfeited the game to Boston. The score in the permanent books is 6–3 in favor of the Red Sox. Appropriately, no pitcher was credited with a win nor tagged with a loss. It didn't really matter in the long run; Boston finished the season 17 games out of first place and the Senators were 31 games out.

In all, there were three games—none of which went against the Sox.

Near-forfeit games

There were near-forfeit games, such as the infamous Seat Cushion Night game in 1982 or 1983 where each fan was given a Red Sox logo'd seat cushion on entering the park. The Sox stunk so badly that evening that literally hundreds of seat cushions littered the field, sailed like Frisbees onto the outfield grass. Sherm Feller warned the crowd that the umpires would forfeit the game to their opponents if the fans couldn't become more ruly. Given that the game was beyond hope in any event, this hardly seemed like a serious threat, but fans did start to behave a bit better (and some of us wanted to take our seat cushions home). There was almost another forfeit in the ALCS in 1999 when umpires made two atrociously bad calls against the Red Sox in the playoffs versus the Yankees and fans began to litter the field with plastic drink bottles and other trash until threatened with a forfeit. The umpires uncharacertisically apologized later for the call—though the Red Sox suffered the loss in this one notwithstanding.

On several occasions, such as in the 1903 World Championship season, there were games that came close. It's one thing to throw out a player, or a group of players, but forfeiting a game is a major decision. Typically, an umpire will give full and final warning before invoking such an extreme penalty. On May 9, 1903, Jesse Tannehill squared off against Cy Young. New York was leading 2–0 after 4½ innings due to some shoddy fielding (Parent made three errors in this game) but Boston had two men on base and Chick Stahl at the plate. Umpire Carruthers called a pitch a ball, which Tannehill thought a strike and when Stahl stroked a run-scoring double on the next pitch, the New York pitcher "indulged in a torrent of abuse of the umpire, couched in the filthiest language" whereupon Carruthers tossed Tannehill from the game. Second baseman Jimmy Williams was also tossed. When the New York players refused to leave, Carruthers pulled out his watch and issued them a deadline on penalty of forfeit. One of the other New York players cajoled them into leaving and the game continued. Howell, allowed virtually no time to warm up, couldn't hold Boston and three more runs scored that inning, five more in the sixth and another three in the seventh. It wasn't the smoothest game but Boston beat New York, 12–5. With all of the scoring, it was the longest game of the year to date—a full two hours and five minutes.

A "no-decision" game

July 28, 1924

When was the last time that you heard of a game being protested—and then found out that the protest was upheld?

In addition to the three forfeited games, there was also one no-decision game. The score was 10–5, but it is listed as, in effect, a 10–5 tie! A no-decision. July 28, 1924 was the date. The game was in St. Louis. The score was Boston's 5–4 after 8½ innings, but St. Louis tied it up in the bottom of the ninth on a double by Gene Robertson. With Robertson on second, Norm McMillan strode up to the plate to hit. Umpire Brick Owens would not permit McMillan to bat, though, and ordered catcher Tony Rego to bat instead. Rego grounded out to short and the game went into extra innings. The Red Sox immediately pounced on the flustered Browns for two walks, a hit batsman, and three hits (and five runs) in the top of the 10th and then held them scoreless in the bottom of the frame. Browns manager George Sisler protested the game, though, citing the umpire's refusal to let McMillan bat. He did get his chance in the 10th; McMillan led off but grounded out. Why would Owens refuse McMillan? McMillan had entered the game in the St. Louis eighth as a pinch runner for Browns catcher Hank Severeid. In the same inning, the Browns also pinch-hit for shortstop Wally Gerber. When the Browns took the field for the top of the ninth, McMillan took Gerber's spot at short and Rego was sent in to catch. When McMillan came to the plate, he was batting in Severeid's slot in the order—Severeid being the player he'd pinch-run for. Apparently the league leadership agreed that Owens erred, and a victory was taken away from Boston, resulting in the game being officially declared a "no-decision." The game was re-played in its entirety as the second game of a September 13 doubleheader. It was a high-scoring 13–11 Red Sox victory.

TIE GAMES

Speaking of tie games, how often are there real tie games? There was one back in 1985. It's hard to remember any others. They used to be not uncommon, though, particularly in the era before ballparks all had lighting. Games were called on account of darkness with some frequency, and sometimes the score was tied at the time the game had to be called. Other times, games were called by curfew either under local statute or because, by pre-agreement, the teams had agreed to end a game by a certain time—most typically because of transportation arrangements.

Often times, the game tied was the second game of a doubleheader, when they just ran out of time—or available light. This happened 17 times in Red Sox history. Of the 82 times the score ended in a tie, fully 20 of them were under manager Joe Cronin. Of course, he did manage almost twice as many games as any other Sox skipper. The highest ratio of ties to games managed belongs to Jack Barry, with five ties in 157 games during the 1917 season.

July 31, 1985

The July 31, 1985 game was the most recent tie game. For the Red Sox, it had been 3,868 games since their last tie—setting a major league record for most consecutive games without a tie. Heavy rains hit Fenway that night. Had they called it after six innings, the White Sox would have won 1–0, but the Bosox tied it in the bottom of the seventh (on a Dave Sax sac fly) and the umpires motioned for the tarp at 10:16, finally calling the game at 11:34. Over a foot of water was reported in the visitors' clubhouse. The individual records stand in the record books, but the game itself was replayed in its entirety at 5:00 p.m. the next day, as part of a night doubleheader. Boston lost that game, 7–2. There hasn't been a tie game for Boston since, and through the end of the 2007 season, the current streak stands at 3,399. Without work stoppages or other interruptions, sticking to a 162-game schedule, sometime early in the 2010 season, they might set the new mark.

June 8, 1961

Twenty-four years earlier was the last time there had been a tie game in which the Red Sox were involved. That game was in Boston on June 8, 1961—a scheduled Thursday doubleheader. Boston won the first game, 6–5, and was leading in game two by a 3–2 score after eight innings. The rains didn't come soon, enough, though, and the Angels tied the game in the top of the ninth. Then, to make matters worse for the remnant of the 11,042 who were still there after 19 innings of ball on a rainy evening, the Angels scored once again in the top of the 11th, putting them up 4–3. Gary Geiger came up with a runner on base in the bottom of the 11th and tripled, tying the score. Unfortunately, Geiger hadn't counted too well—he thought he'd won the game and walked off third base where he was promptly tagged out. With the score 4–4, and the rain coming down harder after 1:00 a.m., the game was called. The game was made up as part of a twinbill the next day, Boston winning, 5–3, then losing, 5–1. Since the tie game was called after midnight and both games on Friday ended before midnight, the Sox thus completed three ballgames on June 8.

In the first half of the 20th century, though, there were quite a few tie games. There was at least one tie game every year for the first 20 years, save 1911 and 1918. Of the 82 tie games, remarkably 41 of them were home games and 41 were away games. Who won the most? Neither team—these were ties! Well, not exactly. Most of them were played out on subsequent dates.

In the first 50 years, there were 76 ties. Since 1950, there have been but six. Two of those six began on back-to-back dates—though in fact they were both called as tie games on the very same day.

July 20 and 21, 1954

In Boston on July 20, 1954 Boston scored twice in the bottom of the eighth to take a 5–3 lead but Cleveland came back with two runs of their own on a two-run homer by Bobby Avila with two outs in the ninth. The two teams then maintained a 5–5 tie until the game was called after 16 innings under a league curfew rule which stated that no inning could be commenced after 12:50 am. In the bottom of the ninth, the Sox had men on first and second with nobody out but Billy Consolo was sent in to bunt for pitcher Willard Nixon and popped up to catcher Ray Narleski who then fired the ball to second, catching Ted Lepcio before he could get back to the bag. After the BIDP (bunt into double play), Milt Bolling singled but it wasn't a deep enough single to score the runner from first. During the regularly-scheduled game the very next day, July 21, the Sox built up a 6–0 lead after three, but the Indians got four in the fourth and three more in the fifth. With Boston scoring once in the sixth, the two teams played to a 7–7 tie. Rains forced the end and it was called during the ninth inning by umpire Red Flaherty. As it happens, both tie games were actually called on the same date—July 21.

After 24 innings without a decision, the Sox made up one of the games on the 22nd. The first makeup game was lost 5–2, the only two Red Sox runs coming on a ninth inning homer by Harry Agganis. The Sox lost game two, 5–3, with all the Boston runs on a Williams homer. The August 29 makeup date was part of another doubleheader which drew a crowd of 36,344, said to be the largest crowd in the Yawkey era since overflow crowds were no longer allowed on the playing field itself. Unfortunately, they saw the Sox drop both games that day to the Indians, the ninth and 10th times in a row the Tribe won in Boston. The next day, Cleveland won again, sweeping all 11 games the Indians played in Boston that year. This was the great Indians team that won 111 games to 43 defeats, but were then swept in the World Series by the New York Giants.

September 13, 14, and 15, 1904

Another time, 50 years earlier, there had been back-to-back-to-back tie games! Sort of. On September 13, 1904 the Boston Americans were in Philadelphia playing the Athletics. The game was 0–0 and ended in a tie after one hour and 15 minutes of heavy mist and a stinging wind, called after seven innings. Despite the mist and mud, neither team made an error—but neither team scored, either. Both pitchers held their opponents to two hits. Boston had to get back home, where they had two games against New York to host the following day. On July 14, Boston's Norwood Gibson and New York's Jack Powell battled to a 1–1 tie in game two of the doubleheader, stopped after the fifth inning. Again, this was a game called due to mist. New York had won the first game, 3–1 (Jack Chesbro over Big Bill Dinneen). The very next day, the 15th, the same thing happened all over again: New York and Boston ended up tied 1–1 in game two of that day's twin bill. The game ran a full nine innings, called due to darkness. Boston won the first game, 3–2 (Tannehill over Orth, with New York making the final out leaving the bases loaded). Game two pitted Powell against Boston's George Winter. That's right, New York pitcher Jack Powell started both games that ended in ties, on two consecutive days. He must have been wondering how long he had to pitch before he got a decision. At least he didn't get a loss! He did win his next start, though he ended up in a third tie in the start following that one. Three ties in four starts. Talk about durable pitchers, though. Chesbro started three times in four days at the end of the season—and beat the world champion Boston team two out of the three.

Other times, other ties

If you like ties, 1907 and 1914 were very good years. Those years are tied for first place in the most ties per year. In 1907, there were six tied games, three of them with Chicago, two with Philadelphia, and one in New York.

October 5, 1907

The complete game pitcher for the New Yorkers was Slow Joe Doyle—maybe one of the reasons the game dragged on for a full two hours and three minutes before it was called at the end of 10 innings due to rain. The Boston pitcher in this '07 game was Joe Harris, whose record for the year was 0–7. Too bad he didn't get a win. It was the last game of the year, and there was no reason for a makeup. It was also the last start Joe Harris ever got; he was 3–30 in three years with Boston. They didn't invite him back—though he'd had a better year than the 2–21 mark of 1906, a year in which he also contracted typhoid fever at the end of the season. He must have been a tough luck pitcher—his 3.35 lifetime ERA wasn't bad at all. The day was doubly odd, in that it was a scheduled doubleheader. The tie was the first game, called after the 10. Everybody stuck around, though, and the weather cleared, so they started the second game—but then had to call it after three innings due to darkness.

In 1914, there were also six ties. The first two were back-to-back ties in Boston, both against Philadelphia. The first was 1–1, the second tie was 9–9.

Back to back ties: April 21, 1914 and April 22, 1914

Boston had just dropped both games of a doubleheader to the visiting Athletics on April 20. Dutch Leonard and Bob Shawkey squared off and both pitchers threw 13 full innings in a 1–1 tie (seven hits apiece) until the game was finally called on account of darkness. It was about as evenly matched a game as there could be. Both pitchers walked four batters. Both teams left eight runners on base. Leonard struck out nine to Shawkey's three, but runs are what counts. Boston got one in the third and Philadelphia got one in the sixth. That was it. Tris Speaker pulled off his first unassisted double play in the top of the 13th. It was Shawkey who was doubled off second, taking the Athletics out of the inning.

After battling to a 1–1 tie on the 21st, the two teams tied at 9–9 on the 22nd. Unlike the pitcher's duel the day before, this one saw "much bush-league stuff pulled" including five Philadelphia errors. This game was stopped after eight innings, "called to catch train" being the reason given. Boston was lucky they got in that final inning. Actually, Boston had been leading 5–1 after the fourth inning, but then Philly got four more runs in the top of the fifth to tie it up. In the seventh, they got another four and led, 9–5. The Federal express left Boston at 5:00 p.m. and both teams were due to take the train—Philadelphia to go home for their home opener against the New York team, and Boston to Washington for the Senators' opening day. Had they missed the five o'clock train, the Boston team would not have arrived in time the next day. After the seventh inning, umpires Connolly and Dinneen figured to get one more inning in. It was Boston's last chance. Philly rightfielder Murphy made a "very rank error" on a play that "any schoolboy" could have made. The inning would have ended on Henriksen's whiff one batter later, and the game in Philly's favor. Instead, it was two out with runners on first and second. Hooper doubled, scoring one. Engle walked on four pitches, loading the bases for Tris Speaker. Plank came on in relief and, on a 3–2 count, Speaker tripled, clearing the bases and tying the score. With 21 straight innings, ending in two tie games, now the two teams had two makeups to fit in.

No one ever did score

July 14, 1916

In a game called on account of darkness after 17 scoreless innings, St. Louis left-hander Ernie Koob blanked Boston, though the Red Sox had 14 hits off him, he walked three, and hit Jack Barry twice. Carl Mays pitched for Boston, even more effectively, but it looked like he'd given up a run in the 15th when Koob came around third base and barreled over Mays at home plate. Koob failed to touch third base, though, and third baseman McNally retrieved the ball Mays had dropped and tagged him out. Mays wasn't hurt badly, but was replaced by Leonard. The game continued, until the lack of light prevented it from going on.

Opening Day in 1910 proved to be a 4–4 tie between the Red Sox and the Yankees, called due to darkness after 14 innings.

In 1921 and 1922, the Red Sox experienced back-to-back years with no ties at all—the first time that had ever happened. It didn't happen again until 1932 and 1933, and then not again until 1950 when the Sox made it four straight years without a tie. 1959 and 1960 were the next back-to-back tieless seasons, but after a 4–4 tie game against the Los Angeles Angels on June 8, 1961, there was not another tie game until July 31, 1985—and there hasn't been one since. Thus, since 1961, there's only been one tie game in over 40 years.

An unusual game, then the anticlimax of a tie

September 29, 1943—St. Louis 3, Boston 3

It was a late-season Fenway doubleheader during wartime. In the first game, Tex Hughson squared off against Nels Potter of the Browns. The score was 2–2 after nine. In the top of the 11th, St. Louis shortstop Vern Stephens hit a solo home run off Hughson to give the Browns a one-run lead. But Boston scored once in the bottom of the inning. Up again in the top of the 13th, with Hughson still on the mound, Stephens did it again—his second extra-inning home run of the game. This time, the Red Sox failed to rally.

The second game was also tied after nine, this time 3–3 (Galehouse for St. Louis and Joe Dobson for Boston). But the umpires deemed it too dark to continue to play, so the second game was called a tie and everyone went home.

Highest scoring tie game

May 3, 1949—Boston 14, Detroit 14 (13 innings)

The highest-scoring tie game was a 14–14 tie in 1949 when the Red Sox played Detroit. 1949 was the year when George Kell (of the Tigers) beat out Ted Williams (of the Red Sox) for the league batting title by just .0001557!

In this game, Kell went 2-for-6 and Ted went 3-for-7 with a home run and a double. Both teams had a good shot at winning. The Red Sox jumped out to a 3–0 lead in the first on Stephens' three-run homer and added another one in the second, but the Tigers came back with one in the second and then broke out for nine runs in the third inning. After three, Detroit held a commanding 10–4 lead, but the Sox kept coming back—with three in the fourth, four in the sixth, and with three more in the seventh, and overtook the Tigers to take a 14–11 lead heading into the bottom of the ninth.

In a game which ultimately saw 11 pitchers in action, Boston's Windy McCall tired and Denny Galehouse came in with the bases loaded and one out. A Pat Mullin pinch-hit triple off Detroit's right-field wall cleared the bases and tied the score.

The Tigers loaded the bases in the 11th but Tex Hughson got Bob Swift to fly out. The same thing happened in the 13th—bases loaded, Hughson got Swift to fly out. The game was called on account of darkness after 13. All that work for nothing—the Red Sox used six pitchers and the Tigers used five. Boston used 15 players in all, and Detroit used 18. Boston had 20 hits to Detroit's 17. There were 19 walks, 13 of them issued by Boston. Even with all the runs that did score, there were plenty of runners left on base: Detroit 16 and Boston 10.

Was this a game that unfairly robbed Williams of the batting title and hence the Triple Crown? If you were to add three hits and seven at-bats to Ted's stats, he'd have hit .3438 and if you were to add two hits and three at-bats to George Kell's stats, he'd have hit .3428! The only problem with this scenario: the hits and at-bats *were* counted. Individual statistics from tie games are always counted; the only statistics a tie game does not yield are those related to winning and losing.

The first tie game at home, in Boston, was a 4–4 tie against Detroit on August 18, 1902. The "Detroits" scored once in the top of the first, but then the "Bostons" scored once, too. Detroit scored another one in the second, and two more in the fourth, but then Boston tied it up with three in the bottom of the fifth on three errors by Detroit. The teams got in six more innings with neither team scoring until finally umpire O'Loughlin called the game on account of darkness. Cy Young pitched all 11 for Boston according to the boxscore, though the accompanying *Boston Herald* article says that Hughes pitched the first two before Collins replaced him with Young. Mullin threw 11 for the visitors. Both teams had nine hits.

It had been in Detroit where Boston tied its first away game. On August 31, 1901, the Tigers won the first game of a doubleheader, 6–5, but the second game was called on account of darkness after a full nine innings with the score knotted 4–4. Boston had had a decent 4–1 lead but the Tigers had clawed back with one in the eighth and two more in the bottom of the ninth.

The Babe versus a couple of Rubes

April 16, 1915—Boston 6, Philadelphia 6

Then there was Babe versus Rube. April 16, 1915. Only the third game of the season, which opened in Philadelphia, and Boston already had a win, then a loss and finally a tie: 6–6, against Philadelphia. Pitching for the Red Sox was Babe Ruth. This young pitcher had only recently turned 19, but he'd shown some promise the year before. Ruth was 2–1 in his rookie year, with a 3.91 ERA. There were signs of shakiness; he had a poor strikeout to walk ratio having walked seven but only struck out three. He'd given up 21 hits in 23 innings. At the plate, he was no great shakes, either. He'd hit .200 with only one extra base hit—a double—and had struck out four of the 10 times he'd batted. He hadn't even worked a single walk. In his first start in 1915, he let up six runs, blowing a 6–1 Boston lead. What did Ruth do when staked to the big lead? He walked the first batter in the fifth. Barry doubled, then Ruth walked the other pitcher, Rube Bressler, loading the bases. He then walked Murphy, forcing in a run. And he walked the next batter after that, forcing in another run. The other Rube in the Philadelphia lineup, Rube Oldring, then singled, driving in one run, and young Ruth was yanked by manager Bill Carrigan. Oldring hit a homer in the seventh to tie the game, which was called after nine. Right after it was called on account of darkness (the street lights had gone on after the sixth inning), it started to rain anyhow. Carrigan gave Ruth another start a week later, and he won that one, 9–2. Then he lost his next four starts, one after another. Was this a player worth keeping?

Short and scoreless

April 14, 1928—Boston 0, Washington 0

It was a cold and dismal day when the umpires called the game after five innings "much to the disgust of the few hundred fans on hand." (Frank Young, *Washington Post*) They'd seen some interesting, if soggy, play. Herb Bradley was the starter for Boston and Milt Gaston started for the Senators. Each pitcher gave up just two hits, despite the conditions, and each pitcher walked just one batter. The game did have two errors, one by each side. Both Red Sox hits (one was by the pitcher, Bradley) were infield rollers to first base. A single and a double off Bradley were both clean hits. The Sox had men on first and second with nobody out in the bottom of the second, but a pop foul, a fly out, and a grounder to third ended that threat. In the top of the fifth, Tate led off with a double for the Senators and reached third on a grounder to the shortstop when the throw was dropped by Boston's third baseman. First and third, but a popup to second base brought about one out. The squeeze was on but the throw home was too high for the batter and a rundown ensued. Two outs, though the man on first scampered around to third during the back and forth. A walk restored the first and third scenario, but Gaston struck out. Boston failed to score. Game called on account of rain. It had lasted only 50 minutes.

Sorry, no more baseballs!

The Red Sox played the Cincinnati Reds to an 18–18 tie during a spring training game on April 6, 1939, the game called off for lack of baseballs. They'd begun the game in Florence SC with a good supply of four dozen balls, but there was a 40-mph "breeze" throughout the game (at one point in the third, Cincinnati shortstop Billy Myers' cap blew off and time was called so he could run and retrieve it). The two teams combined for 46 hits, among which were four home runs and a considerable number of ground rule doubles hit into the stands. A large number of fouls balls were also hit into the crowd of 2,285 and fans held onto them as souvenirs. The field had just been constructed a week earlier and "there wasn't a blade of grass on the diamond" so "great clouds of dust" obscured play despite the local fire department watering the grounds. The game ended in the top of the ninth with a runner on first base, when Harry Craft fouled off the 48th baseball into the crowd.

Almost one year later, almost the very same situation presented itself. The date was April 5, 1940 and the venue was Memorial Park in Greensboro NC. The same two teams were playing, though in the other Carolina. This time they started the game with twice as many baseballs. The score stood 10–8 in Cincinnati's favor when Boston's Leo Nonnenkamp fouled off an eighth-inning pitch. Ready to hit, he could not. All 96 balls had been used.

Other unusual games

36 runners left on base

Speaking of runners left on base, given the number of men on the basepaths, you'd think the August 22, 1951 game would have been a high-scoring affair. When the Bosox visited St. Louis and played the Browns on August 22, 1951, starting pitcher Tommy Byrne gave them just about all the help they could use. He issued 16 walks and 11 hits—but somehow the Red Sox only scored three runs. They left 22 runners on base. Through the first nine, Boston only scored once and the game went into extra innings. In the top of the 13th, after there were two outs and one man on, Byrne walked four Sox batters in a row, forcing in two runs and giving the Red Sox a 3–1 lead. Finally, Byrne was lifted and Mahoney came in and struck out DiMaggio to end the inning.

Byrne's final walk was to Red Sox starter Leo "Black Cat" Kiely, still in the game himself in the 13th. Kiely hadn't been a master of control, either. He'd given up eight bases on balls and 10 hits, and he tired in the bottom of the 13th giving up a walk and a single. Kinder came in and on his second pitch hit a double play ball to Johnny Pesky to end the game. St. Louis had left 14 men on base.

Four times the Red Sox left the bases loaded. The only offensive star was Pesky, who had three doubles and a single but still couldn't get himself either a run scored or a run batted in.

Most runners left on base while being shut out

The Sox were shut out by Oakland, 3–0, on May 16, 1988. With seven hits and seven walks, they got runners on base, but left 14 of them there. Marc Onigman notes that Sox starter Jeff Sellers got pretty poor run support. The year before, he'd lost eight games in which his teammates scored a collective total of 13 runs. At this point in 1988, they'd gotten him three runs in his first 38 innings pitched.

of times left on base

You have to get on base to begin with, of course, and then be stranded. No American League player has been left on base more than Wade Boggs in the last 50 years; Boggs holds two of the top three seasons—if you call it a "top season" to be stuck on base over 180 times when an inning ends.

Ichiro Suzuki was LOB 204 times in 2004
Wade Boggs was LOB 190 times in 1985
Wade Boggs was LOB 183 times in 1988

Shutting down scoring threats

The Yankees put plenty of men on base—enough to score seven runs while still leaving a record 20 men on base during a nine-inning game—but lost the September 21, 1956 contest to the Red Sox, 13–7.

The Red Sox themselves left 16 men on base during a nine-inning game on April 28, 1973. Despite 11 hits, they couldn't push but one runner across the plate and lost to the White Sox, 2–1.

The Sox were 0-for-19 with runners on base—and won the game

In the April 24, 2004 game against the New York Yankees, a Boston Red Sox batter came to the plate 19 times with a runner in scoring position and never once in the game did any one of those batters get a hit. Nonetheless, they won the game, 3–2 in 12 innings.

Fortunately (for Red Sox fans), there were three sacrifice flies.

Earliest game date

The earliest in the year the Red Sox had ever played a regular season game was on March 31, 2003. It was (obviously) Opening Day. That was the only March opener they'd ever had—until they advanced the date to one six days earlier, and opened the 2008 season on March 25, 2008. The game ran into extra innings, and resulted in a 6–5 Red Sox win in 10 innings over Oakland at the Tokyo Dome.

Earliest start time: 10:00 a.m.

Patriots Day games typically start at 11:05 a.m. these days. Back on April 20, 1903, though, Boston's Huntington Avenue Grounds hosted two games on a combined Opening Day / Patriots Day separate admission doubleheader. The 10:00 a.m. first game is the earliest start of any major league game since the start of the 20th century. Some 8,376 up-and-at-'em fans saw Cy Young and Boston beat Philadelphia's Rube Waddell, 9–4. On April 20, 1953 and April 19, 1954, the Sox had 10:15 a.m. starts, again for the annual Patriots Day game.

With the time difference between Boston and Tokyo, the scheduled March 25, 2008 Opening Day broadcast required Hub fans to get up before dawn to see the first pitch at 6:07 a.m. Boston time. There was a bit of a reprieve as the game started three minutes late. Given the International Date Line, however, they were watching—live—a game played that evening, at 7:10 on the evening of March 25th, Tokyo time. Speaking of broadcasts…

The first broadcast of a Red Sox game was of Opening Day 1927, with Gus Rooney of WNAC radio (naturally an AM station, as there were no FM stations in those days). Beginning in 1928, Fred Hoey took over the mike and he covered Red Sox games through the 1938 season. The Sox stuck with WNAC throughout; the station was part of the Yankee Radio Network (no relation to the team from New York). Hoey, Norman Macht has noted, saw his first baseball game in the 1897 Temple Cup Series, and worked all Boston ballgames— Braves and Red Sox, whichever team was home at the time—until he died. During winters he held an executive position at the Boston Garden. In 1931 Fenway Park fans honored him with a special day. Hoey had previously worked at head usher at the Huntington Avenue Grounds.

Was his brother Jack Hoey, who played for the Sox? It could be. Jack was four years older. Or was this Fred related to old Fred Hoey, who was the manager for the New York Giants during part of the 1899 season? A prize to any researcher who can document a family tie.

The first television broadcast was on April 23, 1948, sending the signal from New York. Several hundred watched the broadcast at Boston's Parker House Hotel. The Red Sox beat the Yankees, 4–0. Among those watching the game were the Yawkeys and GM Joe Cronin. The game was sent to Boston by station WABD in New York and was sponsored by the Atlantic Television Corporation. The *Globe* covered the broadcast, noting, "The reception was very clear, and the spectators were able to follow the flight of the ball and the progress of the game, with a running commentary, very easily."

Shortest game ever: 50 minutes long

The shortest game the Red Sox ever played was the five-inning scoreless tie against the Senators on April 14, 1928. The game took just 50 minutes to play before rains prevented its continuation, but lasted just long enough that the team didn't have to refund any money to patrons. There weren't very many people there, though, only a few hundred. For those who were, the next day's *Washington Post* had little sympathy: "It rained at intervals all morning and the air was damp and cold. Folks willing to risk their lives on a day like this deserved some punishment." See the full game account in the preceding section on tie games.

The shortest game the Red Sox ever played against the Yankees was 55 minutes long. It happened on September 5, 1927. It was the second game of a doubleheader, in the days before there was lighting on the field. The first game lasted 18 innings, and Boston beat New York, 12–11. That was the good news. It was a thrilling game. The Yankees had tied it 8–8 in the ninth, and the game went on for eight more scoreless innings. New York scored three times in the top of the 17th, but the Red Sox tied it back up with three of their own. Boston finally won it in the 18th on doubles by Buddy Myer and Ira Flagstead. They wanted to get both games in, so may have played pretty quickly in the second game, which the Yankees won, 5–0. It was called on account of darkness after five innings. That was the bad news.

The Red Sox once played an even briefer affair, but it was in spring training. The April 9, 1918 ballgame in Birmingham between the Brooklyn Dodgers and Red Sox officially lasted 35 minutes (seven innings, 3–1 Brooklyn), though news accounts suggested the game might have been a few minutes shorter. Neither team tried to hard to win, often swinging at first pitches, in an attempt to get back to the warmth of their hotel rooms all the sooner.

An inning longer than some ballgames

The sixth inning of the July 24, 2004 game between the Red Sox and Yankees lasted 1:07—one hour and seven minutes—longer than some entire ballgames in the early years of the franchise. The Yankees scored six runs in the top of the sixth, on six hits and three walks, while the Red Sox implemented two pitching changes to try and stem the bleeding. The Red Sox then scored four runs in the bottom of the sixth, on four hits and two walks. The Yankees used four pitchers. There were 89 pitches thrown in the inning. Both teams left three men on base. This is the game that Bill Mueller won with a homer in the bottom of the ninth, 11–10 Red Sox.

Longest game ever: 395 minutes

In the first nine innings of the August 25, 2001 ballgame in Texas, both the Rangers and Red Sox scored seven times each. In the second nine innings of the 6:35 game (believed the longest ballgame the Red Sox ever played), only one run was scored. Derek Lowe was the losing pitcher, giving up one unearned run on zero hits. It came on two walks, an error, a wild pitch, a steal of third, and then Chad Curtis scored on a ground ball. The Red Sox used nine pitchers in all and Texas used eight. Texas 8, Boston 7.

Longest home game: six hours and one minute

It began as a typical night game at Fenway. September 3, 1981. Seattle scored once in the second and twice in the third, but Boston got two back in the bottom of the third and tied it with a run in the fourth. The Mariners scored four unanswered runs, until Boston got one back in the bottom of the eighth and tied it with three runs in the ninth. Then 10 more innings got played, before the game was suspended at 1:16 a.m. after 19 innings of play. It was the second suspended game of the season, the first being May 4.

For the fans who assembled the evening of September 4 to see the game continue, it was all over in 22 minutes. After Bob Stanley got two outs on grounders, Dave Henderson singled and

Joe Simpson tripled. Stanley was the seventh Red Sox pitcher of the game; the eighth Mariners pitcher similarly retired the first two Red Sox on infield plays—but then Rick Miller singled, Jerry Remy singled, and Dwight Evans walked to load the bases. Jim Beattie, the ninth Seattle pitcher, came in to face Jim Rice (2-for-8 in the game). Rice bounced the ball to the Seattle shortstop, who retired Evans coming into second base. Both teams had used every possible position player except one hitter apiece. The Mariners also won the game that followed, 5–2.

Longest night game ever

The longest night game was played at home: 4:45, on August 18, 2006 against the Yankees. It set a major league record. Unfortunately, for the players, it was the second game both teams played that long day of baseball. There had been a 3:55 afternoon game. Unfortunately, for Red Sox fans, the Yankees won both of them: 12–4 and 14–11.

Latest ending time: 2:32 a.m.

The latest end of a Red Sox game was at Tiger Stadium in a 3–2 loss to Detroit on August 5, 1988. It was a night-time doubleheader, with a 2:22 rain delay mixed in during the first game, all conspiring to push the final ending time to 2:32 a.m. They got in a full 8½ innings in both games—yes, the Tigers took two, 3–1 and 3–2.

The latest-ending home game was a 2:26 a.m. end to another losing game, an August 24, 1977 rain-delayed game that saw the Rangers beat the Red Sox, 6–3.

Longest rain delays

The longest rain delay at home was a recent one, on June 10, 2006. It was a scheduled day game, meant to be the first game of a day/night doubleheader, and pitcher Jon Lester's major league debut. By the time Lester got the chance to throw his first pitch, it was 6:12 p.m. He'd waited out a four-hour, 47-minute rain delay. After 102 pitches, and 4⅔ innings of work, Lester left the game with it tied 3–3. The Rangers won, 7–4.

The longest rain delay the Red Sox have endured on the road was in Toronto (in the days before Skydome a/k/a Rogers Centre). It was September 26, 1985 at Exhibition Stadium, Boston's Jeff Sellers against Doyle Alexander. Both pitchers threw complete games, but only after enduring a 3:18 rain delay at the start of the game. The Red Sox won, 4–1, the game finishing at 1:02 a.m. Mike Greenwell hit a two-run homer and Wade Boggs singled in two more runs, and Sellers spun a three-hitter.

Extended evenings: back-to-back
extra-inning games, 1951

July 12 (+13) and July 13 (+14), 1951

The first extended evening began with a regulation nine-inning affair. In the first game of a twilight-night twinbill, both teams went scoreless through six. Boston got two in the seventh, one in the eighth and then just barely held on in Chicago's home half of the ninth. Bases full, nobody out, Parnell was pooped. In popped Harry Taylor in relief, and he induced a grounder to Doerr, then a grounder to Doerr, and finally a grounder to Doerr. Two runs crossed the plate, in the process, but the third out was made and the third run didn't score. Boston won, 3–2.

The second game on July 12 was 4–4 after 7½ and it stayed that way for a long, long time, with White Sox pitcher Saul Rogovin going the distance. Lou Boudreau's single for Boston started things in the 17th, and he moved to third on a hit-and-run, scoring shortly afterward on Clyde Vollmer's deep left-field sac fly. Ellis Kinder worked the final 10 innings for the Red Sox and got the win, his 16th straight win over the White Sox. The 17-inning game set an American

League record as the longest night game ever. The win catapulted the Red Sox over the White Sox and into first place for the first time in '51. The game ended at 12:45 a.m. on the 13th.

Fortunately, only one game was scheduled for later that night. The record 17-inning game started on the 12th was eclipsed by a 19-inning marathon started on the 13th. Mickey McDermott labored hard for Boston throwing the first 17 innings himself. When he left, the score was 2–2 just as it had been since the fifth inning.

Harry Taylor was back in for Boston in relief, and the whole team was feeling relieved when the Red Sox scored twice in the top of the 19th inning. A Chicago single, anther single and a bunt single loaded the bases for the home team White Sox. Eddie Stewart's pinch-hit single plated two and tied the score once more. Boston began hoping to see the 20th inning at this point, but a deep Don Lenhardt fly to DiMaggio in center scored Nellie Fox on the sacrifice. 5–4, White Sox. 36 innings in two games, and 45 innings in about 30 hours.

The most number of innings played in one game

The September 1, 1906 game at the Huntington Avenue Grounds was tied 1–1 after six innings, and then went on and on and on. Pitch counts were for sissies. Neither starting pitcher (Philadelphia's Jack Coombs and Boston's Joe Harris) ever left the game. Both of them went the distance—24 innings. It was the first game of a doubleheader. The second game never got played. Harris threw 20 consecutive scoreless innings—a one-game record that will likely never be approached. In the 24th, he struck out the first batter, then gave up a single. The runner stole second and Harris struck out a second man. His next pitch hit the bat of Osee Schrecongost as the batter ducked—and bounced over second base, driving in a run. Back-to-back triples followed and Philadelphia had scored three times. Coombs retired the Boston side in the bottom of the 24th and got the win after four hours and 47 minutes. Harris finished the year 2–21, but this was one marathon effort. Coombs went on to a very good career, his best year being 1910: 31–9 with a 1.30 ERA.

The game with the most innings at Fenway was one described above, the 20-inning game of September 3, 1981 that was suspended and completed the following day.

The Boston Americans played another 20-inning game at the Huntington Avenue Grounds on July 4, 1905. Rube Waddell and Cy Young both went the distance, but Cy ran into trouble in the top of the 20th, with "a fumble, a hit by pitched ball, a force out, and two singles" resulting in two runs for the Athletics and a 4–2 defeat for Boston. Boston lost the day's second game, too.

The most innings played in a Red Sox road game

The longest road game the Red Sox ever played, in terms of the number of innings, was also a 20-inning game. There were actually two of them:

1) at Sicks Stadium, Seattle on July 27, 1969, the Red Sox beat the Seattle Pilots 5–3 in a game that took 20 innings and lasted 5:52.
2) Yankee Stadium, August 29, 1967. Yankees 4, Red Sox 3 in a 20-inning game that took 6:09 to complete. There had been another game played that night, and played quickly, too: the evening's first game took only 2:10. The Red Sox won that one, 2–1, on a Jim Lonborg three-hitter.

Other extra-inning extras

We've seen that the Sox opened 1969 with three extra-inning games in a row. In 1943, they played four extra-inning games in a row, all against the St. Louis Browns at Fenway Park, in back-to-back doubleheaders on May 31 and June 2. Boston won three of the four. 45 innings in two days.

A couple of games that took a little extra effort to bring to fruition came on July 9, 1937 and June 18, 1947. In the '37 game, it looked like the Athletics had wrapped it up when they scored six times in the eighth to take an 8–4 lead. But Boston tied it in the top of the ninth—and then scored three more times in the top of the 10th. The A's weren't ready to quit yet, and re-tied the game with three of their own. Finally, in the 12th, Ben Chapman tripled and Joe Cronin doubled, and the Sox scored a run that went unanswered for a 12–11 win. In 1947, playing the Browns in Boston, it was 1–1 after six. Both teams scored once in the eighth. Four scoreless innings followed, then St. Louis scored once in the top of the 13th—but the Sox scored once in the bottom of the 13th. St. Louis raised the stakes, scoring twice in the top of the 14th; the Red Sox matched that with two of their own. When the Browns failed to score in the 15th, the Sox saw their opening and Johnny Pesky singled in pinch runner Eddie Pellagrini with the winner.

Postponements

There are many games that never occurred, postponed due to bad weather or other circumstances. Some games got underway and were called off before becoming an official game. This has sometimes resulted in a lost performance of one kind or another. There are other games that just never began. The reasons for postponement are varied. Typical ones include rain, wet grounds, cold weather (and, occasionally, snow), but newspaper reports also mention Red Sox games called off due to "threatening weather" or climate conditions that were "unsettled."

The first game called off for Boston's AL team was on May 5, 1901, due to rain. As we have seen, games called off were sometimes not made up, frequently resulting in seasons with less than the full scheduled number of games being played. In one 11-day stretch in 1954, nine games were postponed. Despite that, the Sox played a full 154-game schedule—and two more games as well (there were two tie games, on back-to-back days in July).

The first postponement in a World Series game came the year of the first World Series. On October 9, 1903 it was deemed too cold to play ball in Pittsburgh and the day's game was postponed until the following day. Boston won that seventh game…but had to play again three days later in Boston, because the Series was a best of nine in 1903. The Series game on October 9, 1912 had been tied 5–5 after nine, and the Giants took a 6–5 lead in the top of the 10th but Tris Speaker hit what looked like an inside-the-park home run in the bottom of the inning, then looked to be tagged out at the plate—but Giants catcher Art Wilson couldn't hold the ball. With the score re-tied, 6–6, and with starter Christy Mathewson still on the mound for the Giants, the game was called after 11 innings due to darkness.

In the 1975 Fall Classic, there were postponements on three consecutive days. Both teams stood idle on October 18, 19, and 20 before being able to resume play.

Other than weather conditions, games have been called off due to:
— gamblers swarming on the field (June 16, 1917 at Fenway Park)
— the death of President Warren G. Harding (August 3, 1923)
— Harding's funeral (August 10, a day of mourning)
— hurricane (August 31, 1954)
— the funeral of Dr. Martin Luther King, Jr. (April 9, 1968)
— players' strike (The first several games of the 1972 season were never played due to a strike. As we know, the 1994 season was cut short by a strike. The Red Sox had just traveled to Baltimore after losing three in a row in Minnesota. They were playing the Orioles on August 11, and had a 1–0 lead when rains came in the third inning. After a rain delay of two hours and 16 minutes, the game was called off—and so was the season.)
— terrorist attacks (in the aftermath of September 11, 2001)

The 1945 All-Star Game was called off due to war.

There were even games called off in order to boost ticket sales. For instance, the scheduled August 20, 1936 game in New York was "deferred so a doubleheader could be played Sunday, when about 50,000 are expected to sit in." It worked; 63,906 was the Sunday attendance. The August 11, 1939 game against the Washington Senators was deliberately postponed to create a twinbill on August 13. When less than 500 people showed up on a hot and muggy August 20, 1947 in St. Louis, a quick shower provided an excuse. The *Boston Globe* said that "lack of customers, not rain, was the real motive for the quick postponement." Attendance was so poor that the Red Sox hadn't even covered expenses during their stay in St. Louis.

In 1907, Boston called off three exhibition games (in French Lick, Indianapolis, and Cincinnati) due to the suicide of their manager, Chick Stahl. And a postseason exhibition tour of the West Coast by the Red Sox and the Phillies in 1915 was called off for lack of money. The financial guarantees were deemed unsatisfactory. (The Phillies claimed it was due to a banquet commitment they'd made in Philadelphia, but earlier news reports make that excuse look hollow.)

Many games were called off due to darkness in the days before artificial lighting made night games a possibility. That's not to mention games truncated when darkness struck. There are times that a ballclub would try to prolong a game in hopes it would be called before becoming an official game. Occasionally, the efforts resulted in farce.

A game that Boston would have loved to see called was the second one on September 27, 1905 against the White Sox. Boston's Big Bill Dinneen threw a no-hitter in the first game and, with Cy Young starting the second game, the team had to have felt good about their prospects. Chicago batted the same lineup (only changing pitcher and catcher), but piled up nine runs in the top of the first. The game was called after six, Chicago leading 15–1, when it was deemed too dark to continue. Had Boston maybe let the score run to 35–1 through four innings, and dragged out play, none of the runs would have counted and the team would not have suffered a loss.

Such strategies did obtain. The August 5, 1935 game at Fenway Park was washed out after five innings. With the Yankees leading, 10–2, the Red Sox had tried to kill time. Myril Hoag even stole home standing up; the call today would be "defensive indifference." The Red Sox just didn't want to record an out. Yankees runners more than once tried to get thrown out on the basepaths, hoping to move the game along. A week later, the league fined both managers for "highly reprehensible" play.

This may have reminded some fans of the June 22, 1911 game. The New York Highlanders scored four times in the first and thrice more in the second. When rain started falling in the fourth—it not yet an official game—the Boston players "moped along like pallbearers" while the New Yorkers "hustled to beat the band," according to *The New York Times*. In the fourth, NY's Daniels swung wildly at three pitches, hardly intending to hit one. Fitzgerald got wood on one, a routine grounder, but Boston second baseman Engle "faded away from it scandalously" enabling Fitzgerald to reach second base. When Hartzell lofted an easy fly ball to left, Fitzgerald made no attempt to get back to second—he started running and never stopped, giving Boston no choice but to double him off the bag and end the inning. Umpire Connolly pushed the Red Sox to bat and move things along. The game was called after 4½—but New York won 7–0.

As noted above, there was the July 14, 1916 game against the St. Louis Browns that went on and on, and resulted in a scoreless tie after 17 innings and too much darkness. Boston and the Browns played to another scoreless tie, a double shutout after 10 innings, on September 8, 1929, this one called because of Boston's Sunday law that required games to stop at 6:00 p.m.

The following season, 1912, a July 18 game started promisingly for the Red Sox, who scored 10 runs in the bottom of the first—yet the inning never ended. With two outs, the rains came, the field became a lake, and the game was postponed—all those hits and all those runs washed away. The game was made up the following day, and the Red Sox beat Chicago, 8–0.

Starting and stopping. Two months later, on September 19, 1912, the rains may have helped Cleveland, twice, though both games were likely lost causes from the Red Sox perspective. It was a scheduled doubleheader. The Red Sox were trailing 9–3 when rain caused the first game to be called after five innings. Both teams waited around for an hour after that, though, and when the rains let up, they decided to play the second game. Cleveland built up a 6–0 lead through six, when this game, too, was called—though on account of darkness.

In 1944, the Browns wanted badly to get in a game. The Red Sox had lost 10 in a row

Action photograph in the last inning of the July 14, 1916 game, called on account of darkness.

and St. Louis had won each of their last seven. The Browns were tied for first place with the Tigers with just five games left in the season. The game was originally set for 2:30, but heavy rain caused it to be called off at 3:30. The Sox had checked out of their hotel to head out of town, but agreed to reschedule as a night game at 8:00. The game got underway at 9:05 and, despite another rain delay, was completed at 11:09. The Browns lost, 4–1, and could have blown the pennant. Detroit won their game. St. Louis swept the final four from the Yankees, though, while the Tigers lost two of their last three.

Snow caused the 1996 home opener to be postponed. Back in 1953, the first two games of the year had had to be postponed due to snow. In those days, when the game was called off, the Red Sox ticket office would hang out a flag reading "No Game Today."

1964 was a good year in terms of playing out the schedule. The Red Sox almost made it through a full season without a postponement. The first game called was September 29; the Red Sox were shut out twice by Cleveland the following day.

Victims of a perfect game that was deemed not perfect, though still a game, the Red Sox suffered at the hands of Minnesota's Dean Chance on August 6, 1967. Chance retired every Red Sox batter he faced—all 15 of them. It was called after 4½ innings, an official 2–0 win for Chance and the Twins, a complete game, too, but he wasn't given credit for a perfect game. A similar scenario ended the 2006 season when Devern Hansack of the Red Sox threw a no-hitter at Fenway in the October 1 game against the Orioles that was rained out after five innings. He got a shutout, a complete game, the win, and a little glory—but nothing like the immortality that an "official" no-hitter would have provided. Matt Young was denied no-hitter status back on April 12, 1992. He threw a game against Cleveland and never gave up a hit. He lost the game, in Cleveland, by a 2–1 score, only throwing eight innings because, of course, there was no point in the Indians batting in the bottom of the ninth. Since Young only threw eight innings, and since he lost, you won't find his name in the list of Red Sox no-hitters even though he pitched the full game and never gave up a hit.

Lost home runs. Add to the list of disappointed players Joe Pepitone of the Yankees (we feel so sorry for him). He hit a grand slam in the top of the first inning of the June 20, 1969 ballgame in Boston. Rain came, and umpire Hank Soar called off the game. Pepitone was livid, complaining that it hadn't rained that much and, besides, the field needed water.

The day the Red Sox showed up in the wrong city

Then there was the time that Boston didn't play a game, because they showed up in the wrong city. They didn't know they were going to become the Red Sox yet; this was 1901.

Every time you set up a new league, you're bound to have a few problems. The first year of the American League ran very smoothly, considering that it was a new enterprise. Many of the best players from the National League jumped ship for the better financial offers in the new league, and the caliber of play was very high. In many cities which had two teams—such as Boston—attendance at the new American League parks outpaced the established NL teams, often by large margins. Boston's NL team had drawn 190,000 in 1900, but with two teams in town, their 1901 attendance dipped to 146,502. The Boston Americans, however, drew 289,448 and for the next 50 years swamped attendance at the Nationals' field. But there were a few first-year kinks.

A couple of months into the season, on June 26, 1901 Jimmy Collins and his Boston team showed up at Columbia Park in Philadelphia, in uniform and ready to play the Athletics. Umpire Alfred Manassau turned up, too. The problem was—there was no team to play. The Philadelphia Athletics weren't there. They were in Washington, playing the Senators at American League Park. Since the umpire was in Philadelphia, no umpire showed up in Washington—so one catcher from each team was drafted to umpire in that game: Mike Grady of the Senators (who came from Philadelphia) and ex-Senator Tom Leahy of the Athletics (who came from New Haven) umpired the game. "Their work was excellent," wrote the *Philadelphia Inquirer* correspondent. The *Washington Star* added, "Their decisions were unusually accurate and satisfactory." The Athletics may wish they had stayed at home; they were leading 4–1 when Washington scored four times in the ninth to win the game, the final run scoring on a very close play at home plate as Washington's John Farrell slid in with the winning run, ruled safe by Leahy of the Philadelphia team.

Meanwhile, in yet another city—Baltimore—the Orioles sat idle. They were waiting for the Bostons to arrive. Then the Chicago White Sox showed up instead! Balitmore manager John McGraw refused to play Chicago, since it said on his schedule that his team was supposed to host Boston. So Baltimore waited for Boston, Boston was in Philadelphia, and the White Sox had pulled into Baltimore but the Orioles wouldn't play them.

Detroit had just left Baltimore and was on its way home to host Milwaukee. Milwaukee, for its part, played a game against Cleveland as it prepared to head on to Detroit. Cleveland had left Boston and was on its way to Chicago, but paused at home for the game with Milwaukee.

How did this mix-up come about? Three home games in Baltimore had been rained out—those against Boston on April 24 and 25 and the June 15 game against Chicago. Chicago was nearby, having played Philadelphia the day before, on June 25. Boston had a game to make up against Philadelphia and that was scheduled for July 31. The original schedule had Boston at Baltimore on July 3. Then someone in the League office realized that Boston already had a morning game set on the Fourth of July; train schedules being what they were, the Boston team couldn't get back home in time if they'd played an afternoon game in Baltimore on July 3. So League President Ban Johnson re-scheduled Boston to play in Baltimore earlier, on June 26, instead. The problem was that Johnson apparently forgot to tell either Boston or umpire Manassau about the change. Boston (and the league umpire) therefore followed the original schedule and showed up at an empty ballpark in Philadelphia. Johnson also forgot to tell Chicago that plans had changed, so the White Sox kept to their original schedule, too, and traveled to Baltimore. At least there was another team there, but as Johnson had told Baltimore to expect Boston, when Chicago turned up instead, McGraw would not play them.

Somehow the *Boston Herald* had it right; the *Sunday Herald* told readers that Boston was going to play in Baltimore on the 26th, but apparently nobody on the team read the *Herald* or didn't believe everything they read in the papers.

The newspaper boasted a bit, under a story headlined THE HERALD HAD IT RIGHT. "The failure of the Boston American team to appear in Baltimore yesterday can be ascribed to no other cause than downright stupidity. In last Sunday's *Herald* it was announced that the team was scheduled to play in Baltimore on Wednesday, yet, marvellous to say, President Somers, Business Manager Gavin and Jimmy Collins were not aware of that fact. It does look as if it would pay the busy representatives of the local club to read *The Herald* carefully before they go on another trip. It would save them lots of trouble and expense, and enable them to know exactly where they are expected to play."

This was nothing that a cellphone couldn't have fixed.

In a position to win (or lose) on the last day of the season

Despite the Yankees' success at winning pennants and winning World Series, the Red Sox have actually faced twice as many situations where the pennant was on the line the final day of the season.

All three times that the New Yorkers have come to the day game of the regular season in a position to win, they faced the Bostons. They've never found themselves in that situation with any other team. They lost the first time (1904) but won the next two (1949 and 1978). The game in 1978 counts, despite it being a single-game playoff, because that single game is defined as part of the regular season.

Of the six times Boston found itself in this situation, they won three and lost three.

New York

October 10, 1904 Boston 3, New York 2 (there was another game this day, but inconsequential)
October 2, 1949 New York 5, Boston 3
October 1, 1978 New York 5, Boston 4

Boston

October 10, 1904 Boston 3, New York 2
October 3, 1948 Cleveland 8, Boston 3
October 2, 1949 New York 5, Boston 3

October 1, 1967 Boston 5, Minnesota 3
October 1, 1978 New York 5, Boston 4
October 3, 1990 Boston 3, Chicago 1

POSTSEASON

World Series

The Red Sox have gone to the postseason 18 times in the 106 years of American League play through 2007. The postseason used to be just the World Series, until additional rounds of playoffs were added beginning in 1969. As we know, Boston won the World Series every time it played in one, prior to 1946. And, we recall, they failed to win one between 1918 and 2004. But that's ancient history now.

Sox players who played for Boston in more than one World Series:

Harry Hooper—1912, 1915, 1916, 1918
Hick Cady—1912, 1915, 1916
Bill Carrigan—1912, 1915, 1916
Larry Gardner—1912, 1915, 1916

Dutch Leonard—1915, 1916
Carl Mays—1916, 1918
David Ortiz—2004, 2007
Rico Petrocelli—1967, 1975

Olaf Henriksen—1912, 1915, 1916
Duffy Lewis—1912, 1915, 1916
Babe Ruth—1915, 1916, 1918
Everett Scott—1915, 1916, 1918
Dwight Evans—1975, 1986
Rube Foster—1915, 1916
Del Gainer—1915, 1916
Dick Hoblitzell—1915, 1916
Hal Janvrin—1915, 1916

Manny Ramirez—2004, 2007
Curt Schilling—2004, 2007
Ernie Shore—1915, 1916
Tris Speaker—1912, 1915
Pinch Thomas—1915, 1916
Mike Timlin—2004, 2007
Jason Varitek—2004, 2007
Carl Yastrzemski—1967, 1975

Ernie Shore, 1916.

Which Red Sox player appeared in the most World Series games? Harry Hooper, 24 games (1912, 1915, 1916, and 1918).

Given the two rounds of playoffs that precede the World Series today, which Red Sox players appeared in the most playoff games? Note that it is possible to come in first in Red Sox playoff games without ever having played in a World Series itself. The answer to the question: Jason Varitek, who has appeared in 53 playoff games. Trot Nixon appeared in 38.

The Red Sox were denied their World Series rings twice in a row

In the early days, the equivalent to today's championship rings were the world championship emblems traditionally presented to each member of the winning ballclub. The Sox were denied their emblems after both the 1916 and 1918 World Series wins. On October 20, 1916, eight days after Boston had won the World Series from Brooklyn, the National Commission voted to deny World Series emblems to a number of members of the Sox team because the players had participated in an October 15 exhibition game in New Haven. The purpose of the rule, a newspaper report explained, was "to keep the heroes of the diamond from dragging their laurels out on the prairies and letting them trail in the mud for a few extra dollars." The emblems were reported to be worth about $85 wholesale.

Red Sox owner Joseph Lannin objected, suggesting that some other form of discipline be applied and arguing, "No one can take away the glory the Red Sox players earned for their grand ball playing." The Baseball Players' Fraternity objected as well, asserting that baseball can't discipline players for exhibitions after the season was over and after player contracts had expired. On December 8, 10 members of the Red Sox were fined $100 each by the National Commission for participating in postseason exhibitions. Lannin had sold the Red Sox team to Harry Frazee and Hugh Ward on November 1.

The matter of the emblems was worked out and on February 4, 1917 members of the 1916 World Champion Boston Red Sox received special watches engraved with the names of all the players. The players who had dragged their laurels onto the prairies of New Haven were told, though, that they would only receive their watches after they paid the $100 fines. On March 16, it was reported that the watch which would have gone to 1916 owner Joseph Lannin had instead gone to new owner Harry Frazee, at Frazee's request. Lannin huffed that he wouldn't even accept it if one were sent to him at such a late date. So Frazee, who wasn't even in baseball until after the 1916 World Series, got a watch, and Lannin, who had seen the Red Sox to back-to-back World Championships, did not.

Just two years later, the Red Sox won the World Series again. On October 4, 1918 for the second Series in a row, the World Champion Red Sox were to be disciplined for engaging in post-Series play when it was announced that Bush, Schang, Strunk, and Mayer were among those being investigated for having "engaged in a trip under the name of Red Sox." Word was that the National Baseball Commission would deprive several Boston players of the emblems usually presented to World Series winners. On November 16, the National Commission voted to assess fines against Bush, Schang, and Strunk.

The Commission also voted to withhold the world championship emblems from all the World Series participants, because of their role in threatening to go on strike during the Series itself. Only some very last-minute negotiations had averted a mid-Series strike while fans were getting restless in their seats waiting for Game Five to begin. It's a long story we needn't pursue here; *Red Sox Century* presents the details well. In a nutshell, after Game Three, the players learned that the owners planned to reduce the shares to both teams in the Series from what they had historically been. The players only played Game Four when promised a hearing. Come time for Game Five—which would have been the final game should the Red Sox improve on their three games-to-one lead—and the players realized it might be the last leverage they had. Denied a meeting, but again promised one—this time after Game Five—they chose to stay in their clubhouse to force the issue. Word that the players were on strike quickly spread and the assembled fans grew restless as the start time came and went. It was a standoff, but the ballplayers caved and took to the field after being promised that at least there would be no punishment meted out. At the mid-November meeting, the Commission broke that promise and withheld the emblems.

Fans in Boston did hold a Harry Hooper Day on September 17, 1921, however, and bestowed a number of gifts on him. The *Boston Globe* noted that "the oversubscription will be used to buy gifts for some of the other Boston players who were with Hooper on the World's Champions Red Sox team in 1918, when the National Commission failed to give them emblems as had been the custom."

The 1918 team had to wait a very long time to receive the emblems of appreciation. Not one of them received the emblems while they were living, though Harry Hooper battled for them right up to his death in 1974 and his son John continued the campaign afterward.

The injustice was finally righted, but it was righted by the Red Sox and not by Major

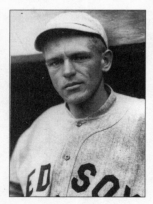

Fred Thomas of the 1918 champions.

League Baseball. It came on the 75th anniversary of the 1918 season. It was only a campaign by baseball historian Glenn Stout that produced the posthumous presentation to their surviving family members on September 4, 1993. An article Stout had written for *New England Sport* started the ball rolling, a sponsor was found, and the Red Sox agreed to honor the men who'd won the team's last World Championship.

Stout tracked down as many family members as he could, including George Whiteman's 95-year-old sister-in-law, Fred Thomas's widow, Dave Shean's son, and John Hooper. Babe Ruth was represented by his adopted daughter Julia Ruth Stevens. The ceremonies were held, a 1918 banner was unfurled from the flagpole, and many family members were at last given recognition of the World Series win. The Red Sox rightfully received credit for their willingness to honor the families of the champions. The guy who initiated the whole thing, though, Glenn Stout, wasn't involved or acknowledged in the on-field ceremony, and had to buy his own ticket to get into the game. Virtue, though, is perhaps its own reward.

Derek Lowe won all three deciding games during the 2004 playoffs

Pitcher Derek Lowe, often reviled during the 2004 season, came in big in the playoffs with an unusual trifecta. He won the third and final game of the American League Division Series against the Angels, pitching the 10th inning in relief. When David Ortiz hit a two-run homer in the bottom of the 10th, Lowe got the win. He won the seventh and final game of the American League Championship Series against the Yankees, starting the game and throwing six innings of one-hit ball while the Red Sox piled up five runs off Kevin Brown and three more off Javier Vasquez. When the Sox won, taking their fourth game in a row from New York, Lowe got the win. Lastly, he won the fourth and final game of the 2004 World Series, in St. Louis, starting and throwing seven scoreless innings while allowing just three hits. When Foulke flipped the ball to Mientkiewicz for the final out, Lowe got the win.

Red Sox elect not to use Babe Ruth in the 1915 World Series

Babe Ruth, despite an 18–8 record during the 1915 season and an earned run average of 2.44, never took part in the 1915 World Series other than to pinch-hit for Ernie Shore in the ninth inning of Game One. He grounded out. During the regular season, Ruth led the Red Sox in home runs (with four) and was ninth in the league. As a pitcher, he was second in the league in hits allowed per nine innings pitched, and fourth in the league in wins percentage—but manager Bill Carrigan chose not to use him in the World Series. For years there were stories that Carrigan was showing Ruth who was boss, a disciplinary matter. Leigh Montville reports in *The Big Bam* that Carrigan explained later that "he never pitched Ruth because he simply had other, better pitchers at the time."

Which Red Sox player recorded the best performance in a World Series?

2007 World Series MVP Mike Lowell signing for young fans. Bill Nowlin photo.

Naturally, that's a debatable point, just as any sort of MVP designation will always be.

The MVP in the 2007 World Series was Mike Lowell, but the honor could well have gone to several other Sox. Lowell hit .400 in the Series, with three doubles, a home run, and four RBIs. With three bases on balls mixed in, he was on base exactly 50% of the time he came to bat. He drove in the winning run in Game Two's 2–1 win. He scored six of Boston's 29 runs. There was little question that he'd been seen as one of the key team leaders throughout the season, and the MVP vote in the Series no doubt was colored by that recognition.

Taking the postseason as a whole, Josh Beckett was 4–0, but in the World Series had only one opportunity to pitch. Interestingly, 2007 was the first time ever that the Sox won the division, the pennant, and the World Series all in the same year.

2004: Manny Ramirez was named the Most Valuable Player in the 2004 World Series. He was 7-for-17 (.412), with an on-base percentage of .500, producing four RBIs and scoring two runs. Mark Bellhorn, though, also had four RBIs and his OBP was .563. Manny's fielding percentage was .750, making six plays and two errors. Bellhorn's was .938, making just one error in 15 chances. Third baseman Bill Mueller hit for a higher average than Manny (.429) and a higher OBP (.556), but he made three errors. His fielding percentage was .850, still better than Ramirez. Registering outs being a key part of the game, both infielders made more outs than Ramirez.

One could rule out Tim Wakefield as the most valuable among the pitchers, but what do you do with these stats?

Derek Lowe—faced 25 batters, ERA: 0.00 Lowe surrendered three hits in six IP.

Pedro Martinez—faced 24 batters, ERA: 0.00 Martinez surrendered three hits in seven IP.

Curt Schilling—faced 24 batters, ERA: 0.00 Schilling surrendered four hits in six IP.

And Keith Foulke was very, very good, facing 21 batters, with an ERA of 1.80.

Give the nod to Lowe because he faced one more batter? But by the time he pitched, the Red Sox already led three games to none, and we know that before 2004 no team had ever come back from being in such a hole to win a championship series. So there wasn't quite the pressure on him that there had been on Game One starter Wakefield or Game Two starter Martinez. It's a tough call, isn't it?

1986: Bruce Hurst was selected as Series MVP in 1986…until the Red Sox blew Game Six and then Game Seven. His name even appeared momentarily in lights on the Shea Stadium scoreboard proclaiming the honor. It was not to be. Marty Barrett was the team's leading hitter (13-for-30, .433, with an OBP of .514). He drove in four runs and was flawless in the field, handling 34 chances without an error. But Dwight Evans drove in more than twice as many runs (nine) and scored four times as many (four to Barrett's one). He made an error, but only one. Dave Henderson hit .500 and led the Red Sox in slugging with .760 to Evans' .615 and Barrett's .500. He was error-free in 22 chances. Hendu was second on the team with five RBIs.

1975: The leading hitter for the Red Sox was Carl Yastrzemski (.310), just as it had been in 1967. Bernie Carbo hit for a higher average but in far fewer at-bats. Carbo and Fisk each hit two home runs. Memorable ones, too! Evans and Lynn led in RBIs (five each), but there were four players with four apiece: Carbo, Fisk, Rico, and Yaz. And Carbo had a really high slugging percentage: 1.429! It would be hard to top Luis Tiant on the mound (2–0, 3.60 ERA). If they'd only won Game Seven, this exercise would be a lot more enjoyable.

1967: Yaz hit an even .400 (10-for-25), had an even on-base percentage (.500), and had a .840 slugging average. That wasn't anything close to Jose Santiago's 2.000 SLG, but factored in a lot more hits. Yaz drove in five runs, two more than the next-closest hitter. Jim Lonborg won two games, but then finally ran out of steam at the end. This one's a pretty easy call for the Sox MVP.

1946: Bobby Doerr hit for the highest average (9-for-22, .409) and he drove in three runs, but Rudy York was no slouch. York drove in five—and scored six. Doerr scored once. York won Game One with a 10th inning homer, and kicked off Game Three with a three-run home run in the very first inning. The Red Sox won, 4–0. Doerr's one homer and two of his three RBIs came late in a game the Sox were already losing 8–1. York made one error; Doerr handled 32 chances without an error. Joe Dobson threw 12⅔ innings without giving up a run, and was credited with one of Boston's three wins. We'd give the nod to Rudy York.

1918: Many people say that George Whiteman was the true hero of the 1918 World Series. Could a guy who batted .250 and only drove in one run be the star of a World Series? Stats alone don't tell the story, but we could point out that only one other Red Sox player had a higher average—Wally Schang—and only one other Red Sox player had as many as two RBIs in the Series—Babe Ruth. As a pitcher, Ruth was 2–0 with an ERA of 1.06 despite walking seven and giving up 13 hits. But Carl Mays was even better; he had the same 2–0 record, but his ERA was 1.00. Mays walked three and gave up just 10 hits—and both of the games he pitched were complete games. Both Mays and Ruth batted .200. So what was it about Whiteman?

In Game One, his single advanced a baserunner, who scored the only run of the game for either team on a single right afterward. The Red Sox lost Game Two, 3–1, but the one Red Sox run came on back-to-back triples by Amos Strunk and Whiteman to lead off the ninth. In Game Three, he was hit by a pitch and scored the first run of the game, a Boston 2–1 win. In Game Six his liner to right field was dropped by Max Flack, driving in the only two runs of the 2–1 game which won the World Series. His five hits were tops on the team, as were his two runs scored in this low-scoring Series. Several times, he made key defensive plays. It was the last major league game Whiteman ever played.

1916: Ernie Shore pitched more innings than any other Boston pitcher, and he was the only one to win two games. His ERA was a wonderful 1.53, though the 1–0 Babe Ruth's ERA was 0.64. Larry Gardner drove in ⅓ of the team's runs: six. No other player drove in more than two. But Gardner only hit .176. Harry Hooper got on base 41.7% of the time, with a .333 batting average, and scored six runs. No other player scored more than three.

1915: Rube Foster was 2–0 (2.00 ERA) in two complete games, and also hit .500 at the plate (4-for-8), with one RBI. There were only 11 RBIs in the entire World Series. Duffy Lewis drove in five of them—in other words, half of the ones not driven in by Foster. Lewis batted .444 and hit one of the three home runs. Harry Hooper hit the other two, and drove in three runs, batting .350. Hooper scored four times, twice as many runs as anyone else. Lewis scored just once, on his home run. Both of Hooper's home runs came in the final game, and the second one gave the Red Sox a 5–4 lead in the top of the ninth inning (and the win—for Rube Foster). Lewis, though, won Game Three and Game Four. Lewis also excelled on defense, and *Globe* sportswriter Tim Murnane concluded, "The all-around work of the modest Californian has never been equaled in a big Series."

1912: Smoky Joe Wood won three games, but it wasn't without giving up a lot of runs. Most of those piled up with the six runs he surrendered in the first inning of Game Seven, bumping up the 2.00 ERA he'd brought into the game to 4.74. Fortunately, this Series had a Game Eight, and Wood threw the final innings. Even then, he almost lost the deciding game, giving up one run in the top of the 10th. Had not Speaker singled in the tying run and Gardner won the game with a walk-off sac fly, Wood would have been 2–2 instead of 3–1. Gardner drove in the most runs—five—and scored the most runs—four, tied with Duffy Lewis and Tris Speaker. Maybe it didn't matter that he only hit .179, because it was clearly a productive .179. Reading the play-by-play, one also finds Steve Yerkes in the middle of things, not only scoring the winning run in the final game but also the winning run in Game Five, and driving in the two runs that won Game One.

1903: Big Bill Dinneen was 3–1 on the mound (his 2.06 ERA wasn't as good as Cy Young's 1.85, but he won one less game—he was 2–1). Young drove in three runs, though. Both pitchers scored once. Hobe Ferris hit .290 and drove in five. He was matched in RBIs by Patsy Dougherty. They both scored three times. Chick Stahl hit .303, and scored six times. He drove in three. Freddy Parent scored the most runs—eight—and drove in four. Stahl didn't make even one error; Parent made three, Ferris made two, and Dougherty made one.

Clutch play in the playoffs

Of course, one doesn't even get to the World Series without winning the pennant, and these days that requires prevailing in the Division Series and the League Championship Series. Looking at the playoff picture as a whole, is there anyone who would deny David Ortiz as the key producer in 2004? He didn't steal second base, like Dave Roberts did. He didn't work the walk, like Kevin Millar did to set things up for Roberts. He didn't pitch with a bloody sock. But he did win three games with walk-off hits, every one of them in extra innings. It's hard to get much more clutch than that. These weren't just three lucky hits, either. Ortiz had the best Red Sox batting average in both the ALDS and the ALCS. His four RBIs in the World Series tied him for tops on the team, and his .308 average wasn't bad. His slugging average of .615 topped everyone but Johnny Damon and Mark Bellhorn.

Clutchest Red Sox hitter of all time

Although in 2005, the Red Sox declared David Ortiz the "clutchest Red Sox hitter of all time" (and indeed, it's hard to imagine him doing better than he did in 2004), the Sox may have forgotten Carl Yastrzemski. In the final 12 games of the hard-fought 1967 season, Yaz was 23-for-44 (.523) with 16 RBIs and 14 runs scored. In the last two games, both of which Boston had to win to win the pennant, Yaz was 7-for-8, with five RBIs—and excelled on defense, too. The Baseball Page summarizes: In his 17 post-season games, the final 12 games of the 1967 season, and the 1978 one-game AL East playoff—the 30 most important games of his long career—Yaz hit .430 (49-for-114) with 10 homers, 29 RBIS, and 31 runs scored.

Postseason hitting streaks

The longest Red Sox postseason hitting streak is held by Manny Ramirez at 17, tying a major league record held by Hank Bauer and Derek Jeter. Manny hit safely in the final three games of the 2003 ALCS against the Yankees and then in all 14 postseason games of the 2004 World Championship season. He failed to get a hit in the first game of the 2005 Division Series.

Manny surpassed Harry Hooper, who had held the prior Sox streak with a hit in 15 consecutive games from October 11, 192 through September 7, 1918. Hooper had been held hitless through nine innings on October 9, 1916 but the game went into extra innings and he singled in the 10th, barely holding onto his streak with a 1-for-6 game.

In 2007, David Ortiz set a major league postseason record by reaching base safely 10 consecutive times. In Game Two of the Division Series, he reached base five times in a row, but then struck out in the first inning of Game Three. He then kicked off another streak with a home run to right field, and in the following nine plate appearances he: walked, singled, singled, was hit by a pitch, walked, walked, doubled, walked, and singled. Ortiz scored five of the 10 times he got on base during the stretch.

David Ortiz and son D'Angelo during Family Day at Fenway. Bill Nowlin photo.

A few other postseason records

The most RBIs in postseason play: 38 (David Ortiz, Manny Ramirez)
The most HRs in postseason play: 11 (David Ortiz, Manny Ramirez)

The most runs scored in postseason play: 35 (David Ortiz)

The most hits in postseason play: 53 (Manny Ramirez)

The most extra-base hits in postseason play: 25 (David Ortiz)

The most singles in postseason play: 36 (Manny Ramirez)

The most doubles in postseason play: 13 (David Ortiz)

The most triples in postseason play: 3 (Buck Freeman, Freddy Parent, Tris Speaker, Chick Stahl)

The most stolen bases in postseason play: 8 (Johnny Damon)

The highest batting average in postseason play (min. 30 at-bats): .429 (Jose Offerman)

The highest slugging percentage in postseason play (min. 30 at-bats): .767 (Todd Walker)

The most wins in postseason play: 6 (Pedro Martinez, Curt Schilling)

The most saves in postseason play: 4 (Jonathan Papelbon, whose ERA was 0.00 in the process)

The most strikeouts in postseason play: 80 (Pedro Martinez)

The lowest ERA in postseason play (min. 15 innings pitched): 0.50 (Hugh Bedient)

Most disappointing Red Sox performance in a World Series?

This one's pretty easy. Sad to say, it really has to be Ted Williams. Here was the Most Valuable Player in the entire American League, but he didn't come through in the World Series. Not that it was his fault. His elbow was severely injured by a Mickey Haefner fastball during a "tuneup" game while the Red Sox were killing time, waiting for the NL pennant winner to be determined. Those who were there say it was swollen to about double size. It clearly hampered Ted throughout the Series. He hit .200, just 5-for-25 and not a single extra-base hit. He drove in a total of one run. What can ya say?

Most frustrating absence from a World Series

The one that cost the Red Sox the most, quite possibly the World Series itself, was Jim Rice's absence in 1975. Like Ted Williams, Rice was hit by a pitch not long before the Series. In Rice's case, he was hit by a Vern Ruhle fastball which broke his hand in the second inning of the September 21 ballgame. Rice necessarily missed the whole Series.

Forced to watch the World Series from an army base

Bill Landis expresses no regrets, but history should nonetheless note that he played the full 1967 season for the 1967 Boston Red Sox, perhaps the most beloved of all Red Sox teams—yet was called into the Army just days before the end of the regular season, departing the team when they had just four games to play. Landis was a relief specialist who won just a single game in 1967—in a season where one win made all the difference. Yet he had to watch the World Series from Fort Polk, Louisiana—and even then was allowed to do so only because the commanding officer of his unit was from Boston.—from the book *The 1967 Impossible Dream Red Sox*.

Unlucky Game Sevens

Every time a World Series ends with a Game Seven, the Red Sox lose. The 1903 World Series lasted eight games. So did 1912. Both the 1915 and 1916 Series lasted five games; 1918 took six. The Red Sox swept the 2004 World Series in four games. Ditto 2007. The ones that lasted seven games: 1946, 1967, 1975, and 1986 all resulted in defeats. Fortunately, League Championship Series seventh games present a different story.

Second-place finishes

Boston had finished first and not made the World Series—in 1904, the National League New York Giants refused to play the Boston Americans. And they've finished second but won the World Series—2004, for example, as the Wild Card Red Sox team swept the World Series.

Naturally, with their 39 pennants, the Yankees lead the AL in first-place finishes. But it's the Red Sox who have finished second most often. This is something to take pride in? Be it as it may, Boston has finished second 22 times. When they came in second in 2007, New York tied the White Sox with 18 second-place finishes. Philadelphia holds the record for last-place finishes (19) and they haven't even existed since 1954; the franchise has 25 last-place finishes.

TRAGEDIES AND ALTERCATIONS

Tragedies—guns, poison, knives, drugs, and the Red Sox

March 28, 1907: Manager (and outfielder) **Chick Stahl** committed suicide in his hotel room during spring training. He played for Boston's National League team for four years, then joined the Boston Americans in the first year of the franchise, 1901, hitting .303. After six seasons, Stahl was asked to take the reins as player-manager of the 1906 team in late season (August 29). The pressure may have been too great. He had apparently often mentioned that managing the team detracted from his ability to play on it.

His personal life was a complicated one, too. Back on January 26, 1902, Lulu Ortman, a 21-year-old stenographer at a Fort Wayne, Indiana lumber company, was arrested as she was drawing a revolver to shoot Stahl. She said he had jilted her for another woman and that she was going to kill him. Researching the Stahl story, historian Glenn Stout believes the besieged Boston skipper was approached by a woman named Barnett who he had impregnated in Buffalo late in the 1906 season and who now demanded he marry her. But Stahl had just married Julia Harmon in November. The team was barnstorming pre-season, and reached West Baden Springs, Indiana, when Stahl drank carbolic acid after breakfast after stepping into Jimmy Collins' adjoining room. The poison killed him. His suicide note read: "Boys, I just couldn't help it. You drove me to it." Several teammates recalled him talking about suicide for much of spring training.

Ironically, Ms. Barnett had tried to kill herself in the New York Central rail depot at Buffalo during what the *Washington Post* termed a "dramatic scene in the waiting rooms…took carbolic acid, with the intention of committing suicide." She was rushed to the hospital and survived. Stahl was said to brood over the scandal. When Stahl successfully committed suicide, he chose the same medium: carbolic acid.

There's not enough information here to draw any conclusions, but a man who was an engineer on the Grand Rapids and Indiana Railroad chose to take his own life in the same fashion just two days after Stahl. David P. Murphy, said to be an "intimate friend" of Stahl's, swallowed carbolic acid and died on March 30, leaving a note which read, "Bury me beside Chick."

On November 15, 1908, Chick Stahl's widow, Julia Stahl, was found dead in a South Boston doorway. Julia's family was convinced that she was the victim of foul play. Her brother-in-law said he believed she had been "drugged, murdered, and then robbed of her jewels."

Stahl's tragic end reminds of another case involving a jealous lover. **Case Patten** wasn't with the Red Sox at the time it happened, but it is worth taking a moment to note a bizarre Kansas City case involving him in 1901. That was his rookie year, playing with Washington as he did all the way through his career until he appeared in just one game for Boston in 1908. Lulu Prince had come to know him while he was still in the minors the year before. On January 10, 1901, she was arrested for murdering her husband of one month, Phillip Kennedy, an agent for Merchants Dispatch Transportation. She pumped five bullets into him, at his office, then kicked him, yelling, "You'll never ruin another girl." She told the policeman who arrested her, "Let go my hands. I want to fix my hair."

One could call the Kennedy marriage a "troubled one" and, it seems, one to which Kennedy only consented when taken to the judge by Lulu's father and two brothers, "compelled at the point of revolvers." There was an understanding that she might have been "in a delicate condition" at the time. This proved not to be the case, but Kennedy likely had taken advantage of her. He apparently refused to live with her, and in a filing for an annulment claimed duress and said he had "lost respect" for her.

After Prince-Kennedy's arrest—her father and brothers arrested as well—testimony at trial by Dr. R. O. Cross said that Miss Prince had told him in November 1900 that she was married to Case Patten, but she did not want it known as he might lose his position on the ball team. Reading between the lines, it is clear she asked the doctor to abort a pregnancy. As with the alleged pregnancy caused by Kennedy, none was ever discovered. Lulu had visited Dr. Cross earlier on January 10, and told him she was now married to Kennedy, not Patten. She claimed insanity, and testified in court that it was Kennedy who had urged her to tell the doctor she was married to Patten. Her brother Albert, out on bond, was a "traveling mandolin player" who came by and gave concerts to Lulu in the jail. Brother Will denied in court that he had ever exercised mesmeric powers over anyone; he also denied that he had been a prizefighter. Father Prince ran a pool hall.

Lulu was convicted of second degree murder and sentenced to 10 years in prison. She secured a new hearing, meanwhile marrying local lawyer John Kramer, and in 1904 was acquitted on grounds of temporary insanity. As it was found that she had since regained her sanity, she was not sent to an asylum, but the newspaper record peters out. No comment from Patten has yet been found.

November 27, 1916: **Bob Unglaub**, infielder and Boston's manager for part of 1907, was severely injured while on his offseason job as a machinist for the Pennsylvania Railroad. Unglaub was managing in Fargo, North Dakota during the regular season. He was struck by a train, sustaining three fractured ribs, a gash across his stomach, and one of his kidneys was cut in half. Unglaub died two days later.

Charley Hall, who played with the Red Sox from 1909–13, let his two sons stay up a little late on the evening of January 17, 1920 in Ventura. Some toys had just arrived from Boston the day before. After his father stepped out of the room, six-year-old Charley climbed up on a trunk in a closet and found a revolver behind some boxes. The gun went off and the bullet struck his younger brother Kenneth, 3, who died in the hospital about three hours later. The Halls later had another son, Marshall.

March 24, 1921: After retiring from baseball, the 6'5" **Larry McLean** was said to have suffered "dissipation"—even becoming (this was apparently shocking in its day) a "Jamaica ginger addict." When McLean tried to climb over the bar of a near-beer saloon on Boston's Washington Street, he was shot to death by saloon manager John J. Conner. The barman was sentenced to a year in jail, even though the D.A. had recommended a lighter sentence.

Secretary of the Boston Red Sox **James R. Price** committed suicide at Fenway Park, slashing his own throat with a razor on one of the runways at the park on January 29, 1929.

Denny Williams had played for the Red Sox in 1924, 1925, and 1928, but any hopes he had of making the team again were wiped out when he was killed in a car crash in San Clemente, California on March 21, 1929.

April 29, 1931: Former owner **James McAleer** shot himself in the head, taking his own life in Youngstown, Ohio.

March 1, 1932: **Big Ed Morris**, Red Sox pitcher, was stabbed twice in the chest by gasoline station operator Joe White during a brawl at a Brewton, Alabama fish fry and peanut boil intended to see him off to spring training. This was Prohibition, but there was apparently a supply of home brew available as well. As the evening progressed, Florida historian Jerry Fischer says, "The boys were enjoying themselves around the campfire when Big Ed stood up and urinated in the peanut pot. Morris thought it was funny, but the other fellas didn't."

Morris died two days later at a hospital in Century, Florida. Morris was initially reported to be recovering, but may have succumbed to infection or pneumonia incurred as he felt into the Escambia River and then crossed it to get to his car and flee his assailant, though accounts of the entire incident are a little murky.

Big Ed Morris, stabbed to death on the eve of spring training. Courtesy of Brace Photo.

Owner Bob Quinn had reportedly been offered $80,000 cash for Morris at one point. Some reports suggest the total might have been higher. Perhaps it was soon after his 19-win season for the 1928 Red Sox—when he won exactly ⅓ of the team's 57 victories.

He was a bit of a character. David J. Krajicek wrote in the *New York Daily News* that as a teenager, he'd been "lured to a small Florida college to pitch. Morris had been on campus for months by the time the faculty realized that he was not enrolled in a single class." When told that education was part of the deal, he's said to have indignantly responded, "I'm here to throw a baseball, not to learn nothing."

Sometime in 1931, Morris apparently entered a hotel elevator and found the operator missing, so he starting running the elevator himself. The elevator boy sounded the alarm, and two house detectives responded and pursued Morris in another elevator. Morris, meanwhile, would open the door at each floor only long enough to give a loud rebel yell. Finally, the detectives sprang on him and wrestled him to the ground, wrenching his shoulder in the fracas. Morris was "practically useless" to the Sox for the rest of the year.

On March 28, 1932, Joe White was sentenced to three years in prison for the fatal knifing of the Boston pitcher, but appealed the conviction on the grounds of self-defense and in the end never served time. During the original trial, Morris' wife Beryl stood up in court, interrupting White's lawyer, and denounced something he had said as untrue. This happening in front of the jury was considered grounds for later vacating the conviction. Testimony indicated that White had initially tried to be a peacemaker in a fight between Morris and a Joe Nolan, but that Morris then pummeled White repeatedly until White grabbed a knife on the ground and stabbed the pitcher. It might not have been the first time Morris had received a knife wound; one unconfirmed account has him being cut by Sox teammate Merl Settlemire in 1928.

Sadly, **Joe Cronin** and his wife Mildred lost twin children, both infants dying at birth on April 8, 1937.

Eric McNair seemed to be surrounded by tragedy. This is the same "Boob" McNair who once boarded the wrong train heading out of Boston's South Station on July 4 after a homestand and wondered why he was surrounded by players from the opposition Philadelphia Athletics. He had lost his wife in January 1937; she died in childbirth less than three months before the Cronin tragedy. McNair was despondent and at one point had to be talked back in from the ledge of the 27th floor hotel room he shared with Sox catcher Johnny Peacock. In December 1938, McNair's brother Pat was at the wheel of a brand new car which crashed into a horse and buggy, killing the horse and smashing the buggy. Neither the farmer driving the horse nor any people were injured. Eric McNair died of a heart attack at the young age of 40, seven years after leaving the majors.

Emmett McCann was found dead in some bushes on a Philadelphia golf course on April 15, 1937. A pistol was found in his right hand.

August 6, 1942: Former Red Sox pitcher **Gordon McNaughton**, working as a postal clerk in Chicago, was enjoying the company of Mrs. Dorothy Moos in a hotel room when his jilted girlfriend, Mrs. Eleanor Williams, entered and shot and killed him. Williams used the service pistol of policeman Barney Towey, who was left sleeping in the hotel room to which he and Mrs. Williams had repaired after night clubbing. Mrs. Williams was a "dice girl in a roadside tavern" and said she shot McNaughton because "he tried to dust me off." Both Williams and Moos said they had left their husbands to be with McNaughton. Though she could have received the death penalty, Williams was sentenced to just 1–14 years imprisonment and, upon losing her appeal for a new trial, said she would remarry her former husband—telegrapher Clarence Williams—in her jail cell. Towey shot himself to death after he was discharged from the police force for negligence in the care of his weapon. Exculpatory testimony on Eleanor's behalf came from other dice girls who said she "was a good girl" until McNaughton came on the scene and "gave her the old pitch." McNaughton had only ever played for the Red Sox, debuting on August 13, 1932 and appearing in just six games. The dead righthander had a record of 0–1, with a 6.43 ERA and an upside-down walks-to-strikeouts ratio based on walking 22 and striking out only six.

Gordon McNaughton, killed by a dice girl in 1942. Courtesy of Brace Photo.

New Brunswick's **Ty LaForest** was never quite accorded the attention that Harry Agganis later received. LaForest came up during the last of the war years, 1945, debuted during a long road trip, and got six hits right away during his first few games. His Fenway debut came on August 26 during a doubleheader against visiting Philadelphia and his ninth-inning homer tied the first game, setting it up for Boo Ferriss to win his 20th game of the year in the 10th with an RBI double of his own. Not content with a 3-for-4 first game, the young third baseman went 2-for-3 in the nightcap, hitting a home run in the game, then breaking a 3–3 tie with a double in the bottom of the eighth.

But when all the veterans came back in 1946, LaForest was sent to Louisville. That next winter, he caught pneumonia and after the third day of spring training he collapsed on the field, never recovered, and died a few months later on May 5, 1947.

This one happened in the press box. On May 8, 1949 the Sox took two from the Browns in St. Louis and *Boston Herald* sportswriter Burt Whitman died covering the game. The first game was a tense 13-inning battle, which ended on a bases-loaded wild pitch, on a two-out 3-and-2 count. Just as the pitch went wild, Whitman fell to the press box floor. "Cover me, Johnny, please. Get the hits, runs and errors." Those were Whitman's last words, spoken to Johnny Drohan of the *Boston Traveler*. A few hours later, he was pronounced dead at a local hospital. Whitman was one of the few "knights of the keyboard" who Ted Williams respected, and when he learned about it afterwards, Ted was reported as "plainly disturbed."

The struggles that **Jimmy Piersall** went through involving mental illness have been documented in his own book *Fear Strikes Out*, and are well enough known that they need not be exhaustively restated here. His "zany antics" sometimes upset the other players, and when he was first shipped out of Boston in late June 1952, the *Washington Post* indicated that Piersall was "in danger of being mangled by players on his own team." Fortunately, his illness was eventually diagnosed and Piersall was able to obtain good treatment and triumph over his affliction.

Harry Agganis appeared in an official capacity at both Braves Field and Fenway Park on the same day in 1954. He hit a game-winning homer for the Bosox and also received his Boston University degree in ceremonies at Braves Field. He'd been offered a contract in the National Football League, but the Lynn native elected to play for his hometown Red Sox instead. The homer was one of 11 he hit in a promising 1954 season. A true local favorite, Agganis was batting .313 in early June 1955 and, on June 2, the "Golden Greek" went 2-for-4 with a double in what proved to be his last game. He entered a hospital in Cambridge and died of complications from pneumonia on June 27th. He is the only Red Sox player to die during the course of the season while on the major league roster.

In the spring of 1965, during spring training in Scottsdale, **Dennis Bennett** was said to have taken two pistols and fired "a half a dozen rounds" at the door of the team's motel. Why? "I had these two pistols and it was Arizona, so why not?" [Ken Coleman and Dan Valenti, *The Impossible Dream Remembered*, p. 105.] And if that wasn't enough of a nightmare, there was also the time that Bennett got into a loud argument with his road roommate Lee Thomas about who should get up to turn off the light. Bennett put out the light with a gunshot, and Thomas lit out from the room.

On October 8, 1971, **Murray Wall** went out hunting rabbits on his farm at Lone Oak, Texas but never came back. He was found in his pickup truck with a handgun in the truck and a bullet wound in his head. UPI initially reported "there was nothing to indicate that a second person was involved" and the cause of death was ultimately ruled suicide.

Leigh Grossman offers the story of **Tom Maggard** in his *Red Sox Fan Handbook*. Maggard was Boston's top draft pick in 1968—a catcher—and worked his way up to Triple A, playing for Pawtucket in 1973. Late in the season, in September, "his arm swelled up after being bitten by an insect. After treatment attempts didn't improve the injury, he was sent home to California, where he died two weeks later." See also the sad story of prospect Andy Yount below.

The low point of **Rogelio Moret**'s 1975 season, Seamus Kearney points out, came on August 5, 1975. He was the scheduled starting pitcher against the Orioles that evening, but at 4:30 a.m., he crashed his car into the back of a parked trailer on I-95 in North Stonington, CT, over 90 miles from Fenway. The Sox had played in Boston the night before. Red Sox manager Darrell Johnson wasn't sure why Moret was (still?) out at that hour, or why he was in southern Connecticut in the first place. Three years later, while with the Texas Rangers, he fell into a catatonic state in front of his locker that reportedly lasted 90 minutes. He was sedated and sent to the Arlington Neuropsychiatric Center.

During 1978 spring training, on March 25, rookie southpaw **Bobby Sprowl** was shot in the right arm while he slept in his Winter Haven hotel room; the gun was fired by a doctor in the next-door apartment who said he thought he heard prowlers. Sprowl was just grazed, and was quickly treated and released at the local hospital. In 12⅔ innings of late-season ball for the Sox in '78, he gave up three homers and nine earned runs.

This one blew over quickly, but shortly after being suspended by the Red Sox for three games after leaving Fenway Park in the wake of an "obscenity-laced tirade" when he found he'd not been named to the AL All-Star squad, **Dennis "Oil Can" Boyd** got in a July 15, 1986 confrontation with Chelsea police about one hour before the game started in Chicago. It was the second time in a few days that he'd had a brush with narcotics cops. Police Det. Sgt. Jack Phillips said he would be charged with assaulting and threatening the police. "He swung on several occasions. He kept insisting he was going to blow our heads off. The last thing he said to me was, 'You're dead meat.'" No guns were found. No drugs were found. Sox GM Lou Gorman said that Boyd felt he was being persecuted by the police. Two days later, Boyd voluntarily checked himself into U Mass Medical Center in Worcester for a "comprehensive examination."

Wade Boggs was a tragedy waiting to happen, but he always seemed to luck out somehow. Late in spring training (March 23, 1991), after a Saturday night out dining at Christy's Sundown Restaurant in Sarasota (and a visit to Christy's Lounge), Debbie Boggs pulled the family's Ford Explorer out of the parking lot—and Wade fell out of the car. Given his sordid affair with Margo Adams just two years earlier, speculation ran rampant that Debbie tried to run over her husband. He had bruises on his elbow and ankle and the elbow bruises were in a "tire-tread pattern, as if a tire ran over his right elbow", reported the *Boston Globe*'s Nick Cafardo. "I didn't have my seat belt on," Boggs commented, noting that he was glad to be alive. Apparently, the back tire of the car did run over his elbow. The story reminded Boggs-watchers of other stories, such as the time he bruised his ribs by falling over when trying to put on his cowboy boots in Toronto, or the time he said he had willed himself invisible to escape a knife-wielding man.

Sammy White died of choking on August 5, 1991, though newspapers termed it an "apparent heart attack" which may indeed have been the precise cause of death.

February 23, 1992: **Carlos Quintana** crashed into a bridge about 80 miles outside of Caracas, Venezuela as he was speeding his two younger brothers to a hospital. Both had been wounded by gunshots during a Carnival party. Quintana's wife had two broken legs; Carlos had his left arm and his right toe broken. Clearly, it could have been worse.

Pitcher **Vaughn Eshelman** sustained second-degree burns during spring training trying to put out a fire in his hotel room started by a candle left burning in the bathroom by his wife. Asked why they had a candle burning at 6 a.m., Esh told Gordon Edes, "Why do women do a lot of things? She likes a good smell when she wakes up, I guess." It was March 19, 1996. He'd heard his wife screaming, woke up, and found the towels on fire in the bathroom with flames licking up the walls. Eshelman used a washcloth to beat out the flames. His hands? "They looked cooked. Real charred. I'd never felt pain like that. It felt like my bones were on fire."

The Red Sox had a wonderful prospect in **Andy Yount**, a first-round pick in the 1995 draft. Yount was playing with the Lowell Spinners in 1996 when his best friend died in a Texas car crash. Unable to attend the funeral during the season, Yount went to visit the grave in September and "flipped out" at the waste of his friend's life; he angrily flung a glass of orange juice at the grave and the glass broke in his hand so badly that it cut tendons in his pitching hand. Nine surgeries later, Yount was released by the Red Sox. He expressed appreciation for the patience the Red Sox had always shown him, a longtime Red Sox fan.

Red Sox outfielder **Wil Cordero** was arrested in the early morning hours of June 11, 1997 and charged with assaulting his wife Ana with a telephone receiver and trying to choke her. She withdrew the complaint and they walked out of court hand-in-hand. D.A. Thomas Reilly decried the quick release of Cordero, and pursued the case despite Ana Cordero requesting the charges be dropped. Despite one ovation he received for a home run in July, Fenway fans never forgave him and showered him with taunts like "Phone call, Will!" He played out the season but under a cloud and didn't last long with the Red Sox after this incident. On November 3, the former Sox player was given a 90-day suspended sentence in the Middlesex House of Correction, after he pleaded guilty to domestic assault in the beating his wife. He was also required to take a 40-week course for convicted batterers. He had faced a prison term of up to eight years. On December 11, 1997 Cordero was served with a restraining order after police in Puerto Rico responded to a call from Ana Cordero that her husband had threatened her and said he would "rip off her head."

Mo Vaughn was arrested in the early morning hours of January 9, 1998 and charged with drunken driving when his Ford pickup truck collided with a car parked and abandoned in the breakdown lane, and flipped over onto its roof. On his way back from a visit to the Foxy Lady, Vaughn failed a number of sobriety tests, according to state police, but pleaded not guilty to a charge of drunken driving at his arraignment. No one was injured, but Mo's reputation was the main casualty. During spring training, he blasted the Red Sox for what he called a "smear campaign" against him.

It was, the *Globe* headlined, "**Dick Williams**' impossible nightmare." In a January 29, 2000 AP story datelined Fort Myers, readers learned that Williams had been "arrested on an indecent exposure charge while attending the World Series of Fantasy Baseball Camp." He may have been involved in a fantasy of his own, or a victim of sorts. He was accused by a woman who worked next door to the hotel; she'd apparently seen him walking in his birthday suit outside of his room. He pleaded no contest and was "released on time served." Asked for a comment, Williams said, "The case has been settled and dismissed. That is all I have to say." Williams is to be inducted into the Hall of Fame in 2008.

In July 2000, **Paxton Crawford** was a promising pitcher who got two spot starts with the Red Sox. He won one and lost one, but had just a 2.19 ERA. Sent back to Pawtucket, after Pedro Martinez recovered from an oblique muscle problem, Crawford suffered a hotel room accident in Ottawa that is still shrouded in mystery. He said he rolled out of bed and fell on a drinking glass he'd left on the floor. It took eight stitches to close the wound. He'd just pitched a seven-inning no-hitter. One rumor was that he'd gotten into an argument with a lady of the night, and fallen on the glass during a scuffle. In June 2006, for no apparent reason, Crawford unexpectedly announced that he had used steroids while a player with the Red Sox. Perhaps it was his way of explaining (and perhaps accurately) why he'd never really made it in major league ball.

News broke on October 10, 2000 that former Red Sox pitcher **Rich Gale** had pleaded innocent in York, Maine, to charges that he had exposed himself to a state trooper at a rest stop in Kittery the previous May. Gale's attorney said there was no basis for the charge and it never would have been brought had not the state trooper "voluntarily stuck his head in the defendant's vehicle."

Federal agents arrested former Red Sox outfielder **Alex Cole** on August 9, 2001, as part of a drug sting. Cole was 35 at the time and playing for the independent Bridgeport Bluefish team, arrested at the stadium prior to a game against Atlantic City, and charged with conspiracy to distribute heroin. Four other men were arrested at the same time. The following year, Cole pled guilty to one charge of conspiring to possess with the intent to distribute heroin, and was sentenced to 18 months in federal prison.

Former major league outfielder **Jeff Stone** was allegedly stabbed by his wife in their Portageville, Missouri home on January 19, 2002. Linda Stone was arrested and charged with first-degree assault. Stone was hospitalized with multiple stab wounds; his wife was released on $100,000 bond.

Yet another Red Sox prospect had his life cut short when **Dernell Stenson** was killed in Chandler, Arizona on November 5, 2003. He'd been a prime prospect for the Red Sox but was placed on waivers in February 2003 and claimed by Cincinnati, for whom he hit .243 in limited action. While having an exceptional Arizona Fall League season, he was carjacked and shot when he attempted to grab a pistol from one of his attackers. A detailed account of the tragic events appears in the *Oxford American* magazine issue #59, 2007.

Two days after Christmas 2005, former Red Sox relief ace **Jeff Reardon** walked into a jewelry store in a Palm Beach Gardens mall, handed a Hamilton Jewelers employee a note that said he was armed and was robbing the store. The employee gave him $170 in cash (after all, who buys jewelry with cash in an upscale Florida shopping mall?) and he left. Police found him nearby in a restaurant and, even though he had no gun, arrested him for armed robbery, and returned the money he'd relieved from the retailer. Reardon said he remembered none of it, and concluded that he'd somehow been affected by the mixture of the 12 different anti-depressant medications prescribed for him in the aftermath of his son's 2004 death from a drug overdose. Nine months later, on August 28, 2006, Reardon was found not guilty by reason of insanity. He began a course of shock therapy and a greatly reduced number of anti-depressants and in late 2006, there were signs that progress was being made.

Stan Grossfeld broke the sad story of **Sammy Stewart** in the October 25, 2006 issue of the *Boston Globe*. Stewart, a very good relief pitcher for a number of teams including the 1986 Red Sox (4–1 in 27 appearances), was serving a minimum of six years in North Carolina's Piedmont Correctional Institution. He'd been charged with 43 crimes in the 26 times he'd been arrested since 1989. He was serving his sixth prison sentence. Stewart had two children born with cystic fibrosis; his son died in 1991. "That's an excuse, not a reason," his ex-wife told Grossfeld. He'd hit bottom, even living under bridges in Asheville. "I would panhandle," he told the writer. "I was one of the best at that." Stewart swore that this time he'd truly reformed and he wanted to show his children that he'd beat back the demons that possessed him.

On March 3, 2008 Red Sox scout **Jesse Levis** was arrested in Florida by Port St. Lucie police and charged with two felony counts of committing lewd and lascivious acts in front of children under the age of 16, in the window of his hotel room which overlooked the Springhill Suites swimming pool. The hotel manager said Levis had been involved in a similar incident in 2007.

The greatest tragedy of all

The greatest tragedy of all in Red Sox history, however, came in the 1940s when the Red Sox had the chance to become the first major league team to hire an African-American, and spurned the opportunity. They could have signed Jackie Robinson and Sam Jethroe on the spot, taken advantage of their working option on Willie Mays, and done a world of good. Instead, they incurred Robinson's wrath for their racism and sank back into mediocrity by the time the Fifties rolled around.

Pinky Higgins

He was a walking tragedy all by himself, one of those who (like Yankees owner George Weiss) swore he'd never have a black player on his ballclub. He held out as long as he could. He was a drinker and a racist, an habitué of The Dugout, on Commonwealth Avenue. *Bostonia* magazine remembered the hangout: "Halfway between Fenway Park and Braves Field—and underground—the bar's name is presumably a play on words in two senses. It was said that Pinky Higgins, Red Sox manager from 1955 to 1962, would be at the Dugout within 15 minutes of the end of a game, and after having a few, would occasionally fall off his stool."

A drinking buddy of Tom Yawkey's, there were allegations that Higgins and Joe Cronin were part of an "Irish mafia" which held back Italian players like Frank Malzone and Jerry Casale.

Pinky Higgins's nickname always seemed very appropriate for a white racist. The Red Sox manager was noted for his statement to writer Al Hirshberg, "There'll be no niggers on this ball club as long as I have anything to say about it," and he stands among the leading suspects in the annals of Red Sox racism. Of course, the buck stopped with Tom Yawkey. The *New York Times* reported that Higgins "intensely disliked his nickname, which was given to him as an infant because of his coloring, and asked the other players to call him Mike."

Pinky was finally let go by the Red Sox in 1965 and Dick O'Connell was made GM, charged with bringing the Red Sox into the late 20th century. Higgins took a position as scout for the Houston Astros. On February 28, 1968 he plowed his car into a northern Louisiana state highway department crew working on the I-20 pavement about five miles west of Ruston, killing one man and injuring three others. George W. Killen, 63, a highway worker from Simsboro, LA., was struck fatally while flagging motorists to slow down and change lanes at a repair site. Frederick Woodard was critically injured, and Joe Felton Ginn and William T. Wiltcher were hurt as well. Higgins was alone in his car at the time and suffered no injury himself.

Joe Ginn, reached in March 2007 six days before retiring from 37 years of later highway work with Lincoln Parish, still remembered the incident. "We was pouring tar in those cracks across I-20, filling in the cracks, then you put sand on it. We had the two flagmen behind us. They were just motioning people over, and he run over George Killen...the first flagman. He killed him and came on down through there and hit us.

"Woodard. He was right with me. We got hit, I think, at the same time. I think it messed his leg up, one of his knees. I don't think he ever did go back to work. The witnesses there said that I was maybe about 6–8 inches off the road, lying there. When I woke up, there was all three of us lying right straight across I-20. They had the whole thing blocked. It knocked my left shoulder completely out, skinned the top of my head." Ginn lost consciousness from being struck. He spent a few days in the hospital, then went back to work, but even today, "the weather can change and that old arm of mine hurts. They say a dislocation is worse than a break."

Ginn heard that Higgins was drinking. "What they told me, they said he got out of the vehicle and said, 'It looks like you all had a bad accident.' He didn't even know he did it." Some authors have mistakenly assumed that the work crew was comprised of black workers; Ginn confirms they were not.

Higgins was locked up overnight in Lincoln Parish Jail, posting bail the next morning. He pleaded guilty in November 1968 to negligent homicide and driving under the influence of alcohol. Lincoln Parish District Attorney Ragan D. Madden said that Higgins was "very cooperative, very penitent."

Sentencing was delayed until January 1969, because of a heart condition; Higgins suffered two heart attacks during this period. He was finally sentenced to four years at hard labor, but released after serving just two months of his sentence. This was apparently not unusual in Louisiana at the time; state law permitted parole for a first offender at any time, if his sentence was for less than five years. Apparently, the charm he worked on Tom Yawkey was put to good use in the Louisiana prison system as well. When released, a "high-ranking prison official who knew him" was quoted as saying, "There are criminals and there are people like Mr. Higgins. I wish we could let all of those like Mr. Higgins go." Harold Kaese did report that his heart condition played a role in his parole.

Higgins was released from the St. Francisville prison on March 20, 1969 but he didn't have much time to celebrate. The same newspapers which reported his release one day reported his death the next. His wife brought him to St. Paul's Hospital in Dallas around noontime on March 21 and died at 2:10 p.m. in the hospital's emergency ward. He is buried in Hillcrest Memorial Park, Dallas.

Joe Ginn still sees the spot on the road when he drives by. "I think about that every time I go down I-20."

Tragedies that could have wiped out the team

Being a little morbid at times, I always wondered about the possibility of an entire major league baseball team being wiped out in a plane crash. Fortunately, this has never happened.

One hopes it never will. There have been a number of fatal disasters befalling other sports teams, though: Torino soccer team (1949), Cal Poly—San Luis Obispo football team (1960), US figure skating team (1961), Bolivian soccer team (1969), Wichita State football team (1970), Marshall University football team (1970), Evansville IN basketball team (1977), US amateur boxing team (1980). In each instance, 14 or more members of the teams involved were killed in crashes. In 2007, five members of the Bluffton University baseball team were among those killed in a Georgia bus crash. Accidents unfortunately do occur.

May 19, 1905: The team was in Cleveland but holed up in the Hotel Euclid while the games were rained out for three days in a row. The weather let up a bit on May 19, so the team boarded a bus to head to League Park. On the way there, a Euclid Avenue streetcar slammed into the bus at the corner of Dunham and Euclid Avenues, overturning the bus. The ballplayers were "badly shaken up" in the collision but fortunately no one was seriously injured. They were, however, "naturally nervous when they arrived at the grounds" and might have affected play. Cleveland scored 11 runs on 16 hits off Jesse Tannehill, and won 11–4.

April 2, 1933: A deadly train wreck killed the engineer and fireman, but the Red Sox team escaped serious injury. The "Cavalier"—the Pennsylvania Railroad's Norfolk-to-New York express train carrying the Red Sox—crashed around 3:12 a.m. in the town of Wyoming, Delaware, derailing the engine and eight cars, including two of the three sleeper cars containing the Red Sox team, and tossing the players about. *Boston Globe* reporter Mel Webb was on

IL 3, 1933—SIXTEEN PAGES   COPYRIGHT 1933, BY   (2)   TWO CE

SOX TRAIN IS WRECKED
PLAYERS NOT INJURED

Boston Team, in Derailed Sleepers, Tossed About
In Delaware Mishap That Kills Engine Crew,
But Wins Afternoon Game at Jersey City

The time the whole team escaped death.

board and provided a graphic account of the twisted wreckage. Doc Woods, the Red Sox trainer, helped administer to some of the wounded passengers on board. Tom Oliver tried to extricate the engineer, but gave up when he realized the man was dead. Only pitcher Bob Klein felt possible effects, to his shoulder, later in the day. Four of their trunks were destroyed, but not even one bat was cracked. Players were relieved at their narrow escape and reacted with some humor; Bob Seeds cracked that at first he had thought the crash was Fatty Fothergill sliding into home plate. The shaken-up Red Sox played an exhibition game against the Jersey City Skeeters later in the day, and won handily, 12–0. The following day, they shut out the Skeeters again, 6–0. [On July 7, 1947, three Phillies were among 100 injured in a train wreck at Chicago's Grand Central Station. Schoolboy Rowe was knocked unconscious but none the the player injuries were serious.]

July 14, 1939: A 2:30 a.m. fire at the Red Sox quarters in Cleveland destroyed 20 awnings. The *Globe* reported that "Elden Auker rushed out in his pajamas, broke into a room in which one of the awnings were aflame and put it out with an extinguisher."

August 27, 1946: It wasn't the whole team, but the Red Sox almost lost their greatest player of all time, Ted Williams, when he was involved in a serious head-on automobile accident in Holliston, Massachusetts. The Sox slugger was on his way to play in an August 27, 1946 exhibition game against the Cleveland Indians in East Douglas, Massachusetts scheduled to celebrate the 200th anniversary of the town.

Ted's car crashed into that of Holliston resident George Doncaster who, it turned out, had no idea who Ted Williams was. Ted was traveling with his wife Doris and with good friend Massachusetts State Police Sgt. John Blake and his wife. Road conditions were not good; in fact, the game was rained out and rescheduled to late in the season. Blake suffered a cut on the head, Ted sustained a slight strain to his leg, and the two wives were shaken but uninjured.

Doncaster took a great deal of ribbing in the weeks to come for not knowing of Ted Williams, and he shot back, "Well, who wants to know him? Certainly not I."

July 28 and 29, 1951: Red Sox fans were involved in deadly accidents on successive days. On the 28th, Delmer Jewett, a pickle company president, and three other men were killed when their single-engine plane crashed on the way home from the Indians/Red Sox game at Fenway. Clyde Vollmer had beaten Bob Feller with a walk-off grand slam in the bottom of the 10th.

The very next day, a chartered bus full of baseball fans were on their way to see the Red Sox and Indians game when the bus crashed into another bus and six automobiles. Eighteen were hurt and two hospitalized, but the fans continued on to see the Indians win a close 5–4 game.

April 19, 1953: The whole Red Sox traveling party—29 players, five coaches, and two trainers, plus two radiomen and a photographer—flew by chartered airplane from Washington to Boston's Logan Airport and had a bit of a scare when the inner glass layer of the plane's windshield shattered, showering the captain and the pilot with glass fragments. The plane landed at LaGuardia to effect repairs, then continued on to Boston.

April 25, 1955: The Sox were traveling by train from New York to Kansas City on the *20th Century Limited*. As they were passing just south of Poughkeepsie, another train shot by heading to the City. Both trains were traveling at about 70 miles per hour when the New York bound train swayed on the tracks and side-clipped a door handle on the Red Sox train, knocking the handle off the car. "I froze," said one man. "I thought the other train was off the tracks."

March 22, 1957: The Sarasota-based Red Sox flew to San Francisco on March 21 for a four-game spring training set against the San Francisco Seals. The morning of their first game an earthquake hit the Bay Area, registering 5.5 on the Richter scale. A series of aftershocks continued throughout the day, the largest being a 3:15 p.m. shock registering at 4 on the scale. The quakes were the "severest barrage of earth shocks since the great earthquake and fire of 1906," reported the *New York Times*. The paper reported that "thousands poured in terror out of the buildings in San Francisco and suburban communities." The shocks were felt as far as 150 miles away. The AP office in San Francisco responded to an inquiry from its Boston office: "The Seals and San Francisco quake neither before temblors nor Red Sox. Game's on." In fact, the Seals didn't appear to be rattled. They won, 5–2.

Much of the above listing of potential team tragedies is drawn from the pages of Day by Day with the Boston Red Sox.

Victoria Snelgrove

October 20, 2004. It was a very real tragedy when Red Sox fan and Emerson College student Victoria Snelgrove, 21, was killed by police who fired a plastic bullet filled with pepper spray into the crowd outside Fenway Park as a very enthusiastic crowd celebrated the come-from-behind victory over the Yankees in the American League Championship Series. The bullet hit her in the eye and exploded inside her skull. She died on October 21. The Boston Police Department later paid over $5 million to her family in a settlement.

Near tragedies

On returning to the Hotel Euclid in Cleveland after the August 2, 1904 ballgame at League Park, pitchers Bill Dinneen and Norwood "Gibby" Gibson, shortstop Fred Parent, and second baseman Hobe Ferris discovered and extinguished a fire, preventing a possible tragedy.

A minor tragedy. March 24, 1929: On Sunday, March 24, playing in a 10-inning spring training game at Winter Haven (the Sox edged the Phillies, 7–6), first baseman Phil Todt and second baseman Billy Regan were so badly burned by the sun that a news report in the March 28 *Boston Globe* said they were "still confined to their rooms because of Sunday's sunburn."

On April 26, 1947, Rudy York's hotel room in Boston's Myles Standish Hotel caught on fire. It wasn't the only time this happened. York developed a reputation for this sort of thing, and was once said to have "led the league in hotel room fires." After retiring from baseball, York worked for a fire department in his home state of Georgia.

The Red Sox came close to losing their biggest star during the Korean War when Marine fighter pilot Ted Williams was hit by enemy fire and crashlanded his Panther jet at a U.S. Air Force base on February 16, 1953. Ted narrowly escaped with his life. See the book *Ted Williams At War* for the full story, as well as information on another time Ted's plane was hit by anti-aircraft fire.

In 1956, Willard Nixon reportedly fell off a circus elephant at Sarasota. In 1960, Bill Monbouquette fell off a horse during spring training in Scottsdale, Arizona. Maybe the pitcher from Medford was tempted by the chance to be a cowboy.

During spring training 1960, Marty Keough and pitcher Dave Hillman were returning to Scottsdale's Safari Hotel, the Cactus League home of the Red Sox, 15 minutes after curfew when their car turned over five times.

With rain, sleet, and temperatures in the 30s, it was so cold at Fenway early in 1974 that some of the Tigers started a fire in the visitors bullpen during the April 13 game. Jerry Moses was the catcher

Ted out West, Scottsdale. Courtesy of The Sports Museum of New England.

in the bullpen for Detroit and knew the Fenway grounds crew from his three seasons with the Red Sox. He dumped out some of the material they used as absorbment matter on the field, then asked one of the crew, "Hey, do me a favor, will you? Go out and get me some wood and we'll have a little fire to keep ourselves warm." The wood arrived. Matches were lit and a fire was built. Smoke began to billow out of the bullpen, documented by newspaper photographs. "It did us some good," said Moses, "But pretty soon the smoke got bad, and we almost choked to death. I expected to see the fire engines come racing into the ball park." Boston won, 8–1.

Mugged! On May 2, 1974 manager Darrell Johnson was robbed in Kenmore Square.

Reggie Cleveland was given 15 stitches in the right side of his face after his car overturned in a Storrow Drive tunnel on Sunday night, June 30, 1975. He'd reportedly been reaching into the back seat for a doughnut. Gordon Edes says the incident inspired this immortal line from Dennis Eckersley: "We need driver's ed, not a pitching coach." Five weeks later, Roger Moret had his own car crash. See August 5, 1975 in the preceding section.

And a few days after that, on August 9, coach Johnny Pesky's electric blanket caught on fire in the team hotel in Oakland.

And who knows what could have happened to pitcher Rick Jones? He missed the team flight to California on August 9, 1976 and was reported wandering around Kenmore Square.

Bobby Ojeda may have beaten the odds when he slipped and fell in the bathtub in an Oakland hotel on August 21, 1982. The Red Sox pitcher was placed on the disabled list. A report in 2001 indicated that bathtubs are one of the five leading causes of accidental deaths in the home.

J. O. Schmidt's 1992 essay "Allergy to venomous insects" reports that approximately 17 Americans die each year after being stung by a bee. Bobby Ojeda may have dodged another one when stung during the National Anthem before the June 22, 1983 ballgame.

September 20, 1989: Mike Greenwell was scratched from the lineup after he was hit by a SkyDome maintenance tractor before the game. The *Globe* notebook reported he had had to sit out due to "bruises he suffered when he was hit by a sweeper while playing catch in the outfield before [the] game. The vehicle, which resembles a tractor, is used to vacuum dirt and other objects off the artificial surface. Greenwell said he was playing catch with a ballboy when the driver of the sweeper swerved and hit him, knocking him to the ground." Greenwell suffered bruises to his pelvis and leg, and had a "slight head injury." He was back the following day.

The *Boston Globe* reported from Baltimore on August 2, 1993 that around 6:00 a.m. the previous day, Roger Clemens had come across a male mixed terrier "lying helplessly on the side of an exit road off the Jones Falls Expressway. Clemens and a couple of other Sox players stopped to check on the animal. "Clemens, who owns several dogs, got out of his rented car to help the injured animal, it bit him on the top of his right thumb, which ultimately sent Clemens to Johns Hopkins University Hospital to receive a tetanus shot."

October 20, 2004. At the same time that Victoria Snelgrove was killed at Fenway Park, six people in the Dominican Republic were injured by falling bullets that had been fired into the air as Dominican fans celebrated the Red Sox winning the pennant. The Associated Press reported "raucous celebrations across the Dominican Republic, home to Boston's Pedro Martinez and David Ortiz, the series MVP." Two were injured in Santo Domingo, two in Santiago, and two in La Romana. All were reported in stable condition.

In 2007, outfielder Coco Crisp was clipped on the leg by an out-of-control mascot driving an ATV at high speed on the field. There was no injury at all, but well could have been. Crisp seemed, if anything, amused.

A tragedy that wasn't—baseball and baked beans in Boston

At a SABR board meeting in 2005, director Norman Macht read a couple of paragraphs aloud from "The Joy of Foul Balls" (*The National Pastime*, #25) and the room convulsed with laughter for a few minutes. The very enjoyable story included this passage on a ballgame from long ago:

> On August 11, 1903, the A's were visiting the Red Sox, then playing in the old Huntington Avenue Grounds. At the plate in the seventh inning was Rube Waddell, the colorful southpaw pitcher for the A's, who was known to run off the mound to chase after passing fire trucks, and to be mesmerized whenever an opposing team brought a puppy onto their bench to distract him. Waddell lifted a foul ball over the right field bleachers that landed on the roof of a baked bean cannery next door.
>
> The ball came to rest in the steam whistle of the factory, which began to go off. As it was not quitting time, workers thought there was an emergency and abandoned their posts. A short while later, a giant cauldron containing a ton of beans boiled over and exploded, showering the Boston ballpark with scalding beans. It is probably safe to say that this was the most dramatic foul of all time.

Certainly so! When laughter subsided, I remarked that I'd contributed a multi-part series of articles for the Red Sox magazine in 2003, recounting each and every game of the 1903 season that culminated in the first victory in a modern World Series for the Boston Americans. I'd not come across any mention of an explosion raining baked beans onto the crowd—it's the kind of thing you'd remember—but I certainly wanted to learn more.

The article's author was Tim Wiles, director of research for the National Baseball Hall of Fame for the past 10 years. I wrote Tim and asked him where he'd learned about this incident and he referred me to Mike Gershman's book *Diamonds*. On page 70, there it was, a story the very respected Gershman titled "The Great Beantown Massacre." Mike gave as his source Charles Dryden who he described as "for years Philadelphia's leading baseball writer." Dryden's rendition was even more dramatic:

> In the seventh inning, Rube Waddell hoisted a long foul over the right field bleachers that landed on the roof of the biggest bean cannery in Boston. In descending, the ball fell on the roof of the engine room and jammed itself between the steam whistle and the stem of the valve that operates it. The pressure set the whistle blowing. It lacked a few minutes of five o'clock, yet the workmen started to leave the building. They thought quitting time had come.
>
> The incessant screeching of the bean-factory whistle led engineers in the neighboring factories to think fire had broken out and they turned on their whistles. With a dozen whistles going full blast, a policeman sent in an alarm of fire.
>
> Just as the engines arrived, a steam cauldron in the first factory, containing a ton of beans, blew up. The explosion dislodged Waddell's foul fly and the whistle stopped blowing, but that was not the end of the trouble. A shower of scalding beans descended on the bleachers and caused a small panic. One man went insane. When he saw the beans dropping out of a cloud of steam, the unfortunate rooter yelled, "The end of the world is coming and we will all be destroyed with a shower of hot hailstones."
>
> An ambulance summoned to the supposed fire conveyed the demented man to his home. The ton of beans proved a total loss. [Dryden's story ran in the *Philadelphia North American* on August 12, 1903]

What a great story! Naturally, I wanted to learn more. I was surprised I hadn't come across such a dramatic event while reading 1903's daily game stories in the *Boston Herald*. I'd read all the usual books about the Red Sox, and hadn't heard this one before. I couldn't find anything on ProQuest, which made me wonder even more. So I took myself off to the Microtext Reading Room at the Boston Public Library. Surely Dryden would not have been the only sportswriter to have noticed 2,000 pounds of boiling baked beans splattering onto the bleachers at the ballpark, or the dozen factory whistles shrieking alarm.

The *Boston Globe* had no mention of any such incident. The seventh inning was a particularly unremarkable inning, about the only inning *not* described in detail in the game account. The *Herald* noted, "Murphy opened the seventh by striking out and Monte Cross drew the first gift of his side, but it amounted to nothing as Powers was out to Dougherty and Waddell fouled to Lachance." Waddell did foul out, but one presumes that Lachance caught the ball somewhere in the vicinity of his position at first base. There was no mention of an earlier foul in the at-bat that went out of the grounds, nor of baked beans cascading onto unwitting patrons of the park, or anything of the sort.

Dryden's piece seemed oddly comic, almost as though it had been written as comedy for a publication such as *The Onion*. There was a particular line that stood out to me: "One man went insane." Though one could imagine losing a grip on reality if suddenly and unexpectedly coated with scalding baked beans and molasses during an afternoon at a ballgame while sirens shrieked from all sides, there was something about that line that raised a red flag.

Reading through the other various Boston newspapers of the day—the *Boston Journal*, the *Post*, the *Record*, the *Daily Advertiser*, and the *Traveler*—not one mention turned up of any exploding bean works or any problems at the ballgame. The *Journal* noted that an earlier explosion (not at a bean company) in Lowell had claimed another victim. After a burglary in Wrentham, the crooks escaped using a stolen railroad handcar. A seven-year-old drowned in

Fall River. A Charlestown woman had been missing for two days. A runaway horse injured two people in Franklin Square when it bolted due to the noise of an elevated train.

There was no ballgame on August 12, but it was not because the park was being cleaned of baked bean residue. The team was simply on its way to Detroit.

The *Boston Post* noted many of the same stories as the *Journal*, and paid particular credit to Reserve Officer Morse for saving several small children by stopping the runway horse. The *Post* offered a sports page cartoon of the ballgame (a 5–1 Boston victory), and depicted four baseballs being lofted off Waddell to various parts of the park, but did not illustrate any explosions, screaming whistles, or rain of beans. A man in Braintree, a hunter, shot himself in the left hand by mistake. John J. Sullivan, a fireman with Ladder 2, caught a 5'4" skate fish off Apple Island. There were any number of stories, but notable by its absence was any account of an exploding baked bean cauldron.

The *Boston Record* offered a follow-up story regarding an accident at the Philadelphia baseball park, the National League park where the Boston Nationals had been playing against the Phillies. The games there had been called off because of an accident that had taken place on August 8. An altercation between two drunks outside the park caused a number of people to rush to the wall overlooking the street, and as people crushed forward to gawk at the disturbance, the wall collapsed, killing a number of people and causing over 200 to be treated for injuries. At least 12 people died in the collapse or in the days that followed. It must be one of the most serious accidents to have occurred at a major league baseball park.

As a reporter from Philadelphia, Dryden had to be aware of the tragedy. This made the Boston story seem more credible, since this was hardly a time for levity. One would have to believe that Dryden didn't just make up the story of the baked beans in Boston. How can we explain this remarkable story that was remarked upon by no other writer?

In e-mail correspondence, Tim Wiles had written me that he thought it might be a good idea to poll SABR and "see if any one knows whether Dryden had a mischievous streak." He added, "This might make a nice little article…on the pitfalls of repeating what others have written without double checking."

First, I decided to look around a bit myself, to see what I could learn about Dryden. The very first item I found showed Charles Dryden enshrined in, of all places, the very Hall of Fame where Tim works. He was a 1965 recipient of the J.G. Taylor Spink Award. Dryden was listed as a charter member of the Baseball Writers' Association of America. What more reliable sources could we hope for than Mike Gershman, Tim Wiles, and a Spink Award honoree?

Oh, oh. There it was. In the next sentence, the Hall of Fame bio provides a crucial bit of information about Dryden: "The humorist was often regarded as the master baseball writer of his time."

It turns out Dryden was the one who coined the phrase: "Washington—first in war, first in peace, and last in the American League." He labeled Frank Chance the "Peerless Leader" and called Charles Comiskey "The Old Roman." The Hall of Fame's website noted of Dryden: "Upon receiving compliments from New York writers on his humor-filled columns, Ring Lardner replied: 'Me, a humorist? Have you guys read any of Charley Dryden's stuff lately? He makes me look like a novice.'"

Further research on Dryden shows that he particularly enjoyed tweaking Rube Waddell. In another story, he claimed that Waddell had once been found taking a bite out of the Washington Monument, but that it was not a serious problem because the Athletics pitcher had rubber teeth. Dryden also informed readers that the reason left-handed pitchers were called southpaws had nothing to do with early 20th century ballparks being positioned in such a way that home plate was toward the west and the late afternoon sun would therefore not be in the eyes of the batter. The truth, Dryden assured his readers, was a simple one: there was a particular left-hander who tried out for the Chicago Cubs and hailed from Southpaw, Illinois. It was as simple as that.

Dryden's account of the August 11, 1903 game reads smoothly enough and contains the expected information about the ballgame. Entitled "Prodigal Waddell Pitched and Lost," it starts on page one and continues inside on page five. It is only in the 11th paragraph that the story about the baked beans turns up, seemingly out of nowhere but seamlessly integrated into the account of the day's game. There was an earlier story of a mascot retained for the game by Lave Cross, a "human reservoir" described as "a colored man who can drink ten quarts of water or any other liquid without removing the pail from his lips." Dryden added, "When Cross engaged the reservoir the teams wanted to know why he did not use 'Rube' for a mascot." Cross did not reply. The story continued on to note Waddell's role "once again…as chief actor in a baseball tragedy"—and then recounts the story of the exploding steam cauldron of baked beans.

The *Philadelphia Inquirer* failed to notice any explosions, but did note that Boston had now taken five out of six from the 1902 champion Athletics. The game had been the final one of a six-game set, with Philadelphia taking the second game but losing all the others including this day's 5–1 defeat at the hands of Long Tom Hughes and the Boston Americans. Boston scored twice in the first, once in the second, and coasted on Hughes' seven-hit pitching, the only run for the visitors coming in the eighth inning. The win left Boston at 60–34 on the season. Philadelphia was 54–41, in second place but 6½ games behind.

And after the game, the Athletics—presumably accompanied by Dryden—caught an 8 p.m. train which in 36 hours would bring them to Chicago.

Two early team mascots, Glennon and Monahan.

Back in 2003, Norman Macht had posted a warning still found today on SABR's website, in a section of guidelines devoted to BioProject: "A writer's credentials do not guarantee reliability. Fred Lieb's books have errors of fact. Charles Dryden, like other reporter-humorists, made up stuff. Jim Nasium had either a porous memory or fertile imagination." Apparently, we knew it all along, but that such a wildly improbable story was reported as fact by both eminent writers Gershman and Wiles is a lesson in double-checking even primary sources and considering the quality of those sources. And a reminder that baseball research can result in some very entertaining forays.

Thanks for help in researching this article to: Nicole DiCicco, Clifford Blau, and Tim Wiles.

A Red Sox player death that wasn't

Bill Henry's wife was sitting at home in Texas when SABR member and genealogist David Lambert called her to offer condolences on Bill's passing. Taken aback, she explained that Bill was sitting right there with her in their living room. Major league pitcher Bill Henry, who debuted with the Red Sox in 1952, was reported as having died in Lakeland, Florida on August 27, 2007. "I've been right here this whole time," Bill Henry—the real left-hander told reporters later. It turned out there was another Bill Henry, the same height, around the same age, also left-handed, and with enough of a knowledge of baseball to have deceived his third wife and family and neighbors around Lakeland, even Prof. Robert McHenry with whom he gave a biannual lecture on baseball at Florida Southern College. Was it a tipoff that the lecture was entitled "Baseball, Humor and Society"? We may never know. The ersatz Henry had baseball cards of the real Bill Henry, and had fooled his wife and friends for many, many years. "I just took his word that that's who he was," explained his wife of 19 years. She'd even painted a portrait of him using an old Bill Henry baseball card as the painting's basis.

Yankee bus catches fire in the Ted Williams Tunnel

It's worth a mention. On May 19, 2002, a few minutes after the Seattle Mariners bus left Fenway Park for Logan Airport, it caught on fire inside the tunnel named after a Red Sox hero. The bus was run by Yankee, a bus company that often transports visiting teams but (for reasons of appearance) can never be the bus line of choice for the Red Sox. The driver suffered smoke inhalation, but no one else was injured.

Fights on (and off) the field

Sometimes the best stories turn out not to be true! Red Sox pitcher Mickey McDermott had been described as "the only 18 game winner ever traded for losing a fight to a sportswriter." Not true, according to Mickey. The story is in his autobiography, *A Funny Thing Happened on the Way to Cooperstown*. As author Howard Eisenberg put it, he "popped a *Christian Science Monitor* writer who said he was afraid to pitch against Cleveland ('the only team I could beat'), when the reason was jock itch from navel to toe. And it was only one of three reasons. The other two were cussin' out Yawkey's wife, and the Sox felt they needed someone to hit behind Ted. But, hey, everyone's entitled to their Rashomon."

The incident happened after the May 10, 1953 ballgame when, in the words of the *Boston Globe*'s Harold Kaese, McDermott "provoked a brief but angry fight with our colleague Bob Holbrook in the clubhouse." According to McDermott, when he struck Holbrook, Ted Williams applauded, saying, "Way to go. You're the first player to pop a writer in 20 years." Harold Kaese heard tell of a time when Stuffy McInnis threw a punch at Paul Shannon of the *Boston Post*.

One story that *is* true, though perhaps harder to believe, comes from the day that Red Sox coach Al Schacht knocked himself out with a punch to his own jaw. It was during between-games entertainment at Yankee Stadium on August 23, 1936. Schacht was a clown as well as a coach, and staged a one-man boxing match with himself—refereed by heavyweight champion Jack Dempsey. He threw a fake "knockout" punch and fell to the ground. Dempsey counted to 10 and counted him out. Schacht then tried to struggle to his feet but was woozy and fell back down again, to renewed laughter. At this point, though, Schacht wasn't laughing. "Taken to the clubhouse in a near state of collapse, [he] learned from doctors that he had snapped a bone in his left shoulder in his fall and had torn several ligaments." [*Washington Post*, August 25, 1936]

Schacht had to wear a sling for some time. The injury sure didn't hurt him financially. Coaching was nowhere near as lucrative as clowning, though. He remarked in September that he had had to turn down over 200 engagements. He was making $6,000 a year as a coach, but by February 1937 he had already booked some $35,000 worth of gigs in the minor leagues.

Some Boston fans were rowdy from the outset. On August 14, 1901 several Boston players rescued umpire Joe Cantillon from incensed Boston rooters, who called him a "robber" and "thief." The *Chicago Tribune* reported, "There was much stupid playing from both teams today and there were also many close decisions against Boston. The crowd started for Cantillon at the close of the game, but the home team kept them back and hurried the umpire off the field." Chick Stahl and Parson Lewis apparently played important roles in the rescue. Cantillon did not umpire after the 1901 season.

Two Boston players were ejected for fighting—with each other! On September 11, 1906, rightfielder Jack Hayden accused second baseman Hobe Ferris of not trying hard enough to catch a fly ball to short right field; the ball got by the right fielder and went for an inside-the-park home run. Ferris fired back a few words and reaching the Boston bench, Hayden struck Ferris four blows to the head. After Hayden was set down, Ferris rushed back and kicked him hard in the mouth. Twelve policemen rushed to restore order, while 500 fans poured onto the field. Both players were charged with disorderly conduct, but neither would press charges against the other.

On Tuesday, October 8, 1912, in New York, the automobiles of Boston's Royal Rooters were "stoned and deluged with dirt by the urchins lined up along the street and avenues leading from the ballpark" to downtown. On the 11th, it was the players themselves who were "bombarded" with dirt and stones; Buck O'Brien was hit in the face and cut by a sharp stone. A few players decried the inaction of New York's finest in "no unmistakable terms." The *Boston Globe* report indicated that police made no effort to stop the rowdyism.

October 14, 1912: Buck O'Brien was the target of another attack, after Game Six of the World Series. He'd given up five runs in the first inning and the Red Sox lost the game, 5–2. This didn't sit well with Smoky Joe's brother Paul Wood, who had bet heavily on the game believing his brother would be pitching. The choice of O'Brien was a surprise—to O'Brien among others. Stout and Johnson report rumors that Buck had been drinking heavily the night

Buck O'Brien boxing with Bill Carrigan.

before, and suggest that Sox owner James McAleer may have put him in hoping to lose the game, both to cash in on some bets himself and to ensure that there would be at least one big gate at Fenway Park. Paul Wood reportedly "sought out O'Brien and blackened one of the pitcher's eyes in a wild fistfight."

Blood was spilled under the Cleveland grandstand and Tris Speaker was spiked three times in a free-for-all fight after the May 7, 1913 game. It all sprang out of Bill Carrigan's block of the plate, which nearly knocked Jack Graney unconscious early in the game. Boston won the game, 4–1. The *Chicago Tribune* noted "several bloody shirts, buttonless sweaters, and torn trousers" in the clubhouse. Boston's catcher Les Nunamaker turned up the next day with his eye swollen shut. The game the next day was "played in silence" (*Tribune*) as not one player spoke to an opponent during the May 8 game, which Cleveland also lost, 3–2. Both Nunamaker and Cleveland third baseman Olson were hit with $25 fines for their role in the fray.

Sox manager "Rough" Carrigan didn't get the nickname from nowhere. He's said to have once "belted Babe Ruth, his young pitcher, and once ended up in a clawing match on the clubhouse floor with Win Green, the team's clubhouse man." Green was the trainer for the Red Sox in the teens. The quote comes from Harold Kaese's *A Rooter's Guide to the Red Sox*.

June 30, 1916: Boston catcher Sam Agnew was arrested for assault and taken to Police Headquarters in Washington DC, as a result of a row in the third inning. After Boston pitcher Carl Mays hit Washington Nationals captain George McBride with a pitch, McBride retaliated, flinging his bat at Mays. Players from both teams rushed onto the field and in the jostling that followed, Agnew punched manager Clark Griffith hard on the nose. Agnew said Griffith had used "vile language" and, furthermore, swung at him first. There was a background to the skirmish;

players throughout the league contended that Boston pitchers were aggressively employing the beanball as a tactic. Both Mays and McBride had had strong words the day before. The first pitch McBride faced was "uncomfortably close" to his head; the second one hit him.

The next day, league president Ban Johnson indefinitely suspended Agnew, McBride, and both managers—Griffith and Bill Carrigan. In a crowded courtroom, Boston owner Joseph Lannin requested that a warrant be issued for McBride's arrest and one was granted, but after the parties conferred, Griffith declined to prefer charges and the case was referred to the United States Attorney's office for further investigation.

On June 23, 1917, Babe Ruth walked leadoff batter Ray Morgan, but was so incensed by the call that he rushed to the plate to argue with umpire Brick Owens. Ruth was ordered back to the mound, and threw a punch that struck Owens on the ear. Ruth was suspended for nine days and had to pay a $100 fine. Ernie Shore was summoned to take Ruth's place on the

Heroes aplenty: Babe Ruth, Ernie Shore, Rube Foster, and Del Gainer in 1914.

mound. Shore said that manager Jack Barry "asked me if I'd pitch until he could get someone else warmed up." Morgan promptly tried to steal second but was thrown out, and Shore went on to retire every one of the 26 batters he faced. While Shore was the pitcher, the Red Sox recorded 27 outs without a single runner reaching base. For decades, his performance was considered a perfect game until a late 20th century ruling declared it otherwise. *The Washington Post* suggested that it was fortunate for Ruth that Owens showed restraint: "Brick has the reputation of being able to 'lick his weight in wild cats' and had he mixed with Ruth there is little question but what the pitcher would have finished second."

August 12, 1917: Chicago's first baseman Chick Gandil claimed that his counterpart, Boston's Del Gainer, tried to spike him as Gainer was doubled off first base in the fourth inning. In the ninth, on a play that wasn't close at all, Gandil slid into first showing his spikes. No harm was done in either case, but the players got into it a bit. Boston pitcher Lore Bader wasn't in the game, but he stuck up for Gainer with a few words of his own. After the game, Gandil lingered on the way to the dressing room and confronted Bader. It was, the *Chicago Tribune* subhead said, a "one punch fight"—Gainer knocked Bader unconscious.

Even team officials got into it, too. During spring training in 1919, Red Sox team secretary Larry Graver was arrested in Spartanburg, South Carolina on April 10 for punching a local resident in the nose when the fan called him a "cheap Northerner" and raised his arm as if to strike Graver.

May 30, 1919: At Philadelphia, during an Athletics rally, fans banged on the roof of the Red Sox dugout. Carl Mays, who'd pitched the day before, became incensed at the incessant pounding, grabbed a baseball and fired it hard into the stands, hitting Bryan Hayes of the Philadelphia customs office in the head and breaking his straw hat. Another Sox player punched the man sitting next to Hayes. Only the intercession of Connie Mack dissuaded Hayes from having Mays arrested. The Sox and Athletics split the day's doubleheader.

Sometime in 1928, Red Sox pitcher Merl Settlemire somehow got into a knife fight with fellow pitcher Big Ed Morris and stabbed him. This was the same Ed Morris fatally stabbed by a gas station operator in 1932.

In another Al Schacht fight, on July 3, 1935, Al Schacht's black eye was not the stuff of comedy; he earned it fair and square, as the Red Sox coach got into a five-minute fistfight after the game with Washington pitcher Ed Linke. The two had exchanged bitter words on at least a couple of previous occasions dating back to the previous season. Schacht had been riding Linke during the game, and Linke sent word he'd meet Schacht under the stands after the game. Schacht sent word back he'd see him then and there. When the game was over, both teams rushed to watch. "It was more of a wrestling match than a fight, and Linke's superior bulk gave him the advantage," wrote the *Washington Post*. The battle was broken up when Washington's secretary arrived on the scene.

Boston right fielder Ben Chapman was angry at being called out on an attempted double steal in the second game of a July 11, 1937 twinbill in Philadelphia. After he'd taken his position in right field, he fired a baseball in, seemingly aimed at umpire John Quinn. Chapman got tossed, became further enraged, and charged Quinn, hitting him this time—by throwing his glove at him. Chapman was restrained and removed from the field of play. Boston won both games.

The day of May 30, 1938 is most noted for the fight between Jake Powell of the Yankees and Boston's manager Joe Cronin. When a pitch from Boston's Archie McKain hit Powell, the batter charged the mound. Protecting his pitcher, Cronin raced to intercede and absorbed Powell's blows. After the combatants were separated, and ejected, Cronin's only exit from the playing field in those days was through the New York dugout. Several Yankees followed him into the tunnel, prompting the three umpires to follow. "Presently all the other players also dashed from view," reported *The New York Times*, "leaving the record crowd to view in bewilderment nothing but the grass while Cronin and Powell renewed hostilities under the stands."

During the war years, on May 9, 1943, while the Senators swept two from Boston, the two catchers—Ellis Clary and Johnny Peacock—got in a "wild-cat melee," a real "snarling, clawing fist fight" in the first game.

Detroit's George Vico wasn't happy to arrive at home plate when Hal White missed the bunt and botched a squeeze play. Vico was dead to rights but tried to bowl over Boston catcher Birdie Tebbetts, and came up swinging to boot—a little foolishly punching Tebbetts in the mask. Birdie threw off the mask, though, and mixed it up. Both were ejected, but had to be separated a second time when they started fighting again in the tunnel on the way to the club-houses. This all happened on May 6, 1948.

Two teammates were sparring with each other, and it well might have cost the Red Sox the pennant. On July 9, 1948, Ted Williams and Sam Mele were rough-housing in the train corridor as the team traveled to Philadelphia and Ted suffered some rib cartilage damage. It cost him 15 games and Mele found himself in the doghouse. One more win in 1948 and the Red Sox would have won the pennant.

May 24, 1952: Barbs tossed during batting practice broke out into a fierce battle between two fiery competitors. The Yankees' Billy Martin had been swapping remarks with Boston's Jimmy Piersall all season long. Martin challenged Piersall to join him under the stands, and a fistfight broke out in the runway between the Red Sox dugout and dressing room. Martin reportedly drove Piersall to his knees. The two were separated, but then Piersall is said to have gotten into another fight with his own teammate, Mickey McDermott, when he was changing his bloodied shirt in the Red Sox clubhouse. Of secondary interest, the Red Sox won, 5–2. Piersall did not play.

May 21, 1955: The game was a 12-rounder and neither team had scored after 11. Tom Brewer started for the Sox and Mickey McDermott started for the Senators. Fisticuffs erupted on the field when McDermott picked Jackie Jensen off first and got him in a rundown, and Jensen knocked McDermott down, knocking the ball out of his glove. McDermott came up swinging, and both benches emptied. Jensen was called out for interference, then thrown out of the game for fighting. A leadoff walk to Pedro Ramos, in for the evicted McDermott, led off the bottom of the 12th for Washington. A dropped ball at third and a hit off Ellis Kinder's glove—neither of which were errors, but both of which might have stopped the winning run—led to the 1–0 Washington win.

June 21, 1967: A battle of beanballs erupts between the Red Sox and the Yankees at Yankee Stadium, as the New Yorkers lose their fifth straight game (and 10 of their last 13). The Red Sox scored four times in the first inning, and Yankees pitcher Thad Tillotson may have felt that Joe Foy had to pay the price for his fifth-inning grand slam the day before. In the second inning, Tillotson's pitch hit Foy on the helmet. This was back before the DH and Tillotson had to bat against Lonborg in the bottom of the second. He was hit in the back, between the shoulder blades and both benches emptied for five minutes. A few punches were thrown and Pepitone had to leave the game with a strained left wrist. No one was ejected, perhaps a mistake. The very next inning, Reggie Smith was floored, buzzed by a close one, and in the fifth inning, pinch-hitter Dick Howser was hit in the helmet by another one of Lonborg's throws. The Red Sox won, 8–1.

July 12, 1970: The Red Sox took two from the Indians, 6–2 and 8–2, but the fireworks started early in the second game—in the top of the first inning. Fred Lasher was pitching, with two outs and Yaz on first. He hit Tony Conigliaro on the arm and Tony charged the mound, kicking him in the thigh and punching him in the nose. Conig was incensed. Not only had he nearly been blinded, or worse, when beaned by Jack Hamilton in August 1967, but just the week before Lasher had threatened Tony saying, "Conigliaro better watch out the next time we meet." Now it was that time, and his first pitch hit Tony, who reacted. Conigliaro was ejected from the game (but had moved Yaz to second, and Yaz scored on Rico Petrocelli's single). In the second, Tony's brother Billy Conigliaro homered.

May 24, 1973: In a game against Milwaukee, Bill Lee threw a pitch that hit catcher Ellie Rodriguez, a former amateur boxer and a player with whom Lee had a history from winter ball in Puerto Rico in 1972. When Lee had hit Rodriguez with a pitch in Mayaguez, the catcher and a couple of friends jumped him after the game and knocked out four of Lee's teeth. It looked like pure malice to observers when Lee picked Rodriguez off first, and then yelled to him, "That's once. I'm going to hit you again!" Reggie Smith saw it in racial terms and called out Lee, and the two of them got into a fight of their own in the Red Sox clubhouse. Lee said he was knocked unconscious by Smith, who hit from behind.

May 20, 1976: In the first meeting of the year between the two rivals, the Yanks were ahead, 1–0. It was the bottom of the sixth at the Stadium, and there were two outs. Lou Piniella was on second when Oscar Velez hit to right field. Even though Dwight Evans had already cut down Fred Stanley at the plate in the third inning, Piniella decided to go for it. Evans cut him down, too, when Fisk held onto the ball (just as he had on August 1, 1973 when Munson tried to bowl him over). Piniella upended Fisk, who bounced up and onto Piniella. Both players got into it, and things seemed to be settling down again when Graig Nettles started punching Sox starter Bill Lee. The fight resumed with redoubled intensity. Nettles later said he'd thrown Lee on the ground, and apparently hurt his shoulder. Then, he said, Lee was yelling at him "until

I couldn't take it any longer. I socked him in the eye, and he hit me." [*The New York Times*] Lee had to leave the game—rushed to Lenox Hill Hospital—suffering a torn shoulder and some torn ligaments and looked to be through for the season. Though Ed Figueroa had kept the Sox scoreless until this time, Boston immediately exploded in the top of the seventh and went on an eight-run rampage over the final three innings. The Sox had never hit a home run off Figueroa, but he gave up a two-run shot by The Rooster (Rick Burleson) in the seventh. Yaz hit homers in both the eighth and the ninth, and Boston won, 8–2.

June 22, 1989: Sox starter Mike Smithson hit Texas' Rafael Palmeiro with a pitch and the Rangers' bench emptied. Coming to Smithson's defense was one Red Sox player—Joe Price. The rest, wrote Dan Shaughnessy the following year, "sat in the dugout like cigar-store Indians" as Price led the "charge up Joe Mooney Hill." (Joe Mooney was the groundskeeper at Fenway.)

June 30, 1990: After June 2, when catcher Tony Peña was flattened by a message pitch, Peña predicted, "Somebody go down tomorrow." The Indians' leadoff batter, Stan Jefferson, was hit by the second pitch thrown by Roger Clemens. Both benches emptied (see June 22, 1989 above) and manager Joe Morgan later crowed, "I loved it. We got even, didn't we?" He said the team had voted 34–0 "that it would be such." Tony Peña said it was the first time he'd thrown a punch in 10 years in the big leagues, but felt good about it: "We did something good as a team." The Red Sox won, too, 8–2. On June 5, Morgan was suspended three games for inflammatory comments.

August 14, 1991: Mo Vaughn and Mike Greenwell's shouts escalated into a fight at the batting cage in Anaheim, to the surprise of fans watching batting practice. Both exchanged punches and Greenwell left with three visible bruises on his face. Others intervened, and the batting cage was nearly knocked down during the scuffle. It apparently started with Vaughn playfully tapping Greenwell, and not knocking it off when Gator asked him to. Videotape shot by a fan showed that Greenwell struck first. The next day's club blackboard bore a coach's message: "Hitting: 11:35. No infield. No fighting."

July 19, 1997: In another incident, a Cleveland man said that Mo Vaughn punched him in the mouth outside an area strip club at 2:30 a.m. This was two years after a fight at Boston's Roxy.

July 24, 2004: Mariano Rivera had successfully converted 23 consecutive save opportunities, but Boston third baseman Bill Mueller hit a three-run homer off Rivera in the bottom of the ninth inning and won the game for the Red Sox, 11–10. Earlier in the game, both benches emptied and punches were thrown, after Boston's Bronson Arroyo hit Alex Rodriguez with a pitch and A-Rod took offence, leading to a little jostling with Jason Varitek, who wound up shoving his glove into Rodriguez's face. Some argue that this was the moment the Red Sox became energized and began to turn the 2004 season around.

One can only guess that there were any number of other fights that were hushed up and never made the newspapers.

Some punches that weren't thrown were Babe Ruth's (he threatened to punch Ed manager Barrow in the nose on July 1, 1918), Wes Ferrell's (on August 21, 1936 he said he was going to punch manager Joe Cronin in the nose), and Bill Lee's (after Bernie Carbo was traded, Lee declared on June 16, 1978 of GM Haywood Sullivan, "I'd like to punch his head off").

A number of the blow-by-blow descriptions above were taken from *Day by Day with the Boston Red Sox*, but it's doubtful the author will sue.

Weekend Yankee killer

Often overlooked in the aftermath of the July 24, 2004 fight between Tek and A-Rod was the work of Kevin Millar that weekend. During the three days the Yankees were in Boston, he only put up the following numbers:

Friday: 3-for-4, three home runs, three RBIs (and obviously three runs scored)

Saturday: 4-for-5, all singles, one RBI, two runs scored

Sunday: 3-for-4, one homer, four RBIs, one run scored. For some reason, the Yankees hit him with a pitch, too.

Make that 10-for-13 with four HRs and eight RBIs.

Obscenity and the Red Sox

The all-time prince of the profane on the Red Sox was—without the slightest #@%^* doubt— one Ted Williams. Although we've offered a lot of lists in this book, one we will forego is a glossary of all the various words uttered by Terrible Ted. It's just a good thing he didn't play for manager Patsy Donovan (1910–11). Donovan, Curt Smith tells us, hated obscenity. "Tish, tish," he told players, or "Tut, tut, boys, please don't say those words."[Curt Smith, *Our House*, p. 17]

The need for gun control at Fenway Park

Gun control at Fenway didn't seem to be an issue way back when.

While researching the 1903 baseball season of the Boston Americans—the first "Red Sox" team to win the World Series—I came across what would seem today a very startling tradition at the ballpark: the firing of pistols and revolvers to celebrate good play. There is no apparent indication that any handgun-waving fanatics ever shouted "Kill the ump!" with malice in mind.

Both incidents occurred on holidays at home—Bunker Hill Day and Independence Day.

June 17—Cleveland and Boston split a doubleheader, Norwood Gibson losing the morning game 3–1, but Tom Hughes getting six runs in support, won the afternoon game 6–1. Cy Young had returned to Ohio, informed of the death of his mother-in-law. Both teams got eight hits in game one, and Gibson only walked three, though he did hit three batters. The Clevelanders just bunched their hits better and drove in three runs to the lone tally by the home team. Parent got three more hits, going 3-for-4 again—and 2-for-3 in the second game.

Gunfire at the game? The *Herald* reported a noisy holiday crowd (a state holiday officially termed Evacuation Day, but locally called Bunker Hill Day) "with revolvers, rattles and bells." Cleveland piled up four errors in the afternoon game.

July 4—Boston, back home again, celebrated Independence Day by winning both games of their a.m./p.m. doubleheader with St. Louis, 4–1 (Hughes) and 2–0 (Dinneen). It was a loud crowd and "about every play of more than usual excellence was accompanied by a salvo of reports of cannon crackers and the discharge of firearms."

In the morning game, umpire Connolly never showed and umpire Hassett showed up late, so Cy Young served as the sole umpire for the first inning, then yielded to Hassett when he arrived. Connolly made it in time to begin umpiring during the second inning of the second game.

St. Louis scored in the second of the first game and the score still held at 1–0 until Boston piled up four runs in the seventh. St. Louis didn't score at all in the second game, as Dinneen only let them have three hits and didn't walk anyone.

Second-place Philadelphia lost the first game of their twin bill at home against the Tigers.

Boston fans are first reported as indulging in what has since become a time-honored practice of scoreboard watching. "A fine large score board is in operation at each game and the scores of the games away are bulletined as they are received," reported the *Herald*.

Was this gunplay a unique situation in 1903? Apparently not. In 1902, both holidays featured home games for the Americans and the *Boston Morning Journal* of July 5, covering the games of the day before, wrote, "Every incident of the game worthy of note, whether performed by home players or the Baltimores, was followed by salvos of blank cartridges and cannon firecrackers, and old men vied with beardless youths in true Fourth of July style. The din was simply deafening at times." The *Boston Post* covered the game as well, and the writer for the

Ted Williams and Cy Young.

Post said, "The joy of the 8000 fans present knew no bounds. Hundreds of revolvers blazed simultaneously, while the din from giant firecrackers was terrific....Almost every play made by Boston in the forenoon game brought forth rounds of cheers, also of blank cartridges, and up to the ninth inning, Baltimore was unable to get a run across the plate." Hundreds of revolvers, in a crowd of just 8000 souls? Thankfully, these were said to be blanks. One would hate to imagine a late-inning Baltimore rally, and a player cut down at the plate by a bullet fired in anger.

Nothing in any of the game accounts indicates surprise at the custom, though newspaper accounts of other Fourth of July festivities don't indicate gunfire as a part of those events.

There was no gunfire reported on Bunker Hill Day in 1902.

The next Fourth of July game was in 1905. Although the Bunker Hill Day games in '05 were particularly exciting ones, with "thrills of delight" from the assembled crowd, and although the Detroit players almost rioted over one bad call, there was no gunfire noted. The Fourth of July saw a 20-inning defeat of the home club at the hands of the Athletics in weather that was so hot many collapsed around the city. If the writer for the *Post* was any indication, the fans were good sports. "Proud in defeat were the champions," he wrote, referring to the reigning AL champs who had lost the game—still, it took the Athletics 20 innings to defeat them and therein lay cause for pride. During the game, countless rounds of ammunition were fired. "Not an inning passed that did not thrill the crowd," he wrote. "After every good play, hundreds of six-shooters barked the gladness of their owners; men, women and children would jump into the air as Boston pulled out of a hole, and in the 19th, when on a double play Hoffman was nailed at the plate, one would think that the crowd had lost complete control of its senses." One can only imagine. These fans did not need a scoreboard urging them to clap hands for their team.

The imagery is disturbing, though, when one reads that, on another play, "Like a shot from a rifle Criger threw the man out stealing second."

The game was a classic, seeing both Cy Young and Rube Waddell both pitch 20-inning complete games. Philadelphia's Waddell attributed some of his success to gunfire from the stands: "The fact that it was the Fourth of July kept me going," he wrote in the *Cleveland Press*. "I guess the shooting of revolvers and the fireworks and the yelling made me pitch better."

There was no Fourth of July game at the Huntington Avenue Grounds in 1906. In fact, the only other years when there were home games on the Fourth were 1907 and 1911, and the tradition seems to have died out after 1905. There was no indication of gunfire—much less from hundreds of guns—in either the 1907 or 1911 games.

We would be remiss, though, if we did not note that New England Patriots scoring is always accompanied by gunfire at Gillette Stadium, with Minutemen in Revolutionary War garb letting loose a volley of musket fire following each touchdown, field goal, or extra point.

On the road to the Red Sox, Carl Yastrzemski encountered a little gunfire during the Triple A Junior World Series championship game against Havana, in Havana. Fidel Castro had just taken over in Cuba earlier in the year, and Yaz and his teammates had to endure one of his two-hour speeches. There were armed guards and soldiers everywhere. In his first autobiography, Yaz remarked, "The guy who wrote that it was the first series with more submachine guns than bats didn't exaggerate. There were submachine guns all over the ballpark, and bats only on the field. Trigger-happy kids wandered around with their guns at the ready, and every once in a while one went off." [*Yaz*, with Al Hirshberg, NY: Viking, 1968, p. 94]

Jonathan Papelbon has been known to bring a fierce-looking crossbow into the Red Sox clubhouse, but growing up around guns in the game is something more typically found these days in, say, Venezuelan Winter League ball. Alejandro Machado, who appeared in 10 games with the Red Sox in 2005 was asked about firearms at the ballfield by prolific interviewer David Laurila. Machado answered, "The culture permits it, so some do. But I don't have one. Not yet, anyway!" Laurila asked because 2004 Pawtucket Red Sox Pitcher of the Year Tim Kester had mentioned players packing guns during his own interview. We followed up with Tim, who wrote back, "Yes, a lot of players carry guns down there for 'personal protection.' As you probably know, there is a lot of crime/poverty down there and baseball players are very recognizable so they are targeted a lot by criminals. You've probably heard stories about players being robbed and even shot down there. Richard Hidalgo was carjacked and shot in the leg. Omar Infante who was on my team had his brother killed a few years ago and there are many more examples. On the team I played on there was a lock box in the clubhouse were everyone would put their personal items while we were on the field and there would be about 6–10 guns in there on any given day. They were all handguns and mostly the kind that you put a magazine in, not the revolver type, although I know at least one guy had a revolver. As far as being too casual with them, that is an understatement. It seemed like someone was always playing around with a gun. The Americans on the team were all a little bit freaked out and the GM had a meeting to tell the players to keep their guns put away because some Americans were threatening to go home. I could tell you a lot of stories about the dumb stuff they would do with guns. I can't verify that the fans had guns but if I had to bet I would say some did. They would blow off firecrackers once in a while and I would always flinch because they sounded like gunshots. It's pretty crazy down there."

Taking some of the fun out of an old tradition, security people at today's Fenway Park check arriving patrons to actually prevent them from bringing handguns to the ballgame: the 2007 regulations specifically state: "No bags or items larger than 16 x 16 x 8, coolers, cans, bottles, flagpoles, firearms, or fireworks will be permitted." Yes, these same vigilant gatekeepers also look to seize soft drink cans or other beverages that fans might bring into the ballpark.

Patting down patrons at Fenway, after September 11, 2001. Bill Nowlin photo.

ROYAL ROOTERS, BLOHARDS, AND FAR-FLUNG FANS

Fans

Red Sox fans follow in the even longer tradition of fanaticism regarding baseball in Boston. One of the reasons the American League determined to place a franchise in Boston was the city's passion for the game. Many of the old baseball boosters switched loyalties when the Americans came to town; many others patronized both ballclubs.

Royal Rooters

There is also a lengthy history of organized fan support, most notably the Royal Rooters in Boston's early days. Peter J. Nash, chronicler of the Rooters, traces the history of Boston "cranks" and fans back into the 19th century in his book *Boston's Royal Rooters*. The Rooters organized travel-ing aggregations which brought 125–130 Boston fans to Baltimore in 1897 to see the Beaneaters beat the Orioles for the National League pennant. When the American League placed a franchise in Boston, the Rooters supported that team as well and a sizable party traveled to Pittsburgh for the four games played

Boston's Royal Rooters cheering on the Sox.

there during the 1903 World Series. It was in Pittsburgh that they truly launched the first Boston victory anthem, "Tessie." They hired bands to play the song—incessantly, so much so that some of the Pirates remembered years later how the constant playing unnerved them.

The Rooters traveled to New York the following year to see the deciding game of the 1904 pennant, the result again going in Boston's favor. Among the more noteworthy leaders were saloonkeeper Michael "Nuf-Ced" McGreevey and Congressman John F. "Honey Fitz" Fitzger-ald, grandfather of President John F. Kennedy. Active throughout was Lib Dooley's father John S. Dooley.

When not at the games—such as during the fallow months known as the offseason—fans organized a series of booster clubs to host dinners and the like. Over the course of time, these booster clubs went by various names such as the Winter League, the Half Century Club, the Bosox Club, and the BLOHARDS.

The Winter League

Overlapping in time with the Royal Rooters, the first of these outside-the-park clubs was the Winter League. The first mention we have found of the Winter League comes in 1908, when the group is said to have held its annual outing at Sunset Farm in Holliston, Massachusetts. That this was already considered to be annual event suggests there were earlier evenings as well. John Campbell was president, and John S. Dooley the vice president and secretary. Mem-bers of the organization included Red Sox owner John I. Taylor, former ballplayer and *Boston*

Globe sportswriter Tim Murnane, former players Hugh Duffy and Tom McCarthy, as well as a number of Boston area businessmen.

What was then called the winter league is what folks for years have dubbed the "hot stove league"—a chance for people to get together and talk about baseball in the off season. John Dooley was not only noted as vice president and secretary of the Winter League, but prized for his drive to build the organization. He'd been the first president and, apparently, the principal organizer as well. An appreciation in a January 1913 issue of the *Boston Journal* referred to "Jack Dooley, secretary of the Winter League Club, by whose efforts the club has nearly doubled its membership in the last six months...." was awarded a diamond ring in recognition of his work. The 1913 dinner honored Hughie Jennings, who pronounced that he'd enjoyed the "time of his life."

John Dooley presents one of the longest threads weaving throughout this book. He had so many interesting connections with the Red Sox that we want to take considerable time to look at his life and his love of baseball here.

Dooley's involvement precedes the Red Sox, helping get the franchise settled and into its first ballpark in Boston, and rooting for Boston baseball teams without missing an Opening Day for three-quarters of a century. According to Jack Mahoney's article in the April 14, 1968 *Boston Herald*, Dooley had seen every opener since 1882. Art Ballou's article in the June 20, 1963 *Globe* dated his Opening Day streak back to 1894—and Dooley added that there were many seasons in which he'd seen every home game. Whichever date one picks, by 1968 he'd been to at least 75 in a row.

John S. Dooley

John Stephen Dooley was born in Somerville, Massachusetts on Christmas Day, 1873. He lived to the age of 96, dying on March 1, 1970.

From a very early age, Dooley had a connection to the game of baseball and as Americans began to orbit in space, he was able to tell people that he had witnessed the very first baseball game ever played under the lights. That newfangled invention the Weston light bulb was but three years old (Edison's first incandescent bulb was invented in 1879) when the first night game was played at Hull, Massachusetts on September 2, 1880. The next day's Boston newspapers tell the story of how two teams from competing Boston department stores (Jordan Marsh Co. and R. H. White & Co.) played a full nine innings in Hull under "a new system of electric lighting" at Strawberry Hill, on the grounds of the Sea Foam House at Nantasket Beach. Three large wooden towers, each 100 feet high, were erected and placed some 500 feet apart. On the top of each were placed 12 "Weston lamps," each grouping providing some 30,000 candlepower of illumination. The system of massed groupings of lights was provided by the Northern Electric Light Company. A 30-horsepower generator powered the array.

The *Boston Post* explained that "on the broad lawn in the rear of the house there was sufficient light to enable a game of base ball to be played, though scarcely [with] the precision as by daylight." The two picked nines squared off, the game tied 16–16 after nine innings and called off so the players could catch the last boat back to Boston. The *Boston Herald* compared the light to that of "the moon at its full" and said that as a result "the batting was weak and the pitchers were poorly supported." And young Jack Dooley was there. His half-brother William Dooley worked for R. H. White and had taken his younger brother to the event.

Dooley was a pitcher himself in his younger days, playing for the Franklins of Egleston Square, according to a May 13, 1956 article in the *Boston Sunday Post*. He also played some semipro ball in Attleboro and made another acquaintance in the process, Chick McLaughlin, captain of the Harvard baseball team. Through McLaughlin, he met Joe Kennedy, who he recalled as "a first baseman, but not too good." Kennedy "played only one game—the last one against Yale—and then only the last two innings to get his letter. But he played for Chick's college all-stars which toured the area after the college season was over. Through my acquaintance with Joe, I met young Jack." Yes, that Jack Kennedy—John Fitzgerald Kennedy, future President of the United States.

In fact, Dooley knew a couple of Boston's major political figures. As a young man growing up in Roxbury, Jack Dooley used to deliver milk on Eustis Street together with a young John Michael Curley. When William Dooley died, Curley was a pallbearer at his funeral. The Dooleys had a summer home in Hull on B Street, just a few houses away from where Joseph P. Kennedy had a home. Honey Fitz had a home in Hull, too.

Not surprisingly, Dooley frequented ballgames of Boston's first team, the Nationals, who played in the late 19th century at the Walpole Street Grounds and, later, the South End Grounds. Dooley recalled visiting the clubhouse in that era, one when "the players had to wait in line for a bath in a flat tin tub. It took them longer to get the bath over than the playing of the game itself." [handwritten notes for a speech found in Katherine Dooley's papers]

Dooley was one of the men to whom Connie Mack turned when Ban Johnson enlisted his help in creating the American League. And Johnson knew Dooley well. Dooley told the *Boston Globe*'s Art Ballou in 1963 that the architect of the American League used to call him "my little Irishman from Boston."

The story, as Dooley set it down, went thus: In the fall of 1900, Johnson came to Boston to see if it were feasible to situate a charter American League franchise in a city already known for its passionate interest in baseball. He set up shop in the Old South building on Washington Street and sought out Hugh Duffy, holding a number of meetings with him. Dooley sat in on a few of the meetings. Lining up the players was easier than finding a suitable location for the ballpark. Duffy had considered a position as a principal with a proposed American Association team to be placed in the area in an attempt to fend off an American League incursion. Duffy declined, arguing, "The grounds are too far out. They are in Cambridge and will not draw from Boston. Harvard students might patronize the club, but that is about all."

"I recall Peter Kelley, an old newspaper man, calling on me at my office," Dooley wrote in a brief account he typed up. Kelley was calling on behalf of Cleveland's Charles Somers, designated as the first president of the Boston American League club. Kelley himself "had an option on the old bicycle track across the Charles River in Cambridge, on a lease calling for a yearly rental of $5,000." Johnson, though, didn't like the Cambridge location recommended by Mack and Clark Griffith. He didn't want a Boston team playing anywhere but in Boston. He kept that information to himself and the small circle of men trying to help situate the team.

Boston was the eighth and final city selected as home for a club in the new American League. Only by finding an appropriate site for a baseball field would the American League truly decide to place a team in Boston. Had the men not found a good location, the league would have placed its eighth club in either Buffalo or Indianapolis. SABR researcher Doug Pappas found that the National League's Arthur Irwin had leased the Cambridge property in a pre-emptive move to try and keep out the upstart league, but the lease was structured such that it would expire if the property was sold.

A location deemed more suitable, however, was a site on Huntington Avenue controlled by the Boston Elevated Railway Company. Duffy showed the site to Kelley and they both recommended it to Johnson. Dooley recalled Durand Associates as the actual owners of the land, but they had leased it to the railway, which envisioned building a terminal there. The car barn wasn't in the cards, but the railway was holding out for a $10,000 a year rental.

Dooley was at the time working for the firm of J. R. Prendergast, brokers in cotton goods and yarn with offices at 87 Milk Street. Prendergast's brother Daniel was in charge of the real estate department of the Boston Elevated. Dooley knew the terminal plan was off—it turned out there was an ordinance that prevented the construction of car barns on the land which, even though it had served as a dump, was still across the street from the opera house—and urged Duffy and Kelley to approach Dan Prendergast, offer $5,000 a year "and mention my name. Under no conditions, I said, were they to go higher than $5,000."

The offer was, Dooley said, "violently refused" and Prendergast called Dooley to complain about the "measly rental" the men had offered. "If you want my advice," Dooley says he told Prendergast, "I'd grab that $5,000 offer because they can get that wonderful site in Cambridge for that figure. You'd better grab them right now before they close with Cambridge."

Prendergast took the bit and a deal was struck. Dooley later told the *Boston Post*'s Gerry Hern, "I suppose I should be a little sorry for what I did to get the American League in here, but when I sit in Fenway Park these days, I figure maybe the good Lord will forgive me. It was in a good cause."

In 1956, Hern wrote, "More than anyone, Jack Dooley is responsible for the American League obtaining the Huntington ave. grounds as their playing field." Had Dooley not helped out, there might never have been a Boston Red Sox. The February 2, 1901 issue of *The Sporting News* records the formal awarding of a Boston franchise to Somers. Three weeks later, the February 23 *Sporting Life* reported that Somers had said the American League would never have invaded Boston if the National League had acceded to its original request for recognition as a major league.

Dooley later went to work for his brother at Wm. J. Dooley & Co., 60 Congress Street. Like Prendergast's, the firm was also a broker in cotton goods and cotton yarns, and did quite a good business at the time serving the mills of New England. Later, in 1912, William Dooley was honored by Pope Pius X, who bestowed on him the title of Knight of the Sword and Cape, carrying the rank of private chamberlain to the Holy Father. At the same time, James Prendergast was made Grand Commander of the Order of St. Gregory.

Soon after the AL franchise was established, the 1903 team won the pennant and Dooley was there in the grandstand watching the first World Series game ever played, on October 1, a member of the Royal Rooters. The following year, Boston won the pennant again, playing the final two games against the New York Highlanders. Dooley was there, too. One finds his name in the October 9, 1904 *Globe*, listed among the Rooters who took two train cars from Boston to see those last two games.

The Winter League, Dooley once said, was organized with a simple purpose: "Its object is to promote better baseball for Boston. In its membership are listed a large number of Boston's royal rooters—most of them daily attendants at the game." Dooley himself didn't just make Opening Day. There were many years in which he never missed a game—and that often meant taking in games with both of Boston's teams. For decades, he made the annual pilgrimage to spring training as well.

The Winter League Club, as it was often called, met with some frequency. Boston newspapers report both a dinner in Holliston to honor Hughie Jennings and a night at the Majestic Theatre in January 1913, a dinner at the Hotel Lenox in April, a trip to Portland in May for the opening game of the New England League season there, a trip to Fitchburg in January 1914, and a February dinner at Hurlburt's Hotel

Hugh Duffy (left) and John S. Dooley board the train to Sarasota, 1951. For Duffy, age 85, it was his 62nd trip to spring training. Courtesy of Katherine Dooley.

honoring Johnny Evers. Dooley and Hugh Duffy were noted as traveling back from a February meeting in New York, and Dooley and several others including Duffy traveled to New York again with the Braves late in September. In December 1914, he began organizing a winter dinner to honor Braves manager George Stallings. Late in the month was "Maranville Night" at the Old Howard Theatre; the *Globe* noted that "Jack Dooley and his Winter League will be on hand." He was spotted in the corridors at meetings of New England League baseball in January 1915 and at a Quincy House dinner where the 125 dined on turkeys sent from Stallings' plantation in Georgia. Dooley was described as the "moving spirit of the Winter League."

He turned up again, involved at an old-time athletes event in Holliston in July. The annual feast was held at Quincy House in February 1916, attended by 150 members. That December, President Dooley announced the annual banquet, this time to honor Rabbit Maranville, who became a longtime friend of the family (when he married, John's wife Winifred Dooley gave the Maranvilles the baby carriage that had held Lib Dooley as an infant).

Dooley continued to play some ball for the enjoyment of it. A 1912 article in the *Boston Post* has him playing third base on the same Winter Club team as two future Hall of Famers (the Hall of Fame wasn't founded for another 20 years). Hugh Duffy played center field and Tom McCarthy played left. Other players known in old-time Boston baseball circles included Jack Barry, Arthur Cooper, Carl Nichols, and Jack Slattery. Both Barry (beginning in 1915) and Slattery (back in 1901, the first year of the franchise, before they were the Red Sox) played for the Red Sox, and Cooper was scouting for the Sox at the time.

The following April, Dooley managed a Winter League team "composed of a number of old-timers, college and semi-professional stars" to play against Hugh Duffy's Portland team of the New England League. Nichols and Slattery were Dooley's choice of batterymates, and Walter Lonergan (1911 Red Sox) and "Chick" McLaughlin were set for the infield. In April 1914, a brief note says that Dooley, president of the Winter League, had umpired a game in Fitchburg between that New England League team and the Boston Pilgrims, "a team composed of former college players." Dooley was "struck by a foul ball behind the right ear, and it was badly lacerated."

That didn't dampen John Dooley's fervor. Dooley had the passion to organize. In July 1914, he was back at Sunset Farm and joined in the founding of the Old Time Athletes' Assocation. Dooley is listed as on the original board of directors. It was apparently not a charitable organization to take care of elderly ballplayers, but instead one to "bring together men for a few more desperate flings at athletic glory," in the words of Joanne Hulbert. Joanne points out that Sunset Farm still exists today with a street address of 320 Chamberlain Street, in the section of Holliston known as—this is for real—Mudville.

In May 1918, Rabbit Maranville, Del Gainer, Mike McNally, Whitey Witt, Herb Pennock, and Leo Callahan—all in the U.S. Navy—set sail under sealed orders, among those who saw them off were John Dooley and former Red Sox manager Jack Barry, now a Chief Yeoman in the Navy himself.

It should be no surprise that when it came time to campaign for Sunday baseball in Massachusetts, John Dooley was in the midst of it, along with his brother-in-law Eugene J. O'Connor. A catcher in his early days, O'Connor played for the Boston Brotherhood Club and the Boston team in the United States League. He was apparently signed by the Boston Nationals at one point but does not appear to have played in a major league game. He covered baseball for the *Boston American* and became sports editor of the paper in 1904. His November 9, 1952 *Boston Globe* obituary deemed him "one of the original advocates of Sunday baseball and also was credited with bringing about twilight baseball." An appreciation written several days later by Victor O. Jones was headlined "Father of Sunday Baseball."

Civil disobedience in pursuit of Sunday
baseball.

With a six-day workweek typical at the time, there were precious few times that workingmen could take in a baseball game.
O'Connor was willing to go to great lengths to help extend baseball's popularity, even though that meant coming up against the
Lord's Day laws of the period with a little civil disobedience. The
October 21, 1912 *Globe* tells how O'Connor got himself arrested
by playing baseball on Boston Common on Sunday afternoon
the day before.

The fight dragged on for years, Sunday baseball not becoming legal until the 1929 season. A more complete story of Bos-
ton Sunday baseball is told elsewhere in this book, but we want to underscore here the role
that John Dooley played in allowing Sunday baseball to be played at Fenway Park. Dooley
reportedly urged an attorney friend of his, Charles Young of Quincy, to approach Lt. Gov.
Leverett Saltonstall, to see what could be done regarding the prohibition against a baseball
game being held within 100 yards of the Church of the Disciples. Saltonstall visited the minister, who had no objection at all and since 1932, the way has been cleared for Sunday games
at Fenway.

In 1951, the *Boston Sport-Light* had Dooley as secretary of the Sarasota Athletic Club and
presented a testimonial to Joe Cronin at their annual gathering. It seems he was active organizing in Florida as well.

Mr. Dooley's son, John S. Dooley, Jr., served as manager of the Boston College baseball
team in 1926. He was a shortstop, but his son John J. Dooley says that he chose not to play
baseball in college so he could concentrate on his studies. John J., grandson to our man,
worked as a professional baseball umpire from 1978 to 2000 after completing a career in the
United States Navy.

The Lido Beachcombers A.C.

The Sarasota Athletic Club referred to above was yet another Red Sox fan club, also referred to
as the Lido Beachcombers A.C. An article in the December 15, 1954 *Sporting News* mentions
Sam Mele being given a "welcome home" party at the Fresh Pond Grill in Cambridge in early
December after he was reacquired by the Red Sox. GM Joe Cronin was a guest as well. The
Beachcombers were referred to as "fans and writers who visit Sarasota when the Sox are training
in Florida." Only a very few old-timers still remember the loose-knit Sarasota aggregation.

The Red Sox One Half Century Club

As the Red Sox reached their 50th anniversary, a group of boosters formed the Red Sox
One Half Century Club. The first honorary
president? John S. Dooley. The club received
a flurry of attention in the years Johnny Pesky managed the Red Sox, with John Dooley
appearing in a sports page cartoon in the *Herald* and with Dooley being presented a silver
cup on September 22, 1963 at Fenway. Photographs from 1963 and 1965 show Dooley with Pesky, Bobby Doerr, Mel Parnell,
Duffy Lewis, writers John Drohan and Jack
Malaney, and fellow booster Dick Casey.

John Dooley, with cup, flanked by Johnny Pesky and Mel Parnell
with other Half Century Club boosters. Courtesy of Katherine
Dooley.

We the People Speak

Even before the Half Century Club, there was another (apparently short-lived) club called "We the People Speak." The group was described in news accounts as "an organization of bleacherites at Fenway Park" which began in 1942 and on September 7, 1944 held its third annual gathering at Boston's Parker House. Guests included Pete Fox, Bob Johnson, and Mike Ryba.

The BoSox Club

The Half Century Club seemed to fade very quickly afterward, because when Ken Coleman first arrived in Boston to broadcast Red Sox baseball in 1966, he was unaware of any recognized booster club. Ken came back home to his native Boston, having worked in Cleveland for several years. While broadcasting for the Indians, he'd been a member of the Wahoo Club. "It was an Indians booster club," he told this author, "and when I came to Boston I spoke with Bill Crowley, who was the public relations director of the Red Sox. He told Crowley about the Wahoo Club and got Cleveland's Gabe Paul and Al Rosen on a speaker phone to talk with Crowley and some other interested people in Boston. They described the club and how it worked. Coleman says it was quite a small club at the time, sometimes only a dozen or two members coming to gatherings.

Ken inspired a group of Red Sox fans—some "50 prominent Boston businessmen"—to organize the BoSox Club and it had its first meeting in early 1967—and what a year that kicked off! The club's first event was a "Welcome Home to the Red Sox" luncheon held on April 10 at Anthony's Pier Four, the day before the home opener. Some 260 members and their guests attended the luncheon and heard Dick Williams introduce the entire Red Sox squad, and outline his plans for the 1967 season. "When we started the club," Ken explained, "we met at first at the Somerset Hotel. Dominic DiMaggio was the president and we had a board of governors. Bob Cheyne was one of them; he was an executive at the old WHDH. Brad Jernigan was in the banking business. They were always lunch meetings. The first year that we had them on a regular basis, Dick Williams never missed a meeting. He was at every one of them. I don't recall how many people came to those early meetings; there were always a lot of people."

The BoSox Club, for years, has been what Coleman was able to describe as "the most successful club in the country." There are close to 900 members at the present time. The Club meets monthly throughout the baseball season, with guests from the Red Sox and the visiting club in town at the time of any given luncheon. The luncheons average around 325 members, though the November 2007 luncheon drew well over 500. The Club also organizes spring training junkets and its 2006 banquet in Fort Myers fed 200 members. The BoSox Club gives out a number of scholarships to baseball camps and other honors to school ballplayers, and organizes an annual spring training jaunt as well. When the Red Sox are in need of additional volunteers to help staff certain events, they will often reach out to the ranks of the BoSox Club as well. Among Red Sox team personnel, Dick Bresciani has been the valued long-time liaison to the BoSox Club.

Visit the club's website at www.bosoxclub.com for more information.

The BLOHARDS

BLOHARDS stands for the Benevolent Loyal Order of Honorable and Ancient Red Sox Diehard Sufferers. This fan club holds meetings twice a year in the heart of the beast—New York City. And an annual bus trip to Boston for Opening Day. Earlier meetings were held at the Park Avenue Armory, but the Yale Club is the venue of choice today. The April 2007 meeting drew 180 to the luncheon and included entertainment by John Pizzarelli. One of the very first places the 2004 World Championship Trophy visited was a specially-convened meeting of the BLOHARDS to celebrate the long-awaited Holy Grail.

The group is said to have been formed in 1960. In a 1979 piece in the *New York Times*, Henry Berry tells of his initiation into the organization. It was 1964 and it happened in the bar car of a Connecticut-bound New Haven Railroad train following a Yankee-Red Sox confrontation at the Stadium. Uxbridge native Jim Powers was on the train with a number of fellow sufferers, and when Jim broke into song: "Who's better than his brother Joe? Dominic DiMaggio...," he captured Berry's attention. They swapped stories and, Berry wrote, "By the time the train reached Darien I was not only a member of the club but its vice president-historian."

Both have passed on. Jim Powers, though, lived to see that trophy brought to the BLOHARDS event. A board of six runs the organization today: Julie Killian, Sarah Powers, Jim Shea, Ray Duffy, Joe Cosgriff, and Peter Collery. Like the BoSox Club, a membership organization, one suspects that collection of dues is not the highest of priorities—witness Jim Shea's response when asked how many members the organization had at the start of 2007: "I'm guessing that there are around 800 hundred on the e-mail list, but I don't know how many are paid up."

Mike Port speaking at a BLOHARDS luncheon at the Armory. Bill Nowlin photo.

Groucho Marx said he'd never want to join a club that would have him for a member. We're not sure what that has to do with anything here, but this is a club which includes among its key events the time in 1992 that "Butch Hobson, newly-appointed as manager of the Red Sox, essentially challenges a by now age-enfeebled Henry Berry to a fist fight during an early April BLOHARD confab at the McGraw Hill building. Berry's crime? Gentle mockery of Hobson's mentor Don Zimmer. In three subsequent seasons as Sox skipper, Hobson fails to ever bring the team in above .500." The assembled sufferers were kinder to Jimy Williams, about whom they graciously comment: "Immensely likeable, during a 45 minute conversation, he never once gives a straightforward answer to any remotely controversial question." Every manager since Dick Williams—except for Kevin Kennedy—has appeared before the BLOHARDS. Of Dan Duquette, the website chronology notes, "Notwithstanding his reputation, he is gracious, relaxed and funny."

Now here's something different. In the *2007 Boston Red Sox Media Guide*, pitcher Javier Lopez lists some personal information—where he graduated high school, his college baseball record, the fact that he was Colorado's player rep for a year, his marriage to Renee, and... "attended luncheons in 2006 for the BoSox Club and the BLOHARDS."

For more information on the BLOHARDS, including a full chronology, please check www. blohards.com.

Bluenose Bosox Brotherhood

The Bluenose Bosox Brotherhood is proof positive that Red Sox Nation has no borders. The BBB is a diehard group of Sox fans from Nova Scotia, "Bluenose" being a nickname for residents of that Canadian province. Launched in 2005 by Annapolis Valley residents Don Hyslop, Dave Ritcey, and Jim Prime, the Bluenose Bosox Brotherhood has grown to approximately 100 members from across the province. The club has become so popular that plans are underway to create BBB chapters in various parts of the province.

Bill "Spaceman" Lee is the BBB's "Emperor for Life," Johnny Pesky is the "Patron Saint," and Dick Gernert is "Ambassador-at-Large."

The latest coup by the BBB was convincing the Red Sox to bring the 2007 World Series trophy to Halifax, the capital city, in January of 2008. The connections between Boston and Halifax are many and varied. In 1917, when the Halifax Explosion devastated the city and left thousands dead and wounded, it was Boston that came to its aid most quickly and effectively. Nova Scotians have never forgotten that act of compassion and every year a Christmas tree arrives in the Massachusetts capital as a token of gratitude. There are numerous historical, cultural, business, and family ties between Nova Scotia and Massachusetts. One of the most enduring is a mutual love of the Red Sox. Prior to the existence of the Montreal Expos in 1969 and the Toronto Blue Jays in 1977, the Red Sox were the "home team" for most Nova Scotia baseball fans. Countless fans of an earlier generation huddled around their radios to pick up scratchy broadcasts of Sox games. Today many people make the annual trip to Fenway Park to see their favorites in action. Countless others have invested in satellite dishes so that they don't miss a game.

The BBB meets on a semi-regular basis to discuss all things Red Sox. There are plans to make road trips to Boston as well as Pawtucket, Lowell, and Portland, Maine. Funds made from auctions and other activities are donated to children's charities such as the Jimmy Fund, the IWK Children's Hospital, and minor league baseball. As this book goes to press, we hear word of a possible Herring Choker branch in neighboring New Brunswick, perhaps to be organized by Bruce MacDonald from Ted Williams' old stomping grounds on the Miramichi River.

Far-flung fans

There are also the unorganized fans, ones that can't effectively be members of a booster club. There are clusters here and there, and Jim Conners has certainly built a strong following in the Los Angeles area centered on his Irish pub and restaurant, Sonny McLean's, located on Wilshire Boulevard in Santa Monica. See www.sonnymcleans.com for more on the club itself. Suffice it to say you could walk off Wilshire and think you were in a time and space warp, back in a comfortable neighborhood bar in any working class area of Greater Boston. For several years now, Conners has organized one or more buses of Sox fans to visit Angels Stadium when the Red Sox come to Anaheim. Angels management has made it more difficult in recent years, and Sonny's is having a harder time getting a bloc of seats. Dick Dodd of the Standells joined the bus ride in 2006, singing "Dirty Water" aboard the bus for good luck. The Sox won—finally breaking a Sonny's losing streak.

Red Sox owner Tom Werner made sure that another one of the very first stops on the 2004 Trophy Tour was all the way across the country—at Sonny McLean's.

There are any number of Red Sox-related listserves and online forums. One of the most venerable is the Bosox List, which has been going for 15 years now. The list has several hundred dedicated participants, a considerable number of whom are from other lands. Some of the stories of these far-flung Sox fans are worthy of attention.

The Bosox List can be reached at: BOSOX@APPLE.EASE.LSOFT.COM

George Kentros / Sweden

George Kentros was born in Worcester, Massachusetts in 1964. In May 1986, he moved to Stockholm, Sweden to play the violin professonally, and now has a family with two young children, Theodor and Sofia. George plays mostly new classical music. His group is the peärls before swine experience.

George follows the Red Sox from Sweden via the Internet. "When the Net came to Sweden I was one of the first to get it at home, and it's extremely important." Following the Sox remains one of his ties to America and to his youth. "One of the advantages of being a freelance is I get to pick my vacations more or less, so I come to New York when the Sox play there and stay with my brother. He and my parents send me a couple of videotapes each season, but I haven't been to Fenway since 1983, and it kills me."

"I am looking forward to learning more about this Internet video thing MLB is making noises about instituting next year, that would be the first thing I would unhesitatingly pay real money for on the Web. I think I can win over my kids to baseball and the Sox, I'm less sure about my Swedish wife...."

George concludes, "As I have always said, sports may not be the same as culture, but the Bosox are definitely culture."

Micke Hovmöller / Sweden

It's one thing to be born in Worcester and move to Sweden, but how did a Swedish native become interested in baseball? Micke is 30, and currently the head of statistics at Stockholmsbörsen, the Swedish stock and derivatives exchange.

"I used to watch it a bit when it was broadcast on a Swedish sports channel in the very early '90s. I remember rooting for Rickey Henderson in general, but not for any specific team. For some reason I then started following baseball closely via the Internet in 1996. I mostly followed it in a statistical way, watching Heathcliffhanger racking up saves (and blowing them with the same intensity) and Mo closing in on the league lead in walks."

The Red Sox were the team which first captured Micke because the firm he worked for at the time, Cambridge Technology Partners, had its headquarters in Boston, "so they were kind of 'the local team,' even though I've never been to Boston (or any part of the U.S. except for Florida, Illinois and Wisconsin)." Micke's visits to Skydome and the Trop unfortunately did not coincide with the Red Sox coming to town. "I tried to book our Tampa vacation so that the Red Sox would be in town but for scheduling reasons that wasn't possible. I saw the Angels and the Rangers instead. I did plan my trip so that we would see the last game in the FSL, Sarasota Red Sox at Lakeland Tigers, but when we got to Lakeland they had moved the game from 6 p.m. to noon, so the game was already played by the time we got there. That gave me some explaining to do to the wife...."

The visit to Toronto was in March, so there were no ballgames. "We did try to take the tour, but Ricky Martin was having a concert later that night so the tours were cancelled. I didn't like Ricky Martin before and now I hate him badly—but technically, I've been 'in' Tropicana Field and 'at' the Skydome."

Micke follows the Red Sox via the Internet, visiting dozens of web sites—primarily the Bosox list. "I'd say I follow them pretty intensely. If there was an important game during the night, the first thing I do in the morning is turn on the computer and look at the box score and read the recap. I listen to most (75%?) of the day games via Internet radio since they start at 7 p.m. local time. The games starting at 1:00 a.m. are too inconvenient, unfortunately.

"I always know what 25 players are on the roster at any one time, but I don't think I'd be able to name all the players on the 40-man roster. When I saw the lineup for a game I would immediately know what most list members would think about it.

"My level of activity on the Red Sox list is pretty much inversely correlated to the amount of work I have to do, but I always read everything. As it happens, the head of market supervision here at the exchange is a huge Yankee fan, so we talk quite a bit. I know of no other Swedes that are Red Sox fans, unfortunately."

Asked if he sometimes sees tourists wearing a "B" cap, and maybe stops them to talk, Micke replies, "No. Baseball caps are, in 99% of cases, worn as "fashion statements" (or lack of such, in the case of Yankee hats which completely dominate the market). I doubt even 50% of the people wearing MLB stuff know what sport it is (seriously!). One can also buy college sports stuff, and I know for sure that that is completely unknown in Sweden). I once saw a proud father wearing some NHL cap with his two sons aged about 8 and 6, one in a Yankee cap and one in a Red Sox cap. That pretty much tells the whole story, I think."

Jonathan Kolodny / Israel

Jonathan tells his own story: "Originally from Sudbury (and later Newton MA), I have been a Sox fan for as long as I can remember—my earliest television memory was watching the '75 Series (age six). We have pictures of me in a Sox cap from age four.

"I was in Cambridge for four years ('90–'94, doing my PhD/post-doc) and London for 4.5 (November '95–May 2000). I moved to Israel to open an office for my firm, and plan to stay out here for the long term.

"Because of the seven-hour time difference, and the fact that NESN isn't part of the local cable package here in Israel, I tend to follow the Sox by 'watching' the broadcasts on Saturday and Sunday nights (for afternoon games) and late-night West Coast games on Yahoo's Sports-Channel, and listening to Web radio broadcasts (though the reception tends to be poor).

"Of course I read the list religiously, and that is often my best source of information.

"Unfortunately, I see more Yankee/Mets caps than Red Sox caps here, primarily because most US expats or emigrants are from the NY/NJ area. Occasionally I stumble across an Israeli Sox fan, who picked up the bug after working in high-tech in the Route 128 area. My eldest son (now age seven) has also become a die-hard fan, and my youngest can also be spotted in a Sox cap."

Darcy Paquet / Korea

"I was born in Hopkinton, Mass. and then moved to Hardwick, Mass. when I was 12, but in my mid-twenties I moved to Korea to teach English. That was in 1997. I had majored in Russian in college, and in graduate school became certified to teach English as a foreign language. My plan after graduating was to teach English in Korea for a couple years, pay off my student loans, and then move on to Eastern Europe. I liked it so much in Korea I just stayed. I married my wife Hyeon-sook, a Seoul native, in 2001 and we had a son Jamie in December 2004 (just a couple months after the Sox won it all).

"In 2001, I moved from teaching to journalism, writing about Korean cinema for a British film magazine. These days I am the Seoul correspondent for *Variety*, the L.A.-based entertainment paper. I also maintain a website on Korean cinema at www.koreanfilm.org, and do advising for various international film festivals.

"My grandfather came to Boston from Italy as a baby, and was a diehard Bosox fan since the 1910s. He later moved to Montreal to start up a factory, and I hear he used to stay up nights trying to get Sox games on the radio (usually it didn't work, which would make him quite upset!) Later he moved to Fort Lauderdale. When I was a kid we used to watch Sox games together, and ever since he died in 1986 (July, a few months before that fateful Series), we've put his old Red Sox cap on the top of the Christmas tree in place of a star.

"For this Red Sox fan living abroad, the internet has been a godsend. I keep up mostly by reading the Bosox list and by visiting sites such as ESPN or Yahoo for scores. Occasionally I read the *Globe* online, but I've become somewhat selective—I prefer actual news to the occasionally hysterical opinion pieces they run.

"Whenever the Sox have a Korean player on the roster (Cho Jin-ho, Kim Byung-hyun, etc.), it ensures that we get to see their games on TV here in Korea. Otherwise we have to wait until the team faces off against Park Chan-ho or some Korean pitcher on another team.

"Tim Savage and I have met up a few times here in Seoul. We share both an interest in Korea and in the Red Sox, so it's always good to see him.

"I never played much baseball as a kid, being more of a soccer person. Baseball is by far my favorite sport to watch and follow, but I prefer playing soccer or ultimate frisbee. Here in Korea, I've unfortunately been too busy with work to play any sports.

"Meanwhile, I hold out hope that one day the Sox will land an ace Korean pitcher who contributes years of a sub-3.00 ERA and ensures that I always have a selection of Red Sox games to watch on Korean TV…."

Mike Trathen / New Zealand's #1 Red Sox fan (and .400 hitter)

Mike Trathen bills himself as New Zealand's #1 Red Sox fan. He's in his mid-30s, and works in Materials Management for the Auckland District Health Board. He first heard about the Red Sox during 5th Form (more or less age 16), and attributes the interest to a history teacher who was knowledgable about a wide range of topics. Studying US history, the discussion went to American sport and the Yankees and Red Sox came up.

Mike played just one season of baseball in New Zealand, in a Sunday morning league during the summer of 1994 for the Howick-Pakuranga Braves. He admits it's difficult to judge the standard of play, but he hit over .400 and his club awarded him their hitter of the year prize. "I played all over the park from 2B, 3B, LF, and CF. I even had a couple of turns on the mound. I don't have any stats but remember one inning where I set them down in order with a swinging strikeout for the third out. That was probably the exception, however, as our team wasn't very good. Only one player had any real experience, and enthusiasm in the team died pretty quickly because we didn't win very often." Mike went back to track, cross-country, and soccer—but still follows baseball.

The first major league game he ever saw was in New York when the Mariners beat the Yankees, 10–3, on August 17, 1996. Then he took Amtrak to Boston and saw seven games in a row beginning August 19. It was a good stretch; the Sox won six out of seven. Mike rented a car and drove to Pawtucket for a game. He still has all his ticket stubs. He returned to Boston in 2000 and stayed at the Howard Johnson Fenway, and took in the game when Carlton Fisk's number was retired. A trip to Cooperstown and then Vermont was followed by a couple more Fenway games. "The most memorable thing I remember is watching a Red Sox fan (girl) laying into a guy Yankee fan and then getting hauled away by the cops. She was still punching at him as they were both led away. Bloody hilarious to watch."

He's able to get all the championship games and a good assortment of games throughout the season as well. "Even when I am at work I will have CBS Sportsline or ESPN Gamecast on for every Red Sox game. I don't have the radio here, but I follow every game."

Keith Willoughby / Wales

Keith is a computer programmer from Pontypridd, Wales. He picked up a library book and read about baseball, then listened to broadcast on a US Forces Radio station broadcasting out of Germany. Not familiar with the game, it was hard to follow so his interest waned until 1997, when Channel 5 in the UK started broadcasting a couple of games a week. The only city in America he'd ever visited was Boston, so it was natural to root for the Red Sox. He admits, though, "I hasten to add that I knew some of the history of the Sox, so I knew what I was getting into beforehand!" The internet helped him become "completely and utterly hooked" and has since made it his business to take in a couple of games at Fenway.

Peter Uelkes / Germany

German by birth, Peter Uelkes has a Ph.D. in physics and used to work in the field of high energy physics (elementary particle physics) but now works as an IT consultant in the financial

industry. He lives in Mönchengladbach, and follows the Sox via Internet, mail order videos, a subscription to *Diehard*, and lots of books. A few years ago, he was able to come to Boston and do the Fenway Park Tour, "a dream come true." He saw the Red Sox beat Chicago at Comiskey, 7–2.

His interest was initially sparked in the late 1980s, watching a weekly broadcast on one of the German TV sations. He first got interested in the Red Sox, watching Game Four of the 1990 ALCS, with its infamous Roger Clemens incident. "I don't know why," he writes, "but I became a Sox fan at that point. I started following the Sox on a day-to-day basis around 1993" which he is able to do through the Internet. He's never played baseball, not even softball.

Peter Uelkes.

Sean McGerty / Australia

Sean McGerty is a computer programmer who was first introduced to baseball as a youngster. "SoftPitch and TeeBall are played as organised sports at Australian schools and it was a Cana-

dian teacher who recommended I try playing for my local baseball club." Sean's father contacted the Australian Baseball League offices and they recommended Ted Williams' book *The Science of Hitting*. He won his team's batting title at the ripe old age of 12. He kept playing, both summer and winter seasons, and back in 2001 hit over .400, following in the footsteps of his mentor. He is also an accredited umpire in Australia.

He fondly remembers a visit to Fenway Park, aware at the time how he'd come from so far and yet for other fans it was just another day at the park. Because a 7:00 p.m. Boston game begins at 9 a.m. local time in Australia, this might present him a little scheduling problem—except that the nature of his job permits him to follow the action pitch-by-pitch. He added this thought

Sean McGerty in Sydney.

a few years ago about the situation where as a fan, in effect, every game was an away game: "While you might think I'm at a major disadvantage (and I am), consider this. I can get more new information about the Sox from these sources on a daily basis than I can about my local Rugby League Football team that I've followed the last 20 years or so. There just aren't the resources here."

Ismael Milach da Silveira / Brazil

Age 29, Izzy thought baseball was "boring as hell." He was a fan of the NBA and NFL, but not of baseball. The only feeling he recalls was "disgust with the Yankees and their fans here…a sport where you can buy your trophies? No, thank you."

Izzy lives in Pelotas, Rio Grande do Sul, in the southern part of Brazil, just a few miles from Uruguay and Argentina in an area he says is known for having the best BBQ in the world. He works at a network administrator for EMBRAPA, a federal government enterprise that translates as the Brazilian Agricultural Research Corporation.

He became a Red Sox fan in 1999 when his brother bought the PlayStation game MLB '99. He admits he didn't know much about the Rivalry at the time, but instinctively chose to play whatever team he thought had the best chance to beat the Yankees in their division. That would be the Red Sox. As he started to play, he was impressed with Pedro Martinez. "I didn't know the rules, tactics, or anything, but with Pedro pitching, I could do no wrong." He started following the season as it developed, and that was an exceptional year for Pedro, one of the best years any pitcher in the game has ever posted. "He became one of my idols. Pathetic as it sounds, MLB '99 is the reason why I'm a Red Sox fan and, God, I thank the game for that."

His brother is an Angels fan, but a casual one. Since 1999, Izzy himself had DirecTV but then moved to MLB.tv and watches or listens to almost every game. He's got a Pedro jersey, a Manny jersey, a Papi jersey, five or six caps, some T-shirts, coffee cups, and more. He's no casual fan.

Far-flung season ticket holders

There are some season ticket holders who live pretty far from Fenway, too.

Certainly there are transplants who live outside New England, but still maintain their ties with the home team. With Red Sox season tickets tough to get, they tend to stay within the family and fans are reluctant to give them up. There are a few who live a very long way from Yawkey Way.

Maui? Bob Straub has lived there since 1988. He's a recreational professional, a supervisor for the County of Maui Parks and Recreation Department, who also owns his own embroidery business. He writes, "I am originally from Pennsylvania and was always a Yankee Hater, so I naturally gravitated to the Red Sox as a kid. They were my American League team and the Phillies were my Nat'l. But upon moving to Spencer, Mass., I gave up my allegiance to the Phillies and concentrated on the Red Sox. That was 1972. I bought my seats as a season tix holder in 1976, and have had the same seats ever since." Bob officiates basketball and umpires softball, serving as the umpire coordinator for the Maui Interscholastic League umpire coordinator. His seats are in section 26, and he springs for the full Plan A—every game. Not surprisingly, he shares the tickets with a regular group, which is helpful since there have been years when he's not been able to make a single game.

Thailand—then there's Robert Kuwada, an international investment counselor with the Ministry of Finance in Thailand. A native of Newton, Massachusetts, he flew back from Bangkok to Boston in October 2004 so he could see the Sox in the World Series. At least that wasn't a fruitless trip!

Ojai, California—Jason Carney is a history teacher at the Thacher School in Ojai. In 2000, he researched the process, secured an early appointment the day season tickets went on sale, and scored a pair of Plan A tickets in the grandstand. The Boston native raised in Wellesley shares the tickets with three friends. He gets to five or six games a year and sells off the rest of his share. He says he got a copy of *Beyond the Sixth Game* for his 12th birthday and has gone through it "too many times to count." He follows the team online, reading the *Globe* sports section every day. Jason was ecstatic when the Red Sox prevailed against the Yankees in 2004. "I had two tickets for Games Six and Seven against St. Louis for my wife and me. Plane tix reserved. So the end was a little bittersweet—but I'm also still living off the high of them winning it all." Sox fans who have lived and died with the team over the years will recognize his postscript to the season: "Of course, given my Calvinist roots, to torture myself I use one of the tickets (Game Seven) as a bookmark."

Internationalism and the Red Sox

Tim Savage sent an e-mail in November 2001 reporting one of the increasing opportunities for following the Red Sox from afar. From his hotel room, he watched an NHK broadcast of a Hideo Nomo start—watching a U.S. baseball game, with Japanese commentary, while in a hotel room in China.

Tony Olsen, born and raised in Canada, worked for the Canadian government from 1985–87. He was able to follow the Red Sox, reporting that "Red Sox games in Bermuda, especially 1986, were easy to pick up on the radio from WTIC Hartford Connecticut. I could golf in the mornings—when I wasn't working—spend the afternoon at the beach, come home and listen to the Sox games on the radio on my porch overlooking Somerset when the tall ships visited. A little bit of heaven…"

Hitting a ball over the Great Wall of China

Speaking of China, Walt Dropo is almost certainly the first (and probably still the only) major leaguer to hit a ball over the Great Wall of China. His brother owned a fireworks company, for which Walt also worked. In an interview, Walt was asked how this came to be. He explained, "About six months before I visited China, Bob Hope went over there and he hit a golf ball with a 9-iron over the Great Wall. I said, I'm going over there with my brother on a buying trip, to buy fireworks, and we were going to do some sightseeing outside of Peking—going to visit the Great Wall—so I just took it on myself to bring a bat and a ball from the United States. I had my little niece throw me a pitch and I hit it over the Great Wall of China. Hope did it and so I figured I'd do it. The Wall wasn't that high." Was there anyone on the other side to catch the ball? "The Mongolians were over there."

Dropo played at Fenway seven years *before* his rookie season

Walt Dropo was Rookie of the Year in 1950, but he first played in Fenway Park way back in

1943—and his manager was Babe Ruth. The game was an exhibition game to raise money for the war effort. Dropo was 20 years old at the time. He played first base, but went 0-for-2 while teammate Ted Williams (also playing for Ruth) took left field, went 2-for-4 and homered, driving in four runs. Dom DiMaggio tripled and drove in two. Ruth's All-Stars beat the Boston Braves, 9–8.

In an interview, Dropo affirmed the finding. "I was on the same team as Ted WIlliams and Babe Ruth. That's a trivia! World War II came about. I was at the University of Connecticut and I was drafted in the ROTC, and I was at Fort Devens. They kept me there in Special Services and I played for the Fort Devens team. They sent down a couple of us to that All-Star game to represent Fort Devens. So I was representing Fort Devens at that time. I was on the team, and they selected a couple of us All-Stars and I was one of them. Ruth was there. Ted was there. Dominic DiMaggio was there."

Walt Dropo on the Great Wall. Courtesy of Joanne Alfieri.

Fan frustration

We'll close this story by touching on a little fan frustration. Most readers of this book are probably Red Sox fans and most of you probably have your own stories. It's amazing, though, how healing the days from October 17–27, 2004 can be.

Paying the ultimate price for Red Sox fandom was William Sickles, a 39-year-old letter carrier who literally lost his life defending the Red Sox. His sad demise came about following an argument in a Brooklyn, NY barroom with a rabid Brooklyn booster no doubt displeased that the Red Sox had beaten Brooklyn in the first game of the 1916 World Series earlier in the day (October 7).

May 4, 2008: Yanks fan Ivonne Hernandez, 43, was taunted with a "Yankees Suck" chant when patrons outside a Nashua bar saw her car's Yankees sticker. She accelerated and drove into the group, killing 29-year-old Matthew Beaudoin. Hernandez was charged with second-degree murder and aggravated DWI.

After the Red Sox lost the 1946 World Series, John McIntyre, 61, of Andover, Massachusetts died of a self-inflicted wound. The *Boston Herald* reported that he had "shot himself when he heard that the Cardinals defeated the Red Sox in the World Series." Relatives reached in 2001 explained that McIntyre had suffered from a number of mental problems.

Cut up pretty badly over a couple of key Red Sox losses was fan Chuck Harrison. He broke his left hand over Bucky and his right hand over Buckner. The story's a little less simplistic, of course, but not much. Chuck remembers, "Strictly speaking, I cut my left hand to the point of stitches when Yaz popped up to Nettles in '78; it's overstating it to say that I actually broke it. I *did* however break my right hand in '86 over the Mookie Wilson groundball, pounding my fist against the wall. When I showed up for classes the next day with my hand in a cast, no explanation was necessary for any of my friends." Even before 2004, though, Chuck had learned how better to deal with disappointment. "The years have served, if nothing else, to teach me a modicum of equanimity and the virtues of patience."

The healing that came from the World Series win in 2004 didn't come soon enough for Jose Rivera, though. After the Sox took Games Four and Five of the ALCS from the Yankees, the Massachusetts man was killed in an argument over the game. A source familiar with the investigation told a *Boston Herald* reporter, "They were arguing over the Red Sox game. The shooter was a Yankees fan."

Carlos Ortez of Quincy was wearing his Red Sox cap when he was assaulted by two men in a Yonkers NY hotel bar on October 3, 2007 and suffered multiple facial fractures that left him hospitalized days later. His co-worker Walter Ostromecki said that they'd been taunted for being Red Sox fans, and that Ortez was attacked later on by one of the men who'd been riding them. A few days later, police asserted that the argument wasn't about baseball, but (believing that or not) the Red Sox nevertheless offered Ortez a ticket to an upcoming 2008 ballgame.

SOX WHO SERVED—RED SOX IN THE ARMED SERVICES

For decades, baseball fans have debated what Ted Williams' statistics might have been had he not lost nearly five full seasons to military service in both World War II and the Korean War combined. Williams served with distinction in both wars, as a U.S. Navy flight instructor in the first conflict and as a Marine combat fighter-bomber jet pilot in Korea. Williams was not alone by any means, though; he was joined in Second World War service by a large number of other Bosox—and there were quite a few Boston players in the First World War as well.

These players helped the cause, their assignments determined by military authorities. Some spent time staging morale-boosting baseball exhibitions, but this was typically ancillary duty. Most were not involved in actual combat, though there were those who were—most notably the thrice-decorated World War II hero, Earl Johnson.

The first war in which Sox players saw action was World War I. With 16 years of play under their belts, the Red Sox had already won five World Championships when the United States went to war, declaring war on Germany in the final days of 1917 spring training, just five days before Opening Day. Earlier that spring, ball teams had begun to form their own military drill units and march around on the ball field.

The World Champion Red Sox opened in New York in 1917, and before the game both the Yankees and Red Sox marched in close order. "The military drill was a much appreciated feature," wrote the *Boston Post*, "and the half hour that the Highlanders spent in evolutions before the game set the crowd on fire with military fervor." Yankees owners Ruppert and Huston marched with their ballplayers. The Red Sox won that game 5–3, with Sox pitcher Babe Ruth yielding but two hits.

Gen. John Pershing and recruit George H. Ruth. Courtesy of Gary Bedingfield.

Among the Red Sox ballplayers who served in WWI were Hal Janvrin in the Army Signal Corps and Dick Hoblitzell in the Army Dental Corps, and Lore Bader, Jack Barry, Del Gainer, Dutch Leonard, Duffy Lewis, Mike McNally, Herb Pennock, Ernie Shore, Chick Shorten, and Fred Thomas—all of whom enlisted in the Navy (and most of whom played for the Charlestown Navy Yard ball team).

Ballplayers, like other American men, were under a "work or fight" order which motivated many—notably Shoeless Joe Jackson, who suffered some criticism in the press—to seek employment in an essential industry, such as a shipbuilding plant or a steel mill rather than be subject to being sent to the trenches overseas. Dutch Leonard quit the Sox in midseason 1918, signed up with the Fore River Shipyards in Quincy and played with the Fore River ball team. Babe Ruth had joined a reserve unit in Boston, the 104th field artillery, and posed for a publicity shot with General Pershing. The publicity may have been Ruth's major contribution to the war effort; he didn't miss any playing time and was never included in *Baseball* magazine's listings of the 140-plus major leaguers who served in the World War.

Jack Barry—later the baseball coach at Holy Cross for 50 years—was player-manager for the Sox in 1917, but in the Navy the next. Star outfielder Duffy Lewis was in the armed services, too, as were several other players. Barry's successor as manager was Ed Barrow; before Barrow began to sell Sox players to the Yankees post-war, it was the call to military duty which stripped the Sox of some of their stars. In fact, the *Boston Globe* reported, before the 1918 season began, that "no club in either major league has been so depleted by the war as have the Red Sox." Fully 20 Red Sox roster players were in military service, including Jimmy Cooney, Wally Mayer, Carl Mays, Stuffy McInnis, Bill Pertica, and Jimmy Walsh and a couple of men who perhaps as a result never saw playing time with Boston: Bentley and Wilder. Nonetheless, as is well-known to virtually every New Englander, the 1918 Red Sox won the World Championship.

The "war to end all wars" did not accomplish its objective, and within 23 years, the U.S. was back at war. Although organized baseball was given the "green light," even in the wake of

Pearl Harbor, the Second World War saw most of the 1942 Sox team enter one branch of the service or another. Virtually the entire 1942 starting lineup was gone within a year, save first baseman Tony Lupien—and he did a Naval stint later in the war.

Emerson Dickman served in the Merchant Marine. Joining Ted Williams in Navy class-room and flight instruction was Johnny Pesky. Other members of the Navy were Mace Brown, Bill Butland, Tom Carey, Bill Conroy, Dom DiMaggio, Freddie Pytlak, and Char-lie Wagner. Wagner was closest to military action, but contracted dysentery while in The Philippines—and the disease may have sapped his strength such that he never recovered his pre-war form. He has continued to serve the Sox ever since, as a long-time scout. Williams naturally received the most publicity, and indeed served with distinction. He was ranked such a good pilot that he was asked to serve as a flight instructor, and he performed that duty until hostilities were ended.

Roy Partee in Leyte. Courtesy of Sue Partee.

Earl Johnson was the real military hero of the WWII group. Johnson served in the Army, as did Paul Campbell, Tommy Carey, Joe Dobson, Bobby Doerr, Danny Doyle, Dave Ferriss, Al Flair, Andy Gilbert, Mickey Harris, Tex Hughson, Roy Partee, Jim Tabor, and Hal Wagner. Partee took part in the invasion of The Philip-pines and served two years guarding prisoners of war on Leyte. Earl Johnson was 10–7 with the Sox in 1940 and 1941, but enlisted in the Army right after Pearl Harbor. He served with the 120th infantry and landed in Europe 21 days after D-Day, several times coming across groups of dead bodies—from both sides—still un-buried. Unfortunately, he witnessed the results of the Malmedy Massacre in Belgium, where 150 American prisoners were killed by Nazis. Johnson took part (as did later Sox manager Ralph Houk) in the famous Battle of the Bulge. For heroism in combat, Johnson was awarded the Bronze Star, a Bronze Star with clusters, and the Silver Star, and received battlefield commissions promoting him to lieutenant.

Johnson's citation for the Bronze Star reads: "On September 30, 1944, in Germany, during heavy concentration of hostile fire, a friendly truck was struck by an enemy shell and had to be abandoned. The fact that the vehicle contained vital radio equipment made it imperative that it be recovered before falling into enemy hands. Sergeant Earl Johnson and several other members of his unit were assigned to this hazardous mission. They courageously braved a severe hostile fire and were completely successful in dragging the vehicle over an area in plain view of the enemy." The Bronze Star with clusters was awarded after he helped urge a tank crew to drive through a minefield on its way to wiping out a German position which had pinned down his men.

"Lefty" Johnson's Silver Star required another soldier to pitch in relief of the Red Sox southpaw. The two were fighting hedgerow by hedgerow in France when they noticed a Ger-man tank laying in ambush—with its hatch open. Johnson threw two hand grenades at the tank—but missed with both. The other soldier—who'd supposedly never thrown a baseball in his life—tossed one and scored a direct hit. "Gee," Johnson remarked later, "If I only had that kid's control, what a pitcher I would be." The blast killed all five German tankers. Johnson's platoon started the Battle of the Bulge with 36 men, but ended with only 11.

There were others who served, thought not in military uniform. Lou Finney, for instance, missed the entire 1943 season not because he was in the U.S. Army, but because he was farm-ing—supplying essential foods for defense. He played some in the second half of 1944, but was then again asked to work the farm in 1945.

Of course, some ballplayers who had served in the war first joined the Red Sox afterwards. Hal "Skinny" Brown pitched for Boston for parts of three seasons beginning in 1953. Brown served 32 months in the Army Air Corps as a gunner and told interviewer Bill Hass that he flew 18 missions providing infantry support starting just six days after D-Day: "I was shot down in the (English) Channel once, but got out. Most of our raids were over the submarine pens around La Havre. We were in medium bombers and would go across the Channel and didn't have any fighter escort. We got hit and didn't make it back to England. We had to bail out. They picked us up after a few hours in the Channel."

There was an even shorter gap between WWII and the Korean War, but that conflict never spread beyond the Korean peninsula. It still reached out its tentacles to ensnare a few Red Sox, though—most notably Ted Williams. Ted's former C.O. in Korea, Art Moran, told the authors of *Ted Williams: The Pursuit of Perfection* that it was almost certainly a clerical error which resulted in the Marines recalling a Theodore Williams (not realizing they were calling back to duty a 33-year old former pilot who'd already served three years during WWII. Ted let it be known that he was not pleased, but once in the Marines he threw himself into the tasks at hand, learning to fly jet aircraft and eventually flying 39 combat missions over North Korea. Williams was considered a good pilot and flew eight of his missions as John Glenn's wingman, the two of them going on fighter-bomber runs to take out enemy factories and attack enemy troop concentrations. Williams was hit twice by ground fire, one time crash-landing his F9F Pantherjet only to see it burst into flames moments after he had fled the jet he'd brought down safely.

Tom Brewer, Dick Brodowski, Leo Kiely, Frank Malzone, Chet Nichols, Karl Olson, Haywood Sullivan, George Susce, and Faye Throneberry all served in the military during the Korean conflict, mostly stateside. Another Sox player recalled to duty in Korea was Jake Jones, who'd joined the Bosox in mid-1947 but was out of major league ball after the 1948 season. Jones was a certified ace, having downed seven Japanese Zeroes during WWII.

Very few baseball players from any team served in Vietnam; Boston's Jim Lonborg, though, served in the Reserves and often had to work his service duties into his pitching schedule as he helped lead the Sox to success in the Impossible Dream year, 1967. Tony Conigliaro did Reserve duty as well, and Bill Landis suffered the sad fate of having to report for six months in the Reserves just four days before the 1967 season ended. He thus missed a shot at pitching in the World Series.

As the U. S. military has become a more professional force and less reliant on conscription, and as the threats facing the United States have generally required fewer combat troops, the likelihood of future Red Sox players (or other American civilians) seeing wartime military service has been—fortunately—greatly reduced.

Japanese soldier asks about Ted Williams

Ted Williams' spectacular 1941 season received attention in another baseball-loving nation: Japan. The season ended two months before Pearl Harbor and the news of Ted's .406 season circulated in Japan. Ted's name cropped up in at least one unexpected quarter in mid-summer 1942.

Ray Makepeace graduated from high school in Minneapolis and had seen Ted play there during the 1938 season, while Ted was with the Red Sox farm team Minneapolis Millers. "We used to go down to Nicollet Park and we'd send one man up a telephone pole behind home plate, and in batting practice he would call the balls that were foul, telling us where they were going. There were four or five of us, and if you got a used ball, you'd get in for nothing." Makepeace played a little ball himself, some Class D ball in the Cardinals system. Well before war broke out, though, he'd signed up with the Army and sought a posting to The Philippines. There he was with an artillery contingent on Corregidor when the island surrendered to Japan in May 1942.

Makepeace found himself in a labor batallion working in the port area of Manila, loading and unloading Japanese ships. At one point in June or July 1942, he was doing temporary duty in a Japanese kitchen and just outside the galley a group of Japanese soldiers was playing some ball. One of the balls rolled over by him, so he picked it up—and threw them back a curve ball. A soldier approached and asked, "You're a pitcher? You play baseball?" He replied yes, he did. Ted's 1941 season must have been fresh in the Japanese recruit's mind, since his next question was to ask if Makepeace knew Ted Williams. Yes, he did, he answered. "Then he asked me if I knew Babe Ruth and I said 'sure' and he said 'F—— Babe Ruth!' I showed him how to throw a curveball." Makepeace was given a pack of cigarettes and had to get back to his duties.

"Red Sox" P.O.W.s in German prison camps

The "Boston Red Sox" also played baseball in at least four German P.O.W. camps—Stalag IIIB, Stalag 383, Marlag und Milag, and Oflag 64. Prisoners of war, using equipment donated by the Red Cross, were permitted to play a variety of sporting events and baseball was among them. Astonishingly, at Oflag 64 (an officers' camp), the POWs even published their own in-camp newspaper, the *Oflag Item*. There one can find news stories and baseball standings of the teams the inmates formed, typically named after major league teams back home. Charles Eberle, one of the POWs, recalls, "We had Yankees. Boston Red Sox. Wherever different guys were from. Softball, mostly, is what we had. I was on the Red Sox, yeah. Catcher. I remember the guys. John Creech. Len Warren. The guys that you got along with, you were on that team together. Early, when we had food and we had energy, we were engaged in softball and touch football and other sports. After a while, we weren't getting food and of course that was dropped."

LIFE AFTER THE RED SOX (HOW EX-PLAYERS KEPT BUSY)

Yes, there is life after the Red Sox—maybe not for the diehard fan but the players—at least in earlier times—typically took up some other work. Many of them worked during the winters as well—Buck Freeman, for instance, worked as a "stoker in the boiler room of a local silk mill" according to biographer Eric Enders, in part to keep in shape. In most cases, the occupations listed below are post-career professions but in some (Waite Hoyt, for instance) they reflect positions that the players held during their playing career. In Freeman's case, Enders also informs us that as a 12-year-old he worked as a slate picker, then was promoted to mule driver in the coal mines near Wilkes-Barre.

In earlier times, and for some players just starting out today, an off-season job can be essential. Sometimes that can lead to post-season work and sometimes it can lead to a post-career profession. In Ellis Kinder's case, the need for a job delayed his becoming a ballplayer for several years. His father died when he was 20, leaving a widow and six children on a farm in Arkansas. Ellis became the sole support of the family working on road construction when the crops were in. At age 23, he lost his mother as well. Offered a position as a pitcher, he had to turn it down; it just didn't pay enough. He told the owner, "Sure I'd like to pitch…but I can't afford to." He played a couple of semipro games a week to make a little extra. Almost two years later, he finally did take a job with the ballclub in Jackson, Tennessee and did well for a couple of years. Then he got a job as a pipe-fitter with the Illinois Central Railroad. Years later,

he told Roger Birtwell of the *Boston Globe*, "Plenty of overtime. I was making good dough."
He sat out another year. He turned 31 the year his major league career finally got underway,
hence the nickname "Old Folks."

Let's look at some of the careers players pursued after they'd finished their time in the
majors.

Jerry Adair—coached for the A's, then served as a security guard for the Lloyd Rader Center in Sand
    Springs, OK, a secure residential treatment facility for juveniles age 13–19 incarcerated for violent
    crimes
Sam Agnew—operated a garage at Boyes Springs, CA
Dale Alexander—tobacco farmer in Greene County, TN
Nick Altrock—coach and clown for 45 years with Washington Senators, and restaurateur in
    New York City
Larry Andersen—works as a broadcaster for the Philadelphia Phillies
Kim Andrew—FedEx truck driver
Ivy Paul Andrews—coached and officiated at numerous high school and coal company team events in
    the Birmingham AL area
Mike Andrews—Executive Director of the Jimmy Fund
Frank Arellanes—"entered business life in this city" (San Jose)
Steve Barr—plumber
James Barrett—senior partner Barrett and Walsh real estate firm
Jack Barry—coach, Holy Cross
Dennis Bennett—owns a cocktail lounge
Moe Berg—spy
Louis "Boze" Berger—colonel, United States Air Force (his Air Force nickname was "Bosey")
Max Bishop—coached at the United States Naval Academy for 24 years
Clarence Blethen—worked at a variety of county jobs including: disposal plant employee, laborer,
    foreman, fireman at Camp Detrick, maintenance man, orderly in Montevue County Home
Harvey "Red" Bluhm—Bluhm was employed by Fisher Body in their Cut & Sew Assembly Schedule,
    and was foreman in that department at the time of his death.
Ed Bressoud—college dean
Jesse Burkett—worked for Massachusetts Highway Dept.
John Burkett—pro bowler
Joe Bush—worked for rubber company
Frank Bushey—grocery store operator in St. Marys, Kansas
Earl Caldwell—manager of Mission (Texas) Citrus Growers, Inc, a co-operative farm association
Ray Caldwell—bartender and railroad worker
Bill Carrigan—president of Peoples Savings Bank, Lewiston, Maine
Tom Carey—After Navy service in the war, he was a city playground leader for several years in
    Rochester, NY for the City Recreation Bureau at Edgerton Park.
Jerry Casale—owned a restaurant business in New York City for many years
Ben Chapman—insurance agent with State Mutual Life Insurance Company
Charlie Chech—life insurance writer (salesman) with Pennsylvania Mutual Life, in Los Angeles
Jack Chesbro—ran a chicken farm
Eddie Cicotte—raised strawberries
Danny Clark—salesman, American Oil Company
Lu Clinton—During his off seasons with baseball he worked for Parkinson Motors and Jack Bowker
    Ford and Cookson Stone Co. After his baseball career he moved to Wichita, Kan., where he was
    owner and operator of a heating oil company, Clinton Productions Corp.
Bill Clowers—oil field worker for Abercrombie, a petroleum company, which was later purchased by
    Amoco
George Cochran—retail clerk at the Jim Dandy Market, Hawthorne, California

Jimmy Collins—worked for Buffalo Parks Department

Ray Collins—farmed in Colchester, VT using a horse-drawn plow, ran a boarding house/B&B, and gathered maple syrup

Gene Conley—owner of Foxboro Paper Company

Jimmy Cooney—worked at Cranston Print Works, a textile concern in Cranston, RI

Doc Cramer—ran a meat market in Manahawkin, NJ

Bob Cremins—cartoonist for the *Philadelphia Bulletin* and a boxing canvas designer

Lou Criger—farmed for a while but moved to Arizona because of his tuberculosis; family ran a bakery in Tucson

Gene Desautels—high school counselor in Flint, Michigan

Al DeVormer—a busy guy, he worked variously as (in this order): city milk inspector, farm inspector, clerk at B. A. Hoxie & Sons pharmacy, guard/watchman at American Seating Co.

Emerson Dickman—manufacturer's rep for furniture company

Bill Dinneen—umpired in the American League for 28 years. He held an interest in a brewery in Syracuse after retiring from umpiring.

Sam Dodge—worked at Earl Fletcher & Company, a scrap metal company in Tupper Lake, currently Fletcher & Son Recycling and Energy

Bobby Doerr—ran a mink farm in Oregon, and worked several years as a major league baseball coach

Harry Dorish—coached and scouted for a number of teams

Patsy Dougherty—assistant bank cashier

Walt Dropo—in the fireworks business and investment work

Jean Dubuc—printers ink salesman

Joe Dugan—worked for Recreation Department of the Boston Park Department

Howard Ehmke—ran a tarp and awning company, making canvas covers for sports fields and other applications

Bill Evans—owned and operated two service stations, and later owned a limousine he drove for Yellow Cab

Homer Ezzell—scale inspector for the Missouri Pacific Railroad

Carmen Fanzone—trumpet player and head of American Federation of Musicians' local in L.A.

Hobe Ferris—mechanic

Lou Finney—farmer

Buck Freeman—umpired, managed, scouted

Curtis Fullerton—worked at Charlestown Navy Yard, Charlestown, Massachusetts

Denny Galehouse—major league scout, and worked for both Ravenna Arsenal and Goodyear Aircraft

Bob Gallagher—high school teacher of history, government, and economics

Bob Garbark—baseball coach at Allegheny College, Meadville PA from 1947 to 1978. Garbark, who retired as Professor Emeritus of Physical Education, also ran a summer youth baseball program for the Meadville Recreation Department for over 20 years.

Larry Gardner—served for more than 20 years as head baseball coach at the University of Vermont

Milt Gaston—sergeant, Tampa FL sheriff's department

Gary Geiger—scout for the St. Louis Cardinals

Norwood Gibson—chair, General and Analytic Chemistry, Wabash College

Don Gile—pharmaceutical salesman and district manager; VP of major national home health care firm

Joe Ginsberg—represented the Jack Daniels Distillery

Harry Gleason—deputy sheriff and process server for Camden County, NJ

Chuck Goggin—special investigator for the FBI in background investigations

Billy Goodman—farming and real estate

Jeff Gray—insurance agent

Mike Greenwell—owns an amusement park

Moose Grimshaw—worked (and died) in a packing plant at Canajoharie NY

Vean Gregg—ran "The Home Plate"—a Hoquiam, Washington shop that sold sporting goods, cigars, and had a lunch counter

Turkey Gross—was "in the drug business" according to his Hall of Fame player questionnaire

Sea Lion Hall—policeman, and later a sheriff and jailer

Harry Harper—started a junk business that grew into a large trucking firm. Set up a contracting company, owned a large supermarket, a food company, and became New Jersey State Labor Commissioner

Ken Harrelson—baseball announcer

Joe Harris—worked over 30 years for the Melrose (MA) Fire Department

Clem Hausemann—worked in the process department at the Enjay Chemical Co.

Richie Hebner—gravedigger

Charley Hemphill—automobile iron master

Joe Heving—pipefitter, Southern Railway

Johnny Heving—"basket room supervisor YMCA Salisbury NC" per his HOF questionnaire

Piano Legs Hickman—scouting 14 years for Cleveland, then coach with U. West Va., served also as Mayor of Morgantown, WV and Sheriff of Monongahela County

Dick Hoblitzell—dentist; baseball coach at West Point; real estate; farmed and raised cattle; wrote newspaper columns; county treasurer and sheriff

Johnny Hodapp—undertaker in Cincinnati

Harry Hooper—postmaster at Capitola, California

Paul Howard—fireman with the Boston Fire Department, 1910–1943

Waite Hoyt—mortician

Ed Hughes—policeman for the Chicago Police Department for 20 years

Tom Hughes—worked in a Chicago tavern and as a groundskeeper in the Chicago parks system

Bill Humphrey—scouting supervisor for the St. Louis Cardinals

Charles Jamerson—high school coach, then head coach at Memphis State and two other colleges. Later in life, he was personnel director for the Burlington Mills plant in Davie County, NC.

Jackie Jensen—in Christmas tree business

Bob Johnson—firefighter in Glendale, CA for a period of time; he also worked as an off-season carpenter at Paramount Studios for a couple of years.

Rankin Johnson—worked for auto dealers as parts manager, salesman, and GM, and in real estate. From 1965–68 he was president of baseball's Eastern League.

Dalton Jones—banker

Jake Jones—farmer; ran flying service doing cropdusting

Rudy Kallio—owned a bar near Aloha, Oregon named the Green Meadows Tavern

George Kell—baseball commentator

Ellis Kinder—worked as a carpenter, roofer, and other construction jobs in the housing field

John LaRose—card dealer at Foxwoods Resort Casino

Dutch Leonard—California vintner

Duffy Lewis—traveling secretary for the Boston Braves for 26 years

Ted Lewis—president of the University of New Hampshire

John Lickert—truck driver

Greg Litton—jeweler and professional speaker

Jim Lonborg—dentist

Harry Lord—Maine state legislator

Tony Lupien—stockbroker, author, and Dartmouth baseball coach

Keith MacWhorter—works in 401(K) and insurance sales

Babe Martin—real estate broker

Wally Mayer—cigar store clerk

Carl Mays—scouted for 20 years and ran the Carl Mays Baseball Camp in Oregon

Dick McCabe—vice-president of the William Simon Brewery in Buffalo, New York

Windy McCall—real estate sales

Tim McCarver—sports announcer

Marty McHale—investment broker

Stuffy McInnis—manager of Phillies, and baseball coach at Norwich, Cornell, and Harvard

Jud McLaughlin—factory worker and clerk for Gillette Safety Razor Company

Andy Merchant—health caretaker

Herb Moford—tobacco inspector

Vince Molyneaux—traveling auditor for the Reconstruction Finance Corporation

Joe Morgan—snowplow driver and baseball manager

Jerry Moses—sports concessions business/Boston Culinary Group

Buddy Myer—banker in New Orleans

Elmer Myers—drove a truck and sold meat products for a New Jersey packing house. Later operated a concession stand on the Atlantic City boardwalk, then ran a tavern on the Black Horse Pike in Collingswood, NJ.

Heber "Dick" Newsome—farmed in the area between Ahoskie and Murfreesboro, NC

Leo Nonnenkamp—worked for the Postal Service

Len Okrie—worked for Fayetteville, NC sheriff's department and for Wal-Mart

Steve O'Neill—scouted and worked for Cleveland Recreation Department

Mickey Owen—Greene (Springfield) County, TN sheriff

Frank Owens—salesman for Minneapolis paper companies. Also worked later in life as a guard.

Al Papai—for 20 years, worked as a letter carrier for the U.S. Postal Service

Fred Parent—managed or coached at Colby College, Harvard, and a number of New England baseball teams, and also ran a gasoline filling station and operated a boarding house

Case Patten—truckman and general hauler

Johnny Peacock—mule trader; owner of lumber and grain companies; vice-chairman Wayne Community College Board of Trustees

Bill Pertica—bartender

Rico Petrocelli—head of Petrocelli Sports, a marketing company

Urban Pickering—police chief, Modesto, CA

Jennings Poindexter—roustabout in Oklahoma oil fields for Pure Oil and Phillips 66.

Nels Potter—proof-press operator. Later, built his own bowling alley, served as Township Supervisor, and sold insurance.

Three Sox with nouns for last names: Peacock, Grove, and Foxx.

Del Pratt—manager, operated bowling alley, coached high school football, ran gas station, managed sporting goods department of a discount store

Lester "Larry" Pratt—city treasurer of Peoria, IL from 1941 to 1945. Investigator for the state's attorney's office from 1924–32 and from 1956–60.

Chuck Rainey—general contractor in San Diego

John Reder—chief engineer at J. J. Corrugated Box Company, Fall River, MA

Bobby Reeves—supervisor of the heating and air-conditioning department, Chattanooga Electric Power Board

Dick Reichle—salesman

Jerry Remy—baseball commentator

Walt Ripley—worked for jewelry company L. G. Balfour

Buddy Rosar—engineer in the powerhouse at the Ford stamping plant, Woodlawn, NY

Muddy Ruel—attorney; later: assistant to the Commissioner of baseball

Bret Saberhagen—head baseball coach at Calabasas High School near Los Angeles

Charley Schanz—drove a delivery truck and worked in warehouse for beer distributor Saccani Distributing, then for Phillips 66 as warehouse manager

Bill Schlesinger—ran his father's hardware store

George Schmees—worked at Bernard Food Industries in San Jose for 32 years, ending up as food processor foreman

Bob Seeds—owner of Amarillo Gold Sox

Dave Shean—ran a poultry business

Al Simmons—coach

Craig Skok—electronics sales rep

Frank "Piano Mover" Smith—in the moving business in Pittsburgh (believe it or not)

Peter Smith—guidance counselor

Reggie Smith—runs Reggie Smith Baseball, a successful baseball clinic near Los Angeles

Bill Schlesinger at the hardware store. Rich Gibson photo.

Mike Smithson—high school athletic director

Wally Snell—chairman of the Botany Department at Brown University

Moose Solters—operated a tavern in Pittsburgh

Tris Speaker—ran Tris Speaker, Inc., a wholesale wine and liquor company, and worked as a sales rep for a steel company

Jake Stahl—president of Washington Park National Bank, Chicago

Jack Stansbury—worked for Magnolia Refinery Company in Beaumont, TX

Dave Stapleton—homebuilder

Elmer Steele—letter carrier Poughkeepsie

Al Stokes—contractor

Amos Strunk—insurance broker

George Stumpf—worked in shipyards and was a bartender at the Southern Yacht Club, New Orleans

Jake Stahl, Chicago banker.

Frank Sullivan—golf pro in Hawaii

Len Swormstedt—worked as a machinist at Atwood & Morrill, Salem, Massachusetts

Jesse Tannehill—worked in Cincinnati machine shop

Luis Tiant—hosts the El Tiante snack bar at Fenway Park and is involved in El Tiante Cigars

Frank Truesdale—mechanic's assistant

Bob Unglaub—machinist for the Pennsylvania Railroad

Bobby Veach—proprietor and owner of the Bobby Veach Coal Company of Detroit

Clyde Vollmer—owner of the Lark Lounge in the Cincinnati area

Jacob Volz—from 1914–1948, worked at Jenner Manufacturing Company, a candy company, variously listed as an employee, a fireman, a boilerman, and an engineer. In the 1951 city directory he was listed as a machinist and in the 1952–53 directory as a mechanic.

Tillie Walker—piano and organ sales; Tennessee highway patrolman

Monte Weaver—a university geometry teacher before becoming a ballplayer, Weaver owned an awning business after baseball, then bought some orange groves.

Earl Webb—mine foreman for Consolidated Coal Company of Jenkins, KY. Webb also managed the company baseball team.

Bill Werber—worked at Werber Insurance Agency

Sammy White—worked gardening in Kauai, Hawaii and helped develop Princeville Golf Course there, becoming the head professional

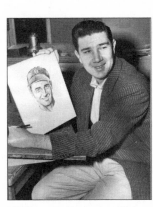

Bill Wight, with his drawing of Ted Williams.

George Whiteman—constable, Houston Police Department

Bill Wight—commercial artist

Ted Williams—had his own fishing line company, and later endorsed sporting goods products for Sears

Jim Willoughby—homebuilder

Jack Wilson—floorwalker at a department store

Clarence Winters—worked in the tool crib for the Ford Motor Company

Joe Wood—coached at Yale for 20 years, then ran a golfing range in California for many years

Pinky Woods—police chief

Rudy York—After he retired from baseball, he served as a firefighter on the Bartow County forest fire unit out of Cartersville, Georgia.

Cy Young—farmed potatoes and raised chickens, hogs, and sheep

Thanks to Jon Daly, Bill Lee of www.baseballundertaker.com, Ray McIntyre, Rod Nelson, Angela Parker, Paul Penta, and public librarians across the country.

Note: needless to say, in many cases, a player will have held more than one position since completing his major league career. This is not an attempt at an exhaustive list, but merely represents a listing kept for interest's sake while assembling other material for this book. Information from many sources, including notes from fellow baseball enthusiasts, is included here, and only occasional attempts have been made to independently verify the information.

Red Sox player sold for one dollar

One bizarre case involving other occupations involved Jack Hoey, who played outfield for Boston from 1906–08. After the 1908 season, Hoey tried to continue as a ballplayer in Connecticut and became the center of a controversy when he was sold by the president of the Waterbury club for one dollar to the New Britain ballclub as part of what appeared to be a side deal in exchange for a vote at a Connecticut League meeting. When the Waterbury club was then sold, the new owners were told that Hoey was not included, even though he'd been on the list of players under contract. Though too complex a story to get into here, the *Hartford Courant* railed in the spring of 1911 that "the player himself…had about as much to say as a slave on the auction block in the south" before the Civil War. As it turned out, Hoey was not in the best of shape. He'd taken an off-season job as a clerk at the Connecticut Hotel in Waterbury, but didn't like the work so he took a position at a lunch room where he apparently impressed patrons by juggling fishcakes. The *Courant* complained that the buyer and seller in the dollar deal both acted as though they personally owned Hoey. The ballplayer refused to report to New Britain and was suspended by the league. Come 1912, he was made player-manager of the New Britain team. Later in life, Hoey worked as a machinist in a Massachusetts watch factory, and then for Connecticut Light & Power and for the U.S. Rubber Co. in Naugatuck, CT.

DENTISTRY AND THE RED SOX

While browsing through Red Sox history, it seemed remarkable that a fair number of Red Sox players also practiced dentistry. So, as it happens, did Dr. Charles Steinberg, recent executive Vice President for Public Affairs who earned his doctorate in dentistry from the University of Maryland, albeit quite a few years after he began working in baseball for the Balitmore Orioles at age 17. Dr. Steinberg continued to work for the Orioles front office while at the same time pulling a little double duty as team dentist. He is a founding member of the National Academy for Sports Dentistry.

Sox players known to have worked in dentistry include the following:

Jack Hayden

On September 25, 1906, Boston's Hobe Ferris was suspended by the American League for the rest of the 1906 season because of a fight with teammate left fielder Jack Hayden. "It was the most cowardly attack I have ever witnessed upon the ball field," said umpire Silk O'Loughlin. "I understand that even Ferris' wife upbraided him for kicking Hayden in the face." Hayden lost several teeth when Ferris, swinging his spikes from the top of the dugout, kicked him in the mouth. Interestingly, Hayden was a dental student at the University of Pennsylvania.

Jim Lonborg

Most recently, we have Dr. James Lonborg, the American League Cy Young winner in 1967 and one of the key figures in the "Impossible Dream" team from that magic year. Jim had taken a pre-med course of studies at Stanford University, graduating with a B.A. in biology before sinking his teeth into a major league baseball career which began with his Red Sox debut on April 23, 1965. After 15 years in the majors, "Gentleman Jim" retired from baseball in 1979, and he began the study of dentistry.

"During the course of my years playing baseball, I always kept in touch with the medical profession," he explains. During the winters, when he wasn't playing winter ball, he often worked with the New England Rehab Hospital, doing adminstrative work in nursing and other areas of hospital work. Red Sox co-owner Buddy LeRoux was a principal at the hospital.

"After I was released in June 1979 by the Phillies, I came home and got settled in for a while," Lonborg explains. My wife and I took a vacation to Stratton Mountain in Vermont and we discussed various career possibilities on the road up. We had quite a number of friends who were dentists and she suggested that I always looked good in a uniform and it would be a way to continue in the health care field, which had always interested me. I talked to a couple of dentists, one who was the team dentist for the New England Patriots and received a lot of encouragement." He interviewed the following week at the Tufts University School of Dental Medicine.

Jim was 37, and he and his wife Rosemary had six children at the time. Tufts had a three-year program. Dentistry offered a shorter professional training period (given that no internship is required) than did going the M.D. route. Baseball salaries were not large ones in that era, and this second career offered Jim the opportunity to gain control over his life within a very few years while working in health care. Jim graduated from Tufts in 1983. (As it happens, he worked on this author's teeth once, while a dental student at Tufts. That was the author's second interaction with him; after the final regular season game in 1967, a young Mr. Nowlin was one of the very first fans to rush onto the field, reaching Jim before he had left the mound and clapping him on the back in celebration of the pennant victory.)

Jim started in practice in Boston with a fellow practitioner, Dr. Stein, but soon opened his own practice in Hanover, Massachusetts, on Boston's South Shore. The Hanover practice developed nicely and after a period of time working from both offices, he concentrated on the thriving South Shore practice. His wife Rosie has for many years been very active at the Jimmy Fund, and since the late 1980s has been one of the most dedicated and beloved volunteers at the Dana-Farber Cancer Institute.

Fred Anderson

The earliest known connection between dentistry and the Red Sox is Fred Anderson, a pitcher. You'll find him in the record books, as playing for the Red Sox in 1909 and then again in 1913. It is said that he passed up an opportunity to join the Red Sox until he finished his dentistry training. A few years later, he joined the team.

John Frederick Anderson was born in Calahan, NC—six miles from Mocksville. He debuted on September 25, 1909—and the Sox swept two from the St. Louis Browns. Edith Anderson, a relative through marriage, reports that when Fred got too old to play ball, he turned to the practice of dentistry for which he had trained. He had a practice in Winston-Salem and Edith still has his dental chair.

A grand-nephew of Fred Anderson, W. Taylor Slye, reports, "He was my grandmother's brother. I'm 60. I knew him. We'd visit him. I was born in Davie County, North Carolina, but grew up in Washington, D.C. In fact, my daddy grew up right across from the old Griffith Stadium and used to work at the soda shop right on the corner of 7th and Georgia Avenue. He told me about Lou Gehrig and Babe Ruth and all these guys who would come over after the ballgame."

Fred Anderson received his degree in dentistry from the University of Maryland, meanwhile setting the strikeout record at the university. He used his mouth in pitching as well. Anderson was a spitball pitcher, a practice legal at the time.

He began his major league career with the Red Sox in 1909 with just one game—a start right near the end of the season. He yielded just three hits and one run in eight innings, with five strikeouts and one walk. He didn't make the team in 1910, and played in the farm leagues for the next three years. Finally, in 1913, he had another shot with the Red Sox and threw 57⅓ innings, but fared not nearly as well (0–6, 5.97 ERA). He played 1914 and 1915 with Buffalo and 1916–1918 with the Giants. In his later years, he sometimes played ball in his area with fellow North Carolinian Ernie Shore.

Anderson quit baseball, the story goes, over a contract dispute with John McGraw and that is when he truly turned to dentistry as a career. He was in his 30s, then, and had played a couple of seasons for Buffalo in the short-lived Federal League, then three years with the New York Giants. His career record was 53–57 with a 2.86 ERA (he led the National League in 1917 with a 1.44 ERA and helped propel the Giants to the 1917 World Series. Anderson was tagged with a Game Two loss after giving up four runs in three innings of relief. Taylor Slye questions the story about the dispute with McGraw: "I personally think that he just said 'It's time for me to get on my career.'"

"He never worked on my teeth," his grand-nephew adds. "We have several dentists in the family. Three of them on my grandfather's side; Fred was the only one from my grandmother's side. Dr. Robert Anderson, from another side of the family, was short of stature, and several people in town tell me, 'Oh, he pulled my teeth, yeah. He was a small man and he'd just get up on my chest….' My grandmother and Fred grew up maybe about 100 yards from my grandfather's house. They lived just up the road there. Fred's practice as far as I can determine began in Statesville, North Carolina, later moved to Charlotte and finally to Winston-Salem before retiring to Davie County where he died in 1957."

Dick Hoblitzell

First baseman Dick Hoblitzell served as a dentist in the military during World War 1. Known as "Doc" Hoblitzell during his playing years, he was born in Waverly, WV and died in Parkersburg WV in 1962.

He played 11 years in the majors, first for Cincinnati and then came over to the Red Sox mid-season in 1914. In 1915, 1916, and 1918, Hoblitzell was on the World Championship Red Sox teams. All three of the last times the Sox won the World Series in the 20th century, Doc Hoblitzell was there. He didn't take part in the 1918 Series, having departed mid-season for military service, but knocked out nine hits in the 1915 and 1916 Fall Classics. Over 11 seasons in major league ball, he compiled a strong .278 average with 1,310 hits in 4,706 at bats.

His daughter Connie Michael still lives in the family home half the year, splitting her time between West Virginia and Florida. She talks about her father: "He got his degree in Cincinnati, at the Cincinnati School of Dentistry. I think it was part of the University of Cincinnati. What he did was go to school in the winter and play baseball during the summer. He opened an office with his older brother William in Cincinnati and they shared the space. That's where he set up his practice. His brother remained a dentist until his retirement and death years later. My dad went more and more into baseball, but he always had the idea that he would more or less retire into dentistry.

"Then he went to Boston and his career went on from there. He was there for 1915 and '16, the World Series, but then the war came along and he became Capt. Hoblitzell of the U.S. Dental Reserve Corps. In 1918, he played in 25 games and then he left Boston for military service partway through the year. He ended up in the Army as a first lieutenant, stationed in Texas for a while, but ultimately at West Point. He was in the Dental Corps, and he did practice dentistry during the war. While stationed at West Point, he also coached for the baseball team. McArthur was the superintendent of the school then. He was very impressed with him. The Army made use of his baseball and his dentistry."

Did he work on players in Cincinnati and/or Boston? One of his relatives believes he served as team dentist for the Reds but his daughter says, "I don't think he practiced in Boston at all. When he went back to West Virginia, it was more for the neighbors and that sort of thing, but he didn't really go back into full practice after he left."

Was it true that the former first baseman occasionally subjected his children to free dental care? Connie responds, "Oh, my, yes. He worked on me. In the little office I have in the house, in the old home, where I was raised, he set up his office with a big old desk. I still have the dental chair he brought from Cincinnati and most of the tools. I had quite a mouthful of fillings that he put in. They didn't have the fluoride back then. I'm 73. I have some old, old fillings. Still have my teeth. He didn't believe in Novacaine. He always had that certain look in his eyes, and I could tell he was thinking…he would say, 'Let me look in your mouth' and, oh, I would shudder."

Dick Hoblitzell prepares to extract Larry Gardner's tooth. Courtesy of Connie Michael.

After the Army, for a while he was player-coach and then managed some ball teams—Reading, Pennsylvania and Charlotte, North Carolina with the Hornets for years. In Charlotte, his daughter Connie was born, and Dick got into real estate. Then during the Depression the family moved back to West Virginia in 1931. He was in real estate, insurance, and managed the family farm. It was a fairly large farm, about 540 acres, most of which Connie still owns. He raised Black Angus cattle. Dick moved into politics and became a local sheriff, then served on the county commission and eventually became county court president. John Hoblitzell is another relative. Dick was first cousin to John's grandfather.

As sheriff of Wood County in the early '50s, he became a political mentor of John Hoblitzell's father, who served in the United States Senate under an interim appointment for seven months. Jennings Randolph won the seat in the next election.

"He had very good memories of the Red Sox, and he used to tell stories," his daughter recalls. "I know the letters he wrote to my mother, he expressed how really it was a difficult profession. The traveling, overnight on the train, then have to get off and play games. It wasn't nearly as glamorous. It was a hard life then, really. And they were rough. They weren't the glamour boys that they are today.

"I remember meeting quite a few teammates. We went back in 1939 to the Old Timers Game. In Boston. I remember meeting Tris Speaker and some of those who were really special. Harry Hooper. They came down and visited down on the farm a lot. They thought that was fun, getting away on an old farm in West Virginia. I never met Babe Ruth, but my brother did. Daddy and Babe Ruth roomed together for years. He had some real stories about Babe… in fact, I think he had some stories that he couldn't tell his daughter."

Dick Hoblitzell is honored with a plaque (of the non-dental variety) in the West Virginia Hall of Fame in Charleston.

Lou Legett

Catcher Lou Legett, who played on both the Braves and the Red Sox in the mid-1930s, was briefly a practicing dentist beforehand. "Doc" Legett was born (1901) and died (1988) in New Orleans. As nephew Ben Legett understands it, he graduated with a degree from the University of Tennessee, and then moved back home to New Orleans where he opened an office in the Maison Blanche Building on Canal Street. He played both football and baseball in Nashville; he had been a four-letter athlete in high school. The football team at Tennessee was a strong one, and had so many dental and medical people on it that it was pegged "the Doctors' Team."

In May 1929, Lou Legett broke in with the Boston Braves. He appeared in 39 games, but only mustered 13 hits for a disappointing .160 average. This was apparently good enough for the Red Sox, who were in the midst of the most dismal stretch in their history. The Sox finished dead last every year from 1922 to 1930 except 1924, when the White Sox were half a game worse. Legett did bat .200 and .289 the next two years but with only 12 hits over the two-year span. In 1934 he appeared in only two games but never had an official at-bat and apparently decided dentistry offered more of a future.

Ben Legett was himself a dentist until he retired in the mid-1990s. He does recall "Doc" Legett and agrees that there might have been some unconscious influence that his uncle may have had on his own choice of career. "I guess my first good catcher's mitt came from him, the worn-out one that had the stuffing come out of it," Ben recalls. "I saw him play when Nashville came down to New Orleans and played the Pelicans one time. It turned out to be a 16-inning game or thereabouts, and I was pretty sleepy when I got to go home, but it was great to have him back with the family afterwards."

Ben noted one benefit that the rough and tumble life as a catcher brought to Lou Legett's practice: "As a dentist and as a baseball player, he had so many broken, crooked fingers, I marveled at the fact that he could practice dentistry at all. On the other hand, with his crooked fingers he could get to places in the mouth that I could not with my straight fingers."

Doc McMahon

Doc McMahon pitched and won the only game in which he ever appeared, a game against the New York Highlanders. The date was October 6, 1908. McMahon threw a complete nine-inning game, striking out three and walking no one. He gave up three runs on 14 hits and ended the season (and his major league career) with an undefeated 1–0 record.

It was the next to the last day of the season. Eddie McMahon faced New York's Andy O'Connor, a "Roxbury lad" who was also making his major league debut. Like McMahon, this was O'Connor's one and only appearance in the major leagues. Another Massachusetts native, O'Connor also threw a complete game. He struck out five, but he walked seven, hit three batters, yielded 15 hits, and was tagged for 11 runs. For the next 72 years (O'Connor died at age 96 in 1980), the New York pitcher must have looked back with regret at his one line in the record books. McMahon, on the other hand, could recall with pride the one shot he had.

He also acquitted himself pretty well at the plate. He went 2-for-5, both singles, and so goes down in history as both an undefeated pitcher and a lifetime .400 hitter.

Henry John McMahon was born in Woburn, Massachusetts on December 19, 1886. McMahon had been one of the outstanding scholastic pitchers in the state, helping bring his team to victory in the old Middlesex and Mystic Valley leagues. After graduating from Woburn High, McMahon attended Holy Cross from 1906 to 1908 where he played ball with Jack Barry, captain of the 1908 team as a sophomore. Holy Cross records indicate that McMahon did not have a particularly impressive baseball career there. He never graduated from Holy Cross; he moved on to Tufts Dental School, where he earned a degree in dentistry.

Nearly 100 years later, how he ended up with the Red Sox remains a bit of a mystery. But he was not only signed, he got a chance to start.

Signed by the Red Sox, Doc McMahon had stayed for much of the year with the Boston team, after which he was sent to minor league teams in Syracuse NY and Reading PA for seasoning. His contract was sold to the Wilkes-Barre club on December 29, 1908, according to the *Woburn Times*. His fellow students at Tufts presented him with a "traveling bag" in March 1909 as he left for Wilkes-Barre, and the *Times* noted that, "He is practically a member of the Boston Americans and may be 'resold' to Boston before too long." He did not rate his prospects highly, though, and before too long "he abandoned his baseball ambitions and took up the practice of dentistry in this city," explained McMahon's obituary. McMahon later became a coach at Woburn High, and continued playing semipro ball. An August 1917 news account had McMahon pitching for Manchester-by-the-Sea, saying he "whipped United Shoe at Manchester" in a 1–0 shutout which ran his scoreless innings streak to 21 straight innings.

The former pitcher turned dentist settled into the family home at 3 Border Street and enjoyed life in his hometown. Doc McMahon died of heart trouble on the couch in his own living room at age 41, leaving a wife and three children.

James Thompson "Doc" Prothro

Doc Prothro spent just one year with the Red Sox, but it was a good year. The third baseman batted .313 with 51 RBIs in 415 at-bats. 52 walks helped him post a .390 on-base percentage. He'd played part-time for the Washington Senators in 1920, 1923, and 1924

The Sox had traded for him in a bit of a complicated way. First they sent infielder/outfielder Howie Shanks to the Yankees, reacquiring Mike McNally, who they'd traded to New York back in 1920. The day after they reacquired McNally, they traded him to the Senators for Prothro. The next year (1926) he was gone, to Cincinnati where he only appeared in three games. He spent most of 1926 and 1927 with the Portland Beavers in the Pacific Coast League. In the late 1930s, Prothro managed the Little Rock team for the parent Red Sox, winning one pennant for them in 1937.

Prothro had never played professionally until age 27. He'd been practicing dentistry in Dyersburg, Tennessee, after having earned his degree at the University of Tennessee Dental School. A scout for the Washington Senators, pitcher Joe Engel, saw Prothro playing shortstop for the town team and recommended him to Clark Griffith. He hit .385 in very limited action late in the 1920 season. When asked to go to Reading in 1921, rather than remain with the big league club, Doc refused to report and went back to dentistry instead. After a couple of years on the ineligible list, he accepted assignment to his hometown Memphis Chicks in 1923, did well, and was brought up again to the Senators in September. He played well enough again, and stuck with the Senators for 46 games (.333) in 1924 before being sent back to the Chicks in favor of Ossie Bluege. The Senators reacquired his contract from Memphis at the end of the season, and traded him to Boston.

In 1926 and 1927, Doc played for Portland in the Pacific Coast League. Beginning in 1928, he managed the Memphis Chicks for seven years. After Tom Yawkey bought the Red Sox, he poured some money into the Sox farm system and hired Prothro away to manage Little Rock starting in 1935, where he reportedly did quite a good job developing young prospects—and earned himself a three-year major league managing stint with the Philadelphia Phillies. After three straight last-place finishes, Phillies owner Gerry Nugent sold the team and Prothro returned back home to Memphis, where he in turn became part owner and manager of the Chicks, retiring after the 1947 season. Bill Weiss and Marshall Wright inform us that Doc's son Tommy Prothro was head football coach at UCLA for many years and coached the NFL Los Angeles Rams in 1971–72.

Jack Slattery

Jack Slattery graduated from college with a degree in dentistry, but never practiced.

There were other Red Sox docs as well, including **Doc Gessler**. When he appeared at "Cy Young Day" on August 13, 1908, newspaper reports wrote that he was dressed as a "country dentist," leading one to suspect he may have been a doctor of dentistry, too.

Other possible dentists include **Pete Appleton**. Pete was reported in *The Sporting News* to have studied law, but in a later issue *Sporting News* editor Spink wrote that Appleton had become a dentist.

MUSIC AND THE RED SOX

The history of music and the Red Sox embraces both the role that music plays at Boston ballgames and the members of the Red Sox themselves who have played or sung over the years. There have always been crowd chants to urge on the team, and anyone who reads about the early days of the team encounters the tale of "Tessie"—the popular song of 1903 that was sung by Boston's Royal Rooters. Even the Pittsburgh Pirates said that the song got on their nerves and may have cost them the first World Series. Today, every fan taking in a game at Fenway hears "Sweet Caroline" in the eighth inning—and hopes to hear "Dirty Water" after the game. The Sixties classic by the Standells—"Dirty Water"—is only played when the Red Sox win.

Chuck Burgess and this author have devoted a full book to the victory song in their book *Love That Dirty Water: the Improbable Anthem of the Boston Red Sox* (Rounder Books, 2007). There is no need to re-tell the story in these pages, but we will touch on several of the highlights in the history of the relationship between the Red Sox and music.

Looking through early newspapers, "Tessie" shows up during the 1903 World Series, the final games of the pennant-winning season of 1904, and the World Series wins in 1912, 1915, and 1916. It became a Red Sox ritual, albeit one that was largely abandoned following the 1916 World Championship. "Tessie" only made a brief appearance during the 1918 World Series, and John Holway is one author who contends that it was turning their backs on "Tessie" rather than selling Babe Ruth to the Yankees that caused the Red Sox to wander in the wildnerness for some 86 years. When Dr. Charles Steinberg, Jeff Horrigan, and the Dropkick Murphys joined forces early in 2004 to try and revive "Tessie," what happened come October 2004? We all know the answer. The story is laid out in detail in *Love That Dirty Water*.

Red Sox pitcher Bronson Arroyo recorded "Dirty Water" as the final track on his CD *Covering the Bases*, released on Asylum in 2005. He wasn't the first Sox player to make music. The earliest team talent that crops up in newspaper accounts was the Red Sox Quartet, a 1911 barbershop-style quartet featuring tenors Hugh Bradley and Marty McHale, baritone Tom O'Brien, and bass singer Larry Gardner. It wasn't even the only vocal quartet on the 1911 Red Sox—another featured Heinie Wagner, Red Kleinow, Bill Carrigan, and Eddie Cicotte. They were popular enough to be booked on the Keith's vaudeville circuit after the season was over.

Other Red Sox players with musical backgrounds include Hubert "Dutch" Leonard (1913),

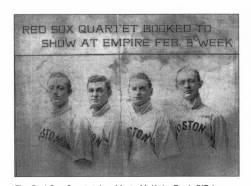

The Red Sox Quartet, L-r: Marty McHale, Buck O'Brien, Hugh Bradley, Billy Lyons.

who was a drummer in a family aggregation and who gave up a musical career to pursue pitching for the Red Sox. Some 45 years later, another pitcher, Mickey McDermott, sang at nightclubs in Boston and even performed duets in the Catskills with Eddie Fisher.

Both Johnny Pesky and Ted Williams were music buffs. Ted enjoyed jazz pianists and Johnny even worked one winter as a DJ on Boston radio station WBMS.

Carmen Fanzone only appeared in 10 games with the Red Sox, in 1964, but he played the National Anthem on his trumpet and his career found him playing in the Jimmy Dorsey Orchestra, among others. Around the same time, Tony Conigliaro released a couple of locally popular 45 rpm rock singles and earned himself a recording contract with RCA Victor.

Fans who came of age in 1967 will never forget the musical *Man of La Mancha* and its hit song "[To Dream] the Impossible Dream."

When Arroyo released his CD in the summer of 2005, Red Sox players Johnny Damon, Kevin Youkilis, and Lenny DiNardo were found on the record as guest singers. The album did well, making the charts in *Billboard* magazine. And the lead guitarist on "Something's Always Wrong" was none other than Red Sox GM Theo Epstein. Epstein also figured in another CD, released in 2006, the debut album by Boston sportswriter Peter Gammons. Entitled *Never Slow Down, Never Grow Old*, the CD is a benefit for The Foundation to Be Named Later, which raises funds for disadvantaged youths in the Boston area. TFTBNL is run by Theo Epstein's brother Paul, and is one of the charities favored by the Red Sox. The July 2006 record features contributions by Arroyo, Red Sox pitcher Tim Wakefield, and backing vocals by a good chunk of the team: Jonathan Papelbon, Lenny DiNardo, Kevin Youkilis, Gabe Kapler, and Trot Nixon, plus Wakefield, and NESN's Don Orsillo. Even Red Sox assistant director of baseball operations Zack Scott helped out on harmonica.

Songs About the Red Sox

There have been numerous songs explicitly about the Red Sox, or songs that mention the Sox. It would be difficult to come up with a comprehensive list, but the following provides a good start.

"Red Sox Speed Boys" sheet music.

The first one found that was devoted to the team was the 1903 "Boston Americans Two Step" written by J. Ignatius Coveney.

The 1908 Sox were known as The Speed Boys. Henry E. Casey (words) and Martin Bennett (music) composed "The Red Sox Speed Boys" and Bennett published it.

Writers Daniel J. Hanifen and Bernard H. Smith lionized right fielder Harry Hooper in 1915 with their song "Hoop, Hoop, Hooper Up for Red Sox."

Babe Ruth was the subject of many a song, but the only one published during his years with the Red Sox was 1919's "Batterin' Babe (Look at Him Now)" with words and music by Jack O'Brien and Billy Timmins. The sheet music promoted the song as "The Home Run Hit Song of the Season" and "Dedicated to our own 'Babe' Ruth." Ironically, part of the decision to sell The Babe to the Yankees may have been New York theater man (and Red Sox owner) Harry Frazee's ongoing desire to raise money for his Broadway musicals.

In 1938, Moe Jaffe's Mills Music folio *Batter Up* included "Root for the Red Sox"—but Jaffe was indiscriminate. He wrote 16 songs, one for each major league ballclub.

Joseph A. McOsker's "Cheer for the Red Sox" was copyrighted on June 14, 1967. The Red Sox were in fourth place at the time and "The Impossible Dream" was right around the corner. McOsker could have used some better marketing. After the '67 season was over, the *Impossible Dream* album sold over 100,000 copies. The Fenway Park organist John Kiley released *Red Sox Organ Music*—and featured Rico Petrocelli on the drums.

In 1968, rock band Earth Opera recorded Peter Rowan's song "The Red Sox Are Winning."

Other songs include:

"Be a Believer in Red Sox Fever" by The Paid Attendance, 1979.

"Bill Lee" by Warren Zevon, 1980.

"Baseball and the Sox" by Terry Cashman, 1982.

"Oil Can" by John Lincoln Wright, 1985—a tribute to Oil Can Boyd. Lincoln wrote a couple of other songs about Fenway and the Red Sox.

Ted Williams' daughter Bobby-Jo cut an EP: *A Musical Tribute: The Ted Williams Story* sung by her and Wayne Edmondson.

There was even a musical—*The Curse of the Bambino*—written by David Kruh and Steven Bergman in 1997–99. It premiered on April 25, 2001 at Boston's Lyric Stage Company and had a run lasting into early June. A compact disc recording of the show was produced and sold. In December 2004, the authors rewrote the work to accommodate the recent World Series win.

There was a band named Carlton Fisk. And there are any number of hopefuls, including some musicians from western Massachusetts who hope to score with "The Red Sox Rock." As 2006 wound down, the Red Sox began discussions with Boston's Berklee College of Music about hosting a worldwide songwriting competition to come up with the next great Red Sox song.

Early rock and roll recording artist Freddy "Boom Boom" Cannon (his biggest hit was "Tallahassee Lassie") released a single in the summer of 2007, which was a new treatment of his old hit "Palisades Park." The song was "Down at Fenway Park" and received some play at Fenway itself.

And did we mention that the book *Love That Dirty Water: The Improbable Anthem of the Boston Red Sox* (Rounder Books, 2007) goes into all this in great detail, while recounting the whole back story of how a California band that had never been to Boston ended up recording the 1966 single that's become the victory song of the Red Sox since Opening Day 1998? Yes, we did.

Marty McHale, the Irish Thrush

Marty McHale was more than a tenor and high baritone in the Red Sox Quartet. In 1910, he pitched three consecutive no-hitters for the University of Maine (and eight shutouts in all). That drew the attention of the Red Sox. (He also hit five holes-in-one as a golfer, but that took him a lifetime.) He was quite a popular player, and a singer to boot, dubbed the "Irish Thrush" by no less than Damon Runyon. Naturally, the players began calling him "Thrush" and the nickname stuck. *Variety* once dubbed him "The Baseball Caruso."

McHale had other talents, too. While in the Air Corps in the World War, Lt. McHale produced a full-length film entited *Baseball Review of 1917*. It was distributed to YMCA's around the country, but McHale went overseas to serve with the Signal Corps in France and by the time he returned in 1919, a film on 1917 was considered too dated for theatrical release. He had a vaudeville routine with Turkey Mike Donlin titled "Right Off the Bat" and otherwise kept himself busy between baseball seasons. McHale told Larry Ritter, "It's about fifty-fifty" when he was asked whether he liked baseball better, or vaudeville.

McHale pitched for the Red Sox in 1910, 1911, and 1916, in between pitching for the New York Yankees (Highlanders) in 1913, 1914, and 1915. He was one of six players the Sox sent to Jersey City to acquire Hick Cady in early January 1912. After just two appearances in his second stint with the Sox, he was sold to Cleveland in May 1916, thereby managing to miss World Series opportunities with Boston in 1912, 1915, and 1916. After 1916, he left baseball. After the war, he became a syndicated sportswriter for the *New York Evening Sun* and the Wheeler Syndicate, became a stockbroker, and eventually founded his own successful investment firm.

Other Red Sox players in film

In addition to McHale, Mel Almada's brother Louis worked for Warner Brothers and Mel was cast in several films (see the section on him under Latinos on the Red Sox). Lou Stringer appeared in a number of Hollywood films, particularly those with baseball themes such as *The Jackie Robinson Story* and *The Monte Stratton Story*. He did a fair amount of acting work but became tired of all the standing around on movie sets. Another Red Sox player who appeared in *The Jackie Robinson Story* was Dick Williams. Greg Beston describes his participation, versatile as it was in the low-budget production: "He is the pitcher facing Jackie at some point in the movie and I believe he allows a home run. While Jackie rounds second base in his trot, we see the same Dick Williams as one of the middle infielders."

Of course, several recent films such as *Fever Pitch* show players such as Johnny Damon, Jason Varitek, and others. And that's not to mention TV shows on which various players have made guest appearances from *Saturday Night Live* to *Queer Eye for the Straight Guy* to Leno and Conan and Letterman.

BOSTON PLAYERS WHO UMPIRED IN GAMES

Although any number of Sox players, coaches, and managers believe they could have called a particular play, or pitch, better than the umpire on the spot, there were a handful of occasions in 1903 when a Red Sox player actually did umpire a game.

May 2—Two players, one from each team, umpired—**George Winter** from Boston and Osee Schrecongost of Philadelphia. Umpire James E. Hassett must have caught cold the day before. Boston and Philadelphia didn't square off again until early August, but May 2's game was the ninth of the young season between the two ball clubs. Boston lost 3–0 as Eddie Plank, pitching on one's day rest, shut out Boston on five hits. Plank pitched the complete game, running his streak to 17 consecutive innings in which Boston batters failed to score off him. Boston had a couple of chances. Twice they had a runner on third with just one out, and in the sixth the bases were loaded. Cy Young gave up but eight hits, and one run each in the first, the fifth and the ninth. Plank sealed the victory in the top of ninth with two outs when he hit a home run to right. Boston tried two pinch-hitters in the ninth, but neither succeeded. The *Boston Globe* praised the work of the substitute arbiters: "Owing to the sickness of umpire Hassett, a player from each team officiated and did well."

July 1—Winter was called on again, in the summer. Umpire Sheridan didn't show for the game in Chicago. The White Sox chose Doc White and Boston chose the now-experienced George Winter. The game was a 1–0 10-inning shutout for Cy Young over Pat Flaherty, efficiently played in 90 minutes without an error on either side. Only one Chicago baserunner reached as far as second base. With one out in the top of the 10th, Hobe Ferris singled for Boston. He advanced to second when Criger hit into a fielder's choice and was out at first. Ferris scored the game's lone run when Cy Young himself doubled down the third base line. The *Chicago Tribune* declared that the two subs had "officiated with entire satisfaction. There was only one protest registered, and that by Ferris when he was retired by a yard on a double play, but claimed not. The crowd got after him for his bad manners, and he shut up quickly."

July 4—Boston was set to play two Fourth of July ballgames against visiting St. Louis, but when it came time for the morning game, umpire Hassett was again nowhere to be found. Neither was Tommy Connolly. **Cy Young** called the balls and strikes, the sole umpire for the first inning until Hassett turned up. Connolly made it in time to begin umpiring during the second inning of the second game. Boston won both games by scores of 4–1 (Hughes) and 2–0 (Dinneen).

July 8—For the second time in five days, **Cy Young** was pressed into duty as umpire—and pitcher Patsy Flaherty of Chicago umpired for the second time in two days. Flaherty had been asked to umpire the day before, July 7, when the White Sox were playing in New York and umpire Jack Sheridan suddenly attacked White Sox right fielder Dan Green with his face mask during the seventh inning. Sheridan was arrested and taken away in a patrol wagon to be booked for assault. (Green refused to press charges, but the police charged Sheridan with disorderly conduct. He was discharged by a magistrate in court the next day after apologizing.) Flaherty from Chicago and Monte Beville of the New York team umpired the rest of the game. In Boston on July 8, the scheduled umpire was Hassett—again, but this time he had an excuse: he'd been ordered to Washington by league president Ban Johnson. This left no umpire in Boston, though, so Flaherty and Cy Young served as arbiters. Boston won the game, 6–1.

George Winter umpired on another occasion, in 1905. It was September 18 in Washington. Umpire Tim Hurst was late showing up for the day's doubleheader and so Winter and Washington pitcher Malachi Kittridge made the calls. Washington won the first game, 4–2. And then Hurst turned up, so he umpired the second game. It was quite a day for Winter. The *Boston Sunday Globe* had borne the news of his engagement to be married and "the modest little pitcher was all smiles." Then he umpired the day's first game. And finally, he pitched—and won—the second game. He gave up three runs on 11 hits, but benefited from terrific run support. He didn't do too badly at the plate, either; Winter was 4-for-5 with four singles and scored four times. The final score was 16–3, Boston.

In 1906, hapless **Joe Harris** served as a substitute umpire on August 23. This was the same Joe Harris who was on his way to compiling the worst W-L pitching record in Boston history; he finished the year with a 2–21 mark. Lack of run support was often the case for Harris; his ERA for the year was a not-that-bad-for-the-era 3.52. On August 23, St. Louis and Boston were set to play a game in Boston, with Winter for Boston and Powell for St. Louis. There was no explanation, but no umpire turned up. "Two players were pressed into service," wrote the *Globe*. "Howell held the indicator behind the plate and Harris was on the bases. Each had some close decisions to make, but the players were good natured and took everything, even the close ones, in good spirit." It wasn't easy umpiring a game your club was in. "The players were able to guess that their teammates were not enjoying themselves…and did not make any effort to make their lot harder." St. Louis won the game, 3–1. Harris pitched the next day. Despite being staked to a 4–0 lead, he lost yet another game.

Back in 1901, **Frank Foreman** had umpired in one game, though it was after he'd joined the Baltimore ballclub. Bill Dinneen was a substitute ump twice in 1907, but he was with the Browns at the time (umpiring became Dinneen's regular gig from 1909 through 1937). At one time or another, wearing other uniforms, Red Sox alumni who had umpired (either before or after their Boston days) also included Nick Altrock, Charlie Berry, Frank Chance, Nig Cuppy, Billy Evans, Duke Farrell, Buck Freeman, Charlie Hickman, Win Kellum, Deacon McGuire, Case Patten, George Pipgras, and Bucky Walters.

We'll leave this section with one thought: imagine Carl Everett being asked to umpire a game.

Thanks to David Vincent and Retrosheet for data to help track down some of these substitutions.

Cy Young's spurt on the basepaths

Anyone who has ever seen a photograph of Cy Young will remember that he was, to put it kindly, "heavy-set." One wouldn't think him particularly fleet afoot. Yet in a game against New York on September 15, 1903, facing Jesse Tannehill Cy stole two bases in the same 12–3 game. They were his only two steals of the season. When Boston played Cleveland just two days later and catcher Charley Farrell singled in the fifth—his first game back from injury— Cleveland captain Larry Lajoie allowed Young to serve as courtesy runner for Farrell twice. The first time, Young went first to third on Dougherty's single to center, then scored easily when Collins tripled. Next time up, Farrell hit safely and Cy came in to run, but was unable to advance as Winter popped up. Boston won the game easily, 14–3.

The time the Red Sox almost got arrested
for playing a game at Fenway Park

There was a time in 1918 that the Red Sox almost got arrested for trying to raise money for the Red Cross. Harry Hooper, Babe Ruth, and company hauled off in handcuffs for violating the Sabbath law in Boston?

Playing baseball on Sundays had long been prohibited in Boston, but a delegation from the American Red Cross visited Fenway Park on May 24, 1918 and came to agreement with owner Harry Frazee that a regular scheduled game would be played on Sunday the 26th against the White Sox. Chicago owner Comiskey was happy to agree to move the Monday game ahead to Sunday instead. The entire proceeds of the game were to go to the Red Cross. Regular ticket prices would apply, but box seats would be auctioned off to the public to raise even more money for the cause. Frazee agreed that the Red Sox would absorb the cost of staging the game. League president Ban Johnson readily agreed as well.

With the World War on in earnest, the Red Cross could use all the money it could raise. It was estimated that between $40,000 and $50,000 would be raised—a major sum by the standards of the day.

The state legislature had passed legislation permitting Army and Navy service teams to play on Sundays, provided no admission was charged, and it was reported that both state and city authorities had given permission for the game.

Massachusetts Governor Samuel W. McCall supported the effort. So did Boston Mayor Andrew J. Peters, who signed a license to permit the game. The Attorney General of the Commonwealth ruled that the mayor had the authority to approve the license. The game was widely advertised in Boston newspapers. Everything looked great—it was motherhood and apple pie and a patriotic fundraiser for a needy cause.

Late on Saturday afternoon, Boston Police Commissioner Stephen O'Meara stepped in with a communique to Superintendent of Police Michael H. Crowley declaring the proposed game in violation of the law, in that admission would be charged, and instructing Crowley that "police procedure should be to secure the names of persons taking part in or promoting it and apply to the court for summonses for them." It was actually a fine line the Commissioner was taking; his lengthy statement in effect passed the buck on to the courts. The two police officials anticipated the possibility that the court would decline to issue summonses "or, having granted them, acquit the defendants." In that case, however, the Superintendent warned, "the police will assume that such games are lawful and will thereafter treat them as games played on weekdays."

No one wanted to see the police taking names, and prosecuting the case, so the game was scrapped and the Monday schedule adhered to with ballclubs agreeing to donate the full proceeds of that game instead.

When the game was held on Monday, only $5,500 was raised and a good half of that was said to have been the result of money bid for Sunday seats in the auction which the winning bidders let ride. Well under $3,000 was raised by virtue of tickets sold for the game itself. To make matters worse, Boston lost, 6–4.

Sunday baseball—banned in Boston

For years, Sunday baseball was banned in Boston—and in most cities around the country. Over the years, various cities began to permit Sunday ball. Boston was one of the last cities to remove the prohibition, with only Philadelphia and Pittsburgh lagging behind among major league cities.

Early 20th century newspapers often featured small news items reflecting the ban. Numerous incidents occurred as players struggled with the prohibition against a game they loved. Indeed, some of the players themselves declined to play on the Sabbath. One such was "Parson" Lewis, pitcher for the 1901 Boston American League club.

On May 29, 1905, New York City's police arrested all the players at a semipro game. The only one not arrested being Giants ace Iron Joe McGinnity, who was scheduled to pitch but was in street clothes at the time.

The issue has never truly gone away; just a few years ago, in 1998, New York's Cardinal John O'Connor complained that too many soccer and Little League games were being scheduled on Sunday mornings and interfering with the availability of altar servers in his diocese.

Feelings were strong. In 1919 the Lord's Day League of New England even published a 28-page pamphlet entitled "SYMPOSIUM: Shall Sunday baseball be legalized in Massachusetts?" The League clearly stood against legalization, stating that there were 170 references in the Bible, among them "Remember the Sabbath Day, to keep it holy." Quoting another passage from Scripture, it spoke out against "lovers of pleasure more than lovers of God." To ensure secular support as well, the League pamphlet assembled quotations from George Washington, Abraham Lincoln, and others. Lincoln is quoted: "As we keep or break the Sabbath-day, we nobly save or meanly lose the last best hope by which man rises." The fight, according to the Speaker of the House of Representatives of Massachusetts, Hon. Joseph Warner, quoted in the same pamphlet, was "against the injection of anything which shall open our Lord's Day to disturbance and Commercialism."

Both personal interests and commercial ones coalesced in the campaign against the Sunday laws. For many fans, it was virtually the only time they could attend games in the era before night baseball. Teams saw important economic benefits in Sunday play. Revenues increased and shares of specific teams often allegedly rose as much as 50% once Sunday ball was approved.

In Boston, the leader of the fight to permit Sunday baseball was Eugene J. O'Connor. The 40-year-old Dorchester resident was arrested for an act of what today we would today call civil disobedience, arrested for challenging the law. On October 12, 1912, the *Boston Globe* reported that O'Connor "began batting a ball to several youngsters at 3:40 and was arrested by patrolman Gallop of Division 4."

Today's Red Sox fans may be interested to know that O'Connor was an uncle of longtime season ticket holder Lib Dooley, the "Queen of Fenway Park"—who held season tickets from 1944 until her death in 2000 and reportedly never missed a home game until her final year. When O'Connor died, the *Globe* ran a brief appreciation entitled "Father of Sunday Baseball."

After many years of effort, the matter was placed on the ballot in a statewide referendum in 1928. The voters chose to permit Sunday baseball throughout the Commonwealth. A proviso in the law, however, stipulated that Sunday baseball was not to be played within 100 yards of a house of worship—apparently it was feared that the distractions of the national pastime might cause worshippers to divert to the ballfield while on their way to church.

Because Fenway Park stood within 100 yards of a church on the corner of Peterborough and Jersey Streets, the Church of the Disciples, no baseball was played at Fenway Park on Sundays until 1932. The Red Sox played at Braves Field on Sundays beginning on April 28, 1929—a 7–3 Sox loss to the Philadelphia Athletics. Red Sox fans wanted to see their team play at Fenway, but they had to wait more than three years.

Finally, an exasperated John S. Dooley (Lib Dooley's father) spoke up and, at his indirect behest, Lt. Gov. Leverett Saltonstall approached the minister of the church, Abraham Rihbany, and simply asked if the minister had any objection. Not at all, was the reply, given that Red Sox games started at 1:00 p.m.

Heading to Fenway in front of the church at the corner of Jersey Street and Peterborough Street, the church within 100 yards of Fenway Park. Bill Nowlin photo.

and the church service was over by noon. The church was a Unitarian one, and a quite liberal congregation. The first Sunday game at Fenway Park was played on July 3, 1932. The Yankees beat the Red Sox, 13–2. From that time forward, Sunday baseball has been played at Fenway.

There was, however, a 6:30 p.m. curfew that obtained until 1946. On May 14, 1946 a bill was introduced in the Massachusetts legislature to repeal the curfew. The reason? On April 21, the Red Sox had hosted the Philadelphia Athletics for a Sunday doubleheader at Fenway. The Sox were losing the first game, 7–0, after five innings of play, but scored sufficient runs to overcome the deficit and gain a 12–11 win in 10 innings (on a bases-loaded single by Ted Williams). Boston was losing the second game, but only by 3–0, when the game was curtailed after the bottom of the fifth and declared a win for Philadelphia. This was, of course, particularly galling because of the come-from-behind success earlier the very same day. This just wouldn't do; the legislature removed the early evening curfew.

The Boston Red Sox and the Boston Braves

A list of Red Sox games played at Braves Field appears in the 2003 *Red Sox Media Guide*, on page 286.

SOX WHO PLAYED FOR THE BOSTON BRAVES OR THE YANKEES

Players who played for the Boston Braves and the Boston Red Sox

Gene Bailey Braves 1919–20 Red Sox 1920

Walter Barbare Red Sox 1918 Braves 1921–22

Frank Barberich Braves 1907 Red Sox 1910

Frank Barrett Red Sox 1944–45 Braves 1946

King Brady Red Sox 1908 Braves 1912

Chet Chadbourne Red Sox 1906–07 Braves 1918

Jack Coffey Braves 1909 Red Sox 1918

Jimmy Collins Braves 1895–1900 Red Sox 1901–07 (player-manager 1901–6)

Gene Conley Braves 1952 Red Sox 1961–63

Jimmy Cooney Red Sox 1917 Braves 1928

Nig Cuppy Braves 1900 Red Sox 1901

Babe Dahlgren Red Sox 1935–26 Braves 1941

Bill Dinneen Braves 1900–01 Red Sox 1902–07

Joe Dugan Red Sox 1922 Braves 1929

Doc Farrell Braves 1927–29 Red Sox 1935

Wes Ferrell (also p) Red Sox 1934–37 Braves 1941

Buck Freeman Braves 1900 Red Sox 1901–07

Charlie Hickman Braves 1897–99 Red Sox 1902

Roy Johnson Red Sox 1932–35 Braves 1937–38

Eddie Joost Braves 1943 and 1945 Red Sox 1955

Andy Karl Red Sox 1943 Braves 1947

Billy Klaus Braves 1952 Red Sox 1955–58

Rube Kroh Red Sox 1906–07 Braves 1912

Lou Legett Braves 1929 and 1933 Red Sox 1934–35

Ted Lewis Braves 1896–1900 Red Sox 1901

Danny MacFayden Red Sox 1926–32 Braves 1935–39 and 1943

Gene Mauch Braves 1950–51 Red Sox 1956–57

Stuffy McInnis Red Sox 1918–21 Braves 1923–24

Marty McManus Red Sox 1931–3 (player-manager 1932–33) Braves 1934

Fred Mitchell Red Sox 1901–02 Braves 1913 (coached Braves 1914–16 and managed Braves 1921–3)

Hap Myers Red Sox 1910 and 1911 Braves 1913

Chet Nichols Braves 1951 Red Sox 1960–63

Frank O'Rourke Braves 1912 Red Sox 1922

Nels Potter Red Sox 1941 Braves 1948–49

Jack Quinn Braves 1913 Red Sox 1922–25

Wally Rehg Red Sox 1913–15 Braves 1917–18

Woody Rich Red Sox 1939–41 Braves 1944

Joe Riggert Red Sox 1911 Braves 1919

Red Rollings Red Sox 1927–28 Braves 1930

Babe Ruth Red Sox 1914–19 Braves 1935

Red Shannon Braves 1915 Red Sox 1919

Al Shaw Red Sox 1907 Braves 1909

Dave Shean Braves 1909–10 Red Sox 1918–19

Al Simmons Braves 1939 Red Sox 1943

Chick Stahl Braves 1897–1900 Red Sox 1901–06 (managed Red Sox 1906)

Jake Volz Red Sox 1901 Braves 1905

Murray Wall Braves 1950 Red Sox 1957–59

Bucky Walters Braves 1931–32 and 1950 Red Sox 1933–34

John Warner Braves 1895 Red Sox 1902

Rabbit Warstler Red Sox 1930–33 Braves 1936–40

Joe Wilhoit Braves 1916–17 Red Sox 1919

Jim Wilson Red Sox 1945–46 Braves 1951–52

Cy Young Red Sox 1901–08 (managed 6 games in 1907) Braves 1911

Hugh Duffy played for the Braves (1892–1900), managed the Red Sox (1921–22) and coached for the Red Sox (1932).

Billy Herman was a Braves player (1946) and a Red Sox manager (1964—66).

Fred Lake managed both the Red Sox (1908 and 1909) and the Braves (1910).

Eddie Mayo played for the Braves (1937–38) and coached for the Red Sox (1951).

Bill McKechnie played for the Braves in 1913 and managed the Braves 1930–37; he coached for Red Sox 1952–53.

Johnny Schulte played for the Braves (1932) and coached for the Red Sox (1949–50).

Jack Slattery played for the Red Sox in 1901 and coached for the Braves in 1918–19, and managed the Braves in 1928.

In many instances, players did not play out the full years cited above but only played part of the year in question. For instance, Doc Farrell opened the 1927 season with the New York Giants and played 42 games with them before coming to the Red Sox. In 1929, he returned to the Giants after only five games with the Braves.

Gene Conley also played for another Boston professional sports team—the Boston Celtics basketball team

Hap Myers played for the Red Sox in 1910 and later in 1911, but in the earlier part of 1911 he was briefly with the St. Louis Browns before being traded back to Boston.

Players who played for the Red Sox and the Yankees

Doc Adkins Red Sox 1902 Yankees 1903

Ivy Andrews Yankees 1931–32; 1937–38 Red Sox 1932–33

Pete Appleton Red Sox 1932 Yankees 1933

Neal Ball Yankees 1907–09 Red Sox 1912–13

Scott Bankhead Red Sox 1993–94 Yankees 1995

Willie Banks Yankees 1997–98 Red Sox 2001–02

Don Baylor Yankees 1983–85 Red Sox 1986–87

Mark Bellhorn Red Sox 2004–05 Yankees 2005

Juan Beniquez Red Sox 1971–75 Yankees 1979

Lou Berberet Yankees 1954–55 Red Sox 1958

Doug Bird Yankees 1980–81 Red Sox 1983

Wade Boggs Red Sox 1982–92 Yankees 1993–97

Darren Bragg Red Sox 1996–98 Yankees 2001

Ken Brett Red Sox 1967–71 Yankees 1976

Hal Brown Red Sox 1953–55 Yankees 1962

George Burns Red Sox 1922–23 Yankees 1928–29

Joe Bush Red Sox 1918–21 Yankees 1922–24

Ray Caldwell Yankees 1910–18 Red Sox 1919

Jose Canseco Red Sox 1995–96 Yankees 2000

Roy Carlyle Red Sox 1925–26 Yankees 1926

Danny Cater Yankees 1970–71 Red Sox 1972–74

Rick Cerone Yankees 1980–84; 1987; 1990 Red Sox 1988–89

Ben Chapman Yankees 1930–36 Red Sox 1937

Jack Chesbro Yankees 1903–09 Red Sox 1909

Jack Clark Yankees 1988 Red Sox 1991–92

Tony Clark Red Sox 2002 Yankees 2004

Roger Clemens Red Sox 1986–96 Yankees 1999–2003; 2007

Tex Clevenger Red Sox 1954 Yankees 1961–62

Lou Clinton Red Sox 1960–64 Yankees 1966–67

Michael Coleman Red Sox 1997–99 Yankees 2001

Rip Collins Yankees 1920–21 Red Sox 1922

David Cone Yankees 1995–2000 Red Sox 2001

Dusty Cooke Yankees 1930–32 Red Sox 1933–36

Guy Cooper Yankees 1914 Red Sox 1914–15

Lou Criger Red Sox 1901–08 Yankees 1910

Babe Dahlgren Red Sox 1935–36 Yankees 1937–40

Johnny Damon Red Sox 2002–05 Yankees 2006–07

Al DeVormer Yankees 1921–22 Red Sox 1923

Patsy Dougherty Red Sox 1902–04 Yankees 1904–06

Joe Dugan Red Sox 1922 Yankees 1922–28

Cedric Durst Yankees 1927–30 Red Sox 1930

Mike Easler Red Sox 1984–85 Yankees 1986–87

Alan Embree Red Sox 2002–05 Yankees 2005

Clyde Engle Yankees 1909–10 Red Sox 1910–14

Todd Erdos Yankees 1998–00 Red Sox 2001

Steve Farr Yankees 1991–93 Red Sox 1994

Doc Farrell Yankees 1932–33 Red Sox 1935

Alex Ferguson Yankees 1918, 1921, 1925 Red Sox 1922–25

Wes Ferrell Red Sox 1934–37 Yankees 1938–39

Chick Fewster Yankees 1917–22 Red Sox 1922–23

John Flaherty Red Sox 1992–93 Yankees 2003–04

Tony Fossas Red Sox 1991–94 Yankees 1999

Eddie Foster Yankees 1910 Red Sox 1920–22

Ray Francis Yankees 1925 Red Sox 1925

Billy Gardner Yankees 1961–62 Red Sox 1962–63

Milt Gaston Yankees 1924 Red Sox 1929–31

Frank Gilhooley Yankees 1913–18 Red Sox 1919

Joe Glenn Yankees 1932–38 Red Sox 1940

Tom Gordon Red Sox 1996–99 Yankees 2004

Randy Gumpert Yankees 1946–48 Red Sox 1952

Chris Hammond Red Sox 1997 Yankees 2003

Harry Harper Red Sox 1920 Yankees 1921

Greg Harris Red Sox 1989–94 Yankees 1994

Joe Harris Yankees 1914 Red Sox 1922–25

Fred Heimach Red Sox 1926 Yankees 1928–29

Charlie Hemphill Red Sox 1901 Yankees 1908–11

Rickey Henderson Yankees 1985–89 Red Sox 2002

Tim Hendryx Yankees 1915–17 Red Sox 1920–21

Butch Hobson Red Sox 1975–80 Yankees 1982

Fred Hofmann Yankees 1919–25 Red Sox 1927–28

Ken Holcombe Yankees 1945 Red Sox 1953

Elston Howard Yankees 1955–67 Red Sox 1967–68

Waite Hoyt Red Sox 1919–20 Yankees 1921–30

Tom Hughes Red Sox 1902–03 Yankees 1904

Jackie Jensen Yankees 1950–52 Red Sox 1954–61

Deron Johnson Yankees 1960–61 Red Sox 1974–76

Hank Johnson Yankees 1925–32 Red Sox 1933–35

Roy Johnson Red Sox 1932–35 Yankees 1936–37

Sam Jones Red Sox 1916–21 Yankees 1922–26

John Kennedy Yankees 1967 Red Sox 1970–74

Red Kleinow Yankees 1904–10 Red Sox 1910–11
John Knight Red Sox 1907 Yankees 1909–13
Andy Kosco Yankees 1968 Red Sox 1972
Jack Kramer Red Sox 1948–49 Yankees 1951
Frank LaPorte Yankees 1905–10 Red Sox 1908
Bill Lamar Yankees 1917–19 Red Sox 1919
Lyn Lary Yankees 1929–34 Red Sox 1934
Louis Leroy Yankees 1905–06 Red Sox 1910
Duffy Lewis Red Sox 1910–17 Yankees 1919–20
Jim Leyritz Yankees 1990–96; 1999–00
     Red Sox 1998
Tim Lollar Yankees 1990 Red Sox 1985–86
Mike Lowell Yankees 1998 Red Sox 2006–07
Joe Lucey Yankees 1920 Red Sox 1925
Sparky Lyle Red Sox 1967–71 Yankees 1972–78
Danny MacFayden Red Sox 1926–32
     Yankees 1932–34
Jeff Manto Red Sox 1996 Yankees 1999
Josias Manzanillo Red Sox 1991 Yankees 1995
Carl Mays Red Sox 1915–19 Yankees 1919–23
Mickey McDermott Red Sox 1948–53 Yankees
     1956
Jim McDonald Red Sox 1950 Yankees 1952–54
Lynn McGlothen Red Sox 1972–73 Yankees 1982
Bob McGraw Yankees 1917–20 Red Sox 1919
Deacon McGuire Yankees 1904–07 Red Sox
     1907–08
Marty McHale Red Sox 1910–11; 1916 Yankees
     1913–15
Norm McMillan Yankees 1922 Red Sox 1923
Mike McNally Red Sox 1915–20 Yankees 1921–24
Bob Melvin Red Sox 1993 Yankees 1994
Ramiro Mendoza Yankees 1996–02; 2005 Red Sox
     2003–04
Doug Mientkiewicz Red Sox 2004 Yankees 2007
Elmer Miller Yankees 1915–22 Red Sox 1922
Buster Mills Red Sox 1937 Yankees 1940
Fred Mitchell Red Sox 1901–02 Yankees 1910
Johnny Mitchell Yankees 1921–22 Red Sox
     1922–23
Bill Monbouquette Red Sox 1958–65 Yankees
     1967–68
Wilcy Moore Yankees 1927–29; 1932–33 Red Sox
     1931–32
Jerry Moses Red Sox 1965–70 Yankees 1973
Johnny Murphy Yankees 1932–46 Red Sox 1947
Rob Murphy Red Sox 1989–90 Yankees 1994
George Murray Yankees 1922 Red Sox 1923–24
Mike Myers Red Sox 2004–05 Yankees 2006–07
Bobo Newsom Red Sox 1937 Yankees 1947
Gus Niarhos Yankees 1946–50 Red Sox 1952–53
Harry Niles Yankees 1908 Red Sox 1908–10

Otis Nixon Yankees 1983 Red Sox 1994
Les Nunamaker
     Red Sox 1911–14
     Yankees 1914–17
Mike O'Berry
     Red Sox 1979
     Yankees 1984
Lefty O'Doul
     Yankees 1919–22
     Red Sox 1923
John Olerud
     Yankees 2004
     Red Sox 2005
Steve O'Neill Red
     Sox 1924 Yankees 1925

Les Nunamaker wearing the garb of the good team he served.

Bob Ojeda Red Sox 1980–85 Yankees 1994
Joe Oliver Yankees 2005 Red Sox 2005
Spike Owen Red Sox 1986–88 Yankees 1993
Ben Paschal Red Sox 1920 Yankees 1924–29
Herb Pennock Red Sox 1915–22; 1934
     Yankees 1923–33
Bill Piercy Yankees 1917–21 Red Sox 1922–24
George Pipgras Yankees 1923–33 Red Sox
     1933–35
Bob Porterfield Yankees 1948–51 Red Sox
     1956–58
Del Pratt Yankees 1918–20 Red Sox 1921–22
Curtis Pride Red Sox 1997; 2000 Yankees 2003
Paul Quantrill Red Sox 1992–94 Yankees 2004
Jack Quinn Yankees 1909–21 Red Sox 1922–25
Jeff Reardon Red Sox 1990–92 Yankees 1994
Bill Renna Yankees 1953 Red Sox 1958–59
Gordon Rhodes Yankees 1929–32 Red Sox
     1932–35
Aaron Robinson Yankees 1943–47 Red Sox 1951
Carlos Rodriguez Yankees 1991 Red Sox 1994–95
Buddy Rosar Yankees 1939–42 Red Sox 1950–51
Braggo Roth Red Sox 1919 Yankees 1921
Muddy Ruel Yankees 1917–20 Red Sox 1921–31
Red Ruffing Red Sox 1924–30 Yankees 1930–46
Allan Russell Yankees 1915–19 Red Sox 1919–22
Babe Ruth Red Sox 1914–19 Yankees 1920–34
Rey Sanchez Yankees 1997 Red Sox 2002
Ray Scarborough Red Sox 1951–52 Yankees
     1952–53
Wally Schang Red Sox 1918–20 Yankees 1921–25
Johnny Schmitz Yankees 1952–53 Red Sox 1956
Dick Schofield Yankees 1966 Red Sox 1969–70
Everett Scott Red Sox 1914–21 Yankees 1922–25
George Scott Red Sox 1966–71; 1977–79 Yankees
     1979
Bob Seeds Red Sox 1933–34 Yankees 1936

Howie Shanks Red Sox 1923–24 Yankees 1925

Rollie Sheldon Yankees 1961–65 Red Sox 1966

Ben Shields Yankees 1924–25 Red Sox 1930

Ernie Shore Red Sox 1914–17 Yankees 1919–20

Bill Short Yankees 1960 Red Sox 1966

Norm Siebern Yankees 1956–59 Red Sox 1967–68

Camp Skinner Yankees 1922 Red Sox 1923

Elmer Smith Red Sox 1922 Yankees 1922–23

Lee Smith Red Sox 1998–90 Yankees 1993

J. T. Snow Yankees 1992 Red Sox 2006

Jake Stahl Red Sox 1903; 1908–10; 1911–12
Yankees 1908

Mike Stanley Yankees 1992–95; 1997 Red Sox
1996–97; 1998–00

Mike Stanton Red Sox 1995–96; 2005 Yankees
1997–02; 2005

Tom Sturdivant Yankees 1955–59 Red Sox 1960

Frank Tanana Red Sox 1981 Yankees 1993

Jesse Tannehill Yankees 1903 Red Sox 1904–08

Lee Thomas Yankees 1961 Red Sox 1964–65

Jack Thoney Yankees 1904 Red Sox 1908–11

Hank Thormahlen Yankees 1917–20
Red Sox 1921

Luis Tiant Red Sox 1971–78 Yankees 1979–80

Bob Tillman Red Sox 1962–67 Yankees 1967

Mike Torrez Yankees 1977 Red Sox 1978–82

Frank Truesdale Yankees 1914 Red Sox 1918

Bob Turley Yankees 1955–62 Red Sox 1963

Bob Unglaub Yankees 1904 Red Sox 1904–08

Bobby Veach Red Sox 1924–25 Yankees 1925

Sammy Vick Yankees 1917–20 Red Sox 1921

Jake Wade Red Sox 1939 Yankees 1946

Jimmy Walsh Yankees 1914 Red Sox 1916–17

Roxy Walters Yankees 1915–1918 Red Sox
1919–23

Pee-Wee Wanninger Yankees 1925 Red Sox 1927

Gary Waslewski Red Sox 1967–68 Yankees
1970–71

Bob Watson Red Sox 1979 Yankees 1980–82

David Wells Yankees 1997–98; 2002–03 Red Sox
2005–06

Billy Werber Yankees 1930–33 Red Sox 1933–36

George Whiteman Red Sox 1907; 1918
Yankees 1913

Mark Whiten Red Sox 1995 Yankees 1997

Bill Wight Yankees 1946–47 Red Sox 1951–52

Stan Williams Yankees 1963–64 Red Sox 1972

Archie Wilson Yankees 1951–52 Red Sox 1952

Harry Wolter Red Sox 1909 Yankees 1910–13

John Wyatt Red Sox 1966–68 Yankees 1968

Bill Zuber Yankees 1943–46 Red Sox 1946–47

Larry Gardner and Harry Wolter.

As with the Braves / Red Sox listing, we have employed the names "Red Sox" and "Yankees" for convenience, even while recognizing that the teams were originally known as the Boston Americans and the New York Highlanders.

George Whiteman—first Boston, then New York, then back to the Red Sox

One of the more unusual situations of a player who played for both Boston (before they were called the Red Sox) and New York (before they were called the Yankees) is that of George Whiteman, who never played for any other major league team. The Boston Americans wanted to sign Whiteman out of the Texas League, but the Houston team wouldn't sell him unless Boston also bought another player named Tris Speaker. Whiteman appeared in four games for Boston, debuting in left field on September 13, 1907 and going 1-for-6, in a 13-inning tie game against Philadelphia. His spectacular catch in the bottom of the 11th spared Boston from defeat. He was 1-for-4 on the 17th, and he "starred in the field by going under the trees in the northwest corner of the field and stabbing a clout off Jones' bat which, in nine cases out of ten, would have been good for a home run." Two pinch-hit roles on the 14th and 24th were fruitless. He wound up 2-for-12, for a .167 average.

After the 1907 season, the Boston franchise became the Red Sox and sold Whiteman in February 1908. He played for Houston, Montgomery, Missoula, and Houston again. After five years in the minors, he was acquired by the New York Highlanders late in the 1913 season. He appeared in 11 games and batted .344, but apparently didn't make a sufficient impression; they released him in October. He was picked up by Montreal and played there for a couple of years, then in Louisville and Toronto. After four more seasons in the minor leagues, the Red Sox signed him for the 1918 season. Back with Boston, he got 214 at-bats in 71 games and hit a decent .266, driving in 28 runs and contributing to the winning of the pennant. Some argue that he was the unexpected star of the 1918 World Series. He toiled 11 more years in the minor leagues, often as a player-manager, and put up some good numbers, but he never played another major league game.

Speaker? He got three hits in 1907, hit .224 in limited action in 1908, but went on to play in 20 more seasons and compile a lifetime .345 average, fifth best all-time.

SOX PLAYERS IN OTHER SPORTS

It's fairly well-known that Sox pitcher Gene Conley also played pro sports as a center for the Boston Celtics of the NBA, Bill Russell's backup. Make that the World Champion Boston Celtics. Conley was on the 1959, 1960, and 1961 champion teams. Because he'd also been on the 1957 World Champion Braves, Conley remains the only professional sports player on champion teams in two sports. He also won the 1955 All-Star Game (in baseball). Conley had played for the Boston Braves before the team relocated to Milwaukee, thus making him also the only pro to play for three professional teams from the same city—Braves, Red Sox, Celtics.

On April 27, 1963, for at least a moment in the fourth inning, two NBA players (Gene Conley of the Celtics and Dave DeBusschere of the New York Knicks) each pitched for their respective Sox (Conley for the Red, and DeBusschere for the White). It was a 9–5 game, and Boston won it. Conley was half of the December 1960 trade that still stands as "the biggest trade in history"—the Red Sox traded 6′6½″ pitcher Frank Sullivan to acquire the 6′8″ or 6′9″ Conley.

There were many Red Sox players who were multi-sport athletes in high school or college. Some, like Jackie Jensen and Harry Agganis (a first-round pick of the Cleveland Browns in the 1952 draft), played football. Johnny Pesky skated with the Boston Bruins and there were murmurs of a contract offer—before the Red Sox told him not to be found scrimmaging on the ice.

Infielder John Reder's obituary from the *Fall River Herald News* states that he "was also considered one of the top professional soccer players in the country and was named a soccer All-American." Reder played first base and third base for the Red Sox in 1932. In the world of soccer, he

Dick Radatz, Bill Monbouquette, and Gene Conley, 1962. Courtesy of Katie Conley.

had been a goalie for the New York Marksmen (1929–30) and for the New York Yankees (!), who were also called the New Bedford Whalers, in 1931. Reder of the Red Sox batted .135 in 37 at-bats, with one double and three RBIs. He was born in Lublin, Poland.

It's with pro football, though, that the greatest overlap occurred. A full six Sox also played in the NFL:

1921: **Jack Perrin** played for the Red Sox for two days in 1921, but appeared in four games. The outfielders played in back-to-back doubleheaders on July 11 and July 12, batting .231 (3 for 13, all singles; he also struck out three times) with one RBI. He was the Big Ten All-Star left fielder for Michigan that year, but he only got one chance in the field for the Red Sox. He recorded a putout. It was his only time in major league baseball—but five years later, he got into six NFL games as a blocking back with the 1926 Hartford Blues. He kicked one field goal and also kicked for three extra points.

On April 20, 1923 **Dick Reichle** hit his one and only major league homer off Waite Hoyt, a two-run bounce home run to left field, part of a three-run first inning for the Red Sox. Babe Ruth's double with the bases loaded in the ninth gave the Yankees the win. Reichle appeared in 122 games that year, but the next time he played major league ball it was in the NFL—as an offensive end for the 1923 Milwaukee Badgers.

Hoge Workman had his major league debut with the Red Sox on June 27, 1924. Workman walked one Yankee and surrendered three hits in 1⅓ innings and then was lifted for a pinch-hitter. He threw 18 innings in 11 appearances in 1924, but by year's end was playing in the National Football League for the Cleveland Bulldogs. His 11 MLB games were overshadowed by his 19 NFL games. Workman's best work was for Cleveland, where he threw nine touchdown passes in nine games in 1924. He put in time as a quarterback, end, fullback, and halfback. After six years out of major league sports, he resurfaced for nine more games with the 1931 Cleveland Indians NFL team, and the following year he played in one game for the New York Giants, gaining one yard in one attempt.

Charlie Berry might have played football against either Perrin or Reichle, or both. It was a busy year for the MLB/NFL nexus. In 1925–26, he played in 20 games as an offensive end for the NFL's Pottsville Maroons, 10 games in 1925, and nine in 1926; he scored nine touchdowns—four receiving, four rushing, and one off a fumble. Berry also kicked three field goals and 29 extra points during his gridiron career. In baseball, Berry was a catcher for the Red Sox for several years, from 1928–32, and played in 709 major league games for the Athletics, Red Sox, and White Sox, from 1925 through 1938, batting .269. Babe Ruth might have known better than to have tried to bowl over Berry, attempting to score on a sac fly on April 22, 1931. Later in the same inning, after he'd taken his place in the field, Ruth strained a ligament and ended up being carried off the field. Cause and effect? Perhaps not. Berry's post-playing days saw him a two-sport man as well: he was an American League umpire from 1942 through 1962, and also served as a referee in the NFL for 24 seasons.

Bill McWilliams got into two games and had two at-bats for the 1931 Red Sox (see his story elsewhere in this book). He never got a hit. He got into five NFL games in 1934 as a wingback and halfback for the Detroit Lions, where he recorded 16 yards rushing in six attempts.

Carroll Hardy played for the Sox from 1960 through 1962. He'd been a halfback, appearing in 10 games for the 1955 San Francisco 49ers, recording 37 yards rushing on 15 attempts, with 12 receptions for 388 yards, an average of 28.2 yards per reception, scoring four touchdowns. With Boston, Hardy is best known as the only man to pinch-hit for Ted Williams. He also pinch-hit for both Carl Yastrzemski and Roger Maris (with Cleveland). After baseball, Carroll Hardy served a stint as director of player personnel and assistant general manager for the Denver Broncos, spending 20 years in the Broncos front office.

Thanks to Brian McKenna for helping with some of the information on other sports.

After **John Burkett** finished 15 seasons of major league baseball, he finally achieved his first sports ambition—to become a pro bowler. Burkett told the *Reno Gazette-Journal* that he'd worked at a bowling alley for $1.50 per hour during high school. "I wanted to turn pro out of high school. Baseball just kind of came along. I was drafted in the sixth round (out of high school) and they gave me 13 grand and I thought I was rich and wouldn't have to work. I gave baseball a shot thinking I could always come back to bowling later if it didn't work out." It was bowling that didn't work ouy, but he finished 32nd in the 2000 Brunswick Pro Source Don Carter Classic, while still pitching, winning $1,040. In 18 games he averaged 217.28. After his final season, 2003, he tried to go pro full time, but in January 2004 he fell short of making the first cut at the American Bowling Congress Masters.

Golf? **Ken Harrelson** broke his leg in spring training 1970 and missed almost the entire season. In mid-1971, he decided to take up pro golf. He told biographer Alex Edelman, "I just lost my desire to play baseball. I was still a competitor…but I didn't want to play baseball anymore." Harrelson sadly announced that he would quit the game he had loved for so long to pursue a professional golfing career. That pursuit ended badly, and Harrelson turned back to baseball once more in 1975, coming back to Boston—this time as an announcer." Harrelson spent three years on the Tour, even competing in the British Open. He found that golf was much tougher than baseball. "In baseball, you react to the pitcher," he said. "In golf, it's just you. The mental part is what gets you." [www.golfschool.com]

Researcher Brian McKenna found two Red Sox players appearing in National Basketball League games, **Ernie Andres** (1939–43 for Oshkosh) and **Lou Boudreau** (playing briefly for the NBL's Hammond, Indiana Ciesar All-Americans prior to World War II). In his autobiography, Boudreau wrote, "I was pretty good, though I wasn't very tall, and I probably could have continued to play in that league for a few years." But the Cleveland Indians asked him to concentrate on baseball and give up the hoops. Other pro basketballers before World War II who have Red Sox connections are: **Bucky Harris**, **Bucky Walters**, and Negro Leagues and Red Sox farmhand **Piper Davis**.

In the winters of 1967 and 1968, **Ferguson Jenkins** kept in shape playing for a while with the Harlem Globetrotters. They were always in a league of their own.

Jimmy Piersall was not only signed by the Red Sox right out of high school, but drafted by the Boston Celtics as well.

Harry Agganis was another player with two-sport potential. Billy Consolo roomed with Agganis the year before Harry's Red Sox debut. Consolo recalls the Cleveland Browns calling him up. They told him, "Otto Graham has retired and you're our number one draft choice. You don't want to play baseball." Consolo says, "I heard all those conversations, man. He could have been a professional football player, quarterback for the Cleveland Browns." But Agganis did want to play baseball and was off to a strong start before his tragic death.

There were two Sox players with two-sport potential on the 1929 team: Bill Barrett and Ed Morris. In the off-season, both applied for licenses to box professionally—hoping to cash in on some of the money that White Sox infielder Art Shires was earning in the ring. A match at the Boston Garden, pitting Barrett or Morris against Shires was contemplated. Commissioner Landis stepped in and announced that "any ball player engaging in the so-called manly art of boxing would be considered retired from baseball." That was that, other than the Benevolent Association of Boxers retaliating by banning boxers from playing professional baseball.

A two-sport man signed by Boston but who never made the team. There are bound to be a few of them. Perhaps the first was reflected in this brief note in the April 10, 1901 edition of the *Washington Post*: "The Boston American League team has signed Dr. Harley Parker, the Chicago billiard expert and ball player." Billiards was another sport that tracks play by innings. Parker had appeared in 18 games for the Chicago Colts (precursor to the Cubs) in 1893, 1895, and 1896, pitching in 17 of them. He was 4–2 in 1895 but fell to 1–5 in 1896. He did play in one major league game in 1901, but it was for Cincinnati on June 21. He pitched eight innings and gave up 21 runs, 14 of them earned. Apparently, Boston made the right choice not throwing him out there on the mound. Later in the year, Parker wound up pitching for Buffalo. He later umpired 28 AL games in 1911, but none involved the Red Sox. Parker was active in billiards tournaments for at least the next couple of decades.

In 1941, former Red Sox farm director **Billy Evans** (1936–40) was the general manager of the NFL's Cleveland Rams. But maybe we're getting too far afield here.

Other sporting events held at Fenway Park

Speaking of fields, over the years there have been a number of other sports played at Fenway Park besides baseball. The American Football League franchise Boston Patriots, who began play at the former Braves Field, leased Fenway Park beginning with the 1963 season after Boston University began to build dormitories on the old Wigwam site. "Red Sox Agree to Shelter Homeless Patriots" read the headline in *The Sporting News* (January 19, 1963). It was likely Dom DiMaggio who was key to the initial two-year lease; he was one of the 10 original owners and vice president of the Patriots. Back in 1956, Tom Yawkey had banned football games at Fenway in order to protect the playing surface for his baseball team. Given the possibility of the Patriots being homeless, Yawkey showed a sense of "civic responsibility" in offering the lease, in the words of GM Dick O'Connell. When Yawkey had banned football at Fenway, he had the special field seats that had been used during gridiron games gathered together, and donated them to the Baseball Hall of Fame.

Some 1953 Sox clowning around with a football at Sarasota.

Fenway Park configured for Patriots football. Courtesy of Gino Cappelletti.

The franchise's first home game was played at Boston College's Alumni Stadium (the Red Sox season was still underway); the first game at Fenway came on October 11, 1963—a 20–14 Patriots win over the Oakland Raiders. The last football game played at Fenway came on December 1, 1968—a 33–14 defeat for the Cincinnati Bengals.

The Pats weren't the first pro football team to play in Fenway Park, though. The Boston Bulldogs had played at Braves Field in 1929, then renamed themselves the Braves. They switched venues to Fenway Park after the 1932 season and took on another, somewhat related name, the Boston Redskins (later the Washington Redskins). After the Redskins left town, the Boston Shamrocks (AFL) were organized and in 1936 won Boston's first football championship, in a complicated scenario that helped contribute to a fairly quick dissolution. In 1940, the Boston Bears were born, but lasted just a year. The Boston Yanks were another football team that played at Fenway for five seasons, beginning in 1944; the Yanks eventually morphed into the Indianapolis Colts after franchise stops in New York, Dallas, and Baltimore.

Interestingly, one of the players for the Yanks was named Ted Williams. Former Gloucester High and Boston College footballer Theodore P. Williams later played for the other Eagles, the NFL Philadelphia Eagles, and also played for the Washington Redskins.

A sampling of some of the other sports events staged at Fenway include:

November 11, 1919: It was BC High 10, Boston English High 0
in a football game played before 6,000 spectators. Four days
later, on November 15, some 15,000 saw B.C. beat Holy
Cross 9–7. After that win, some 800 students and alumni
snake-danced all the way from Fenway to Boston Common.
On November 29, BC beat Georgetown 10–7 on a dropkick
to win the Catholic collegiate conference, also at Fenway.

July 10, 1929: Wrestler Gus Sonnenberg's famous flying tackle
defeated Ed "Strangler" Lewis, enabling Sonnenberg to
retain his heavyweight title.

August 10, 1929: In the opening game of the American Soccer
League season, Boston beat New Bedford, 3–2.

November 30, 1929: Boston College 12, Holy Cross 0 before
30,000 college football fans. Just the week before, B.C. had
beaten B.U. 33–0.

Ted Williams with Boston's Richard Cardinal
Cushing.

September 2, 1930: a heavyweight boxing match drew 15,000 to
a night bout at Fenway. Babe Hunt outpointed Ernie Schaaf.

September 6, 1932: junior lightweight boxing champion Kid Chocolate retained his title against chal-
lenger Steve Smith, taking every round of the 10-round event.

September 13, 1932—in another another bout just a week later, Unknown Winston—"Negro heavyweight from Waterbury, Connecticut"—knocked out Walter Cobb of Baltimore in the second
round of a scheduled 10-round fight.

October 8, 1933—in their home opener, the Boston Redskins beat the New York Giants, 21–20, before
15,000 fans for the National Professional Football League game.

June 27, 1935: Some 30,000 fans saw Dan O'Mahoney (formerly a soldier in the Irish Free State) take
the title away from the St. Louis Greek Jimmy Londos, thanks to a flying body scissors after one
hour and 16 minutes of "rugged grappling."

July 20, 1937—Steve Casey from County Kerry beat Danno O'Mahoney of Ballydehob before 8,000
for the "Celtic championship of the wrestling world." The turnout was deemed disappointing.

April 26, 1968: the Los Angeles Wolves beat the Boston Beacons, 4–0, in a North American Soccer League match. Fenway was home park for the Beacons, starting with some 1967 exhibition
games. The team only lasted a year, but did draw 18,000 patrons to one game against a visting
club featuring Brazil's Pele.

Larry Lucchino, festooned with championship rings

They weren't all earned at Fenway, but it's worth noting that Red Sox President and CEO
Larry Lucchino not only boasts his 2004 and 2007 World Championship rings, but has a Super
Bowl ring from working with the Washington Redskins in 1983, and a Final Four watch from
being on the Princeton basketball team. Lucchino also has another World Championship ring,
from the Baltimore Orioles in 1983. Observant readers will note the two rings from that one
special year.

Other events at Fenway

July 22, 2002: a ticketed event, the evening memorial service for Red Sox star Ted Williams
drew over 20,000 to Fenway Park. During the day, another 10,000 people visited Fenway to
pay tribute.

Other baseball games have been held at Fenway Park, too, and not just the Beanpot games
or other amateur games. Tufts and Harvard have played intercollegiate games there as well.

A few years before Jackie Robinson, Sam Jethroe, and Marvin Williams tried out at Fenway, there was a Negro League game played there. On September 8, 1942 the Philadelphia Stars beat the Baltimore Elite Giants, 8–7, in what the *Boston Herald* termed "the first Negro major league exhibition game in Boston." Bill Wright hit a pair of doubles and helped contribute to a three-run seventh inning rally by the Elite Giants, but the eight runs the Stars scored in the top of the third saw them through the rally in a game that was called after seven innings due to weather. Both of the Baltimore middle infielders—Tom Butts and Sam Hughes—were purportedly being given tryouts by the Pittsburgh Pirates, and it was expected the game would draw a larger crowd but only about 1,000 fans turned up.

In 1943, there was a series of four games held at Fenway Park where Quincy's Fore River Shipyard All-Stars played a succession of Negro League teams: the New York Black Yankees, Cuban All-Stars, Kansas City Monarchs, and the Birmingham Black Barons, who played the final game in the series to a 2–2 tie on September 3, 1943. Again, it was a raw weather day; one of Boston's black newspapers, the *Chronicle*, noted that "only fifty fans were white out of a total of five hundred." There haven't been very many events at Fenway Park where whites only comprised 10% of those in attendance.

Various exhibition ballgames between touring teams kept coming, though, over the years. Notable among them was the July 11, 1950 game between the New England Hoboes and Satchel Paige's team, played while the All-Star Game was on in Chicago. Satch and the Hoboes played to a 3–3 tie, the game called after nine. Some 27,418 paid to attend the Mayor's Charity Field Day event, and 10-year-old Jim Welby Jr. of Roxbury won a Cadillac convertible. A somewhat over-the-top Gene Mack Jr. wrote in the *Globe* that it was "one of the greatest entertainment programs in the city's history."

There was even a time the Cleveland Indians played an intrasquad game in Boston. This happened on May 8, 1944. The Indians had hosted St. Louis on May 7 and were due to play in Boston on May 10, so the Indians came on ahead and while the Red Sox were in Rhode Island for an exhibition game at the naval air station at Quonset, the Indians played a pickup game as the home team at Fenway Park before heading to Davisville, Rhode Island for an exhibition doubleheader of their own.

Needless to say, there have been any number of high school, Beanpot, Cape Cod League, and other charity baseball and softball games held at Fenway Park over the years. The Boston Park League, to name just one such event, held the final game of its seven-game championship series at Fenway on September 10, 1942. The Dick Casey Club of Dorchester beat the Navy Yard A.A. of Charlestown behind the pitching of Pete Cerrone, a Red Sox equipment man who often threw batting practice at Fenway Park and boasted 425 career wins in his semipro baseball career. Cerrone also worked selling men's suits at Filene's department store.

One possibility that never did come to pass: David McDonald reports that in 1919, Babe Ruth, in a contract tussle with the Red Sox, announced he was thinking of becoming a professional boxer. He claimed a Boston promoter had offered him $5,000 to fight heavyweight Gunboat Smith. Ruth even went as far as working out at a gym. It's doubtful, though, that Fenway would have been the venue.

Pros from other sports have been enlisted from time to time to help out the Red Sox. In April 1955, for instance, welterweight champion Tony DeMarco sold tickets for the Red Sox from a special stand set up at City Hall. [See the April 21, 1955 *Globe*.]

Is politics a sport?

Among the politicians who have given speeches at Fenway Park are: Theodore Roosevelt (August 1914), Franklin D. Roosevelt (the final speech of his 1944 re-election campaign), Barry Goldwater (September 1964), and Eugene McCarthy (1968), as well as Irish Prime

Fenway Park, 1914.

Minister Eamon DeValera (June 1919). The crowd greeting DeValera was estimated as "at least 50,000." Gene McCarthy drew the largest outpouring of his antiwar Presidential campaign, variously estimated as an overflow crowd of some 40,000 to 45,000. It was a ticketed event and tickets had sold out a few days in advance. Some 6,000 or so watched the speech on 200 televisions set up outside the park.

Music at Fenway

There was a touring jazz festival announced to visit Fenway in July 1973, but (despite it not being that long ago) we've not been able to find any indication the event ever occurred.

In the 21st century, Fenway Park has hosted music concerts by Bruce Springsteen, the Rolling Stones, Jimmy Buffett, The Police, and more. Both The Standells and Dropkick Murphys have become regulars performing at the park or at related events such as "Rally Monday" 2007 prior to the playoffs. The long history of music and the Red Sox has been dealt with at length in the book *Love That Dirty Water: The Standells and the Improbable Victory Anthem of the Red Sox* (by Chuck Burgess and Bill Nowlin), and inquisitive readers are recommended to that book for more on the subject. Nowlin and Red Sox Manager of Fenway Affairs Beth Krudys combined to write a two-part feature on the subject of music at the park in *Red Sox Magazine* during the 2007 season.

The annual Hot Stove Cool Music event has been held at Fenway in the early years of the new century, and—needless to say—the National Anthem is performed by an amazing array of performers throughout each season.

In 1914, Fenway was host to a carnival to raise money for children made destitute by a major fire in Salem. In 1919, some 6,000 members of the Triple Link League of Odd Fellows held their annual Church Day event at the ballpark in what was described as a religious and patriotic service. In February 1935, Shubert International announced plans for a series of outdoor operetta revivals at Fenway Park to be staged during the summertime. The Tigers had already agreed to provide Navin Field for the purpose and Shubert was negotiating with several other ballclubs with an eye toward developing a touring company. We have yet to confirm whether operettas were staged at Fenway; if not, there's still time.

Exotic dancers at Fenway

You really never know what you might find at Fenway Park, or outside it. This was hardly an occasion where the venue was rented to present a non-baseball event. It's more along the lines of parasitism—taking advantage of the crowd collected for a game.

Prior to the August 31, 2001 Red Sox/Yankees game which opened a crucial three-game series in the battle for the American League East title, outside the park there was the usual heightened commotion and bustle which characterizes visits from the Yankees. Radio station WEEI was giving away posters for fans to wave from their seats—one side reading "Yankees Suck" and the other reading "I Hate Roger"—a reference to Roger Clemens, New York's starting pitcher of the evening. WEEI often distributed such signs—they'd begun with large "K" cards on days when Pedro Martinez pitched. Over time, they created signs with other slogans, such as "Trash the Tribe" when the Indians came to town and so forth.

The slogans were usually mild, fun for fans. This was the first night they had distributed a poster which expressed hatred on one side and what is effectively an obscenity on the other.

Apparently, radio station WFNX wanted to get in on the action, as well. But they decided to one-up WEEI in tastlelessness. Their signs also read "Yankees Suck" on one side, but they also mounted a "Yankees Suck" parade which made its all the way around the park. The focal point of the parade were 10 "exotic dancers" which they had hired for the occasion. Dressed in the skimpiest of outfits, the young ladies carried signs and attracted gapes from families, fans, and stunned police officers who talked into their walkie-talkies but took no action. The "dancers" were supplied at WFNX's request by Shamrock Entertainment, which bills itself as "New England's All Nude Party Favorites."

"No one got in any trouble for it," said someone at Shamrock reached a few days later. "It was a promotion set up through the radio station. There were no difficulties. None at all." Told that the police seemed not to know what to do about this, the Shamrock man replied with a chuckle, "We probably do a lot of parties for those guys."

Radio personalities Storm and Birdsey explained, "We hate the Yankees. We're Red Sox fans. We're in New England and it's hard not to be part of hating the Yankees if you're a Red Sox fan.

"We thought, let's do this up right. Let's have a 'Yankees Suck' broadcast at Bill's Bar on Lansdowne Street. For a month leading up to it, we invited Yankees Suck song submissions—a contest, who could come up with the best Yankees Suck songs. We had over 30 submissions, the top three we had perform the song live. One man had to fly in from California.

"And we thought, what Yankees Suck broadcast would be complete without a Yankees Suck bikini parade? You know what, they weren't exotic dancers. They were all people that volunteered for it. Shamrock provided four of the girls, but the other eight girls there just showed up wanting to be in it. We provided them with bikinis. We had a secret webcam set up where they changed [joking]. Absolutely a successful promotion. The bar was absolutely packed. From 3:30 until about ten of 7:00, it was packed. It was like New Year's Eve."

Other sports *under* Fenway Park

After the Charles River Press vacated the underworld at Fenway, it was replaced by an auto garage and ultimately a bowling alley. From the 1960s until early in the 21st century, the Kenmore Bowladrome (later Ryan Family Amusements) inhabited the space with a 20-lane bowling alley. There was also a video game room, until renovations under new ownership converted the area to help house the growing Baseball Operations department and to permit the growth of the Game On restaurant.

RECORDS

Red Sox players and Red Sox teams hold any number of records, many of which we will touch on here. The annual *Red Sox Media Guide* updates their list each year and constitutes the best comprehensive source to consult for a listing of the many records in detail. Rather than be duplicative of this material, we simply urge you to check the *Media Guide* for a full list.

PITCHING

It is neither desirable nor possible to try and cover everything about Red Sox pitching without this book becoming completely unwieldy. That could be a book or two or three. Let's explore a few items, though.

The first truly great Red Sox pitcher was one who only wore the "Red Sox" in his final season with the team—Cy Young. By the time he did, though, he'd thrown a perfect game and won 171 games. He won 21 more in 1908, and so compiled a total of 192–112 with Boston. In just his first two years pitching for Boston, he won 65 games (33 wins in 1901 and 32 wins in 1902).

In 1904, the entire Boston pitching staff pitched a phenomenal 148 complete games (and this was when there were only 154 games each year—though there were three tie games as well, all in a three-day stretch!) Bill Dinneen, for instance, started 37 games and completed 37 games. The *team* earned run average was a stunning 2.12 and the moundsmen only surrendered 233 walks in 1,406 innings of play. The pitchers recorded 21 shutouts. Forty one (yes, 41!) of the complete games were by Cy Young. At one point, Young retired 76 consecutive hitters without a hit over 25⅓ innings, as part of a stretch in which he threw 45⅔ consecutive scoreless innings. During that stretch, Young threw four straight shutouts, three of the wins by the score of just 1–0. The 1904 Red Sox didn't need 25 players, or 40 players or 50 players, to do this. They only used 18 players all season. And only five pitchers all year long. There were only nine times in the 157 games that a relief pitcher was used.

The last time that more than half the games in the season were complete games came in 1946, when the staff threw 79 complete games. The team played 156 games, including two ties. Boo Ferriss had 26, Tex Hughson had 21, and Mickey Harris had 15.

Cy Young performed a number of other roles while with Boston: he served as a coach, a ticket taker, an umpire (by mutual consent of the other team), and even was a pinch-runner— twice in the same game!

Cy's teammate George Winter, though, once led the pitchers in the league (in 1904) with three pinch-running appearances.

Cy Young's worst game

July 29, 1903—It was a seesaw of a slugfest, New York winning in the ninth inning, 15–14. The Highlanders jumped out to a 6–0 lead off Cy Young. Young gave up 15 runs on 18 hits. There were fully seven triples in the game, but only two home runs, by Boston's Dougherty and O'Brien. Why Young was not relieved after giving up three runs in both the first and second innings is unknown, but he labored through to pitch a complete game. Boston tied the game 7–7 in the fifth. New York added three more runs in the sixth, but Boston came back with three, too. In the seventh, New York scored four more times and one more in the top of the ninth. Despite being down by five, Boston pushed across four runs in the bottom of the ninth, falling just one run shy. The game featured two pinch-hitters named Stahl: Chick hit for Criger in the eighth and Jake hit for Young in the ninth. Chick made an out; Jake tripled. Jack Chesbro was the winner, and he clearly didn't have that much better a day.

Fewest walks per nine innings, for a season

Until the unheralded Carlos Silva of the Twins topped it in 2005, Cy Young held the American League record for over 100 years, which he'd set in 1904—with only 29 walks in 380 innings pitched, that was an average of well under one walk per nine-inning game: 0.69 walks per game, to be precise. Young also held the second-lowest average, 0.78 in 1906. And the fourth lowest and the sixth lowest. With Silva's remarkable season, Cy dropped down a notch.

Cy Young—20-game loser

In 1906, despite a decent 3.19 ERA, Young was a 20-game loser with a record of 13–21. Of course, the rest of the team were losers, too—which was much of the point. The team posted an awful record of 49–105. They allowed 706 runs but only scored 463. They were equally bad at home and away: 22–54 at home and 27–51 on the road.

Just as a side note, in his days as a pitcher for the Red Sox, Babe Ruth was known to help out bagging peanuts on Saturday mornings, according to former peanut vendor Tom Foley, interviewed in 1985. None of the other players had arrived yet, but Ruth would help out. "Then he'd toss a $20 bill on the table" as he left.

Other 20-game losers

Young wasn't the only 20-game loser in 1906. Joe Harris was 2–21 (and Bill Dinneen fell just short, with a mark of 8–19). Holding the dubious distinction of losing more games in a season than any other Red Sox pitcher of all time is Red Ruffing, who was 10–25 in 1928 (and was 9–22 in 1929) on his way, over six-plus seasons, to a 39–96 record with the Red Sox. You might say it turned his career around when he was sent to the Yankees in early 1930. All he did was win 234 games to 129 losses and get elected to the Baseball Hall of Fame in 1967.

Big Bill Dinneen lost 21 games in 1902, but also won 21. Slim Harriss lost 21 games in 1927, but only won 14. The four other 20-game losers were: Sam Jones (12–20, 1919), Howard Ehmke (9–20, 1925), Milt Gaston (13–20, 1930), and Jack Russell (9–20, also in 1930). Since 1930, no Red Sox pitcher has lost as many games.

100 wins/100 losses

Through the 2007 season, the Red Sox have won 8,540 regular season games. The only pitchers who have won 100 or more games for Boston are these 10 pitchers: Cy Young, Roger Clemens, Mel Parnell, Luis Tiant, Pedro Martinez, Joe Wood, Bob Stanley, Tim Wakefield, Joe Dobson, and Lefty Grove.

The Sox have lost 7,960 games. Only three pitchers have lost 100 or more: Tim Wakefield (134), Cy Young (112), and Roger Clemens (111).

Being in the right place at the right time

Rule 10.19(c)(4)—The winning relief pitcher shall be the one who is the pitcher of record when his team assumes the lead and maintains it to the finish of the game.

The White Sox had a 4–0 lead after four innings at Fenway Park on May 4, 1962. Sox starter Don Schwall didn't seem to have it. After two singles, a three-run homer, and a one-out double, he was pulled in the top of the fourth; he'd given up the four earned runs on six hits and four walks. Mike Fornieles came in and got two outs on a couple of grounders. Fornieles retired the side in the top of the fifth, but was taken out for a pinch hitter in the bottom of the fifth. Nothing was happening. Carroll Hardy had walked and Pumpsie Green flied out to center. Russ Nixon batted for Fornieles and singled. Then the next nine Red Sox reached base. There were four changes of pitcher. The runs kept coming. By the time the inning was over, the Sox had scored 12 runs. The final score was Boston 12, Chicago 6. And Mike Fornieles booked an unexpected win.

Brother, can you spare a run?

One of the worst stretches in Boston baseball history came during the disastrous 1906 season, when the team was shut out for four games in a row, all on the road. Chicago won the first three: August 2 (Doc White), August 3 (Ed Walsh), and August 4 (Roy Patterson). After a day off, Cleveland's Addie Joss shut out Boston again. Boston's pitchers only gave up 11 runs in the four games, but that proved to be more than enough. Finally, in the third inning of the first August 8 game, Boston scored three runs for Cy Young and he held Cleveland to one. Joe Harris won the day's second game, 1–0. It was one of his two wins.

See also below how Joe Wood had a 1.68 in 1910—but lost 13 games.

20-game winners

The Red Sox have had 47 pitchers win 20 or more games in a season, most recently Curt Schilling's 21–6 season in 2004 and Josh Beckett's 20–7 season in 2007. Cy Young did it six times—in 1901, 1902, 1903, 1904, 1907, and 1908. Luis Tiant did it three times, as did Roger Clemens. Bill Dinneen did it twice, and so did Jesse Tannehill, Joe Wood, Babe Ruth, Wes Ferrell, Tex Hughson, Dave Ferriss, Mel Parnell, and Pedro Martinez. Only New York (57) and Cleveland (55) have had more 20-game winners.

Complete game leaders

In 1902, Cy Young pitched 41 complete games. Two years later, in 1904, he pitched 40 complete games. Others who have thrown 30 or more complete games in a given season are: Bill Dinneen (39 in 1902), Cy Young (38 in 1901), Bill Dinneen (37 in 1904), Joe Wood (35 in 1912), Babe Ruth (35 in 1917), Cy Young (34 in 1903), Cy Young (33 in 1907), Bill Dinneen (32 in 1903), Ted Lewis (31 in 1901), Cy Young (31 in 1905), and Wes Ferrell (31 in 1935), Cy Young (30 in 1908), and Carl Mays (30 in 1918).

In 1902, Cy Young won 10 consecutive complete games. Joe Wood (1912), Joe Bush (1921), and Boo Ferriss (1946) each won nine. Young threw complete games in 275 of the 297 games he started for Boston, an astonishing 92.5%. There were just 22 starts he didn't finish.

As of this writing, through the first seven years of the 21st century, the Red Sox team collectively has a total of 31 complete games.

Consecutive innings without relief

How do you spell relief? In 1904, Bill Dinneen may not have known. He started 37 games and threw 37 complete games, without ever needing a relief pitcher. He lost 14 of the games (23–14 was his record), yielding as many as eight runs in one game and six runs on four occasions, but his overall ERA was still a stellar 2.20. The total number of innings pitched without relief: 335⅔. It remains, not surprisingly, a league record. The NL record was set the same year; John W. Taylor of the Cardinals threw 39 complete games and 352 consecutive innings. (Taylor kept going; he finished every game he started—34—in 1905, and finished all 17 of his starts for St. Louis in 1906, too—as he had done for the Cubs in 1902 and 1903.) It's too bad Dinneen was out of action for almost a month (June 24 to July 19) or he could have given Taylor a run for the major league single-season mark.

Dinneen threw six extra-inning games during the year, the longest one running 16 innings on June 12, a 2–1 win over St. Louis. He may have come back too quickly on July 19; he lost a 12-inning game that day, 3–1. His next two starts were extra-inning losses, too—an 11-inning one on July 23 and a 10-inning loss on July 29.

Dinneen had finished the 1903 regular season with 10 complete games, adding another 88 innings to his overall mark. He'd been pulled after just one inning in the August 17 game. He started 1905 but only got in one complete game—an 11-inning win. He was relieved in the seventh inning of the April 25 game against Philadelphia; Grimshaw pinch-hit for him in the bottom of the sixth. Adding an even 17 innings in 1905 to the accumulated 423⅔ innings gave Dinneen a total of 440⅔ consecutive innings before he left a game.

Was he Dinneen or was he Dineen? It's a good question. All the newspapers at the time he played ball spelled his name Dineen. Most of today's books spell it Dinneen. To help this book get it right, Gene Carney went to check out his gravestone in Utica and that's spelled Dinneen. While he umpired for so many years, it was spelled both ways, but more often than not as

Dinneen—and one even finds more than one occasion (like the September 20, 1925 double-header boxscores in the *New York Times* where he was Dinneen in the first game and Dineen in the second!) This scribe hangs his decision to use the longer name—Dinneen—on an article in *The Sporting News* following his retirement as ump. The April 28, 1938 article reported that Dinneen "had quite a time getting scribes to place three 'n's' in last name and who labored several seasons before attaining waivers on title of 'Wild Bill.'" OK, Bill.

Strikeout leaders

Pedro Martinez struck out 313 opponents in 1999, by far the most K's recorded in a single season by a Red Sox pitcher. Roger Clemens ranks second with 291 (1988). Pedro comes in third, with 284 in 2000. Fourth was Smoky Joe Wood with 258, one ahead of Clemens' 257 in 1996 and two ahead of Clemens' 256 in 1987. The most Cy Young ever struck out were the 210 he whiffed in 1905.

The Sox who led the league in strikeouts were: Cy Young, 1901 (with 158 Ks); Tex Hughson, 1942 (113); Jim Lonborg, 1967 (246); Roger Clemens, 1988 (291); Roger Clemens 1991 (241); Roger Clemens, 1996 (257); Pedro Martinez, 1999 (313); Pedro Martinez, 2000 (284); Hideo Nomo, 2001 (220); Pedro Martinez, 2002 (239).

When a foul ball was not a strike

In the American League's first two seasons, a foul ball was not counted as a strike. This, quite obviously, made it a lot more difficult to strike out batters until the rule was changed in time for the 1903 season. Nevertheless, despite being hampered by this rule, Cy Young led the league by striking out 158 batters during his first season with Boston. In 1902, he struck out 160 (and Bill Dinneen struck out 136) but Philadelphia's Rube Waddell led with 210.

The team as a whole registered 396 K's in 1901 and 431 in 1902. With foul balls counting as strikes (unless there were already two strikes on the batter) beginning in 1903, the totals increased—but not by as much as one might have anticipated. Boston struck out 579 batters in that championship season. The total surpassed 600 in 1904, when Boston won the pennant again (612 strikeouts). Annual totals have tended to increase progressively over the decades, but the average from 1911 through 1920 was only 571 per season. And the figure in 1919 was even lower than back in 1901—the Red Sox staff only whiffed 381 opposing batters. Herb Pennock led the team with 70. In all, there were nine years (the war-shortened season of 1918, and the unfortunate seasons of 1919, 1920, 1925, 1926, 1927, 1930, 1931, and 1932) in which the Red Sox couldn't even record as many as the 396 strikeouts the staff posted without benefit of the foul strike. The worst year of all was 1925, with just 310 K's. Howard Ehmke's 95 led the team.

The most strikeouts in a season came in the first year of the 21st century, 2001. The Red Sox struck out 1,259 opponents. Of course, they had a few more games in which to do so in that the season expanded to 162 games beginning in 1961. The first time the Sox struck out more than 1,000 batters was 1963. Bill Monbouquette struck out 174 and reliever Dick Radatz was second with 162. By the 1990s, the average K-per-year figure was 998.5 and that includes the strike-shortened year of 1994 when the Red Sox only played 115 games. Adjusting for that year puts the average annual total over 1,000—and, as it happens, the only year since 1998 that the Red Sox struck out less than 1,000 batters came in 2005 when they punched out 959. Tim Wakefield led with 151. Of the 1,259 strikeouts in 2001, Hideo Nomo led the team (and the league) with 220. Twenty pitchers struck out 10 or more opponents during the course of the campaign.

10-strikeout games

The list of Red Sox pitchers who have thrown the most 10-K games in a given year is dominated by two men:

Pedro Martinez (19 games in 1999 and 15 in 2000, nine in 2001 and 2002, and eight in 1998) and Roger Clemens (12 games in 1988, nine in 1987, eight in 1986 and in 1987). Jim Lonborg threw eight in 1967.

On August 1, 2004, when Martinez struck out 11 batters, it was the 68th time in his Red Sox career that he had struck out 10 or more batters in a game. He thereby tied Roger Clemens for the club record in 10-K games. On August 12, Pedro did it again. 10 K. For the third game in a row. By the time his Red Sox run was complete, he had done it 72 times in all.

No strikeout games? There are quite a few of those, but it's unusual to win back-to-back complete games without striking out a single opponent. Charlie Wagner did it in 1942 and Mel Parnell did it in 1956.

Strikeout-to-walks ratio

Through 2007, Curt Schilling had the best ratio of strikeouts to walks (4.38 to 1) of any major league pitcher since 1900 who had thrown at least 2,000 innings. Second on the list is Pedro Martinez with a 4:28–1 ratio.

The worst ratio was Ted Wingfield's 1 to 27, in 1927. Wingfield pitched 74⅔ innings and struck out—yes—just one man all year long. He faced 346 batters, walked 27, and allowed 105 hits. No wild pitches all year. No balks. Just one strikeout, on August 10—Athletics shortstop Chick Galloway.

Most walks ever for a Red Sox pitcher

When he walked Bobby Abreu in the first inning of the April 28, 2007 ballgame, Tim Wakefield became the all-time leader in terms of doling out free passes among Red Sox pitchers, dethroning the reigning Roger Clemens who had the mark of 856. Wakefield continues to build on his lead. Wakefield is third all-time among Red Sox strikeout leaders, but only moved within 1,000 of Clemens during the '07 season. He's just three behind Pedro Martinez for second place, though, and likely to make that mark early in 2008. He's second in starts to Clemens' 382; Wake had 337 through the 2007 season.

An awful lot of walks in one game

Buck Newsom walked 10 White Sox in the June 16, 1937 game—and won. Fortunately, he also struck out eight, and didn't allow even one extra-base hit. Boston 3, Chicago 2.

Ken Chase walked 11 Senators in just four innings of relief on June 13, 1943. He also gave up five hits. For some reason (maybe it was his 0–4 record), this interested the New York Giants enough to trade for him the next day. He was 4–12 for the Giants.

Emmett O'Neill walked 10 Tigers on July 14, 1945 but won the game, 7–1. He only gave up three hits, and benefited from two double plays.

May 20, 1948—Red Sox pitchers Mickey Harris (7) and Mickey McDermott (11) combined to walk 18 Indians. Guess who won the game? Yes, Cleveland. 13–4.

Just standing around doing nothing paid off for the Red Sox, in the August 22, 1951 game at St. Louis. Tommy Byrne was pitching for the Browns and in the course of 13 innings of work, he walked 16 Red Sox batters. A Ted Williams single and three consecutive walks forced in the go-ahead run in the top of the 13th. The Red Sox left 22 men on base.

That'll show him! April 23, 1954. Bill Werle threw nine balls in a row, so Bosox manager Lou Boudreau replaced the catcher! Del Wilber came in for Sammy White.

Even though he was pitching a no-hitter, Earl Wilson was pulled from the July 31, 1959 game in the fourth inning; he'd already walked nine batters and had the bases loaded at the time.

Then there were the six walks Lefty O'Doul issued in just one inning. July 7, 1923. Lefty was left in to take a pounding. He gave up 11 hits in three innings, too, and 13 runs in the sixth inning alone. The Red Sox lost that game, 27–3.

He'd rather forget it, for sure. Bucky Brandon walked the leadoff batter in the bottom of the 11th in Chicago (August 27, 1967). After a sacrifice bunt, he intentionally walked the next batter. And walked two more, though there was a wild pitch and a fielder's choice mixed in. Game over. The White Sox won it in 11, 1–0. Argh.

One too many walks to start a game

Starting the second game of the April 21, 1946 doubleheader, Jim Bagby Jr. walked the first four Athletics he faced. He was pulled from the mound, but had already forced in the run granting Philadelphia all the edge they needed in a 3–0 ballgame. The A's had not officially registered even one at-bat against Bagby.

Balks

One of the most costly balks for Boston was Diego Segui's in the top of the 13th inning at Fenway on the evening of May 9, 1974. Minnesota had runners on first and third with one out when Segui balked in Rod Carew as the Twins' Jerry Terrell reached down for some dirt and Segui interrupted his delivery. Though Terrell struck out, his action brought home the tie-breaking run.

Eight years earlier, also in top of the 13th inning, Jim Lonborg was pitching in relief during the April 12, 1966 game against the Orioles. With two outs and the bases loaded, and Luis Aparicio at the plate, Lonborg balked and brought in the ultimate winning run, for a 5–4 loss.

Perhaps the most notorious balk was prompted by a Francona. Earl Wilson was pitching for the Red Sox with the bases loaded (Tito Francona on first). Just as Wilson began his delivery, Francona shouted, "Hold it, Earl!" Earl did, and the Indians got a run out of it. It was their first of the game, but they won it, 10–0. The date was June 11, 1962.

The only run of the game scored by either team on August 18, 1943. Boston's Yank Terry walked Detroit leadoff batter Doc Cramer, then balked him to second. Cramer reached third on a sacrifice, scored on a sacrifice, and Terry lost the game, 1–0.

Just dropping the ball by accident produces a balk. Sparky Lyle did it against the Yankees in 1969: oops! It was the top of the eighth on June 21, 1969 and the resulting run tied the game, 2–2. The Yankees took a 5–2 lead in the top of the 11th, despite losing a baserunner to a hidden ball trick. The Red Sox scored four times in the bottom of the 11th, winning it on George Thomas's two-run single to center field.

A decade earlier, on August 20, 1959, there were runners on first and second and two outs (there would have been three, but when Casale picked Kansas City's Jerry Snyder off first base, Boston first baseman Vic Wertz dropped the ball). Unnerved a bit? Casale walked the next man and then gave up a homer to Bob Cerv. After another walk and a single, Nelson Chittum came on in relief. He walked the first batter, intentionally, then dropped the ball, balking home another run. For an encore, Sammy White allowed a passed ball for yet another run before the fire got put out. In the end, the Red Sox won, 11–10.

In 1962, on the 19th of August, Bill Monbouquette managed to balk by falling down on the pitching rubber with the ball still in his hand, setting up the run that proved the winner when the next batter hit into a run-producing fielder's choice.

Balk, balk, balk. Washington's Camilo Pascual balked three times on May 22, 1959—in the first, second, and fifth innings. Only the fifth-inning balk ultimately cost him, but it was a one-run game, a 4–3 win for the Red Sox.

Two balks which helped the Red Sox win: Atley Donald balked in the go-ahead run during the sixth inning on June 26, 1943 and Joe Coleman balked in the run that proved the difference in the May 7, 1968 game in Washington. We'd prefer to downplay Andy Karl's ninth inning balk in 1943 and Mickey Harris's game-deciding balk in 1948.

The Red Sox had a 4–0 lead against the Angels on May 2, 1970 and Jim Fregosi was struck out for the second out of the fourth inning. Wait a minute! No, he wasn't. It was called a balk. Reprieved, Fregosi singled and drove in the baserunner who'd been advanced to second base. It was the first run of a three-run inning, the first three of eight unanswered runs that gave California the 8–4 win.

A balk that was a walk and not a balk

Harold Kaese recounts the amusing tale that helped the Red Sox. June 6, 1973, in the fifth inning in Boston. Tommy Harper was due up and Ken Wright had just walked two Red Sox, so the Royals brought in Charlie Bird to pitch. He threw three balls to Harper, then dropped the ball. Kaese says, "When the ball rolled towards third base, it was ruled ball four, not a balk. The umpire thought it had missed the inside corner by 80 feet." The net result was even better—the bases were loaded and a subsequent sacrifice fly scored a run. The Red Sox won it in the 10th on Bob Montgomery's home run.

Wild pitches that won pennants for Boston

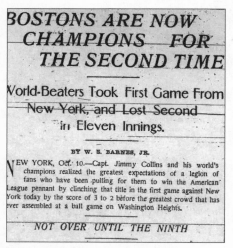

BOSTONS ARE NOW CHAMPIONS FOR THE SECOND TIME

World-Beaters Took First Game From New York, and Lost Second in Eleven Innings.

BY W. S. BARNES, JR.

NEW YORK, Oct. 10.—Capt. Jimmy Collins and his world's champions realized the greatest expectations of a legion of fans who have been pulling for them to win the American League pennant by clinching that title in the first game against New York today by the score of 3 to 2 before the greatest crowd that has ever assembled at a ball game on Washington Heights.

NOT OVER UNTIL THE NINTH

Winning the pennant in 1904. The Giants refused to play the A.L. champions.

The first was in 1904, when Happy Jack Chesbro uncorked a ninth-inning wild pitch over the head of New York catcher Red Kleinow. Lou Criger scored from third base and Bill Dinneen held the New Yorkers scoreless in the bottom of the ninth. The win gave Boston the pennant.

Then, in 1967, on the final game of the year, Minnesota's Al Worthington came on in sixth-inning relief of Dean Chance. The Sox had just scored three times to overtake the 2–0 Twins lead on Lonborg's bunt single, Adair's single, Dalton Jones's single, and Yaz's single, and Harrelson's reaching on a fielder's choice. Worthington threw a wild pitch, letting Yaz take third, then threw another wild pitch, letting Yaz score with the fourth of the five runs the Sox scored. Boston won the game, 5–3.

The final game might not have been so fateful if the Red Sox hadn't already lost three games that year due to the wild pitch—each one at Anaheim Stadium to the Angels: Jim Lonborg's in the bottom of the ninth on May 3, 1967 in Anaheim (a 2–1 loss), Lee Stange's fourth-inning wild pitch on August 11, 1967 in Anaheim (which gave the Angels the only run in a 1–0 game), and Jim Lonborg's fourth-inning wild pitch just two days later—on August 13, 1967 in Anaheim—which gave the Angels the third run of their 3–2 win.

And back in 1949, the Red Sox might have won the pennant if Mel Parnell hadn't thrown a September 28 wild pitch with two outs in the bottom of the ninth inning and the based loaded with Senators. The score was tied, but the wild pitch cost the Sox the ballgame.

Some other wild ones, all in the '60s

Billy Gardner scored on Hoyt Wilhelm's 10-inning wild pitch on June 22, 1962. Boston 2, Baltimore 1.

Ramon Mejias, pinch-running for Bob Tillman who had tripled, scored on Whitey Ford's April 16, 1964 11th-inning wild one. Boston 4, New York 3.

June 24, 1964. After giving up a single to White Sox leadoff hitter Don Buford, Ed Connolly (1–5 on the season) threw a wild pitch and Buford took second. Then he threw a wild pitch and Buford took third. With two more wide of the strike zone mixed in, Floyd Robinson walked. Connolly then threw another wild pitch and Robinson took second. Buford held at third, but scored on a sac fly. A single brought in Robinson, and Connolly recorded another out. Then Ron Hansen hit an inside-the-park home run. After a walk and a single, manager Johnny Pesky had seen enough. Connolly was taken out of the game, but he took with him a 1–6 record at day's end.

Unable to cash in were the Red Sox on August 29, 1965 at Comiskey. Eddie Fisher came on to defend a 3–2 White Sox lead after Boston's first batter in the eighth singled. He promptly threw a wild pitch and Frank Malzone scurried to second. He walked the batter, Tony Conigliaro, and then threw another wild pitch. Both runners advanced. Felix Mantilla hit one hard to second baseman Buford, who threw home to get Malzone. Tony C took third. Fisher threw a third wild pitch and Mantilla took second, but Conig was held at third. A grounder to first base resulted in Conigliaro being thrown out at the plate. Yaz grounded out. The score held, 3–2, despite three wild pitches all in the same inning with runners on base each time.

Dave Morehead threw one wild pitch, but saw two runs score. What the heck, it was already a 9–0 game, with the White Sox batting in the bottom of the eighth. Tommie Agee walked. Don Buford singled. The two executed a perfect double steal, and then both scored on Morehead's wild pitch. 11–0. Morehead retired the next three batters in order. May 30, 1966.

ERA leaders

Dutch Leonard's 0.96 ERA in 1914 set the all-time major league mark. Red Sox pitchers with low ERAs include Joe Wood (1.49 in 1915, 1.68 with a losing record in 1910, and 1.91 in 1912). Cy Young had a 1.62 ERA in 1901, 1.97 in 1904, 1.82 in 1905, 1.99 in 1907, and 1.26 in 1908. That makes five seasons of ERA's under 2.00 (his entire career with Boston saw him with an ERA of exactly 2.00).

Eddie Cicotte posted a 1.97 ERA in 1909 and Ray Collins posted a 1.62 in 1910. Four years in a row, the Red Sox had a sub-2.00 pitcher: Rube Foster recorded a 1.65 ERA in 1914, Ernie Shore recorded a 1.64 ERA in 1915, Babe Ruth recorded a 1.75 ERA in 1916, and Carl Mays recorded a 1.74 ERA in 1917. In 1915, with both Smoky Joe Wood and Ernie Shore under 2.00, the Sox had two. The only other Red Sox pitchers who achieved sub-2.00 ERA seasons were Luis Tiant (1.91 in 1972), Roger Clemens (1.93 in 1990), and Pedro Martinez (1.74 in 2000).

Through 2007, Jonathan Papelbon's career 1.62 ERA is the lowest earned run average of any pitcher in major league history, based on throwing 150 or more innings.

No-hitters and near no-hitters

Cy Young—May 5, 1904 (perfect game) [catcher: Lou Criger]
Jesse Tannehill—August 17, 1904 [catcher: Duke Farrell]

Bill Dinneen—September 27, 1905 [catcher: Lou Criger]
Cy Young—June 30, 1908 [catcher: Lou Criger]
Joe Wood—July 29, 1911 [catcher: Bill Carrigan]
Rube Foster—June 21, 1916 [catcher: Bill Carrigan]
Dutch Leonard—August 30, 1916 [catcher: Bill Carrigan]
Ernie Shore—June 23, 1917 (perfect game)* [catcher: Pinch Thomas]
Dutch Leonard—June 3, 1918 [catcher: Wally Schang]
Howard Ehmke—September 7, 1923 [catcher: Val Picinich]
Mel Parnell—July 14, 1956 [catcher: Sammy White]
Earl Wilson—June 26, 1962 [catcher: Bob Tillman]
Bill Monbouquette—August 1, 1962 [catcher: Jim Pagliaroni]
Dave Morehead—September 16, 1965 [catcher: Bob Tillman]
Matt Young—April 12, 1992* [catcher: John Flaherty]
Hideo Nomo—April 4, 2001 [catcher: Jason Varitek]
Derek Lowe—April 27, 2002 [catcher: Jason Varitek]
Devern Hansack—October 1, 2006* [catcher: Jason Varitek]
Clay Buchholz—September 1, 2007 [catcher: Jason Varitek]
Jon Lester—May 19, 2008 [catcher: Jason Varitek]

*No matter what the Commissioner may rule, pitching a complete game without allowing any hits is here considered a no-hitter. Matt Young only threw eight and Devern Hansack only threw five; in each case, though, they threw a complete game. And didn't allow a hit. Ernie Shore came into the game with a man on first base, and recorded 27 consecutive outs. You can't throw a more perfect game.

Leonard's no-hitter was an interesting one in that it came in his second start of the day. He began the first game, but "I didn't even last an inning, or even what might be called part of an inning. They made four runs against me, and I couldn't get one of them out. Perhaps Carrigan was peeved. I would not have blamed him if he was, but he never showed the least sign. 'Get into a dry shirt,' said he, 'and be ready to pitch the second game,' as he waved me out of the box. An hour and a half later, I came back and pitched my first no-hit, no-run game. Wasn't that giving a fellow a show?" [*Boston Globe*, August 27, 1924]

Buchholz's no-hitter came in just his second major league start.

Catching no-hitters

An integral part of any no-hitter is the the man who's calling the pitches: the catcher. To better acknowledge this, we've added the names of the catchers to the no-hitters in the list presented above. We can easily see that two Boston catchers have each caught three no-hitters: Lou Criger and Bill Carrigan. Jason Varitek has caught four, and by our more accurate definition, Varitek has in fact caught five.

Monbo's turnaround

Prior to Monbo's 1962 no-hitter, he'd yielded 17 runs in his previous four starts, throwing just a total of 10⅔ innings. Fifteen of those runs were earned. For years, he held the Red Sox record for most strikeouts in a game—17 (May 12, 1961), but he never struck out more than seven batters in any of his games the rest of the season.

Near no-hitters

In an August 29, 2000 contest with Tampa Bay, Pedro Martinez hit the first Devil Rays batter he faced, Gerald Williams. Williams charged the mound and and knocked down Pedro before Jason Varitek intervened. A running game-long war between the two clubs resulted in eight ejections, but as the game wore on, Pedro mowed down batter after batter, including 13 who struck out. He had a no-hitter going after eight innings. John Flaherty was the first batter up in the ninth and after a few pitches to Flaherty, the religious necklace Pedro wore came apart. He took it off and stuffed it in his pocket. Next pitch? A clean single.

The *Red Sox Media Guide* lists more than 25 one-hitters thrown since 1950. Some notable earlier one-hitters were George Winter (4/18/1905), Cy Young (5/30/1908), Frank Arellanes (9/4/1908), Charley Hall (8/27/1910), Ray Collins (8/30/1910—just three days after Collins), Joe Wood (7/7/1911—just three weeks before his no-hitter), Babe Ruth (7/11/1917) and Rube Foster (8/6/1917). Foster's one-hitter was a 2–0 loss; he walked two, gave up a two-run double, and then never yielded another hit.

A perfect game within a game?

Late in the 1919 season, Waite Hoyt pitched nine perfect innings against the Yankees, but only after he'd given up a run in the second. Boston tied the game in the top of the ninth, 1–1, on Babe Ruth's majestic home run that cleared the right-field roof at the Polo Grounds. It was the first one to ever clear the roof—and was Ruth's 28th homer of the year, setting a new major league record. Hoyt didn't let a single runner reach base from the fourth through the 12th innings, but when Boston failed to score in the 13th, he faltered. Wally Pipp tripled and scored on Pratt's sacrifice fly to Boston's Babe Ruth in left. Hoyt had pitched nine perfect innings, but lost the game.

Pedro's masterful year

After his 1999 season, people thought Pedro Martinez could hardly have a better season. He'd won the Cy Young Award, was the MVP of the All-Star Game, and was named AL Pitcher of the Year by *The Sporting News*. His 313 strikeouts led the league with an average of 13.2 Ks per nine innings pitched. His 23–4 record was best in baseball. So was his 2.07 ERA. Pedro only allowed 6.75 hits per nine innings pitched, and his WHIP (walks plus hits per innings pitched) was just .923, in part reflecting his strikeouts to walks ratio of 8.46.

What did he do the following year? He didn't win as many games (he was 18–6), but then again neither did the Red Sox, winning 86 games instead of the 92 they'd won in 1999. Pedro arguably pitched better, though. His ERA was just 1.74 (compared to 2.07 the year before and compated to a league average of 4.91), his WHIP was only .737 (compared to .923), his strikeout to walks ratio was 8.88 (better than 1999's 8.46), and he only allowed 5.31 hits per nine innings pitched. Pedro only allowed opposing batters to hit .167 off him, the stingiest performance by a major league pitcher since records began to be kept in the 1800s. His on-base percentage against was .213, the lowest since 1884 (and conditions were so different then as to be questionably comparable). He won himself another unanimous Cy Young Award.

In seven seasons pitching for the Red Sox, Pedro only lost 37 ballgames. And several of those were due to exceptionally poor run support. He won 117. With a 78–22 record in his first 100 decisions, he established a mark for the best start, ever, of any pitcher in his first 100 decisions with a single team.

The best start ever for a Red Sox rookie pitcher

You can't hope to start much better than did Boo Ferriss in 1945. After walking the bases loaded in his first inning of major league ball, Ferriss managed to recover and shut out the Philadelphia Athletics. His second outing was at Fenway and he shut out the Yankees. He'd pitched two complete games in the major leagues and still not surrendered a run. After four scoreless innings, making it 22⅓ consecutive scoreless innings at the start of a career, he finally gave up a run, about halfway into a game in Detroit. He won it, though, 8–2, and he kept on winning—eight straight games, beating every team in the league the first time he faced them.

Four of them were shutouts. Ferriss finished 1945 with a 21–10 record and a 2.96 earned run average, pitching for a seventh-place ballclub.

Ambidextrous pitchers

Like Greg Harris some years later, Boo Ferriss was ambidextrous. Like Harris, Ferriss never had the chance to try going both ways with the Red Sox. Despite batting left-handed, Ferriss only threw right-handed throughout his career, which was exclusively with Boston. The other one in the Ferriss/Harris duo, Greg Harris, pitched for the Red Sox 1989–1994 and apparently not one of his managers had enough of a sense of adventure to let him throw left-handed if only to one batter.

Harris signed with the Expos in 1995, and Pedro Martinez was pitching for Montreal on September 28, 1995. The Expos were in last place, but with four games left to play still had a chance to take fourth place from Florida. The score was 9–3 Cincinnati after eight innings, and Greg Harris came in to pitch the ninth. He got Reggie Harris to ground out, then turned around and pitched left-handed—and walked Hal Morris. But he stuck with the southpaw style and got Eddie Taubensee to ground out weakly, catcher to first. Then Harris turned back around and threw righty to Bret Boone, who grounded back to the mound. The last time an ambidextrous pitcher had worked in a major league was apparently Elton "Ice Box" Chamberlain of the 1888 St. Louis Browns. The Red Sox had it in their power to do it with two different pitchers, and blew it both times.

Was Bill Dinneen ambidextrous? Maybe not, but he did bat left-handed once in a 1904 ballgame.

Pitchers who hit batters

Bronson Arroyo tied a Red Sox record in 2004, hitting an even 20 opposing batters. The team record had stood since 1923, when Howard Ehmke accomplished the same feat.

Pitchers who hit walk-off HRs

As best we can reconstruct, it has only happened four times in the first 107 years of Red Sox history, and all four times were packed into the space of 377 days.

Wes Ferrell—August 22, 1934   Wes Ferrell—July 22, 1935
Wes Ferrell—July 21, 1935   Jack Wilson—September 2, 1935

And guess who the starting pitcher was the day Jack Wilson hit his? Wes Ferrell.

In the first of the four games, Ferrell hit a homer in the bottom of the eighth to tie the game against the White Sox, 2–2. He came to bat again in the bottom of the 10th. Again, he faced righthander Les Tietje and again he hit one out. The *Chicago Tribune* noted, "Both sailed over the left center field wall, the final one being such a long drive that the Chicago outfielders were on their way off the field before it disappeared from view."

The next year, he did it two games in a row. On July 21, he came to bat as a pinch-hitter. It was the bottom of the ninth and the Tigers had a two-run lead. There were two runners on base, but there were two outs, and Lefty Grove was due up. Ferrell was sent in to face Tommy Bridges. Mickey Cochrane told Bridges to walk Wes—since three times before Ferrell had homered against Bridges in key situations. Bridges argued that it couldn't happen four times, and Cochrane relented in the conference at the mound. Bridges' first pitch was hit over the left-field Wall for a three-run homer to win the game.

The very next day, now facing the St. Louis Browns, Ferrell got the start. Both he and Browns pitcher Dick Coffman pitched wonderful games, and the score was tied 1–1 after 8½ innings. Up in the bottom of the ninth, Ferrell hit another walk-off, another one high over Fenway's left-field Wall. The Red Sox would not win back-to-back games on walk-off homers until May 10 and 11, 2005—some 70 years later, and neither of those was hit by a pitcher.

Wes Ferrell was the starter on September 2, 1935 but had no chance at late inning heroics since he was drummed out of the box in the third inning. It was 7–0 Washington, all the runs charged to Mr. Ferrell. Jack Wilson took over for the Red Sox. The Sox scored once in the fourth, twice in the sixth, and five times in the eighth (Joe Cronin's grand slam the big blow). Tied in the 11th inning, Red Sox rookie righthander Wilson greeted Senators reliever Phil Hensiek with a "screaming home run into the right center field bleachers." [*Washington Post*]

And we've been waiting more than 70 years for another walk-off home run from a Red Sox pitcher.

Last pitchers who hit a home run for the Red Sox

In the last 35 years, there haven't been all that many home runs hit by Red Sox pitchers, primarily (of course) because of the advent of the designated hitter in 1973. And there was a huge gap from September 1972 (when three were hit—the last without the DH) until May 2006 when Josh Beckett hit one out. Here's the list of all the ones hit from 1971 forward.

Sonny Siebert 4/08/1971	Sonny Siebert 9/02/1971
Sonny Siebert 4/28/1971	Marty Pattin 7/01/1972
Sonny Siebert 5/23/1971	Sonny Siebert 9/07/1972
Sonny Siebert 6/26/1971	Bill Lee 9/11/1972
Ken Tatum 8/12/1971	Marty Pattin 9/26/1972
Gary Peters 8/25/1971	Josh Beckett 5/20/2006
Sonny Siebert 9/02/1971	

Beckett's home run came in a game against the Phillies in Philadelphia. He'd singled and driven in a run in the sixth to tie the game, and then scored a few batters later on a David Ortiz sacrifice fly. Up again against Phillies starter Brett Myers, Beckett homered to left-center field with one out in the seventh. He won the 8–4 game. It was his second career home run.

With seven of the 14 homers since 1971 coming from Sonny Siebert, it's a fair guess that he hit pretty well. He only had a .173 career average, but hit 12 home runs in all, half of them in 1971.

Red Sox pitchers are going to be lucky to hit homers in the years to come. During spring training 2007, both Josh Beckett and Daisuke Matsuzaka were instructed not to even swing at pitches during their interleague at-bats against the Mets and Dodgers for fear they might strain a muscle. While very understandable, and perhaps a wise precaution, imagine if pitcher Babe Ruth had abided by those instructions during the regular season.

Declining to swing the bat doesn't necessarily hurt you, though. In the March 16 exhibition ballgame (called due to rain), Matsuzaka kept the bat loosely on his shoulder. After two quick strikes, the Dodgers pitcher walked him, and he scored shortly afterward on a Hinske homer. Then the game got rained out. Daisuke swung at a pitch in the 2007 World Series, though, and singled to left field to drive in two runs.

Most hits by a relief pitcher who didn't start a game:

Dick Radatz 19, 16 of which were during his years with the Red Sox	Cecil Upshaw 12
Sparky Lyle 15, eight of which were during his years with the Red Sox	Kent Tekulve 10

Most HR by a relief pitcher who didn't start a game? There are quite a few with one home run. Dick Radatz is among them.

Pitchers with infinite ERAs in their Red Sox career

Left-handed pitcher Matt Perisho recorded an earned run average of infinity in 2005 while pitching for the Red Sox. Many of us could probably have done the same. After six innings, Baltimore led Boston 4–3 in the September 2 night game at Fenway Park. Lenny DiNardo was done for the night, and Terry Francona asked Chad Harville to take over. He walked first baseman Chris Gomez. Harville then got Luis Matos to hit one back to the mound, and he threw out Gomez at second. Matos reached first on the fielder's choice. Switch-hitter Brian Roberts was up next, and the Sox turned to Perisho. Roberts doubled to center field and Matos scored. Chad Bradford came in to pitch to the next batter. Melvin Mora grounded out 5–2, but Miguel Tejada singled to center, scoring Roberts. That was the only time Perisho pitched in all of 2005. Charged with one earned run in zero innings pitched (he only faced the one batter), that left Matt with an infinite ERA. He'd appeared in 177 major league games, with a career ERA of 6.39, but with the Red Sox he achieved a certain sort of perverse perfection.

One of the easiest saves ever

Willie Banks really lucked out on July 23, 2002. Tampa Bay was visiting Boston, and Red Sox starting pitcher Tim Wakefield had given up four runs through five innings. The Sox, though, had a 16–4 lead at the time. In came Banks to start the sixth. Of course, Wakefield got the win. Under the save rules, Banks earned the save by pitching three innings (in fact, he pitched very well—two hits and no runs in four full innings). But it wasn't exactly the same as coming into a bases-loaded situation in a 1–0 game in the bottom of the ninth and holding the lead for your team.

A save of a different sort

Actually, more than Al Nipper, it was more that the Twins' desire for extra revenue cost them a win. The Red Sox were retiring the numbers of Ted Williams and Joe Cronin in a pregame ceremony on May 29, 1984. With the tribute to Ted and Joe, they figured it would take an hour and the game would get underway at 8:30. But it was a rainy evening and Cronin, who was feeling ill, did not speak. The ceremony ended before 8:00, and both teams were ready to play, anxious to get the game in before the rains came in earnest. But the Twins TV station had rejiggered their programming and sold the time up to 8:30, and so that's when play began. Minnesota held a 5–0 lead, driving starter Mike Brown from the mound with one out in the top of the fourth. Al Nipper, on in relief, was poised to start the fifth. Assessing the situation, he made sure he gummed up his spikes with mud and then complained that the mound was unplayable. Drying agent didn't work, and (after a delay of 101 minutes) the game was called. Good acting on Nipper's part, but had the whole game not been delayed at least an extra 15 minutes, the fifth could likely have been played and the Twins would have had a W.

Holding a lead

The 1950 Red Sox never lost a game when leading after eight innings—not once.

Three pitches, three outs

It's only happened about three dozen times in major league history. Sonny Siebert did it for the Red Sox on May 11, 1969, throwing three pitches in the second inning of the game against California. The Sox were victims once, too, on April 14, 1910 when Hippo Vaughn retired three Red Sox in the 10th inning.

A steal of home does in Dutch Leonard

Maybe Dutch Leonard needed to work a bit on his move to the plate. In the eighth inning of a tie game on July 11, 1913, Cleveland's Ray Chapman tried to steal home and almost made it. Almosts don't count, though. He was out. The game remained tied until the top of the 15th, the score 5–5.

Cleveland had the bases loaded and two outs. Ivy Olson was the runner on third. All three runners started "doing a lot of hopping around"—hopping, hoping to distract the left-handed Leonard who inevitably had to have his back to third base while making his delivery. Olson in particular faked a run in towards the plate on each of Leonard's first three pitches to the batter, Jack Graney. Leonard, for whatever reason, "persisted in taking a long windup on every ball pitched." On the fourth one, with the count 2–1, Olson broke for the plate and "beat the ball to the plate by a yard." The Indians took the lead, and Graney worked a walk. With the bases loaded once more, Grover Land singled in two more runs while Graney took third. Then Graney ran to try to steal home, but he left a split-second too soon and Leonard caught him heading for the plate. A rundown ensued, but Graney scored. The 9–5 lead held, and Leonard lost.

Best winning percentage by a Red Sox reliever (25 or more decisions)

Charley "Sea Lion" Hall (24–4) .857   "Smoky" Joe Wood (20–8) .714
Rich "El Guapo" Garces (23–8) .742

Most wins in a row

The longest streak of consecutive victories by a Red Sox pitcher came in 1912 when Smoky Joe Wood won 16 in a row. After a 4–3 loss to Philadelphia on the Fourth of July, Wood won 16 in a row beginning with a 5–1 win over St. Louis. He beat the Browns, then Detroit, Chicago, Cleveland, Chicago, St. Louis, Cleveland, Detroit, St. Louis, Detroit, Cleveland, Chicago, New York, Washington, Chicago, and St. Louis. There were six shutouts in the streak, and over the 16 games Wood yielded just 27 runs.

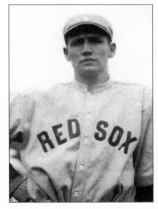

Smoky Joe Wood.

The second longest Sox streak was by Roger Clemens, kicking off the 1986 season. He didn't lose a game in April, nor in May, nor in June. After the first half of the season, Clemens' record was 14–0. It was only on July 2, and only in the top of the eighth in a 4–2 game against Toronto, that Rocket Roger lost his first game. Clemens finished the season 24–4.

Ellis Kinder won 13 games in a row in 1949. He'd won 12 starts in a row, starting on July 19, and every one was a complete game win—one of them a 12-inning game. On top of that dozen, he won yet another game he'd entered as a reliever. The opposition was getting desperate. New York's Ralph Houk invited Kinder out the night before the September 24 game and got him totally drunk. It didn't matter. He never let the Yankees get more than one hit an inning and shut them out, 3–0, for his 13th consecutive win. On the year, he had 30 starts and 13 relief appearances. 19 complete games and a league-leading six shutouts.

Cy Young (1901), Dutch Leonard (1914), and Boo Ferriss (1946) each won an even dozen in a row. Tex Hughson (1942), Jack Kramer (1948), Roger Moret (1973), and Bob Stanley (1978) each won 11 straight. The ones who won 10 in a row were Cy Young (1902), Boo Ferriss (1946—one of two long streaks in the same year), Ike Delock (1958), Dick Radatz (1963), Mike Boddicker (1990), and Tim Wakefield (1995).

Most wins in a row against a given team

Ellis Kinder holds this record. From July 22, 1948 until he finally lost one on May 12, 1953, Kinder won 18 decisions in a row against the Chicago White Sox. That was more than four full years of wins without a single defeat. Almost overlapping with Kinder, Mel Parnell won 17 decisions in a row against the Washington Senators from July 8, 1948 until he lost one on September 20, 1952.

Smoky Joe Wood won 15 in a row against St. Louis back in 1911–14.

Most wins in back-to-back seasons

Babe Ruth won 23 games in 1916 and 24 in 1917. Not one Red Sox pitcher has matched the total of 47 in back-to-back seasons since Ruth. Clemens came closest with 24 in 1986 and 20 in 1987. Of course, not even Ruth could top Cy Young, who won 33 in 1901 and 32 in 1902, for a total of 65! And then won 28 in 1903 and…obviously continuing to decline from one year to the next, only 26 in 1904.

Most losses in a row

Joe Harris won not one of his first 15 starts in 1906. He'd won his last game in 1905. After his August 8, 1906 win he lost his next 13 decisions and the team finally decided it had seen enough. Harris finished his major league career with a lifetime record of 3–30. That's not a typo. That is three wins and 30 losses.

Most saves in a month

Bob Stanley had 12 saves in August 1980. It was a month in which the Sox played well, winning 20 games and losing only seven.

Most saves in a month by a rookie

Jonathan Papelbon, 10, in 2006. Papelbon also holds club records for the most saves in a row to start a season: 20, and the most saves in his rookie season, 35, both in 2006. Thought of as a starter beginning in 2007, the idea was abandoned before the season began and he recorded an ERA of just 1.85, while saving 37 games for the championship team. In the postseason, he was 1–0, with four saves (including three of the four World Series games).

Saves to wins

Derek Lowe was a reliever when he first came to the Red Sox in 1997. He was given 10 starts the following year, but ended with a 3–9 record in a year the Red Sox made the playoffs (albeit briefly). From 1999–2001, he was a very successful reliever—only starting three games, all in 2001—recording 15 saves, a league-leading 42 saves, and 24 saves, respectively. His record over the five seasons with the Sox was 20–34. Then he was made into a starter, and posted a 21–8 mark with a 2.58 ERA in 2002. The 20-plus wins made him the first pitcher ever to save 20 or more games one year, then win 20 or more the next.

A win, a loss, a save, and a blown save all in the same series

Collect the Whole Set Department: In the same Yankees-Red Sox series in July 2003, Byung-Hyun Kim had a win, a loss, a save, and a blown save. The night of July 25 at Fenway, Kim came into a 3–3 tie to pitch the ninth inning and gave up a run, taking the loss. During the July 26 day game, Kim came into the eighth inning of a game the Red Sox were winning, 4–3, allowed an inherited runner to score (thus tagged with a blown save), but pitched 1⅓ innings and earned a win when David Ortiz singled in Jeremy Giambi to win the game in the bottom of the ninth. July 27, he came into the game the Red Sox were leading 6–4 and only gave up one run; he earned a save.

Beating the same team in three different parks, all in the same season

Ray Culp of Boston beat the White Sox on 6/21/1968 at Comiskey Park, on 8/8/1968 at County Stadium in Milwaukee, and on 8/12/1968 at Fenway Park.

A different number of runs every game, for 13 consecutive games

Starting on July 16, 2007, the Red Sox scored a different number of runs in each of the next 13 games they played: 4, 3, 5, 2, 10, 11, 8, 6, 1, 0, 14, 7, 12. Fans avidly following the scoring in this streak were sorely disappointed that they failed to score 9, 13, or more than 13 runs on July 29, when they lost to Tampa Bay, 5–2.

Worst run support for a Boston pitcher

When Joe Harris lost the September 22, 1906 game to Cleveland, 7–0, it was the eighth shutout he'd lost in 1906. None were close-scoring affairs. Harris ended the season 2–21. The two wins came in the middle of the season, on July 30 (Harris pitched well but was yanked in the sixth after walking three batters on 12 straight pitches) and on August 8, when he threw an astonishing four-hit 1–0 shutout of the Cleveland club. Harris had an acceptable earned run average of 3.52, but some truly terrible run support.

Worst won-loss record despite truly excellent pitching

What can you say about Smoky Joe Wood in 1910? His ERA was 1.68. But he lost more games than he won. The Red Sox as a team won 81–72, but Wood was 12–13. The team scored more runs than its opponents, both at home and on the road, 640–565. But things just didn't fall right for Wood, who finished the season 12–13. He was only one of three Sox starters with ERAs under 2.00. Ray Collins posted a 1.62 ERA and Charley Hall a 1.91. Neither of them won all that many games, either. Collins was 13–11 and Hall was 12–9. Wood's problem was more in terms of defensive support: In the 10 starts he lost, the Sox scored just 17 runs total, but Smoky Joe saw 19 errors committed behind him.

Wakefield surrenders six HR in one game, but wins

Tim Wakefield let the Tigers maul him for six home runs in five innings of work on Sunday, August 8, 2005—but Boston beat back Detroit 11–9 and Wakefield got the win. Wakefield tied a major league record (post-1900) in the process. The last time another pitcher had given up six homers was when George Carter of the Philadelphia Athletics did so September 24, 1940, in the first game of a doubleheader. (Guess who was hitting then? The Boston Red Sox.)

Wake's ERA rose a bit, with seven earned runs, but they were all solo shots but one. He gave up one in the first, two in the second, two in the third, and one in the fifth.

The Sox scored early and often enough, so when Wakefield left after five, he left with the lead and wound up with the win. "I was very lucky," he said after the game.

The most extra-base hits given up by a pitcher in one game

It's a fair guess that Curt Schilling would rather not hold this American League record: 10, August 10, 2006 in Kansas City.

Red Sox rookie pitching records

Most wins ever by a Red Sox rookie pitcher: 21, by Boo Ferriss in 1945. This despite surrendering more hits (263) than any before or since.

Most losses ever by a rookie pitcher: 19, by Frederick Davis "Ted" Wingfield, in 1925. It was his fifth year with major league appearances but officially his rookie year. Wingfield lost 16 more the following year, on his way to a 24–44 career record. It didn't help that his 1925 strikeout-to-walk ratio was upside-down; walking 92 while only striking out 30. His ERA wasn't disastrous, though, at 3.96—but that was a function of his pitching so many innings. He also holds the rookie record for the most runs allowed in one season: 145. A lot of those runs were unearned runs; he was charged with 112 earned runs. This was a year the Red Sox were pretty poor competitors, finishing last with a 47–105 record.

Most strikeouts by a rookie pitcher: 201, by Daisuke Matsuzaka in 2007—shattering the old mark of 155, by Ken Brett in 1970. Brett had appeared in the 1967 World Series and had five decisions in 1969, but 1970 was his official rookie year and he struck out 155 while walking 79 batters. He posted an 8–9 record with a 4.07 ERA. Brett was a left-hander. The record for right-handed K's by a rookie (144) was shared by two pitchers, both Red Sox righties: Dutch Leonard (1913) and Dick Radatz (1962).

The rookie record for the most walks ever? Don Schwall, 110 in 1961. Despite that, he had a successful W-L mark of 15–7 (3.22 ERA).

Best ERA by a rookie pitcher: Ernie Shore's 2.00 in 1914.

Buck O'Brien holds two rookie records: most innings pitched (275⅔) and most games started (34), both naturally from the same year, 1912.

Two pitchers share the complete game record for rookies, with 26 apiece: George Winter (1901) and Boo Ferriss (1945). Buck O'Brien was just one behind, with 25 in 1912.

The most games in which a Red Sox rookie appeared: 66, Hideki Okajima (2007). The mark for a right-hander is held by Jonathan Papelbon: 59, in 2006.

Shutouts in major league debut

There are seven Red Sox pitchers who threw a shutout in their major league debut. The last one was Billy Rohr, who one-hit the Yankees in New York on April 14, 1967. No one's done it for the 40 years since.

First up was Floyd Myron "Rube" Kroh of Friendship, New York. On September 30, near the end of the worst season in team history, Kroh threw a 2–0 two-hitter in St. Louis. It took one hour and 26 minutes, and his name appeared spelled as Crow in a number of the next day's boxscores. His first start of 1907 came on August 18, and was a 2–1 win over St. Louis, a seven-hitter. He lost his next four starts and found himself on the Cubs come 1908.

Larry Pape won his first game on July 6, 1909. It was also a 2–0 game, against Washington. Pape gave up four hits. His catcher was Tom Madden, catching his first full game for Boston, too.

He won his only other start of the year, six-hitting Washington in an 11-inning 3–1 win. The only run the Nationals scored in that one came on an error Pape himself committed. Oddly, the winning hit came off the bat of Doc Gessler, who had been traded to Washington *before* the game but was allowed to play for Boston nevertheless.

Thomas J. "Buck" O'Brien, the pride of Brockton, arrived in Philadelphia from Denver and won his first game the very next day, like Kroh and Pape by a 2–0 score, on September 9, 1911. The Philadelphia Athletics got six hits off Buck.

In a September 17, 1934 road game, rookie lefthander George Hockette allowed St. Louis two singles (one in the eighth and one in the ninth) and no runs. The Red Sox won, 3–0.

Boo Ferriss threw his first game on April 29, 1945. As outlined above, he walked the bases loaded in the first inning, pitched out of trouble, scattered five hits, and won the game, 2–0.

Dave Morehead, a graduate of the same Hoover High School in San Diego as Ted Williams, threw his shutout (3–0) in Washington on April 13, 1963. It was a five-hitter. The 19-year-old struck out 10 Senators at D. C. Stadium.

There were three other Sox pitchers who threw a shutout in their first starts, but who didn't make the above list because they'd been used in relief prior to that first start. They are:

Ben Flowers, who beat St. Louis 5–0 on eight hits on August 5, 1953,

Russ Kemmerer, who beat Baltimore 4–0 on just one hit on July 18, 1954, and

Jim Wright, who beat Chicago 3–0 on seven hits on May 6, 1978.

Throwing a complete game shutout in your last major league appearance

Even rarer than hitting a home run in your final at-bat in the major leagues is throwing a shutout in your last game. Brian Denman is one of just five pitchers to do this. Denman shut out the Yankees, 5–0, on October 2, 1982. It was a six-hitter at Yankee Stadium. Denman improved his record to 3–4 and closed his only major league season with a 4.78 earned run average. He pitched 49 innings in all, and was 0-for-9 at the plate. He never returned to the big leagues.

The longest shutout

The longest Red Sox shutout came on May 11, 1904. Cy Young pitched 15 innings and won the 1–0 game against the visiting Detroit nine. Opposing pitcher Ed Killian merits a nod as well, though he gave up 10 hits to Cy's five. It was the last three Boston hits that did Killian in—a single to Ferris, a single to Ferrell, and a single to Dougherty.

Young also threw a 13-inning shutout. It was on September 9, 1907 against Philadelphia—and no one won. The game ended in a 0–0 tie. Rube Waddell matched Young's work. Boston had four hits; Philadelphia had six. Boston made two errors; Philadelphia made five. Neither pitcher walked a man. Darkness forced an end to the game.

Babe Ruth threw himself a 13-inning shutout, too, on August 15, 1916. Both he and Washington's Walter Johnson allowed eight hits. Johnson walked five, Ruth walked three—but balked once and struck out two to Johnson's five. It was Johnson who gave up the game's lone run, though. Jack Barry singled, but Johnson got the next two batters. Tillie Walker singled to center, and then Larry Gardner singled through the gap in right center for the walk-off win.

The other 13-inning complete game shutout was Ed Durham's, also at Fenway, against the Tigers on September 12, 1931. Durham held the Tigers to five hits, and the Red Sox won it 1–0 when Bill Sweeney doubled to right and took third on a bad throw. Tom Oliver's sacrifice fly scored the winning run.

The most recent extra-inning shutout was Bruce Hurst's, on August 7, 1988. Boston beat Detroit 3–0, in 10 innings in Detroit. Tigers pitcher Jeff Robinson threw an excellent scoreless game through nine, but had to leave after giving up a leadoff double to Mike Greenwell and a bunt single to Ellis Burks. Reliever Guillermo Hernandez let both runs in, and then another one.

Most shutouts in a season

Cy Young won 10 shutouts in 1904 and Joe Wood won 10 in 1912. Babe Ruth won nine in 1916. Carl Mays won eight (1918) and Roger Clemens won eight (1988). Sox pitchers who spun seven shutouts each were Cy Young (1903), Dutch Leonard (1914), Joe Bush (1918), Luis Tiant (1974), and Roger Clemens (1987).

World Series shutouts

There have been 93 World Series shutouts. The only two thrown by pitchers born outside of the US did it for the Red Sox (Cuba's Luis Tiant, 1975) and the White Sox (Venezuela's Freddy Garcia, 2005).

Other shutouts of note

Cy Young had 38 of them. So did Roger Clemens. Smoky Joe had 28 and Tiant 26. The lefty with the most shutouts is Dutch Leonard with 25. Parnell was second with 20. In these days of carefully-monitored pitch counts, shutouts become increasingly rare. Even during his best season, Pedro Martinez only had four—which was enough to lead the league in 2000. Through the 2007 season, Pedro is tied with Babe Ruth for career shutouts with 17.

A double shutout day came on July 17, 1956 when Tommy Brewer shut out Kansas City in the first game, 10–0, and Bob Porterfield shut them out in the second, 1–0—the one run coming on a Ted Williams homer.

In 1940 and in 1964, the Sox were shut out twice in the same day by visiting teams (the White Sox and Indians, respectively).

Three shutouts in a row? On September 19, 20, and 21, 1958, Tommy Brewer, Frank Sullivan, and Ike Delock shut out the Senators three games in a row—each game by the identical 2–0 score. From August 8–11, 1962, Gene Conley, Bill Monbouquette, and Ike Delock whitewashed the opposition three games in a row, and kept it going for the first five innings of the second game on the 11th.

In 1968, Ray Culp threw four shutouts in a row, and by declining scores: September 13 (3–0), September 17 (2–0), September 21 (2–0), and September 25 (1–0). Culp allowed just 18 hits in the four games combined. In 1972, Luis Tiant threw four, too: August 19, August 25, August 29, and September 4.

Charlie Wagner threw back-to-back 1–0 games on June 19 and 24, 1942. Willard Nixon did the same on April 20 and 24, 1955. Cy Young, though, threw three 1–0 games in a row, during just nine days (June 23–July 1, 1903), and his 7–0 shutout on June 13 made it four consecutive shutout starts.

Four shutouts in one season against the Yankees! Mel Parnell, in 1953, shut out the Yankees on July 1 and 9, and September 19 and 25. Not bad! He only started one other game against NY that year, and won that one, too. Bill Monbouquette shut out the Senators four times in 1964, but somehow that doesn't seem to bear the same sense of gravitas.

Tex Hughson threw six shutouts in 1946, and four of them were 1–0 shutouts. The last one, on September 13, clinched the pennant. Joe Bush won five 1–0 games in 1918.

The highest career winning percentage in post-season history

Through 2007, Curt Schilling holds the record for the highest winning percentage in the postseason among pitchers with 10 or more decisions. Schill was 11–2, for an .846 winning percentage. Other pitchers have more wins, but no other has a higher percentage of wins.

Perhaps not surprisingly, among pitchers who have thrown at least 100 innings in the postseason, Mariano Rivera's astonishing 0.77 through 2006 is the lowest ERA ever. Christy Mathewson is second with 1.06, and Schilling is third with 2.23.

The losingest bullpen in Red Sox history

One of the reasons the 1966 season was so bad, and the team lost so many games, was that the bullpen was one of the "losingest" in team history. There were only four bullpens in baseball that were equally as bad during the decade of the Sixties. The 1997 Sox, though, topped the chart with 31 losses ascribed to the pen.

1997 Red Sox (31)   1966 Red Sox (30)   2001 Red Sox (30)

It could be worse, though. There are five teams in history that have topped 35 bullpen losses, with the 2002 Rangers holding the AL record at 38 and the 2004 Rockies holding the major league record with 39.

Thanks to SABR's Malcolm Allen for this tidbit.

A disastrous doubleheader

Be glad if you weren't born yet when this day dawned. The day was June 23, 1931. This was one of those years for the Sox; they finished 45 games out of first place, winning 62 while losing 90 (.408—hey, isn't that at least higher than Ted Williams hit in 1941?) Remarkably, they finished in sixth place and only missed fifth by .001—Detroit and Chicago were even worse. The Cleveland Indians finished 30 games behind—but this day, the Tribe ruled.

It was a doubleheader, in Cleveland. The Indians took the first game 13–0 and won the nightcap 10–0, for a total score on the day of 23–0. Not once, but twice, Boston had batted in vain. They mustered six hits on the day, all singles—five in the opener off Clint Brown and but one hit in the nightcap off Willis "Ace" Hudlin, a single by Earl Webb. Cleveland had 16 hits in game one and 12 more in game two. Brown walked three and Hudlin walked four. Cleveland's shortstop Burnett made three errors, and Boston left 12 on base, but you really don't want to know any more about these games. You really don't—unless you're an Indians fan.

Winning both games of a doubleheader

Two Red Sox pitchers have thrown and won complete games in both games of a doubleheader: Ray Collins on September 22, 1914 (5–3 and 5–0 against the Tigers in Detroit) and Carl Mays on August 30, 1918 (12–0 and 4–1 against Philadephia at Fenway). Others have tried but fallen short, including Mays against the Yankees in 1919, and Buck Newsom against the Athletics in 1937. Ex-Red Soxer Wilbur Wood tried to do it to the Red Sox for Chicago in 1971—but when Wood gave up four runs in the top of the first, left after seven innings, and lost the game, there was no point trying for the second game.

Red Sox ERA champions over the years

1901: Cy Young 1.62	1938: Lefty Grove 3.08	1991: Roger Clemens 2.62
1914: Dutch Leonard 0.96	1939: Lefty Grove 2.54	1992: Roger Clemens 2.41
1915: Joe Wood 1.49	1949: Mel Parnell 2.78	1999: Pedro Martinez 2.07
1916: Babe Ruth 1.75	1972: Luis Tiant 1.91	2000: Pedro Martinez 1.74
1935: Lefty Grove 2.70	1986: Roger Clemens 2.48	2002: Pedro Martinez 2.26
1936: Lefty Grove 2.81	1990: Roger Clemens 1.93	2003: Pedro Martinez 2.22

Strikeout Champions

1901: Cy Young 158	1991: Roger Clemens 241	2000: Pedro Martinez 284
1942: Tex Hughson 113	1996: Roger Clemens 257	2001: Hideo Nomo 220
1967: Jim Lonborg 246	1999: Pedro Martinez 313	2002: Pedro Martinez 239
1988: Roger Clemens 291		

Cy Young Award winners

1967 Jim Lonborg RHP

1986 Roger Clemens RHP [unanimous choice]

1987 Roger Clemens RHP

1991 Roger Clemens RHP

1999 Pedro Martinez RHP

2000 Pedro Martinez RHP [unanimous choice]

Note: the Cy Young Award was initiated in 1956. Starting in 1967, one was presented in each league.

Cy Young.

We couldn't resist adding this, from Bill Deane of the Society for American Baseball Research, regarding Pedro Martinez in 2003: "Pedro Martinez was summarily dismissed by the voters, presumably due to his meager total of 187 innings pitched. Here's another way to look at it. Suppose Martinez had pitched an additional 79 innings for the Red Sox, and in those innings been slammed for 106 hits, including 19 homers, giving up 50 earned runs for a 5.67 ERA.

Would that have made him a more viable Cy Young Award candidate?

Apparently so, because that would give him statistics identical to Roy Halladay's. The writers, in their wisdom, voted for Halladay.

Hit by pitch—in the days before warnings were issued

There were at least three occasions when Red Sox pitchers blew a game by hitting a batter. Way back in 1926, on Memorial Day in the Nation's Capital, Red Ruffing hit Washington's Bucky Harris in the bottom of the 11th inning. The bases were loaded. The Senators won the game, 4–3. It was a bit of a bitter pill; the Red Sox had taken a 3–2 lead in the top of the 11th. After starter Hal Wiltse wilted and walked the first batter of the bottom of the 11th, Sox manager Lee Fohl sent in reliever Ted Wingfield who secured two outs, but also allowed two hits and one run, and intentionally walked the next man, setting the stage. In came Ruffing, who pitched to just the one batter—and hit him.

Yankee Stadium hosted a bruising ballgame on April 19, 1945. Going after Leon Culberson's second-inning fly ball were New York outfielders Johnny Lindell and Herschel Martin. The two collided and Martin "all but had the top of his nose shorn off by Johnny Lindell's gleaming spikes." Yankees physician Robert Emmet Walsh had to put several stitches in Martin's nose. In the seventh inning, Dr. Walsh was called upon again when Red Sox player/manager Joe Cronin broke his right leg sliding hard into second base. And in the bottom of the ninth, with the bases loaded and the score tied 3–3, Boston pitcher Mike Ryba cracked Lindell hard on the wrist as he ducked to avoid one headed for his head. Lindell's wrist was unbroken, and the Yankees won the game.

It was only the second inning when Luis Tiant hit Mike Epstein with a pitch on August 26, 1973. Epstein took his base, moved up a base on a grounder back to the mound, then scored on Leroy Stanton's single to center. It was the only run the Angels scored in a 1–0 loss dealt the Red Sox.

Hitting a batter in a World Series game could be really bad news, but when Rube Foster's pitch hit Philadelphia's Milt Stock during the 1915 World Series, plate umpire Cy Rigler denied Stock the bag since he'd not tried hard enough to evade the pitch. Remembering some later times with regret, Jim Rice never played at all in the 1975 World Series after his wrist was broken late in the season by Vern Ruhle. Jim Ed could have made all the difference in the tightly-fought Series. One wonders, of course, how Boston would have done in 1967 had Tony Conigliaro not been so severely injured on August 18 by Jack Hamilton's pitch that Tony missed the rest of the season. Or whether the 1946 Sox would have prevailed in another seven-game World Series had Ted Williams not suffered a bad injury to his elbow in the days just before the Series.

The Red Sox just missed making the World Series in 1949; one more win during the year would have propelled them to a pennant. Umpire Bill McKinley ruled that a ball which appeared to hit Dom DiMaggio on the hand was a foul ball, and denied him first base. DiMaggio was out the next five games with an injured thumb.

HBP x 3

New York's Tom Morgan put two Red Sox on base in the third inning on the last day of June in 1954. Then he hit Billy Goodman to load the bases. Two runs scored on a ball that rolled through Rizzuto. Morgan then hit Ted Lepcio to re-load the bases—and then hit Milt Bolling to force in a third run. It took Morgan a total of nine pitches to hit the three Boston batters.

On August 26, 1945, going for his 20th win, Boo Ferriss walked five, threw a wild pitch, surrendered six hits, and hit three Philadelphia batters. He hit Ernie Kish once, and hit Irv Hall twice. With the game tied in the bottom of the 10th, Ferriss doubled home the winning run in a walk-off.

Willard Nixon must have wondered if White Sox catcher Sherm Lollar was wearing something magnetic that attracted baseballs—he hit Lollar three times in the June 8, 1956 game—with a fastball, a curveball, and a slider. The last batter hit three times had been Mel Ott in 1938. Jim Lonborg hit Detroit's Bill Freehan (also a catcher) three times in the August 16, 1968 game.

Most batters hit in a ballgame

Looking at just the past 50 years, the most batters hit in a ballgame featuring the Red Sox is six. It happened twice. On May 24, 1998, David Cone of the Yankees hit Troy O'Leary, Mike Benjamin, and Jason Varitek, and Willie Banks hit Lou Merloni. Red Sox pitchers Tim Wakefield and Ron Mahay hit Tim Raines and Chuck Knoblauch—but not, it should be pointed out, until after three Red Sox had first been hit. On July 16, 2002, playing in Detroit, Damion Easley got hit three times (hey, back off the plate!), twice by John Burkett and once by the same Willie Banks (now pitching for Boston), while Varitek, Nixon, and Offerman were all hit by Tigers pitchers.

BATTING

We've seen above the stories of three Red Sox players who homered in their last at-bat: Chick Stahl, Ted Williams, and Don Gile. And that of Calvin Pickering, who hit one in his last Red Sox at-bat, but came back three years later to play a few more games with Kansas City and sully his own stamp on the record book.

Home runs in their first at-bat

Making a good impression from the get-go…

June 10, 1938: Lefty Lefebvre was a rookie Red Sox pitcher signed out of Holy Cross on June 9. He swung at the first major league pitch he ever saw and homered in his first (and only) major league at-bat in 1938. It was the only pitch he saw all year long. His pitching wasn't as good that day; he gave up six earned runs in the game's final four innings, surrendering two home runs. He played in 87 games over four seasons, but never hit another fourbagger.

April 22, 1946: Local boy makes good. After Johnny Pesky was beaned by a Sid Hudson fastball, Boston's Eddie Pellagrini made his major league debut. Pelly came up in Pesky's slot in the lineup

Lefty Lefebvre. Courtesy of Lefty Lefebvre.

in the seventh inning and hit a game-winning home run over the left-field Wall in his first at-bat. The Red Sox beat the Washington Senators, 5–4.

May 10, 1960: Vic Wertz hit a first-inning grand slam for the Red Sox, but the White Sox tied it up as the game progressed. Teammate Rip Repulski, in his first American League at-bat (he'd spent parts of seven seasons in the senior circuit), pinch-hit an eighth-inning grand slam which proved the game winner.

May 19, 1962: Bob Tillman homered in his first official major league at-bat. It was his third game and his third plate appearance—he walked in his first two plate appearances—and it left the park in the fourth inning of a game against the Los Angeles Angels.

August 29, 1967: A Yankee Stadium doubleheader saw Boston win the first game 2–1, but lose a 20-inning nightcap, 4–3. The second game saw Ken Harrelson's first time up for the Red Sox; he hit a solo homer in the second inning off Bill Monbouquette of the Yankees.

July 5, 1970: John Kennedy, just acquired from Milwaukee, entered his first game in a Red Sox uniform as a fifth-inning pinch-hitter. The Sox were trailing, 3–2, but Kennedy hit a drive to right field off Rich Austin that got by Roy Foster and rolled to the wall. Kennedy circled the bases for a game-tying inside-the-park home run. The Sox went on to win, 8–4.

August 22, 1993: Recently-acquired right fielder Rob Deer hit a second-inning solo home run in his first plate appearance for Boston, part of a 3-for-6 debut.

September 19, 1997: It was 1–0 in Boston's favor through eight innings, but in the top of the ninth Chicago's Albert Belle hit a grand slam. In his first plate appearance for the Red Sox, pinch-hitter Curtis Pride hit a solo home run. Three batters later, Scott Hatteberg hit a two-run homer to tie the game. Boston lost it in the 10th, but Pride made his way into this book.

May 15, 1998: He'd played in three games on the road, and came into his hometown ballpark batting .143, but Framingham's Lou Merloni hit a home run in his first at-bat at Fenway, against KC's Jose Rosado. Making the experience particularly sweet is that it was the 33rd anniversary of the marriage of Lou's parents and he'd arranged to bring them and a few others from the family to the game in a limousine. His three-run homer provided all the difference in the 5–2 final.

August 1, 2004: Newly-acquired shortstop Orlando Cabrera, replacing fan favorite Nomar Garciaparra, didn't waste time attracting the attention of Fenway fandom as he hit a home run in the first inning of his first game at Fenway Park. The victim was 2004 Cy Young winner Johan Santana of the Minnesota Twins.

Postscript: Kevin Youkilis played his first game on May 15, 2004 in Toronto. He popped up to shortstop his first time up. He homered his second time up. It was his first game, but not his first at-bat. Hence, he's relegated to this postscript.

Leading off a game with a home run

First time up—pow! Home run! It's a nice way to start a game. Nomar Garciaparra did it seven times for the Red Sox in his rookie year, 1997, the one year he was leadoff hitter for the Red Sox. Dwight Evans hit five of his seven leadoff homers in 1985. He also did it on the very first pitch of the season in 1986. Mike Andrews, Ellis Burks, Bernie Carbo, and Kevin Youkilis did it four times—as did Tommy Harper, who did it four times in back-to-back seasons (1972 and 1973). Over the course of his career, Harper hit a home run first time up nine times, tying him with Dom DiMaggio for tops on the Red Sox. Mike Andrews was second with eight. Garciaparra and Evans each had seven, tied with Harry Hooper—who had the distinction of once homering to lead off both games of a doubleheader (May 30, 1913) in Washington. The two homers constituted half his home run output for the year.

Debuting in the World Series with a home run

The voting was already in for Rookie of the Year when Dustin Pedroia came to the plate to lead off the bottom of the first inning at Fenway Park, facing starter Jeff Francis of the Colorado Rockies in Game One of the 2007 World Series. Swinging at the second pitch he saw, the Red Sox second baseman hammered a pitch that just cleared the Wall and landed in the Green Monster seats in left-center field for a home run. Pedroia drove in 10 runs in the postseason, hitting .283. Pedroia won the AL Rookie of the Year Award with 24

Peter Gammons and 2007 Rookie of the Year Dustin Pedroia. Bill Nowlin photo.

of the 28 first-place votes, despite playing the last several weeks of the season and throughout the playoffs with a broken hamate bone in his hand which required surgery in early November. He'd finished 10th in the league with a .317 batting average.

The most home runs in postseason play

In the same 2007 postseason, Manny Ramirez hit four home runs, bringing him to 24 postseason homers—more than any other player in history.

A slam was all it took

You can't lead off the game with a grand slam, but Bobby Doerr's first-inning grand slam was all it took to do in the St. Louis Browns on July 19, 1948. 4–1 was the final.

Carroll Hardy did it at the other end of a game, on April 11, 1962: a walk-off grand slam in the bottom of the 12th to end a scoreless duel between Cleveland's Ron Taylor (in his major league debut) and Bill Monbouquette. Both pitchers went the distance. Boston 4, Cleveland 0.

Then there was the game that started on June 13, 1968 and ended on August 4. The June game was called with a 1–1 tie in the middle of the sixth inning because the Angels had to catch a plane back home (these were the days before team charters). When play resumed a month and a half later, Boston's Lee Stange pitched three no-hit innings and California's Andy Messersmith pitched to one batter in the bottom of the ninth. With the based loaded, Hawk Harrelson hit a grand slam.

Seconds

Twice in two days, Joe Lahoud hit one-out home runs in the top of the first. On June 14 and 15, 1971, John Kennedy grounded out to lead off the game but Lahoud followed with a solo home run both times.

Winning a World Series game with a home run

Hooper also hit two home runs in a very important game. It was the fifth and final game of the 1915 World Series against the Philadelphia Phillies. His ninth-inning homer was the first time a World Series game had been won with a home run. Harry hit two in the game, the second one breaking a 4–4 tie in the top of the ninth inning. Both homers were "bounce home runs"—until the rule was changed in 1931, a fair ball bouncing over the fence was scored a home run. Today these would be ground-rule doubles. But they were home runs at the time.

When we note the low home run totals of early baseball, and realize that a good number of them weren't what we would call a home run today, we understand that a ball truly hit out of the park was even rarer than it first would appear. Under today's rules, they might still be playing that 1915 World Series game.

Most extra-inning home runs by a Red Sox player

One expects David Ortiz might have a chance to get there some day, though we're only talking regular season here. Ted Williams hit 13 extra-inning homers, a full five more than the eight apiece hit by Jackie Jensen, Jim Rice, and Carl Yastrzemski.

Walk-off home runs

Among Red Sox batters, the player with the most game-ending home runs in a single season is Jimmie Foxx (1940)—four. They came on June 2, June 6, July 3, and August 16. Foxx won a few other games with home runs, too, like the May 14 win—but that was an away game and his game-deciding homer came in the top of the 10th. It made the difference, but wasn't truly a game-ending home run.

Foxx is tied with Ruth, Musial, Mantle, and Frank Robinson for 12 in the course of their career. Bobby Doerr hit seven for the Red Sox. David Ortiz has hit eight for Boston.

Fred Lynn hit three in 1985. And we all know about David Ortiz, who hit just one during the regular season in 2004 but two during the 14 games of that year's postseason.

Foxx's most dramatic one may have come on August 23, 1938. With two outs in the bottom of the ninth and the Red Sox down 12–10, Double X hit his second home run of the game—a grand slam—and Boston beat Cleveland.

A pinch-runner who hit a walk-off homer was Mickey Owen. On July 19, 1954 Owen came into the game in the eighth inning to run for fellow catcher Sammy White. He stayed in the game and capped a six-run Red Sox rally in the bottom of the ninth, beating Baltimore with a grand slam.

Last-inning home runs

Ted Williams hit but two true walk-offs in regular season play at Fenway Park, but on the road there were 11 times he hit a game-winning homer in the final inning of play. Two of them were grand slams (off Pete Appleton in 1939 and off Al Aber in 1955).

The most home runs in a month

In June 1958, Jackie Jensen hit 14 homers. Jimmie Foxx impressed teammate Ted Williams by hitting 13 in July 1939, and then hit 13 again in August 1940. Clyde Vollmer hit 13 in July 1951. Jim Rice hit 13 in May 1978. And Dwight Evans hit 13 in August 1987.

More home runs every year

Every year he played in the majors, and hit a home run, David Ortiz hit more homers than he did the year before. Starting in 1997, his totals are: 1, 9, 0, 10, 18, 20, 31, 41, 47, 54. This couldn't keep up…could it? [In 1999, he only had 20 at-bats.] All good things come to an end. In 2007, Big Papi hit "only" 35 homers, perhaps due to damaged knees which required postseason surgery.

Only three other players can match a streak of seven seasons with increasing home run totals: Cy Williams (1917–1923), Darrin Fletcher (1991–1997), and Jim Thome (1991–1997). Fletcher topped out with 17 homers his last year. Cy Williams wound up with a league-leading 41 back in 1923. Thome's top mark, capping his streak, was 40.

Homer-hitting pairs

In 2004, Manny Ramirez (43) and David Ortiz (41) set a club record with 84 homers between them, breaking the mark set by Ted Williams and Vern Stephens in 1949. Ramirez led the American League in home runs and in slugging average, with .613. David Ortiz led the league in extra-base hits with 91. That was one short of the Red Sox team record of 92, held by Jimmie Foxx since 1938. Because Ortiz hit 47 doubles and Manny hit 44, they set a new major league record—the first set of teammates ever to hit at least 40 home runs and 40 doubles in the same season. In 2005, the pair beat their own record, combining for 92 home runs (45 by Ramirez and 47 by Ortiz). In 2006, Ortiz hit the all-time Red Sox high in homers (54), but Ramirez hit just 35.

Fewest team home runs hit at home in a given year

Incredible but true! The 1916 World Champion Red Sox hit only one home run all year long in their home ballpark.

Tillie Walker, playing for the St. Louis Browns had hit one on September 24, 1915—and that was the last home run hit at Fenway until June 20, 1916. Oddly enough, it was Tillie Walker who hit the June 20 one—although now he was playing for the Red Sox. Walker hit three in all during 1916, but this was the only one he—or any Red Sox player—hit at Fenway.

Tillie Walker.

Walker's homer accounted for the only run in a 4–1 loss to the Yankees. New York's Ray Keating pitched a complete game scattering just seven hits. "Tillie Walker showed the local fans how he could clear the left field fence with a drive. His home run over the score board in the seventh was a terrific clout. It is the third circuit drive Walker is credited with over the same barrier," wrote the *Boston Herald* sportswriter. Walker led off the ninth with a "blow that came near to driving Keating to cover" (*Boston Post*) and Gardner followed with a double but neither scored. In fact, the Sox left the bases loaded in both the eighth and ninth innings.

Walker's was the only Fenway homer for the Red Sox all year long. As it happened, the Sox also only yielded one home run all year at home. It was an inside-the-park homer by Bobby Veach of the Tigers, and that involved Walker as well. Batting in the second inning of the first game of a July 19 doubleheader, Veach banged a Carl Mays offering over Walker's head to the flagpole in deepest center field. Tillie badly misjudged the ball, actually running in on it. Veach scrambled around the bases while Tillie reversed direction to retrieve it. Veach had a double in the ninth, but the Red Sox won 4–2 and took the second game that day, 9–5.

Hy Myers hit a homer for Brooklyn in the World Series that year, but the Red Sox played both the 1915 and 1916 World Series at Braves Field, since it had greater seating capacity. In 1914, though, the Braves were in the Series and they played at Fenway. In the 1914 World Series, the Braves' Hank Gowdy hit a bounce home run. That was the last World Series homer hit at Fenway until Rudy York hit one in 1946 during Game Three. Doerr hit one in Game Four and Culberson hit one in Game Five. The next one started to build a streak—Jose Santiago's in Game One, 1967. Yaz hit two in Game Two and another one in Game Six, 1967 (while Reggie Smith hit one and Rico Petrocelli hit two). Unfortunately, the Sox streak of home runs at home during Series games stopped at six games as they were held homerless in Game Seven.

After Veach's July 19, 1916 home run, the next homer hit at Fenway was Wally Pipp's for the Yankees on April 23, 1917. The next Red Sox to hit a home run at Fenway was Larry Gardner, on May 31, 1917, more than 11 months after Walker's June 20 homer.

How long had it been prior to Walker's homer? Since September 23, 1915 when Dick Hoblitzell hit one.

Babe Ruth led the league without ever hitting even one home run at home

In that same year, 1916, George Herman Ruth threw a league-leading nine shutouts. With a record of 23–12, Ruth also led the league in ERA (1.75) and fewest hits per game (6.40). Opponents hit just .201 off the Babe. And in 323⅔ innings pitched, he didn't give up even one home run. He hit three, though. When it came to the World Series, though, it was Ruth who gave up that first-inning homer to Hy Myers—an inside-the-park job. In the third inning, Ruth drove in the tying run, then held Brooklyn scoreless until the Red Sox won the game in the bottom of the 14th inning, to take a two-games-to-none lead.

In 1918, when he led the American League with 11 home runs, Babe Ruth hit every one of them on the road.

For a while in 1919, Babe Ruth was the only Red Sox player who seemed able to hit a home run. In between homers by his teammates, Ruth hit 14 home runs in a row. By year's end, the Babe had hit 29 of Boston's 33 homers.

Ruth was the only player to win both an ERA title and a batting crown in his major league career. He only won one of each. Ruth won the above-mentioned ERA title in 1916, and his batting championship with the Yankees (.378 in 1924).

The fewest home runs hit by the Red Sox team leader

There were three years when the leading home run hitter for the Red Sox only had three homers, and three years in which the leader only hit four.

Three-homer leaders
1908 Doc Gessler / 1916 Del Gainer, Babe Ruth, and Tillie Walker / 1917 Harry Hooper

Four-homer leaders
1913 Harry Hooper / 1914 Tris Speaker / 1915 Babe Ruth

Two grand slams in same game

Four of the 11 players to do it have been Red Sox players. One, Tony Cloninger, later became Red Sox pitching coach. The non-Red Sox players are: Tony Lazzeri (May 24, 1936), Jim Gentile (May 9, 1961), Tony Cloninger (July 3, 1966), Jim Northrup (June 24, 1968), Frank Robinson (June 26, 1970), Robin Ventura (September 4, 1995), Chris Hoiles (August 14, 1998), and Fernando Tatis (April 23, 1999).

Representing the Red Sox, we have:

Jim Tabor—July 4, 1939. It was the second game of a doubleheader in Philadelphia. Boston won the first game 17–7 with home runs by Ted Williams, Joe Cronin, Bobby Doerr, and Jim Tabor. A good day got even better for third baseman Tabor in the nightcap, as he slugged three more home runs, two of them with the bases full. The third-inning and sixth-inning grand slams and a solo shot gave Tabor nine RBIs in the game and 11 on the day.

Rudy York—July 27, 1946. Rudy York's 10 RBIs made a big difference in Boston's 13–6 win over the Browns in a St. Louis night game. He had a shot at even more, after going 3-for-3 with two grand slams and a two-run double, but struck out with a man on in the seventh and grounded into a double play with two men on in the eighth. All in all, though, one suspects he was pleased with his performance.

Nomar Garciaparra—May 10, 1999. No one had knocked in 10 runs in an American League game since 1975, and Nomar had never hit three homers in a game—not even in Little League. He entered the game with just two home runs on the season, but then hit a slam in the first, a two-run homer in the third, and another slam in the eighth. The Red Sox won with runs to spare, 12–4 over the Mariners.

Bill Mueller—July 29, 2003. With the Red Sox down, 2–0, Mueller hit a solo homer to lead off the third inning and put the Red Sox on the board. The Sox had just taken a 5–4 lead in the seventh when he came up with the bases loaded facing Aaron Fultz. Mueller stepped into the box batting right-handed and hit a grand slam. The very next inning, he found the bases full but facing right-hander Jay Powell, so the switch-hitting Mueller batted from the left side—and did it again. It was the first time in major league history that a batter had hit two grand slams in one game, one from each side of the plate.

Inside-the park home runs

The inside-the-park home run is one of the more exciting plays in baseball. In Red Sox history, the team has hit 350 IPHR's. His first time at bat in 1919, with Jack Barry on base, Babe Ruth hit one to deep center which became an inside-the-park HR as Ruth "tore around the bases, galloping like mad" (*Globe*) with what proved the winning run in an Opening Day 10–0 shut-out of the New York Yankees.

John Kennedy hit an inside-the-park HR his first time up as a Red Sox rookie.

Mike Greenwell hit an inside-the-park grand slam at Fenway, against the Yankees no less, on September 1, 1990. It was part of a rather convincing 15–1 win. New York right fielder Jesse Barfield was hurt on the play, which was a good part of the reason Greenwell was able to circle the bases. Barfield was the second Yankees outfielder who had to leave the game that inning. Mel Hall had come out two batters earlier when he'd crashed into the wall trying to play Wade Boggs' double. Greenwell's IPHR was hit off Greg Cadaret. It was his second inside-the-park job. The earlier one had been hit the year before, on July 7, 1989, also at Fenway. The pitcher? Greg Cadaret.

One of the more exciting IPHRs was a grand slam, but sadly a slam in vain. The date was August 8, 1961, with Boston at home playing to a family night house. Camilo Pascual was pitching for the Twins and gave up a double to Jackie Jensen, then walked Don Buddin. Bill Monbouquette bunted, but Pascual cut down the lead runner, Jensen, at third base. Runnels walked, and **Gary Geiger** stepped into the box. He was batting around .240, but on a 1–0 count he drove the ball down to the Pesky Pole in right field where it hit the low wall and shot past Bob Allison all the way out to the Minnesota bullpen. As Allison chased after the ball, all four runners chugged around the bases, Geiger just beating the relay to the plate. It was reported by historically-challenged writers as the first inside-the-park grand slam in Fenway history. The Twins rallied from a 4–0 deficit, though, and won the game 6–5.

Another Fenway grand slam IPHR (predating Geiger's) was hit by **Don Lenhardt** on April 19, 1952 against Dick Fowler of the Philadelphia Athletics, helping the Red Sox to a Patriots Day doubleheader sweep.

The most famous inside-the-parker was, of course, that hit in the first inning by **Ted Williams** on Friday the 13th, September 13, 1946—which clinched the American League pennant, providing the only run in a 1–0 Boston win. It was hit against the Williams Shift, but that wasn't why Ted called it the most difficult of the 521 homers he'd hit in his long career. It was the only IPHR he'd ever hit. But why was it the most difficult? "I had to run." Ted told the writers, "I want you to make it clear that all the credit goes to Hughson. He pitched a helluva game. My home run didn't mean a thing when I hit it."

Joe Foy won the game on July 17, 1966 when his inside-the-park homer off KC's Ken Sanders broke a 2–2 tie in the top of the 10th and won the game for Boston.

One of the more improbable IPHR's came off the bat of the somewhat plodding **Dick Stuart**—and apparently also off the head of center fielder Vic Davalillo. August 19, 1963. Harold Kaese says it "hit the Fenway wall and then Vic Davalillo's head before bouncing into the left field corner." It was reported at the time as the first inside-the-park home run to left field at Fenway, and the AP wrote that Stuart "careened around the bases like a runaway truck."

There were back-to-back IPHR's, in a way, on July 26, 1998 when **Nomar Garciaparra** hit a three-run homer at home against the visiting Toronto Blue Jays. After a travel day, **Darren Lewis** hit one in the next game the Red Sox played, in Oakland on July 28—another three-run inside-the-park job.

The very last home run of **Bill Buckner**'s long (1969–1990) career was an inside-the-park home run—hit by perhaps the last man you'd think could leg it around the bases before the ball was thrown home. At Fenway Park on April 25, 1990 the 41-year-old player hit a drive off Kirk McCaskill of the Angels. It was a drive to right, and Claudell Washington crashed into the stands, hurting his knee so badly he later had to leave the game. The *Globe's* Frank Dell'Apa wrote that it was "likely the first homer in which the ball remained in play and the fielder went over the fence."

Many years earlier, the Sox suffered a surprising inside-the-parker. It was June 27, 1911 and the Philadelphia Athletics were winning 6–3 after seven. Tris Speaker had grounded out to end the seventh, and then turned to walk to his position. Boston pitcher Ed "Loose" Karger had reached the box and, with rookie Les Nunamaker behind the plate, he saw that his fielders were taking their time taking their positions, most of them still in the diamond, so he took a warmup toss to the plate. Gloucester, Massachusetts native Stuffy McInnis of the A's hopped into the batter's box and poked the ball over second base. A sports page cartoon showed the ball skipping over second and skittering into shallow center field. He may have just been funning with Karger, because he never left the plate until he heard the other Athletics yell to him to run. Then he scampered around the bases, while the Red Sox protested (in vain) to the umpires. The Sox were so startled that Speaker didn't even make a move to get to the ball until McInnis was well underway.

Earlier that season, Ban Johnson had ruled that pitchers should not be permitted warmup pitches—in order to shorten the games. Remarkable, in that not that many games ran much over two hours in those days. The *Boston Post* called the McInnis IPHR "one of the queerest home runs ever made in professional baseball." The *Post's* Paul H. Shannon deemed McInnis "rather unsportsmanlike" and added, "he need not labor under the impression that any halo will surround his head for the achievement…McInnis is welcome to all the bases and all the glory he gets from this hit." Tim Murnane of the *Globe* added his own comment, writing that umpire Egan's ruling that the play stood "was against all baseball law and Umpire Egan failed to show the spirit of fair play. The unfortunate incident spoiled what was a fine game by the visitors, who clearly outhit, outfielded and outpointed the home team from every angle."

The next year, Boston's Larry Gardner hit a total of three home runs. Every one of the three was of the inside-the-park variety, and two of them came on the same day against the same pitcher. On July 2, 1912 Gardner hit one in the second and one in the eighth, both off Russ Ford of New York. A month later, on August 1, Gardner hit another IPHR off Mack Allison at Sportsman's Park in St. Louis. Russ Ford surrendered 11 home runs all year long, six of them hit by Red Sox batters.

They just don't make 'em like they used to

Inside-the-park home runs are rare today. They used to be more common. Hobe Ferris and Tris Speaker each had 25 IPHR's for the Red Sox, Buck Freeman had 22, and Jimmy Collins had 21. In fact, Ferris hit nine home runs in 1903 and every one of the nine was an IPHR, the first one hit in Washington and the final eight all hit in Boston. In the first five seasons of the franchise, the Boston Americans hit 182 home runs and a full 125 of them were inside-the-park homers. Nearly 69%. It helped that they played their home games in the Huntington Avenue Grounds where a ball hit to center field could roll nearly forever; *Green Cathedrals* reports a distance of 530 feet to center. The best day of all at the Grounds for inside-the-parkers came on June 11, 1901 (only the 12th home game in club history) when three Boston batters (Freeman, Hemphill, and Ferris) each hit clean drives to center field, making for a frustrating day for Milwaukee pitcher Bill Reidy and center fielder Hugh Duffy. Boston beat the Brewers, 8–4. It was the only game in which Boston recorded three IPHR's, though on September 28 that year, they hit three during a doubleheader—and two of those were off Bill Reidy as well. Dowd hit one in the first game off Bert Husting, and Jimmy Collins collected two off Reidy in the final game of the 1901 campaign for the 25th and 26th inside-the-park home runs of the season. Boston hit 11 of what we now seen as traditional home runs—out of the park.

Hal Janvrin.

The last time someone hit two in the same game for the Red Sox was when Hal Janvrin did so on October 4, 1913 but that was kind of a "joke game" (*Boston Globe*) that saw Washington's star pitcher Walter Johnson playing center field when Janvrin hit his first one and manager Clark Griffith insert himself in center (his one appearance of the season) in time to see the second one skip by him. The pitchers were Mutt Williams, throwing his first-ever major league game, and veteran infielder Germany Schaefer, appearing in only his second (he'd faced three batters the year before). The *Globe* called the game "probably the most farcical exposition of the National game that was ever staged" but said the Washington crowd enjoyed the "frolic."

There was one notable stretch of six games in a row (September 15 through 21, 1903) in which Boston hit 10 IPHRs, at least one in every game.

By decade, through the 20th century, the Sox have seen the numbers of IPHR's regress as follows:

1901–1910: 195	1941–1950: 10	1971–1980: 2
1911–1920: 75	1951–1960: 6	1981–1990: 7
1921–1930: 26	1961–1970: 11	1991–2000: 3
1931–1940: 11		

Hobe Ferris alone hit more than the entire team has since 1963.

Ferris comes first on the list of the most IPHR's in a single season, with the nine in 1903. Buck Freeman hit seven that same year. Speaker hit eight in 1912. Freeman also had two years with six (1901 and 1902) and so did Speaker, with six in 1909.

The Sox have hit four in the 21st century: Kevin Millar, Pokey Reese, Trot Nixon, and Kevin Youkilis being the batters.

Bounce home runs

Even some of the home runs that were not inside-the-park home runs were ones that did not go out of the park, on the fly. A bounce home run was a ball that hit fair and bounced out of the field of play—what we would today call a rule book double. The rule was changed in 1931; the Red Sox hit their last bounce home run in 1926. In their first decade, 19 of the home runs were bounce home runs—the highest total being the six hit in 1910, two of which were hit by Duffy Lewis. Two of Ferris's non-IPHR's were bounce home runs, both in 1907. Speaker had two as well, both in 1911. Freeman had a couple. So did Jake Stahl. Jake Stahl hit 10 homers in 1910—nine were IPHRs and the other one was a bounce home run. And Harry Hooper's

Duffy Lewis, 1912.

home run that won the World Series for the Red Sox was—you guessed it—a bounce home run (one of two bounce HRs he hit in the fifth and final game).

The player with the most bounce four-baggers was the same: Duffy Lewis, who benefited four times—twice in 1910 and twice in three days (June 19 and 21, 1912), both hit in New York. Other players with multiple bounces are Tris Speaker with three, and Buck Freeman, Heinie Wagner, Jake Stahl, and Clyde Engle—each of whom hit two.

Hitting three home runs, all in the same inning

In Olathe, Kansas on June 26, 1944, a former catcher in the Red Sox system, Bob Jenkins, hit three home runs all in the same inning as his Naval Air Station Clippers defeated the Kansas City National Distillers, 35–0. Maybe the National Distillers had been sampling their own wares? Jenkins had never made the Red Sox team, but he still made this book.

Hitting four home runs, all in the same inning

This one was a group effort. The Red Sox have done it 10 times in their history, but on April 22, 2007 they hit all four in back-to-back-to-back-to-back fashion. Only four other major league teams had ever done it: hit four home runs in successive at-bats. Manny Ramirez, J. D. Drew, Mike Lowell, and Jason Varitek hit the four, all of them off Yankees rookie pitcher Chase Wright at Fenway Park. It took Wright 10 pitches to serve up the quartet of four-baggers.

Back-to-back-to-back in the World Series

With back-to-back-to-back homers in Game Six against St. Louis in 1967, the Red Sox tied a World Series record. They all came in the fourth inning—Rico, Yaz, and Reggie Smith.

Red Sox pitchers batting in runs

It was a long, dry spell. Not dating back to 1918, but 1972 was the last season in which a Sox pitcher knocked in a run—until July 4, 2004. In the '72 season, Red Sox pitchers knocked in 31 runs (Pattin and Siebert with nine each, Tiant and McGlothen four apiece, Culp with two, and then Curtis, Lee, and Peters with one each). Then came the DH, and until interleague play, Red Sox pitchers simply didn't hit during the regular season. Even when interleague play was brought in, Boston pitchers were more often put out.

The last RBI by a Red Sox pitcher in the 20th century was Lynn McGlothen's, on September 27, 1972, in the bottom of the second inning of a Wednesday day game at Fenway. Reggie Smith walked to lead off the second. Petrocelli struck out. Fisk walked, and then Evans singled, scoring Smith and moving Fisk to third. Griffin walked and the bases were loaded. McGlothen grounded out, 6–3, but Fisk came in to score. Harper then made an out. Two runs on one hit, and McGlothen was 0-for-1 on the game.

When the Brewers scored four times in the top of the third, McGlothen was pulled and out of the game. The Sox won the game in the end, 7–5, so that was nice, but McGlothen's RBI was the last time a Red Sox pitcher knocked in a run for almost 32 years.

The drought was finally broken by Derek Lowe, who hadn't yet been born when McGlothen knocked in that run. D-Lowe doubled in the top of the second in a Fourth of July game against the Atlanta Braves, and drove in his batterymate, Jason Varitek. Bill Mueller tried to score, too, but was cut down at the plate or Lowe would have had two RBIs. The run put

Boston on top of the Braves, 1–0. Unfortunately, Lowe, who had retired the first seven Braves batters in order and only surrendered three hits in the first four innings, got hammered for seven earned runs in the fifth and was excused from further play that day.

The following year, 2005, Tim Wakefield drove in a run and so did David Wells. And in 2006, Josh Beckett drove in three, two on May 20 and another one on June 17. Daisuke Matsuzaka drove in two runs in Game Three of the 2007 World Series.

Of course, it wasn't as though the Red Sox didn't have some good-hitting pitchers over the years. Mickey McDermott hit well enough that he was known to bat seventh in the order at times (May 30, 1954, for example), and even sixth (one year earlier, on May 30, 1953). In 1953, McDermott was a .301 hitter in 93 at-bats. Batting seventh in the order was shortstop Johnny Lipon (.214), catcher Gus Niarhos (.200), and third baseman Billy Consolo (.215). In the second game of the Memorial Day doubleheader, pitcher Willard Nixon also batted sixth in the order. Nixon, however, hit just .190 that year. Boston won the first game, but lost the second.

In terms of RBIs, Cy Young drove in 15 runs in the first year of the franchise, 1901. That stood as the Red Sox record until Babe Ruth drove in 21 in 1915. The all-time high was Wes Ferrell's 32 in 1935.

The RBI totals:

Wes Ferrell—32 (1935)	Wes Ferrell—24 (1936)	Babe Ruth—21 (1915)

19 each by Red Ruffing (1928), Dave Ferriss (1945 and 1947), and Gary Peters (1971).

17 each by Cy Young (1901), Red Ruffing (1929), and Wes Ferrell (1934).

Hitting for the Cycle

Patsy Dougherty July 29, 1903	Lu Clinton July 13, 1962
Tris Speaker June 9, 1912	Carl Yastrzemski May 14, 1965
Roy Carlyle July 21, 1925	Bob Watson September 15, 1979
Moose Solters August 19, 1934	Fred Lynn May 13, 1980
Joe Cronin August 2, 1940	Dwight Evans June 28, 1984
Leon Culberson July 3, 1943	Rich Gedman September 18, 1985
Bobby Doerr May 17, 1944	Mike Greenwell September 14, 1988
Bob Johnson July 6, 1944	Scott Cooper April 12, 1994
Ted Williams July 21, 1946	John Valentin June 6, 1996
Bobby Doerr May 13, 1947	

Two of these were hit in the precise order: single, double, triple, and home run. Those were the ones by Leon Culberson and Bob Watson.

As the chart indicates, Hall of Famer Doerr hit for the cycle twice. He also broke up three no-hitters.

Two of the Red Sox batters who hit for the cycle also did so for another team. Joe Cronin had previously cycled for Washington (against the Red Sox, in a September 2, 1929 game played at Braves Field) and Bob Watson had done so for the Astros in 1977. Only two players other than Watson (Babe Herman and Chris Speier) have cycled in both leagues.

Yaz's cycle included a second homer, for 14 total bases, but the Red Sox lost the game, 12–8 in 10 innings. Clinton's cycle included two singles; the second one was a slow roller to third base but sufficient to score Yaz all the way from second base with the go-ahead run in the 15th inning of the game in Kansas City.

Then there was the cycle that wasn't. In modern major league history, there are only two players who have managed three hits in the same inning. They were both Red Sox players. Gene Stephens got three hits in the seventh inning on June 18, 1953 against the Tigers. Johnny Damon equaled that mark on June 27, 2003 against the Florida Marlins, when he doubled, tripled, and singled—all in the first inning. By the time he came up again in the third, he had a shot at hitting for the cycle by the third inning. Alas, he struck out. Damon had three more homerless chances but did end the game 5-for-7. It was quite a game. There were two other Red Sox players (Bill Mueller and David Ortiz) who could have cycled but did not. They each lacked a triple. The very next evening, again in a Red Sox-Marlins game, another Boston batter fell a hit shy. It was Gabe Kapler in his first-ever game for the Red Sox. He'd just joined the club a few hours earlier, and banged out a single, two doubles, and a triple but couldn't rack up a round-tripper.

Speaking of breaking up no-hitters, Shannon Stewart himself broke up two Red Sox no-hit bids. With two outs in the bottom of the ninth inning, Curt Schilling had a no-hitter going in Oakland on June 7, 2007. Shannon Stewart singled to right field. Schilling got the win, thanks to a first-inning David Ortiz home run. It was the second time that Stewart got the only hit in a game against the Red Sox. On May 25, 2001, Stewart doubled for the Blue Jays to lead off the fourth. It turned out to be the only hit of the game off Hideo Nomo, he who had already no-hit the Orioles earlier in the season on April 4.

Ted Williams wins five 1–0 games with home runs

It doesn't really matter that much how you win, but winning a 1–0 game with a home run does have a special kind of feel to it. Ted Williams won five of them, more than any other player in baseball history—until 2007, when Barry Bonds won the April 21 game against Arizona with a solo home run. And we know about Bonds. Bobby Grich, Dwight Evans, and Jim Wynn each did it four times.

June 24, 1942: In a twilight game at Ted's favorite park, Briggs Stadium, Williams hit a seventh inning shot off Virgil Trucks into the upper level seats in right field. Charlie Wagner held the Tigers to just three hits and got the win for Boston, facing just 28 batters in all.

September 13, 1946: the only inside-the-park home run of Ted's 521 homers came in Cleveland, in the first inning off Red Embree, and clinched the 1946 pennant for the Red Sox as Tex Hughson threw a three-hit shutout for the Red Sox. Embree only allowed two hits, total, but one was Ted's IPHR poked into left field against the Williams Shift, rolling all the way to the fence.

September 14, 1949: this one was also hit to left, but up into the netting at Fenway. Hal Newhouser was the victim, pitching for the Tigers and having completed 18 consecutive scoreless innings. Ellis Kinder got the win, his 20th of the season for Boston.

July 17, 1956: the Red Sox won the first game, 10–0, but only managed the one run—it was #400 of Ted's career—against the visiting Athletics at Fenway. Tom Gorman's first pitch of the sixth inning was banged out over the visitors' bullpen into the seats in right field. Pitcher Bob Porterfield was the beneficiary.

August 28, 1957: Jim Bunning was pitching for Detroit, in Detroit, and only gave up two hits. But one of them was to Ted, a seventh-inning homer that gave Frank Sullivan a victory and was the last one that Ted hit in a 1–0 win.

Other games won, with all the Red Sox runs scored by a home run

Needless to say, Ted won other games in which his home run provided all the Red Sox runs of the game—most notably the August 27, 1955 game in—surprise—Detroit. Despite only managing two hits in the entire nine-inning game, the Tigers had scored once in the first and twice in the third. They led 3–0 after eight innings. Frank Lary had a shutout going, scattering six hits. He gave up singles to Eddie Joost, to Faye Throneberry pinch-hitting for Boston pitcher Tommy Hurd, and to Billy Klaus. The Sox had the bases loaded, but they also had two outs.

Detroit brought in Al Aber in relief, to try and get the one out they needed to win the game. Ted hit a grand slam. The Tigers got to bat again, but Kinder shut them down. Ted's homer provided all four runs in the 4–3 win.

There were four other Red Sox wins in which a Ted homer accounted for all of Boston's runs.

August 15, 1942: The Sox took two from the visiting Senators. In the first game, Ted's two-run third-inning homer off Sid Hudson combined with Tex Hughson's 10-hit effort gave Boston a 2–1 win. Washington got their run on a steal of home by George Case. Boston scored two in the bottom of the ninth to take the second game, 7–6. The HR was Ted's 25th of the season.

August 2, 1947: For the third time, Tex Hughson won a game in which a Ted Williams roundtripper provided every one of the Red Sox runs. Sam Mele tripled to lead off the bottom of the first, and Ted homered. Hughson allowed the Tigers one run on seven hits and beat Virgil Trucks by a score of 2–1. It was the second time Ted had taken Trucks deep for all the runs of the game.

September 17, 1953: Near the end of the season, after Ted had returned from the Korean War, he hit a two-run homer off Ned Garver in Detroit. The eighth-inning home run was all Ellis Kinder needed for a 2–1 win in his 67th appearance of the season, the number setting a new league record at the time.

September 17, 1960: Home run #520, the next-to-last one of Ted's career, flew over the 31-foot-high right-field fence and out of Griffith Stadium, as Boston beat Washington, 2–1. The only two hits in the game off Pedro Ramos were Willie Tasby's single through the box followed by The Kid's long shot. Billy Muffett got the win for Boston; he only gave up three hits.

In all, Ted won 10 games for Boston with home runs that plated all the runs the Red Sox scored in the game. Carl Yastrzemski did this six times (June 2, 1967; April 18, 1971; September 4, 1972; May 25, 1976; June 6, 1977; and September 6, 1978). Dwight Evans did it five times. Manny Ramirez has done in three times. Tony Conigliaro and Jim Rice both did it four times. Bobby Doerr and Orlando Cepeda did it twice each. In all, it's been done 83 times by Boston ballplayers. The others who did it more than once: Harry Hooper (both in May 1913), Jimmie Foxx (both in the first week of June 1940), Reggie Smith, George Scott, Troy O'Leary, and Trot Nixon. One-timers are: Jake Stahl, Del Pratt, George Burns, Ira Flagstead, Bobby Reeves, Billy Werber, Dom DiMaggio, Leon Culberson, Sam Mele, George Kell, Jackie Jensen, Dick Gernert, Frank Malzone, Carroll Hardy, Lou Clinton, Joe Foy, Dalton Jones, Sonny Siebert, Rico Petrocelli, Butch Hobson, Dave Stapleton, Tony Perez. Mike Easler, Don Baylor, Carlos Quintana, Phil Plantier, John Valentin, Tom Brunansky, Jose Canseco, Mo Vaughn, Nomar Garciaparra, Midre Cummings, and David Ortiz.

There were five times that Ted's home run scored all the runs in the game, period. The opposition score no runs at all. Carl Yastrzemski ties Ted with five such wins. Dwight Evans has done this four time. Manny Ramirez and Jim Rice did it three times. Conigliaro (Tony), Doerr, Petrocelli, and Scott have done it two times apiece. The one timers naturally include many of those on the list above. In chronological order: Hooper, Burns, Flagstead, Reeves, Foxx, DiMaggio, Culberson, Mele, Kell, Gernert, Malzone, Hardy, Jones, Smith, Cepeda, Stapleton, Quintana, Plantier, Valentin, Brunansky, Cummings, O'Leary, Nixon, and Ortiz.

Pitchers with game-winning homers

Only twice has a pitcher stopped the Sox cold with a game-ending homer, and—wouldn't you know it?—both times it was a Yankee pitcher who did it.

The first time it was Red Ruffing, who broke in with Boston in 1924 and appeared in 189 games until he was moved to New York early in 1930. Ruffing had a rough time with the Red Sox, going 39–86. For New York, he won 231 games. One of which was on April 14, 1933. It was the second game of the season. Ruffing actually started the scoring with a double to right-center in the bottom of the third, moving up a base on a single and scoring on a sacrifice fly to left. The Red Sox responded with two in the bottom of the fourth, on a bases-loaded single by Johnny Hodapp. The Yankees tied it up in the sixth on a Lou Gehrig solo home run. Gehrig had homered to win New York's Opening Day game just the day before. In the bottom of the ninth inning, the Yankees loaded the bases. A Rabbit Warstler error let Lou Gehrig take first. Chapman sacrificed him to second, so Sox pitcher Bob Weiland intentionally walked Lazzeri. Bill Dickey popped up to short and there were two down. Frankie Crosetti walked, the bases were loaded, and the pitcher was up. Red Ruffing was a good hitting pitcher; he hit 36 home runs lifetime. Boston manager McManus came out and talked with Weiland, who said he could take care of Ruffing—but Ruffing swung at the first pitch and it was a game-winning grand slam into the stands over the right-field fence. 6–2, New York.

The other time was in 1957 and the pitcher was Bob Grim. It was September 5 and the Sox were 13 games behind the league-leading Yankees. Again, the score was tied 2–2 and again there were two outs in the bottom of the ninth in New York. Willard Nixon went the distance for Boston. He'd been up 2–0 through seven, courtesy of a two-run Jackie Jensen homer off Bob Turley in the fourth. Nixon faltered in the eighth, walking three New Yorkers and then seeing two score on Gil McDougald's "roller" which ran into right. Berra started off the ninth with a single but then, with one out, overslid second base on a stolen base attempt and was tagged out. Momentum might have shifted, but Jerry Lumpe singled and Enos Slaughter walked on a 3–2 pitch. Grim appeared in 46 games in 1957 (he finished the season 12–9 and led the league with 19 saves) but as of September 5 he hadn't had a hit all year. Batting .000, and down in the count 0–1, he hit a three-run homer into the first row of the seats in right field to earn the win. Red Sox rightfielder Jensen said he easily could have caught it but had never seen Grim hit to right field before and he was playing far too shallow.

One of the slams that stung the most may have been Mel Stottlemyre's on July 20, 1965, because he was a Yankee and a pitcher, and because it gave New York all the runs he needed to win the game, 6–3. Though it was a fifth-inning slam, it still stung just as badly.

OK, now let's get to the good stuff. As we saw above, there were four times that Red Sox hurlers homered to win. August 22, 1934 was Wes Ferrell vs. Toots Tietje, and the White Sox were up 2–1 heading into the bottom of the eighth inning when Ferrell hit a solo shot over the left-field fence to tie the game at two runs apiece. Chicago's first run came in the third when a two-out single was followed by an error on a fly to left-center. They added a second run the next inning on two singles by Appling and Dykes, Appling scoring on an out to first. Boston's run came in the fifth after Moose Solters singled and Morgan doubled. Rick Ferrell was at bat, and a pickoff attempt at third saw the ball hit the bag and bounce out to left as Solters scored. In the bottom of the 10th inning, two outs and nobody on, up came Wes Ferrell once more, and once more he hit a home run—his second of the game. The first one tied the score; the second one won the game. The hard-hitting pitcher also singled in the sixth, going 3-for-4 on the day and leaving with a "W" as well. Boston 3, Chicago 2. In 10 innings.

Less than a year later, brother Wesley did it again. The date was July 22, 1935. The score was 1–1, in the bottom of the ninth inning. St. Louis had scored its run in the top of the fifth, when it grouped three of its seven singles. Coffman, pitching for the Browns, was Ferrell's equal in that both had given up but seven hits. The Sox scored their run in the sixth on a walk, a single by Almada that let Cooke scoot around to third base, and a sacrifice fly. Babe Dahlgren flied out to lead off the bottom of the ninth, and Coffman had Ferrell down 1–2 when

Ferrell guessed right and hammered the curve ball over the Wall in left. 2–1 Boston. It was the second game in a row that Wes Ferrell won with a walk-off home run. The very day before, on one of the first Sunday ball games played at Fenway Park, he'd been put in as a pinch-hitter with two men on and won the game for Lefty Grove, 7–6. Maybe that one doesn't count as a pitcher hitting a game-ending homer, though, since Ferrell wasn't a pitcher in that game. He was a pinch-hitter. A good hitting pitcher, for sure. The fact remains, though, that two games in a row Wes Ferrell hit game-winning home runs in the bottom of the ninth inning.

And Wes drove in all six runs for his 6–4 win over Philadelphia on August 12, 1936—with a two-run homer in the third and a grand slam in the fourth. Hod Lisenbee was Ferrell's victim of the day.

Just a few weeks later, another Boston pitcher won a game with a roundtripper. This time it was Jack Wilson winning the game on September 2 (1935) in the bottom of the 11th. This time there were 25,000 fans filling Fenway for a doubleheader, both games going into extra innings. Boston dropped the second game 3–2, but forget about that. It was the first game that featured the most fun for the fans. Washington scored early (four runs in the top of the first) and often, and held an 8–1 lead after 5½. It was Wes Ferrell who'd been hit the hardest. He was gone by the third, relieved by Jack Wilson. Cronin singled in Almada in the fourth; Almada had doubled. A walk, a double by Cronin, and a single by Johnson drove in two runs in the sixth to bring the score to 8–3. Cronin featured again in the bottom of the eighth, his grand slam pulling the Sox within one. Cronin knocked in six of the nine Red Sox runs and was reportedly a star defensively, too. An error, a stolen base, and a single scored the tying run and the Senators and Sox were knotted 8–8 until the bottom of the 11th. Jack Wilson was batting in his first major league game. He'd hit the ball hard to right and walked, but in his third at-bat and on a 3–2 count he hit the ball into the center-field bleachers, a feat that only Jimmie Foxx and Billy Rogell had reportedly done at the time. Wilson won the game, and then 67 more, but he probably never had the satisfaction of this win, pitching a full nine innings and homering to earn the win. 9–8, Boston.

Most multi-home run games

In his years with the Red Sox, Ted Williams hit two or more home runs in the same game on 37 occasions. Jim Rice is second on the Sox with 35; he played in about 200 fewer games than Ted. Through 2007, David Ortiz has done it 28 times for the Red Sox and Manny Ramirez has done it 26. Carl Yastrzemski's in between them, with 27.

Three-homer games? Ted Williams had three of them, Nomar had two (both at home, one of them on his 29th birthday), and Mo Vaughn had two (also both at home). So did Jim Rice, once at home and once on the road. The hitters with one are (going back in time): Kevin Millar, Bill Mueller, Jason Varitek, Trot Nixon, John Valentin, Jack Clark, Tom Brunansky, Carl Yastrzemski, Fred Lynn, Joe Lahoud, Ken Harrelson, Norm Zauchin, Clyde Vollmer, Bobby Doerr, and—the first to ever do it for the Red Sox—Jim Tabor in 1939. Harrelson's three home runs on June 14, 1968 accounted for all the scoring in the 7–2 victory over the Indians.

After Nomar's July 22, 2002 three-homer game, Michael Gee of the *Boston Herald* wrote: "Garciaparra won the Player of the Week award in one hour of yesterday afternoon's game."

A few more home run stats

A few selective stats. The *Red Sox Media Guide* is a good source for more detailed Red Sox home run records.

Most home runs in a game by the team: eight, against Toronto on July 4, 1977.

Most home runs in an inning: a major-league record tying two, by Bill Regan (June 16, 1928), Ellis Burks (August 27, 1990), and Nomar Garciaparra (July 23, 2002). Regan hit an inside-the-park and a conventional home run in the same inning.

Most home runs in a season by the team: 238 (2003)

Most grand slams in a season: 11 (2005)

Most home runs by pinch-hitters in a season: six (1953)

Most home runs in consecutive games: five, by Jimmie Foxx, Ted Williams, Dick Stuart, George Scott, and Jose Canseco.

Most home runs in one month: 14, by Jackie Jensen in June 1958 and David Ortiz in July 2006.

Home run #10,000

Kevin Millar's home run in the bottom of the eighth inning on August 9, 2003 was home run #10,000 hit at Fenway Park. Two innings earlier, Manny Ramirez had hit #9,999 to tie the game. Over the Green Monster. Millar came up to bat with the score tied 3–3, and runners on first and third. Baltimore's pitcher Travis Driskill uncorked a wild pitch and a run scored. With pinch-runner Gabe Kapler on second, Millar hit the next pitch over the Monster as well. It proved the margin of difference in the 6–4 Sox win. Millar showed some humility: "I'm also the guy who was the 300th guy to strike out against Randy Johnson two straight years."

Who's hit the most homers at Fenway?

Red Sox batters

		Visitors
1 Ted Williams 248	6 Rico Petrocelli 134	1 Babe Ruth 38
2 Carl Yastrzemski 237	7 Manny Ramirez 128	2 Mickey Mantle 38
3 Jim Rice 208	8 Jimmie Foxx 126	3 Harmon Killebrew 37
4 Dwight Evans 199	9 Mo Vaughn 118	4 Al Kaline 30
5 Bobby Doerr 145	10 David Ortiz 92	5 Joe DiMaggio 29

Every starting player hit 10 or more home runs

It had never been done before in the 103-year history of the Red Sox. A new club record was set August 27, 2003 when Todd Walker hit a two-run homer in the seventh inning to put the Sox ahead in an important game against the Blue Jays, 5–3. Every starting player on the team had then hit at least 10 home runs on the season.

The first homer hit by a player in a Red Sox uniform

We already know that Buck Freeman hit the first homer for the franchise and that Hugh

Harry Lord and Babe Ruth.

Bradley hit the first at Fenway, but who hit the first home run for the Red Sox? Readers will recall that 1908 was the first season the team was known by that name.

The first homer hit by a ballplayer wearing a Red Sox uniform was hit by leftfielder Gavvy Cravath, a "handsome drive" in the March 6, 1908 intrasquad game at the expense of Elmer Steele. Cravath was hitting for the Regulars and Steele pitching for the Yannigans.

The first one hit against an opponent was third baseman Harry Lord's drive into the left-field corner in the fifth inning of the 6–0 defeat of the Little Rock Travelers, in Little Rock on March 17, 1908. The two-run homer extended the Sox lead to 4–0.

The first Sox homer hit in a regular season game came on April 23 in Washington, with two outs in the top of the fourth inning when Doc Gessler "poled a low smash to center and crossed the plate before the ball was relayed in." It was one of 14 homers hit by the Sox that first year as the Sox. The victim? Washington pitcher Bill Burns.

The first Red Sox homer hit at a home game was Gavvy Cravath's, on May 29 in a game against Washington.

RBIs

When it comes to offense, driving in runs is the name of the game.

The most runs batted in during a single season by a Red Sox batter was 175 (Jimmie Foxx, 1938). Second was the Williams/Stephens combo in 1949—159 RBIs apiece—a quick calculation shows a total of 318 combined. David Ortiz comes next, with his 148 in 2005. The highest total not to win the RBI crown was the 144 Manny Ramirez drove in that same year, 2005—because Ortiz drove in four more.

Nine times, Ted Williams drove in 100 or more runs. Appearing in only 89 games in 1950, due to breaking his elbow in the All-Star Game, Williams still drove in 97. Had he played every game of the year, as he had in 1949, and produced at that rate, Ted would have driven in 167—still not as good as Foxx's 1938 season. Jim Rice had eight years when he knocked in 100 or more runs during his decade of dominance. Bobby Doerr, Jimmie Foxx, and Manny Ramirez all have six 100-plus RBI years with the Red Sox. (Foxx had seven with the Athletics before coming to Boston, and Ramirez had five with the Indians before he joined the fold.) With RBI #100 on August 20, 2006, Manny had six 100-RBI seasons in a row for the Red Sox. Previously, only Foxx had accomplished that.

And Foxx was astonishing in his 1938 season, in that he hit over 100 RBIs at Fenway Park alone! His totals for the year were 104 RBIs at home and 71 RBIs on the road. Foxx hit for a .402 average at Fenway with 35 of his 50 homers. In just nine home games, in which he hit two home runs each time, he racked up 18 of those homers and 40 runs batted in. Talk about home field advantage.

Mike Greenwell's 23 game-winning RBIs in 1986 remains the American League record for this statistic, which remains difficult to mine over time (it was only an "official statistic" for around 10 years). Big Papi watchers will be interested to know that David Ortiz had 21 game-winning RBIs in 2005. Any way you look at it, official or not, that's good!

The most RBIs by a Red Sox batter in a single game is 10 and that's been done four times:

Rudy York—July 27, 1946
Norm Zauchin—May 27, 1955 (10.75% of his year's production all in just one day)
Fred Lynn—June 18, 1975
Nomar Garciaparra—May 10, 1999

In post-season games, John Valentin drove in seven runs against Cleveland on October 10, 1999. The very next day, Troy O'Leary drove in seven runs against Cleveland.

The most runs driven in during one given month was 41 by Ted Williams in May 1942. In June 1950, Ted drove in 40. The surprising flash-in-the-pan Clyde Vollmer drove in 40 during July 1951. Talk about anomalies—he'd only driven in 37 total the year before, and only drove in 50 total the following year. The 40 in the one month was 47% of his 1951 production of 85 RBIs.

Both Carlton Fisk (September 1977) and Nick Esasky (August 1989) drove in 35 runs in a given month; so did David Ortiz in July 2006. Nomar Garciaparra twice drove in 33 during a month (July 1998 and May 1999). Jim Rice drove in 33 twice, too, in the same year: May 1978 and August 1978.

For a career, Carl Yastrzemski drove in 1,844 runs—five more than the #2 man, Ted Williams, who drove in 1,839. (Of course, Ted did miss most of five seasons while serving in the military and suffered more from injury than Yaz. Yaz had 11,968 at-bats to Ted's 7,706. Ted averaged an RBI every 4.19 at-bats, while Yaz averaged one every 6.49. But who's counting? Driving in over 1,800 runs is a great accomplishment. Third on the Red Sox list is Jim Rice with 1,451, fourth is Dwight Evans with 1,346, and fifth is Bobby Doerr with 1,247.

They played every game all year long

We just saw that Ted Williams played every game in 1949. How often has a Red Sox ballplayer appeared in every game, all year long? You can be sure no pitcher ever has, but 25 players have—some of them more than once. Everett Scott did it five times, from 1917 through 1921. Early Boston Americans ballplayers Buck Freeman and Candy LaChance both did it in the years 1902, 1903, and 1905—and Freddy Parent did it in 1901, 1902, and 1905. The only one to do it three times since 1921 is Dwight Evans who played in every game in 1981, 1982, and 1984.

Twice each Hobe Ferris, Frank Malzone, Jim Rice, Chick Stahl, Vern Stephens, and Carl Yastrzemski played every game. Other men to do it once were: Jimmy Collins, Dom DiMaggio, Bobby Doerr, Tommy Dowd, Jimmie Foxx, Harry Hooper, Duffy Lewis, Tom Oliver, Jimmy Piersall, Del Pratt, George Scott, Phil Todt, Bill Wambsganss, and Ted Williams.

The best year for such constancy was the first of the franchise, 1901: four different men played in every single game: Collins, Dowd, Ferris, and Parent. The most recent year to feature two Sox players in every game was 1981, when both Evans and Rice patrolled right field and left field, respectively. Of course, this was a strike-shortened season, so each only played 108 games with 59 days off between halves of the interrupted season.

The closest to complete in a long time was Mo Vaughn in 1996. He played 161 of the team's 162 games, missing only the July 25 game in the Hubert H. Humphrey Metrodome in Minneapolis. He'd hurt his knee sliding into home plate the previous night at Fenway Park; he needn't have extended himself so much—the Red Sox won that game, 12–2. The soreness was sufficiently gone by the following day and Vaughn finished out the year. The closest we've seen since has been David Ortiz, who played in 159 games in 2005.

Six RBIs in one inning

Six runs batted in during one inning remains the major league record. It was tied by Carlos Quintana on July 30, 1991 helping the Red Sox break out of their worst home slump in over 60 years. The Sox had suffered nine straight home losses; they hadn't won a game at Fenway since July 6. And earlier that day, Red Sox reliever Jeff Gray suffered what appeared to be a stroke in the clubhouse.

Former Bosox Oil Can Boyd was pitching for Texas and Quintana was playing left, subbing for Mike Greenwell, out with a sprained wrist. Quintana hadn't had a hit in days. In the first inning, he popped up to the catcher. But in the third inning, Boyd walked the bases loaded and the Q hit a grand slam. "I looked for the slider and I got it," Quintana said afterwards. Later in the inning, Carlos doubled off reliever Wayne Rosenthal and knocked in two more, accounting for six of the 10 Red Sox runs. Final score: Boston 11, Texas 6. "The sarsaparilla should taste better tonight," said manager Joe Morgan.

Tom McBride did it for the Red Sox, too, back on August 4, 1945. It was in the second game of a doubleheader; the Senators had shut out the Sox in the first game, 4–0. McBride was 0-for-1 in a pinch-hitting role. He played both first base and left field in the nightcap (no, not at the same time), and drove in half the runs in the 12-run top of the fourth, twice batting with the bases loaded and twice clearing the bases—once with a double and once with a triple. McBride added another RBI later in the game, which the Red Sox and Boo Ferriss won, 15–4.

Six RBIs in a game—by a pitcher

That's a lot of runs batted in by anyone, but even in the days before the DH it was a lot of runs for any pitcher. Mentioned elsewhere in this work, Wes Ferrell hit two home runs, a two-run shot and a grand slam, in successive innings on August 12, 1936—accouning for every one of the runs in Boston's 6–4 win over Philadelphia.

Ellis Kinder threw a five-hitter in the first game of August 6, 1950 against the White Sox. He hit a grand slam and drove in two more runs, providing more than enough runs for Boston's 9–2 victory.

Six RBIs on one hit

Rico Petrocelli was 1-for-5 on Wednesday afternoon, June 21, 1972—but drove in six runs. Four came on the fifth-inning grand slam he hit off Bill Gogolewski of the Texas Rangers. In the third inning, he'd hit into a force play, Reggie Smith cut down at second base, but with Yaz scoring. In the seventh inning, with Yaz again on third, he grounded out and Yastrzemski scored. It's not quite as hard if you can bookend a slam.

The most runs batted in during a single postseason

The record is 19 and it's held by three ballplayers: Sandy Alomar Jr. with Cleveland in 1998, Scott Spiezio with the Angels in 2002, and our own David Ortiz with the Red Sox in 2004. Remember that year?

RBIs in consecutive games

Joe Cronin drove in one or more runs for 12 games in a row—20 RBIs from June 27—July 9, 1939. Taking notes, perhaps, was rookie Ted Williams, who matched the 12-game stretch, driving in 18 runs in the 12 consecutive games from August 31-September 13, 1942. Ted later had an 11-game streak in 1950. The league records are 13 (AL, Taft Wright in 1941) and 17 (NL, Oscar Grimes in 1922).

Runs scored

Scoring runs is pretty important, too. Getting on base and being in a position to score—setting the table, so to speak—is a key ingredient in a successful offense. Dom DiMaggio and Johnny Pesky knew their job was to be the table-setters during the era they played, with Ted Williams coming up behind them. There were more than a few times the speedy Pesky held up at first, rather than trying to stretch a single into a double. Man on second, first base open—opposing managers would be more likely to work around Williams, or just walk him intentionally. Unless it was a sure thing, Johnny knew he'd be taking the bat out of Ted's hands if he went for the two-bagger.

#1 in runs scored for the Red Sox—again, reflecting his longevity, was Carl Yastrzemski. Not that there's anything wrong with longevity; they're not going to pay your salary if you aren't producing. Yastrzemski scored 1,816 runs for the Red Sox. #2 was Ted Williams, with 1,798. (Of course, he scored 521 of those on his own home runs, but there's nothing wrong with that.) #3 was Dwight Evans, with 1,435. Rice was #4 with 1,249, and Bobby Doerr came in fifth with 1,094. Seeing how Doerr stacks up in many of these departments lends more support to his inclusion in the Baseball Hall of Fame. The only other two Red Sox with more than 1,000 runs scored are Wade Boggs (1,067) and Dominic DiMaggio (1,046).

119 runs scored in a nine-game stretch

Between June 2 and June 10, 1950 the Red Sox scored a total of 119 runs—and still lost three of the games.

Scoring lots of runs for several games in a row: The scores were 8–2, 9–0, 9–3, 10–3, 10–8, and 10–2 as for six games in a row, Boston scored eight or more runs in a game, the streak coming on six consecutive days between June 1 and June 6 in 1903.

Going a long time without being shut out

From April 26 through September 20, 1950, the Red Sox played 136 games without being shut out. Maybe an even more impressive streak, though, ran from May 30, 1938 through July 25 that year: the Sox scored more than one run in every one of the 45 games played.

Twice in the same year—1936—the Sox scored more than two runs in each one of 23 consecutive games. From May 19 through June 11, and then again from June 22 to July 18. And for the first of those two 23-game stretches, the Sox scored three or more runs in every game.

Failing to record a shutout ate up almost one entire season, 153 games in all after July 24, 2005 until July 14, 2006. When Curt Schilling, Manny Delcarmen, and Craig Hansen combined to shut out Oakland 7–0 on July 15, it was the first time the team had shut out the opposition since Curt Schilling closed out a 3–0 shutout of the White Sox started by Wade Miller on July 23 the year before.

In the interest of fairness, we should probably acknowledge that the team was itself shut out four times in a row, on August 2, 3, 4, and 6, 1906. Moving on...

Not getting totally blown out

If you call not giving up 10 or more runs an accomplishment, then please note that for 181 games in a row, the Red Sox never gave up as many as 10 runs, the streak running from the 11–6 defeat to Chicago on August 18, 1916 until losing to New York on September 13, 1917.

The day a pitcher with only one leg held the Red Sox to a run

Just about everyone who's read a little baseball history has come across the story of Eddie Gaedel, the 3-foot, 7-inch pinch hitter who drew a walk in his only plate appearance, on August 19, 1951. Gaedel's at bat was a publicity stunt by Bill Veeck and nothing but a novelty. Gaedel seems to have stolen the retrospective limelight from Bert Shepard, a Second World War hero who played a major league game against the Red Sox with an artificial leg.

Shepard had played some minor league ball pre-war before being drafted in 1942. He volunteered and trained as a pilot flying P-38 Thunderbolts. His 34th mission proved to be the first daytime bombing raid over Berlin. Other missions followed that one, but his last one was on May 21, 1944. Shepard came in on a run towards a Berlin aerodrome at an altitude of just 20 feet, following other Allied planes attacking the field. One or two hundred Nazis on the ground were firing automatic weapons as the warplanes swept in, and as Shepard approached the airfield his foot got shot off by groundfire, he got hit in the chin, and his plane crashlanded and burst into flames.

Regaining consciousness quite some time later, he found himself in a German hospital, with his right leg amputated below the knee. After eight months as a prisoner of war, and deemed unlikely to return as a combatant, the Germans sent him home in a swap of P.O.W.s in early 1945.

Bert Shepard had worked out in prison camp, playing catch and practicing his fielding. He got around on an artificial leg crafted by a fellow prisoner. While at Walter Reed Hospital after returning Stateside, he was being fitted with a new leg when Secretary of War Robert Patterson toured the facility, chatting with various patients about what they planned to do after they were discharged. Patterson was surprised that Bert Shepard said he wanted to play pro ball, and the Secretary placed a call to his friend Clark Griffith of the Washington Senators.

Not much was made of the leg and fans watching him pitch as spring training progressed had no idea Shepard was an amputee. As a pitcher, he drove off his rear foot, which in this case—as a left-hander—meant using his good leg.

Tellis interviewed Shepard for his book *Once Around the Bases*, and recounts an amazing incident which stunned Red Sox fans. Shepard was pitching batting practice at Fenway. After a few pitches, his leg cracked, amplifying a smaller crack he'd sustained doing some running a couple of days earlier. Shepard recalled, "I made another pitch, and the leg turned sideways. So I straightened it up and threw another pitch, and by now the leg is almost at a 90-degree angle. So I straightened it up again and made another pitch, and this time the foot broke completely off inside my sock."

Tellis says the fans at Fenway "saw Shepard's foot, still in its sock and shoe, dangling loose as the batting-practice pitcher went into his next windup, brought his leg up, kicked back toward center field to get his momentum, and began his pivot toward the hitter—only to have the shoe and the foot fly off and head toward center field. 'I just turned around casually and made another pitch,' Shepard says, 'and the players were lying around on the ground laughing. But think of the fans! They didn't know I had an artificial foot.'" Catcher Rick Ferrell said, "The crowd gasped. They thought it was his real foot."

Shepard had been signed with the Senators as a coach, but manager Ossie Bluege promised him a shot in a game. On July 10, he got a start in a war-relief exhibition game against the Dodgers. Shepard walked the first two batters on eight pitches, but then settled down and retired the side and pitched through three innings yielding but one hit.

On August 4, 1945 Shep got his chance to appear in a regular season game, in Washington. It was the second game of a doubleheader against the Red Sox and Boston had pushed across 12 runs in the top of the fourth inning. Bluege, looking to spare the rest of his staff, brought Shepard in.

Carlos Santiago "Sandy" Ullrich had started the game and given up seven runs, five of them in the fourth (which he started by walking the bases loaded) when Bluege brought in Joe Cleary. Cleary managed one strikeout, but walked three more Red Sox himself and gave up five hits and seven runs. Joe Cleary, the departing pitcher, had left Shepard with the bases loaded. There were two outs and Catfish Metkovich was at the plate, a decent .261 lifetime hitter over a 10-year career. The count ran to 3-and-2, but Shepard got him swinging on a fastball inside. It was quite an inning. Boston's Tom McBride batted in six of the 12 runs with a triple and a double.

Shepard finished the game, throwing 5⅓ innings and pretty much shut the Sox down, holding them to just one more run on three hits. He struck out two, walked one, and picked up a couple of assists on balls hit back to the mound. At the plate, he went 0-for-3, batting against Boo Ferriss (a 21-game winner that year). First time up, he struck out, then he hit into a doubleplay and finally rolled out to Ferriss on the mound.

The Senators were in the 1945 pennant race right into the final days, finishing just 1½ games out. Despite Shep's successful stint (he boasts a career 1.69 ERA), Bluege never saw fit to give him another shot. That was Cleary's only major league appearance as well, and

Cleary's lifetime ERA is 189.00. It would have been higher still, had Shepard not struck out Metkovich and seen the three inherited Red Sox runners stranded.

Oddly, the story did not receive much play in the *Boston Globe*. Shepard was not even mentioned in the game story, and the only coverage he got was about a 1½ inch insert box headlined "One-Legged Shepard Pitches in First Major League Game." No interviews, no other coverage, nothing.

Bert Shepard continued in the minors, playing here and there, off and on for another 10 years. He retired after the 1949 season, but then came back again in 1952—often appearing as a novelty player. He quit for good in 1955. Author Todd Anton interviewed Bert Shepard at length and presents his life story in the book *No Greater Love*.

Biggest game-to-game shift in winning margin

The most runs scored by one team in a major league game were the 29 runs scored on June 8, 1950. When the Red Sox lost by five runs the following day, 12–7, it represented a shift in winning margins of 30 runs. This fell one run short of the record, though, set on July 13 and 14, 1904 after Cleveland beat New York 16–3 one day, only to get skunked by the New Yorkers the next day, 21–3.

Consider the FOUR games, though, that the 1950 Red Sox played at the time. On top by 49–8 in the first two, then down 30–15 in the two that followed.

June 7, 1950 Boston 20, St. Louis 4   June 9 St. Louis 12, Boston 7
June 8 Boston 29, St. Louis 4   June 10 Detroit 18, Boston 8

Of the 29 games the Red Sox played during that June, there were 14 games in which one team or another scored 10 or more runs.

Walks and walks percentage

A walk's as good as a hit. Well, not necessarily. It does get you on base and increases your team's chances of scoring. But given that some hits are home runs, some are triples, and some are doubles, one would probably prefer an extra-base hit almost all the time to a single. A single can be more productive than a walk, too—certainly a good number of singles will score a runner from second, move a runner from first to third—or even first to home. A walk can't do any of those things.

Getting on base is good, though. And no one walked any better than Ted Williams. His lifetime walks percentage of 20.75% is tops in baseball history—more than one out of every five times Williams came up to bat, he got on base with a base on balls. He walked 2,019 times in his major league career. A number of those were intentional walks, of course. The Kid holds the American League record for most intentional walks in a season, and he earned it in the year he turned 39. He drew 33 intentional walks in 1957, a figure matched by John Olerud with Toronto in 1993. Olerud appeared in 36 more games than Williams, though, for whatever that's worth.

A case can be made that sometimes a walk is better than a hit. It's a question of psychology, and baseball is often a game of psychology in the one-on-one challenge between pitcher and batter. A hit can often be a lucky fluke, a ball that drops in perhaps. A walk represents four failures to get the ball over the plate in a given at-bat and reflects more of a failure on the pitcher's part than one of those fortuitous fluke hits. A walk—a free pass—is typically an unintended gift to the offense. "Those walks'll hurt you every time," broadcasters will say. Clearly, that's not true, but it happens often enough that pitchers hate to give up a walk. Working a walk, maybe fouling off several pitches in the process, can do a number on a pitcher.

Yaz drew 1,845 walks, Evans drew 1,337, and Boggs drew 1,004.

And Tracy Stallard never did walk, not even once. In 265 plate appearances, never once did Stallard draw a base on balls. He had 27 hits in 247 at-bats, executed 11 sacrifice hits (and one sacrifice fly), he reached on an error seven times, and he was hit by a pitch once. He whiffed 88 times. As a pitcher, he doled out 354 bases on balls. But as a batter, he never once worked a walk.

Most walks by a rookie: 107, by Ted Williams in 1939—still a major-league record.

Most intentional walks to a rookie: 13, to George Scott in 1966.

Walking men

On July 8, 1934, Max "Camera Eye" Bishop walked eight times in a doubleheader, four times in each game.

Pitcher Chuck Stobbs walked four times in the first four innings alone of the June 8, 1950 game. The Red Sox were busy that day; they also registered 28 hits and beat the Browns, 29–4.

From 2005 through 2007, David Ortiz recorded more than 100 walks, 100 runs, and 100 RBIs for three seasons in a row. The only other Red Sox player to hit these heights was Ted Williams, who did it six seasons in a row (1941–49, despite missing three years during WWII). Ortiz led the AL in walks in the latter two years, the first Sox player to lead in back-to-back seasons since Ted Williams, 1946–49.

An intentional walk with the bases loaded?

David Kaiser, author of *Epic Season*, a book on the 1948 season, authored an e-mail telling of an event that happened on September 24 that year. "The Red Sox, tied with the Indians for first place, played the Yankees, a game back, at the Stadium. They had the kind of back-and-forth high-scoring game that the contenders had so often that year. In the fourth inning, with two on, two out, and the Red Sox leading, Joe Page relieved for the Yankees with Johnny Pesky up. Pesky grounded to the right side, Page failed to cover, and Pesky was safe to load the bases and bring up Ted Williams. Williams had hit a two-run double with the bases loaded earlier in the game. Page walked him on five pitches. It wasn't intentional, technically, but newspaper accounts suggested he just didn't want to let Ted hit. He was rewarded when Junior Stephens popped out to end the inning down 5–3, and the Yankees eventually won the game, 9–7."

Fake intentional walks

It can be a risky move, but it can work, too. On September 10, 1954, with a man on second base but first base open, Hal Brown on the mound for the Red Sox and a 3–2 count, Sammy White put on an act, stepping out of the box to take what looked to be a concession to Vic Wertz by putting him on base to set up a play for the next batter. Brown fired the ball right down the middle and struck out Wertz. It wasn't the first time that year the Sox tried the trick, but the time before Frank Sullivan missed the strike zone and walked Gene Woodling.

On June 7, 1968, though, Yaz was up. He'd already been walked intentionally twice in the game, and the White Sox had thrown two pitchouts during his seventh-inning at-bat. It didn't stretch credulity to think they'd give him another IBB. Joel Horlen tried to slip the pitch by him, but Yaz pounded it out of the park.

Another twist

Three years earlier, Lee Thomas was up for Boston with Baltimore's Stu Miller pitching. The count ran to 3–0 and Miller decided to walk Thomas—who swung at the pitch despite it being far out of the zone. Then Miller tried again, and Thomas again swung at the intentionally wide pitch. And fouled out when Miller had to pitch to him on a 3–2 count.

STRIKEOUTS

Sox players who struck out the least often?

Based on a minimum of 350 at-bats, the walks to at-bats ratio of Jack Tobin was the best of any Red Sox player ever—Tobin struck out just 12 times in 583 at-bats. Over a much more extended period, one has to be impressed by Stuffy McInnis. In over 2,000 Red Sox at-bats, he struck out only 49 times. And Doc Cramer had over 3,000 at-bats, but struck out less than 100 times (just barely).

A low strikeouts to at-bats (K/AB) ratio is obviously the best.

The best nine

Player	At-bats	Strikeouts	K/AB ratio
Jack Tobin	583	12	.0206
Les Nunamaker	356	8	.0225
Stuffy McInnis	2,006	49	.0244
Del Pratt	1,128	30	.0266
Lou Finney	1,930	60	.0311
Tom Oliver	1,931	61	.0316
Doc Cramer	3,111	99	.0318
Johnny Hodapp	413	14	.0339
Ossie Vitt	997	34	.0341

The worst nine

Billy Consolo	618	168	.2718
Bernie Carbo	986	256	.2596
Marc Sullivan	360	92	.2556
Brian Daubach	876	222	.2534
Mo Vaughn	3,828	954	.2492
Phil Plantier	512	127	.2480
Lee Tinsley	677	166	.2452
Jose Canseco	756	175	.2315
Damon Buford	513	117	.2281

Pitchers who whiffed a lot

Lefty Grove	516	233	.4516
Bill Monbouquette	498	221	.4438
Jim Lonborg	354	154	.4350
Ike Delock	352	150	.4261
Danny MacFayden	384	142	.3698

Lefty Grove.

Joe Dobson, Jack Russell, Frank Sullivan, and Earl Wilson would round out the nine striking-outingmost pitchers.

Five and even six strikeouts in one game

Five strikeouts in one game: Boston's Phil Plantier did it October 1, 1991. The Red Sox were 3½ games out of first place with six games to play. Plantier struck out in the first, fourth, sixth, seventh, and ninth innings—each time except the fourth with men on base. The Red Sox lost, 8–5, to the Tigers—and lost four of the next five games, too.

Six strikeouts in one game: Cecil Cooper did it on June 14, 1974—but he had 15 innings to pull off the feat. It wasn't his best day. He was Boston's leadoff batter but went 0-for-8 in the game. We could perhaps be a bit understanding; the opposing pitcher was Nolan Ryan and he struck out 19 Red Sox in 13 innings of work. Luis Tiant went the distance for Boston, but lost 4–3 to the Angels in Anaheim.

Both records are shared by several other players.

A few selected single-game strikeout situations

What a way to start a season. Opening Day 1911, Walter Johnson struck out four Red Sox in the first inning. The catcher dropped a third strike, prolonging the inning.

George Scott once struck out five times in an April 1966 game in Cleveland. He had 12 innings in which to do so. He walked once, too. The team as a whole struck out 17 times that day, and 16 times the next day—33 times in two days. Both games went into extras and Boston dropped both.

Rico Petrocelli struck out six times in a row, but spread it over two games. Pitchers Darrell Brandon (seven times, in 1966) and Ray Culp (eight times, in 1971) both had long streaks of strikeouts.

Most hits / runs by the team in a season

The 1997 Red Sox averaged more than 10 hits a game, with 1,684 hits in 162 games. That's a 10.395 average. In the days of the 154-game schedule, the 1,665 hits in 1950 was an average of 10.8 per game. Even without the additional eight games, the 1950 Red Sox scored the most runs ever: 1,027.

Fewest hits / runs in a season? The fewest runs scored was 463 by the Boston Americans in 1906—even lower than the 473 scored during the war-shortened 1918 season or the strike-shortened seasons of 1981 (519) and 1994 (552). The fewest hits in a season came during the 1994 strike year—just 1,038 hits. In a non-shortened season, the 1,179 hits in 1905 was the all-time low total.

Most Red Sox hits in a game: 28

The Red Sox record for most hits in a game is 28, on June 27, 2003. They beat the soon-to-become World Champion Florida Marlins, 25–8. For an account of this game, see "Big Innings/ Big Scores" below.

Most Red Sox hits in a game they lost: 23

September 3, 1981. The game ended just about 24 hours after it began; it was suspended after 19 innings as a 3–3 tie, then re-started the following day. In the top of the 20th inning, Seattle scored one run when the Mariners' Dave Henderson singled off new reliever Bob Stanley and Joe Simpson tripled him in. The Red Sox failed to score in the bottom of the 20th. The Red Sox had 23 hits, but Seattle had 24. Seattle used nine pitchers; the Red Sox used seven. Seattle left 22 men on base; the Red Sox left 17.

The largest negative hit differential in a game the Red Sox won

June 8, 1958: The Red Sox only made five hits in the game, while the White Sox got 19. Guess who won? It might have been the largest negative hit differential (or whatever you want to call it), but Boston won the game, 6–5. Boston's first three hits were all solo home runs and they were the only three hits Boston had until the ninth. Chicago tied it up in the ninth and took a 5–4 lead in the top of the 10th. Then Jackie Jensen hit a two-run homer into the net in left to win the game. The Sox won the second game, too.

Run differentials

Seasons in which the Red Sox scored 200 or more runs than they allowed:

1912—255	1950—223
1949—229	1903—204

Negative run differentials for the Red Sox include five seasons best forgotten:

1932—<349>	1926—<273>	1906—<243>
1925—<283>	1927—<259>	

A lot of singles

In the first game of two, the Yankees hit safely 18 times against Boston pitching—every hit a single. Despite the absence of extra-base power, New York easily won the September 3, 1947 game, 11–2.

Using the Wall to effect

In the September 26, 1961 doubleheader at Fenway, the White Sox and Red Sox made good use of the outfield fences—of the combined 52 hits (each team won one game), a full 19 of them were off the wall and another six went over it.

Doubles

Most doubles in a season by a player: Earl Webb, 67 (1931)—a major-league record.

Most doubles in a season by a rookie: Fred Lynn, 47 (1975)—an AL record.

Most doubles in a season by the team—a major-league record 373, which the Red Sox have done twice, in 1997 and 2004.

Most doubles in a game by a player: a major-league record four by Billy Werber (July 17, 1935), Al Zarilla (June 8, 1950), Orlando Cepeda (August 8, 1973), and Rick Miller (May 11, 1981). Werber hit his four in consecutive at-bats.

Most doubles in a game by the team: 12 (July 29, 1990 against Detroit)—tied for the American League record.

Most doubles by a player in one inning: two, and the first time it was done, it was done by a pitcher (Joe Wood, July 4, 1913). Since Joe did it, so have Hal Janvrin (June 9, 1914), Grover Hartley (May 28, 1927), Joe Cronin (August 3, 1939), Jody Reed (September 8, 1991), and Mo Vaughn (June 21, 1994). Players from other teams are tied for this major-league record.

Most doubles in an inning by the team: five (twice), both times against the Blue Jays (June 21, 1994 and June 1, 2003).

Triples

In earlier days, when overflow crowds were permitted behind ropes to stand in the outfield, balls hit into the crowd were typically scored as either doubles or triples through the ground rules announced before the day's game. The ground rule helped Patsy Dougherty hit three triples in one game (he hit two singles, too) on September 5, 1903—and this was in a game called due to rain after 7½ innings.

On May 6, 1934, the Red Sox hit four triples all in one inning and without even the benefit of a ground rule. Much of the credit went to Detroit pitcher Firpo Mayberry, not having one of his better days. The Red Sox scored 12 runs in the fourth inning, with consecutive triples contributed by Carl Reynolds, Moose Solters, Rick Ferrell, and Bucky Walters. As Boston batted around, all four came up again in the same inning and they added two singles, a walk, and a double.

Most triples in a game by a player: a major-league record three, by Patsy Dougherty, as presented above.

Most triples in a game by the team: Ferris hit a triple, too, in the September 5, 1903 game, so that makes four for the team. There were the four consecutive triples in one inning on May 6, 1934. The Sox also hit four against Kansas City (Athletics) on August 3, 1965 and against Kansas City (Royals) on August 24, 1971. That's the most we've been able to find so far, but we suspect there might be a Deadball Era game with five or more. Anyone got one?

Most triples in an inning by a player: one, tied by lots and lots of people.

Most triples in a season by a player: 22, by Tris Speaker in 1913.

Most bases loaded triples in a season: three, by Jackie Jensen in 1956, tied for the major league record.

Most triples in a season by a rookie: 17, by Russ Scarritt in 1929.

Most triples in a season by the team: 113 (1903), which is tied for the AL record. Fewest triples in a season: 16 (2006).

In 1940, Ted Williams alone had 14, and Lou Finney had one more.

Because of ground rules in the 1903 World Series, Boston had 16 triples and Pittsburgh had nine. Balls hit into the overflow crowds on the field counted as triples.

A few big triples

Leading off the third inning of Game Five in the 1912 World Series, Harry Hooper tripled and Steve Yerkes tripled back-to-back. Both scored—Hooper obviously coming in on Yerkes' three-bagger—and the Red Sox beat Christy Mathewson, 2–1.

Yaz hit what should have been a triple against the Tigers in 1972, but Aparicio fell down rounding third and Yaz couldn't stop, steaming into the bag at third. With two runners on third, Yaz was ruled out, with a double. The Red Sox lost the October 2 game, and the Sox lost the pennant by a half a game to the Tigers.

In mid-September 1967, in the bottom of the eighth of a 1–1 game, after Mike Ryan singled with one out, Jose Tartabull came in to run for Ryan, and Jim Lonborg tripled off Catfish Hunter driving in what proved to be the winning run.

May 10, 1969 in the top of the 10th in a 3–3 game, Tony Conigliaro tripled with the bases loaded giving the Red Sox a 6–3 lead and the win.

A foul dribbler becomes a triple

When Jake Jones dribbled a weak little ground ball down the third base line and saw it roll foul, little did he know that he'd wind up with a triple. It was July 27, 1947, in the sixth inning of the first game of a Fenway doubleheader against St. Louis. Starting pitcher Fred Sanford threw his glove at the ball between third and home. Third baseman Bob Dillinger was about to scoop up the ball, which was about six inches in foul territory at the time.

"Aghast at having to make a silly decision, the four umpires looked sorrowfully at each other for several long seconds," wrote Harold Kaese in the *Globe*. "Then Cal Hubbard, chief umpire, did his duty by holding aloft three banana-like fingers."

The two leagues had different rules at the time. In the National League, there was no penalty assessed for throwing equipment at a foul ball. Sanford didn't have that excuse. He'd never played in the National League.

The AL rule dated back to 1939, when another play at Fenway prompted the rule. It was when Gene Desautels fired his catcher's mitt at a similar foul dribbler. There being no rule against it, there was no penalty, but among the spectators that day was Tommy Connolly, league umpire-in-chief. He, quite reasonably, wondered why a player could throw a glove, a mask, a cap, or anything at a ball that still might roll fair without any penalty. Hence the AL rule was implemented that any batted ball, fair or foul, interfered with in such a way would result in an automatic triple. In the NL, it was apparently not uncommon for fielders to throw stuff at a foul ball, but if they inadvertently knocked the ball fair, it would be ruled a triple.

Jones scored a bit later. Sanford left for a pinch-hitter in the seventh. "Giving Jones a three-bagger on a 60-foot foul was like standing Sanford before a firing squad for illegal parking," wrote Kaese. Still, he should have known better. Boston won both games of the doubleheader.

Fenway Park, 1947.

Extra-base hits

Most extra-base hits in a game by the team: 17, a major league record (June 8, 1950)

Most extra-base hits in an inning by the team: 7, tied for the AL record (September 24, 1940)

Most extra-base hits in a season by a player: 92, by Jimmie Foxx in 1938 (David Ortiz hit 91 in 2004, and also holds third and fourth place with 88 in 2005 and again in 2007.)

Most extra-base hits in a season by a rookie: 86, by Ted Williams in 1939

Most extra-base hits in a season by the team: 649, a major-league record (2003)

Leading the league in both on-base percentage and slugging in the same year

Two players have done it nine times apiece:

    Babe Ruth—1919, 1920, 1921, 1923, 1924, 1926, 1927, 1930, 1931
    Ted Williams—1941, 1942, 1946, 1947, 1948, 1949, 1951, 1954, 1957

Rogers Hornsby did it eight times and Barry Bonds did it six times.

Ted Williams still holds the record for the most games in a row to reach base safely

A lot of initials are familiar to baseball fans. Even casual fans know what RBI and ERA stand for. Many have become familiar with OBP and OPS. But what about CGOBS? That's not an oft-recognized set of initials, and yet it may represent one of the greatest accomplishments in baseball history. CGOBS stands for Consecutive Games on Base Safely.

Ted Williams once said, "I believe there isn't a record in the books that will be tougher to break than Joe's 56-game hitting streak. It may be the greatest batting achievement of all."

Williams's last written words were, "I really do know how lucky I've been in my life. Get a good pitch to hit!" The words appeared in February 2002, concluding his remarks in the *Ted Williams Museum* magazine. [Disclosure: Ted's final words were ghostwritten by the author of this book.]

The Red Sox star, who died in July 2002 at the age of 83, both preached and practiced what Hall of Famer Rogers Hornsby had taught him in 1938 when Williams was with the Minneapolis Millers: "Get a good ball to hit."

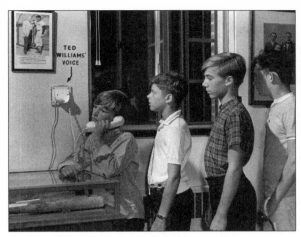

Hear Ted talk. Exhibit at the Hall of Fame, Cooperstown.

Williams sometimes was criticized for taking too many walks and not offering at pitches perhaps just outside the strike zone, but he believed if he started going for bad pitches and had any success, he'd begin swinging at ones even farther outside. It was important to maintain a disciplined approach. Don't go for the ball the pitcher wants you to chase.

The primary task of a hitter is to get on base, and nobody did that better than Williams. He believed that a walk was—in many ways—as good as a hit. In addition to putting a runner on base, he knew a walk could advance a runner and unnerve the pitcher. Williams had a career on-base percentage of .482—in other words, he reached base 48.2 percent of the time.

As we have seen, Williams walked more than 20 percent of the time—a higher percentage than any other hitter in history. He drew so many walks that his lifetime batting average of .344 (sixth best in the history of the game) became that OBP of .482, the best of any player ever.

Herm Krabbenhoft is the researcher who boosted Ted's 1941 OBP of .551 to .553 when he discovered two previously-uncredited bases on balls while researching CGOBS. Krabbenhoft was intrigued by something. He knew that Yankees star Joe DiMaggio had hit safely in 56 consecutive games in 1941, failed to hit in game #57, and then hit in 16 more in a row. But DiMaggio had walked in game No. 57, so he had reached base safely in 73 straight games; in fact, he walked in the game before his streak started, thus compiling a streak of 74 games in which he reached base. Had anyone topped that?

After weeks of checking thousands of players' statistics, Krabbenhoft found that one hitter had topped that mark: Williams had a consecutive games on base safely (CGOBS) streak of 84 in 1949. Starting July 1, Williams got on base in every game through September 27.

Consistency was a Williams characteristic. Throughout his entire career, if one excludes games in which he had only one plate appearance, as a pinch hitter, there were only seven times from 1939 through 1960 that he failed to get on base safely two games running. And only once (in 1939) did Williams fail to get on base three games in a row (May 23–25, 1939). On August 20, 1939, Williams didn't get on base in either game of a doubleheader. In 1940, he failed in the second game of a July 13 doubleheader and in the first game of the next day's doubleheader. Both days he reached safely in the other game.

From July 14, 1940 through September 26, 1950—more than a full decade—Williams never once had back-to-back games without reaching safely, if a pinch-hit appearance in 1941 and another in 1948 are discounted.

But on September 27, 1950, he failed to reach base in a doubleheader—again, his lapse confined to one day. It was nearly four years later, in September 1954, that he went two straight games without reaching base. It happened just twice more, once in 1958 and once in his final season, 1960.

There were not even many single games in which Williams failed to get on base. In 1948, excluding two pinch-hit appearances, there were only three games all season when he was kept off the bases. In 1949, it only happened five times. Over the 292 games in which Williams appeared in those two years, there were only 10 games (two as a pinch hitter) in which he didn't reach at least with a hit or walk.

As it happens, Williams holds three of the four longest CGOBS streaks:

Ted Williams (1949)—84	Ted Williams (1941)—69
Joe DiMaggio (1941)—74	Ted Williams (1948)—65

In 1957, soon after he turned 39, Williams reached base in a record 16 consecutive plate appearances:

Sept. 17 vs. KC—pinch-hit home run	Sept. 21 at NY—home run, three walks
Sept. 18 vs. KC—pinch-hit walk	Sept. 22 at NY—home run, single, two walks
Sept. 20 at NY—pinch-hit home run	Sept. 23 at NY—single, three walks, hit by pitch

SABR's Cliff Otto points out this string includes four home runs in four consecutive official at-bats. Pretty good for an old man, who hit .388 that year, just a handful of hits short of another .400 season. A younger, faster Williams might well have beaten out a few infield hits and made the magic mark once more.

So Ted holds nearly every significant "on base safely" record there is:

Highest single season on-base average of the 20th century—.553 (1941)*
Highest career on-base average—.482
Most seasons leading league in on-base average—12
Longest consecutive plate appearances on base safely streak—16 (1957)
Longest consecutive games on base safely streak—84 (1949)

*In 2002, Barry Bonds had an on-base percentage of .582, setting the single-season mark in the year after he hit 73 home runs. Indicted by a Federal grand jury in November 2007, it remains to be seen whether allegations of cheating through the use of illegal steroids tainted several of the records set by Bonds. We're not hesitant to use an asterisk to draw attention to the question.

Was Ted right, though? Would hitting in 56 consecutive games be the most difficult record to break? Pete Rose came the closest of any major leaguer, in 1978, when he hit safely in 44 straight games. How close is that? As Krabbenhoft has pointed out in more recent research, 44 is 78.6% of the way to 56.

Ted didn't even have the opportunity to learn of his own 84 CGOBS streak; he died before Krabbenhoft's work was published. Who's come close since 1949? In one season, the closest was Duke Snider's 58 CGOBS streak of 1954. 58 is 69.0% of the way to 84. If you were to look at a streak spanning more than one season, Mark McGwire had a 62 CGOBS streak from the end of 1995 into the beginning of 1996. 62 is 73.8% of the way to 84.

Pete Rose got significantly closer to matching or beating DiMaggio's mark than anyone has come to Williams' 84 CGOBS streak.

Krabbenhoft proposes that Teddy Ballgame's 84 consecutive games on base safely streak "may be the greatest batting achievement of all."

Williams hit for power as well as average. He hit 521 home runs, despite losing nearly five prime seasons to military service. Williams was an early member of the 500 home run club. He remains the last man in the .400 club. And he is one of the very exclusive members of the Triple Crown club—leading his league in average, runs batted in, and home runs. He earned membership twice, while missing by the thinnest of margins in 1949.

One would be hard pressed to find a better hitter. Williams could well have achieved his childhood dream, to have people say, "There goes the greatest hitter who ever lived."

Top Red Sox hitting streaks

The longest hitting streak in Red Sox history was set in 1949 by Dominic DiMaggio, some 34 games. There were two who hit in exactly 30 consecutive games: Tris Speaker in 1912 and Nomar Garciaparra in 1997. Johnny Damon hit in 29 straight games in 2005, and Wade Boggs hit in 28 straight in 1985. Two players have hit in 27 games in a row: the same Dom DiMaggio (in 1951) and Manny Ramirez (in 2006). Buck Freeman (1902), Johnny Pesky (1947), and Nomar Garciaparra (2003) each have 26, while George Metkovich (1944) and Wade Boggs (1987) each had 25. Tris Speaker, incidentally, had hitting streaks of 20, 20, and 30 in 1912—the only player in the majors to have three 20-plus game streaks in one season.

In 2007, Kevin Youkilis tied a team record with nine consecutive multi-hit games (May 20–May 29), matching Jim Rice's nine (May 1–9, 1978).

Worst slumps in Red Sox history

George Scott suffered an 0-for-36 slump in September 1978. He was starting to close in on Luis Aparicio's 0-for-44 slump that ended June 1, 1971—Aparicio's was such a bad slump that President Richard Nixon famously offered a little empathy.

Worst to start the season was probably Rich Gedman in 1987, who was 0-for-20 in his first eight games until he hit a ninth-inning single—and then went 0-for-10 in the week that followed. Starting the season 1-for-31 (an average of .032) put him at a disadvantage in the quest for an American League batting crown. Gedman finished the season batting .205.

Researcher Cliff Otto notes, "There are many players who went through an entire season without a hit. The most notable performance was that of pitcher Bob Buhl, who was 0-for-70 in 1962 (one game with the Milwaukee Braves and the remainder with the Cubs). He struck out in 36 of those at-bats. Pitcher Bill Wight had the next worst single-season performance, 0-for-61 with the White Sox in 1950." He was acquired by the Red Sox that winter (not for his offense), along with pitcher Ray Scarborough, for pitchers Joe Dobson and Dick Littlefield and outfielder Al Zarilla. Wight got three hits in 41 at-bats the following year—maybe it was friendly Fenway!

Righthander Ellis Kinder was 0-for-32 with the 1952 Red Sox (with 10 strikeouts). It was a tough year on the mound as well. After going 11–2 in 1951, he was 5–6 in 1952—though his ERAs were virtually identical (2.55 and 2.58 in the two years). Come 1953, Kinder improved to 10–6 (1.85 ERA) on the mound and boosted his average from .000 to .379! Kinder had 11 hits in 29 at-bats.

Season-starting slumps? Chuck Schilling started 1962 going 0-for-25. The season was nine days old before he got his first hit, a single with two outs in the seventh inning of the April 19, 1962 game against the visiting Tigers. He was promptly picked off first to end the inning.

Catfish Metkovich hit an Opening Day triple in 1944, but then racked up 40 more at-bats before hitting safely again. Gene Stephens suffered an 0-for-21 start in 1953, and Rico Petrocelli an 0-for-19 start in 1965 before singling and doubling in his seventh game of the season.

Breaking out of a slump sometimes came by the long ball. Jim Kaat unintentionally helped Lou Clinton out of an 0-for-21 slump by serving up two gopher balls in back-to-back at-bats on August 12, 1963. And Joe Lahoud one-upped Clinton after going 1-for-24, and hitting .083 at the time. On June 11, 1969, he hit three home runs off three different Twins pitchers at Metropolitan Stadium.

Even great hitters like Yaz hit slumps. He homered to hit out of an 0-for-17 slump in the June 2, 1963 game in Chicago, homered to hit out of an 0-for-18 slump in the 11th inning of the August 30, 1967 game at Yankee Stadium, and homered off Dick Bosman to break an 0-for-20 slump on May 25, 1970 at Fenway.

Power burst

On Independence Day, 1951 Clyde Vollmer homered off Morrie Martin of the Athletics in the top of the ninth, capping a 9–0 shutout for Mickey McDermott. It was the first of 13 home runs that Vollmer hit in the month of July, an astonishing burst of power from someone with 797 at-bats and just 23 home runs in the years before 1951. After July was over, he hit four more homers the rest of the year, and just 24 in the 775 at-bats in the years that followed. Vollmer's second home run in the string was a first-inning grand slam off Allie Reynolds. His last was another grand slam in the bottom of the 16th inning off Bob Feller. In between, he managed to hit homers off quite a selection of pitchers including Vic Raschi, Joe Dobson, Billy Pierce, Bob Lemon, Early Wynn (two on July 19), Virgil Trucks, and more. On July 26, he hit three of them off three different White Sox pitchers. The Red Sox needed the three of them; it was a 13–10 win and his three-run homer provided the final three runs.

And that wasn't all. On July 6, his triple clinched a win over the Yankees. His July 12 sacrifice fly in the 17th inning won the second game of two against the White Sox (his two-run homer in the first game helped Boston to a 3–2 win). Two days later, he won another game against the White Sox, singling in two ninth-inning runs for another 3–2 victory. On July 19, his second homer of the game came in the top of the 11th inning and would have won that game, too, except that—hardly his fault—the Indians scored twice in the bottom of the 11th.

Big innings / big scores

The largest amounts of runs scored by the Red Sox in single innings were the 17 runs scored by the Red Sox on June 18, 1953 and the 14 runs scored in the very first inning of the June 27, 2003 ballgame against the team that became that year's World Champions, the Florida Marlins. Tell us it isn't fun to wallow in the surfeit of scoring in these two big innings.

June 17 and 18, 1953: Sox score big over Tigers, two days in a row 17–1, 23–3

The Tigers lineup featured Johnny Pesky, Walt Dropo, and Matt Batts—all former Red Soxers—but on June 17, the Boston crew showed no mercy for the visitors. Willard Nixon only let them have five hits, and just one run (a ninth-inning unearned run coming in with two outs on a pinch-hit single by Mullin). Boston scored two runs each in the first and second, seven in the fourth, and added one in the fifth and five more in the eighth. Gernert hit two home runs. Umphlett had four hits, Sammy White had three, and Billy Goodman had three as well, plus three walks. Boston 17, Detroit 1.

This was just a warmup. The very next day, Boston scored 17 runs all in one inning! Apparently, the Tiger bench had decided to give it to the Red Sox and try to shake them, and they heckled like hell. Gene Stephens had been 0-for-5 the day before—but in the seventh inning of the June 18 game he made three hits in a single inning—setting a modern record.

The game had been close, 5–2 Boston after six when the Red Sox just broke it open. The Red Sox got 14 hits and six walks—and 17 runs—all in the seventh inning. George Kell made two of the outs. The Red Sox half of the inning took 47 minutes to play. The whole game, though, only took 3:03. Just for kicks, they added one more in the eighth. Boston 23, Detroit 3. The game either set or tied 16 records—possibly itself a record.

Oh, go ahead, feast on this:

White singled to short right.
Stephens singled to right, White taking third.
Stephens stole second.
Umphlett singled to left, scoring White and Stephens
Lipon struck out.
Kell doubled off the left-field wall, Umphlett taking third.

Goodman walked to fill the bases.

Piersall singled to right, scoring Umphlett and Kell.

Gernert hit his 12th homer into the left-field screen scoring Goodman and Piersall.

Kinder singled to right.

White walked.

Welk replaced Gromek on the mound for Detroit.

Kinder and White advanced on Welk's first pitch, which was wild.

Stephens doubled to short right, scoring Kinder and White.

Umphlett walked.

Lipon singled to left, scoring Stephens.

Kell lined to Lund for the second out.

Goodman singled to center, scoring Umphlett.

Lepcio ran for Goodman.

Harrist replaced Welk.

Zarilla batted for Piersall and walked.

Gernert walked, forcing in Lipon.

Kinder singled to center, scoring Lepcio and Zarilla.

White singled to center, scoring Gernert.

Stephens singled to right, scoring Kinder.

Umphlett singled to center, scoring White.

Lipon walked, filling the bases.

Kell flied to Lund.

—*from the* Boston Globe

June 27, 2003: Sox score 14 times in the first inning, to beat the Marlins 25–8

The 2003 game came in the midst of a six-game stretch in which Boston scored 72 runs. Byung-Hyun Kim started for the Red Sox and allowed Florida one run on two hits in the top of the first. Then Carl Pavano took the mound for the Marlins. He'd been a draft pick of the Sox in 1994, packaged to the Expos as part of the trade for Pedro Martinez in December 1997. Johnny Damon doubled to right, and was singled in by Todd Walker. The score had quickly been tied. But that was hardly the end of it. A full 10 runs scored before a Red Sox player made the first out. That set a new record. Two pitchers had come and gone without recording an out: Pavano (six hits, six runs) and Michael Tejera (four hits, a walk, ultimately charged with five runs). Allen Levrault finally retired the side, but not before he'd been tagged for three more runs. Nomar Garciaparra popped up to the catcher for the first out. The second out came three batters later, but was a run-producing sacrifice fly. And the third out in the inning came when third base coach Mike Cubbage sent Bill Mueller home from second on a Johnny Damon single to left. Mueller didn't have a chance. One suspects Cubbage might have had mercy in mind.

Damon had doubled, then tripled, then singled—he was ¾ of the way to a cycle in the first inning. Here's the summary from the next day's *Globe*: Damon doubled to right. Walker singled to center, scoring Damon. Garciaparra doubled to left, sending Walker to third, Ramirez homered (17) to left. Ortiz doubled to right. Millar singled to center, scoring Ortiz. Tejera relieved Pavano. Nixon singled to right, sending Millar to second. Mueller walked. Varitek singled to center, scoring Millar and Nixon and sending Mueller to second. Damon triped to right, scoring Mueller and Varitek. Walker singled to right, scoring Damon. Levrault relieved Tejera. Garciaparra popped to the catcher. Ramirez singled to right, sending Walker to third. Ortiz walked. Millar hit a sacrifice fly to center. Nixon walked. Mueller doubled to left, scoring Ramirez and Ortiz and sending Nixon to third. Varitek walked. Damon singled to left, scoring Nixon. Mueller out advancing, left fielder to catcher.

The Red Sox continued to score, in every inning but the sixth. Perhaps no surprise: they won the game. The final score was 25–8, and Boston manager Grady Little apologized to Marlins manager Jack McKeon before the next game for breaking the unwritten rule about running up the score. Red Sox principal owner John W. Henry expressed shock that Little would apologize; might he have had a glimmer right then and there of the events to befall Little in the seventh game of the 2003 League Championship Series? The Red Sox scored nine runs that next game—but lost, 10–9. The Marlins didn't mind scoring sufficiently. Boston recovered and took the third game of the set, 11–7.

Before the 2003 game, the Red Sox record for first-inning runs had come at Fenway on the Fourth of July, 1964. It started simply enough, with an error, a single, and a walk. Dick Stuart walked in the first run, then Lee Thomas hit a grand slam. OK, that got the Angels' attention. After two outs, the scoring resumed with a walk, a single, a single, a single, and a single before Stuart hit into a force play to end the inning. 9–0, Red Sox on their way to a 13–5 win.

We could travel way back to 1901 to revisit the time that Boston scored 19 runs in two consecutive innings. It happened in Philadelphia on May 2—only the sixth game ever played in the history of the franchise. The game account noted, "Just now manager Mack's pitching department is very weak." Tell us about it! Starting pitcher Ivan "Pete" Loos got through the first inning only allowing two runs, but walked the first four batters of the second—and never appeared again in major league ball. Bill Bernhard took over and walked the first man he faced. A fly ball dropped by a showboating Fred Ketchum let three runners score and the floodgates were open. Boston scored nine times in the second, and 10 more in the third. Mack let Bernhard absorb the pounding; the final score was 23–12. The 11 runs scored in the first two frames were clearly not enough.

One month later, to the day, another big inning provided a few insurance runs. Boston was already ahead, 4–2, playing in Milwaukee. Top of the ninth, two outs, when Ben Beville doubled into the crowd (his first of two in the inning—the only two major league hits he ever had) and Boston was off to the races, scoring nine times and presenting Milwaukee with a 13–2 score, against which they failed to respond.

There was another 14-run inning, one that made all the difference on the Fourth of July, 1948. At the time it tied the major league mark. Philadelphia had tied the game, 5–5, in the top of the seventh, but lost it when the Red Sox scored 14 times (12 of them off reliever Charley Harris) in the bottom of the seventh. The inning included two walks by Ted Williams and two by Bobby Doerr, two singles by Johnny Pesky and by Ellis Kinder, and a few other treats as well.

Breaking open an extra-inning game big-time were the Bosox of 1973. On July 8, in Chicago, the score was tied 2–2 after nine. The Red Sox were worried about dropping a doubleheader, having lost the first game, 6–1. By the time Bob Montgomery hit his grand slam, the Red Sox had already scored four times. The slam made it eight and Buddy Hunter scored for the second time in the inning when Tommy Harper singled him in. The final was 11–2.

Once upon a time, the Indians scored 13 runs in an inning against the Red Sox. If look it up you must, check the scores for 1923. You'll find it.

Runs scored

The most runs scored in a Red Sox game were 36, back on June 29, 1950. The Red Sox beat the Philadelphia Athletics 22–14. There were 39 hits, 21 walks, 18 different players had hits, nine different Red Sox scored two or more runs apiece. There was but one homer—by Ted Williams. The Red Sox got six in the top of the first, but Philadelphia scored four. Boston added eight more in the second; Philadelphia added three. The only inning in which neither team scored was the third.

The Fourth of July often seemed to bring fireworks. The most runs scored in a single day came on the Fourth in 1939. The Red Sox won the first game, 17–7, and the second game, 18–12. Red Sox pitchers surrendered 15 hits in the first game and 15 hits in the second game, and walked five total. But Philadelphia pitchers allowed 20 in the first game and 15 in the second—including four home runs to Jim Tabor alone (this is the game in which he hit two grand slams in the same game—the second). Despite all the home runs clearing the bases, and the record 54 total runs scored, there were 32 men left on base—16 by each team.

The most runs the Red Sox scored by themselves in one game was the noted June 8, 1950 game where they eclipsed the hapless St. Louis Browns by a full 25 runs, winning 29–4.

June 8, 1950: Boston 29–St. Louis 4

Early June 1950 was a special time to be a Sox fan. In a one-week stretch, the Red Sox scored 104 runs. They beat the Indians 11–5 and then again 11–9. Taking on Chicago, Boston came out on top 17–7 and then 12–0 before dropping a game 8–4 to the White Sox. When the St. Louis Browns came to town, though, they really feasted with a 20–4 win one day followed by a 29–4 rout the very next day.

June 8 was the big day. The Red Sox broke five major records all in one game—runs scored (29), runs batted in (29), total bases (60!—the previous record was 55), and runs scored in consecutive game (49), and most hits in two consecutive games (51). With the seven runs they scored the next day, they set another record—56 runs in a three-game series.

Look at the composite line score for that week of Boston baseball up through June eighth. It's a marvel to behold for any Beantown booster:

	1	2	3	4	5	6	7	8	9
OPPONENTS	6	0	6	7	4	3	7	3	5
RED SOX	21	15	14	18	9	7	7	13	0

And all the runs scored despite the Red Sox typically batting in only eight of the nine innings.

The Red Sox batted in the ninth inning only once, in the 8–4 loss to Chicago. They didn't score in that frame.

On June 8, Chuck Stobbs was on the mound for Boston and gave up four runs on eight hits, three of them in the third inning and one in the ninth. Browns pitcher Cliff Fanning held Boston scoreless in the first inning, but in the second they scored eight times. The Red Sox added three more in the third and another seven runs in the fourth. With the score 20–3 after four, the Red Sox public address announcer invited the bleacherites to move out of the sun and enter the grandstand. There were but 5,105 fans at the game. "They should invite the Browns into the grandstand instead," someone cracked.

This was all hitting. The Browns only committed one error, didn't hit a batter (such restraint), and Fannin only walked one. Fannin was lifted in the third, after giving up the eight runs in the second. The box score noted that pinch-hitting pitcher Ned Garver—sent in to bat in the nine hole—"fanned for Fannin" in the third. Cuddles Marshall took over and he walked five while Sid Schacht walked two. Stobbs, meanwhile, walked seven. With all the scoring and with three pitching changes for the Browns, the game still only took 2:42 to complete.

Bobby Doerr hit three home runs and drove in eight. Walt Dropo hit two home runs and drove in seven. Ted Williams hit two home runs and drove in five. Clyde Vollmer was the weak spot in the Boston lineup; the leadoff hitter went just 1-for-7 with a double, though he walked once. Stobbs himself was 2-for-3 with a couple of singles.

St. Louis right fielder Dick Kokos complained afterwards, "The way they make outfielders chase the ball, you can't catch your breath when it's your turn to bat." Browns manager Zack Taylor, learning that Johnny Pesky had hurt his side during the game and would have to miss one or more games, muttered, "That's a tough situation. The Red Sox lose a regular who is hitting .358 and the guy they have to replace him with [Billy Goodman] is only hitting .359."

The Red Sox once lost by a 24-run margin; it was that same 1923 game against the Indians mentioned above—the score was 27–3.

Scoring and scoring and scoring—
3, 2, 2, 2, 2, 3, 1, 1, 3, 1, 1, 4, 1, 1, 2, 5, 1, 0

Not as well known as the 1, 4, 8, 9, 27, 42 numbers that currently adorn the right-field roof façade at Fenway, what do those numbers represent? The Boston Americans scored three runs in the sixth, two in the seventh, two in the eighth, and—because they were home and ahead of New York, 12–3, they didn't have to bat in the bottom of the ninth. The date was September 15, 1903. Cy Young got the win. On the 16th, Cleveland came to town, and Boston scored in every inning of the eight innings it took to win, 14–7. They'd now scored 11 innings in a row.

Boston scored in every inning of the September 17, 1903 game except the seventh and final one when Cleveland's Dusty Rhoads, who went the distance, somehow retired the side without a run. Boston had scored for a total of 17 straight innings. When bad weather became too hard to bear, umpire Silk O'Loughlin called the game after 7½ with Boston winning, 14–3.

High-scoring shutouts

By definition, only one team scores runs in a shutout. The Sox suffered a bad one when they couldn't score even once off Herb Score and lost the May 18, 1955 game, 19–0. An even worse day was the June 23, 1931 doubleheader in Cleveland. We couldn't even bear to look this one up—the Red Sox lost the two games by scores of 13–0 and 10–0. There was a similar doubleheader that we did look up, though: July 11, 1954. Pitching in Philadelphia for the last-place Red Sox, Frank Sullivan threw a 18–0 five-hit shutout in the first game and Tommy Brewer threw an 11–1 five-hitter in the second.

Bunting

There are few plays in baseball more exciting than the successful squeeze bunt. One of the most dramatic ones in recent years—in the limelight since it was the deciding act in a playoff game—went the wrong way for the Red Sox. It came in the first game of the 2003 Division Series, in Oakland, in the bottom of the 12th inning of a 4–4 tie. With two outs and the bases loaded, A's catcher Ramon Hernandez laid down a perfect squeeze and Eric Chavez scored with the winning run. Fortunately, the ALDS ended well for Boston.

Three times the Yankees got squeezed include the September 26, 1949 game when Bobby Doerr squeezed and scored Johnny Pesky giving the Red Sox a 7–6 win at Yankee Stadium, and a one-game lead over New York with just five games to play. In September 1962—hardly a pennant race for the Red Sox—Boston took two games from the Yankees on 9/9 in New York. After winning the first game, 9–3, the two teams were tied in the top of the 16th inning. Bob Tillman doubled, then took third on Marshall Bridges' wild pitch. After Chuck Schilling struck out, Billy Gardner—who the Yankees had traded to Boston in mid-June—pinch-hit for Dick Radatz and laid down a squeeze, scoring the less-than-swift Tillman. The Sox held on to win, 5–4. Playing at home on May 16, 1968, the Red Sox were down 10–5 after 7½ innings. In the bottom of the eighth, the Red Sox scored five runs and had Hawk Harrelson on second and Reggie Smith on third. Shortstop Jerry Adair laid down a squeeze bunt back to the mound, and Smith scored the go-ahead run. And Lee Stange got the save in the ninth.

Another squeeze that won came on July 23, 1947. The White Sox took a 7–6 lead in the top of the ninth, but the Red Sox tied it. In the bottom of the 14th inning, with the bases loaded and one out, Don Gutteridge successfully squeezed and the near-capacity crowd went home happy.

"Don't look back. They may be gaining on you," said Satchel Paige. Twice, the Red Sox stole a game from Satch with a last-inning squeeze. First, Lou Boudreau won one in Boston, dropping down a bases-loaded squeeze to break a 1–1 tie in the bottom of the 10th inning and pay back Paige for the 2–1 10th-inning defeat he'd dealt them in May. Second, in St. Louis, Johnny Lipon laid one down to score the second run for the Sox in a come-from-behind 7–6 win.

One failed squeeze benefitted Boston. It was the bottom of the first inning during Game Five of the 1915 World Series, and with the bases loaded and nobody out, it looked like the Phillies might have a big inning. Gavvy Cravath bunted into a 1–2–3 double play. They still scored two runs, but lost the game—and the World Series—on a 5–4 game after Harry Hooper hit a tie-breaking bounce home run in the top of the ninth.

With a tie game, top of the ninth, at Yankee Stadium on April 29, 1963, Dick Williams squared to bunt but didn't put the bat down. Harold Kaese said Williams admitted that he froze at the plate. He may have confused New York catcher Elston Howard in the process, though, and the ball got by Howard allowing Eddie Bressoud to come home with the go-ahead run.

1969 wasn't a good year for the Sox to squeeze. In the third inning on April 30, with one out and a man on third, pitcher Lee Stange bunted into a double play—and lost the game, 1–0. The very next day, Ray Culp was up in the identical situation in the top of the fourth. He missed the sign and struck out, leaving the on-rushing Joe Azcue a dead duck at the plate.

Harold Kaese tells of a weird at-bat for Russ Gibson in 1969 when he tried a squeeze; the ball bounced off the ground and hit his bat a second time—so he was called out for interference.

It was the first of August in 1973 when Gene Michael missed a squeeze in the top of the ninth during a 2–2 tie game, as his Yankees roommate Thurman Munson came barreling home—and found himself facing an immovable Carlton Fisk waiting at the plate, ball in hand. Fisk was flattened, then flipped Munson off him, and the two tangled in a commotion that resulted in both catchers being ejected. Munson later said, "There's no question I threw the first punch, but he started it." In the bottom of the ninth, Mario Guerrero singled home new Boston catcher Bob Montgomery for the 3–2 Red Sox win.

To the extent that laying down bunts can provoke the opposition, Bill Monbouquette may have been the most provocative of Red Sox pitchers when three times in a row (the fifth, sixth, and eighth innings of the June 15, 1961 game at Briggs Stadium, he bunted and three different Detroit fielders committed errors. But a bunt can certainly backfire. Ask Karl Olson. Early in 1954, Olson had hit into a triple play. On April 24, though, at Griffith Stadium, he was up in the third inning with runners on first and second. He tried to bunt to advance the runners but popped up to Washington pitcher Mickey McDermott instead. McDermott threw the ball to the shortstop who doubled off Tommy Brewer at second base, then fired to first to nip Billy Goodman.

Occasionally, a player can take two bases on a bunt. Jimmy Piersall bunted once for a double on July 4, 1953; the next year, he scored from second on a bunt. Ted Williams did it once in 1951 against the Yankees, and (after the Red Sox scored 19 runs in the first game on August 27, 1938) Ben Chapman scored the only run of a 1–0 game when Red Sox pitcher Bill Harris laid down a bunt in the seventh inning of the second game; Chapman rounded third and scored on the bunt and run play.

Many know Carroll Hardy as the only man to ever pinch-hit for Ted Williams. What he did in that 1960 game was to line back to the pitcher to start a 1–3 double play.

Two big bunts for the Red Sox were: (1) Ted Williams' safe bunt in the 1946 World Series. The injured Williams only managed five hits; the one against the Williams shift stole headlines away from the Cardinals' Joe Garagiola, who went 4-for-5 with three RBIs as St. Louis won, 12–3. "Williams Bunts" read the headlines. (2) Jim Lonborg's bunt single that started a come-from-behind five-run rally in the sixth inning of the last game of the 1967 season, which gave the Red Sox the pennant.

A couple of bunting sprees:

(1) The Yankees may have thought Babe Ruth needed a little exercise, and was perhaps a little hampered from a night out on the town. For whatever reason, on May 4, 1918 they laid down bunt after bunt—in the third inning alone, they lay down three successful bunts in a row. In all, Ruth fielded 13 balls, committing two errors—one of which allowed two runs to score. Ruth hit a double and a home run, but lost the game, 5–4.

(2) The Red Sox tried the same tactic against Cleveland's Allen Sothoron on September 22, 1921. He was "notoriously weak in fielding bunts" so the Sox laid down 10 of them in the 3⅓ innings he was on the mound. In the third inning, every single Boston batter bunted—though no one scored. Cleveland won the game, 9–8, in the 12th inning.

Sacrifices

The most sacrifices in one game may have been that very September 22, 1921 game against the Indians. Red Sox batters sacrificed eight times in the game: two each by Leibold, McInnis, and Scott, and one apiece by Shano Collins and Eddie Foster.

There's no question that the most meaningful sacrifice fly has to be the one that won the 1912 World Series, when Larry Gardner's 10th-inning fly brought in the final run to beat the Giants.

There have been some notable sac flies that produced unexpected results. One we'll mention here was the April 19, 1918 ball hit by Babe Ruth deep into the outfield, deep enough that after the catch, Boston's Everett Scott scored all the way from second base.

Bunting to sacrifice a runner across was something Bill Monbouquette was particularly good at; he did it 14 times in 1961.

Russ Nixon only hit three sac flies in all of 1965—but he hit all three in the same game: an August 31 night game at D. C. Stadium. The catcher singled his first time up and flied out to left his second. In the fifth inning, he drove in Felix Mantilla. In the seventh, he drove in Lee Thomas. And in the ninth, he drove in Tony Horton. The last one tied the game, 5–5. The Sox scored three times in the top of 10th and took the game, 8–5.

The most sacrifices by one player in a game that we can find are the four hit by Jack Barry (0-for-0 in the August 21, 1916 boxscore)—the only four sacrifices in the game, by either team. Cleveland pitcher Guy Morton made three errors, and threw a wild pitch, helping the Red Sox to a 4–0 win.

Robbed of three sacrifice flies, all in the same game

George Scott may have set a record in frustration in the July 3, 1977 game against the Orioles when in the second, fourth, and sixth innings he came up with Carlton Fisk on first base. Three times in a row,

George Scott's BBQ, Greenville MS. Photo by Ron Anderson.

he hit a ball so deep to the outfield that Fisk was able to tag up and take second. The first two times, Yaz was on second base and tagged up, too. Though he had advanced five baserunners, three of whom later scored, Scott was never credited with even one sacrifice fly. The following day, Scott hit two homers and drove in three.

Pinch hitting

June 17, 1943: Twice in the same day, **Joe Cronin** of the Red Sox hit a pinch-hit homer. Both were three-run blasts, one in each game of the doubleheader against St. Louis. Just two days earlier, he'd hit another pinch-hit three-run homer. By year's end, he had five pinch-hit four-baggers. As player-manager, it was his choice to decide whether to put himself into games; in 42 pinch-hit at-bats, he racked up 18 hits and a major-league-leading 25 pinch-hit RBIs.

On the other hand, **Billy Hitchcock** went 0-for-16 as a pinch-hitter for the 1949 Red Sox.

Del Wilber pinch hit for the Sox in 1953 and hit a home run off the first pitch thrown to him. Next time up, same thing: one pitch, one pinch-hit homer. That's a pattern that's a little hard to maintain. Wilber did hit three pinch-hit homers in five plate appearances, though.

In so doing, Wilber had bettered **Charlie Maxwell** who hit three pinch-hit homers in eight appearances in 1951—two came off future Hall of Famers Feller and Lemon, and the third was a grand slam off Satchel Paige.

Vic Wertz hit two pinch-hit grand slams in 1959.

Who hit the most pinch-hit homers for the Red Sox? That would be Ted Williams, with seven. Joe Cronin had five and Del Wilber had four in all. With three apiece, not counting the postseason, we have Bernie Carbo and Rich Gedman.

When a pinch-hit grand slam is only a single: Dalton Jones, playing for Detroit on July 9, 1970, came in to pinch-hit for catcher Jim Price with the bases loaded. Facing Vicente Romo, he slammed the ball into Tiger Stadium's upper deck—but was called out for passing base-runner Don Wert. The other three runs scored, breaking a 3–3 tie and ultimately giving the Tigers a 7–3 win.

In 1962, **Russ Nixon** hit two pinch singles in one inning for the Red Sox. It was in the fifth inning of the May 4 game, the Sox losing 4–0. Starter Mike Fornieles was pulled in favor of pinch-hitter Nixon, who singled and scored three batters later. The Sox batted around and Nixon came up again, facing the fourth White Sox pitcher of the inning, and singled again, this time driving in two runs. The Red Sox won the game, 13–6, thanks to a 12-run fifth.

Most pinch hits by the team in one inning? On September 8, 1995 facing the Yankees, the Red Sox had four pinch-hits in one inning, tying the major league record. And it paid off. It was the top of the eighth inning and the Yankees had an 8–0 lead. David Cone was pitching for New York. After Tim Naehring struck out to lead off the inning, manager Kevin Kennedy gave **Scott Hatteberg** his first major league at-bat, pinch-hitting for Bill Haselman. Hatteberg singled to right field. Luis Alicea reached on a fielder's choice. **Lee Tinsley** batted for Willie McGee and singled, scoring Hatteberg. **Carlos Rodriguez** batted for John Valentin and he, too, singled, driving in another run. **Chris Donnels** then hit for Mo Vaughn—and he singled, driving in a third run. Jose Canseco, hitting for himself, singled and made the score 8–4. Mike Greenwell, hitting for himself, grounded out to the pitcher. Troy O'Leary, hitting for himself, grounded out to the shortstop. In the bottom of the eighth, the Red Sox made six defensive changes. They still lost, 8–4.

The Sox have had a number of pinch-hit specialists—**Tom Wright**, for instance. Some years that's just about all he did.

The Sox have also had some good-hitting pitchers—**Boo Ferriss**, for instance. Despite a career .250 batting average, Ferriss was used a number of times as a pinch-hitter. As a pitcher, he appeared in 144 games; as a ballplayer, he appeared in 194 games. Of those 144 games he pitched in, Ferriss says he was never once taken out for a pinch-hitter. He must have forgotten the September 26, 1948 game, but even pitcher Babe Ruth was pinch-hit for a couple of times.

Pinch hitting in the postseason

Probably the biggest pinch hits in Red Sox history came in 1912, 1916, and 1975. The latter was Bernie Carbo's Game Six eighth-inning blast into the center-field bleachers with two on and two out, and the Red Sox losing to the Reds, 6–3. Batting for Roger Moret, Carbo homered to tie the score and set the stage for Carlton Fisk's dramatic bottom of the 12th inning walk-off home run.

In 1912, in the deciding game of the World Series against the Giants, it was the bottom of the seventh with two outs and runners on first and second in a game the Red Sox were losing 1–0. Pinch-hitting for pitcher Hugh Bedient, Olaf Henriksen doubled off the third-base bag, driving in the tying run. In the top of the 10th, the Giants scored a run off Smoky Joe Wood, who was due up to lead off the bottom of the inning. Clyde Engle pinch hit for Wood and reached on the error known forever as "Snodgrass' muff"—two batters later he scored the unearned tying run on Speaker's single and two batters later a sacrifice fly brought in the deciding run.

Four years later, in the bottom of the 14th inning of Game Two of the 1916 World Series, pinch-hitter Del Gainer singled in pinch-runner Mike McNally with the winning run—winning the 2–1 game for Babe Ruth, who'd pitched all 14 innings.

Ruth's first World Series at-bat had come the previous year—1915—as a pinch hitter. He grounded out unassisted to the first baseman for the next-to-last out of the game. It was his one and only at-bat of the Series.

In the very first game when "Mr. Ruth, one of the Baltimore recruits" first played, he was the starting pitcher. The score was tied—Cleveland 3, Boston 3 when Ruth (0-for-2 at the plate) was due up to hit, so manager Bill Carrigan had Duffy Lewis pinch hit for Ruth. Lewis singled.

Pinch running in the postseason

That belongs to Dave Roberts. 2004. Nuf ced.

Pinch-hitting leaders

If you had to pick the best pinch-hitter the Red Sox ever had, it would probably be Rick Miller. In 1983, Miller pinch-hit 35 times and posted a .457 batting average as a pinch-hitter (16-for-35). His overall average for the year was .286, meaning that when not hitting in the pinch, he hit .2599.

The most pinch-hits in a single season was 18, by player-manager Joe Cronin in 1943 (.429) while future manager Dick Williams recorded 16 pinch-hits in 1963, tying with Miller for second place. Rick Miller also holds third place, with the 14 pinch-hits in 1984. Miller had a team-leading 53 pinch-hit at-bats in '84, but was unable to repeat at the 1983 level; Miller only batted .264 in 1984. That was still better than his average when not hitting in the pinch, which was .257.

Over the course of their Red Sox careers, though, Dalton Jones (56) had more pinch-hits than Miller (49), followed by Russ Nixon (43), Ted Williams (33), and Joe Cronin and Olaf Henriksen (29 each). Climbing on the list is current Red Sox catcher Jason Varitek. He's got 28, one ahead of Jack Rothrock's 27, and within easy striking distance of Joe and Olaf.

Joe Cronin hit five pinch-hit homers in 1943, three of them being three-run homers in a three-day stretch—and two of them on the same day. Cronin hit pinch-hit three-run homers in both games of the June 17 doubleheader against the visiting Athletics, following up the one he'd hit on June 15.

Pinch-hit game-ending home runs

This is not an area of great historical strength for the Red Sox. On five occasions a Red Sox pinch-hitter has hit a game-ending home run. On 11 occasions, though, the Sox have lost a game to a pinch-hit homer.

Let's get the bad news out of the way first.

4/22/1950—Paul Lehner pinch-hit for Philadelphia pitcher Alex Kellner, who'd thrown all 15 innings for the A's. Ellis Kinder, starting his sixth inning in relief, was the victim of Lehner's home run over the right-field wall. Philadelphia 6, Boston 5 (15 innings).

5/28/1958—Pinch-hitter Gail Harris stroked one into the upper deck in Detroit, a two-run homer that broke a 2–2 tie in the bottom of the ninth. Willard Nixon took the loss.

4/11/1968—Gates Brown, pinch-hitting for Detroit, won a game that had been tied since the sixth with a home run off Red Sox reliever John Wyatt. 4–3 final.

8/11/1968—Gates Brown, pinch-hitting for Detroit, won a game that had been tied since the eighth inning with a solo home run off Earl Wilson in the bottom of the 14th inning. Starting to look like déjà vu. It was Brown's third home run of the year. Every one of them had been a pinch-hit homer and every one had been at the expense of the Red Sox (he'd crunched one off Lee Stange just two days earlier, too). There was a second game on August 11. The Red Sox took a three-run lead in the top of the ninth, but the Tigers came back with four to win it—the final run coming on a single in the bottom of the ninth by…left fielder Gates Brown.

9/15/1970—After five errors practically handed the Yankees a win in the first game, Mike Nagy and the Red Sox shut out New York through eight in the second game. Until Curt Blefary pinch-hit for pitcher Steve Kline and hit a three-run homer to right field. 3–2, Yankees.

6/15/1971—Boston had a 4–3 lead over California, but the Angels had a man on base. Fireman Sparky Lyle came in with one out and a runner on second. Syd O'Brien pinch-hit for right fielder Gonzalez and hit out a game-winning two-run homer.

5/23/1979—Bob Stanley started for Boston and was still pitching in the bottom of the 10th when Orioles pinch-hitter Pat Kelly—just barely—popped one out over the Red Sox right fielder and the right-field fence, a three-run homer that gave Baltimore a 5–2 win.

4/30/1983—It was 1–1 in the bottom of the 11th in Anaheim Stadium. Pinch-hitter Daryl Sconiers batted for Rob Wilfong, who'd come in as a pinch-runner for Reggie Jackson. Sconiers banged a three-run blast off Mark Clear and gave Doug Corbett his first win since May 28, 1982. Corbett was 1–9 in 1982. Now he was 1–0 in 1983.

9/28/1987—The Red Sox were leading 7–3 after 8½ innings, but the Yankees started scoring runs. They'd already tied it off Wes Gardner and Joe Sambito, when Calvin Schiraldi got the call. New York's Mike Easler pinch-hit for Gary Ward and hit a two-run homer.

6/21/2003—In interleague play, the Phillies and Red Sox were tied after 11. Boston scored once in the top of the 12th, but the Phillies scored once, too. So the Red Sox ratcheted up the ante, scoring twice in the top of the 13th. The Phils scored once and had a runner on second. Rudy Seanez came in to pitch to announced pinch-hitter Todd Pratt, who hit a two-run homer to win it.

4/22/2005—The Red Sox scored twice in the top of the ninth at Tropicana to tie it, 4–4. Alan Embree came in to pitch the bottom of the ninth, but the first batter he faced—Eduardo Perez—hit a pinch-hit home run for a 5–4 Tampa Bay victory.

Now for the nice ones:

One story we've already told above, **Wes Ferrell**'s pinch-hit three-run ninth-inning homer off Tommy Bridges winning the July 21, 1935 game against the Tigers. And then Ferrell hit another game-winner the following day—but then he was the pitcher and not pinch-hitting. On July 21, Lefty Grove got the 7–6 win.

It was Bill Monbouquette for the Red Sox, and the May 23, 1964 game against Kansas City was tied 3–3 after eight. Dick Radatz came in to relieve and was set to take a loss after giving up a run to the Athletics when Ed Charles singled in Dick Green in the top of the ninth. John Wyatt was meant to close the game for K.C., but walked Bob Tillman. He recovered and got Ramon Mejias to ground out to the shortstop, with Tillman forced out at second base. **Felix Mantilla** pinch-hit for Radatz—and hit a two-run game-winning home run. Radatz gladly scarfed up the win.

Just about a month later, **Russ Nixon** was the pinch-hitter. June 26, 1964. Dave Morehead pitching against Cleveland's Tommy John. It was 1–1 after six innings, but the Indians scored once in the top of the eighth. Radatz came in to pitch the ninth. It stayed 2–1. Tommy John was still pitching for Cleveland; he'd given up one run on seven hits. Chuck Schilling grounded out, short to first. Felix Mantilla singled. Yaz made the second out with a fly ball to left field. Down to the final out, Radatz was again removed for a pinch-hitter. Russ Nixon homered, the Sox won 3–2, and Radatz picked up another win.

Twenty years later, **Reid Nichols** came into the June 11, 1984 game against the Yankees. Bruce Hurst had started the game, but didn't have one of his better games. Hurst was hit for six earned runs on 12 hits in 8⅔ innings. Mark Clear came on to get the final out in the top of the ninth; two Yankees were left on on base, but they had a 6–3 lead. Jackie Gutierrez singled to start off the bottom of the ninth. Wade Boggs walked. Jay Howell replaced Ray Fontenot on the mound for New York. Dwight Evans singled to load the bases. Jim Rice singled, driving in Gutierrez but leaving the bases still loaded, nobody out, and the score now 6–4. Tony Armas grounded out to shortstop, and the runners held. Bob Shirley came in from the bullpen. Mike Easler also grounded out to shortstop; no run scored, the bases remained loaded. Bill Buckner singled, driving in two runs and tying the game. Reid Nichols was sent in to pinch-hit for Rich Gedman and won the game with a three-run homer. Red Sox 9, Yankees 6, the Sox having scored six runs in the bottom of the ninth inning.

May 9, 1995. Mo Vaughn homered in the first to give the Sox a 1–0 lead over the visiting Orioles. Chris Hoiles hit a two-run homer off Rheal Cormier in the top of the second to give Baltimore the edge. Ben McDonald loaded the bases in the third, then walked Mo Vaughn and hit Jose Canseco. That gave Boston a 3–2 lead. Jeff Pierce relieved for the Red Sox, walked two and then gave up an RBI single to Hoiles. The O's had tied it in the top of the sixth. It was still tied in the bottom of the ninth. Jesse Orosco took over for Baltimore and struck out Troy O'Leary. Wes Chamberlain was asked to pinch-hit for Luis Alicea. The Orioles countered with Armando Benitez. Chamberlain hit a home run. 4–3, Red Sox.

Pitchers who pinch hit

Wes Ferrell, Boo Ferriss, Mickey McDermott, Gary Peters, Red Ruffing, and Earl Wilson all were pitchers who could hit well enough to be used as pinch hitters on occasion. Lefty Lefebvre even beat the Yankees once in a 1939 ballgame.

Pinch hitting for Ted Williams and Babe Ruth

We know that both Babe Ruth and Ted Williams pitched in major league ballgames, and that Joe Glenn is the only man to catch both of them. We know that Carroll Hardy is the only man who ever pinch-hit for Ted Williams. There were at least four men who pinch-hit for Babe Ruth at one time or another in The Babe's Red Sox years: Duffy Lewis (July 11, 1914), Hick Cady (April 24, 1915), Del Gainer (June 29, 1915), and Olaf Henriksen (July 7, 1916). Word is that Mike McNally pinch-hit for the Babe, too, but we've been unable to confirm that. Of course, Babe sometimes turned up for work a little "under the weather."

Most games by a Red Sox player without an at-bat?

The all-time leader is Bob Stanley, who played in 637 games without an at-bat. He did have one at-bat in Game Two of the 1986 World Series. It was the top of the ninth inning, with runners on first and second and nobody out. The score was 8–3 in favor of the Red Sox, so it wasn't a pressure situation. Stanley struck out. Wade Boggs, up next, doubled. Boston won, 9–3.

The worst hitter in Red Sox history?

Who was the worst hitter in Red Sox history? We posed the question to Clifford Otto, who came up with three answers. First, based a minimum of 350 at-bats, using OPS (on-base percentage plus slugging) as the criterion, the worst three single seasons were by two players named Scott:

		AVG	SLG	OBP	OPS
Scott, Everett	1915	.201	.231	.237	.468
Scott, George	1968	.171	.237	.236	.473
Scott, Everett	1918	.221	.269	.242	.510

In terms of full career, with a minimum of 1,500 at-bats, and excluding pitchers, Lou Criger ranks highly:

	AVG	SLG	OBP	OPS
Criger, Lou	.209	.279	.275	.555
Scott, Everett	.246	.306	.276	.584
Burleson, Rick	.274	.362	.324	.686

Cliff points out that special consideration might be given to Dick Ellsworth, who never had an extra-base hit for Boston. He drew one walk and was hit by a pitch once in 83 plate appearances while striking out an astonishing 62.7% of his times at bat.

Some great come-from-behind finishes

May 13, 2007: One of the most improbable comeback wins in Red Sox history unfolded at Fenway after Baltimore's Jeremy Guthrie had held Boston to just three hits in 8⅓ innings. And the Sox had matched that by committing three errors. It wasn't a good game. The Orioles led 5–0. With one out and nobody on in the bottom of the ninth, a sky-high popup in front of the plate was dropped by the O's catcher. No big deal, right? Manager Sam Perlozzo panicked and turned to the bullpen. There followed: a double by David Ortiz that scored a run, a single, a walk, another walk that forced in a run, a Varitek double that scored two more. The Orioles walked Hinske to load the bases. Alex Cora pinch-hit and grounded into a fielder's choice— Youkilis was out at home (according to the umpire). The lightning-fast Julio Lugo then hit another infield single and barely beat the tag, as the tying run scored—and bounced off closer Chris Ray's glove as the winning run scored. 6–5, Boston.

May 30, 1931: The Fenway faithful saw quite a doubleheader. The first game pitted Philadelphia's Lefty Grove against Boston's Jack Russell, and neither team scored through 11 full frames. Suddenly, Mule Haas hit a homer into the right-field bleachers and Russell crumbled;

before the inning was over, the defending World Champion Athletics scored five times and won game one, 5–0. In game two, the Athletics scored in four of the first five innings and the score stood at 5–0 heading into the bottom of the ninth. Finally, Philadelphia's Roy Mahaffey tired, and neither he nor Eddie Rommel nor even Rube Walberg could stem the Sox, who poured on six runs to overcome and take the game.

June 18, 1961: One of the greatest games in Red Sox history (plug: to learn more about it, read *The 50 Greatest Red Sox Games*) saw the Sox down by seven runs in the bottom of the ninth, in part because Willie Tasby had hit a grand slam for the Senators in the top of the ninth. Boston was losing 12–5, with two outs and one man on. They won the game. They scored three runs, then Jim Pagliaroni hit a grand slam to tie the game. Bases cleared, the Sox started populating them once more with a Wertz walk, a Buddin single, and a pinch-hit walk-off from Russ Nixon. And then the Sox won the second game that day, 6–5, in 13 innings.

Overcoming some other seemingly insurmountable leads

Give Bob Feller a 7–0 lead, you've got a sure win, right? Not on August 27, 1950. In the bottom of the third, Feller walked three batters and gave up three hits, one of them a three-run Walt Dropo homer. The Sox scored five times to put the Indians lead in jeopardy. Reliever Al Benton saw his teammates commit three errors in the bottom of the seventh, and he served up a grand slam gopher ball to pinch-hitter Clyde Vollmer. Boston 11, Cleveland 9.

The very next day, future Hall of Famer Bob Lemon was staked to an even larger lead, 10–0. Boston got one measly run in the bottom of the third, so the Indians doubled that with two, giving them an 11-run lead. Batting in the bottom of the fourth, the Red Sox singled six times and walked twice before Lemon left—in favor of Al Benton, who gave up a three-run homer to Billy Goodman. The Sox scored eight times. In the sixth, they scored two more until Bob Feller was brought back. Yet they got to Feller in the eighth and pushed four more across for a 15–14 win. Al Zarilla's two-run homer was the capper.

By August 20, 1967, in the year of the Impossible Dream, it had begun to seem that anything was possible—including overcoming the 8–0 lead the Angels had built through 3½. Jerry Adair's solo home run in the eighth tipped the scales for a 9–8 triumph.

The Senators led 7–0 at the midway point. Before it became an official game, Boston scored four in the bottom of the fifth, then four more in the seventh (a three-run homer to Rico Petrocelli was key). Washington scored once in the top of the ninth to tie the game. A walk, an error, and an intentional walk filled the bases with Red Sox in the bottom of the ninth—and Darold Knowles walked Rico, forcing in the winning run.

Losing 10–1 after five, and 10–4 after eight, the 1911 Red Sox scored seven runs in the top of the ninth to take an 11–10 lead. The Tigers tied it, sending the game into extra innings. Boston scored twice to win it, 13–11. It was May 13.

If you want the other side of the story, there was the 8–1 lead that Jack Wilson had on September 8, 1937 heading into the ninth inning at Yankee Stadium. Harold Kaese remembered that one: "With two on and two out, the Yankees preceded to score eight runs. With a 3–2 count on Lou Gehrig, Wilson was relieved by Tommy Thomas. One pitch and the game ended with Gehrig's three-run homer." [*Rooters Guide*, p. 11] Or you could read about how Mel Parnell had a 9–0 lead against the Yankees on Opening Day 1950, and lost 15–10. You can read about it someplace else, though.

Sometimes you just can't win

There were back-to-back games in Boston on August 16 and 17, 1966 when the Orioles scored five runs in the ninth to take both games.

A 4–1 lead is hardly insurmountable, but on April 28, 1930 the last-place Red Sox were feeling good about their chances against the reigning World Champion Philadelphia Athletics. Ed Morris had a five-hitter going. He didn't give up a hit, but the A's scored four times without a hit in the top of the ninth and won the game.

Start to finish

Sam Mele hit the first Baltimore pitch of the game for a home run in the bottom of the first, and the last Baltimore pitch of the game in the bottom of the 11th inning, an RBI single to break a 2–2 tie. It was August 28, 1854.

The weirdest walk-off ever?

Let's finish this section recounting what might have been the weirdest walk-off ever. It happened on May 18, 1986, with the Texas Rangers playing in Boston. The score was Texas 3, Boston 2 until Marty Barrett and Wade Boggs hit back-to-back doubles to lead off the bottom of the ninth. Score tied, the game went into extra innings and the Rangers scored once in the top of the 10th. Greg Harris was pitching for Texas and got Ed Romero on a fly ball to left field. With one out, Steve Lyons singled to center field. The pitcher had him picked off first, but his throw went astray and Lyons took second on the play. Then Marty Barrett hit a flare to right field that George Wright dove for. Lyons was already at third, but backtracked when it looked like Wright had made the catch. He just missed the catch and the ball got away. Barrett meanwhile, with little to lose, was chugging all the way around first base to second. Both Lyons and Barrett slide into second base at the same time, both of them doing a pop-up slide. Lyons picked himself up and took off for third, while Wright picked up the ball and fired it in—all the way out of play!

Since Barrett was on second base at the time of the throw, he was awarded home plate. So was Lyons. Both runners scored and the game was over, 5–4 Red Sox.

Thanks to Wayne McElreavy for remembering that one.

BASE-RUNNING

It's not really a sub-set of hitting, but it's an element of the offense. The Red Sox have never been known as a base-stealing team, typically choosing to go for the big bang. There have been eras, though, such as the "Speed Boys" of 1909. Harry Lord stole 36 bases, one more than Tris Speaker, and the 1909 Red Sox set a club record of 215. That was the only year they hit the 200 mark; there are by far more years under 50 than there are over 100. The nadir of base thefts came in 1964 when they stole just 18 bases all year long, with Carl Yastrzemski and Dalton Jones tied for the team lead with six apiece. Second place for Sox sluggishness was in 1951, when Billy Goodman stole seven of the team's 20 SBs. Only once has a Red Sox team led the league in stolen bases—1935 (91 steals).

The most bases stolen by a Red Sox player in a single season remains the 54 stolen by Tommy Harper in 1973. He beat the old record (52) set by Tris Speaker back in 1912; Speaker also holds third and fourth place on the list, though he's tied for fourth with Otis Nixon (42 in 1994).

Harry Hooper stole more bases than any other Red Sox player—a total of 300. Speaker ranked second with 267. Yaz came in third, 99 behind Speaker with 168. Fourth was Heinie Wagner's 141. And fifth came Larry Gardner with 134. Tommy Harper stole 54 in the one season, but just fell short of doubling that total for full (abbreviated) career with the Red Sox: he stole 107 bases. In all, Harper swiped 408 in his career; Speaker took 432.

Probably the most famous stolen base in 107 years of franchise history came in 2004. Dave Roberts. To some extent, that erased the memory of the three bases Lou Brock stole in Game Seven of the 1967 World Series.

Billy Werber pulled off four steals of home during his nearly four seasons with the Red Sox (1933–36). His most entertaining steal may have been the one he took on August 21, 1934. The Tigers were visiting Fenway and Schoolboy Rowe was pitching. Before the game, umpire George Moriarty was killing time and talking with Werber about stealing bases; he mentioned how a player could steal second on a base on balls. Rowe walked Werber later in the game. "Jogging to first, I looked at Bill Rogell at shortstop and Charlie Gehringer at second. Both had their backs to the infield, tapping clods of earth with their spikes. About fifteen feet before first, I put it into high gear and touched the base under a full head of steam. The crowd roar could probably be heard all the way to the Back Bay station. Ray Haworth, the Tiger catcher, still had the ball in his hand and threw to second, which was covered by no one. The ball bounded out to JoJo White in center field while I slid into second, bounced up, and scurried to third." [Werber, *Memories of a Ballplayer*, p. 116] Werber says he later pulled the play three more times.

It wasn't, strictly speaking, a stolen base, but it was alert base-running that saw Werber take home from second base as New York's Bill Dickey fired a ball to first base on a fielder's choice; Werber scored the only run in the 1–0 defeat of the Yankees, at Yankee Stadium, on Opening Day 1935.

May 28, 1973. Sixth inning, in Kansas City at Royals Stadium, in what was ultimately a 5–4 game when every run counted. With two outs, Tommy Harper singled, then stole second off Dick Drago. Catcher Carl Taylor's throw to second was off the mark and Harper took third. On the very next pitch, he stole home. The Red Sox won.

Wally Moses, playing for Chicago, stole home in the bottom of the 14th inning of the July 7, 1943 game in Comiskey. There were runners on first and third with one out. Mace Brown came in to relieve Mike Ryba and walked Luke Appling to load the bases. He got a second out, but while facing the next batter, Moses stole home and won the game. Billy Hitchcock won an August 12, 1949 game against Washington with an eighth-inning steal of home that made the score 12–11 in Boston's favor.

Harold Kaese remembered some other notable steals—Bert Campaneris took third one time while the Red Sox were intentionally walking a Kansas City batter. Reggie Smith stole five bases on August 29, 1967 against the Yankees—twice in the first game and thrice in the second.

Top of the ninth in the July 2, 1974 night game, it was tied 4–4 Baltimore-Boston. The Red Sox pulled off two double steals in the same half-inning, the second one being the first of Dwight Evans' two steals of home in an eight-day stretch. The twin double steals ignited a four-run Red Sox rally that saw them win the game, 9–5. On this July 2 date, Evans stole home against Baltimore's Bob Reynolds (Elrod Hendricks catching)—and on July 10 he repeated the trick against Texas's David Clyde (Duke Sims catching).

The Sox pulled off a few triple steals, too. In 1909, the afore-mentioned Harry Lord led one with Tris Speaker and Doc Gessler trailing. In 1914, the whole Red Sox outfield combined on one—Harry Hooper, Duffy Lewis, and Tris Speaker.

On July 22, 1909, Ty Cobb embarrassed the Red Sox by stealing second base, third base, and home—one after the other—in the seventh inning. Armando Marsans tried the same thing in July 1916, but was thrown out at the plate.

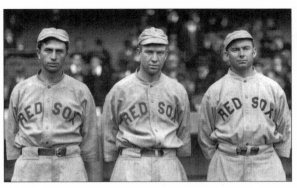

The Golden Outfield: Harry Hooper, Tris Speaker, Duffy Lewis.

Motoring on the basepaths

Everett Scott once took *two* bases on Babe Ruth's deep fly ball on April 19, 1918. Yaz did it once, too, in the second of two games at Yankee Stadium on July 9, 1961. He'd already driven in the third run of the fourth inning. After a double steal, Gary Geiger was on third and Yaz was on second when Jim Pagliaroni hit a fly ball to left field. Geiger scored on the fly, and Yaz behind him. Yogi Berra had fallen while catching the ball.

Scoring from second base on a bunt was Ben Chapman on August 27, 1938—the seventh-inning "double squeeze bunt" by pitcher Bill Harris won the game for the Red Sox, 1–0.

Stolen bases in four decades

The first major league ballplayer to steal a base in four different decades, and the only one to do so through the year 1999 was, of all people, Ted Williams. There are now two more: Rickey Henderson, then Tim Raines. Two of them played for the Red Sox, Henderson's tenure being a very brief and under-utilized 2002 season, while Raines was understood to have routinely demanded a no-trade clause in his contracts ensuring that he would never play for Boston. Henderson stole eight bases for Boston, and was caught just twice.

In their careers as a whole, Rickey Henderson stole 1,406 bases, Tim Raines stole 808, and Ted Williams stole…24. Ted stole two in 1939, 14 in the 1940s, seven in the 1950s, and one in 1960. He was caught stealing 17 times, once in the 1930s and once in the 1960s, and 15 times in between.

Slow steals?

One of the slowest men on any team, Cy Young once stole two bases in one game—September 15, 1903. "When huge Cyrus made the second steal, the earth must have quaked and the sun must have blinked bewildered."—*Chicago Journal*

Three stolen bases five years in a row

Dwight Evans, 1980–1984—for each of those five years in a row, Dewey stole exactly three bases.

Triple steals

One of the most exciting plays in baseball is the steal of home. Typically executed as part of a double steal, with runners on first and third, the runner on first will break for second and draw the catcher's throw, while the runner on third will delay just long enough for the catcher to make the throw to second, then streak for the plate. What about a triple steal, though, with runners in motion all over the place? Harry Hooper led one on May 28, 1914 against the Cleveland Indians—and not that big a fuss was made over it in the Boston newspapers. Tim Murnane of the *Boston Globe* called it a "great steal home" noting that Cleveland catcher Carisch "had the ball at the plate but failed to appreciate Hooper's very clever wide slide." He didn't even comment on the fact that three bases were stolen in one play. The *Boston Post* provided details of the "pretty triple steal"—Thomas beat out an infield hit. Bedient, trying to sacrifice, popped up to the pitcher. Hooper dropped a Texas Leaguer into short right. Everett Scott walked. Duffy Lewis hit to second, forcing Scott there. Lewis then stole second, and Speaker was intentionally walked ("purposely passed" wrote the *Herald*). With two strikes on Janvrin, Hooper stole home to score the first run of the game. Lewis stole third and Speaker stole second. It was a close play at the plate and the *Herald*'s writer said that it looked to him as though Hooper was out. Carisch thought so, too, and argued with umpire Chill—who didn't ("Umpire Chill Gets Heated" noted a *Globe* subhead)—resulting in Carisch's first ejection from a major league game in six-plus seasons. Indians manager Joe Birmingham kicked up some chalk and was tossed, too—he created a little more controversy after he changed and took a box seat behind the Red Sox dugout. Ivy Olson was a little too loud as a bench jockey, and he was thrown out as well. Janvrin then grounded out.

Cleveland won the game 5–2 with three runs in the top of the ninth inning, despite the Sox sending up four pinch hitters in the bottom of the ninth, one of whom was manager Bill Carrigan, who drew a walk.

Nine times, Ty Cobb stole home against the Red Sox

July 22, 1909 against Harry Walter and Pat Donahue. In fact, during the seventh inning, he stole
    second, third, and home.
August 18, 1911 against Jack Killilay and catcher Bill Carrigan as the front end of a triple steal
June 9, 1915 against Ray Collins (and, for the second time, catcher Bill Carrigan)
August 23, 1919, against Waite Hoyt and catcher Roxy Walters, also as the front end of a triple steal
September 18, 1920 against Elmer Myers and Wally Schang
May 8, 1922 against Allen Russell and catcher Muddy Ruel
August 10, 1924 against Buster Ross and Val Picinich
April 26, 1927 against Tony Welzer and Grover Hartley
July 6, 1927 against Del Lundgren and Grover Hartley

The dying art of the Red Sox steal of home

It's just something the Red Sox rarely try any more. The last successful steal of home came in 1999 (there were two that year), when Jose Offerman took home during a double steal on August 30. The other time was earlier that year, on June 4, when Jeff Frye stole home against Tom Glavine; it was meant to be a suicide squeeze but the pitch was too far off the plate for Darren Lewis to lay down a bunt. The Red Sox tried to steal home in 2001, 2002, 2003, and 2004—and then just quit trying. The last straight steal of home was Billy Hatcher's on April 22, 1994.

"Upside-down baseball"—purposely letting the Yankees steal home

August 5, 1935. It was a rain-shortened five-inning game, described by a photo caption in the *Boston Globe* as "upside-down baseball." The Yankees scored once in the top of the second inning, when Fritz Ostermueller walked in a run, but Boston scored twice to take a brief lead. Ostermueller wasn't very effective—to put it mildly. He issued another walk, three singles, and a double in the top of the third, and the Yankees were up 4–2. After walking two more Yankees in the top of the fourth—bringing his total to six free passes—relief pitcher George Hockette came in and gave up a single, a single, and a single. That earned him a shower, too. In the five innings of the twice-interrupted game, the Sox brought out three more pitchers as well. Five pitchers in five innings. And the score was 10–2, New York, after 4½ innings. There had been a 20-minute rain delay in the fourth and with more rain on the horizon in the fifth inning, the Red Sox began trying to delay, stall, and generally s-l-o-w the game down in hopes it would be canceled before they completed the bottom of the inning and it became an official game.

As Dick Thompson put it, in an informal writeup of the game, both *The Sporting News* and the Boston papers commented on how farcical the "comical contest" became. "The Yanks were trying hard to make three outs and the Red Sox were trying just as hard not to make them. The Yanks stole four bases because [Sox catcher] Rick Ferrell wouldn't throw the ball. Myril Hoag, who stole four bases all season, was credited with a steal of both second base and home in the inning." Hoag stole second, but as he approached third base on the next play, Sox third baseman Billy Werber could have easily tagged him out and Hoag even stopped to make it easy for Werber, who "refused to tag him and Hoag finally stepped on the bag. A moment later he ran to the plate as though he were trying to steal, but stopped standing up before he got there. The *Globe* wrote, "Mr. Ferrell is juggling the ball all over the lot while Mr. Hoag is pausing a foot short of the platter....Ferrell finally had his way and they had to give Hoag a stolen base, of all things!"

Thompson reports that both managerial Joes, McCarthy and Cronin, were later fined $100 apiece by the American League office for the delaying tactics.

Courtesy runners

In earlier times, if a player was injured, but perhaps not enough to have to leave the game were he given a few minutes to recover, the opposing manager would sometimes permit a courtesy runner to take his place. The original player would then re-enter the game on defense.

Cy Young was a pinch-runner TWICE in the same game!

September 17, 1903—This is the same game noted above, wherein Boston completed a streak of scoring in 17 consecutive innings. No one had more than two hits for Boston, but in fact everyone for Boston got two hits with the exception of Hobe Ferris, who had to be content with his second home run in as many games, and pitcher George Winter, who was 0-for-4. Charley Farrell played the whole game, his first game back from injury. As a courtesy, captain Larry Lajoie allowed Cy Young to run for Farrell both times he hit safely. 14–3 was the final score.

Cy Young, a pinch-runner?

This was apparently just two days after he stole two bases in the same game, on the 15th.

Lewis runs for Lewis, then Lewis re-enters the game

Right at the end of the year in 1911, Boston visited New York for the last time and swept all three games. The first two wins were both halves of an October 3 doubleheader, Boston winning 4–1 and 7–0. In the first game, Duffy Lewis singled and Engle followed with an out. Second baseman Jack Lewis then singled, putting runners at first and third. Bradley struck out for the second out of the inning. With catcher Rip Williams up (he was finishing up a year he hit .239) the two Lewises tried a double steal—and pulled it off, Duffy Lewis scoring successfully on the throw down to second. Jack Lewis was badly shaken up in a collision at second base with New York's shortstop Hartzell covering the bag. Duffy Lewis received permission to run for his namesake (there was no relation between the two Lewises) and trotted back to second base—the same sack he'd just rounded on Jack's single two at-bats earlier. Williams disappointed and Lewis (Duffy, running for Jack) did not advance. As *BaseballLibrary.com* notes, "Apparently, one Lewis is as good as another."

Later in the game (it's not clear how much later), Jack Lewis came back in the game, and got another hit. He also played game two that day but went 0-for-4. Duffy Lewis stole another base in game one, and went 1-for-4 in the second game, a double.

Morgan, beaned, replaced by Cooke, who leaves game when Morgan returns—but then reappears later on

The Sox slapped St. Louis with two losses at Fenway Park on June 18, 1934, 6–5 and 14–9, which lifted Boston over .500 (29–27). Ed Morgan, Boston's first baseman, batted third in the order. In the bottom of the fourth frame, Morgan was beaned by a fast curve ball and laid low. He left, feeling a little woozy. Dusty Cooke came in as a courtesy runner for Morgan, stole second, and scored on Indian Bob Johnson's double to right. The Sox sent up seven more batters, scoring four runs in all. With nobody out, they were getting pretty close to when Morgan would be due up again, but then the pitcher Welch grounded into a double play and leadoff batter Cissell fouled out to the catcher, ending the inning. Given time to clear the cobwebs, Morgan shook them off and took his position again in the fifth. It was an active game for him; he made 11 putouts in all. Cooke re-entered the game later on, taking Reynolds' place in center field.

Morgan was OK; he played game two, as did Cooke. Morgan had a hit in the finale, and Cooke went 2-for-3, scoring three times.

Pinch-run and steal two bases in the same inning

In the game on September 23, 2003, Adrian Brown pinch-ran for Manny Ramirez in the eighth and stole second and third. He became the first Red Sox player ever to pinch run and steal two bases in an inning.

Pinch-ran, then hit a grand slam in the same inning

In the sixth inning of the July 13, 1959 game against the Yankees, Gene Stephens pinch-ran for Ted Williams after Ted had singled in Jackie Jensen. Two batters later, he was thrown out at the plate on Sammy White's grounder to third base. The Red Sox batted around, though, and Stephens came up with the bases loaded and hit a grand slam to give the Red Sox four more runs in a nine-run inning.

Four pinch runners in the same game, and one of them a pitcher

It was Friday night, April 17, 1998 at Fenway Park, with the Cleveland Indians in town. Jimy Williams was Boston's manager—and he made some moves that paid off. The Red Sox came up to bat in the bottom of the ninth, trailing 2–0. Scott Hatteberg singled off starter Charles Nagy to lead off. Damon Buford was the first pinch-runner, in for Hatteberg. Darren Bragg struck out. But Jim Leyritz pinch-hit and singled to right, Buford taking second. Midre Cummings was put in to run for Leyritz. Varitek pinch-hit and singled to drive in Buford (Varitek was pinch-hitting for Mike Benjamin, who had pinch-run for Mark Lemke back in the seventh; Benjamin then played second base.) Michael Jackson took over for Nagy and gave up a single to Garciaparra, who loaded the bases for Reggie Jefferson, whose sac fly to center scored the other pinch-runner, Cummings. The Sox had tied the score, and the game went into extra innings.

Tom Gordon was pitching for the Red Sox. Buford took over at second. After Cleveland's Manny Ramirez singled, with Jim Thome coming up, Buford was waved over to play third base while John Valentin played second. After Thome singled, Buford and Valentin switched back again. Sandy Alomar struck out, but when Brian Giles came up, Jimy had Buford go back to third base. Giles struck out, at which point Buford and Valentin switched yet again. Whether all this defensive maneuvering paid off is hard to determine; none of the infielders were ever involved in a play despite the fact that in just the half-inning, Buford had played 2b,3b,2b,3b,and 2b.

In the bottom of the 10th, Mo Vaughn singled and in came pitcher Steve Avery to pinch-run for him. Troy O'Leary singled, then Buford was walked on purpose, loading the bases. Bragg singled and the pinch-running Avery scored the winning run.

Then there is the baserunning gaffe that can cost a game

The evening of May 11, 2001 at Fenway ended anti-climactically. Oakland led 4–0 after two innings, and 6–3 after 7½, but the Red Sox tied it up with three in the bottom of the eighth. The A's scored one run in the top of the ninth. Mike Magnante came in to pitch the bottom of the ninth for Oakland. He walked Nixon, then got Offerman on a fly to right. Carl Everett singled, sending Nixon to second. Jeff Tam came on in relief and hit Manny Ramirez, loading the bases for the Red Sox with one out. Troy O'Leary then lifted a fly ball to left field—game tied! No, wait a minute. Nixon just trotted home as the throw went to second base. Everett was tagged out at second before Nixon crossed the plate. Game over. Had Nixon either *run* to home, or had Everett managed to get himself into a rundown, the Red Sox would have tied the game with John Valentin coming to bat. Instead, Val watched from the on-deck circle, and then went back to the dugout and something on the order of 32,000 fans went home.

A baserunning oddity

It doesn't happen that often, but most baseball fans know that if a baserunner is hit by a batted ball, that runner is out. It happened to Ernie Shore twice in one game. The Sox swept a doubleheader on July 28, 1917 from the Browns. Shore pitched the second game, but was erased on the basepaths in the third inning by a ball hit for a single by center fielder Jimmy Walsh. Then, in the fifth, he bunted and, while running to first base, "caressed the pill" (in other words, he was hit by his own ball). Out. The only other time this had occurred twice in a game to the same baserunner was apparently back in the 19th century.

Hit by batted ball

Aside from Shore's misfortune indicated above, there have been a few other instances in which batted balls have hit players—in recent times, Sox fans recall both Matt Clement and Bryce Florie being struck in the head by balls hit by opposing batters. Hank Greenberg himself hit both Fritz Ostermueller, breaking his cheekbone and some teeth on May 25, 1935, and Jack Wilson, who suffered a fractured skull on August 8, 1945. Yaz singled off Dick Drago's jawbone on September 1, 1972, and (after Drago left the game) scored the only run of a 1–0 game, charged—of course—to Drago. The Red Sox lost in the 10th inning of the July 30, 1950 first game when Larry Doby slammed a ball into Joe Dobson's stomach (the AP said it struck him over the heart); while he was stunned, the ball laying at his feet, Dale Mitchell scored all the way from second base to walk off with a win. It was the year after Al Zarilla hit Bob Kuzava with a liner, after the young White Sox pitcher had just tied a league record by striking out six Red Sox in succession during the August 26 game.

Perhaps two of the more unusual instances were when the Yankees' Babe Dahlgren hit himself in the eye with his own foul ball, and had to leave the August 6, 1940 game, and when Ted Williams slammed a line drive off returned war hero Lou Brissie's shrapnel-injured and plastic-protected leg during the Patriot's Day doubleheader opening the 1948 campaign. Brissie stayed in the game and won it, a four-hitter, just one of which was Ted's. Brissie had survived an attack that killed 11 of his fellow infantrymen during combat in Italy. (The Athletics won the first game, too, behind the pitching of former P.O.W. Phil Marchildon.)

What do you hope for when there are two runners on second and one on third?

It's maybe too much to hope for, but the 1935 Red Sox found themselves in just that situation on April 23, playing the Yankees. Moose Solters doubled and Mel Almada walked. Babe Dahlgren hit a ball sharply to left, and the throw came home to Bill Dickey. Fortunately, the pileup on the basepaths proved advantageous when the throw bounced over Dickey's head and *two* runs scored.

Stolen bases

When he stole his 30th (and final) base of the year on September 23 against the Orioles, Johnny Damon became the first Red Sox player to record back-to-back 30-steal seasons since Tris Speaker had done it in 1914. Speaker had stolen 52 in 1912, 46 in 1913, and 42 in 1914—more than 40 per year. Damon stole 31 bases in 2002 and 30 in 2003.

In 2007, speedster Julio Lugo set a team record, stealing 20 bases in a row without being caught. Jacoby Ellsbury reached 25 times without being caught, in 2007–08. Lugo's thefts helped the Sox establish a team high 80% success rate in steals—with 96 stolen bases in an even 120 attempts.

It was Coco Crisp, also in 2007, who raised the bar in terms of stolen base percentage in a given season. Of all baserunners with at least 50 attempts, Crisp succeeded 83.3% of the time (50 steals in 60 attempts.) He'd had an even higher percentage (84.6%) in 2006, but in just 26 tries.

FIELDING AND DEFENSE

The year 2006 saw the best-fielding infield the Red Sox have ever fielded. Three of the four infielders set team records for defensive play, all in the same season. Second baseman Mark Loretta wound up with just four errors for a fielding percentage of .994. (He also handled 83 chances without an error playing first base.) His play at second gave him the edge over Bobby Doerr's team record, set in 1948 (.9925, six errors).

Alex Gonzalez ended the year with a league-leading .985 fielding percentage, with only five errors all year long, at shortstop. Vern Stephens (1950, .982, 13 errors) held the previous Red Sox record.

Mike Lowell held down the hot corner at third base, making just six errors and posting a .987 mark, easily eclipsing Rico Petrocelli's .976 mark, set when Rico only made 11 errors in 1971. Lowell's career .976 fielding percentage is best of any third baseman in major league history (minimum 1,000 games).

Errors were far more common in the American League's early days, given the condition of the fields and given gloves that were primitive by today's standards. Of the 138 games played in 1901 by the Boston Americans, there were 337 errors committed—an average of 2.44 errors a game. Freddy Parent led with 63 errors at shortstop. In 2006, the team as a whole only committed 66 errors, despite playing a full contemporary 162-game schedule—an average of 0.41 errors per game.

Best team fielding percentage in major league history

As it happened, the entire 2006 Red Sox team was a great fielding team—so good that they set the major league record for best fielding percentage ever. The team collectively committed just 66 errors; the next-closest teams of the year were Oakland and Minnesota, which both made 84. Boston's team fielding percentage was .989096316.

The previous record was set in 2003 by the Seattle Mariners, who broke the team defensive record set by the New York Mets in 1999 (.98886605 to .988751034). The Mariners only committed 65 errors, but the Red Sox still ecliped Seattle by .000230266. Boston's was a short-lived record, however. The 2007 Colorado Rockies posted a team fielding percentage of .9892.

Handling 668 chances in a row without an error

Errors really aren't that rare. Stringing together 10 or more errorless games is. In 2006, the Red Sox team set the all-time major league mark by playing 17 consecutive error-free games. First baseman Kevin Youkilis made an error on the second batter of the game during June 11's home day game against Texas. The Sox didn't make another error all month, the next one coming on July 1 when Marlins leadoff batter Hanley Ramirez stole second and catcher Doug Mirabelli's throw to second was errant (allowing Ramirez to scurry to third). In between, Boston handled 668 chances in a row without one miscue.

In the very same first inning of the July 1 game, the Red Sox committed a second error but it was the only other one of the game. In the entire 2006 season, they never made more than two errors in a game. The Sox played 108 games that were completely error-free.

Not handling any chances at all for more than seven games

There are plenty of games in which a right fielder might not field a ball. Baby Doll Jacobson, though, trudged back and forth to right field for more than seven games in a row (64⅓ innings in all) from June 17 through June 25, 1926 without recording either a putout or an assist. Basically, he just went out to right, stood around, and then came back to the dugout—for more than a week of steady (in)action.

Perhaps not having to focus on his fielding freed up Baby Doll to better performance at the plate. Over the same seven-game stretch, he was 15-for-28 (.536) with seven singles, seven doubles, and a home run.

To be in the middle of the action and never see any action at second base is very unusual, but for a full 15 innings in the June 11, 1913 ballgame, Steve Yerkes never had a single fielding opportunity—no assists, no putouts, not even an error. He did get a double, though, one hit in seven at-bats.

TRIPLE PLAYS

The steady everyday fielding was much appreciated by Red Sox fans, but defensively there's nothing more spectacular than the triple play.

Unassisted triple plays

There have been 11 unassisted triple plays since 1901, six of them in the 1920s. Two were pulled off by Red Sox players, George Burns in 1923 and John Valentin in 1994. Less than three weeks after Burns' triple play, another Boston player executed one—but the second Boston ballplayer was a Brave, Ernie Padgett. The first one ever saw the Sox as victim. Two (or three) on, nobody out—that's the formula for any triple play. It's the ultimate rally killer.

In the top of the second, first game of a doubleheader on July 19, 1909, Cleveland's shortstop Neal Ball grabbed a line drive by Amby McConnell, stepped on second base to put out Heinie Wagner, who was unable to get back to the bag on time, and then tagged the oncoming Jake Stahl, who was running from first to second. Ball batted in the bottom of the second inning and hit an inside-the-park home run. What an inning for Mr. Ball! Cleveland won the game, 6–1, thanks as well to a fine pitching performance by a former Boston pitcher named Cy Young. Frank Arellanes won the nightcap for Boston, 8–2.

Cleveland's second baseman Bill Wambsganss pulled off an unassisted triple play in the 1920 World Series versus Brooklyn. The Indians' monopoly on unassisted triple plays, though, was snapped by Boston's George Burns on September 14, 1923—though Cleveland was involved. Burns, oddly, was a first baseman. It was the top of the second inning, the same half of the same frame as Ball's play. The Indians also had runners on first and second and, of course, there was no one out. Riggs Stephenson was on second, having singled to center and moved up a base on Rube Lutzke's walk. Frank "Turkeyfoot" Brower lined a ball that was heading to right field, but Burns snagged it about 15 feet from first base. He ran the rookie, Lutzke, down and tagged him, then saw that Stephenson was most of the way to third. Instead of just flipping the ball to Norm McMillan or Johnny Mitchell at second base, maybe Burns saw his place in history. He ran to second, sliding into the bag just a few feet ahead of Stephenson, who slid in from the other direction.

Never heard of either McMillan or Mitchell? These were not the best years for the Red Sox. Jack Quinn was the winning pitcher for Boston, who won the game 4–3 in 12 innings. The Indians had taken a 3–2 lead in the top of the 12th. Al DeVormer doubled in a pinch-hitting role, and Joe Harris was walked to set up possible force plays. Howie Shanks got on with a hit and a throw that was off the mark. With the bases loaded, Ira Flagstead faced a relief pitcher. After 11 innings and with three men on base, the Indians decided to go to their bench. Guy Morton's first pitch was banged into left and two runs scored, tying and then winning the game as the throw from left sailed over the catcher's head. Burns singled once, going 1-for-4.

Glenn Wright, Jimmy Cooney, and Johnny Neun also executed unassisted triple plays in the Twenties, but then we had to wait for Ron Hansen (1968) and Mickey Morandini (1992) for the next two. On July 8, 1994, John Valentin was at shortstop. Seattle had men on first (Keith Mitchell had walked) and second (Mike Blowers had singled) in the top of the sixth, and already led 2–0. The DH (they didn't have those in Burns' day) Marc Newfield hit the ball sharply—on a line right to Valentin. Valentin stepped on second, retiring Mike Blowers who was off the bag and "trotted a few steps to tag the runner (Keith Mitchell) coming from first—all very nonchanlantly," wrote Nick Cafardo in the next morning's *Globe*. "EASY AS 1-2-3" headlined the paper's sports section. Valentin admitted that he'd thought there was already one out, and that probably contributed to his nonchalance. He said, a little sheepishly after the game, "Keith Mitchell wasn't really running. I looked over at the scoreboard and saw that there was one out and my teammates reminded me to tag him." In the bottom of the same inning, Valentin followed the example of Neal Ball, who he'd probably never heard of before, homering to lead off the inning. Val was first up and he sent a 3-2 pitch over the left-field wall. Two more homers in the bottom of the sixth plated four, and the Sox won 4–3.

Of the triple play, John Trainer (another *Globe* writer) said that it unfolded rather slowly, and looked so routine, that "it took the Fenway fans a full two minutes" to realize what they'd just witnessed. Valentin, thinking there was already one out—the catch apparently resulted in the first out being registered on the scoreboard—was trotting toward the dugout when he came across Mitchell, who had "slowed to a walk, and Valentin tagged him as he jogged by."

Valentin has the ball. He told SABR's David Vincent that he threw the ball back to the mound while leaving the field, but that it was retrieved by one of the umpires who gave it back to him later.

Hitting into a triple play on the first ball put in play in the ballgame

Gary Waslewski just didn't have it on July 15, 1967. Catcher Russ Gibson warned Sox manager Dick Williams, but he had Gary start anyhow. He walked Aparicio. He walked Russ Snyder. When the count reached 2–1 on Paul Blair, Johnson called in Jose Santiago. On a 3–2 count, Blair put bat to ball and lined to Joe Foy at third. He fired to Mike Andrews at second who, despite being bowled over by the onrushing Snyder, held the ball and had time to fire to George Scott at first.

Regular old run-of-the-mill triple plays
August 7, 1901

It didn't take long before Boston's AL team pulled off its first triple play. It came in Baltimore (against the team that became the New York Yankees) on August 7, 1901. With runners on first and third and nobody out, Roger Bresnahan bunted back to pitcher Nig Cuppy, who started what evolved into a 1–5–2*–6*–1* triple play (the asterisks indicate who made the putouts) due to some bad decisions made on the basepaths. The next morning's *Boston Globe* suggested that Baltimore's baserunners proved that "experienced baseball players can sometimes act as though their brains have been transformed into cottage cheese."

June 6 and June 7, 1908—triple plays two days in a row

The Red Sox were in Detroit, down 2–1 after two innings. Boston's first two batters of the third, Harry Lord and Amby McConnell, both singled to left. Gavvy Cravath lined a shot directly at the third baseman who started a 5–6–3 triple play, the first ever at Bennett Park. Boston took the game, though, 10–5. The very next day, still in town, the Red Sox wasted no time putting runners on base. Jack Thoney swung at the first pitch of the game and singled. Lord singled and the Sox had runners on first and second. McConnell's foul ball smashed the Tigers' catcher's finger, and he had to leave the game. McConnell singled and Thoney scored. Cravath singled, and Lord scored, McConnell taking third—then coming home on Cobb's error as Cravath took second. Unglaub reached first on a bounder back to the pitcher. An infield single loaded the bases. Heinie Wagner's roller to second base scored Cravath from third, but helped trigger the second triple play in two days as the second baseman tagged out the runner coming into second and threw Wagner out at first. The first baseman fired to the plate just in time to get Unglaub trying to score the fifth run.

May 6, 1911

The Yankees pulled off their first-ever team triple play at the expense of—who else—the Red Sox, on May 6, 1911 at Hilltop Park in New York. The "walk-off" triple killing doused a dangerous Red Sox rally in top of the ninth inning. New York was ahead 6–3, and neither team had scored since the fifth. Russell Ford had held Boston to five hits, but then surrendered singles to both Rip Williams and Les Nunamaker. Bill Carrigan was sent in to pinch-hit for pitcher Eddie Cicotte, and when "Ford buzzed a jump ball at the Maine grocer," Carrigan "swung at it like Flanagan waving the 16-pound hammer."

Shortstop Wilbur Roach, though, leapt high in the air and snared the liner, fired to second to get Williams, and then Earl Gardner threw to Chase at first to double off Nunamaker. It was the second time Nunamaker had been doubled off by second baseman Gardner; just two innings earlier he'd been unable to get back to second base in time after Gardner had gone after a fly ball to short right.

August 11, 1922—two pitches to retire the side

After the Senators singled twice to lead off the ninth, the Sox brought in a new pitcher, Allen Russell. On his second pitch, batter Howie Shanks laid down a sacrifice bunt but Boston catcher Muddy Ruel scooped it up in front of the plate and fired down to third base to force out the man on second. Third baseman Pinky Pittenger fired across the diamond in time to get Shanks out, and first baseman George Burns returned the throw to Pittenger to cut down the oncoming Bucky Harris, who'd tried to go first to third while the play was unfolding. The Red Sox bats couldn't create any magic, though, and Boston lost, 5–4. It was a 2-5-3-5 triple killing.

September 26, 1927

The Sox hosted the Washington Senators for a doubleheader and started the afternoon pulling off a triple play in the top of the first inning of the first game, a very unusual 8-4-2 play, Flagstead to Regan to Hartley. It was all downhill from there. It was a sacrifice fly with runners on first and second. Both runners tagged up, but the runner at second was out. Quincy, Massachusetts native Foster "Babe" Ganzel, who'd tagged and gone to third, saw an opportunity when he saw the ball being thrown to second and tried to score on the play, but both runners were thrown out instead. Despite that excitement, the Red Sox lost the game as it played out, 4–2.

The Red Sox seemed to try for a record in the second game, but fell short: they only committed 10 errors in the one game. Catcher Bill Moore led the way with four of his own. They lost, 11–1.

September 7, 1935

One of the most noteworthy triple plays in Red Sox history was dubbed "the freakiest triple play in big league annals" by the *Boston Herald*. Sox shortstop (and player/manager) Joe Cronin was up in the bottom of the ninth inning, first game of the September 7, 1935 doubleheader against the Indians. Cleveland had scored twice in the top of the ninth, running the score to 5–1, but the Bosox battled back. "Ski" Melillo singled, as did pinch-hitter Bing Miller and right fielder Dusty Cooke. One run was in and then Billy Werber singled to short right, loading the bases. With nobody out and suffering four straight singles, Indians manager Steve O'Neill yanked starter Mel Harder and inserted Oral Hildebrand in relief. Mel Almada singled off him, but the runners all moved up just one base. 5–3 Indians, bases still loaded, and still nobody out.

Cronin, a good man in the clutch, slammed a hard drive toward left field, but third baseman Odell Hale lunged and got a bit of his glove on the ball. The *Herald* reports, "The ball caromed off his mitt, hit him not too heavily on the left side of the head over the hair, and then still without hitting the ground, arced coyly over toward shortstop, where the alert Knickerbocker picked it gayly out of the air, retiring Batter Cronin." The runners took off when they saw the ball carom off Hale's glove, before he gave it the header, and it was an easy thing for Knickerbocker to toss to Roy Hughes at second. Hughes had time to spare, as he threw to Hal Trosky at first to double off Almada. Three outs, rally snuffed out, game over.

Hale had done well in game one, homering as part of a 2-for-4 opener. He suffered a "wee lump" on his head, but played the second game, going 2-for-4 again, with a double, helping Cleveland take two on the day.

April 28, 1938

Another ninth-inning triple play, but this time it favored the Red Sox. The early-season Yankee Stadium game saw a Lefty vs. Lefty faceoff. The 1937 World Champion Yankees put up Lefty Gomez (18–2 lifetime against the Sox) against Lefty Grove for the visiting Red Sox. Grove held the New Yorkers to five hits, while Boston piled up a 6–1 lead through four innings, then held it until the bottom of the ninth. The only NY run had come on a sac fly by Gomez back in the third. Neither Joe DiMaggio nor Bill Dickey had been able to play.

Doerr misplayed a ball, and Grove walked Joe Gordon, so New York had two on and nobody out. Catcher Joe Glenn hit a hard shot toward right field, but Jimmie Foxx "glove-stabbed the ball, and quick as a cat, flipped it toward unguarded second base. Joe Cronin reacted quickly enough to reach the ball and the bag a split second before Twinkle Toes Selkirk could return. Almost in the same motion, Frisco Joe rifled the ball over to Foxx, where Jumbo received it flush on the cushion with young Gordon still frantically scrambling back." Arthur Sampson noted that it happened so quickly it was several minutes before everyone realized the game was over. Three outs in the space of perhaps three seconds.

April 24, 1954—Karl Olson brings about five outs in his first two at-bats

Boston's Mel Parnell, a 21-game winner in 1953, had a bone in his left forearm broken by a Mickey McDermott pitch in the third inning of a game in Washington. This was the same year that Ted Williams broke his collarbone in spring training. When Parnell was taken to the hospital, Tommy Brewer took first base to run for him. Billy Goodman singled to right and Brewer held at second. Left-fielder Karl Olson (Ted's replacement) had already grounded into a double play as the second batter up in the top of the first. Now, he tried to sacrifice the two runners, but popped up the bunt to McDermott, who wheeled and fired to second base, getting Brewer before he could get back to the bag. Mel Hoderlein, who took the throw, then fired to Roy Sievers at first and they got Goodman. It was pretty much a disaster all the way around. For Olson, it was two at-bats and he'd brought about five outs. Olson popped up leading off the sixth. But in the eighth inning, he tripled and kicked off a rally that led to four runs. Boston scored twice more in the ninth and won the game for Skinny Brown, 6–1.

September 28, 1963—bunting into a triple play

The last game of the year saw the Angels at Fenway, with a 3–2 lead after six. They threatened to add an insurance run or two when Charlie Dees doubled to lead off the seventh and Lee Thomas walked. Trying to advance the runners, Felix Torres bunted but hit it too hard and Sox pitcher Pete Smith caught it, then fired to third baseman Frank Malzone to get the advancing runner. Malzy threw to Eddie Bressoud at second to tag out Thomas as he came into the bag. Boston scored once in the eighth to tie it and Lou Clinton's bases-loaded single in the bottom of the ninth won it, and the season was over.

July 17, 1990—two triple plays in one game

Tom Bolton was pitching for Boston against Scott Erickson for the Twins. In the bottom of the fourth of a scoreless game, Wade Boggs walked. He took third on Jody Reed's double to right, and then Carlos Quintana walked to load the bases with nobody out. Twins third baseman Gary Gaetti says he always anticipated the possible triple play. Tom Brunansky hit a hard grounder to him. Gaetti stepped on third, and then started your classic 5-4–3 triple play. The Fenway faithful started buzzing when a similar situation presented itself in the bottom of the eighth. Tom Naehring had doubled and Boggs had, again, walked. Gaetti was ready, and when

Jody Reed grounded to him, he did it again: step on the bag, fire to second, watch the relay to first. 5-4–3. Fenway was stunned for nearly a full minute, then burst out into applause for what we had all witnessed. Boston fans went home happy; Tim Naehring had singled in a lone unearned run in the fifth and the Red Sox the game, 1–0.

August 6, 2001

It was described as "from the outhouse to the penthouse." It happened in back-to-back at-bats. Boston held a 4–2 lead in the fourth inning, with two men on base and nobody out. Scott Hatteberg lined into a triple play. The Rangers then scored five runs to take the lead. In the sixth inning, Hatteberg came up again, this time with three runners on base—and nobody out. He hit a grand slam home run to put the Red Sox in the lead, a lead they maintained.

DOUBLE PLAYS, TOO

When one thinks of the two Gaetti-initiated triple plays, there are a few double plays that come to mind as well, namely the very next day when the Twins and Red Sox combined to set a major league record for the most twin killings in one game. The date was July 18 in the year 1990. Though they had won the game, the Sox were no doubt still shaking their heads over the day before. Gunning for another record, they grounded into six double plays—and won again, 5–4. "We're on a roll," cracked Wade Boggs after the game.

The Red Sox win featured not only the six GIDP for themselves, but they turned four. The total of 10 double plays by both teams broke the old major league mark, but the Sox fell short of the single-team mark of seven (set by the Giants in 1969). The Red Sox got off to a good start, grounding into double plays in the first inning, the second, the third, the fourth, and the fifth—though the one in the fifth inning only came after they'd driven in four runs. You had to think they were indeed on a roll, but in the sixth they grounded out, grounded out, and struck out. They never got a runner to first base, and having a baserunner is a prerequisite to a double play. Leading 5–4 after the seventh, Boston never got to bat in the bottom of the ninth, thereby missing a chance to dig a deeper hole for the next contestant to overcome.

Manager Joe Morgan remembered a minor league game in Burlington NC—the first game of a doubleheader, a seven-inning game—where one team hit into seven double plays. "We can hit into 15, as long as we win," said Kevin Romine, who'd hit into two of them, in the second and fourth innings.

A double play with one sweep of the arm

August 25, 1925: After scoring nine times in the bottom of the first inning, the Tigers were running away with the game, but Boston catcher Al Stokes got in a little playing time later in the game and made a nice little play—tagging out two Detroit runners with one sweep of his arm. It was the seventh inning and Johnny Bassler was on second, with Fred Haney on first. Topper Rigney hit a long fly to center. Ira Flagstead ran it down but dropped it. Bassler had held up, but Haney had not, and so was hard on Bassler's heels as both men ran to home plate. Flagstead picked up the ball, threw to the cutoff man, Rothrock, who fired the ball home to Stokes. Bassler slid to the inside of the plate while Haney slid to the outside. Both Tigers "hit the dust simultaneously. Stokes stood his ground, and with one sweep of his arm, tagged them both before their spikes hit the rubber. Not to be outdone, the umpire shot both arms upward, indicating the double play." [*Washington Post*] Stokes recorded the two outs, but also made two errors in the same game. Boston lost, 14–4. [From *Day by Day with the Boston Red Sox*]

Most double plays in a single season

The Red Sox player who took part in the most double plays in a single season was first baseman Rudy York, who took part in 154 in 1946. That was one more than Jimmie Foxx's 153 in 1938.

Rick Burleson holds the major league record for shortstops with 147 in 1980. Bobby Doerr holds eight of the top nine seasons for Red Sox second basemen; his best year was 1949 when he took part in 134 twin killings. Johnny Pesky, moved over to third base against his inclination, leads with 48 in 1949 (that was enough to lead the league that year as well).

Outfield double plays? Tris Speaker took part in an even dozen—twice. He did it first in 1909, then did it again in 1914. Speaker even pulled off five unassisted double plays for the Red Sox, including two in 1914 alone, one on April 21 and one on August 8.

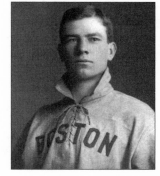

Tris Speaker, author of five unassisted double plays.

A couple of catchers who completed unassisted double plays are Charlie Armbruster (April 26, 1907) and Sammy White (September 13, 1953). White tied a major league record on May 25, 1954 by hitting into three consecutive double plays, his first three times up. The fourth time up, there was no one on base. It was in the top of the ninth. He hit a home run that won the game, 3–2.

The Sox combined as a team to hit into double plays eight innings in a row on May 1, 1966. In the day's doubleheader, they hit into six DPs beginning with the fourth through the ninth innings of the first game (which they lost, 6–1). In the second game, they hit into two more, in the first and second innings. The second of two first-inning runs scored on the first DP, though, and that was sufficient for a win, the final being 9–1 Red Sox.

It cuts both ways: a run the Angels scored on a first-inning double play beat Sonny Siebert in California, 1–0, on August 27, 1971.

Catcher Muddy Ruel helped pull off 17 double plays in 1922. Tony Peña was second with 15, in 1991.

Pitcher Boo Ferriss helped record 10 double plays in his rookie year, 1945.

Grounding into double plays

In 1984, Jim Rice grounded into a record-setting 36 double plays. It was one of four seasons that Rice led the league. The previous record of 32 had been set by another Red Sox batter, Jackie Jensen, in 1954. In the process of hitting into so many double plays, though, Rice drove in 122 runs and Jensen drove in 117.

HIDDEN BALL TRICKS

In the hidden ball trick department (even in the early days of the last century, this was always referred to as the "old hidden ball trick"), the Red Sox have pulled off 17 of them, while only being caught 11 times. Johnny Pesky pulled off three of the 17 and Marty Barrett pulled off three more. It's been more than 50 years since a Red Sox player has been caught.

Boston player as perpetrator

Candy LaChance caught Baltimore's Billy Gilbert on May 2, 1902
Harry Lord caught St. Louis's Tom Jones on August 29, 1908
George Burns caught New York's Chick Fewster on June 24, 1922
Danny Clark caught Chicago's Roy Elsh on May 17, 1924

Marty McManus caught Cleveland's Earl Averill on August 21, 1933
Oscar Melillo caught Detroit's Billy Rogell on August 22, 1936
Johnny Pesky caught Washington's Bill Zuber on May 31, 1942
Johnny Pesky caught New York's Tommy Henrich on July 4, 1942
Bobby Doerr caught St. Louis's Denny Galehouse on June 2, 1943
Johnny Pesky caught Washington's Buddy Lewis on July 6, 1947
Joe Foy caught Baltimore's Merv Rettenmund on September 18, 1968
George Thomas caught New York's Jerry Kenney on June 21, 1969
Jackie Gutierrez caught Minnesota's Tim Teufel on August 17, 1984
Marty Barrett caught California's Bobby Grich on July 1, 1985
Marty Barrett (to Glenn Hoffman) caught California's Doug De Cinces on July 21, 1985
Marty Barrett (to Jody Reed) caught Baltimore's Jim Traber on September 5, 1988
Steve Lyons caught Chicago's Ozzie Guillen on May 13, 1991
Julio Lugo caught Arizona's Alberto Callaspo on June 8, 2007

Boston player as victim

Patsy Dougherty was caught by Washington's Bill Coughlin on June 25, 1902
Fred Parent was caught by Washington's Hunter Hill on April 29, 1905
Hobe Ferris was caught by Detroit's Bill Coughlin on May 12, 1905
John Knight was caught by Detroit's Charley O'Leary on August 19, 1907
Amby McConnell was caught by Bill Coughlin on May 13, 1908
Les Nunamaker was caught by St. Louis's George Stovall on May 11, 1912
Wally Schang was caught by St. Louis's Jimmy Austin on June 18, 1919
Stuffy McInnis was caught by Detroit's Babe Pinelli on June 19, 1920
Shano Collins was caught by Washington's Joe Judge on April 24, 1922
Jimmy Piersall was caught by St. Louis's Billy Hunter on June 21, 1953
Sammy White was caught by Chicago's Chico Carrasquel on June 24, 1955

Doerr's play was notable in that Galehouse was the baserunner on first base at the time and second baseman Doerr had to keep creeping over to get close enough to tag him before Galehouse suspected anything.

His humiliation was perhaps so deep that he fled to center. Jimmy Piersall was on second base with two outs during the June 21 game in 1953. Billy Hunter said, "Give the bag a kick for me, it's out of line and I want to straighten it." Piersall replied, "Straighten it out yourself." "I can't. You're standing on it." Piersall stepped off and Hunter tagged him out. Piersall left without saying a word and trotted out to his position in the field. [*Washington Post*, June 30, 1953]

The Fenway faithful were at fever pitch on June 24, 1955. The Sox had won 14 of their last 16 games, and came into the bottom of the ninth just trailing by one run. Sammy White singled, and Faye Throneberry bunted over the pitcher's head for a single. Grady Hatton flied out, and then White found himself tagged out when he stepped off second base—shortstop Chico Carrasquel had retained the baseball. Even then, there was a chance to win the game. Pitcher Sandy Consuegra slipped and fell on top of the ball when he went to field Piersall's slow grounder, hurting himself so that he had to leave the game. Morrie Martin struck out the final man.

Some HBT's require more cleverness than others. Lugo's teammate Mike Lowell said of the 2007 trick Lugo pulled: "That's not a real hidden-ball trick, although I'm sure the stats say it is." And they do. What Lowell meant was that there was no real deception involved; the pitcher didn't have to "sell" the trick in some fashion. Callaspo just took his hand off the bag a little too quickly to dust himself off and Lugo still had the ball in his glove, reached down, and touched him with it.

Thanks to Bill Deane, who has located more than 250 hidden ball tricks in major league history.

Note: After Marty Barrett pulled the hidden ball trick on 16-year major league veteran Bobby Grich, he says that Grich calmly told him that if he *ever* tried it again, he would rip Barrett's eyes out.

Catching no-hitters

Bill Carrigan caught three—Smoky Joe Wood, Rube Foster, and Dutch Leonard.

Jason Varitek caught five, if you count Devern Hansack's October 1, 2006 complete game with no hits (which we do, even if MLB does not). Tek's other three: Hideo Nomo (2001), Derek Lowe (2002), Clay Buchholz (2007).

Lou Criger caught three, two by Cy Young, and one by Bill Dinneen.

Bob Tillman caught two, too—Earl Wilson, 1962 and Dave Morehead, 1965.

Dutch Leonard with Bill Carrigan.

Other Sox catchers who caught Boston no-hitters:

Duke Farrell (Jesse Tannehill, 1904)

Charlie Armbrister (Bill Dinneen, 1905)

Sam Agnew and Pinch Thomas (Ernie Shore, 1917)—not only were there two pitchers in this game that Babe Ruth started, but there were two catchers as well.

Wally Schang (Dutch Leonard, 1918)

Val Picinich (Howard Ehmke, 1923)

Sammy White (Mel Parnell, 1956)

Jim Pagliaroni (Bill Monbouquette, 1963)

John Flaherty (Matt Young, 1992)

Time elapsed between Ehmke's no-hitter (1923) and Mel Parnell's (1956) = 33 years

Morehead (1965) to Nomo (2001) = 36 years

A fan who saw three no-hitters in a row at Fenway

There aren't too many who could have seen both the 1965 Morehead no-hitter and the Nomo one, in part because of the 36 years that elapsed. There were also very few fans at the Morehead no-no (just 1,247), which further reduces the chances simply because the pool of possibilities is that much smaller. As far as has been determined, the only fan who was at both was the author of this book. Dick Radatz and Lee Thomas were at both of them, but neither was at Hansack's no-hitter. Because the start time of the 2006 game was delayed 3:23, the author of this book was able to complete a family obligation, make the game, and catch the third consecutive Fenway no-hitter over the elapsed 41 years.

This doesn't count another no-hitter thrown at Fenway on April 27, 1997—when Scott Barnsby of U. Mass. no-hit the Northeastern Huskies, 1–0, in a Beanpot semi-final game.

The author watched the end of Clay Buchholz's 2007 no-hitter from a restaurant lounge in Cambridge, though. Streak snapped. But a new streak began with Lester's May 2008 gem.

Outfield assists

The classic Red Sox outfield of Harry Hooper in right, Tris Speaker in center, and Duffy Lewis in left may never have been topped. In terms of outfield assists alone, be it noted that in the five seasons 1910 through 1914, the three of them generated 396 outfield assists, each one of them recording 20 or more assists every single year. In 1913, Speaker had a league-leading 30 assists, Lewis had 29, and Hooper had 25—84 outfield assists in all.

In just one season, 1909, centerfielder Tris Speaker recorded 35 outfield assists. And then he did it again, with 35 more in 1912. These days, runners won't test the arm of an outfielder who develops a reputation for making assists, but Speaker played such a shallow center that it wasn't really an option. More than once, he'd field a ball on one hop and throw to first base in time to retire the batter. "The Grey Eagle" was credited as a "fifth infielder" by none other than teammate Babe Ruth, who pitched for the Red Sox for six seasons. Five times Speaker made unassisted double plays by grabbing liners or low flies and running in to step on second in time to record a second out on the play. After his 22 years in the majors, Speaker accumulated a grand total of 449 outfield assists. (He also had 12 as a first baseman and one as a pitcher.)

Ira Flagstead had 31 assists in 1923 and Harry Hooper had 30 assists in 1910.

In 1940, **Dom DiMaggio** led all outfielders in assists (with 16) despite appearing in only 94 games. It was one of three years he led the league.

Carl Yastrzemski was no slouch in the outfield. Not counting his time playing first base (or the 33 games he played at third), Yaz made 195 outfield assists. His first nine years, he reached double digits in assists. Seven times in his career, he led the league in the category.

Ted Williams, considered by some to be sub-par defensively, threw out 140 runners. His teammates never saw him as sub-par.

A reputation helps at times. Not everyone is a Yaz or a **Dwight Evans**, on whom runners worried about taking a chance. Evans led the league in assists three times, but the number of baserunners who chose not to challenge his arm surely ran into the hundreds. In 2005, **Manny Ramirez** led the major leagues in outfield assists with 17, five of which retired players trying to take an extra base.

Assists from all over

By just his 16th game in the 2003 season, utilityman Damian Jackson had already recorded assists from left field, center field, right field, shortstop, and second base. Later in the year, he picked up seven more from third base.

Three outfield assists in one game

On April 19, 1926, Sox centerfielder **Ira Flagstead** started three double plays in a 2–1 Red Sox win. It was the second game of a Patriots Day doubleheader against Philadelphia. Twice he gunned down Athletics trying to score at the plate. The third time, he initiated an 8-5-4-2 double play that squelched a rally.

On September 8, 1923 playing right field, against the Yankees, Flagstead had earned three assists, cutting down three Yankees. Babe Ruth was the first Yankee retired. He'd tried to move up after a fly out; nothing doing. In the sixth inning, Flagstead ranged near the right-field foul line and snared Schang's line drive, wheeled and turned to double Ward off first base. In the bottom of the eighth inning, Meusel had singled but when he tried to take third on Schang's single, Flagstead fired in time to gun him down. Flagstead had recorded two putouts and three assists.

Three assists by the same infielder, all in the same inning

This could equally well have been titled "three putouts by the same pitcher, all in the same inning." But the fact that the infielder was first baseman "Old Stonefingers" Dick Stuart seems more unlikely than that the pitcher was Bob Heffner. The inning was the first one of the June 28, 1963 game at Yankee Stadium. Tony Kubek grounded out, Stuart to Heffner covering. Roger Maris grounded out, 3 to 1. And Joe Pepitone grounded out, 3 to 1. In between, though, Bobby Richardson singled, Heffner threw a wild pitch, and Tom Tresh doubled in Richardson. The Sox won in the end, though, 4–3. 1963 was the sixth of seven consecutive years in which Stuart led the league in errors at his position.

Most assists in a nine-inning game

Pitcher: Jesse Tannehill had 10 assists in the April 27, 1905 game, tied by Carl Mays with 10 on August 26, 1916.

Catcher: Wally Schang had eight assists in the May 12, 1920 game.

First base: Stuffy McInnis had six assists on August 22, 1918 and Bill Buckner had six on June 14, 1986.

Second base: Hobe Ferris recorded 11 assists in the first game on September 23, 1905; he had just three in the second game.

Third base: Three third basemen each reached the 10-assist mark for Boston: Vern Stephens (May 23, 1951), Frank Malzone (September 24, 1957), and Freddy Sanchez (June 14, 2003).

Shortstop: Topper Rigney helped put out 11 on July 15, 1926. Eddie Bressoud helped put out 11 on September 18, 1962. And Rick Burleson helped put out 11 on May 7, 1977.

Outfield: The most in a nine-inning game is six. Flagstead's two games are reported above. The most recent player to record three assists in a game was Reggie Smith on September 23, 1972.

Two outfield assists by the same fielder in the same inning.

The two throws tied a major league record. They came on back-to-back plays. Unfortunately, the Red Sox were on the wrong end. Tampa Bay's Rocco Baldelli cut down both Kevin Millar and Jason Varitek of the Red Sox in the bottom of the fifth inning on August 12, 2004. Not to worry; the Red Sox still won, 6–0.

10 assists in one inning

Tying a major league record set in 1921 by Cleveland against Philadelphia, the Red Sox recorded 10 assists in the fifth inning of the May 10, 1952 game against the Yankees. The final score in this game was Yankees 18, Red Sox 3.

Combining the accounts provided by Retrosheet and *The Sporting News*, this looks to be the play-by-play of the inning in question:

YANKEES 5TH: H.Bauer homered; P.Rizzuto walked; I.Noren was hit by a pitch [P.Rizzuto to second]; Y.Berra singled to right field (F.Throneberry to B.Goodman to J.Piersall to G.Niarhos to V.Stephens to G.Niarhos) [P.Rizzuto out at home, I.Noren to third (on throw), Y.Berra to second (on throw)]; G.Woodling reached on a fielder's choice (J.Piersall to G.Niarhos) [I.Noren out at home, Berra to third]; G.McDougald reached on a fielder's choice; Piersall threw wild past first base after fielding McDougald's grounder, Berra scoring and Woodling reaching third on the play. With Johnny Hopp at bat, McDougald broke for second base. Niarhos threw the ball back to Maury McDermott, who wheeled and picked Woodling off third. Woodling was run down and tagged out. The play: Niarhos to McDermott to Stephens to Niarhos to Piersall to Niarhos to McDermott. Whew! 2 R, 2H, 0 E, 1 LOB.

A little bit of help, please?

George Scott picked up an assist on 9/9/1970 when Jim Northrup popped up foul to third base. Scott saw the ball glance off his glove, but Rico Petrocelli grabbed it before it hit the ground. Assist: Scott. Harold Kaese says that four years earlier, Scott was saved by an alert Joe Foy in a similar situation where Foy got the assist and Scott the putout.

Can readers help?

Maybe readers of this book can help. Harold Kaese wrote about a play: "Johnny Peacock once lost his catcher's mitt starting for a foul fly, but he kept going and caught it barehanded." That would have been one to see. We can't pin down the date. We wish we'd seen Smead Jolley back in the early days running up "Duffy's Cliff" in left field on July 19, 1932, catching Wes Ferrell's fly ball and tumbling down after. Ferrell shut out the Sox, though, on four hits.

And for fun, it might be hard to match Billy Goodman's hit on September 11, 1948—which hopped inside shortstop Eddie Joost's shirt. Joost apparently had no idea where the ball was, and only after looking around did he realize it was inside his shirt.

It's a little hard to win a ballgame without any gloves

All of the gloves of the Red Sox were stolen from the visitors' locker room in Chicago, so they all had to come up with new gloves for the August 5, 1964 game against the White Sox. They lost the game, 5–1. Police later spotted a couple of 10-year-old boys carrying expensive gloves, who said they were given them by older boys. The gloves were found in a barn on 31st Street in Chicago.

Most putouts in a nine-inning game

Pitcher: Al Nipper twice recorded eight putouts in a game (July 15, 1984 and September 18, 1985). He was preceded by Elmer Steele (September 14, 1908) and Bill Butland on August 30, 1942.

Catcher: Not surprisingly, it was the 20 putouts that Rich Gedman recorded, every one on a Roger Clemens strikeout, on April 29, 1986. When Clemens struck out 20 on September 18, 1986, catcher Bill Haselman only recorded 19 putouts on strikeouts, since he dropped the third strike on Travis Fryman's second-inning strikeout and had to throw to first base to get him.

First base: Stuffy McInnis had fully 21 putouts in the July 19, 1918 game. So did Bill Sweeney on June 24, 1932.

Second base: Hobe Ferris put out 10 opponents in the May 13, 1901 game. Max Bishop matched the number on April 30, 1934.

Third base: Eight different Red Sox players hold the team record for six putouts in a game. The most recent one was Wade Boggs, who did it on May 2, 1988.

Shortstop: Heinie Wagner put out 10 on July 27, 1907 and Vern Stephens put out 10 on June 25, 1950.

Outfield: Speaking of Ted Williams on defense, The Kid still leads the Red Sox with the most putouts in a nine-inning game ever recorded by a Red Sox outfielder: Ted garnered 10 putouts in the September 4, 1948 ballgame. Three other outfielders tied Ted in more recent years: Tommy Umphlett in the second game on August 16, 1953; Fred Lynn on June 4, 1978; and Lee Tinsley on August 14, 1995.

Games without an outfield putout

The whole Twins outfield stood around doing next to nothing on September 13, 1968. Not a single Twin outfielder made a putout, though Bob Allison did record an assist, and there were five singles to the outfield which—had the outfielders truly done nothing—would have surely changed the score from the 3–0 Red Sox win. A similar thing had happened on June 14, 1962, when the Orioles outfield failed to record even one putout or one assist. They were hopping all day, though, as the Sox pounded out 12 hits (and not one homer) in a losing 7–4 effort.

Other putout trivia

Ben Chapman couldn't have been too much busier in Fenway's right field, though, on June 25, 1937. The Boston outfielder recorded seven successive putouts in right, and a total of nine in one game, both marks setting records at the time. We've seen how Stuffy McInnis made

21 putouts at first in one game. First baseman Babe Dahlgren only made two during a 1935 game, tying the record held by Dick Hoblitzell since 1914.

Wally Schang, though, worked all 14 innings behind the plate, on September 13, 1920 without ever recording a putout. His triple tied the game in the seventh and Hooper's sacrifice fly won It in the 15th.

For 16 innings on July 21, 1954, Jackie Jensen stood around in center field without catching a single fly ball. The 5–5 game with Cleveland ended in a tie. At least he got in a little running, with a base hit, a stolen base, and scoring one of the runs.

Twice, though, Red Sox pitchers made three putouts in just one inning. Randy Heffner did it on June 28, 1963 at Yankee Stadium. Every one of the three first-inning putouts came on a 3–1 grounder (Dick Stuart to Heffner). Jim Bagby did it once in 1940.

The Red Sox were victimized by Yogi Berra in just one inning, when the Yankees catcher made all three outs in one inning during a 10–9 Red Sox win at Yankee Stadium, May 23, 1954.

When a putout sank a team

Rocky Colavito let his instincts take over as he chased down a ball off Jackie Jensen's bat. The score was tied in the bottom of the eighth, with one out and runners on second and third. Had he let it drop foul, Jensen would have had to face another pitch. Colavito caught it, though, and Gene Stephens tagged and scored the go-ahead (and, soon, winning run) of the June 5, 1958 game against the Indians. Harmon Killebrew did the same thing in the top of the first inning of the May 28, 1962 game in Minnesota. He caught Frank Malzone's foul fly to left and Carroll Hardy scored. It was the winning run (the final score was 3–0).

Most double plays in a nine-inning game

The magic number is five. Mo Vaughn and 12 other first basemen each participated in games when they took part in five double plays. Bobby Doerr was involved in five at second base on August 8, 1946. Vern Stephens, Rico Petrocelli, and Mario Guerrero each have five-DP games.

Ira Flagstead's three is the most in one game by an outfielder.

Even given extra innings in which to work, no Red Sox player ever took part in six.

Who played the most games for the Red Sox at each position?

Carl Yastrzemski played in 3,308 games for the Red Sox, far and away more than any other player. However, the player who played the most games at a given position was Ted Williams, who played 2,151 games at outfield (all in left field except for the 149 games he played in right field his rookie year).

Yaz played 2,077 in the outfield, 1,913 in left, and 757 at first. He was DH in 414 games, played center in 166, third base in 35, and right field for eight games.

Bobby Doerr played in 1,852 games, at second base. Wade Boggs played in 1,521 games at third. Everett Scott played 1,093 games at short. George Scott played 988 games at first base, Carlton Fisk caught 990 games, and Bob Stanley appeared in 637 games on the mound.

Played all nine positions in the field

Though he broke in as a shortstop, playing 22 games in 1925 (and two in 1926), by 1927 Jack Rothrock had become more versatile and played 13 games at first base, 36 at second, 40 at shortstop, and 20 at third. The next year, he added the outfield to his repertoire—26 games in

Jack Rothrock. Courtesy of Brace Photo.

left, 12 in center and 19 in right field. Not one to leave any stone un-turned, Rothrock also caught in one game and pitched in another—both in 1928. Career totals on defense:

1B: 38 games; 2B: 63; SS: 28; 3B: 48; LF: 138; CF: 194; RF: 311; C: 1; P: 1

Steve Lyons, who served three separate stints with the Red Sox, got off to a good start his rookie year (1985), playing five positions (LF, CF, RF, 3B, SS—he also DH'd in five games). He added 1B with the other Sox (playing for Chicago) in 1986, added 2B in 1987, caught two games in '88, and finally got the chance to pitch in 1990 (with Chicago) and again in 1991 (back with Boston).

Nine shortstops in nine years

Think we've had an unusual number of shortstops early in the 21st century? Come Opening Day, the man holding down the #6 slot on the starting nine changed for nine years in a row in the 1950s:

1950 Vern Stephens / 1951 Lou Boudreau / 1952 Jimmy Piersall / 1953 Milt Bolling / 1954 Ted Lepcio / 1955 Eddie Joost / 1956 Don Buddin / 1957 Billy Klaus

In 1958, the starting shortstop was Buddin again, as in 1959. Strictly speaking, because Klaus played in between 1956 and 1958, there were nine years in a row when the starting #6 was different from the year before. 1949 had also been Vern Stephens.

Twelve second basemen in 12 consecutive years

1994 Scott Fletcher / 1995 Luis Alicea / 1996 Wil Cordero / 1997 John Valentin / 1998 Donnie Sadler / 1999 Jeff Frye / 2000 Jose Offerman / 2001 Chris Stynes / 2002 Rey Sanchez / 2003 Todd Walker / 2004 Mark Bellhorn

In 2005, Bellhorn repeated, momentarily breaking the string. With Mark Loretta at second, come Opening Day 2006 and Dustin Pedroia there in 2007…but then Pedroia repeated.

Fourteen right fielders over 14 years

We can top that, though, by heading out to right field. Consider the Red Sox right fielders on Opening Day from 1988 through 2000:

1988 Mike Greenwell / 1989 Dwight Evans / 1990 Kevin Romine / 1991 Tom Brunansky / 1992 Phil Plantier / 1993 Andre Dawson / 1994 Billy Hatcher / 1995 Mark Whiten / 1996 Troy O'Leary / 1997 Rudy Pemberton / 1998 Darren Bragg / 1999 Trot Nixon / 2000 Darren Lewis

In 2001, Trot Nixon was back in right once more.

Consecutive starts at the same position

When Jason Varitek started the 2008 season behind the plate, it was the ninth Opening Day in a row he'd manned the position. No other Red Sox player has started as many as nine consecutive openers at the same position.

Two totally different lineups in the same day

Eddie Kasko started totally different lineups in both halves of the September 6, 1971 double-header. The Boston Red Sox played a twinbill against the Yankees in New York. The game one lineup for Boston was Kennedy (2b), Aparicio (ss), Yaz (lf), Smith (cf), Conigliaro (rf), Fiore (1b), Gagliano (3b), Montgomery (catcher}, Culp (p), and Lee (p). The game two lineup for Boston was Griffin (2b), Miller (cf), Lahoud (rf), Petrocelli (3b), Scott (1b), Oglivie (lf), Beniquez (ss), Fisk (catcher), Curtis (p), Tiant (p).

Best fielding percentage at each position—Red Sox career

Pitcher: Bill Monbouquette .985
Catcher: Tony Peña .994 (but Jason Varitek is at .993 and has a shot to unseat him)
First base: Kevin Youkilis .998 (Stuffy McInnis was .996 and, impressively, Yaz comes in second with
.994 playing a position that was not his primary one. Of course, for that matter, the 2007 season in
which Youkilis set his mark was his first full year playing first base.)
Second base: Marty Barrett .986
Third base: Mike Lowell .975 (Rico Petrocelli is second at .970)
Shortstop: John Valentin .972
Outfield: Jimmy Piersall .989
(Minimum 250 games)

Perfect in the outfield

In 1977, Carl Yastrzemski handled 366 chances without committing a single error. His 1.000 fielding percentage included 285 putouts in left field, two in right field, and 57 at first base. Yaz had a league-leading 16 outfield assists, and added six more assists from first base.

Ken Harrelson also posted a 1.000 fielding percentage in the outfield, in 1968. He made 241 putouts, almost all in right, and had eight assists, without making an error. The Hawk also played first base, and handled 144 chances successfully— but made three errors at first.

Wilson glove executive showing the company's wares to Ted Williams.

Perfect at first

Kevin Youkilis played the full 2007 season without making an error at first base, even though given 1,080 chances in which to do so. Filling in 13 games at third base, he committed three errors there—even though that was his traditional position before being asked to play first base beginning in 2006. But what we want to focus on is his work at first base—flawless! Youk ended the regular season having played 190 consecutive games at first base without even one error, dating back to July 4, 2006.

Best single-season fielding percentage

Aside from the outfield, there have been two catchers who had perfect seasons—based, per the *Red Sox Media Guide*, on catchers who played in at least half the team's games. In 1957, catcher Pete Daley recorded 289 putouts and made 20 assists. In 1988, Rick Cerone recorded 471 putouts and made 28 assists. Each hold the 1.000 percentage mark. Cerone played a major-league record 159 games (896 chances) before making an error on May 9, 1989.

Based on handling at least 50 chances in a season, 11 Red Sox pitchers have 1.000 seasons. The first pitcher to do it was Ed Morris in 1928 (four PO, 48 A), followed by Jack Russell the very next year (15 PO, 69 A). Gordon Rhodes, in 1934, had five putouts and 47 assists. In 1942, two pitchers each had perfect seasons: Joe Dobson and Charlie Wagner. Dobson had 17 PO and 42 A, while Wagner had 9 PO and 46 A. Mel Parnell had two perfect years—1949 (eight PO and 53 A) and 1953 (15 PO and 38 A). Bill Monbouquette had two perfect years, too, back-to-back: 1963 (a league-leading 31 PO and 37 A) and 1964 (15 PO and 38 A). In 1976, Rick Wise made 23 putouts and had 36 assists. The only pitcher to have a 1.000 season since Wise was Derek Lowe, whose 2003 season saw him record 20 putouts and have 45 assists.

The best-fielding Boston first baseman ever—before 2007—was Stuffy McInnis. He recorded a near-perfect .999 year in 1921: just one error in 1,652 chances. That translates to 0.999394673123. But 1.000 tops that, and Kevin Youkilis played first base without even one error in 2007.

Bobby Doerr had a .993 season at second in 1948, with 366 putouts and 430 assists, while only making six errors. Doerr led the league in fielding four times; this wasn't one of those years, though. Snuffy Stirnweiss had an ever-so-slightly better year. As noted above, Mark Loretta posted a new record .994 in 2006.

At third base, the hot corner, Rico Petrocelli's .976 in 1971 ranks tops, just beating out Grady Hatton's .976 from 1955, .976242 to .9757576. As noted above, Mike Lowell posted a new record .987 in 2006.

Shortstops Rick Burleson, Rico Petrocelli, and Vern Stephens all show .981 percentages in the books, in 1978, 1969, and 1950 respectively. Extending the calculations, we find:

Stephens (1950) .9814815   Petrocelli (1969) .9813085   Burleson (1978) .9808185

As noted above, Alex Gonzalez posted a new record .985 in 2006.

Worst at their position in all of baseball?

Since 1950, two Red Sox fielders hold the unwanted distinction of being the worst fielder at their position in the major leagues. Dick Stuart (a/k/a "Dr. Strangeglove") committed 29 errors at first base in 1963. Why was he allowed to play 155 games that season? He also hit 42 homers and led the league in runs batted in with 118.

Across the diamond in 1978, third baseman Butch Hobson made 43 errors, for an .899 fielding percentage. He only hit .250. The Sox just didn't have anyone better.

That was pretty bad—the worst fielding percentage ever for a Red Sox player? Patsy Dougherty just barely edged out Hobson, with an .898 mark in 1902. He just made 21 errors, but with fewer chances.

Errors

It's quite hard to play several ballgames in a row without anyone making an error. The first time the Red Sox ever played nine games in a row without an error came in 1951. Even very steady fielders can suddenly start fumbling.

The most errors by a Red Sox second baseman in a single season were the 61 by Hobe Ferris in 1901. Only one player stood in the way of him holding the all-time league record for errors by a second baseman: Kid Gleason, who committed 64 errors that very same year for Detroit.

Six errors in one game?

The errant player was Bill O'Neill, and the game of shame was on May 21, 1904. Boston was hosting St. Louis, and shortstop O'Neill's "ragged work" gave the visitors a 5–3 win. Committing a full six errors in one game, it still took him 13 innings before finally giving the game away when the pitcher Howell tripled in the two go-ahead runs. In one game, O'Neill had committed as many errors as 2006's Mike Lowell committed in a full year of 153 games.

Six errors in two games? Shortstop Juan Beniquez did it, with back-to-back triple-error games on July 13 and 14, 1972. All but the second one came on errant throws.

Twelve errors in one day? It took the whole team to do it, and the Red Sox were the benefi-ciary. During the July 16, 1939 doubleheader, Detroit committed eight errors in the first game, and four in the second. The Sox made just one, and won both games.

Ten errors in one game! Noted above in the section on triple plays was the 1927 date when the Sox committed 10 errors all in the same game. They'd been error-free in the first game of the September 26 twinbill. Despite all the miscues, they managed to pull off three double plays in the 11–1 loss.

Two notable errors in Red Sox / Yankees games: when Tom Oliver knocked the ball out of catcher Arndt Jorgens' grip in the bottom of the eighth in the second game on August 2, 1931, the Red Sox won a 1–0 game, and Allie Reynolds had a no-hitter going with two outs in the ninth when Yogi Berra dropped Ted Williams' foul popup, giving The Kid another chance—but he fouled out again.

Four Indians errors in the ninth inning gave the Red Sox three runs and a 5–3 win on July 30, 1944. Lou Boudreau hit a walk-off double to win the day's second game for the Tribe.

The Red Sox made four errors in both the first and second games of the 2004 World Series, but won both games, and even though Boston made four errors in the last game of the 1912 World Series, they won that one, too.

Every run in the game scored because of an error

There are a number of 1–0 games where the run scored on an error, but Boston's 3–1 win over Philadelphia on April 17, 1917 saw every one of the four runs come in on errors. The Red Sox committed three errors and the Athletics committed five. Everett Scott's error at short and Duffy Lewis's off-the-mark throw home allowed Philadelphia to score once in the bottom of the first. Three boots by the A's let the Red Sox score once in the second, and two errors by infielders let the Sox put both runners on base in the sixth, and two singles brought them in.

Walk-off errors?

Johnny Damon's momentary bobble of Omar Vizquel's hit on August 31, 2002 in the bottom of the ninth in Cleveland allowed the Indians to win a 8–7 game. The Sox were down 6–0 early in the game, but fought back, eventually tying the game at 7–7 in the top of the eighth. It was Damon's first error in over two years—he'd set a league record by handling 592 chances flaw-lessly over 249 games.

Even worse was Arnold Earley's error in the August 13, 1961 ballgame. Orioles pitcher Steve Barber had gone the distance, despite giving up six hits, 11 bases on balls, and hitting Pete Runnels twice. The game was tied after nine, but Boston took a 4–3 lead in the top of the 10th. The O's re-tied the score. Then Boston took a 5–4 lead in the top of the 11th. Mike Forn-ieles was pitching in relief of starter Bill Monbouquette. He let the first two Orioles get on, so the manager called on Earley to put out the fire. The first batter he faced, Russ Snyder, tried to move the runners along with a sacrifice bunt, but Earley tried to cut down the lead runner but threw the ball well over third baseman Frank Malzone's head and both baserunners scored, which first tied and then won the ballgame for Baltimore.

Buckner's error

We don't at all want to dwell on it here, but the most infamous error in all of Red Sox history was the one charged to Bill Buckner. For those who don't know, it happened in Game Six of the 1986 World Series. You can look it up—Buckner should never have been on the field de-fensively at that point. Were it not for a pitch that went astray…were it not for the fact that the Red Sox blew a lead in Game Seven…well, we really don't want to dwell on it here. But we're very pleased to note that the Red Sox invited Buckner back to throw out the first pitch at Boston's home opener in 2008, following the presentation of the World Championship rings to the 2007 Red Sox team. He accepted, and was accorded a prolonged standing ovation.

Pesky's NON-error

Mr. Red Sox, Johnny Pesky. Bill Nowlin photo.

One of the most notorious non-errors in Red Sox history was the notion that "Pesky held the ball" in Game Seven of the 1946 World Series. Did he hold the ball? That's a long story, and people who have seen the two films come to different conclusions. Read the book *Mr. Red Sox: The Johnny Pesky Story*. Was Johnny charged with an error? Nope. The only error in Game Seven was Whitey Kurowski's. Did a run score, enabling the Cardinals to win the game and the Series? Undoubtedly.

Catfish Metkovich makes three errors in one inning

Opening Day 1945 got off to a rocky start for Catfish Metkovich; the Sox first baseman committed three errors all in the same inning—only the second major leaguer to do so. Playing at Yankee Stadium, the Red Sox jumped off to a three-run lead in the top of the first inning. And Metkovich was looking good early; he "made a fine back-handed catch of Martin's grounder over first" in the bottom of the first. Rex Cecil was pitching well for Boston, only having given up two hits in the first six innings—though one of them was a home run by Russ Derry, a former farmer who'd joined the Yankees in August 1944. Boston added another run in the top of the seventh, and suddenly everything unraveled. A double followed by two singles brought in one run. Cecil's pickoff attempt shot past Newsome covering second base and both runners moved up on the throwing error.

Then Metkovich swung into action. Yankee catcher Garbark hit an easy hopper, but Metkovich missed the tag when he tried to get Garbark coming into first. He fired home to cut down Buzas coming in from third, but the throw went wild and two runners scored. Two errors were assessed—one for the missed tag and one for the errant throw. Garbark, who'd stayed at first, moved up on the pitcher's sacrifice. Stirnweiss walked. Leftfielder Martin hit a sharp grounder, which Metkovich booted, loading the bases. Third error, setting the stage for another home run by Russ Derry, this one a grand slam. With seven runs, Clark came in to relieve Cecil but the game was over. Final score, Yankees 8, Red Sox 4.

On May 11, 1949, Bobby Doerr was an open door, making three errors in the second inning. Rico Petrocelli, another exceptionally steady fielder, made three miscues in the nine-run bottom of the fifth on July 29, 1966.

Passed balls

Catfish made three errors in one inning, but Doug Mirabelli more or less matched that with three passed balls in the sixth inning of the May 23, 2006 ballgame against the Yankees. He had been "recalled" from San Diego—actually, a hastily-arranged trade that sent pitcher Cla Meredith and catcher Josh Bard to the Padres for Mirabelli after Bard struggled trying to deal with Tim Wakefield's knuckleball. Mirabelli arrived at the ballpark on May 1, just 13 minutes before first pitch, actually changing into his uniform in the back seat of a State Police cruiser that whisked him to Fenway from the airport. No separation of baseball and state when it comes to the Red Sox.

The major league record, post-1900, is four PBs in one inning shared by the Giants' Ray Katt and the Rangers' Geno Petralli.

Bard's offense? He allowed 10 passed balls in five games of trying to catch Wakefield. Fortunately, not one of them led to a Red Sox loss.

Passed balls can hurt, though. One that hurt badly was the time Johnny Peacock failed to glove Joe Dobson's pitch properly on September 12, 1942—the ball banged off the heel of Peacock's glove, hit him in the forehead, and caromed back to the screen behind home plate. "Joe Cronin almost fell off the bench laughing," Dobson told Harold Kaese, explaining, "He switched signs and forgot to tell me." The official scorer didn't know the full story, though, and Dobson was the one penalized, charged with a wild pitch.

Boston benefited from a few notable passed balls. On May 25, 1972, the game's winning run scored when Baltimore's Elrod Hendricks allowed a passed ball to elude him and Luis Aparicio scored from third. The very first of the 1,798 runs Ted Williams scored in his career came on a passed ball, courtesy of Philadelphia catcher Frank Hayes on April 21, 1939.

Was it a passed ball or a wild pitch?

It's always a debate. Fans are still arguing the question regarding Game Six of the 1986 World Series. Was it a Bob Stanley wild pitch or a Rich Gedman passed ball? It's a dispute that once embroiled their two wives, each one standing by her man. In 1935, Billy Werber kept the Yankees on their toes. On Opening Day, April 16, Werber doubled and took third when Gomez threw wildly in a pickoff attempt. He raced home when Bill Dickey dropped the third strike on batter Carl Reynolds. Dickey threw to first to retire Reynolds, and Gehrig's return throw to the plate was off the mark and got away from Dickey. On June 8, in the second game, Werber was on second—the bases were loaded—when Gomez threw a wild pitch (as per the box-score) and Boston pitcher Ostermueller scored. While Gomez and Yankees catcher Jorgens were "commiserating for the oversight…the fleet-footed Bill Werber" also scored. Werber's run proved the one that won the game. Kaese says that twice in 1969 passed balls by the rival catcher led to Red Sox wins, but even after checking the boxscores for every win, we can't find even one. Maybe it doesn't matter in the long run; they'd still have had to win 23 more games that year to win the pennant.

An unusual error that helped the Red Sox score the last run of the year

It was 1973, the last game of the year. The Brewers were at Fenway that Sunday afternoon. The house was about ⅓ full. Milwaukee took a 2–1 lead in the top of the eighth. The Red Sox were in second place and the Brewers were in fifth place. No team was close enough to either that their respective places in the standings would change as a result of the game. Reggie Smith singled to start the bottom of the eighth, then Danny Cater singled to put runners on first and second. Fisk flied out deep enough that Tommy Harper (running for Reggie) tagged and took third. Ben Oglivie then hit a sacrifice fly to center field and Harper tagged and scored the tying run, but Brewers catcher Charlie Moore was so incensed at Harper being called safe that he fired the ball into the ground while arguing (forgetting to call time) and as the ball skittered away, Cater ran in and scored, too, giving the Red Sox a 3–2 lead and—after four defensive changes in the top of the ninth and a succession of three consecutive Milwaukee pinch hitters failed to produce a run—the win.

Another throw in anger cost the Red Sox a run

One of the Tigers' six runs came in on what a *Chicago Tribune* photo caption dubbed the "comedy play of the year." August 28, 1956, in Boston. Top of the sixth. Al Kaline hit a homer, and then Bill Tuttle doubled. Red Wilson hit a high hopper to second that was hit so high that Tuttle scampered all the way around to score on a close play at the plate. Boston catcher Sammy White became so enraged at Frank Umont's call that he was ejected. In anger, he threw the ball to left-center field. Ted Williams retrieved it and tossed it back in, but everyone was so transfixed by White's ongoing tantrum at the plate that Wilson was able to make his way around the bases without anyone noticing and came all the way around from first to score. Sox manager Pinky Higgins argued that White's ejection meant that time was called and protested the game. League president Will Harridge disallowed the protest, explaining that the umpire couldn't call time while there was still a chance of continued action and that White's throw put the ball back into play. The Red Sox only scored three runs that day.

Left fielder Ted Williams makes putout at second base on play involving every infielder

The Red Sox trampled Philadelphia 13–5 before 18,979 at Fenway on June 26, 1951. Both Pesky and Doerr made errors, but the defensive gem of the game was a "hard way double play" which accorded an assist to every infielder and to catcher Les Moss to boot. And the putout was made by Ted Williams, right at the second base bag. Joe Astroth was on second base in the top of the eighth, the score 9–5. Ray Murray pinch-hit for pitcher Johnny Kucab, and grounded out, shortstop Pesky to Goodman. Astroth, though, was in between second and third and Goodman fired back across the infield to Vern Stephens at third. Astroth reversed direction, heading back to second so Stephens threw to Doerr. Now Les Moss had come all the way from behind the plate to back up Stephens at third, and when Astroth headed back toward third, he took Doerr's throw. Astroth doubled back to second, but Ted Williams had scooted in and was waiting for him just about 18 inches off the bag and doubled him up. The play went 6-3-5-4-2-7.

A catcher catching three consecutive pop-ups to start a game

First inning, September 25, 2004. Doug Mirabelli behind the plate, personal catcher for knuckleballer Tim Wakefield. Yankees leadoff hitter Derek Jeter fouled out to Mirabelli. F2. Next up was Alex Rodriguez, and he hit one higher, but still foul. Mirabelli came back and caught it. F2. Number three batter was Gary Sheffield. Would he foul off a pop-up, too? The crowd was waiting in anticipation. He did foul one back but it came down on the screen behind home plate. Close call. Mirabelli told reporters later, "I said something about what was happening to the umpire as I was walking back. It could have happened right there." Moments later, Sheffield popped one up, fairly high and right in front of home plate. There was little breeze, and the ball pretty much went straight up and then came straight down. Though many fans were calling for the ball to twist foul, Mirabelli caught it about one foot in fair territory, maybe two feet up the first base line from home plate. Record that one as a 2.

Three putouts for the catcher. Three popups, three down. Mirabelli later had four runs batted in, and the Red Sox won 12–5.

Five glove changes in one inning

It was, as Brian MacMillan termed it, a bit of a Three Stooges routine as Kevin Millar and David McCarty kept changing gloves in the bottom of the 12th inning of the July 1, 2004 game at Yankee Stadium. The game was obviously tied, 3–3. Curtis Leskanic came in to pitch for the Red Sox and Miguel Cairo led off with a triple. Jason Giambi was sent in to pinch-hit for Derek Jeter. Kevin Millar came in from right field and played near third base for Giambi's at-bat. Giambi struck out. With Gary Sheffield up, Millar was moved from third over to first base, grabbing his first-baseman's glove, while David McCarty exchanged his for a regular glove, moving to a spot between first and second. Leskanic hit Sheffield with a pitch and now had to face Alex Rodriguez with runners on first and third and one out. Millar returned to right field, after turning in his first-baseman's glove. McCarty went back to play first, and re-acquired his glove for that role.

A-Rod walked. Bases loaded. Millar came in again at first (another glove change) and McCarty took the position between first and second once more (he had to switch gloves, too) for Bubba Crosby's at-bat. With the expanded infield playing in, Crosby grounded out to Pokey Reese at short. With two outs, the Red Sox went back to a regular defense with Millar and McCarty each doing glove swaps again as Bernie Williams came up. Bernie struck out.

In the top of the 13th, the Yankees made defensive moves at six of the nine positions, but Manny Ramirez hit a home run—against which no defense worked. Sadly for Sox fans, the Yankees scored twice in the bottom of the 13th.

Grounding out for the cycle?

This must have happened before, but it was still remarkable. In the April 16, 2004 Red Sox/Yankees game, New York's Kenny Lofton grounded out for the cycle. He was up five times and every time he grounded out to a different infielder. First, to each of the four position players. Then, last time up, in the ninth inning, he grounded back to reliever Keith Foulke on the mound. The next day Lofton was put on the disabled list. Stiff quad muscle.

Dick Stuart

Any discussion of Red Sox fielding has to mention "Old Stonefingers"—Dick Stuart. Was his reputation as a poor fielder exaggerated? He led the league in errors by a first baseman in each of his first seven years, including his rookie year, 1958. He led the league with 16 errors that year, despite playing in well under half the games (64 games).

A few notable fielding gaffes

The *Washington Post*'s Shirley Povich commented on Boston's bush-league play in the September 25, 1936 game in the Nation's capital. Sox starter **Jim Henry** got knocked out of the box in the third inning after giving up just one hit. He walked two men, hit a third, and then gave up a two-run single to Johnny Stone. With runners on first and third, he walked behind the mound and dropped the ball. The two runners broke from their respective bases, pulling off a double steal as a befuddled Henry picked up the rosin bag by mistake and threw it to second. On the next pitch, Stone stole third. There was still nobody out. Joe Cronin had seen enough; he brought in Jack Wilson to pitch. But Cronin hadn't seen the end of it. In the fifth inning, Wilson gave up a single and walked two batters—and then, in Povich's words, "performed the trick of losing his balance on the rubber, falling to the ground and committing an automatic balk which permitted DeShong to score from third unmolested."

It was June 10, 1964 in the second game of two against the Yankees at Fenway. **Russ Nixon**, behind the plate for Boston, thought there were two outs when he caught a ball in the dirt on a third strike. He flipped the ball to the batter, Yankee relief pitcher Phil Mikkelsen, and trotted back to the dugout. The whole Red Sox team, responding to Nixon's gesture, started to run in as well. Mikkelsen tossed the ball into fair territory, towards the mound, and ran all the way around to second before the Red Sox recovered. Mikkelsen later scored an unearned run on Tony Kubek's double.

Talk about a bad day. On May 9, 1968 with **Jerry Stephenson** on the mound, Ed Stroud of the Senators bunted safely, and then stole second. Stephenson balked and Stroud strolled to third. Stephenson got an out, but then threw a wild pitch and Stroud scored safely.

We could go on and on. We could probably write a whole book on errors and misjudgments. But that would be depressing. Let's end on a better note, a personal reminiscence by Clifford Otto:

"The Red Sox were in RFK on on July 26, 1968 with Dick Ellsworth on the mound. He had a no-hitter through four and a 2–0 lead with one out in the bottom of the ninth, having given up just four singles. A single, a strikeout by Frank Howard, and two more singles brought the Senators within one. Hank Allen, who batted for his brother Bernie in the previous inning and stayed in the game at second, proceeded to hit a blast to deep center field. **Reggie Smith** leaped high, reaching well over the seven-foot chain link fence, the crowd going wild. When he came down, he trotted halfway back to the infield before opening his glove and showing the ball to the umpire who had run out to center. There was a stunned silence, then a mighty cheer for Smith."

Red Sox (opponents) errors in the postseason

1903 World Series—14 (19)	1986 ALCS—7 (8)	2004 ALDS—1 (3)
1912 World Series—14 (16)	1986 World Series—4 (5)	2004 ALCS—1 (4)
1915 World Series—4 (3)	1988 ALCS—1 (3)	2004 World Series—8 (1)
1916 World Series—6 (13)	1990 ALCS—5 (1)	2005 ALDS—2 (1)
1918 World Series—1 (5)	1995 ALDS—4 (6)	2007 ALDS—1 (0)
1946 World Series—10 (4)	1998 ALDS—0 (1)	2007 ALCS—3 (4)
1967 World Series—4 (4)	1999 ALDS—5 (3)	2007 World Series—2 (0)
1975 ALCS—4 (5)	1999 ALCS—3 (5)	
1975 World Series—6 (2)	2003 ALDS—5 (5)	
	2003 ALCS—3 (5)	

Total: 118 Red Sox errors and 125 errors by opponents

Most career putouts for a Red Sox player

Not surprisingly, first basemen lead the list for the most putouts recorded by Red Sox players. The following list show the top 10 Red Sox in terms of putouts recorded, through 2006.

Carl Yastrzemski 10,437 (6,459 at 1B; 3,941 in the outfield; 37 at 3B)
George Scott 8,740 (8,560 at 1B; 180 at 3B)
Phil Todt 8,676 (8,675 at 1B, one in the outfield)
Mo Vaughn 7,842 (all at 1B)
Jimmie Foxx 7,311 (7,126 at 1B; 178 as catcher; nine at 3B)
Jason Varitek 7,646 (all as catcher)

Most career assists for a Red Sox player

Bobby Doerr 5,710—more than 2,000 above the second-ranked fielder

Everett Scott 3,394	Rick Burleson 3,247	Hobe Ferris 3,064

Most career assists by a Red Sox pitcher

Cy Young 689	Carl Mays 450	Bill Dinneen 397
George Winter 468	Joe Wood 402	

Make you realize they kept the ball down better 100 years ago?

Most putouts by position

Pitcher: Roger Clemens 214 (second place: Tim Wakefield 146)
Catcher: Jason Varitek 7,646 (second place: Carlton Fisk 5,111)
First base: Phil Todt 8,676 (second place: George Scott 8,560)
Second base: Bobby Doerr 4,928 (second place: Hobe Ferris 2,411)
Third base: Frank Malzone 1,270 (second place: Wade Boggs 1,165)
Shortstop: Everett Scott 2,310 (second place: Heinie Wagner 1,919)
Outfield: Dwight Evans 4,255 (second place: Ted Williams 4,158)

The greatest catch of all time?

Tris Speaker saw a lot of baseball in his life. In the December 16, 1954 *New York Daily News*, Jimmy Powers cited Speaker as having said that Harry Hooper's catch in the 1912 World Series was "the greatest catch of all time, and greater than Mays' straightaway gallop."

Gold Glove Award

Rawlings has sponsored a Gold Glove Award since 1957 to honor the best defensive player at each position. In the earlier days of the award, more Red Sox fielders shone defensively and third baseman Frank Malzone won the very first one presented—in the year that only one was awarded for the major leagues. Since that time, there has been one Gold Glove given at each position in each league, and at least one Red Sox player has won it for each position. Malzone also won the American League award in 1958 and again in 1959. Carl Yastrzemski won it seven times as an outfielder, but Dwight Evans topped that with eight wins. Other multiple winners are Fred Lynn at outfield (four times) and George Scott at first base (three). After Tony Peña won it at catcher in 1991, it was a full 14 years before another Red Sox player won at any position. When one did, it was another catcher—Jason Varitek (2005).

Gold Glove Awards won by Red Sox players:

1B George Scott 1967, 1968, 1971 (Scott won it five more times with Milwaukee)
Kevin Youkilis 2007
2B Doug Griffin 1972
SS Rick Burleson 1979
3B Frank Malzone 1957, 1958, 1959
OF Carl Yastrzemski 1963, 1965, 1967, 1968, 1969, 1971, 1977
OF Dwight Evans 1976, 1978, 1979, 1981, 1982, 1983, 1984, 1985

OF Jimmy Piersall 1958
OF Jackie Jensen 1959
OF Fred Lynn 1975, 1978, 1979, 1980
OF Reggie Smith 1968
OF Ellis Burks 1990
C   Carlton Fisk 1972
Tony Peña 1991
Jason Varitek 2005
P   Mike Boddicker 1990

AWARDS AND HONORS

Most Valuable Player

Nine Sox players have won the MVP award, as voted by the Baseball Writers Association of America. They are:

1912—Tris Speaker
1938—Jimmie Foxx
1946—Ted Williams

1949—Ted Williams
1958—Jackie Jensen
1967—Carl Yastrzemski

1975—Fred Lynn
1978—Jim Rice
1995—Mo Vaughn

Ted Williams came close other times, but even winning the Triple Crown in 1942 and again in 1947 was apparently not good enough. At least one voter in 1942 couldn't see fit to list Ted in his top 10 (each voter lists the top 10 in order of priority).

Pedro Martinez had a good shot at the MVP in 2000, but two writers chose not to give him a chance, either, their argument being that he was a pitcher who only played every five days or so and not a day in/day out ballplayer. The voting instructions clearly state that pitchers are supposed to be considered as potential MVP candidates, but these writers chose to follow their own rules.

Rookie of the Year

The rookie of the year award only began in 1947, or else surely Ted Williams would have won it in 1939 and Johnny Pesky would have won it in 1942 (Pesky was third in MVP voting in his rookie year). The Red Sox rookies who earned the BBWAA votes as Rookie of the Year are:

Walt Dropo, 1950

Don Schwall, 1961

Carlton Fisk, 1972 (unanimous)

Fred Lynn, 1975

Nomar Garciaparra, 1997 (unanimous)

Dustin Pedroia, 2007

Fred Lynn, as we can see, won both the
    MVP and ROY in his rookie year

Second-place rookie of the year finalists were: Tom Umphlett (1953), Billy Klaus (1955), Frank Malzone (1957), Reggie Smith (1967), Mike Nagy (1969), Jim Rice (1975), Dave Stapleton (1980), and Rich Gedman (1981).

Rookie batting leaders

The most home runs hit by a Red Sox rookie is 34 by Walt Dropo in 1950. Ted Williams hit 31 in his rookie year, 1939. Nomar Garciaparra hit 30 in 1997. Norm Zauchin and George Scott each hit 27, in 1955 and 1966, respectively.

The most RBIs by a Red Sox rookie is 145, hit by Ted Williams in 1939. In fact, that remains a major league rookie record. Walt Dropo got as close as you can without matching it with his 144 in 1950. The National League record is 130, set by Albert Pujols in 2001.

Silver Slugger Award

This award is presented by *The Sporting News*, initiated in 1980. Manny Ramirez won it five years in a row, from 2001 through 2005. His 2002 award was won as DH, the other four as leftfielder.

Wade Boggs won six Sliver Sluggers with the Sox: 1983, 1986, 1987, 1988, 1989, and 1991.

Dwight Evans won two, Jim Rice won two, and David Ortiz has so far won four.

American League batting champions

The Red Sox have done well in producing batting champions. In the 107 seasons of the franchise, they have produced 25 batting champions—and that's without having even one at all the first 31 years. Remarkably, even with one of the greatest hitters for average of all time (Tris Speaker) on board, he never won a batting title with the Red Sox. Even in 1912, when Speaker hit .383, that was only good enough for third place; Ty Cobb hit .409 and Joe Jackson hit .395. He did lead in on-base percentage that year. The one year Speaker did lead the league, 1916, was his first year with Cleveland.

Of the 25 Boston Red Sox batting champions, only six of them batted right-handed. One (Bill Mueller, 2003) was a switch-hitter. Mueller's league-leading batting average was .326. He hit .342 at home and .309 on the road. The right-handed champions were the first two— Dale Alexander and Jimmie Foxx, Carney Lansford in 1981, and the more recent ones Nomar Garciaparra and Manny Ramirez. Ted Williams won six titles, and only a series of strange

Ty Cobb with Ted Williams.

Boston's first batting champion,
Dale Alexander.

circumstances prevented him winning at least a couple more. Wade Boggs won five and Carl
Yastrzemski won three.

1932 Dale Alexander .367	1960 Pete Runnels .320	1985 Wade Boggs .368
1938 Jimmie Foxx .349	1962 Pete Runnels .326	1986 Wade Boggs .357
1941 Ted Williams .406	1963 Carl Yastrzemski .321	1987 Wade Boggs .363
1942 Ted Williams .356	1967 Carl Yastrzemski .326	1988 Wade Boggs .366
1947 Ted Williams .343	1968 Carl Yastrzemski .301	1999 Nomar Garciaparra .357
1948 Ted Williams .369	1979 Fred Lynn .333	2000 Nomar Garciaparra .372
1950 Billy Goodman .354	1981 Carney Lansford .336	2002 Manny Ramirez .349
1957 Ted Williams .388	1983 Wade Boggs .361	2003 Bill Mueller .326
1958 Ted Williams .328		

American League home run champions

The Red Sox have also done pretty well with home run championships, too—without the taint
of steroids. Nineteen times a Red Sox player has ranked first, though four times tied with a player
from another team. Buck Freeman was the first, with a league-leading 13 homers in 1903. The
lowest total to win for a Boston batter was 10 homers—twice. Jake Stahl hit 10 and won the title
in 1910, and Tris Speaker hit 10 and shared the title with Home Run Baker in 1912.

Babe Ruth won the title twice, the first time coming with just 11 home runs in 1918. (It
was a short season due to the war.) Most recent, of course, was David Ortiz who hit 54 in
2006, surpassing the 50 Jimmie Foxx hit in 1938 as the most ever by a Red Sox batter. And Foxx
didn't win the home run crown that year. (Hank Greenberg hit 58.) Ortiz's 2006 total was
more than that of the first four champions combined (Freeman / Stahl / Speaker / Ruth). Ted
Williams won the title four times. Jim Rice won it three times.

1903 Buck Freeman 13	1942 Ted Williams 36	1978 Jim Rice 46
1910 Jake Stahl 10	1947 Ted Williams 32	1981 Dwight Evans 22
1912 Tris Speaker 10	1949 Ted Williams 43	1983 Jim Rice 39
1918 Babe Ruth 11	1965 Tony Conigliaro 32	1984 Tony Armas 43
1919 Babe Ruth 29	1967 Carl Yastrzemski 44	2004 Manny Ramirez 43
1939 Jimmie Foxx 35	1977 Jim Rice 39	2006 David Ortiz 54
1941 Ted Williams 37		

American League RBI champions

The Red Sox have produced 21 leaders in runs batted in. Buck Freeman won it in 1902 (with
121) and 1903 (with 104) and David Ortiz has won it the last two times (with 148 in 2005 and

137 in 2006). Odd though it may seem, even though Manny Ramirez has one batting title with Boston (2002) and one home run crown (2004), the only RBI crown he's ever won was with Cleveland in 1999.

Ted Williams won four RBI titles. Jackie Jensen won three, hitting behind Williams in the lineup. Oddly, there were two years in a row when two Red Sox players shared the crown. In 1949, both Vern Stephens and Ted Williams drove in 159 runs. In 1950, both Vern Stephens and Walt Dropo drove in 144 runs. Neither Stephens nor Dropo ever won it outright.

1902 Buck Freeman 121	1958 Jackie Jensen 122
1903 Buck Freeman 104	1959 Jackie Jensen 112
1919 Babe Ruth 114	1963 Dick Stuart 118
1938 Jimmie Foxx 175	1967 Carl Yastrzemski 121
1939 Ted Williams 145	1968 Ken Harrelson 109
1942 Ted Williams 137	1978 Jim Rice 139
1947 Ted Williams 114	1983 Jim Rice 126 (tie)
1949 Vern Stephens 159	1984 Tony Armas 123
Ted Williams 159 (teammates tied)	1995 Mo Vaughn 126 (tie)
1950 Vern Stephens 144	2005 David Ortiz 148
Walt Dropo 144 (teammates tied)	2006 David Ortiz 137
1955 Jackie Jensen 116 (tie)	

The Triple Crown

The Triple Crown is an indication of baseball royalty. Leading your league in batting average, home runs, and runs batted in constitutes winning the Triple Crown. Since 1903, the year many suggest was the first year of baseball's modern era, there have only been 10 batters to win the Triple Crown. Ted Williams did it twice, and just missed doing it a third time in 1949 by the slimmest of margins. Carl Yastrzemski did it once, in 1967, and for 40 years since, no one has done it in either league.

Year	Batter	League	AVG	HR	RBI
1909	Ty Cobb	AL	.377	9	107
1922	Rogers Hornsby	NL	.401	42	152
1925	Rogers Hornsby	NL	.403	39	143
1933	Jimmie Foxx	AL	.356	48	163
1933	Chuck Klein	NL	.368	28	120
1934	Lou Gehrig	AL	.363	49	165
1937	Joe Medwick	NL	.374	31	154
1942	Ted Williams	AL	.356	36	137
1947	Ted Williams	AL	.343	32	114
1956	Mickey Mantle	AL	.353	52	130
1966	Frank Robinson	AL	.316	49	120
1967	Carl Yastrzemski	AL	.326	44	121

Clearly, the degree of competition matters. Cobb won the Triple Crown with just nine home runs. He led the majors that year, with only Tris Speaker (7) and Red Murray (7) coming close. No one approached him in average or RBIs. Cobb not only won the Triple Crown in his league, but in all of baseball. Being the best in both leagues in a given year is termed the Major League Triple Crown.

You'd figure that Hornsby's .401 was the best in the majors that year, but George Sisler hit .420 for St. Louis in the American League, and Ken Williams (also with St. Louis) led the AL in RBIs. Nonetheless, Hornsby led his own league by margins of 47 points in average, 20 runs in RBIs, and 16 homers—dramatically better than the second-place batter in each of the three areas.

Three years later, Hornsby won the Major League Triple Crown.

1933 was quite a year—a Triple Crown winner in each league! Even more remarkably, both played for Philadelphia teams—Foxx for the Athletics and Klein for the Phillies. Foxx won the AL by 20 points in average, 14 homers, and 24 RBIs, but Klein was clearly better in batting average.

The very next year, there was another Major League Triple Crown winner—Lou Gehrig of the New York Yankees. Gehrig had healthy margins in HRs and RBIs, but he was just one percentage point above Paul Waner's .362 average. Nonetheless, Gehrig accomplished something Ruth never did—for that matter, think of the many great hitters baseball has seen and realize the many who never won the Triple Crown: Willie Mays, Babe Ruth, Stan Musial. The list is a long one, but those three names alone provide another indication of how rare a feat winning the Triple Crown truly is.

The last National Leaguer to win the Triple Crown was Joe Medwick, who won it in 1937. Medwick tied with Mel Ott in the home run race, but hit 10 points above Mize in average and drove in a full 41 more runs than the #2 man in the NL. Joe DiMaggio hit 46 homers and Hank Greenberg drove in 183 runs, but Medwick topped his own league in all three Triple Crown categories.

In 1942, Ted Williams saw his average plummet from 1941's .406, but he handily won the Major League Triple Crown, by margins of 25 points in average, six homers, and 27 RBIs.

After three years of military service, and a serious elbow injury that might well have cost the Red Sox the 1946 World Series, Ted Williams won the Triple Crown once again in 1947. In no category did he lead the majors, but against the competition in the American League, no one was better. He hit 15 points higher in average, hit three more home runs, and drove in 16 more runs than any other batter.

Williams and Hornsby are the only two players to ever win the Triple Crown twice—and Ted very nearly won it a third time in 1949. Ted hit four more homers than teammate Vern Stephens, the #2 American Leaguer. He drove in the exact same number of runs as Stephens. But he lost the batting title to George Kell, even though both are shown with .343 averages. Kell's was .3429118 and Williams' was .3427561. That's a difference of .0001557, one thousandth of a point. The slightest mistake in the calculations (a walk mistakenly listed as an at-bat) and the balance shifts. And Ted walked 162 times in 1947; Kell walked 61 times. Ted reached base via hit or walk 356 times. Kell reached base 240 times. Ted's on-base percentage was .490 to Kell's .424.

Mickey Mantle took the Triple Crown in 1956, the last time any player has won the Major League Triple Crown. He outhit Ted Williams by eight points in average, but he hit 45 points more than Hank Aaron in the National League. His margin in homers was nine and in RBIs was 21.

Ten years later, Frank Robinson won handily against his AL peers, though Aaron drove in more runs in the NL and both Alou brothers hit for higher averages in the senior circuit.

Then came 1967, just a year later. Yaz had his sights set on it before the season began. Red Sox third base coach Eddie Popowski told Steve Cady of the *New York Times* in 1983, "He told me in spring training that year he thought he had a shot at it. He said, 'It's going to be great when every hit means something, when every putout means something.'" Yaz beat out Robinson for the AL batting total .326 to .311, and hit even more home runs than Hank Aaron (44 to 39), though he tied for the home run lead with Harmon Killebrew. Yaz's 121 RBIs topped Killebrew's 113, and was 10 above NL champion Orlando Cepeda. He didn't win the Major

League Triple Crown, though, because the National League had a lot of very hot hitters. Roberto Clemente hit .357 to lead the league, and there were four other National Leaguers who hit for higher averages than did Yaz: Tony Gonzalez (.339), Matty Alou (.338), Curt Flood (.335), Rusty Staub (.333). Against the competition that really counts, to get your team to the World Series, Carl led his league.

Yastrzemski also led the American League in runs scored, hits, total bases, runs produced, on-base percentage, slugging average, and a number of more sophisticated statistical categories. It was very definitely a very good year. Yaz also won batting titles in 1963 and 1968, but 1967 was the only year he led the league in either home runs or RBIs.

The OBP Triple Crown

It's an article of faith these days that batting average is an old-fashioned statistic and that the new Holy Grail for batters is OBP—on-base percentage. The "walk's as good as a hit" approach has a lot to recommend it. After all, the hitter's goal is to get on base and, if possible, help score runs. The argument becomes complex, of course. Was Ty Cobb right in criticizing Ted Williams for taking a base on balls rather than trying harder to drive in a run, or was Williams right in insisting on the plate discipline which he felt made him the hitter he was—by refusing to swing at a bad pitch?

Others will argue that focusing on on-base percentage is also too simplistic, and that a more sophisticated array of statistics is necessary to truly rank the best performance by hitters in a given year. There are also arguments that OBP should really be stated as OBA—on-base average.

Leaving all those aside, and just considering on-base percentage instead of batting average, would there be a different set of Triple Crown winners if the three criteria were: OBP, HR, and RBI? Yes, there would. Beginning with the year 1903, there are 12 seasons in which a player has led his league in batting average, home runs, and runs batted in all in the same year. Two players have done it twice: Rogers Hornsby and Ted Williams.

A player who draws a lot of walks is going to produce a much higher on-base percentage than his batting average alone. Barry Bonds set the major league record for single-season OBP in 2002 (.582) in large part due to the large number of intentional and semi-intentional walks he drew: a record 198. Though thought to have done so using illegal substances, Bonds shattered Ted Williams' long-established record of .553, set in 1941. Bonds led the league in batting average in 2002 as well, but was second in home runs and only sixth in RBIs (in good part because the bat was taken out of his hands so many times by pitchers working around him).

Replacing batting average as one of the three criteria for the Triple Crown, and using on-base percentage figures instead, we find 21 seasons in which a batter has won the alternative Triple Crown. Babe Ruth, who never won the standard Triple Crown even once, ranks first with five of those 21 seasons.

Rogers Hornsby still has his two, but on the strength of his 1949 season, Ted Williams has three. No other player has more than one, but we find that Jimmie Foxx, Joe Medwick, and Mickey Mantle lose their Triple Crowns, while Gavvy Cravath, Willie McCovey, Harmon Killebrew, Dick Allen, Mike Schmidt, and Barry Bonds each win one apiece.

Triple Crown winners, substituting OBP for AVG

Year	Batter	League	OBP	HR	RBI	OPS
1909	Ty Cobb *	AL	.431	9	107	.948
1915	Gavvy Cravath	NL	.393	24	115	.903
1919	Babe Ruth	AL	.456	29	114	1.113

1920	Babe Ruth	AL	.533	54	137	1.382
1921	Babe Ruth	AL	.512	59	171	1.358
1922	Rogers Hornsby *	NL	.459	42	152	1.181
1923	Babe Ruth	AL	.545	41	131	1.309
1925	Rogers Hornsby *	NL	.489	39	143	1.245
1926	Babe Ruth	AL	.516	47	150	1.253
1933	Chuck Klein *	NL	.422	28	120	1.024
1934	Lou Gehrig *	AL	.465	49	165	1.171
1942	Ted Williams *	AL	.499	36	137	1.147
1947	Ted Williams *	AL	.499	32	114	1.133
1949	Ted Williams	AL	.490	43	159	1.140
1966	Frank Robinson *	AL	.410	49	122	1.047
1967	Carl Yastrzemski *	AL	.418	44	121	1.040
1969	Willie McCovey	NL	.453	45	126	1.109
1969	Harmon Killebrew	AL	.427	49	140	1.011 (#2 in OPS)
1972	Dick Allen	AL	.420	37	113	1.023
1981	Mike Schmidt	NL	.435	31	91	1.079
1993	Barry Bonds	NL	.458	46	123	1.135

*was Triple Crown winner with either BA or OBA

If one wanted to pose the higher standard of a Quadruple Crown, requiring leadership in both batting average and on-base percentage, the asterisked players would have won this notional Quadruple Crown: Hornsby (twice), Williams (twice), and Klein, Gehrig, Robinson, and Yastrzemski.

Because OPS (on-base percentage plus slugging) has become such a fashionable statistic in recent years, we added OPS to the new table and find just one instance in which the OPS leader was other than the OBP leader. In 1969, Killebrew was #2 in OPS behind Reggie Jackson, who posted a 1.018 OPS that year.

Clearly, the large number of walks drawn by Ruth and Williams has boosted their OBP figures. Ruth only won one batting title (.378 in 1924), but he led the American League in on-base percentage in 10 different seasons. He holds the third-highest walks percentage of all time (.194), behind Max "Camera Eye" Bishop (.200) and Ted Williams (.206).

Williams ranks first, having walked in 20.6% of his plate appearances. The additional walks boosted Ted over George Kell for the OBP lead in 1949.

While Ted just barely lost the battle for average (his .343 was really .3427 to Kell's .343, which extends out to .3429), Kell's on-base percentage was .424 to Ted's .490. In fact, Kell only ranked fourth in OBP that year, behind both Luke Appling (.439) and Eddie Joost (.424) as well as Ted. Williams had walked (or been walked) 162 times; Kell didn't even rate in the top 10. Despite almost the same number of at-bats (Kell had 522 and Williams had 531), Kell walked only 71 times—less than half as many as Williams. Kell hit only three home runs in 1949, to Williams' 43 and drove in just 59 runs, exactly 100 behind Williams' 159 (Williams' teammate Vern Stephens also drove in 159 that year). Had Williams made just one less out in 1949, all else being equal, he would have won the batting title, too—but, of course, he did not.

Bishop? Despite his high percentage of walks, he only

Mrs. Babe Ruth reading the *Boston Record-American* about Ted Williams.

led his league once (1928) and never once ranked higher than third in on-base percentage. For his career, he ranks 13th in OBP among players since 1903.

Babe Ruth ranks second with a lifetime on-base percentage of .474, while Williams ranks first with .482. Over the course of a career that extended from 1939 to 1960, and despite twice interrupting his career for military service, almost half the times Ted Williams stepped into the batter's box, he reached base safely.

The pitching Triple Crown

To lead your league in wins, in strikeouts, and earned run average is pitching's triple crown. Boston has only had two, and they more or less bracketed the 20th century. Cy Young achieved the feat in 1901 and Pedro Martinez did it in 1999. The very first year of the franchise, after 11 years in the National League, Cy Young was enticed over to join the Boston Americans. He already held a career mark of 286–170. He was coming off a 19–19 year with the St. Louis Cardinals, but posted an outstanding 33–10 mark for Boston, with a 1.62 ERA aided by his 158 strikeouts. Young had 41 starts and threw 38 complete games. He relieved two times. In every game he appeared, he was credited with a win or a loss. He had seven more wins than the second-place finisher, 31 more strikeouts, and the next-closest ERA was almost a full run higher: 2.42. He held batters to an opponents' batting average of .232 and on-base percentage of just .256.

The next Red Sox pitcher to win the Triple Crown was Pedro Martinez, who did so in 1999. Pedro struck out almost twice as many batters as had Cy, whiffing 313 batters. He had an astonishing year, relative to other pitchers in the league. His 23 wins were five more than the second-winningest pitcher, Cleveland's Bartolo Colon. His 313 strikeouts were more than 100 above the #2 man, Chuck Finley, who struck out an even 200 opponents. His ERA of 2.07 was more than a run higher than David Cone of the Yankees, who finished second with 3.44. He posted a strikeouts-to-walks ratio of 8.46; the next closest wasn't even half that, at 3.44 (Felix Heredia). He struck out an average of 13.20 batters per nine innings. Finley came the closest: 8.44. His WHIP (walks plus hits per innings pitched) was .923. Eric Milton's 1.226 was as close as anyone approached Pedro that year.

Pedro also set a couple of other records in the process. He fanned at least one batter in 40 consecutive innings between August and September of 1999. As far as SABR researchers have determined, the previous record was 25 innings. To exceed 25 and go all the way to 40 is to truly topple an older mark. There was also a stretch of eight games in which he struck out 10 or more batters. The old record of seven was set by Nolan Ryan in 1977. In early 1999, Pedro tied the mark between April 15 and May 18—but then he beat the record in eight straight starts from August 19 through September 27. Had he not come in to pitch one inning in relief of brother Ramon in the October 1 game, he would have had 10 10-K consecutive starts.

After his first three seasons with the Red Sox, Pedro had a record of 78–22, the best start for any pitcher ever in his first 100 seasons with a given team. Unfortunately, though, he lost a game on April 15, 1999. That put his record for the year at 2–1. In 2002, with a 5–0 start (later improved to 7–0), Pedro Martinez became only the second pitcher in major league history to begin a season with a 5–0 record or better in three consecutive seasons. Dave Stewart was the first, with Oakland from 1988–90. In Pedro's case, though, he also had an 8–0 start in 1997 and a 5–0 start in 1998, but in his Triple Crown year of 1999 he lost his third decision, that April 15 game, largely due to lack of run support. Pedro gave up two earned runs in seven innings, but Boston batters never scored even once. Pedro ran his record to 11–1 before incurring his second loss. Had he not lost that one game, he would have won his first five or more in six straight seasons.

While we're talking about Pedro, let's also note that on May 18, 2002, Pedro Martinez opened the ballgame against the Seattle Mariners with nine straight strikes. This is not an easy thing to do. There can be foul balls, of course, but never a foul on the third pitch of the at-bat, unless it's a foul right into the catcher's mitt. He's the only pitcher in American League history ever to have opened a game with three straight strikeouts on nine pitches. Sandy Koufax did it once in the National League. All in all, there are 34 times it's been done at some point during a game, but only once in each league to start off a ballgame.

Back to the pitching Triple Crown, though, it's been won 15 times in American League history, most recently by Johan Santana in 2006. Renegade Roger Clemens did it twice—but only after leaving the Red Sox. The Rocket did it in back-to-back years, 1997 and 1998, for the Toronto Blue Jays. Another pitcher with a Red Sox pedigree won it twice as well, but Lefty Grove won it before coming to Boston, in 1930 and 1931 for the Philadelphia Athletics.

Martinez didn't win the honor in 2000, which would have given him back-to-back Triple Crown seasons. He led in strikeouts, 284 to Colon's 212. His ERA was much lower than in 1999, just 1.74. Roger Clemens, #2, was almost two full runs more—3.70. Pedro's WHIP was an astonishing .737. But he only won 18 games, fourth on the list. Tim Hudson and David Wells each had 20. Andy Pettitte had 19. Pedro had 29 starts, same as the year before, but his teammates didn't score as many runs and so he wound up with a record of 18–6 rather than the 23–4 of the year before.

.406 and 406

The number 406 pops up at least twice in Red Sox history. With a decimal point in front of it, it shows up as Ted Williams' .406 batting average in 1941—the last time any major leaguer hit over .400 for a single season. Had it not been for the temporary suspension of the sacrifice fly rule that year, Ted would have hit .411—and there wouldn't have been such suspense on the final day of the year, which Ted wouldn't have entered with a .399 average.

Without the decimal point, it's the 406 total bases that Jim Rice reached in 1978 (46 home runs, 15 triples, 25 doubles, and 127 singles). The closest to Rice that year was Baltimore's Eddie Murray with 293 total bases. Rice was the first right-handed hitter in the American League to pass the 400 mark since Joe DiMaggio had 418 total bases in 1937.

Another .400 hitter?

Wade Boggs actually hit over .400 for a season's worth of 162 games; it was just his historic misfortune that he didn't do it within one calendar year. From June 13, 1985 through June 8, 1986, Boggs hit over .400. In 1985, he hit .418 at Fenway (130 hits in 311 at-bats) but just only .322 on the road (110 hits in 342 at-bats). The next year, though, he hit almost exactly the same at home and away, .357 at Fenway (99 hits in 277 at-bats) and .356 on the road (108 hits in 303 at-bats).

Team average of over .300

The last TEAM to hit over .300 was the 1950 Red Sox—and that's with Ted Williams only batting a subpar .317.

"The Best Player Not Yet in the Hall of Fame"—Dom DiMaggio

During the years he played, 1940–52, if one excludes the war years, Dom DiMaggio had more total hits than any other player. Only Ted Williams and Stan Musial had more doubles over that same stretch. Only Ted scored more runs than Dom in the same period.

Dom averaged 104.6 runs scored per season over his career. He is the only player NOT in the Hall of Fame to have such a high total. In the Hall of Fame, only Lou Gehrig and Joe DiMaggio rank higher.

American League records held by Dominic are all as an outfielder: total chances per game (2.99), chances accepted per game (2.92), and putouts per game (2.82). He also holds two single-season records—most chances accepted (526, in 1948) and putouts (503, also in 1948). He is only one of five outfielders ever to have more than 500 putouts in a season.

Dom DiMaggio started seven double plays in 1942, from his position in center field, one of them an unassisted double play.

Dom D led the American League in stolen bases in 1950—with only 15 (it's the lowest leading total ever, but was still enough to lead the league that year).

He also holds the record for the longest hitting streak in Red Sox history, 34 games in 1949.

"The greatest satisfaction I have in baseball is that I broke in wearing glasses, and in those days, an athlete wearing glasses was a no-no. You couldn't be an athlete and wear glasses, so when I was successful, I helped open the floodgates and I feel I gave other glass-wearing athletes the courage to stick it out and play." *Chronicles*, p. 109

The only Red Sox player to play before the President of the United States and the King of England, and also have an audience with the Pope.

On February 11, 1914, Tris Speaker was among touring major league ballplayers granted an audience at the Vatican before Pope Pius X. This was particularly ironic in that Speaker was one of the Masons on a Red Sox team that bristled with division between Catholics and anti-Catholics.

Fifteen days later, Speaker appeared in a game watched by King George V at the Stamford Bridge Grounds in London, home of the Chelsea football (soccer) team since 1905. It was an 11-inning game, and the king stayed for the whole game. Tom Daly, who later served as a Red Sox coach from 1933 through 1946, hit a home run in the game.

Speaker also played in the first World Series game ever attended by a sitting U.S. president, on October 9, 1915. It was Game Two, a 2–1 Red Sox victory at Baker Bowl, Philadelphia. The first hit of the game was Speaker's single in the top of the first. And Woodrow Wilson was watching.

The world tour also brought Speaker to Australia, Hong Kong, The Philippines, Ceylon, Egypt, and Japan. In a December 6, 1913 game against Tokyo's Keio University, he hit two home runs. Jim Elfers has written up the tour in his book *The Tour To End All Tours,* and both Timothy Gay and Charles Alexander have written Speaker biographies.

When former Red Sox player Stuffy McInnis met Pope Pius XI in 1924, one can almost imagine the introductions: "Pope, meet Stuffy. Stuffy, Pope."

100 Wins in a Season

Year	Record	Manager
1912	105–47	Jake Stahl
1915	101–50	Bill Carrigan
1946	104–50	Joe Cronin

100 Losses in a Season

Year	Record	Manager
1906	49–105	Jimmy Collins, Chick Stahl
1925	47–105	Lee Fohl
1926	46–107	Lee Fohl
1927	51–103	Bill Carrigan
1930	52–102	Heinie Wagner
1932	43–111	Shano Collins, Marty McManus
1965	62–100	Billy Herman

Red Sox players with a higher batting average than the team's winning percentage

Based on a minimum of 200 at-bats, there have been some good batters in some bad years.

Team winning percentage in 1925 = .309	Team winning percentage in 1932 = .279
Ike Boone .330	Dale Alexander .372 (won batting title)
Roy Carlyle .326	Smead Jolley .309
Doc Prothro .313	Roy Johnson .298
Tex Vache .313	
Baby Doll Jacobson .305	

Hopefully, we'll never see years like those again.

Most consecutive years without the lowest winning percentage

The last time the Red Sox had the lowest winning percentage in the league was in 1932, when they won 27.9% of their games. 43–111 was the final mark that year.

The Yankees were worst in the American League as recently as 1990. What a good year that was—until the playoffs, anyhow.

MATCHUPS AND FURTHER FENWAY FACTS

Red Sox / Yankees matchups

Over the years, there have been many historic matchups between the two rivals. There's no question that the Yankees hold the edge in games won. Even as they remain without a World Series victory in the 21st century, the Yankees had still finished ahead of the Red Sox for 11 years in a row before. The last time until 2007 you'll find Boston above New York in the standings was 1995. Even when they finished with the precise same number of wins and losses in 2005, New York wound up on top because they took 10 of the 19 games against the Red Sox that year. But in 21st century championship rings….

Since 1901, the Boston Americans / Boston Red Sox have won 915 of the regular season head-to-head games while the Baltimore Orioles / New York Highlanders / New York Yankees have won 1,099. It's going to take a while to catch up.

The longest winning streak for Boston against New York is 17 games, ranging from October 3, 1911 to July 1, 1912. The longest winning streak for New York against Boston is 12, twice, from May 27, 1936 to August 23, 1936 and also from August 16, 1952 to April 23, 1953.

The most runs scored by the Red Sox against the Yankees is 17 and it happened twice the same summer: May 28, 2005 and July 15, 2005. The high for the Yankees against Boston was 24, on September 28, 1923.

The longest game in the rivalry: 20 innings (August 29, 1967), a game that took 6:09 to play to completion. New York won, 4–3, in the second game of a doubleheader. Boston won the first one, 2–1, in a brisk 2:10 as Jim Lonborg three-hit the Yankees. Despite losing the second game, the Red Sox took over first place in the American League standings due to a Twins loss to the Orioles.

The Yankees have shut out the Red Sox 148 times; the Red Sox have shut out the Yankees 109 times.

First time in history Sox have allowed
12 or more runs in three straight games

An unfortunate low point occurred in mid-August 2006. It was the first time the Red Sox had allowed a dozen or more runs in three consecutive games.

August 18: 12–4 loss to NY
August 18: 14–11 loss to NY in the day's second game
August 19: 13–5 loss to NY

They only let the Yankees score two runs in the game that followed, but Boston only scored once, so lost again.

This section may seem kind of short, but hasn't it been written about enough? For more on the rivalry, see the entire book on the subject by Bill Nowlin and Jim Prime, *Blood Feud: The Red Sox, the Yankees, and the Struggle of Good Versus Evil.*

Matchups with all teams (1901–2007)

	Wins	losses	win%	RS	RA	W-L(home)	W-L(away)
ANA	307	264	.538	2569	2396	172–115	135–149
ARI	2	4	.333	25	28	0–3	2–1
ATL	20	25	.444	190	218	7–14	13–11
BAL	1104	911	.548	9566	8737	594–407	510–504
CHC	1	2	.333	20	22	0–0	1–2
CHW	945	906	.511	8040	7868	546–380	399–526
CIN	3	0	1.000	23	4	3–0	0–0
CLE	938	1008	.482	8795	9091	506–467	432–541
COL	4	5	.444	40	44	3–3	1–2
DET	999	941	.515	9203	8966	546–426	453–515
FLA	13	8	.619	140	102	7–5	6–3
HOU	3	0	1.000	15	9	3–0	0–0
KCR	195	205	.488	1860	1812	108–92	87–113
LAD	2	4	.333	23	33	2–1	0–3
MIL	213	184	.537	1923	1833	113–84	100–100
MIN	934	910	.507	8314	8123	524–394	410–516
NYM	10	8	.556	78	59	6–3	4–5
NYY	915	1099	.454	8831	9663	507–507	408–592
OAK	1034	845	.550	9114	8207	570–376	464–469
PHI	18	13	.581	190	159	11–6	7–7
PIT	4	2	.667	37	19	2–1	2–1
SDP	6	3	.667	29	25	2–1	4–2
SEA	195	144	.575	1773	1568	105–65	90–79
SFG	4	2	.667	38	26	3–0	1–2
STL	2	4	.333	34	34	1–2	1–2
TBD	111	58	.657	978	694	61–23	50–35
TEX	308	272	.531	2827	2644	183–106	125–166
TOR	239	192	.555	2167	2008	119–96	120–96
WSN	11	7	.611	101	78	9–0	2–7
Total	8540	8026	.516	76943	74470	4713–3577	3827–4449

Note: this table includes franchises that moved—for instance, Twins embraces the Washington Senators, Orioles includes the old St. Louis Browns, etc.

Some other franchise facts

Home winning percentage: 56.85%   Road winning percentage: 46.24%

The Red Sox have played 14 more home games than they have played games on the road, a statistical oddity attributable to the number of games in earlier years when they never played out the full schedule or didn't make up all the postponed games.

Best home record in a given year: .792 (61–16) both in 1946 and 1949

Best road record in a given year: .640 (48–27) in 1912

Worst home record in a given year: .289 (22–54) in 1906

Worst road record in a given year: .208 (16–61) in 1932 (the exact opposite of the 61–16 home seasons in 1946 and 1949)

Last five years the Red Sox played below .500 ball at home: 1966, 1980, 1983, 1994, 1997

The seasons in which the Sox played better on the road than at home: 1906, 1908, 1914, 1917, 1928, 1939, 1953, 1975, 1980, 1984, 1995, and three years in a row: 2000, 2001, and 2002.

Greatest gap between winning percentage at home and away: 1949 (337 points—.792 at home, .455 on the road)

The only year the team won exactly the same number of games at home and away: 1997 (39–42 at home, and 39–42 on the road)

The only year the team had the same record in the first half and the second half: 1968 (43–38 in the first half of the season, and 43–38 in the second half)

There's a feeling among Red Sox fans that the team tends to do well early in the season and then fade—a September swoon. This seems not to be the case, overall. Of the 107 seasons played through 2007, the Red Sox had a better record in the first half 51 times and in the second half 55 times. And then there was 1968, when the records were identical.

The biggest improvements from the first half to the second half:

1996 (first half .424, second half .636, a 212-point improvement)

1948 (first half .527, second half .704, a 177-point improvement)

1949 (first half .538, second half .711, a 173-point improvement)

The biggest collapses from the first half to the second half:

2006 (first half .616, second half .434, a 182-point decline)

1990 (first half .630, second half .457, a 173-point decline)

1978 (first half .687, second half .525, a 162-point decline that ended with Bucky Dent's homer)

The winningest months and the losingest months

Based on winning percentage, and at least five regular season decisions in a given month, the best and worst months in Red Sox history are:

Month	Best	Worst
April	11–2 (1918) .846	2–10 (1925) .167
May	21–6 (1946) .778	4–22 (1906) .154
June	20–5 (1901) .800	4–24 (1927) .143
July	20–7 (1993) .741	6–24 (1925) .200
August	24–6 (1950) .800	7–22 (1964) .241
September	19–5 (1949) .792	7–20 (1952) .259
October	7–0 (1905) 1.000	1–6 (1910) .143

A particularly bad month

August 2006 was a particularly bad month for Boston. The Red Sox only won 30% of their games, winning nine while losing 21 (.300). The team was decimated with injuries. In the process, the Red Sox tied a major league record for the most defeats in a month when they'd begun in first place. After July 31, the Sox were 63–41 and in first place in the AL East, one game ahead of the Yankees. After losing 21 of their next 30, just one month later they were 72–62 and a full eight games behind those same Yankees. Only five other teams in history saw such a precipitous fall from first place over the course of one month. Each of them lost exactly 21 games in the month in question. The other teams are listed in the *2007 Red Sox Media Guide,* on page 300.

Shutouts

The Red Sox shut out their opponents 1,113 times through 2007, and were shut out 1,046 times.

Their best year was 1995; they were shut out only one time, on August 2 in Detroit when the Tigers' Sean Bergman threw a four-hit shutout and beat Roger Clemens in a 5–0 game. The next-best seasons were 1950 and 2004. Both years, the Sox were only shut out three times.

Looking at lopsided years, the best year for Boston was 1903 when they shut out their opponents 20 times but were only shut out seven times. The worst came three years later, in 1906, when they were shut out 28 times but only shut down the opposition six times. The 28 shutouts were the most suffered in a single season. The most times the Red Sox shut out the opposition in a year were 24, both in 1914 and 1916. The best stretch was June 21–23, 1916 when the Red Sox scored a total of four runs and won three games, 2–0, 1–0, and 1–0 against the Yankees, Yankees, and Athletics.

For whatever it might be worth, here are the decade-by-decade totals:

Years	Red Sox shutouts	Games the Sox were shut out
1901–10	127	143
1911–20	182	118
1921–30	66	115
1931–40	62	89
1941–50	115	79
1951–60	85	97
1961–70	94	109
1971–80	124	90
1981–90	97	94
1991–2000	90	71
2001–07	71	41

Runs scored / runs allowed

The Red Sox scored 1,027 runs in 1950, by far the most ever. 2003 came next, with 961.

The fewest runs scored were the 463 scored by the 1906 team.

The largest difference between runs scored and runs allowed was in 1949. The Red Sox scored 896 runs but only allowed 667, a difference of 229 runs. The 1932 aggregation, which we've identified as the worst team in Red Sox history, allowed 915 runs while only scoring 566, a difference of 349 runs.

High-scoring games

Was there ever a year in which the Red Sox never saw 11 or more runs scored against them? There was not. In every year of their existence, even in the Deadball Era, there was at least one game in which the opposition scored 11 or more runs. In 1916 and 1923, that was the high total. In every other year, the opposition had a game scoring at least 12 or more runs.

The Red Sox always had at least one such high-scoring game, too. In 1914, 1923, and

1992, the highest-scoring game was 11 runs. In every other year, they had at least one higher figure.

In 2007, the Sox tied the team record for the most consecutive games in a row with 10 or more runs scored: four, sweeping an August road visit to the Chicago White Sox with scores of 11–3, 10–1, 14–2, and 11–1. The 46–7 run differential was larger than the two times they'd done it before, in 1912 (49–16) and 1950 (51–21).

Blowout games

Defining a blowout as a game in which one team scored at least five more runs than the other, the Red Sox won the most blowout games in 1903 (39–13), 1948 (39–21), and 1950 (39–15). Given the team's performance in 1906 and 1932, one might guess that one of those years had the fewest blowouts. One would be correct: the 1906 team only managed seven.

The most unbalanced year in Boston's favor was the 26–8 campaign of 1942. The worst was 1932 (7–45). A full 45 times in 1906, the team was dealt losses of five or more runs. Discouraging, and reflective of the 105 losses that year.

One-run wins and losses

The most one-run wins in a single season came in 1953: 35. 2002 came second, with 34.

The most one-run losses were the 36 losses in 1930. Frustrating.

The most favorable split was in 1986, with a 24–10 record in one-run games. Second came the 35–16 season of 1953. The worst split was in 1933 (14–33).

Longest winning streak in team history

The Boston Red Stockings once started off a season winning the first 26 games—the only problem was, this was not the Red Sox. It was the National League team, and the year was 1875. Quite a way to start a season. It's a streak that has never been topped, though John McGraw's New York Giants tied it in 1916. The Giants' streak was at the end of the season, and they lost the chance to beat the Red Stockings' streak on the final day of the 1916 season, playing the Boston Braves. Despite the streak (and an earlier 17-game streak in the same season), they wound up in fourth place.

The American League record for consecutive wins by a team (19) is shared by the White Sox (1906) and the Yankees (1947).

The best streak for the Red Sox was 15 straight wins in 1946, from April 25 to May 10. In 1948, the Sox put together a 13-game win streak from July 18 through July 27. "Morgan Magic" in 1988 saw the Sox win 12 in a row, and 18 of 19—which was pretty darn good! There have been six 12-game winning streaks in Red Sox history—and one of them was in 1946, starting up not long after the 15-game streak stopped. They are:

July 28—August 8, 1937
July 4—July 16, 1939
May 29—June 11, 1946

July 15—July 25, 1988
August 3—August 14, 1995
June 16—July 29, 2006

Let's shoot for 16. If not 162. But even a modest seven- or eight-game winning streak can be immensely rewarding (viz., the postseason both in 2004 and 2007).

NUMBERS AND UNIFORMS

Uniform numbers

Just as the Red Sox never played the National Anthem at Fenway before 1931 (they played the "Star Spangled Banner" often, but it was not designated as the National Anthem until 1931), neither Babe Ruth nor Cy Young nor Tris Speaker nor any Red Sox player before 1931 ever wore a number. The Red Sox did not wear uniform numbers prior to the 1931 season.

Since that year, Red Sox players have worn numbers ranging from #1 (the first to wear it was Bill Sweeney in 1931) through #84 (J. T. Snow in 2006). Coach Jason LaRocque wore #88 in both 2005 and 2006. Johnny Lazor had a 63-year streak going; when he wore #82 back in 1943, it was the highest number ever worn by a Red Sox player—but Snow wanted to honor his recently-deceased football-playing father and the Red Sox let him wear #84. When asked in a December 2001 interview why he'd worn #82, Lazor said he didn't know—and that he thought he'd worn #29! He didn't recall any particular reason why he'd worn #82. He passed away one year later, so was spared the knowledge that his streak was snapped. (Lazor was also #14 in 1943 and kept that number through 1945.) In 2007, when Eric Gagne came to the Red Sox he found his usual number, 38, was taken by a guy named Schilling so he reversed those numbers and wore 83.

The following numbers have never yet been worn by a Red Sox player: 69, 70, 71, 72, 72, 73, 74, 75, 76, 78, 79, 80, and numbers 85 and higher. The only number in the 70s even worn was 77, worn by Josh Bard in 2006.

Always striving for a lower number? Billy Consolo was #11 in 1955, #7 in 1956–1957, and #1 in 1957–1959. Disrupting the pattern a bit was that he started off as #8 in 1953–1954.

The most popular number of all—the number worn by more players than any other number, that is—is #15, which has been worn by 51 players. It was also worn by hitting coach Ron "Papa Jack" Jackson in 2006.

The most popular number among coaches is #32, worn by 18 different coaches from Shano Collins in 1931 to Bill Haselman in 2005–2006. Only 14 players have worn #32, and the only one to do so for more than two full years is Derek Lowe who wore it for seven seasons, 1998–2004.

Not a single coach or manager has ever worn #19—but exactly 50 different players have.

The #12 was worn by 43 different players (the Grover Cleveland of Red Sox uniform number wearers, Ted Lepcio, wore it during two different stretches). Not to be outdone in terms of the number of times wearing the same number, Johnny Pesky was #6 on four oc-

Father Guido Sarducci attempts to exorcise the curse at Fenway. Courtesy of Don Novello.

casions—in his rookie year of 1942, again after he came back from the war in 1946–1952, as a coach from 1981–1984, and in the 21st century as an Instructor. Johnny wore #22, though, when he was Red Sox manager in 1963–1964 and wore #35 when he was a coach in 1975–1980. Why did he select #22 when named manager? "I just wanted a double number. I liked the infielders to have single numbers. That's the way I was raised."

Perhaps a little preditably, the #13 has been worn least frequently among the lower numbers. The nine players who have defied any curse associated with #13 are, in order: Elden Auker, Reid Nichols. Billy

Joe Robidoux, John Valentin, Rey Sanchez, Lou Merloni, Doug Mientkiewicz, Roberto Petagine, and Alex Cora. The other low number only worn by nine players was #9, the reason being that Ted Williams started wearing it as early as 1939 and no one has worn it since.

For a venerable founding franchise in the American League, the Red Sox have retired a very small number of numbers on their own: #1, 4, 8, 9, and 27. Bobby Doerr, Joe Cronin, Carl Yastrzemski, Ted Williams, and Carlton Fisk.

Red Sox players who wore numbers that were later retired

#1—before Bobby Doerr's #1 was retired in 1988, it was also worn by the following ballplayers:

Bill Sweeney (1931), Al Van Camp (1932), Ed Gallagher (1932), Rabbit Warstler (1933), Max Bishop (1934–35), Mel Almada (1936), Ben Chapman (1937), Bobby Doerr (1938–1944), Ty La-Forest (1945), Ben Steiner (1945), Bobby Doerr (1946–1951), Fred Hatfield (1952), George Kell (1952–1954), Grady Hatton (1954–1956), Billy Consolo (1957–1959), Herb Plews (1959), Jim Mahoney (1959), Don Buddin (1960–1961), Eddie Bressoud (1962–1965), Joe Foy (1966–1968), Joe Azcue (1969), Tom Satriano (1969), Luis Alvarado (1969–1970), Phil Gagliano (1971–1972), Bernie Carbo 1974–1978), Jim Dwyer (1979–1980), and Chico Walker (1981–1984). Manager John McNamara wore #1 from 1985–1988.

Note: when one or more players in a given year is listed with the same number, they are listed in the sequence they wore the number (in 1932, for instance, Van Camp played his final game on June 23 and Gallagher played his first game on July 8).

#4—before Joe Cronin's #4 was retired in 1984, it was worn by these ballplayers:

Rabbit Warstler (1931), Hal Rhyne (1932), Smead Jolley (1933), Roy Johnson (1934), Joe Cronin (1935), Eric McNair (1936), Joe Cronin (1937–1947), Sam Mele (1948–1949), Ken Keltner (1950), Lou Boudreau (1951–1954), Jackie Jensen (1955–1959), Lu Clinton (1960), Roman Mejias (1963–1964), Rudy Schlesinger (1965), Jim Gosger (1965), Don Demeter (1966–1967), Norm Siebern (1967–1968), Billy Conigliaro (1969), Tom Satriano (1969–1970), Ben Oglivie (1971), Tommy Harper (1972–1974), Butch Hobson (1976–1980), and Carney Lansford (1981–1982).

Interestingly, Cronin switched to #6 for the 1936 season and McNair wore #4. In 1937, McNair wore #6 and Cronin reverted to #4.

#8—before Carl Yastrzemski's #8 was retired in 1989, it was worn by these ballplayers:

Urbane Pickering (1931), Bennie Tate (1932), Otto Miller (1932), Johnny Gooch (1933), Bucky Walters (1934), Red Kellett (1934), Babe Dahlgren (1935), Doc Cramer (1935–1940), Lou Finney (1941–1942), Al Simmons (1943), Bob Johnson (1944–1945), Hal Wagner (1946–1947), Birdie Tebbetts (1947–1950), Mike Guerra (1951), Tom Wright (1951), Aaron Robinson (1951), Hal Bevan (1952), Billy Consolo (1953–1954), Sammy White (1955), Pete Daley (1958–1959), and Ed Sadowski (1960). Carl Yastrzemski wore #8 from 1961 through 1983.

#9—before Ted Williams' #9 was officially retired in 1984, it was worn by these ballplayers:

Charlie Berry (1931–1932), Smead Jolley (1932), Merv Shea (1933), Rick Ferrell (1933), Gordie Hinkle (1934), Dusty Cooke (1935–1936), Bobby Doerr (1937), and Ben Chapman (1938). Ted Williams wore #9 from 1939 through 1960 and no one has worn it since.

#27—before Carlton Fisk's #27 was retired in 2000, it was worn by these ballplayers:

Jim Brillheart (1931), John Michaels (1932), manager Bucky Harris (1933), Dib Williams (1935), coach Bing Miller (1936–1937), Dick Midkiff (1938), Yank Terry (1940), Charlie Wagner (1940–1942), Leon Culberson (1943), Tex Hughson (1944), Bob Garbark (1945), Charlie Wagner (1946), Tex Aulds (1947), Ed McGah (1947), Bill Butland (1947), Johnny Ostrowski (1948),

Lou Stringer (1949–1950), Fred Hatfield (1951), Leo Kiely (1951), Dick Brodowski (1952), Al Benton (1952), Skinny Brown (1953–1955), George Susce (1955–1958), Bill Monbouquette (1958–1965), Darrell Brandon (1966–1968), Sonny Siebert (1969), Ed Phillips (1970), Carlton Fisk (1971–1980), Mike Brown (1982–1985), Jeff Sellers (1985), Pat Dodson (1986–1988), Greg Harris (1989–1994), Stan Royer (1994), Mark Whiten (1995), Dave Hollins (1995), Butch Henry (1997–1998), and Kip Gross (1999).

#42—before Jackie Robinson's number was retired throughout Major League Baseball on the 50th anniversary of his entry into the major leagues in 1997, it was worn by these ballplayers:

Babe Barna (1943), Tom McBride (1943), Andy Gilbert (1946), coach Oscar Melillo (1952–1953), Dick Brodowski (1955), Herb Moford (1959), Hal Kolstad (1962), Dick Stigman (1966), Ken Brett (1969), Sonny Siebert (1970–1973), Lance Clemons (1974), Bobby Darwin (1976–1977), Chuck Rainey (1979–1982), Doug Bird (1983), Rob Woodward (1985–1986), Dave Henderson (1987), John Trautwein (1988), Greg Harris (1989), Larry Andersen (1990), Jim Pankovits (1990), and Mo Vaughn (1991–1998). Vaughn was grandfathered in to be able to continue to wear #42—which he consciously requested knowing it had been Robinson's number—throughout his career.

Unofficially retired is **#21**. No one has worn it since Roger Clemens last wore it in 1996.

In some years, more than one player has worn a given number. For instance, in the very recent World Championship year 2004, the number 36 was worn by three different players: Bobby Jones, Orlando Cabrera, and Mike Myers. And the number 37 was worn, in the same season, by Frank Castillo, Earl Snyder, and Adam Hyzdu.

The most players to ever wear the same uniform in a given year is four—and it's occurred three times, twice with the same number. In 1951, Tom Wright, Aaron Robinson, Mel Hoderlein, and Karl Olson all wore #28. And then in 1980, Allen Ripley, Jack Billingham, Bobby Ojeda, and Steve Crawford all wore #28, too. In 1959, the #39 was sewn to the jersey backs of Dave Sisler, Billy Hoeft, Jack Harshman, and Jerry Mallett.

Which pair of Red Sox relatives wore the highest sum of uniform numbers?

It certainly wasn't the Barrett brothers—Marty wore 17 and Tommy wore 33. Or the Conigliaros (Tony wore 25 and Billy wore 4). The Ferrells were even lower: Wes wore #12 throughout, while Rick was one of those guys always going for the lower number (he started with #9 in 1933, went to #7 the next year, and got all the way to #2 by 1936).

It wasn't Marc Sullivan (#15) or his father Haywood (#16).

The lowest combination was set by Roy Johnson (#3) and brother Bob (#8). Roy did add a digit when he increased his number to #4 his second year on the job, but even then, it only adds up to 12. But whose jersey numbers added up to the highest sum?

Hint: their surnames ended in -artinez, but they weren't Pedro (#45) and Ramon (# 49) even though that adds up to a solid 94.

Here's the answer, and it's tough to top: Sandy Martinez wore #58 and his cousin Anastacio Martinez wore #67, both in 2004, for a grand total of 125.

Highest two uniform numbers to play in the same game back to back?

It happened on April 9, 2006. The two jersey numbers totaled 161: J. T. Snow (#84) led off the fifth inning with a single off the right field wall in Baltimore, followed by a single by catcher Josh Bard, wearing #77.

The day Roger Moret wore Luis Tiant's number

Rogelio Moret wore #29 but after the game on May 12, 1975, according to the book *Diary of a Winner*, "thieves robbed the Sox clubhouse during the night" and made off with 17 jerseys and four pairs of pants—among the jerseys was Moret's. It had been Half-Price Night at the Oakland Coliseum, but someone simply helped themselves to the uniforms. Rick Wise started for the Red Sox the next night, May 13, and went 6⅓ innings, when Moret came in to relieve—wearing Luis Tiant's #23. Tiant's talent didn't rub off on Moret. There was a runner on second with one out. Moret got Reggie Jackson to pop up, and then walked Joe Rudi intentionally. But then Billy Williams homered, Sal Bando walked, and pinch-runner Matt Alexander stole on Moret. He walked Gene Tenace on purpose, then retired Claudell Washington to close the inning. The Red Sox lost, 9–5, the loss charged to Wise.

The Red Sox had reportedly also had a few uniforms stolen out of the clubhouse in Anaheim in the series that immediately preceded the Oakland games.

For a complete listing of numbers worn by Red Sox players over the decades, see Bill Walsh's work at *www.redsoxdiehard.com.*

The day Coco Crisp wore Jackie Robinson's number

Beginning in 1997, Jackie Robinson's #42 was retired throughout Major League Baseball. Only those ballplayers then wearing the number (which included Boston's Mo Vaughn, who had consciously chosen to wear Robinson's number) were permitted to continue to wear the number. By 2007, only New York's Mariano Rivera was still wearing a 42 jersey. On April 15, 2007 MLB celebrated the 60th anniversary of Jackie Robinson's debut and gave each team permission for a player to wear Robinson's number on that one day. Boston's game was postponed, but they celebrated the day a week later on April 22. Though the Red Sox were a truly international team, with players from the Dominican Republic, Venezuela, Japan, Puerto Rico, and more, only center fielder Coco Crisp and third base coach DeMarlo Hale were African Americans. Crisp wore the jersey number, as did David Ortiz and coach Hale. Every Red Sox player wore a #42 patch on his cap.

The wearing of the green

It was quite a weekend for tinkering with uniforms. Two days before Crisp and Ortiz wore #42, the whole team wore green jerseys in tribute to the recently-deceased Red Auerbach of the Boston Celtics. With green jerseys and caps but red longsleeve undershirts, red piping, red warmup jackets, and red socks, it looked like Christmas in April on the 20th day of the month, 2007. Though green "B" caps, pink "B" caps, and other variations had been available to fans for a few years, it was the first time the players had worn green. It was also, for no apparent reason, the first time that Sox home jerseys bore the names of the players on the back.

The day the players refused to put on their designated uniforms

When interleague play began in 1997, one of the most anticipated games in Boston was when the Red Sox hosted the Atlanta Braves. Even when the Braves had been the Boston Braves, the two teams never played each other during the regular season, though for many years they held a "city series" exhibition game each year for charity. For the 1997 interleague game, both teams wore old-fashioned uniforms to pay tribute to the past.

Other teams also wore different uniforms of one sort or another. It was inoffensive fun. When 1999 rolled around, the real estate firm Century 21 developed a co-promotion with Major League Baseball it coined "Turn Ahead the Clock." For the September 18 home game against the Detroit, the Red Sox and Tigers were both supposed to wear futuristic uniforms—what someone imagined baseball uniforms would look like in the year 2021.

Some players were heard to grumble about wearing what was in effect an advertisement for a real estate company. When both teams took the field, not a futuristic uniform was to be seen. According to sources, the uniforms "failed to show up" on time. Funny—the same thing happened to eight teams, not just these two.

Will Red Sox uniforms one day look like those of racing car drivers?

Creeping commercialism? MLB still doesn't permit the practice in the United States, but the Red Sox wore the corporate logo of data storage company EMC on their uniforms when they opened the 2008 season with two games in Tokyo. Though there have been numerous patches of one sort or another over the years, this was the first time that the Red Sox uniform bore the patch of a private company or sponsor.

WE COULDN'T LEAVE THIS STUFF OUT...

Favorite seats at Fenway

Admittedly a fully subjective subject, my own favorite seats at Fenway—besides the ones I call my own—include:

Of course, the red seat—which these days even has a website named after it. The seat is high up in section 42 of the right field bleachers, the 21st seat in the 37th row. Fourteen rows from the top. Its place in Red Sox history was immortalized when the "seat" was a number on a thick plank upon which patrons sat until chairs were brought in after the 1977 season. One such patron was Joseph A. Boucher, a construction engineer from Albany who never expected to be hit on the head with a baseball, being some 502 feet from home plate. It was a warm Sunday afternoon in the late spring—June 9, 1946. Boucher should have been awake; it was only the bottom of the first inning of the second game, and Ted Williams was up with a runner on base. But the late afternoon sun was in his eyes and he never saw it coming. Fred Hutchinson pitched and—bang!—Ted hit the longest home run ever hit at Fenway (according to the Red Sox, who later measured one of Manny Ramirez's shots at 501 feet, conveniently just one foot short). Bam!—it bounced off Boucher's straw skimmer, punching a hole in it, and bounced away. "They say it bounced a dozen rows higher," Boucher told *Globe* reporter Harold Kaese. In the seventh inning of the first game, Ted had hit one off reliever Tommy Bridges. The Red Sox took both games from the Tigers.

Another seat with a great vantage point is the seat *right* behind home plate where Senior Advisor for Baseball Projects Jerry Kapstein sits for every game. In years gone by, before two rows of extra seats were added, the front row seats were often available shortly before game time for the fortunate fan who might stumble upon it minutes before the game. I sat in the front row center seat on four or five occasions, once (in May 1978) right beside Mrs. Bob Bailey.

Once upon a time, I was also fortunate to sit with Lib Dooley for a game. A season ticket holder since 1946, and a Boston public schoolteacher with a long family history in Boston baseball (see references to her father elsewhere in this volume), I typically sat about a dozen rows behind her and a little more toward home plate but we often talked before or after games. Her seat was in the very front row, right behind the Red Sox on-deck circle—which was itself moved to be closer to her seat (and watchful eye) after the day a fan reached over and stole a ball from the bag of balls when the batboy was away from his position. Ms. Dooley put out a small plastic tray, which seemed to have been "borrowed" from an airline, and placed some cookies on it for the batboys—or a player—to munch on. After the sixth inning, she broke out some bite-size Three Musketeers and Snickers bars, and explained that she didn't put them out earlier because she didn't want to "spoil" the batboy. You could hardly have a better seat—though John Henry's seats aren't bad!

Lib Dooley's cookie tray. Bill Nowlin photo.

I can't say I ever sat in John Henry's seat, but I did sit in the one immediately behind it with my friend Mark Fischer one night in the first year of the "dugout" seats when we decided to splurge. It was well worth it. Turning to the right, you could look right into the Red Sox dugout—this was before the bench was installed where Terry Francona and bench coach Brad Mills sit during games. More than one ballplayer looked over and nodded while in the hole, waiting to take his place in the on-deck circle.

Then there are the quirky seats—the front row of section 28 has exactly one seat in it, but it's not that comfortable a place from which to watch the game. The seat's a "double-wide"—well, not exactly, but it's much, much wider than your typical blue slatted seat. Perfect for the 300-pound fan. But maybe not for someone afraid of heights. It's not that it's high; it's just that there is all this yawning space in front of you from where two aisles converge to form the triangle wedge section that is section 28. You feel exposed sitting there. You could almost get vertigo and pitch forward and tumble down the steps.

Section 33—one of the alcohol-free sections—has a nice solo seat in the very last row. Another quirky place from which to watch a game, though you can't lean over the wall toward the field and wave at Manny Ramirez in left. Front row Green Monster seats let you do that. They're the only seats on the Monster really worth having; sitting in the second or the third row robs you of the chance to see as much as 25% or more of all of left and left-center field. Anywhere on the Monster is a great spot, though, for batting practice. Back in the days when there was a net atop the Wall, no fan could ever get up there and hope to snag a souvenir.

The right-field roof box seats let you see pretty much the entire park, albeit from a high perch. The view, though, is arguably even better than the bleachers despite being so much higher—and having virtually no chance at all of ever having a ball hit off your hat.

Red Sox fans will sometimes take perverse pride at their obstructed view seats; it can be quite an adventure to watch a game from behind a pole! Bend this way or that, to get ready for the pitch, or to hope to see the Sox execute a double play.

Speaking of poles, right next to the Pesky Pole can be a nice seat. Keep your hands in so as not to interfere with balls in play!

Some of those twisted seats in the right field corner can be pretty uncomfortable, directed at odd angles to almost face each other and wedged in tight. That's an adventure of another kind. But they're always sold out.

Hey, for that matter, I'd be glad to sit in the top row of the bleachers. I did it often enough as a kid. For many people, ANY seat at Fenway is a favorite seat—just being able to get into the park and sit down can be an accomplishment.

Obstructed view, 2007. Bill Nowlin photo.

Another one who got away

When Clark Griffith sold son-in-law Joe Cronin to the Red Sox, Cronin should have known baseball was a business. About nine years later, before the 1944 season, Griffith's Washington Senators showed Cronin that you've got to close the deal. The Red Sox had brought talented youngster Eddie Yost to Boston for two weeks of workouts and Cronin was suitably impressed by the young 17-year-old third baseman. Cronin assumed that the front office had signed up Yost. They had not, and he was scooped up by Senators scout Joe Cambria. Shirley Povich wrote in the *Washington Post*, "All that the Sox acquired from Yost's tryout was a whopping two-week board bill at one of Boston's fancier-priced hotels." Yost played 18 seasons in the major leagues, and finally joined the Red Sox as a coach from 1977 through 1984.

The best Bosox that got away

Several years ago, Keith Woolner was ruminating on the reputation the Red Sox have for letting some of their best players get away (e.g., Carlton Fisk) or sending them away (Babe Ruth comes to mind). He decided to approach it scientifically using a statistical ranking he created known as VORP (Value Over Replacement Player). For a full explanation of how VORP works, please consult: www.baseballprospectus.com/statistics

Keith began by looking at the player's stats in his last season with Boston, then added up his production numbers for all the teams he played after he had left the Red Sox and ranked those by VORP. In the rare case of a player like The Boomer (George Scott) who had two stints with the Red Sox, he only totaled the figures for those years after his final stint with the Sox.

The data provided here should be mostly self-explanatory, with the additional exception of MLV, defined as "the number of additional runs a team would score with the player in question instead of an average batter."

Top 10 careers by position players after they left the Red Sox

	AVG	OBP	SLG	MLV	VORP
Babe Ruth	.347	.480	.708	1617.9	1589.8
Tris Speaker	.349	.433	.512	667.1	640.0
Ellis Burks	.299	.377	.546	289.5	361.6
Cecil Cooper	.302	.339	.470	228.6	353.6
Gavvy Cravath	.290	.378	.486	299.7	332.1
Buddy Myer	.304	.393	.412	168.5	323.1
Lefty O'Doul	.353	.413	.539	316.9	319.3
Brady Anderson	.258	.366	.432	92.7	312.8
Reggie Smith	.294	.379	.510	254.1	263.1
Carlton Fisk	.257	.329	.438	63.7	250.6
Ben Oglivie	.276	.340	.457	169.3	229.6

Top 10 careers by pitchers after they left the Red Sox

	W-L	SV	ERA	VORP
Red Ruffing	219–124	7	3.47	771.1
Waite Hoyt	227–170	51	3.57	603.4
Eddie Cicotte	147–95	21	2.21	433.8
Sam Jones	161–149	23	4.02	388.1
Wilbur Wood	164–149	57	3.18	372.0
Carl Mays	126–72	19	3.44	356.4
Bobo Newsom	151–152	11	3.80	306.8
Frank Tanana	134–148	1	4.03	284.4
John Tudor	78–40	0	2.66	259.8
Sparky Lyle	77–59	169	2.89	220.8

Once they officially retire, there is no doubt that Roger Clemens and Jamie Moyer will crack the "Top 10." Clemens will likely come in at #3 on the list, and Moyer as #5.

The worst Red Sox club ever

The worst Red Sox club ever? That's what the *Globe*'s Harold Kaese called the 1932 team in a June 18, 1959 article. It would be hard to argue otherwise. The team won just 43 games, and lost 111 for a winning percentage of .279. Batting .300 is one thing. Winning less than 30% of your games is another. The 1932 club is the only Sox team to finish below .300. The Sox finished a mere 64 games out of first place (occupied by the 107–47 New York Yankees).

The Red Sox started by losing their first four games. By May 7, they were 3–16. They were 2–11 on their first long homestand, only winning the second time in the final game of the 13-game stretch. After losing both halves of the June 2 doubleheader, they still had five times as many losses as wins (7–35). They only won their 20th game on July 16, the 30th on August 18, and the 40th on September 11.

The team batting average was .251—despite the presence of Dale Alexander, who won the American League batting championship with a .372 average. Why opposing teams didn't pitch around him remains a bit of a mystery. They scored 566 runs, but allowed 915—not a formula for success. Smead Jolley led in RBIs with 99, and home runs with 18. The only other player with double digit home run figures was Roy Johnson, who hit 11. Alexander's 56 RBIs was second to Jolley.

The team ERA was 5.02, which might not seem so bad today, but was pathetic at the time. Junior Kline, who weighed a reputed 280 pounds according to some contemporary reports, was the winningest pitcher, with 11 wins. He was 11–13, with a 5.82 ERA. Of the 18 men who pitched for the Red Sox at one time or another throughout the season, the only one with a winning record was 8–6 Ivy Andrews. He had a 3.81 ERA. Ed Durham boasted a slightly better ERA—best on the team at 3.80—but his W-L record was 6–13.

The team drew 182,150 patrons—for the whole year.

Lowest attendance at Fenway Park

For a park that routinely sells out every game and hopes to set the consecutive sold-out game record in 2008, it's a little sobering to remember that there were times the team hasn't drawn as well. It seems a little hard to pin down precise figures, but these look to be the lowest attendance dates in Red Sox history.

October 1, 1964 (Cleveland Indians at Boston)—306 fans. Boston 4, California 2
September 28, 1917 (St. Louis Browns at Boston)—356 fans. St. Louis 2, Boston 1
September 29, 1965 (California Angels at Boston—409 fans. Boston 2, California 1
September 28, 1965 (California Angels at Boston)—461 fans. California 4, Boston 3

The two games played on September 28 and 29, 1965 represented the full homestand against the visiting Angels. Total attendance for the homestand came to 870. These games came less than two weeks after the September 16, 1965 Morehead no-hitter attended by just 1,247 fans (including the author of this book). The games featured Yaz, Tony Conigliaro, Dick Radatz, and other Sox stars—but still failed to draw.

The *Chicago Tribune* reports that only 68 fans attended Fenway Park on July 14, 1922. "Exactly sixty-eight people, and the figures are not exaggerated, sat in the grand stand this afternoon…the turnout was the smallest of the season. This small attendance was approached other days during the year." However, not one of five daily papers in Boston indicates any less than 2,800 in attendance. One must be skeptical that the 1922 count is valid.

Largest crowd before which the Red Sox played

It was 83,533 (paid attendance of 81,891)—though *The New York Times* reports that an additional 511 paid to get in but had their money refunded to them because they simply couldn't find a vantage point to watch the game. On top of that, the paper said that another "five or six thousand fought a hopeless battle to get in after the ticket booths were ordered closed." The date was May 30, 1938. It was a doubleheader at Yankee Stadium. The Red Sox lost both games, 10–0 and 5–4.

Of course, one needs to note the largest crowd at an exhibition game. Strictly speaking, the largest crowd before the team—or any team in the world—has ever played was the one totaling an official 115,300 sold tickets on March 30, 2008 at the Los Angeles Coliseum. The Red Sox beat the Dodgers, 7–4.

Largest crowd before which the Sox played in Boston

It was, of course, the Yankees that helped draw the crowds. Newspaper reports indicate that 48,000 people crammed into Fenway Park—somehow—on August 12, 1934, of which 46,766 paid. Those who could see saw the Sox beat the Yankees 6–4 in the first game, but drop the second, 7–1. In addition to those inside, *The New York Times* informs that "outside the portals of the park some 15,000 more stormed and fumed in the streets because they could get no nearer to the scene."

There have been even larger numbers on a given day, but on dates with two separate admission ballgames.

Lengthy games

When Cleveland defeated the Red Sox at 1:36 a.m. (a 5:14 game) on October 13–14, 2007, the Sox pulled into a tie with the New York Yankees for most games lasting 5:00 or more. Both teams have 25.

It was the 30th time the Red Sox have had a game end after 1:00 a.m., a major league record. The NL record rests with the Phils at 23.

A shorty

September 29, 1923, the Yankees at Fenway. The pitching matchup was Waite Hoyt vs. Jack Quinn and the game was completed in 1:03!! The *New York Evening Telegram* reported it as "one of the fastest games of the year." Incredibly there were nine runs scored on 24 hits. Wayne Townsend's reaction was: "ONE of the fastest??? Maybe time ran slower back then."

Red Sox palindrome

Snafu? Oy, Boston! O, do not sob, you fans!

THANKS

Joanne Alfieri
Todd Anton
Mark Armour
Rachel Bachman
Jerry Beach
Gary Bedingfield
Uri Berenguer
Greg Beston
Dick Beverage
Charlie Bevis
Peter Bjarkman
Maury Bouchard
Bob Bowen
Bob Brady
Patrick Brennick
Dick Bresciani, Boston
    Red Sox
Dr. Robert S. Brown
Chuck Burgess
Frank Caprio
Bill Carle
Gene Carney
Sabina Carroll
Joe Castiglione
Jim Charlton
Jason Christopherson
Ken Coleman
Colleen Couture,
    Woburn Public
    Library
Michael Creamer
Mary Kay Daughters
Bill Deane
Dan Desrochers
Dennis Dillon
Dom DiMaggio
Bobby Doerr
Bob Donaldson
John Dooley
Katherine Dooley
Walt Dropo
Saul Dunn

Edwin Fernandez-
    Cruz
Merrie Fidler
Jerry Fischer
Ted Fischer
Sean Forman
Nomar Garciaparra
Dick Gernert
Elizabeth Gillis
ReBecca Glidewell-
    Brown
Alison Gordon
Barbara Gregorich
Dick Guest
Mark Halfon
Lois Hamill, Holy
    Cross
Chuck Harrison
Otis Hart
Bill Hickman
Sean Holtz
Micke Hovmoller
David Kaiser
Maxwell Kates
Dave Kaszuba
Pat Kelly
David King
Terry Kitchen
Marc Kligman
Graham Knight
Gregory Korte
David J. Krajicek
Justin Kubatko
Mary Leary
Don Lee
Len Levin
John Lickert
Phil Lowry
Melissa Ludtke
Ed Luteran
Norman Macht
Peter Mackie

Kenneth Matinale
Elizabeth McLeod
Debbie Matson, Bos-
    ton Red Sox
Tony McClean
Wayne McElreavy
Brian McKenna
Paul McNeeley
John Merian, El Tiante
    Cigars
Gerry Myerson
Rod Nelson
Steve Netsky
David Nevard, *A Red
    Sox Journal*
Alan O'Connor
Marc Onigman
Cliff Otto
Doug Pappas
Angela Parker
Roger Parmelee
Mark Pattison
Hayford Peirce
Johnny Pesky
Tom Powell
Jim Powers
Jeffrey Powers-Beck
Mary Pratt
Rocco Pravidica
W. Mike Presz
Jim Prime
Dave Raglin
Joe Ramirez
Jose Ramirez
Bob Reed
Retrosheet.org
Ric Russo
Mary Jane Ryan, Bos-
    ton Red Sox
Jorge Sainz
Ken Samelson
Tim Samway

Chris Savage
Tim Savage
Bob Schaefer
Kevin Schanz
Diane K. Shah
John Shiffert
Tom Simon
Barry Singer
David Smith
Jessica Smith, Boston
    Red Sox
Lyle Spatz
Ted William Spencer
John Harry Stahl
Bob Sullivan
Steve Steinberg
Rock Swaine
Fred D. Taylor
Josh Tenisci, Boston
    College
Bob Thompson, *Oflag
    64 Item*
Dick Thompson
Rick Thurston
Bob Timmerman
Noe Torres
Ted Turocy
Jules Tygiel
Frank Vaccaro
David Vincent
Bill Walsh
Joe Walsh, Harvard
    University
Ted Williams
Walt Wilson
Saul Wisnia
Ray Wittenberg
Linda Wobbe, St.
    Mary's College
Tim Wolters
Keith Woolner
Pete Zenardi

The following newspapers and magazines were consulted frequently:

Boston Globe	*Boston Post*	*Sport*	*Sports Illustrated*
Boston Herald	*Diehard*	*The Sporting News*	

…for which we also thank the Boston Public Library and the Tufts University Library.

We particularly want to thank the various members of the Society for American Baseball Research (SABR) who would often chase down answers to the most obscure of questions—for instance, coming up with a boxscore of a postseason exhibition game in Manchester NH in 1901 upon request. SABR is a community of some 7,000 members who truly enjoy baseball in all its dimensions. Contact SABR via its website at www.sabr.org.

Information on ejections comes courtesy of SABR's ejection database, compiled by Doug Pappas. Thanks to David Vincent.

As always, www.retrosheet.org was a prime source of data. Dave Smith and David Vincent both fielded a fair number of inquiries. Another prime site for baseball data is: www.baseball-reference.com, and thanks to Sean Forman for help as well.

SOURCES

All quotations from ballplayers are from original interviews conducted over the years by Bill Nowlin, except as noted. All photographs are from the collection of Bill Nowlin unless otherwise noted.

AN APPEAL FOR MORE ODDS AND ENDS

After years of working on this book, assembling all the bits and pieces, I have no doubt that there are hundreds of other stories out there. When you smack yourself on the forehead and exclaim, "How could he have missed THIS one?"—tell me about it.

I would welcome ideas from readers about anything at all that comes to mind—wacky or factual. And to correct any mistakes I've made.

Please don't hold back -- send me your ideas, your musings, your corrections.

Bill Nowlin
bnowlin@rounder.com
1 Rounder Way
Burlington MA 01803

BIBLIOGRAPHY

Abrams, Roger, *The First World Series and the Baseball Fanatics of 1903* (Boston: Northeastern University Press, 2003)

Adelman, Tom, *The Long Ball* (Boston: Little, Brown, 2003)

Alexander, Charles C., *Spoke: A Biography of Tris Speaker* (Dallas: Southern Methodist University Press, 2007)

Auker, Elden, *Sleeper Cars and Flannel Uniforms* (Chicago: Triumph, 2001)

Baldassaro, Lawrence, *Ted Williams: Reflections on a Splendid Life* (Boston: Northeastern University Press, 2003)

Balf, Todd, *The Story of Manny Being Manny* (Beverly, MA: Joga Press, 2006) children's book

Ballou, Bill, *Behind the Green Monster* (Worcester, MA: Ambassador Books, 2005)

Baseball Prospectus, The Writers of, ed. Steven Goldman, *Mind Game* (NY: Workman, 2005)

Baseball Writers of The New York Times and The Boston Globe, *The Rivals* (NY: St. Martin's Press, 2004)

Berry, Henry, *Boston Red Sox* (NY: Collier, 1975)

Bevis, Charlie, *Sunday Baseball* (Jefferson, NC: McFarland, 2003)

Boroson, Melinda, *86 Years: The Legend of the Boston Red Sox* (Waltham, MA: Brown House Books, 2005) children's book

Boston Globe, *Believe It* (Chicago: Triumph Books, 2004)

Boston Globe, *So Good! The Incredible Championship Season of the 2007 Red Sox* (Chicago: Triumph, 2007)

Boston Herald, *Boston Red Sox, 2004 World Champions* (Champaign, IL: Sports Publishing, 2004)

Boston Herald, *Boston Red Sox, 2007 World Series Champions* (Champaign, IL: Sports Publishing, 2007)

Boston Red Sox, *Boston Red Sox Media Guide* (Boston: Boston Red Sox, 2005)

Bradford, Rob, *Chasing Steinbrenner* (Dulles, VA: Brassey's, 2004)

Browning, Reed, *Cy Young* (Amherst: University of Massachusetts Press, 2000)

Bryant, Howard, *Shut Out* (NY: Routledge, 2002)

Buckley, James Jr., *Perfect* (Chicago: Triumph, 2002)

Buckley, Steve, *Red Sox: Where Have You Gone?* (Champaign: Sports Publishing, 2005)

Burgess, Chuck and Bill Nowlin, *Love That Dirty Water* (Burlington, MA: Rounder Books, 2007)

Campbell, Peter A., *Old-Time Baseball and the First Modern World Series* (Brookfield, CT: Millbrook, 2002)

Castiglione, Joe and Doug Lyons, *Broadcast Rites and Sites: I Saw It on the Radio with the Boston Red Sox* (Lanham, MD: Taylor, 2004)

Cataneo, David, *Tony C.* (Nashville: Rutledge Hill Press, 1997)

Catsam, Derek, *Bleeding Red* (Washington, DC: Vellum, 2005)

Chadwick, Bruce and David M. Spindel, *The Boston Red Sox* (NY: Abbeville, 1991)

Chapman, Con, *The Year of the Gerbil* (Danbury, CT: Rutledge Books, 1998)

Christoper, Matt, *On the Mound with…Curt Schilling* (NY: Little, Brown, 2004) youth book

Cinquanti, Michael, *A Year's Worth of Red Sox Birthdays* (Amsterdam, NY: Genium, 2005)

Clark, Ellery, *Boston Red Sox 75th Anniversary History* (Hicksville, LI: Exposition Press, 1975)

Clark, Ellery, *Red Sox Fever* (Hicksville, LI: Exposition Press, 1979)

Clemens, Roger and Peter Gammons, *Rocket Man* (Lexington, MA: Stephen Greene, 1987)

Cole, Milton and Jim Kaplan, *The Boston Red Sox* (North Dighton, MA: JG Press, 2005)

Coleman, Ken with Dan Valenti, *Diary of a Sportscaster* (Pittsfield, MA: Literations, 1982)

Coleman, Ken with Dan Valenti, *The Impossible Dream Remembered* (Lexington, MA: Stephen Greene Press, 1987)

Coleman, Ken, *So You Want To Be A Sportscaster* (NY: Hawthorn, 1973)

Coleman, Ken with Dan Valenti, *Talking On Air* (Champaign: Sports Publishing, 2000)

Conigliaro, Tony with Jack Zanger, *Seeing It Through* (NY: Macmillan, 1970)

Conley, Kathryn R., *One Of A Kind: The Gene Conley Story* (Advantage Books, 2004)

Connery-Boyd, Peg and Brendan Fitzgerald, *Red Sox Coloring and Activity Book* (Hawks Nest Publishing, 2007) childrens book

Corbett, Bernard, *March to the World Series: The 1986 Boston Red Sox* (Boston, Quinlan Press, 1986)

Creamer, Robert, *Babe: The Legend Comes to Life* (NY: Simon & Schuster, 1974)

Creamer, Robert, *Baseball in '41* (NY: Viking, 1991)

Crehan, Herb, *Red Sox Heroes of Yesteryear* (Cambridge: Rounder Books, 2005)

Crehan, Herb and James W. Ryan, *Lightning in A Bottle* (Boston: Branden, 1992)

Dawidoff, Nicholas, *The Catcher Was A Spy* (NY: Vintage, 1994)

DiMaggio, Dom with Bill Gilbert, *Real Grass, Real Heroes* (NY: Zebra, 1990)

Dolan, Edward F., Jr. and Richard B. Lyttle, *Fred Lynn: The Hero from Boston* (NY: Doubleday, 1978)

Doster, Rob & Mitchell Light, *Game Day: Red Sox Baseball* (Chicago: Triumph, 2006)

Dunn, Jimmy, *Funnyball: Observations from a Summer at the Ballpark* (Portsmouth, NH: Peter E. Randall Publisher, 2007)

Enders, Eric, *100 Years of the World Series* (NY: Barnes & Noble, 2003)

Femia, Vin, *The Possible Dream* (Worcester, MA: Chandler House Press, 2004)

Fenway Park: The Fan Navigator to Fenway (Chicago: Wise Guides, 2007)

Ferroli, Steve, *Hit Your Potential* (Indianapolis: Masters Press, 1998)

Foulds, Alan, *Boston's Ballparks & Arenas* (Lebanon, NH: Northeastern University Press, 2005)

Frisch, Aaron, *The History of the Boston Red Sox* (Mankato, MN: Creative Education, 2003) children's book

Frommer, Harvey, *Baseball's Greatest Rivalry* (NY: Atheneum, 1982)

Frommer, Harvey and Frederic J. Frommer, *Red Sox vs. Yankees: The Great Rivalry* (Champaign: Sports Publishing, 2004)

Frommer, Harvey, *Where Have All Our Red Sox Gone?* (Lanham, MD: Taylor Trade, 2006)

Gammons, Peter, *Beyond the Sixth Game* (Lexington, MA: Stephen Greene, 1986)

Gay, Timothy, *Tris Speaker* (Lincoln: University of Nebraska Press, 2005)

Gillette, Gary and Pete Palmer (eds.), *The Ultimate Red Sox Companion* (Hingham, MA: Maple Street Press, 2007)

Glebe, Iris Webb, *The Earl of Dublin* (privately printed, 1988)

Golenbock, Peter, *Red Sox Nation* (Chicago: Triumph, 2005)—an updated version of his book *Fenway*

Goode, Jon and Lauren, *Pitching with the Papelbons* (no publisher indicated, 2007) childrens book

Gorman, Bob, *Double X* (NY: Bill Goff Inc., 1990)

Gorman, Lou, *One Pitch from Glory* (Champaign: Sports Publishing, 2005)

Gowdy, Curt, *Cowboy at the Mike* (Garden City, LI: Doubleday, 1966)

Grossman, Leigh, *The Red Sox Fan Handbook* (Cambridge: Rounder Books, 2005)

Halberstam, David, *Summer of '49* (NY: William Morrow, 1989)

Halberstam, David, *The Teammates* (NY: Hyperion, 2004)

Halloran, Bob, *Destiny Derailed* (Salt Lake City: Millenial Mind Publishing, 2004)

Hanson, Geoffrey, *Curse to Verse* (no location indicated: October Publishing, 2005) childrens book

Harrelson, Ken with Al Hirshberg, *Hawk* (NY: Viking, 1969)

Hirshberg, Al, *The Red Sox, The Bean, and The Cod* (Boston: Waverly House, 1947)

Hirshberg, Al, *What's the Matter with the Red Sox?* (NY: Dodd, Mead, 1973)

Holley, Michael, *Red Sox Rule* (NY: Harper Entertainment, 2008)

Holway, John B., *Ted the Kid* (Springfield, VA: Scorpio Books, 2008)

Holway, John B., *The Last .400 Hitter* (Dubuque: William C. Brown, 1992)

Honig, Donald, *The Boston Red Sox* (NY: Prentice-Hall, 1990)

Hornig, Donald, *The Boys of October* (Chicago: Contemporary, 2003)

Johnson, Bobby, *What Curse?* (NY: iUniverse, 2004)

Johnson, Dick and Glenn Stout, *Ted Williams: A Portrait in Words and Pictures* (NY: Walker, 1991)

Kaese, Harold, *A Rooter's Guide to the Red Sox* (privately printed, 1974)

Kaiser, David, *Epic Season: The 1948 American League Pennant Race* (Amherst: University of Massachusetts Press, 1998)

Kaplan, Jim, *Lefty Grove: American Original* (Cleveland: Society for American Baseball Research, 2000)

Keene, Kerry, Raymond Sinabaldi and David Hickey, *The Babe in Red Stockings* (Champaign: Sagamore, 1997)

Kemmerer, Russ with W. C. Madden, *Ted Williams: 'Hey kid, just get it over the plate!'* (Fishers, IN: Madden Publishing, 2002)

Kettmann, Steve, *One Day at Fenway* (NY: Atria, 2004)

Krantz, Les, ed. *Not Till the Fat Lady Sings: The Most Dramatic Sports Finishes of All Time* (Chicago: Triumph Books, 2003)

LaHurd, Jeff, *Spring Training in Sarasota* (Charleston, SC: Arcadia, 2006)

Lally, Dick, *The Boston Red Sox* (NY: Bonanza, 1991)

Latchford, Jennifer and Rod Oreste, *Red Sox Legends* (Charleston, SC: Arcadia, 2007

Laurila, David, *Interviews from Red Sox Nation* (Hingham, MA: Maple Street Press, 2006)

Lautier, Jack, *Fenway Voices* (Camden, ME: Yankee Books, 1990)

Lee, Bill with Dick Lally, *The Wrong Stuff* (NY: Viking Press, 1984)

Lee, Bill with Jim Prime, *The Little Red (Sox) Book* (Chicago: Triumph Books, 2004)

Leiker, Ken, Alan Schwartz, and Mark Vancil, *Red Sox: A Retrospective of Boston Baseball* (NY: Sterling, 2005)

Lieb, Frederick, *The Boston Red Sox* (Carbondale: Southern Illinois University Press, 2001) orig. published 1947

Linn, Ed, *The Great Rivalry* (NY: Ticknor and Fields, 1991)

Linn, Ed, *Hitter* (NY: Harcourt, Brace, 1993)

Liss, Howard, *The Boston Red Sox: The Complete History* (NY: Simon & Schuster, 1982)

Longest, A. Knoefel, *Idiot-Syncrasies: How the Red Sox Were Smart Enough to Win the World Series* (Avon, MA: Adams Media, 2005)

Lowry, Philip, *Green Cathedrals* (Reading, MA: Addison-Wesley, 1992)

Lyle, Sparky with Peter Golenbock, *The Bronx Zoo* (NY: Dell, 1979)

Lyne, Mike, *Fourteen Games in October* (Bloomington, IN: Author's House, 2005)

Lyons, Steve, *PSYCHOAnalysis* (Champaign, IL: Sagamore, 1995)

Maple Street Press Red Sox Annual 2006-2008

Markusen, Bruce, *Ted Williams* (Westport, CT: Greenwood Press, 2004)

Massarotti, Tony, *Dynasty: The Inside Story of How the Red Sox Became a Baseball Powerhouse* (NY: St. Martin's, 2008)

Massarotti, Tony and John Harper, *A Tale of Two Cities: The 2004 Yankees-Red Sox Rivalry and the War for the Pennant* (Guilford, CT: Lyons Press, 2005)

Martin, George I., *The Golden Boy* (Portsmouth, NH: Peter E. Randall, 2000)

Masur, Louis P., *Autumn Glory* (NY: Hill & Wang, 2003)

McCarney, Tim and Tom Deady, *Surviving Grady* (San Francisco: AiT/Planet Lar, 2004-05)

McDermott, Mickey with Howard Eisenberg, *A Funny Thing Happened on the Way to Cooperstown* (Chicago: Triumph, 2003)

McGrath, Patrick J. and Terrence K. McGrath, *Bright Star In A Shadowy Sky* (Pittsburgh: Dorrance, 2002)

McSweeney, Bill, *The Impossible Dream* (NY: Coward-McCann, 1968)

Miller, Jeff, *Down to the Wire* (Dallas: Taylor Publishing, 1992)

Millikin, Mark, *Jimmie Foxx, The Pride of Sudlersville* (Lanham, MD: Scarecrow, 1998)

Mnookin, Seth, *Feeding the Monster* (NY: Simon & Schuster, 2006)

Montville, Leigh, *The Big Bam* (NY: Doubleday, 2006)

Montville, Leigh, *Ted Williams* (NY: Doubleday, 2004)

Montville, Leigh, *Why Not Us?* (NY: Public Affairs, 2004)

Nash, Peter J., *Boston's Royal Rooters* (Charleston, SC: Arcadia, 2005)

Neft, David S., Michael L. Neft, Bob Carroll, and Richard M. Cohen, *The Red Sox Fan Book* (NY: St. Martin's Griffin, 2005)

Nemec, David and Scott Flatow, *The Ultimate Red Sox Baseball Challenge* (Lanham, MD: Taylor Trade Publishing, 2008)

Neyer, Rob, *Feeding the Green Monster* (NY: Warner Books, 2001)

Nowlin, Bill, *Day By Day with the Boston Red Sox* (Burlington, MA: Rounder Books, 2007)

Nowlin, Bill, *Fenway Lives* (Cambridge: Rounder Books, 2004)

Nowlin, Bill, *Mr. Red Sox: The Johnny Pesky Story* (Cambridge: Rounder Books, 2004)

Nowlin, Bill, *Ted Williams At War* (Burlington, MA: Rounder Books, 2007)

Nowlin, Bill, ed., *The Kid: Ted Williams in San Diego* (Cambridge: Rounder Books, 2005)

Nowlin, Bill., ed., with Mark Armour, Len Levin, and Allan Wood, *When Boston Still Had the Babe: The 1918 World Champion Red Sox* (Burlington, MA: Rounder Books, 2008)

Nowlin, Bill., ed., with Mark Armour, Bob Brady, Len Levin and Saul Wisnia, *Spahn, Sain, and Teddy Ballgame: Boston's (almost) Perfect Baseball Summer of 1948* (Burlington, MA: Rounder Books, 2008)

Nowlin, Bill and Jim Prime, *Blood Feud: The Red Sox, The Yankees, and the Struggle of Good versus Evil* (Cambridge: Rounder Books, 2005)

Nowlin, Bill and Jim Prime, *The Red Sox World Series Encyclopedia* (Burlington, MA: Rounder Books, 2008)

Nowlin, Bill and Jim Prime, *Ted Williams: A Splendid Life* (Chicago: Triumph Books, 2002)

Nowlin, Bill and Dan Desrochers, *The 1967 Impossible Dream Red Sox* (Burlington, MA: Rounder Books, 2007)

Nowlin, Bill and Mike Ross with Jim Prime, *Fenway Saved* (Champaign: Sports Publishing, 1999)

Nowlin, Bill and Cecilia Tan, eds., *The Fenway Project* (Cambridge: Rounder Books, 2004)

Nowlin, Bill and Cecilia Tan, eds., '75: The Red Sox Team that Saved Baseball (Cambridge: Rounder Books, 2005)

O'Nan, Stewart and Stephen King, Faithful (NY: Scribner, 2004)

Ortiz, David with Tony Massarotti, Big Papi: My Story of Big Dreams and Big Hits (NY: St. Martin's, 2007)

Pachter, Adam (ed.), Fenway Fiction: Short Stories from Red Sox Nation (Cambridge MA: Rounder Books, 2005) fiction

Pachter, Adam (ed.), Further Fenway Fiction (Burlington, MA: Rounder Books, 2007) fiction

Pahigian, Joshua R., The Red Sox in the Playoffs (Jefferson, NC: McFarland & Co. Inc., 2006)

Pesky, Johnny with Maureen Mullen, Diary of a Red Sox Season—2007 (Chicago: Triumph Books, 2007)

Petrocelli, Rico and Chaz Scoggins, Tales from the Impossible Dream Red Sox (Champaign, IL: Sports Publishing, 2007)

Piersall, Jim and Al Hirshberg, Fear Strikes Out (Lincoln, NE: Bison Books, 1999)

Prime, Jim with Bill Nowlin, Tales from the Red Sox Dugout (Champaign: Sports Publishing, 2000)

Prime, Jim and Bill Nowlin, More Tales from the Red Sox Dugout: Yarns from the Sox (Champaign: Sports Publishing, 2002)

Prime, Jim, Red Sox Essential: Everything You Need to Know to Be a Real Fan (Chicago: Triumph Books, 2006)

Prime, Jim and Bill Nowlin, Ted Williams: A Tribute (Masters Press, 1997)

Prime, Jim and Bill Nowlin, Ted Williams: The Pursuit of Perfection (Champaign: Sports Publishing, 2002)

Purciello, Gerard, The Year They Won (Weston, CT: Brown Barn Books, 2005)

Redmount, Robert, The Red Sox Encyclopedia (Champaign: Sports Publishing, 1998)

Reis, Ronald A., Baseball Superstars: Ted Williams (NY: Chelsea House, 2008) youth book

Remy, Jerry, Hello, Wally! (Chantilly, VA: Mascot Books, 2006) children's book

Remy, Jerry with Corey Sandler, Watching Baseball (Boston: Globe Pequot, 2004)

Reynolds, Bill, Lost Summer: The '67 Red Sox and the Impossible Dream (NY: Warner Books, 1992)

Riley, Dan. ed., The Red Sox Reader (Boston: Mariner/Houghton Mifflin, 1999)

Rucker, Mark and Bernard M. Corbett, The Boston Red Sox, From Cy to The Kid (Charleston, SC: Arcadia, 2002)

Ryan, Bob, When Boston Won the World Series (Philadelphia: Running Press, 2003)

Sammarco, Anthony Mitchell, Boston's Fenway (Charleston, SC: Arcadia, 2002)

Sampson, Arthur, Ted Williams (NY: A. S. Barnes, 1950)

Schrafft, Nichole Wadsworth, A Field Guide to Fenway Park (Rockport, MA: Twin Lights, 2005)

Schwartz, Jonathan, A Day of Light and Shadows (Pleasantville, NY: The Akadine Press, 2000)

Scoggins, Chaz. Game of My Life: Boston Red Sox (Champaign, IL: Sports Publishing, 2006)

Seidel, Michael, Ted Williams: A Baseball Life (Chicago: Contemporary, 1991)

Shafer, Scott P., What Dreams They Have (www.lulu.com, 2006) poetry

Shaughnessy, Dan, At Fenway (NY: Three Rivers, 1996)

Shaughnessy, Dan, The Curse of the Bambino (NY: Penguin, 1991)

Shaughnessy, Dan, The Legend of the Curse of the Bambino (NY: Simon & Schuster, 2005) childrens book

Shaughnessy, Dan, One Strike Away (NY: Beaufort, 1987)

Shaughnessy, Dan, Reversing the Curse (Boston: Houghton Mifflin, 2004)

Shaughnessy, Dan and Stan Grossfeld, Fenway: A Biography in Words and Pictures (Boston: Houghton Mifflin, 1999)

Shea, Tim, Fenway! The Ultimate Fan's Guide to the Nation's Ballpark (Minneapolis: Tasora Books, 2007)

Shea, Tim, Fenway Pole Finder (Minneapolis: Itasca Books, 2006)

Sheldon, Heather Barlow, Seymour's Soaring Red Sox (Acton, MA: Cassiopeia Press, 2005) childrens book

Simmons, Bill, Now I Can Die in Peace (NY: ESPN Books, 2005)

Smith, Curt, Our House (Chicago: Masters Press, 1999)

Snyder, John, Red Sox Journal (Cincinnati, OH: Emmis Books, 2006)

Soos, Troy, Before the Curse (Hyannis, MA: Parnassus Imprints, 1997)

The Sporting News, Curse Reversed (St. Louis: Sporting News Books, 2004)

Stout, Glenn and Richard Johnson, Red Sox Century (Boston: Houghton Mifflin, 2004)

Stout, Glenn, ed., Impossible Dreams (Boston: Houghton Mifflin, 2003)

Sugar, Burt, The Baseball Maniac's Almanac (NY: McGraw-Hill, 2005)

Sullivan, George, The Picture History of the Boston Red Sox (Indianapolis: Bobbs-Merrill, 1979)

Sullivan, Robert, Our Red Sox (Cincinnati, OH: Emmis Books, 2005)

Tan, Cecilia, The 50 Greatest Yankee Games (NY: John Wiley, 2005)

Tan, Cecilia, and Bill Nowlin, *The 50 Greatest Red Sox Games* (NY: John Wiley, 2006)

Tebbetts, Birdie with James Morrison, *Birdie* (Chicago: Triumph Books, 2002)

Tiant, Luis and Joe Fitzgerald, *El Tiante* (Garden City: Doubleday, 1976)

Thompson, Dick, *The Ferrell Brothers of Baseball* (Jefferson, NC: McFarland, 2005)

Thorn, John, Phil Birnbaum, and Bill Deane, *Total Baseball* (Toronto: Sport Classic, 2004)

Tsiotos, Nick and Andy Dabilis, *Harry Agganis, The Golden Greek* (Brookline, MA: Hellenic College Press, 1995)

Underwood, John, *It's Only Me: The Ted Williams We Hardly Knew* (Chicago: Triumph Books, 2005)

Valenti, Dan, *Clout!* (NY: Stephen Greene, 1989)

Valenti, Dan, *From Florida to Fenway* (Pittsfield, MA: Literations, 1982)

Walton, Ed, *Red Sox Triumphs and Tragedies* (NY: Stein and Day, 1980)

Walton, Ed, *This Date in Red Sox History* (NY: Scarborough, 1978)

Werber, Bill and C. Paul Rogers III, *Memories of a Ballplayer* (Cleveland: Society for American Baseball Research, 2001)

Williams, Dick and Bill Plaschke, *No More Mr. Nice Guy* (NY: Harcourt, Brace, Jovanovich, 1990)

Williams, Ted and David Pietrusza, *Teddy Ballgame* (Toronto: Sport Classic Books, 2002)

Williams, Ted and Jim Prime, *Ted Williams' Hit List* (Indianapolis: Masters Press, 1996)

Williams, Ted with John Underwood, *My Turn At Bat* (NY: Fireside, 1988)

Wood, Allan, *1918* (Lincoln: Writers Club Press, 2000)

Yastrzemski, Carl and Gerald Eskenazi, *Yaz: Baseball, The Wall and Me* (NY: Doubleday, 1990)

Yastrzemski, Carl and Al Hirshberg, *Yaz* (NY: Viking, 1968)

Zingg, Paul J., *Harry Hooper* (Urbana: University of Illinois Press, 1993)

No author or editor listed:

2007 World Champions: Boston Red Sox. Boston Sweeps Again! (Tinton Falls, NJ: 106 Apple Street, 2007)

Williams and DiMaggio: The Stuff of Dreams (Chicago: Rare Air Media, 1999)

INDEX

It would have taken a whole season to index this book, if every mention of every player's name was included. What we have done instead is to index the names which attach to what we thought to be an interesting story, or something which someone might want to look up, rather than every time every name appeared in a list or table or even in the text. We confess, though: the index is about as idiosyncratic as the book.